"Henry Mayer's remarkable study of Garrison is a great achievement.... Impressive for its deft examination of many complex issues of the period...enlivened by the masterful use of colorful detail. Henry Mayer has written one of the best accounts we are ever likely to have of how one man's idealistic belief in the possibility of moral regeneration and political transformation came to be realized....A monumental work of historical biography."

— Michael Winston, *The Washington Post Book World*

"Henry Mayer's excellent new life of William Lloyd Garrison...has a depth of character that previous treatment never quite accorded him...[and] opens up a view of...the quality, the rhythms, the hardships, and most of all the satisfactions, of an entire life dedicated to the unswerving promotion of an extremist cause.... Mr. Mayer is a man of broad culture and a wide store of reference, which combine with literary verve to give depth, proportion, and continuity to the successive scenes in the life and times of an extraordinary particular person."

— Eric L. McKitrick, *The New York Review of Books*

"A magnificent portrait of Garrison, filled with fresh insight into the man and his movement and written with unsurpassed narrative elegance. It is the best biography of the great abolitionist crusader I have ever read."

— Stephen B. Oates, author of
The Approaching Fury: Voices of the Storm, 1820–1861

"This eloquent, powerful biography by Henry Mayer should restore [Garrison] to the position he held in the country before the Civil War—a thundering voice challenging the conscience of white America. It is a book that may well encourage and inspire the coming generation to do for our time what Garrison did for his."

— Howard Zinn, author of *A People's History of the United States*

"William Lloyd Garrison...stirred the conscience of millions and—more than anyone—helped move the issue of slavery to the top of the political agenda. Without him, Lincoln might not have had his chance for greatness. This comprehensive work, for the first time, does him justice—beautifully."

— Mario M. Cuomo, former governor of New York and author of
Lincoln on Democracy

"This is a masterpiece. Brilliantly written and intelligently constructed, Mayer's elegant presentation rightly places William Lloyd Garrison at the forefront of America's greatest heroes."

— Annette Gordon-Reed, author of *Thomas Jefferson and Sally Hemings*

"Fluently and fascinatingly rendered...Mayer has an especially strong sense of place."

— Carla Davidson, *The New York Times Book Review*

"The narrative pace of the story and the fine writing style provide us with an excellent portrait not only of Garrison, but of all of the other people whom he affected."
— John A. Garraty, author of *The American Nation*

"[A] marvelous new study…Henry Mayer has rescued this nineteenth-century abolitionist from common distortions."
— Alvin S. Felzenberg, *The Weekly Standard*

"[A] massive and glorious biography…Mayer gives us a heroic example of the biographer's art, bringing his subject vividly to life…. *All on Fire* is an obsessively readable work of prodigious scholarship and enormous narrative power, marked at every turn by subtlety and insight."
— Daniel Akst, *San Jose Mercury News*

"[Mayer's] big, bold, revisionist view of Garrison is, in a word, masterful. The author never loses control of the complex material, and skillfully weaves the facts of his hero's life into the tumultuous events of his time is a prose style that is clear, detailed and compellingly readable."
— William F. Gavin, *Washington Times*

"Henry Mayer restores to Garrison his rightful place in the American pantheon…. *All on Fire* does an outstanding job of placing Garrison in the context of the great events and issues of the era."
— *Chicago Tribune*

"Engaging…William Lloyd Garrison, whose anti-slavery crusade helped right the most fundamental wrong in American history, comes in for a richly deserved biographical treatment."
— *Philadelphia Inquirer*

"Richly researched…Mayer does a superb job of putting Garrison in his rightful place at center stage of American life in the nineteenth century."
— *San Francisco Examiner & Chronicle*

"Henry Mayer's massive, clearly written, often gripping biography of Garrison is a great story…. None of [Garrison's] earlier chroniclers matches Mayer's writerly skill and sure narrative sense."
— Benjamin Schwarz, *Los Angeles Times Book Review*

"[A] truly inspiring work…Mayer masterfully and seamlessly integrates all the dimensions of Garrison's life. Indeed, the author's eye for detail, from the drudge tasks of an apprentice printer to the warm family life of a prominent agitator, makes this one of the most realistic, authentic biographies I have ever had the pleasure to read…. One of the best narrative histories of abolitionism overall."
— Jeffrey Rogers Hummel, *The American Enterprise*

WILLIAM LLOYD GARRISON
CIRCA 1850

Daguerreotype, artist unknown; tarnish mark across brow
(Collection of Marc and Mona Klarman)

ALL ON FIRE

William Lloyd Garrison and the Abolition of Slavery

HENRY MAYER

W. W. NORTON & COMPANY
NEW YORK • LONDON

For information about permission to reproduce selections from this book, write to
Permissions, W. W. Norton & Company, Inc., 500 Fifth Avenue, New York, NY 10110

For information about special discounts for bulk purchases, please contact
W. W. Norton Special Sales at specialsales@wwnorton.com or 800-233-4830

Manufacturing by RR Donnelley, Harrisonburg
Book design by Diane Hobbing of Snap-Haus Graphics
Production Manager: Devon Zahn

Library of Congress Cataloging-in-Publication Data

Mayer, Henry.
All on fire : William Lloyd Garrison and the abolition of slavery / Henry Mayer.
p.   cm.
Includes bibliographic references (p. 633) and index.
ISBN 0-312-18740-8 (hc)
ISBN 0-312-25367-2 (pbk)
1. Garrison, William Lloyd, 1805–1879. 2. Abolitionists—United States—Biography.
3. Antislavery movements—United States—History—19th century. I. Title.
E449.G25M39   1998
973.7′114′092—dc21
[B]   98-19406
CIP

First published as a Norton paperback 2008
ISBN 978-0-393-33236-0 pbk.

W. W. Norton & Company, Inc.
500 Fifth Avenue, New York, N.Y. 10110
www.wwnorton.com

W. W. Norton & Company Ltd.
Castle House, 75/76 Wells Street, London W1T 3QT

1 2 3 4 5 6 7 8 9 0

FOR ELLEN AND BILL SEWELL

The voice of him that crieth in the wilderness, Prepare ye the way of the Lord, make straight in the desert a highway for our God.

Every valley shall be exalted, and every mountain and hill shall be made low; and the crooked shall be made straight, and the rough places plain:

And the glory of the Lord shall be revealed, and all flesh shall see it together. . . .

Isaiah 40:3–5

I have need to be all on fire,
for I have mountains of ice about me to melt.

William Lloyd Garrison, 1831

CONTENTS

BOOK FOUR
A HEAVENLY RACE DEMANDS THY ZEAL
1844–1858

BOOK FIVE
AND AN IMMORTAL CROWN
1859–1879

PREFACE

ALL ON FIRE IS A BOOK ABOUT AN AGITATOR, AND ITS ARGUMENT CAN BE SIMPLY STATED. WILLIAM LLOYD GARRISON (1805–1879) IS AN AUTHENTIC AMERICAN HERO WHO, WITH A BIBLICAL PROPHET'S POWER AND A PROPagandist's skill, forced the nation to confront the most crucial moral issue in its history. For thirty-five years he edited and published a weekly newspaper in Boston, *The Liberator,* which remains today a sterling and unrivaled example of personal journalism in the service of civic idealism. Although Garrison—a self-made man with a scanty formal education—considered himself "a New England mechanic" and lived outside the precincts of the American intelligentsia, he nonetheless did the hard intellectual work of challenging orthodoxy, questioning public policy, and offering a luminous vision of a society transformed. He inspired two generations of activists—female and male, black and white—and together they built a social movement which, like the civil rights movement of our own day, was a collaboration of ordinary people, stirred by injustice and committed to each other, who achieved a social change that conventional wisdom first condemned as wrong and then ridiculed as impossible.

Unlike most public men, Garrison pointedly encouraged conflict. He believed that agitation began with conviction of personal duty, and he consistently advocated the highest (some would say impossible) standards of moral citizenship. Most significant, Garrison did not shrink from the realization that the assault upon slavery would require a direct confrontation with American assumptions of white supremacy. He boldly coupled his demand for immediate emancipation with an insistence upon equal rights for black people, a principled stand whose moral clarity eluded every prominent political figure of his era. When emancipation finally arrived, it came therefore by indirection as a consequence of civil war and was accomplished in a halfhearted revolution that failed to achieve fully the moral transformation Garrison envisioned. In bitter irony, the end he most fervently desired—the abolition of slavery—came by the means—the physical coercion of warfare—that, as a pacifist, he most consistently abhorred. Even more ironic, Garrison the agitator found himself hailed in triumph as the moral symbol of a nation made virtuous by victory in a cause belatedly embraced and quickly abandoned.

The tension created by significant social movements is always resisted and condemned during the struggle and invariably forgotten afterward. Now that we are all abolitionists, a special effort must be made to understand the depth of opposition Garrison encountered. Let us remember that in 1831, thirty years before the firing on Fort Sumter, when Garrison founded *The Liberator* and dedicated it to the immediate abolition of slavery and the realization of equal rights for all, the president of the United States—like all but two of his predecessors—owned black people as property, every presidential candidate belonged to a philanthropic organization committed to freeing only those slaves who would resettle in Africa, and every politician believed strongly that, as a matter of both constitutional law and social reality, the question of slavery in the states stood outside the competence of the national legislature.

Against the advancing nineteenth-century concept of the American nation as a mystical union which expected deferential allegiance from its citizens as the price of sharing its bounty and grandeur, Garrison counterposed an older eighteenth-century idea: the republican and revolutionary spirit of civil liberty as manifested in a skeptical and assertive citizenry committed to questioning the exercise of power. His career is a landmark in the American dissenting tradition and exemplifies the fault line that in democratic politics separates the insiders, who think progress comes from quiet lobbying within the halls of power, from the outsiders, who insist that only public manifestations of dissatisfaction can overcome institutional inertia. Garrison audaciously believed that a citizen could be more influential by deciding not to vote and that a leader could be more faithful to his constituency by refusing to hold office. He took Biblical injunctions seriously enough to incur the wrath of clergymen, and he pressed the claims of the American revolutionary creed with an insistence that put him at odds not only with conventional politicians but with the convention of political compromise itself. He defied public opinion in an effort to change it, condemned political parties and the churches in an endeavor to influence them, and once publicly burned the U.S. Constitution—at a picnic on the Fourth of July, no less!—to dramatize his conviction that citizens had a profound duty to resist unjust laws. His action was in the long tradition of the politics of prophetic witness that reaches from Martin Luther to the eighteenth-century Quaker agitators like John Woolman and Benjamin Lay and the twentieth-century activism of Daniel Berrigan and Dr. Martin Luther King, Jr. (That Henry David Thoreau, one of the few Americans who had an affinity with Garrison's understanding of citizenship, also spoke at the event and had his text published in *The Liberator,* is generally overlooked.)

Our political culture is not kind to those who challenge its norms, and as abolition has come to seem inevitable, so has Garrison's nonconformist agitation come to seem shrill, weird, and counterproductive. That is how the critics of his own day portrayed him, and some charged that his behavior retarded the very movement he helped create. It is unfortunate that the stereotype of Garrison as the lunatic fringe personified has become history's vantage point, because from the margins—using spiritual ideas as his lever— he managed to shift the political center in a manner seldom matched in our history. Third parties in the United States are viewed as hornets that sting and die, but as a party of one, Garrison thrived as a gadfly for thirty-five years and set the political agenda for a generation.

From his tiny printing office in the shadow of Boston's Faneuil Hall the editor challenged the "great triumvirate" of antebellum politics. He blasted Henry Clay for the sham reform of colonization; he countered John C. Calhoun's defense of slavery as a "positive good" and confronted the South Carolinian's threat of secession with a principled repudiation of his own; his agitation so altered the framework of politics that Daniel Webster's once powerful paean to "Liberty *and* Union" eventually rang hollow as a craven submission to tyranny. As each new set of converts to the antislavery movement expressed fresh outrage at the republic's denial of its ideals, the pressure mounted for the national redefinition that Garrison had long advocated and that Lincoln, in a wartime climate heavily influenced by abolitionists, so memorably articulated at Gettysburg. It comes as a surprise to realize that of all the antebellum political conceptions about slavery that contended for supremacy—states' rights, three-fifths clause, Missouri Compromise, toleration but nonextension, popular sovereignty—it was Garrison's program of immediate emancipation through the repudiation of the proslavery constitutional compromises and a union dissolved and reconstructed that prevailed.

As so often happens in reform movements, the questions multiplied. When cautious souls challenged the participation of women in the abolitionist movement as improper and unnecessarily provocative, Garrison leaped to the defense of women's rights, and he supported the demand for suffrage that inevitably followed. Philosophical questions ensued as well, about the propriety of legislating benevolent moral reforms, the effectiveness of the two-party system as an instrument of social change, the role of religion and the church in shaping public policy, the legitimacy of the U.S. Constitution, and the conflicting obligations of citizens toward legislative statutes and the mandate of conscience. Garrison's willingness to face these questions and the unconventional answers he proposed for them brought the editor into the "original relation to the universe" that his great contemporary Ralph Waldo Emerson extolled as the highest striving of the human intellect and soul.

Garrison was one of the first Americans, after Thomas Paine, to make agitation his professional vocation, and he became a prototype of the New England "reformer" regarded with bemused tolerance by Emerson and ambivalent disdain by Nathaniel Hawthorne and Henry James. The abolitionist was a sweet-faced scold, however, punning and wisecracking his way through the movement's endless meetings, bustling about his kitchen serving food to his young children when his wife's injured arm made domestic work too burdensome, remarking when his daughter Fanny warmed her hands on his great bald head that a hot-blooded fanatic was at least good for something.

The editor tuned his life to the sound of Jubilee's trumpet. Even as a little boy he loved to sing in his mother's Baptist prayer meetings, and in later years the zealous editor would rouse his family on Sunday mornings by banging out on the piano favorite hymn tunes from his childhood. The call he felt, however, pulled him toward neither the new birth nor the ministry, but toward the great work of making the evangelical impulse felt in society. Immediate abolition became his gospel, and the antislavery movement became his household of faith. Garrison and abolitionism drew upon the nineteenth century's last great outpouring of rural Protestant revivalism, and he used the language of repentance and conversion to exhort America to save its soul and avert the wrathful judgments that lay in wait for oppressors.

The Garrisonian spirit, however, had secular roots also in both the natural rights tradition that fueled the great revolutions in Britain, France, and the United States and the romantic idealism that grew out of them. It was no accident that Garrison located his press within sight of Faneuil Hall and the Bunker Hill Monument or that two of his major essays are deliberate variations on the form and style of the Declaration of Independence. His preoccupation with individual assertion on behalf of fundamental principles and with the relationship between personal freedom and public liberty makes the Garrisonian spirit part of the grand movement of western Romanticism that finds its expression in the Beethoven of *Fidelio,* in the Wordsworth of *The Prelude,* and in the Hugo of *Les Misérables.* Garrison was also swept along by the rising tide of Victorian confidence in industrial and material progress. He was born in the age of Jefferson, Pitt, and Bonaparte, and he died in the era of Grant, Gladstone, and Bismarck. He began his career as a printer's apprentice, setting type by hand and printing gazettes one sheet at a time, and at his retirement, sixty years later, huge steam presses turned out newspapers at the rate of ten thousand sheets an hour. He went to his first antislavery meeting by packet boat and his last by railroad in one-third the time, and he occasionally fancied himself as an engineer for the "moral railroads" that would transform the soul of the century as profoundly as the steam engine had reshaped the economy. Garrison believed in progress, but understood that moral advance required as much application of energy as did the physical feats that so gripped the midcentury imagination. His belief in the power of the word and his faith in moral regeneration became the touchstones of his politics, and the themes of suffering and love, of apocalyptic change and millennial hope, suffused his thought. The editor knew what Martin Luther King, Jr., knew: that "the moral arc of the universe is long, but it bends toward justice."

I became interested in Garrison after writing the biography of another political agitator, Patrick Henry, whose consciousness was formed in the culture of evangelical Protestantism. Like Henry, Garrison turned religious energy toward secular ends, and the careers of both men provide striking examples of the ways in which the power of an outsiders' movement can reshape the agenda of an entrenched elite. However, in writing about Henry, a slaveholder, and the political conflict that led to the adoption of the U.S. Constitution and the Bill of Rights, I felt the unfinished nature of liberty's story. The noxious three-fifths clause, which laid the basis for the slaveholders' domination of antebellum politics, received scant attention in the debate on ratification that formed the climax of Henry's political career; to explore further the racial contradictions that underlay the American founding and to consider slavery as a constitutional problem required another book and, ironically, led me to the agitator who burned the Constitution.

As a man whose political consciousness was shaped in the civil rights and antiwar movements of the 1960s, I was readily intrigued by this agitator who abhorred party politics and called out the transformative energies of the beloved community. Historians' focus in recent years has turned not only from Garrison but from abolition itself as a social movement, and an important story has been lost. Garrison himself has not been the subject of a full-scale biography for more than thirty years, and of the two studies published in 1963, one, *Against Wind and Tide* by Walter Merrill, underplays Garrison's politics, while the other, *The Liberator* by John Thomas, reacts so negatively to Garrison's rejection of traditional party politics that it misses the brilliance of Garrison's moral agitation. Despite their publication dates, both these books are essentially works of the 1950s, conceived in the stark polarities of the Cold War and suspicious of departures from the social norm. I have tried to bring a fresh perspective born of my own acquaintance with movements for social change. No one who participates in a social movement is ever quite the same again, and I think that it helps to see Garrison not as an isolated freak, but as the inspiring leader of a diverse group of people whose consciousness had broadened and whose growing sense of collective power had emboldened them to act. From this perspective, too, I have regarded *The Liberator* not simply as a source, but as a rightful character in the story, taking my cue from the editor's sons, who observed that "to an extent seldom witnessed in journalism, *The Liberator* involves at once the biography and the autobiography of its editor."

Most revisionists set out to deflate a reputation; my task, however, is to reinvigorate one. In reconstructing a less stereotyped version of Garrison's life, I don't expect most readers to agree with everything he thought or wrote, but I want them to profit by the challenge of encountering his ideas with, I hope, something of their proponent's integrity and power. I also want them to take advantage of the opportunity to experience the deepening sectional crisis of the 1850s from the perspective of the radical fringe rather than from that of the moderate politicians who dominate the point of view of the conventional narratives. Because one finds but scattered references to Garrison in a book as brilliant and at the same time as popular as James McPherson's *Battle Cry of Freedom* (1988), it is easy to conclude that the abolitionist was irrelevant to the final phase of the struggle when, in fact, his movement had helped define the framework in which the political contest took place.

The reader may be disappointed that I have not given either the internal history of the South or the complex relationships of masters and slaves the attention that they deserve. There are many fine books that do this; mine attempts rather to attend to the reverberations of Garrison's moral case against slavery, and its focus is perforce more Northern than Southern. If I have tended to reflect Garrison's oversimplified view of the Southern experience, it is, in part, a consequence of the monochromatic view the South had of Garrison. For all the subtleties of Southern culture and politics and all the genuine ambiguities of its predicament, the inescapable truth is that the slaveholding South would not relinquish its property in human beings and chose instead to close itself off from abolitionist influences and compound its oppression with the crime of silence. Northerners shared in this acquiescence and this guilt for many decades, as Garrison tirelessly pointed out, and one intent of this book is to trace the way in which his agitation gradually changed the paradigm of Northern politics to admit the moral argument against slavery that the South would never acknowledge.

To say all this is not to speak from a lack of personal sympathy with a people under duress. I spent my adolescent years in a small Southern town whose municipal park contained the traditional Confederate monument, with the inscription "Not for wages, not for glory, 'Twas for home and right they fell," and when I went to college at Chapel Hill, I met a student from my town whom I had never known at home and whose race excluded him from playing in that park. This book was born in the contradictions of that experience. In coming into the civil rights movement as a college student, I felt the exhilaration of participating in a righteous cause but also the anguish of knowing full well how hard it is for a people schooled in one way to heed history's mandate to alter their behavior, if not their hearts. What distinguished the South of the 1950s and 1960s from the 1840s and 1850s is that its people, white and black, were in active and productive argument with each other and ultimately achieved a social transformation, though not without violence, bloodshed, and martyrdom. In the antebellum South the internal quarrel was quickly and effectively suppressed, and the region resolutely set itself against the change demanded by people they perceived as outsiders, though Northerners and Southerners shared a profound political identity as Americans. Had the South conceded the moral force of Garrison's argument, ironically, it would have secured for itself more control over the dissolution of chattel slavery; in choosing defiance, however, it bred a cataclysmic destruction.

The sentimental strain in our culture has turned our thinking about the Civil War into a pageant of heroism and a threnody of grief that separates the sacrifice from the cause. It allows us to regard the conflict as a tragedy of flag without acknowledging that it was equally a tragedy of race in which Northerners died to preserve a political system that had failed to solve the gravest moral issue in our history and Southerners shed their blood in a desperate counterrevolution to ensure that it never would. Even today there are people who believe that they can fly the Confederate flag as a tribute to gallantry untainted by the white supremacy for which it stood. They are deceiving themselves and playing false with history. It seems to me indisputable that the defense of slavery was the fundament of the Confederacy, and to expunge slavery from the history of the Civil War is to produce *Hamlet* without the Prince. To write of the Civil War without Garrison, however, is to write of the American Revolution without Tom Paine, the labor movement without Eugene Debs, the civil rights movement without Bob Moses, or feminism without Elizabeth Cady Stanton.

As I set out on this venture nearly a decade ago, many good people tried to warn me off. One of the scholars I most admire told me with regret that Garrison appealed to the artist in me rather than the historian; he didn't think there was much left to be said about the abolitionists. A New York publisher told me that Garrison didn't have much to do with the abolition of slavery, and an editor in Virginia thought it would be tedious to have an entire book devoted to "a Johnny one-note." (But what a note!) A North Carolina classmate of mine advised me to think twice before I committed myself to spending so much time in the company of a person like Garrison. While the previous comments whetted my appetite, this one did give me pause. To live with a hortatory and self-righteous presence might well be a gloomy experience, yet I had an inkling that there was more to Garrison than the caricature permitted, and my hunch was verified. The agitator turned out to be a far more good-natured, practical, and agreeable companion than either my friend or I had anticipated. People remark at the discrepancy between the pariah and the pussycat because they assume that Garrison's righteous public attack must originate in a private unappeasable anger; it is clear to me now that he became an agitator as much out of love as hate, as much from plenitude as deprivation, and that his vision cannot be understood outside the context of the Christianity that was its inspiration.

At the outset I thought it would be accurate to say that Garrison had "secularized" the religious impulse and made it serve political ends, but I now think that is an inadequate and perhaps condescending formula. Garrison and his colleagues were believers who challenged the institutional church and evolved a creed of their own, but who never lost their faith in the redemptive power of Jesus Christ. Although contemporary liberals are suspicious of religious fundamentalism and prefer to emphasize the secular dimensions of our national experience, we nevertheless need to remember that in the first half of the nineteenth century Americans experienced a profoundly democratic religious transformation that brought the energy of the Protestant Reformation directly to bear upon social concerns; radical popular religion helped eradicate an evil with which socially liberal theological opinion had learned to coexist. Evangelical piety is a challenge to understand, but it helps explain Garrison's self-conception as a fanatic. He lived in the realm of italics and exclamation points, but his exaggerations were rather those of heightened focus than untruth, and he wielded the typestick and toiled at the press with a sense of mission not unlike that of the printers of Puritan England who manufactured the tracts that would reform a commonwealth.

To contemplate Garrison's career is thus to ponder both the role of the agitator in a democratic polity and the tragic contradictions that underlay the failure of the Constitution and the necessity of reconstructing it. The plain truth is that antebellum America did not have political leaders able to "negotiate a revolution to avoid a civil war," to use the Rev. Jesse Jackson's description of the extraordinary transfer of political power from the white minority to the black majority in South Africa. Given our political system's inability to consider moral questions and the narrowness of the political spectrum Americans find tolerable, it is not hard to understand why Garrison was destined to be a pariah. The slaveholding class in the United States became the only ruling elite in the world to resist the international tide of abolition with all-out warfare, and we have fashioned a powerful myth of political collapse and rebirth to explain the tragedy in a way that minimizes both the failure of the 1787 Constitution and the revolutionary quality of the Civil War Constitution that supplanted it. It is sobering to realize, however, that if the political leaders of the 1850s had succeeded in averting war, it would have been at the cost of an emancipation deferred into the twentieth century and perhaps not fully accomplished—to use Lincoln's prediction in the debates with Douglas—until the 1950s. That abolition now seems an event of the distant past and not an event in living memory is part of the legacy of moral vision and free expression that should make William Lloyd Garrison an honored name in our history.

When Garrison first sounded his note of Jubilee in a Fourth of July sermon at Boston's Park Street Church in 1829, he regarded his address as "the preface of a noble work," but did not anticipate that it would take his working lifetime to accomplish the task of abolition. In 1835 a Boston mob would nearly lynch him in front of Faneuil Hall and the governor of Massachusetts would consider extraditing him to Georgia on charges of sedition. Thirty years later he was engulfed affectionately by crowds of liberated black people in the war-ravaged streets of Charleston, South Carolina, and when the Stars and Stripes was raised once more over the reconquered Fort Sumter, Garrison had his hand on the halyards by invitation of the president of the United States. Yet, for all its ironic reversals, his was a career in civic idealism and intellectual heroism, for he had the humanity to imagine a radically different society, the courage to insist upon its principles, and the faith to persist in agitation until his vision became manifest and the slaves went free. This book tells his story. That the Garrisonian vision of a nation that has transcended racial prejudice seems clouded and impolitic today reminds us that our story is not yet finished.

HENRY MAYER

Berkeley, California
1 May 1998

ALL ON FIRE

BOOK ONE

AWAKE MY SOUL

1805–1830

GARRISON AT TWENTY

Engraving based on a portrait by William Swain, Newburyport, 1825
(Library of Congress)

CHAPTER ONE

A PRAYING PEOPLE

THE ABOLITIONIST'S FOREBEARS CAME TO AMERICA AS BOUND LABORERS. ON A SQUALLY DAY AT THE END OF MARCH 1770, STEWARDS FOR CAPTAIN WILLIAM OWEN OF THE ROYAL NAVY MUSTERED A COMPANY OF THIRTY-eight indentured servants, including William Lloyd Garrison's maternal grandparents, aboard a two-hundred-ton Liverpool square-rigger berthed in the Mersey River. The ship, which Owen had recently purchased and re-christened with his own name, stood ready to depart for Canada, where the naval officer turned "lord of the soil" by a land grant from the Crown planned to employ his gang of seafarers, craftsmen, and farmers in founding a proprietary colony on an island at the entrance to the Bay of Fundy. The laborers, most of whom were unemployed Merseyside linenworkers and weavers, had temporarily bargained away their freedom in exchange for pas-sage to Britain's latest North American frontier and the promise of eventual leaseholds on fresh and bountiful land.

When the servants, who had endured the humiliation of a forced march from Owen's estate fifteen miles upriver, found themselves herded into a cargo hold with barely five feet of headspace and tiers of wooden slabs jammed in as sleeping pallets, their spirits sank, for they had not signed away their liberty to be stabled like livestock. While the ship heaved and groaned, straining at its ropes in the stiff wind, the bondsmen became "riotous and disorderly," and Captain Owen—a fierce-looking officer who had lost an eye in a brawl and had his right arm shot off while capturing a French warship off Pondicherry—had to be summoned from a farewell dinner with his busi-ness partners to quell the disturbance personally.

The gale blew itself out a few days later, and the *Owen* weighed anchor and dropped down past the great South Dock, where one hundred vessels a year readied for the "African trade" that supplied a different form of labor—slave labor—to the New World. Thousands of yards of English cal-icos and linens, tons of wrought iron and brass, and thousands of pounds of gunpowder sailed off to West African trading depots, where they were ex-changed for shackled human cargoes to be crammed 'tween-decks and trans-ported to British plantations in the West Indies and on the North American mainland. There enslaved laborers—bound not for a term of years but for a lifetime and, with their progeny, beyond as legal chattel—cleared the land and grew the cash crops whose transport back to England completed the vicious triangle. The business had grown so large that a wholly new dock that would enclose five acres of water was under construction at the Mersey shoreline just for Guinea-bound ships. Their cargoes brought such lavish profits—as much as thirty percent on each voyage, people said—to Liverpool's carriers and merchant brokers that most had cast a cold eye upon Owen's little farming scheme. They would leave Nova Scotia to small-time proprietors like Owen and the distressed English laborers who, as one editor scoffed, sailed off dreaming of "mountains of roast beef and rivers of rum." Yet, in the course of colonial development, the small shiploads of indentured servants in quest of land had peopled North America as surely as the slave traders and planters in search of profits. In the fifteen-year period between the end of the Seven Years War on the American continent and the outbreak of the Revolution, the transatlantic movement westward reached new heights, as a quarter million people—half from the British Isles and almost that many from West Africa—found themselves uprooted from one world and transplanted into another. People shaken out of the Hebrides or the Hausa villages along the Niger became part of vast labor systems that, within another century, would contend for supremacy on the battlefields of Virginia.

For the first three weeks of their voyage, those in steerage endured mountainous waves from "a high cross and confused sea" that poured into the hatchway of their gloomy quarters, drowning the cooking fire in the galley and prompting Owen to log woefully, "My landmen Sea-sick & sick of the Sea." Once they found calm sailing, however, Mary Lawless and Andrew Lloyd found each other. Mary was the daughter of the soldierly John Lawless, who had crossed the North Atlantic a decade earlier and fought on the Plains of Abraham (1759) under the martyred General Wolfe to wrest Canada from the French and now sought to partake of the fruit of that victory as a British settler. He had indentured himself as Captain Owen's barber and signed up his wife and daughter to cook and wash for the proprietor. Andrew Lloyd was a young Welshman who had grown up in a Protestant enclave in County Cork, as had Mary's mother, Catherine, and had come on board apprenticed to the *Owen*'s master, Captain Plato Denny. By the end of the voyage in June 1770, friendship had ripened into romance, a romance so intense, the Garrison family tradition has it, that the couple rushed to marry on the day their ship landed in North America. In truth, they waited for the better part of a year, until the company's strenuous labor had raised on spacious Campobello Island in Passamaquoddy Bay a settlement that could boast marshland drained for hayfields, sturdy houses roofed with fine blue slate, and a prosperous trade in cordwood and codfish. Captain Owen presided over the work and, in the tradition of the country squire, served as both justice of the peace and chaplain. On March 30, 1771, Owen united Mary Lawless and Andrew Lloyd in marriage and genially presided over what he termed a "real and genuine Yankee frolic" with plentiful food, jigs and country-dances, and "much social glee."

Andrew Lloyd had made himself into a first-rate pilot in the notoriously tricky waters of 'Quoddy and the Bay of Fundy, and before the decade ended he had become master of the schooner *Managuash* and a prosperous carrier of salted fish, lumber, and furs in the trade among the provincial merchants of St. John, Windsor, and Halifax. While Mary's parents turned to farming land they had acquired on neighboring Deer Island, she and Andrew grew a family, eventually numbering thirteen children, on Campobello. They named their firstborn son Plato, to honor Andrew's former master, and they took great pride in their bevy of daughters, the eldest of whom, Frances Maria—the abolitionist's mother—proved to be both the family beauty and the source of its heartache.

Born in 1776, as the 'Quoddy folk tried to keep clear of the rebellion brewing in the older mainland colonies to the southwest, Frances Lloyd grew into a tall and sturdy young woman, as fully capable of butchering a moose or sailing a skiff as baking bread or sewing the clothes for her numerous younger sisters and brothers. She had a quick mind and, despite a lack of schooling, learned to love literature and write with fluency. The Lloyd children knew the spare rewards of a frontier household that grew its food, spun its wool, made its candles, sat on its hand-hewn maple benches, and slept under hand-sewn downy comforters. "I had enough to attach me to this world," Frances later told her own daughter, scarcely realizing what an isolated corner of the world she inhabited.

The 'Quoddy islands had floated in political limbo for many years after the American revolt. Since boundary commissioners appointed jointly by the Crown and the new U.S. government could not trace a continuous line through the tangled channels of Passamaquoddy Bay, the communities remained virtually autonomous enclaves. Frances had reached courting age by the time a settlement in 1798 allowed the Stars and Stripes to be raised over nearby Eastport and Moose Island, just a few hundred yards across the water from her home. Campobello and Deer islands were supposed to become part of the United States, too, but John Lawless and Andrew Lloyd joined a petitioning chorus that successfully kept them Britons and placed their land under the jurisdiction of the newly formed Canadian frontier province of New Brunswick.

Not until the preachers came to Passamaquoddy did Frances Lloyd realize that there could be satisfactions beyond the unchanging round of island life. As if to compensate for their disinclination to political upheaval, Nova Scotians underwent a religious revolution in the 1780s that awakened unchurched frontier families into a "pious frenzy" marked by what the Episcopal bishop of Nova Scotia ridiculed as a "rage for dipping." Baptists preaching the pietistic gospel—the belief that salvation could be obtained through an emotional "new birth" in loving fellowship with Jesus Christ—had roused the western counties with prayer meetings of unparalleled excitement. By the light of blazing birchbark torches repentant sinners groaned and sang and cried out in religious ecstasy, and people rode twenty, thirty, even fifty miles to join their brethren in such wondrous outpourings of the spirit.

The revival, which spread from maritime Canada across the hinterland of northern New England, had begun with Henry Alline (1748–1784), the frail son of a Rhode Island family that had sought opportunity in Nova Scotia. Young Alline had scanty schooling and worked off and on as a tanner and currier, until he experienced a religious conversion that suffused "his whole soul with love" and propelled him into a strenuous preaching career in which he traveled hundreds of miles every year by boat, horse, and snowshoe, stirring religious fervor across the province and leaving, like trail blazes, hosts of converted sinners and scores of independent churches.

Frances Lloyd was only eight years old when Alline sailed her coast on his final tour in 1784, but other itinerant preachers came in his wake. Their appearances became great religious festivals. Families came from all over the bay, lodging in their boats for the several nights of a revival meeting. There were only three ordained ministers in the vast tract between Campobello and the Penobscott River, and these stolid Anglicans had a disinclination to travel. The "New Lights" kindled by Alline, however, would take the gospel anywhere, especially to unchurched districts like 'Quoddy, and they remained less concerned about the form of the new churches that sprang up than they did about the drama of salvation that brought souls back to Christ and the redemptive power of perfect love. The nascent religious community at 'Quoddy remained an ecumenical one for many years; when the first church was convened, on Moose Island in 1794, it imposed no sectarian tests for membership and called no permanent minister to its pulpit.

Frances Lloyd heard her first preaching in meadows and barns. She went with the other young women of the island, wearing short loose gowns and aprons tied about their heads, in a frolicsome spirit, as much to socialize as to pray. The boisterous and proud Frances, indeed, scoffed at those folk who were so easily overcome and fell to shouting and confessing their sins. Yet she felt her own stout heart beginning to melt under the heat of the preaching, and one night she began to weep. Her soul grew restless, her discontent palpable; she came to sense the power of that majestic God who divided the flames of fire and shook the wilderness. She, too, groaned in sin and cried out for mercy. For the peace of her soul she called on Christ to be her Savior, and, in the words of an Alline hymn, her cutting anguish ceased and she found a strength divine.

Frances embraced the "personal religion" of the dissenters and broke the binding ties with her parents. She seldom spoke of it again, but a family legend grew up that Mary and Andrew Lloyd, who had remained partial to the Anglican orthodoxy that had come over with them on the *Owen*, would not recognize the workings of grace. They regarded Frances's conversion as another unbecoming, even dangerous, outcropping of her willfulness and pride. Turning their headstrong eldest daughter out of their house, they sent Frances to live with her grandparents on Deer Island.

She also spent a good deal of time in Eastport, where she taught in the community school and conducted prayer meetings. Occasionally she read from the printed sermons of the evangelical leaders, but more often she spoke extemporaneously from the promptings of her heart. The gatherings were popular, and the powerful young woman at the pulpit attracted not only the faithful, but the restless sparks of the neighborhood. One night as she was leaving prayer meeting, her shoulders wrapped in a woolly coat against the chill, a young man she had never seen before came up to her and boldly asked, "Miss Blue Jacket, may I walk you home?" Frances re-buffed him, but when a few weeks later she received a letter, fervent in both poetry and piety, from this erstwhile escort, whose name was now revealed to be Abijah Garrison, she had no trouble remembering the way he had looked at her and she hesitated not a bit before accepting his invitation to correspond.

Abijah Garrison was no stranger either to prayer meetings or to strong-willed women. His mother, Mary Palmer Garrison, had defied her family by leaving the Congregational Church, where her father was a deacon, to take up with the Baptists, and when the Rev. Henry Alline came up the St. John River to preach at her little village of Maugerville, New Brunswick, Mary Garrison could be counted as part of the rejoicing company "that went with [him] from place to place, sometimes six or seven boats loaded with people." Abi-jah himself, born in 1773, was old enough to remember how the fervent crowds lined the riverbank during Alline's visit in 1779 and pressed their little children toward the Gospel messenger.

Like Frances Lloyd, Abijah had grown up in an isolated but determined farming community that counted his parents among its pioneer settlers. They had built their township along a remarkably fertile alluvial flat running be-tween the St. John River and a parallel smaller stream, the Jemseg, that poured out of a large backwoods lake. The Palmers had come to the Jemseg region in 1764 from Newbury, Massachusetts, in association with nearly one hundred other Essex County families drawn by generous land grants that had enticed them into believing that "a new New England" could arise in the fruitful valleys of maritime Canada. At the outset of the enterprise, daughter Mary had married Joseph Garrison, a thirty-year-old migrant prob-ably descended from Huguenots who had crossed the Atlantic to escape French persecution. This long-faced quiet man lived contentedly in the Palmers' shadow. He had a township allotment of five hundred acres upriver by one tract from his father-in-law's; he let his wife name the children (there would be nine all told) with Palmer names; the children all looked like Palmers, too, fair-skinned and fair-haired, with the jolly air and sanguine temperament of their mother and her adventurous kinfolk.

The Yankee settlers prospered in the new country of lush grainfields, rivers abundant with salmon, trout, and sturgeon, and extensive forests of conifers and hardwoods that afforded a cash crop. Maugerville monopolized the trade in naval masts that made New Brunswick a valuable province, and squadrons of men labored intensively to bring down the mighty trees and haul the tall trunks to the river. Abijah and his brothers also went with their father on lumbering expeditions that hewed smaller white oak timber for barrel staves, which they sold in St. John. A few pennies went to the deacon's son who kept school several months each winter, and Abijah learned to read and write with tolerable grace. He did not learn to accept the life of a farmer and lumberjack, however, and by the early 1790s he had left the Jemseg to work as a seaman with a firm of St. John merchants who kept a few vessels busy in regular trade with their old hometown of Newburyport in Massachusetts.

Soon he was sailing under two flags. After 1793, with Britain and France at war and the neutral Americans grabbing more and more of the carrying trade with the West Indies, the seaports of the United States did their best to entice British sailors into the American merchant service. American seaman's papers, which might protect a British tar from being impressed into the Royal Navy, could be obtained in such an easy charade that, like many of his shipmates, Abijah Garrison found it prudent to get himself "naturalized." On a voyage into Newburyport in March 1797, he strolled over to the Custom House and enrolled under the U.S. Seamen's Protection Act. The clerk neatly inscribed his name in the huge folio registry and, inquiring as to Garrison's place of birth, ambiguously recorded the mumbled answer as "Brunswick," adding one more "ditto" to a long column labeled "Nativity in the United States." Garrison received certificate number 427, which described the young sailor as twenty-four years old, five feet ten inches in height—tallish compared to other registrants on the page—and of "fresh" complexion, a term that politely melded the Palmer fair skin with the blood-red birthmark that blotched Abijah's face and ran under his chin like a muffler.

Garrison eventually worked his way up to become a capable pilot and a "sailing-master" in charge of navigation in the merchant fleet. In July 1798, while working on the schooner *Boyne*, Abijah put in at 'Quoddy, telling a friend that he'd come in search of "Lady Fr____s," the young woman with whom he had corresponded. Having duplicated Andrew Lloyd's rise in the world, the young mariner proposed to take Lloyd's feisty daughter in marriage. The 'Quoddy captain assented, and after their marriage in December 1798, Abijah brought his bride. whom he dotingly called Fanny, back to the

Jemseg to live among his kinfolk during his absences at sea. Joseph Garrison had died in 1783 when Abijah was ten, and his mother had supported her family as a midwife, an occupation she continued after remarriage to another quiet farmer, Robert Angus. Theirs was a hospitable and pious home, and Fanny was grateful for their sympathetic care, especially after her firstborn child, a daughter named for Abijah's mother, died in infancy.

Later, with Abijah content for a time to work as a pilot in the Bay of Fundy, the Garrisons set up for themselves in rooms on Duke Street in the little seaport of St. John, where a son, James, was born in 1801 and a daughter, Caroline, in 1803. It became harder and harder to supply his family, Abijah found, as the maritime provinces suffered under wartime trade restrictions and the sluggish economy was worsened by a severe drought that made even bread and vegetables scarce. Having floated hither and yon in search of the right situation, the navigator decided upon a course correction. "I have been following the rule of false position, or rather permutation, these seven last years, and have never been able to solve the question to my satisfaction till now," Abijah wrote. This time, however, he was sure that the answer lay in relying upon his American sea papers to make a permanent move to Newburyport, a thriving place where he had good connections and high hopes for promoting his family's welfare.

Newburyport lay in the northeasternmost corner of Massachusetts at the mouth of the Merrimack River, tucked into a long crescent on the south riverbank. The town's spires glittered white against water dark with silt from distant New Hampshire hills. To go from the thin harvests and somnolent wharves of eastern Canada to prosperous Newburyport, with its mile-long waterfront a forest of masts and its docks piled high with cargoes from the Indies, East as well as West, seemed to these immigrants from isolated New Brunswick to be like a voyage to London itself. Newburyport was the third-largest place in Massachusetts, with only Boston and Salem outranking it in both tonnage and people. As home to five thousand souls, Newburyport had the attributes of a real town, with church towers and crisscrossing streets (some paved with stones and illuminated by torches at town expense), a public market noisy with vendors and redolent of beef on the hoof and oysters in the shell, and a new courthouse designed by the same man who had done the State House at Boston. There were fine mansions on the high street, an elegant mall lined with poplar trees where the "topping folks" could promenade, blocks of brick buildings filled with shops, booksellers and printing offices, and enterprising merchants who subscribed to the grand projects—an arched bridge across the river, a turnpike running straight as an arrow all the way to Boston—that would earn the town an even brighter mark on the map of commerce. The delighted Abijah took a good look around and exclaimed, "Money is as Plenty here as goods."

Opportunity drew Garrison to Water Street, where two dozen merchants had broad wharves—each a commercial village unto itself—jutting out into the Merrimack. In 1805 Newburyport had at least 176 vessels registered to its townsfolk, and in the month of Abijah Garrison's arrival, this fleet had brought freight valued at more than $800,000 into the port. English woolens, Russian linen sheetings, Swedish iron, French glassware, and Dutch gin each had a place in the trade, along with paint and ribbons and cheese and nails and parasols and writing paper. For all these goods, and more, Newburyport had shipped out vast quantities of dried fish, planks and shingles, bricks, candles, cordage, corn, and rum distilled directly at Coffin's and Brown's docksides from molasses brought up from the West Indies, along with sugar to be reexported to the Baltic. The town also built the ships it sailed, using stout timbers from the Merrimack back country and equipping the vessels with sails and rigging, pumps and blocks, and iron fixtures all done in the port's workshops. "Come here if you can," Abijah urged his brother Joseph. "There is more than fifty ways you might find employment, and always have the Cash as soon as the work is done."

Roaming the docks in search of a suitable berth, Abijah spurned opportunities to work in the waters he knew best. He declined good wages for piloting Newburyport traders through 'Quoddy's vexing currents and not even thirty dollars a month could tempt him into the Labrador fishery. More could be made by sailing toward the tropics. He made short voyages to Virginia for loads of corn and flour (buying and selling part of the cargo himself at a tidy profit) and longer ones to Guadeloupe for molasses, sugar, and crates of oranges, tamarinds, and other tropical bounty. At last, it seemed, he had found his way.

Fanny Garrison, too, had found opportunity in Newburyport, and hers was an abundance of the spirit. For several years before her arrival, the Baptists had excited some interest. A revival, originating in the Prospect Street Congregational Church in 1802, had spread through town and rekindled interest in evangelical religion. Weekly prayer meetings sprang up: kindred spirits gathered in someone's house to exhort each other with phrases of Scripture twined around the testimony of their hearts. The Baptists—with their fervid piety and ecstatic worship forms, their voluntary submission to each other's loving concern, and their eagerness to keep faith with the gospel rules of the early church—offered a striking contrast to the staid and settled ways of the town's Congregational churches. The port's leading ministers, whose sermons on "commonplace topics in commonplace language" had bored the young law student John Quincy Adams when he had clerked in the town in 1786, still held their pulpits two decades later and shook warning fingers at the "flimsy sect" of Baptists who challenged them.

Newburyport was feeling the reverberations from the religious tumult Henry Alline had created in the Nova Scotia of Fanny Garrison's childhood. That awakening had prompted two decades of religious revivals all across

northern New England, which had led to the rise of hundreds of loosely
organized dissenting groups that abandoned orthodox Calvinism and the established Congregational Church for an evangelical religion directly attuned
to the new birth and open to charismatic preaching and spontaneous, communal expression. In one region it would be itinerant Methodists or Baptists,
in others it would be Universalists or Freewill Baptists or zealous preachers
simply calling themselves Christians, but everywhere the awakening was a
populist insurgency that elevated the individual conscience and disdained
the ordained clergy, cherished the words of the Bible and spurned formal
theology, gave ordinary people a voice and challenged traditional church
organizations.

The Baptist revival that drew Fanny Garrison into its company was taking
place within earshot of the tomb of the eighteenth century's most celebrated
evangelist, the Rev. George Whitefield, who had preached three times in
Newburyport and had collapsed and died there in 1770. A woman named
Martha Farnham held prayer meetings in her modest house on School Street
behind the big Federal Street Presbyterian Church where Whitefield lay
buried. Across the way a group of artisans prayed at the house of carpenter
Moses Short, and by the spring of 1805, just at the time the Garrisons moved
to town, the two meetings had gathered themselves into a church, issued a
call for a minister, and found a regular place of worship in a schoolhouse
on the river flats below the port.

Like her Biblical namesake, Martha Farnham knew how to minister to
people's needs. ("Her friends knew her worth" would be engraved on her
tombstone.) She found room in the house on School Street for the Garrisons,
and she took Fanny, with two toddlers to care for and a third child expected
by winter, under her wing. Two years younger than Fanny, Martha was
married to a mariner fifteen years her senior, and with their husbands both
absent for long periods, the women's friendship easily ripened. Martha had
an infant daughter, Harriet, and when Fanny gave birth on December 12,
1805, to her second son, named William Lloyd—to honor both Abijah's
youngest brother, a gravely pious schoolteacher, and her own family—the
women cared for the babies together.

They also became sisters in Christ ("the best of bonds"), sharing conduct
of the weekly prayer meetings on School Street, where Fanny's strong voice
led hosannas to the Lamb of God. "My heart grows warm with holy fire and
kindled with a pure desire," she would sing; "Come my dear Jesus from
above and fill my soul with sacred love." In the cramped house of Martha
Farnham—"the tender sympathisizing friend of my Bosom"—Fanny Garrison declared that she had found a "happy Mansion."

Abijah Garrison missed the vitality of the Farnham house. "It seems seven
years to me since I saw you last," he complained to Fanny in November
1806 from Guadeloupe; "I cou'd with pleasure this moment give all I shall

earn this voyage to be present with you and my children. May God bless you [and] preserve you in health is the prayer of your affectionate husband." Heartfelt words no doubt, yet when wages dried up a year or so later, Abijah found family life impossibly burdensome.

It was Abijah's misfortune to have left Nova Scotia just before its hard times eased and to have resettled in Newburyport just before its trade collapsed. This was less a function of the rule of false position than it was the reverberations from the Napoleonic Wars. As France and Great Britain entered the final phase of their struggle for European domination, each sought to cripple its opponent by economic warfare. While the United States made sophisticated legal claims for a neutral party's right to trade with all belligerents, the warring nations preyed on American ships and sailors and adopted regulations intended to drive Americans from the lucrative carrying trade they had developed since they had become independent. Britain now took steps to promote Halifax and St. John as major distribution points for North American trade, and as Nova Scotia flourished, New England's West Indian trade greatly suffered. In response, the Jefferson administration, hoping both to vindicate neutral rights and to avoid expensive and degrading involvement in the sordid wars of the Old World, undertook a high-minded diplomatic policy of peaceable coercion that culminated in December 1807 with a complete embargo on U.S. trade with Europe. The boycott placed few immediate burdens upon the agrarian heartland that supported Thomas Jefferson, but it stifled the seaports of Federalist New England.

Abijah Garrison and hundreds like him lost their livelihoods. By springtime Newburyport counted seventy idle vessels laid up in port, and its newspaper editor grouchily named the grass growing up on the wharves as the chief product of "Farmer Jefferson's embargo." In December 1808 the muffled drums and tolling bells of a funeral procession marked the first anniversary of the embargo in Newburyport, as shabbily dressed sailors dragged a dismantled ship through the streets, its helmsman carrying a placard with the pathetic inquiry "Which way shall I steer?"

Fanny's husband did not march in the protest, for by that time he had chosen a different course. Enforced idleness in a house with four children under the age of seven (and an infant daughter born to the Garrisons in July 1808), seemed less attractive in reality than it had from distant Guadeloupe, and the fervor of the Farnham prayer meeting did not provide him the satisfaction that it gave his wife. Trouble further mounted when five-year-old Caroline, impelled by hunger as much as curiosity, ate some poisonous spring shrubbery and died in an agony of convulsions.

The succession of events overwhelmed the self-pitying Abijah. He lost his faith, fell away from the temperate path, and spent his days and the few dollars he could scrounge from day work drinking in waterfront saloons. Family legend recounts that Sister Garrison once quite literally broke up her husband's drinking party by smashing the offending bottles, and this is sometimes taken to mean that Abijah Garrison was driven to desert his family by his termagant of a wife. Yet no one knows precisely when Abijah walked out, much less the circumstances. She may have thrown him out; he may have stormed out, or, just as likely, weaseled away with the promise that he would search for work again under the Union Jack at 'Quoddy or St. John and then send for the family. No summons ever came, and although occasionally there was a rumor—he was teaching school in New Brunswick, he was voyaging again in the tropics, he was bigamously married in St. John—the family on School Street never saw him again.

His wife seldom spoke of her absent husband and in subtle ways tried to obliterate his imprint. She dropped the affectionate diminutive Fanny and became known to her pastor and friends as Maria. She also habitually called her second son Lloyd, after her own family name. The children remembered nothing of Abijah, and when William Lloyd Garrison, as an old man, diligently searched through the Newburyport shipping archives he could find not a trace of his father's presence. A distant cousin eventually turned up an hourglass, crudely cut with the initials A. G., that the son gratefully accepted as tangible evidence of his progenitor.

Lloyd did remember his tall, raven-haired mother as a vigilant guardian with a "vigorous, lustrous [mind] sanctified by an ever-glowing piety." Her frontier-bred determination never faltered, he thought, as he watched her march through life with "high views" of its duties and, with the firmness of a Christian soldier, boasting that only a cannonball could lay her low.

Sister Garrison gave her son lessons in relentless but cheerful combat. She taught him to anticipate the day when "the palm shall be put into our hands and we triumphantly shall cry victory," but she admonished, too, that in the struggle against sinfulness, "we have need to be equipped with the whole armour of God." His mother's was an active religion, an endless battle in which combat was conducted in volleys of words as well as deeds. The son remembered that powerful voice in its torrents of pious exhortation, a fervent pastiche of lines from hymns, passages of Scripture, and the promise that in the pietists' continuing drama of sinfulness and salvation "God himself shall wipe all tears from his dear followers' eyes when their warfare is accomplished." With her voice—"one of the best," her son would say—raised in song, his mother enacted the mighty scenes of combat and praise, of struggle and deliverance, that made a lifelong impression upon the child at her knee.

And what mother could resist the little boy who walked around singing, in a sweetly piping voice, "Through all the changing scenes of life, in trouble and joy," the first psalm tune he'd ever learned? Garrison never lost his affection for the favorite hymns of his childhood and the dramatic feelings they stirred in him. He loved the vigorous procession of "Coronation," with its many repeated notes that hailed "the pow'r of Jesus' name!" and led to the marching, full-throated "Bring forth the royal diadem and crown Him

Lord of all." He always found new energy and freedom in "Majesty," whose
driving, fugal phrases told of how the Lord mastered the tempest and drove
the darkness from the sky. To the plaintive shepherd's tune from Handel's
Messiah, Garrison sang his favorite hymn, "Awake my soul/ Stretch every
nerve/ and press with vigor on/ A heavenly race demands thy zeal/ and an
immortal crown."

The grand drama of deliverance and the sound of the celestial choir enabled
the little family to cope with the harshness of daily life. Abijah Garrison's
desertion had left his wife and children nearly destitute. They got along with
the help of the Farnhams and others in the Baptist society. Sister Garrison
worked intermittently as a "monthly nurse" who tended newborn infants and
their mothers in the first four weeks after delivery, but to do so she had to
leave her own baby behind to be cared for by Martha. The pint-sized boys,
Jemmy and Lloyd, gathered clams on the river flats and sold sticks of homemade molasses candy on the street. Sometimes they fetched leftovers from
their mother's charitable employers or collected soup from the mariners'
relief kitchen set up in 1809 at town expense, enduring the taunts of street
kids as they carried their tin pails home like pig swill.

Sister Garrison seemed indomitable to her son, but her churchfolk knew
the heaviness of her heart. Her sorrows and her faith made her eloquent in
prayer, and she became a familiar voice in the community. "God's people is
a praying people," she believed, and the weekly female prayer meetings
stood as "the very gate of Heaven to our souls." When she felt cold, she
wrote, "the flame of Jehovah's love" warmed her, and when she felt "barren
and dead," Jesus revived her in prayer meeting with the feeling that God's
grace was as sweet as "the Dews of Heaven."

The tender care she received from Martha Farnham and their pastor,
Elder John Peak, demonstrated the mercy of "an invisible power" that held
the promise of eventual peace in Christ. An itinerant preacher in the Alline
tradition who had first received the call in a New Hampshire field in 1785,
Peak had also known sorrow. Rheumatic fever had crippled him as a young
man, one daughter had died of a fever on the journey to accept Newburyport's call in 1805, and another languished a winter before recovering her
health. Though lame and halt in body, with sad, dark eyes and a mournful
face, Peak proved an inspiring, affectionate "brother in adversity," and Sister
Garrison said that she would always remember the way he calmed her afflicted mind with "the consoling and heart cheering promises of the Gospel."

John Peak preached in all neighborhoods, but, insisting upon a central
location for the church, he persuaded the faithful to march from the outlying
river chapel into the town proper, where they gathered in the loft of a vacant
town building whose boarded-up windows made it an odd place, Newbury-
porters said, in which to find new light. To embody their unity he led the

processions himself. Glowing with piety, walking on streets Whitefield had trod, and singing the hymns Alline had sung, these evangelicals felt themselves "wrapped up in God . . . ravished with a divine ecstasy beyond any doubts or fears." In her church Sister Garrison found "rapture, extacy, and joy," and amid sisters and brothers "dear to me in Bonds of Spiritual Union," she made a home for her children.

"The good work progressed," Elder Peak wrote, as more inquiring meetings and prayer sessions took place in houses like Sister Farnham's and Sister Garrison's. The Baptist society prospered "in a great rain of righteousness" that increased the church to about eighty members by 1809 and permitted the construction of a trim brick meetinghouse on a corner of Liberty Street behind an important block of stores. Then, on the night of May 31, 1811, earthly vanities went up in smoke. A large column of fire burst through the roof of a stable down on Merchants' Row and, fed by a dry wind, rapidly spread toward the market house and the ferry wharf. Although the volunteer companies quickly reached the scene and long lines of townspeople formed to pass buckets of water to the firefighters, the conflagration soon engulfed the "most ancient, wealthy, and commercial" part of town. Families in the path of danger threw their belongings into wagons and, clutching their bedclothes about their shoulders, tried to get their children and goods to places of safety, including the sturdy Baptist church, which appeared to be well beyond the limits of the blaze. An abrupt change in the wind, however, pushed the fire across State Street, where it began to devour the large brick buildings that everyone had counted on to protect the lower end of town.

Elder Peak saw the fire entering his street and ran home, where he found his daughter Ploomy packing crockery and bedding. He took down his clock and had a few minutes to throw volumes from his library into a wheelbarrow before the fire bit into his roof. Somehow they made their way to the Farnham house, where Ploomy fell sobbing uncontrollably upon the piles of goods. From the roof the minister could see the vast column of cinders and flames and watched, with sinking heart, as the roof of their new church collapsed and sank into ashes. "We should suspect some danger nigh, where we possess delight," he reminded himself.

At Farnham's, where many refugees gathered, the spectacle could be observed in all its terror. The five-year-old William Lloyd Garrison would never forget being held aloft to watch the leaping flames that seared the sky. The glare of light was intense, yet smoky clouds obliterated the moon and the night air became as sultry as a summer's noon. Firemen's trumpets rang out over the crash of chimneys and the cries of distress, while explosions of stored powder and spirits from the wharfside distilleries gave off thunderous sounds of war.

Shortly after dawn, when a cooling fog helped quench the blaze, the fire at last came under control, and Newburyport stared devastation in its grimy, acrid face. Two hundred and forty buildings destroyed, thirteen wharves consumed, ninety families homeless, every dry goods store a wreck, the town library a ruin, and the Baptist meetinghouse in shambles. A visitation without parallel, the fire burned the heart out of the town and broke up forever the possibility of family life for Sister Garrison and her children.

CHAPTER TWO

THE ART AND MYSTERY OF PRINTING

"WE APPOINT AND GOD DISAPPOINTS," SISTER GARRISON LIKED TO SAY, AND WITH HER PATH GREATLY STREWN WITH THORNS IN THE AFTERMATH OF THE GREAT FIRE OF 1811, SHE FOUND HERSELF "A WOMAN OF SOR-rowful spirit" indeed. Times stayed hard in Newburyport. Rebuilding could not proceed quickly in an economy weakened by the restrictive trade policies continued under President Madison and disrupted further by the war with Great Britain that began, after diplomatic failure, in 1812. Martha Farnham began to press her friend for more contributions to the household accounts, and Maria decided that she could better herself by working in another town. Some of the brethren in Lynn, thirty miles to the south, thought they could find a place not only for her, but for twelve-year-old James, who had grown rowdy and needed to be fixed in a trade. So, in the early winter of 1814, Sister Garrison and her elder son moved away, leaving the younger children under "Aunt" Farnham's care.

Lloyd wept bitterly when his mother left. "God measures out our affliction and more than balances the cup with mercies," she reminded the disconsolate boy. Through her own scalding tears she told him that she felt "all the tender care that was in the power of a mother to feel." Their separation would be temporary, she was sure, and he could best endure the trial by obeying his elders and minding his books.

The youngster tried, but he had trouble applying himself to his lessons at the little school across the way. Inclined to write with his left hand, Lloyd endured many an improving slap with the ruler and watched his little sister Elizabeth surpass him in penmanship before he got the hang of it. From the time-tested *New England Primer,* Lloyd practiced reading didactic verses— "Job feels the Rod yet blesses God"—and reciting, by syllables, memorized spelling words whose associations only accentuated his plight. "Ab-sent Bold-ly Con-stant Fa-ther . . . A-bu-sing Be-witch-ing Con-foun-ded Drun-ken-ness." Beyond the primer, Lloyd absorbed the words and cadences of hymns and Scriptures by osmosis. These verses so permeated everyday conversation that, like most of his generation, Lloyd learned to speak and write in a manner that employed, almost unconsciously, the rhythms and motifs of the Bible and moved in and out of direct quotation without any need for attribution.

From Lynn, where his mother at first found only demeaning jobs that called more for servants' work than nursing, there came a steady stream of little bundles and letters with uplifting remarks for the children that concealed her own low spirits. Lacking a gospel sister in Lynn with whom she could "converse on the things of the kingdom" as she used to do on School Street, Maria would sit alone in her room at midnight, imagine herself talking with her friend Martha, and pour her heart into writing meditations that she only occasionally sent to her friend.

Martha Farnham felt downcast, too. She missed her dear friend, but she also missed the money that Maria, now regularly employed, was supposed to be contributing to the household. Martha's renewed complaints deepened Maria's sorrow and led to much protestation of her gratitude and a suggestion that, to ease the burden, one child be moved to another family. "If you can get dear Loyd a place until a door will be opened hear [sic] then I will send for him," she promised.

Aunt Farnham moved quickly. She soon found an older couple in the church who were willing to take the boy. Ezekiel and Salome Bartlett, like humble grandparents in a fairy tale, lived in a tiny cottage at the foot of Summer Street, near the river. Each having lost a spouse, they had married in 1796 and raised two daughters of their own. Brother Bartlett wrung a spare living by cutting wood, sharpening saws, and selling apples and kindling from his doorstep. How they could afford to keep a growing boy in such narrow circumstances, with scanty support from his own mother, was not clear, but Sister Bartlett, who had grown close to Maria in prayer meeting, was a charitable soul and took the task on faith.

Lloyd went to live with the Bartletts in the summer of 1814. His mother wrote affectionately from Lynn, asking him "to be a good boy and mind what Uncle and Aunt Bartlett tell you. Don't neglect your book and do mind that bad boys does not lead you astray to play truant." That the ramshackle Bartlett place sat right on the riverfront worried her greatly. "Don't go near the water," she warned Lloyd, "for should you be drowned your soul must go to God to be judged." She said nothing about his coming to Lynn, although she reported that James, "a good boy and a great comfort to me," had become an apprentice cordwainer and was making thirteen pairs of shoes a week. Schooling, however, was uppermost in her mind, both for Lloyd and Elizabeth, for she told Martha Farnham that while the girl could be boarded in Lynn for what she was now trying to contribute to the Farnhams, the cost of schooling there was very high.

Newburyport, however, prided itself on its public schools. Lloyd, now almost nine years old, went to the big grammar school building up on High Street near the courthouse. The little boys sat on hard slab benches, where they endured surreptitious kicks and pinches from bigger boys behind them and tried to keep still as the older students went through their recitations. The younger pupils read and spelled aloud twice a day from Noah Webster's blue book, which resembled *The New England Primer* in its long lists of divided words, its woodcuts that turned virtues into emblems, and its sternly moralistic fables. Once out of the speller, they used a motley collection of gazetteers to supply the rudiments of geography and history and a few broken-backed copies of *The Columbian Orator* to acquaint them with the dramatic verse of Addison and the grave eloquence of Pitt and Washington. The masters typically were divinity students in hopes of something better, and none lasted too long at the lectern of what one of them, Ralph Waldo Emerson, recalled as "the hot, steaming, stove-ed, stinking, dirty, a'b'spelling-school room."

Outside the classroom Lloyd eagerly joined in the crosstown snowball fights between the "up-alongers" of his new neighborhood and the "down-alongers" from the lower riverfront. He skated exuberantly on the river and the ponds, and he fondly remembered flying kites, jumping hopscotch, batting a ball, and playing marbles in warmer seasons. Once he gained celebrity for a daring swim—so much for his mother's warning—across the Merrimack to "Great Rock" and a tough return against the tide.

The idyll could not last. Lloyd had to drop out of school in order to work alongside impoverished Uncle Bartlett, and the boy, overcome by misery, tried to run away. "Poor Loyd," his mother wrote. "How I want to see him." Sister Garrison found herself in a quandary. She longed to return to Newburyport but despaired of finding work there, whereas she felt miserably lonesome in Lynn but had plenty of work, although she detested her well-to-do employers. If Lloyd could not go to school in Newburyport, his mother reasoned, then he might as well learn a trade in Lynn, and she could ease both their hearts by bringing her unhappy child to her bosom. She managed to find him a place with Gamaliel Oliver, a cordwainer who belonged to the Society of Friends, and early in 1815 Lloyd packed his few possessions at Bartlett's and set off for Lynn.

Visitors to Lynn all remarked upon the peculiar little shacks that seemed to sit out on the grounds of many houses in that town. Larger than privies or chicken coops but smaller than tenant cottages, these "ten-footers" held the key to the town's prosperity, for within their cramped quarters workmen annually made thousands of pairs of shoes. Lloyd scurried to make himself helpful in the Oliver ten-footer by stoking the stove, waxing thread, and running back and forth to the family's house, where the womenfolk bound the uppers that the journeymen would attach to the lowers they had made in the shop. The men joked that Lloyd was hardly bigger than the last he was learning to pound, and in truth the lapstone and hammer were much too heavy for him. His sore knees ached continually and his fingers grew stiff, but the youngster was proud that he learned to make a "tolerable" shoe.

Employment in Lynn did not lead to a resumption of family life. Lloyd stayed with the Olivers, who treated him well; his mother had steady work as a live-in nurse for a succession of women, each haughtier and more pre-occupied with "fripperies and parade" than the one before, while James, who had changed masters, could seldom be found in his appointed abode. Now fourteen and quite wild, James had developed a taste for the local "black strap" cordial composed of New England rum sweetened with a dollop of molasses, and he frequented a seedy tavern on the edge of town. Then he ran off with a girl to a more infamous roadhouse on the Salem highway, where they stayed drunk for two days, and James had to be forcibly removed by his master after the carousing apprentice had tried to break up the place in a brawl. After remonstrances from his master and his mother, James made promises that he could not keep, and the drinking and fighting continued. Soon James had lost his job.

Maria Garrison decided to remove her sons from Lynn. They would go far away, to Baltimore, with a local businessman, Paul Newhall, who intended to establish a shoe factory and wanted Mrs. Garrison to supervise the workers' dormitory. The prospect of having her sons directly under her care outweighed the pain of leaving her daughter in Newburyport and abandoning the company of Baptists who had been so dear. Elder Peak supplied their departing sister with a letter of dismission attesting that "Mrs. Francis Meriah Garrison is a regular member of the Baptist Church of Christ in Newbury & Newburyport, in good standing, & as such she is hereby recommended the fellowship and ocasional communion of any sister church of the same *Faith & Order*."

The boys and their mother, who felt herself "sick in body, dark in mind," sailed from Salem on October 9, 1815, on the brig *Edward*. The trip took fourteen days and the hauls of "fine codfish" did little to cheer the seasick Lloyd, who was accompanied in misery by two dozen fellow passengers. His mother, however, had not lost her sea legs, and having written so often of her storm-tossed soul, she took pleasure now in keeping a nautical log, filled with notations about winds, course bearings, sails and rigging, and the "very palatable" porpoise she managed to eat for breakfast amid heavy seas and the penetrating smell of bilge. Yet as the sailing finally turned pleasant in Chesapeake Bay, Sister Garrison's mood darkened again. "Everything seems to look beautiful, but alas my mind is not congenial with the scene . . . I see nothing before me but troubles and trials," she sighed, consoling herself with an old hymn: "And let our bodies part/ To different climes repair/ Inseparably joined in heart/ The friends of Jesus are."

Although Baltimore—then the third-largest city in America with nearly sixty thousand people in 1815—seemed "a place of confusion" to Maria Garrison, she maintained herself reasonably well in the booming seaport. The Newhall shoe factory failed after several months, but she found nursing work in the homes of a succession of respectable merchants. In the summer of 1816 she attended a woman at a country estate, Harmony Hall, where she ate her fill of rich people's food ("You won't recognize me," she confided to Martha. "I weigh 162 pounds") and was treated "like a lady" herself by the retinue of servants. "The birds sing so finely that it often gives me a faint idea of the paradise of our first parents," she said.

Sister Garrison went to Baptist services three times every Sunday, walking the length of Baltimore Street to get there, but she missed the society in Newburyport. The local minister, though "an excellent man and a good preacher," was no match for her shepherd on the Merrimack. "Give me my dear old father Peak," she pined. To improve her opportunities to discourse on the things of the kingdom, she established a women's prayer meeting— the first among evangelicals in Baltimore—and presided over it with passion and eloquence. Lloyd accompanied his mother to church, walking several miles in each direction, and Sister Garrison anticipated that her younger son ("a fine boy, though he is mine," she would say modestly) "will be a complete Baptist as to the tenets."

Her hopes for Lloyd rose as James's situation declined. The older boy drank rum in the sailors' dives of Fells Point until he found something he liked better: whiskey. Drunkenness and brawling cost him several clerking jobs his mother had obtained for him. Each time there would be a tearful scene, a lecture, and the inevitable promise, only to be broken by another round of misbehavior. Eventually, like his father, Abijah, James disappeared, presumably into a life at sea.

The spectacle of James's disgrace may have kept Lloyd on the straight and narrow path, but virtuous conduct did not make him happy. The boy was miserable. Freed from a cordwainer's arduous labor by the failure of Newhall's factory, Lloyd worked at store-clerking jobs arranged by his mother, but her frequent absences on jobs of her own left him lonely and homesick. "He is so discontented," Maria told Martha in April 1816, "that he would leave me tomorrow and go with strangers to N.P.; he can't mention any of you without tears." Since, above all, his mother wanted Lloyd to remain "steady," she eventually acceded to her son's desire to return "home" and go to school for at least one more year "until a door should open" for an apprenticeship in Baltimore. Canvassing her patrons until someone found passage for Lloyd under an obliging captain's supervision, Sister Garrison entrusted her young son to the keeping of God and the brethren of Newburyport.

Uncle and Aunt Bartlett welcomed eleven-year-old Lloyd back, and he resumed his place in school and church. Listening at night as the family read from John Bunyan's account of Christian's tribulations, Lloyd must have felt that he had made his own pilgrimage over the Hill of Difficulty and the Slough of Despond. Yet he still faced trials, for the Bartletts could not keep him indefinitely. His mother missed him terribly and tried to entice him back to Baltimore by finding him a clerking apprenticeship as she had for

James. Lloyd resisted. As a clerk he would have no capital at the end of his time, whereas if he learned a trade like carpentry he would be able to set himself up as an artisan and, he added coyly, help support his mother. "Your good behavior will more than compensate for all my troubles," his mother replied. "Only let me hear that you are steady and go not in the way of bad company, and my heart will be lifted up to God, for you." Along with her blessing went a grim reminder: "I have heard nothing from James. I do not know whether he is dead or alive."

Despite Lloyd's professed interest in carpentry, he lasted only a few weeks when Uncle Bartlett tried him with a cabinetmaker, Moses Short, in nearby Haverhill. Homesickness drew him like a magnet back to Newburyport. Lloyd climbed out a window and ran off to hitch a ride on the back of the daily mail coach, but his master took a "short" cut, as Garrison liked to pun in telling the story to his children years later, and recaptured the runaway. As an understanding father and fellow Baptist, however, Moses Short released Lloyd from his indenture and allowed him to return to Bartlett's without penalty.

No clerking, no carpentry, no job at all for poor Lloyd, it seemed, until in October 1818 someone saw a "Boy Wanted" placard in the office of the *Newburyport Herald* and thought of old Bartlett's lad. The boy could read; perhaps he would like to work with words more than wood shavings. Without consulting Sister Garrison, Uncle Bartlett went ahead. The door had opened; the cherubic Lloyd would become a printer's devil.

The *Herald* office on State Street was one of the nerve centers of Newburyport. From it there issued a large four-page newspaper on Tuesdays and Fridays, and in it on almost any day there could be found a merchant arranging his advertisements for new flour or Leghorn bonnets, an attorney's clerk seeking printed forms or placing an auction notice, a boy from the Custom House with news of the week's arrivals and departures, a citizen concerned that his latest disquisition had not yet seen the light of day, or a few of the Federalist Party brethren chatting with the editor, Ephraim W. Allen, about the next election or the one just past.

Allen had come to town at the turn of the century, an ambitious journeyman printer who had learned his craft in the celebrated Boston house of Thomas & Andrews, the largest printing establishment in America, with five presses and a staff of ten. Within a year of taking a job on the *Herald,* Allen had become its co-owner. Within a few more years, Allen had married his partner's youngest sister and was well launched on a printing and publishing career that would last four decades. A two-press shop like Allen's took some capital—perhaps as much as $500—to establish, but the combination of newspaper subscribers and advertising, job printing, and an occasional small book venture could yield a modest profit. Allen had done quite well for a printer; the tax collector rated his printing office as worth $1,000 in 1811, while his house and lot in Liberty Street was assessed at twice that amount.

Prosperous or not, country printers and small-town editors like Allen had become one of the bulwarks of the young republic. A free press had burgeoned during the Revolution and bloomed profusely in the ensuing generation. In 1775 the British colonies had only thirty-seven newspapers, though Lord North might have wished for even fewer, but by 1800 the United States had at least 150 newspapers, and the number had more than doubled by 1810, with no sign of letting up. By 1820, Massachusetts alone had more than fifty daily or weekly newspapers and more than 120 printing offices.

As Newburyport's editor, Allen labored on the premise that "an independent press is the surest safeguard of freedom," and he took pleasure in promoting the town's enterprises, because he believed that "commerce and the press seem to bring mankind, however distant in residence, together in one great family. . . ." No one ever called Ephraim Allen a genius, but everyone appreciated his probity, his energy, his civic-minded decency, and the cautious judgment that, in the words of a neighbor and town historian, allowed him to "keep up with the times without committing himself to the support of mere specious novelties."

To this hardworking, upright citizen fell the care of William Lloyd Garrison. For the young boy it was an opportunity as grand as Benjamin Franklin's, a move from the fringes of town life to its center, a rescue from the stark poverty that had haunted him at Bartlett's and Farnham's, a chance to learn a respectable trade and, perhaps, move into the world of letters. Yet Lloyd was overwhelmed by what lay ahead. Even sixty years later, celebrating his retirement from printing, Garrison could remember how miserable he felt upon walking into the *Herald* office for the first time: "My little heart sank like lead within me."

This would be his last chance to make good at a trade in town. If he failed or ran away, he would never be more than a day laborer unless he went off to sea like his father and brother or tried his luck out west. Lloyd knew how to be useful, and he obligingly kindled fires, swept the floor, and fetched buckets of water for his master. New boys in printing offices, however, had some especially noisome tasks. Lloyd had to tend the kettle of varnish and lampblack that boiled up into an ink that left its sticky smudges everywhere and gave the shop its oily aroma. Worse yet, Lloyd had to soften the sheepskin used for covering the rag-and-wool balls with which the ink was applied at the press. To become sufficiently pliable ("as soft as a lady's glove" was the measure) the pelts had to be soaked in urine for a fortnight, but each day the apprentice had to pull the skins out of the reeking pail, twist them in his hands to wring out some of the moisture, roll them in old newspapers, and stomp on them with his feet until they were dry enough for the next night's soaking. "Treading out a pair of skins," one apprentice recalled, "was an epoch in a printer's devil's life which he will always remember until *odor* is lost in forgetfulness."

All winter the despondent Lloyd gave good service, but he dreamed of escape. Finally, in March 1819, he told Mr. Allen that he missed his mother and wanted to return to Baltimore. Allen remonstrated with him—"I've never had a better boy," he said—and pointed out that he'd gone to some expense over the months and would have to be compensated before Lloyd could leave. By the time Maria Garrison gathered the necessary money, however, the boy had changed his mind. Lloyd could not bring himself to leave the security of Newburyport for the uncertainties of Baltimore, and surprisingly, his mother concurred. Prospects in Baltimore were "not the best," she said, and the chances of falling in with bad company were greater in the rowdy city than in straitlaced and watchful Newburyport. He had "acted wisely in staying and learning your trade," she said. "If you should meet with some things that are not so agreeable, remember that in all situations in life there is a something that is not congenial to our mind." (When yellow fever swept Baltimore a few months later, Maria was even more relieved; the boy who had taken the place she had wanted for Lloyd died in the epidemic.)

Spurred, perhaps, by the threat of losing a promising lad, Allen accelerated Lloyd's training. As Lloyd worked at his menial chores he had heard the buzz of strange words—*tympan, frisket, platen, pica, octavo, brevier*—and common words—*chase, stick, bed, quire, furniture, pie*—used strangely, and he had despaired of ever penetrating what the master called "the art and mystery of printing." Then one day, when a galley tray filled with lines of type spilled to the floor, the printer pointed to the jumble and asked Lloyd to sort the mixed-up (hence "pied") type and "distribute" each letter to its proper place in the "case."

"It seemed to me that I never should be able to do anything of the kind," Garrison recalled. The pieces of metal type had to be sorted into a pair of wooden boxes that rested on a high sloping stand at hand level. The upper case, divided into ninety-eight separate compartments, held the capital letters, numerals, various accented letters, and ornaments, while the lower case sorted the small characters into fifty-six compartments of varying sizes, the largest placed near the middle and reserved for the most frequently used letters. Lloyd proved quick, however, at the job, and from sorting pied type he moved to the comparatively easier task of "taking up," line by line, the columns of type used in Tuesday's paper so that they could be distributed and recomposed for the Friday edition. The work required intelligence and dexterity, not strength, and Lloyd found that he enjoyed grabbing the shanks of the letters, running his hand along the boxes, and, having learned to tell a *d* from a *p* and an *n* from a *u*, deftly dropping the letters into their proper places.

Once he had learned the case, Lloyd faced the challenge of the stick. With written copy in front of him, the compositor reached into the case with his right hand, selected the required letters, one at a time, and set them into a small metal tray, or composing stick, held in his left hand. Long years of learning hymns and listening to chapters of the Bible read aloud had given Lloyd the compositor's first asset, a good memory; the longer the phrase he could hold in his head, the faster his eye and hand could select slugs of type from the case. Nimbleness in grasping and placing the letters had to be matched by attentive regard for the insertion of spaces between words for legibility and to maintain the column width of the line. Lloyd had to learn to avoid the twin pitfalls of leaving so much white space that more experienced hands teased him for making "pigeon holes" or spacing so closely that the words ran on each other. Such "close setting" had another hazard: if Lloyd had inadvertently omitted a word or two, he'd have no room to maneuver it into the line and might well have to take up and reset a good bit of work in order to make things right.

He practiced first on simple jobs—forms and handbills—and then moved on to setting squares of advertisements. Then the lad tried his hand at lengthier matter, literary or historical selections that did not have to be prepared in a hurry: the account of the latest expedition to the Yellowstone River, perhaps, or the description of John Trumbull's "magnificent" new painting of the signing of the Declaration of Independence

Lloyd became an expert compositor who could, as one admiring journeyman recalled, "easily set a thousand ems an hour for several successive hours" and make only "two or three slight errors" in a whole column of matter. In learning to work to high standard with pleasure and equanimity, Lloyd had the example of a young journeyman named Tobias Miller, to whom he was "drawn magnetically from the beginning." Miller was the perfect older brother for Lloyd, who admired the man's good sense and calm spirit. Nothing could rattle him. If bad proof had to be corrected late into the night, Miller would murmur, " 'Tisn't as bad as it would be if it were worse," and a dropped paragraph or pied form would elicit only the reassuring "Never mind! 'Twill be all the same a thousand years hence!" Working alongside Toby Miller, Lloyd Garrison learned the patience and good cheer that ever afterward characterized his own work.

Lloyd grew proud of his craftsmanship, and as the months and years went by, he matched his mastery of composition with competence at makeup and presswork. Each time the typesetter had filled his stick, he transferred the lines of type to a shallow wooden "galley" tray until he had assembled enough type to form a page. Then the block of type had to be "tied off" with a piece of string and transferred onto the "imposing stone." When Lloyd first worked at the flat marble table he was still so short that he had to stand on one of the press weights in order to take proofs from his galleys. Then, after correcting the errors, he watched as Allen or the shop's foreman placed a rectangular iron frame or "chase" around the type, arranged the columns and pages to their satisfaction, and then "locked up" the form with wooden blocks ("furniture") and wedges ("quoins") that would prevent the blocks of type from sliding or falling out of place.

Slender young Lloyd did not have the strength at first to pull the levers of the large wooden press (pressmen had to weigh at least 160 pounds), but he learned the complicated fiddling maneuvers by which the form was "made ready" on the press so that the printed impression would come out evenly on the paper. Apprentices like Lloyd also learned to work alongside the "puller" at the press, applying the ink, feeding the sheet of dampened paper onto the tympan, and taking it up to dry after the pressman had pulled hard on the lever that screwed the weighted platen down onto the form to make the imprint. Gutenberg had first taken impressions of movable type in order to make a Bible, and every printer knew there was still something holy about that transforming moment when blankness turned to words. Lloyd had penetrated the mystery after all.

After the form was printed, it was cleaned and unlocked, and the type was taken up line by line and distributed into the cases, to be used on the next job. It took part of two days to print an edition of the *Herald*. At top speed an efficient team at the press could turn out a "token" (250 printed sheets) an hour, but that was considered an exhausting pace; 200 sheets an hour was more likely. With five hundred subscribers and at least another hundred sent (free, on exchange) to other editors, it would take several hours to print the *Herald*'s outside pages (one and four), which would then hang up to dry overnight, before the inside pages (two and three) could be printed on the reverse side. Since advertisements—many of which continued unchanged from one issue to the next—covered all of the front page and a good portion of pages three and four, the composition work for each issue was not overwhelming, and some job printing could be scheduled for the intervals.

The shop's foreman apportioned the time and supervised the making up of the pages. Like most country papers the *Herald* ran all its news in long single columns, broken up only by standard headings—"By the Mails," "Foreign," "Ship News," "Auctions," "Hymenal," "Obituaries," "Literary"—and the titles of the few signed communications. The editor had a column or two for his own commentary, which generally included both formal remarks upon a topic of importance and short squibs—often marked by the admonishing finger known as the printer's "fist"—that addressed the reader, or other editors, in a direct, conversational style. There were no headlines in the modern style and no attempt to present the news in order of priority. The Brighton livestock show and damage reports from the hurricane two months ago in Martinique (a local story, given Newburyport's far-flung commerce) would run alongside President Monroe's message to Congress; a dispatch from the Court of St. Petersburg would mix with an essay on the merits of fattening cattle on potatoes.

Editors counted upon their readers to pay close attention. Newspapers "were not toys and pastimes, taken up every day, and by everybody, in the short intervals of labor, and then hastily dismissed, like waste paper," the Boston journalist Samuel Goodrich, one of Garrison's contemporaries, recalled. Reading the newspaper was a respectful, even a grave occasion, to be approached with deliberation and a ceremonial affixing of the spectacles.

Along with the tricks of the trade, then, Lloyd acquired a solemn sense of vocation. The most powerful stand was no longer the inkstand but the printer's stand, Ephraim Allen liked to say, and in looking over the stories about the independence movement in South America, the editor would observe that it had taken so long because for generations there had been "but one Printing Press from Buenos Aires to Lima and that had belonged to the Jesuits. . . ." Allen reminded his boys that *The Federalist* had first appeared "in the columns of a newspaper," and he insisted that a newspaper "ought to aspire to something higher than merely pampering the public appetite for news." The newspaper, Garrison learned, "ought to be made the vehicle, and a most effective one, too, for disseminating literary, moral and religious instruction."

Although no formal articles have ever come to light, Allen accepted the paternal role masters assumed for apprentices like Lloyd and always said he felt "very partial" to the boy. Lloyd moved into the Allens' home on Summer Street—just a block or two up from the Bartletts', but a world away in material abundance. There he had the companionship of Will Allen, the printer's oldest son, who was just Lloyd's age, amid the hubbub of three younger boys and two babies whom the friendly apprentice loved to dandle on his knees. As a printer and occasional publisher Allen had books on hand, and in Lloyd's spare hours over the next five years he undertook an assiduous campaign of reading and self-education. Late into the night he read Shakespeare's plays and Milton's poems over and over until he had memorized long stretches of verse. The Allens, of course, read aloud from the Bible and sang Dr. Watts's hymns (from an edition Allen himself had published), but as a family with some literary aspirations, the household found pleasure in Robert Burns's humane songs, Thomas Moore's graceful Irish lyrics, and Walter Scott's ballads, especially *The Lay of the Last Minstrel* and *Marmion*.

After the virtuous classicism of *The Columbian Orator* and its celebrations of parliamentary eloquence and patriotic sacrifice, this heartfelt modern poetry seemed sweet indeed to adolescents like Lloyd. In it he heard, as Wordsworth taught, "the still, sad music of humanity," and from it he learned that emotions could overflow in nature's realm as well as God's. His favorite writer, Felicia Hemans, the most popular English poet of the day, allowed him to reconcile the two kingdoms. Lloyd adored Hemans's lyrics with their exquisite combination of secret sorrows and Christian piety, and he retained a fondness, too, for her predecessor William Cowper, whose gently modulated verses found both the poetry and the morality in ordinary life. Lloyd also enjoyed the evangelical novelists, such as Hannah More and Maria Edgeworth, who perfected the art of giving "instruction in the dress of innocent amusement."

This literature acted as a conservative counterweight to the more extravagant literary impulses symbolized in word and deed by Lord Byron. Like so many of his contemporaries in the English-speaking world, Lloyd fell under Byron's volcanic influence. (Byron could "no more be kept at bay than the cholera," shuddered the Boston publisher Samuel Goodrich.) The literary shock tactics of *Childe Harold*—with its wild address and outrageous reach—made a profound and lasting impression on the printer's apprentice. Lloyd read the stanzas on the Battle of Waterloo over and over again until he was "weary with excitement." Byron's verses, he thought, were "unsurpassed" for "rousing the blood like a trumpet call." Yet Lloyd managed to heed that clarion voice of liberty without succumbing to the gloomy despair of the poet's outlaw heroes or the scoffing at conventional morality that made Byron a byword for blasphemy and Satanic defiance. This was the result, perhaps, of absorbing Byronism as domesticated by Mrs. Hemans, whose long verse dramas, *The Vespers of Palermo* and *The Siege of Valencia*, depicted, with operatic grandeur, episodes of heroic insurgency and religious sacrifice.

The self-assertion that found its most titanic expression in Byron received historical grounding for readers of Lloyd's generation in the many novels by Sir Walter Scott, whose brooding, outcast heroes set their worlds aright, always by force of character and sometimes with blood shed in the name of justice. From Scott readers felt that they were getting what Lloyd called "the lights and shadows of real and varied life" instead of the creaking doors, clanking chains, and other "phantasms" of "moonstruck" romances. History itself spoke to Lloyd in the conflicts portrayed in Scott's novels as Scotch Covenanters tried to preserve their religious integrity against royalism and episcopacy (*Old Mortality*, 1816) or a devout young woman, elevating conscience above law, walked from Edinburgh to London to prevent her sister's execution by a vengeful court (*The Heart of Midlothian*, 1818).

Lloyd's education was primarily a literary one. Unlike his wellborn ally in abolitionism Wendell Phillips, a Harvard College graduate, Garrison had no grounding in Greek and Latin, no readings in history and philosophy, no courses in mathematics or natural science. To the drama of salvation he experienced in his mother's church, the printer's apprentice overlaid the melodrama of self-assertion inspired by works in his master's library. An education so radically pious on one hand and emotionally extravagant on the other intensified his faith in words as moral weapons and made him, like Childe Harold, unwilling to "yield dominion of his mind/ To spirits against whom his own rebell'd." Here was forming an agitated literary consciousness that aspired to glory and the greatness of truth, a sensibility ready to turn the moral imagination into a literary force and act upon the great Romantic credo that poets are the unacknowledged legislators of the world.

Lloyd may have aspired to poetry, but when he inevitably tried his hand at writing, he chose the more traditional form of epistolary satire and the persona not of a prophet but of a crank. In May 1822, he wrote out in disguised longhand an essay about a recent spate of breach-of-promise suits, signed it "An Old Bachelor," and slipped it under the door of the printing office. When the playful piece—executed in a mannered style Garrison had perhaps learned by copying over Franklin the way Franklin had once copied Addison—caught Allen's fancy, Lloyd rapidly set it into type and felt himself bursting with secret pride when he gazed upon his work in the *Herald*. In a day or two he had another comic diatribe from the bachelor ready, and it, too, ran in the paper directly. A week later, the anonymous correspondent, now signing himself by initials alone, "A. O. B.," tried his hand at a genuine literary sketch. "The Shipwreck" did not have much nautical verisimilitude, but its lurid drama won the editor's favor. In its description of the writer, plunged from a sound sleep in which he was dreaming of reunion with his happy family and forced onto the dark and perilous seas in a lifeboat, one senses something of the adolescent sexual urges that gripped the young artisan. "A. O. B." describes the groans of his companions and his fear that some terrible monster of the sea would swallow him. He vividly relates how he grew dizzy and felt his senses "completely worked up to a frenzy," only to climax with a "piercing shriek" and a final swoon onto the beach where, the writer says, he later awoke, relieved, "with my oar firmly grasped between my hands."

So emotional an outpouring may have frightened the young author, who remained silent for a month before slipping another batch of work under the door. The anonymous correspondent had become a fixture on the paper. Lloyd just had to tell someone of his triumph, and so he wrote a proud letter to his mother in Baltimore. She was concerned that his writing might open him to ridicule or jeopardize his job, but then added, more kindly, that she was "pleased with the idea, provided that nothing wrong should result from it." Send me the pieces, she joked, so that I can "give you my opinion whether you are an old bachelor, or . . . A may stand for Ass, and O for Oaf, and B for Blockhead."

His mother's "quizzing," as teasing was then termed, had its effect. Lloyd stopped writing. The old bachelor disappeared from the *Herald*'s pages. When local politics inspired Lloyd to take up his pen again in March 1823, he opted for a fresh *nom de plume*: "One of the People." "Rather a great signature, to be sure, for such a *small man* as myself," Lloyd humbly told his mother this time, and to forestall more quizzing, himself observed, "You will undoubtedly smile at my turning politician at the age of *eighteen*. . . ."

Maria Garrison had little patience with her son's literary ambition. Authors "generally starve to death in some garret or place that no one inhabits," she jibed, "so you may see what fortune and luck belong to you if you are of that class of people." Even worse, she considered politics a monstrous snare and warned her son that he might find himself in the grip of the Hydra. "Had you been searching the Scriptures for truth, and praying for the direction of the holy spirit to lead your mind into the path of holiness," Sister Garrison felt obliged to point out, "your time would have been more wisely spent, and your advance to the heavenly world more rapid." Yet she would not be too harsh. "I love you as dear as ever," his mother told Lloyd; if he could visit her, "be so kind as to bring on your pieces that you have written for me to see."

By 1823 Lloyd's mother was dying, and both mother and son knew it. She had written frequently of her wasting disease. She had been in the "agony of death" for forty-eight hours in November 1822, and her friends had said her pulse had actually stopped. Then she had "a shitting blood," but the Lord had spared her just so she might see her dear boy once more. Surely, she pleaded, Mr. Allen would allow Lloyd, after a separation of six years, to visit his disconsolate mother's bedside.

Allen did not want to lose his best worker for a minimum of five weeks. He had balked at previous requests for leaves, most notably in 1820 when the mother, having finally felt able to relieve the Farnhams of caring for her daughter Maria Elizabeth, had wanted Lloyd to escort his sister to Baltimore. Again, in September 1822, with news that his sister and mother were both desperately ill, Lloyd once more sought permission to visit, but this time Allen said that the young man could not be spared, as the firm was hurrying to print a book. He would allow Lloyd to go in the spring, Allen promised, but in December 1822, the master went off to settle business affairs in Mobile, leaving Lloyd as shop foreman.

Month after month went by, with Lloyd knowing that his sister had died and his mother could not survive much longer, before Allen tardily returned at the end of May. Lloyd spoke with him privately and received no sympathy. Lloyd might have gone, Allen said, if he had not been so long delayed at Mobile, but now he needed Lloyd to work on the long-planned and much-postponed expansion of the paper and would have to pay a journeyman to do it in the youth's absence. Couldn't Lloyd settle his mother's affairs without the "trouble" of a visit? his employer wondered, but finally agreed that he would write to Sister Garrison to confirm the need.

Lloyd raged privately at his master's selfishness and groused that the money saved on the apprentice's board would readily pay for the substitute. Warning his mother that Allen would feign affection and cite "fallacious obstacles" in the way of his leave, Lloyd advised his mother to press for the visit "not merely as a boon, but as a just right. . . ." She should "faithfully portray to him the feelings of a mother . . . put the case home to his own conscience, and ask him to draw the parallel, what would *he* think were he to be refused in such a case."

Seeking justice through a direct appeal to the emotions and the sympathetic appreciation of the victim's plight would always be Garrison's editorial style. Sister Garrison wrote as instructed, describing her "lonesome solitary situation" and pleading in her own forthright voice the case of the poor boy who was trying with his good behavior "to soothe his mother's path to the grave." Allen relented. He allowed that Lloyd might be spared for a short visit in June, after the newspaper's changes were in place, and asked only that he stop in Boston first in order to investigate some new type for the remodeled newspaper. Into Lloyd's head came a verse from the Psalms: "Oh! had I the wings of a dove, then would I soar away, and be with you."

Lloyd got lost in the twisting streets of Boston and never found the shop his master had asked him to visit. Then boisterous headwinds slowed his ship's passage, and it was an unbearably tedious fourteen days before the anxious young man landed in Baltimore on July 5, 1823, and made his way to the sickroom. "O God, so altered, so emaciated," Lloyd thought when he beheld his mother at last. Instead of the tall, robust, blooming woman he remembered from childhood, he found a bent and bedridden creature, "pined away to almost a skeleton" and propped up on pillows to ease her choking cough. He would never have recognized her, Lloyd said later, but there was no one else in the room.

His mother gazed upon a son also greatly changed. The scrawny eleven-year-old she had sent back home in 1816 had returned to her a grown man, and a handsome one, too, long-faced like his father, but with her own glowing eyes and lustrous brown hair. With his neat cravat, ruffled shirt, and decent coat, her Lloyd looked prosperous, even elegant, and he carried himself with a dignity that testified to his good character.

She had lived in dread that Lloyd would fall into bad company and, like poor James, lose his livelihood and become a prisoner of drink. But now Lloyd stood before her, well-mannered and well-spoken, as tender and as affectionate as a son could be. Mother and son read from the Scriptures, sang the old hymns, settled some "trifling matters" about her few possessions, and passed the time in quiet talk. She had one sister in Nova Scotia, another on Deer Island; her brother might still be alive, but the rest of Lloyd's aunts and uncles on her side were dead. She was dying virtually penniless and would leave him only a legacy of the spirit. On his father's side there remained his uncles Silas and William on the St. John River, she thought, but she had heard nothing lately about his father. (A few years earlier she had cautioned Lloyd not to give away her whereabouts, "for should your father be alive he might come on here [to Baltimore].")

Her son need worry no longer about that. Lloyd would soon be alone in "a wicked and unfriendly world," and she yearned to know that he was impressed about the salvation of his soul. She told him how piously his poor little sister had met her death, and she wished, oh how she wished, that Lloyd, too, would find grace in the Lord. His mother so wanted Lloyd to be good and to do good; she worried that his fluency with the pen would distract him into seeking "the applause of mortals." Excessive ambition in Lloyd might prove as dangerous as poor James's profligacy. Lloyd replied that writing, like his other endeavors to cultivate "the seeds of improvement," kept him from becoming a "giddy youth," but his mother was not impressed. "Dear Lloyd," she urged, "lose not the favour of God; have an eye single to his glory, and you will not lose your reward."

Well cared for by her Baptist friends, who would bury her in their churchyard, Lloyd's mother fixed her eyes firmly upon the mansions of paradise and in her fevered, weakened state saw the conducting angel "set the captive free." "Glory Glory to his name," she murmured, "a few more struggles and sighs then I shall be at rest." Lloyd had not been back in Newburyport more than a month when, in early September 1823, the final word came. Sister Garrison's boy went to the case and made up a notice (with a tidied account of the family history) to insert in the *Herald*.

> DIED. In Baltimore, 3rd inst., after a long and distressing illness, which she bore with Christian fortitude and resignation, Mrs. Frances Maria Garrison, relict of the late Capt. Abijah G., formerly of this town, aged 45.

Then William Lloyd Garrison, the budding editor, applied for the professional courtesy that would, at no additional expense, inform the distant relatives of his mother's demise: "The printers of the *Eastport Sentinel* and *St. John Star* are requested to copy this death into their respective papers."

CHAPTER THREE

A New Race of Editors

In the last years of his apprenticeship, young Garrison became a man-about-town. His circle of artisans and shopkeepers knew him for his careful dress, his extravagantly genteel manners, and his chipper, jaunty bearing, which made him a favorite at picnics, musicales, and sleighing parties. He enjoyed making puns and reciting poetry, especially his own, and his propensity for earnest, high-flown talk led some folks to twit him as "M' Lord Garrulous." His conduct verged upon the giddiness his late mother had feared, yet he seemed to be rising in the world.

Although still a youth and bound to his master, Garrison enjoyed considerable freedom. He had become the foreman of Allen's printing office, supervising the job printing as well as production of the newspaper, which put him in the thick of the town's business and politics. He had caught the editor's enterprising spirit, too, and brought together a number of rising young men into a self-improving reading circle. Garrison had "a passion for reading," another member recalled, and "borrowed books from everyone he knew even slightly."

Eventually the group institutionalized itself as the Franklin Debating Club, and in 1824 extended its founder the honor of making the club's Fourth of July Address. The jubilant salute of cannon and church bells made the morning vibrate with excitement as Garrison rose in the meeting room above Gilman's store to make his debut as a public speaker. Though he was not tall, his foursquare stance and compact physique gave him a formidable look, as did his long, earnest face, with its prominent nose, thin-lipped straight mouth, firmly molded chin, and thrust jaw. He stood, as was his habit, "as erect as an Indian," his cheeks glowing pink against his parchment-pale skin, his new silver spectacles glinting in the morning light as he spread his arms wide and rapturously praised the occasion, the flag, and the mighty sound of "freedom's awakening trumpet-call."

This was a young man's speech to a young man's group, and Garrison felt obliged to affirm his generation's willingness to make sacrifices in freedom's name as the Revolutionary Fathers had done. Instead of rehearsing the well-known drama of the independence saga, however, the young orator pursued a more contemporary theme: how the Revolution's torch had "illumined, electrified, and warmed the world!" The past few years had witnessed national revolutions in South America, uprisings—in the name of liberal constitutionalism—in Portugal, Piedmont, Sicily, and Spain itself, and a Greek insurgent movement that sought independence from the Turkish overlord. Everywhere, it seemed to idealistic young men like Garrison, Liberty and Equality did battle against Throne and Altar in a contest for which America stood as "the splendid, immaculate guide." He painted a harsh picture of the "leagued Banditti" of conservative European powers which had executed Riego, the Spanish officer who had led the uprising at Cádiz, and massacred or enslaved thousands of rebellious Greeks on the island of Chios. These forces of reaction, Garrison told his fellow patriots, would be vanquished by "heaven's artillery," as nature, reason, and a just God awakened slumbering peoples and inspired them to "thunder 'Equality' through the land." With Byronic fervor he quoted the poet as his ultimate inspiration: "For Freedom's battle once begun,/ Bequeath'd from bleeding sire to son,/ Though baffled oft, is ever won."

For a boy of limited experience and even less education, Garrison had made a remarkably self-assured address. It confirmed the young printer's intuition that he could put his most ardent hopes into words, and it linked his own ambitious striving with the world's forward march. Although the talk was a sideshow to the procession and pulpit orations staged by the town elders later in the day, Garrison's performance superbly vindicated the Franklinesque method of self-improvement. The club members so much admired it that they took up a subscription for its publication, and the orator had the exquisite pleasure of personally composing and printing it at the *Herald* office.

The spirit of the Revolution manifested itself before him when the Marquis de Lafayette, the transatlantic avatar of liberty who was touring the United States as "the guest of the nation," visited Newburyport a few weeks later. The selectmen ordered a great triumphal arch of flowers erected across State Street, and a festive banquet for *le bon ton* took shape at Wolfe's Tavern. Garrison stood with hundreds of others along State Street for hours on August 31,1824, awaiting "the hero of two continents," whose party was delayed by festivities at nearly every crossroads on the post road from Salem. A drenching rain began to fall, the floral arch sagged, but no one gave up his place. Late in the evening, finally, the signal gun roared from Oldtown Hill, and the townsfolk lit their torches and illuminated their windows with candles. Lafayette arrived in a low carriage that enabled him to reach out to well-wishers without leaving his seat. The marquis—his face puffy and his paunch substantial, but a living link to the Revolution nonetheless— looked at the people with inexpressibly Gallic tenderness, and Garrison never forgot how the old hero's big, mournful eyes brimmed with tears at their devotion. The inclemency and the late hour made a reception impossible that evening, Lafayette was understood to have said, but the general would be pleased to greet them all in the morning at his lodgings. Although the rain curtailed the morning's marching and testimonials, Garrison was among the hundreds of citizens received at the Tracy mansion on State Street. He felt as if he had touched the hand of George Washington himself.

Seven years earlier, in August 1817, Garrison had lined up with his fellow schoolboys to strew flowers in the path of President James Monroe, who passed through town on an inaugural tour of New England. The new president, though a Virginia Republican like his predecessors Jefferson and Madison, wanted to ease the strains of the late war, and the commercial-minded Federalists of maritime Massachusetts responded well to Monroe's gesture, so effusively greeting the man who had helped shape the ruinous commercial boycott and war that a Boston editor gushed that "the era of good feelings" had dawned. The phrase had caught on, and despite the stresses of a severe economic depression in 1819, the old party tensions had subsided so much that "Federal Republicans" and "National Republicans" seemed to be amalgamating into one party united in pursuit of economic growth and republican virtue.

Not in Newburyport, however, where partisanship never subsided. For many of Newburyport's old Federalists the political clock had stopped with the War of 1812. They refused at first to support New England's favorite, John Quincy Adams, in the presidential contest of 1824 because sixteen years earlier that apostate had supported Jefferson's Embargo Act as the diplomatic alternative to war. Although they still believed that government should be conducted by the wisest, most public-spirited, and—like as not—the wealthiest men of the community, the Federalists had organized themselves to exploit the modern vote-gathering techniques of popular meeting, leafleting, precinct mobilization, and partisan argument in the newspapers. Campaigning for Harrison Gray Otis, the high-toned Federalist candidate in the 1823 Massachusetts governor's race, Garrison had styled himself "One of the People," in a nod to the emerging new style of popular politics. These were the articles that had so worried his mother, but the young man persisted, for he believed the Federalists to be "the friends and disciples of Washington," who were defending "correct principles" against the blight of deistical Republican office-seekers. No matter that Washington had died a quarter century earlier or that the Republicans ran a man friendly to the evangelical sects while the Federalist Otis had ties to the Unitarian rationalists of Harvard. The *Herald* and its employees hewed to the Federalist cause. Eventually they mustered some tepid support for Adams in the 1824 contest against the popular military hero Andrew Jackson, though Garrison's articles merely parroted the arguments of others. When the deadlocked race was broken by the choice of Adams in the House of Representatives, even the most bitter diehards, including editor Allen, conceded that the ascension of the "National" Republicans, as opposed to Jackson's "Democratic" Republicans, and the continued drift of Massachusetts factions into an amalgamated statewide "unity" ticket signaled the end of Federalism.

Garrison's political pamphleteering subsided. He had demonstrated that he could mount the barricades with Lord Byron or shadow-box with political ghosts with equal facility, and in the excitement of wielding the pen he seemed unaware that his ideas were inconsistent and naive. In the last few months of his apprenticeship he wrote only a few pieces on bookish topics, save for one more satire on marriage by the old bachelor, which allowed the young man on the verge of independence to vent his hesitations and revived, perhaps, some long-buried recollections of his earliest years: Socrates and Xantippe as surrogates for Abijah and Fanny.

Then, at last, in December 1825, Garrison was twenty-one, or thought he was,° and hailed his coming-of-age in eight stanzas of fervent Byronic address on the front page of the *Herald*. Resolved to stand against the material temptations of the world, the poet depicted himself as "the *Spirit of Independence*," a proud and glorious being, eagle-eyed beneath a mild and open brow, who would never cringe before temptation or oppression. "Nor wealth shall awe my soul, nor might, nor power," he declared, "And should thy whelps assail—lank poverty!/ Or threatening clouds of dark oppression lower,—/ Yet these combined—defied! shall never make [me] cower." Although he had "turned author" against his mother's wishes, Garrison was groping for a literary credo that would nonetheless honor her spirit of moral warfare.

He had celebrated the end of his apprenticeship by allowing his friend William Swain, an aspiring artist who had a tiny studio above the *Herald* office, to practice on his countenance. The result was predictably pedestrian as a likeness—though the artist caught the gleam in Garrison's eye and the high blush to his cheek—but as a portrait of a young man poised for success, it is revealing. Garrison's dark hair was already receding from his high forehead, but he wore it in a Byronic upsweep. He eschewed the poet's famous open collar, however, for the tightly wrapped cravat favored by genteel ministers and politicians. His face bore an earnest expression, yet the artist found some hesitation in it, as if the young printer were wearing borrowed clothes that he had not yet made his own.

What would this Yankee Childe Harold do with his newfound independence? He dreamed of sailing off to Greece to join the fight against Turkish tyranny and wrote a poem in the voice of a Grecian youth "fired with Freedom's flame." The prospect looked glorious, complete with "a Spartan maid" ready to shed tears over the martyred soldier's grave, but in practice the idea proved too daunting for a just-released apprentice who became deathly seasick on even a coastal schooner. He thought, briefly, of trying for an

---

°Garrison's apprenticeship of seven years and two months was fixed to end on December 10, 1825, a date that both Deacon Bartlett and E. W. Allen had believed to be his twenty-first birthday. The matter remained confused until Garrison accepted 1805 as his birth year after a visit to his Nova Scotia relatives in 1834.

appointment to the military academy and becoming an army officer, but a penniless orphan with the most tenuous political connections had no chance. Garrison really wanted to start a newspaper of his own fearlessly dedicated to independence and truth, but he had no capital and no place to start. Until a door should open for him, he prudently decided to stay on as a journeyman printer at the *Herald*. He would work for straight wages, of course, and since Allen no longer had any obligations to provide room and board, Garrison would move back to "Aunt" Farnham's house.

The Baptist Society had grown but fitfully in the years after Sister Garrison had departed, but the Farnham household remained a center of faith. Martha Farnham still conducted prayer meetings, now assisted by her daughter Harriet, Garrison's childhood playmate. She had married Jacob Horton, a steady mechanic, in 1824 and had a daughter of her own, for whom Garrison became a playful "Uncle Willy."

The young man had never really left either the Farnham family circle or the Baptist fellowship. Elder John Peak had exhausted himself in raising funds to rebuild the church, this time on Congress Street in the town center, and in 1818 he had accepted a call to another pulpit. Several fervent young men had succeeded him, and while the number of conversions never approached the earlier rain of righteousness, the society remained a source of light for the children who had grown up in it. Garrison had regularly attended services during his apprenticeship; he called himself "a *dry* Baptist by education," a religiously inclined individual, that is, who was zealous for immersion as the acceptable sacrament, but who had never received it himself. His close friends—Isaac Knapp, William Cocker, Tobias Miller—also stayed in the church, and the young men began to think of ways in which their piety might make itself felt in works of religious benevolence.

Garrison felt no call to preach the gospel, but, like many other pious folk of New England, he heeded the mandate to be his brother's keeper. To protect the Sabbath Day from profanation, to bring Bibles and Sunday schooling to the unchurched, to spare families from the decay caused by drink, to aid the work of charity in the crowded cities and the spread of light in heathen lands across the sea all seemed worthy endeavors to idealistic young men still unsure of their vocations. Toby Miller was thinking about becoming a "city missionary" somewhere, and Will Cocker wondered about a gospel mission to Liberia, and Garrison, whose growing inclination toward a Quakerlike pacifism was further cooling his ardor to take up the sword in Greece, mused about a Christian calling for the work of uplift and improvement.

Garrison continued to work at the *Herald* until springtime, when opportunity's door opened right up the street. His friend Isaac Knapp had taken over the *Northern Chronicler,* a National Republican sheet that had flourished briefly during the Adams campaign and had unsuccessfully tried to attract an independent readership under the fresh name *Essex Courant.* If

Garrison wanted to take over the small printing office a few doors up from the *Herald* and try his hand at newspapering, Knapp would gladly sell. The putative buyer knew himself to be a better writer and compositor than Knapp, whose columns tended to be made up clumsily with thick display types scattered like ink blots across the page, and he jumped at the idea of an editorial chair of his own. He broached the idea with Allen, who endorsed it and, eager to have one of his own pupils at the helm of a formerly Republican paper, agreed to lend Garrison the purchase money.

Allen gave his protégé a nice send-off in the *Herald*, which announced on March 17, 1826, that Isaac Knapp's ill health had prompted him to relinquish his newspaper to "Mr. William L. Garrison, who enters upon this undertaking with a full knowledge of the business and with such talents as, we think, cannot fail to ensure an estimable journal." But the editor's real tribute had come the previous week, when the *Herald* had carried an advertisement seeking "a smart, active, & intelligent boy of 14 or 16 years of age, as an apprentice to the printing business."

Garrison did not like to be beholden to anyone, and his arrangement with Allen remained confidential. To dispel, even from his own mind, the notion that he might be someone's cat's-paw, however, Garrison would call *his* paper the *Free Press*. In a salutation to his subscribers (a list "by no means bulky," the editor conceded), Garrison admitted that his extreme youth made him less than "fitly qualified" for the task at hand, but hoped that earnest determination and integrity would compensate for a lack of worldly experience. Yet for all the protestations of independence, Garrison devoted the leading space in his first issue to an old Federalist gripe: the reluctance of Congress to repay Massachusetts the money the state had advanced to defend the coastline during the War of 1812. By dredging the issue up all over again and giving much space in subsequent numbers to the official correspondence and debates that reiterated the old arguments over the legitimacy of the Hartford Convention, Garrison's *Free Press* was declaring its interest as clearly as if it had pinned the old Federalist black cockade to every sheet.

With its banner proclaiming "Our Country, Our Whole Country, and Nothing But Our Country," Garrison intended his newspaper to be a vehicle of the patriotic renewal he had hailed in his Fourth of July Address two years before. Although he knew the old political landmarks were fading, Garrison nonetheless tended to equate "lynx-eyed" patriotic vigilance with the Federalism he had absorbed from his town. He consistently warred against opportunism and professed the old-fashioned Federalist's dislike for the political horse-trading he derided as "You scratch my back, and I'll tickle your elbow."

The *Free Press* had a bold ring, but it looked a good deal like the comfortably familiar *Herald*. Like Allen, Garrison laid out his pages neatly, with the matter sorted into various "departments." Like the *Herald*, the *Free Press* offered extracts from important speeches, kept track of the port's traffic, advertised the local grocers' latest wares, and offered its readers an entertaining miscellany of geographical curiosities, home remedies, and literary anecdotes. Garrison had learned his trade well. He put out an attractive sheet, folded once to make four eleven-by-seventeen-inch pages, nicely printed and composed so cleanly that he could jest in his columns about the occasional typographical howler that turned someone's *claims* into *clams*. When a dropped word made it appear that Nathaniel Macon had been chosen president of the U.S. (instead of the U.S. Senate), Garrison indulged his fondness for puns in a playful paragraph about the "C of troubles" he had encountered for elevating Macon above Clay, Calhoun, Clinton, and Crawford. He composed his own editorials—about twenty-five column inches weekly—at the case, and he spoke in a lively and self-assured manner from the outset, writing with more flair than his mentor and indulging, as Allen never did, in humorous turns: "We never penned a paragraph with greater warmth of feeling," Garrison began a column on July's heat wave. "Fat people seem as if they would melt, and lean ones look as if they would dry up."

The *Free Press* took a decided interest in poetry. The editor decorated his essays with quotations from Shakespeare and Pope, and he scanned the literary magazines for the best of modern poetry. In the easy days before international copyright, Garrison could simply clip the poems he liked and reprint them. He ran Byron's aching lamentation "To Thyrza," and many poems about innocence and loss, fidelity and truth, by the enormously popular Felicia Hemans. Although Garrison affected disdain for "newspaper poetry," he almost at once became a sponsor of local talent. He printed a lament about the slave trade, out of concern for the subject, but also with interest in the "young lady of fine talents" who submitted it. Then, in early June 1826, the editor found an envelope slipped under his door. Inside lay a poem, "The Exile's Departure," a Scott-like song about isolation and patriotism, written in pale ink by a timid hand, signed only "W. Haverhill." Recalling his own surreptitious effort to break into print, Garrison read the work with sympathy and published it straightaway with a note inviting the anonymous contributor to continue the favor. The next post brought "The Deity," a blank-verse tribute to the "still, small voice of conscience," and the post after that brought a sweet reminiscence of youth.

The editor could not contain his curiosity. He badgered the post rider for information and learned that the correspondent was a young Quaker shoemaker, only a year or two younger than the editor, named John Greenleaf Whittier, whose sister, it turned out, had found the boy's poems stashed away in the attic and, from motives only a sibling can understand, sent one in to the newspaper. Whittier found himself speechless with embarrassment and pride when he saw his efforts in print, and he had to wriggle into his Sunday coat when his parents called him from the workshed to meet the lordly editor himself.

Garrison had driven out to Haverhill to give the shy bard encouragement.

The boy's father, a poor farmer, was no more impressed with "W." 's poetry than Garrison's mother had been about "A. O. B." 's sketches, and to Friend Whittier the dandified, bespectacled editor seemed an emissary from the nether world. Garrison spoke earnestly of the need to nurture talent and predicted that the young shoemaker, with more education and encouragement, could become as famous in America as Bernard Barton, the gentle Quaker poet, had become in England. Whittier's father replied, "Sir, poetry will not give him *bread.*"

For once in his life Garrison was silenced. As he rode home to Newburyport his departed mother's warning that starving authors would be lost to God rang sharply in his ears. He was struggling himself to attain influence and celebrity without losing the piety that his mother cherished. He had to believe himself called to "the station of an editor" as powerfully as others felt called to the pulpit. He would be part of a "new race of editors" who would be neither "political adventurers" nor "loose moralists," but men of "nobler views" who would give their voice to "every moral enterprise" and "fearlessly maintain the truth." That was why he often recited aloud and repeated in print Shakespeare's credo "What stronger breastplate than a heart untainted!/ Thrice is he armed that hath his quarrel just,/ And he but naked, though locked up in steel,/ Whose conscience with injustice is corrupted." And that was why he filled his poetry column with the unaffected, heartfelt verses that continued to come in a trembling hand from Haverhill.

Although friends treasured his sweet temper and sympathetic understanding, Garrison deliberately created for his readers the editorial personality of a tiger who loved nothing more than a good fight. He would learn how to inspire with his eloquence, but from the outset he seemed instinctively to know how to pick an editorial quarrel, how to annoy, to agitate, to grab hold of any issue and worry it column after column, issue after issue, as each week's pile of newspapers exchanged through the mail brought replies from the editors attacked and fresh retorts and counterarguments from Garrison. It was a stylized combat known as "slang-whanging"—intensely partisan and often laced with personal invective—in which men wielding type sticks in widely distant towns provided an invigorating spectacle for their readers and gave freedom of the press a robust and exhilarating definition.

One of the first to feel the sting of the editor's pen labored at the case just down the street. Garrison suddenly turned on his former master (and lienholder), E. W. Allen, and mocked "the panegyrics" the *Herald* had indulged in at the simultaneous deaths—on the Fourth of July, no less—of Thomas Jefferson and John Adams in 1826. That their demise occurred on the fiftieth anniversary of American independence struck the public mind as the most remarkable coincidence in the nation's short history, and the newspapers could not print enough in the way of eulogies, anecdotes, correspondence, and biographical sketches of the two statesmen. The *Free Press* offered its readers a generous measure of extracts, including the much-praised eulogy delivered in Newburyport by the rising young attorney Caleb Cushing, but Garrison editorially took a jaundiced view of the crocodile tears many editors now shed and declared that he would not "bedaub the grave of either of these men" with flattery, falsehood, or hypocrisy. Editor Allen, in his pupil's view, had indulged in this trio of vices, canonizing Jefferson without acknowledging that he had abhorred the man for years and denounced him many times over in his apprentice's hearing as "the Great Lama of Infidelity." Allen's "burlesque" picture of "all heaven" rejoicing at Jefferson's arrival "prostituted" the language; if the editor of the *Herald* now found that he had mistaken Jefferson's character all these years, perhaps next week he would "renounce the sin of Federalism," chided Garrison. That stung Allen, who replied that he needed no "schooling" from "the young gentleman" up the street in the defects of Jefferson's administration. " 'So ripe a scholar, and yet so young,' " Allen clucked, warning Garrison not to make his reputation at his mentor's expense.

However driven by the young editor's accumulated resentments, the quarrel became more than a personal matter when Garrison realized that Allen was indeed getting right with Jefferson in order to cast off his own settled political identity. Something was afoot in the old precincts of Newburyport's Federalists, and Garrison had got wind of it. He published a warning to the incumbent Federalist congressman, an attorney from Haverhill named John Varnum, that a "little knot" of politicians in Newburyport, prominently connected by interest and family, had "secretly consolidated" against him and would defy custom by putting forward a candidate of their own. The "honest substantial yeomanry" of the district, said Garrison, were about to be victimized by "a set of interested jugglers."

Bringing the scheme to light, however, cost Garrison his editorial chair, for the local candidate was, much to his surprise, Caleb Cushing. The son of a prominent shipping merchant, Cushing had charming manners, a Harvard education, a quick pen that produced literary essays and legal briefs with equal facility, and an ambition so ill concealed that tart-tongued Hannah Gould, the town poetaster, wrote one of her sportive "epitaphs" mocking it: "Lie aside all ye dead/ For in the next bed/ Reposes the body of Cushing/ He has crowded his way/ Through the world as they say/ And even though dead will be pushing." Cushing had run the *Herald*'s editorial affairs in 1822–23 while Garrison, only a few years his junior, still worked as shop foreman. The apprentice disliked the arrogant newcomer, who had taken over Garrison's place as Allen's trusted lieutenant and whose pedigree, poise, and learning accentuated Garrison's feelings of inadequacy, but Mr. Allen admired him greatly. So much so that now, in September 1826, he quietly supported the idea of denying reelection to the Federalist incumbent by running Cushing for Congress on a local "amalgamated" ticket of Republicans and Federalists.

Garrison's jibes, it turned out, had struck more deeply than he had first realized. Allen *was* changing his political tune, and it seemed that his mentor had expected Garrison to sing from the same book. If Allen had assumed the *Free Press* would become a pro-Cushing sheet, however, he had seriously misread its editor. When Garrison alerted the Federalist regulars to the brewing revolt, he embarrassed the Cushing people and turned his "brother editor" Allen into an outraged creditor.

Garrison abruptly announced in his September 14 editorial column that "influenced by considerations of importance only to himself and wishing to alter his present line of business," he was putting the *Free Press* up for sale. Since he had only the week before taken encouraging note of his six months' tenure and expressed satisfaction at the "regular and flattering increase in subscriptions," it seems inescapable, though no proof exists, that Allen called in his loan to Garrison and forced the young editor into a quick sale to the friends of Cushing.

The very next issue, on September 21, announced that Garrison had transferred the newspaper to John H. Harris, a journeyman from Gloucester. Harris declared that he would revert to the original design "established by republicans" for a second newspaper in town and that with "the efforts of those gentlemen from whom he has the expectation and promise of assistance" he would be altering "the general tone" of the sheet. For a weathervane, however, the reader needed to look no further than the paragraph hailing Caleb Cushing's brand-new history of the town, just published by E. W. Allen.

Word went around town that Garrison, being "no friend" to Cushing, had been "displaced," but Garrison kept publicly to the story that he had decided to "sell" for wholly personal reasons. "Displaced" sounded as if he had not operated independently in the first place. He didn't want anybody to think "that any man or set of men, had the control of the Free Press while I published it," he explained. Yet he did not pass up any opportunity to point out that anyone who endeavored to maintain a truly *free press* in Newburyport could not count upon "speedy wealth or preferment."

Garrison's protests could not turn the town against Cushing, but the candidate's own opportunistic maneuvers seriously discredited him in the rest of the district, and he lost by more than a thousand votes. The *Free Press* shut down after the election; the hapless Harris, who had anticipated a longer tenure, lamented that he was not "sufficiently forewarned of the consequences of his undertaking."

The election imbroglio had soured Garrison on politics. The spectacle of high-minded men modifying their principles while ridiculing their opponents for apostasy is seldom edifying, and Garrison had come up in a particularly rigid and unbending school. To hear the town leaders apply the new rationale—the temper of the times did not warrant maintenance of the old party distinctions—in support of a self-aggrandizer like Cushing was more cant than Garrison could bear. The real problem, though, was that Federalism had collapsed, and the emerging political identities all seemed rooted in a scramble for economic advantage that repelled the idealistic young printer.

Garrison found himself out of work, but he had gained a sense of the editor's calling on the *Free Press* and knew that his future lay in that direction. While he might have to labor as a journeyman at someone else's case for a while, he had done well enough to harbor aspirations for another printing office and editorial chair of his own. As his mother had hoped, he had gained the respectability of the printer's trade, but as his mother had feared, he still dreamed of the poet's influence and glory. He had found his vocation in "thoughts that breathe, and words that burn," to use Thomas Gray's much-quoted phrase. Yet writers, as Whittier's father had so tersely observed, had to earn their keep; if Garrison were not to succumb to the first bites of lank poverty's whelps, he would have to find work—any kind of work—before he could contemplate any more political or moral warfare.

CHAPTER FOUR

MY SOUL WAS ON FIRE THEN

GARRISON HAD ONLY ONE PLACE TO TURN: BOSTON. THE CITY WAS THE CENTER OF THE PRINTING TRADE AND THE PIVOT OF THE GATHERING BENEVOLENCE MOVEMENT; BOSTON WAS SO MUCH THE INTELLECTUAL AXIS of New England that its proudest citizens nurtured the conceit that the State House dome atop their Beacon Hill was "the hub of the solar system." Boston! Garrison had gone there only twice. The first time, on his way to Baltimore in 1823, he had gotten lost in the old town's mystifying cobweb of streets, and the second time, on a larky summer's outing with Isaac Knapp, he had walked the forty miles to the city in boots so tight that he lay in agony in their cheap lodgings and could not bear to step out for a look at the capital's attractions. The third time would have to be different.

Boston had nearly sixty thousand inhabitants in 1826, which made it ten times as large as Garrison's Newburyport, but only one-third the size of New York and Philadelphia—the nation's largest cities. In many respects Boston was an overgrown maritime town, but unlike Newburyport, which seemed to be suffocating in the amber preserve of the eighteenth century, Boston possessed a vital energy that would propel it into the steam age and, by 1860, make it a metropolis of 180,000 people and the center of New England's industrial revolution. The pulse of new ideas that would soon generate a renaissance in American letters also beat strongly in Boston, although the city's ruling class—the braided aristocracy of Quincys, Appletons, Otises, Cabots, and Lowells—brooked few challenges to its tastes and remained more suspicious of intellectual and social innovations than it did of fresh ways of making money. Yet, paradoxically, there was much in the New England tradition that supported change: the Puritan method of literate argument in the service of spiritual examination, the moral idealism of the American Revolution in pursuit of human rights, and the stubborn, even cranky insistence, common to both movements, on the necessity of self-expression for conscience' sake. The Puritan tradition of authoritarian rule, best exemplified by generations of Mathers, coexisted uneasily with the heritage of outspoken Protestant dissent, and the provincial Toryism of Boston's nineteenth century elite contrasted sharply with the Revolutionary heritage of the ancestors it worshiped. In such a crucible of incompatible elements William Lloyd Garrison would attempt to forge his career. Between 1826 and 1829, Boston framed the path that led him from a benign interest in human betterment to a burning concentration on racial injustice, from a diffuse ideology of benevolent uplift to the pointed one of immediate abolition of slavery, and from the limited horizons of a small-town printer to the ambitious universe of a crusading national editor.

Garrison rose before dawn one day in December 1826 to catch the stagecoach, which kept him shivering and jouncing all day on a miserably hard seat before depositing him at nightfall in Dock Square, adjacent to the patriot's Mecca, Faneuil Hall. With the square's customary hubbub now stilled in the freezing darkness and the stalls of the huge granite Quincy Market shuttered against the night, the city hardly seemed hospitable to a red-cheeked boy from the provinces. Fortunately the young printer had a nearby destination: a boardinghouse in an alley off Union Street kept by Thomas Bennett, a Baptist man of letters and journeyman printer, who had worked on the *Herald* and would help Garrison get started in the city.

The newcomer lived on Bennett's charity while he scoured the printing district, going "from office to office day after day, week after week," Garrison recalled, in a desperate search for work. Boston had dozens of periodicals—several daily sheets, a number of weekly religious heralds and commercial gazettes, and a crop of monthly literary reviews—along with numerous job printing firms and several type foundries. Garrison got acquainted with many of them, filling in at a shop when a regular employee was sick or drunk, or when an extra man was needed for an urgent piece of work. Eventually he found a regular place as a compositor in Eastburn's book and job office on Congress Street, repaid Bennett, and settled into his new city.

With a population ten times that of Newburyport packed into an area only three times as large, Boston proved formidable. The city's wrinkled topography, its unceasing traffic, and its hordes of people made the place cramped and difficult to negotiate. Although Newburyport had its wealthy neighborhood and its waterfront dives, its regular street plan made it a simple business to walk from one to the other in a very few minutes and to have a complete view of the town in mind. Boston, by contrast, had distinct neighborhoods, which the labyrinthine streets kept as social islands, and one had to walk farther to get anywhere. It was at least fifteen minutes from the docks up the hill to the Common, a vast parkland compared to Newburyport's narrow mall, and an even longer walk back to Dock Square if one crossed the brow of Beacon Hill past the State House and came down the back side of the hill and across the triangular expanse of the old Mill Pond, now nearly filled with gravel excavated by land developers and tons of oyster shells, manure, and offal dumped in by the municipal street cleaners.

The old colonial town had, by Garrison's day, spread across a low-lying peninsula that thrust out into the Charles River like a clenched fist; in the past two decades well-constructed bridges had opened the fist and given the booming city extended fingers into the New England hinterland, and day after day bulky wagons filled with country produce rumbled into town intent upon sales at the market or the long wharves that jabbed eastward into the harbor. Freight from the ocean-borne commerce intensified traffic in the opposite direction, sending an endless cargo of European comforts into Yankee cabins, for only New York and New Orleans outranked Boston among American ports for tonnage. The two streams mingled in Dock Square, while the proceeds from the transactions fueled the exchanges in adjacent State Street, where nearly a dozen new banks and insurance companies had sprung up to gain a share of the trade and underwrite new lines of development, especially in the textile mills powered by the waterfalls of Garrison's much-loved Merrimack.

Above the square lay the North End, the oldest part of the city, where the Mathers lay buried on Copps Hill and Paul Revere had watched for signal lanterns in the needlelike spire of Christ Church. Once home to the leather-aproned artisans who had formed the backbone of the Sons of Liberty, the North End had declined since the days of Revere and Sam Adams. The master carpenters and masons, the cabinetmakers, the hatters, the lace-makers, the silversmiths, and other specialty craftsmen had moved into better sections to the west and south, leaving the North End's narrow alleys to less well paid maritime and market workers, while the cheap rooming houses along Hanover and Ann streets sheltered an amorphous mass of young men drawn to Boston in hopes of making their fortunes.

Catching the ambitious drift, Garrison did not stay long with Brother Bennett. As soon as his finances permitted, he found a more genteel situation at 30 Federal Street, just below Milk Street, on the southern edge of the business district and not far from the birthplace of Benjamin Franklin, the prototype of the American self-made man, who had learned the printing trade in the neighborhood in which Garrison now tried to make his way. He moved into a boardinghouse run by the Rev. William Collier, a Baptist preacher who published several religious newspapers and had become a gospel missionary to the poor families of Boston. Collier had known Elder Peak of Newburyport, and Garrison had the opportunity for a tender reunion with his mother's beloved pastor when Peak spent five weeks in Boston filling the pulpit of an indisposed colleague.

At Collier's Garrison found himself among people whose minds were "awake to the moral movements of the world." Collier himself was an amiable and generous soul, self-effacing yet fatherly, who attracted a coterie of young men eager to improve society. The talk lasted long into the night as the boarders and their guests probed the issues of war and peace, poverty and plenty, the proper organization of school and church and society. In this milieu of printers and preachers Garrison found not only a more abundant version of the Baptist fellowship he had enjoyed in Newburyport, but a city so alert to spiritual issues that Garrison and his friends considered preaching to be "the most interesting entertainment that Boston had to offer." Taking inspiration wherever they could, they made regular rounds of the city's pulpits and witnessed the latest phase in New England's long-standing battle between orthodoxy and liberalism.

New England had been born in separatism and nurtured in piety, but each generation had contended with dissenting concepts of faith and the "hiving off"—or casting out—of those souls who yearned for a more perfectionist and anti-institutional Christianity. The seventeenth century had seen its greatest challenge from Quakers and Anabaptists, the eighteenth century had endured itinerant Baptist and Methodist revivalists, and the most recent generations struggled with Universalists and Shakers and Mormons and Disciples of Christ and dozens of ephemeral sects that gathered for a season under a charismatic shepherd, then dispersed or merged with others. As Garrison came to manhood, however, the most compelling threat to New England's traditional religious order came not from the mystics, but from the rationalists. Under the influence of Enlightenment ideas and their own material prosperity, more than 125 Congregational churches had by the 1820s renounced the Holy Trinity and embraced a Unitarian creed that emphasized genteel moralism over fervent piety as a sign of one's salvation and permitted the commercial and professional elite to feel less dependent upon God and more impressed with its own power. Garrison observed the religious upheaval from the populist side of the denominational spectrum, a more antinomian vantage point well to the left of the contending parties, yet as he made the rounds of Boston's pulpits with his Baptist friends he became caught up in the competition between the orthodox champion Lyman Beecher and the Unitarian eminence William Ellery Channing. Each had an enriching influence upon Garrison's commitment to benevolent reform, though the young man would quickly surpass both in the application of their teachings.

Beecher, a rotund and somewhat absent-minded soul in his early fifties, had come to the capital in 1826 from a series of country pastorates to reinvigorate orthodox Christianity in the city whose churchmen had done the most to justify the region-wide declension from the stern commands of Calvinist piety to the rationalist mildness of Unitarianism. Yet Beecher also sought to vindicate the patient, intellectually rigorous methods of the Puritan fathers and avoid the revivalist excesses of itinerant preachers who would rouse and manipulate their congregations with extravagant dramatic devices that Yale-trained theocrats like Beecher considered impious or heretical. They were particularly concerned by the astonishing popularity of Charles Grandisson Finney, an upstate New York attorney-convert who claimed that he had received a retainer to plead Christ's cause and was leading remarkably successful revivals across western New York that portended another great awakening and rearrangement of the institutional church. Beecher and his colleagues thus wanted to revive orthodoxy without igniting the revivalist enthusiasm that might jeopardize their control of the church.

It was a tall order, but somehow Beecher managed it. He conducted week-long prayer meetings, preached with enormous vigor, and initiated what his wife called "a season of wonderful talking" that brought piety and soul-searching to the forefront of religious experience. He also advanced the benevolent idea that "the way to get good was to do good"—a concept that had once offended the stern Calvinism of the Mathers, but one that the New England theology had gradually accommodated—and he considered a sermon that did not induce anybody to do anything as a waste of time. Beecher, too, liked to demonstrate vitality in his person. He walked briskly, enjoyed fiddling a tune he called "Go to the devil and shake yourself," and ostentatiously "worked off the energy" generated by his preaching by sawing huge loads of wood in his front yard or doing chin-ups in his cellar.

The Unitarian leaders regarded Beecher as a bumpkin and buffoon, but there was no denying his power. He had converted hundreds. Church membership rolls were swelling in all the Congregationalist meetinghouses, and when a prominent merchant named Lewis Tappan—disgusted by liberal worldliness—reconverted from Unitarianism to the orthodox faith of his youth, it was clear that Beecher had accomplished his mission in Boston. He had restored "the spirit of the pilgrims" and dramatized the connection between religious piety and civic health, insisting that Christians could not, by their inaction, remain accessories to social evils. Indeed, it was Beecher's emphasis upon "disinterested benevolence" that had fetched Tappan, who explained in a very popular pamphlet that he had realized that the liberals were puffed up by "Pharisaical pride" and indifferent to the needs of others. Tappan, who would soon join his wealthy brother Arthur as a major director and benefactor of charitable reforms on a nationwide basis, declared that in contrast to the Unitarians' cold and self-centered ethic, the orthodox "stand up for morality and piety, fearlessly, and at the risk of unpopularity."

Like other newcomers struggling to avoid urban temptations, Garrison found himself drawn to the twice-weekly meetings at Beecher's Hanover Street Church in the North End. Secure in his Baptist tenets, though not born-again, Garrison was attracted more by the preacher's moralism than by his theology. He heard in Beecher's emphasis upon the Scriptures as "a code of laws" a mandate for Christians to fashion a system of moral government that would reveal "the glory of God in the salvation of man" and found himself ready to enlist in the benevolent enterprises that Beecher liked to describe as "a disciplined moral militia."

Ironically, Garrison's embrace of evangelical uplift also led him to appreciate the sermons of Beecher's *bête noire*, William Ellery Channing, the Unitarians' most eloquent spokesman, who held forth at his Federal Street Church a few blocks south of Collier's house. Channing was Beecher's opposite in every way. While Beecher, a blacksmith's son, had worked himself up from the humble country of western Connecticut, Channing had grown up in cultured Newport, the son of a prominent attorney, and had taken his degrees at Harvard. Beecher would boom out the words of "Old Hundred," while Channing would gently quote Wordsworth. (Both, though, had a sneaking admiration for Byron's powers; "What a harp he might have swept for Christ," Beecher mused.) Beecher projected the bumptious enthusiasm of a promoter, Channing the fey studiousness of the poet. Garrison feasted on the "skillful swordplay" generated between Beecher, whom Garrison found simple but vigorous, and Channing, whom he considered beautiful but superficial. If Beecher gave benevolent reform a gospel imperative, then Channing imbued it with a romantic aesthetic of self-reliance.

In the pure atmosphere of Beecher's and Channing's Boston, the moral renovation of the world seemed close at hand, and the idealists at Collier's house believed that they could see "the light of the sun of righteousness" rising over their city. With impious exuberance Garrison declared that if Adam and Eve had only been driven from Paradise to Boston, "their deep woe [would have] lost its keenness," for there could be no more worthy place to live on earth. For young men uncertain of their futures in a jangling and crowded city, the triumphant unity of a moral crusade had a strong personal appeal. It gave Garrison and his companions both a spiritual anchor and an intellectual direction. They would call themselves *philanthropists*— lovers of humanity—who would combat sinfulness, conquer suffering, and make earthly improvement a signal for the Christian kingdom to come.

Organized benevolence—tracts and agents to spread the word, local societies to raise the funds, a swelling tide of public opinion to convert the nation— would be the method, but for an eager reformer, yearning for greatness as was Garrison, the goal had to be more than a soup kitchen on every corner or a Sunday school tract on every doorstep. Inspired by Lyman Beecher's powerful lectures on intemperance and goaded by the specter of his own insecure childhood and his brother's alcoholic excess, Garrison put his efforts into the burgeoning temperance movement as the most important and vital philanthropy of the age.

Garrison had no difficulty heeding Beecher's call to suppress spirituous liquors. The Rev. William Collier conducted his boardinghouse on "cold-water principles," and Garrison enthusiastically took the American Temperance Society's pledge. To promote the cause, which had spawned a thousand local societies and a hundred thousand members, Collier had gotten up a temperance newspaper, ambitiously called the *National Philanthropist,* which straggled along like most of Collier's good-hearted efforts until he realized that an energetic editor sat at his own breakfast table and invited Brother Garrison to take it over in January 1828.

Fifteen months had passed since Garrison had lost the *Free Press* to partisan wrangling, and he resumed his place in an editor's chair with his customary enthusiasm and grandiose ambition "to raise the moral tone of the country." Pinning to his masthead the slogan "Moderate Drinking Is the

Downhill Road to Intemperance and Drunkenness," Garrison declared himself an absolutist prepared to destroy the practice root and branch. By experience and temperament Garrison was not one for halfway measures; he joined Beecher in a campaign for a ban that would be "Total with a capital Tee." Garrison's editorials praised the grocer who refused to sell liquor and the housewife who declined to serve whiskey punch to callers. His columns told of the road builder who paid top wages to those who pledged abstinence and the barn-raising accomplished in record time when the laborers declined to lubricate the process with rum. He printed stories of horrifying deaths from indulgence, and he tried the humorous tack of listing the chemical analysis of ardent spirits and asking, "Will you take a glass of gum-dragon and salt-tartar?"

The new editor brought to the *Philanthropist* the aggressive and contentious editorial style he had developed on the *Free Press*. He reprinted a speech in one column and attacked it in the next. He studded a text with asterisks and daggers pointing to footnotes in which he queried and corrected and rebutted in paragraphs twice as long as the original. Garrison also gave the *Philanthropist* a weightier and more influential look. He enlarged the sheet from four columns to five, arranged his matter under neat departmental headings, and gave over his fourth page to literature, especially devotional tales and uplifting poetry. Professing a distaste for those editors who "diluted" their columns with "mawkish romance, incredible recitals and accumulated wonders," he would no longer go for the farmer's almanac material that was the staple of country journalism. A newspaper had to be instructive, Garrison insisted, and "one column of sound morality is worth a page of doubtful miscellany."

His work on the *Philanthropist* drew Garrison's energies away from partisan politics. Within days of his arrival in Boston the year before, Garrison had tried to speak in a nominally Federalist caucus at Faneuil Hall, but he could not fully comprehend the entrepreneurial and personal alliances that cut across party lines in the city and found himself in over his head. His efforts to interject himself as a participant, moreover, met with immediate rebuff. A critic in the *Boston Courier* complained of the "impudent" young man, whom nobody knew, yet who had taken the floor and spoken with much "verbosity" from "copious notes" crammed into his hat. Garrison resented the insinuation that he was endeavoring "to write himself into notice," and he railed against the clannish rivalries that suppressed independent-minded voices. Men like Garrison did have an ambitious, abrasive quality that the genteel mercantile elite did not like to admit into their councils until it was softened by the accumulation of wealth. He might not have found himself shut out by the more bumptious and unsettled Democratic Party, which was building a local organization on the strength of grassroots enthusiasm for the resurgent candidacy of Andrew Jackson, but Garrison shared the traditionalists' disdain for the grasping opportunism and naked partisanship of the opposition. Mocked for his own ambition, yet desperately eager for a success that would not violate his stern code of conduct, Garrison mocked his critics and boastfully announced, "My name shall one day be known to the world."

If a corrupt society disdained him, Garrison would vindicate himself by winning fame as an apostle of public virtue. Politics, he declared in one of his first editorials for the *Philanthropist,* in January 1828, also required a moral reformation, for partisanship had itself become an intoxicating spirit. From this insight flowed an important strategic principle that would guide him for decades: reformers must accumulate "a great moral influence sufficient to control the strongest efforts of party intemperance and enhance the value of public opinion." Political parties had too many selfish concerns to be accurate barometers of civic morality, Garrison insisted, and the public interest had to be protected from their tendency to turn all issues of principle into instruments of private advantage.

Within a few weeks of writing this editorial, Garrison had the opportunity—right at Collier's table—of meeting an extraordinary practitioner of moral politics. Benjamin Lundy, a Quaker harness maker who had learned the printing trade in order to give himself a forum for denouncing the evil of slaveholding, had come to Boston in March 1828 to raise money for his one-man newspaper, the *Genius of Universal Emancipation.* Garrison had seen Lundy's publication in his exchange pile, and though his craftsman's eye considered it "a little dingy sheet," its overflowing feeling of "earnestness and zeal" had offered such powerful inspiration that he was surprised to find the trumpet-tongued editor resembled the frail apostle Paul more than the muscular Hercules. A wispy little man with thinning hair and a quiet voice, Lundy did not look as if he could stand up to a gust of wind, Garrison thought, much less the tide of adverse public opinion. Yet the more he heard from Lundy the stronger his character and the firmer his mettle seemed to be, until Garrison decided that behind Lundy's meek exterior lay "the boldness of Luther."

The editor listened raptly as Lundy unfolded his story. Born into a New Jersey Quaker family in 1789, he had lost his mother when he was very young, and his difficult childhood had been marked by long bouts of feverish illness that kept him from school and left him partially deaf and spiritually inert. He left home at nineteen, traveled across Pennsylvania and western Virginia, and found a place as a saddler's apprentice in Wheeling, where he recovered his faith and found a direction for his life. The sight of fellow human beings chained in Wheeling's slave pens while awaiting shipment down the Ohio River "grieved my heart," Lundy told Garrison, and "the iron entered my soul." Over the next few years he married and established himself as a harness maker across the river in Mount Pleasant, Ohio, but the memory of those slave coffles nagged at his conscience until he vowed that he would "break at least one link" of the oppressive chain. In 1816, Lundy sold his business to become a witness and prophet, as the Quakers John Woolman and Benjamin Lay had done in the years before the American Revolution, on behalf of emancipation and the Golden Rule.

Lundy was demanding attention to an issue that had lain dormant for a generation. The contradiction between creed and practice had made some Americans uncomfortable enough in the Revolutionary decades to abolish slavery by statute or judicial interpretation in the Northern states, which accounted for only six percent of the enslaved population. Massachusetts had immediately swept it away under its state constitution in the 1780s, two decades before Garrison's birth, while New York's gradual abolition law, not passed until 1799, only freed slaves born after the act's passage at age twenty-five for females and twenty-eight for males, which meant that emancipation had taken effect there only the year before Garrison met Lundy in Boston. A liberalization of manumission procedures in Virginia and Maryland proved the only public steps yet taken against slavery in the Southern states, though most Revolutionary leaders, including Thomas Jefferson and Patrick Henry, had written feelingly of both the moral blight of slavery and the paralysis of will that prevented them from acting upon their sympathies. Only among the Quakers did antislavery advocacy persist into the nineteenth century; when Lundy began his mission, he drew support from Friends in tiny manumission societies across the upper South. For most Americans, however, a fatalism had set in that regarded slavery as an immutable feature of the landscape, an unlooked-for evil that had been fastened upon them by generations long past and whose resolution had to be left to enlightened generations not yet born.

Lundy wrote antislavery articles for a friend's newspaper and, upon the editor's death, learned the mechanical aspects of printing well enough to issue the newspaper himself. Next he traveled across Tennessee and North Carolina like an itinerant preacher, holding meetings wherever he could, encouraging the formation of societies, and borrowing time in a friendly printing office to print the next issue of his paper as "an ensign" around which emancipationists could rally. Thinking that he could extend his influence by publishing on the eastern seaboard, Lundy moved to Baltimore in 1824, where he tried to make the *Genius* a weekly instead of a monthly and hired a printer (with funds begged from sympathizers) in order to free his time for lecturing and organizing. Lundy personally inspired dozens of slaveholders to manumit their slaves, sometimes with the proviso that they be relocated to the black republic of Haiti, in which case Lundy then escorted them to the Caribbean to ensure that they indeed received the land subsidies promised by the Haitian government. When Lundy returned from one such errand of mercy in 1825, he learned that his wife had died in childbirth and that his three older children and his infant twins had been sheltered with friends and relatives pending his return. Lundy made a fateful decision to permit his children to remain with their foster families and free himself completely for the cause.

"Nothing is wanting . . . but the *will*," Lundy insisted, and he frequently printed a crude sketch of a slave coffle under the title "Hail Columbia!" with the injunction "LOOK AT IT, *again* and *again!*" That would be his mission: to open America's eyes. His newspaper, his impromptu meetings, his long evenings of counsel with a conscience-stricken slave owner, his petitions, and his endless journeying (the man had labored in nineteen of the twenty-four states, Garrison marveled, and had traveled more than twelve thousand miles) were all aimed at rousing the "slumbering faculties of a humane people." In those earnest hours of conversation at Collier's, Garrison remembered ever afterward, Friend Lundy "opened my eyes" and "inflamed my mind" on the subject of slavery. When Lundy declared, "I shall not hesitate to call things by their proper names, nor yet refrain from speaking the truth," a thrill went through Garrison, and when Lundy added, "Take right hold! Hold on! And never abandon an inch of ground after it has been taken," Garrison's soul burned with desire to do battle.

Lundy personified the visionary "new race of editors" to which Garrison aspired. He saw in Lundy a middle-aged version of himself: slender and quick, with abundant energy and sharp talk that testified to his righteousness with every gesture and syllable. Their faiths stood upon the same twin rocks—the Bible and the Declaration of Independence—and their hands knew the bonds of a shared craft. Impressed that Lundy had taught himself the "art and mystery" of printing, Garrison declared (correctly) that not even Woolman or Lay or Benezet had realized "the all-shaking power" of the press for moral witness the way Friend Lundy had. Lundy had suffered the wrath of slave traders, had endured a beating on the streets of Baltimore, and had weathered an effort by a Baltimore judge to suppress his paper on trumped-up charges of libel. Nothing could stop him, Garrison believed, and the younger man listened with admiration to Lundy's quiet vow that he would never abandon his newspaper even if his hands could produce but one issue a year. In the very next issue of his own paper, Garrison saluted Lundy's "unwearied efforts" and esteemed the *Genius* as "the bravest and best attempt in the history of newspapers."

Garrison's conversion proved the only harvest of Lundy's trip. In New York he had received good wishes, but no contribution from Arthur Tappan, brother of the reconverted Lewis and a wealthy merchant who had underwritten many other benevolent causes. In Providence, Lundy had found the reformer William Goodell "slow of speech" on the slavery issue, and the eight Boston clergymen he met in Collier's parlor listened politely, but declined to help. They found Lundy's fanaticism more alarming than stirring, and Dr. Channing, who heard things only at second hand, was concerned enough to write privately to Massachusetts's new senator, Daniel Webster, that "the rashness of enthusiasts" could make slavery a socially disruptive issue unless political and religious leaders exercised careful management.

Where the ministers sensed trouble, Garrison felt hope. "Have we not reason to exult in the prospect before us?" Garrison inquired of his readers on March 21, 1828, the week after Lundy's visit. "The reign of perfectibility" had not yet arrived, Garrison conceded, but "the seeds of an immortal harvest" were beginning to bud. Rehearsing much of Lundy's message about the 130 antislavery societies that the Friends had organized in the border states, the tradition of private manumissions there, and the work of colonization groups that promoted voluntary emigration of freed slaves to Africa and Haiti, Garrison insisted that antislavery could be an organized force along the lines of the temperance and peace movements. "Emancipation alone will preserve the life of the republic" and restore the luster of the American character far more successfully than military laurels or material gain, Garrison insisted. "The struggle is full of sublimity," he concluded, and "the conquest embraces the world."

The enthusiasm with which Garrison endorsed antislavery not only testified to Friend Lundy's inspiration; it revealed Garrison's deepening commitment to the vocation of reform. The next week he printed the prospectus for the *Genius,* offering to receive subscriptions on its behalf, and reiterated his admiration for Lundy's pilgrimage for justice. Garrison quoted the tribute paid the Quaker by *Freedom's Journal,* the country's only newspaper edited by black men—John Russwarm and Samuel Cornish—who wondered aloud where "another Lundy" could be found "to bear the buffeting and scorn of an unfeeling world for the sake of injured humanity." Where indeed? Garrison began to think of himself as Lundy's "coadjutor" almost at once, and Lundy promised that after a few months' work in Baltimore he would resume, perhaps with Garrison's help, his canvass of the northeast.

Meantime, Garrison gave the *Philanthropist* a broader sound. His editorials concentrated upon preserving morality in politics. "Liberty does not consist in dropping a piece of paper into a certain crevice, though thousands who are the mere automata of political jugglers have no better conception of the term," Garrison observed, as the spring elections approached. Citizens with aspirations for human betterment could not be held in thrall to a political party's lust for victory and the spoils of patronage; they had to vote with candor and discernment, and always in conformity with their ideals. As the themes of liberty and slavery, reformation and struggle, preoccupied his mind, Garrison transformed himself from a Federalist partisan into a Christian patriot; he could readily endorse the credo put forward by the Rev. Lyman Beecher's journal, *The Spirit of the Pilgrims*: "There is no safety for republics but in self-government, under the influence of a holy heart, swayed by the government of God."

On July Fourth, 1828, however, the Christian patriot left his post. Having completed his six-month contract, Garrison resigned from the *Philanthropist* without a hint about his plans. For the second time he had left an editorial desk abruptly; for the second time, too, he had to combat rumors that he had been sacked. John Neal, the vain and intemperate editor of a Portland paper with whom Garrison had often jousted, lumped him with other editorial critics of Neal's who had recently lost their jobs, and Garrison defended his reputation in a lengthy, abusive letter insisting that his "retirement" was voluntary and that Neal could not have missed the publisher's effusive tribute to his valuable labors. "The task may be yours to write my biography," Garrison taunted, adding that he spoke "in the spirit of prophecy, not vainglory,—with a strong pulse, a flashing eye, and a glow of the heart." Once again, the self-confident Garrison trumped his critic with a proclamation of his own historic destiny. Opposition always intensified his defiance and heightened his own sense of worth. Like his mother, Garrison took pleasure in feeling embattled. While Sister Garrison engaged in the pietist's combat with earthly weakness, however, her son fought against the deprivations of a wretched childhood and the social obscurity of the compositor's trade. Yet he seemed driven less by material wants than the desire for attention and influence. His soul had embraced large truths, and he yearned to make a spiritual mark upon the world.

Garrison plunged directly into antislavery work. Friend Lundy arrived back in town at the end of July 1828, having held large and successful meetings in New Haven, New Bedford, Andover, Salem, and Lynn. Garrison worked hard with him to organize a public gathering in Boston, but it proved difficult to find a hall and an hour not taken up by other benevolent groups. "Negroes are every where and always the last to be thought of or noticed," Lundy grumbled. They finally secured the use of the vestry room at the Baptist church near Collier's, and on August 7, Garrison had the great satisfaction of seeing the aisles crowded and every seat filled by the time Lundy rose to speak.

In his earnest and calm manner, Lundy made an appeal to both reason and conscience, admitting candidly that little could be accomplished until "the great body of the people" became interested in the work of abolition. Having lived in the South, he could say confidently that the majority of the people there, including slaveholders, desired to have the slave system abolished, though he believed that it would take a national "spirit of inquiry" to strengthen the will necessary for the Southern states to adopt gradual emancipation laws as had New York and Pennsylvania. Confronting his listeners with the "constitutional" truth that slaveholders would ultimately depend upon "physical force at the north" to protect them in case of insurrection, Lundy emphasized that New Englanders could not "supinely fold their arms and imagine they have no interest in this matter." Form an antislavery society in Boston; petition your representatives and rally the public, Lundy urged, for "the ultimate liberation of every slave in the republic" depended upon assertions of moral strength.

It was a thoughtful speech, though hardly a provocative one, and the audience seemed receptive. However, the pastor of the church, Dr. Howard Malcolm, rose to take issue with Lundy's prescription. Malcolm, a Philadelphia commission merchant who had renounced the market for the Baptist ministry only a few years earlier, thought it might be meddlesome and provocative for New Englanders to organize agitation on the subject. "Natural causes" would circumscribe the evil, he thought, for the border states of Kentucky, Maryland, and perhaps Virginia were selling their large supply of slaves to the cotton states farther south; gradually they would abolish slavery and add to the free-state influence in Congress, and North Carolina and Tennessee would become the vulnerable border states and subject to the same process. This should relieve our feelings somewhat, Malcolm said, about the internal slave trade, for we see in this an example of the manner in which "God overrules events in themselves evil, for the promotion of ultimate good."

When Garrison and Lundy indignantly tried to debate Malcolm's argument, the minister gaveled them down and adjourned the proceedings. The editors then held forth in the hallway, scandalized that "trafficking in human flesh" could be advanced as a surer and more humane remedy than "the voice of a contrite people" working its will upon the legislatures. The "perverseness" of the minister's argument, Garrison predicted, would rouse "the friends of universal emancipation" to form an antislavery society at once.

Meeting with such "friends" a few nights later, however, they encountered much resistance. Excuses came tumbling forth. "It would terribly alarm and enrage the South to know that an antislavery society existed at Boston!" Garrison recalled mockingly. "But—it would do harm, rather than good, openly to agitate the subject! But—we had nothing to do with the question, and the less we meddled with it the better!" One or two individuals favored decisive action, but they lacked "station and influence." The "wise and prudent" element, including several ministers, would concede only that "*perhaps* a *select* committee might be formed, to be called by some other name that would neither give offence, nor excite suspicion as to its real design."

"My soul was on fire then," Garrison remarked, when he recalled the "moral cowardice" and "cruel skepticism" of Boston's would-be reformers. Lundy, however, was used to such setbacks. He knew that "philanthropists . . . think forty times before they act," and he reminded the disappointed Garrison that their public meeting had at least broken the "stupid spell of apathy." A committee was "a nucleus," Lundy said, and if Garrison remained active and persevering—mark that *if,* warned Lundy, who had seen many warm hearts grow cool after an initial setback—they would gain a full-fledged organization. "Precept upon precept, line upon line," he chanted from the Book of Isaiah (28:10–11). "Here a little *and* there a little: For with stammering lips and another tongue will he speak to this people." *Mark that!*

If Garrison had left his job on the *National Philanthropist* in hopes of forming a collaboration with Lundy, he was disappointed. After the Boston lecture in August 1828, Lundy picked up his knapsack and walked off toward Worcester on an expedition of quiet agitation that would take him all the way to Buffalo before he turned south toward Baltimore and his newspaper. If Garrison had thought he would work as the Massachusetts agent for the petition campaign against slavery in Washington, D.C., he was equally frustrated. Boston's "select" committee never met again.

So Garrison executed a startling about-face. He took a job as a political hack. Some National Republican Party men in Bennington, Vermont, had come all the way to Boston in search of an editor; their local paper had gone over to the popular Democratic candidate, Andrew Jackson, and they needed a rival voice to sound the argument for President Adams's reelection. The 1828 campaign had only a few months left to run, but Vermont, they believed, could easily be brought into the Adams fold if newspapers rallied the faithful. Stymied in Boston with high ideals, no rostrum from which to advocate them, and no money to pay his room and board, Garrison accepted their offer—which included a hundred-dollar advance—with the proviso that in addition to the Adams line he be permitted to discuss "moral subjects" in his columns. "They gave me *carte blanche*," Garrison told his friends, thus satisfying his conscience that he was not so much doing ignoble party work as regaining a valuable forum. A village newspaper, he reminded himself, "revolutionizes more minds in a month than would the most complete library in a year."

For the third time in three years Garrison threw himself into the task of starting up a newspaper. He called his new vehicle the *Journal of the Times* and chose for its motto the high-sounding declaration "Reason shall prevail with us more than popular opinion." This was a knock at the emotional mania for Jackson that sedate politicians everywhere deplored, and the editor of the rival *Vermont Gazette* lost no time in ridiculing the pretensions of "the Boston man, or babe" who had come to set Vermonters straight. Although he ran a long front-page article comparing the merits of the two candidates and continued weekly to contrast the intelligent, upright, and commercially responsible Adams with the slave-mongering, whiskey-drinking, sword-wielding Caesar who challenged him, Garrison insisted that he was not conducting a "hireling press" or taking advice from a partisan sect. "We should like to see the man, or body of men . . . that would *dare* to chalk out our limits, or dictate our words . . ." he wrote; he was "no time-serving, shuffling, truckling editor . . . [who] has not enough courage to hunt down popular vices, to combat popular prejudices, to encounter the madness of party, to tell the truth and maintain the truth."

The political promoters who had invited him to Bennington had no cause for complaint, however, and the six hundred friends of Adams who ponied up subscriptions after the first issue of October 3,1828, received full value, not only in regular editorials that sustained their political cause, but in lively introductions to their editor's numerous other concerns. The *Journal* proved to be the most attractively laid out and exuberantly conducted of Garrison's three newspapers; no less an editor than Horace Greeley remembered it from his own New England apprentice days as "about the ablest and most interesting newspaper ever issued in Vermont." Until Garrison got his own exchange list underway, he begged his printer friend Stephen Foster to send him armloads of papers from Boston, and before long Garrison had happily stirred up prolonged arguments with editors from Salem to Schenectady. "There is *nerve*" in Garrison's pen, wrote an admiring Benjamin Lundy from Baltimore.

Garrison did his partisan work with flair and humor. He now extolled Adams, whom he had deemed insufficiently Federalist four years earlier, as the true heir of Washington, and he summed up the case against Jackson with a parody of a popular Scotch song that predicted "Slavery's comin', Knavery's comin'/ Plunder's comin', Blunder's comin'/ Robbin's comin', Jobbin's comin'—An' the plague of war is comin' on." Although Adams carried New England and stayed even with Jackson in the middle states, the South went so overwhelmingly for Old Hickory that for only the second time in the republic's history an incumbent president—each an Adams from Massachusetts—was denied reelection. In the closely contested election of 1800 the "federal ratio" that augmented the South's electoral votes by three-fifths the number of slaves had proved the margin of John Adams's defeat, and in 1828 John Quincy Adams was equally certain that his own repudiation marked the revival of a Democratic coalition pledged to the protection of Southern slaveholders. Within a few years the embittered and irascible Quincy Adams would return to Congress to agitate the slavery question for a constituency roused to concern by Garrison's abolitionist journalism, which itself received fresh impetus from the Southern electoral triumph.

Of the many reforms for which Garrison had promised to contend— temperance, pacifism, practical education, and "the gradual emancipation of every slave in the republic"—antislavery inspired his most persistent efforts. Two weeks after arriving in Bennington, Garrison had organized the first in a series of meetings to consider petitioning Congress for the gradual abolition of slavery in the District of Columbia. He sought support from "all who are honest in their republicanism, all who are willing that every man, black or white, should live as God made him—FREE." Such citizens should not cede their principles to slaveholders like Andrew Jackson, who ought to be exhibited in a sideshow, Garrison railed, "manacled with the chains he has forged for others and smarting under the application of his own whips." In fantasizing a public humiliation and punishment for the figure who embodied, at least for white men, the expansion of democracy, Garrison revealed his bold iconoclasm and the intensely personal anger that fueled it. Throughout his career the Puritan avenger and the Christian pacifist would coexist uneasily in Garrison's imagination.

The editor brought Bennington to a surer exercise of duty than Boston; by mid-December 1828, the statewide drive had collected the signatures of 2,300 Vermonters. The *Vermont Gazette*'s editor made fun of the manner in which the young interloper, "a pair of silver-mounted spectacles riding elegantly across his nose," dominated the petition meetings with "the pert loquacity of a blue-jay," but Garrison took pride in his first venture at organizing a moral constituency. The *Journal*'s critics branded Garrison as an insurrectionary whose advocacy of immediate abolition would bring on a bloodbath in the South and destroy the Union. The editor, however, forswore immediatism as "visionary" and "out of the question." The edifice of slavery would have to be dismantled, "brick by brick, and foot by foot," though generations might pass to their graves in the endeavor, Garrison said, "so that it may be overturned without burying the nation in its ruin." Only complacency and inaction could be more ruinous, he added, promising New England would not be permitted to sleep "while we have the management of a press, or strength to hold a pen."

Not an idle boast, to be sure, but one that raised the very real question of whether Garrison intended to transform the *Journal* from a deliberately short-lived campaign sheet into a steady enterprise. The editorial exuberance and literary output—Garrison wrote dozens of poems as well as personally composing (at the case) many inches of editorial matter each week—testified both to his drive and the congenial setting. Garrison boarded at a church deacon's home and became friends with the head of the Bennington Classical Seminary, and his poetry lauded the inspiration of the encircling mountains and the luminous stars at night. Country life, he thought, could provide "all the necessaries without the temptation" of the noisy, smoky city.

Garrison, however, had no natural constituency in Bennington, and the entrenched *Gazette* continued to berate his ambition and self-importance as "windy, vain, arrogant, and depraved." Worse still, the *Journal*'s printer-proprietor, Henry Hull, had turned nasty about finances and stuck Garrison with bills that the editor had understood would be met as part of the arrangement. As the working conditions soured, the editor began to feel himself in exile. He missed his mutually admiring circle of printers, philanthropists, and aspiring writers in what they humorously called "the literary emporium" of Boston. Although the *Journal* had proved a far superior achievement to the *Philanthropist*, when news came that John G. Whittier—now headed for the literary career his father had feared—would become that paper's new editor, Garrison's yearning increased.

In one important dimension, Garrison's heart had never left Boston. He had met a young lady named Mary Cunningham at a holiday promenade on the Common during his first Boston summer, and they had seen each other again at the Athenaeum, an intellectually respectable venue where young men and women could pass the afternoon discreetly admiring each other while viewing the paintings in the gallery. From distant Bennington the lonesome Garrison unburdened his pent-up feelings in poetry that artlessly charted the fever of young love. Posing once more as the old bachelor, Garrison declared—in the inaugural number of the *Journal*—that Cupid had conquered his once-stubborn heart and made him "Hymen's partisan." "My bachelorship I throw aside—/ My haughtiness—my lofty bearing—/ Sweet Mary! wilt though be my bride?/ To thee I bow—thy chains I'm wearing."

Miss Cunningham's response, if any, evidently did not satisfy the poet, for two weeks later, "A. O. B." gave the *Journal* a poetic lament on earthly vanity that sounded like a case of unrequited love, though phrased abstractly enough that Lundy—surely unaware of its subtext—reprinted it in the *Genius*. More of Garrison's poetry followed, but when the young woman, who evidently did not appreciate courtship by newspaper, broke things off, the editor vented his feelings by printing some sad verses by Mrs. Hemans.

Self-pity soured into frustration, however, and when Garrison's friend Stephen Foster passed along some gossip in March 1829 about the young woman's use of cosmetics, Garrison exploded. "So!—Mary Cunningham *'paints'*—does she? Never mind, my dear fellow, it shall be at her own expense," he told Foster. "I'll be the painter," he wrote, indulging himself in an angry fantasy. "Hold your head steadily, dearest . . . a little more vermilion, a denser flame of health on this cheek—I like to see the *blood*, Mary, mounting up to the very temples . . . shut your mouth, and draw back that little saucy tongue, you pretty witch, for I'm going to put a ruby blush upon your twin (not thin) lips, *after I've kissed them*—there—softly—smack goes the brush°°°°*Cetera desunt.*"

Garrison knew by this time that he would be coming back to Boston. Although he was "proud of the paper" and its "quick reputation" for active philanthropy, he had resigned his post with the *Journal* at the end of his six-month term. As before, he imagined himself called to higher duty, when in fact he had quarreled with his boss and reached a dead end. Garrison's valedictory claimed that he had been "invited to occupy a broader field— the whole country, and to engage in a higher enterprise . . . in behalf of the slave population." Privately, however, Garrison told his friends that he was "truly miserable" and "half resolved never to write another editorial . . . [or] make another effort to gain either money or applause." (This was the first admission that he might have gone to Vermont in search of them.)

In truth he had no immediate prospects. Early in December, 1828, Lundy had turned up in Bennington in the midst of another of his onerous pilgrimages. Legend later held that the Quaker editor had walked all the way from Baltimore to propose a collaboration with Garrison, but the truth is more prosaic. Friend Lundy had come up from New York City on the Hudson River steamboat, caught the stage in Albany, and hiked only the last twenty miles. He shook off his young friend's effort to stage a public meeting, but doubtless met privately—as he had all along his route—with people involved in the current petition campaign. The two men had evidently planned a joint venture to begin at the conclusion of Garrison's contract, but then Lundy had suspended publication and gone off in mid-January on an expedition to Haiti from which he had not yet returned. In the meantime, Collier, who promised to help Garrison find work if he gave up the grandiose idea of going south, charitably welcomed him back to Federal Street. He shared a room with the saturnine Whittier, who spent a good deal of time staring out of the window biting his pencil or complaining about the frosty formality of Boston social life. "I cannot love this city," the poet said dolefully.

Garrison, by contrast, continued to adore Boston. Even though Collier could not come up with a steady job for him, he cheerfully returned to working "like a tiger" at piece rates, kept his eye out for a journeyman's berth, and still hoped for a firm call from Lundy. Meanwhile, he "lounged" a good deal at the Athenaeum, where he gave not "a fig for canvass faces" but enjoyed "the fresher, and merrier, and prettier ones, all glowing with life, having most dangerous eyes and bewitching forms." Although Whittier—certain that he was fated to "marry a Quakeress with her bonnet like a flour dipper, and a face as long as a tobacco yawl"—got "the hypos" lounging in the gallery, the ambitious and confident Garrison was soon in love again. Whittier thought him "imprudent," to say the least, calling upon his beloved nearly every night and reciting exuberant verses of his own composition. "The girl must be a singular piece of housing-stuff if she can swallow all that," Whittier scoffed. "I wouldn't give him a pinch of snuff for his chance." Six weeks later, Garrison was still visiting "his Dulcinea every other night, almost," Whittier gossiped, "but is fearful of being 'shipped off,' after all by her. Lord help the poor fellow, if it happens so."

Garrison was in the toils of literary composition as well as courtship. He had received an invitation to address the afternoon church services jointly held by the orthodox Congregationalists at Park Street Church on the Fourth of July. In the denomination's annual cycle of charitable giving, July was the month devoted to African missions, and capitalizing upon this, the American Colonization Society had, over the course of the decade, succeeded in making Independence Day church services a time for special emphasis—and a collection—on its behalf. The sanctity of the day, its partisans argued, made it appropriate to demonstrate to the Almighty that freedom-loving Americans extended their sympathy and charity to "a long divided and suffering people whose destinies seem by Providence entrusted to their hands." Although the ACS would be extending its reach by holding its own service at the Methodists' Bromfield Street chapel on July Fourth, its adherents expected to take up a collection at Park Street as well.

That social custom now sanctioned some discussion of slavery on the Fourth of July made Garrison's choice of topic inevitable. He had never ranked colonization very high on his list of practical remedies, however, and he knew from the addresses he had heard on such occasions how complacent they could be. As a reform-minded editor who had written eloquently of the need to bring piety into politics, Garrison had seemed a reasonable choice for the event, though the invitation committee undoubtedly lacked awareness of the radical direction the editor's thinking had taken during his sojourn in Vermont. For Garrison the call to speak at Park Street Church offered a public forum just at a time when he lacked an editorial column of his own, and he was determined to make the most of it. Because the colonizationists had appropriated the holiday to their own uses, historians have made the double mistake of assuming that the ACS sponsored Garrison's pulpit appearance and that he therefore shared its views. On the contrary, as a disciple of Lundy, who viewed colonization more as a measure of individual relief than the preferred means to emancipation, Garrison regarded the Park Street service as an opportunity to make his most radical statement yet on the necessity for abolishing slavery in the name of equal rights, not racial separation. He deliberately slighted colonization in his remarks and called public attention afterward to the omission.

The speaker spent more than a week writing his address. Whittier watched the text swell into many pages of foolscap on his roommate's writing desk, and he heard the author despair of condensing an argument that threatened to consume nearly an hour in delivery. The speech would be severe, long, and likely to give offense, Garrison warned his friends, but he insisted that the subject justified the strict course he had chosen. His theme would be "national danger," and his method would be "plain truth told in a plain manner." The service would be Garrison's first major opportunity to speak out beyond his own circle of readers and reformers to people of consequence from Boston's self-satisfied religious community, and he was determined to sound "a new tone" in platform discourse, just as he had roused once-drowsy newspapers with what fellow editors termed his "bold, abrupt, and original" style. The committee would regret its choice from the moment that the speaker began by denouncing the holiday as "the worst and most disastrous day in the whole three hundred and sixty-five."

Saturday, July Fourth, 1829, dawned cloudy, windy, and chilly. The flag-lined streets did not seem as thronged as usual, and the traditional clutch of refreshment booths, tables, and tents on the Common had dwindled markedly, owing perhaps to Dr. Beecher's success in suppressing sales of alcoholic beverages there. After the ritual cannon salute and procession from Faneuil Hall to Old South Meeting House, a rising attorney, Colonel James T. Austin, gave the municipal oration, which the *Columbian Centinel* judged "a production of no ordinary merit" but the *American Traveller*'s reporter considered pompous and long-winded. The other speakers of the morning hardly made a better impression. At Federal Street Church, Dr. Malcolm stayed away from controversy and confined himself to a bland discourse on the importance of history. At Bromfield Street Church the ACS lecturer proved a poor speaker and difficult to hear, though he sought to convince the congregation that "the sublime spectacle" of Americans purging themselves of the curse of slavery by repatriating the slaves to Africa would be "a moral painting on the canvass of time" worthy to set alongside scenes of the Crucifixion and the signing of the Declaration of Independence.

By the time Garrison and his circle of printer friends set out to walk the six blocks uphill from their downtown rooming house for the four-o'clock lecture, the afternoon had turned wet with "a dank, dreary, dismal, drizzling rain." They did not often visit the fashionable precinct on the slope of Beacon Hill where Park Street Church loomed high over the northeast corner of the Common. Along one side of the edifice a mall of graceful elm trees swept the long block up Park Street past the town houses of the Quincys and Eliots and Ticknors to the steps of the august red-brick State House; on the other, the gracious facades of Tremont Street manses, with another mall of trees and the greensward beyond, added to the air of prosperous tranquillity. Park Street Church was a new edifice with an old look; built twenty years earlier in the Georgian style Thomas Bulfinch had made popular, it was a large structure of painted yellow brick, whose boxy proportions were relieved by two curved vestibules and a slender colonnade that embellished the entrance. Its steeple was the tallest in Boston and echoed the English design with its stack of octagons—windowed, columned, and pedimented—crowned with a graceful spire and a weather vane shaped as a blazing star.

On the inside, however, the austere auditorium had a minimum of drapery and decoration, other than a gleaming mahogany baptismal stand and a set of curved stairways leading to the elevated pulpit. From that privileged vantage point, Garrison looked out upon a sizable audience—the church could easily seat fifteen hundred people—and felt his knees "knock[ing] together at the thought of speaking before so large a concourse." He sat quietly through the opening exercises. A young woman from his hometown of Newburyport had composed a poem for the occasion, which was read between prayers. Park Street's renowned choir then performed, with a fervor that Garrison found "beautiful and thrilling," an antislavery ode—"Hearest thou, O God, those chains,/ Clanking on Freedom's plains,/ By Christians wrought!"—composed by a liberal minister friend and sung to the tune of "America."

At last the time came. Garrison stepped up to the desk ready for combat. His black suit could not dull his flashing dark eyes or the youthful pink glow of his cheeks, both accentuated by his decision to appear more like a poet than a preacher, as the *Traveller*'s man noted, "with his neck bare, and a broad linen collar spread over that of his coat," in the popular Byronic style. It was a signal that iconoclasm would provide the salient quality of the address, as Garrison excoriated the inadequacy of the American political culture and the racism that prevented full realization of its egalitarian promises.

He began with a startling attack upon the Fourth of July itself as a day of intoxication and hypocrisy and declared that the shameful toleration of the crime of slaveholding ought to "spike every cannon and haul down every banner" in the holiday salute. The annals of history held no parallel for the "glaring contradiction" between our creed and our practice, he said, and left him "ashamed" of his country. The congregation stirred and murmured as its lecturer declared himself "sick" of "hypocritical cant about the rights of man" and "unmeaning declamations in praise of liberty and equality." He could not stand up before Europeans still under the sway of monarchy and exult in his American citizenship without blushing with embarrassment, Garrison said, while the *Traveller*'s reporter furiously scribbled in his notebook the distorted charge that the speaker had refused to acknowledge himself an American citizen.

Though people did not like to talk about slavery, they recognized its baseness. Garrison did not think he had to explain why slavery was a curse or attempt to freeze his auditors' blood with a depiction of "the immense wilderness of suffering" that slavery had created. "I take for granted that the existence of these evils is acknowledged, if not rightly understood," he said. "My object is to define and enforce our duty, as Christians and Philanthropists." To do this Garrison bravely confronted the racist assumptions that underlay slavery and chilled any serious discussion of its abolition. His case rested upon four dramatic propositions that defined new ground for an antislavery movement and made the Park Street Address an epochal moment in the history of freedom. Speaking with greater reach and a boldness that no critic had ventured before, Garrison insisted that enslaved Americans had the strongest possible claims for redress and that the people of the non-slaveholding states had a righteous duty to break the political silence that prevented the slaves' cause from being heard. He argued further that the degrading consequences of slavery could not be used to justify a denial of liberty to its victims and that black people could—and should—rank equally with whites as citizens.

Although Garrison spoke to an audience disposed to acts of benevolence, he based his argument not upon charity, but political philosophy. The great majority of the slave population was American-born and "entitled to all the privileges of American citizens," he emphasized, while their children "possess the same inherent and inalienable rights as ours." (Garrison was speaking to an audience of white people; Boston's small free black population did little to observe the Fourth of July, and the high-toned Park Street congregation was not hospitable to people of color. A few months after Garrison's address the congregation would be scandalized when a black merchant acquired title to a Park Street pew in a business settlement and froze him out while its real estate committee inserted restrictive covenants in the pew deeds.)

Having referred to the sacred phrases of the Declaration of Independence, Garrison drove his point home by asking his listeners to imagine the language that American slaves would use in justifying to the world a rebellion of their own. In the cadences of Jefferson's declaration, Garrison then catalogued a long course of usurpation and tyranny: "They have invaded our territories. . . . They have wedged us into the holds of their 'floating hells.' . . . They have sold us in their market-places like cattle . . . driven us in large droves from State to State, beneath a burning sky. . . . They have lacerated our bodies with whips. . . . They would destroy our souls. . . ."

Not only did the slaves possess inherent rights, Garrison insisted; the states had a democratic right to voice the concerns of the nonslaveholding majority in the counsels of the nation. We have "a common interest . . . as members of one great family . . . to demand a gradual abolition of slavery," he said. Even if one were to disregard the Golden Rule and "the common dictates of humanity," Garrison reasoned, the free states had a stake in the matter "because by [slavery's] continuance, they participate in the guilt thereof, and are threatened with ultimate destruction."

There were also sectional political concerns. New England Federalists had complained for years about the Southern weight in national politics, owing to the extra representation granted to slaveholders by the three-fifths clause in the U.S. Constitution, but Garrison gave the congregation a fresh lesson in political arithmetic. Though the free states had a population twice as large as the slave states, they wielded only twenty-two percent more of the electoral vote and had to suffer the "anti-republican" absurdity of slaveholders reducing men to property while claiming that they should be counted as constituents. The "price of Union," Garrison said bluntly, was too high if it silenced the voice of an "overwhelming majority" and required tacit approval of a soul-destroying evil.

Yet the abolition of slavery had to be a moral endeavor before it could be a political one. Only an aroused public conscience could persuade legislators to withdraw protection from slavery, the speaker contended, and he admonished the evangelically minded congregation that Christians could not, in fairness, strive to liberate other lands from darkness and superstition, yet make no impression upon the laws at home. Agitation would inevitably be noisy and disruptive, he acknowledged, but slavery could not be abolished without a collision "full of sharp asperities and bitterness" that would confront "the worst passions of human nature." The conflict, furthermore, would have to begin in their own communities, for "the prejudices of the north are stronger than those of the south; they bristle, like so many bayonets, around the slaves. . . ."

To reinforce the point, Garrison again chose the technique of imaginative substitution. "Suppose that . . . the slaves should suddenly become white," he bade the silent hall.

"Would you shut your eyes upon their sufferings and calmly talk of constitutional limitations?

"No," he roared, "your voice would peal in the ears of the taskmasters like deep thunder." Boston would rock more violently than it had during the revolt against Great Britain, the pulpits would shake with holy zeal, and the charge that such white slaves are "degraded" or "inferior," and therefore undeserving of freedom, would be dismissed outright.

This startling confrontation with racial bias brought Garrison to his final thesis: the equal citizenship of black and white. He condemned as a "pitiful subterfuge" the common argument that slavery had incapacitated black people for freedom and would thus make their liberation a curse rather than a blessing. He also condemned the racist corollary, advanced most prominently by Thomas Jefferson in *Notes on the State of Virginia,* that differences of color, as well as capacity, loomed as powerful obstacles to emancipation and an egalitarian society. Look at the achievements of Carthage in ancient days and Haiti today (and perhaps the infant colony at Liberia, Garrison said, in his only, passing reference to the colonization scheme) to see what free black citizens might accomplish. If slavery had reduced black men and women to "a level with the brutes, is it a valid argument to say that therefore they must remain brutes?" Freedom and education would be the proper remedies to "elevate them to a proper rank in the scale of being," he said, though it would be "a wild vision" to think that such could happen overnight. Emancipation would have to come gradually, but it had to begin at once. "Our choice is simply between virtuous and quiet freemen and desperate and degraded slaves," he said, and asked, "Whose society is the more preferable?"

"Let us not shackle the limbs of the future workmanship of God," he pleaded. "Let us, then, be up and doing." Slavery was "a national sin" that all Christians in America had a duty to subdue. The clergy should "light up a flame of philanthropy" and, in the words of Isaiah, "proclaim liberty to the captives, and the opening of the prison to them that are bound." Women should form "charitable associations" for prayer and relief; auxiliary colonization societies should support those who chose emigration; newspaper editors should "sound the trumpet of alarm and plead eloquently for the rights of man"; the American people should choose representatives courageous enough to abolish slavery where no constitutional compromise restrained them, in the capital city itself. Christians must "shake off their slumbers and arm for the holy contest," Garrison concluded, for "I will say, finally, that I tremble for the republic while slavery exists." The paraphrase of Jefferson was deliberate—and telling. Garrison had nailed the flags of freedom, citizenship, and equality to the antislavery standard, and he would never lower

them again. He had, in Park Street Church, rewritten the Declaration of Independence to include African-Americans.

Whittier realized immediately what his friend had done. "The best since '76," the poet told the speaker as they walked out of the church together. Garrison could look with satisfaction up Tremont Street and across the city toward the thin spire of the Old North Church where the Revolutionaries had hung their lanterns. Now he had placed a new generation's signal lamp in a Boston steeple to warn the nation of a danger that loomed neither from land nor from sea but from within its vain and complacent soul. Yet if Garrison had tried to recall the idealism of the Revolution, he had also endeavored to reinvigorate the religious legacy of New England. Like the Puritan settlers of old, Garrison, echoing John Winthrop and others, sought the reformation of a corrupt world by a return to fundamental principles. Though he had delivered a jeremiad worthy of the divines who had once held sway in Boston's pulpits, he had more in common with the antinomian dissenters such as Anne Hutchinson and Roger Williams who challenged the keepers of the moral law in the name of the inspired private conscience. Nonetheless, he emerged from Park Street Church as a visionary, who yet regarded Boston as the city on a hill, a moral beacon as well as a political one, and who summoned the citizens of a Christian republic to honor their covenant with God and with themselves.

As he evoked the grand spiritual drama of abolition for the first time, Garrison's sense of himself as a social redeemer received its most fervent expression. In one passage he likened himself to an attorney, pleading in the solemn court of public opinion, not for thousands of dollars in damages, but for the liberation of two million beings in bondage. In another passage he became a giant-killer, facing down the gorgon of slavery as David had triumphed over Goliath, and in his peroration he spoke as a prophet of the Lord, proclaiming, "Thus saith the Lord God of the Africans, 'Let this people go, that they may serve me.'" He had issued an unprecedented call for a moral revolution in America and revealed the deep wellsprings of feeling that made him willing to lead it. As the most forthright and extensive statement of American egalitarian principle written between the Declaration of Independence and the Gettysburg Address, the Park Street Address deserves more recognition than it has received as a notable state paper. As a harbinger of Garrison's commitment to agitation—and the considerable courage and skill he brought to the task—the Park Street appearance was equally momentous, for it demonstrated that Garrison did not fear, and perhaps actually preferred, to build his reputation as an iconoclast willing to defy conventional wisdom.

His eloquent sermon, however, inspired no immediate activity in Boston, and by mischaracterizing it as dealing with colonization, the newspapers indeed seemed at pains to deny its radical thrust. Only Garrison's former paper, the *National Philanthropist,* reprinted the complete text, and no other newspaper picked it up on the exchange circuit. The ACS leaders realized what had happened, however, and the following year made sure that their own Fourth of July service took place at Park Street Church.

Since the Park Street Address did not open the wider national field that Garrison desired, he remained stymied in Boston, with neither a vantage point for reform nor a steady job. By midsummer of 1829 he told friends that he might be forced to return to Newburyport and *"dig on* at the case for Mr. Allen." Why he thought Allen would have him back remains a mystery, as does Garrison's confidence that he could work peaceably for his old master without suppressing his militancy.

Radical as it was, Garrison quickly moved beyond the position he had staked out in Park Street. Ten days after the address he attended a freedom jubilee marking the anniversary of Great Britain's abolition of the slave trade in 1807. The sponsoring African Abolition Freehold Society, a black benevolent association with an interest in the purchase of real estate, had organized a large procession composed of leaders of the self-improvement societies, Masonic lodge members, and schoolchildren, which was followed by a convocation at its meetinghouse, also the home of the black Baptist church, on the north slope of Beacon Hill. The program featured a temperance address by a white clergyman—probably an acquaintance of Garrison's who had invited him to come along—who irritated his audience by venturing the passing opinion that the emancipation of the Southern slaves was neither safe nor desirable without a long period of preparation that would "qualify" them for freedom. "A very audible murmur ran round the house," Garrison recalled, "which spoke a language that could not be misunderstood." When an ACS agent jumped up to reiterate the speaker's point with more "ingenious" language, an even more decisive and earnest rumble of dissatisfaction welled up. At Park Street Garrison himself had insisted that it would be "a wild vision" to think that the transition from slavery to freedom could occur within a single generation, but he refused to regard the disabilities of slavery as a reason to defer a commitment to the goal. Now he realized that even his own hedging tended to undercut the moral argument for abolition, and he knew that if he were black, he would also make his disapproval vocal. The chorus of protest, Garrison said, spoke "the language of nature—the unbending spirit of liberty," and it struck him with undeniable force that there could be no just middle ground between slavery and freedom.

That Garrison attended such an event, let alone that he experienced an emotional revelation, demonstrates just how far he stood from the center of public opinion. For most of Boston, the small black community of nineteen hundred remained invisible, save when its people entered wealthy homes as domestic workers or the selectmen were importuned to shut down the roistering seafarers' gaming houses, brothels, and taverns that crowded Cambridge Street along the West Boston riverfront. The annual July 14 procession—a traditional undertaking among the politically assertive black Masonic lodge—attracted its share of pamphleteers who mocked the "bobalition annibersary fussibles" in minstrel show dialect and racist cartoons. Yet there was Garrison in attendance, along with an invited white clerical speaker, and with a mind open enough to appreciate the power of the collective black claim to equal citizenship. He had asserted the abstract right in his own address, but he heard the call sounded with emotional depth in the African Meeting House as he had never heard it sound before.

Or had he? Is it possible that Garrison, through his preacher friends Collier and Peak, had a more continuing acquaintance with the black Baptist church and had learned something of black political activities even before he spoke at Park Street? No evidence exists, yet it remains a distinct possibility. Garrison later acknowledged that, growing up unaware of slavery, he had shared the "ordinary prejudices" of the commonwealth toward free blacks, but he said little about how he had overcome them. Newburyport, he recalled, had but a tiny black enclave, a remnant population composed of freed slaves and marine castaways, who lived on "the outskirts of town in a place contemptuously styled 'Guinea'—despised, forsaken, uncared for by the people generally" and thus easy objects of ridicule by schoolchildren. Yet his mother had provided him with a powerful counterexample in writing of the kindly care she had received from a black woman named Henny. "Although a slave to man, [she is] yet a free-born soul by the grace of God," Sister Garrison declared, and she admonished her son to "remember her for your poor mother's sake." Once Lundy had opened his eyes to the horror of slavery, Garrison turned his mother's injunction into a social imperative and came to an even deeper appreciation of the truth that "God hath made of one blood all nations of men." He did so with a passion and a sympathy that seems too fervent and unique to be solely a product of abstract thought; direct personal experience is frequently the strongest solvent for inherited biases. Yet only his account of the July 14 celebration—which he sent at once to Lundy's newspaper—survives as a tantalizing indication of the political education he may have acquired on the margins of the color line in 1820s Boston.

While the issue of gradualism nagged at his conscience, Garrison found an old tract, *The Book and Slavery Irreconcilable*, which deepened his conviction of the sinfulness of slavery. Written in 1816 by the Rev. George Bourne, a Presbyterian minister who had been hounded out of Virginia for his forceful advocacy of emancipation, the pamphlet boldly declared that every slaveholder who considered himself a Christian or a Republican was "either an incurable Idiot who cannot distinguish good from evil, or an obdurate sinner who resolutely defies every social, moral, and divine requisition." Garrison had chosen to say very little about the sinfulness of slavery at Park Street, but Bourne's work—"the more we read it, the higher does our admiration of its author rise"—returned him to first principles. Taking to heart Bourne's maxim "Moderation against sin is an absurdity," Garrison realized that gradualism was untenable on religious as well as political grounds. "I saw there was nothing to stand upon, if it could be granted that slavery was, for a moment, right," he said. If human beings could be justly held in bondage for one hour, he reasoned, they could be held for two, and so on through the generations to eternity. Yet if slavery was a sin, like robbery and murder, then it ought to cease at once.

"Immediatism," as Garrison was coming to understand it, was not so much a political tactic as an expression of the evangelical consciousness Dr. Beecher had done so much to cultivate. With its emphasis upon repentance and reformation, immediatism issued the come-outer's call to "touch not the unclean thing" and upheld a perfectionist's standard in the march toward social and political reformation. An English Quaker, Elizabeth Heyrick, put the case with an eloquence that inspired Garrison's soul. In a pamphlet that circulated widely in benevolence circles and that Lundy had reprinted in the *Genius,* Heyrick expressed the outsider's impatient view of the British antislavery reformers' preoccupation with Parliamentary maneuvers. Gradualism in politics was "the very masterpiece of Satanic policy," she said bluntly, for the fear of losing everything by asking too much intimidated reformers into prolonging sinfulness by asking too little. "Truth and justice make their best way in the world when they appear in bold and simple majesty," she wrote, and insisted that abolitionists had to conduct themselves "with more the spirit of Christian combatants, and less of worldly politicians."

Garrison's embrace of immediatism completed his equivalent of a religious conversion. He felt himself purged of sin, ready to testify about his convictions, and eager to exhort others to repentance. In Boston and Bennington he had served what amounted to a second apprenticeship as a crusading editor and he had found a cause that desperately required his talents. The vocabulary of immediatism gave Garrison new words for his mother's vision of spiritual warfare, but it also heightened his own yearning, heretofore more poetic than religious, to transform the world by liberating the inner moral force of every human being. "Extended ages consist of accumulated moments," Mrs. Heyrick had written, and Garrison felt keenly that his hour—and the slaves'—had come. When, at last, Lundy called in mid-August 1829, Garrison heeded him at once.

CHAPTER FIVE

IN BALTIMORE JAIL

BALTIMORE, WHERE GARRISON JOURNEYED IN THE SUMMER OF 1829, WOULD OFFER HIM A MEASURE OF EXPERIENCE IN A SOCIETY SHAPED BY THE PECULIAR INSTITUTION AND PROFOUNDLY TEST HIS METTLE AS A CRU-sading editor. In the months since he had agreed to collaborate with Ben-jamin Lundy, Garrison had experienced a pivotal transformation from gradualism to immediatism and felt more disposed than ever to attack the inadequacies of colonization as an antislavery measure. He had realized, moreover, that the question of emancipation could not be addressed without considering the status of black people in America and the process by which racial prejudice retarded equal citizenship. It was by no means clear that Lundy shared these enlarged views, nor did Garrison know how far he could press them in Baltimore, which, after all, was an entrepôt for slavetrading and the largest commercial city on the slaveholding eastern seaboard. His six months on the *Genius* in 1829–30 would both confirm Garrison's identity as an implacable social critic and push him to the margins of American political society.

Boston had recently gained regular steamboat connections that could have put Garrison at Lundy's side in forty-eight hours, but the young editor could not afford the ticket. He sailed instead on the first available packet, an econ-omy measure that cost him dearly, for the vessel lay becalmed for days with its sails flapping inertly under a broiling August sun. The voyage took as long as the trip young Lloyd had made from Salem to Baltimore with his mother in 1815, and Garrison vowed that next time he'd put a pack on his shoulders and "trudge on foot"—as Lundy did.

The city had grown substantially in the six years since Garrison had visited his dying mother. The harbor seemed even more crowded with fleet clipper ships, prosperous-looking houses climbed farther up the hillsides, the public buildings had acquired a dignified grandeur, and the city exuded a bustling air of enterprise and culture. The tracks of the pioneering Baltimore & Ohio Railroad extended many miles into the western market, and the monument to George Washington on the city's highest hill was about to receive its statue, though Garrison shared the common complaint that the sculpture was an inferior likeness.

When the Rev. Waldo Emerson had visited Baltimore the year before, he had bestowed upon the city a Yankee's ultimate accolade: "It looks like

Boston." The similarity proved painful for Garrison, however, who complained to Whittier of "low spirits" in his new situation. "He says he is homesick," Whittier told their Boston friends, "and what is worse, *love-sick*. . . ." The editor had renounced his latest Dulcinea for the cause.

Journalistic challenge roused Garrison from the doldrums. Though he modestly styled himself the "assistant editor," Garrison boldly took charge of the *Genius*. He installed a fierce-looking American eagle across the masthead in place of the pallid sketch Lundy had used of sunbeams emanating from the Capitol dome. He also freshened the newspaper's appearance; with a tighter four-column layout, cleaner type, and better paper it radiated energy and proved easier to read than the old gray sheet.

Lundy made no objection to any of this; he had brought his young friend to Baltimore precisely to invigorate the newspaper and free himself for the missionary work he much preferred. He would travel for several weeks at a time, hoping to plow new antislavery territory and to open the eyes of others as he had Garrison's, before returning to Baltimore with whatever he had collected in information, inspiration, and new subscriptions. Lundy had always seen his newspaper as an adjunct, a tool in the cause of his itinerant work as a Quaker witness; he was an editor by necessity, not vocation. Garrison, however, had chosen to make his career as a journalistic advocate, and the newspaper, not the face-to-face meeting, was his true metier. It was not surprising, therefore, that after publishing 226 numbers of the *Genius of Universal Emancipation* at great personal sacrifice over the previous eight years, Lundy readily stepped aside after three meager paragraphs in the editorial column of September 2, 1829, to make way for sixteen from his new collaborator.

Garrison wasted no time in declaring that immediate emancipation had become his watchword. Since his Boston address, Garrison explained, "mature reflection" had convinced him that "no valid excuse can be given for the continuance of the evil [of slavery] a single hour." To those who argued, as he had at Park Street and as Lundy still did, that it was impractical and visionary to consider such a prospect, Garrison answered that "the question of expedience has nothing to do with that of right." Those who tyrannize had no more right to decide when to break the chains of their subjects than a thief had to pick the day on which he might safely give up the practice. Garrison now likened gradualism to dipping out the ocean. Only a decisive stroke, he insisted, could end the evil.

His embrace of immediatism led Garrison to speak more harshly of colonization as an "exceedingly dilatory and uncertain" project that could not accomplish any substantial reform. As an "auxiliary" mode of relief, the voluntary removal of some emancipated slaves to Liberia or Haiti deserved "encouragement," Garrison said, but as a remedy, it was "altogether inadequate." Voluntary emigration would never run ahead of population growth,

Garrison pointed out, and coercive deportation would violate the rights of free black citizens.

Despite his deepening opposition to colonization, Garrison publicized Lundy's humanitarian efforts to relocate manumitted slaves in Haiti—on a voluntary basis—and maintained the senior editor's practice of offering one page of the newspaper in French for the benefit of Lundy's Haitian constituency. For his part, Lundy held to the insistence that colonization alleviated distress in individual cases and brought the issue of emancipation into general discussion, but Lundy never accepted the ACS arguments that justified mandatory deportation on the grounds that the slaves were too degraded to be prepared for freedom or that black and white could never live equally together in America. Indeed, his senior partner fully shared Garrison's insight about the politics of race. "The odious distinctions between white and black have been created by tyrants . . . for the express purpose of acquiring and preserving their *unjust authority*," Lundy wrote. "That is the Alpha and Omega of it."

The two men decided from the outset that, in the Quakerly tradition, their editorial voices would remain separate. "Thee may put thy initials to thy articles, and I will put my initials to mine," Friend Lundy said, "and each will bear his own burden." In his old age Garrison claimed that this practice reflected the disparity of their views and joked that his radical columns could scare off a dozen subscribers for every one attracted by Lundy's moderation. The senior editor, however, actually did very little writing for the *Genius*. In six months, Lundy's only major editorial contributions would be a long front-page account of private manumissions directed by the wills of two exemplary planters, an extended review of a report on conditions in Haiti, and several prescient warnings that Southern politicians were plotting to take over the Mexican province of Texas, since that nation—in the aftermath of declaring its independence from Spain—had abolished slavery within its borders. For the most part the *Genius* reflected Garrison's immediatism, not Lundy's gradualism. Lundy never challenged Garrison in print, and Garrison never attacked Lundy for not measuring up to his immediatist's yardstick. The system of signed contributions, in fact, protected Garrison's advocacy as much as Lundy's conscience and set a high standard of cooperation for radical journals.

There was little likelihood that these strong-minded individuals could have reached common agreement and much to be gained by letting their individual voices be heard. Lundy had "a choleric side," Garrison learned, and deafness made it difficult to have a protracted conversation with him. With Lundy, it was best to listen and draw inspiration. Garrison, too, liked to hold forth, but he relished cut-and-thrust debate in a way that Lundy—whose mind Garrison considered "active, but not robust"—did not.

In their concepts of activism the two men were very different. Lundy practiced a benevolence of charitable deed, while Garrison had emerged as an exponent of the prophetic word. Lundy hoped to persuade individuals to emancipate slaves; Garrison wanted to persuade the nation to abolish slavery. Lundy still hoped for political action in the South; Garrison aimed to shock the North into moral awareness. Lundy tended to emphasize the satisfaction that would come from taking benevolent action, Garrison the disaster that would punish a failure to act. Lundy shared Garrison's belief in the sinfulness of slavery, but the younger man's evangelical fervor and melodramatic style went against the Quaker grain. Lundy winced whenever Garrison referred to slaveholders as "man-stealers," even though he advanced Scriptural warrant for the term; indeed, Lundy would rather say "advocates of slavery" than "slaveholders," hoping thereby to separate (for purposes of conversion) the sinner from the sin.

Though Garrison defended his radical views on religious and moral grounds, they were also a response to changing political conditions. For most of the decade the nation had lapsed into the complacent belief that the great debate over Missouri statehood in 1820–21 had settled the slavery problem forever. The famous compromise line drawn at latitude 36°30' fixed the limits of expansion for slavery to the remaining territory owned by the United States south of the line and allowed people to indulge further the illusory notion that the institution would eventually wither away. Yet under the spur of a booming cotton market, settlement of the southwestern territories had proceeded so rapidly that slaveholders now entertained designs on Mexican Texas, a foreign land where the writ of the Missouri agreement did not necessarily run. Individual manumission, with or without colonization, had done nothing to reduce the growth of the slave population, which in 1830 amounted to two million souls, including 700,000 children below the age of ten. The domestic slave trade between the older seaboard states and the new cotton lands still flourished in Baltimore, in Richmond, and in Washington, D.C., literally within sight of the nation's Capitol, while Andrew Jackson—the fifth slavemaster among the seven presidents—had flamboyantly taken over the White House. The vice-president, South Carolina's John C. Calhoun, was a crafty architect of constitutional doctrines that elaborated a state's right to "nullify" federal legislation—against the interstate slave trade, for example—that infringed on its "sovereignty" or that adversely affected its interests.

Our politics are "rotten," Garrison said bluntly, and opponents of slavery could place no "cheering reliance on 'the powers that be.'" Slavery was expanding and the federal government seemed ever more firmly in the grip of slaveholders; the Jackson administration had countenanced the forcible removal of the Cherokee and Choctaw from vast tracts of Southern land fraudulently obtained by speculators; colonizationists sought a government subsidy, while antislavery petitions received summary rejection; Southern "hotspurs" demanded that Texas be rescued from the abolitionist decrees of the Mexican government and added to the domain of slavery. With all this occurring, who could say that anything but the clearest, most forceful and dramatic rejection of the entire system could make an impact? "*We* boast of our freedom, who go shackled to the polls," Garrison had complained in his Park Street Address, and there is little doubt that the triumph of the Jacksonian party in the election of 1828 had helped propel him into anti-slavery militancy.

Garrison endeavored to make his one little newspaper a counterweight to the entire burden of political practice in the United States, and he cheerfully agreed with those friends who warned him that his "wild notions" of immediate and complete emancipation would only provoke more hostility. "That they will create much opposition, I cannot doubt; that *therefore* they should be abandoned, I cannot admit. . . . New truths, like new improvements, are slowly adopted," he explained; they are always "disorganizing in their operation." He *wanted* controversy and considered it a vital social process; "let us all begin to talk . . . and depend upon it, something noble will be done—and not till then."

To impress his readers with the gravity of the evil, Garrison revived one of Benjamin Lundy's most provocative features, a column entitled "Black List" that catalogued "Horrible News—Domestic and Foreign." In it Garrison printed atrocity stories culled from other newspapers, public documents, and private correspondence. The first week's list reported on the discovery of the bodies of kidnapped Negro children in Delaware and the murder of a runaway slave in Georgia. When a critic objected that "a *bad* white man" would have met a similar fate, Garrison expressed incredulity. A delinquent white runaway shot in the back? Surely the correspondent knew "that where a *white* skin is hardly indictable, a *black* one is deemed worthy of the most aggravated punishment."

The column aimed volley after volley in the editors' continuing campaign against the "abominable traffic" in slaves. Garrison wrote of setbacks to the planned suspension of the slave trade by Brazil, gave reports about the smuggling of captives into Cuba, and presented a graphic description of slave traders' "pens" in Alexandria, Virginia. The "Black List" contained statistics on the thousands of slaves being shipped from the Chesapeake region to Louisiana and related dreadful instances in which free blacks from Northern cities had been kidnapped and sold into bondage. He also chastised the other Baltimore papers for accepting advertisements about the local slave auctions, reasoning that as "accomplices to the crime" those editors were as guilty of "grasping avarice" as the slavetraders whose money they accepted.

Garrison was raising the alarm about the relatively new phenomenon of the long-distance forced migration of slaves that saw more than one million slaves transported from the older Southern states to the new southwest between 1790 and 1860. While possibly one-third to one-quarter of these slaves moved with their owners as part of family decisions to relocate, the majority were shipped in profitable transactions by commercial traders. The business was large enough that in 1830 an adolescent slave in the upper South had a ten percent chance of being traded to the southwest, and historians estimate that by 1860, the cumulative risk was thirty percent, as Kentucky, Tennessee, and northern Georgia joined the Carolinas, Virginia, and Maryland as net slave exporting areas.

The repetitive attacks in the "Black List" provoked a roaring controversy with Austin Woolfolk, "the most notorious of the Baltimore Negro-buyers," who two years previously had physically attacked Lundy on the street for making aspersions upon his character in print. (Lundy had sued Woolfolk for assault, and although the editor won his verdict, the unsympathetic judge had awarded only token damages of one dollar and tried, unsuccessfully, to have Lundy indicted for libel.) When Woolfolk rumbled about taking further action against Lundy for the latest criticism, Garrison jibed that the trader ought to be able to tell a "G." from an "L." and invited him to call at his boardinghouse for a public debate on the wickedness of the traffic. Woolfolk did not appear.

Garrison pounced with especial delight when he learned—through a black informant on the waterfront—that a Woolfolk-brokered cargo of seventy-five slaves shipped from Baltimore for New Orleans had sailed in the ship *Francis* owned by a merchant, Francis Todd, from Newburyport and skippered by another 'Porter, Nicholas Brown. "So much for New England principle," Garrison wrote, citing the incident in the "Black List" for November 13, 1829, along with figures that demonstrated Woolfolk's position as the "largest shipper" of slaves in Baltimore. Returning to the incident in the following week's column, Garrison declared his intention "to cover with thick infamy all who were concerned in this nefarious business." Men who participated in the wicked trade "for purposes of heaping up wealth should be ☞ SENTENCED TO SOLITARY CONFINEMENT FOR LIFE ☜," he said, for they were no better than "highway robbers and murderers." About his townsman, Garrison added, "I recollect that it was always a mystery in Newburyport how Mr. Todd contrived to make profitable voyages" when others failed, but now "the mystery seems to be unraveled. Any man can gather up riches, if he does not care by what means they are obtained."

Garrison coupled his attacks on the slave trade with concentrated attention to the increasing volume of proslavery apologetics. In the Revolutionary generation, defenders of slavery—including Thomas Jefferson and Patrick Henry—had emphasized the practical difficulties of emancipation while professing their abhorrence of slavery and their moral discomfort at the incongruity of maintaining it in a nation founded upon the philosophy of natural rights. In the 1820s, however, a new generation of slaveholders— concerned by the rising tide of abolition in the newly independent nations of Latin America, the renewal of the campaign to end slavery in the British

West Indies, and the stirrings of antislavery activity in the United States—refused to concede the moral issue and began to defend slavery in far-reaching terms as a humanitarian institution. Charles Cotesworth Pinckney, one of South Carolina's wealthiest rice planters and the scion of a political family that included signers of both the Declaration of Independence and the U.S. Constitution, told an agricultural society in his state in 1829, for example, that he could not admit that the condition of slavery was "a greater or more unusual evil than befalls the poor in general." He suggested that under the paternal care of their masters the slaves had fewer worries than the Old World poor or free laborers in the North, not only because their material needs were well met, but because they were relieved of anxiety about the future; their families would be cared for, even unto sickness or death, and they had been rescued from pagan Africa and given the Christian hope of a blessed immortality. With Garrison's familiar jabbing notes attached to the printed extract, the editor deftly exposed the racial prejudices that underlay Pinckney's claims and wondered if he proposed to fetter the white laboring classes "and place them under the domination of iron-hearted task-masters, as it would be immensely better for their bellies." More such "benevolent" and "disinterested" theorizing from slaveholders, Garrison declared, would open the public's eyes as nothing else could.

The prickly defensiveness of the slaveholders afforded Garrison an irresistible target, and he taunted and baited them mercilessly in his columns, hoping that the embattled masters would further embarrass themselves in the court of public opinion. When, however, Southern leaders pointed to Northern examples of racial hostility in order to condemn advocates like Garrison as meddlesome hypocrites, the editor confronted the issue candidly and declared that whether "the curse of deep-rooted prejudice" could be surmounted was "a question which our northern people must answer." Could black people ever be on a level with the whites in this country? "Not if we perpetuate their slavery—not if we deprive them of the benefits of instruction—not if they are denied the privileges of citizenship," Garrison said. "But snap their chains asunder—give them a fair start—and nothing but our prejudices will prevent them from standing eventually 'on a level with the whites.'" To those colonization-minded critics who persisted in referring to the free black population as "foreigners," Garrison replied that most were born here. Though in their color they resembled Africans, they were as much American citizens as those whites who looked like Englishmen. "Does *our* color make us subjects of George IV?" he asked.

Garrison's platform of immediatism and equality squarely challenged the sham reform of colonization and shattered the establishment's liberal and philanthropic self-image. He boldly challenged even Henry Clay, whose political program of economic development Garrison had long favored, for allowing the delusion of colonization to "seal up his lips" on the subject of slavery itself. Early in 1830, Garrison reprinted long extracts from Clay's address to the Kentucky Colonization Society in order to attack what he called Clay's preference for "eternal slavery" over an emancipation that was not accompanied by deportation. In Clay's eyes, said Garrison, "a free black is a nuisance—and a community of slaves more tolerable than a community of colored freemen."

Garrison's willingness to criticize Clay, the politician whom he considered the "tallest and most majestic figure in the nation" and the only plausible candidate to reclaim the presidency from Jacksonian "anarchy, corruption, and [mis]rule," is a striking example of the editor's iconoclasm and his insistence that politics had to be subordinated to moral principle. Clay had served as Speaker of the House for much of Garrison's lifetime, and he had won a national reputation as the "great pacificator" for securing passage of the Missouri Compromise. Garrison had long admired Clay, both for his advocacy of national economic development and his support for the emerging republics of Latin America, and although the editor conceded that Clay's social position as a Kentucky slaveholder "detracted immensely" from his merits, he nonetheless considered the veteran politician "a friend to the cause of emancipation." Clay's latest address, however, put that estimate in doubt. Garrison did not expect the Kentuckian to denounce the slave system with his own fiery intensity, but he had hoped for "deeper sympathy" and some recognition of "the awful guilt of . . . defiling the moral workmanship of the great God." If a man of Clay's talents could remain so insensitive, Garrison concluded, then it was "morally impossible for a[ny] slaveholder to reason correctly on the subject." A slaveholder's vision was warped by the belief that one race was born to serve another, and even if his conscience "detects the absurdity" of the doctrine, as an interested party he was "never at a loss to find palliatives for his conduct" and, like all tyrants, was ready to plead the welfare of his subjects as a justification for his rule. Clay's insistence that it would be a national blessing to have the two races "separated . . . in distinct and distant countries" grieved Garrison as a surrender to injustice and a "shocking" failure of moral leadership. If men of "high standing and extensive influence . . . shrink from the battle," he asked, "by whom shall the victory be won?"

Garrison would eventually take pride in the idea that the antislavery crusade might be waged by outcasts and apostles through "the foolishness of preaching," and his disillusionment with Henry Clay marks an important way station on his journey from a strategy based upon an appeal to benevolent leaders to one that sought to change the climate of opinion in which leaders had to operate. His break with Clay also marked the end of his search for a political hero; henceforth he would regard politicians as craven opportunists in thrall to expediency and reserve his praise for those who risked their reputations in defiance of political conventions. Garrison's editorials in the *Genius* express a gathering anger at the political silence of the establishment and a growing resolve to challenge it at any cost. In them, too, lies a keen awareness—as his distress with Clay's separatism makes clear—that the debate over slavery could not be resolved without addressing the issue of racial prejudice and the widespread assumption that black people stood outside the American polity.

Garrison had become more sensitive to the issue of color prejudice because, for the first time in his life, he lived in a racially mixed society. Although he had at least a passing acquaintance with the strivings of Boston's black community, Baltimore offered a dimension of social experience that Garrison had not previously known. One out of every four people in Baltimore was black. In Boston, blacks composed only three percent of the population and scarcely registered as a collective presence; in Baltimore, the black population was a palpable entity—not only as laborers in nearly every facet of commercial and social life, but as a troublesome and vexing issue for the political establishment. In Boston, Garrison lived on the fringes of the black enclave, but in Baltimore he lived within the black community and came to know its people and its perils at first hand.

Ties with the antislavery Friends facilitated the young editor's entry. For many years, Quaker philanthropists in Baltimore, led by the much-admired Elisha Tyson, a retired flour miller and community patriarch, had promoted both manumission and freedmen's protective legislation, and they had forged a tiny biracial political coalition that became Garrison's base in the city. He and Lundy boarded at the home of two Quaker women, Beulah and Sarah Harris, at 135 Market Street, and they found their social circle in the side streets and alleys of the southwest side, where the Friends Meeting House and the black Methodist church stood within a few doors of each other on Sharp Street. In this neighborhood, as in Fells Point, Old Town, and several other sections of the society, black and white working people—sailmakers, milliners, cooks, blacksmiths, seamstresses, teamsters—lived jumbled together on unpaved blocks in narrow two-story frame houses that were sometimes no bigger than one square box set upon another. Substantial houses coexisted side by side with shacks, water had to be carried from the public pump, and chickens pecked in the hard dirt yards.

Garrison had known these neighborhoods briefly in his youth, for his mother had conducted her prayer meetings in such back streets and had died among her Baptist sisters in a black woman's arms. Now Garrison became friendly with the Quaker John Needles, a cabinetmaker who had assumed the late Elisha Tyson's place as the philanthropists' leader. Needles had purchased the type for Lundy's printing office, concealed antislavery tracts in the furniture he shipped south, and allowed his warehouse to be used for a school for black children. Garrison also met the schoolteacher William Watkins, a tall bespectacled black man who, like Garrison, had begun his working life as a shoemaker. He worked with the whitewasher Jacob Greener and his sons, the trader Hezekiah Grice, and other leaders in the black community. He sang with these families in church, heard their children's recitations in their volunteer-run schools, shared their suppers, and sold the *Genius* door-to-door with them. Theirs was the fellowship of a reform movement—self-conscious, tentative, and undoubtedly strained by subterranean anger and guilt—but a sustaining community nonetheless.

Although it is commonplace to say that in Baltimore the Yankee editor had a direct opportunity to observe the institution of slavery at first hand, what he actually observed on a daily basis proved to be the precarious situation of black citizens in a political culture dominated by white supremacists. Maryland, and Baltimore especially, had changed dramatically since the Revolutionary era, as wheat (which required less intense cultivation and could be tended by hired day-workers) had replaced tobacco as its staple crop, and the mills and factories of the booming city had become a magnet for cheap immigrant labor from Europe. Once manumission had been made easier during the period of Revolutionary idealism, the combined shift in economics and morality meant that Maryland's population of free blacks quadrupled between 1790 and 1810 and continued to grow rapidly enough for the state to have the largest free black population in the Union for the remainder of the antebellum era. In Baltimore free African-Americans had increased their numbers from eight thousand to fifteen thousand between 1820 and 1830, while the number of slaveholding households dropped nearly in half. When Garrison came to Baltimore in 1829, there were barely five thousand slaves in the city, the majority of them working as domestics in the homes of the well-to-do. Only the large shipbuilding concerns employed as many as ten slaves at a time, and often their owners rented them out to other businesses on an interim basis. In addition, planters from the lower Chesapeake frequently allowed some of their skilled slaves to "hire out" their labor in the shipyards, ironworks, or brick factories in the city, which meant they lived independently and saw their masters or a deputy only weekly to turn over their wages. (The slave Frederick Douglass worked in Baltimore on such a basis only a year or two after Garrison's stay there.) Slave and free labor proved indistinguishable in Baltimore, for free blacks also had domestic and shipyard employment and slaves mixed easily in their neighborhoods and institutions.

The substantial presence of free black people in Baltimore, including a large number of manumitted slaves, contradicted the idea that slavery was the naturally ordained condition of the African race. No one walking on the streets, dining in the hotels, supervising a cargo on the wharves, stabling a horse, or shopping in the market could distinguish a black slave from a black citizen, and neither abolitionists nor apologists for slavery had trouble understanding that this ambiguity threatened the racist foundation on which the peculiar institution was built. The more that African-Americans established their identity as a free people by owning property, founding schools, churches, and benevolent associations, and raising their voices in politics, the more uneasy whites became. Black citizens, though free, faced grave political disabilities—disenfranchisement at the polls, exclusion from juries and even from testifying against whites—and lived on the dangerous edge of freedom, subject to kidnap by slave traders and, after 1826, to a Maryland law requiring those without visible means of support to post bond or be jailed for vagrancy. Garrison emerged as a champion of social improvement and civil protection for the free black community, whose rise in the world would refute the commonplace assumption that slavery had so degraded black people that they could never live on a plane of equality with whites.

The necessary relationship between abolition and civil rights proved an enduring lesson of Garrison's sojourn in Baltimore. The city's leadership had "no strong attachment to slavery" and objected to the efforts of southern Maryland planters to secure protections for slavery at the expense of the commercial legislation favored by urban entrepreneurs. Baltimore looked ahead to steam power and had begun to regard slave power as no longer compatible with progress. Yet being against slavery meant little, as Garrison realized, if political enmity extended to free blacks. The growing numbers of free African-Americans in the city raised the specter for white politicians that at some not-so-distant day Maryland might be dominated by a black majority. "You can manumit the slave, but you cannot make him a white man," declared Robert Goodloe Harper, a prominent supporter of the colonization movement which, in his view, would remove "an idle, vagabond, and thieving race" from America. The city's chief judge, Nicholas Brice, had publicly complained to the governor that the laws governing free blacks ought to confine them more strictly in a subordinate position. He also opined that "injudicious manumissions" had placed a heavy burden of poverty, insubordination, and criminality upon Baltimore, where freed slaves (especially old people released by economy-minded masters) tended to congregate. Manumission, suggested Brice, who was an officer in Maryland's ACS affiliate, ought to be restricted by the legislature only to "those Negroes consenting to go to our African colony."

Against the city's leadership, whose moral and economic condemnation of slavery was matched by a racist hostility to black citizenship, stood the "saving remnant" that supported the *Genius*. Daniel Raymond, an attorney who had defended Lundy and written extensively against slavery, challenged Harper's view of black incapacity: "The industrious thrive and increase," he wrote, and "their offspring, accustomed to liberty, acquire the habits of the whites, and make equally as good citizens." Garrison's friend Jacob Greener had disrupted a citywide colonization meeting to demand that "the first object" of the group's efforts be support for the education of Baltimore's black children. Wash the stain of prejudice from the Stars and Stripes, Greener challenged, and cease to inflame opinion against us by complaining of our lowly status.

Garrison opened the *Genius* to these militant black voices and supported
their arguments. He urged critics to visit, as he had, the schools established
by Greener and others and "try if they can argue against fact." He published
letters from a black advocate of colonization and encouraged the schoolteacher William Watkins to contribute a series of rebuttals (published under
the *nom de plume* "A Colored Baltimorean") insisting that black citizens
would rather struggle against injustice at home than suffer exile. When a
New Bedford, Massachusetts, editor crudely attributed Garrison's interest in
black welfare to his status as a bachelor, the editor would not rise to the
bait, but he did find an occasion to declare, with reference to reports that a
Haitian leader's daughter had married a Prussian colonel, that "the time is
to come when all the nations of the earth will intermarry, and all distinctions
of color cease to divide mankind."

Although Garrison had demonstrated his flair for independent journalism
on his three previous newspapers, the *Genius* matured his talent as an editorial crusader. "We call things by their right names, in plain language," he
said with pride, and "no man's power shall awe us into submission." He grew
more proficient at extracting material from the mainstream press and public
record that offered opportunities to expatiate on his themes, and he spared
no one, harassing governors and senators with the sharp repartee he had
honed in years of combat with rival small-town editors. At times it seemed
a quixotic tilting at windmills, as Garrison cheerfully conceded, yet each mail
bag yielded a letter or two that confirmed the editor's impact not upon
official leaders but upon his true constituency, the ordinary citizen with a
troubled conscience. From Garrison's old stand at Bennington, Vermont,
came news that student orators at the local seminary had taken up the cause
of immediatism and decried those who counseled an expedient delay. An
Ohio correspondent affirmed Garrison's insistence that justice must be done
regardless of the consequences, and a writer from Sudbury, Pennsylvania
declared that if "somebody must suffer in consequence of the liberation of
the blacks, then I would say, let the whites suffer, for the blacks have suffered long enough."

Garrison's was not the only voice raised against oppression. A black minister
in New York, Samuel Cornish, who had published *Freedom's Journal* until his
coeditor had given it a colonizationist tinge, launched another newspaper, *The
Rights of All,* dedicated to race advancement at home. More dramatically,
however, David Walker—a free black man from North Carolina who in the
mid-1820s had migrated to Boston, where he ran a used clothing store and
gained a reputation as an eloquent lay preacher—converted his forceful talks
into a blistering seventy-six-page pamphlet, *Walker's Appeal . . . to the Colored Citizens of the World,* which put the case for black liberation in its stark-
est form.

Walker's exhortation, which drew upon the powerful incantatory rhythms
of the Bible and the Methodist pulpit, insisted that black people in the

United States endured more "wretchedness" than any other people in history. He attributed their misery to four causes: the barbarity of slavery, a cringing and servile attitude—even among free blacks—that perpetuated ignorance, the indifference of the Christian clergy, and the colonization scheme that insulted black citizenship and aspirations. Walker explicitly attacked Thomas Jefferson's racist assertions about black inferiority, and he urged black men to give *Notes on Virginia* to their sons to inspire their anger. He deplored submissiveness among blacks, contended for the right of self-defense, and raised a prophetic voice for a rebellion in the name of the Lord's justice. Walker balanced his rumbling insinuations about slave revolt, however, with the prospect of racial harmony should slaveholders cease their oppression without bloodshed and white Americans forsake racism and avarice for the true practice of Christian charity.

Walker's Appeal gave vent—for the first time in U.S. public discourse—to the depths of black rage at the crimes of slavery and prejudice, and he insisted that the day of domination of the *whites* (a term he used interchangeably with *Americans*) would soon end. The pamphlet was published in September 1829 and went through two more editions over the next six months. Walker circulated his work among the black civic associations in the northeastern seaboard cities, and he adopted various stratagems, which included the stitching of pamphlets into the lining of the jackets he sold to black sailors, for getting the word into the slave states.

The editors of the *Genius* had *Walker's Appeal* on their table by midautumn, and it provoked much discussion. The animus and implacability of the pamphlet gave the shudders to Benjamin Lundy, whose efforts Walker had previously lauded, and the Quaker considered it too inflammatory to notice in print. Vengeful feelings had to be repressed and physical force eschewed for the sake of the cause, Lundy argued, but Walker's outburst of rage appealed to the worst passions in human nature and could lead to nothing but catastrophe. Garrison, however, had a more mixed response. He considered the text as one of "the most remarkable productions of the age" and admired its "impassioned and determined spirit." Each of Walker's main points touched a theme Garrison had pursued in his own writing, and both men had drawn deeply from the inspirational wellsprings of evangelical Christianity and natural rights philosophy. As a black man Walker engaged in more racial self-criticism than Garrison would ever attempt and exhorted an angry people to revolt with a prophetic grandeur that both appalled and fascinated Garrison.

Walker's pamphlet flared as the American manifestation of the "black Jacobin" spirit that had overthrown French colonialism and slavery in the Caribbean. The San Domingo revolution, which began in 1791 and continued until Haitian independence was achieved in 1804, was a seminal event in New World history—the first expulsion of a European colonial power by people of color—though Americans generally regarded it only as a nightmarish spectacle of racial savagery, and the U.S. government refused to extend diplomatic recognition to Haiti until after the Civil War.

As a Christian who believed in turning the other cheek and forsaking
vengeance, Garrison could never endorse a slave uprising, yet he always
insisted that such bloodshed would be the ultimate outcome of a failure to
enact abolition. Walker was paying white Americans "in their own coin,"
Garrison thought, in extending the logic of the revolution to the oppressed
slaves. However "injudicious" the call, there could be no doubt that Walker's
exhortation was "warranted by the creed of an independent people." Yet
Garrison paid close attention to the ambivalent emotions that swirled
through the *Appeal* and appreciated Walker's "seasonable warnings" that an
uprising could be averted through white repentance and the abolition of
slavery. Most whites, however, were more anxious to silence the tocsin of
slave revolt than to listen for the subtle harmonies of racial reconciliation,
and they condemned the work as sedition.

Perhaps in deference to Lundy's condemnation, Garrison did not comment on *Walker's Appeal* in the *Genius* until January 1830, after a strenuous
campaign to suppress it had begun. New Orleans had arrested four black
men who had copies in their possession, Richmond had become jittery after
thirty copies were found in the home of a free black laborer, vigilantes
harassed the free black enclave in Walker's hometown of Wilmington, North
Carolina, and Savannah prevented black seamen on incoming vessels from
landing in the city after dozens of smuggled copies were discovered in the
port. The legislatures of Virginia and Georgia considered repressive laws,
including one that would make "the circulation of pamphlets of evil tendency
among our domestics" a capital offense. No one ought to be surprised at the
uproar, Garrison noted; if the South did not have reason on its side, it would
of course employ oppressive power. The editor couldn't help but observe
that the ready circulation of a pamphlet by an obscure black man from
Boston demonstrated "that the boasted security of the slave states is mere
affectation, or something worse."

The furor over Walker may have jeopardized the future of the *Genius,*
for suddenly, in February 1830, Garrison and Lundy were indicted by a
Baltimore grand jury on the chilling, seldom-used criminal charge of having
published "a gross and malicious libel" against Francis Todd. The trouble
stemmed from the articles in the "Black List" in which Garrison had censured the Newburyport merchant for his connection to Woolfolk and the
slave trade. Todd's local attorneys had filed a civil defamation suit a few
weeks previously that sought $5,000 for damages to his reputation, and the
editors worried that, given their precarious finances, the expense and travail
of that suit might well drive them out of business. That they now also faced
a criminal prosecution and possible jail sentence meant that they had antagonized many more people than a shipowner in a distant town; the local
authorities had decided to silence them.

The crime of libel derived from the common law of England which held that, in Blackstone's words, one could be prosecuted for "malicious defamations of any person, and especially a magistrate, made public by printing . . . in order to provoke him to wrath, or expose him to public hatred, contempt, or ridicule." Blackstone did not believe that libel prosecutions infringed freedom of the press, which he construed as a protection against laws intended to prevent matter from being published. Whether the First Amendment to the U.S. Constitution carried over this English common law understanding of freedom of the press as merely a guarantee against prior restraint or rested upon a broader libertarian foundation has long preoccupied constitutional scholars. Libel suits were used as a political weapon against colonial newspapers, although beginning with the Zenger case of 1735, important modifications, especially the concept that the truth of the matter could be used as a defense against the charge, weakened the force of the common law. The Sedition Act of 1798, in practice a national criminal libel statute, proved the high-water mark of such prosecutions in America, although both Federalists and Jeffersonians continued for a few more years to muzzle their political critics by invoking state libel laws against them. Such prosecutions declined, however, as many states, including Maryland in 1804, enacted laws that explicitly made truth a "good" defense, thus superseding Blackstone and extending greater protection to the press.

Maryland's decision to prosecute Garrison was therefore unusual in several respects. Political defamation cases had always arisen from cases in which newspapers had criticized public officials, not private citizens, and no such prosecution had taken place in Maryland for a generation. Although most historians have regarded the criminal proceeding as an inevitable and justifiable result of Garrison's intemperate style, the affair actually bears the hallmarks of a politically inspired prosecution. It is impossible to reconstruct how the proceeding was instituted. Pressure may have come from the influential slave trader Austin Woolfolk, who likely had something to do with encouraging Todd's civil suit, and it is certainly curious that Todd's attorney for the damage suit—a well-connected lawyer named Jonathan Meredith who had once practiced law with Maryland's attorney general, Roger B. Taney—sat at the prosecution's table during the criminal trial and argued a major portion of the case for the state. The criminal proceeding may also have grown out of the political anxieties generated by *Walker's Appeal*. Woolfolk's friend on the bench, Judge Nicholas Brice, had referred Lundy's attacks on the slave trader to the grand jury once before, and perhaps he sensed that the climate had become more favorable to repression. One of the most influential Jacksonian editors in the country, Thomas Ritchie of the *Richmond Enquirer*, had loudly insisted that a systematic design existed to circulate seditious papers among the slaves, and Taney, who was in the process of relinquishing his state office in order to accept the equivalent post in Jackson's cabinet, may have heeded the call for greater vigilance against every kind of antislavery journalism. Lundy and Garrison certainly believed that the full weight of the Baltimore "Jackson party" tipped the scales of justice in their case.

The editors had no money for their defense, but Charles Mitchell, a Connecticut judge's son who had established his own practice in Baltimore, volunteered to take their case pro bono. Mitchell had a brilliant reputation as an advocate, although the senior members of the local bar qualified their praise with murmurs that implied unsoundness in Mitchell's politics, and was active in the benevolence movement and sympathetic to abolition. Mitchell first succeeded in getting Lundy's case severed from the prosecution. Since the traveling senior editor had not even been in Baltimore when the offending issue was published, the court agreed to continue his case indefinitely, which meant that Lundy would not have to stand trial with Garrison, though the threat of a later prosecution hung over him. Lundy made plain his anger at the blatant attempt to "muzzle the press," though he wryly told friends that he couldn't say that he would have used exactly the same words that his partner had. He publicly rejoiced, however, at the exposure of "the *Slave-Freighter, Todd*" and groused that never had there been "a more labored attempt . . . to give a coloring to a charge of libel."

In legal terms Mitchell did not think Garrison's case difficult to defend. Under the 1804 statute a showing that Todd indeed owned the vessel—and that it had in fact carried a cargo of slaves—would demonstrate that Garrison's column had made a truthful report and could not be considered libelous. Mitchell might have had a more difficult time demonstrating the truth of the later passage insinuating that Todd had made more money than his fellow townsmen because he had plied the slave trade. However, the state's attorney had neglected to prosecute this arguably defamatory passage, although Garrison later learned that it had in fact antagonized Todd more emphatically than anything else in the paper. The hastily drawn indictment cited only the first eight sentences of the long article, and Mitchell intended to argue that although Todd's name appeared in them (albeit in boldface capital letters) as the owner of the vessel *Francis,* the burden of these sentences had to be construed as a general condemnation on slave traders that Garrison had perfect editorial freedom to proclaim. Even the indictment had to reach for one parenthetical reminder after another—"(meaning that the said Francis Todd, amongst others, had the wickedness)"—to link the editor's diatribe to the merchant, and Mitchell thought the prosecution would be hard pressed to argue that an editor could be punished for expressing a generally held moral view about the slave trade, much less for reporting that an individual had engaged in a form of domestic commerce that was—however regrettably—still protected by law.

Yet when Garrison and Mitchell walked up Calvert Street from the printing office to the imposing brick courthouse on the Lexington Street hill on the wintry morning of March 1, 1830, they knew that, however strong their legal case, the politics of abolition were really at issue. The libel prosecution was intended, as Garrison charged from the outset, "to stifle free inquiry, to dishearten every effort of reform, and to intimidate the conductors of newspapers."

The metallic gray sky could be seen through the tall windows of the courtroom, and the damp chill that precedes a snowstorm still clung to their shoulders as Garrison and his attorney settled themselves at the defendant's table. The chief judge, Lundy's old antagonist Nicholas Brice, had assigned the case to himself. Fifty-nine years old, brought up in the common law traditions of Coke and Blackstone, married into a well-to-do family from the tobacco region of the eastern shore, presiding officer of the temperance and colonization societies, Brice enjoyed a distinguished reputation and thought of himself as a humanitarian. He had personally manumitted four "valuable" male slaves, as well as a female slave and her children, and had extended legal assistance in many other private manumission cases. Garrison knew, however, that Brice hewed to the Jackson party line that kept slavery off the congressional agenda and that he had blatantly sided with Austin Woolfolk—praising the slave trader's "beneficial" occupation for removing "nuisances and vagabonds" from the region—when Lundy had sued the slave trader for assault in 1827. Brice had "all the humanitarianism of a shark," Garrison said.

The editor listened intently as the clerk read out the indictment declaring that he "unlawfully, wickedly and maliciously . . . did print and publish . . . false, scandalous, and malicious matter and libel . . . to the great scandal, damage, and disgrace of the said Francis Todd, to the evil example of all others in like manner offending, and against the peace, government, and dignity of the state."

"*Not guilty*," Garrison replied. He had summoned Todd to the bar of public opinion and for that he found himself called to the bar of justice! Garrison insisted that in publishing such strictures he had not "exceeded the freedom of the press, or the legitimate province of an independent editor." To heighten the public debate he had sent Todd a copy of his remarks—that was Garrison's established practice, not mere bravado—with the invitation to take as much room as he cared to have in the *Genius* to account for his conduct. (Garrison said later that he harbored no personal hostility toward Todd, but wanted to show that "a New England assistant was as liable to reprehension as a Maryland slaveholder" and, perhaps, to deter Yankee merchants from future traffic in human beings.)

"Not guilty," the clerk repeated, then, at the judge's bidding, he summoned the jurors to be sworn: Bond, Bradshaw, Dukehart, Ford, Hutchins, Jarrett, Magauran, Palmer, Parker, Scott, Waggoner, and Wilson. It was a jury composed nearly equally of commercial men and artisans, all of whom later swore that they considered slavery a great evil, held no such property themselves, and hoped that someday the blight might disappear. *Someday!* That little word epitomized for Garrison the gulf that stretched between himself and a jury of his peers.

The prosecutor, a long-faced lawyer named Jonathan Meredith who also represented Todd in the pending civil suit, had the allegedly libelous matter in the indictment read for the jury. Then Meredith, a courtly and elegant gentleman much loved in polite society, casually offered to help the jury understand the case by reading the remainder of the article as well. It would demonstrate, he said, the writer's "malicious intent."

"Objection," roared Garrison's attorney. "No one can be compelled to defend himself against charges *not set forth* in an indictment," Mitchell said, as he launched into a long and learned argument on the subject. He cited authorities that upheld the *defendant's* right to read "material and qualifying parts of the same publication" in exculpation, but emphasized that there was no precedent in Anglo-American jurisprudence that gave such liberty to the *prosecution*. The indictment before them contained no libel on Francis Todd and *upon that indictment alone* the defendant was entitled to be judged. He fervently prayed that the court would pause "ere it allowed such a strange and unwarrantable procedure."

"Overruled," Judge Brice said without pause. "The right of the plaintiff to read extraneous and corroborative material is as ample as the defendant's," he held, nodding to Meredith to begin the prosecution's reading of the disputed passages.

Then the state called its first witness, Henry Thompson. A plump and prominent merchant who had handled Francis Todd's Baltimore business for many years, Thompson told the court that he had contracted to transport the slaves on the *Francis* without consulting the owner but had immediately informed him of the contract and conditions. Asked if Todd had responded, Thompson said, "Yes. Mr. Todd replied that he should have preferred another kind of freight; but as freights were dull, times hard, and money scarce, he was satisfied with the bargain." Although hearsay, and unsubstantiated by the introduction of the letter into evidence, this information actually supported a "truth is no libel" defense. The prosecution, however, embarked on the diverting strategy of arguing that Garrison had wrongfully charged Todd and the skipper Nicholas Brown with having treated their cargo cruelly. (Those passages were not part of the indictment either.) Thompson testified that he had stocked the ship generously and that he knew Brown to be "a humane man." He knew further that the purchaser of the slaves, a New Orleans planter named Milligan, had done much business in Baltimore and was known to be an honorable gentleman.

Garrison, who was certain Milligan was a slave trader, squirmed in his seat as Judge Brice joined in "warm panegyrics" about the Louisianan's character. (That the cargo had been purchased from his friend Woolfolk only increased the hypocrisy of the judge's remarks.) The laudatory talk grew thicker as the pilot of the *Francis* was sworn and testified that the slaves— eighty-eight in all, or thirteen *more* than Garrison had reported—had come on board not at Baltimore, but at *Annapolis*. They were not chained as the article had alleged, but enjoyed free use of the decks, along with plenty of fine food and clothing courtesy of Captain Brown, "the best of shipmasters." A friend of Garrison's, appalled at the pilot's flattery, whispered that the man must have been bribed to go on so effusively.

The prosecution next called E. K. Deaver, a printer who said out loud that he had no great relish for lawsuits and didn't want to be tortured by questions. Asked if he had printed the paper named in the indictment, Deaver said he couldn't swear that he had printed "that identical number." Deaver was excused. Meredith tried again with Deaver's partner, James Lucas, who said he felt the same embarrassment. He was certain that their office had printed the paper, though when Meredith asked if Garrison had seen the issue, Lucas said he couldn't swear to that.

"Did Mr. Garrison correct the proof sheets thereof?" Meredith asked.

"I couldn't swear to it," Lucas said.

"Did the editors Lundy and Garrison generally correct the proof sheets?" Meredith persisted.

"Yes."

Meredith felt that he had made his case and called no further witnesses to establish either the damage caused by the article to Todd or the alleged disruption of the peace.

On Garrison's behalf, Mitchell called only a single witness, Dr. McCulloh of the Custom House, who verified that the clearance papers of the *Francis* showed that she had cleared in October 1829 from the port of Baltimore *direct* for New Orleans, with an assorted cargo, but no slaves. Mitchell then introduced written testimony (accepted by Meredith) from the Collector of the Port of Annapolis that explained a new clearance had been issued there after the *Francis* had taken on a cargo of eighty-eight slaves from a plantation some miles down the bay from Baltimore.

These discrepancies in the facts, however, could not materially disturb the conclusion that Garrison had truthfully stated that Todd's ship had carried slaves. Indeed, it seemed that the "Black List" had pointed its finger at a particularly sordid transaction in which Woolfolk had sold a wholesale lot of slaves to a New Orleans trader and had engaged in some shady practices to conceal the dimensions of the transaction. Later Captain Brown would even insist that he was merely transporting "passengers," since Milligan already owned the slaves when they boarded the ship and had told him that they would not be resold. All of this dissimulation also suggested that slave traders labored under a good deal of public opprobrium even before Garrison had written a word about it.

How could Garrison's article be considered libelous, Mitchell asked in an eloquent summation that would last nearly two hours, when the postulate he assumed—"that the domestic slave trade is as heinous as the foreign"— was "an opinion shared by a multitude of good men [who] had a right at any time, publicly or privately, to declare [it]"? As long ago as 1808, Congress had condemned the African slave trade as piracy and made transportation of slaves from an American port to the West Indies a crime, but in "stamping the seal of infamy" upon that traffic, Mitchell contended, Congress had also "fixed it indelibly" upon the domestic trade, which was tolerated only because it lay under the cognizance of the individual states, beyond the authority of Congress to control. Indeed, the state's evidence showed that Todd had "severe twinges of conscience" himself.

Mitchell argued that the state had entirely failed to convict the defendant of having either written, printed, or published the article. He condemned the introduction of the unindicted portion of the article as a desperate maneuver to take the defendant by surprise and deny him time to prepare evidence that the omitted parts were true. The law of libel itself was "the last and most successful engine of tyranny," Mitchell concluded, and had done "more to perpetuate public abuses, and to check the march of reform, than any other agent." Instead of having their words tortured into criminal conduct, the editors of the *Genius of Universal Emancipation* deserved praise for their efforts and ought to have their freedom sustained, "not only by the jury, but by their country."

In rebuttal for the state, the deputy attorney general, R. W. Gill, English by birth and a distinguished scholar, took over from Meredith. The diminutive Gill darted back and forth as he spoke and made Garrison think of an irritating, buzzing fly. Slaveholders had a right to be secure in their property, Gill said, and toward that end so "fanatic and virulent" a publication as the *Genius* ought to be placed under "wholesome restraint." (This was a reversion to the older view of libel and ignored the standard of proof laid down in the 1804 statute.) He asked the jurors to consider the "malicious intent" of the "Black List" article and expressed confidence that they would do their duty. As the prosecutor passed to the jurors copies of the entire November 20, 1829, issue of the newspaper, Judge Brice leaned forward to caution the jurors that they must acquit or convict upon the matter contained in the indictment. However, he added, they might "derive auxiliary aid" from the remainder of the submitted material.

No one doubted the outcome. The jury retired and returned fifteen minutes later with a verdict of guilty.

Mitchell immediately filed with Judge Brice several motions appealing the verdict. They would not be heard for several weeks, so Garrison was able to leave the courthouse on his attorney's bond. "Power and not justice has convicted me," Garrison thought, knowing that the verdict sounded the death knell for the *Genius*. He would have to walk back through the chilly streets to write his newspaper's obituary. The snow had fallen steadily all day, and a crowd of eager children on sleds had taken possession of the Lexington Street hill.

Exactly six months after it began, Garrison and Lundy's brave partnership came to an end with the edition of March 5, 1830. This time Lundy took the lion's share of the space to mourn that their "prodigality of labor . . . and liberal increase of expenditure" had not borne more fruit. To the usual difficulties of "scanty patronage" had to be added "others of the most aggravated character" intended to destroy the establishment. Lundy wanted it understood that "persecution . . . threats, slanders without number or qualification, as well as libel suits and personal assaults" could not silence the *Genius,* and he would revert to solo publication on a monthly basis with absolutely no change of principles. Lundy would say nothing critical of his besieged partner, the junior editor, who had proved "a faithful and able coadjutor" and demonstrated "his strict integrity, amiable deportment, and virtuous conduct." In a few instances, "as might have been expected," Lundy said, articles appeared that "did not entirely meet my approbation," but they did not prevent the editors from cherishing "the kindliest feelings and mutual personal regard." Garrison added but three paragraphs to Lundy's valedictory, regretting the painful but unavoidable collapse of the partnership and vowing that he would continue to perfect his ideas and protest with severity as long as two million "fellow beings" remained enslaved.

To no one's surprise, the editor's legal appeal failed, and Judge Brice sentenced him to serve six months in jail or to pay a fine of fifty dollars and court costs that brought the total to nearly seventy dollars. Since journeymen printers earned about six dollars a week, Garrison would have had to raise a sum equal to three months of steady work. He couldn't pay the fine, even if he had wanted to, but, privately, he preferred to be jailed in a righteous cause. Although the Baltimore papers had carried not one word about the trial, they now nastily described Garrison as a "voluntary inmate" of the county facilities. They took their cue from Judge Brice, who went around saying that Garrison "was ambitious of becoming a martyr." If so, Garrison retorted, "His Honor is equally ambitious of gathering the faggots and applying the torch."

The unrepentant Garrison entered Baltimore Jail on April 17, 1830. The large brick building, surrounded by a high stone wall, occupied six acres of ground on the slope behind the courthouse, and the editor mockingly thanked Judge Brice for "the preferment" of being lodged in such an "imposing tenement." "I pay no rent," Garrison joked. "I am bound to make no repairs and enjoy the luxury of independence. . . ."

Under the supervision of its new warden, David Hudson, the jail, however, was in the midst of receiving a new slate roof and a fresh coat of whitewash to erase from its walls the gloomy streaks of soot from the prisoners' cooking fires. Hudson, who had replaced a drunken and sadistic keeper only a few months earlier, had ordered an up-to-date steam cooker from the Sing Sing prison in New York, and the prisoners now took turns boiling up a communal pot of beef for breakfast and thickening the leftovers into a vegetable soup for dinner. Hudson's reforms had met with approval from the jail's governing board, which also wanted him to take better care to classify and separate the prisoners. Debtors and youthful offenders had, for too long, mingled to no good end with hardened criminals, the board of visitors believed, and they expected Hudson to use his discretion to remedy the situation.

The warden designated the four large (twenty-foot-square) prisoners' "apartments" into separate accommodations for debtors, criminal offenders, women, and those denied walking privileges within "the bounds." Youths, however, would stay within the Hudson family's own quarters, at least until the new warden's promised separate cottage could be built. Although the city had judged the fierce-sounding Garrison a pariah, Mr. and Mrs. Hudson took one look at the sweet-faced scold, who had turned twenty-four but retained a fledgling's appearance, and decided that, under the board's mandate, they had better keep him within their own nest.

In the greatest of ironies, Garrison's pen had brought the writer to the end his mother had dreaded, "the place no one inhabits," and there he had found a family. Garrison ate at the Hudsons' own table, received his visitors (the faithful Lundy came every day) at their door, and had a desk in their parlor. Indulged as a writer, admired for his notoriety, protected as a victim, Garrison felt himself suffused with a humanitarian glow. "Love to the whole world," he saluted.

"I am as snug as a robin in his cage," Garrison reassured his childhood playmate Harriet Farnham, "[and] I sing as often, and quite as well, as I did before my wings were clipped." Harriet had written to upbraid her Lloyd for censuring Francis Todd, but Garrison, awash in Newburyport memories and the confirming security of the jail, brushed her complaint aside. "Ah! Harriet, that was not written like a mother," he replied, revealing whose blessing he wanted to possess.

As a journalist Garrison took a special interest in the captured runaway slaves who lived at the jail until reclaimed by their masters or purchased by slave traders for resale. He listened patiently to their stories, which he would later retell in his lectures, and remonstrated with the dealers who preyed on them. He counted it a victory that Austin Woolfolk, who usually visited the jail in search of bargains, stayed away so long as Garrison remained in residence.

Incarceration heightened Garrison's sense of power. "The court may shackle the body, but it cannot pinion the mind," he proclaimed. "My soul flames as intensely, in prison, as out of it." He flaunted "Baltimore Jail" as his address and took an almost manic pleasure in writing letters, including mock greeting cards to his "persecutors." "Beware of my pen," he warned

Gill. "I will give you a deathless notoriety," he told Brice. "Consult your bible and your heart," he advised Todd.

Although he was comfortably housed and indulgently treated, Garrison inevitably likened himself to Byron's "Prisoner of Chillon," the Swiss patriot incarcerated on the rocky shores of Lake Geneva for attempting to liberate his country. In emulation of Byron's sonnet ("Eternal Spirit of the chainless Mind!"), Garrison wrote his own hymn to intellectual freedom that depicted the mind as "swifter than light" and brighter than the stars, rapidly encircling the world and leaping from earth to heaven. He also spent the first two weeks of his confinement writing an account, which ran to eight printed pages in Lundy's quick pamphlet edition, that gave particulars of the trial and defended the principles of a free press. Every libel prosecution tested how far "that freedom has been restricted by power on the one hand or perverted by licentiousness on the other," Garrison suggested, and readers would be able to judge for themselves whether he had exceeded the bounds of editorial freedom or the Baltimore court had conducted "a burlesque upon the Constitution."

The pamphlet did not change the verdict, but it did get Garrison out of jail. When the New York philanthropist Arthur Tappan, whose generosity sustained many benevolent reform efforts, finished reading it at the end of May 1830, he went directly to his desk to write a letter to Benjamin Lundy. "If one hundred dollars will give [Garrison] his liberty, you are hereby authorized to draw on me for that sum," Tappan said. He also offered another hundred to "aid you and Mr. G. in re-establishing" the *Genius*.

One week later, on June 5, Garrison walked out of Baltimore Jail after forty-nine days' imprisonment. He tucked away Warden Hudson's receipt for the fees as a keepsake, for in Baltimore Jail he had—in the deepest sense—liberated himself. Writing from prison to his former master E. W. Allen, Garrison insisted that "everyone who comes into the world should do something to repair its moral desolation, and to restore its pristine loveliness; and he who does not assist, but slumbers away his life in idleness, defeats one great purpose of his creation." Even worse than those who do nothing toward reform, he added, are those "barbarians" who "discourage the hearts of the more industrious and destroy their beautiful works." With a poet's intuition he had come to an understanding that would inform his entire career as a writer and agitator. His would be the dual mission of letting in the light and attacking the forces of darkness. Garrison had learned to speak the truth, come what may, and he had turned the state's stigmata into a badge of honor. Maryland had convicted him for libel, yet he had permanently forged in his soul a conviction that he could say anything he wanted. Many had censured him for his severity, Garrison said, but "thank God! none have stigmatized me with luke-warmness."

As with many prisoners of conscience, Garrison's jail term more thoroughly bound him to his cause. Nothing else in his life seemed as worthwhile or compelling. He had lost his newspaper and his income, he had antagonized his hometown, and he had failed his mother's desire that he remain steady and respectable. His brother had gone bad through drink and dissolution, but Lloyd had become bad by doing good. He had forsaken the conventional pieties of the small-town editor, disdained the opportunist practicalities of the conventional politician, and become defiant, even contemptuous, of unresponsive institutions. The humiliating poverty of his boyhood became a badge of honor, a token of his antagonism toward commercial society and its sordid compromise with slavery. He had refashioned himself as a mixture of the Byronic hero and the Biblical prophet, the purist who lived by the commandments that others only invoked with hypocrisy. He had become an outcast with a daring vision and a ferocious clarity of expression, and he cast his fortune with those whom society had excluded. "It is my shame that I have done so little for the people of color," Garrison wrote from Baltimore Jail. "A few white victims must be sacrificed to open the eyes of this nation, and to show the tyranny of our laws. I am willing to be persecuted, imprisoned and bound for advocating African rights, and I should deserve to be a slave myself, if I shrunk from that duty or danger." That offering would be his vocation and his glory.

BOOK TWO

STRETCH EVERY NERVE

1831–1835

GARRISON AT THIRTY

Mezzotint by John Sartain from a portrait by Manessah C. Torrey
(Courtesy of the Trustees of the Boston Public Library)

CHAPTER SIX

A NEW ENGLAND MECHANIC

BOOMING CANNONS WOKE THE CITIZENS OF BOSTON ON THE MORNING OF
SEPTEMBER 17, 1830, WITH A SALUTE TO THE TWO HUNDREDTH ANNIVER-
SARY OF THE TOWN'S FOUNDING. BY SEVEN O'CLOCK, THE DAY ALREADY
glowing with autumnal brilliance, the fire companies began to gather on the
Common, and promptly at eight they staged a review to the "enlivening
strains" of Professor Zeuner's "Grand Centennial March." At nine the procession of civic dignitaries and massed bands formed at the State House on
Beacon Hill. Led by the Ancient and Honorable Artillery Company in its
plumed hats and sky-blue coats, the parade crossed the Common through a
double line of three thousand cheering schoolchildren and wound its way to
the squat red-brick building at the head of State Street that had served as
the capitol during the American Revolution. There, the city council re-
dedicated the venerable Old State House as the new City Hall. "We are
now before the altar whence the coals were taken which have kindled the
flame of liberty in two hemispheres," Mayor Harrison Gray Otis intoned,
and, changing the figure, he prayed that the civic machinery perfected in
Boston might now propel the nations of the world "on the railroad which
leads to universal freedom."

From the gaily decorated hall the procession moved up Washington Street
to another hallowed landmark, Old South Meeting House, where Sam Adams had once presided over the popular assemblies that had launched the
revolt against British rule. There the crowd settled itself for what proved to
be a two-hour-long oration by their former mayor, Josiah Quincy, who had
gone on to the only office of comparable prestige, the presidency of Harvard
College. Though some smart young lawyers found Quincy's remarks "rather
ill-digested," the majority of the audience listened raptly as Quincy reminded
Boston that its historic distinction lay in the city's "bold vindications of right,
[and its] readiness to incur danger and meet sacrifice in the maintenance of
civil and religious liberty." Townsmen now had the duty of enlarging "the
temple" of American freedom with the sublime proportions of "intellectual
and moral architecture" that would redound to the glory of Boston and New
England. The audience crowned Quincy's address with a massed rendition
of Handel's "Hallelujah Chorus" and filed out into the invigorating splendor
of a Boston autumn afternoon.

Then came the dinners—the city council at Faneuil Hall, the Historical

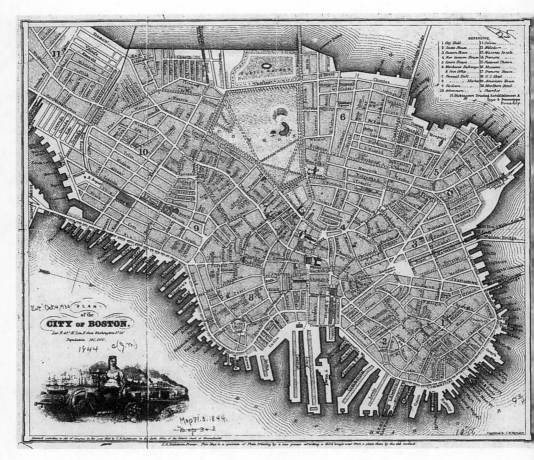

Boston in 1844. Garrison lived in various locations in the South End, Wards 10–11, shown at the left on this map.

Society at the Exchange, and thousands of citizens spread out upon the green. Toasts rang out—to the city, the founders, the flag, the fire companies, the revolution then unfolding in France, the glorious Lafayette, the free press, and "the day" itself. Bands filled the air with "Hail Columbia," "La Marseillaise," and "Yankee Doodle." At nightfall, finally, came the fireworks—streaming and sparkling to the delight of "an innumerable congregation" on the Common and the bedazzled pride of the *Evening Transcript*. Its editor, a Harvard man named Lynde Walter, looked at the world that night and found it much to his liking. Feeling the weight of writing for posterity, for he felt certain that some would preserve his newspaper as a souvenir of the joyous day, the editor surveyed "the progress of free institutions" and found the United States most blessed. The only political controversy he could discern lay in a serious sectional disagreement over the tariff and a partisan difference over the right of the national government to make expenditures for internal improvements. Religious sects were "numerous," and the march of benevolence was continuous, though the removal of the southern Indian nations to far western lands had "excited much attention." "Philanthropists labor to effect the gradual extinction of slavery," Walter said approvingly, and "Free Blacks are conveyed away gratuitously and colonized in Africa." Education was widespread, books were cheap, steam power had come into general use to drive ships, and while horses and oxen remained common modes of transport, "locomotive engines are highly approved." Only "undistinguished ripples in the tide of affairs" ruffled the surface of the prosperous seas on which Bostonians could expect to sail until the celebrating generation was gathered to its fathers and "an unborn people" would read and learn of its calm and steady progress.

Even if Lynde Walter had known that the notorious William Lloyd Garrison—just returned to Boston after three months of lecturing and seeking support for his next antislavery newspaper—had so enjoyed the festivities as to consider anew making Boston his home, Walter's serenity would not have been shaken. Indeed, several weeks later, after meeting his fellow journalist, Walter welcomed him to town with praise for the young man's "noble and visionary enthusiasm." Garrison had concentrated his talents upon "the accomplishment of a stupendous project which he can never hope to see perfected," the editor ventured, "but of which he will be long remembered as an early and laborious pioneer." Walter had misjudged his man, for Garrison intended to witness the Jubilee himself. He had become the advocate of a new principle—immediatism—and a consummate agitator who had already suffered for his beliefs. Nothing would stop him from holding Boston to every word of its loftily spoken creed.

Garrison had ended up in Boston almost by default, after three hectic months in the summer of 1830 shuttling along the eastern seaboard in search of support for another newspaper. In Baltimore Lundy had equipped a tiny printing office by spending the balance of Arthur Tappan's June gift, but he could only afford to publish the *Genius* monthly as a tract-sized pamphlet and told Garrison that he would not resume the weekly edition until subscriptions "enable us both to remain at home to superintend it." Nor would Lundy reconsider their idea of setting up a branch office in Washington. It seemed clear that he no longer wanted to work with Garrison.

To make a fresh start single-handedly, the young editor decided to work up a series of public lectures that would press the cause personally to the reform-minded in the other major cities, but the pending civil suit had undergone so many postponements that Garrison thought the court was dallying with him in order to keep him pent up and silenced without the martyrdom of prison. He boldly decided to leave Baltimore and let the lawsuit go uncontested. "I give Mr. Todd every advantage," he laughed. "Let the court have all the sport to itself." Such insouciance shocked Friend Lundy, but the impatient crusader did not want to waste his time in a fruitless, even contemptible forum after his sights had shifted elsewhere. The editors had come to divergent paths, but they parted as friends. Lundy took avuncular pride in Garrison as his "philanthropic ex-apprentice" ("a fine lad who conducts a fearless press," he would say), while Garrison always saluted Lundy as the elder statesman of the antislavery movement. The two men, however, never met face to face again.

Garrison had wanted to raise the abolitionist flag directly in the nation's capital, which he thought might become "the first citadel to be carried," since Congress could legislate for the federal district without infringing upon states' rights. Early in August 1830, he wrote out a proposal "for publishing a weekly periodical in Washington City, to be entitled 'THE PUBLIC LIBERATOR, AND JOURNAL OF THE TIMES' " and dedicated to "the abolition of slavery" and the "elevation of our colored population." The paper would "exercise a strict supervision" over Congress and would be—in the words of Isaiah—" 'a terror to evil-doers, but a praise to them that do well.' " Friendly editors, he anticipated, would follow the custom of inserting his prospectus into their own columns for several weeks running, and interested readers could subscribe through their local postmasters.

He also sought private subsidies, sending a copy of the proposal to the wealthy silk-jobber who had paid his Baltimore fine, Arthur Tappan, but with scant hope, since the only meeting with his benefactor after his release from jail in June 1830 had been frosty. (Tappan kept no chairs in his office for visitors, disliked small talk, and frequently became so overcome by his waspish temper that he had to lie prostrate for a half hour with a wet cloth upon his face. In such an atmosphere, Garrison was barely able to express his gratitude before the interview ended, though Tappan's brother Lewis found himself charmed by the young editor and cheerfully told him that he recalled Garrison's nemesis Francis Todd from former times in Boston and had always thought the man had a "sharp look" and a "fox-like" manner.)

Within a week of making the request, however, Garrison had a positive, if graceless, reply. Tappan's inquiries had turned up reports that Garrison had abundant talent as a writer, but lacked business acumen. "I am not sufficiently acquainted with you [to judge] whether you possess the various qualifications that must be concentrated in the editorial and publishing departments to insure success to a paper," Tappan said. The enterprise being a noble one, however, he would risk offering $100 in "cheerful" aid.

Tappan's gift allowed Garrison to think seriously about buying the printing office of the *Washington Spectator,* a paper favorable to the American Colonization Society, whose editor, Walter Colton, had run into the usual fiscal difficulties. The ACS leadership had kept an eye on Garrison, however, and did not want to let him into Washington. "For heaven sake do not let Colton sell out to that Bedlamite Garrison," an ACS agent advised. "The board had much better buy C. out and break up the establishment" rather than let it get into the hands of "a second Walker."

Stymied in Washington, Garrison turned north. He used Tappan's advance and another gift of $100 from an admirer in Maine to travel and lecture while scouting out another location for a newspaper. He stopped first in Philadelphia, where Lundy's old friends among the Quaker antislavery leadership arranged three nights of lectures, August 31–September 2, 1830, at the Franklin Institute. With "great plainness of speech" Garrison candidly laid out his doctrine of immediate abolition and attacked colonization as a false reform before a small audience composed entirely of Friends and the leaders of benevolent societies in the black community, including the wealthy sailmaker James Forten. The *Philadelphia Inquirer* found Garrison a little stiff as a speaker, but admired his literary composition and "philanthropic" concern. With more lectures in New York, New Haven, and Hartford, Garrison improved his delivery until he rose to his themes with the intensity of a revival preacher and spoke so powerfully that listeners came away feeling that they had "heard the groans and viewed the lacerated bodies of the poor sufferers."

The force with which he addressed the issue of racial equality struck responsive chords in the black churches he visited, especially in New Haven and Hartford, where a friend, Simeon Jocelyn, a white engraver and printer turned preacher, had temporary charge of the United African Society. Wherever he spoke, Garrison made "converts and friends" and promoted his twin goals: building support for his projected newspaper and founding a national antislavery society that, like other benevolent agencies, could circulate tracts and promote missions throughout the country.

He also stalked the opposition. "Do you know that I have taken up a crusade against the American Colonization Society?" Garrison queried Lundy. "Perhaps I am as mad as was the chivalrous Don Quixote," he mused, but he felt obliged not only to criticize the concept, but to attack its organized advocates. In New Haven he had a "prolonged" interview with the Rev. Leonard Bacon, a leading Congregational minister and a special champion of the ACS, but could not draw the wary clergyman into a public debate. In Hartford, Garrison tried the same tactic on another of the society's advocates, T. H. Gallaudet, who reassured national headquarters that he had maintained "a perfect silence" toward the belligerent editor.

In Newburyport, Garrison's former master, E. W. Allen, had declined to reprint Garrison's account of the trial ("an *ex parte* statement," Allen sniffed), but then tried to argue Todd's case by drawing a casuistical distinction between "trafficking" in slaves and merely "transporting . . . certain blacks." Where Garrison saw the criminal laws being used in "a flagrant infringement upon liberty of the press," his former master saw only the "private" issue that his ex-apprentice had carelessly attacked a gentleman and was now "browbeating" him for taking lawful steps to vindicate his character. Though it pained Allen to repudiate a young man who had lived in his family, he would not condone Garrison's "rashness and indiscretion." The town concurred, and some people said they had always regarded the boy as a show-off whose impetuousness would get him into trouble. When Garrison tried to schedule a talk, church trustees friendly to Francis Todd shut their doors. With an indignant note to the *Herald* denouncing those "who have exerted their influence . . . in order to seal my lips," Garrison left Newburyport, not to speak there publicly for thirty years.

Once more Garrison set out from his birthplace to Boston, hoping to find in the metropolis the vindication and the influence that he could not obtain in his hometown. He began his Boston campaign by gaining access to the *Evening Transcript*. Editor Walter, eager to demonstrate that Bostonians reproved the "selfish indifference" that had shut Garrison out of Newburyport, opened his columns to the newcomer, who immediately contributed two pieces in contrasting styles. One retold, with scarcely a rhetorical flourish, the sad story of two runaway slaves who had hidden themselves on a Boston-bound vessel only to have the city magistrates bind them over, under the Fugitive Slave Law of 1793, for return to their owner in New Orleans. The other—more flamboyantly entitled "Ought We Not to Blush!"—pointed to the "republican blasphemy," especially among the Richmond, Baltimore, and Charleston papers, of cheering the advance of liberal sentiments in France while their own subscribers held thousands of black people in a "despotism" crueler than that of the deposed Charles X.

Boston, however, appeared no more eager than Newburyport to hear Garrison speak. An exasperated Garrison had to place a "Wanted" notice in the *Courier* threatening to hold forth on the Common if he could not secure a meeting hall or church in which "to vindicate the rights of TWO MILLIONS of American citizens." This desperate move prompted an invitation to speak, not in a church, but in the room used by Abner Kneeland's Universalist Society, whose free-thinking ideas skirted the dangerous ground of agnosticism. Given Garrison's own skepticism about prevailing ideas, the venue was an appropriate one, and it is a measure of the young agitator's ability to manufacture attention that when he stood up in shabby Julien Hall on Friday evening, October 15, 1830, he faced an audience that not only filled the room, but conferred some prestige upon the occasion. Tradition claims that Lyman Beecher himself turned out to hear one of his young men, and Dr. Channing's assistant, the Rev. Ezra Gannett, represented the Unitarian establishment. Several important merchants—Deacon Moses Grant and John Tappan, an elder brother of Garrison's benefactor—had come to monitor the event for the Colonization Society. (Afterward, the infuriated Tappan said that he wished brother Arthur "had let Garrison lay in Baltimore Jail.") Samuel Sewall, a well-regarded young attorney and scion of one of the Bay State's oldest families, had come at the behest of his cousin Samuel J. May, a Boston-bred Unitarian minister from Connecticut, and May's brother-in-law, the idealistic educator A. Bronson Alcott.

Conscious that he was addressing the most influential audience he had ever faced, Garrison spoke that night with calm determination and an uncommon eloquence that, as Alcott put it, was "full of truth and power." He began by thanking his hosts for the lesson in charity and tolerance they had offered the Christian churches to whom Garrison had vainly appealed for a forum, but he made plain that, far from sharing Kneeland's skepticism, he believed that slavery could only be ended through the power of the gospel. Garrison shaped his discourse around the fundamental premise that "immediate, unconditional emancipation, without expatriation, was the right of every slave, and could not be withheld by his master an hour without sin." He considered the concept of a "republican or Christian slaveholder" as much a solecism as the contradictory notions of "a religious atheist, a sober drunkard, or an honest thief," and he admonished his audience that by "holding fellowship with slaveholders" in their political parties, church associations, and commercial alliances, the people of New England gave a moral sanction for the entire system. Nor did their support of colonization help matters. ACS agents in the free states, he charged, diligently misrepresented the society's goal as an antislavery enterprise, but his residence in Maryland had taught him that the "especial intentions" of the Southerners who supported the plan were to remove free black people from the country. Colonization, he insisted, would only perpetuate slavery and did not deserve the support of genuine reformers.

Garrison made a particular effort to describe the cruelty of slavery. He had scanted the topic in his Park Street Address, but on his eastern travels in the summer of 1830, he had found people "strangely indifferent" to the subject of slavery and fatalistic about its continuance. Judging that callousness stemmed from ignorance, he worked up material that offered a vivid, even sensational account of black bondage. He described the slave pens of Woolfolk, the runaways he had met in jail, the badly beaten men who had sought help at the printing office, and the wretched separation of families, to which, as the child of a broken home, he always brought special poignancy. Garrison contrasted his own incarceration in prison with the unremitting confinement of the slave whose fetters would be broken only by the ultimate liberator, Death itself. If public sympathy was excited because "justice has been denied me in a single instance," he urged, "how ought it to flame for two millions of as valuable and immortal souls, who are crushed beneath the iron car of despotism? . . . O that my countryman might feel as keenly for a black skin as for a white one!"

At the end of the lecture an irresistible emotion propelled Samuel J. May to the front of the hall, where he embraced Garrison as a prophet. "I am sure you are called to a great work," May told him, "and I mean to help you." The men talked until midnight at Alcott's lodgings, and May felt his ministry had gained new purpose. "That night," May liked to say, "my soul was baptized in his spirit, and ever since I have been a disciple and fellow-laborer of William Lloyd Garrison." The lecturer could not have made a more valuable convert. Eight years older than the editor, May had grown up in the comfort and security of a Boston mercantile family well connected by descent and marriage to the Sewalls, Hancocks, and Coffins. He had studied with Channing before taking his degree at Harvard and, after ordination, returned to Channing's pulpit as the great man's assistant. In 1823 May had accepted a call to an isolated Unitarian church in Brooklyn, Connecticut, where he had become active in temperance and peace organizations and had met Benjamin Lundy in 1828 when the Quaker itinerant had spoken in Brooklyn during his northern tour. A thoughtful, considerate, sweet-natured man, May proved an ideal parish minister. He dispensed with the formal preaching gown and stiff white bands, which, in his view, set religion apart from ordinary life. Fair-minded and sympathetic, May proved "the best of comforters," his congregations agreed, and Alcott dubbed him "the Lord's Chore-Boy" for the agreeable competence with which he attended to the details of organizing benevolent reforms.

Garrison needed a friend with May's blend of conviction and practicality. "I learned that he was poor, dependent upon his daily labor for his daily bread, and intending to return to the printing business . . . for his own support," May recalled, and he promised to rally influential friends to the editor's cause. May went right to work and arranged for Garrison to repeat his lecture at a very respectable location: the Athenaeum. He also added an appeal for immediate abolition to the guest sermon—fortuitously on the subject of prejudice—he was scheduled to preach at Summer Street Church. The well-to-do congregation stirred uncomfortably as May explained that his prompting to bold speech had come from a young man whom God had called "to do a greater work for the good of our country than has been done by anyone since the Revolution." The preacher urged his listeners to attend the Athenaeum lecture and asked the congregation to sing Garrison's favorite hymn, "Awake my soul, Stretch every nerve, and press with vigor on."

A few people clustered about May to express gratitude for his testimony, but the general mood proved frosty. State Street buzzed so with the story the next morning that May's father warned his son at luncheon that he would lose all influence with gentlemen of standing if he pushed too quickly against an evil that could be ameliorated only in the fullness of time. May stood fast, but a few days later when the editor of the Unitarian tract series told May that he had to remove the interpolations on slavery from his sermon on prejudice or suffer its rejection, the clergyman toned down his work. "He would not have done this, nor should I have consented to it, a few years later," May recalled, "but we were all in bondage then."

Garrison, meanwhile, found the orthodox as cool as the liberals. He sought Dr. Beecher's support, but the great preacher claimed that he had "too many irons in the fire already." Beecher indulgently praised the editor's zeal but advised him to stay within the established boundaries of the benevolence movement and the colonization society. "If you will give up your fanatical notions and be guided by us," Beecher said, to Garrison's disgust, "we will make you the Wilberforce of America."

The chill deepened a few weeks later, despite the success of the Athenaeum lecture, when Garrison had a falling out with Lynde Walter of the *Transcript*. Walter had published a "fair offset" from the *Charleston City Gazette* that objected to Garrison's jibes at Southern hypocrisy and wondered aloud if this man "who has been lately punished in Baltimore for similar impertinences . . . [could] be provided with some decent honest employment at the plough or any other vocation which will keep him out of mischief." Defending his right to agitate the issue, Garrison drafted a thunderous reply warning the Charleston editor "that before he again recommends a particular avocation to a *New-England mechanic who is not ashamed of his trade*," he ought to find honest work for the indolent slaveholders in his midst. The heated exchange was standard journalistic "slang-whanging," but Walter grew faint-hearted and published Garrison's riposte with extreme "reluctance." He sourly advised the reformer to "temper his zeal with discretion" so that he might "make friends, and not lose them." Taking his cue from State Street and Beecher, Walter insisted that New England was "bound in Christian charity to avoid all intemperance in writing or speaking upon a subject so intimately connected with the existence of our Southern Brethren."

Garrison's insistence upon discussing racial matters had touched a raw nerve, but he had also challenged the powerful watchword of political union. The year's greatest best-seller had been the pamphlet edition of Daniel Webster's reply to Senator Hayne, in which the Massachusetts orator had contrasted the South Carolinian's emphasis on state supremacy and weak central government with the splendid vision of a growing nation—its prosperity boosted by national support—bound in perpetual constitutional union. Northerners and westerners were too busy and well-off to worry about slavery, Webster had declared, and Southerners ought to stop suspecting that their brethren in the free states would use federal powers to mount an attack upon what was most assuredly a local matter. "I go for the Constitution as it is, and the Union as it is," Webster said, and his memorable peroration—"Liberty *and* Union, now and forever, one and inseparable"—captured the minds of a generation. It assured the triumph of the nationalist ideal over the compact theory that Hayne, a colleague and disciple of John C. Calhoun, had promulgated as necessary for the South's "protection" in a hostile political climate.

The Webster-Hayne debates of January 1830, which prefigured the sectional issues that would surface again in the aftermath of the Mexican War, had percolated through the nation's newspapers throughout the spring, overshadowing, among other events, coverage of the editor's troubles in Baltimore. Even Garrison, in the final issue of the *Genius,* had printed excerpts from Webster's speech and hailed its "masterly exposition" as a constitutional textbook for all posterity. Now, however, he began to have doubts about the spell Webster had created and realized the powerful sanction it gave to complicity with slaveholders. His growing skepticism would soon expose him to charges of treason, but Garrison would so profoundly reshape the contours of debate that when Webster restated his position during the momentous debates of 1850, a once-admiring New England public would condemn him as a proslavery apologist.

With the *Transcript* now closed to him, Garrison intensified his efforts to acquire a forum of his own. His interest in Washington, D.C., had waned over his weeks of touring New England, where "contempt [seemed] more bitter, opposition more active, detraction more relentless, prejudice more stubborn, and apathy more frozen" than he had anticipated. Garrison lacked experience in the capital, but he knew the Boston printing trade and had grown absorbed by the challenge the city presented. If Dr. Beecher could walk in the Pilgrims' footsteps, Garrison reasoned, he himself could follow the revolutionary path of Adams and Otis and inspire a moral reformation in the shadow of Faneuil Hall.

Garrison first talked over his freshly invigorated idea for *The Boston Public Liberator* with his circle of friends, who had tried unsuccessfully to launch a local antislavery society. Collier thought he could find Garrison some space in Merchants' Hall, where so many of the benevolent papers were issued. Isaac Knapp, his boyhood chum and predecessor at the *Free Press,* volunteered to give Garrison some help at the case, and Stephen Foster, their friend at the *Christian Watchman,* thought he could print the work in spare hours at his press until Garrison could buy a secondhand one of his own.

The editor next talked to his small cadre of well-connected admirers.

Samuel J. May agreed with Garrison that New England's insensibility was a "moral phenomenon" that ought to be addressed directly from Boston, as did his cousin Samuel Sewall, whose namesake and ancestor had written one of the earliest-known antislavery tracts, *The Selling of Joseph,* in 1700. Another of May's Harvard classmates, David L. Child, who had fought in Spain against the Bourbon monarch and endured two libel prosecutions for his newspaper attacks upon Jacksonian politicians, encouraged Garrison's venture from his post as editor of the *Massachusetts Journal,* the very first newspaper on which Garrison had worked in Boston. Child's wife, the prominent author Lydia Maria Child, whom Garrison admired for her humanitarian views and fiction sympathetic toward Indians and slaves, at first thought the idea was too provocative, but soon came around, deciding that "it would take live fish to swim upstream."

For all his goodwill, however, the circumspect Sewall also worried about giving unnecessary offense. A name like *Public Liberator,* with its evocation of Bolívar and the South American revolutions on the one hand and the Irish defiance of Daniel O'Connell on the other, might be too readily construed as an invitation to slave rebellion. Wouldn't a milder name, perhaps *The Safety Lamp,* more accurately reflect the editorial philosophy and intentions? Garrison did not agree. He meant his paper to concentrate public attention upon the slaves' liberation, and he meant to uphold a universal standard of freedom. Indeed, he planned to subjoin to the title (which would be *The Liberator,* with no city name affixed) the motto "Our Country is the World— Our Countrymen are Mankind." With a boldness quite striking for one dependent upon subsidies, Garrison made it plain that the conduct of the paper would be his alone, and with a deference not always apparent in benefactors Sewall accepted the editor's judgment.

The firm support of a handful of strong-minded rebels among the elite, however, would not be enough. Having learned in Baltimore how significant the black community could be in sustaining a radical newspaper, Garrison would not begin *The Liberator* until he had gained the confidence of black Bostonians. Compared to Baltimore's 15,000 blacks or Philadelphia's 22,000, the black population of Boston—1,875, according to the 1830 census— seemed minuscule, but for Garrison they stood large as the living embodiment of the cause. The city had always had a black presence. The ship *Desire* had landed a parcel of slaves along with a cargo of tobacco in 1638; the western end of the Copps Hill burial ground contained the graves of generations of black mariners and domestic workers, both slave and free; a black sailor, Crispus Attucks, had fallen in the Boston "massacre" of 1770; a black minuteman, Peter Salem, had killed the redcoats' Major Pitcairn on Bunker Hill; a black domestic servant, Phyllis Wheatley, who had been baptized in Old South, had received a commendation from General Washington for her patriotic verses. Just before the Revolution, the town's 1,500 blacks (whose freedom was confirmed by Massachusetts constitutional enactments in 1780) had accounted for nearly ten percent of the town's population, but by Garrison's time, the spectacular growth of the city had reduced the black segment to only three percent of the total.

Black people lived on the margins of Boston municipal life. Though eligible to vote, they stood excluded from juries and the militia and found themselves confined to the lower echelon of available jobs. Seasonal laborers, such as black dockworkers and sailors, lived close to the wharves, in large boardinghouses that functioned as fraternal associations and social clubs. Workers with steadier jobs, such as sawyers, teamsters, cooks and maids, or those with valet-related occupations such as barbers, hairdressers, seamstresses, laundresses, and clothes merchants, tended to leave the rowdy North End for the upcoming West End, where small row houses on the north slope of Beacon Hill afforded two or three families shared dwelling space. (When a man married and left one of the North End halls, his friends termed him "lost to the hill.") The families on "the hill" had founded a Baptist church on Belknap Street, a Methodist church on May Street, and a temperance boardinghouse on Southac Street, though these reputable establishments could not overmatch the gaming houses and bordellos on nearby Buttolph and Cambridge streets that provided less savory income opportunities for the neighborhood. "The hill" was not a ghetto, however. Some black families, especially mulattos of Caribbean ancestry, with a little more property than the others, lived quietly on streets south of the commercial center, and white artisans also took advantage of the cheap housing in the spreading West End.

The black community took care of itself. Its grocers served as informal bankers; its social clubs, which dated back to the African Society of 1796, brought food and firewood to the sick; its barbershops became bulletin boards; and the African Society's Meeting House (where the Baptists worshiped and a school for black youth flourished) became the community's town hall. Although Boston had a tolerant reputation, black people faced racial abuse, the indignities of segregated schools and churches, and a citizenship decidedly second-class if not as precarious as that endured by their counterparts in Baltimore, where the legal machinery of slavery might readily entrap them again. Yet leaders in Boston's black community felt confident enough to raise their voices politically, not only against slavery, but against the prejudiced conditions of their own lives. In 1826, Boston took the lead in forming the General Colored Association of Massachusetts as both a philanthropic and protest organization, and in 1828, David Walker had used the association's forum to articulate the position that later formed the basis of his visionary pamphlet. In August 1830, however, Walker—a robust man in his midthirties—died, apparently of a lung disease that also claimed his baby daughter, but the loss was devastating enough to generate community suspicions that he had been a victim of foul play. No evidence could be found to substantiate the charge, and the police would not take up the case.

When Garrison made overtures to the black community five months later, no one else had come forward to speak or publish as forcibly as Walker had. Nor had anyone come forward with a plan for a black-run newspaper, for Boston's small black population could not have sustained a venture by itself even if the city's printing trades had not shut out people of color. (Walker had his pamphlet printed clandestinely in New York and had served as the Boston agent for Samuel Cornish's newspapers, *Freedom's Journal* and *The Rights of All*, which had gone out of business.)

Garrison had a ready access to "the hill" through two preacher friends, his landlord, William Collier, and his mother's beloved pastor, John Peak, who had come to Boston to share with Collier the task of ministering to the black Baptist congregation until the vacancy in its pulpit created by the resignation of its founding pastor, the Rev. Thomas Paul, could be filled. The ailing Paul—along with his Methodist counterpart, the Rev. Samuel Snowden—blessed Garrison's endeavor. The two black ministers, indeed, had called out hearty amens during the editor's talk at the Athenaeum, and Paul had warmly embraced the young man at the lectern afterward.

On December 10, 1830, two days before Garrison's twenty-fifth birthday, he spoke to a group of black leaders and expressed his deep sympathy for those "struggling against wind and tide," as he always put it, to advance their rights and defend their character. Garrison often said that he never rose to address a black audience without feeling ashamed of his own color, and he hoped that he could atone for the wrongs done to blacks by devoting his life to the struggle for liberty and equal citizenship. He intended his newspaper to support them in maintaining self-respect, educating their children, fighting for their constitutional rights, and organizing an assault upon the monstrous and tyrannical slave system. Such forthrightness and simplicity won him many friends that night. One of the meeting's organizers, James G. Barbadoes, a hairdresser whose name bespoke his West Indian origins, later praised him for remarks "full of virtue and consolation . . . [that] furnished a rule to live by and die by." Ever since Garrison's imprisonment in Baltimore, Barbadoes said, he had known the editor to be "God's servant," and he expressed gratitude that this young man had not perished in the South, but had been spared to bring his "precious fruit" to the benefit of Boston. Although some leaders, notably the Masons' John T. Hilton, nursed suspicions born of long experience, most of the activists followed Barbadoes in regarding the young printer as "a Daniel come to judgment." They would make the newspaper their own, and a committee of black women headed by Elizabeth Riley and Bathsheba Fowler began to raise a few dollars to support it.

Garrison decided to go ahead with a "specimen number"—printer's lingo for a sample—which he intended to publish on New Year's Day, 1831. Relying upon the "truck and dicker" system, he and Knapp gathered their equipment and traded their manual labor for office space and some case and press time at Foster's *Christian Watchman* in Merchants' Hall. Knapp canvassed for supplies: potash and lime for cleaning type, lamp oil, and charcoal for ink, brushes and rollers and blotters, baskets for papers and twine for bundling stacks for the post office. Garrison, who would have sole billing as editor though he shared the publisher's title with Knapp, began the task of typesetting copy and composing the pages. By the end of December 1830, Garrison had made ready an issue of four pages, with four columns laid out neatly on a modest fourteen-by-nine page. He faced only one more obstacle: a lack of paper.

The partners had hoped that Deacon Moses Grant, a paper supplier and a fellow in the temperance movement, would extend them a few reams on credit, but Grant declined. He knew them to be reputable, the story went; he worried less about his money than about the fanatical notions they proposed to advance—he wanted no part of those. The project seemed stalled until Knapp found another firm that would advance a small quantity of paper on seven days' credit. They went ahead with the press run, assuming that money somehow would turn up in time. On the day the bill was due Garrison went to the post office and found a check for fifty-four dollars from James Forten, the black leader from Philadelphia, who asked the editor to consider the money as advance payment for twenty-seven subscriptions. Names and addresses were carefully enclosed, along with Forten's ardent hopes that Garrison's efforts to combat slavery and prejudice would not be in vain. The editor had appealed to Forten a few days after the meeting with Boston's black leaders, and he always credited the wealthy sailmaker's prompt and generous response with making *The Liberator* a reality.

On the afternoon of Saturday, January 1, 1831, the first issue came off the press. Block capital letters proclaimed THE LIBERATOR across the banner. The front page offered a poetic salutation, reports on the campaign to abolish slavery in the District of Columbia, and the customary address "To the Public," which Garrison turned into an editorial manifesto. In August he had issued proposals for establishing a journal in Washington, D.C., he said, but the enterprise "was palsied by public indifference." Having become convinced that the free states, especially New England, required "a greater revolution in public sentiment" than he had previously realized, he would now "lift up the standard of emancipation in the eyes of the nation, *within sight of Bunker Hill and in the birth place of liberty.*"

Judging it unnecessary to republish his August manifesto, Garrison emphasized only his reliance on the Declaration of Independence and a nonsectarian intention to enlist all religions and parties in "the great cause of human rights." He would "strenuously contend for the immediate enfranchisement of our slave population," Garrison promised, and he repudiated what he called his "unreflecting" assent to the "popular but pernicious doctrine of *gradual* abolition" that he had expressed at Park Street Church in July, 1829. "I seize this opportunity to make a full and unequivocal

THE LIBERATOR.

VOL. I.]   WILLIAM LLOYD GARRISON AND ISAAC KNAPP, PUBLISHERS.   [NO. 1.

BOSTON, MASSACHUSETTS.]   OUR COUNTRY IS THE WORLD—OUR COUNTRYMEN ARE MANKIND.   [SATURDAY, JANUARY 1, 1831.

recantation," he wrote, "and thus publicly ask pardon of my God, of my country, and of my brethren the poor slaves, for having uttered a sentiment so full of timidity, injustice and absurdity."

The Liberator, he promised, would make slaveholders and their apologists tremble. He would redeem the nation's patriotic creed by making "every statue leap from its pedestal" and rouse the apathetic with a trumpet call that would "hasten the resurrection of the dead." He would speak God's truth "in its simplicity and power," and he would speak severely. He would also speak from the heart, in his own voice and in the first person singular rather than the more distant and aloof editorial plural. "I *will be* as harsh as truth, and as uncompromising as justice," Garrison pledged. "On this subject I do not wish to think or speak, or write, with moderation. No! No! Tell a man whose house is on fire to give a moderate alarm . . . but urge me not to use moderation in a cause like the present." He drove the point home with staccato phrases: "I am in earnest—I will not equivocate—I will not excuse—I will not retreat a single inch." Then he reached into the upper case and added one more promise: "—AND I WILL BE HEARD."

Thus began one of the most remarkable ventures in the history of American journalism. No editor has ever produced a newspaper of agitation for longer than Garrison sustained *The Liberator*, which appeared weekly without interruption for thirty-five years and did not cease publication until the ratification of the Thirteenth Amendment constitutionally abolished slavery in December 1865. When the twenty-five-year-old Garrison started his newspaper, Abraham Lincoln was a twenty-one-year-old sodbuster on the Illinois prairie, Jefferson Davis was a newly commissioned U.S. Army officer fighting the Sauk and Fox on the Wisconsin frontier, and Davis's West Point classmate Robert E. Lee was building federal batteries on the Georgia coast. Ulysses S. Grant and William T. Sherman were still schoolboys in Ohio, and Harriet Tubman was a ten-year-old field hand on a Maryland slave plantation. John Brown was teaching school and running a tannery in Pennsylvania, Stephen A. Douglas was reading law in western New York, Frederick Douglass was learning to read as an adolescent slave in Baltimore, and Harriet Beecher Stowe was teaching composition in her sister's Hartford Female Seminary. Their careers a generation hence would each be profoundly shaped and, in some cases, redirected by the process Garrison set in motion in 1831. With ferocious determination, Garrison broke the silence and made the public listen in a way that his predecessors had not. He employed a writing style of extraordinary physicality—in his columns trumpets blare, statues bleed, hearts melt, apologists tremble, light blazes, nations move— that animated the moral landscape as the Romantic poets had spiritualized the natural world, and he made the moral issue of slavery so palpable that it could no longer be evaded. "Surely, no man yet/ Put lever to the heavy world with less," the poet James Russell Lowell wrote in 1848. "What need of help?—He knew how types were set,/ He had a dauntless spirit and a press."

When Garrison said that he unfurled the standard of liberty within sight of Bunker Hill, he meant it literally. Merchants' Hall, a large, plain, brick structure, rose four stories high at the corner of Congress and Water streets in the heart of the city, and from its attic rooms one could peer through grimy windows for a view across Dock Square and Faneuil Hall to the obelisk rising on the Charlestown battleground across the river. An elegant market—filled with bakeries, oyster bars, and fish and produce stands and lighted with gas—had taken over the ground floor of the building, but the others housed printing offices, stationers, and related trades. *The Liberator* used No. 6 as its address the first week, but then Garrison worked his way along the corridor under the eaves, using borrowed space in No. 8 the second week and No. 9 the third, before settling down into cheap quarters at No. 11, the very room in which he had begun his Boston editorial career on the *Philanthropist* just three years earlier.

With that fourth issue, Garrison and Knapp assumed responsibility for printing their own newspaper, since Foster, under pressure from his clerical publishers, could no longer lend them his press and had to take his name off the masthead. They rescued a font of worn, secondhand type from a foundry, turned up a well-used Ramage handpress, and set up a printing office. No. 11 was a spacious room, large enough to accommodate the typecases, the sturdy oak table topped with a gray stone slab on which Garrison made up—"imposed"—his pages, and another long table for folding, sorting, binding, and mailing. Though the greasy walls and ink-spattered windows gave the place an air of what even friendly visitors termed "slovenly decay," No. 11 proved homey enough for Garrison and Knapp, who decided to economize by moving out of Collier's and laying sleeping pallets on the floor of the office. "We found our own provender," Garrison recalled, "living chiefly upon bread and milk, a few cakes and a little fruit" cadged from the downstairs shops.

Garrison's life was completely defined by *The Liberator* and the abolitionist cause. He worked at odd jobs by day so that he could produce the newspaper at night. He had his circle of printers and reform-minded friends, but he hardly had a social life beyond church suppers or musicales in the black community and an occasional call upon the few well-to-do families who patronized the paper. No more lounging at the Athenaeum or paying court to his Dulcinea. Garrison never wrote a word about it, but—as he had done in Vermont—he used his newspaper's poetry column to hint at his frustrations with poem after poem about unrequited love. His bouts of self-pity faded, however, as he grew ever more absorbed in the work and attracted a notoriety that pleased the agitator in him if not the swain.

The venture took more time than expected, however, and Garrison regretted not being able to pay more attention to the editorial department. People think that "I have six days each week to cater for it, when, in fact, scarcely six hours are allotted to me, and these at midnight," he lamented to Samuel J. May. The "mechanical part" of the paper required "the most unremitted labor," he added. For every issue Garrison and Knapp composed and distributed one hundred thousand types, performed the presswork, folded, bundled, and mailed the papers, dealt with correspondence, and scanned the exchanges for possible material.

For an editor preoccupied with technical matters Garrison nonetheless displayed great literary facility. For the first four issues of *The Liberator,* he personally wrote enough copy to fill six columns each week: several editorials, many headnotes and pugnacious footnotes, book notices and reviews, innumerable squibs and fillers, and nearly a dozen poems. In the remainder of the paper Garrison provided a lively mixture of excerpts from the religious and temperance press, factual material on slavery, reports of meetings held to protest the slave trade or register opposition to colonization schemes, inspiring verses from Cowper and Byron and the black literary societies, and provocative letters from readers and the editorial fraternity—along with the editor's annotations and rebuttals. Endeavoring "to diversify the contents of the Liberator, as to give an edge to curiosity," Garrison brought all his training in the roles of a country editor—the wry observer, the humorist, the booster, the partisan—to the more complex task of reaching a diverse national audience on the most explosive issue of the times. The first issues of *The Liberator* looked no bigger than a pane of window glass, Garrison liked to say, but they certainly "let in the light," combining high purpose with a zestiness that in retrospect made Garrison's work on the *Genius* seem gray and ponderous.

The Liberator picked up, however, almost exactly where the *Genius* had broken off—with an account of the Baltimore trial of Francis Todd's civil suit, which had taken place without Garrison in October 1830. A jury of merchants had found Garrison guilty of libel and ordered him to pay one thousand dollars in damages, a penalty that the editor disregarded as an infringement upon the right of inquiry and that Todd never tried to collect. Taking the opportunity to tell the entire story over again, Garrison reiterated his attack upon New England's complicity with the slave system, but conceded that he had no specific information about Todd's previous ventures into the trade. "He says that this was his first cargo of souls . . . and I am almost as sure that it will be his last," the editor said pointedly.

From the outset, *The Liberator* attacked racial prejudice and political hypocrisy with as much force as it directed toward the peculiar institution itself. Garrison blazoned the front page of his second issue with two dozen "truisms" that mocked the paralyzing contradictions of American society: "All men are born equal, and entitled to protection, excepting those whose skins are black and hair woolly . . ." Garrison's satiric catechism began. "If white men are ignorant and depraved, they ought freely to receive the benefits of education," he continued, "but if black men are in this condition, common sense dictates that they should be held in bondage and never instructed." Yet Garrison could not remain sour for very long. He followed these caustic columns with a paragraph entitled "Our Trust" in which he refused "to give up our country as sealed over to destruction" and declared that "as long as there remains a single copy of the Declaration of Independence, or of the Bible, in our land, we will not despair."

An improvement in the condition of black citizens formed an essential element in Garrison's abolitionist strategy. Advancing the cause of civil rights would further undermine the rationale for slavery and would offer a vision of peaceable emancipation. "The toleration of slavery at the South is the chief cause of the unfortunate situation of free colored persons at the North," *The Liberator* maintained. "It is this institution which brought their color into contempt and still perpetuates the feeling." White people would have to "take our free colored and slave inhabitants as we find them," Garrison said, "[and] . . . respect them as members of one great family, who may be made useful in society, and honorable in reputation." In a series of articles addressed directly to black Americans—perhaps the first ever by a white writer to employ the salutation "countrymen"—Garrison emphasized the need for united political action to challenge "every law which infringes on your rights as free native citizens." Racial discrimination in the election and judicial codes and in the laws regulating transportation, schooling, the issuance of business permits, and marriage licenses were all "gross and palpable violations" of the U.S. Constitution, the Bill of Rights, and the constitutions of every state, he said. From his second issue onward Garrison campaigned for repeal of an archaic Massachusetts statute that forbade ministers from marrying a white person to a Negro, Indian, or mulatto. The argument that the personal right to marry should not be abridged by the state epitomized Garrison's willingness to stand against the inhumanity of racism even at the explosive frontier of sexual relationships. Despite some editorial sneers at the editor's personal interest in amalgamation and the sanctimonious objection that liberalization in Massachusetts would be an affront to the laws of other states, Garrison's relentless logic carried enough force to secure repeal in the lower house of the legislature.

The editor wanted his newspaper to be a forum for black activists and a vehicle for a biracial political coalition, and he set a militant tone by devoting at least ten column inches over the first few months to notices and correspondence about David Walker's *Appeal*. Though Garrison would not endorse violent resistance, he made sure that the black community understood his regard for forthright expression. "Let your voices be heard," Garrison urged, and he welcomed black writers to *The Liberator*'s pages. His Baltimore friend William Watkins indignantly denounced the timidity of editors of religious papers who ignored the plight of the free black population out of deference to their slaveholding subscribers. The Philadelphia leader James Forten, who had fought in the Continental Navy and whose own family had lived freely in Pennsylvania since the days of William Penn, passionately attacked the colonization principle that "a man is an alien to the country in which he was born." "To separate the blacks from the whites is as impossible as to bale out the Delaware with a bucket," Forten jibed, and he suggested that if the Colonization Society spent its money on offering premiums to master mechanics to take black apprentices, they would do far more to uplift the race and overcome prejudice. (The publishers of *The Liberator* did their part without a cash incentive: they hired the Rev. Thomas Paul's youngest son and namesake as an apprentice in February 1831. The boy, however, did not remain in the trade, but went on to college—Dartmouth '41—and became a teacher.)

His sympathetic vision made Garrison a hero to his black readers. "How sweetly sounds the name of 'Liberator,'" a Bostonian wrote, with a prayer that the editor's mission would "prove as fruitful as the coming of Titus into Macedonia." Black subscribers proved to be the sustaining force of *The Liberator*'s first year, with over five hundred subscriptions sold by midsummer, though the newspaper's readership—given that copies were passed around by hand and posted in reading rooms and barbershops—was considerably greater. Garrison especially took heart from the meetings of black political associations that sprang up to denounce the colonization scheme. *The Liberator* hailed each one with a ritual headline—"A Voice from New Bedford!" "A Voice from Providence!"—and a full report.

Garrison traveled to New York and Philadelphia to meet with the larger black political groups, and he turned the speeches he had made into a twenty-four-page pamphlet, *An Address to the Free People of Color*, that reiterated the themes he had pressed in *The Liberator*—an emphasis upon equal treatment, self-advancement through the acquisition of literary and mechanical skills, united political action, and a thorough repudiation of colonization. The *Address* sold out its first edition of one thousand copies before the end of July 1831, and, though it taxed their little office to the utmost, Garrison and Knapp immediately undertook a second printing. By August 1831, they would have three thousand copies in circulation. In Boston, Garrison's forthright address and widening offensive won over the previously skeptical elements on "the hill," led by J. T. Hilton, who now professed themselves convinced of Garrison's commitment and wrote publicly to claim him proudly as "their advocate." Their expression of trust, the editor replied, "outweighs in consolation all the abuse which has been heaped on me." Privately Garrison told Samuel May that if he proved unable to do much toward abolishing slavery, at least he would have had a hand in raising the political stature of the free black population.

Garrison had aimed his newspaper at five constituencies—which he enumerated as the religious, the philanthropic, the patriotic, the tyrannical, and
the free people of color—but only the last two had responded, black people
affirmatively and slaveholding editors and politicians with abuse. Unlike the
Genius, which had representatives in the upper South, *The Liberator* had
no agents and few subscribers south of Washington, D.C., yet through the
medium of newspaper exchange, Southern editors not only saw the paper
but reprinted material from it—accompanied by bitter condemnation—
which was then picked up by other papers and eventually worked over again
by Garrison in a lively cycle that kept his name and cause before the public
and enabled *The Liberator* to make a noise out of proportion to its size or
subscription base.

There was one constituency, significantly, that Garrison did not name: the
growing number of mechanics' unions and workingmen's parties, especially
in the largest cities, that had organized themselves in an effort to protest
the trend toward mechanization and monopoly that was leading to a growing
maldistribution of wealth, declining control over the workplace, and a lack
of political power for once-influential artisans and journeymen. Garrison retained enough of his Federalist and Whig assumptions about the harmony
of interests that theoretically united capital and labor in prosperous enterprise to express suspicion of what he regarded as a class-based politics of
envy. In the very first issue of *The Liberator* he sharply criticized efforts to
"exasperate our mechanics" into anti-aristocratic party organizations, and this
attack has led historians to portray the editor as wholly unsympathetic to the
plight of free labor in the North. It is true that Garrison—as an artisan
turned small proprietor—understood freedom in the nineteenth-century
sense of self-ownership rather than as the traditional craft ideal of owning
the means of production. This definition illuminated the contrast between
Northern free labor and Southern slavery, but minimized for him the significance of "wage slavery" as a political critique. Nonetheless, Garrison reacted with heartfelt sympathy and anger when he saw firsthand, during a
tour of Rhode Island cotton mills in 1832, the severity of the regimen imposed on the operatives, including women and children. In a long report to
The Liberator he spoke feelingly about the need for the ten-hour day and
delivered a stern warning to "our rich capitalists" about the dangers inherent
in oppressing labor. He followed up the warning that fall by printing several
more pieces depicting the evils of the factory system and child labor.

Garrison looked at free labor issues, as he regarded slavery, through the
lens of religious reformation. His Rhode Island reports emphasized that he
had "long since withdrawn from the field of politics," and he saw the workingmen's parties and their electoral and legislative agendas as part of the
scramble of materialist issues that he had repudiated. As the labor groups
became absorbed into the radical wing of the Jacksonian movement against
economic privilege, Garrison increased his distance, for the overall logic of

the Jackson party exempted slaveholders from its own critique. The editor instead absorbed the question of economic inequality into his larger preoccupation with the spiritual quality of American life. By the mid-1830s he bitterly denounced clergymen like Beecher for slandering working people as poorly behaved. The real issue, charged Garrison, was that the rich were no longer regarding laboring men "as brothers" and were not granting "due estimation" to the working population, whether white or black. "They are generally overtasked; they are seldom adequately remunerated . . . they are valued according to the strength of their bodies, rather than to the intelligence of their minds and the improvement of their hearts." All religious-minded people, Garrison insisted, had to protest the rising tendency toward aristocratic privilege and a consequent denigration of workers; "an equality of rights," he said, "must beget an equality of conditions. . . ." Here, in embryo, was the appeal to the free labor ideology that would become the backbone of the Republican Party in the 1850s.

Although Garrison had hoped to reach reform-minded benevolent leaders through *The Liberator,* their initial apathy changed into hostility as he increased the tempo of his attacks, especially against the ACS. Lyman Beecher, among others, felt obliged to warn his congregation to disregard the "few foolish whites" who opposed the benevolent plan of repatriation and "recklessly" advocated immediate abolition. (It was the first time, said Garrison, that Dr. Beecher had advised "a gradual abolition of wickedness.") The ACS national secretary, Ralph R. Gurley, who had earlier dismissed Garrison as "a rash and deluded youth," now denounced him as a "mad incendiary . . . scattering firebrands from Boston" and emphasized the point at the lectern by crumpling a folded sheet of *The Liberator* like kindling. Shortly after Gurley's return to Washington, D.C., from a New England tour, anonymous letters advised Southern postmasters that a newspaper called *The Liberator*—"published in Boston, or Philadelphia, by a white man, with the avowed purpose of inciting rebellion in the South"—was openly circulated among the free blacks in the capital. No one could prove that the ACS had begun the hostile campaign, but it seemed likely. Garrison himself received a nasty letter from Washington warning that his paper would not be "much longer tolerated" and advising him to "go to Africa" with his "flat-nosed" friends.

Unlike the self-effacing Lundy, Garrison had deliberately chosen to make himself an issue. "There shall be no neutrals; men shall either like or dislike me," he announced. The editor—and the newspaper as an extension of himself—would draw energy, like a lightning rod, to galvanize the cause. His statements poured forth with an intensity that seemed more like a spontaneous eruption than a composed literary style, which was precisely the effect Garrison wanted. He could have been "as smooth and politic as anyone," the editor once observed, but declared that he much preferred "nature to art." It was nonetheless a deliberate decision, not an irresistible impulse, that led him to write as he did. He chose his words, one close friend said, with the care of a pharmacist weighing out a prescription.

Nearly every visitor commented upon the surprising contrast between the private Garrison and the public firebrand. People walked in expecting to find "a stout, rugged, dark-visaged desperado," as one guest put it, and found instead "a pale, delicate, and apparently over-tasked gentleman" scurrying from desk to case to imposing stone, making light of the work with an unending series of hymn tunes and jokes, and stopping occasionally to stroke the pussycat stretched out affectionately on the periphery of the work space. Never too busy to talk, it seemed, Garrison stimulated an unending flow of conversation—copious, strong-minded, and fervent—that often turned the printing office into a seminar or Sunday school. The self-effacing Knapp formed a silent backdrop to conversation, as he struggled with the ledgers, the slips of paper containing fragments of subscription information, and the stack of bills. Knapp worked hard, spoke little, and quietly nursed the petty resentments that would one day rupture the bond with his more exuberant partner.

Each week Garrison took a perverse delight in reprinting the jibes of editors who called him everything from an "officious and pestiferous fanatic" to a "mawkish sentimentalist" who wept over "imaginary suffering" like "boarding school misses and antiquated spinsters." The insults, he said, "are like oil to the flame of my zeal." When New York's Mordecai Noah, one of the most caustic editors in the country, dismissed Garrison as "a printer by trade and a reformer of empires by profession," he accepted the sneer as a compliment. He had less patience, however, with people who professed sympathy for the cause but insisted that he moderate his conduct before committing themselves. Such demands came, significantly, from well-to-do whites; the editor's black constituents seldom found his language too harsh or angry. A pinch of practical help—donations, subscribers, a supply of larger paper—would do more for the cause than all the admonitions "to reform the reformers," Garrison said. It was not his language that caused offense, for virtually every editor engaged in the freewheeling style that seemed the essence of a bumptious and aggressive free press, but rather the subject to which Garrison applied his words.

Yet even Samuel May, who understood more than most the dramaturgy of Garrison's editorship, once entreated him to be more temperate. While out for a walk in early spring, Garrison listened "patiently and tenderly," May recalled, as the older man rehearsed the concerns of their more timorous friends. Then, however, Garrison exploded, insisting that he would only soften his language "when the poor downtrodden slaves tell me that I am too harsh."

"O, my friend," urged May, "do try to moderate your indignation, and keep more cool; why, you are all on fire."

Garrison stopped walking and looked straight at his beloved friend. He laid his hand upon May's shoulder with "a kind but emphatic pressure" and, speaking "slowly, with deep emotion," said:

"Brother May, I have need to be *all on fire*, for I have mountains of ice about me to melt."

The two friends stood there in the street, silent for a moment, and May could feel the pressure on his shoulder long after Garrison had withdrawn his hand. "From that hour," May wrote forty years later, "I have never said a word to Mr. Garrison in complaint of his style."

Garrison found himself so busy that he let a milestone go by unremarked: for the first time in his career he had sustained a venture for longer than six months. Yet before the year ended he faced a major effort to suppress his paper as the instigator of slave revolt. At the end of August 1831, the dread words "INSURRECTION IN VIRGINIA!" jumped from the pages of every newspaper in the country. Dispatches from Richmond related the blood-soaked tale: a contingent of slaves in "Southampton County had risen against their masters, killing seventy white people, before being subdued by the state militia. Over the next several weeks the "Southampton Tragedy" deep-ened as more than one hundred black people died at the hands of soldiers and vigilantes in reprisals across the county. A manhunt for the leader of the uprising—a visionary slave preacher named Nat Turner—kept much of southeastern Virginia and North Carolina in an uproar over the next seven weeks until he was captured and jailed in Jerusalem, the county seat, where he was hanged on November 11, 1831.

"We are horror-struck," Garrison wrote upon receiving the first reports from Virginia. Recalling his prophetic verse in the opening number of *The Liberator* that depicted the slaughter of innocents if emancipation came not peaceably but by the sword, Garrison said gravely, "What was poetry—imagination—in January, is now a bloody reality." As a pacifist who sought "to accomplish the great work of national redemption through the agency of moral power," Garrison would not condone the calamitous massacre, but neither would he ignore its underlying causes. "In his fury against the re-volters," the editor asked, "who will remember their wrongs?" He had put the same question to critics of *Walker's Appeal*, but what had been intellec-tual debate two years earlier now had become the most urgent political question of the generation.

Garrison faced the pacifist's quandary about revolutionary social change. He did not want to condemn the ends because he disapproved of the means, and he especially wanted white Americans to realize that their own political experience sanctioned Turner's course. "The slaves need no incentives at our hands," he pointed out to those who would "slander . . . pacific friends of emancipation" as provocateurs. Scarred backs and endless labor were spurs enough, he argued, as was the credo of liberty espoused by those "patriotic hypocrites" who refused to recognize that oppressed black people "rise to contend—as other 'heroes' have contended—for their lost rights." Yet Garrison had moral reservations about the violent legacy most Americans accepted. "I deny the right of any people to *fight* for liberty, and so far am a Quaker in principle," Garrison told a friend privately. "I do not justify the slaves in their rebellion; yet I do not condemn *them*, and applaud similar conduct in *white men*." Few editorial writers beyond his immediate circle endorsed Garrison's view of the insurrection as an apocalyptic warning or shared his willingness to sympathize with the oppressed despite their turn to measures he deplored. Although his former sponsor, the *Transcript's* Lynde Walter, found himself shaken enough to urge Virginians to consider a gradual abolition plan, most commentators took the violent affair as a sign of a residual black barbarism that made emancipation a practical impossibility.

Southerners, predictably, saw a conspiratorial dimension in the uprising and directed their anger toward free Negroes, especially peddlers and preachers, whom they suspected of spreading seditious ideas in pamphlets and newspapers. The *Richmond Enquirer* asked its readers to supply information about the circulation of "Garrison's 'Boston Liberator' (or Walker's Appeal)" in the state, and Virginia's governor, John Floyd, established a separate file folder for information on meddling agitators. In the anxious weeks following the bloodshed he rapidly filled it. Floyd received letters from all over the South describing suspicious events and the malign influence of Quakers, itinerants, and "fanatical" Yankee editors. "Much mischief is hatching here," said one informant from Philadelphia; articles from *The Liberator* were being read aloud at conclaves in black churches. One Virginia postmaster after another confiscated copies of *The Liberator* and mailed them to the governor as evidence.

Garrison received abusive and threatening letters from the South (the postage due hurt worse than the warnings, Garrison joked) and not a few hints of assassination from New England. A friendly minister advised the editor that he had overheard men in the Andover stagecoach talking of Garrison being "taken away, and no one be the wiser," a remark, given the mysterious fate of David Walker, that should have given him pause. The editor remained unfazed. "I hold my life at a cheap rate," he replied gratefully to his friend, for "if the assassin take it away, the Lord will raise up another and better advocate in my stead." Upon learning of the death threats, Arthur Tappan sent $100 to Garrison so that he could mail *The Liberator* to national leaders, adding with untoward jocularity, "As I see your life is threatened, I feel anxious to have all the advantage of it while you live. . . ." Some of the free copies Garrison sent to legislators and college presidents wound up in Governor Floyd's dossier.

While the Virginia leader pondered legal moves against "the club of villains" at Boston, public opinion convicted Garrison as the hidden architect of the Southampton Tragedy. The editors of the most influential newspaper in Washington—the *National Intelligencer*—declared in an article destined to be reprinted all over the country that publishing and circulating a paper as "diabolical" as *The Liberator* constituted "a crime as great" as poisoning a community's water supply. They called upon the mayor of Boston and the Massachusetts legislature to suppress the paper and punish the "instigator of human butchery" who produced it. In a blistering reply Garrison laid bare the politics of repression. The clamor against him was intended "to prevent public indignation from resting upon the system of slavery." The institution brewed its own destruction, yet its partisans attributed the explosion to "a foreign and an impossible cause." He employed no secret agents, Garrison jibed, for his paper "courts the light, and not darkness. . . . Tell me not that an evil is cured by covering it up . . . that if nothing be said, more will be done." He conducted *The Liberator*, Garrison emphasized, in order "to *prevent* rebellion" and save lives by overthrowing the blood-drenched slave system "by moral power, by truth and reason." He filled his letter with extracts from his previous editorials and the speeches of British abolitionists in the hope that the editors around the country who had copied the attack would also pick up his rebuttal from the *National Intelligencer* and thus give the material wider circulation. *National Intelligencer* editors Gales and Seaton, however, foiled him by spiking the piece. They judged its language "too severe" for their newspaper and publicly admonished Garrison to cease his "misguided crusade against a relation of society which he does not comprehend and must aggravate by intermeddling." Furious at this departure from journalistic custom, Garrison printed his rebuttal across the width of his own front page, hoping to get other newspapers to copy it directly from him. None did.

The outcry against Garrison continued throughout the fall, but the editor would not let himself be silenced. He had a riposte for each attack, and his confidence swelled with each outburst of hostility. In early October 1831, the town of Georgetown in the District of Columbia passed an extraordinary law prohibiting free Negroes from taking copies of *The Liberator* out of the post office under penalty of a twenty-dollar fine and thirty days in jail, as well as the threat of being sold into slavery for four months if the fines and jail fees went unpaid. ("An outrage," stormed Garrison; the law must be challenged in the U.S. Supreme Court.) In Raleigh, North Carolina, a grand jury indicted Garrison and Knapp for distributing incendiary matter on the strength of a reference to *rumors* of a Carolina insurrection that a postmaster had found in a confiscated copy of the newspaper, and in Columbia, South Carolina, a vigilance association posted a $1,500 reward for the apprehension and conviction of any white person circulating *The Liberator* or other publications of a "seditious tendency." ("A pretty liberal sum," Garrison joked, "but we think we are worth more.") In Georgia the legislature upped the ante by offering a reward of $5,000 for anyone who arrested Garrison and brought him to the state to be tried for seditious libel. (That was not a joking matter. "A bribe to kidnappers," he raged, "a price set upon the head of a citizen from Massachusetts! . . . Where are the immunities secured to us by our Bill of Rights?")

The question was not a rhetorical one. Some Southern officials worked hard to make suppressing *The Liberator* an issue of interstate comity. For the sake of harmony in the Union, they argued, Northerners had to silence the fanatics who would disrupt the social fabric of the Southern states. Whether this was a rhetorical point or an actual legal mandate occasioned much discussion in Richmond, and when it ended inconclusively, Governor Floyd groused that "this Union is at an end [if we are] tied up . . . from doing ourselves justice."

Meanwhile, Boston's Mayor Otis heard an earful from his Southern friends. A courtly South Carolinian, Benjamin Faneuil Hunt, whose Yankee connections went back many generations, suggested that the city's tolerance for "seditious" journalism would jeopardize its commercial relations in Southern ports. From Alexandria, Virginia, Nelly Custis Lewis, granddaughter of Martha Washington, told Otis that Garrison merited the death penalty for making "innocent" Southerners feel as if they were sitting on "a smothered volcano." South Carolina's Senator Hayne, in receipt of a "gratuitous" copy of *The Liberator,* suggested that Mayor Otis, with whom he had served in Congress, ought to exercise his power to suppress a contagious newspaper in the interest of public health. Otis felt obliged to send someone around to Merchants' Hall to see who had sent a copy of *The Liberator* to Senator Hayne, but Garrison challenged his authority to investigate and showed Otis's deputy the door. No matter. The mayor quietly assured his correspondents that the newspaper had "insignificant countenance" in Boston. "It is edited by an individual who formerly lived at Baltimore, where his feelings had been exasperated by some occurrences consequent to his publications there," Otis reported, doubting that "the new fanaticism" would ever be taken seriously by respectable people, who shared the mayor's own view that emancipation should be left "to yourselves, to time, to the Providence of God."

The proximity of Garrison's rise and Turner's rebellion unmasked for a new generation the intransigence of proslavery politicians and their Northern allies and allowed Garrison to dwell upon the darker side of the constitutional compromises Americans accepted as fundamental. It is too much to say—as some commentators do—that Nat Turner made William Lloyd Garrison's reputation, but by making a scapegoat of *The Liberator,* Southern leaders played into Garrison's hands and enhanced his sense of power. The attacks revealed the dynamic that would underlie the tempestuous events of the next three decades. At each challenge Southerners would emphasize that their commitment to the Union was contingent not only upon protection of their property in human beings, but upon protection from criticism of their

peculiar institution. As long as Northern public opinion valued the political
and commercial stability epitomized by the Union more highly than the
moral and spiritual precepts of the abolitionists, it would accede to the slaveholders' demands. When the president of Brown University, Francis Wayland, wrote to Garrison asking that "the paper you very politely sent me" be
discontinued, he gave as his reason the need to preserve harmony in the
Union. *The Liberator's* "menacing and vindictive" attitude toward slaveholders, Wayland admonished, "prejudices their minds against a cool discussion
of the subject" and, not incidentally, threatened to aggravate the slaves' hard
lot. The editor of the *Boston Courier,* Garrison's old friend Joseph Buckingham, went even further, suggesting that newspapers could be restrained
from antagonizing the South on the old common law principles that made
sedition and treason appropriate grounds for restricting press freedom. As
"a New England editor" Garrison could not countenance Buckingham's cen-
sorious view and retorted that if Buckingham were branded, whipped, and
sold at public auction, he might amend his definition of sedition.

Here, in essence, lay Garrison's understanding of his task as an agitator.
He was determined to put a lurid cast upon the landscape of compromise
and concession, to heat up the issue until the public felt ashamed of its
connection to slavery and angry at granting political privileges to slaveholders. While public officials spoke glowingly about the harmony of the
Union, Garrison encouraged the testimony of religious-minded people who
no longer wished to "remain constitutionally involved" in the guilt of slavery,
and in defending *their* right to be heard, the editor believed that he was
doing no more than meeting his civic obligation.

Garrison used his newspaper to reformulate the spiritual identity of the
nation. He contrasted the social visions of an open-handed and charitable
Christian republic with the closed and impious world of the slaveholder. He
wanted "to extract a root of bitterness, which is poisoning the whole nation,"
he emphasized, ". . . [and] to preserve the Union by removing an evil, which,
if suffered to grow, must inevitably produce a separation of the States." The
visual ornament to *The Liberator's* masthead in April 1831 presented the
stark alternatives. It held up a social mirror to the conscience by presenting
a picture of a slave auction situated in front of the nation's Capitol with
liberty's flag atop its dome and a whipping post in its plaza. The details were
those of a livestock market, save for a sorrowing slave family in the foreground and, for good measure, Indian treaties lying in the dust. The appeal
was not simply to individual sympathy but to collective identity, and it so
offended Southerners that Senator John C. Calhoun attempted—unsuccessfully—to ban newspapers with "pictorial representations" of slavery from the
mails. Garrison broadened the message in 1838 with a second panel that
depicted free labor and emancipation and in 1850 linked the two vignettes
with a medallion of Christ rebuking the master and uplifting the slave.

The artwork illuminated the direction Garrison sought for the nascent abolition movement as the catalyst of collective moral power. Unlike Lundy, who worked from the Quakerly assumption that the spread of light would raise the number of individuals ready to accept emancipation as their Christian duty, Garrison envisioned a decisive moment of social reformation. Lundy's viewpoint is epitomized in the popular medallion of the fettered black slave pleading, "Am I not a man and a brother?" which Garrison, too, used for sympathetic effect. Yet while Lundy looked to charitable acts, Garrison sought crisis and transfiguration. From the very first issue of *The Liberator* he insisted that slavery could not endure indefinitely in a Christian democratic country. He often quoted the passage from Christ's parable—"a house divided against itself cannot stand"—and, a quarter-century before Abraham Lincoln's celebrated speech, invited Americans to ponder the fate of a polarized nation.

Garrison's social vision, however, could not be separated from his eschatological one. He understood emancipation as a transfiguring moment—a collective Jubilee—that would bring America into a millennial age. Inescapably, then, emancipation had to be the work of Christianity and the churches. "Nothing but extensive revivals of pure religion can save our country," Garrison wrote in April 1831. "All reformations, whether political, civil, or religious are . . . the result of long accumulating causes [and] are the harvests of the spiritual husbandmen, who have tilled the ground and scattered the good seed. . . ." These were not simply metaphors for agitation. Garrison believed that only by purging itself of the sinful practice of slavery could his society attain the Christian purity its religious leaders advocated. He lovingly called *The Liberator* "a root out of dry ground," an allusion to a striking passage from Isaiah (53:2–4) that is the Old Testament's most vivid evocation of the Messiah, and Garrison felt a kinship with the righteous servant— "despised and rejected of men"—whom the Lord had chosen to bear the transgressions of the heedless and point the way to redemption. Yet the greater the sin, the greater the glory of those who suffer to extirpate it. Garrison could revel at times in the abuse he received because the epithets of the unrighteous confirmed his own sense of moral grandeur. The abolitionists knew themselves to be heroes and looked to the postmillennial day— as a fantasy in an April *Liberator* had it—when Christian principle had overthrown prejudice, a black president ruled the country, the capital had changed its name from the slavemaster Washington to the abolitionist Wilberforce, and "wonder-working time" had at last honored "the noblest efforts of the noblest minds which our county has produced."

In twelve months of unflagging labor and furious controversy, Garrison had taken up the mantle of Walker and tried to make his countrymen understand the message of Turner. Sustained by the hard-earned contributions of hundreds of black people and a handful of well-to-do reformers, *The Liberator* had withstood its enemies and thoroughly defined itself as a radical messenger by the end of its first volume. In December 1831, Garrison promised to enlarge the newspaper and urged each friend of immediate abolition to bring in a new subscriber for the ensuing year and to "agitate the subject on every suitable occasion, and among all classes of people." He now could describe the dynamic of a gathering social movement: "talking will create zeal—zeal, opposition—opposition will drive men to inquiry— inquiry will induce conviction—conviction will lead to action—action will demand union—and then will follow victory." *The Liberator,* he vowed, "shall yet live to hail the day of universal emancipation."

CHAPTER SEVEN

SCATTER TRACTS LIKE RAINDROPS

GARRISON OUTLASTED THE NAT TURNER FUROR, BUT THE HOSTILITY DI-
RECTED TOWARD HIM EMPHASIZED HOW DESPERATELY THE ABOLITIONISTS
NEEDED AN ORGANIZATION. THE EDITOR WOULD DO THE FIREBRAND'S
work, awakening the sleepers as if they were at a torchlight camp meeting,
but once roused, the moral strength of the converts had to be concentrated
and directed. For most of 1832 and 1833 Garrison linked his agitation to
the process of building an abolitionist movement—articulating its vision and
negating the influence of the colonizationists who stood in its way. He sought
an organization that possessed the relentless force of an oceanic wave, he
said, in which no separate drop was more important than another, yet achieving it paradoxically enhanced his own stature and enlarged the scope of his
leadership.

The Liberator first broached the idea for a national antislavery society in
March 1831, when Garrison declared that abolitionists needed to mobilize
themselves on the model of other benevolent organizations. They ought to
put agents in the field in order to build a network of local groups and "scatter
tracts like raindrops, over the land, filled with startling facts and melting
appeals on the subject of Negro oppression. . . ." He had made some headway in meetings with leaders in New York and Philadelphia during a lecturing trip in June 1831 and returned convinced that an "energetic"
American antislavery society would soon be formed, under either Tappan's
aegis in New York or the Friends' banner in Philadelphia. The post-Turner
attempt to suppress Garrison, however, intimidated supporters of the em-
bryonic association, and even Arthur Tappan felt discouraged enough to tell
Garrison that he didn't want his name attached to any copies of *The Liberator* directed to Southern leaders. "My ability to do good" would be "considerably diminished by the loss of my Southern customers," he said. Only
Garrison refused to bend. If a national society was sidetracked, he would
start a regional one. If Turner's uprising had given a new impetus to arguments that emancipation could only be accompanied by deportation, he
would hurry to complete his book-length attack on the whole colonizationist
delusion.

For a man whose name had become a byword for headstrong provocation,
Garrison's role in the formation of the New England Anti-Slavery Society—

the first association in the country pledged to immediate emancipation as its platform—proved a triumph of several months' patient diplomacy. He had expected the group to coalesce at a meeting scheduled for Samuel Sewall's law office on November 13, 1831, but the way proved unexpectedly thorny. The gathering brought together members of Garrison's two circles—the ardent journalists and reformers who frequented *The Liberator*'s office and the genteel young professionals who contributed steady financial support and opened new forums for the editor—but the fit proved less than fully compatible.

From the first group Garrison had recruited the quietly faithful Isaac Knapp, the printer Oliver Johnson, the editor Moses Thacher, and the schoolteacher Joshua Coffin, who had taught Whittier in Haverhill and now sought to open a school for black youth in Boston. Johnson—an earnest, handsome fellow whose long face was saved from somberness by a perpetual smile at the corners of his mouth—also worked in Merchants' Hall and had shyly admitted that he had gone into the printing trade after admiring Garrison's work on the *Journal of the Times*. The "quickening power" of the editor's conversation, the incandescent zeal of his craftsmanship, and his "mightiness in Scripture" all inspired Johnson, who became a lifelong friend and colleague, and the abolitionist's first biographer. Thacher was one of the first orthodox ministers in eastern Massachusetts to repudiate Beecher's colonization views and turn his religious paper into a voice for immediatism; he also had become deeply involved in the egalitarian anti-Masonic agitation and had served a term in the state legislature.

From the second group there came the forthright Samuel J. May, whom Garrison cherished as the kindest of brothers and admired as the wisest of fathers; the attorneys Samuel Sewall and Ellis Gray Loring, who had risked their reputations to support *The Liberator;* and their friend David L. Child, whose gifts as an intellectual and political analyst paled next to the editorial and expressive powers of his author wife. Though excluded by custom from the meeting, Lydia Maria Child exerted a strong influence nonetheless, for under Garrison's inspiration she had increasingly turned her professional talents to abolitionist ends. Also present, with ties to each group, was a Quaker importer and hat manufacturer named Arnold Buffum—a solemn bundle of energy lately returned from a trip to England—who enjoyed holding forth on transatlantic developments and reciting the verses of the British antislavery poets Cowper and Montgomery in a rich, mellow voice.

Seated amid the comfortable appointments of State Street, however, instead of in the sparsely furnished Merchants' Hall, even Garrison's close friends hesitated. Everyone acknowledged slaveholding to be sinful, agreed that the slaves should be freed at once, regarded colonization as a fraud, and defended the principle of civil equality, but some doubt arose about the wisdom of stating such principles in the articles of incorporation, as Garrison—following the model of British groups—had proposed. For two

hours the roomful of earnest souls considered the issues. Would an immediatist statement and accusatory language "excite prejudice" and place unnecessary stones in their path, or would a frank avowal of principles set the
necessary courageous standard? Would it be better to accept gradualists—
but not colonizationists—as members until public opinion grew more enlightened, or would this so blur the movement's commitments as to render
organization futile? When the passionate discussion cooled and the time had
come to count heads, the room divided nine to six in favor of Garrison's
motion. The vote spelled defeat, not victory, however, for the company
had previously agreed that it wanted at least twelve men—the "apostolic"
number—ready to take associated action. Now they would have to reconvene
after a month's reflection.

Garrison went back to Merchants' Hall disheartened. *"Expediency!"* he
railed, was "the deadliest word in our language." Yet Garrison knew that
people do not want "to give up their prejudices at once," and he could not
help but wonder if he had overreached himself. In an unguarded moment
Garrison had admitted that no matter how zealously he contended for immediatism, "it will, alas! be gradual abolition in the end." Yet even if slavery
would not be overthrown by a single blow, he reasoned, shouldn't abolitionists always contend for what "ought to be"? Of course they should, Sam May
reassured him and "the first step . . . is to make the public feel there is need
of improvement." May counseled Garrison as he would a parishioner to
realize that great moral changes in the world neither come about at one
blow nor occur in "precisely" the way pointed out by those who first insist
upon them. "You and I will continue to cry 'woe, woe, woe' . . . until the
Channings and Beechers . . . in the land are roused to answer the demand
of the people . . . ," he said. The idea that radical pressure would redefine
public opinion in a way that "leaders" would be obliged to recognize was
Garrisonian, yet the tone was not. Just as Garrison had a talent for what his
friends called "hitting the nail on its head," May had a gift for making the
hammer stroke sound reasonable and appropriate.

Buoyed by May's support, Garrison returned to the December meeting
and another round of inconclusive discussion. Though he missed May's conciliatory style (the minister, now that winter had set in, could no longer make
the eighty-mile journey up to the city from his pastorate in eastern Connecticut), he had instead the practical talents of Joshua Coffin and the support of three new recruits: Alonzo Lewis, a teacher and poet, who promoted
Garrison's work in the *Lynn Mirror* and arranged for the abolitionist to
lecture in the town where he once had served as a shoemaker's apprentice;
another poet and literary editor, William J. Snelling; and a ministerial colleague of Thacher's, the Rev. Abijah Blanchard, who also doubled as an anti-
Masonic editor. Nevertheless it took three more meetings marked by Coffin's
artful pleading and a brilliant tactical stroke by Garrison to bring the group
to a decision.

Coffin reminded the group that gaining members by making concessions to their prejudices would be like having subscribers to a newspaper who never paid their bills—a figure that Garrison heartily approved—and gradually nudged the moderates' draft away from the indeterminate language the attorneys favored. "While we should take care so as not to give offense," the schoolteacher said disarmingly, "equal care should be taken that . . . no indifferent, lukewarm, or 'dough-faced' New Englander would be induced to join the Society." To avoid any confusion with the colonizationists, Coffin suggested, the proposition to call themselves a "Philo-African" association should be replaced by a more explicit name: "The New England Anti-Slavery Society." With that suggestion adopted in a spirit of practical accommodation, the group went on to approve draft articles that established the governing process for the society and by January 1, 1832, had, in effect, formed an organization without having agreed on a statement of principles. Garrison then made an audacious move. He arranged for the next discussion of the draft preamble to be held not in Sewall's office but in the basement of a black church. If the young white men feared the criticism of their elders on State Street and in the fashionable pulpits, Garrison would coax them into action through direct acquaintance with the community on "the hill."

The African Meeting House—a tall red-brick building with a peaked roof and simple lines, save for the decorative touch of four arched doorways across its facade—stood in a cul-de-sac off Belknap Street in the heart of the black community. A Baptist congregation had worshiped in the spacious two-storied sanctuary since its completion in 1806, and the ground floor had space for benevolent societies and classrooms for black children, who were excluded from the city's grammar schools. A fierce northeast storm brought freezing rain and snow to Boston on Friday evening, January 6, 1832, and Garrison, Knapp, and Johnson made the long walk from Merchants' Hall through "sloppy streets" into the West End. The group met in the basement schoolroom, with "a number of colored citizens" as interested observers. The black leadership evidently intended to remain within its own Massachusetts General Association—for the time being, at any rate—but in a remarkable gesture of support for Garrison offered the room to his little band and came out to witness the debate.

The latest version of the preamble breathed no more fire than its predecessors, though its draftsman, William Snelling, had tried to weave the legal, rationalist, and religious strands of the argument into the text. Its first sentence broached immediatism in the most legalistic manner possible: "We, the undersigned, hold that every person, of full age and sane mind, has a right to immediate freedom from personal restraint of whatsoever kind, unless imposed by the sentence of law for the commission of some crime." Someone suggested that the word "bondage" be substituted for "restraint," and the change was readily made. The legalistic tone broadened somewhat in the second sentence, which held that "man cannot, consistently with reason, religion, and the eternal and immutable principles of justice, be the property of man," and nodded to Garrison in the third sentence by asserting that "whoever retains his fellow-man in bondage is guilty of a grievous wrong." This was not the strong denunciation of *sin* the editor sought, but he would accept it.

Mild as it was, the preamble occasioned yet another discussion. The young Unitarian attorneys Sewall, Loring, and Child still hung back, but with the silent influence of their black hosts and the embarrassment of indecision weighing over them, the rest of the group voted to accept the preamble and go ahead. Coffin turned a page in his minute book and copied out the now-complete constitution in a clear hand. The members stepped up to sign their names, and the New England Anti-Slavery Society came into being, committed both to abolition and the establishment of equal rights. In a curious minuet, whose choreography can no longer be reconstructed, the black elders evidently decided not to become "founders" of what appeared to be a young men's benevolent organization on the evangelical model, but in a gesture of collective support enrolled their names in Coffin's book in a parallel column. Black people subsequently participated in the NEAS, after their own association dwindled away, though their vital role in the founding remained obscure.

Garrison rejoiced that, at last, his solitary efforts would be reinforced by an organization. The twelve founders constituted not only an apostolic number for preaching, he thought, but a proper-sized jury "to sit in judgment on the guilt of the country." Walking out into the storm, Garrison looked up at the building and then gestured eastward over the brow of the hill toward the city's center. "Friends, we have met tonight in this obscure school-house," the apostles remembered him saying, "but, before many years we will rock Faneuil Hall."

The NEAS swiftly launched a petition campaign against the slave trade and formed committees to inquire into the problem of segregated schooling, to protect free colored people from the danger of kidnappers, and to develop opportunities for young black youths as apprentices in the skilled trades—all under the aggressive presidency of Arnold Buffum, who said he had become an abolitionist in his youth after hearing about the horrors of captivity at the knee of an African-born fugitive slave whom his father had helped to a fresh start in the North. Garrison took a lesser post as corresponding secretary and unofficial publicist who gave full voice to the society's pronouncements in *The Liberator*. With others now sharing the work of agitation, Garrison could concentrate his efforts first upon his newspaper and then upon his long-promised treatise on the Colonization Society.

When Garrison had announced that he would expand the size of *The Liberator*, an editor in Hartford had gibed that the Georgia legislature ought "to enlarge their reward accordingly." The Georgians ought to go after their "incendiary" colleagues in the Virginia legislature, Garrison riposted, for in Richmond they were "seriously talking of breaking the fetters of their *happy* and *loving* slaves." Although Governor Floyd had advised his state's lawmakers to tighten the legal restraints on slave conduct and the circulation of provocative literature, the assembly found itself—under the combined pressure of post-insurrection hysteria in the slaveholding eastern counties and political and economic resentments in the more egalitarian western regions—making an unprecedented examination of slavery as an institution.

For several months in the winter of 1831–32 one Virginian after another rose to criticize the institution and to consider—for the first time in public— measures similar to the *post nati* laws enacted in New York and Pennsylvania after the Revolution that would free slaves born after a certain date. By Garrison's standard the proposals proved hopelessly compromised: too limited, too slow, too much dependent upon the safety valve of colonization and the infamy of compensating slaveholders, not the slaves, for losses. Yet, as the spectacle of a society in ethical turmoil, the debates fascinated Garrison as a vindication of open discussion and a rebuke to "shameless apologists" who urged silence in the North.

The Virginia debate ended badly. The legislature rejected every antislavery measure, passed a stringent new slave code, and recommended that free Negroes be expelled from the commonwealth. Garrison nonetheless celebrated the event as "an entering wedge" that demonstrated the planters' alarm and put "on record, never to be obliterated" the masters' unequivocal admission that their system merited destruction. Ironically, many Southern politicians saw Garrison's point, and never again would the slaveholding leadership permit such extensive public discussion. The press, the pulpit, the colleges and seminaries, the bar and the courts all collaborated to suppress dissent about slavery and close the South to all the " 'isms" that the evangelical and benevolence movements had generated north of the Potomac. "We must satisfy the consciences, we must allay the fears of our own people," John C. Calhoun's editorial spokesman asserted. "We must satisfy them that slavery is of itself right—that it is not a sin against God—that it is not an evil, moral or political. . . . In this way, and this way only, can we prepare our own people to defend their institutions."

Calhoun's task would prove a formidable one. One of the paradoxes of the antebellum South was that two-thirds of free Southern whites were not slaveholders. Only thirty-six percent of Southern households owned slaves in 1830, and among the slaveowners, moreover, a concentration of ownership prevailed. Three-quarters of the masters owned fewer than ten slaves, while three-quarters of the slaves lived on plantations that employed twenty or more slaves. In the cold figures of the 1830 census, this meant a half million slaves owned by small farmers, one million slaves owned by planters with land ample enough to require gang-style labor, and a half million slaves in thrall to a planter aristocracy of ten thousand families owning more than fifty slaves each. Over the next thirty years, as a booming cotton market kept the price of slaves high, the size of the slave-owning class contracted to only twenty-five percent of the white households, while the area of "black belt" plantation agriculture expanded, pushing poor whites onto poorer land and setting up major internal political controversies within Southern states over land and credit policies, taxation, suffrage, and reapportionment. The wealth and power of the slaveholding aristocracy enabled it to mute the brooding conflict between King Cotton and the democratic yeomanry with the ideological weapon of racism and the political demonology of outside agitators. That fanatical abolitionists might turn degraded blacks loose to compete with white labor, unsettling both the economy and the social hierarchy and blocking a small farmer's rise in the world, became the specter that rallied majority support for the slaveholding minority.

Garrison never fully comprehended the degree of conflict within the South and often spoke as if every white Southerner were a slaveholder. Not until the 1850s, when a few Southern critics of the system broke the prevailing silence, did some abolitionists consider an appeal to the interests and sympathies of nonslaveholding whites, especially in the border states. By then Garrison had given up all hope of voluntary emancipation by Southerners and was urging a national political reconstruction that would break the power of the South. Yet his principal concern was neither sociological nor political, but moral, and from the standpoint of conscience, every white Southerner was indeed complicit with oppression, especially as Calhoun's "positive good" defense began to permeate the discussion. In the 1830s, however, Garrison did not yet frame his attack in sectional terms. While he vigorously challenged Calhoun at a time when politicians acquiesced in suppressing dissent, Garrison did not spare Northerners from the charge of moral complicity with an inhuman system.

The Virginia debate may have presaged the closing of the South, but for the editor of *The Liberator* it demonstrated the need for more, not less, discussion. Garrison endeavored to make the debate a national one. He had begun the second volume by printing his newspaper on a twenty-by-twenty-five-inch "Royal" sheet which allowed five columns instead of four and thus increased the reading matter by twenty percent. The roominess allowed him to offer substantial weekly excerpts from the Virginia debates and much commentary from the South, and by appending his customarily contentious footnotes, Garrison sparked dialogue over the span of a thousand miles.

The expanded *Liberator* also gave increasing prominence to women's voices, both black and white, and Garrison devoted some of his increased space to a weekly column of news about female antislavery societies. He headed it with the British icon of the pleading slave, altering the inscription, however, to read, "Am I Not a Woman and a Sister?" He reprinted many poems by Phyllis Wheatley, and he published—in both column and pamphlet form—the formidable black exhorter Maria W. Stewart, who preached and wrote for Boston audiences with an urgency that had gone unheard since the death of David Walker. The editor's collaboration with Mrs. Stewart, who spoke in the overflowing and voluble pietistic style Garrison knew so well in his own mother, attests to his standing in the black community and the influential role of his newspaper. "God has raised you up a Walker and a Garrison," Stewart would say as she urged her black audiences to exercise their political and intellectual powers. "The Americans have practiced nothing but head work these 200 years, and we have done their drudgery. And is it not high time for us to imitate their examples and practice head-work, too, and keep what we have got, and get what we can?" That the young white editor and the young black woman, whose husband—a ship's chandler—had died several years earlier, could confer about her articles across a desk demonstrates how the nascent abolition movement forged new roles and creative opportunities for people on the margins of American political culture.

The Liberator could boast the names of forty-seven agents on its masthead and several thousand subscribers enrolled in Brother Knapp's ledger by spring 1832, and the furor had so thoroughly subsided that Garrison joked that the paper must have lost some of its original fire. A Boston judge tried to rekindle the argument when he hinted to a grand jury that he would regard as a breach of the peace the publication of newspapers intended to excite hatred against the people of another state or provoke rebellion among their slaves. The jury made no moves toward Garrison, however, and some distinguished members of the bar wrote lengthy objections to the judge's reasoning. Garrison had not become popular by any means, but it appeared that he had gained some breathing room.

Garrison took the opportunity to complete the book-length refutation of the colonization doctrine he had begun the previous summer but laid aside when the Turner affair intervened. He went after the ACS with the readiest tools at his command: scissors, paste pot, and composing stick. Night after night, week after week, Garrison assiduously read the society's annual reports and its monthly magazine, the *African Repository,* and clipped out every statement that demonstrated either the proslavery bias of the organization or its racial prejudices. He sorted the clippings into neat, fan-shaped piles that by mid-April 1832 had burgeoned into a ten-part indictment, the outline for a polemic so extensive that Garrison and Knapp would need nearly two months to print it.

Although Garrison prepared a forty-page introductory essay of his own, his strategy, inspired by the debates in Virginia, required that the colonizationists testify against themselves. Christ's maxim "Out of thine own mouth will I condemn thee" became Garrison's literary imperative and eventually graced the title page of the book. Over the next six weeks, as the spring evenings afforded longer hours of decent light, Garrison cadged time from *The Liberator's* production schedule to set a batch of quoted material in agate type. He added sentences of his own to provide continuity, and, given the controversy he expected to spark, proofread his galleys with exquisite care. He then imposed the matter into a signature—a section of eight pages—which he printed in quantity and stored until he eventually had the makings of a bulky tract with twenty signatures. He did not stop there, however, but added nine more signatures containing the resolutions and addresses of all the recent public meetings at which black people had condemned the colonization plan. Including them would increase the cost of the book, but greatly enhance its moral power and enable a collective black voice to reach the clerical and political establishment.

By mid-May 1832, he was folding the sheets, stitching them together, and binding each unit with a soft-papered, sepia-toned cover until he had an edition of 2,750 copies, which he officially published on June 1, 1832. For sale at sixty-two cents each (or two for one dollar), it was a 236-page book entitled *Thoughts on African Colonization: or An Impartial Exhibition of the Doctrines, Principles and Purposes of the American Colonization Society, together with the Resolutions, Addresses and Remonstrances of the Free People of Color*. It was to be Garrison's only book-length work, and it so thoroughly accomplished its polemical task that it has disappeared into the same oblivion as the organization it attacked. This is a backhanded tribute to Garrison's talent, but it also means that the eloquence with which the editor defended racial equality is also forgotten. *Thoughts* was more than a work of negation; it offered the vision of a society that transcended race.

The ACS had acquired its reputation for benevolence largely by hearsay and the endorsements of prominent politicians and clergymen. Founded in 1816 by a Virginia congressman, Charles Fenton Mercer, who candidly saw a colony in Africa as "a drain for pauperism" among the South's free people of color, the idea was taken up by a Princeton theologian, Robert Finley, who had persuaded himself that it would be an act of benevolence to offer an African asylum in which black people could rise from the degraded position they were inevitably destined to occupy in America. In appealing to Congress for federal support in the acquisition of land and the transportation of colonists, Mercer, Finley, and their allies—most notably two Maryland Federalists, the congressman Robert Goodloe Harper and the attorney and patriotic poet Francis Scott Key—employed a variety of arguments. They reassured slaveholders that colonization would offer a safety valve for troublesome elements, while they opened for Northern humanitarians the vague but beguiling prospect that the success of a settlement in Liberia (whose capital, Monrovia, would honor the incumbent president) would exert a moral influence on behalf of voluntary manumissions in the South. To the evangelical clergy they emphasized the missionary appeal of bringing Christianity to Africa, a theme that some British abolitionists, including Wilberforce, also had found attractive.

Although the ACS had transported only a token number of 1,400 settlers to Liberia during the 1820s, the friends of colonization had assumed prominent positions in the pyramid of benevolent societies, which gave the amorphous ACS program the added luster of the temperance, Bible tract, and Sunday school movements. Given its diverse constituency, the ACS never issued a systematic exposition of its views and only began to publish a magazine in the late 1820s, when, after hopes for federal support had waned, it organized local societies and the Fourth of July collection services. The ACS had attained its standing largely because most people thought very little about the slavery problem, and those who did accepted as axiomatic the underlying assumption (which went back to Jefferson) that abolition had to be accompanied by the physical and political separation of the races. That this principle had acquired a humanitarian aura—and the support of the Northern clergy—most roused Garrison's ire, and he aimed his attack not only at the organization, but at the idea of white supremacy it fostered.

"Many innocent birds have been decoyed into the covey," Garrison lamented, and the depth of his complaint may be appreciated by realizing that Garrison's staunch friend, Samuel Joseph May, supported the ACS as a benevolent "introductory to more efficient measures." "I can almost see the kindling of your eye and the quivering of your lip," May wrote at the outset of an eight-page letter to his friend in which he tried to explain his view that the ACS at least opened "a channel of information" about the condition of black people in America. Much about the ACS was "derogatory," May admitted, and he would never endorse the idea of forcible repatriation, but if voluntary colonists could make Liberia "a beacon and a model"—as the Puritans in New England had done for their faith, May added—that endeavor would help dispel "the vapours of prejudice" and clear the air for the necessary work of abolition.

Garrison paid "no attention to the seven pages you wrote him on African colonization," their young friend Henry Benson told May, but as the editor matured the plans for his book, he realized that he would have to address himself to good souls like May and demonstrate clearly that the principles of the ACS did not accord either with the gospel or with the American creed. "I dedicate this work to my countrymen," Garrison wrote at the outset of *Thoughts*, "in whose intelligence, magnanimity, and humanity I place the utmost reliance." He rooted his crusade upon the belief that white people had the character and faith to surmount the prevailing "wicked prejudice" toward blacks, and indeed, of all Garrison's iconoclastic principles, this one was the most idealistic. He brushed aside technical issues such as the alleged prosperity of Liberia and its putative influence upon manumission to concentrate upon the immoral connection between color and prejudice. *"This is the question—and the only question,"* Garrison declared: "whether it is not the sacred duty of the nation to abolish the system of slavery now, and to recognize the people of color as brethren and countrymen who have been unjustly treated and covered with unmerited shame."

The words seemed aimed like an arrow at the conscience of Samuel Joseph May. Yet, as a good evangelist, Garrison first made an example of himself. He, too, had once considered the ACS a praiseworthy organization, Garrison admitted, largely because he had followed the opinions of influential clergymen and had not studied the society's statements for himself. "I was then blind," he declared, "but now I see." Now his book would show the great mass of colonization supporters in the North that "the omnipotent power of men and wealth and station" had concealed the society's "sinful palliations . . . and unrelenting prejudices," and he invited his readers to share the experience of conversion.

Few "can hamma as loud as Garrison," his Yankee admirers liked to say, and *Thoughts on African Colonization* struck one thunderous blow after another. Garrison offered twenty-two pages of quotations to substantiate his first charge that the ACS was "pledged not to oppose the system of slavery" and an equal number in support of the collateral ideas that the society apologized for slaveholders, recognized slaves as property, and actually enhanced their value by making the system more secure. He pounced on speech after speech from the minutes of the annual meetings that struck variations on Henry Clay's founding statement that the society intended no interference with the existing property relations in the South, and he reprinted appeals for patience from slaveholders who felt trapped in a centuries-old problem. He would not "arraign them for the crimes *of their ancestors,*" Garrison retorted, but for perpetuating them: did inheriting stolen property convert it into an honest acquisition?

The second half of Garrison's book concerned racism. He charged that the ACS encouraged prejudice, intended to expel the free black population, and—worst of all—"denie[d] the possibility of elevating the blacks in this country." The "agony of soul" Garrison had experienced in the course of his study now reached "the acme of intensity." He quoted the national executive of the society, the Rev. Ralph R. Gurley, who advised black people to bend their hopes to Africa and "*not* regard our country as their permanent residence, or as that country in which they will *ever,* as a people, enjoy equal privileges and blessings. . . ." Garrison countered such prejudice with poetic vision. "I rejoice that God has made one star to differ from another star in glory," he wrote, "and that He presents to the eye every conceivable shape, and aspect, and color, in the gorgeous and multifarious productions of Nature." All God's creatures can dwell "in harmony together. . . . Of this I am sure."

Equality required that the black voices in his book be "tenderly regarded," the author emphasized. He had said little about the Liberia colony itself, partly because he considered it peripheral to the principles at stake, but mostly because the black organizations he quoted had repudiated the idea so thoroughly. "They are as unanimously opposed to a removal to Africa, as the Cherokees from the council-fires and graves of their fathers," Garrison said, drawing a sharp parallel with a cause that had attracted sympathetic attention in benevolence circles. He had devoted regular attention in both *The Liberator* and the *Genius* to the shameful case of Indian removal in which the Jackson administration deported the Cherokees and Creeks from their settlements in the southeastern states to arid reservations in Oklahoma. Indian removal was Jackson's major reward to the states' rights advocates who had backed his candidacy and a reliable barometer of the president's racism. The Cherokee had made themselves into useful citizens on the whites' terms, Garrison wrote, but in a grievous "breach of faith" they were being driven away by "the exercise of a despotic power, to gratify the avarice of Georgia" and its land speculators. Garrison held proslavery apologists "answerable" for the injustice done the Indians. "It is this wicked distinction of color in our land," he emphasized, "which finds so many strenuous advocates even among professing Christians, that has robbed the red men of their rights"—and given black removal a cloak of plausibility.

Thoughts on African Colonization may have been an ungainly work, festooned with long ribbons of quotations and fragmented into an excessive number of sections, but the tract spoke truth in heartfelt tones. Garrison took fierce pride in his work and staked his reputation on it, insisting that he had made it "as fair in its quotations, and as correct in its typography, as possible." In the dual role of agitator and publisher he shipped books on consignment to his agents, and within a week he had Arthur Tappan's "truly liberal" order of one hundred copies, ten for himself and ninety for complimentary distribution to college libraries and influential clergymen. Black opponents of the ACS circulated the book through their own networks; thirty years later one of Philadelphia's abolitionist leaders still remembered being handed the tract as a young man by his barber in Carlisle, Pennsylvania, who had previously introduced him to *The Liberator*. A black minister from Middletown, Connecticut, Amos Beman, recalled hearing passages from both *Walker's Appeal* and Garrison's works read aloud again and again in community meetings until "their words were stamped in letters of fire upon our souls."

Thoughts captured the attention of the humanitarian public with a force unmatched in American journalism since Tom Paine's *Common Sense*. It "kindled a fire," a young divinity school professor in Ohio recalled, at a time when it seemed "the whole business of the press, the pulpit, and the theological seminary, was to reconcile the people to the permanent degradation and slavery of the negro race." Garrison intended to make his *Thoughts* into "a textbook for abolitionists," and he succeeded.

Buttressed by the book, the apostles of the New England Anti-Slavery

Society launched a concentrated assault upon the ACS. Refusing to concede the Fourth of July, the NEAS organized rival meetings that undermined the traditional ACS fund-raising service. (Garrison gleefully reprinted the letter from a Providence man who subscribed to *The Liberator* with money he had withheld from the ACS collection plate.) On Arnold Buffum's summer-long lecture tour across Massachusetts and Rhode Island, he found the clergy hostile, but the public well disposed to the Garrisonian argument that the ACS was *not* an antislavery society. Shut out of the Congregational or Unitarian meetinghouse, Buffum would raise his stentorian voice in a Baptist or Methodist chapel and interpret the barred door as a sign of the ACS intent to suppress criticism of slavery in the interest of social peace. The colonizationists would "excuse me," Buffum liked to say, "for having an opinion of my own upon this subject . . . and for [living] in a land where everyone has an equal right to think for himself, and to present his thoughts to others."

Class tensions underlay the controversy. At a citywide meeting of ministers in Boston, a convert said later, all but two clergymen agreed with the contention that the abolitionists were "beneath notice" and came from "the poorest, obscurest, and most ignorant" segment of the population. Garrison, morever, was dismissed as "a low-lived, ignorant, insignificant mechanic . . . connected with no church, and responsible to nobody." Misled by such intelligence, the ACS agent for New England, the Rev. Joshua Danforth, a Princeton man who had formerly pastored a Presbyterian church in Washington, D.C., deliberately ignored Garrison's book and failed to appreciate the popular power that the NEAS mobilized. When he finally embarked upon a series of lectures late in the summer, Danforth compounded his problems by insulting his challengers as "unlicensed" preachers and impetuous nonentities led by a mere "Quaker hatter," in contrast to the judges and divines who graced his organization's offices. How could Buffum—"a small mouse trying to crawl over a great mountain"—and Garrison—"an upstart with a price upon his head"—carry more weight with the public than the Lyman Beechers and the Harry Otises? he asked aloud.

Danforth had a stuffy, punctilious air that grated on New England audiences. Though only thirty-four years old, he adhered, like many colonizationists, to an old-style politics of deference, which the abolitionists effectively likened to the haughtiness of the slavemaster. His attempt to pitch the battle on class lines placed him in opposition not only to the nascent abolition movement, but to the widespread anti-Masonic agitation then sweeping New England. The two insurgent forces drew upon similar emotional wellsprings—an evangelical opposition to deistic religion, a moral reformer's reaction to the alleged libertine excesses of the Masonic order, and a democratic hostility to aristocratic privilege and secret societies—and manifested rising hostility to established institutions and settled social practice. Danforth could not have picked a worse moment to malign the humble origins of his antagonists, and *The Liberator* made sure that New England's mechanics did not forgive the insult. The editor scoffed at the "miserable pride" with which Danforth and his allies put on the airs of "the 'good-society-folks' [who] cannot stoop to the *canaille*," while Buffum (who now happily signed himself "The Hatter" and joked that his power would be *felt*) reminded his audiences that "men of little estimation"—fishermen, he believed—had once taken "quite an active part in benevolent enterprises."

Garrison himself went out on the hustings, participating at an anti-Masonic convention in Worcester, urging the formation of an antislavery society in Providence, and undertaking in October 1832 a three-week intensive tour of Maine. Portland's entire black community turned out in force for his inspirational talk in the Friends Meeting House and then demanded a second address from him in their own chapel. Meanwhile, Garrison's host, the Quaker merchant Nathan Winslow, whose generous contributions helped sustain *The Liberator* and underwrite the publication of *Thoughts,* so successfully promoted the editor's lecture that more than two thousand people crowded into the Unitarian church to hear it. One distinguished auditor, Judge Samuel Fessenden, found himself moved to tears and returned to the Winslows for conversation that went on past midnight. Fessenden repudiated his connection with the ACS, successfully urged his colleagues on the bench to read Garrison's *Thoughts,* and shortly presided over the formation of a state antislavery society.

As he traveled across Maine, Garrison found at least a minister or two in each town ready to turn away from the colonizationists and circulate *Thoughts* to their colleagues. At Colby College in Waterville, after he complied with the students' request to contrast the two societies competing for their allegiance, they enthusiastically voiced their support for the NEAS. Similar events were taking place at colleges from New Jersey to Ohio, where students and faculty—using *Thoughts* as the basis of argument—debated the issues and renounced the ACS. At Western Reserve the trustees fired two faculty members who had publicly repudiated colonization. While Gurley congratulated the college for thwarting a plot to subvert it into "a seminary for educating Abolition missionaries," Garrison opened the pages of *The Liberator* to the beleaguered immediatists, who could not get a hearing in their local papers.

Everywhere the editor went, people pressed forward to tell him how his book and *The Liberator* had opened their eyes and rekindled their hopes. They told him, too, of the subtle pressures they encountered: the mother who had urged them to hide *Thoughts* before her guests arrived or a neighbor who recoiled at the sight of Garrison's newspaper in the post office and urged them "to keep better company." Abolitionism began with resistance to conventional ideas, Garrison knew, and in meeting his readers face to face, he encouraged them to emulate the "village Hampden" of Gray's beloved elegy "that with dauntless breast/ The little tyrant of his fields withstood." Slowly they would build a movement upon hundreds of individual acts of conscience.

Garrison had gone out on the lecture circuit, he admitted, partly "to do justice" to himself. With the exception of two brief trips to Philadelphia, he had worked without surcease at *The Liberator* and on his book for nearly two years. Although he always maintained his proud demeanor in the face of abuse, Garrison felt the wounds nonetheless, and it pleased him to see the surprise on strangers' faces when they realized they were conversing with the notorious firebrand. "They had almost imagined me to be in figure a monster of huge and horrid proportions," Garrison wrote, "but now finding me decently made, *without a single horn*, they take me cordially by the hand, and acknowledge me 'a marvellous proper man.' " (The phrase—from Shakespeare's *Richard III*—underscores the poignancy of Garrison's feelings, for it is spoken as the villainous prince assumes a lover's part.)

Garrison would often begin a lecture with the salutation "Ladies and gentlemen, I am the peace-disturber Garrison—the fanatic Garrison—the madman Garrison," and he would take great delight as the audience first tittered nervously, then laughed and applauded at the preposterous notion that this pink-cheeked, bespectacled young man with his beaked nose and balding dome could be an incendiary. By unmasking himself before an audience Garrison invited its love and he received it. Yet this ploy was not merely a bid for attention; it had a didactic purpose as well. He wanted to inspire his listeners with his ordinariness and demonstrate to them that even the mildest-looking soul could stand up for truth. He invited them to join him in what Harriet Beecher Stowe later called a "grand Miltonic poem, in which . . . otherwise commonplace lives shone with a solemn splendor."

Garrison and Buffum had done their work well. With ACS support dwindling everywhere from New England to Ohio, Gurley's strategy of ignoring Garrison had clearly failed, and in November 1832, the ACS leadership finally broke what Garrison called its "death-like silence" about his treatise. In a lofty six-page statement that subtly reformulated the ACS position while it condemned the editor's extremism, Gurley tried to redirect the argument. Of course, "all good men agree[d]" that the condition of the colored population was "miserable" and that "immediate" efforts should be made to relieve and improve it, Gurley wrote in the *African Repository*. Christians must decide if voluntary colonization was a benevolent means of extending such assistance and creating the "gentle and persuasive influence" necessary to melt away slavery without the horror of civil war. Gurley contrasted the ACS honey with Garrison's gall at vilifying the South and reproaching "the wisest and best men" of the North "all because we do not say, that an evil system . . . which has been fortified by time, and prejudice, and habit and law, can be, and ought to be entirely, and completely, and instantaneously

demolished." No Christian would deliberately sacrifice "the substantial interests, both of individuals and the community, to any unsubstantial theory
of the rights of man," Gurley declared. If this explicitly conservative rebuttal
to Garrisonian radicalism were not enough, Gurley added the credo of the
master: "It is not right that men should possess that freedom, for which they
are entirely unprepared, [and] which can only prove injurious to themselves
and others." So long as blacks remained in the country the masters would
still have rights over them, "growing out of circumstances resembling that
of parents over children," which might be innocently and legitimately exercised "on principles of Christian charity." Gurley had confirmed Garrison's
insistence that the deepest fault line in American society ran not between
immediatists and gradualists, but between egalitarians and racists, and this
was a line that did not coincide with sectional boundaries.

Gurley's review signaled a counteroffensive for the colonizationists that
attacked immediatism and Garrison in equal measure. Danforth charged that
Thoughts combined "the most disgusting egotism [with] the grossest mis-
representation." Some writers pounced upon the few errors in citations,
while others claimed that Garrison had unfairly assumed that every partisan
of colonization spoke officially for the organization. The prominent Congregational minister Leonard Bacon insisted that the ACS had "no confession
of faith," and appropriately so, in the interests of sectional harmony. Bacon
pronounced Garrison's style "not one to do good with" and suggested that
he "let alone controversy and stick to his poetry."

The ACS offensive gave fresh momentum to the debate, however, and
refocused it on Garrison's terms. Over the winter of 1832–33, with nearly
two thousand copies of *Thoughts* in circulation and Northern humanitarians
debating the issues in forum after forum, colonization receded from view,
as Garrison had hoped, and immediatism came to dominate the agenda of
reformers. In New England the turning point came when *The Liberator*
bedeviled Danforth into the public confrontation he had long avoided, and
the occasion—at Salem, in February 1833, with Buffum pressing Danforth
from the pulpit and Garrison adroitly managing the resolutions offered from
the floor—proved a triumph for the abolitionists. Danforth condemned their
"recklessness" and said he would debate no more. He did, however, organize
a large meeting in Boston's Park Street Church at which Garrison's old
nemesis, the politician Caleb Cushing, and an influential theologian, the Rev.
Calvin Stowe, soon to be Beecher's son-in-law, said little about colonization
but professed themselves equally opposed to slavery and those radicals who
would threaten the Union.

The colonizationists had chosen a bad moment to divert the debate with
the specter of disunion, however. South Carolina had recently culminated
its long quarrel with the federal government over tariff rates by passing an
ordinance of "nullification" in November 1832, an assertion of state sovereignty that all parties understood as applying to the slavery controversy as

well. If the nation divided, it would not be their fault, the abolitionists argued, for the slaveholders had revealed two essential principles: they would
hold the Union hostage to their peculiar institution, and they would oppose
all commercial measures, such as the tariff, that increased the power of the
North and enhanced its antislavery potential. Although John C. Calhoun and
other nullifiers opposed government support for colonization measures for
fear that *any* federal involvement on the slavery question would eventually
threaten them, Garrison perceived both nullification and colonization as
forms of slavery protectionism.

Yet there were many ironies in the nullification controversy. The states'
rights advocate President Jackson sternly rebuked the nullifiers with a proclamation that partook so fully of Daniel Webster's nationalism that Boston
beamed its approval and Harvard gave Old Hickory an honorary degree,
while Garrison, a strong critic of Calhoun's constitutional theorizing, wrote
his own attack upon the tendency to regard the U.S. Constitution as a sacred
document. The nullification doctrine had to be repudiated, but that did not
mean that the Constitution stood above reproach or did not need repair. "It
was a compact formed at the sacrifice of the bodies and souls of millions . . .
for the sake of achieving a political object—an unblushing coalition to do
evil that good might come," Garrison wrote, insisting that the people of the
North should not be intimidated into silence by veneration of a document
"dripping as it is with human blood." Whether slavery could be abolished
within its confines would preoccupy the reformers for two decades once the
obscurantist shadows of nullification and colonization were dispelled.

Thoughts on African Colonization accomplished its mission, but the book
nearly cost the author his newspaper. When Garrison returned from Maine
in mid-November 1832, the morose Knapp told him that they had no cash
and that a quarter's worth of operating capital was tied up in the pile of
more than twelve hundred unsold copies of Garrison's book. "We cannot
live upon air," he said. When it came to money matters, however, Garrison
had a Micawberish confidence that "something would turn up." Within a
few days he had dispatched a circular letter to his warmest patrons—the
Tappans, the Winslows, the Fortens—who not only agreed to buy up the
wholesale stock and redistribute the book through their own commercial
networks, but offered cash donations as well. The edition was sold out by
mid-December 1832, and Garrison had enough money to buy a load of fresh
type on which to print the next volume of the paper.

The successful effort to raise money for *The Liberator* left Garrison feeling depleted. "My life seems to me to have been a blank," he confided to a
friend on his twenty-seventh birthday in December 1832. "The older I grow,
the less do I seem to accomplish." He had staked his identity on the
cause, yet its advance did not fully satisfy him. Garrison was lonely. His
friend Oliver Johnson had left their bachelors' hall at the printing office in

September 1832 to marry Mary Ann White, a happy event that made the self-pitying Garrison feel that romance would never come his way. He had pined for years after Mary Cunningham, but she had irrevocably closed the door by marrying a gent named Horace Porter in the previous spring. His interest had quickened in the young Winslow sisters down east in Portland, but he did not pursue it. When three young women from Haverhill started writing to him under the collective name "Inquirers after Truth," he brightened, however, and replied at length. Eventually, in April 1833, Garrison contrived an occasion to visit Haverhill for a lecture and declared that the village had "stolen his heart." "My spirit was as elastic as the breeze," he wrote in gratitude to his young and eligible hostess Harriet Minot, declaring that after only one day back home he "sighed at the separation, like a faithful lover absent from the mistress of his affections." The shy Garrison probably meant such extravagant words as a hint to Miss Minot, but, for all his public eloquence, he found himself struck dumb when it came to voicing his feelings directly to a woman. The yearning ran so deep and the fear of rejection loomed so large that Garrison, who enjoyed taunting society for its rejection of his values, lacked the confidence to risk the same dynamic in courtship.

No such inhibitions governed his expressions of fraternal affection, however. In thanking his hostess profusely for having arranged a reunion with their mutual friend John Greenleaf Whittier, whose morose disposition and preoccupation with politics had led to several years of silence between the two men, Garrison told Miss Minot that "to see my dear Whittier, once more, full of health and manly beauty, was pleasurable indeed." Ostensibly he hoped that her circle could draw the popular author into writing for the cause, but he also sought emotional reciprocity from his once-close friend. In asking another of the "Inquirers" for help in restoring ties with the poet, he urged, "Tell him that my love to him is as strong as was that of David to Jonathan." Given Garrison's penchant for Biblical language and his absorption in the rituals of primitive Christianity, it would be a mistake to take the remark as evidence of a homosexual relationship between the two men. Strong emotional bonds among evangelical men who had rejected the competitive commercial ethic were well recognized in the movement and, far from carrying an assumption of overt sexuality, were considered an aspect of the apostolic union in *agape* or the Christian love Christ and His disciples bore for one another. The Garrisonian men, indeed, developed an ideal of Christian masculinity that in its tenderness and sympathy, its disposition toward pacifism, and its willingness to accept women as equal participants in both social reform and personal relationships subjected them to cultural ridicule as well as political hostility. That this untraditional identity extended to sexual relationships among men remains a highly speculative proposition, however, and one that in the case of the reticent Garrison and the even more repressed Whittier seems highly unlikely.

Although the "Inquirers" wanted the editor to pay a return visit to Haverhill, he could not readily comply. Garrison was on the verge of departing for England on an anticolonization mission for the NEAS, and by the time he returned in October 1833, his romantic interests had shifted in another direction. The NEAS had first suggested that Garrison go abroad to solicit funds to support a project much discussed in benevolence circles, an institute for black students that would blend the liberal and mechanical arts and help enlarge the black leadership class, but political urgency soon changed the focus of the mission. The ACS had stolen a march with the wealthy reformers of Great Britain, especially the venerable Thomas Clarkson, by misrepresenting itself in London as an antislavery organization working "to assist the emancipation of all the slaves in the United States," and the NEAS leadership considered it imperative to send an agent of its own to unmask the deception. Only Garrison—the movement's most redoubtable figure and author of the devastating *Thoughts*—could perform the work. Though it would take "great self-denial" to tear himself away from *The Liberator,* the editor said, the prospect of a glorious mission excited him. It would be a grand opportunity to dramatize the American cause, to forge an alliance with British abolitionists and study their methods, and to gain transatlantic recognition of his leadership. He accepted the assignment, though it would be several months before the NEAS could arrange a letter of credit from Arthur Tappan and Garrison could install Oliver Johnson as his substitute.

While the editor readied himself for departure, a bitter commotion arose, over a Connecticut teacher's plan to conduct a school for blacks, that gave Garrison an opportunity to dramatize the themes of his forthcoming mission: the infamous connection between colonization and racial prejudice and the necessity for black education and equal treatment. The schoolteacher, a determined woman named Prudence Crandall, had grown up in a Quaker farming family and received her education at the Friends' much-admired Brown Seminary in nearby Providence, Rhode Island. She had taught at several academies in eastern Connecticut before being appointed by the prominent citizens of Canterbury—a Windham County village six miles south of Samuel J. May's town of Brooklyn—as the headmistress of their new young ladies' seminary in 1831. The trustees helped her finance the purchase of a spacious and handsome house on the village green, and the school flourished until the autumn of 1832, when Crandall incurred displeasure by allowing Sarah Harris, the younger sister of the teacher's black household helper, to attend classes as a day student.

Sarah Harris wanted to become a schoolteacher herself to aid the cause of racial uplift she had read about in *The Liberator*. Her father, one of a dozen black farmers in the neighborhood, had become the paper's agent, and through his daughters, the abolitionists' arguments had come to Crandall's attention. They reinforced the teacher's own principles, and she became convinced by Garrison's argument that both men and women had underestimated the power of female activism. Crandall resisted her trustees' pressure to have Sarah Harris dismissed, but this firsthand acquaintance with oppression quickened her conscience and prompted her to contemplate a more dramatic witness on behalf of the people of color.

Crandall wrote a confidential letter to Garrison in January 1833, asking his advice "respecting changing white scholars for colored ones." Did he think such a step would benefit the cause? If so, would it be possible for her to attract two dozen students from Boston and the other seaboard cities? She cautioned Garrison to say nothing about the contemplated change, for any hint of her idea would ruin her present school. The journalist did not have to keep silent for long. Ten days later, before Garrison had replied to the letter, a note was handed into his office: "The lady that wrote you a short time since would inform you that she is now in town, and should be very thankful if you would call at Mr. Barker's Hotel and see her a few moments this evening at six o'clock."

William Lloyd Garrison had never kept a political tryst before, and Prudence Crandall had never made one, but the high cause quieted whatever misgivings they might have entertained, and the rendezvous at the perfectly respectable temperance hotel was accomplished. Garrison's moral intensity made his mild appearance all the more remarkable upon first acquaintance, and his courteous, even stiff demeanor reassured Crandall that she had not misplaced her confidence. Looking at the schoolteacher, dressed with becoming plainness, sitting with studied calm—her brown hair drawn tightly in a bun and her pale face bearing witness to the gravity of her mission— Garrison knew her at once as a worthy coadjutor. They put their heads together and talked seriously. Crandall had told people in Canterbury that she was going to Boston to appraise new teaching material, and in the broadest sense of the term, she was doing so. She asked Garrison for introductions to appropriate black families in the eastern cities, which he provided, along with the suggestion that she pursue two likely allies: Simeon Jocelyn in New Haven and Arthur Tappan in New York. He thought her school would complement the institution the NEAS planned, but cautioned her that hostility in New Haven had already scotched efforts to open the school there, and they had to be prepared for more trouble. Crandall declared that she would bear whatever injury duty required.

The teacher soon told her white students and trustees that she would terminate their arrangement at the end of February 1833. She had experienced a conversion and intended to devote her vocation to the betterment of the oppressed. Her *new* school would commence on April 1 with twenty black girls scheduled to enroll. A notice in *The Liberator* soon made her plan public, along with a paragraph from Garrison describing the "rush of pleasurable emotions" with which he endorsed the venture. The advertisement described a traditional course of studies at a cost of twenty-five dollars per quarter for tuition and board and gave as references not only Garrison,

Buffum, and Arthur Tappan, but the black leaders James Forten and Samuel Cornish.

It did not require much perspicacity for the burghers of Canterbury to conclude that their teacher had become an abolitionist, and the next week's *Liberator* carried an anguished report from the Providence leader George Benson about an outburst of "unholy prejudice" in the town. A delegation had warned Miss Crandall that her action would "bring disgrace and ruin" upon the village and give unseemly airs to the local black people. Her callers did profess concern for their education, however, "provided it could be effected *in some other place!*—a sentiment, you will say, worthy of a true colonizationist."

Colonization and "Negro-phobia" worked hand in glove, Garrison knew, and in Benson's account of the town's intention to call an emergency meeting and invoke obscure vagrancy statutes against visiting students, the editor saw the enemy's face revealed in all its ugliness. He insisted that the proscriptive spirit had to be resisted. Miss Crandall "must be sustained at all hazards," he told Benson, for "if we suffer the school to be put down in Canterbury, other places will partake of the panic. . . ." The cause could not afford another New Haven–style setback, Garrison warned, and he vowed that if "self-respect" and the patient counsel of Samuel J. May, who had agreed to represent Miss Crandall at the town meeting since its rules forbade the floor to women, could not "make the town ashamed of its conduct," he would use his press "to bring them to their senses."

The editor had an opportunity the very next week to wield his typestick against Crandall's opponents when he learned that the Canterbury town meeting had gone very badly for the schoolteacher. The town voted an official warning that ancient vagrancy laws prohibiting "the introduction of *foreigners*" would be invoked against her. The one brave soul who rose to defend Crandall was shouted down, and May and Arnold Buffum were first denied the floor and then ordered out of the building by the town clerk, Andrew T. Judson. An attorney with aspirations for higher office, Judson turned the event into a demagogic triumph in which he raised the specter of miscegenation, predicted that if the school went into operation Connecticut would become "the Liberia of America," and accused Miss Crandall of being the tool of outside agitators bent on jeopardizing the town's property and purity in the name of immediate abolition and benevolence toward "nigger girls." "He twanged every chord that could stir the coarser passions of the human heart," Samuel J. May recalled with a shudder of distaste.

In printing Benson's report under the headline "Heathenism Outdone," Garrison termed the "scandalous affair" a "genuine flower from the colonization garden" and endeavored to heap "infamy" upon the prominent persecutors by setting their names—especially Judson's, which appeared several times—in huge block characters that jumped from the page. "To colonize these shameless enemies of their species in some desert country would be a relief and blessing to society," Garrison wrote. His typesetting and sarcasm, however, alarmed Crandall, who implored him "to handle the prejudices of the people of Canterbury with all the *mildness* possible, as everything severe tends merely to heighten the flame of malignity amongst them."

Garrison could write no more about the affair because he had become enmeshed in the preparations for his trip abroad, but he decided to add a visit to the embattled schoolteacher prior to the series of farewell ceremonies he had planned to exhort the faithful and raise money for the journey. The obsequies began at an NEAS quarterly meeting in the State House and continued with a service in the plainer habitation of the African Meeting House, where a group of black youth, who had organized themselves into the Juvenile Garrison Independent Society for self-improvement, presented their patron with a heart-shaped silver medal inscribed to "the fearless, faithful, and eloquent vindicator of the rights of the people of color." Their parents kissed and hugged the editor to wish him godspeed, and one tearful woman pressed a dollar into Garrison's hand along with a cake to eat upon his way.

Departing Boston on April 5, 1833, Garrison went only as far as Providence, where he spoke in a black church and told the assembly that *The Liberator* would help them bring down the great "Bastille" of slavery and build "the beautiful temple of freedom upon its ruins." Sobbing black people crowded around him afterward, as eager to shake his hand as Garrison had once been to touch Lafayette's. Henry Benson thought it an "affecting" tribute, and his younger sister Helen, who was hearing Garrison for the first time, thought the editor had "the soul of poetry" about him.

The next morning, after some pleasant conversation with Miss Benson, an amiable and hearty person whose name he misheard as "Ellen," Garrison went off in a chaise with her brother George to the family homestead at Brooklyn, Connecticut, twenty-eight miles away. The senior George Benson, a retired merchant who headed the local peace society and had befriended Benjamin Lundy, apologized for the "Egyptian darkness" that presently clouded his community, and the family eagerly told Garrison that Miss Crandall had defied the town of Canterbury by opening her school. Her friends anticipated more harassment, however, for the townspeople had resolved to close their shops to the teacher and her allies, and the grim threat of vagrancy proceedings—which could be punished by a public flogging—hung over the students. Crandall's supporters, however, thought that "a bold front" would enable them to prevail; if necessary, they had money to mount a court case if Judson obtained new repressive state laws against the school. But Almira Crandall, the teacher's sister, gloomily remarked that "it is the age of Goths and Vandals here."

The Rev. Samuel J. May, happily reunited with his friend, prevailed upon Garrison to speak in his meetinghouse on Sunday evening, which the editor willingly did, and he "removed a mountain of prejudice," people said. Prudence Crandall herself came up from Canterbury for the service and stayed on at the Bensons to talk with Garrison. "It was a source of great joy," she said, and he praised her as "a wonderful woman . . . as undaunted as if she had the whole world on her side." Everyone agreed that the opposition had made "a woeful mistake" in appealing to colonization principles as the basis of opposition, and May acknowledged, at last, the force of Garrison's objections to the ACS. (A private conversation with Judson, May said, had revealed depths of prejudice that left the minister deeply offended. When the minister promised to challenge discriminatory laws all the way up to the U.S. Supreme Court, Judson snorted that the Constitution had already settled the status of the blacks: they belonged to Africa and could either "be sent there or kept as they are here.")

The Hartford stage driver mysteriously failed to call for Garrison as promised early the next morning, and the editor had to jump into "a common wagon" and chase the coach for seven miles before climbing aboard soaked to the skin and bespattered with mud. Thirty minutes after Garrison's hasty departure, the Bensons discovered the sinister reason for the driver's default. The sheriff arrived at full speed, bearing writs sworn out by Andrew T. Judson and his cohorts that sought to detain Garrison on charges of libel. While the lawman fruitlessly chased after the editor, the Bensons successfully dispatched warnings to Hartford and New York that the writs were a trick to capture Garrison and ship him off to Georgia.

Alerted to the danger, Garrison hid out with friends in Philadelphia and New York until Tappan and Buffum managed to get him safely aboard a Liverpool-bound vessel on May 1, 1833. No sooner had they returned to Tappan's warehouse than an attorney's clerk turned up to inquire of the editor's whereabouts. "You're a little too late," Buffum laughed, but the tension in Canterbury was no joking matter. It epitomized the conflict Garrison had forced into the open, and it demonstrated that, however mighty in spirit, the abolitionists lacked the political power to protect themselves from determined opponents. The struggle might be far uglier—and exact a higher personal cost—than the editor had first imagined.

Though Garrison would, as he advised others to do, "speak always confidently of success and glory in the name of abolitionist," he had inwardly grown anxious at the magnitude of the task and the extent of his responsibility. Shortly before his departure he had experienced a dreamlike vision of himself upon an eminence that afforded him a panorama of worldwide suffering. He saw the ravaged villages of weeping Africa and heard "a voice from Heaven" crying, *"Plead for the oppressed!"* He tracked "the paths of the slave ships" across the ocean, wincing at the cries of the "suffocating victims" in "an African golgotha" as the heavenly voice again commanded, *"Plead for the oppressed!"* A "sickly sensation" passing over his frame, Garrison felt himself surrounded by the two million slaves in the United States— "debased, weary, famishing, bleeding, and bound"—whose cries wounded his ears and melted his heart. Behind them "unborn generations of victims stalked like apparitions," and once more Garrison heard the voice of Heaven, "in a tone awful and loud, with increasing earnestness," commanding, *"Plead for the oppressed!"*

Few men in the United States had ever taken so comprehensive a view of slavery's horrors, much less seen its victims in such an imploring light or felt the spiritual call to abolition with such physical power. He had a historic mission to perform and would judge himself harshly if he averted his eyes from the landscape of misery and did not advance the work of redemption. Garrison never recounted a religious conversion, but this melodramatic vision of himself as a prophet of liberation comes as close as he ever did to revealing the charismatic, spiritual gifts that impelled him. He had warned John Neal years earlier that his would be a biography worth writing, but what had seemed thwarted personal ambition in the neophyte of 1828 had deepened into a powerful sense of religious, even apocalyptic destiny. No longer a provincial, he was hardly of this world at all, but rather a prophet of the millennium to come. His newspaper, his book, his voyage to England were the measures of the moment; he believed his soul to be the true and everlasting instrument of the Lord's great cause.

CHAPTER EIGHT

AMBASSADOR OF ABOLITION

——•◆•——

GARRISON, LIKE SIMÓN BOLÍVAR OR THOMAS PAINE, WAS A PATRIOT WITH COSMOPOLITAN ASPIRATIONS. "OUR COUNTRY IS THE WORLD—OUR COUNTRYMEN ARE MANKIND" WAS THE MOTTO HE AFFIXED TO THE MASTHEAD of *The Liberator* from its first issue to its last, and he always understood emancipation as a "universal" ideal. That he happened to work in the most obdurate slaveholding country in the Americas did not blind him to the progress of abolition elsewhere. Racial slavery had been a fundamental element in the European exploitation of the New World, but by 1833, more than one-third of its slaves had gained freedom. The revolution in Haiti had liberated eighty percent of French colonial slaves—the only instance in which a violent military uprising by the slaves themselves accomplished the work of abolition—and slavery would be abolished in the remaining French possessions by 1848. Three-quarters of the slaves in the orbit of Hispanic colonialism had been freed by 1830, primarily as by-products of the two decades' worth of national revolutions that had liberated Argentina, Colombia, Chile, Central America, Mexico, and Bolivia from Spanish rule. Abolition would occur in Spain's largest remaining colony, Cuba, during its long-delayed independence movement of the 1870s, as it would come to Brazil, the former Portuguese colony, during its own internal upheaval of the 1880s. Only in the United States had former colonies mounted an incomplete revolution that gained independence from their European metropolitan power without relinquishing the labor system that had generated a large portion of their imperial value, and only in the United States would the masters resort to warfare rather than negotiate some form of emancipation. Although Americans seemed disinclined to model themselves after the Catholic countries and concentrated solely upon the dread example of the Haitian uprising, Garrison hoped that the long history of British antislavery efforts, which would shortly culminate in the abolition of West Indian slavery, might be more influential with his countrymen.

It was a celebrated story, extending back nearly a half century to the test cases Granville Sharpe argued in court and the public campaign against the slave trade initiated by Quakers and led by Thomas Clarkson and William Wilberforce, and Garrison told it often in his lectures. He hailed the British abolition of the slave trade in 1807 as an epochal victory of "right over wrong, of liberty over oppression" and marveled at the prodigies of organizational effort that, after the interval of the Napoleonic Wars, marked a resurgent effort against slavery itself. Interestingly, Garrison and his colleagues never extended more than a passing nod to the simultaneous 1807 prohibition by Congress of the U.S. overseas slave trade, a "silent abolition" that took place as a grudging fulfillment of the bargain struck at Philadelphia in 1787 and, in the ugly shadow of the domestic slave trade Garrison had protested in the *Genius,* glowed but dimly as a moral beacon. No heroes emerged from the U.S. action, and no movement took wing from it. When Garrison wanted to identify himself with the tradition of humanitarian success, he hailed Wilberforce and Clarkson and declared, as he did before a black society in Boston, that he had dedicated himself to a lifelong effort in their spirit.

When cutting off the trade did not improve the prospects for emancipation in the British West Indies, since even the higher price of slaves did not disturb the sugar planters' judgment that it was "cheaper to buy than breed," the reformers began a fresh campaign for legislation that would ameliorate the slaves' condition—and prepare for a gradual transition to a free labor system—through establishment of nutritional standards, limitations on permissible punishment, and careful regulation of work hours. Such proposals rested upon field studies conducted by religious missionaries and government inspectors and blended empirical social science and evangelical sentiment with the long-standing English approach of centralized administrative relief. Over the course of the 1820s the inadequacies of these measures became more and more obvious, especially after an uprising of Jamaica's slaves in 1831 and reprisals by the planters that included attacks upon Methodist and Baptist missionaries revealed the stark polarities of a slave society and the planters' obdurate opposition even to gradual change.

The worsening situation in the Caribbean fatefully intersected with a growing insurgency in British politics. To stave off the menace of revolutionary action by discontented industrial laborers at home and the disaffected Catholic majority of colonial Ireland, the British political establishment felt obliged to repeal the discriminatory legislation against evangelical dissenters (1828) and Irish Catholics (1829) and to enlarge and reform the electorate (1832) by admitting urban and entrepreneurial influences to a political system traditionally dominated by the landed gentry. In the new calculus of British politics the special interests of the West Indian planters (who represented a declining sector of the national economy) had become secondary to the fate of the system itself. Even a distant observer like Garrison recognized the momentous 1832 Reform Bill as "the certain forerunner" of an abolitionist victory.

When Garrison landed in Liverpool—the port from which his grandparents had set out for Nova Scotia sixty years before—on May 23, 1834, he made the journalist's natural move: he rushed immediately across the quay to obtain an armful of newspapers. Just ten days earlier, the Whig government led by Earl Grey had finally brought into Parliament a bill for the gradual abolition of slavery in the nation's colonies. The proposal Garrison reported at once to *The Liberator*, was "a kind of *go-between* the planters and the abolition party, and of course, gives satisfaction to neither." It would require the freed slaves to work as their masters' "apprentices" for a large portion of their day while extending a "loan" of £15 million to cushion the West Indian proprietors' eventual loss of property. Whatever the shortcomings of the bill, and the immediatist Garrison thought them considerable, he nonetheless preserved for *The Liberator* his first excited impression of a people who had arrived at the "universal feeling" that slavery must end. Parliament was overwhelmed by petitions, the editor reported; four members had to carry in one mammoth roll, while the House of Lords received an even larger document—"signed by EIGHT HUNDRED THOUSAND ladies!!!"—that was said to be larger than the lord chancellor's ceremonial woolsack.

Garrison found Liverpool to be like New York—too large, too busy, too absorbed in commerce, and hence too disagreeable to warrant close inspection. Feeling the solemnity of his mission, moreover, Garrison resolved not "to act the mere tourist," and he forswore writing the customary traveler's reports unless the scenes bore upon the subject of emancipation. Thus, when after four days of meetings with prominent Quaker abolitionists in Liverpool he left the city by the novel means of its railroad, Garrison noted only that he "was almost *too* impetuously conveyed to Manchester." That "dense and bustling" city detained him only long enough for a transfer to the more conventional stagecoach and the thirty-hour ride to "the capital city of mankind."

Though the editor chose not to report his observations, Garrison could see in the coal-blackened valleys of Lancashire, the dark ironworks of the upland towns, the vast cotton mills of Manchester, and the whizzing railroad itself the underpinnings of the industrial transformation that had diminished the significance of the West Indies and turned the eighteenth century's age of trade into the nineteenth century's age of production. Ironically, while the rise of industrialism had made the West Indies less important as both producers and consumers in the overall economy of Great Britain, it had enhanced the role of the United States. Slave-grown U.S. cotton accounted for seventy-five percent of Britain's imported supply of 248 million pounds in 1830, and this total would swell to more than ninety percent of the one billion pounds imported in 1860. Moreover, the United States had become Great Britain's largest single customer of manufactured goods, accounting for an annual trade of £6 million in the late 1820s and growing steadily larger. If West Indian planters had lost their political and economic clout, it was in part because the masters of the American South had taken their place; in seeking an international antislavery alliance Garrison would be mobilizing against an international economic partnership knit in cotton thread.

Garrison made his way to Finsbury Square, an elegant gaslight enclave off the Moorgate Road just north of the London Wall, not far from the Bunhill Row neighborhood where Milton and Bunyan had written their great Protestant epics and Wesley had preached his evangelical Methodism. Garrison would be the guest of James Cropper, a Quaker merchant whose studies and pamphlets of the 1820s added an economic dimension to the moralists' antislavery argument and who served as *The Liberator*'s London agent. The next morning Cropper escorted the editor into the City. Their destination was a coffeehouse in the shadow of the vast medieval Guildhall, which along with the neighboring Bank of England and St. Paul's Cathedral formed a trio of monuments to London's history and influence. About sixty delegates, representing many of the antislavery societies in the kingdom, took breakfast together every morning, Cropper explained, to monitor the progress of the abolition bill, whose controversial details were still being furiously negotiated in Parliamentary committee and the cabinet; later the abolitionists would adjourn to work in the antislavery offices around the corner or engage in lobbying efforts of their own.

Garrison walked into a roomful of the British equivalents of Arthur Tappan —wealthy bankers, shippers, and manufacturers of evangelical or Quaker bent who had labored for a decade or more in the cause of abolition and now had victory in their grasp. Unlike Garrison's American patrons, who had only moral influence to wield, these men had acquired political power. The Reform Bill of 1832 had broadened the franchise and reapportioned the House of Commons to reflect the growing strength of commercial Liverpool and industrial Manchester and Birmingham, where dissenting religion ran deep and moral reformers held sway. At least forty of the new constituencies grew from medium-sized and middle-class English and Welsh towns that supported abolitionist activities, while a dozen of the "rotten boroughs" wiped out by reform had previously returned members with a West Indian interest. The abolition movement—the men and women who had petitioned and paraded and turned out by the thousands for the Anti-Slavery Society's traveling lecturers—had demanded emancipation pledges from candidates standing for the reformed Parliament and had elected more than one hundred of their number to office, thus paving the way for action. Even so, the government had so long postponed its promised introduction of an emancipation bill that the abolitionists had undertaken a whirlwind petition campaign that culminated shortly before Garrison's arrival with five hundred petitions delivered to the Commons and six hundred to the Lords on the single day of May 14. The government submitted its draft bill that very evening, conceding at last that slavery had become politically untenable.

The coffeehouse caucus began its morning with prayer and Scriptures, followed by a convivial breakfast discussion and a generous welcome to Garrison as the ambassador of American abolition. He quickly learned, however, that the proposed manual training school "excited admiration," but raising money for it would be impossible while the public was preoccupied with the abolition bill. Garrison readily laid the project aside and turned with relief to the more dramatic and satisfying portions of his commission: counteracting the fraudulent representations of the ACS, studying the British abolitionists' methods, and laying the foundations for a transatlantic alliance.

On these points he found the British leaders remarkably open-handed. They welcomed him to join their private counsels, escorted him to the visitors' gallery of the House of Commons, and made sure that New England's plenipotentiary would be privately received by their political allies. Thomas Fowell Buxton, Wilberforce's successor as the antislavery political chieftain, invited Garrison to breakfast, but greeted him blankly, for Buxton had supposed the redoubtable advocate from Boston, in the United States, to be a black man. (It was the only compliment, said Garrison, that he ever cared to remember.) Daniel O'Connell, the "Liberator" who would repay the reformers' support of Catholic emancipation with Irish votes on the abolition bill, greeted the American exuberantly and promised to speak for him whenever necessary.

Garrison found his internationalist sentiments fully reciprocated. He heard many people echo the sentiments of the West Country minister who declared, "True charity begins at home, but it is a very false charity that stops there," and he happily reported to the NEAS that societies for worldwide abolition were in the offing. The British felt accountable for the origins, if not the continuance, of American slavery, the abolitionist Charles Stuart told Garrison, and owed their cousins "all the amends which holy love can make." Stuart, a flamboyant former army officer who always dressed in kilt and cape, seemed an improbable companion for the self-conscious Garrison, whose concern for propriety was heightened by the gravity of his mission and the social standing of his new acquaintances, but the old soldier with a newfound evangelical streak took the editor in hand and brought him into the swirl of abolitionist politics.

To beard the ACS agent, Elliott Cresson, Garrison and Stuart developed a two-pronged strategy. First, they would discredit Cresson either in public debate or for his refusal to engage in one. Second, they would demonstrate through the newspapers and a vast array of speakers at London's palladium of reform, Exeter Hall, that the giants of the ascendant Whig Party and the bulwarks of the benevolence movement endorsed American immediatism and believed that the ACS had abused their confidence. This approach combined the tactics the NEAS had employed to smoke out Danforth with a matchless British resource—readily mobilized public opinion—that the editor could only dream about creating in the United States.

Garrison invited Cresson to debate seven propositions that arraigned the ACS as a tool of slaveholders and the enemy of immediate abolition. Cresson dodged the offer—preferring, he said, a private meeting to clear up misconceptions without imposing upon the public—but Garrison rejected the "ruse." His business was "exclusively with the British people" and with Cresson as an official agent who had "dealt falsely" with that public, Garrison replied, and he renewed his challenge as a paid notice in the *Times*. The frugal editor found himself aghast at the cost of the maneuver; he paid out the equivalent of thirty dollars for an advertisement that would have cost no more than two in Boston. When the ACS spokesman did not reply ("too pusillanimous, or too wary," Garrison judged), Stuart gloated that they had Cresson on the run.

Cresson was following in Great Britain the same strategy the ACS had employed in the United States, endeavoring to isolate and smear Garrison while attracting endorsements from the elite that he assumed would be weighty enough to impress the public and obviate the need to debate. The ACS agent had told British leaders flatly that no one in America endorsed immediatism. When pressed by someone who had plainly heard of Garrison, Cresson conceded that there was an incendiary paper "printed by a madman in league with a man named Walker," but emphasized that Southern legislators had denounced it and posted a reward for its editor, who was himself a convicted felon. Yet, just as Danforth had underestimated the force of popular opinion in New England, so did Cresson fail to appreciate how fully a decade's worth of antislavery agitation had taken the British public beyond the pious gradualism the ACS professed. Neither did Cresson realize that the racism the ACS manifested had little resonance for a public eager to purge itself of sin by emancipating slaves who lived quite far away. In tactical terms, moreover, Cresson did not realize how skillfully the British abolitionists could manage a public meeting to create an impression that would then be transmitted—by published minutes, pamphlets, and visiting speakers— across the network of local and regional societies. He was, however, about to learn.

Garrison announced a public lecture of his own, scheduled for June 10, 1833, at which he would present his well-honed indictment of the colonization idea and distinguish the platform of the organization he represented—the NEAS—from the sham reformers of the ACS. The meeting took place in the largest Baptist chapel in London, situated in Devonshire Square, on the edge of Spitalfields, whose weavers and artisans had made the district a stronghold of religious nonconformity for more than a century. Warmed by an audience several thousand strong, Garrison spoke in blistering tones that mocked the affinities between slaveholders and colonizationists and castigated the ACS agent for misrepresenting the object of the society as the abolition of slavery. Cresson ought to be grateful, he said, that "you did not arrest him on the charge of collecting money upon fraudulent pretexts."

Aware that Cresson was in the audience, the chairman, James Cropper, sprang the abolitionists' trap. He solemnly declared that he felt obliged to allow the ACS representative an opportunity to refute so grave a charge, even though the meeting had not been organized for a debate.

Cries of "Hear! Hear!" rang through the hall as George Thompson, the most vigorous and celebrated of the lecturers dispatched throughout the kingdom by a committee of the Abolition Society, jumped up and declared that he had heard the ACS agent make such claims and wanted the chairman to see a pamphlet in which Cresson had put them in writing. When Cropper handed the text to Garrison to read aloud, Cresson's companion jumped up and objected, "I think this is calculated to cause a discussion."

"We want discussion," Cropper interjected. "When a charge is fairly brought against an individual, we want to give him an opportunity of denying it, if he can. . . ."

Cresson sneered that he would not demean himself by entering a discussion with "such a chairman, such a lecturer, and such a meeting."

"I'll give him two hours to my one," Thompson called. "That's all I require."

The congregation laughed and jeered while Cresson sat stony-faced and silent in its midst, and Garrison knew that he had accomplished his task in England. As the meeting turned into a jubilant abolitionist rally, which had to be continued over a second night to accommodate a surge of speakers, Thompson offered a resolution declaring that Garrison had proved his case against the ACS and entreating "all the friends of civil and religious liberty to withhold their sanction and assistance" from it. The meeting roared its approval and gave Garrison the ceremonial three cheers. The editor had heard strong amens in black churches and felt warm surges of sympathy from his lecture audiences, but never before had so many prosperous and influential white men given him a hero's accolade.

Garrison immediately followed up his London advantage by calling upon the personification of British abolition, William Wilberforce, to counter Cresson's misrepresentations and to secure the old hero's blessing for his own humanitarian program. Accompanied by the effervescent George Thompson, Garrison set out for Bath, where the aging Wilberforce hoped to find ease for his infirmities in the famous spa's salubrious waters. They had not helped much, and Garrison was amazed to discover that Wilberforce, the spiritual giant, had the body of an ancient pygmy. He was shorter even than Benjamin Lundy and frailer yet than Dr. Channing, and his back had become so crooked over the years that it took a great bodily effort to keep his head raised while speaking. His face, however, had a radiant smile, his voice a silvery cadence, and his bright eyes gave evidence, said Garrison, that his mind remained "a transparent firmament, studded with starry thoughts."

Born in 1759 to a Yorkshire family whose prosperity rested securely in the Baltic trade, Wilberforce had come under the evangelical influence of both Whitefield and Wesley, but did not undergo a spiritual rebirth of his own until after he had entered the cozy London social whirl and assumed a seat as one of Pitt's supporters in the House of Commons. Unlike Garrison, who built the nucleus of a movement in the cramped rooms of Collier's boardinghouse and the attic of Merchants' Hall, Wilberforce had a "chummery" at a mansion at Battersea Rise, just off Clapham Common, where his evangelical friends gathered to prepare their articles, plan their strategy, and make themselves into a community of Christian politicians. Wilberforce finally carried a successful bill against the slave trade through Parliament in 1807, but by then he had also encouraged "bettering societies" to attend to prison conditions and the suppression of drunkenness and vice.

"Factories did not spring up more readily in Leeds and Manchester than schemes of benevolence under his roof," James Stephen said of Wilberforce, and all England profited from his sunny disposition and incessant energy. This scurrying figure—dressed in a dingy black suit and wearing his hair powdered long after fashion had moved toward poetic, flowing locks—served as an officer on sixty-nine different committees for the public good and, even after his retirement in 1825, kept up a tireless correspondence, especially with respect to the renewed campaign for abolition. Although Wilberforce had a career in politics, his vocation was a spiritual one, and like Garrison, he saw the creation of a moral climate—"the kindling of the flame," he called it—as the vital basis for reform.

Wilberforce's eyes sparked as Garrison described the progress of his band of coadjutors in New England, and the venerable champion asked searching questions that delighted Garrison. They talked for hours, with Wilberforce recumbent upon the sofa but springing up with "youthful freshness" to emphasize a point or, sweet man, to retrieve a thimble his wife had dropped upon the carpet. When Garrison told him of the grief that American abolitionists, especially the free people of color, felt at seeing Wilberforce's name enrolled among the friends of the ACS, the old man grew very agitated. He had commended only the idea of a missionary enterprise in Liberia, insisted Wilberforce, who had once supported an evangelical venture in Sierra Leone. He never regarded colonization as remedy for slavery, and what's more, he had told Elliott Cresson that he abhorred the ACS insistence upon the immutability of racial inequality and regarded it as "false and UNCHRISTIAN" doctrine.

To combat Cresson's misrepresentations Wilberforce gave Garrison "three queries" that he might direct at the ACS agent or use elsewhere in debate. Dictating rapidly as he rallied to battle, Wilberforce concocted rhetorical questions that set forth his true position and projected his vision that blacks and whites "might and ought to live together as one mutually connected and happy society." This was a less direct method than the personal statement Garrison had sought, but the editor took the paper gratefully. With the old man's strength obviously failing, Garrison ventured to excuse himself, but Wilberforce insisted that they walk out upon the South Parade and enjoy the classic perfection of the townscape. "We begged him not to make the effort," Garrison said, and they compromised by standing at the front window while Wilberforce pointed out objects of interest. Then the hallowed figure gave Garrison his benediction, and the American—so much Wilberforce's heir in spirit, vision, and dedication—took his leave.

In addition to Wilberforce's paternal blessing Garrison came away from Bath with an equally valuable treasure, the enduring friendship of George Thompson. Only eighteen months older than Garrison, Thompson inspired the editor with a fraternal admiration that equaled his feelings for his first abolitionist brother, Samuel J. May. Like Garrison, Thompson had neither pedigree nor much formal education. The son of a Liverpool bank clerk, Thompson had come under the influence of Dr. Ralph Wardlaw, an important Scottish evangelical leader, and, again like Garrison, had taken up reform as his profession. A tall man with raffish good looks and a prizefighter's combativeness, Thompson seemed too much the adventurer for some of the aristocrats in the movement, who detected a vulgar tinge in the intense devotion Thompson inspired, especially among the ladies. Yet his honeyed voice—Garrison found it "irresistible"—and his daring, quick-witted platform manner made Thompson an invaluable asset.

Thompson had gravitated, naturally enough, to the young militants who had formed the "Agency Committee" in 1831 to make a more aggressive appeal to the public than the national society, preoccupied as it was with Parliamentary politics, thought advisable. "Sin will lie at our door if we do not agitate, agitate, agitate," they told each other. "The people must emancipate the slaves for the Government never will." Thompson covered thousands of miles in the cause, achieving special acclaim for the slashing series of debates he held with Peter Borthwick, an agent of the West Indian planters opposed to emancipation. In addition to escorting Garrison to Wilberforce, Thompson had come to Bath to beard Borthwick in his hometown, and Garrison could only marvel at "the masterly effort" with which Thompson, having passed a sleepless night in the stagecoach, completely won over "a severely critical and highly intellectual assembly in the Athens of England!" By the time Garrison and Thompson returned to London, the two men had become soul mates, two Christian rebels on a spree. They shared a dedication to reform, a strategy of belligerent popular agitation, and a refusal to be cowed by their social superiors. Oh, thought Garrison, if only I could bring *you* back with me to America.

With Cresson "skulking about London" in retreat after his meetings attracted scant support, the abolitionists went ahead with planning an "off-set" meeting of their own. When the idea had first come up, Garrison had wondered whether they could draw yet another crowd on the subject of colonization, but O'Connell blithely advised him not to worry: "I'll come and make a speech for you," he promised. George Thompson, too, would speak, but the morning would belong to Garrison, who had gained a large public in only a few weeks. "The people, as they become acquainted with him, love and admire him," Stuart reported to Arnold Buffum, for Garrison was "laboring like himself . . . zealous, uncompromising, untiring."

On Saturday morning, July 13, 1833, the customary crush of pedestrians in the Strand was increased by many hundreds of people converging on Exeter Hall, a bright new building with a classical facade squeezed into a narrow lot across the roadway from the Savoy. "What are you called for together today?" George Thompson asked the thousands who had crammed the hall to overflowing. "To countenance WILLIAM LLOYD GARRISON . . . the devoted friend of the free persons of color and of the slaves of the United States . . . be it yours to cheer his heart . . . be it yours to send him back fortified with your blessings and your prayers. . . ."

An ovation greeted Garrison. "I have crossed the Atlantic on an errand of mercy," he told the throng, as he proclaimed the end of "complexional prejudice" and "the narrow boundaries of a selfish patriotism." In an eloquent passage that drew both tears and applause, Garrison mingled his Byronic and Christian voices into a choral portrait of a loving world. Quoting the famous British abolitionist slogan "Am I not a man and a brother?" Garrison reminded his listeners that "whenever, in all time, a human being pines in personal thralldom, the tones of that talismanic appeal uttered by him shall be swiftly borne by the winds of heaven over the whole earth, and stir up the humane, the brave, the honorable, the good, for his rescue; for the strife of freedom is no longer local, but blows are struck for the redemption of the world."

From this powerful opening, which John G. Whittier would later term "a specimen of beautiful composition I have rarely seen excelled," Garrison moved into the more familiar vein of scathing attack upon Cresson's misrepresentations. He skillfully turned the queries he had obtained from Wilberforce into severe strokes against the agent who dared not show his face to the abolition public. He upbraided the American Colonization Society as "the Bastille of Oppression" and urged the British public "to assail it with the battle-axe of justice" and set free the captives within. Thousands of people in America had "caught a portion of your zeal," he said, and while the ACS was "falling like Lucifer, never to rise again," Britons would be cheered before year's end to learn that a national abolition society—modeled on their own—had come to life in the United States.

Borne along by the emotional tide of the meeting, however, Garrison launched into a denunciation of American slavery that inverted the high-minded internationalism with which he had begun. Professing admiration for his country, Garrison nonetheless tendered a long list of "accusations" against the United States, charging it with perverting its highest principles and insulting the majesty of Heaven by the crime of slavery and the pro-scription and banishment of the free people of color. America "falsifies every profession [of its creed] and shamelessly plays the tyrant," Garrison declared. He capped his own indictment by quoting O'Connell's stark injunction to Americans: "Dare not to stand up boasting of your liberties and your privi-leges, while you continue to treat men, redeemed by the same blood, as the mere creatures of your will."

Just as Garrison completed reading O'Connell's rebuke to a guilty nation, the man himself entered the hall to deafening shouts and applause. The spectacle of the two "Liberators" united in their denunciation of America as "the vilest of hypocrites—the greatest of liars" (in O'Connell's phrase) so scandalized the friends of colonization, including some visiting Virginians, that they immediately wrote letters to U.S. newspapers to broadcast their outrage at Garrison's having curried favor with foreigners by violating the taboo against speaking ill of one's country while abroad. Yet there was noth-ing in the speech that Garrison had not already said in *The Liberator;* and he had, at the outset, pledged in Park Street Church that he would not stand before kings without professing embarrassment at slavery's profanation of American values.

The Exeter Hall meeting confirmed Garrison's stature in British eyes as the most fearless and dedicated of the American abolitionists. The mass meeting, too, administered a death blow to the colonizationist attempt at transatlantic fundraising. "It is our duty," said George Thompson in closing, "to regard the ACS as the hateful bantling of a fiend-like prejudice, and to boldly tell brother Jonathan that if he thinks, *by means of an agent with a face of brass,* to dupe us out of any more of our money, he is mistaken; that we will speedily send his base metal away, and keep our own precious coin for worthier and nobler purposes."

Only one figure among the British luminaries, Thomas Clarkson, had kept silent during Garrison's tour, and the American finally decided to apply di-rectly to the great man, whom he considered the grander British equivalent of Benjamin Lundy. Clarkson had initiated the campaign against the slave trade, gathered the facts into tract after tract, fought mightily against a re-pressive government until the streams of benevolence and politics had con-verged in triumph, and then written an eloquent history of the movement that occupied an honored place in the hearts of abolitionists on both sides of the ocean. Now seventy-three and very infirm, Clarkson, like Wilberforce, nonetheless maintained an active correspondence, and his name remained one with which to conjure. Knowing that Cresson had gotten to Clarkson by exploiting his association with Philadelphia's most conservative Quakers, Gar-rison realized that his would be an uphill battle, but buoyed by the Exeter Hall reception, he decided to undertake it.

Garrison chose as his traveling companion to Clarkson's Ipswich estate the black American minister Nathaniel Paul, who had fortuitously come to England on a mission to raise funds for the Wilberforce settlement, a group of fugitive slaves making a fresh start for themselves in Canada. The British abolitionists had welcomed Paul and incorporated him into all of the anti-colonization meetings. Following the scheme of carefully planned oratory that the British societies had pioneered, Paul had received two assignments. He would tell meetings, including the huge Exeter Hall gathering, of the overwhelming opposition to colonization among American blacks, and he would defend his fellow citizen Garrison from Cresson's smears that he was a mere pamphleteer who lacked standing in the United States because he had served a jail term on a libel charge. Had Wilberforce or Clarkson arraigned the slave trade in Baltimore, Paul told his audiences, they, too, would have found themselves indicted, convicted, and jailed.

Garrison and Paul, who would shortly marry an Englishwoman, marveled at the lack of prejudice they had encountered in traveling about London: no arguments over seats in the coaches, no separate tables in restaurants, no indignities in church. He had known it would be thus, Garrison remarked, "but the novelty of the spectacle called up involuntary surprise, as well as pleasurable emotion." Both Garrison and Paul found it difficult to convince their British friends of the magnitude of discrimination in the United States, and Garrison tried to explain it as a matter of both racial and class prejudice. No one objected to a black servant accompanying his aristocratic master in a stagecoach; it was the independent black man who appeared clothed in the raiment of citizenship that evoked rudeness and hostility, he said.

When the two Americans arrived at Playford Hall, Ipswich, on July 14, 1833, they had to stroll about the grounds for half an hour while Clarkson's associate Richard Alexander, a wealthy Quaker with close ties to Cresson's colleagues in Philadelphia, prepared the great man to conduct a "strict examination" of Garrison. Finally, a servant called the visitors indoors, and Alexander led the blind and tottering Clarkson forward. The venerable reformer seemed in distress, but grasped Garrison's hand and said gravely, "I cannot see you—I have now wholly lost my sight, but . . . I believe I have lost it in a good cause." Garrison, who had prepared an effusive greeting, found himself "awed into silence."

Clarkson told himself that he remained "open to conviction" by the editor though so much American intelligence ran against him, but the patriarch hardly gave his guest an opening to speak. Vividly and minutely reciting the substance of his conversations with Cresson and explaining the nature of his endorsement of the American Colonization Society, Clarkson said that he approved of the scheme so far as it related to Liberia itself, but did not regard the society as being more than an "auxiliary" in the work of abolition. If he thought that compulsion were being employed, even indirectly, to effect the removal of the free people of color or such blacks as were manumitted, he would deprecate the measure as "unspeakably cruel and wicked." When Garrison interjected that compulsion and prejudice had marked the scheme from its inception, Clarkson would not credit the point. The editor presented only "vague report or hearsay," Clarkson retorted, and not even Paul's account of how black people felt injured by colonizationist prejudice could dissuade Clarkson from his belief in Cresson's more benign portrait of the ACS.

The men talked past each other. Clarkson said that by refusing either to accept Cresson's invitation to head a British colonization society or to endorse the immediatists' critique he would show his impartiality. Garrison, however, replied that since the United States regarded Clarkson as the "unfaltering friend" of the ACS, he could hardly be considered a neutral unless he formally repudiated his previous endorsement.

"Tell the people of the United States, Mr. Garrison, that Thomas Clarkson is now resolved not to give any countenance to the American Colonization Society," the old man said with great emphasis. "Tell them that *I occupy neutral ground*." He would put nothing on paper, however, and the Americans left in frustration. (Clarkson later told Cresson that Garrison had not "satisfied" him on many points and that he regretted the man's imprudence in raising black people to a plane of impossible expectation.)

William Wilberforce had come up to London in late July, suffering from pneumonia, but grateful to Providence for sustaining him until the Commons had given the emancipation bill its third and final reading. Though the House of Lords had yet to act formally, the venerable leader died on July 29, 1833, secure in the knowledge that his life's mission had been fulfilled and that three-quarters of a million blacks in the British West Indies would be freed from bondage. Though the long-dreamed-of action would not occur for another five years—August 1, 1838, was the date specified—the abolition bill was a landmark in social history, for the world's leading colonial and industrial nation did what would have been unthinkable fifty years earlier and repudiated the labor system that had laid the foundation of its wealth and power. As the radical leader John Bright had said of the 1832 Reform Bill itself, if it was not a good bill, it was most assuredly a great bill when passed.

When Britain paid its respects to Wilberforce on August 5, 1833, Garrison walked with George Thompson in the funeral procession that accompanied the leader's body—borne on a black-plumed hearse with horses caparisoned in black velvet—to Westminster Abbey. Immense but silent crowds lined the streets, as the hearse, the chief mourners, the members of Parliament in deep mourning dress, and the nation's preeminent abolitionists—and their American friend Garrison, the grandson of British indentured servants—joined the Duke of Wellington and the Archbishop of Canterbury in the final tribute.

Garrison finished off his trip by gaining reinforcements for the movement at home. When asked by Buxton how best the British could help the American cause now that theirs had triumphed, Garrison jauntily replied, "By giving us George Thompson!" When the laughter had subsided, the abolitionists looked at each other and mulled the prospect seriously. Although some wondered whether an English lecturer would not excite more prejudice than the trip would be worth, Garrison replied that New England would take Thompson to its bosom. He could teach the Americans much about the latest organizational techniques, and his visit would symbolize the international alliance as nothing else would.

"Then, you may have Thompson, and all our other lecturers, too," Buxton said.

There remained the delicate question of money. The NEAS could probably board the visitor and cover his local travel expenses, though Garrison had no authority to make a commitment, but passage money would have to be found elsewhere. Thompson, who was eager to make the trip, promised to raise a subsidy through a local society. The two friends embraced and looked forward to a reunion in Boston in a year's time.

There would be one more gift. James Cropper and Zachary Macauley surprised Garrison with a farewell present: a letter to take back to the United States that protested the "delusive claims" of the American Colonization Society to antislavery principles and denounced both its roots in prejudice and its unchristian widening of the breach between the races. This would be "a millstone" that would drown the society "in an ocean of public indignation," the American said. With the exception of Clarkson, the most influential British abolitionists had signed it, and most precious of all, Wilberforce's signature—in a firm and plain hand—crowned the list. "His testimony is almost like a voice from the grave," Garrison whispered.

The editor could count his work in England a great success. He had awakened a general interest in the American question, "dispelled the mists" with which Cresson had "blinded the eyes of benevolent men" with respect to colonization, and laid down the ground of "efficient cooperation" with British abolitionists. He had attracted the support of able writers and editors, as well as the female antislavery societies, and he had procured a large collection of abolitionist tracts, pamphlets, and documents that would provide "an inexhaustible supply of ammunition." He had seen firsthand how the careful planning of a central committee combined with extensive canvassing by paid lecturers and voluntary work by local legions of women had brought public opinion to bear upon Parliament. Yet he had seen, too, how countervailing political pressure could severely compromise the result. For all its inadequacies, however, an abolition bill had passed, the nation cheered, and the world took heart. Garrison would bring the encouraging message of perseverance and success to his American colleagues, and having shared the historic moment at the highest echelons of the British movement, he would speak with the enhanced authority of firsthand knowledge. He had come to London as a New England editor of some notoriety, but through his own talents and the subtle process of historical alchemy he would return as Wilberforce's heir.

CHAPTER NINE

THE MOST EVENTFUL YEAR IN MY HISTORY

THE HERO RETURNED HOME TO A NIGHTMARE. WHEN GARRISON PICKED UP THE NEW YORK NEWSPAPERS AT QUAYSIDE ON OCTOBER 2, 1833, HE READ WITH AMAZEMENT THAT "THE NOTORIOUS GARRISON"—JUST RE-turned from London—had organized a meeting in Clinton Hall that very evening to form a citywide antislavery society. As he made his way from the docks up toward Printing House Square and the political heart of the city at Park Row, it became clear to Garrison that hundreds had taken the news-papers' broad hints to subdue abolition fanaticism and were bent on mobbing the meeting. New York's streets, always crowded with draymen and vendors and commercial men walking in the tense and hurried manner travelers had learned to recognize as peculiar to the city, seemed edgier and more ma-levolent than usual, filled as they were with swaggering drunkards and gangs of Bowery "b'hoys" out for mischief. The current of traffic bore the editor to the columned arcade in front of the auditorium, where thousands milled noisily, demanding that Garrison be snatched out of the meeting and extra-dited to Georgia. It seemed as if Garrison had entered a madhouse, having left an England warmed by the glow of humanitarian success only to be standing unseen—like a spectral presence—in the midst of an American crowd bent on destroying him.

The crowd seemed composed both of men "in good clothes" and "the very sweepings of the city," and it verged on becoming a drunken and in-furiated mob. Clinton Hall, men were saying, had closed its doors to the abolitionists, who had presumably gone home, but with the cry of "On to Tammany Hall," the crowd surged to the imposing town house two blocks away that served as the Democratic Party headquarters. Several thousand strong by now, they crammed into every seat in the place, filled the aisles and stairwells, and still left some of their number roaring and stamping in the street. After an hour's denunciation of Garrison and his ilk, the crowd roared approval of a resolution that condemned agitation of the slavery ques-tion as perilous to the Union and commercial prosperity.

An electric shock went through the crowd when scouts came bursting in with news that the abolitionists had begun their meeting in Chatham Street Chapel, an evangelical hall near the wharves. Garrison, who had gained similar intelligence and hurried toward the relocated meeting, found him-self overrun by his second mob of the evening, and he once again stood unrecognized on its edge, as the drunken crowd banged on the gates of the chapel, hooting angrily as they saw the lights being extinguished inside. Breaking in, but finding their quarry departed, the ruffians made sport of a sodden black man in their midst by placing him in the chair as a mock Arthur Tappan and running a burlesque antislavery meeting with many ribald speeches and racially abusive resolutions.

Garrison never caught up with the Tappans that night. He took shelter with friends and went directly to Boston, but it did not take long to ascertain what had happened. Elliott Cresson and his friends had filled the newspapers for several weeks before Garrison's return with spicy and malicious reports of the editor's Exeter Hall speech, branding him a demagogue and traitor who had pusillanimously gone to Great Britain to preach the overthrow of the American government. When the Tappans and their friends announced their meeting, five days before the editor's return, the newspapers leaped to stigmatize their effort as part of Garrison's fanatical design. The party press expected New York's Democratic regulars to protect their powerful alliance with Southern Jacksonians with a ferocious outpouring of disapproval.

The New York uproar was a counterattack intended to rob the editor of his newly acquired English prestige before he could capitalize upon it among American humanitarians. "This misguided young gentleman who has just returned from England, whither he has recently been for the sole purpose of traducing the people and institutions of his own country . . . will act wisely in never to attempt addressing a public meeting in *this* country again," crowed one New York editor after the Clinton Hall fracas, while Garrison countered that the mob scene "furnish[ed] the blackest page in the history of party fury in this country," save only the proceedings of "the barbarians in Canterbury." The only note of consolation proved to be editorials from two important newspapers—the *Journal of Commerce* and the *Workingman's Advocate*— that defended the abolitionists' rights of speech and assembly, though the businessmen considered their objectives "unconstitutional" and the labor journal deplored the prosperous evangelicals' lack of interest in the lot of free labor.

The uproar forcibly reminded the editor of the contrast between Great Britain, where public opinion had crowned abolition with legitimacy and success, and the United States, where the abolitionists still found themselves a tiny minority obliged to defend the very idea of discussing the issue. Yet even in Britain, where the parliamentary system made it easier to formulate a national plan, it had taken a movement of well-to-do outsiders at least a decade to persuade an aristocratic government to address the issue of emancipation and shunt aside—with the aid of a multimillion-pound grant—the interests of an important bloc of West Indian planters. These slaveholders, unlike their U.S. counterparts, were generally absentee owners who left their Caribbean plantations in the hands of overseers and passed their careers in society and politics at home. Equally pertinent, Parliament abolished slavery in distant overseas colonies, thousands of miles from London, where the threat of Haitian-style racial reprisals in the aftermath of abolition seemed both remote and fanciful.

How different was the situation faced by Garrison in the United States, where the national Capitol stood within sight of slave pens and auction blocks, where a federal system of divided sovereignty severely limited the national legislature's jurisdiction over the problem, where the abolitionist leaders were dissident printers and preachers instead of powerful aristocrats or urban capitalists, and where the slavemasters lived among their chattel laborers. "It is a totally different thing to be an abolitionist on a soil actually trodden by slaves," the English radical Harriet Martineau wrote after visiting the United States for nearly two years. Concluding that slavery dominated American society as thoroughly as "the aristocratic spirit" pervaded Britain, Martineau believed that one could not compare the two abolition movements directly, but rather had to understand that the Americans faced a task and an opposition equivalent to what would beset British reformers who at once attacked the monarchy and the poor laws.

In building a movement against a deeply rooted and rapidly growing slave system, Garrison faced a number of daunting obstacles. The first was the sheer size of the problem. Of the ten most populous states in the Union, which together accounted for three-quarters of the 1830 national population of twelve million, six were slave states. Within the South, thirty-six percent of the households owned one-third of the region's inhabitants, a total of 1.98 million people. In three Southern states—South Carolina, Mississippi, and Louisiana—a black majority was held in thrall to a minority of whites, while in four others—Alabama, Georgia, Virginia, and North Carolina—blacks averaged forty percent of the population. During the 1830s, moreover, the booming southwestern cotton states would double their populations; the cotton crop, which had accounted for only eleven percent of the slave labor force in 1800, would employ two-thirds of the South's slaves by 1850, when the enslaved population would exceed three million.

In emancipating 750,000 slaves in the West Indies, Great Britain approached the problem as an economic conversion to a free labor system, but from his study of the colonization movement Garrison knew that American slavery was a racial caste system as well as a means of production and profit. The racist ideology that made black people seem fit for enslavement in the South and a degraded and threatening element in the North loomed as a second, and truly formidable, obstacle for the nascent abolitionist movement. Mob hostility revealed the poison at its most virulent, but it is important to appreciate the extraordinary resistance in all sectors of society to abolitionists' summons to transform American society by transcending the prejudice of skin color.

If the sheer number of enslaved black people and the prevailing racist animosity were not obstacles enough, the abolitionists faced further barriers in the workings of the American political system. The Constitution itself—with its addition of slave property to the calculus of representation, its pledge to defend states against insurrection and assist in the recapture of runaways, and its guarantee that each state had control over its domestic concerns—produced a "federal consensus" that slavery had a protected status in American politics and could not be regulated or abolished in the states where it already existed. The most serious national crisis thus far over the problem, the Missouri statehood controversy of 1819–20, dealt not with abolition but with the territorial expansion of slavery, and it ended with a series of compromises that reinforced both the federal consensus and the belief that accommodating the slaveholding class was essential to the stability of the nation.

The political parties of the Jacksonian era, moreover, with their concern to build the intersectional coalitions necessary for winning the presidency, fastened onto this philosophical consensus a practical code of silence. Slavery became known as the "peculiar" institution, not because it offended morals or theology, but because it was held to be the local and particular concern of the masters, and Southerners conditioned their participation in national politics on the assumption that the slavery question would remain off limits. Jefferson had built a Democratic Party coalition on this premise, and in the aftermath of the Missouri Crisis, the Democrats rebuilt their coalition on the traditional Virginia–New York axis with the timely addition of a redoubtable southwestern candidate, Andrew Jackson, and a renewed understanding that the price of Southern support would be a protective silence on slavery. In the view of the brilliant New York strategist Martin Van Buren, the arrangement was an ongoing electoral bargain that ensured the fruits of victory for all its participants, but the most ideological Southerners, led by John C. Calhoun, would endlessly attempt to augment their practical veto power with the constitutional theories of nullification and secession. This would complicate the Democrats' internal politics and, ironically, enhance the slaveholding Jackson's credibility as a nationalist defender of the Union.

By 1833 the Jacksonians had consolidated their political dominance, and although a Whig opposition had emerged against the strong-willed president, the differences between the parties—the laissez-faire, egalitarian, states'-rights, strict-constructionist Democrats and the development-minded, elite-minded, subsidy-minded, nationalistic, and moralistic Whigs—were less significant to Garrison and the abolitionists than their common need to placate their Southern constituencies and allay sectional tensions in the interest of party harmony and national victory. Between the patronage and spoils system that greased the party machinery and the veto power exercised by slaveholders, the political system seemed a morass of corruption and compromises inimical to the claims of morality or religion. To break the federal constitutional consensus and the binding cords of party, the abolitionists would have to rebuild the climate of opinion and replace pragmatic tests with principled ones.

The height of the barriers only enhanced Garrison's zeal for assaulting them. Intrepid as ever, the returning editor took the outpouring of hostility as a sign of the movement's growing strength. The NEAS had three full-time agents in the field during the summer of 1833, and they had harvested several thousand new members and a dozen local affiliates. The NEAS model, in addition, had served as inspiration for nearly fifty local groups distributed over the northern tier of states from Bangor, Maine, to Paint Valley, Ohio. By contrast, the ACS collections had declined dramatically, rumor held that the organization was thousands of dollars in debt, and its New England agent, the Rev. Joshua Danforth, verged on resignation.

Two literary figures had given their pens to the cause. The poet John Greenleaf Whittier had turned away from party politics to write a stirring tract on immediatism, *Justice and Expediency,* and Arthur Tappan had subsidized a run of five thousand copies for national circulation. Lydia Maria Child—the best-selling author of domestic fiction and editor of a very popular juvenile magazine—declared herself an abolitionist in a two-hundred-page volume, *An Appeal in Favor of That Class of Americans Called Africans,* that addressed the evil effects of slavery and racial prejudice in the common-sense style that had already made her a household favorite. The *Appeal* provided readers with a terse review of slavery's history and its appalling physical and moral abuse, along with a cogent account of how the "undue advantages" of the three-fifths clause had given slaveholders the means of dominating American politics. Not only did all important questions have to be treated "in pairs . . . like Siamese twins," but by giving more votes in the national councils to the masters on the basis of the chattel they held, the slaves, figuratively speaking, "are made to vote for slavery." Child also condemned colonizationists for accepting racial prejudice as immutable when it so obviously stemmed from the degradation imposed by slavery. The colonizationists are "always reminding us that the *master* has rights as well as the slave," while the abolitionists "urge us to remember that the *slave* has rights as well as the master." With the tartness of a New England schoolmistress she added, "I leave it for sober sense to determine which of these claims is in the greatest danger of being forgotten."

On only one key measure—a national organization—had Garrison's coadjutors fallen short. In his absence the evangelicals in New York and the Friends in Philadelphia had warily jockeyed for preeminence all summer, though Arthur Tappan had hired the hard-driving Elizur Wright, a militant professor who had resigned from Western Reserve College rather than be silenced, as his personal antislavery secretary to build a network of likely participants. The Clinton Hall riot and an attendant wave of what Garrison called "Negro-phobia" in Philadelphia, however, caused more hesitation, and the Tappans favored a postponement until May 1834, when the major benevolent societies would hold their annual New York conventions.

Garrison, however, insisted that the movement could not bow to intimidation and had to attain "strength in union" while the example of British emancipation remained luminous and fresh. By early November 1833, Garrison had prevailed. A call went out—in the form of private letters signed by Arthur Tappan—for leading abolitionists to meet in Philadelphia on December 4 to "take counsel together and *go forward*" in a national organization. It would be a quiet occasion, lacking in any "show" that might cause "the physical interruption of the mobocracy," Elizur Wright explained, but influential nonetheless.

Garrison, meanwhile, had a good deal to do in recruiting a delegation from New England and getting his newspaper's affairs in order. Yet he had supervised only two issues before he rushed off to visit one of the movement's prime battlegrounds, Prudence Crandall's school in Canterbury. The schoolteacher had endured much since Garrison left Windham County with Andrew T. Judson's minions on his heels. In June 1833, Crandall, who had thirteen pupils, including several from New York and Rhode Island, was arrested for violating a repressive new statute that punished anyone who maintained, taught in, or boarded students at a school for the instruction of colored persons who were not inhabitants of Connecticut. Bound over to county court on $150 bail, the schoolteacher spent a night in jail, and *The Liberator* spread word of her martyrdom up and down the seaboard. Her attorneys regarded the law as an infringement upon Article IV, Section 2, of the Constitution, which guaranteed the citizens of one state "the privileges and immunities" of citizens in other states where they may temporarily reside, but the key question of whether black people were to be regarded as citizens was not reached, because the jury divided on the evidence and did not reach a verdict. The October 1833 retrial took place in the hate-filled atmosphere generated by the Clinton Hall riot, and Crandall was easily convicted. The judge had blunted the constitutional challenge by charging the jury that blacks should not be considered as citizens; even if they were, however, he ruled that the law was a legitimate exercise of the state's power to regulate education.

Although Crandall remained free, pending an appeal on technical grounds, the townspeople renewed their campaign of intimidation. Shopkeepers would not sell her supplies, the churches had closed their doors, the physician would not treat the boarders' ailments, and, at the end of a long hot summer in which water ran low, someone had fouled the school's well with a load of manure. One evening, during prayer service, a rock had come sailing through the small-paned window in the parlor. Undaunted, Crandall saved the missile as a mantelpiece curio, but she knew that her venture had come upon "the weary, weary days."

Garrison, it seemed, had come to cheer her up. They walked all about the handsome house, an eight-room dwelling as elegant as the Federal dwellings on Newburyport's High Street, with fanlights and pediments and Palladian windows. The place seemed a mansion both to editor and schoolmistress, who had grown up in humbler circumstances, and to the young pupils as well. A two-story ell attached to the kitchen served as their dormitory, along with a cozy attic. Afternoon sunlight streamed through the many-paned windows as Garrison looked at the textbooks, the telescopes, the chemical equipment, the maps and globes, and the portable writing desks in the classrooms, and he sat beaming with pleasure in the front parlor as the young ladies recited poetry, read their compositions, and sang their favorite hymns. The school was in "the full tide of successful experiment and worth a trip across the Atlantic to visit," Garrison assured his readers, with an eye out to the British women's groups which had taken a special interest in the venture.

Crandall had often said that while she had expected opposition, she had never thought Christians would behave as outrageously as her townspeople had done. She showed Garrison the infamous stone resting on the narrow mantel above her fireplace, the curtains stained with rotten eggs, and the cracked windowpane. Through the glass Garrison thought he had a glimpse of Andrew T. Judson, glowering and red-faced in his yard across the road, endeavoring to confirm the rumor that Garrison himself had come to inspect his abolition academy. Though her situation remained grim, Crandall vowed that she would "never *no never*" reverse her course.

Since it was out of the question for Garrison to spend the night at the school, he rode down the long hill to the valley of Blackwell's Brook and up the opposite ridge to Brooklyn. He passed a pleasant evening with the Benson family, only to have the household awakened at midnight by the deputy sheriff with freshly sworn indictments for Garrison's alleged libel of the Canterbury selectmen. Judson had nabbed his quarry, but the harassment had scant effect. The court date was put off several times, and, in fact, the case never came to trial.

The local newspaper, however, crowed that the editor and "the Canterbury heroine" might take "pleasure" in standing together before the bar of judgment in their holy cause. The jailbirds could well be lovebirds, village gossips cooed; that would explain a great deal of the trouble. Although Garrison and Crandall had met but three times, celebrity had linked their names and presumed an attraction that neither ever acknowledged. Crandall maintained a grave and circumspect attitude toward Garrison, and if the exuberant editor felt more than a spiritual respect for his colleague in reform at Canterbury, he remained far too shy to express it. His heart, moreover, seemed drawn to Brooklyn. To George Benson, Jr., he confided that among the "delightful attractions" of his father's household "the soft blue eyes and pleasant countenance of Miss Ellen are by no means impotent or unattractive." While he concentrated upon the movement's organization, gossips in Canterbury made Crandall out to be a slave of love, and Helen Benson quietly hoped that she would have an opportunity to set Mr. Garrison straight about her name.

Garrison had extravagant hopes for the Philadelphia meeting. The outspoken Joshua Coffin agreed to go, as did Garrison's chief black ally, James G. Barbadoes; Arnold Buffum would be there, as would Amos A. Phelps, a fresh voice among the Boston clergy, and a Presbyterian minister named Nathaniel Southard who had started another school for black youth in Boston. More gratifying still would be the presence of John G. Whittier, whose expenses would be underwritten by Samuel Sewall, who probably subsidized Garrison as well. The editor especially wanted Whittier along because he expected the poet to influence the cautious Friends in Philadelphia.

Traveling by stagecoach and packet boat, it took Garrison six days to get from Boston to Philadelphia, a pace closer to the one Sam and John Adams had kept on their trips to the Continental Congress sixty years earlier than to the speeds railroad builders anticipated reaching before the decade ended. Philadelphia, however, was no longer the gracious tree-lined seaport with its neat checkerboard of red-brick houses that the Revolutionary generation had known. Smokestacks vied with steeples on the skyline, coal barges from the Lehigh Valley crowded the west side docks, and iron works, textile mills, breweries, and locomotive foundries now outnumbered the craft shops, shipyards, and wholesale houses that had once dominated the town's economy. The city still retained a quieter flavor than rival New York, and the broad streets running straight as arrows across town made the place feel less crowded than Boston, though Philadelphia had twice as many people living in it.

Of the 163,694 people enumerated in the 1830 census, 14,554 were people of color, and among them resided a propertied class led by the sailmaker James Forten, the caterer Robert Bogle, the barber Robert Douglass, the grocers Joseph Cassey and James McCrummell, and the baker Cyrus Bustill. In visits with these families Garrison found in their company "a river of delight." Sitting at Forten's cultivated table, guests laughed uproariously when their host observed that after his family had lived four generations in Philadelphia the colonizationists could hardly expect to set him on the shores of Africa and watch him "run at once to the old hut."

Black Philadelphians, more fully than their counterparts in Boston, had claimed many craft jobs in shoemaking, carpentry, and cabinetry and had long dominated the food and service trades from bakeries and oyster shops to dressmaking and barbering. Steam-powered industry, however, had displaced many artisans, both black and white, just at a time when the tempo of European immigration, especially from Ireland, was quickening, and the size of the black community was swelling with refugees from Chesapeake slavery. Competition for jobs and partisan jockeying on sectional issues had inflamed racial tensions in the city. In cartoons lampooning the emerging black middle class the Jacksonian caricaturist Edward Clay had caught the popular mood. One widely reprinted sketch depicted a black dandy greeting a young woman in a gaudy dress and bonnet. "How you find yousef dis hot weader Miss Chloe?" he asks, and she replies, "Pretty well I tank you Mr. Cesar only I aspire too much!"

In such an atmosphere the abolitionists had no hope of popular success. The public halls and churches shut their doors when the police declared that feelings against "the amalgamationist conclave" ran so high that they could not be responsible for the safety of a meeting that ran past dark. The militants found support only in the black community. Most of the delegates, Garrison included, boarded with its families, and one of its societies—the Adelphi—lent the convention its meeting hall, a little building adjacent to the oldest black church in the city.

When the assembly convened on the morning of December 4, 1833, none of the timid Philadelphia elders would take the chair and the militant younger generation instead chose one of its own, Beriah Green, a theologian who had resigned in protest at Western Reserve and then become president of the biracial Oneida Institute. He followed Quaker precedent, however, with an interval of meditation and felt prompted himself to recite one of Garrison's favorite texts, Isaiah 58:1: "Cry aloud, spare not, lift up thy voice like a trumpet, and show my people their transgression, and the house of Jacob their sins."

Though a guard was posted at the door, the meeting was not a secret cabal, as the colonizationists later charged, but open to spectators, among whom were prominent ACS officers, Southern medical students, and a number of women, including the staunch Lucretia Mott, herself a Quaker lay minister, whose husband, James, was one of the convention's elder statesmen. From ten states, sixty-three delegates—all pledged to "immediate emancipation, without expatriation"—had braved the wintry roads to attend the convention, and several hours of the first morning were consumed by reading spirited letters from dozens more, including thirty students from Maine's Waterville College, who could not attend but endorsed the goal.

The delegates represented the grassroots militancy of Garrison's New England and Ohio's revival-dominated Western Reserve, along with the traditional Quaker reformers, the prosperous evangelical gentlemen led by the benevolent Tappan brothers, and the idealists of the manual labor movement, in which students at schools such as Oneida and Oberlin took on work projects that reduced their costs, elevated their respect for physical labor, and promoted a communal ethic that served as antidote to commercialism and a foundation for interracial education. (Oneida students had read aloud Garrison's *Thoughts on Colonization,* the story went, in between deliveries of gravel at a road-building site.) Despite their denominational and social differences, the delegates shared the fundamental conviction that slavery was a sin and that the nation had to be called to repentance. They understood, with Garrison, that their campaign would amount to nothing less than a revival of religion and would have to be done, in effect, outside the institutional church, for all the considerations that influenced the political parties also operated upon the national religious denominations and made them obliging partners in the company of silence. From the three big cities also came a handful of black leaders; though they were not destined to play a central role in the organization, they would influence the white abolitionists' understanding of the racism that underlay slavery and the necessity for maintaining an emphasis upon the realization of civil rights. Unrepresented at the meeting, though their influence had already made itself felt in the local societies, were abolitionist women, whose subsequent participation in the movement would both enlarge its radical vision and fracture its organization.

Assigned to a ten-member drafting committee, Garrison retired to his room in James McCrummell's attic to write the document that would provide the dramaturgical framework in which the fledgling organization linked itself to the American revolutionary tradition. May and Whittier remembered leaving him there at ten o'clock and returning early the next morning to find the shutters still drawn, the lamp still blazing, and Garrison applying some finishing touches to his declaration. "More than fifty-seven years have elapsed since a band of patriots convened in this place to devise measures for the deliverance of this country from a foreign yoke," Garrison began. "We have met together for the achievement of an enterprise, without which, that of our fathers is incomplete, and which for its magnitude, solemnity, and probable results upon the destiny of the world, as far transcends theirs, as moral truth does physical force." Contrasting the principles of a bloody war for territory and sovereignty with a spiritual war for universal freedom, Garrison maintained that the revolutionaries' grievances seemed trifling in comparison "with the wrongs and sufferings of those for whom we plead. . . . Our fathers were never slaves," he said pointedly.

Garrison's document conceded that Congress had no power *"under the present national compact"* to interfere with slavery in the sovereign states though it had adequate power over the territories, but his use of italics indicates a readiness to challenge the federal consensus and reconstruct the fundamental law. He pronounced the three-fifths clause, the Fugitive Slave Law, and other supports as a "criminal and dangerous relation to slavery that MUST BE BROKEN UP." To that end the American Anti-Slavery Society would pledge itself to organize abolition groups "in every city, town and village of our land" that would sponsor agents, circulate tracts, purify the churches, enlist the press, and act upon the Christian and constitutional duty to "remove slavery by moral and political action. . . ." "The guilt of [the nation's] oppression is unequaled," the text asserted; ". . . it is bound to repent instantly . . . to break every yoke, and let the oppressed go free." In a stirring conclusion, Garrison, following his model, submitted the declaration to the "candid examination" of both the American people and "the friends of liberty" throughout the world. "We plant ourselves upon the truths of Divine Revelation and the Declaration of our Independence as upon the EVERLASTING ROCK," he wrote, and pledged the signatories "to deliver our land from its deadliest curse . . . and to secure to the colored population of the United States all the rights and privileges which belong to them as men and as Americans, come what may to our persons, our interests, or our reputations—whether we live to witness the triumph of JUSTICE, LIBERTY and HUMANITY, or perish ultimately as martyrs in this great, benevolent and holy cause."

Garrison had sounded the call for a second American revolution. His colleagues on the drafting committee applauded it, but did not relinquish their obligation to discuss it at length. The process, Garrison well knew, would bind the group all the more tightly, and he balked only at the need to cut a page-long disquisition on the wickedness of colonization. May broke the impasse by suggesting that the lead sentence—which put the society on record against "schemes of expatriation" as a substitute for total abolition— be retained, along with a slam against the compensated emancipation for which the British had settled. The rest of the passage could be safely deleted, May soothed, because it was not worthwhile to perpetuate the memory of the dying American Colonization Society in this immortal document. "Brethren, it is your report, not mine," said Garrison, acceding.

At the plenary session Garrison received an artist's ultimate accolade: several minutes of profound, heart-stopping silence followed a reading of the draft. Then one of the Quaker brethren, citing the Friends' doctrine "First impressions are from heaven," proposed immediate adoption, but the body nonetheless weighed each sentence carefully. Lucretia Mott rose from her seat in the gallery to recommend that the pledge of faith would be stronger if they transposed phrases so that the delegates planted themselves *first* on the Declaration of Independence and *then* on Divine Truth as the Everlasting Rock. Garrison accepted the proposal, though thirty years later Mrs. Mott still remembered how one of the youthful members turned "to see what woman was there who knew what the word 'transpose' meant."

The balance of the proceedings took up measures that charted the American Anti-Slavery Society's course: the adoption of a formal constitution; addresses to the church denominations; formation of affiliate groups, including female societies; a new petition campaign against slavery in the District of Columbia; an attack upon discriminatory state laws, especially in education; the favoring of products made by free labor; the preservation of the alliance with friends of abolition in Great Britain. A formal signing of the declaration took place at the concluding session on December 6, 1833. One of the delegates had the text engrossed upon parchment, and Samuel May read it aloud once more, "his sweet, persuasive voice faltering with the intensity of his emotions" as he repeated the solemn pledges. Then, one by one, the delegates stepped up to the writing desk, a tilted wooden box resting on copper-ball legs, and solemnly affixed their signatures. There were a total of sixty-three, and Garrison was only half joking when he remarked that this was seven more than the Declaration of Independence had received. Four years after Garrison had sounded the alarm in Park Street Church, three years after he had vowed to make *The Liberator* heard, and less than two years since he had published his *Thoughts on African Colonization,* the abolition movement had organized itself for a national campaign that would confront the deepest contradictions in the American political tradition.

Garrison would continue to play the role of abolitionist agitator, but the organization would be managed by the Tappans and their friends. The editor was awarded a seat on the executive committee by being named to a minor post—secretary for foreign correspondence—that acknowledged his success in England, but most of the AAS offices (including the presidency for Arthur Tappan) went to New Yorkers anxious to restrain the Boston hotheads who had propelled them into organizing sooner than they had preferred. Garrison seemed not to mind playing second fiddle and accepted one friend's advice that it would be prudent to "give in to some of their *notions*" for a time. The executive committee did agree to buy up half the remaining stock of the pamphlets Garrison had printed (an infusion of cash that the editor later said "saved the life" of *The Liberator*), and Elizur Wright, the national executive secretary, offered him a position as a field agent for eight dollars a week and traveling expenses, the same rate of pay offered by the Bible societies. Garrison, who had seen the fruits of agency work in England, considered it the most crucial tool in the struggle, yet he declined the call. The editor did not want to jeopardize *The Liberator* for a temporary job. The newspaper had become an extension of himself, and he valued the autonomy and the prophetic voice it gave him. Rather than become an organization's emissary, he would remain the movement's symbol.

Garrison simultaneously launched a private campaign that would keep him close to home. On January 18, 1834, he sat down to write a letter to his friend's sister in Brooklyn, Connecticut. Having finally corrected his misimpression, he saluted her abruptly—"Miss Helen"—then stopped. What could he say next? He, who composed columns of editorials with lightning fingers at the case, scratched and bit his quill and took a whole hour to fill both sides of his sheet of writing paper. He began with a long rhapsody on the springlike weather ("Yesterday, my feelings were as rigid as the weather—today, they are gushing forth like an unsealed fountain") and portrayed himself as a bird who had taken wing, flying first to Brooklyn and

Providence, then to the friends of the slave in New York and Philadelphia and across the ocean, and finally soaring to "the heaven of heavens" where he had "communed with Him whose name is Love."

A letter, he explained to his recipient, was "a strong token" of his esteem, for he hated writing them, and would do so only from necessity or out of "very ardent" friendship. Was that too forward? Should he have asked her permission to correspond? Perhaps he ought to remain businesslike? Observing that seventy ladies in Amesbury had organized themselves into an antislavery society, Garrison told Miss Benson that he hoped she would stimulate such a venture in Brooklyn or Providence, where Helen frequently visited her brother George or her married sister Charlotte Anthony. He asked for the latest news from Canterbury, sent warm regards to her family, and carefully signed himself "your friend and well-wisher."

It took Garrison several weeks to work up nerve enough to mail his epistle, and after a suitable interval he received a courteous but cautious reply. "Mr. Garrison," Helen Benson began her letter on February 11, "Your very interesting letter was duly received and I should answer it with more alacrity than I can at present command, did I feel myself fully competent to sustain a correspondence with one whose talents and attainments are so superior to my own; but if you will allow friendship to supply the place of a gifted mind, perhaps my communication may not be wholly unacceptable."

On the verge of twenty-three, Helen Benson had been educated entirely at home under the watchful eyes of four older sisters. She felt inadequate in elevated company but she could write with becoming gravity. Her letter replied carefully, in turn, to each point of Garrison's letter. Yes, she agreed that life in the countryside (Garrison had moved into a boardinghouse in Roxbury, a village south of Boston) offered more opportunity for "serious reflection" than the distracting city. No, she couldn't possibly organize a society, for her influence was "extremely limited" and her efforts would be "inefficient." Since Garrison's remarks in a Providence lecture about masters taking sexual advantage of their slaves, she pointed out, women had shied away from talking about slavery; "whether the ladies are more fastidious here than elsewhere I know not," she added, in a tactful display of her own frankness. As for Canterbury, there had been a small fire at the Crandall house—arson, presumably—that did little physical damage but severely tried the poor teacher's soul. (In a postscript Helen added the fresh news that Miss Crandall had become engaged to a Baptist minister, Calvin Philleo, of Ithaca, New York!) As for Brooklyn, did he think that the Benson farm deserved the title "Friendship's Vale . . . the asylum of the oppressed," bestowed by the grateful teacher? Closing with her "warmest wishes" for his happiness and the success of "the noble cause," she signed herself, "Your friend, H. E. Benson."

Modest and self-effacing, yet not lacking in candor, Helen's letter perfectly fit the style of epistolary courtship. She professed herself unworthy,

then displayed the tenderness that made her desirable. She discussed matters they had in common, including friendship with a woman in the public
eye, and attended carefully to everything Garrison said. She made no reference to the act of correspondence itself, yet by coyly asking him a question,
she gave him implicit permission to write again.

Garrison did so. He loved the "frankness" and "contemplative spirit" of
her letter, he said, and dared to add that it felt "exactly in unison" with his
own. He thought the women of Providence would regret their "heartless
refinement," and he hoped the fire at the school would yet prove an accident.
His whole soul responded "YES!" to the dauntless teacher's designation of
the Benson home as a freedom-loving haven. Closing with affection for the
entire family, the writer bade her "take for yourself as much as you will
from, Your sincere friend, Wm. Lloyd Garrison."

Before Miss Benson could compose a reply, the writer was on her doorstep. He had to make a court appearance in Brooklyn, but that was the least
of his reasons. Although the abolition cause flourished, Garrison felt
"crowded and crushed" by his office duties and confided to friends that he
felt "dissatisfied with almost every thing" he did. Whittier would have di-
agnosed it as another bad case of "the hypos," and it seemed plain that the
editor had fallen into a lovelorn despair. He had to see if the emotions hinted
in his letters were anything more than a literary conceit.

Garrison had already fallen in love with the Benson family. He felt refreshed in their "quietude of spirit," their cheerful and generous philanthropy, and the security and repose of a family life he had never known. As
a surrogate family, moreover, they completely accepted—indeed, admired—
what he had made of himself. Father Benson (George Sr.), still vigorous at
eighty-two, had retired many years earlier from a successful mercantile career in Providence to devote himself to philanthropic causes and had just
been reelected to the presidency of the New England Anti-Slavery Society.
Mother Benson (née Sarah Thurber), a religious woman who shielded her
oval face with the traditional lace cap of her Puritan ancestors, leavened her
piety with a generous hospitality, remaining unfazed and serene amid the
comings and goings of a large household. They had lived for many years in
a handsome house on Providence's College Hill, where all seven children—
five girls and the two boys, George Jr. and Henry—were born and raised,
but moved to the farm at Brooklyn in 1824. The senior Bensons had been
Baptists, but after falling out with their minister, had gravitated toward the
Quakers, though in Brooklyn they comfortably worshiped with the Rev. Samuel J. May. Two of the older daughters, now in their thirties, had joined the
Society of Friends.

Helen—the youngest girl, born on February 23, 1811—had made no
profession of faith, but had absorbed the religiosity of the family and radiated
such a calm and good-hearted spirit that the family liked to call her "Peace
and Plenty." With her rich brown hair framing an oval face like her mother's,

Helen Benson had, without being coquettishly pretty, a fresh and pleasant air about her that Garrison found irresistibly comforting. He had fantasized about a woman more nurturing than the strident Sister Garrison, and in a curious transposition, sent Helen a poem which he claimed to be a description of his mother that he had actually published in 1831 as a portrait of Mary Cunningham.

The editor quickly obtained the court postponement he sought (in a strategy of delay until the Crandall furor eased) but lingered from Tuesday to Friday, March 3–7, 1834, at Friendship's Vale. The house was a big comfortable place, a larger but less ornamented "four [rooms] above four" than Prudence Crandall's house, with a kitchen ell—actually the oldest part of the house—and a huge attic and cellar with unmortised stone walls that testified well to Connecticut craftsmanship. Garrison paid what he hoped was unobtrusive court to Helen Benson as they walked up to visit the farm's "never-failing" springs and rambled in Kingsley Lane and on Gray Mare Hill, but then one morning he slept late, and rather than appear to be waiting for him (she said later), Helen took her walk alone. Garrison thought this a discouraging sign, and though he yearned to "disclose" his feelings (he said later) as they rode over to Canterbury in a carriage, he felt "tongue-tied and timorous" and so kept his peace. He didn't want to take her "by surprise," he told himself, and if he had misperceived her feelings, he would spare both of them embarrassment by writing her a letter instead.

He did so, the minute he returned to Boston, on March 8, 1834, admittedly "very tired" yet compelled by "gratitude, affection, and duty" to send "a hasty note" that embodied his "whole heart, that you may divide it among all the members of that most estimable family residing in 'Friendship's Vale.'" But how could he send what he had already left in Brooklyn? he asked, for "all of you have got possession of my heart." Referring to a medallion of liberty that the family had given him, Garrison said coyly that the "pretty little gift" was in "a *circular* shape." "Have you anything to give me *in the shape of a heart,* Helen?" he asked. "Just examine carefully, if agreeable, and let me know hereafter."

Ten days later he had an answer, the one he had feared. "Shall I say to you I feel highly complimented on possessing the esteem of one I so highly and justly value, and one every way my superior?" Helen Benson wrote. "I should be ungenerous to you did I not say I fear your short acquaintance has not made you a sufficient judge of my inferiority. *I must say you do not know me!* and I fear that you are too sanguine in your expectations and that disappointment would inevitably be your portion, were I to accept of as much friendship as you have . . . offered, and which my friend I scarcely dare trust my heart to cherish."

Did she, then, reciprocate his affections, but hesitate out of humility, or did she think them unsuited to each other? Garrison couldn't be sure, and the rest of the letter, which described in some detail an earnest—and con-

fidential—conversation Helen had had with Prudence Crandall only heightened the ambiguity. The teacher had heard many bad reports about the Rev.
Calvin Philleo's character, and she wanted to know if Helen had heard anything adverse. Feeling "absolutely obliged" to tell Prudence that the Bensons
(and Garrison) had indeed privately discussed rumors of Philleo's instability
and lack of probity, Helen now said that she felt "rather a weight off my
mind," though she doubted that "anything I said made the least difference
to her for love you know heightens every virtue." Prudence received the
message kindly and told Helen confidently that although she had pledged
herself to Philleo, "still she had so *perfect a control* of herself that she could
withdraw her affections at a moment. Wonderful woman! not one of a thousand could have said as much," Helen said, without remarking that she was
exerting a similar self-discipline.

Her rejection—if that was what it was—crushed Garrison. Yet he responded at once, on March 19, 1834, bravely declaring that her letter had
come like "a gleam of sunshine" into his clouded and melancholy life. He
chatted on, praising her candor with Crandall, and indicating that he did not
expect her to answer every one of his letters, since he had no claim upon
her attention. Then he launched into a paragraph about the friends he had
made in the abolition cause, both in America and England, that ended with
the self-pitying remark that amid his reflections "a tear would frequently
start unbidden to my eye, from a melancholy consciousness that, among
them all, there was not *one* who cherished toward me aught beyond 'friendship's affection.' " Quoting stanzas from Byron and Hemans, to improve the
theme of loveless solitude, he threw himself upon her mercy. "Alas! all may
be mated but me—I have no attractions to enkindle or secure love—there
is none in the wide world whose heart I am authorised to claim—none, into
whose bosom I can pour the wealth of my affections." This was not the
crusading editor talking, but the child abandoned at the poor woodcutter's
cottage. If Helen had thought Garrison had mistaken her for the public
stalwart she knew that she would never be, it was now plain to her that he
sought—and needed—a kind and nurturing soul mate. Though he could not
force the words out, he wanted Peace and Plenty.

"My Dear Friend," Helen rushed to reply on the afternoon (March 21,
1834) that she received his letter "frought with so many melancholy sentiments." "I am grieved, exceeding *grieved* to think my letter conveyed to
your mind such unpleasant reflections, for I surely did not intend it, and
thought I said sufficient to convince you that I felt *deeply interested* in your
welfare," she wrote. "Yes indeed I do! and *nothing* but the knowledge of
your superior attainments arose as an obstacle to preclude the gratification
of accepting your proposal." Helen took a deep breath and then wrote,
gravely and formally, "Sincerely do I reciprocate the affectional feelings of
your heart and am happy to know that I am the favored one whom you have
selected; and in whose heart, you may pour the wealth of your affection."

She had indeed said it for both of them, and now her tone melted. "Well my kind friend," Helen went on, "I do not mean there shall be anything in *this* letter if it is in my power to prevent it, that shall cast the least sadness over your wounded heart and I cannot bear to think that I so innocently inflicted pain on one, whom of *all* others, I should be the most unwilling to injure." "Oh! that touching sentence of yours—'I have no attractions to enkindle or secure love'—I *never saw one* that *possessed* more," Helen insisted, "for they have completely entwined themselves around my heart. . . ."

There was more—a lot more—chatter and poetry, and an anecdote about wishing for his company at a wedding she and sister Anna had attended that morning. She added one more apology for the sadness her previous letter had brought him and asked him to burn it. In that letter she had been too cautious; in this one she feared that she had erred on the other side. "I have opened my heart to you, perhaps have expressed too much. . . . But do accept the right, the *wrong forgive*," she asked, and closed, "Believe me ever yours with unceasing affection, Helen E. Benson."

Garrison received the letter ecstatically ("Oh! generous, confiding, excellent girl! do you then reciprocate my *love?* Yes, my fears are dispelled—my hopes are confirmed—and now I can shed delicious tears of joy!") Unfortunately, the vagaries of the postal service—it took a minimum of three days for letters to travel between Boston and Brooklyn, which meant that a full week passed between question and answer—put his beloved in a state of extreme agitation. Nine days after writing, time enough for a reply, Helen received a short note from Garrison which made no mention of her sentiments. (Written only hours before her key letter arrived, it was an addendum intended to lighten the mood of the previous melancholy epistle.) Helen was frantic with thoughts that either her letter had miscarried or, worse, that now *she* had misunderstood *him*. She wrote him an urgent note, intending to post it, but upon learning that Prudence Crandall was off on business to Boston, Helen disguised her letter as one from her brother Henry and asked Prudence to deliver it by hand.

Two very long days later she received the overdue reply expressing Garrison's joy, and the day after that she received a second letter, prompted by the message Prudence had carried, with further expressions of bliss and the news that he had formally written to her father. The Bensons, of course, had already guessed the secret and happily blessed the union. With "joyful anticipation," Helen told "Dear Lloyd" that she accepted the happiness awaiting her and would confide in his "kind and gentle love." What time did he leave Boston for Roxbury? she asked, for she liked to think of him at twilight, sitting in his little cottage, writing to her. And write he did, several times a week, long rhapsodic expressions filled with extracts of poetry and the exquisite nothings that lovers treasure. "You have made me fall in love, not only with you, but also with my pen," Garrison exclaimed, and he treasured her replies as a "mirror" in which he could see her face."

Two weeks later, on April 20, 1834, en route to New York for the first annual meeting of the fledgling AAS, Garrison returned to Friendship's Vale as its daughter's swain. For three days Helen and Lloyd walked and talked and sighed and looked, and they parted "sighing and kissing," he remembered, with a lock of her hair resting against his heart.

Garrison had told her during the visit that his financial prospects would never be great. He would reconsider taking up the AAS lectureship (at $1,000 a year) if that would enable him to support her more comfortably, but he hated to give up his newspaper, and she wouldn't hear of the idea. Helen urged him not to be anxious on her account, for she was not extravagant and would live "exactly as you see proper." Her worry was that he would be too distracted by domestic concerns to maintain the vigor of the crusade; she begged him to forget about her and Friendship's Vale while "fighting the abolition cause" in distant cities.

"Dear Helen," he answered on April 24, "am I not a strange compound? In battling with a whole nation, I am as impetuous, as daring, and as unconquerable as a lion; but in your presence, I am as timid, and gentle, and submissive, as a dove." It would be a conundrum of his character that would persist for forty-two years of marriage. Many abolitionist friends, having read his sonnet to an unnamed woman in *The Liberator,* had assumed that he was marrying Prudence Crandall, especially as he had been observed squiring the schoolmistress about Boston and dancing attention upon her like a man taken with love. When they heard that it was George Benson's daughter instead, people laughingly said, "She [must be] a good abolitionist." Garrison always replied that he could never have chosen anyone other. While Helen of course shared his "benevolent feelings," she was no activist, and Garrison knew it. He was marrying "for domestic quiet and happiness," as he later told his brother-in-law George. Helen "is one of those who prefer to toil unseen . . . and to sacrifice in seclusion," Garrison recognized from the outset, and he was confident that she would offer "no trifling support to abolitionism" by enabling him "to find exquisite delight in the family circle, as an offset to public adversity."

Helen Benson was one of the few people in the world who actually saw and appreciated Garrison in his entirety. She fell in love with both the poet and the prophet, and she enabled him to stay balanced. He did not have to play the fanatic at home, but could express the tender, sweet-natured side of his character, and she could do what she did best without feeling pressure from her husband to emulate the women who assumed public roles for which she felt unsuited. He brought drama to her life; she brought security to his. Their relationship gave confidence and plenitude to the editor's visionary labors, and theirs would be a great though unheralded collaboration.

For Garrison to marry a woman as decent, generous, and wholehearted as Helen Benson, was the greatest good fortune, and an outcome that fit the upward trajectory of his career. He was marrying into a family that had financial means but was distinguished for its philanthropy, and he had fallen in love with exactly the sort of plainspoken, conscientious country woman who formed the backbone of the abolitionist effort. The proximity of Prudence Crandall to the courtship, however, has led some writers to speculate on Garrison's "choice" and to decide, on the basis of his stereotyped reputation for intolerance, that he wanted a traditionally compliant woman who would nurture him without being as domineering as his mother. The argument does a disservice to all four parties. Garrison was hardly a male chauvinist; Helen Benson was hardly a wallflower; Prudence Crandall was no Mary Wollstonecraft, but rather more a Dorothea Brooke whose ideals stirred her to a solitary act of protest; Frances Maria Garrison hardly suffocated her son—rather he suffered more from their separation than her dominion.

Prudence Crandall had more formal education than Helen Benson and had acquired a professional vocation before her conscience had prompted her into the moral witness of the Canterbury struggle. That Garrison met her in her moment of inspiration made her, in an important sense, unavailable to him—even if she had been interested in him, which seems improbable given her simultaneous, though ambivalent, attraction to the older and choleric Calvin Philleo, a Baptist minister. As the village gossip indicated, a romance between the editor and the teacher would have compromised her independence and made her seem his cat's-paw. Garrison may indeed have been too shy to approach the strong-willed Crandall, but he was almost too shy to approach Helen Benson, who, after all, had a firm and upright sense of herself and knew perfectly well what she wanted. Helen and Lloyd, it turned out, had well-matched temperaments and tried very hard to be agreeable with each other. The editor's stubborn and quarrelsome public image, again, belies the conciliatory and tactful disposition he brought to personal relationships. Since Garrison worked extremely well with two generations of female activists in the movement without becoming either domineering or submissive, however, one may imagine that a marriage with Prudence Crandall would not have been all that different from the one with Helen. Perhaps Crandall, who deferentially permitted Samuel May to speak for her in public, might have run an interracial school in Boston or become active in the antislavery movement, but there is much to suggest that she would have settled gratefully into a supportive role not much different from Helen's. In fact, the cruel attacks upon her school broke the teacher's spirit, and although she retained her convictions, she took no active part in the struggle for many years and was ensnared in the pain of an unsuitable marriage to a harsh and oppressive man. The Garrisons would lose contact with the schoolteacher for many years as she migrated west to Illinois and Kansas, but in her old age, after reading the funeral tributes to Helen, Crandall wrote

Garrison a touching note of condolence. Yours, she said, was one of the "few such perfect unions" she had ever known.

As the wedding day approached, Helen worried about her "incapacity" to serve Garrison as she ought, especially as he began to urge abolitionist friends to stop off at Brooklyn and acquaint themselves with his bride-to-be. Was she going to be the movement's hostess? Would she have to worry about her wardrobe and be expected to set an example, like a preacher's wife? "Be assured that nothing arduous, or excessive, or difficult, will be required of you as the wife of W. L. G.," he said, for they would live quietly "without any parade." "I am a plain man . . . my habits are, like yours, very simple and abstemious . . . my *visiting* acquaintance is extremely limited; and I shall aim to be very domestic."

Yet as they began to discuss wedding arrangements Helen might have paused at Garrison's injunction to avoid both "extravagance and eccentricity" because the style of their wedding would be "widely told, especially among the colored population." No "rich and showy" wedding cake, he requested, and Helen—having heard similar injunctions from Prudence Crandall—readily agreed. No wine, he added. As a temperance family, Helen replied, the Bensons would never have considered that. No large crowds, he cautioned, but could he invite his aunt, his lamented mother's only sister? Of course he might invite guests of his choice, she answered, adding, "I never knew you had an aunt. . . . I have always intended to ask" about his relatives. Garrison suggested an October wedding date, after his trial, but Helen wanted it sooner, in early September, when the weather would be better. As you please, he said; why not September 1?

Prudence Crandall's legal appeal did not succeed. The judges dodged her substantial constitutional arguments and dismissed the verdict on a technicality, which meant that the abolitionists could not take the case up to the U.S. Supreme Court. With the "Black Law" still in force, the school remained subject to prosecution, and although Crandall had become an international heroine, she felt distraught, discouraged, and unsure of her next step. She broke off her engagement (to Helen's relief), but then in August she surprised her friends by suddenly marrying the dubious Calvin Philleo after all. He seemed disposed to continue, and perhaps expand, the school. Garrison had heard the man preach twice before black congregations in Boston and decided that though Philleo might be covetous and eccentric, he could not judge him a bad man. Helen did not agree; "Love is blind," she said.

"So, my dear, they have got the start of us by almost a month!" Garrison told Helen. He had escorted the visiting Philleos out to Roxbury and showed them the house—dubbed Freedom's Cottage—that he had rented for his own bride a short distance from Boston. The lovely trees, the soft hills, and the fields of berry bushes, moreover, would remind her of Friendship's Vale, he reassured her, and Helen happily exclaimed that the arrangement ideally afforded "the city and country *combined*. . . . we can mingle in society when we please without being obliged to conform to all the feelings and fashions of life."

Garrison ticked off the remaining weeks and busied himself with furnishing the house and unpacking the boxes that Helen shipped off, filled with the linens and clothes that she and her sisters had passed the summer sewing, and with the crockery and kitchenware that Mother Benson had gathered. ("Housekeeping is a much more formidable enterprise than I had anticipated," he wrote.) The Bensons would give them a wedding set of Lowestoft ware engraved with a dove and branch above a crowned heart. When he unpacked a china tea set Helen had bought, his heart sank, for he had purchased "a beautiful set" in London, replete with antislavery emblems. "We can keep the latter more for show," he said gallantly.

Finally, at the end of August 1834, Garrison bundled his aunt Charlotte and his partner Isaac Knapp and Knapp's sister from Newburyport into a chaise, and the party set off for Brooklyn. Exactly one year ago, he mused, he had been halfway across the Atlantic, "as little dreaming that I should be a married man within twelve months, as that I should occupy the chair of his holiness the Pope." Since then he had seen New York turned "upside-down" by a mob intent on his head, realized his hopes for a national abolition society, and written what he hoped would be its "imperishable" declaration, and "in the midst of these mighty movements . . . wooed 'a fair ladye' . . . and found that which I have long been yearning to find, a home [and] a wife. . . ." Truly, he thought, "it has been the most eventful year of my life."

At eight o'clock on the morning of Thursday, September 4, the tiny Garrison party stood with the large contingent of Bensons and some of the Canterbury friends in the handsome front parlor at Friendship's Vale to witness the wedding ceremony. The morning proved overcast and muggy, but thanks to the house's Newport-style hatchways in attic and cellar a lovely breeze circulated through the rooms. In traditional country manner the bride and groom sat facing the minister, their close friend Samuel J. May, who stood behind the improvised pulpit of a chairback. He asked the couple to rise, bade them join hands, and led them through the exchange of vows. May remembered that Garrison was very nervous, while Garrison recalled that "the dear minister's heart was deeply affected, and almost too full for clear, unembarrassed utterance." Neither man managed to note anything of the bride's demeanor, which in all likelihood was calmer than the groom's, or her dress, which, following custom, was probably a dove-colored silk. After a brief period of felicitations, some cups of fruit punch, and a hearty breakfast, the party ended. By nine o'clock Mr. and Mrs. Garrison had climbed into their cariole (with Helen's best friend, Eliza Chace, at the reins and Lloyd's aunt Charlotte as her companion in the driver's seat) and were ready to travel forty miles north to Worcester, where they would stop for the night. The Bensons waved their farewells, and amid laughter and shouts the vehicle pulled away. Lloyd and his beloved Peace and Plenty were riding happily into a life that would have precious little of either.

CHAPTER TEN

BRICKBATS IN THE CAUSE OF GOD

THERE WOULD BE NO HONEYMOON RESPITE. THE ABOLITIONISTS CARRIED ON WHAT GARRISON CALLED "THE STRIFE OF CHRIST AGAINST THE EMPIRE OF SATAN," AND IN 1834–35 THE MOVEMENT FOUND ITSELF IN A CYCLE of attack and counterattack. For almost every assertion of conscience, every instance of racial integration, and every organization founded, the crusaders could expect acts of ostracism, verbal retaliation, or physical abuse. There were enclaves of relative safety and neighborhoods of extreme danger, but success in one town often generated hostility in another, and a violent outbreak in one place had a deterrent effect upon organizing in another. Only by revealing the full extent of malicious "heathenism" in the society, however, could "the genuine disciples of Christ" carry on their crusade "skillfully and understandingly," Garrison insisted, and he reached deeply into the Dissenting tradition to compare their moral warfare with Christian and Faithful's passage through Vanity Fair, the market of worldly corruptions laid out by Beelzebub on the path to the Celestial City.

So "forcibly" did Bunyan's allegory strike Garrison as applicable "to the case of modern abolitionists" that in November 1834 he reprinted the entire episode from *Pilgrim's Progress* across three columns of *The Liberator*'s front page. With the excitement that comes from seeing familiar words in a fresh light, readers contemplated the spectacle of the pilgrims, who spurned the Fair with avowals to purchase only the truth and consequently were beaten and jailed for disturbing the peace. At their trial Faithful testified that laws and customs that "were flat against the Word of God" deserved no loyalty and pronounced his judges more suited to the government of Hell. The jury, headed by Mr. Blind-man and Mr. Implacable, ordered Faithful burned at the stake. Yet the pilgrims saw a chariot carry him to the Gates of Heaven, and Christian, later escaping his jailers, cried out, "Sing, Faithful, sing, and let thy name survive/ For though they killed thee, thou art yet alive." A new traveler, Hopeful, joined Christian in "a brotherly covenant" and "thus one died to make testimony to the truth, and another rises out of his ashes to be a companion. . . ."

Like Bunyan's valiant pilgrims, the abolitionist apostles would endure the violence as they would a purge, in hopes that it would make the inherent brutality of the slave system visible and more amenable to healing. "Be of good cheer," David Child told Garrison, for "the Devil comes not out without much tearing and rending and *foaming at the mouth*." These words would be severely tested, for as the abolitionists made their own tumultuous passage through the Vanity Fair of American politics, the struggle exacted a physical price that broke Prudence Crandall's spirit, torched Lewis Tappan's house, and brought Garrison face to face with a lynch mob in front of Faneuil Hall.

The Garrisons had hardly settled themselves in Freedom's Cottage before word came that vandals had once again struck the school in Canterbury. On the night of September 9, 1834, just a few days after the teacher and her new husband had attended the Garrisons' wedding in Brooklyn, the sounds of smashing glass and cracking wood roused the household. A band of toughs had broken in and destroyed the furniture in the front rooms while they yelled crude oaths and so frightened one student that she coughed up blood.

The end had come. The girls' safety could no longer be assured, and Crandall finally surrendered. She asked Samuel J. May to explain to the students that she would close the school and return them to their parents' homes. "The words almost blistered my lips," the minister told Garrison afterward. The Rev. Calvin Philleo, who under state law now controlled his bride's property, drafted an advertisement for *The Liberator* that put the house up for sale. (The couple would retire to his farm in central New York, but the marriage soured and in the 1840s Prudence migrated to the Illinois prairies with her brother.) "Human endurance has its bounds," Garrison wrote in an editorial sympathetic to the teacher's desire for surcease, but privately he told May that the movement ought to keep reminding the public about the shameful episode.

The Canterbury outbreak was the climax of a violent summer. In July, mobs had besieged three black churches in New York, attacked black people on the streets, and set fires at a dozen houses, including Lewis Tappan's. In August, an even more virulent outbreak in Philadelphia had taken the life of one black man, who drowned when he tried to swim across the Schuykill River to escape a hostile mob that in the course of three riotous nights damaged the homes of forty black families.

With an agitator's resiliency, however, Garrison kept himself looking ahead. " 'Let us never be weary in well-doing,' " he would recite, as his mother had before him, " 'for in due time we shall reap.' " In the fall of 1834, Garrison could point to many favorable "signs of the times." The women of Boston had organized a female antislavery society that within a few months attracted a broad-based membership from both races. Equally cheering, Amos A. Phelps had found more than one hundred New England clergymen willing to endorse the published version of his bold and candid sermons on the sinfulness of slavery. Earlier in the year a group of divinity students at Lane Seminary in Cincinnati, led by Theodore Dwight Weld, had held a mighty eighteen-day revival on the question of slavery which had ended in the conversion of virtually the entire student body to the tenets of immediate abolition. Speakers from Lane had thrilled huge gatherings in New York and Boston with reports of the manner in which abolition had seized their consciences and prompted them both to form an antislavery society and to volunteer to teach in Cincinnati's black community. No longer could immediatism be regarded as the peculiar frenzy of Boston hotheads. The triumph was especially sweet because the president of Lane, who tried to suppress the student agitation, was none other than Dr. Lyman Beecher, who had left Boston to heed the call of religious education in the west.

The drama of the Lane revival epitomized the struggle against colonization that had taken place over the past several years, and the climax came when James Gillespie Birney, an outspoken Kentuckian who had emancipated his slaves, became so impressed by the Lane actions that he resigned his post as an agent of the American Colonization Society and, under Weld's aegis, agreed to work instead for the American Anti-Slavery Society. The defection of Birney, combined with the disclosure that the ACS stood $40,000 in debt, capped the immediatist triumph. Garrison filled his columns with Birney's apologia and mocked the ACS financial woes by finding a new occasion each week to print the debt figures in oversized display type. Across New England the ACS clergy delivered a unanimously gloomy report to headquarters: "Colonization is dead."

The cause received another boost when Garrison's English friend George Thompson, with a stipend from the antislavery women of Glasgow and Edinburgh, came to the United States in October 1834 for an indefinite stay as an abolitionist agent. The troublemaking New York papers predicted that mobs would hound Thompson wherever he went, for "if our people will not suffer our own citizens to tamper with the question of slavery, it is not to be supposed that they will tolerate the officious intermeddling of a Foreign Fanatic." Testing the waters, however, Garrison brought Thompson to an antislavery meeting in Groton, Massachusetts, where the Englishman spoke with an eloquence and intensity that won the hearts of his audience. "All eyes are now turned upon the United States," Thompson said, after recounting the history of the British movement, but cautioned that far from meddling in American politics, he had come as a citizen of the world to expound universal principles of Christian charity.

Before the week was out, Thompson had repeated his speech in Lowell, accepted a series of engagements in the state of Maine, and made the first of many talks in Boston, where the abolitionist faithful gathered, despite a severe rainstorm, in the new antislavery office—a loft above a bookstore at 46 Washington Street. Within a short time Thompson was speaking eight or ten times a week in towns throughout New England and thrilling his listeners as he drew the lessons of immediatism from the text "Execute justice in the morning," making the words ring like an alarm bell in the crowded meeting halls. He regaled his audiences with firsthand anecdotes drawn from Garrison's mission to London and spoke meltingly, as a representative of British abolitionism, of their shared mandate from heaven to purge America of the guilt of slavery and prejudice. Though nasty editorialists derided Thompson as "a clubroom declaimer" and the pet of "a bevy of old maids" in Scotland, his meetings proceeded without disruption, and everywhere he brought fresh recruits into the burgeoning number of antislavery societies. Or almost everywhere. In Concord, Ralph Waldo Emerson, under pressure from his abolitionist aunt, endured a private breakfast at which the young essayist found himself outtalked by Thompson. The man is "vanity-stricken" and "inconvertible," Emerson complained afterward: and "what you say or what might be said would make no impression on him. . . ." The discussion did more for Aunt Mary Moody Emerson, who heard from the visitor enough about Garrison to lay aside her prejudices and promise that she would tell her friends to take up subscriptions to the paper she had previously advised them to shun.

Garrison would have loved to travel with Thompson, feeling his surge of energy and savoring the acclaim for having secured so valuable an emissary, but pressing business—domestic and professional—kept the editor at home. Although he liked to joke that "the honey-moon has not yet waned with us," the young husband worried a good deal about his bride that autumn. Most men in that era accepted the social role of making their wives comfortable, but Garrison—having abjured material success—assumed more responsibility than was common for his wife's emotional well-being. "I am almost afraid to receive you," he had confided to Helen during their courtship, "lest I shall fail in making you happy."

On the surface all was well. Helen loved the picturesque setting of Freedom's Cottage, tucked "up in the woods" on a backstreet above the village of Roxbury. Lloyd had furnished the old farmhouse—a lean-to, originally, with a steep back roof to shed the winter's snow—with inexpensive but attractive pieces, and the size of the woodpile testified to Helen's husband's energetic care. Their evenings by the fireside, reading aloud or taking quiet delight in each other's companionship, answered all her expectations. Yet she was homesick. A letter from her sisters in Brooklyn sent her upstairs in fits of weeping, and "the troops of talkative abolitionists," as Garrison called them, who stopped by to visit left Helen feeling tongue-tied and inadequate. Isaac Knapp's sister, whom the men expected to be Helen's female companion, proved disagreeable and went back to Newburyport, and until Anna Benson could come up from Brooklyn for an extended visit in November, the anxious Garrison would not leave his bride in melancholy solitude. "I have been quite a *homebody*," the editor told his friends. "Morning, noon, and night, I am generally to be found here [at Freedom's Cottage], poring over my editorial budget, or scribbling letters to friends, or reading newspapers or books. . . . Mr. Knapp is indeed very kind to spare me so much from the office." While the impetuous lion in him sought warfare and, perhaps, a combatant's glorious death, the tender dove wanted only to be nestled with his heart's desire amid the consolations of poetry and love. His friends saw in him Wordsworth's "Character of the Happy Warrior" (1807) "whose high endeavours are an inward light/ That makes the path before him also bright . . . embued as with a sense/ And faculty for storm and turbulence/ Is yet a soul whose master-bias leans/ To homefelt pleasures and to gentle scenes."

To walk from home to office epitomized the conflict. Garrison sauntered downhill through woods and hayfields along the narrow highway, startling coveys of quail, to the country village with its meetinghouse facing the common, a thicket of shops, a gristmill, and small fishing craft moored along the harbor flats. If the weather was poor, the editor would wait at the town hall for the horse-drawn omnibus that carried passengers to the center of Boston in thirty minutes. If the day was fine, however, he would stride off himself for the mile-long walk across the narrow neck of land that separated the Charles River from Boston Harbor.

The crossing took Garrison from the bucolic past to the industrial future. Once so wind-swept that it became impassable at high tide, the neck had become a paved causeway broad enough to carry the traffic of both Tremont and Washington streets. Landfills on the seaward side had made place for country houses, but as Garrison drew close to the city, he could see the development of South Cove rising before him: a large depot for the brand-new Worcester railroad and fifty-six acres of adjoining shops, houses, a four-story hotel, and the largest merchandise depot in the country. On the river side he could see the black plumes of smoke from the locomotives crossing the Mill Dam; the causeway had turned the Back Bay into a polluted basin of turbid water, less hospitable to huge flocks of shorebirds than to the mills and foundries that lined its banks. When he entered Boston, the ring of hammers and the whine of saws could be heard everywhere, as the Pearl Street area witnessed the pulling down of its old sea captains' houses and the creation of a new factory district of sugar refineries, textile warehouses, foundries and tool works, shoe and clothing mills, and manufactories for household luxury goods such as Chickering pianos and Singer sewing machines. The editor disliked walking down by the wharves, perhaps because the acrid odors of creosote and fish reminded him of his desperate childhood on the edge of the Merrimack, but the long piers and sprawling sheds of the nation's second-largest port held the raw materials of the city's prosperity. Ninety thousand bales of Southern cotton were unloaded in Boston in 1835, double the amount of five years earlier. Arrayed in bulky stacks that stood higher than houses, the crop symbolized a commercial alliance with slavery that turned the staple crop into factory-milled textiles for the inland market, with the Boston Lowells and Lawrences profiting not only from the work of the mill towns that bore their names but the railroads that carried the products across the region. Rail lines to Worcester, Lowell, and Providence all began operations from Boston in 1835 that would soon give the city a western rail connection to Albany and Buffalo and put the market of the Great Lakes basin within its reach. When Garrison first came to Boston in 1826, the place had still retained the stolid character of a provincial trading town, but by 1835 it had become a brisk commercial and manufacturing city of eighty thousand people, not as furious in its pursuits as New York, which was more than twice Boston's size, but so crowded and pulsating an emporium that the bellwether Lynde Walter of the *Transcript* decried the city's metamorphosis from "social family to bustling multitude . . . where we have to ask, who is my neighbor." The more radical Garrison, by contrast, took the city's advances as a metaphor for the rapid transformation he sought in the moral sphere. Abolitionists, he liked to say, had to dig and drill and blast until they had built a level track for "the great locomotive engine of Truth."

Brother Knapp had found cheaper quarters for *The Liberator* above a bookstore at 25 Cornhill, a long street curving down from Scollay Square to Faneuil Hall and filled with bookshops, stationers, and printing offices. Visitors to the antislavery office around the corner at 46 Washington often made a pilgrimage to the newspaper's headquarters, where they expected the editor to educate them personally and save them the trouble of perusing the pamphlets and documents he urged upon them. (The problem would become aggravated in later years when the organization shared the Cornhill office—and the rent—with *The Liberator*.) From the literary standpoint, Garrison's seclusion at Freedom's Cottage was a boon; working with fewer interruptions allowed his editorials to grow into essays and gave more thematic coherence to his selections from the exchange pile. From the business point of view, however, *The Liberator* suffered from its editor's domestic preoccupations. Although 1834 had begun with nearly six hundred new subscriptions, the money for them had never arrived, and Knapp's accounts had grown so tangled—and his relations with business-minded agents like Arnold Buffum so sour—that even well-meaning friends despaired of restoring order. By autumn the deficit approached $1,700, and Garrison feared that he would either have to give up the paper entirely or compromise his independence by running it as the salaried employee of an antislavery society.

George Thompson spared Garrison from drastic measures. As soon as the Englishman learned the details of his friend's business predicament, he bent his talents to the task of fund-raising. Writing on oversized sheets in a bold hand that epitomized his platform style, Thompson inspired *The Liberator*'s friends to redoubled efforts. No other paper, Thompson insisted, could hold the movement to the high ground of immediatism. No other paper had the esteem of abolitionists in Great Britain, and no other paper urged the cause of black people with more courage and candor. At every stop on his tour, moreover, the Englishman persuaded people to take responsibility for a fixed number of copies and remove the "incubus" of financial worry from the Boston pioneer.

Defending *The Liberator* as the bastion of radical abolition was more than a rhetorical flourish. The Tappan brothers were not happy with Garrison's penchant for criticizing the halfway views of the benevolent gentlemen and clergy they were cultivating as potential resources for the movement. When the former ACS leader Leonard Bacon of Hartford tried to recruit the Tappans into a gradualist alternative to the AAS, the editor felt vindicated in his vigilance. Garrison's uncompromising style provoked a fresh round of argument over his vehement language. Arthur Tappan thought that Garrison had dealt too harshly with the influential Bacon and his coterie of orthodox ministers and groused that the editor ought to consider "whether his 'holy indignation' is always as holy as he appears to think it." Garrison was their Luther, Maria Child countered, and was justifiably "injudicious" in his truth-telling: "where an evil is powerfully supported by the self-interest and prejudice of the community, none but an ardent individual will venture to meddle with it."

The issue was "not *phraseology, but principles,*" Garrison maintained. Complaints about his language were intended to stigmatize as *"Garrison men"* all the immediatists—whose prose styles varied with their personalities, the editor observed—and thus denigrate a broad movement as a personal faction.

The conflict over Garrison's language—"a *wordy* matter," the editor later joked—prompted him to resume his lecturing and travel. Helen had a cheering visit with her family at Friendship's Vale in March 1835, while her husband at last had an opportunity to accompany George Thompson on a major series of lectures in Philadelphia and New York. The Englishman made a soul-stirring appearance before three thousand people in Philadelphia's Bethel Church, the citadel of black Methodism, and also preached in a staid Presbyterian church for two hours to a crowd so large that the gallery threatened to give way under the crush. In New York the two men addressed three churches in one day, and Garrison also spoke in two black congregations, taking inspiration from his favorite texts: "Break every yoke, and let the oppressed go free" (Isa. 58:6) and "Remember them that are in bonds as bound with thee" (Heb. 13:3).

At a special gathering at Lewis Tappan's house, where the visitors could still see the relics of the past summer's attack, Garrison had an opportunity to improve relations with the New York leaders of the AAS, long a delicate issue among the Boston people. With the rise of other state societies in New England, the NEAS could no longer serve as the region's only voice, and in February 1835, the pioneering organization bowed to its own success by agreeing to become a state auxiliary of the AAS and renaming itself the Massachusetts Anti-Slavery Society. A "plan of cooperation" had emerged to govern the protocol of fund-raising and the dispatch of agents, but direct discussion between Garrison and Elizur Wright, the sharp-faced former professor of divinity who directed the AAS office, helped smooth the path.

Garrison found the usually dour Wright in an ebullient mood, because he had, at long last, hired the two most eloquent of "the Lane rebels,"° Theodore Dwight Weld and Henry B. Stanton, as lecture agents for the AAS. Equally exciting, Wright, who was a shrewd man with figures, had calculated that the AAS could publish nine times the literature for only five times the cost. He and Lewis Tappan had devised a plan to issue twenty thousand to fifty thousand copies a week of tracts that would saturate the country with the abolitionists' message. The AAS would spend far more on printing than on lecture agents, but the pamphlets would, with the help of new railroads and improved postal service, carry the word faster and prepare the ground for the organizers. Use of the mails, moreover, would enable the AAS to get its message to ministers, legislators, and editors in the South, where—all agreed—it would be too risky to assign field agents.

Garrison appreciated the boldness of the publication plan. He knew, of course, that a quiet revolution had overtaken printing technology in the past few years, with the introduction of stereotyped plates, cheap rag paper, and steam presses. Just outside the AAS office on Nassau Street he could see for himself how the Harper Brothers had installed behemoth power presses in a four-story building on Printing House Square to produce a million books a year, and he could hear talk of how the New York daily newspapers had—with the conversion to steam—gone from two hundred impressions an hour on the handpress to a thousand an hour on Hoe's single-cylinder machine. Soon, perhaps, even an edition of *The Liberator* might roll quickly from a steam press in a few hours instead of being printed one sheet at a time by hand over the course of two days. The editor enthusiastically led the endorsement of Wright's plan at the annual meeting in May 1835, and the press orders went out at once.

The trip reinvigorated Garrison for the struggle, but he experienced terrible misgivings about leaving his wife and slept very poorly on the first night of their separation. He'd had a nightmare, Lloyd told Helen, in which he thought "you and I had been to ride in a carry-all, with two horses—'twas late at night—after letting you get out, away went the horses with me at full speed, and forty times at least I came within a hair's breadth of losing my life." He could not remember the final outcome, Garrison said, but he took the dream as a signal to fuse his public and private lives. He and Helen,

°After the celebrated revival, the Lane Seminary trustees, with the concurrence of Dr. Beecher, had tried to expel Weld and issued new regulations that forbade abolition activities at the school. When a winter of protest failed to sway the obdurate Beecher, the abolition-minded students—most of whom were young ministers in their mid-twenties—resigned in a body, vowed to found a new seminary (later Oberlin College) committed to free speech, and took to the road as abolitionist lecturers.

who had been feeling poorly all spring, decided to move into Boston, where she would find acceptance and support in the abolitionist social circle and he could more closely align the protecting comfort of domestic life with his responsibility as the movement's leader.

Though Garrison had cherished the romantic ideal of Freedom's Cottage, he gave it up without a pang when it proved less than idyllic for his wife. It took two days and five wagonloads to move the couple's household furnishings ("everything but the cat," Garrison joked) from Roxbury to the duplex they had rented at 23 Brighton Street near the new Lowell Railroad Station in the West End, a neighborhood of cheap workingmen's houses that had sprung up along the riverbank beyond Beacon Hill in the past few years. Garrison himself put down straw summer carpets in the four rooms, and with freshly whitewashed walls and the drafty hole in the attic boarded up, the place would do tolerably well, they thought. The only drawback, especially after the rural solitude of Roxbury, proved to be the ease with which conversation and noise passed through the wall of the adjoining apartment. "Every movement seems to be as if we were living together with them in common," Garrison groused. They would be patient about the problem for a few months, however, and then, Helen knew, their side might become the noisier portion. She expected to give birth to their first child shortly after the New Year.

Garrison was overwhelmed by the news and could barely let Helen from his sight. When he was compelled to go with his aunt Charlotte to Nova Scotia in July 1835 in pursuit of a rumored legacy from the Lloyd family, his letters complained of "dreadful" homesickness, and he sent to Helen "a thousand kisses for each of your fair cheeks, and twice ten thousand for your pretty strawberry lips." Though the editor enjoyed meeting some of his forgotten kinfolk, the trip was not a fruitful one. The inheritance—some land on Deer Island—had been appropriated by Uncle Plato Lloyd and could be recovered only through expensive litigation that the editor could not afford. From all the family talk Garrison gained only a new birthdate. Aunt Catherine—"infallible as to these facts," he told Helen—insisted that he had been born in December 1805, not 1804 as his apprenticeship papers had claimed; he was still only twenty-nine years old. "Have you any objections, my dear, to my growing younger?"

By midsummer the abolitionists' new campaign had generated so powerful and far-reaching a counterattack that Garrison did not hesitate to brand it "a reign of terror." A mob in Charleston, South Carolina, had broken into the federal post office and seized several mailbags from New York containing AAS pamphlets. A crowd of three thousand people watched the captured documents fuel a bonfire while effigies of Tappan and Garrison cast hanging shadows over the lurid scene. In Nashville, Tennessee, a gospel messenger named Amos Dresser, one of the Lane rebels, was given twenty lashes in the public market for having AAS pamphlets in his satchel. In Georgetown, D.C., Dr. Reuben Crandall, the younger brother of the oppressed school-teacher, was jailed when he went to the post office to pick up some botanical samples that a vigilant postmaster had found wrapped in antislavery newspapers. In Canaan, New Hampshire, after the selectmen ordered the inter-racial Noyes Academy removed from its jurisdiction, a crowd yoked one hundred oxen to the building and literally dragged it out of town.

Local committees to censor the mails sprang up from Tuscaloosa to tide-water Virginia, where U.S. Senator John Tyler warned that "a powerful combination" in New York—taking advantage of cheap printing, the post office, and the soft hearts of women—had "sprung up . . . to despoil us of our property." Holding up before a hometown crowd an AAS pamphlet, Tyler railed that its cover depicted slavemasters as "demons" while "here stands Arthur Tappan, Mr. Somebody Garrison, and Mr. Foreigner Thompson, patting the greasy little fellows on their cheeks and giving them most lovely kisses . . . and [posing as] the only legitimate defenders of the religion of Christ."

As in the Nat Turner furor, Southern leaders demanded Northern support for federal laws that would exclude from the mails "all printed papers *suspected of a tendency* to produce or encourage an insubordinate and insur-rectionary spirit among the slaves of the South." From Philadelphia to Bangor, anti-abolition meetings sponsored by party politicians and conser-vative merchants readily endorsed the Southern view, and they found sup-port from the Jackson administration. Although the president believed that the federal government lacked power to censor the mail, he concurred in his postmaster general's suggestion, with a wink to the mob, that the mail need not be delivered in the face of community opposition. After protesting crowds filled the streets in New York, the city's postmaster declined even to receive abolitionist material. With rumors flying that assassins had come from New Orleans to kill Tappan, Elizur Wright barricaded the AAS office doors with iron bars and inch-thick planks and hid his stock of pamphlets.

In Boston, death threats against Thompson could be heard in every street. The mischief-maker should be tossed, like the odious British tea, into Boston Harbor, people said, and feeling ran so high that the leadership felt obliged to hide him. A group of abolitionist women swarmed around Thompson after an August 1 lecture in Julian Hall and surreptitiously edged him toward a curtained side exit, from which he was hurried into a waiting carriage bound for New York. Although civic leaders denied permission for an abolitionist meeting in Faneuil Hall, they filled the hallowed venue themselves for a meeting on August 21, 1835, that, in the *Transcript*'s words, would consider how far the "guaranteed rights" of the South should be "marred, mutilated, and brought into contempt . . . by infatuated madmen . . . and reckless ar-guers on abstract principles." Not far at all, the throng resolved, as it called for new laws to punish acts that tended to coerce any of the states into abolition.

The meeting was intended to protect the mercantile elite's trading and political connections with the South, and the abolitionists feared a violent aftermath. "If the mob should break into our office now they would have some luck," Henry Benson whispered, "as we have a great amount of publications on hand." John G. Whittier thought there was an element of "wire-worked manipulation" in the situation. Both political parties in the North were using a combination of high-toned resolutions and mob action "to gull the South" into thinking slavery was safe, though he believed that few politicians would actually vote for the repressive legislation demanded by the slaveholders. If the opposition to the postal campaign became a form of political theater, however, the abolitionists would take the roles of martyrs. Garrison vowed that "if we are beaten with many stripes, and thrust into the inner prison, we trust, that like Paul and Silas, we shall pray and sing praises unto God."

Despite the high talk, the abolitionists thought it prudent to make few public appearances until the fever abated. Thompson, whose safety in New York seemed precarious found better refuge at Whittier's farm outside Haverhill, while Garrison accompanied Helen to Friendship's Vale. Electing to remain there for several weeks, the editor sent twice-weekly packages of "incendiary matter . . . hot enough to melt at least one chain" back to Boston. He advised Knapp to put the paper to bed on Fridays instead of Thursdays, so as to accommodate the circuitous delivery system the editor had devised.

The Faneuil Hall meeting kept Garrison's pen busy for many days as he vigorously replied to the "truly diabolical" remarks of the featured speakers, Harrison Gray Otis and Peleg Sprague. Distinguished for decades in public office, the two venerable figures had extolled the gallant cooperation of South and North in founding the republic and defended the constitutional compromise that—in Otis's candid words—had accepted "the South's claim to consider their slaves as cyphers or nonentities . . . and allow the masters to exercise . . . all the political rights of the slave." This compact, Otis emphasized to ringing cheers, "speaks to every man's understanding, and binds every man's conscience by all that is sacred in good faith, or sound in good policy . . ." Incredulous at Otis's claim that conscience obliged Massachusetts to defend slavery, Garrison jammed a printer's fist in front of the offending paragraph and denounced his onetime hero's patriotism for "exclud[ing] one-sixth portion of your countrymen from its embrace." Against the old-style politics of union and compromise, Garrison eloquently counterposed a politics of universal justice. No government could impose limits upon his moral obligation to repudiate slavery, he said, even "if the whole world is to be changed" before the slaves went free.

Although Garrison challenged the morality of the constitutional compact, he tried to reclaim guardianship of the Declaration of Independence. The Otises and the Spragues would take the document as an artifact of nationhood and a symbol of the practical alliance with the South, but Garrison wanted it regarded as "a beacon light for the oppressed." Though it had been written by a slaveholder and signed by "fallible" men, Garrison insisted that its "sublime" assertion of equality was "a noble sentiment, written by the finger of God in legible characters upon the heart of man." By its lights, race or color could not be made "the test of liberty," Garrison emphasized; whatever their physical disparities, God had made people "equal in value, in dignity, in existence, in immortality" and none could be made political ciphers or be treated by anything less than the Golden Rule. Garrison glossed the lesson by quoting Shylock's plea from *The Merchant of Venice* ("Hath not a Jew eyes?") and Robert Burns's "A man's a man for a' that," from one of the editor's favorite poems.

The violence penetrated the Garrison circle. A stone-throwing crowd in Haverhill broke up a speech by Samuel J. May, and a few days later a drunken gang—"at a certain place misnamed *Concord*"—mistook Whittier for Thompson and pelted him with rotten eggs and brickbats. Then the "agents of Beelzebub" came to Brighton Street in the midnight darkness of September 10, 1835, and erected a macabre gallows on Garrison's own doorstep. Made of five-inch-thick maplewood joists and gruesomely draped in seaweed from the nearby tidal flats, the structure had a note affixed from "Judge Lynch" and two ropes at the ready. No doubt intended to execute "those twin monsters, Slavery and Colonization," Garrison joked.

Despite his insouciance (easy to maintain, perhaps, from the safety of Brooklyn), Garrison was worried. "Be *very* careful all of you," he warned Henry Benson and Knapp, who were staying at Brighton Street, "especially about venturing out late at night." Yet to spike rumors that he dared not show his face in Boston, the editor returned to the city from Brooklyn after the gallows incident. Though greatly alarmed, Helen would not stay behind. "Probably there is less danger than [you] imagine," Garrison told her, but if violence were to occur, "there is a whole eternity of consolation in this assurance—he who loses his life for Christ's sake shall find it." Unbeknownst to them, however, sentinels from the black community kept an eye on their house at night.

The city had grown quiet, almost ominously so, though the abolitionists hoped that the vicious mood had broken. A Thompson meeting had been attacked at Abingdon on September 27, but the town authorities prosecuted the ringleaders for disturbing the peace, and the Englishman returned a week later to speak unmolested. Public opinion, moreover, seemed to be shifting on the postal controversy. The influential *New York Evening Post,* edited by a stalwart Jacksonian, the poet William Cullen Bryant, had sharply condemned the administration for "truckling" to slaveholders and permitting a form of "practical nullification" in which "every two penny postmaster" could censor the press as his whim or the mob dictated. In provoking a defense of free speech, May told Garrison, their opponents had not realized how "the heat of persecution nurtures the very plants it would extirpate."

The calm in Boston did not last, and Garrison had to face the purgative violence that he had so frequently extolled and—his critics said—desperately craved. The lingering fuse set by the anti-abolitionist Faneuil Hall meeting smoldered for two months before bursting into an explosion of mob action in October 1835. The final spark was struck by the announcement that on October 14, George Thompson would address the first anniversary meeting of the Boston Female Anti-Slavery Society. The newspapers, however, set up such a roar—warning that ladies' petticoats could not protect the bullying foreigner from community outrage—that the usual churches and meeting halls either closed their doors or required the posting of prohibitively expensive bonds against property damage.

"Not a place can be found for love or money," an abolitionist woman wrote in her diary. After many conferences at the home of Maria Weston Chapman, the merchant banker's wife whose firm bearing and fierce conviction typified the organization, the leaders rescheduled the session for October 21 at their own headquarters at 46 Washington Street. They told the newspapers that they would maintain "with Christian constancy" their right to meet and to invite the lecturers whom they considered most able to advance "the holy cause of human rights." Because the group had announced no speakers' names for the meeting, rumors quickly spread that the ladies would be hearing from "their handsome Mr. Thompson." Not wanting to risk their English guest's life, however, the women had accepted Garrison's offer to speak in Thompson's place.

On the morning of October 21, 1835, merchants on Washington Street, fearing a riot that would damage their property, petitioned the mayor's office to prevent the meeting. Mayor Theodore Lyman, once a brigadier general in the militia and always a firm friend of the city's mercantile elite, had presided over the repressive Faneuil Hall meeting, and although he affirmed the abolitionists' rights of speech and assembly, he tried at every turn to dissuade them from exercising them. Lyman sent a deputy marshal, Charles M. Wells, around to the antislavery office to assess the situation. Wells encountered Garrison himself, who bristled at the inquiry, but after Wells informed him that the mayor contemplated deploying extra constables if Thompson was to be present, Garrison grudgingly told the marshal that the Englishman was not even in the city and said the mayor could announce that fact in the interests of deterring violence. Wells left, but fired a parting shot indicating the mayor's displeasure with zealots who persisted in holding meetings during such times of community irritability.

Unperturbed, Garrison saw an ailing Henry Benson off on a therapeutic visit to Friendship's Vale and put a note in his hand for Father Benson declaring that as Christ's disciples, the abolitionists—like Gideon's band—

would carry on the war against unrighteousness. The editor then walked home to Brighton Street for an early dinner with his houseguest John B. Vashon, a Pittsburgh black leader who had generously supported *The Liberator* from its inception.

While Garrison dined with his patron, another Boston editor, James Homer of the *Commercial Gazette,* conferred at Cochran's with his supporters, all merchants from Central Wharf, about the handbill they had ordered. They wanted something that "would wake up the populace," and Homer quickly produced a flyer that urged "the friends of the Union" to rally that afternoon at 46 Washington Street "to snake out . . . the infamous foreign scoundrel Thompson." A group of "patriotic citizens," it promised, had offered a purse of $100 to the man who first laid "violent hands on Thompson, so that he may be brought to the tar-kettle before dark." By noon, Homer's apprentices had struck off five hundred copies of the handbill, and within the hour, they had distributed it in insurance offices, hotels, and reading rooms all along State Street and in the North End.

By midafternoon the streets in the neighborhood of the antislavery office—just a short block along Washington Street from where Court and State streets debouched into the small square around the oblong red-brick City Hall—had filled with commercial men from the surrounding offices, truckmen and food handlers from nearby Quincy Market, and apprentices and clerks who had slipped out for the excitement. The weather was "positively hot" and the mood equally sultry and disagreeable; when some in the crowd passed the word that the mayor had discovered Thompson had fled, one gentleman told another, "Well, Garrison is here," and his companion replied that he would gladly pay $5,000 to ship the editor to Savannah.

Their putative cargo had arrived at 46 Washington early, accompanied by C. C. Burleigh, a long-haired, bearded abolitionist agent from Connecticut who had befriended Prudence Crandall during the Canterbury struggle. The street had not yet filled, although a score of youths had come up the two flights of stairs in an effort to block the entryway to the meeting hall. They taunted Garrison, but made no serious effort to molest him, and the editor went into the auditorium, which looked like a schoolroom, with its rows of wooden benches, a raised platform for the speakers, and abolitionist banners hanging along the far wall. He found twenty-five or thirty women already present, including Mary S. Parker, the society's president, Mrs. Chapman and two of her sisters, the black schoolteacher Susan Paul, and the redoubtable Henrietta Sargent, a generation older than the others but resolute in rising up against what she decried as the "ignorance, indifference, prejudice, and worldly interest" that had shut Boston's heart to "the pure spirit of universal emancipation."

Other members—more than one hundred were expected—were reported on the way, but the few who straggled in amid shouts and insults from the lads out on the landing reported that the streets were so thronged and threatening that many of the women, Helen Garrison among them, had no choice but to turn away. Maria Chapman, whose silvery voice and blond ringlets made her seem more the socialite than the shrewd commander she proved to be, said that she had asked the mayor's office for more protection, but was told, "You give us too much trouble."

Garrison tried to calm the ruckus in the corridor, but his lame joke, "If any of you gentlemen are *ladies* in disguise . . . give me your names . . . and you can take seats in the meeting," further dramatized the issue as one that pitted Christian meekness against established power, feminine sentiment against masculine patriotism, with Garrison identified with the women. The "brazen-faced crew" responded by throwing orange peels over the transom, pounding on the thin doors, and hooting and hollering with redoubled energy. It became apparent that if Garrison spoke, a riot would ensue, and Miss Parker urged him to leave, "for the peace of the meeting and the safety of all." The society, she assured him, would calmly transact its business "and leave the issue with God."

The editor withdrew from the hall into the abolitionists' office, a partitioned space in the rear corner of the room; from its window he could see that Washington Street had become completely choked with a crowd several thousand strong, respectably dressed, but rudely shouting for Thompson like "a troop of ravenous wolves." He sat down at the desk to write a description of the scene, while Burleigh guarded the door in case the gang out front decided to rush the office to get at its supply of pamphlets. The two men strained to hear the meeting over the noise.

Miss Parker opened with a verse from Scripture—"Remember those in bonds, as bound with them"—and a prayer of gratitude that "while there were many to molest there were none that could make them afraid." It was a "sublime and soul-thrilling" moment, Garrison said afterward, to hear "that Christian heroine above the growls of the ruffians." Though Maria Chapman bowed her head, she kept an eye cocked on the doorway, where she could hear boards being pried away and see hostile heads poking up above the partition. She thought of Schiller's deathbed words, "Many things now are clear," and steeled herself to listen to the secretary's report.

Miss Mary Ball stood to read, but her soft voice could not be heard above the din. It scarcely mattered, though, because at that moment Mayor Lyman burst into the hall shouting, "Go home, ladies, go home." (He had taken control of the stairs and passageway with the aid of several constables, but had failed to disperse the crowd.)

When Miss Parker questioned the need to leave, Lyman answered, "I cannot now explain, but will call upon you this evening."

At this, several members stood up to remonstrate with the mayor.

"Mr. Lyman, your personal friends are the instigators of the mob," Mrs. Chapman said. "Have you used your personal influence with them?"

"I know no personal friends," Lyman retorted. "I am merely an official. Ladies, you must retire. It is dangerous to remain."

Several members called out that if they must die in the cause, it might as well be now, but the mayor smiled condescendingly and said, "At any rate, you cannot die here."

In the hubbub Miss Parker asked if the mayor could guarantee their safety upon leaving. "If you go *now*, I will protect you," he replied. To secure the mayor's protection for even a portion of their proceedings would be a modest victory, Miss Parker thought, so she called the question. The group voted to adjourn to a private home to complete its business.

Two by two, white arm in arm with black, the abolitionist women walked up Washington Street through a narrow lane the constables had pushed open for them. Hisses, sarcastic cheers, and racial epithets assailed the procession, which gradually doubled in size as some of the members detained in the crowd broke free to join their sisters on the march to Mrs. Chapman's house, just off the Common on West Street, seven blocks south. They did not realize that Garrison remained in the building, however, and maintained afterward that they would not have complied with the mayor's orders had they known Garrison had been left to bear the anger of the mob alone.

The gentlemen in the street began howling for Garrison just as soon as the women were gone.

"Out with him!"

"Lynch him!"

"Turn him a right nigger color with tar."

For a moment the crowd turned its attention to the large antislavery sign suspended from the windows of the meeting hall and shouted for its removal. Two of the ringleaders—Dimmock and Williams—swaggered up to the mayor, who had come downstairs with the women, and demanded the sign. The mayor, thinking to prevent rock-throwing that would inevitably break windows along with the sign, acquiesced and dispatched a constable with them to remove the sign from its hooks. Although Lyman insisted later that he intended to avert violence by having the sign stored in the hall, Dimmock and Williams, predictably, hurled the hated signboard to the street, where it was quickly smashed to splinters.

As the crowd began shouting once more for Garrison and the owner of the building hurried up to demand protection for his property, the mayor raced back to the meeting hall, hoping to be able to dispel the crowd with a report that Garrison was not on the premises. Instead Lyman came face to face with the editor himself, looking very composed, even cheerful, standing in the center of the room, conferring with Burleigh and Samuel Sewall, who had pressed past the constables to see to his friend's safety.

The mayor expostulated that he had no way of protecting either the building or Garrison and simply urged him to flee. The editor's companions were explaining that they could find no rear exit when John Reid Campbell, a young abolitionist who had somehow slipped into the hall, came up with a scheme for dropping out a second-floor window onto the roof of an adjoining shed and thence out the back alley (Wilson's Lane) and away from the crowd out front.

While Campbell took Garrison by the arm to make the escape, the mayor engaged in a little charade. He bade the sheriff go to the window and tell the crowd that after diligent search no sign of Garrison could be found in the building, and then Lyman went downstairs and repeated the message himself. The crowd groaned and stood still, unsure of its next move. The mayor was mentally congratulating himself on having diminished the danger of a "boisterous night" when a huge shout arose from around the corner, and the crowd surged toward the noise.

"They've got him! They've got him!," ran the cry.

The mayor hurried along, following his people, toward City Hall.

When Garrison and Campbell dropped from the window to the shed roof, they had hoped to run out into Wilson's Lane, but the alleyway proved clogged with people. They ducked instead into a carpenter's shop on the corner. The sympathetic proprietor quickly barred the door. The editor said that resistance was futile and he would give himself up, but Campbell insisted that Garrison had a duty to evade capture as long as he could, and with the help of the shop's apprentice, they tucked him in a corner of the upstairs loft and piled planks in front of the hiding place.

Ruffians soon broke in the door, grabbed Campbell, and pummeled him to divulge Garrison's whereabouts. The young man remained tight-lipped, but one of the shop lads silently pointed to the loft, and in an instant Garrison was pulled from his corner and a rope fastened three times about his chest. Accomplices outside thrust a ladder up to the loft window, and his captors ordered Garrison to step onto the sill and go down the ladder while they held him, leashed like an animal, by the rope.

The editor bowed to the crowd as he crouched, sitting forward, on the ladder and began his descent. Hatless, with wood shavings clinging to his bald head, and his arms askew as he gripped the ladder, Garrison looked the epitome of Christian suffering as he slowly lowered himself toward the mob, waiting in the late-afternoon gloom for its prize.

The hastily looped rope slipped from Garrison's body as he gained the final rung, and the editor hunched himself against the expected rain of blows. Instead he felt himself grabbed by two muscular men, Daniel and Buff Cooley, truckmen not previously noted for their antislavery views, but who were somehow moved to pity by Garrison's plight and repelled by the cries of the lynch mob around them. Shouting, "You can't hurt him," the Cooley brothers propelled Garrison by his shoulders and charged up Wilson's Lane toward State Street. Angry men yelling "Hang him on the Common" and other threats grabbed at Garrison, rending his clothes and breaking his glasses as they sought vainly to dislodge the editor from the Cooleys' grasp. The rescue party pressed through the mob into the square where British soldiers had killed five colonists in the infamous Boston Massacre of 1770. Now the grandsons of patriots were howling for the blood of the agitator who demanded fulfillment of the Revolutionary creed.

Rounding City Hall, the Cooleys saw Mayor Lyman on the south steps with two constables, and in a last stumbling rush, they shoved Garrison over their shoulders into the arms of the officers, who backed into the building, bundling the editor and mayor together as they stumbled over the threshold and shut the doors. The constables hurried Garrison up to Lyman's office, while the mayor told the crowds at the north and south doors that he would maintain law and order at all hazards.

For the second time in an hour the mayor and the editor faced each other in an upstairs room while a potential lynch mob yelled its fury in the street below. Disheveled, breathless, and disoriented owing to the loss of his spectacles, Garrison stood silently as Lyman told him that his presence made the building unsafe. With the city records to think of, and the main post office on the ground floor, the mayor explained, he could protect Garrison only by lodging him overnight in the city jail.

"I am passive in your hands," the editor said, keeping the pressure on Lyman, who proceeded to work out a double ruse. He had the sheriff swear out a warrant—"a mere matter of form," they said—and ordered two coaches, one for each entrance. Dressed in a borrowed coat and pantaloons, Garrison would be hustled out the north door while a few constables faked his departure on the south side of the building.

The feint worked only long enough to get Garrison into the coach. Just as the driver cracked his whip and lurched forward, the alarm went up. Men proceeded to throw themselves on the wheels while others drew knives and attempted to cut the horses' traces. Freely striking his whip at the crowd, the driver—a black man, though his name was never recorded—broke free of the melee and headed at a breakneck pace toward Bowdoin Square and the Charles River Bridge, only later doubling back toward the jail in Leverett Street, situated in the West End only a few blocks from the Garrisons' flat on Brighton Street. A small crowd had gathered in front of the somber brick building, but Garrison was easily whisked through it and lodged in a cell by suppertime. The mayor posted extra guards along Washington Street and near *The Liberator*'s office on Cornhill, but there proved to be no further trouble.

Garrison recovered his spirits in the course of the evening. Knapp, Whittier, and Bronson Alcott all came to visit, and the editor joked that the mayor had certainly removed some incendiary matter from the post office. Later came John B. Vashon, who brought the editor a new hat and the news from

Helen. She had left Caroline Weston in Court Street when they could not get through the crowd and, after checking in vain for Garrison at *The Liberator's* office, had prudently gone home. She had wanted to rush down to City Hall when news came of the mob attack, but some abolitionist friends, the John Fullers, had taken her home with them instead. She knew that Garrison would be true to his principles, she said, but felt chagrined that she had not joined the other women at Mrs. Chapman's house. (The lamps at West Street blazed until nearly midnight as the excited abolitionists reviewed the day's events and debated furiously with callers who tried to dissuade them from further activity. When one pompous friend intoned that he spoke "as a man just from a *mob*," Maria retorted, "And I listen as a *woman* just from a mob.")

His brush with martyrdom left Garrison elated. "Give me brickbats in the cause of God, to wedges of gold in the cause of sin," he said. With spiritual ardor he inscribed a message on the jailhouse wall: "William Lloyd Garrison was put into this cell on Wednesday afternoon, October 21, 1835, to save him from the violence of a 'respectable and influential' mob, who sought to destroy him for preaching the abominable and dangerous doctrine that 'all men are created equal' and that all oppression is odious in the sight of God. 'Hail Columbia! . . .'"

Taken before the magistrates for a *pro forma* hearing, however, Garrison was outraged to discover that the mayor's complaint had actually pressed criminal charges against himself "and thirty or more unknown persons" for an unlawful and riotous assembly that disturbed the peace. The judge dismissed the charges, but joined the mayor and the sheriff in earnest solicitations that Garrison leave the city until tempers cooled. They offered to drive him to Dedham, where he would be reunited with his wife and put on the train for Providence. (Mayor Lyman had paid a "cold and unsympathetic" call, Helen said later, to inform her of the plan.) By nightfall the young couple had taken refuge in Friendship's Vale, leaving what Garrison called "the Ephesian uproar" behind.

Thursday's papers said "what might have been expected of them," Mrs. Chapman's sister, Deborah Weston, groused. The *Daily Advertiser* regarded "the assemblage not so much as a *riot* as the *prevention of a riot*," while the *Atlas* reported that the abolitionists had willfully caused a disturbance that culminated with Garrison being properly jailed as "a public agitator." The *Patriot* deplored the unpleasant consequences that ensued "when women turn reformers," and the *Transcript* expressed satisfaction that Boston had put forward a respectable mob that did not reek of the *canaille* who gave a bad odor to such business in other cities. Homer's *Commercial Gazette,* however, coined the tag phrase that the abolitionists would sarcastically repeat for a generation: the scene in Washington Street and at City Hall, the paper said, was nothing but "a meeting of *gentlemen of property and stand-*

ing from all parts of the city" determined to preserve the peace against domestic incendiaries.

Some Bostonians tried to pretend that nothing had happened. At a Beacon Hill soirée that night, Edmund Quincy, who had seen the mob from his State Street office window, heard nothing from his dinner partner but a chatty account of her European wedding tour. The English radical writer Harriet Martineau, who spent a good deal of time in Boston in the autumn of 1835, commented that she heard "very striking facts which had taken place in broad daylight vehemently and honestly denied" by local residents, whose "ignorance and unconcern" she considered "one of the most hideous features of the times." "I suppose, while Luther was toiling and thundering, German ladies and gentlemen were supping and dancing as usual," Martineau sighed.

The Liberator broadcast the story as only it could. For three days, Knapp, Burleigh, and the apprentice Thomas Paul worked like fury to get the paper out with as much fresh material as they could obtain on short notice, including a graphic account of the scenes inside 46 Washington from Burleigh himself. At the height of the rush, however, Garrison and Knapp's landlord developed a sudden concern about fire and summarily evicted the printers from their Cornhill office. The paper, which normally came out on Saturday, was delayed until Monday afternoon, as Knapp scrambled to have another shop complete the presswork. "Where the Liberator press is we can't tell," Anne Weston told a correspondent, "but it is somewhere or other printing away."

As for the editor, the Bostonians wanted him back, but the Bensons wished him to stay in Brooklyn, where Helen, everyone agreed, would remain until after the baby's birth. Brother George soon worked out an acceptable compromise: the editor would dispose of the Brighton Street house and store the furniture, but visit the city at regular intervals to attend to business and give the lie to critics. On Wednesday, November 4, 1835, exactly two weeks after the uproar, Garrison returned to Boston. Though he ordered the coachman to drop him at the Fullers' instead of 23 Brighton, there was scant need for caution. "I did not prove to be so great a curiosity, as I anticipated," Garrison reported to Helen. He walked the streets unmolested, slept peaceably at home with the cat curled up on Helen's side of the bed, had long and happy evenings socializing with abolitionist friends, and made a quiet visit to George Thompson's hideout at the Southwicks' for a farewell embrace with his friend, who had clearly outlived his usefulness in America and needed to be safely dispatched for home. Thompson had written an eloquent public letter against mob rule, but Garrison cherished even more the sound of his friend's laughter as he boomed from the Southwicks' staircase, "*Such* a mob—30 ladies routed and a 6×2 board demolished by 4,000 men!" (In New York gents of property and standing laughed at their side's version of the affair: a commemorative lithograph depicting a top-hatted crowd denouncing a roped and cowering Garrison while "the Scotch Ambassador" Thompson flees the scene disguised in a woman's plaid cloak and frilly bonnet.)

Having no printing office, Garrison conducted his editorial business from 46 Washington, while Knapp got the paper "set up in driblets," as best he could, in other establishments. "Impossibilities must not be expected of us by our subscribers," Garrison said, though he groused about Knapp's sloppy proofreading. " 'Tis a blundering world," he sighed to Helen and invoked the old catchphrase from his *Herald* days, " 'twill all be the same in a thousand years." Nonetheless, *The Liberator* in those trying weeks never missed an issue and kept up a lively debate on the mayor's conduct in the affair, with some writers emphasizing that Lyman had saved the editor's life and others criticizing the mayor's indulgence of violence. The discussion illuminated both the abolitionists' insistence upon their civil rights and the nefarious alliance between slavery's apologists and the civil authorities. The mob had created "a thousand debaters in place of one," said Garrison. It also made new abolitionists. Some of the editor's most steadfast colleagues in later years, including the patricians Edmund Quincy and Wendell Phillips, dated their "conversions" from the day of the mob. A prosperous broker, Francis Jackson, who would become Garrison's ardent champion and patron, made a grand public gesture by opening his handsome house in the South End to the women's November meeting. Pledging that "one house at least" in the city should be consecrated to free speech even if it courted mob attack, Jackson declared that his roof and walls could not "crumble in a better cause. . . . As slavery cannot exist with free discussion, so neither can liberty breathe without it." Jackson's words deserved "to be printed in letters of gold," Garrison said.

Garrison capitalized upon the uproar so well that Harriet Martineau, who had passed most of her Boston visit among the Unitarian liberals in the Channing circle, insisted upon meeting him. She had heard "every species of abuse" about him and thought "in fairness" that she ought to judge him for herself. As a much-applauded writer of tracts on political and moral economy, Martineau would be an important catch for the movement. In her twenty months in America, she had toured the plantations of the South and supped with the courtly leaders, including former president James Madison, who held black people in bondage, and she shared her observations with the college presidents and clergymen who were her hosts in New England. Despite her formidable reputation and forbidding appearance—jut-jawed and stiff-necked—people enjoyed talking to her. Though quite deaf, she used an ear trumpet with dexterity and confidence and charmed people with her pleasant, even gossipy conversational style.

At the end of December 1835, while Garrison was in Boston on what would likely be his last trip before Helen's confinement, he met with Martineau at the home of Dr. Channing's assistant pastor. Garrison seldom ventured into such elite parlors and initially put off the Englishwoman with "excessive agitation" over her willingness to meet one " 'so odious' " as himself. (She shrewdly judged, however, that Garrison had more difficulty accepting kindness than abuse and settled him down to chat.) Martineau found Garrison's talk to be "as gladsome as his countenance, and as gentle as his voice," she wrote, "and completely lacking in the deliberate harshness" that she disliked in his writing. "He gives his reasons for his severity with a calmness, meekness, and softness which contrast strongly with the subject of the discourse, and which convince the objector that there is principle at the bottom of the practice." They spoke for several hours, after which Martineau pronounced Garrison "an original" who was, by far, "the most bewitching personage" she had met in the entire country.

In Martineau's estimation, Garrison ranked as the "master-mind of the revolution" that would transform the intensely materialistic, slave-ridden culture of Jacksonian America into a truer realization of republican freedom. He had molded the abolitionists into a "a body of persons who are living by faith" and goading America into a new "martyr age" of reformation. Their advanced views had cut them off from ordinary society, she observed, but their commitments had enriched their lives and ennobled them as the "spiritual potentates" of the era.

Martineau understood what many closer to home had not yet realized. Garrison had made himself into a new kind of American agitator who sought political ends through spiritual means. He drew upon the egalitarian ideology of the American Revolution as well as the Romantic disposition to grasp large truths intuitively and embody them in personal action, yet he animated his enterprise with the fervor of militant, messianic Protestantism. He was, variously, a pamphleteer, a prophet, an apostle, and a poet, and at times of highest controversy, all of these at once. It was as if he had put a Bible in the hands of a defiant Byronic hero who condemned conventional society in the name of Christian purity rather than demonic self-indulgence.

In the five years since Garrison had established *The Liberator* he had accomplished exactly what he had promised to do. He had made himself heard on the subject of slavery and made the issue one that Americans could no longer ignore. In 1831 his paper had been half its present size and the only one in the country to advocate immediate emancipation. In December 1835, Garrison boasted, thirty-six papers "openly defended" the doctrine and many others felt obliged to print articles favorable to the cause. In 1831 no organization in the country supported immediatism; now, in addition to the American Anti-Slavery Society, there were seven state societies and more than five hundred local auxiliaries, all stirring up the issue and awakening their churches, their political parties, and their governments to the requirements of racial justice.

Just as Garrison's Baltimore imprisonment had confirmed his personal character as a dissident, his Boston mobbing symbolized the dedication of the movement. As Christian and Faithful had suffered for Christ's vision, so, too, would the abolitionists suffer and bear witness for the slaves. They would make themselves into weapons, and people who remained unpersuaded by their arguments would be shamed by their willingness to endure abuse. Another quarter century would pass, and other martyrs would fall, before Boston would send its sons away to war singing, "As He died to make men holy, let us die to make men free," but the preparation for that grave hour began on the afternoon when William Lloyd Garrison walked down a carpenter's ladder with a rope around his body.

BOOK THREE

AND PRESS WITH VIGOR ON

1836-1844

GARRISON AT THIRTY-FIVE

*Lithograph c. 1840 by P.S. Duval from a daguerreotype by T. B. Shew
(Sophia Smith Collection, Smith College)*

CHAPTER ELEVEN

A UNIVERSAL EMANCIPATION FROM SIN

THE SALEM ARTIST WHO PAINTED WILLIAM LLOYD GARRISON'S PORTRAIT
IN 1835 PLACED HIM AT A WRITING DESK WITH A SHEET OF NEWSPAPER IN
HIS HAND. THE EDITOR, DRESSED IN HIS PLAIN WHITE SHIRT AND BLACK
coat, is sitting face-forward in a red upholstered chair in front of a large
window. On the desk are displayed several gilt-bound books and a quill pen,
and through the window can be seen a parklike estate, complete with a pond
and a turreted mansion house. Despite the incongruous setting, more flattering to the materialistic aspirations of the seaport's merchant elite than to
the visionary editor, the artist—M. C. Torrey—caught something of the
ethereal mildness that always confounded people expecting to meet a monster. Garrison's intent, wide-open eyes stare directly at the viewer, not in
confrontation, but brimful of sympathy, and his straight full lips verge on a
warmhearted smile. The high forehead and wire-rim spectacles give him a
studious air, though he is sitting very erect, head pressed forward, in a manner that hints more at restless energy than intellectual reflection. Yet there
is an appealingly gentle aura about this man, his pale face glowing with a
light that seems to come from within, that sets him apart from the prosperous businessmen who formed the artist's usual clientele. Most striking of all,
however, is how young Garrison looks. Despite the early baldness, his
smooth skin (bluish at the jaw from his closely shaved dark beard), his thick
black eyebrows, and his remnant of brown hair all indicate his youth. He
did not turn thirty until two months after the mobbing. To a striking degree,
his mild countenance matches his confident belief, inspired by the apostle
Paul, that the abolitionists would prevail through "the foolishness of preaching."

The mob confirmed Garrison's identity as a holy fool and prompted him
toward ever more radical expressions of a faith in "practical holiness" that
challenged the established institutions of church and state. As his career in
agitation deepened, he saw his task as raising "the standard of Christian
revolt against the powers of darkness" and came more and more to insist
that the clergymen and politicians who made their compromises with social
evil were as much Satanic agents of misrule as the slaveholders themselves.
He had felt the necessity—in John Milton's phrase—for "reforming the Reformation" and thought of himself as an apostle of radical Christian liberty
in the Miltonic tradition. The bedrock of his faith remained the Protestant's

right of private conscience, but he began to put the abolitionist argument in the context of a perfectionist quest to establish the Kingdom of God on earth and to profess a religious faith unburdened by formal theology or ceremonial practices.

Garrison's vision proved immensely appealing to many conscientious souls, already discontented in belief and searching for higher truths in an America where the values of a self-sufficient agrarian society were yielding to the complex ways of an urban, commercial, and industrial age. For the rest of their lives the men and women who became abolitionists in the 1830s cherished memories of "the missionary work of the old *Liberator* days" when, as Lydia Maria Child put it, "the Holy Spirit did actually descend upon men and women in tongues of flame" and prompted them to act joyously together "in a glow of faith." Theirs was a religious fellowship, and for many individuals the decision to join the movement proved an epochal manifestation of the spirit in their lives. At the very end of the nineteenth century an elderly Boston woman reminded the Garrison children that for sixty-eight years she had regarded their father as her "savior from a cold and selfish life" and believed that she owed more to him "for spiritual joy and growth than all other influences combined."

Yet Garrison's growing personal power in spiritual matters threatened the established clergy, and his growing alienation from the American mainstream alarmed political leaders, who had begun to assess the potential weight of an antislavery voting bloc. If Garrison and his coadjutors thought of themselves as apostolic bearers of new light that would transform their sufferings into a new dispensation, their antagonists regarded them as fanatics, in the strict religious sense of the epithet, which, ever since the English Civil War, had characterized sectarian dissenters whose mistaken enthusiasm bred a mania that jeopardized the safety of church and state. While the abolitionists likened Garrison to a Luther or a Knox, their opposition portrayed him as a deluded Anabaptist, Ranter, or Fifth Monarchy man from the mystical fringe of antinomian heretics. For Garrison's temerity in branding the church complacent and unfeeling and seeking to revitalize it from the outside, the Northern clergy condemned him as a usurper. For his skepticism about politics as the vehicle of moral reform and his spiritual vision of an unselfish, loving society, party-minded managers and aspirants scorned him as an anarchist.

Garrison's insistence upon speaking his mind on all issues raised fresh and provocative questions about the relationship between the abolitionist vanguard and the established institutions of American life. Over the decade from 1836 to 1846, the conflict both broadened and deepened. To the Garrisonian attack upon the slaveholding South and its Northern apologists there was added a profound quarrel with moderate clergymen and their nationally organized church denominations and a prolonged internal struggle in the movement to identify the points of leverage, if any, upon the two national political parties, whose shared need to suppress all discussion of slavery had thus far kept the abolitionists at bay. The editor's role would be to take abolition to the farthest reaches of the political community and dare his countrymen to follow. Even when they remained behind, Garrison's effort changed the contours of the landscape they inhabited. To those who complained that the editor's innovations retarded the antislavery cause, he would reply that it made about as much sense to claim that Fulton's steamboats had injured navigation or the growth of railroads obstructed transportation. To the onrushing technological forces that had so rapidly transformed commercial society Garrison would supply the sweeping and irreversible moral power of an abolitionist movement committed to righting the wrongs of a disordered world.

It took some time for the editor's deeper vision to express itself. His brush with martyrdom had shaken Garrison, who despaired of a society that found itself more willing to direct violence at Christian prophets than to address the evils against which they preached, and he wondered how else it might be called to account. With his mind heaving on many questions, Garrison on New Year's Day 1836 acted upon a friend's suggestion that he begin a diary, for in the solitude of Friendship's Vale he anticipated an opportunity for serious reflection. Yet Garrison's slender leather-bound booklet saw little use. Lacking the pressure of strict deadlines, Garrison found it difficult to write. He procrastinated. He became tongue-tied and distracted; he made a few entries in the first week that might have served as the opening sentences for essays, but he failed to pursue them. He picked up the book only to put it down again after writing the date and a bit about the weather. The diary proved so uncongenial a form that by January 16 he had stopped his daily efforts and made only sporadic efforts at fresh starts on the first of February and March. In April he ceased to do even that.

Garrison never wrote in a quest for self-knowledge, but in an effort to persuade others of what he already knew. Neither a formal nor a systematic thinker, he had no bent for introspection. He was not a philosopher, but a journalist and polemicist who improvised variations on a few grand themes as the moment required, caring less for logic than effect and cutting so bold a public figure as "the happy warrior" that he found it difficult, except in communion with his closest friends, to probe his private doubts. His fresh thoughts tended to be expressed piecemeal, as specific instances in the course of agitation provoked first a few remarks, then an editorial column, and finally an extended rebuttal to critics.

Garrison worked best in his capacity as the editor of *The Liberator*. Even in absentia, he took an aggressive interest in the paper. Though he wrote nothing himself for several months, he had liberal amounts of contradictory advice for his deputies Henry Benson and Charles Burleigh, telling them first to *make everything else give way* to full coverage of the debates on the abolitionists' petitions in Congress, then reminding them to run shorter articles that would not tax the reader's patience. Into each mailbag from Brooklyn, Garrison stuffed a fat bundle of clippings he had compiled from the exchange newspapers. The editor's workrooms always overflowed with newspapers waiting to be digested, and the sight of Garrison, shears in hand, making neat fan-shaped piles of material became a characteristic memory to his children.

The editor did not find his voice again until what he called the "important question of *domestic emancipation*" was resolved at Friendship's Vale. Not even the annual MAS meeting could draw him away from his wife's side as her confinement approached. The days dragged into weeks. When the prospective father grew more anxious than the expectant mother herself, Helen ordered him to Providence for the Rhode Island state antislavery convention, which provided a distracting tonic. Even after Garrison hurried back on the frozen roads, however, he had to wait another week before his wife's labor commenced in the middle of a wintry night. At last, on February 13, 1836, he made a heartfelt entry in his diary: "A fine little son was born to me, this day, at 12 o'clock, for which precious gift I desire to thank God. The mother and child are doing well. The latter weighs 8 pounds, and shall be named George ~~Benson~~ Thompson Garrison." They had compromised on the name so as to honor both the family patriarch and their nonconformist principles, though the substitution irked Helen's father, especially after a caustic editor in Norwich suggested that they name their next son after Benedict Arnold.

Cradling his child, the besotted father felt overwhelmed by "streams of emotion," which he channeled into verse. With his own child pressed to his bosom, the grief of enslaved fathers and mothers pierced Garrison's heart as never before. Five sonnets flowed from his pen quickly enough to be published in the very next *Liberator,* where they drew tears from Samuel J. May, Bronson Alcott, and many other readers. The poems dedicated the baby to the fight for Liberty and Truth and drew a sympathetic bond between free- and slave-born infants and their claim to birthrights of equal dignity and power. Promising to brave any danger to rescue all the children of bondage, the poet anticipated that if he fell a martyr, the babe would "early fill my vacant post/ and . . . Charge valiantly OPPRESSION'S mighty host." Yet Garrison scarcely imagined that his son would be grown to manhood and standing by his side in a soldier's uniform when the day of liberation finally arrived.

Garrison's interval of silence ironically coincided with a period of growth and acceptance for the movement. On the very day of the Boston attack, vigilantes had also mobbed an abolitionist meeting in Utica, which regrouped in even greater numbers in Peterboro to form an organization for all of New York, the largest state in the Union. (The mob had finally pushed into the immediatist camp the erratic philanthropist Gerrit Smith, who had contributed nearly $10,000 to the ACS and not long before had considered both Lundy and Garrison too radical; over the next ten years Smith would contribute more than $40,000 to the immediatists' cause.) From Ohio, Theodore Dwight Weld reported that the rowdies who disrupted his meetings with drums, tin horns, and sleigh bells "ding dong'd like bedlam let loose," had "mobbed *up* the cause vastly more than I could have *lectured it up*." Abridgments of free speech had prompted many editors and citizens to think more favorably about the abolition question, and so many antislavery societies sprang up in the little towns that stretched from New England to the Great Lakes states that by May 1836, the AAS had doubled in size, with a roster of more than five hundred local auxiliaries in fifteen states. In county after county men and women asked their neighbors to sign petitions calling upon Congress to abolish slavery in the District of Columbia. "Keep the mill a-going," Garrison cheered, as the crudely stitched booklets and crinkled rolls of paper chugged into the capital on every postal car. (The petition signed by the Garrisons in Brooklyn stood little chance, however, for it had to be sent to their bitter antagonist Andrew T. Judson, who had parlayed his attacks upon integrated schooling into a seat in Congress.)

The groundswell of abolitionist support accelerated when Congress responded to Southern pressure by refusing to receive the carloads of antislavery petitions. After acrimonious debate the House adopted a "gag rule" that forbade printing or discussing petitions relating to slavery; such documents would be silently consigned the oblivion of being "laid on the table." The AAS held the Northern supporters of the rule up to obloquy in a huge broadside, "Slave Mart of America," that defended "the right to interfere" and contrasted, in *The Liberator*'s familiar style, scenes of the Framers reading the Declaration of Independence and a coffle of slaves appealing for justice in front of the Capitol. Editors once hostile to the cause now denounced the suppression of public opinion, and John Quincy Adams, the former president now returned to the House of Representatives, made himself memorable for his fervent efforts in opposition to the rule, which would be renewed by a coalition of Southerners and Northern Democrats at every session of Congress until the mid-1840s. No equivalent antislavery voice emerged in the Senate, where Henry Clay insisted that the body had no right to discuss what it had no power to decide and that abolitionists could not challenge in the North what were constitutionally protected property relations in the South. Of course free speech was a sacred privilege, he conceded, but when fanatics extended discussion to matters beyond the concern of their own states they twisted the principle of political freedom into unwarranted "propagandism." Attending to so specious an argument, Garrison could hardly believe that he had once considered Clay an avatar of liberty.

Yet the Kentuckian's position seemed mild next to the proposals of South Carolina's John C. Calhoun, whose bill to punish federal postmasters who delivered material deemed incendiary by state officers came within four votes of passage. Calhoun wanted Congress to reject the petitions "preemptorily," for the charade of tabling would breach the slaveholders' "frontier," he argued, and give the abolitionists a foothold that could be manipulated into a claim of "permanent jurisdiction." Abolition had passed from the hands of "harmless Quakers" and become the business of "ferocious zealots" with unlimited funds, Calhoun warned, and he urged Southerners to defend slavery as "a good—a great good" and counter the malign influence of Northern extremists whose "misguided and false humanity" would sever the Union and ignite a deadly race war.

The Liberator gave extended space to Calhoun's speeches, and Garrison recognized him at once as the most implacable and determined of slavery's advocates. Indeed, the editor came to respect Calhoun's bold and forthright defiance and preferred his candor to the equivocal positions taken by men like Clay, who harbored hopes of maintaining a national Whig constituency for another presidential campaign. Calhoun, too, nursed his political ambitions, but pitched his strategy upon a polarized situation that would unite the South behind his sectional candidacy. In Calhoun Garrison found the perfect Satanic antihero—"his conscience is seared as with a hot iron, his heart is a piece of adamant"—whose powerful talents made him "the champion of hell-born slavery" even as Garrison marshaled his forces in defense of equality. The two men proved so well matched in their absolutism that it has tempted posterity to condemn them equally as extremists, but as Wendell Phillips later emphasized, in the 1830s Garrison was the only man north of the Mason-Dixon line willing to challenge Calhoun's brazen logic and declare the issue to be one of right and wrong. When Calhoun insisted slavery was *right*, Phillips said, Webster and Clay "shrank from him and evaded his assertion. Garrison, alone . . . met him face to face, proclaiming slavery a sin and daring all the inferences."

While Northern opinion might share Garrison's view of the monomaniacal Calhoun, it still proved unwilling to accept the editor's own righteous logic. Though Calhoun's aggressive "positive good" position gave the lie to gradualism, many of the people who defended the abolitionists against the gag rule and the mobs nonetheless remained hostile to immediatism, and Garrison worried that the surge of new friends would moderate the platform and take the movement out of the radicals' hands. "We have blasted the rocks . . . and macadamised the road," Garrison wrote, "and now the big folks are riding upon it in their coaches as proudly as if they had made it all. . . . they mean if possible to monopolize it all, and to transfer the credit of its design and completion to themselves!"

He needed to look no further than Boston's Federal Street Church for an example of the threat. The august William Ellery Channing had broken his years of silence in December 1835 with a 160-page pamphlet that both made a compelling philosophical case against slavery and condemned abolitionist methods for bringing it to a speedy end. Channing dismissed the concept of slave property as a "false and groundless" claim against "the essential equality of men" and insisted that no law could make slavery morally acceptable. The sacrifice of one human being to another's will "is the greatest violence which can be offered to any creature of God," Channing wrote. Yet the Unitarian leader refused to "pass sentence on the character of the slaveholder" or advocate any action that would "put in jeopardy the peace of the slave-holding States." Although Channing criticized the suppression of abolitionist speech "by lawless force" as "a worse evil than abolitionism," he did not spare the immediatists. He condemned their principle as "a precipitate action" that would hurt the slaves, and he advised abolitionists to abandon their "showy, noisy" societies and pursue "wiser and milder means" of expression that relied instead upon "the voice of the Individual . . . and not the shout of a crowd." He especially hoped that they would refrain further from reaching out to the multitude of "excitable and unenlightened" colored people who might thereby be prompted to organize a slave revolt.

The immediatists divided in their response to Channing's effort. Samuel J. May contended that the pamphlet, though flawed by inconsistency, brought the antislavery argument into parlors and counting rooms that the apostles could not enter. Others, however, groused that it only gave new sanction to timidity, and they pointed to the high praise Channing garnered from orthodox church leaders such as Dr. Leonard Bacon, who praised the Christian spirit with which the essay had distinguished between the immediatists' provocative demand and what Bacon lauded as "the *immediate duty*" of "commencing a process" which should result in the slaves' liberation "at the earliest date consistent with their well-being." Such tepid reformulations seemed a poor harvest for abolitionist labor. Maria Child, rueing the hours of vaporous talks with Channing she had endured, wrote a public letter defending Garrison's "honest enthusiasm" against the ineffectual "graceful flickerings of Northern Lights" such as Channing, but the newspapers spiked it. *The Liberator,* however, tweaked the minister when it ran, under the dry heading "Severity of the Abolitionists," a passage from Channing's earlier essay on John Milton in which he had defended the Puritan writer's strong language with the argument that "God's most powerful messengers" had to speak in "piercing and awful tones" because nations could not be shaken with "soft and tender accents."

Garrison urged people to think for themselves and not to be gulled by Channing. If abolitionists allowed "a great doctor-of-divinity-worshipping public" to believe that Channing had "discovered" truths they had preached for years, they would forfeit their identity as a movement and find themselves silenced on the great points—immediatism and equality—that Channing had not yet accepted. "The Dr. is still for *gradualism,*" the editor emphasized in a two-column *Liberator* editorial that enumerated twenty-five objections to the work. Channing's book lacked "reforming power" because it was "a work in active collision with itself" and separated "the sinner from his sin" with extenuating arguments that paralleled those of slaveholders and colonizationists. In a mocking litany beginning "the Dr. says . . ." Garrison demonstrated that Channing's condescension toward black people and his injunctions to disband the antislavery societies, abandon immediatism, and cease from agitation could hardly be distinguished from the demands of Senator Calhoun himself. " 'He that is not with us is against us,' " Garrison warned.

The editor's blast quickened his friends' hopes that Garrison would resume his residence in Boston, but he remained sequestered in Brooklyn, preoccupied with the baby and his thoughts. "Dordie Tompit"—as the doting parents called him—had "no lack of attendants," Garrison told friends, and "we think he is a pretty child, *of course.*" He diverted himself with merry games with the baby, sometimes carrying him into town to weigh the boy on the grocer's scale, and delighted in long walks with Helen and the affectionate warmth of the Benson family circle.

Garrison's associates, however, grew impatient with his prolonged "rustication." "Your child—the Liberator—your eldest child, is suffering, as all children do, by the Father's absence," Henry C. Wright told the editor in April 1836, and all his associates wanted to see him at "the famous 46" when they went to the office. The friends speculated among themselves that Garrison was remaining in Brooklyn either as an economy measure or in deference to Helen's wishes. If expenses were the issue, Wright hinted, the MAS board would find a way to help Garrison "think, speak, write, and thunder in Boston." If the problem was an emotional one, Wright advised, "Tell your dear wife she must consider that you were wedded for life or death to another, before you gave her your heart and soul." Brother Wright, an itinerant minister who had grown impatient with the orthodox church, may have spoken with such presumption because he largely lived apart from his own wife, a Newburyport widow some years his senior. Garrison took his plea kindly but explained that Wright had to understand that Friendship's Vale was "indeed a *home,* most desirable in itself, suited to my love of retirement, and of course peculiarly endearing to my dear Helen," though she would follow wherever he needed to go.

It seemed that Garrison was stepping aside. He made several visits to the city as spring came on, but he complained of the crowded streets and "the din of enterprise" in his ears. Although he attended the major spring meetings in New York and Boston, Garrison deliberately kept himself in the background, refusing invitations to speak or manage the proceedings. "We have now so much talent enlisted on our side that I am actually needed no more than a fifth wheel to a coach . . ." he confided to Helen. "Besides, I am an old hack in the cause, and as a new broom sweeps clean, it is better to let some of our new converts have a chance."

Garrison did promise his friends that he would be more industrious about material for *The Liberator,* but despite his avowals that bucolic peace facilitated his writing, he contributed comparatively little to the newspaper. It was not for lack of topics. In 1836, for the first time in the fifteen years since the Missouri Compromise, the nation faced the admission of new states to the Union and another potential crisis. Michigan had grown large enough for statehood, but its recognition, which would give the North two more votes in the Senate, was obstructed by Southern leaders until the admission of Arkansas, the last slave territory in the Louisiana Purchase, could also be approved as a counterweight. The insistence upon a paired admission in deference to the protocol of the Missouri Compromise infuriated the abolitionists precisely because it had the practical result of keeping the slavery issue out of national politics. "Delivering twins" honored the prior agreement to tolerate slavery south of the 36°30' line and accepted sectional balancing as the price of union.

Just as the Arkansas issue faded, however, the antislavery movement faced an unprecedented and far more threatening situation in the Mexican province of Texas, where insurgent American settlers had revolted against the central government and in 1836 declared themselves an independent republic. Southern politicians at once urged an expansion of the Union to include Texas, a vast territory of uncertain boundaries, but lying outside of the Louisiana Purchase and presumably not subject to the compromise line. Partisans of Texas annexation loudly declared that anywhere from five to nine new states could be carved out of this southwestern domain, and slavery could be lawful and profitable in every single one of them.

Abolitionists immediately countered with a blunt attack on the Texas rebels, whose defeat at the Alamo in March 1836 and subsequent victory at San Jacinto six weeks later had attracted sympathetic press coverage as the triumph of a Protestant minority over Catholic despotism. Texas freedom meant Southern slavery, charged David L. Child, in a series of articles based on a study of the American penetration of Texas. The rebels—most of whom were slaveholding planters from the lower South—sought escape from Mexico's abolition law of 1829, which had rendered their investments precarious, and Child claimed (accurately, it turned out) that they had the backing of land speculators from Nashville to New York, proslavery politicians in Washington, and the covert support of President Jackson himself, whose Tennessee protégé and comrade-in-arms Sam Houston had led the revolt and become the Texas president. Much the same story emerged from confidential letters sent to John Quincy Adams by Benjamin Lundy, who had spent several years in Texas hoping to gain land for a settlement of manumitted slaves. Adams worked Lundy's material into powerful speeches in Congress that rallied so strong an anti-Texas view in the Northern states that Jackson, whose term was coming to an end, felt obliged to back away from the much-bruited annexation proposal in order not to fracture the Democratic Party and jeopardize the succession of his vice-president, New York's Martin Van Buren. The abolitionists kept up a steady anti-Texas noise in their petition campaigns of 1836–37, and once in office, Van Buren, who had no personal ties with the Texans and a necessarily high regard for party unity, discouraged the annexationists.

The issue remained in abeyance for almost a decade, but it had demonstrated beyond a doubt that the slavery question, once it got onto the agenda, would disrupt the national party system. The Texas furor also suggested that the abolitionists could make more headway with the Northern public on questions involving sectional power and the extension of slavery than they could upon immediate emancipation. The ramifications would take some time to work out, and Garrison, who had given extensive coverage to Texas without writing much about it himself, found antislavery politics a challenging puzzle. This is a problem abolitionists must overcome, Garrison thought, without becoming politicians themselves.

Garrison wrote little on antislavery because he was ruminating on "other great subjects . . . which are of the utmost importance to the temporal and eternal welfare of man." Though he never acknowledged it explicitly, Garrison underwent an intellectual and religious transformation during his interval of seclusion in Brooklyn that turned him more iconoclastic than ever and pushed him further into a life of opposition to the American social institutions: the church, the law, the political party. Staring into the violent face of the mob in October 1835 made him deeply aware of the rawness of American society, and he began to think about pacifism as a rule for living. If Christians endured barbarous treatment unresistingly, "without resorting either to their own physical energies, or to the force of human law, for restitution or punishment," would this exert a transforming influence upon the world? For two hours one evening in December 1835, he earnestly discussed this question in Boston with Henry C. Wright, who had launched his own pilgrimage after growing disgusted with the complacent orthodox clergy. Garrison's views "are not yet clear and enlarged," Wright noted, "though he has got hold of the right principle."

Garrison had considered himself a pacifist for most of his adult life. He had paid fines for refusing to attend militia exercises, though he groused that his nearsightedness, if not his conscience, should have exempted him from service. He had admired the "peace principles" of his father-in-law, George Benson, had joined the American Peace Society, which opposed international war as an instrument of policy, and had supported the "ultra" argument that the APS ought to oppose "defensive" war as well. In his conversations with Wright, moreover, who had lectured for a season under the APS banner, Garrison had become convinced of the relationship between abolition and pacifism. It was a "glaring absurdity," they said, for Christians to condemn war and uphold the violent authority of the plantation master. "What is slavery," Wright asked, "but the carrying out of the war principle and spirit to the end?" Over the next few years, as Garrison pondered the Biblical injunction to "resist not evil" (Matt. 5:38–39) as a rule for abolitionists, the more willing he became to explore its application to other temporal spheres and embrace a form of Christian anarchism. If human beings were to live by Christ's axioms alone and " 'render unto God the things that are God's,' they would not need a Caesar to rule over them," Garrison thought, and worldly society would conduct itself as the Lord's own kingdom on earth.

Even before he took inspiration from the powerfully iconoclastic Wright, Garrison had thought about the tension between secular law and the Christian spirit. Sometimes the questioning took a humorous form, as when Garrison gibed at the state-sanctioned capital punishment that put roast fowl on the Thanksgiving table. Yet, as was often the case with Garrison, there was a point behind the joke. A civil officer should not compel a thanksgiving, which ought rather to be a free outpouring of the soul; the custom of setting aside one day, moreover, implied that one's gratitude to the Lord during the rest of the year was "immaterial."

"I am growing more and more hostile to outward forms and ceremonies and observances, as a religious duty," Garrison said. He found himself pondering the apostle Paul's injunction to be a minister "not of the letter, but of the spirit: for the letter killeth but the spirit giveth life" (2 Cor. 3: 6). He had heard this passage often from his good friend Lucretia Mott, the Philadelphia Quaker who enjoyed a high reputation as a lay preacher and Biblical scholar and whom Garrison especially admired as "a bold and fearless thinker." Mrs. Mott, along with her husband, James—a textile merchant who had renounced the cotton business as immoral—offered a parental model of dignified goodness and spiritual integrity, and Garrison drew lasting inspiration from one of her favorite mottoes: "Truth for authority, not authority for truth." The Motts had endured a long decade of strife within the Society of Friends that had culminated in the institutional separation of Orthodox and Hicksite tendencies, with the Motts taking the part of the more mystical and radical Elias Hicks (1748–1830) against the increasingly rigid ceremonial practices of conservative Friends who had reverted to a more traditional Calvinism. Hicks spoke forcefully against slavery and spurned the elements of organized religion in favor of what Walt Whitman—whose parents were Hicksites—called "the universal church . . . the soul of man, invisibly rapt, ever-waiting, ever-responding to universal truths . . . in noiseless secret ecstasy and unremitted aspiration."

Though Garrison never formally joined the Society of Friends, his religious views had steadily evolved in a Quakerlike direction, a move which paralleled Helen's and the Benson family's shift a decade previously from a formal Baptist affiliation toward a more generalized respect for the inner light. Garrison always responded warmly to the familial and communal dimension that he took to be the heart of "primitive Christianity," and he shared the Hicksite perspective that ideals of justice and character could not be tailored to formal creeds, but flowed from the inward, God-inspired promptings of the soul. Like the Motts, he saw the dogma of ritual suffocating expressions of faith in the religious community, while in civil society he felt a narrow legalism thwarting the actions of conscience.

Garrison had committed himself to a life of radical defiance, and the gagging and mobbing of the abolitionists made him realize that he could no longer accept the "prevalent heresy . . . that what the law allows is right, and what it disallows is wrong." Massachusetts had once "*lawfully* hanged Quakers, wizards, and witches," he observed, and South Carolina's *laws* transformed people into chattel. Congress had used its rule to silence antislavery voices, public meetings had used their lawfully sanctioned prestige to foment mob violence, and civil officers had become their willing accomplices. Writing a decade before the Concord philosopher Henry David Thoreau lectured his townspeople on "resistance to civil government," Garrison now asserted that he did not care what "the law" allowed or forbade. "If I violate it, I will submit to the penalty, unresistingly, in imitation of Christ, and his apostles, and the holy martyrs," he said. In discerning his duty, however, Garrison would "consult no statute-book than THE BIBLE," and he would disobey legal requirements that conflicted with the spirit of the gospel, "according to the monitions of his conscience and the dictates of his understanding." The issue, Garrison now believed, was personal freedom in the service of divine justice. All public reform comes about through the "interrogation" of the law by morality, he argued; "if we are not to travel beyond 'the strict line of the law' in moral reform, then . . . a gag is put in the mouth, personal freedom is lost, and human improvement is at an end."

Garrison's iconoclasm had brought him to the verge of what Protestant theology condemned as the antinomian heresy, a belief that the workings of the indwelling spirit could place a Christian beyond the need for the moral law. Antinomianism reached as far back as the Gnostics of the second century, though New England knew it best as the challenge posed by the dissenter Anne Hutchinson to the Puritan divines of the Massachusetts Bay Colony. In the religious upheavals of the 1820s and 1830s, an antinomian tendency grew directly out of the Finneyite revival and called itself "perfectionism." Finney had insisted that sinners could be responsible for their own sins and depicted the struggle for salvation in a metaphor drawn from American politics. Sinners campaigned for the election of Satan as ruler of the world, Finney declared, but with a change of heart they could choose Jehovah as their supreme governor and consecrate themselves to His laws of love. A conversion was, in effect, a vote for God's administration and a shift from selfishness to benevolence. Finney's approach suffused Protestantism with the insurgent Jacksonian temper, and it did not take long for some of his disciples to take the great evangelist's ideas farther down the path of individual self-assertion. Could not the special workings of the spirit, they asked, bring an individual who had chosen God into a state of sinlessness, a perfect Adamic obedience to God's laws? And would not this gift of perfect holiness—"a universal emancipation from sin"—allow an individual to travel a highway over the chaos of modern life and bring the Kingdom of God into being as if the Second Coming—the millennium—had already occurred? If sin could be transcended, then the rationale for hierarchical and coercive institutions would dissolve. In such a state of perfect holiness, a young enthusiastic minister, John Humphrey Noyes, told Garrison, humankind could "abandon human government and nominate Jesus Christ for the Presidency, not only of the United States, but of the world."

Such extravagant talk in the language of Christian millennialism exerted its pull on many circles of individuals, and coincided with the increasing spread of various utopian communities. Several congregations of "perfectionists" grew up in western New York under the leadership of the former Finneyite revivalist Luther Myrick, who became an independent-minded editor whose work Garrison often excerpted. Other groups formed themselves in New England, especially in New Haven, where Noyes, a conservatively trained minister whose new views had cost him his license to preach, collaborated with another Finneyite disciple, James Boyle, on a monthly newspaper. *The Perfectionist* laid out the case against the institutional church for disregarding "the personal union of believers with Christ" and exalting instead "legal righteousness" and ritualized observances such as the Sunday Sabbath. While the perfectionists excoriated the established clergy as Pharisees and came to view the organized church as "the anti-Christ," their opponents condemned the perfectionists as "modern antinomians" whose vanity had led them into the passionate error of presuming "superior light and unusual intercourse with God."

In such a contest Garrison had no trouble choosing sides. His nonresistance principles embodied much of the "holiness" ideal, and his own condemnation of suffocating legalisms and self-righteousness in the clergy paralleled the attack mounted in *The Perfectionist*. Noyes, especially, offered the dazzling example of a defiant young man who had broken through the conventional pieties of Andover to declare himself independently ready to assist God in overthrowing corrupt governments and installing Jesus Christ on the throne of the world. He would "come out" of the world and "cease to do evil," he told Garrison in an afternoon of earnest conversation in the editor's office, and he advised Garrison to do the same. Garrison was not quite ready to take such a step, but he found powerful stimulation in the idea—derived from both Noyes and Henry C. Wright—of "practical holiness

. . . the doctrine that total abstinence from sin, in this life, is not only commanded but necessarily attainable." This was anathema to "the religionists of the day," and Garrison knew it. Perfectionism was not Garrison's private lunacy, as his critics implied, but a religious current that suited his messianic personality and gave a theological dimension to his political critique. Garrison never fully declared himself to be in possession of the perfectionist's "spiritual gifts," but he regarded such a mystical relation to the world as both plausible and necessary. The editor said with satisfaction that his views "make havoc of all sects." He was on his way toward repudiating the City of Man for the Kingdom of God and envisioning a standard of citizenship based more in Scripture than the Constitution.

It was not like Garrison to ruminate in seclusion until he could produce a systematic statement of his views. With characteristic bravado Garrison broke his long silence in midsummer 1836 with three long blasts against the aging but still formidable Lyman Beecher that occupied ten full columns of *The Liberator*. The orthodox minister had launched a fresh campaign of suppression against "he-goat" abolitionists and perfectionists "who think they do God service by butting every thing in the line of their march which does not fall in or get out of the way." With the help of Hartford's Leonard Bacon, Beecher had persuaded associations of Congregational ministers in Connecticut and Massachusetts to exclude from their pulpits all itinerant speakers whose "erroneous or questionable views" the ministers deemed "dangerous to the influence of the pastoral office and fatal to the peace and good order of the churches." Then, speaking in Pittsburgh at the Presbyterian General Assembly, he counseled against any discussion of slavery and made a widely reported address that upheld traditional authority by lauding the sanctity of the Sabbath, the leadership of the ordained clergy as enforcers of the moral law, and the "silken ties" among Christians—of the South and of the North—that made the church a national bulwark against Sabbath-breaking and abolitionist fanaticism.

Garrison took Beecher's attacks as evidence of the spiritual morbidity of institutional religion and bitterly criticized the minister's formalism. He lambasted Beecher's readiness to denounce Sabbath-breaking while ignoring the slaveholders' disregard, not only for "the fourth commandment, but THE WHOLE DECALOGUE!" The minister "goes with the South" and its churches "clotted with innocent blood" by willfully refusing to put slavery on his list of dangers to the national morals; those "silken" ties Beecher lauded were "literally the chains of slaves," Garrison seethed. Beecher and his ilk were "selling indulgences" for sin and "lulling consciences" across the country as they had previously stifled the inquiring students at Lane. Only the church that severed its ties with "traffickers in souls" could recover its gospel purity; the others, he said, with perfectionist fervor, had to be regarded as infidels in league with Belial.

Never before had Garrison made so pointed an anticlerical attack, never before had he depicted the clergy as the obliging accomplices of "the profane, the oppressive, the aristocratical" elements in society, and never before had he broadened his critique to link the working classes of the North with the slaves of the South. How could Beecher berate working people for breaking the Sabbath and becoming more disrespectful of property, when it was evident that a greater danger stemmed from the growing tendency of the rich to regard them not as brothers, but as "mere implements"? "All classes *know* and some *feel* that there is a growing aristocracy in our land," Garrison said, and "that privileges are granted to the wealthy few, to the injury and impoverishment of the laborious many," white and black, who were overworked, underpaid, and not treated according to the Golden Rule. "An equality of rights must beget an equality of conditions," Garrison wrote, and if the Beechers were to be true ministers of the gospel, they could no longer "side only with the rich and powerful."

Though diffuse, the essay pointed more clearly than before to Garrison's concern for a "whole-souled" religion that applied a personal understanding of the gospel to social concerns. That his remarks set off "fluttering" among "the *pious* opposers of the anti-slavery course" did not surprise Garrison, and his editorial rebuttals over the next several weeks demonstrated anew his flair for agitation. His remarks on "the Sabbath question" were "incidental" to his main purpose of exposing clerical inconsistency, Garrison maintained, but his critics had so distorted his position that he would have to explain his views at greater length! Armed with copious extracts from both Luther and Calvin, supplemented by references to Paley and Fox, the editor insisted that the Sabbath question was one not of denominational ceremony, but of depth of religious commitment. Only the narrow-minded made "strict outward observance a test of Christian character" and called people infidels for insisting that *"all our time* should be sanctified by works of righteousness."

Garrison sought to uphold a higher standard in religion as in politics, and he risked the charge that he was diverting *The Liberator* from "the one great cause" in order to do so. Yet he considered it a "public calamity" that so many religious newspapers were controlled by people in opposition to social reform and felt obliged to express himself on spiritual matters. When church leaders grew indignant at his presumption and tried to discredit the editor among their parishioners, Garrison nobly defended the right of private judgment in a spirit that harked back to John Milton's memorable argument against censorship in *Areopagitica* (1644). Since bearers of new light could arise in the meanest of places and from the lowliest of callings, Milton emphasized, and truth itself could take so many forms, no office-holder in church or state ought to force "the iron yoke of outward conformity" upon a Christian conscience. "Give me the liberty to know, to utter, and to argue freely according to conscience, above all liberties," Puritanism's great poet declared, in words that Garrison made the bedrock principle of his career in agitation. If his readers found him in error, Garrison declared, they could tell him so and he would publish their dissent. His columns would always be open to his dogmatic critics as well; indeed, he would rather publish the Beechers and the Bacons than have them interdict the newspaper.

The plunge into renewed controversy coincided with a return to Boston. Garrison lodged his little family at the congenial boardinghouse in Hayward Place run by the Parker sisters, the eldest of whom had presided at the Boston Female Anti-Slavery Society meeting on the day of the mobbing. At first they crammed themselves into a single room, but soon the doting landladies made up a suite, and the Garrisons brought some furniture out of storage. They had to buy a new crib for the babe, who was now seven months old and weighed seventeen pounds. Dressed in his best buff-and-blue French print gown, little Dordie resembled the editor only in his baldness, and though the antislavery friends fussed over him no end, a friend of the Weston sisters gave the acerbic verdict "looks tolerable but nothing remarkable."

The tempo of life quickened for Garrison in Boston. He resumed direct charge of *The Liberator*, with all that entailed in sorting articles and correspondence, maintaining the editorial columns, making up pages and reading proof, and he engaged in endless hours of discussion with visitors to the office, went to meetings of numerous associations, and attended lectures at the city's churches and lyceums, as well as the elocution contests, piano recitals, and choral concerts undertaken by the black improvement societies. Helen joined him at some of these events, and they were both swept up in the social current of the abolition friends, with tea at the Southwicks' or Miss Sargent's one afternoon, a gathering at the Chapmans' or Francis Jackson's in the evening, day-long excursions to an outlying farm for visiting or organizing efforts in a nearby town. His homecoming seemed complete when the abolitionists held an anniversary service on October 21 at 46 Washington Street and ceremoniously replaced the sign that the mob had splintered the year before with a larger and "more conspicuous" one.

As the unofficial mayor of Boston's abolitionist community, Garrison had a supportive constituency ready to buoy him against attack. His circle of printer friends stood by him, as did other spiritual seekers like Henry C. Wright and Charles Burleigh, whose long ringlets gave him a Christlike appearance and made him the butt of hecklers, who advised him to cut off his hair and make Garrison a wig. The editor also had a strong following among those who did not share his religious strivings yet admired his fiercely independent advocacy. Renegade Boston Brahmins like Maria and Henry Chapman, Francis Jackson, the Mays and the Alcotts, the Lorings and the Sewells found Garrison's iconoclasm a heartening sign of progress toward the higher plane their Unitarian faith anticipated. The latent conflict between their secular humanism and Garrison's pietistic holiness went unnoticed in their common devotion to abolition and their shared antagonism toward antediluvian clergymen in every denomination. Boston's black people, comfortable within their own churches and disinclined to sectarian polemics, respected Garrison's religious demeanor, if not his perfectionist ideas, and remained unswerving in their defense of the nation's most conspicuous advocate of racial equality. Only Moses could approach Garrison in greatness, an aged black man, John J. Smith, declared on the centennial of the editor's birth, recalling how as a refugee from slavery he had thrilled to visit the *Liberator* office upon arriving in Boston in 1840. "Coming from the South and being a barber I had heard Mr. Garrison spoken of in the barber shop . . . and I wanted to see this wonderful man that there was so much talk about," Smith said. He recalled the long colloquy he had held with the editor about whether any slaveholder could be considered a good person (the editor held not), and he marveled anew at the devotion Garrison enkindled.

The force of Garrison's inspirational leadership could scarcely be separated from the influence exercised by *The Liberator*. The newspaper was essential to the cause, one reader declared, because it was "always a little ahead of public opinion," and without its high standards public opinion would never "go ahead at all." Garrison created so much thunder in *The Liberator* that neither its supporters nor its critics realized the shakiness of the paper's financial base. While other antislavery newspapers had funding from their local or regional abolition societies, Garrison and Knapp had always tried to sustain themselves on the precarious combination of subscriptions and gifts. A committee of sponsors led by Francis Jackson and Samuel Sewall had raised a private subscription to liquidate the newspaper's $3,000 worth of debts early in 1836, but by the end of the year the publishers faced a new batch of unpaid bills. Yet Garrison wanted very much to expand coverage by going to a six-column format and printing upon a larger-sized sheet. Instead of approaching his patrons, hat in hand, for another round of donations, Garrison reversed his previous course and risked his independence by seeking support from the Massachusetts Anti-Slavery Society at its annual meeting in January 1837.

Every church in Boston closed its doors against the MAS in conformity with the Beecher mandate. The state society had to open its annual meeting in the loft of a horse barn attached to the Marlboro Hotel, which prompted Garrison to remark that at last the movement had gained "a *stable* foundation." The "gag" imposed by the city's churches shocked enough consciences to secure the society permission to use a hall in the State House for its evening meetings. More than a thousand people crowded the venerable building for the week's zealous oratory, and several of Garrison's leading supporters worked tributes to the editor—"a poor and solitary individual of the working class," as Loring noted—into their talks. Samuel J. May successfully engineered the delicate matter of a subsidy for *The Liberator*, which was extended upon the understanding that Garrison would retain full control over the editorial department and that no one would regard *The Liberator* as the society's official organ or hold the MAS responsible for sentiments expressed by the editor.

These would prove extravagant and costly expectations, but the arrangement went swimmingly at first. Garrison enlarged the sheet as promised and filled each issue with an overflowing budget of news, documents, essays, and exchanges that by June 1837 had reached a record number of subscribers. The abolitionist host—embodied in more than a thousand local affiliates of the AAS—had succeeded in obtaining a half million signatures on antislavery petitions to Congress protesting the existence of slavery in the District of Columbia and opposing the acquisition of Texas. *The Liberator*'s readers eagerly followed John Quincy Adams's exertions to condemn and evade the gag rule, and the MAS mounted a triumphant campaign to put the state legislature on record against the suppression of the abolitionist voice in Congress.

Making headway at last, the AAS decided to press its advantage by putting an unprecedented number of agents into the field. Though the national office had always tried to keep its distance from Garrison, there was never any question that the editor would attend the agents' three-week New York training session in November 1836. Nonetheless, Garrison was overwhelmed by a chance encounter with Lewis Tappan in Providence, where Helen and the baby were to change cars for Brooklyn, during which that staid orthodox gentleman offered to pay the whole family's steamboat expenses to New York and put them up at his house to boot. To her own surprise Helen found herself accepting the offer (she had never seen the metropolis), and despite a bout of seasickness, she satisfied her curiosity. With Dordie crawling mischievously into everything and her husband too absorbed in the sessions to promenade, however, she returned to Boston a week before the meetings ended. It was well that she had taken the outing, for she was returning to a time of sorrow; both her aged father and her ardent but tubercular young brother Henry died within a few weeks of each other at the turn of the year.

Garrison considered the gathering of "the seventy" apostlelike agents to be the most important convocation abolitionists had held since the American Anti-Slavery Society founding in Philadelphia in 1833. The group held three sessions a day—four hours in the mornings, then two-hour sessions in midafternoon and early evening—at which they worked through an abolitionist curriculum that addressed slavery as a moral wrong, the shortcomings of colonization and gradualism, conditions in the South, the needs of the free black population, and the relationship between prejudice and abolition (a discussion led by two black ministers from New York City). Garrison's remarks were well received, but the leading part in most of the sessions was taken by Theodore Dwight Weld, a brilliant organizer who had recruited fully one-third of the agents from his brethren among the Lane rebels. Weld inspired the gathering with his insistence upon the main point—the sinfulness of slavery—and exhorted the agents to create "an abiding, inwrought, thoroughly intelligent feeling" that would make peoples' hearts ache for the slave and "leap into our ranks because they cannot keep themselves out."

Garrison appreciated the wisdom of bringing the agents together to build the communal spirit so necessary for their dangerous work. Though he was brooding upon religious matters that would isolate him from many of his colleagues, Garrison felt relieved to be treated as "a brother beloved." A concerned Lewis Tappan did take him aside for an earnest chat, but they "harmoniously agreed to differ," the editor said. Ironically, however, Garrison formed a friendship with two abolitionist women at the convocation that would soon raise yet another heretical "question" and disrupt the movement more profoundly than the shock waves generated by his perfectionism. Though not of "the seventy," two Philadelphia Friends, Sarah and Angelina Grimké, participated in all the sessions by special invitation of Weld and the AAS executive committee in recognition of the strong-minded pamphlets they had written and the speaking they had privately done in women's circles. The sisters had chosen Northern exile over the South Carolina plantation society in which they had grown up, which gave weight to their remarks; that they were feminists on the verge of a political challenge to patriarchal authority not even the sympathetic Garrison discerned, for they had only just begun to realize it themselves.

Though their speech bore the soft drawl of the Carolina low country, the sisters spoke the language of "thorough" abolition and buttressed their personal accounts of slave society with learned analysis of Scriptural texts and legislative enactments. Sarah had carefully studied the Virginia abolition debates of 1831–32, and Angelina had filled her stirring *Appeal to the Christian Women of the South* (1836) with examples of heroic female action from the Bible's Deborah, Esther, and the women who ministered to the outcast Jesus to the Friends' Elizabeth Heyrick and the Boston women who had faced down the mob.

Sarah Grimké was forty-four, and her long face bore the lines of middle age, but her inquisitive eyes and the thoughtful tilt of her head gave evidence that she was a power to reckon with. Her father had once told her that she could have been the greatest jurist in the country, had she only been a boy, and her sense of thwarted talents had fueled her conversion from Presbyterianism to the Friends and her rejection of plantation society. Sarah had raised Angelina, the family's youngest child, born in 1805, who devotedly called her "sister mother." At thirty-two, Angelina was an exact contemporary of both Garrison and Maria Chapman, and she matched them in eloquence and flair. Slight of build and dressed in the Friends' mousy gray habit, Angelina might have been overlooked in company but for her earnest, self-assured speech and her dark, soulful eyes. She carried herself with assertive vigor and had, in fact, led her older sister in rebellion, joining the Hicksite Friends and Mrs. Mott's female antislavery society after she had heard George Thompson speak in Philadelphia. In the midst of the terror directed at the postal campaign in August 1835, Angelina had publicly declared abolition "a cause worth dying for" in a letter to Garrison on Christian heroism that the editor pronounced "a soul-thrilling epistle" and published, first in *The Liberator* and then in a pamphlet on the Boston mob. At first despairing at the condemnation her public advocacy had drawn from the Friends, Angelina reasoned that such contumely would be her own abolitionist trial and began to write and organize more extensively. Sarah overcame her own reluctance and joined in her sister's work, saying, "What thou doest, I will do my utmost to help thee in doing."

The sisters had the tacit support of the AAS in organizing their New York meetings, though Elizur Wright and Gerrit Smith cautioned against any public exposure which might bring the opprobrium of having conducted "Fanny Wright meetings" upon them. (With the exception of Wright, a Scotswoman who had tried to organize a socialist labor colony as a gradualist abolition venture in Tennessee in 1824, no women had made platform appearances before mixed audiences on political issues. The Grimké sisters did not plan such a radical step, but the trajectory of their work was leading straight toward it, and when the moment came, they would not hesitate.) For the Grimkés, the convocation of "the seventy" proved "a moral and intellectual feast" that bound them irrevocably to the cause and brought them into the male-dominated abolitionist milieu and a rich acquaintance with Garrison and Weld. For Garrison, the Grimkés offered an example of female activism on a greater scale than Prudence Crandall's solitary testimony, and he returned to Boston eager to have the MAS invite the Grimké sisters to visit the women of New England.

It took nearly six months to complete the arrangements for such an "agency." Meanwhile, the Grimké sisters' New York meetings soon outgrew private parlors and took place in rooms offered by sympathetic church members. Once a man slipped into a back row and remained even after being informed by the minister that the gathering was "exclusively for ladies." Angelina went on unperturbed. "Somehow I did not feel his presence at all embarrassing," she said afterward. The sisters collaborated with the Boston women leaders in organizing a national convention of women abolitionists in May 1837. Garrison, who had signaled the importance of a female constituency for the movement as far back as his Park Street Address in 1829, attended, but he did not address the gathering of two hundred delegates, black as well as white, from nine states. Its most electrifying moment came when Angelina Grimké moved that "to plead the cause of the oppressed . . . the time has come for woman to [assume] the rights and duties common to

From the Old Family Bible

Joseph Garrison was Born 14th August, 1734

Mary Palmer was Born 19th January, 1741.

Joseph Garrison and Mary Palmer were married in the year 1764 the 14th day of August.

Hannah daughter of the above was Born July 16th 1765.

Elisabeth daughter of the above was Born July 15th 1767.

Joseph son of the above was Born April 26th 1769.

Daniel son of the above was Born April 6th 1771.

Abijah son of the above was Born June 18th 1773.

Sarah daughter of the above was Born May 8th 1776.

Nathaniel son of the above was Born July 9th 1778.

Silas son of the above was Born September 16th 1780.

William son of the above was Born May 6th 1782.

Garrison's paternal grandparents used the Bible from which this leaf has been copied. His father, Abijah, born in 1773, was the fifth of nine children.
(Courtesy of Sophia Smith Collection, Smith College)

Garrison was born on December 12, 1805, in the house in front of the Presbyterian Church on School Street, in Newburyport, Massachusetts, shown here in a photograph from the 1890s.
(Courtesy of Newburyport Public Library)

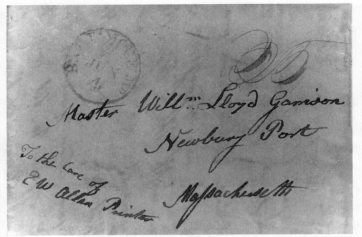

This envelope, postmarked "June 4 [1823] Baltimore," contained the last letter Garrison's mother wrote to her son, who was apprenticed to E. W. Allen, the Newburyport printer. (Courtesy of Department of Special Collections, Ablah Library, Wichita State University)

Elder John Peak led the small Baptist community in Newburyport and became a paternal figure for Maria Garrison and her children after Abijah Garrison abandoned them. (Courtesy of the Library of Congress)

A printing office of the 1820s, with an up-to-date Stanhope iron press in front of the traditional typecase and imposing table. (Courtesy of the Smithsonian Institution)

FIFTY FEET WEST OF THIS SPOT
WILLIAM LLOYD GARRISON
EDITED
THE JOURNAL OF THE TIMES
OCTOBER 3, 1828 – MARCH 27, 1829
HITHER CAME
BENJAMIN LUNDY DECEMBER 6, 1828
TO ENLIST HIM IN THE CAUSE OF THE SLAVE.
GARRISON DEPARTED HENCE
TO LIFT UP IN BALTIMORE
THE BANNER
OF IMMEDIATE EMANCIPATION

This plaque in Bennington, Vermont, commemorates the partnership with the Quaker agitator Benjamin Lundy that brought Garrison into abolitionist journalism. (Courtesy of the Massachusetts Historical Society)

The Park Street Church in Boston, where Garrison delivered his landmark antislavery address on the Fourth of July, 1829. (Courtesy of the Boston Athenaeum)

Many young readers remembered the pictorial headings of The Liberator—*shown here as they first appeared on April 23, 1831, and March 23, 1838*—as their introduction to abolitionist ideas. (Courtesy of the Boston Athenaeum)

THE LIBERATOR

Is a periodical, published every Saturday morning, in Boston, Massachusetts, by WM. LLOYD GARRISON and ISAAC KNAPP, and devoted to the ABOLITION OF SLAVERY, and the CAUSE OF THE FREE PEOPLE OF COLOR. Price $2 per annum, payable in advance. Subscriptions gratefully received.

This advertisement for The Liberator *appeared on the back cover of Garrison's "An Address Delivered Before the Free People of Color in Philadelphia, New York & other cities during the month of June, 1831."* (Courtesy of the Massachusetts Historical Society)

Oliver Johnson, *trained as a printer in Vermont, assisted* The Liberator *in the 1830s and later became editor of the* National Anti-Slavery Standard.
(Courtesy of the Massachusetts Historical Society)

William C. Nell, *a long-time associate in* The Liberator *offices, wrote several pioneering books in black history and led the 1850s fight to desegregate the Boston public schools.*
(Courtesy of the Massachusetts Historical Society)

Francis Jackson, *a Boston businessman and president of the Massachusetts Anti-Slavery Society, served as Garrison's patron for years, giving him financial and moral support.*
(Courtesy of the Massachusetts Historical Society)

Isaac Knapp, *Garrison's boyhood friend, was his business partner and co-publisher of* The Liberator *in the 1830s.*
(Courtesy of the Massachusetts Historical Society)

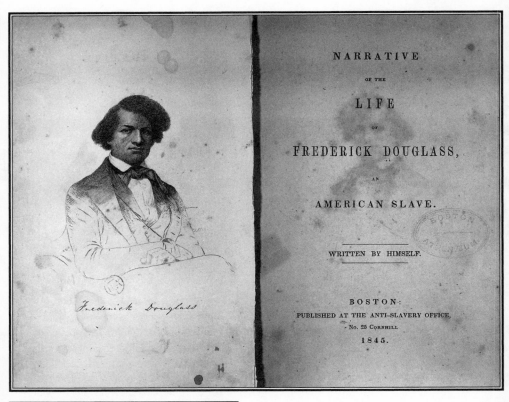

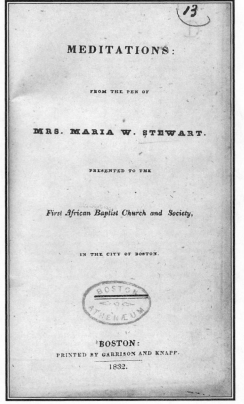

In addition to the newspaper, Garrison's office printed many pamphlets and books, including these important works. Douglass expanded his narrative in 1855, and it has become a landmark in American literature. (Courtesy of the Boston Athenaeum)

This table was used for imposing in the printing office of The Liberator.
(Courtesy of the Massachusetts Historical Society)

The African Meeting House, still standing on Joy (formerly Belknap) Street in Boston, was a center for black community life and the abolitionist movement. The New England Anti-Slavery Society was founded there in January 1832. (Courtesy of the Boston Athenaeum)

Kingsley's Lane, Brooklyn, Conn.

Boston abolitionists commissioned a portrait of the schoolteacher Prudence Crandall in 1834, shown here as copied in 1971 by Carl Henry after the original by Francis Alexander.
(Courtesy of the Prudence Crandall Museum)

Garrison and Helen Benson used to stroll in Kingsley's Lane near Friendship Vale, her parents' home in Brooklyn, Connecticut, which became a center for Prudence Crandall's defenders.
(Courtesy of the Sophia Smith Collection, Smith College)

Crandall declared her intention to open her school to black students in this advertisement from The Liberator, March 2, 1833. (Courtesy of the Prudence Crandall Museum)

PRUDENCE CRANDALL,
PRINCIPAL OF THE CANTERBURY, (CONN.) FEMALE
BOARDING SCHOOL.

RETURNS her most sincere thanks to those who have patronized her School, and would give information that on the first Monday of April next, her School will be opened for the reception of young Ladies and little Misses of color. The branches taught are as follows:— Reading, Writing, Arithmetic, English Grammar, Geography, History, Natural and Moral Philosophy, Chemistry, Astronomy, Drawing and Painting, Music on the Piano, together with the French language.

☞ The terms, including board, washing, and tuition, are $25 per quarter, one half paid in advance.

☞ Books and Stationary will be furnished on the most reasonable terms.

For information respecting the School, reference may be made to the following gentlemen, viz.:—

ARTHUR TAPPAN, Esq.
Rev. PETER WILLIAMS,
Rev. THEODORE RAYMOND
Rev. THEODORE WRIGHT, } N. YORK CITY.
Rev. SAMUEL C. CORNISH,
Rev. GEORGE BOURNE.
Rev. Mr. HAYBORN.
Mr. JAMES FORTEN, } PHILADELPHIA.
Mr. JOSEPH CASSEY,
Rev. S. J. MAY.—BROOKLYN, CT.
Rev. Mr. BEMAN.—MIDDLETOWN, CT.
Rev. S. S. JOCELYN.—NEW-HAVEN, CT.
Wm. LLOYD GARRISON } BOSTON, MASS.
ARNOLD BUFFUM,
GEORGE BENSON.—PROVIDENCE, R. L.

Helen Eliza (Benson) Garrison was born and educated in Providence, Rhode Island, and married the editor in 1834. She is pictured here circa 1853. (Courtesy of the Sophia Smith Collection, Smith College)

Public images of Garrison included both ennobling portraits and racist caricatures.

Leopold Grozelier portrayed Garrison in a noble light in this 1854 lithograph. (Courtesy of the Library of Congress)

A radical British magazine included the visiting Garrison in its "People's Portrait Gallery," London, 1846. (Courtesy of the Library Company of Philadelphia)

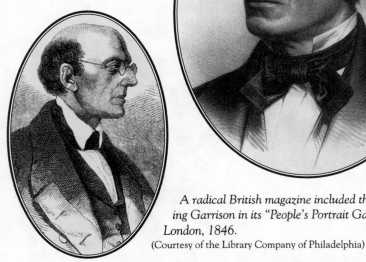

Boston Oct. 21ˢᵗ 1835.

THE ABOLITION GARRISON IN DANGER, & THE NARROW ESCAPE of the SCOTCH AMBASSADOR.

This anonymous caricaturist applauded the editor's near lynching by a Boston mob in 1835. (Courtesy of the Library Company of Philadelphia)

Garrison, as sketched by Robert Douglass, a black Philadephia artist, in 1835. (Courtesy of the Historical Society of Pennsylvania)

PRACTICAL AMALGAMATION.

Edward W. Clay's 1839 cartoon, "Practical Amalgamation," attributes Garrison's abolitionism to lustful self-gratification and expresses the popular fear that civil equality would lead to miscegenation.
(Courtesy of the Library Company of Philadelphia)

E. C. Del's "Practical Illustration of the Fugitive Slave Law" (1851) mocks the controversy and, in this detail, lampoons the pacifist Garrison as a defender of black runaways.
(Courtesy of Wichita State University)

ANTI ANNEXATION PROCESSION.

H. Bucholzer's 1844 cartoon, "Anti-Annexation Procession," mocks those who protested the annexation of Texas as a slave state. Garrison is depicted to the left, leading the hair-shirted abolitionists. (Courtesy of the Library of Congress)

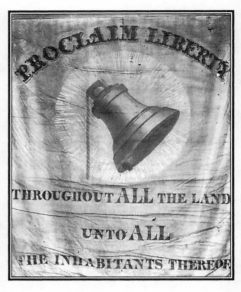

Banners like these often decorated the walls at abolitionist meetings.
(Courtesy of the Massachusetts Historical Society)

Abolitionists added pertinent new verses to favorite hymns and patriotic airs, as shown in this revision of "America," from the Hingham Anti-Slavery Society's 1843 songbook.
(Courtesy of the Library Company of Philadelphia)

Abolitionist women organized drives to send petitions, such as the 1843 ones depicted here, to Congress and the state legislatures demanding action against slavery. (Courtesy of the Boston Athenaeum)

Maria Weston Chapman (left) and Abby Kelley Foster were two of the many feminists who got their start in the abolitionist movement.
(*Left:* courtesy of the Trustees of the Boston Public Library; *right:* courtesy of the American Antiquarian Society)

The Grimké sisters, Angelina (left) and Sarah exiled themselves from their South Carolina slaveholding family and became abolitionist organizers in Philadelphia and New England. (Courtesy of the Massachusetts Historical Society)

American activists added a second figure emphasizing the awareness of women's rights that developed in the movement. (Courtesy of the Boston Athenaeum)

Garrison looked to the Philadelphia leaders,
Lucretia and James Mott, as spiritual mentors.
(Courtesy of the Massachusetts Historical Society)

Sojourner Truth fled from slavery in 1827
and became a leading advocate of abolition
and women's rights, frequently lecturing on
behalf of the American Anti-Slavery Society.
(Courtesy of the Massachusetts Historical Society)

THE LEGION OF LIBERTY.

Philanthrophy imploring America to release the Slave and revive Liberty

The engraving, "Philanthropy Imploring America to release the Slave and revive Liberty," depicting
slavery shielded by the three-fifths clause, is one of the few visual representations of the power granted
to slaveholders in the U.S. Constitution. (Courtesy of the Library Company of Philadelphia)

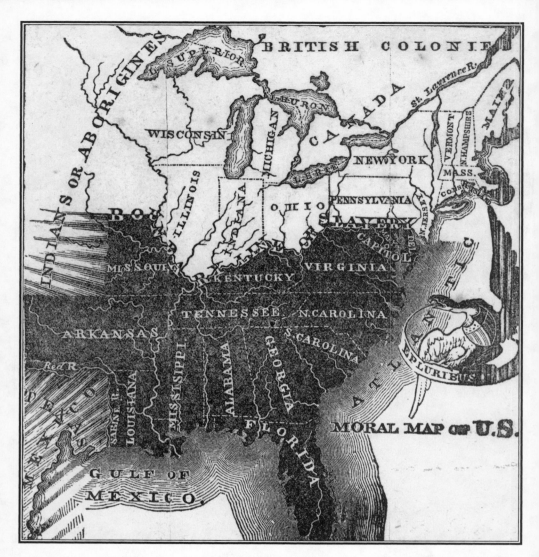

A "Moral Map of U.S." appeared in an abolitionist tract, The Legion of Liberty, in 1847 and illustrates the growing convergence of antislavery and sectional identities. (Courtesy of the Library Company of Philadelphia)

all moral beings . . . and no longer remain satisfied in the circumscribed limits with which corrupt custom and a perverted application of Scripture have encircled her. . . ." The resolution passed, though not unanimously, and it became apparent that the more assertive women became as abolitionists, the more they would be contending for their own civil rights.

That another great reform had taken hold of them seemed natural to the sisters, but they could not help but worry that it would affect their agency. When they arrived in Boston in late May 1837, however, they found themselves in long evenings of conversation at the Chapmans', the Jacksons', and the Philbricks', on common ground. These were "conclaves of brothers and sisters" who shared the view that "a new order of things is very desirable," Angelina said with pleasure. When the sisters drew more than four hundred women to their first talk at "good old 46," it became clear to Angelina that their lectures had to advance not only the cause of the slave "but the cause of woman as a responsible moral being," yet she feared entering such an "untrodden path." Garrison, who had blazed his own trail for years, promised that *The Liberator* would fully support them against the anticipated criticism. "Pray for us," Angelina said; "we see only in a glass darkly what results are to grow out of this experiment."

The visiting agitators went directly to work. Over the next month, Angelina and Sarah Grimké lectured seventeen times in ten different towns to more than eight thousand people, some of whom had walked miles on muddy roads to hear "Carolina's high-souled daughters" testify firsthand about slavery and appeal for the "reading, praying, thinking, and action" that would purify public life and purge the nation of this sin. Not all the Grimkés' auditors were women, however. Men came to hear them in Roxbury, crowded the gallery of a Salem hall, and composed a goodly proportion of the thousand who jammed the largest house in Lynn and hung outside the windows to hear the talk. Angelina marveled that the Lord had "opened the way for us to address *mixed* audiences, for most sects here are greatly opposed to public speaking for women, but curiosity in many & real interest in the anti-slavery cause in others" had broken the traditional barrier and forged a new community of feeling.

They also encountered opposition, not of the mobbish sort that had greeted George Thompson, but rather the silent treatment from ministers who would neither read notices of their lectures nor open their meetinghouses to them. They also heard, more times than they could bear, the words of Saint Paul from 1 Corinthians 14:34 that bade women "keep silence in the churches." Clergymen regarded the Grimké visit with the hostility they had historically directed against itinerant revivalists, and they moved swiftly to check this latest threat. At the end of June 1837, the association of Massachusetts clergymen met at Brookfield and issued a "pastoral letter" to be read from every Congregational pulpit in the state that condemned the forcing of "perplexing and agitating subjects" upon the churches by zealous outsiders. *"Your minister* is ordained of God to be your *teacher,"* the congregations were reminded, and if certain topics are not presented to your satisfaction, it is nonetheless "a violation of sacred and important rights to encourage a stranger to present them." To allow women to intrude worsened the insubordination. "We appreciate the unostentatious prayers and efforts of women . . . in leading religious inquirers to the pastors for instruction," the ministers said, "but when she assumes the place and tone of man as a public reformer . . . her character becomes unnatural." Reformers of both sexes would be well advised to confine themselves to "private efforts for the spiritual good of individuals."

The oleaginous letter ignited burning debates on the rights of women and abolitionist tactics. Garrison condemned the statement as "popery" and printed a long poem by Whittier that mocked "the Brookfield bull." Sarah Grimké condemned "the *usurped* authority" the clergy employed "to crush the immortal mind of woman," and predicted that one day the sentiments contained in the document would be regarded with as much astonishment as the opinions of Cotton Mather on witchcraft. In an eloquent series of letters on the "equality of the sexes" that were published in *The Liberator,* Grimké insisted that God had made no moral distinction between the sexes and that "whatsoever it is morally right for a man to do, it is morally right for a woman to do."

As had happened in the 1835 postal campaign, the clerical attack heightened interest in the cause. The Grimkés' lectures drew significantly larger crowds. In July 1837, the sisters made nineteen appearances in fourteen towns before audiences that totaled twelve thousand people, and though illness forced a curtailed schedule in August, by the end of September they had made twenty-eight lectures in twenty-three towns to more than thirteen thousand people. Men came in their shirtsleeves directly from fields and workshops, Angelina observed with satisfaction, and women flocked to the talks, many carrying small children in their arms. From the rostrum the sisters could see how mothers struggled to keep their children quiet, nursing, dandling, or even walking them to and fro in the lobbies.

The most profound reaction came from the young women who had heard the ministers' condemnation read from the pulpit. A nineteen-year-old schoolteacher named Lucy Stone—recalling how she squirmed and suffered that morning—said that "if I had felt bound to silence before by interpretation of Scriptures, or believed that equal rights did not belong to woman, that 'pastoral letter' broke my bonds." Stone would later earn her way through Oberlin College and become one of its first female graduates, a paid abolitionist field agent and editor, and a national leader in the women's suffrage movement. Abby Kelley, a young Quaker schoolteacher whose organizing skills had underpinned the Grimkés' huge success in Lynn, felt her "moral thermometer" rising and realized, as she soon told Garrison, that the movement would have to take "a decided stand for *all truths,* under the conviction that the whole are necessary to the permanent establishment of any *single* one." Lidian Emerson found herself after a talk with the Grimké sisters determined to find some way of acting in the cause, though her husband, Waldo, continued to hold back. "A man can only extend his attention to a certain finite amount of claims," he said.

Although the pastoral letter had laid down a serious institutional challenge to the abolitionists, it had not indicted anyone by name. A few weeks later, however, in July 1837, five Congregational ministers published "An Appeal of Clerical Abolitionists on Anti-Slavery Measures," which attacked *The Liberator* for its "abuse" of ministers who would not act against slavery to its editor's satisfaction. Garrison's "unparalleled railing" on the Sabbath and his "perfectionist effusions" meant that *The Liberator* could no longer be circulated by gospel-loving abolitionists and that the MAS had forfeited the public trust by subsidizing the newspaper. Other clergymen echoed the charge that Garrison wanted to foist "his peculiar theology" upon the movement and insinuated that those who supported Garrison had become "idolators" of a false prophet. Garrison's lack of formal church membership was said to have disqualified him from any criticism of the clergy. Others condemned *The Liberator*'s "mobocratic" spirit and warned that Garrison verged on demagoguery.

That men who had played only nominal roles in the movement now sought to censure his conduct drove Garrison into a furious front-page reply that ridiculed the "sacerdotal" nature of the appeal. "Abolition brings ministers and laymen upon the same dead level of equality," he insisted, and he decried the offensive "spiritual supremacy" of the attempt to dominate "in an oracular tone as Clergymen." In the quest for justice the editor would bow to no one, and if it took the downfall of "the crazy superstructure . . . [of] man-enslaving religion" to abolish slavery, he would rest content in the belief that a redeemed "spiritual house" would arise from "the ruins of the various religious sects." As the attacks intensified, he responded with a predictably hot mixture of outrage and defensiveness. "You are striving to stab me . . . with a sectarian dagger, a viler weapon than a Bowie knife," he told one critic, and admonished another for having employed "the spirit of an Inquisitor." In a long, self-justifying editorial that recounted his origins as "a poor, self-educated mechanic," Garrison emphasized that he had forged his reputation by "being utterly regardless of the opinions of mankind." Spiritual independence had given him the lever by which he had raised the abolitionist movement, and he would not lightly surrender it.

Garrison had made himself an easy target, yet the argument went far beyond personalities to reveal a divergent understanding of the gospel mandate within Christian denominations. To condemn the editor as a heretic was more than an attack upon Garrison's own beliefs; it was a deliberate effort to undermine the religious foundations of the movement and discredit a spiritual community that, as in every revival, hungered after more soulful nourishment than the incumbent clergy supplied. The radical abolitionists were, in effect, calling for theological reformation within the church by insisting that slavery be attacked as vigorously as other sinful conduct, and the clerical opposition was, in effect, challenging both the intentions and the standing of the reformers. Critics charged that the abolitionists, especially those who tilted toward perfectionist holiness, acted in the name of a "different gospel" that undermined the structure of internal authority both by discrediting the clergy *and* by failing to distinguish genuine religious feelings from transitory emotions aroused by fanatics to gratify their lust for excitement and personal attention. Conservatives had, in fact, opposed every evangelical revival since Whitefield and Edwards on precisely those grounds. The abolitionists could have no claim on Christian congregations, the critics insisted, because the antislavery societies were not doctrinally homogeneous confessional groups, but ad hoc gatherings preoccupied with a particular sin rather than "the whole Gospel." Abolitionism, in their view, weakened the church and retarded the religious progress necessary for emancipation.

The movement worked quickly to avert a takeover by the moderate clergy. Boston's black community held a public meeting—the notices having been read in all three of its churches—that resolved that anyone "who set Garrison at naught" could not be considered a "genuine abolitionist." The clergy's silence *did* uphold slavery, the meeting affirmed, and the clerical "fluttering" proved that the editor had "struck the right nail upon the head." The MAS issued a statement that politely termed the appeals "unkind, unjust, and inconsiderate" and reaffirmed both Garrison's editorial independence and the absence of a religious test for membership. The editor tried to insulate the organization from attack by announcing that he would forgo further subsidy, but he bluntly warned that the cause *"must be kept in the hands of laymen. . . ."*

Though Garrison and his allies had mounted an effective counterattack, they knew that they faced a struggle on more than one front. While the angry ministers remained caucusing, corresponding, and "laying plots" in Boston to undo the editor, the contest threatened to become a national one, for it became increasingly clear that the AAS executive committee in New York wanted—as the clerical protesters whispered—to "cast off Garrison." Significantly its newspaper—*The Emancipator*—made no rebuttal to the clerical protests, an approving silence, it seemed, by comparison to the strong denunciations issued by the rest of the abolitionist press. From the New York office, moreover, both Weld and Whittier were pressuring the Grimké sisters (who had no official connection to the AAS) to stop writing on "the woman question" in order to safeguard the abolitionist cause from criticism. Lewis Tappan publicly decried Garrison's penchant for taking up questions "that had better not have been discussed," though he piously declared that the AAS executive committee viewed the "Boston controversy" as a lamentably personal one that should not be dignified by national notice. Elizur Wright, the AAS executive secretary, also maintained a public facade of "neutrality," stating that the society would not "sit in judgment" upon "sentiments being promulgated in some antislavery papers" that could prejudice the cause, but he made no secret of his own expectation that the clergy's goading of Garrison would eventually provoke the editor into such extravagance that he would have to "leave us . . . and save us the time and trouble of doing anything against him."

The Grimkés and Garrison strengthened each other's resolve against the insidious criticism. When they met for a day of conversation, it was "as iron sharpeneth iron," Angelina said, for they fully agreed that "*the time* to assert a right is *the* time when *that* right is denied." The editor urged them not to silence themselves on the issue of women's rights, and the sisters, who had been reading *The Perfectionist* and discussing the issues of practical holiness with Henry Wright, hoped that Garrison would be "divinely directed" to make *The Liberator* the vehicle for "all the grand principles of reform." Their critics did not understand that the issues of human rights "blend with each other like the colors of the rainbow into . . . pure *practical* Christianity," Angelina said; the Lord had raised up "men and women not to proclaim *our* truth only, but to cry aloud against *all* the sins of our guilty land. . . ." Sarah was equally determined. "My brother," she told Weld, "we have planted our feet on the Rock of Ages."

Just as the abolitionist movement faced its first major internal strain, it received a grim reminder of its position on the perimeter of American politics. In November 1837, a mob killed Elijah Lovejoy, an antislavery editor in Alton, Illinois, and the shocking news of martyrdom in the west intensified the national antislavery controversy once more. With *The Liberator* framed in thick black borders, Garrison mourned the fallen editor: "In destroying his press, the enemies of freedom have compelled a thousand to speak out in his stead. . . ." Yet the circumstances of the printer's death proved troubling. Lovejoy, a Presbyterian minister only a few years older than Garrison, had suffered the destruction of several printing presses in slaveholding Missouri before moving across the river into the nominal freedom of southern Illinois. Since the civil authorities in Alton could not preserve the peace, they had armed and deputized Lovejoy and his supporters as a militia; the tragedy had occurred as the abolitionists repelled a firebombing assault on their office by a rifle-wielding mob.

Garrison was "shocked" that Lovejoy and his coadjutors had allowed the provocations to justify taking up arms in self-defense. They had set a dangerous precedent for the cause, Garrison believed, and though Lovejoy "was certainly a martyr—strictly speaking—he was not . . . a Christian martyr." Below his own remarks, however, the editor felt obliged to report that the

MAS board of managers, while acknowledging the feelings of pacifist members like Garrison, defended Lovejoy's conduct as justified by "the example of our revolutionary fathers" and the "patriotic sacrifices" sanctioned by the Declaration of Independence.

The murder shocked the consciences of many moderate Northerners. Editors who had turned a blind eye to the mobs of 1835 now recognized, as William Cullen Bryant put it, that retaliatory violence threatened to muzzle the press and posed a free speech issue even for people unsympathetic to abolition. In Boston, Dr. Channing himself called for a meeting in Faneuil Hall, and when the city fathers denied his petition, Channing's outraged protest won even Garrison's praise for its "spirit-stirring nobility."

Public opinion forced the authorities to back down, and five thousand people jammed Faneuil Hall on December 8, 1837, in the nation's largest demonstration against the Lovejoy murder. For the first time Boston's elite crowded into the Cradle of Liberty on an antislavery mission, though Channing wanted the meeting confined to a defense of free speech and abjured Garrison not to "mix up the meeting with Abolition."

The editor didn't have to, for a member of Channing's congregation, the hot-tempered attorney general James T. Austin, forced the issue by denouncing Lovejoy and other abolitionists for frightening slaveholders with the prospect that black people would be turned loose like the wild beasts of a menagerie. People rose up in self-protection against such a prospect, Austin said, and for exciting the passions of men by his rash conduct, Austin charged, Lovejoy "died as the fool dieth." In a memorable reply, the attorney Wendell Phillips—the scion of an aristocratic family whose speech that night propelled him into the forefront of abolitionist orators—shamed Austin for calling the murderers patriots who had defended the American Union and insisted that Lovejoy, like those who died in the Boston Massacre, was the true patriot and martyr to liberty.

Phillips's eloquence carried the meeting, which was an implicit act of atonement for the earlier violence against Garrison, and the editor pronounced the affair "a signal triumph for our side." Yet Garrison and his closest friends still had their own reservations about Lovejoy. "The pouring out of [Lovejoy's] blood . . . will not make *Christian* abolitionists," Sarah Grimké observed, and Samuel J. May told Garrison that he feared that slavery could not be abolished by "moral conflict only."

Garrison now believed it imperative to devote himself to "universal emancipation" as a means of maintaining the ethical imperatives of the movement. He would use the term in "the widest latitude" to mean liberating the human race from "the dominion of man, the thralldom of self, from the bondage of sin—and bringing them under the dominion of God, the comfort of an inward spirit, the government of the law of love, and into the obedience and liberty of Christ. . . ." Having served a "regular [seven years'] apprenticeship in the name of Liberty," Garrison wrote in his first issue of 1838, he would now pursue the topic on a more "extended scale" by opening *The Liberator* to discussions about "the cause of peace" and "the perfect government of the most High," questions upon which "the principles of abolitionists seem to be quite unsettled." As for the "woman question," which the Grimké sisters had raised in the course of their powerful agency, Garrison insisted that there could be no doubt that a belief in universal emancipation required one to "go for the rights of woman to their utmost extent."

A new season of agitation had brought women more fully into the cause and had clearly identified a fracture in the movement between those willing to embrace radical social change and those who wanted the slavery question addressed without overturning the established structure of power. Yet Lovejoy's murder epitomized the violence that lay barely below the surface of the argument and reinforced the need to keep Christian ethics at the center of the movement's appeal. What kind of abolitionist movement could exist if people lauded the printer who died with a rifle in his hands and shunned the printer who upheld the Bible as the standard of government? Garrison's own encounter with the mob had sent him into a reexamination that had deepened his radicalism, but it remained to be seen whether his new vision—and the new agitators it had attracted—could persuade the growing numbers attracted to the movement that immediate emancipation for the slaves had the necessary correlative of spiritual transformation for the nominally free.

CHAPTER TWELVE

THE EDITOR AS ISHMAELITE

GARRISON LIKED TO DESCRIBE THE ABOLITIONIST MOVEMENT AS A PROCESS OF SOWING SEEDS OR SPREADING LIGHT, BUT ITS WORK CAN ALSO BE UNDERSTOOD—IN A PHRASE HIS MOTHER USED—AS A SERIES OF DOORS to be opened. At first the editor was shut out everywhere, but found pathways into black communities, the Friends, and the benevolence societies. Though the institutional doors of the church denominations remained closed, a number of ministers and congregations had admitted immediatist advocates, and a few cautious clergymen like Channing had allowed their study doors to crack open a few inches. The chambers of Congress remained firmly closed, as did the national political parties, but several state legislatures had become receptive to abolitionist petitions and a few politicians from those states had begun to think that an open door policy toward antislavery might serve their interests. Reactionary elements still did not shrink from rousing mob violence to block the entryways, though such tactics antagonized a substantial number of fair-minded citizens and opened a few more routes of advocacy. The growing shrillness of the Southern slaveholders' demands to shut the doors of press, post office, and pulpit against the abolitionists testified to their success, and it seemed by spring 1838 that the abolitionists verged on a major breakthrough in public opinion.

The American Anti-Slavery Society had developed a good deal of momentum in 1837–38, with thirty-eight agents in the field, the addition of more than 350 new societies (one for every day of the year, people bragged), 600,000 pamphlets in circulation, and 400,000 petitions forwarded to Congress with nearly a million signatures protesting the gag rule, the potential annexation of Texas, and the continuation of slavery and the slave trade in the nation's capital. A number of men had begun to talk about making the weight of abolition felt in election campaigns, but most abolitionists still considered the broader moral education of the citizenry to be the movement's most urgent political task. Yet the organization faced several new doorways at once. Those who wanted to reach out to a freshly receptive moderate electorate looked in one direction, while those who wanted to enlarge the base of grassroots agitation looked in another, and each wanted to keep the organization's own doors shut against the other's potential allies. Men like the Tappans feared an influx of outspoken women who shared

Garrison's radical views, while Garrison and his supporters dreaded an influx of ambitious office-seekers who would dilute the argument for their own gain. The AAS executive committee, dominated by wealthy evangelical philanthropists like Lewis Tappan and the former slaveholder James G. Birney, believed that the society should be run with the centralized coordination that had well served the benevolent societies of the 1820s, a point of view shared by the clergymen who had turned against Garrison. Aggressive managers like the executive secretary Elizur Wright and the organizer Henry B. Stanton had more appreciation for the popular roots of the movement, but thought the national office might exercise a counterweight upon the radical tendencies represented by Garrison in Boston and his like-minded friends in Ohio, New Hampshire, and other states. The Massachusetts leaders knew it, too, and they began to speak darkly about the danger of concentrating power in any select body of men. Now that the organization was "a prize worth seeking," it had to guard against falling prey to what Garrison termed "political buccaneers and clerical letters of marque." The conflicting tendencies within the AAS would engender a passionate feud and fracture the organization by the end of the decade. In the process, however, Garrison consolidated his position as a universal reformer.

The turmoil over the editor's radicalism erupted fitfully, with periods of rancor followed by intervals of reconciliation. In May 1838, with the clerical opposition temporarily quiescent in Massachusetts, Garrison found himself a welcome participant at the annual AAS meeting in New York despite the strains occasioned by the Grimké campaign. His resolution declaring that "we meet each other, not as members of any religious party, but as abolitionists, on the broad ground of common brotherhood and humanity, as moral and accountable beings, entitled to equal rights and privileges" passed easily, though it might have been construed as opening the "woman question." Even more encouraging from the point of view of the Massachusetts Anti-Slavery Society, the state societies secured greater autonomy in a delicately arranged compromise that permitted them to control fund-raising and organizing within their domain in exchange for a pledge that each would raise a fixed sum for the national treasury. "Every body seemed delighted with the meeting," Garrison blandly reported to Helen.

The good feelings prevailed as most of the leadership went on to Philadelphia for the dedication of Pennsylvania Hall—a new citadel of free speech—where they found themselves frustrated by the limitations of moderate opinion and received a forceful reminder that a door could be slammed shut more quickly than it could be pried open. The building itself, a three-story classical edifice with a facade of marble columns, stood as a reformer's temple that John G. Whittier's celebratory poem predicted would someday outrank the Parthenon as a monument to liberty. Financed by the contributions of working people and open to advocates of all causes, the hall was not explicitly an abolitionist undertaking, but the evil of slavery proved the theme struck most often during the three-day exercises.

The cautious managers had not invited Garrison to speak, and Weld, whom they did ask, excused himself because of a throat ailment that would keep him from public speaking for many years. The committee had sought a dedicatory address from John Quincy Adams, but "Old Man Eloquent" had declined with some blunt remarks about the hypocrisy of celebrating free speech in Philadelphia while Pennsylvania's Democratic congressional delegation supported the gag rule in Washington. Eventually the honor went to a reliable local attorney, David Paul Brown, whose reputation as a humanitarian arose from his defense of runaway slaves. Brown's address, which lasted several hours and ran to twenty-two printed pages, made a notable argument for the injustice of slavery and the right of abolitionists to protest it. Yet he characterized the controversy with slaveholders as a "fraternal struggle" and declared that despite his abhorrence of the peculiar institution he would rather suffer it indefinitely than endure the "dismemberment" of the Union. If that Channing-like equivocation wasn't enough to make Garrison squirm in his seat, the attorney went on to suggest that abolitionists not insist upon the "mere" word *immediate*. "We will not quarrel as to a month, or a year, or twenty years," Brown said, if the slaveholders would only promise emancipation by a date *certain*. He went on to examine the possibilities for compensated emancipation on the British model, the need for an interval of preparatory education, and the prospects for adopting *post nati* laws on the Pennsylvania model of 1780, which had freed—at age twenty-eight—the children born to slaves after that date. That Brown explicitly renounced colonization as a remedy came as cold comfort to the AAS brethren, especially Garrison, who left the hall fuming at its profanation by the "worst heresies" of gradualism.

The next morning several AAS speakers not known for their sympathy toward Garrison defended the moral urgency of immediatism, and at the conclusion of their remarks the editor himself seized an impromptu opportunity to "rebaptise" the hall. From several parts of the auditorium, which held more than two thousand people, a cry went up for Garrison to speak, and in a flash the entire house rang with loud calls for a speech. From his seat in the rear of the gallery, Garrison walked down to the balcony railing and said that he had not intended to speak, but since he had been called upon, there were a few necessary observations to make about the meeting. "At the sound of that voice . . . there was a burst of rejoicing and applause from the congregation," an abolitionist woman from Fall River, Massachusetts, reported, and the cheering throng called for Garrison to come to the rostrum. He seemed reluctant, but the quickening applause gave him no option. The audience would not be denied "seeing freedom's champion occupying the highest place in freedom's hall," and Garrison made his way to the platform, half embarrassed, half vindicated, pressing his hands down to quell the outburst.

The editor had not spoken in Philadelphia since he had appeared with George Thompson in 1835, and he seized the moment with his matchless ability to charm and challenge an audience simultaneously. He regretted the absence of black speakers during the exercises and chided the planning committee for its timidity. He deplored the "squeamishness" he had detected on the subject of immediatism in Brown's speech. He knew such sentiments would be defended as necessary to demonstrate the abolitionists' "prudence and judiciousness," Garrison said, but he retorted that abolitionists had to learn "to hate these words." Slavery could not be overthrown without "a most tremendous excitement" that would awaken the timid and the apathetic and force a social conflict that he likened first to "a moral earthquake," then to a hurricane that roiled the waters, and finally to the martyr age of Christianity. He had given sacred purpose to an audience more ready to be roused than the managers of the event realized, though it seems likely that some of the strongest voices cheering for Garrison belonged to the one hundred or more women from the seaboard states who had come to Philadelphia for the concurrent national convention of female abolitionists. Indeed, it is possible—though no evidence exists—that the entire episode was a neat bit of "wire-working" on the immediatists' part that exploited Garrison's celebrity and his ability to take control of a meeting. Whether calculated or spontaneous, the little drama enhanced the editor's stature and emphasized, for once, the major principle upon which the feuding AAS men emphatically agreed.

The immediatists engaged in another ritual of reconciliation after the meeting, as the leading lights—Tappan, Stanton, Garrison, Wright—all attended a private event that united a Garrisonian perfectionist with an evangelical leader. Angelina Grimké, who had culminated the sisters' New England journey with an appearance before the Massachusetts legislature and a mighty series of lectures in Boston's Odeon Theater, had accepted an offer of marriage from Theodore Dwight Weld! Ever since the meeting of "the seventy," each had secretly cherished thoughts of the other, but only recently had the turbulent Weld declared himself. Although Garrison hailed the match as "a splendid alliance of mind," he candidly told Angelina that he feared that Brother Weld's sectarianism "would bring her into bondage, unless she could succeed in emancipating *him*." She had already agreed to formal "family worship" with daily prayer night and morning, Garrison reported to Helen, so Sabbatarian churchgoing would likely come next, and the formal observances—he feared—would hobble the work of the spirit. Angelina had smiled at Garrison's concerns and told him that she trusted " 'the experiment' would prove mutually serviceable."

For once in his life, Garrison had to hold his peace. The wedding took place on the evening of Monday, May 14, 1838, in the presence of thirty or forty guests, abolitionists all, who had walked the few blocks to the Grimké sisters' cottage on Spruce Street from Pennsylvania Hall. "What a motley crew did you assemble to witness the solemn scene," Angelina's mother wrote unhappily from Charleston when she learned that the salt-and-pepper guest list had included Garrison and Sarah Douglass, a black schoolteacher. The wedding couple had planned their own ceremony. Because Angelina was marrying outside her faith, there could be no Quaker service, nor could Friends attend without risking expulsion from their meetings. Lucretia Mott felt obliged to stay away, though Abby Kelley, the young Quaker teacher and convention delegate from Lynn who had organized Angelina's first successful lecture, bravely entered the parlor. John Greenleaf Whittier, nervous and shy under the best of circumstances, compromised by positioning himself in the hallway, just outside the door but within earshot.

His roommate Weld, smartly turned out in a brown coat and fresh white vest and cravat, opened by solemnly informing Angelina that he would abjure "the unrighteous power vested in a husband by the laws of the United States" and would honor only "the influence which love would give to them over each other." Angelina, dressed in a plain beige gown, promised to honor and love her husband, but pointedly omitted the traditional "obey." The company knelt with the couple for prayers, first by a black minister and then a white one, after which Sarah Grimké poured out her heart in a meditation of thanksgiving. Garrison then came forward to read the wedding certificate and pass it around for the guests to sign. Since Pennsylvania law did not require the presence of a magistrate, Garrison, the movement's leader, epitomized communal sanction for the vows. "It was an abolitionist wedding," Maria Chapman said gaily during the social hour. "A more interesting service I have never seen."

The Weld-Grimké nuptials proved to be a wedding within a war. Although Philadelphia had a reputation for orderliness, the visitors from Boston could recognize the signs of impending trouble. Posters called upon property-loving citizens to disperse the convention. Nasty leaflets, filled with racial abuse, swirled in the streets, and the sight of blacks and whites walking together provoked insults and menacing behavior toward the "amalgama-tionists." (Racist feeling in Pennsylvania had intensified as black people acquired a higher political profile in the abolition struggle, and a state constitutional convention had recently recommended restricting the suffrage to whites. An "Appeal of Forty Thousand Citizens," drafted by Garrison's friend Robert Purvis, sparked a protest campaign that contributed to the furor.) Yet the abolitionists went about their business, accepting the threat of violence as their due and, indeed, expecting it after Garrison had baited the venomous forces in his call for excitement.

The abolitionists applied even more pressure by deciding to hold a public meeting—and a "mixed" one, at that—on Wednesday evening, May 16,

1838, to demonstrate their steadfastness. They secured permission to move from one of the hall's ground-floor rooms, where the convention of women had met all day, to the "grand saloon" on the second floor—a luxurious auditorium filled with row upon row of blue plush chairs and brilliantly illuminated by gaslit chandeliers. Three thousand people had crowded into the hall, and many more had to be turned away. The audience remained orderly, but commotion could be heard outside, as Garrison opened the affair with a prepared speech that reiterated his objections to David Brown's gradualist propositions and insisted that God required principled and unremitting opposition to slavery and its apologists. A mob suddenly broke into the lobby, yelling and shouting so furiously that the editor thought "the very fiends of the pit had suddenly broken loose." Those seated in the back barred the doors and kept the rowdies at bay, while Garrison finished his speech with "great coolness and deliberation." He then introduced his dear friend, Maria Weston Chapman, who had shared that fateful October day of the mob at 46 Washington. For the first time in her life, Mrs. Chapman rose to speak before a mixed assembly of men and women, and while Garrison said she "acquitted herself nobly," the truth is that her brief remarks could scarcely be heard against the din. She waved her hands weakly and summoned Angelina Grimké Weld, whose experienced voice stood more chance of prevailing in the uproar.

With her husband, no stranger to mobbings, listening from the wings, the new Mrs. Weld made the speech of her life. "Do you ask, 'What has the North to do with slavery?' " she wondered. "Those voices [outside] tell us that the spirit of slavery is *here,* and has been roused to wrath by our conventions; for surely liberty would not foam and tear herself with rage, because her friends are multiplied daily, and meetings are held . . . to set forth her virtues and extend her peaceful kingdom." Angelina considered it every person's duty to show that abolitionists did not fear the mob. With brickbats flying and glass shattering against the blinds, she declared that even destroying the hall could not prove the abolitionists wrong or make slavery a wholesome institution. The mob carried on a frightful din as the speaker spent an hour telling of her painful exile from the land of her birth and the "horrors and pollutions" of slaveholding she had witnessed there. With the practiced speaker's confidence she did not neglect the details of organization, urging her audience to buy the pamphlets, subscribe to the newspapers, circulate the petitions, and in every way "come up to the work." When the shrill screams intensified outside, people stirred as if on the edge of panic, but cries of "Order!" throughout the house prevented a rising and fused the audience into a congregation of martyrs. "Her eloquence kindled, her eye flashed, and her cheeks glowed," Garrison said, and no one remained unmoved. At the end, strengthened by Angelina's heroic stand, the audience peaceably filed out into the street, where remnants of the crowd, its numbers diminished over the several hours, allowed the abolitionists a morose, generally unmolested passage, though some toughs harassed a black man in a side alley. Black neighborhoods remained on alert all night, but no more violence occurred.

Crowds of "profane ruffians," however, milled about the hall when the women returned the next morning, May 17, 1838, to their convention room, and as the day wore on, the throng swelled into a concourse of thousands. With rumors sweeping the city that the hall would be torched, Philadelphia's mayor asked the women to adjourn, and, toward evening, they complied, walking bravely from the building in a solemn procession, black and white together, with the "fierce, vile-looking men" sullenly parting to make a narrow path for them. Making a show of locking the doors, the mayor asked the crowd to retire, but when an abolitionist called out, "Get the militia," the mayor winked at the crowd and said, "We don't need the military here. You are my police." With cheers and applause echoing in the street, the mayor went home.

Within minutes a gang had bashed the doors in with axes and rushed into the hall, overturning chairs, smashing desks, and piling broken furniture and papers from the antislavery office in the center of the ballroom. Someone cut the gas pipes and applied a torch that set the temple of free speech ablaze. The famous "liberty bell" atop the Pennsylvania State House tolled the alarm, but the leaping flames could be seen across the city as the hall's zinc roof burned with a hot blue flame. Firemen poured water on the adjacent structures but did not turn their hoses on the burning edifice. Within an hour the roof had caved in, then the floors, and by midnight only the blackened granite walls remained. Old Benjamin Lundy, again toiling in Philadelphia, rushed to the hall to save his lifelong accumulation of papers from the antislavery office, but nothing was left. In the hulking ruin, Lundy said, he "could read . . . the woeful destiny of this nation of oppressors."

"Awful as the occurrence [was]," it would "do incalculable good to our cause," Garrison told friends when he returned to Boston. The destruction of the hall became the latest potent symbol of the violence perpetuated by slavery and the abolitionists' willingness to suffer for its demise. It seemed altogether fitting that Garrison received a poignant note from Lundy, reassuring his former partner that the files of their old *Genius* had, after all, survived the conflagration. "They have not yet got my *conscience*," Lundy said. "They have not taken my heart." The spectacle of the hall in flames—made vivid in a much-reprinted engraving—shocked public opinion and secured protection for the abolitionists. At the end of May the New England Anti-Slavery Convention met unmolested in Boston's recently built Marlboro Chapel, thanks to the firmness with which the city's new Whig mayor forestalled a rumored assault upon the dissenters' forum.

With more than five hundred people attending from every corner of the region, the gathering offered a high-spirited answer to the Philadelphia attack and provided an unrivaled opportunity for rallying the movement's "bone and muscle." Garrison took great delight in the mingling of country farmers and village mechanics with urban professionals, the blue-jacketed cordwainer from Lynn with the black caterer from New Bedford, the salty editor from New Hampshire with the minister from Vermont. With such raw materials, joked William Goodell, "the manufactory of finished fanatics is going on, hour after hour." The current batch included more than sixty women, for Garrison and his friends, inspired by the Grimkés' example, put forward a resolution that admitted them to the convention on an equal basis. The motion passed unanimously only because some of the more conservative "clerical abolitionists" had not yet arrived; later they would spare no effort to reverse the decision. Meanwhile the convention cheered Nathaniel P. Rogers, the editor of the popular *Herald of Freedom* in Concord, New Hampshire, for his comic exposition of another inequality: the "base, low, vulgar ailment . . . color-phobia, [or] dread of complexion" that "old Doctor Slavery" had injected in the public's veins. It is a disease, said Rogers, that makes people shout "darkey, darkey, darkey" and shut up meetinghouses, break school windows, and sneer at female speakers unless they simper. The only known remedy, *anti-slavery*, Rogers said, was discovered by "Dr. William Lloyd Jenner-Garrison" and "somehow changes and redeems the constitution." Garrison riposted that black people ought to get the credit, as "*Nature* taught them."

The good humor subsided when Abby Kelley, who had emerged as the Grimkés' indomitable successor in New England, was named to a working group charged with drafting an abolitionist call to the churches. The clerical caucus tried to intimidate Kelley by insinuating that it would be "disreputable" for her to be closeted with two men in committee. Any document they produced would have to be regarded as "unscriptural" by the bodies being addressed. Kelley held her ground, proving so assertive a speaker that no less a judge than Theodore Dwight Weld urged her to become a paid abolitionist lecture agent. When the ministers lost votes to discharge the committee and to reconsider the admission of women, they stormed out of the assembly to protest the introduction of a "foreign" issue that would injure the slave's cause.

The sectarian lull had ended. Whittier reported to Pennsylvania that the women's issue, despite its intrinsic merit, had "nothing to do" with the goal of the convention and "a discussion of the merits of animal magnetism, or of the Mormon Bible would have been quite as appropriate." This was no idle joke. Some ministers greatly feared that Garrison might turn into the prophet of some new perfectionist sect and lead decent people into the deserts of heresy and unbelief. For others, the woman question posed too severe a challenge to traditional authority. From Philadelphia, James Mott remarked to the Boston friends: "Verily some of our northern gentlemen abolitionists are as jealous of any interference in rights they have long considered as belonging to them exclusively, as the southern slaveholder is in the right of holding his slaves." Both orders must be "broken up," he added, and "*human* rights alone recognized."

Garrison exerted some special effort to advance the theme of racial equality in the aftermath of the Philadelphia violence. He was especially distressed to learn from Lucretia Mott that some "timid ones who are quaking with fear" had taken the terrible climate in Philadelphia as a sign that white abolitionists should not press too hard for social relationships between the races or protest the inequalities that their black colleagues daily faced. Such "half-way abolitionists," Mott wrote, were also trying to discourage black people from participating in the movement, a course that "*thorough* anti-slavery friends" should not countenance. Garrison fully agreed, and to emphasize the point, he offered a major address in New York's majestic Broadway Tabernacle to commemorate the final end of slavery in the British West Indies on August 1, 1838. Since Parliament had mandated emancipation five years earlier, black communities had pointedly ignored the Fourth of July in favor of First of August ceremonies, and the New York celebration would be the largest event yet in the series.

As was his custom, Garrison stayed in the home of the caterer Thomas Van Rensellaer, an agent for *The Liberator* and prominent in vigilance committee work, and he made a special point of recognizing how black participation sustained the movement. Even with his iconoclastic views Garrison exerted a magnetic appeal among black people. Frederick Douglass, a recently escaped slave who had been relocated in the North with the help of the New Yorkers, remembered how *The Liberator* had become his "meat and drink" and taken "a place in [his] heart second only to the Bible." When Douglass first heard the editor speak in New Bedford, the dilapidated hall with its cracked windows and half-sprung doors only enhanced the powerful impression made by the editor who aimed to triumph by conviction alone. His words seemed to glow with "holy fire" and so thrilled the former slave's heart that he looked upon Garrison as "the Moses raised up by God to deliver his modern Israel from bondage."

An audience of nearly four thousand people (two-thirds of whom were people of color, with New York's most influential black minister presiding) crowded into the Tabernacle to hear *The Liberator*'s editor. He had never spoken in such a reverberant hall, a circular auditorium with steeply banked seats personally designed by the great evangelist Charles G. Finney so that each place would have a close and uninterrupted view of the pulpit to facilitate the direct communication that inspired conversions. The audience listened raptly as Garrison hailed abolition as the "brightest triumph of humanity" and rebuked the gradualists who predicted that "turning loose" the slaves would lead to an orgy of bloodshed and the destruction of the plantation economy. The islands that had already ended the transitional period of apprenticeship had fared very well, Garrison argued, and only the most stony-hearted racist could not fail to be moved by the breaking of chains. When the slave system fell in the South, he predicted, the "moral aspect" of the region would change, for "the tide of western adventure and northern capital" would run "in southern channels" to build railroads and factories, establish schools, and awaken enterprise. (He had recently altered his newspaper's masthead to reflect this commercial vision by adding to the familiar woodcut of the slave auction a contrasting panel that depicted emancipation as a radiant hour of gospel preaching and unshackled labor.) Garrison concluded his ninety-minute talk with an anecdote about Grandfather Jacob, an Antiguan freedman who, when told there were still slaves in America, declared, "Ah, de Saviour will make dem free too. *He come to Antigo first— HE'LL BE IN 'MERICA SOON.*" "HE WILL BE IN AMERICA SOON!" Garrison shouted, as the hall rocked with cries of amen, and he cried out, "Come, come, Lord Jesus, come quickly, and bind up the broken-hearted, and set the captive free!"

The celebration proved to be another of the regenerative moments in which the abolitionists fused the idea of slave emancipation with the Christian vision of redemption and resurrection. In Garrison's mind, there was no more powerful justification for ending slavery than the Golden Rule, and he often emphasized his belief that abolition was "the spirit of Jesus" manifest first in the individual—be it apathetic Northerner or slaveholding Southerner—and then in the state and nation. Even people close to the Tappans and concerned about Garrison's radicalism appreciated his achievement. The movement had "morally revolutionized the nation," exclaimed the editor Samuel Cornish in the *Colored American,* having dragged slavery from its lair and confronted its apologists with "a CONSCIENCE . . . which will never sleep, until every slave is emancipated, and every colored man acknowledged as a brother."

Garrison's vision of the transfigured society received its fullest expression a few weeks later in September 1838, when he engineered the creation of a Christian nonresistance society. As Garrison's own thinking moved toward a philosophical concern about the role of force in all spheres of life, he began to regard the American Peace Society as too timid an agency for reform. Just as immediatists had taken on the colonizationists, so radical pacifists would have to challenge the cautious views of the APS leadership, which, not coincidentally, turned out to include some of Garrison's antagonists among the Congregational clergy. Over the course of the summer, May, Wright, and Garrison managed to attract support for an ad hoc convention that would discuss matters that the APS leadership considered too provocative, including the dangers of a standing army, the legitimacy of conscientious objection to military service, the evil of capital punishment, and the question of whether conscientious pacifists could vote for officials whose authority rested ultimately upon physical force.

Several hundred people helped found the New England Non-Resistance Society in Boston's Marlboro Chapel on September 20, 1838, a date that Garrison predicted would one day rival the Fourth of July as the herald of a new epoch for humanity. The majority of delegates were from Massachusetts, with a good handful from Rhode Island and a sprinkling of New Hampshiremen and Pennsylvanians. Although some were Quakers and a few belonged to orthodox churches, most were, as Lydia Maria Child described it, "swinging loose from any regular society [as] I and so many hundred others are doing at the present day" in search of greater spiritual freedom. (The quest was not confined to the radical fringe. In an address to the senior class at the Harvard Divinity School in July 1838, the Rev. Ralph Waldo Emerson had spoken of "a decaying church and a wasting unbelief," pointing to neighborhoods in which "half parishes are *signing off* . . ." Emerson's call for "new revelation" and his injunction that each graduate consider himself "a newborn bard of the Holy Ghost" who would "cast behind . . . all conformity and acquaint men at first hand with Deity" caused such commotion in religious circles that Emerson left the Unitarian ministry and was not invited back to Harvard for thirty years. Maria Chapman had sent Garrison a copy of the talk with a note describing how Emerson had incurred "the wrath of the Cambridge powers.")

The equal participation of women in the nonresistance meeting caused a stir, and when Abby Kelley gaveled to order a minister who happened to be the head of the APS board, he and seven offended colleagues walked out. Garrison produced a constitution ("radical in all things," he told Helen) that took its mandate from the Sermon on the Mount: "Ye have heard that it hath been said, An eye for an eye, and a tooth for a tooth: But I say unto you, That ye resist not evil: but whosoever shall smite thee on thy right cheek, turn to him the other also" (Matt. 5:38–39). Members of the New England Non-Resistance Society would promote the peaceable kingdom and abjure force; they would abstain from militia service, they would neither serve in offices that executed penal laws nor vote for officials whose authority derived from physical force; they would endure suffering for Christ's sake, and bear testimony against sin "until righteousness and peace shall reign in all the earth." Despite urging that governments be "overthrow[n] by a spiritual regeneration of their subjects," Garrison disavowed any "jacobinal" intent. Although nonresistants would neither hold office nor vote as a conscientious protest against the inherent violence of the state, they would "obey all the requirements of government, except such as we deem counter to the commands of the gospel; and in no case resist the operation of law, except by submitting to the penalty of disobedience."

Garrison had put "all the fanaticism of [his] head and heart" into a declaration of sentiments which went beyond the convention's preoccupation with the "inviolability of human life" to project a vision of Christian utopia. It was a striking illustration of Garrison's insistence upon establishing a new frontier before territory previously surveyed had been fully settled. Although he was no philosopher and had no formal education, Garrison was doing the work of an intellectual by questioning prevailing standards of moral judgment and envisioning a society that adhered to different principles. He refused to weigh the impact of his views upon the quest for political power—a refusal that infuriated his critics at the time as well as subsequent historians who find it difficult to fathom public discussion that is not keyed to the tactical constraints of the two-party system. In its millennial yearning, Garrison's nonresistance vision, indeed, can be seen as a confession of powerlessness, a blissful vision of transformed life to set against the cruelty of a society that sics mobs on outspoken editors, burns down halls in which men and women denounce social evils, permits churches to shelter slaveholders, and grants masters extra political power in proportion to the number of their slaves.

That the convention reached for perfect holiness reminded Garrison of abolition's earliest days and exalted him, though he knew that, as with antislavery, there would be no rush to join the new crusade even if people privately conceded the validity of the principles. Yet he insisted that nonresistance threw "a new light upon the atrocities of slavery" and charted a fresh path toward overcoming them through the power of Christian love. Lydia Maria Child, heartsick that her tight budget prevented attendance at the meeting, told Abby Kelley that "little as will be thought of it at present, the Peace Convention is unquestionably the greatest event in the 19th century. . . . Posterity will marvel at the early adoption of such transcendental principles, looking down on all the wider as well as narrower forms of human selfishness. . . ." Indeed, in 1904, Leo Tolstoy wrote of the "spiritual joy" he had experienced upon learning of Garrison's pioneering advocacy of the law of nonresistance and the repudiation of coercion in human affairs. "For the purpose of combatting slavery he advanced the principle of a struggle against all the evil of the world," Tolstoy said in admiration, and therefore he deserved to be remembered as one of "the greatest reformers and promoters of true human progress." Garrison had taken on the burden of the Christian witness who would offer faith against force and meekness against might and expect to prevail through "the foolishness of preaching." As would later be true of Mahatma Gandhi and Martin Luther King, Jr., however, nonresistance did not mean retreat, but conflict, for pacifist protest could draw out and expose the angry violence of a society and compel humanity to alleviate the suffering it caused.

While in Boston, Garrison found his family a new place to live. Helen could not face another cramped winter at Miss Parker's, with Dordie T. having become a rambunctious three-year-old and a new baby—William Lloyd Garrison, Jr., born January 19, 1838—already on the verge of walking. The editor took over the lease on a house rented by the Rev. Amos Phelps (a recent widower), which proved to be a roomy three-story tenement at 2 Nassau Court, a cul-de-sac off Tremont Street in the newish working-class district south of Boylston Market. Fully furnished, with five bedrooms and a small fenced yard, the house would be ample enough for the Garrisons and their anticipated visitors. At twenty-five dollars a month (including the furniture), all the friends pronounced it "a rare chance." Helen recalled it as a gloomy house, but Garrison brushed her reservation aside as the memory of visiting the late Mrs. Phelps's cheerless sickbed. Both house and street had a pleasant air and seemed "as quiet as the country," he said, and Helen yielded. Garrison got to work on the woodpile and laid in stores of potatoes and flour, and on October 1, 1838, the family moved in.

Their entourage included several of Helen's sisters, with their widowed mother expected later in the season, and a free black woman—who would cook at Nassau Court as she had for some years at Friendship's Vale—and her small child, Frederick, young Dordie's playmate.

Helen never pretended to be an activist like Maria Chapman or Abby Kelley; she lacked the confidence to speak or write in public, although she did devote hours to gathering signatures for petitions. Yet she shared Garrison's strong convictions on immediatism and nonresistance and spoke her mind in private gatherings with her customary grace. She lent her name publicly only to the petitions and the Anti-Slavery Fair, a regular part of the December holiday calendar, which the female abolitionists ran as a fundraising bazaar and a device, as Mrs. Chapman put it, "to keep the subject before the public."

With Marlboro Hall trimmed with evergreens and glowing in candlelight, the 1838 fair proved a popular and financial success, raising a record $1,100 for the cause and broadcasting antislavery seed in the form of hand-crafted objects affixed with appropriate mottoes. Pot-grabbers were called antislaveholders; needle books summoned the purchaser to "prick the conscience" of the master; bunches of decorated quills bore the label "Twenty-five weapons for Abolitionists." Many tables displayed imported gifts from English sympathizers, and a "post office" allowed ladies and gentlemen to exchange billets-doux and "sentiments" on antislavery themes. White and black families mingled sedately at the refreshment tables, and the Garrisons found themselves the happy center of attention. The women at Lynn, the editor heard with pleasure, would donate the proceeds of their own local fair to *The Liberator*.

The gift would be welcome, for Garrison once again had to alter the newspaper's arrangements. Realizing that he needed more help, he hired a bookkeeper, but he also wanted to make Oliver Johnson the "general agent" who would order supplies, undertake the weekly mailing (itself a three-day job of wrapping, addressing, bundling, and delivering to post office and quay), and take on a subeditor's chores of writing and proofreading. Garrison despaired, however, of convincing prospective donors that three positions— editor, agent, and bookkeeper—were needed in addition to a printer to make *The Liberator* a going concern.

Then there was Knapp himself—boyhood friend and cofounder of the paper, always ready to stay up late to finish a press run or to print another pamphlet without hope of remuneration, yet growing less competent and efficient by the month, attributable in part to his chronic sickliness and possibly, though no one would talk about it, to the printer's occupational hazard, a craving for alcohol. For years Garrison had known that Knapp's sloppiness in financial matters had cost the paper dearly, both from lost subscription revenues and the reluctance of donors to put money into a badly managed enterprise. No one ignorant of "the losses and crosses of every newspaper concern" could fairly judge Knapp's record, Garrison had loyally insisted, but the time had come to face facts. He decided to supplant Knapp's business role by inviting a reputable committee of staunch abolitionists—the real estate broker Francis Jackson, the patrician Edmund Quincy, and the outspoken Quaker merchant William Bassett of Lynn—to supervise the newspaper's finances. The trio would receive all money—donations as well as subscriptions—and pay all the bills (though without personal liability for them), guaranteeing that Garrison "shall be entirely free and untrammeled in the performance of his editorial duties" and that Knapp would be hired to print the paper at going rates. The committee would settle on the last Saturday of each month, first taking care of money owing for supplies, postage, fuel, the city carriers, and the bookkeeper. From the remaining receipts, the committee would pay, in order, Knapp's printing bill, the agent's salary, and finally the editor's monthly stipend, but upon reflection, all agreed that, in case of shortfall, it would be better for each man to receive a proportional share of the available money.

The agreement "very much relieved" Garrison's mind, he said, as did the committee's successful appeal for funds; with regular small donations of one to five dollars, and some generous $100 boosts from several of the female societies and Jackson himself, the committee tallied nearly $1,500 in gifts by September 1839. The outpouring embarrassed Garrison, who hated to compromise his independence with anything that smacked of charity or selfseeking, and he thanked the donors as their self-denying "anti-slavery steward." He expected to be poor all his life, the editor told them, because "my spirit yearns too strongly over a world involved in misery and ruin by its alienation from God, to be tied down to the gainful pursuits of a grovelling age."

Just as Garrison worked to lay a new foundation for his newspaper, a determined coalition of opponents labored hard to undermine it. Some reopened the attack upon Garrison for introducing extraneous issues into the paper. This time the problem was nonresistance, a spiritual vision that his critics reduced to a slogan by calling Garrison a "no government" man who would loose anarchy upon the land. "Truly, Jack Cade is come again," shuddered one critic, while others warned that Garrison would wreck the movement by forcing abolitionists to repudiate both the Sabbath and the ballot box. Personal attacks also intensified, with the editor being vilified as negligent, polygamous, imperious, and the pawn of a female "prime minister." Mrs. Chapman was "a talented woman with the disposition of a fiend," Lewis Tappan said, who could control Garrison "as easily as she could untie a garter."

In the swirl of rumor and distortion Garrison discerned a "clerical snake . . . coiling in the grass for a spring," and by the beginning of January 1839, he warned his friends that a "plot" existed to subvert both the Massachusetts Anti-Slavery Society and *The Liberator* by supplanting the pro-Garrison board at the annual meeting and voting to subsidize a rival paper. He suspected collusion among the instigators of the 1837 appeal and some of the ministers who served as lecture agents for the state society, who now lobbied for "political action *as a Christian duty*." That Ralph R. Gurley, still banging the colonizationist drum, turned up to lecture in Boston that very week only deepened Garrison's concern, especially when Gurley warned that Garrison had the power of "a Moses or a Mahomet . . . to effect a great revolution in civil society and to be the founder of a new basis of civil and social institutions."

The editor also surmised that the dissidents were being aided by the machinations of the national office. Birney's social distaste for Garrison had long been known, and he made no secret of his desire for a different newspaper in Massachusetts. Wright believed that Garrison had been "sucked into the vortex of spiritual Quixotism" and had urged him since 1837 to withdraw voluntarily from the movement. Stanton went even further and argued that it would be no bad thing to purge the eccentric and difficult Massachusetts leadership from the American Anti-Slavery Society. Stanton, who had read law in the highly political atmosphere of New York's Mohawk Valley towns and would shortly marry Elizabeth Cady, the daughter of an influential upstate judge, thought the time had come for abolitionists to work more directly to influence party nominations and election campaigns. With Garrison's contempt for conventional politics and philosophical opposition to voting looming as major obstructions, Stanton quietly collaborated with the editor's clerical opponents on the attack.

With Birney's help he contrived the specious argument that the AAS constitution mandated abolitionists to exercise the franchise, which meant that Garrison had forsaken its original principles and therefore had to be purged. Had not the editor earlier urged abolitionists to go to the polls, Stanton crowed, and had not Garrison himself voted in the congressional election of 1834 for the pacifist Amasa Walker? Of course he had, Garrison replied, and what of it? "Whereas we were then blind, now we see; and greatly do we rejoice in the light," he said. Voting per se was not the issue; it was, rather, the misguided effort to exclude from the movement those who did not choose to vote or did not want to devote their antislavery effort to electioneering.

Although Garrison joked with Knapp about the clergy's efforts to cast him out as "an Ishmaelitish editor," he took the threat of "internal sedition" very seriously and tried to head off some of the criticism. He had given only two columns on the back page to nonresistance topics, but supported the Weston sisters' idea to subsidize a separate monthly, *The Non-Resistant,* as a more appropriate vehicle for such exploration. He also came up with a plan to condense the best of the antislavery material from *The Liberator* into a dollar-a-year monthly magazine—to be supported by the MAS—that might meet the critics' stated objections.

Friends who could not attend the crucial annual meeting sent public letters of support. From Northampton, Maria and David Child prayed that the society not "stop to settle creeds while our brother lies wounded and bleeding by the way." That Garrison entertained "some views peculiar to but few in the religious world" had nothing to do with the objective of immediate emancipation, they said; if Clarkson had been "a Jew or a Mahometan, would it have been less the duty of Christians to work with him in his great labor of benevolence?" From Scituate, where a full household and an empty purse kept him from traveling, Samuel J. May took the opposite tack of defending Garrison's broadening interests by saying that as the cause advanced, "many things have come up for consideration which were not thought of in the beginning." The churches naturally had to be criticized for their unexpected silence, and women's voices inevitably had to be raised. The "catastrophe at Alton," May insisted, forced abolitionists to consider the issue of nonresistance to evil in its broadest forms. If the South were to resist antislavery measures in the District of Columbia, speculated another writer, then every abolitionist—not merely the nonresistants—would face the moral question of whether to shoulder a musket and march south to enforce the law. Such questions could not be avoided, but the abolitionist vanguard seemed intellectually strong enough to cope with Garrison's provocations, which, after all, probed the heart of the American polity. Only the "technical abolitionists" with their fretful desire to limit the issues, Maria Chapman warned, risked separating "the locomotive from the train."

The annual meeting proved the largest and most dramatic event in the seven-year history of the Massachusetts Anti-Slavery Society, for it irreversibly laid bare the divisions within the movement. When Francis Jackson called the session to order promptly at ten o'clock on the morning of January 23, 1839, Marlboro Chapel seemed to vibrate with suppressed excitement. For Garrison there was the "noble sight" of several thousand people—old and young, male and female, black and white—in the service of the cause. His legions of friends greeted the editor with "the right hand of fellowship," and many took him aside to press a few dollars into his pocket or tell him of their own spiritual pilgrimages. Looking over the hall, Garrison could not help but remember the snowy night when the society, one dozen strong, had held its first meeting in the basement of the African Meeting House on Belknap Street. During these three days of meetings they would hold one public session in Faneuil Hall and another in the State House, and each would be a convocation of thousands.

Buoyed by the large and enthusiastic turnout, Garrison's friends believed they could withstand the virulence directed against the editor by the clerical abolitionists. The Rev. Amos Phelps, who had resigned his MAS agency, angrily pronounced Garrison a wicked man who was unfit to lead any moral enterprise, while the Rev. Charles T. Torrey scoffed at the idea of an officially sponsored digest of *The Liberator* as warmed-over Garrisonism that would be politically offensive. If the MAS were to sponsor a paper, they said, Whittier or Elizur Wright ought to edit it.

Then Stanton spoke up. Strictly speaking, the New Yorker was not an MAS member, but the MAS board had recently offered him the general agent's post in place of Phelps, which gave him standing enough. Stanton was an energetic talker in small groups and a magnetic public speaker who claimed that he only followed Dr. Beecher's rule: pump yourself full of your subject until you can't hold another drop, then knock out the bung and let nature caper. What now flowed from Stanton's mouth, however, confirmed Garrison's worst fears about the coalition that opposed him. Stanton insisted that a new paper was indispensable. Garrison only published political material when the agents worked it into their own articles "sideways," he complained, and then tried to offset it in other columns of his own. "It is not that other subjects are introduced into The Liberator," Stanton said piously, "it is that *such* other subjects are introduced [that are] so injurious to the cause." Garrison might be "nearer right than I am" on the peace question, Stanton allowed, but by taking up nonresistance the editor had "lowered the standard of abolition" and become "recreant to the cause." He had to be replaced.

The editor and his friends sat thunderstruck at Stanton's "treachery." Garrison had known that his critics wanted a paper that "will be less offensive to the clergy, and less free in its spirit, and that will not dare to utter a word upon any other question of reform—*unless it be popular*." That the clerical opponents, however, had found so prominent a layman willing to read the editor out of the ranks came as a grievous blow, especially since Stanton had stayed with the Garrisons and given no hint of his shift in allegiance.

Garrison jumped up grim-faced to say that he had been regarded as the friend of the black man and the slave and hoped he still had their confidence.

"You have! You have!" the galleries roared.

"Am I recreant to the cause?" he called out.

"No! No!" came the answering shouts. When the noise subsided, Garrison went on to say that he had always urged men to be consistent. If their consciences permitted them to go to the polls, he hoped they would vote in support of their abolition principles without regard to party needs. The point, he believed, was "not to prove it the duty of every abolitionist to be a voter, but . . . the duty of every voter to be an abolitionist."

"Let me ask him a question," Stanton interrupted. "Mr. Garrison! Do you or do you not believe it a sin to go to the polls?"

The question stunned the audience. No abolitionist had ever before presented "a creed-measure to his brethren," Maria Chapman said later. Stanton appeared ready to don the Inquisitor's robes and "lord it over the consciences" of the movement, Garrison thought. He would not fall into the trap. In the hushed auditorium, his answer rang out with bell-like simplicity.

"Sin for *me*."

Stanton would not accept the answer. "I ask you again," he roared. "Do you or do you not believe it a sin to go to the polls?"

With surpassing sweetness, Garrison again replied, "Sin for *me*."

He had honored his own scruples without starting a side debate on non-resistance or reading anybody out of the movement. If Garrison had answered more prescriptively, however, Stanton was ready to lead a purge himself. He had a resolution in his pocket that declared that every eligible abolitionist had a duty to vote and termed those who refused—*"under any pretext"*—to be "guilty" of deviating from "the original and fundamental principles of the antislavery enterprise." The New Yorker wisely kept this inflammatory resolution from the floor, but a milder one by one of his clerical allies was voted down as a harbinger of "spiritual tyranny."

The opposition—an obviously slender but exceedingly vocal minority—tried stratagem after stratagem. They asked to divide the resolutions. They challenged the propriety of women voting on them, but Francis Jackson sternly rebuked the ploy. They filibustered until the body imposed a fifteen-minute time limitation, whereupon Stanton cried that they were being "gagged." Eventually the proposal for a different newspaper was defeated and the incumbent board triumphantly reelected, but not before the black clothes dealer John T. Hilton made the meeting's most eloquent defense of Garrison.

He had stood by Brother Garrison, said Hilton, when the young man was living on bread and water to sustain *The Liberator*. He had stood by Brother Garrison when the editor was dragged through the streets by the gentlemen of property and standing. He had known Brother Garrison for eight long years and had never seen him waver from principles. "If Brother Garrison was not a simon pure, sincere abolitionist," Hilton concluded, "than neither he nor his colored brethren would ever trust or confide in a man with a white face again." "This was received with a response that made the Temple shake," said a stunned reporter for the *Ipswich Register*. In the back of the hall John E. Fuller, the only founding member to turn against the editor, groused that when Garrison went to hell, the colored people would undoubtedly follow him there, too.

While Garrison's friends celebrated their victory at a testimonial dinner for *The Liberator,* a distorted version of the meeting went back to the New York office. Stanton told his politically minded friends that Garrison had "made a desperate push to sway the Society over to his nonresistance views [and] succeeded." This was exactly what they wanted to hear about the demon editor, but the statement was a distortion. Actually, Stanton had made a desperate push to have Garrison condemned for his nonresistance views—and failed. Although most of the state society's members did not, in fact, subscribe to nonresistance principles, they nonetheless cherished Garrison's leadership and did not share the New Yorkers' belief that the editor had to be jettisoned to maintain the movement's advance. Garrison was "an historical fact in the annals of antislavery," proclaimed the New Hampshire editor Nathaniel P. Rogers, and his newspaper was "the Ithuriel's spear" that stripped the enemy of disguise and exposed its real shape and dimensions.[*]

In movement discourse, henceforward, the "enemy" included sectarians as well as slaveholders. The hostile ministers soon got up a newspaper, the *Massachusetts Abolitionist*, that condemned the MAS for becoming "a woman's rights, no-government organization" and ridiculed Garrison as "the reformer-general of humanity." Charles Torrey took to calling Garrison's newspaper *The Lying-Berator*, and Amos Phelps loftily proclaimed that "we are where we are because Mr. Garrison is not where he was."

As the personal and ideological controversy intensified, fresh voices tried to calm it. From Northampton, Maria Child bemoaned the arcane nature of the argument, reporting that people in her region had only "a vague notion that it is a squabble between Presbyterians and Quakers, and of course side with the former." With her customary aplomb, Child had found the most pertinent metaphor for a quarrel between institutional authority and antinomian vision, and she urged that "somebody explain in a few brief clear words that the Massachusetts Board . . . [is] . . . not seeking to sustain Garrison, or Perfectionism, or any other ism" but appreciated *The Liberator* "because it represents a *principle of freedom*." The argument, however, had passed beyond patient distinctions. The dissenters had so scapegoated Garrison that nothing would satisfy them short of his repudiation of nonresis-

---

[*]In Milton's *Paradise Lost* the angel Ithuriel found a toad squatting at Eve's side and with a touch of his spear revealed the creature to be Satan himself.

tance, while the majority no longer wanted to "hold fellowship with that opposition to slavery which only manifests itself by opposing abolition."

"Pierced to the heart" by the breach, Garrison's mentor George Bourne thought it would be wise to bring "some of us *Aboriginals*" up to Boston to mediate what seemed to be a family quarrel. When John G. Whittier, however, made a personal appeal not to let "trifling" differences obscure the depth of shared devotion to "the vital principles of universal liberty," an exasperated Garrison complained in print that Whittier approached pacification in "the Henry Clay style" by refusing to recognize issues of conscience. With comparable irritation the Quaker poet professed himself sick of "this everlasting dingdong" about conscience and declared that he would rather Garrison and Phelps have "a regular set of fisticuffs" in the street than continue their incessant skirmishing in the newspapers. If people could not agree on "a harmony of measures" for concerted action, "the sooner we scatter, each man to his tent, the better."

The poet had a point. The argument had become so obscured by personal animosity that no one asked whether the sides could pursue their objectives simultaneously. Yet the clergymen and the politicians had deliberately invited a struggle over personalities by keeping their agenda concealed behind "the Garrison question." Though Phelps and Torrey insisted that they could readily advance abolitionism within their denomination once the radical editor of *The Liberator* was suppressed, this was an argument based on no discernible evidence. It is difficult to avoid the conclusion that the clerical abolitionists were being used by the most conservative clergy to divide the abolitionist ranks, silence Garrison, and preserve their Beecherite position as apologists or gradualists. (Indeed, several years later, one of the ministers who had signed the clerical abolitionists' appeal, Charles Fitch, publicly apologized to Garrison for having joined the attack for selfish reasons of professional advancement.)

Sadly enough, Garrison's long friendship with Whittier became a casualty of the quarrel. The editor had broken with his mentors, but this was the first time he had become estranged from a friend and brother. Though they continued to exchange views in public, they would be old men before their fellowship was restored. Whittier despaired that Garrison had become "a Robespierre" who had "a perfect incapacity of tolerating those who differ from him." Hurt and infuriated, Garrison could not understand why the poet could not see through the campaign of contrivance and distortion intended to drive the editor from the movement. Their breach prefigured the next eighteen months of conflict as the coalition of Garrison's antagonists labored against him. "The split is wide, and can never be closed up," Stanton declared, relishing a contest in which "Garrisonism and Abolitionism" would contend for "mastery." Though they accused the editor of a tyrannical attempt to impose his views, they were actually being more proscriptive, and

while his critics believed that they were ridding the movement of its alba-
tross, many others believed that they were attempting to purge its greatest
asset. To deride Garrison publicly as a traitor to the cause his stubborn
independence had done so much to advance, however, proved a severe mis-
calculation. The editor's very real need for vindication meant that he would
neither moderate his views nor quietly stand aside. The polarization that
ensued—a division of the abolitionist host into separate and mutually hostile
organizations—would take on the fearful name of *schism*.

CHAPTER THIRTEEN

SCHISM

—•◆•—

IN CHURCHES AND REVOLUTIONARY MOVEMENTS, SCHISM HAS HISTORI-
CALLY BEGUN WITH A CONTROVERSY OVER HERETICAL IDEAS AND REACHED
A CLIMAX ON MATTERS OF ORGANIZATIONAL DISCIPLINE AS ONE SIDE TRIED
to impose its beliefs upon the other as a condition of membership. In the
case of the abolition movement, Garrison insisted upon the right to advocate
his ideas but made no attempt to enforce them as a creed. His opponents,
however, found both his principles and his advocacy so threatening that they
tried to drive him from the organizations, or failing that, to found new and
more restrictive ones for themselves. The ostensible issues in 1839–40 were
perfectionism, political action, and the participation of women, and Garrison's antagonists maneuvered to use each as a weapon against him in the
AAS meetings. Underlying the substantial ideological differences there lay
the questions of how much agitation any cause could sustain and whether
the movement was in fact subject to any kind of central discipline or control.

When the aristocratic James G. Birney published a harsh attack upon the
nonresistant abolitionists just before the annual meeting in May 1839 that
once again challenged their right to remain members of the AAS, he sounded
like any conservative defender of traditional society. An Alabama planter who
had emancipated his own slaves, lectured for the AAS, and published an
antislavery newspaper whose press was destroyed by a mob in Cincinnati,
Birney had mounted his own challenge to the prevailing order. Yet he belonged to what Maria Child called the "stop there" party, and he depicted
Garrison and those sharing his views—the "go ahead" party, in Child's
terms—as infidels and anarchists who would "strike at the very root of the
social structure and tend to throw society into entire confusion. . . ." Just as
abolitionists had gained the strength necessary to exert a salutary influence
upon Congress, these wild men—espousing ideas that were modern excres-
cences sprung from the "fungi" of Reformation sects—denounced all governments as tools of the devil and deprived us of our efficiency, Birney
lamented. We are like two physicians, he suggested, one of whom prescribes
restoratives while the other insists upon medicines that will destroy the patient; how can we proceed together?

"When abolition doctors disagree . . . ask the *patient* to decide," retorted
William Powell, who ran a New York boardinghouse for black seamen and
typified the grassroots radicalism essential to Garrison. As "one who has been

sick *all* his days, and knowing that the [slavery] *disease* still continues to make sad havoc among my colored countrymen," Powell advised "all true-hearted abolitionists to buy and circulate the genuine medicine . . . immediatism . . . to be had only at No. 25 Cornhill. . . ."

In practice, the attempt to purge Garrison as a perfectionist or nonresistant foundered on the movement's respect for individual conscience. "If impudence ever reached the point of sublimity," Oliver Johnson declared, "it was when Birney told Garrison that 'it was his duty, being a non-resistant, to leave the movement he had founded.' " Antislavery gatherings had a robust and contentious atmosphere that the participants greatly enjoyed; people appreciated the opportunity to give their testimony and ponder the speculations of their comrades. Garrison's conviction that universal reform could be gained only through the medium of free discussion was, in fact, widely shared throughout the movement; hardly a week passed without his receiving several letters from people, who ostensibly inquired after the editor's views while taking the opportunity to inform him—at some length—about the progress of their own thoughts. "Let every man be fully persuaded," Garrison liked to say, quoting Saint Paul (Rom. 14:5), as he marked many passages of correspondence for insertion in *The Liberator*. Garrisonian abolitionism grew out of the fundamental Protestant ideal of the right of private judgment, but it also was premised upon a deep-seated belief in the autonomy of communities, be they religious congregations or town meetings. The very idea that one ought to surrender one's moral autonomy for the central organization's sake struck Garrison as analogous to compromising with slavery for the sake of union, and he valued the abolitionist organization as a voluntary, constituent-based enterprise of many units.

Though the New Yorkers on the executive committee thought of themselves as national leaders, they were actually not much more than managers of the national publishing program and the agency system; these were vitally important, to be sure, but they offered reciprocal support and stimulus to the array of energetic local and state societies. The annual national meeting in May passed policy resolutions, of course, but it often seemed that they served simply as the scaffolding for discussion, rather than a platform or contract to which agents and members were pledged. The meetings seemed more significant as emotional rallying points, celebrations of the movement's gathering strength, and efforts to attract the notice of the broader public gathered in New York for the conventions of other reform groups.

The schismatics' efforts, therefore to impose ideological tests upon abolitionists affronted both the individual religious conscience and the popular, localist nature of the movement. "Even while professing to be laboring for emancipation, they have always been careful to express their hatred of the *free spirit* in which abolitionists carry on the enterprise," Maria Chapman observed. The antislavery cause would remain safe just so long as "farmers, mechanics, and workingmen are allowed a full and unobstructed participation in all its proceedings," Garrison predicted. "Limit this right to the few, instead of extending it to the many, and courage will give place to timidity, principle to expediency, integrity to corruption, and liberty to conservatism." One would have, in other words, a managed party caucus, not a popular insurgency.

The editor did not raise the specter of party dictation lightly, for his antagonists' call for political action at the ballot box seemed directed at making the AAS into a partisan instrument. Of Birney and Stanton's ambitious intentions he had little doubt, though the pious Lewis Tappan was known to have strong reservations about the organization's involvement in the inevitably sordid business of politics. Yet it was Tappan who tried to put into the society's 1839 annual report an insistent argument that all abolitionists must vote. The report maintained that because Congress ignored petitions and consigned them "to the dust and cobwebs of oblivion," abolitionists could influence the legislature only by using the ballot to alter its composition. "If the ballot-box be given up," Tappan wrote, "the cause is given up with it." Indeed, Birney added in a presumed blow at Garrison, it would be inconsistent of AAS members to argue against voting.

Garrison did not let such prescriptive statements go unchallenged and prevented, by a large majority, the 1839 national meeting's adoption of any test for membership. Birney's statement misrepresented the radicals' position, for they never sought to limit the actions of others; they opposed only those measures that would make the AAS "a thoroughly political organization," preoccupied with the machinery of nominations, platforms, and electioneering and the need to purify itself of elements that might frighten away votes. Garrison insisted that voters and conscientious objectors could "rally together, *en masse*," to alter public opinion so thoroughly that "a rectified political action is the natural consequence." In his view political *influence* could be exercised in many ways, even by those who declined to *create* a Congress by casting votes in an election. After all, he said, the law prohibited women, minors, and aliens from voting, but that did not disqualify them from participation in the abolitionist enterprise.

Garrison declared that he always expected "to see abolition at the ballot box" in ways that would dispel "the sorcery influences of party," stir up the "torpid consciences" of voters, substitute antislavery representatives for proslavery ones, and rescind all the laws that sanctioned slavery. He insisted, however, that such a "political reformation" could only come about "by a change in the moral vision of the people." The voters had first to accept immediatism as their soul-force; then they could be counted in politics. To expect people to vote with antislavery gestures before they had become abolitionized would be to risk a dilution of principle and open the way to the gradualist talk that he had heard at Pennsylvania Hall in 1838. Without a change in moral sentiments, especially on the issue of racial equality, any electoral changes would be superficial and useless. "It has never been a difficult matter to induce men to go to the ballot-box," Garrison argued in words that anticipated Thoreau's, "but the grand difficulty ever has been, and still is, to persuade them to carry a good conscience thither, and act as free moral agents, not as the tools of party."

In his advocacy Garrison thus emphasized the political necessity of moral criticism. His devotion to nonresistance became a demonstration of soul-force, an embodiment of truthful witness that M. K. Gandhi would, a century later, describe as *satyagraha*. In this he acted upon the ethics of absolute conviction rather than upon a sense of practical politics. Given all the in-ducements—both noble and ignoble—to compromise, given all the coun-sels—both wise and self-serving—of expediency, someone, Garrison believed, had to stand for the ideal and move the society toward it by making people feel the shameful gap between the truth and the tolerable. When such protest had gathered enough new elements to make itself felt in society, power would be reconstituted on a more just basis. For Garrison, politics had to be understood in a moral framework, and the abolition movement had to remain a religious enterprise that opened hearts to the imperatives of Christian love. Rather than purge its perfectionists, the movement ought to take inspiration from their temperament, for—in Garrison's view—the redemption of the slave ultimately depended upon the regeneration of the free.

When the conservatives found that they could not purge Garrison on the issues of nonresistance or political action, they deepened the schism on the one controversial issue that did not originate in the editor's "peculiar" views: the woman question. The issue of female participation in the antislavery societies did not, in fact, arise on its own merits, but as a facet of "the minister question" posed by the clerical abolitionists' efforts in 1837–38 to dampen antislavery agitation in the interests of church unity. When the Mas-sachusetts clergy's pastoral letter fulminated against female lecturers in an effort to silence the Grimké sisters, the issue was joined, and Garrison and his friends promptly met it as a denial of the universal principles of equality.

Women had participated in the antislavery activities in both Great Britain and the United States for several decades, but always in the framework of private associations that did not break the boundaries of the domestic sphere in which women were confined by ideology and tradition. Female partici-pation in the Finneyite revivals had led, in fact, to the rise of missionary and benevolent societies for women that addressed a host of social problems, including intemperance and urban vices such as prostitution. Prevailing ide-ology endorsed such endeavors with the assumption that women brought to the work of uplift their special talents for compassion, generosity, and love. Even the conservative clergy could endorse female charity and reform work as long as they remained separate and private activities that did not infringe upon the masculine domains of politics and power and violate the purity of "true womanhood" by dragging the fairer sex into the competitive and selfish ways of men.

The boundaries of women's sphere became harder to respect, however, as antislavery women organized their own societies, wrote polemical essays and published magazines, put on fund-raising fairs, sold newspaper subscriptions, and went door-to-door to gather petition signatures. It seemed absurd, for example, that Prudence Crandall, when challenged for radical work within her own sphere of schoolteaching, had to rely upon men to speak for her in the public meetings that sought to repress her. It seemed equally wrong for tradition-bound ministers to endeavor to silence the Grimkés because their call to deliver their special testimony about slaveholders became powerful enough to attract mixed audiences to the largest meeting halls in every town they visited. Since ministers had encouraged women to take up the work of reform, they could not criticize the momentum that had taken it in new directions. It was like the case of the sorcerer's apprentice, Maria Child dryly observed. "They have changed the household utensil to a living, energetic being; and they have no spell to turn it into a broom again."

For Garrison the woman question clearly demonstrated how the logic of reform united all good causes and carried them to radical new ground. If in their endeavors to break the chains of slavery women discovered, as Abby Kelley put it, that "*we* were manacled *ourselves,*" then abolitionist principle required a defense of equal rights without regard to sex or race. Realization came slowly, however. Despite the feminist inquiries advanced in Sarah Grimké's essays of 1838, it took another decade before a vanguard could launch at the first women's rights convention in Seneca Falls, New York, in July 1848, a direct challenge on the issues of discrimination in voting, education, and property rights.

A defense of the right to be public abolitionists proved one of the crucial steps in laying the basis for a feminist ideology as well as raising the consciousness and liberating the energies of a significant number of pioneers. A generation of female Quaker speakers, for example, helped forge the activism of a Lucretia Mott, who in turn gave heart to Sarah and Angelina Grimké, whose 1837 tour called Abby Kelley to her vocation as abolitionism's most militant and indefatigable lecture agent. A tall and sturdy farmer's daughter from Worcester, Massachusetts, who had come into the movement after hearing Garrison speak in 1832, Kelley had become a schoolteacher and activist among the Friends in reform-minded Lynn and followed the same path as had Garrison and the Grimkés in reaching a perfectionist's concern for "the truth at whatever cost." She attended the female abolitionist conventions of 1837 and 1838, helped to found the Non-Resistance Society with Garrison, and had become the target of clerical abuse for her willingness to serve on a mixed business committee at the New England convention. Taking inspiration from one of Garrison's favorite texts, "God hath chosen the weak things of the world to confound the things which are mighty" (1 Cor. 1:27), Kelley renounced schoolteaching and dedicated herself not only to abolitionist organizing but to taking on the hardest assignments in previously unvisited areas. There she risked physical harm and endured verbal abuse as a temptress and a harlot who would beguile men's minds and work a female's sorcery upon the body politic.

By 1840 Kelley had forged a courageous and remarkable record that Garrison saluted in *The Liberator* as undeniable proof that the antislavery field was her eminently "appropriate sphere." The editor saw the woman question as another instance in which the right of private judgment and impartial liberty had to prevail over conventional arrangements, and it was not at all difficult for him to absorb nascent feminism into his budget of heresies. Although Garrison had married a woman whose quiet nurturance provided a level of security he had not received from his combative mother, he seemed more exhilarated than threatened by strong-minded women and cooperated readily with them in movement activities. Prudence Crandall and Maria Stewart had sought him out for support, and he had collaborated comfortably for years with a diversity of female colleagues ranging from the aristocratic and judgmental Weston sisters to briskly practical Maria Child and the militant Abby Kelley. From the very beginning Garrison had identified a female constituency as essential to the movement and fully agreed with Maria Chapman's observation that women whose efforts could not be hindered by men were more valuable to the movement than men whose "dignity" forbade them to accept women as colleagues. It is a measure of both his intellectual honor and tactical flexibility that he understood and turned to advantage the unprecedented convergence that made twin issues of abolition and women's rights.

It came as no surprise that the anti-Garrison coalition included many who objected to female participation in politics and tried to put the lid back on Pandora's box by blocking their membership in the AAS. Though the MAS and the New England Anti-Slavery Convention had previously recognized women as voting members, the AAS had not formally addressed the issue before 1839. Women had held their own convention concurrently with the AAS in 1837 and 1838, but in 1839 women expected to participate in the annual meeting despite a looming challenge. One Massachusetts minister reported himself "sickened" to see that the MAS was sending women to New York as delegates and wondered that "any female can have effrontery enough to go. . . . I am for having women enjoy their rights, but do not wish to have them claim the prerogatives of men." Elizur Wright agreed; he was "opposed to hens crowing," he said, and thought "the tom turkeys ought to do the gobbling." A shrewd manager, however, he thought that little would be gained (and much harm done) by straining to interpret the AAS constitution in a manner that would exclude women. His cohorts attempted it anyway. Birney, Tappan, and others feared that Garrison would use the women's vote to dominate the organization and fasten his other heretical ideas upon it. On the woman question, as with nonresistance, Garrison symbolized the possibility of a more thoroughgoing social transformation than the conservative abolitionists were prepared to accept. In order to suppress or purge the socially disruptive Garrison, they realized, they would have to bar women.

The 1839 meeting witnessed a two-day debate over whether the membership roll should be made up of *men* or *persons*. Delegate after delegate—including Abby Kelley and Eliza Barney, a Quaker from Nantucket—rehearsed arguments sharpened in the two years since the Grimké sisters' lectures had first provoked opposition. (Neither sister was present, however. Angelina Weld was in the throes of a difficult pregnancy and had exhausted herself combing Southern newspapers—more than twenty thousand issues, her sister had estimated—for stories of abuses that Weld could use in his best-selling compilation *Slavery As It Is*. Sarah Grimké had stayed home to nurse her sister, but some women feared that Brother Weld had heavily pressured them to stay clear of the growing factionalism.) When, finally, the convention voted to admit male and female delegates on an equal basis, Garrison exulted that to have the issue "irrevocably" settled was worth "all the money in the treasury." However, Lewis Tappan nonetheless got up a starchy "protest" which condemned the "repugnant" admission of women as "an expression of local and sectarian feelings . . . well suited to bring *unnecessary* reproach and embarrassment to the cause of the enslaved, inasmuch as [it] is at variance with general usage and sentiments of this and all other nations. . . ." The woman question refused to subside and became the proximate cause of the schismatics' withdrawal from the AAS the following year.

What the conservatives could not accomplish nationally at New York, they tried at the state level in Massachusetts. While the popular movement gloried in its annual New England convention at the end of May 1839, the dissident clergymen and their politically minded allies met privately at the Marlboro Hotel to form a new statewide organization. The MAS, they said, had allowed its destinies "to be moulded at will by a little minority of nonresistants" and had consequently become preoccupied with extraneous subjects "foreign to our original objects, not necessary to their attainment, and in the view of the reflecting, *fatal to our prospects of ultimate success*." Their address to the public made it plain that their association—officially called the Massachusetts Abolition Society, but known everywhere by the sobriquet "new organization"—would be open only to gentlemen ("sober, serious, and prayerful," as Phelps put it) and would make electioneering incumbent upon its members. Its business meetings, the leaders promised, would be strictly confined to the officers and agents, supplemented by one delegate for every twenty-five members of an auxiliary, the same ratio employed in composing the state legislature. (Privately, its adherents told potential members that such tight control would keep "disorganizers" and "Amazons" from railroading the meetings toward "the ulterior ends" of William Lloyd Garrison.)

Old-line abolitionists promptly denounced the new organization men as schismatics who were imposing a proscriptive creed upon the movement. The executive committee of the MAS—the "pioneer" society, it said pointedly—argued publicly that "the real ground of division" was not that the MAS sanctioned "peculiar doctrines" but that "it has refused to condemn them." Boston's black leaders emphasized, too, that the new organization had grown out of "the very root" of the 1837 clerical abolitionists' appeal and was "tainted too much with Colonization." Others contended that the Massachusetts secessionist group was little more than Stanton and Birney's stalking horse and a pawn of the New York committee. The new organization put no agents in the field, collected very few signatures on its petitions (1,200 to the MAS 37,000), attracted few subscribers to its newspaper, and, if anything, boosted *The Liberator's* readership. At the end of 1839, Garrison reported, with slight amazement, that his subscription list had never before contained so many names.

The attack on Garrison had manifestly backfired. The mean-spirited ministers such as Torrey and St. Clair, who thought that purging Garrison would enhance their own reputations, found themselves stranded between the radicals they had schemed against and the conservative denominational leaders who still refused to join the cause. The new organization had neither a clear program to contrast with that of the MAS nor a visionary spokesman to match Garrison. Birney's style retained too much of the oligarchic planter's hauteur, and he disdained the popular base of the movement. Though Stanton appreciated grassroots organizing and knew how to rouse a crowd, his transparent ambition and reputation for mendacity tainted any inclination he might have had for spiritual leadership. Elizur Wright's administrative talents far exceeded his literary gifts and he could do little with the rival newspaper, while the hot-tempered Phelps was too preoccupied with petty grievances to offer much direction or inspiration. His only success came, ironically, given his conservatism on the woman question, in the manner in which he encouraged some of the women in his church—and those of his closest associates among the schismatics—to carry the fight into the Boston Female Anti-Slavery Society, which became rent by schism even before the national society. "The *Liberator* folk" in the BFAS found themselves outmaneuvered by their conservative officers, who were close to Phelps, and it took an extraordinary mobilization of black women members to preserve the society in the face of the high-handed new organization attempts to dissolve it. The carryings-on enraged everybody, including the normally placid Helen Garrison, and made the schism loom larger in Boston than anywhere else.

Although the incessant quarreling taxed Garrison's patience ("all his Welsh blood is up," the Weston sisters told each other gleefully), the editor checked the urge to publish the lengthy and defensive personal replies to critics that had wearied both sides during the clerical abolitionists' appeal. Instead he left most of the editorial counterpunching to Oliver Johnson and Maria Chapman, while the MAS board of managers replied publicly to the misrepresentations of the schismatics. Though the board's statements bore the signs of the editor's pen, they had an institutional weight and credibility that protected Garrison and allowed him to concentrate upon providing the visionary leadership that no one else could supply.

As the controversy swirled through 1839, its acrimonious nature took its toll on the Garrison family. The spring had not, in fact, been a happy few months at Nassau Court, with both children sick for weeks with whooping cough and young George—a "difficult to manage" three-year-old—causing his fretful parents no end of trouble. "He has a tremendous will of his own, and he is very passionate," Garrison told friends, adding with rueful candor that in his obstinacy the boy was " 'a chip off the old block' and something more." There was, moreover, no prospect of sufficient time or money for the usual summer's respite in Brooklyn. Worse yet, the lease on Phelps's house would expire at summer's end, and rather than negotiate a renewal with his nemesis, Garrison would be looking for new accommodations.

The family moved in September 1839, to cheaper and smaller quarters—one half of a house across the Charles River in Cambridgeport. Even then, to make it go they had to take Oliver and Mary Ann Johnson along as paying boarders. "The omnibus goes in and comes out every half hour, and will leave any one at our door," Garrison said wistfully, but the new place was more like Aunt Farnham's crowded tenement of his boyhood than the bucolic Freedom's Cottage of his honeymoon. Their section of Cambridgeport was a neighborhood that developers had conceived as the American Venice—with canals connecting warehouses, shops, and homes along the river—but financial reverses had left a dispiriting marshland of decrepit houses and decaying wharves.

Moving entailed extra expense that Garrison could ill afford. With his salary two months in arrears, he had to ask Francis Jackson and Samuel Philbrick for emergency loans of $100 apiece to furnish the kitchenware, coal grates, carpets, and supplies for the new house. Then he had to borrow from his brother-in-law George to clear the short-term debt and started one of those anxious spirals that habitually afflicted the editor's accounts and forced Helen to become a paragon of frugal household management.

The financial scramble was intensified by the sudden reappearance of Garrison's seafaring brother. One day in late September 1839, the editor received a pathetic summons from the Charlestown Navy Yard, where he found a weather-beaten sailor who introduced himself as Garrison's long-lost brother James. While Lloyd had made his name protesting the lash, James had suffered under it, enduring abuse in the merchant marine and the U.S. Navy that, in its physical cruelty and denial of rights, rivaled anything that Garrison had published in *The Liberator* about slavery. Alcohol had eased James's pain and contributed to his ruin. Confined now to the infirmary on the U.S.S. *Columbus,* James looked wretched, with shaking hands, the drunkard's splotched face, and a gaunt frame bent nearly double with a spinal complaint. The man was obviously a hardship case, and Garrison asked his captain for permission to take James home to procure him medical treatment and extend him such nurturing care "as a brother's affection could prompt." The officer agreed, but insisted that the editor post a forty-dollar bond against the enlisted man's return. (Subsequently Garrison had to forfeit the bond in order to obtain his brother's discharge in a bureaucratic quarrel that only reinforced his antagonism toward "heartless" government.)

Brother Jemmy turned out to be another child in their midst. By turns self-pitying and quarrelsome, the shattered man would listen humbly to Garrison's high-minded lectures on the path of Christian reformation and submit to the courses of homeopathic medical treatments that his brother prescribed. As soon as he recovered some strength, however, James would start roaming the waterfront and, falling in with old shipmates, reacquaint himself with "the fatal poison." Thereupon the brothers would reenact the old scenes of remonstrance and abnegation that Sister Garrison had conducted with her prodigal son, and the remorseful James would bless the Garrisons for their kindness and resume his place as a melancholy invalid on the fringe of the household.

If the editor felt embarrassment at the presence of his reprobate brother, he never voiced it. James became both a burden and an opportunity, and there were evenings when "old Sinbad"—as James liked to style himself—held the antislavery social circle transfixed with stories of the horrifying abuse American sailors endured at the hands of their officers. James's most serious illness—a "fistulous abscess at the base of the backbone," in Garrison's words—seemed related to the many whippings he had suffered, and the editor encouraged his brother to write an account of his experience that might serve as both personal confession and social polemic. Though James produced a vivid account of his descent into drunkenness and the floating hells on which he labored, the editor, in the end, made no effort to publish the testimony.

While Garrison took on the burdens of one alcoholic, he shed himself of another. Isaac Knapp had gone from being a quiet tippler to a noisy drunkard and gambler who had run up large bills and let the newspaper accounts grow more muddled than ever. Some blamed Knapp's decline on his wife—"a mere doll, feeble in mind and fond of dress," Garrison judged, whom his old friend never should have married—while others, including the editor himself, made allowances for Knapp's chronically poor health and melancholy disposition. Whatever the cause, the gentlemen of probity who now supervised *The Liberator*'s finances concluded that Knapp was a liability who cost the paper at least $1,500 a year. Since donors had contributed that amount, the year would end squarely, but Francis Jackson informed Garrison in October 1839 that Knapp would have to go.

The editor winced. He could not forget the ink-stained nights spent with Knapp under the eaves of Merchants' Hall publishing the first issues of their incendiary sheet. However, when it became clear that the committee would withdraw its own indispensable support if Knapp remained on the payroll, Garrison reluctantly bowed to their judgment. Knapp left with a "goodwill" payment of $175 and many hard feelings. Some of Garrison's critics swooped in and offered to underwrite "Knapp's Liberator" as a rival paper, but such a venture never stood a chance, and Knapp continued in the alcoholic tailspin that would lead to his death in 1843. "My friends would be his friends," Garrison said sadly, if Knapp "would only respect himself."

Garrison had never wanted to believe that Knapp had deterred people from contributing to *The Liberator,* but no sooner had the incubus been removed than the committee easily rounded up donations of $1,200 to refurbish the equipment and procure new types. It hired Royal Porter to do a larger press run (3,750 copies) for less than it had being paying Knapp. With three young women compositors working efficiently in the printing office at 25 Cornhill, the cost of producing *The Liberator* fell below the committee's estimate by $1.48 per week during the first quarter of 1840 and $3.79 per week during the second. The committee's "rigid regard" for economy had already yielded the dividends respected in New England's counting houses, but the newspaper's custodians realized the uniqueness of their product. "At a time when a prostituted press panders to the depraved public sentiment of a servile and sensual age," the committee declared, it felt honored to sustain the "independent career . . . of one print which is true to the great ends of freedom and progress. . . ."

"The new year finds us . . . happy in mind, though empty in purse," Garrison reported to his brother-in-law, along with the less happy news that it would be a few weeks yet before he could repay his outstanding debt. He withheld the even more personal news that Helen expected to deliver another child at the end of May, saying only that she was in excellent health and anticipating Mother Benson's next visit.

The delights of family life obviously helped Garrison cope with the steady assaults he endured from his public critics. He could regard the attacks as a perverse vindication of his commitments, but they galled and frustrated him nonetheless. His convictions never wavered, and his pen never weakened, but his body frequently laid him low. The editor seemed subject to ailments; his letters are filled with reports of scrofula and coughs and bilious pains that interrupted his work and sometimes put him out of commission for a week or two at a time. Some of his friends considered him a hypochondriac and gently mocked his fondness for patent elixirs—remedies that Garrison was at pains to ensure did not contain alcohol.

To his other "heresies" Garrison added health cures and innovative medical regimens. The family drew upon the services of a homeopathic physician
and followed the vegetarian simplicities of Dr. Sylvester Graham's popular
diet, whose staple was bread made from traditional whole-grained flour instead of mass-produced white flour. Garrison also tried the radical alternative
of Thomsonian medicine. Samuel Thomson, a self-taught herbalist who had
evolved a system of botanic family medicine as a deliberate challenge to the
learned profession's reliance upon bleeding, blistering, and opiates, had attained a wide vogue among religious dissenters in Garrison's boyhood Essex
County. "As in religion and politics, the people should in medicine act for
themselves," Thomson insisted, and by the late 1830s the Thomsonian system of plant and steam therapy had attained a sufficiently large number of
adherents to hold national conventions and provoke efforts by orthodox physicians to suppress it by law. There could not have been a more sympathetic
affinity between patient and cure. At intervals, Garrison would check into a
Thomsonian "infirmary" on Pleasant Street where he would first drink a
"coffee" laced with lobelia and cayenne to induce sweating and vomiting and
then relax in a perpendicular steaming box, and finally—dripping with per-
spiration—take a nap. After another herbal drink and a second steam bath
and cold shower in midafternoon, the patient dressed and went home feeling
restored to health and ready to tout the benefits of medical "fanaticism."

Garrison needed all his strength for the continuing struggle within the movement. The real battle of summer and fall 1839 proved to be not the intra-
mural quarrel in Massachusetts but a protracted national argument over
political strategy. Garrison and his friends devoted more attention to the
clerical dissidents than their shallow support warranted because through the
smokescreen of organizational politics they discerned the more threatening
question of party organization itself. Historians have oversimplified the issue
as a contest between the "political action" favored by Garrison's opponents
and the "moral suasion" advocated by the editor, but the controversy—and
Garrison's position within it—actually involved antagonistic concepts of political action, one rooted in the quadrennial rhythms of a presidential campaign, the other in the continuing effort to uplift public opinion. Stanton,
Birney and their friends wanted to use candidates "pledged to human rights"
as a rallying point for abolitionism, while Garrison feared such a tactic would
"adulterate" the cause by turning the antislavery societies into "party engines" that would be expected to supply funds and workers for office-seekers
of many stripes.

The editor's suspicion of "the sorcery of party" reached back as far as
his encounter with the ambitious Caleb Cushing in Newburyport and his
engagement in the partisan newspaper warfare of the Adams–Jackson campaign in 1828. From the outset of his career as a reformer, Garrison had
contrasted the "disinterestedness" of philanthropy with self-aggrandizing and

materialist partisanship, and he took virtually no notice of the vicissitudes of party politics in *The Liberator*. Someone who had read no paper but *The Liberator* during the 1830s would have obtained only the scantiest impression of the controversies—the basic stuff of today's textbooks—that raged over banking and tariffs and internal improvements during the Jackson presidency, or the intense jockeying among Clay, Calhoun, and Van Buren to become Old Hickory's successor. Only those issues that had some bearing on the abolition movement—the nullification crisis, the suppression of the mail, the inhumanity of Jackson's Indian removal policy—attracted Garrison's attention. Yet while the editor concentrated upon the sinfulness of slaveholding, the political life of the nation had been transformed in ways that the abolitionists had, belatedly, to take into account.

The Jacksonian insurgency had dramatically increased participation in politics and changed the ways of conducting elections. In the decade following the War of 1812 that culminated in the one-party "Era of Good Feelings" under President James Monroe, closed caucuses of officeholders had nominated candidates and only a quarter of the adult white male population had voted. The grassroots movement of the late 1820s that had propelled a political outsider like Andrew Jackson into office brought previously excluded ordinary citizens into coalition with a new class of state politicians and created a larger, more demanding electorate and—as interest groups scrambled for support—more competitive elections. Turnouts increased dramatically— passing fifty percent in the Jackson landslide of 1828—and would reach a high of seventy-eight percent in the impending presidential election of 1840. Though the Jacksonian Democrats had first perfected the techniques of drawing voters to the polls through colorful campaigning, sensationalized writing in cheap pamphlets and newspapers, songs and sloganeering, and a generous distribution of the spoils of office, those who opposed various elements in Old Hickory's program gradually coalesced into a new opposition Whig party and learned to employ the same techniques. Open conventions chose the candidates for local, state, and national office, and the party organization mounted elaborate barnstorming efforts in support of "the ticket, the whole ticket, and nothing but the ticket." (The "ticket" was not a metaphor, but a brightly colored strip of paper supplied by the party that the voter publicly submitted to the election judges; the secret ballot—with nominees grouped alphabetically by office—did not come into use until the late nineteenth century.) If the sedate politics of Federalist Newburyport had offended Garrison, the gaudy, sensational, and corrupt spectacle of the late 1830s—with its shifting alliances, horse trading, allegiance to party over principle, and public voting process that rewarded conformity over conscience— made him weep.

The abolitionist movement had also employed cheap printing and faster communications to great advantage, and by adroit public questioning of congressional candidates in a district had occasionally made antislavery an important element in the election. John Quincy Adams had returned to the House on the strength of abolitionist voters, as had Joshua Giddings in Ohio and William Slade in Vermont. That abolitionists could apply their test to national candidates, however, remained an unproved assumption. Henry Clay, the Whigs' putative nominee, sought to head off the looming menace of political abolitionism by warning that the "ultraists" in the movement would turn to bayonets when frustrated at the ballot box. Seeking to shore up his Southern support, Clay out-Calhouned his rival by declaring that no amount of benevolent-minded philosophy about slavery could overturn the realities of power; he insisted, "That *is* property which the law declares *to be* property." Even if the abstract right to freedom was conceded, Clay emphasized, "the liberty of the descendants of Africans in the United States is incompatible with the safety and liberty of the European descendants." The speech proved wildly popular, and one admirer hailed it as a "funeral sermon" for "Amalgamation Abolitionists" and "the generalissimo of traitors and white niggers Billy Lord Garrison."

The editor had, of course, long since given up on Clay as a humanitarian, but he reprinted the speech and pronounced the Kentuckian suitable only for the presidency of the Colonization Society. While a jubilant Calhoun rejoiced that Clay had assumed high Southern ground in giving the "finishing strokes" to abolitionism, the Kentuckian's risky attempt to forge a coalition between Southern slaveholders and Northern Whig investors—an alliance of "the cotton bale and the bank note," a Democrat sourly observed—did not materialize. Clay sufficiently offended the gathering moralism in Northern Whig opinion to deny him the 1840 nomination, which went instead to an old soldier and conqueror of Tecumseh, William Henry "Tippecanoe" Harrison, a nonslaveholder whose white supremacism could nonetheless be safely assumed.

The failure of Clay's high-stakes gamble demonstrated that antislavery had made an impression upon the political consciousness of the free states. Seeking to capitalize upon this, Birney, Stanton, and other party-minded abolitionists argued that the movement should advance "a system" of independent candidates so that antislavery voters could choose the best men rather than putting up with weak nominees like Harrison. This would uplift the system and give "radical reformers" a basis for entering the campaign. Eventually one of the parties—presumably the Whigs, since the Democrats had their strongest base in the South—would adopt the abolitionist candidates as their own and give immediatism the balance of power in Congress. This scenario depended, however, upon counteracting the impression of fanaticism. To attract the support of "the great mass of the intelligent mind of the nation," Birney said, abolitionists had to demonstrate "the reasonableness, the *religion,* of our enterprise. To multiply causes of repulsion is but to . . . ensure our own defeat."

The argument quickly shifted from ideology to tactics. Birney now wanted to dissociate Garrison from the movement not because he opposed voting, but because he would frighten voters away. Garrison opposed independent nominations not because he thought all government corrupt, but because he thought a direct appeal to voters would corrupt the movement. The electorate would want to know where the candidates stood on a plethora of issues and the movement had no business writing an all-encompassing political platform. Ironically, though Garrison had been pilloried for his interest in extraneous issues, he wanted to maintain the AAS as a "one-idea" organization; he would confine the program to immediate abolition but keep the membership open to anyone who would pursue the goal in whatever way possible for them. Those who favored independent nominations wanted, it seemed, to narrow both the AAS membership and the activities they would be expected to pursue, yet open themselves to the questions of expediency and compromise on other issues that electoral politics would inevitably generate. To vote for a candidate was the work of a moment; it was "abolition made easy," Abby Kelley said. To bear faithful testimony for immediate abolition and equal rights, as Garrison had said in a speech at Plymouth on the Fourth of July, was the work of a lifetime, for it required one to stand up when a black person was denied a place in the steamboat cabin or when a minister refused to read notices of an antislavery meeting from his pulpit or when a legislator refused to receive the petitions of his constituents. Abolitionists, he insisted, had to be the leaven of fanaticism that would alter the political system and raise every corrupt or indifferent institution to a higher standard of responsibility.

While the advocates of independent nominations, led by New York's Alvan Stewart and using the executive committee of the AAS as their sponsor, convened a series of conventions in New York and Ohio to generate support for their plan and possibly agree upon candidates, Garrison mobilized the MAS to lead the state societies in opposition. Not only would a move into partisanship be premature and divisive, he argued, but it would bring into the ranks "a swarm of unprincipled aspirants" and make abolition "a marketable commodity to be sold to the highest bidder." Campaigning for office, moreover, would forfeit the high ground of disinterestedness and open abolitionists to the charge of cloaking ambition and selfishness in the garb of philanthropy. Even worse, it would seemingly deny the power of moral suasion to overcome prejudice; their object ought to be the conversion of all parties rather than the withdrawal into an enclave of their own. (Taking the reformers out of the major parties, Judge William Jay said, would deprive them of "the little salt that keeps them from utter putrefaction.")

Other writers in *The Liberator* extended the argument. A third party would find itself in a dilemma: if people could not be persuaded to abolition by moral means, how could they be reformed by a party too feeble to distribute the loaves and fishes of office? Yet if the new party held out mercenary rewards, what would become of its moral stature? Even worse, it would be a mistake to become too preoccupied with numbers. If abolitionists got themselves "prematurely counted," David Child warned, the justice of the cause might be wrongly estimated by turnout instead of truth. No one thought that abolitionists could count upon even a tenth of the electorate, "A Plain Man" wrote, and to increase the proportion, "*moral suasion . . .* [has to remain] the chief instrument of *political action.*"

The practical arguments were reinforced by the inescapable fact that a great number of abolitionists, especially in Massachusetts, were Whigs who did not want to leave their party—which had coalesced over the decade in opposition to Jackson but had not yet won a national election—just as it seemed capable of unseating Van Buren and the Democrats with the popular Harrison. One required no more ample proof that party loyalties ran deep, even among men of conscience, than to listen to abolitionist Whigs rationalize their desire to vote "the whole Whig ticket" just this once, despite its traditional avoidance of the slavery question. Even Stanton, who pushed as hard as anyone for independent nominations, realized that the Whigs would "wade to their armpits in molten lava to drive Van Buren from power" and advised Birney that they ought to defer their campaign to another year, for a poor showing would only give more credence to the Garrisonian argument.

The editor himself declined to berate his friends for their political infatuation but downplayed the significance of the election. One could not expect a political transformation to occur any faster than a moral reformation. It was not worth much of an abolitionist's time to be concerned about who occupied the presidential chair, he said, for there was not even a remote possibility that a bill to abolish slavery in Washington, D.C., would be clearing Congress in the next four years—but when one did, whoever was president would not dare to veto it because it would have been passed in response to the popular will. The president was only an indicator of "the direction of popular sentiment," he insisted. "There is no need to trouble ourselves about the *vanes;* let us raise the winds."

Disapproval of independent nominations was so widespread that by the end of 1839 many state societies in both New England and the northwest had condemned the idea of fashioning "a party yoke" for the movement, and the only antislavery newspapers to endorse the idea were *The Emancipator,* published by the New York office, and the new organization's Boston sheet, which had been definitively exposed as a tool of the third-party men. Its editor, Elizur Wright, had confided to Stanton that independent nominations would be the only thing that could keep the new organization alive in Massachusetts. Conceding that the anti-Garrison effort had been "shockingly mismanaged" and "everything made to turn on the confounded woman question," Wright insisted that they had to shift the issue to politics in order to isolate Garrison and give Christian abolitionists "something practical to do." Otherwise Massachusetts would be "a gone case," Wright predicted. Stanton carelessly mislaid the letter, which fell into hands friendly to Garrison, who reprinted it seven or eight times as the schismatics' *coup de grâce*.

Yet the advocates persevered. Although Stewart and his colleague Myron Holley of Rochester, an old hand whose political credits included the leadership of New York's Anti-Masonic Party and the lobbying campaign for the Erie Canal, had failed to nominate candidates at their series of winter meetings, they pressed on until by April 1840 they stage-managed a convention of approximately one hundred New Yorkers at Albany into nominating Birney as an abolition candidate for president. (Later the group would name itself the "Liberty" Party.)

Garrison spoke irritably of the "small but talented body of restless, ambitious men . . . determined to get up a third party, come what may—in the hope, doubtless, of being lifted by it into office." Of even more concern were reports from Henry C. Wright, who had been scouting the New Yorkers' meetings, that Stewart and Holley were bent upon turning the New York state society into an overt political party, just as Elizur Wright had sought to do with the new organization in Massachusetts, and then making the AAS into a central committee for the candidates. They didn't even call it "an abolition party," he wrote in disgust to *The Liberator*, or say that it was for the purpose of advocating abolition principles, but talked merely of "an independent political party" that would nominate candidates to support "the great civil and religious rights of the American people." So vague a mandate, thought Wright, could cloak many personal ambitions. They were "determined to make a desperate push at the [annual meeting] in May [1840]," Wright warned privately. "If they cannot convert the Parent Society into a political party, they will move to form another American Society . . . and proceed to form State societies for the purpose of nominating candidates. . . . Thus matters stand."

Wright's analysis seemed to be confirmed by the actions of the AAS executive committee at New York. The national treasury had dwindled away, as state contributions tailed off, and early in 1840, Lewis Tappan, himself disgruntled at the third-party movement, indicated that he and his brother— who had suffered business reverses in the Panic of 1837 and now had more financial headaches and fewer resources for benevolence—no longer wanted to subsidize associations with "unholy men." He wanted to lay off the paid staff, settle the debts with back stocks of booklets and office furniture, and ready the society for liquidation. In its place he would prefer a self-perpetuating national board of commissioners along the lines of the old-style evangelical missionary efforts, a plan consistent with the social snobbery evinced by Birney and others toward the Garrisonians. The editor's supporters suspected that the financial troubles, though real enough, were being used as a pretext for dissolving the society on political grounds. When the executive committee in April 1840 suddenly transferred ownership of the AAS newspaper, *The Emancipator*, to Joshua Leavitt—another of the clerical abolitionists and a strong third-party advocate—Garrison and his friends no longer doubted that their opponents intended to disband the national society if they could not control it. They learned from Maria Child that Stanton and Phelps had spent most of the spring covertly preparing the ground for dissolution with a whispering campaign that supplied "every minister, influential deacon, or active sectarian, for miles and miles and miles around . . . with the N. York side of the case."

Garrison also mobilized. The MAS put out a nationwide distress call in late April 1840 that enumerated all the stratagems the "disorganizers" might employ to undermine or thwart the original purposes of the AAS. They would seek to reconsider the admission of women, Garrison predicted, or to limit the number of delegates to the annual meeting, or to form an independent board of commissioners, or propose that the society disband itself because it had become a house divided, or effect a secession from the AAS in order to form a society on a narrower, partisan basis. "If you would preserve our noble organization from the spirit which is seeking to dash it into fragments," Garrison wrote, "then you will throng [to New York] in such numbers as to put down all machinations for the dissolution of an organization, which is the terror of oppressor and bigot alike. . . ."

The abolitionist faithful heeded the call. On Monday, May 11, 1840, an immense noontime crowd overwhelmed the Boston & Providence rail depot at the end of Boylston Street, spilling out of the little station house and onto a platform already crowded with satchels and bedrolls and eager travelers. One chartered locomotive with a train of wooden cars waited on the track, but a clanging bell and a great blast of smoke and ash announced the arrival of a second train just behind it. The passengers pressed aboard with joyous disregard for the signs that distinguished the "gentlemen's," "ladies'," and "colored" cars, and soon filled the seats on both sides of the narrow aisles. Amid cheers that could scarcely be heard above the screeching and hissing of the locomotive, the caravan jolted into motion and inched onto the causeway that bore the railroad across the Back Bay.

Garrison's heart stirred as more loyalists crowded aboard the train. The scene was reenacted at every stopping place on the way to Providence, where they had excursion tickets for the overnight boat to New York. Not even the optimistic editor had anticipated the astonishing turnout. Joining the Boston contingent—which included a great gathering from Lynn and dozens from the surrounding counties—were tribes from Plymouth and the Rhode Island towns, along with a delegation from eastern Connecticut rallied by Abby Kelley, who had spent the winter lecturing in their midst. (After hearing one of her powerful speeches, James Garrison declared that Kelley could put the navy's boatswains to shame.) More than 450 people jammed onto the capacious boat to form what Garrison exuberantly termed "a mass of 'ultraism' afloat." People clapped and sang and cheered the "spirited addresses" people felt moved to deliver during the deckside antislavery rally that took place against the background of a dramatic sunset. "A happier crowd I never saw," Oliver Johnson said.

When the meeting subsided the company prepared itself for sleep. After the double tiers of berths in the men's and ladies' cabins were filled, folks spread pallets on the floor and used blanket rolls and carpetbags for pillows. Attracted by the moonlit night and tranquil water, some opted for space out on deck, where they wrapped themselves in waterproofs and shawls against the briny chill. Garrison slept badly. He had embarked on a longer voyage than his companions and brooded all night about the three months' separation from his wife and children he now faced.

The editor would be sailing for England immediately after the annual meeting to attend an international antislavery conference—the first ever—scheduled to open in London in mid-June 1840. Saluted in a poem by Whittier as "the world's convention" that would mobilize "the pledged philanthropy of Earth" in the sacred enterprise, the meeting naturally attracted Garrison's attention, and the MAS agreed to underwrite his expenses. As the months wore on, however, he wavered. With Helen expecting the new baby in early June 1840 and James demanding a good deal of regular care and supervision, Garrison doubted that he could leave. Then arrangements for the convention became embroiled in the sectarian argument, as its evangelical sponsors in London (advised by correspondence with Lewis Tappan) maneuvered to confine the roster of delegates to "gentlemen." Alarmed by this development, Garrison once more decided that he ought to make the trip. He certainly did not want his domestic opponents to dominate the international discussion or undermine his financial connections in Great Britain. Helen assured him that her sisters and mother would see her through the delivery, and George Benson invited James to spend the summer in the salubrious air of Friendship's Vale. Withal, as late as one week before his departure, a close family friend reported Garrison still uncertain about attending that "half-souled *moldy* convention." However, when the editor learned that despite its protestations of insolvency the AAS executive committee was subsidizing the attendance of Birney and Stanton in London, Garrison realized that he could not stay away. Although neither Maria Child nor Maria Chapman could attend from the MAS, Lucretia Mott had agreed to represent the Pennsylvania society, and Garrison told Helen that the "woman question" would be high on the convention's agenda. "The subject cannot be agitated without doing good," he said.

When the *Rhode Island* steamed down the East River at daybreak and tied up at the Catherine Street slip, the "antislavery boatload" had a rude awakening. The proprietor of the cheap hotel on nearby Frankfort Street where mass lodging had been arranged took one look at "the large body of abolitionists from the East, of all colors and sexes, and some of no sex at all," as one reporter described the scene, and declared that he wouldn't stand for such jumbling and amalgamation. He shut the door against "his curly customers," said the *New York Sun*, and threatened to have the local b'hoys run them off. The "woolly flock" had repaired to 63 Barclay Street, the paper hinted, and sure enough the next night rock-throwing vandals broke a few windows at the house, but no tumult ensued.

The newspapers likened the impending showdown to a fight among alley cats. It appeared that Arthur Tappan & Co. "are not up to the latest humbugs by a long way," reported the *Journal of Commerce*. "They can't go perfectionism . . . they do not denounce the clergy . . . they are not in favor of dressing out women in boots and spurs . . . therefore they must be ousted." "The Lie-berator" had mustered hundreds of fanatics from New England to "revolutionize the Society," the paper added, "so here she goes." The *Journal* and the *Herald*, which served up the same interpretation with a racist dressing, had long been hostile to Garrison, but even an old friend like William Goodell, now firmly in the third-party camp, had published warnings that "Pope" Garrison was bent on taking over the AAS with his imported horde of "non-resistants and whole-Whig-ticket abolitionists." (Brother Goodell was in "a most rabid state," Henry Wright told Garrison. "Politics have made him mad.")

The Garrisonians, for their part, could see that those partial to reorganization had also rallied, "pretty numerously," the editor judged by the numbers of New York clergymen suddenly visible in their ranks. The meeting place—the Fourth Free Church Madison and Catherine streets, just up from the East River piers—proved small and became "crowded to suffocation" by the time the business meeting opened on Tuesday afternoon, May 12, 1840. Along with the pious businessmen and grave clergymen customarily in attendance sat more than the usual handful of black men and vastly more women—of both races—than ever before. Garrison looked out upon the rows of earnest people and saw a "Gideon's Army" of whole-souled abolitionists. His rivals, who had spared no effort themselves to bring on their supporters, charged that the ultras had packed the house with Lynn shoemakers on holiday, while the *Herald* poured racist abuse upon "the particolored cabal."

When the church bells rang the hour, the conclave fell silent and waited for the gavel to fall. No chairman, however, stood at the desk. A messenger shortly arrived from Arthur Tappan's office with word that the philanthropist, who disliked commotion, was retiring from the presidency and would not be attending the meeting. Tappan's withdrawal meant that Garrison's staunch friend Francis Jackson, the AAS vice-president, would take the chair, and people looked around to watch Lewis Tappan's reaction as Massachusetts assumed the command forfeited by New York. Was this a step toward reconciliation or a signal for an immediate dissolution? Lewis's habitual thin smile, however, gave no hint of what lay ahead.

After the opening prayer, Jackson picked his way carefully through the presiding officer's first task, the nomination of a business committee that would screen all resolutions submitted and fix the agenda for the meeting. To no one's surprise, he proposed Garrison as chairman, but then submitted a conscientiously balanced list that included Lewis Tappan and Amos Phelps, for the conservatives, and Abby Kelley and Charles C. Burleigh, for the ultras. Jackson called for a voice vote to confirm the membership of the committee, but someone requested that it be taken *seriatim*, one name at a time. Though the intent of the maneuver was plainly hostile, there was no way to avoid it. The vote "went on swimmingly till it came to A. Kelley," recalled Anne Warren Weston. "Then there was first, an immense *yes*—then a superb *no*. . . ." The chair ruled the nomination approved, but the hall erupted in shouts of "Doubted! Doubted!" and called for a division. The moment of truth had arrived.

Jackson asked those who favored Miss Kelley's nomination to stand, and the floor shook as hundreds thundered to their feet. There were so many standing in each pew and against the walls that the tellers had trouble counting, but eventually they announced a vote of 571 in the affirmative. Then Jackson asked the opposition to stand, and a very substantial crowd of nays arose, hundreds indeed, though perhaps thinner than the ayes. One minister jumped up to say that the ladies should not be so modest as to refrain from voting *in this case* ("Poor man!" sighed Parker Pillsbury), while Phelps shouted that women should not be voting on either side. Hissing erupted, which Garrison tried to shush in his quarter, and eventually the final tally was announced: 451 negative, 571 affirmative.

Waves of applause and jeers rolled across the house, while both Garrison and Lewis Tappan struggled to be recognized. The editor spoke briefly against demonstrative behavior, but Tappan would not be mollified. He huffily announced that he declined to serve on a mixed committee, and his friends on the carefully balanced slate one by one rose to echo his statement. To conduct *business* on so "promiscuous" a basis, they said, defied Scripture and ran counter to both the charter of the society and the customary usages of the civilized world.

Volleys of complaints came from all sides of the house.

"Stereotyped objections," groused Pillsbury.

"Slavery is the customary usage of five-sixths of the world," said Ellis Loring, "yet we attack that."

"In Congress the masters speak while the slaves are denied a voice," said Abby Kelley. "I rise because I am not a slave."

As the meeting threatened to become a shouting match, Jackson—citing the lateness of the hour—declared the session adjourned until the next morning. The move foreclosed the possibility of a dramatic walkout, though no one doubted that the conservatives, obviously lacking the votes to dissolve the society, would now withdraw from it. Oliver Johnson wistfully thought that if Jackson had only appointed a second woman as a companion for

Kelley on the committee the issue would have not have arisen in so nasty a form. The morning papers would luridly portray "a blooming young lady" closeted with ten bearded men, while others privately ridiculed Kelley as a Delilah who had shorn the AAS of its power. "Well, there is no knowing what people may come to in this world," John G. Whittier remarked to his sister. "Our friend Abby . . . was the bombshell that *exploded* the society."

Lewis Tappan insisted that the woman question was merely the occasion, not the cause, of the breach. The real issue, he told Weld, was Garrison's desire to "make an experiment upon the public" by foisting a host of radical issues upon the society. Tappan met with thirty friends at his home later in the evening and read them a sketch for a new organization that, in his draft, would forswear any effort "to break up existing organizations in church or state" and would only "give impetus to the usual forms of social action." (Their caution, Lydia Maria Child observed, "will make a kind of abolition that the slaveholder may either laugh at, or compliment, but which he will never fear enough to hate.")

When the meeting resumed on Wednesday morning, May 13, 1840, the dissidents were still in attendance, but grim-faced and silent. They sat through the reading of some relatively mild resolutions on political action that condemned both Van Buren and Harrison as proslavery candidates and deplored the independent nominations made at Albany as a "waste of energy." Though candidate Birney had already departed for the London convention, his party-minded supporters chose to regard the swipe as a full-scale assault upon "voting" abolitionists and protested the "incongruity" of naming their principled candidates in the same resolution as the major parties' dough-faces. (That, retorted Oliver Johnson, was what happened when men stooped to compete on political grounds.) Then Lewis Tappan asked all those who had objected to placing a woman on the business committee to meet in the church basement at four that afternoon for the purpose of forming a new "American & Foreign Anti-Slavery Society." This time the dissidents managed to walk out before the gavel dispatched everyone to lunch.

The afternoon bore witness to a ludicrous spectacle. Upstairs, Garrison moved a tribute to Arthur Tappan for "his long continued and faithful services as President of the Society." Downstairs, Lewis Tappan nominated his brother as president of the new organization and led the secessionists in a booming rendition of the hymn "Lo! what an entertaining sight/ Are brethren who agree." The breach had become formal, but it would take some time to test the capacity of the rival organization to harmonize the Tappans' board-of-missions structure with the Birney candidacy and Liberty Party ideas.

Edmund Quincy's merry jest "After tea we went to a caucus at Thomas Van Rensellaer's to see what we should do with the Society now we have got it" gave a misleading impression of what had occurred; the Garrisonians had not taken over the AAS but resisted an attempt either to oust them or dissolve the organization. The only institution over which the Garrisonians gained power they had previously lacked was the AAS executive committee. Left to themselves, they quickly confirmed their commitment to equal participation by revising the committee's membership to include three women (Chapman, Child, and Mott) and the black caterer Thomas Van Rensellaer. The committee then endorsed Garrison, Rogers, Lucretia Mott, and Charles Lenox Remond, the scion of an important black family in Salem, as its delegates to the imminent world's convention and prayed that the convention would "fully and practically recognize . . . the equal brotherhood of the entire human family." A respected Quaker activist, Lindley Coates of Pennsylvania, replaced Arthur Tappan as the AAS president, and the new officers quickly initiated efforts to recover the organization's assets, including *The Emancipator,* from the private individuals who had received them. Having endured the gravest challenge yet to their leadership, the radical abolitionists did little crowing and gave the lie to their antagonists' charges by abjuring policy statements that might have proclaimed Garrison's views on the so-called extraneous questions.

"We have made clean work of everything," Garrison exulted to Helen at the end of the week. "It was our anti-slavery boatload that saved our society from falling into the hands of the . . . *disorganizers,*" he said, and achieved "a glorious triumph." On Saturday morning, May 16, the editor watched his friends board the *Rhode Island* for the return trip, and his eyes filled with tears at their readiness to drop everything for the cause. Caught up in the spirit of the moment, and overwhelmed anew at the idea of the long separation from his family, Garrison resisted the impulse to jump aboard and return to Boston for more embraces with his wife and children before sailing to Liverpool. Instead, feeling both exhilarated and sad, he stood on the Fulton Street ferry dock and watched the *Rhode Island* get underway, waving and calling out blessings and farewells until its smoke had dwindled to a speck and the friends had vanished from his sight.

Garrison's victory had once again maintained his position as a moral agitator who could not be deterred by the pressure of social conformity. Though modern commentators are wont to condemn both sides as too absolutist to bend for unity's sake, Garrison regarded the long and bruising fight with the schismatics as a living demonstration against the tendency to idealize political unity above moral principle. He skillfully turned the preoccupations of tactical infighting into another drama of pure conscience in combat with the seductions of political expediency. The struggle also vindicated the editor's faith in the spiritual value of free inquiry. *The Liberator* "did not bring [other questions] into anti-slavery," Maria Child emphasized; rather "they *came* in, simply because everything in God's universe is linked with every other thing." No more than Luther, when he set his face against the sale of indulgences, could have envisioned the *Mayflower* setting sail or the First Amendment's bar against religious establishments could the abolitionists have realized from the outset how deeply they would shake the foundations of their society. "Yet *every* road leads to the end of the world," Child said, quoting Carlyle, "if you do but follow it."

The schism thus became another of the passages by which Garrison and his radical colleagues vindicated their position on the margins of American society and made a virtue of their nonconformity. Elizabeth Buffum Chace, the daughter of the first NEAS president and herself a close associate of Garrison's, spoke for many when she explained that she had committed herself to the moral reformers because they were people "who, living in the world, have yet . . . lived apart from it, bearing before it, in their lives, a continual testimony against its evil habits." One might say that the dissidents, too, dramatically defined themselves by stating that they would only consider how slavery might be abolished without challenge to other American institutions. The reformers had broken their association on the thorniest of questions: the relationship between tactics and principle. The conservatives flirted with the dangers of opportunism, the radicals with the pitfalls of self-righteousness; one group risked finding itself with too little to say, the other with speaking only to themselves. To the degree, however, that the schism allowed Garrison to be Garrison, who was unsurpassed at gaining attention for his extremism, it would prove a liberating phenomenon. In endeavoring to narrow the editor's range, his opponents had ensured that his concerns would gain a wider currency; in disassociating themselves from his vision, they condemned themselves to obscurity and allowed Garrison—as they would learn soon enough in London—to put his heroic stamp upon the age.

Chapter Fourteen

Garrisonized to the Backbone

——————•◆•——————

For the second time in his career, Garrison had the opportunity to enhance his stature at home by taking his agitation abroad. In 1833 he had associated himself with the triumph of British abolitionism to vanquish the claims of the colonizationists and promote the formation of an American national organization dedicated to immediatism. Now, seven years later, abolition had become strong enough to contend for a place on the country's political agenda, though its critics remained legion and the era of antislavery unity had given way to a bitter quarrel over both the contours of the reformers' beliefs and their strategic assumptions. Garrison had found himself maligned not only by slavery's apologists but by men he had once considered coadjutors, and he had encountered increasing difficulty in making his own views clear amid the din of poisonous personal controversy. In London he hoped to find an opportunity to define the special character of his leadership once again.

He would have to work quickly, however, for the new organization had put him in a tactical fix. While he had concentrated all his efforts on sustaining the AAS at the annual meeting, his opponents had cleverly divided their troops. Lewis Tappan superintended the walkout from the AAS and the formation of the new American & Foreign Anti-Slavery Society, while Birney and Stanton sailed ahead to forge an alliance with the British & Foreign Anti-Slavery Society, sponsors of the London convention. By making common cause with the British leaders on the woman question, they could continue their campaign against Garrison's radicalism and portray him as a power-mad outsider bent on having his own way.

Since the schismatics had reopened the woman question in New York, Garrison believed that he had to follow it up in London as a matter of principle. Friends warned him that there was no chance that the American women would be seated at the convention, since "such a thing was never heard or thought of in any part of Europe," and even as militant a spirit as George Bourne thought it best not to disrupt what was, after all, something of an experiment in international philanthropy. No one, however, could tell the editor of *The Liberator* to gag himself. If outvoted, he would "lodge a protest," Garrison said, but joked that he wouldn't "secede or 'new organize.'" Yet he ran the risk that if Birney and Stanton could give an American blessing to the exclusion of female delegates before Garrison's arrival, any disruption of the proceedings by the Boston firebrand would only confirm their characterization of him.

He had an indication, moreover, during the long weekend in New York awaiting his ship, that the politics of schism would not be easy. The editor's host, Thomas Van Rensellaer, who had been elected to the AAS executive committee, got up a farewell meeting to secure resolutions of support for the old organization's delegates. Garrison made a passionate two-hour address in which he went into the circumstances of the separation "root and branch," which Lewis Tappan, also in attendance, chose not to contest. Several black ministers, however, with close personal ties to the Tappans, objected to Van Rensellaer's "illiberal" motion to endorse only the AAS delegation, while others suggested the compromise of expressing confidence in all the American abolitionists who would be in London under the auspices of the various state and local societies. Garrison, who generally stayed in the background during such maneuvers, made a personal objection to having his name linked with men like Birney and Stanton who had deviated so greatly from true abolitionism. This was a petty and unwise move that irritated the meeting and led to a postponement of the whole subject. N. P. Rogers stormed out, saying that nothing showed the insidious effect of the new organization more than its attempt to bring sectarian prejudice into the black community and alienate its affection for Garrison. Although it was easy to blame all setbacks on the organizational feud, the meeting signaled that some black abolitionists wanted to preserve a measure of political independence. "Our good feeling is scattered upon all our active Friends," the editor of the *Colored American* wrote, and "we hope our American delegation will meet together in London and . . . bury the hatchet."

Everything depended on a prompt arrival in London, and Garrison grew so anxious about the sailing that he could not sit still long enough to write an account of the New York meeting for *The Liberator*. He packed and repacked his trunk several times over, had the pantaloons of his olive suit shortened at the last minute, and mocked his fretfulness by admitting that he would wear his comfortable old black suit as often as possible. His edginess increased as two days of hard rain and wind and another of interminable "drizzle, drizzle, drizzle" postponed his sailing on the *Columbus* from Tuesday until Friday, May 22, 1840. The delay made Garrison even more regretful that he had not dashed back to Boston on the abolitionists' steamboat, and feeling lonely and morose, he wrote a long letter home filled with loving greetings for Georgie and dear "Willie Wallie"—"kiss him morning, noon, and night," Papa ordered. Even a day's absence from Helen felt like "a bereavement," he said, and in reply to her sad lines on the subject of their separation reassured her that he loved her "far more than words can express."

In a public farewell message dispatched to *The Liberator* via a black deckhand on the pilot boat, Garrison declared that he was making for "the old world, which, under God, is yet to be renovated and made wholly new." Rogers wrote a note to his paper that warned of the "moral hurricane" that would devastate European philanthropy if the women were silenced and promised that the true American abolitionists would demonstrate "a democracy in morals as well as a republicanism in politics." In *The Emancipator* Joshua Leavitt ridiculed these statements as "reckless adventuring" and tasked Garrison and Rogers with a "fatuous desire to carry an irrelevant and party point." Privately, Leavitt drew snickers with smutty remarks about Garrison's thrust to " '*organ*'-ize the convention."

The voyage started badly with a bout of seasickness and grew interminable when the winds died for more than a week. The thirteenth day, June 4, found them off the Grand Banks of Newfoundland—barely one-third of the way—and Garrison feared that he would miss the entire conference. Facing the prospect of a vain mission, he lay awake at night thinking of Helen. "In airy visions I embrace you, but feel only the more wretched as I awake to a sense of my loneliness. . . . Sometimes you have hinted that I was too ready to go away from home," Garrison wrote, in one of the very rare allusions either of them ever made to strain in the marriage, but insisted that he traveled only when "duty and friendship imperatively demanded the sacrifice." Aware that his wife had likely "passed through the perils of child-bed," he dwelt lovingly on the image of another "new-born babe" and wished that a carrier pigeon could bring him news of a safe delivery.

The shipboard climate grew distasteful. Their cabinmates proved "a prayerless, godless, drinking, low-minded set . . . disposed to make light of every thing serious and sacred," he told Helen, and included some loud defenders of slavery. The captain, a "free and easy" Virginian, indulged the raucous atmosphere, while the second mate was a brute. When William Adams, a Pawtucket Quaker representing the Rhode Island state society, reproved the mate for cruelly abusing a seaman, the mate retaliated by trying to have Adams and his bunkmate Lenox Remond expelled from their cabin. Ordered to sleep "with his nigger" on a narrow pallet at the end of a gangway, Adams successfully held his ground, but the ruckus contributed to the strained and anxious mood.

"My situation would be intolerably irksome without Rogers," wrote Garrison, and the friendship with the New Hampshire editor ten years his senior proved the trip's emotional dividend. Rogers had exchanged an established law practice for abolitionist journalism in the aftermath of George Thompson's 1835 lecture tour, and like Garrison he harbored a ferocious editorial personality within a mild and sentimental character. The two men quickly became soul mates. They recited poetry and Scripture to each other, and lying on their hard plank beds, passed the time sharing stories of their lives and families and dreaming of peaceful walks together in the White Mountains when their labors ceased.

Not an hour after arriving in London more than a week late on June 17, 1840, Garrison made an impromptu decision that he would never regret. Calling first at the British organization's office to check for mail from home, he learned that after a long debate five days earlier on June 12, the convention—at the London committee's behest—had voted to exclude the American women from membership. Garrison did not hesitate. He would not sit in a convention that dishonored his colleagues, the editor said, but would bear silent testimony against it from the gallery. He had not heard anything of the circumstances or consulted with anyone else, but had made an impulsive decision that epitomized his genius as an agitator. He had missed half the meeting and his side had lost the vote, but he would dramatize the convention's error in an act of moral witness and dominate the proceedings without saying a word.

Rogers, Remond, and Adams agreed that they would sit out with Garrison, and by the time the quartet arrived at their boardinghouse at 6 Queen Street Place, Cheapside, they had worked themselves up into high dudgeon. "New Org has found a snug abode in London," Rogers groused, certain that the convention had become the tool of sectarians who shared the biases of their American cousins. Many American delegates were lodged at No. 6. Most were friends of Garrison's, including Lucretia and James Mott, Emily Winslow and her father Isaac, one of Garrison's earliest patrons, and a trio of Philadelphians who formed the backbone of the women's society there. There were less friendly faces as well. Henry Stanton was also stopping there, with his young bride Elizabeth Cady, the daughter of a prominent upstate New York judge and a cousin of the wealthy philanthropist Gerrit Smith. James G. Birney had also occupied a room at No. 6, but after several days of barbed exchanges with the scorned women the Kentuckian had fled to a less disputatious abode.

In a long evening's discussion among the friends, Garrison learned what had happened. Even before the convention opened, Joseph Sturge and his colleagues on the London committee had made it plain to the Motts and Wendell Phillips (conveniently an MAS delegate—along with his wife Ann—since they were already in London on an extended European trip) that the sponsors had never contemplated anything so foreign to custom as the seating of women. The London committee, which had planned the symposium-like agenda, would rope off a side chamber adjacent to the floor so that the ladies might listen to the proceedings, but English usage could accommodate them no further. When the Americans replied that they had come to a *world*'s convention, not one to be measured by an English yardstick exclusively, they were laughingly told that the sponsors considered that sobriquet merely "a poetical flourish of Friend Whittier's." Theirs was a general conference of the British society and its invited guests, not a convention that would make up its own roll.° Mrs. Mott asked if arrangements might be made for the American women to meet with their British counterparts, and Sturge replied that he would consult his colleagues about "a social party for Ladies."

"Are the B&F efforts all based upon the idea of immediate emancipation?" the exasperated Mott asked. When Sturge replied affirmatively, she pointedly reminded him that the idea originated with an individual who was both a woman and an English Friend, Elizabeth Heyrick of Leicester, and the interview ended. (Afterward, the story went around that the problem with Lucretia Mott was her commitment not to women's rights but to the Hicksites, which ran counter to the Orthodox beliefs of Sturge and the other Friends who dominated the conference.)

Although the American women encountered no obstacle to speaking at the informal meetings—the breakfasts and teas Garrison had found so invigorating on his 1833 visit—held in the antislavery rooms, they could make no breach in the wall of the convention itself. The Philadelphian Sarah Pugh drafted a protest in which the women thanked the committee for its private hospitality, but deplored its refusal to recognize women as "co-equals in the advocacy of Universal Liberty." At the opening session, against strenuous objection that it would be rude and divisive, Wendell Phillips asked the convention to overrule the London committee and admit all *persons* delegated to the meeting. A raucous debate ensued, filled with many cries of "order" and "division," in which Phillips received support from Garrison's British and Irish friends, who mocked the hypocrisy of seeking universal reform by "disenfranchising one-half of creation." James G. Birney, however, skillfully insinuated that the woman's question—an issue by no means settled among the American societies, he claimed—was but the first of the Garrisonian heresies that would distract the British efforts, as they had already disrupted and divided the American. After Phillips's motion failed by a large margin, loud cheers erupted—just like the House of Commons, the Americans were told—and Phillips had to go through the ritual of promising "utmost cordiality" now that the issue had been heard. It made us "miserable" to see the men smiling and bantering after the meeting, wrote one of the young women at No. 6.

Lucretia Mott returned to the Queen Street Place lodgings after the Garrison party had arrived and greeted them "in joy and sorrow too," she recalled, when she learned that they had resolved not to enter the convention. "Reasoned with them on the subject—found them fixed," Mrs. Mott noted

---

°Of the five hundred delegates named in the convention proceedings, approximately 425 represented antislavery societies in the British Isles. Other than the Americans, many of whom were carried on the roll though they did not attend, the only international representatives were a quintet of Frenchmen, including two members of the Chamber of Deputies, and one Spaniard.

in her diary, though it is not clear whether she was probing their motives or actively disputing the decision. Nevertheless, Garrison and Rogers remained firm. With only six days remaining of the conference and the agenda rigidly set as a series of presentations on the status of abolition around the world, there would be no chance of reopening the woman's question on the floor; they could do it more successfully from the balcony. "There is no World's Convention," Garrison maintained. The clinching argument came from Lenox Remond, who said that he was indebted to the women of Portland and Bangor and Newport for his travel expenses and could not sit in a meeting that had shut out their sisters.

A sentry was guarding the delegates' entrance to Freemasons' Hall, just off Drury Lane, when Garrison and his companions arrived for the convention's morning session on June 18, 1840. When they refused to produce their credentials, an usher pointed the way to an outside staircase that led up to a small gallery like a choir loft (some folks at home would call it "the Negro pew," Friend Adams said), where the Americans took seats on the front bench. They had a superb view of the glittering ceiling, with its embroidered circles of stars and a huge sun of burnished gold. Large semicircular windows spilled sunshine down the columned walls and across the magnificent chamber, nearly one hundred feet long and forty feet wide, where delegates gathered in knots and the platform grew crowded with committeemen, secretaries, and officers.

Garrison and company sat unnoticed for a time. Then Ann Phillips, who keenly resented being snubbed as a delegate, came up to greet the newcomers and pointed out various gentlemen to them. Soon Lucretia Mott and her party arrived, chatted for a time, and then descended to take their roped-off place on the edge of the meeting floor. Ann Phillips accompanied them, as she liked to pass Wendell notes and suggestions during the debates. Word spread that Garrison had arrived, and delegates turned surreptitiously to catch sight of the controversial American.

A procession of visitors began to make its way to the Americans' perch. First came Lady Byron, whose short, unhappy alliance with the poet did not diminish her ability to lend the luster of his name to her many humanitarian pursuits. Byron's widow embraced Garrison, a moment he surely had never imagined when, as a printer's apprentice, he had read *Childe Harold* over and over again by lamplight in Master Allen's attic. Then, to increasing consternation on the floor below, Lady Byron took Remond by the arm and embraced him as well. When Joseph Sturge called the meeting back to order, Lady Byron sat among the protesters, identifying the speakers and making sure that eyes kept turning up toward their obscure corner. By the end of the day other celebrated writers and humanitarians had trooped up to the balcony to pay their respects, and even the great Daniel O'Connell, who had given the women a letter of support in which he declared that "mind has no sex," came to honor the editor of *The Liberator*. He had first considered the exclusion politically prudent, O'Connell told Garrison, but now he repudiated it as "a cowardly sacrifice of principle to a vulgar prejudice."

The American quartet presented a picture that no one ever forgot. There was Garrison, radiant in his dissent, his gold spectacles glinting in the light, with a beatific smile upon his face, flanked by Rogers, the bluff and hearty Yankee; Remond, his handsome ebony face set in a stern expression of reproach; and Adams, in his broad-brimmed Quaker hat and simple gray habit, a silent rebuke to the lofty airs of Joseph Sturge and the other high-toned English Friends. "Long life to these American abolitionists," wrote Maria Waring, a sister-in-law of the Dublin leader Richard Webb, after watching the day's extraordinary proceedings. "They are a glorious crew. Garrison is one of God's nobility. I don't think I ever saw such an angelic, holy-looking face." The Garrisonians, she concluded, "are strong and fine and firm . . . a new race of beings . . . they regard women not as dolls but as human beings."

That night the London committee hastily met and extended handwritten personal invitations to Garrison and the others to attend the sessions. If they would drop by the committee offices, special cards of admission would be provided. The quartet passed up the offer of house seats in favor of their crowded little balcony. "We would not go in as a matter of favor," Garrison explained, when he returned to the hall the next morning. Emissaries came and went from the committee, entreating Garrison to come down to the floor, though when Phillips tried to read Garrison's credentials and explain his absence for the record, the maneuver was blocked in a short and angry scene. Every time Garrison's name was mentioned in a speech, however, the whole conference would applaud "as if they thought they could *clap* him down," said Rogers. "But they might as well have expected to remove the pillars upon which the gallery stood. They could not argue away what they had done. . . ."

The convention had sacrificed its moral authority to "English usage, American new organization, and sectarian prejudice," as Lucretia Mott summed up the unholy influences, though the body pressed on through its stated agenda before final adjournment on June 23, 1840. Phillips tried once more to file a protest signed by the Garrison-minded delegates in support of women's rights, but the B&F officials had the statement tabled and later deleted from the printed report. The committee squelched protest one last time by excluding Garrison and Phillips from the speakers list at a postconference rally in Exeter Hall, though Birney and Stanton both were assigned parts in the program. Remond, however, "stepped forward of his own accord," Garrison said, to deliver a scorching address on "the grand handmaid of slavery—prejudice" that the audience loudly cheered.

At a "tea" afterward in the Crown & Anchor Tavern, which turned out to be a meeting of four hundred guests invited by a coalition of liberal abolitionists from Ireland and Scotland, both Lucretia Mott and Garrison spoke for the first time. She emphasized the importance of boycotting the products of slave labor, while he touched upon women's rights, Irish suffrage, the poor laws, antimilitarism, temperance, and his fond hope that one day humanity would end the Babel of tongues and speak a universal language. The polished London gentlemen snickered at Garrison's enthusiasms, Birney reported, while Elizabeth Cady Stanton grumbled that when Garrison finally opened his mouth, "forth came, in my opinion, much folly." Friend Adams, however, praised Garrison's "faithful testimony" and noted that "our new organizers made no reply."

The Philadelphian Abby Kimber acidly complained that "the *man* question" had split the American organization and the London committee had favored the Birneyites without having heard the other side at all. The Garrisonians considered the idea of holding a public meeting to explain the AAS position more fully, but logistical problems led them to give it up. Their Scottish and Irish friends, however, more radical than the leaders in the metropolis, promised to organize meetings in their principal cities over the next few weeks if Garrison and the others would visit. Though he had hoped to leave for home in early July, Garrison agreed to a brief tour.

Meanwhile the old abolitionists made their case at the many dinners and soirées held in their honor by their British friends. On June 21 they went in two cabs for "a real English dinner" at William Ashurst's estate at Muswell Hill, where Garrison met a number of liberal journalists, made inquiries about the poor laws, read extracts from the *Non-Resistant* to an attentive audience, and interested the host—an admirer of Tom Paine and a friend of the socialist Robert Owen—in a subscription to *The Liberator*. (Ashurst would later write a column on English news for Garrison under the pseudonym "Edward Search.") On June 29 the Quaker banker Samuel Gurney sent seven barouches to convey the American contingent to his magnificent estate in Essex (the grass was "soft as velvet & swept clean as a floor," noted Mrs. Mott), where Garrison happily "sifted in" his views on temperance and other "extraneous topics" before a gathering that included the Duchess of Sutherland, one of the nobility's leading patrons of philanthropic causes.

The duchess asked Garrison to sit for a likeness she had commissioned from the celebrated painter Benjamin Haydon, and the editor rushed off the very next morning to comply. Haydon, who was working on a large-scale painting of the convention, had sketched a great many delegates already, and he toyed with Garrison by asking him if he would object to being placed next to a prominent Negro delegate from Jamaica, an honor (Haydon said cunningly) from which the B&F secretary, John Scoble, had shrunk. Garrison replied that of course he had no objections, but that truth required that he should be placed in the background among the women. Haydon told Garrison that he did not want to sacrifice his "*fine* head" to a background, but, if he came again to sit, Haydon would do him "*life* size, still with the women," as he planned to give Lucretia Mott a prominent place in the spectator's gallery next to the revered Thomas Clarkson. Either the painter was "having him on" or the London committee intervened, for Haydon later decided that Mott had "infidel notions" and blurred her face while excluding Garrison entirely. Gossips, however, said that the two radicals were so eager to appear in the painting that they importuned Haydon for conspicuous places. Birney transmitted the canard to Leavitt, but then discovered he was misinformed and tried to quash it.

Garrison was susceptible to flattery from the well-to-do, especially when he was in the midst of controversy, and he did not always know when he was being patronized. On this trip, however, he developed a more measured view of both Britain and its antislavery leaders. He saw that the English poor labored under more grievous burdens than their white counterparts in America, and, for the first time, he evinced sympathetic interest in the working-men's protest gathering under the Chartist banner. England *looked* beautiful, Garrison told Samuel J. May upon his return, but it was "sitting on a volcano" created by the stark contrasts between the opulence of aristocratic life and the suffering and degradation of the operatives who made it possible. There might be anger enough to overthrow the monarchy, Garrison thought, and reason enough, too. "To think that God . . . has filled this earth with abundance for all, and yet that nine-tenths of mankind are living in squalid poverty and abject servitude in order to sustain in idleness and profligacy the one-tenth!" he wrote.

The British abolitionists turned out to be more domineering and narrow-minded managers than Garrison had previously suspected, and their meetings—with the carefully composed speakers list, obeisance to prominent guests, and continuous cheering and heckling—seemed closer to the mood of American political party gatherings than the atmosphere of "devoted seriousness" that marked the movement's conventions at home. British abolition, Garrison decided, had not been "tried in the same fire" as the Americans had faced, and its leaders still "walked in silver slippers." Birney made more headway with the B&F gentlemen, Rogers observed, because he was more "the Old-England type than the New," an enlightened aristocrat who had exhausted himself as a reformer when he freed his own slaves. The planter might *emancipate,* the two editors concluded, but a general *abolition* required the sterner spirit of "the converted, flinty New England heart." If they wanted a genuine world's convention, they had better hold it in Boston.

The social whirl continued for several weeks after the convention adjourned. The Americans became tourists. Garrison gazed admiringly at Westminster Abbey and St. Paul's, shivered with horror at the execution block in the Tower, and marveled at the perfect likenesses of Scott and Byron, Luther, Calvin, Knox, and Penn in Mme. Tussaud's waxworks. He went to the picture galleries and down the long corridors of the British Museum, persevering longer than Lucretia Mott, who preferred conversation to curiosities and sat down on a bench for a nap. Eventually Garrison, too, admitted that his eyes were "weary of sight-seeing," and the pace eased. He was evidently spared the tours of schools that their hosts thought the ladies must see (and where Mrs. Mott observed girls "too much confined to stitching and other non-sense"), but Garrison was called upon to attend a juvenile choral concert whose evangelical director successfully promoted his own composition "God Speed the Right" as an abolitionist anthem.

While the convention had deepened the factional division within the movement, it also drew the Garrisonian group more closely together as the New Englanders and Philadelphians socialized among themselves and with kindred spirits like the Richard Webb family from Dublin and the Joseph Pease contingent from Manchester. Garrison and Rogers, who would take over the AAS national newspaper upon his return, had developed a remarkable rapport, and Lucretia Mott found that she liked Rogers more and more, too. She also took a special interest in Elizabeth Cady Stanton, though her new husband was squarely in the rival camp, and the two women had long and searching talks on their afternoons together in schools and museums. Stanton appreciated Mott as "a peerless woman . . . [who] opened a new world of thought" for her, and the friendship forged in London would have important ramifications for the women's rights cause in America. They would all leave the convention, Richard Webb declared, "Garrisonized to the back-bone."

When the editor learned on July 2 that Helen had safely delivered a third son on June 4, 1840, he felt so awash with homesickness that he seriously considered racing to Liverpool to catch a vessel scheduled to depart for Boston the very next day. Only with great reluctance was he persuaded to go along with the northern tour then being planned for him. Birney and Stanton had set off on a mission to visit every shire in the country with Scoble and Sturge of the British society, and Garrison admitted that he could not let "the spirit of new organization" take the field uncontested. He promised Helen that he would book space on the new government steamer *Acadia*, leaving Liverpool on August 4 and *scheduled* (no need to be at the mercy of the wind!) to land in Boston on August 20. Fondly he stroked the lock of infant hair that Helen had sent and fancied that he could hear the youngster exercising his lungs across the ocean. How could he be the father of three boys, Garrison marveled. "Why, it was only the other day that I was a babe myself! . . ."

The speaking tour began in Edinburgh with a huge temperance rally and a breakfast for civic leaders at the Royal Hotel. There Garrison narrated the progress of the cause in America and received loud cheers for emphasizing how the "humble and poor" had prevailed against the opposition of the wealthy, respectable, and powerful. Rogers characterized abolition as a universal rather than a national endeavor and underscored the need to end slavery in order to eradicate racial prejudice. Remond then spoke movingly of the black person's half-caste situation in America and heaped much praise upon Garrison for his own suffering in the cause.

The editor felt enraptured to be in the land of Scott and Burns and greatly enjoyed an excursion through the highlands between Edinburgh and Glasgow. His pleasure at the scenic inspiration for the tales of Rob Roy and the verses of "The Lady of the Lake" was diminished, however, by recollections of the suffering he had seen in the industrial society below. At a great public meeting in Glasgow's leading chapel, he felt obliged to take notice of a Chartist placard—"Have we no white slaves?"—he had seen in the entryway and insisted that abolitionists had to be the enemies of economic and political oppression as well as slavery. Cheers rang out again, but there were some ready to chide the visitor for meddling in domestic matters. In general the Scots welcomed Garrison more warmly than the English, and the editor reciprocated by comparing his audiences favorably to New Englanders for their sturdy independence and vigorous consciences.

Garrison's party scarcely had time to wander Glasgow's narrow streets before they departed for Dublin, where Richard Webb had organized private meetings for the group with important Irish abolitionists. After three days of nearly nonstop conversation and visiting in the Webbs' home on Great Brunswick Street, the Americans had indelibly impressed themselves on Irish hearts. A self-educated printer like Garrison, Webb promised to reprint a few nonresistance tracts "just to raise a little bit of a row, and to set people thinking." The Irishman told Garrison that he seemed "to breathe a freer air when you are with me," and the two men laid the basis for a friendship, largely epistolary, that would last their lifetimes.

The favorable impression Garrison made upon the leadership in the principal cities beyond the metropolis paralleled his course in the United States, where he enjoyed far more support in the provinces than in the commercial capital of New York. From an organizational standpoint, the lecture tour probably did more for the AAS—and its fund-raising—than the editor's boycott of the convention, though the moral leadership he displayed in London obviously laid the groundwork for his acceptance. The purity of Garrison's vision and the simplicity of his manner proved fascinating and convincing. "It is no longer surprising that his influence should be so powerful," Webb said, "or that tens of thousands of the most enlightened, most pious and most devoted of the American abolitionists should stand faithfully by him, as their head . . . unawed by sectarian clamor, or the fears of the timid or the insinuations of envy . . . or by the boldness and originality of his own views. . . ." Webb's wife disagreed slightly with her husband. Garrison was "not an innovator," she thought, but simply intent upon "reviv[ing] and enforc[ing]" gospel truth.

The *Acadia,* its funnel belching smoke and its side paddle splashing furiously, made the westbound crossing in a record twelve and a half days. Its sister ship, *Britannia,* had inaugurated the new era of direct steam connection between Liverpool and Boston with an impressive fourteen-day crossing only a month before, landing at specially constructed new docks amid cheers and fireworks from Boston's mercantile leaders eager to celebrate the remarkable commercial advance. Garrison always took pleasure in comparing the momentum of social reform with the pace of technological change, and it was perhaps fitting that, having symbolically broadened the ideal of emancipation in London, he returned to the United States on the latest emblem of the modern industrial transformation.

Though it lacked a pyrotechnical display, Garrison's homecoming certainly proved more festive and less violent than his return in 1833. The editor's friends in the black community, led by John T. Hilton, had planned a welcoming reception for August 20, 1840, but when news came that the *Acadia* would be arriving early, they sent an interracial delegation to the Cunard dock to bring Garrison and Rogers triumphantly into the city. Hundreds turned out for an impromptu parade, and Garrison said that he "could not help weeping like a child for joy" at the demonstration.

The official ceremonies—the first organized by the black leadership at the Marlboro Chapel—came off splendidly. Two thousand people crammed into the room, its unadorned walls a far cry from the splendor of Freemasons' Hall, and Garrison had to choke back tears when Hilton, his own eyes brimming, fervently grasped the editor in "the right hand of fellowship" as waves of applause welled up from the benches. Francis Jackson yielded his customary place in the chair to James G. Barbadoes, who recalled how the black community had rallied to support the young printer at the outset of his career in Boston a decade earlier.

Garrison told of Charles Remond's success in England, where he had remained to lecture, and laughingly expressed surprise that someone had hailed the Salem man as the "only representative of the colored population" in London. Remond was the only delegate of color, to be sure, but he was "not your only representative," said Garrison to strong applause. The editor recounted the story of the "*pseudo* convention . . . a mere automaton in the hands of a self-constituted body in London" that claimed it could not consider "other questions." Yet by excluding women, he emphasized, they had judged the question and discredited themselves as abolitionists by reaching the wrong conclusion, for women and slaves had identical claims to equal rights. "*Human* rights," shouted Garrison, "*that* is the great question which agitates the age."

The Boston editor had "hit the nail on the head again," Rogers exulted.

Critics had already charged them with a foolish idealism for sitting out because all the world was not there, Garrison went on, after the cheering subsided, but he would answer that they sat out simply because some of

those "who *were* there, were denied admission." "If there be any one act of
my life, of which I am particularly proud," he added, "it is in refusing to
join such a body, on terms which were manifestly reproachful to my constituents, and unjust to the cause of liberty."

Garrison's decade of agitation—his jail term, his steadfast conduct of *The
Liberator* during the Nat Turner furor, his mobbing, his courageous embrace
of nonresistance—had prepared him well for his dramatic stand in London.
The short-term tactical advantage he might have secured over the schismatics paled next to the glowing statement he had made about the historic
change his century was making in the conditions of freedom. A vast sea
change in public opinion had begun, an alteration that when complete would
leave people aghast that they had ever thought otherwise, and though only
the vanguard was willing to credit Garrison for it, his insistence upon principled action supplied the vital energy for the process. The editor's great
French contemporary Victor Hugo (1802–1885) would shortly declare that
there is no power to rival an idea whose time has come, and in making his
entire career the agitation of a compelling idea, Garrison—from his obscure
corner of Boston—embodied the credo as few other Americans have ever
done.

The editor returned to a city overheated by politics. In the crisp autumn
weeks of September and October 1840, crowds gathered in front of every
newspaper office in search of the latest intelligence from the presidential
campaign, while the journals themselves teemed with speeches, election reports, and insistent editorials. The Whig Reading Room in Scollay's Building,
just up the street from *The Liberator*'s office, was wreathed with flags and
pennons, while knots of earnest party workers roamed the streets with placards and promises of hard cider for the supporters of "Tippecanoe, and Tyler
too."

The fervid campaign atmosphere—once the hallmark of the insurgent
Jacksonians—offended some high-minded Whigs, who disdained such emo-
tionalism in the civic process and feared "a Saturnalia of spoils and vulgarity."
A great many staunch Whigs, including abolitionists, got caught up in the
excitement, however, and readily stooped to conquer. "The whole nation is
politically insane," Garrison declared, and predicted that the abolitionists
would be "addressing bare walls" until the frenzy subsided. *The Liberator*
did what it could to keep the cause alive. Its columns overflowed, not to
press a candidate's case, but to question the preoccupation with electoral
politics. Garrison lost no opportunity to publicize that two-thirds of the abolition journals and all the state societies (except New York, where party
men had "gagged" the dissenters) opposed the Birney candidacy. "Third
party is only another name for new organization," he warned.

Birney drew the paltry numbers (fewer than seven thousand votes nationwide) that his critics had predicted, while the Whigs carried all but six

states. Garrison editorially welcomed the end of the campaign "as we would the disappearance of the Asiatic cholera from our shores." No previous election had proved so "degrading," he said, in the crudeness that had "literally *manufactured* Harrison into office . . . by all sorts of claptraps, tricks, and devices." As for the "useless third party contrivance," Garrison said, it was an attempt "to propel a locomotive engine without steam." Only the truth, not the ballot box, could set the captives free.

Though Garrison scorned the presidential campaign, he fell victim to its pace. "It is with me all the time, hurry, hurry, hurry," he fretted, and he drove himself so distractedly that he frequently mislaid papers and, on a quick lecture trip to Worcester, lost his wallet, containing fifty dollars in cash and a money order for thirty more. "I feel like an animal that has been denuded of its fur," Garrison said, for he could scarcely afford the loss of nearly a month's salary.

"The Lord is my shepherd," he told Helen, "and he will not fail to watch over me and mine." Friends shared their harvest bounty with the Garrisons; barrels of apples came from brother George in Brooklyn, quinces from another Connecticut friend, sacks of cornmeal and tubs of butter from nearby folk, and a Thanksgiving turkey from Francis Jackson. Georgie and Willie, "rousing lads, full of life and spirit," seemed to enjoy their baby brother, though George still proved "somewhat hard to manage" and loudly declared that he preferred the farm at Friendship's Vale to nursery school in Cambridgeport.

They named the baby Wendell Phillips Garrison, once again passing over the Benson family names to honor an abolitionist friend. It proved a fortunate choice, since the wealthy Phillips, who had no children, took a godfatherly interest in young "Wendy" and later underwrote his education. (When the Phillipses, still traveling in Europe in search of a cure for Ann's increasingly severe nervous ailments, heard the news, Wendell promptly urged his mother to send the Garrisons a gift for his namesake. "A kindness from you & *in your name*" would mean a great deal to this "noble-hearted man," he explained, but the elder Mrs. Phillips, a Beacon Street grande dame who disapproved of her son's turn to ultraism, kept a frosty silence.)

Wendy was, of course, "one of the best babes in all creation," his papa boasted. "He sleeps quietly all night long, is afraid of nobody, and is decidedly pretty." Yet maintaining a household with three children under five on a straitened budget in a crowded duplex taxed even Helen's considerable talents, and by November 1840 she put out a distress call for Grandmother Benson to help them through the winter. "I am at a loss to know how we can do without her," Garrison told his brother-in-law.

The editor, meanwhile, with his penchant for anniversaries, observed a double one. On December 12, 1840, Garrison celebrated his thirty-fifth birthday, and on New Year's Day 1841, *The Liberator* began its eleventh volume. "We are ten years nearer the glorious day of emancipation than when we began," Garrison said, proudly adding that for almost all of that time—spanning 511 issues of a newspaper steadily struggling "against wind and tide"—his critics had charged him with retarding the cause! In the aftermath of the schism he found himself readier than ever to press his vision of the humane life, and his heroic action in London epitomized his genius for turning a protesting gesture into a statement of affirmation.

It was more than coincidence, surely, that the English philosopher Thomas Carlyle gave his celebrated lectures on heroes and history in London only a few weeks before Garrison's arrival. In lauding the power of individuals to influence history, Carlyle emphasized the roles of prophets (Mahomet), priests (Luther), and poets (Dante, Shakespeare) over the customary adulation of generals and statesmen, and even his lecture on heroic monarchs focused, significantly, upon Cromwell as the political embodiment of a religious vision. For Carlyle heroism lay with the iconoclasts whose religious or artistic enthusiasm he comprehended, in the Romantic fashion, as a sign of emotional depth and power. "Is not every true Reformer, by the nature of him, a *Priest* first of all?" Carlyle asked, in appealing "to Heaven's invisible justice against Earth's visible force." Although Victorian culture would eventually turn hero worship into a cult of power, Carlyle's intended emphasis lay upon the sincerity of ideas and the individuals who embody them in both word and gesture. For Carlyle, as for Garrison, the process of modern historical progress originated with Luther and the Protestant conscience. "A man protesting against error is on the way towards uniting himself with all men that believe in truth," Carlyle emphasized, and he pronounced Luther's nailing his theses to the cathedral door as the "greatest moment" in modern history, the harbinger of the great revolutions in England, America, and France.

In making his own agitation—from the founding of his newspaper to his boycott of the London convention—Garrison understood himself to be the prophet who would break through the shadows and silences to the divine truth of things. Garrison was "working for a new world," Hannah Webb wrote after all the heady talk the abolitionists had shared in London and Dublin in the summer of 1840: "A world in which there would be no slavery, no king, no beggars, no lawyers, no doctors, no soldiers, no palaces, no prisons, no creeds, no sects, no weary or grinding labor, no luxurious idleness, no peculiar sabbath or temple . . . no restraint but moral restraint, no constraining power but love. Shall we judge such a man because he may go a little further than we are prepared to follow?"

CHAPTER FIFTEEN

NO UNION WITH SLAVEHOLDERS

IN THE EARLY 1840s, GARRISON RESUMED THE SPIRITUAL JOURNEY INTER-
RUPTED BY THE SCHISM. HOWEVER MUCH THE EDITOR'S DETRACTORS
NEEDED TO ACCUSE HIM OF FOMENTING SOCIAL UPHEAVAL SINGLE-
handedly, Garrison was hardly alone in his challenge to orthodoxy. The abolitionist leaven had done its work, as had the Jacksonian insurgency, the
Romantic movement in poetry and letters, the Owenite and Fourierist socialists, the perfectionists, the nonresistants, and the discontented souls from
genteel Ralph Waldo Emerson to the bearded millennialist Joseph Palmer
and the ecstatic Mother Ann Lee of the Shakers who had "come out"* from
the straitjackets of their denominations to search for more satisfying forms
of religious expression. All over New England and the Western Reserve, it
seemed, there were groups of seekers enthralled by fresh visions of an ideal
society. "A revolution of all Human affairs is now in progress," exulted Bronson Alcott, the teacher who had long ago shared his own dreams with Garrison and their fellow boarders at the Rev. William Collier's on Federal
Street. "There is nothing deemed true and sacred now that shall pass this
time, unharmed."

Religious radicalism came with the smell of leather and sawdust. This was
"predominantly a people's movement," recalled the reform-minded young
clergyman Thomas Wentworth Higginson, "based on the simplest human
instincts, and far stronger for a time in the factories and shoe-shops than in
the pulpits or the colleges." These seekers of the New Kingdom were responding to the call that had reverberated among dissenters ever since John
Bunyan's time. Theirs was the pilgrimage that had inspired Whitefield and
Alline, and theirs was the vision of the celestial city that Sister Garrison had
summoned for the women in her prayer meetings and the children at her
knee. When Garrison had the opportunity of worshiping with some come-
outers in Concord, New Hampshire, in 1841, he extended an editorial salute
to the "little *heretical* meeting" in a small hall over the bank for its "very
simple exercises—untrammeled, spontaneous, after the apostolic pattern"
and went back a second time to share in the hymns, readings, exhortations,

---

*The term derived from the verse "And I heard another voice from heaven, saying, Come out of
her, my people, that ye not be partakers of her sins, and that ye receive not of her plagues" (Rev.
18:4).

and prayers that made up the observance. Such worship and fellowship touched Garrison's earliest memories, for it resembled the spiritual life he had shared with his mother in the Farnhams' house and the meetings Father Peak had conducted for the Baptist faithful in Newburyport. The company of believers—united in the bonds of faith, not creed—remained his spiritual ideal, and in the early 1840s he began to ponder how to apply the come-outers' vision to the politics of antislavery agitation.

Garrison published the call for the universal reformers' most ambitious undertaking—a three-day convention at Boston's Chardon Street Chapel in November 1840 to examine the validity of prevailing views on Sabbath observance and the organized authority of the ministry and the church—and, as a man who respected talk as a source of light, he eagerly attended the meeting. Long before the scheduled hour, the nondescript little building on a side street behind fashionable Bowdoin Square had filled with more than five hundred people representing "every shade of opinion, from the straitest orthodoxy to the wildest heresy, and many persons whose church was a church of one member only," Emerson observed. There had never been such a "picturesque" gathering of the tribes, whose dialects, dress, and eccentricities powerfully displayed the cantankerous independence of New Englanders, yet evoked for Emerson the heady era of English radical Puritanism. "Dunkers, Muggletonians, Come-outers, Groaners, Agrarians, Seventh-day Baptists, Quakers, Abolitionists, Calvinists, Unitarians, and Philosophers—all came successively to the top, and seized their moment, if not their *hour*, wherein to chide, or pray, or preach, or protest," he said.

One may ask what the fastidious Emerson was doing there. Since his controversial Divinity School Address in 1836 he had pursued his inquiries through the medium of the Transcendental Club, a select gathering of open-minded Unitarian ministers and an occasional guest that met regularly to ponder questions such as "Wonder and Worship," "Miracles and Mysticism," "Pantheism," and other issues of spiritual philosophy. Only once had an abolitionist minister, such as Samuel J. May, joined the discussion; only in 1840 had the group devoted any attention to "the doctrine of reform" and the question of "organizing a new church," which the group addressed twice in September 1840, before breaking off, never to meet again. In his lectures Emerson generally looked down upon "the faithful men of one idea" ("these poor Grahams and Garrisons," he had called them in his notebook) and proclaimed the intellectual superiority of "wise passiveness" over the creation of new institutions. Yet his curiosity got the better of his strictures, and he went to Chardon Street to observe at first hand the gathering stream of plebeian religious radicalism.

There was so much talk that the nominal chair, Edmund Quincy, could not bring the congregation to order and indeed found himself admonished by several speakers that an organized meeting would itself be an affront to the spirit. Somehow the meeting agreed to devote its three days to "the Sabbath question" alone and hold a second convention six months later to weigh the issues of ministerial and Scriptural authority. Not all speakers, of course, adhered to this decision about the agenda, but the move pleased Garrison, who vigorously urged his case for making every day a sacred one. The defenders of traditional worship included some of his clerical opponents, notably A. A. Phelps and a Baptist colleague, Nathaniel Colver, whom Garrison accused of subverting the philosophical discussion to party purposes.

The gathering was too heterogeneous to bend in any single direction, an outcome which did not perturb Garrison, who suggested that local conventions take up the issues and enable laymen "to search the scriptures afresh, for *themselves*." The doctrinal achievements of the Chardon Street convention were less important than the spirit of inquiry it represented and the egalitarian manner in which it conducted itself. Even the snobbish Emerson found himself captivated. To have members of the old aristocratic families mingling with people without pedigrees and encountering "clownish faces lit with sacred fire" produced memorable conversations, Emerson said. "These men and women were in search of something better and more satisfying than a vote or a definition, and they found what they sought . . . in the prophetic dignity and transfiguration which accompanies . . . a man whose mind is made up to obey the great inward Commander. . . ."

Emerson had finally felt the pulse of the movement that sustained Garrison. It did not take long for Garrison's detractors, however, to promote the canard that he had presided over "an infidel convention," and the meddlesome Nathaniel Colver, who had allied himself with Birney and the English evangelicals at the London convention, funneled the Chardon Street proceedings abroad in order to breed doubts among the editor's British friends. Garrison made rebuttals that, as was his custom, restated his views with even greater intensity. "I believe in an indwelling Christ, and in his righteousness alone," Garrison explained to Elizabeth Pease. Though he belonged to no church, he maintained that his views "harmonized" with much in the tradition of the Society of Friends. Yet his thought had absorbed a perfectionist quality that took him further. Rejecting the Calvinist principle of predestination, he contended that individuals could "put on Christ" themselves and "exercise that faith which overcomes the world" by living the sinless life. This was the perfectionist's antinomian conviction of the indwelling spirit, and it separated Garrison from both the orthodox and the evangelicals led by Charles G. Finney at Oberlin, who had evolved their own "Arminian" version of a perfectionism based upon an individual's *willingness* to be free from sin. The religious imperative was always more important to Garrison than the theology that explained it, however, and he buttressed his views with little more than quotations from the prophets and apostles. In opposition to the sterile formalism of the existing denominations, he had formulated an activist's religion of "vital godliness" and "practical holiness" that transcended doctrine and merged with "the righteous reforms of the age."

Spiritual restlessness strengthened the rising voice of abolitionist protest within the churches as well. Some Quakers, notably Garrison's supporter William Bassett of Lynn, were expelled for publicly challenging the Friends' hostility toward agitation, while others, including Arnold Buffum and his family, withdrew under pressure. In March 1841, Abby Kelley told her Uxbridge (Massachusetts) Monthly Meeting that she felt obliged to "come out and be separate" because the Friends had elevated "forms" over "vital religion" and frowned upon those activists who had "mingled" with other denominations in antislavery organizations. Hoping to dissuade Kelley, the Uxbridge Friends kept quiet about the letter for six months, which provoked her into giving it to Garrison for publication in *The Liberator*. Her restlessness inevitably had repercussions. When a Presbyterian woman named Rhoda Bement rebuked her minister for failing to read notices about a series of lectures by Kelley in Seneca Falls, New York, and then skipped church to attend them, the elders of her church tried to discipline her. The four-month-long ecclesiastical trial became, in itself, a major organizing tool for Kelley, and Mrs. Bement ended up in a breakaway Wesleyan Methodist sect that supported abolitionism.

Perhaps as many as half a million people found spiritual homes in new church groupings, such as the Progressive Friends, the Baptist Free Mission Society, the Union Church, the Free Presbyterian Church, and the Indiana Yearly Meeting of Antislavery Friends. Uncounted thousands more came out of their old churches but entered no new one, taking their spiritual nourishment privately in the company of abolitionist friends and, like Garrison, partaking of the practical holiness of reform while maintaining a Christian but not a denominational identity. A person who withdrew from a church's fellowship gave "the strongest proof of his sincerity," a come-outer wrote in *The Liberator*, "and the very fact of his departure will call . . . attention more effectually to its cause than anything he could say while yet a member." By the mid-1840s the upheavals among Baptists and Methodists over their policy toward slaveholders would split these denominations on sectional lines.

Even within Unitarianism, breakaways took place, giving abolitionism one of its most influential new voices. Theodore Parker preached about the contradictions of Scripture to his West Roxbury congregation and outraged Boston with a lecture, titled "The Transient and Permanent in Christianity," that distinguished between mutable creeds—"the robe, not the angel"—and the permanent spiritual state of "perfect obedience to the great law of God." Not long after, the renegade preached the first of many sermons on slavery, and—unlike his mentor Channing—Parker defended the intensity of abolitionism and spoke about the need to challenge existing social institutions in the name of "remedial justice." The Unitarian establishment froze him out of its pulpits, but Parker, who came from a solid Yankee family and had steeped himself in both classical and modern philosophy and criticism, withstood the pressure and continued to advocate what amounted to another version of Romantic perfectionism. Like Wendell Phillips, Parker had repudiated his patrimony of high-toned conservatism and attracted an egalitarian-minded following, who convened an independent church around him in Boston. By the winter of 1841–42 the religious press had firmly linked "Parkerism" with "Garrisonism," and the minister had become another leader in the gathering congregation of universal reformers.

Parker had become the mildest sort of abolitionist come-outer, but others exerted a more flamboyant defiance. In New Hampshire one of the state society's agents, Stephen S. Foster, undertook a personal campaign of church disruptions, standing up in a meetinghouse as the minister's sermon began to declare that, as a Christian, he had come to say a few words on behalf of millions of their kidnapped and enslaved brethren. In denouncing the complicity of the denomination with slaveholders, he would often cap his charges with the well-honed accusation that by allowing thousands of slave women to be held in concubinage, the church was worse than any brothel in the city of New York. Commotion often ensued, and Foster—a tall, lean man with flashing eyes, a sonorous voice, and a carpenter's rough hands—would keep speaking no matter what followed. He would ignore the minister's remonstrance, bellow denunciation over the choir's hastily rendered hymns, enter a colloquy on the few occasions when the congregation insisted that he be welcomed, or sit limply and continue speaking while the deacons dragged him from the church. By the end of 1841 Foster had been ejected from twenty-four churches, twice from the second story, and jailed four times. Another New Hampshireman, a former minister named Parker Pillsbury, joined Foster as a "steeplehouse troubler" and later became an agent for the AAS. A third New Hampshireman, Thomas Beach, another minister who had resigned his pulpit to take up itinerant agitation, was arrested in Newburyport for disrupting a Friends' meeting, and rather than pay the fine, he spent his days in jail sending fire-breathing articles on come-outerism and free speech to *The Liberator*. Garrison did not endorse their disruptive tactics, which he considered too coercive, but he gave a wider voice to such witnesses against Northern complicity. In a rare instance of moderation the editor confided to Helen that while he wished "bro. Foster would exercise more judgment and discretion in the presentation of his views," he had found it "useless to reason with him."

Religious upheaval and come-outerism formed one strand of Garrisonian moral suasion; direct social protest formed another as the ultra-abolitionists continued to bear witness against racial injustice. In July 1841, *The Liberator* carried several complaints from David Ruggles, a militant abolitionist from

New York, about "Jim Crow" mistreatment, first on a Nantucket steamer, whose captain refused to allow him a place in the cabin and forcibly threw him from the boat, and then on the New Bedford & Taunton Railroad, whose conductor ordered him to move to "the dirty car" set aside for travelers of color. When Ruggles refused, the conductor tried to rally the crowded carful of passengers to support the ouster, but an abolitionist minister spoke up instead for the black man's rights. The angry conductor then went into the depot and returned with the superintendent, who dragged the nearly blind Ruggles from the train and dispatched it to Boston with his suitcase still aboard.

A printer and organizer who headed the vigilance committee that rendered protection to fugitive slaves in New York, Ruggles was no stranger to protest. He promptly sued the railroad for assault, but the judge upheld the authority of a private company to regulate seating and found no evidence to support a damage claim. Garrison denounced the decision as "unspeakably atrocious" in an account headlined "Lynching in New Bedford." The local black community organized protest meetings, more accounts of "Jim Crow" mistreatment began to surface, and the Boston abolitionist community organized a fête in Ruggles's honor that even Helen Garrison, normally reluctant to attend public events, attended with pleasure. Her husband "rejoiced" at the affair—one of the first instances in which a large number of Boston blacks and whites had ceremonially dined at the same table—since it drove "another nail into the coffin of prejudice."

Since many abolitionist leaders—including Garrison—had agreed to attend a midsummer convention on Nantucket, they immediately protested Ruggles's mistreatment. By gathering first in New Bedford and boarding the island-bound steamer in a large and determined interracial group, the abolitionists provoked a wharfside argument that breached the wall of segregation and won them unrestricted use of the upper deck, where they drew a crowd and conducted an impromptu debate with holiday travelers, including a New Orleans slaveholder and an Episcopal clergyman. "All that occurred in the boat was eminently calculated to aid the cause of abolition," Henrietta Sargent told Maria Child, who promptly published her correspondent's report in the *National Anti-Slavery Standard*.

The Nantucket convention met for three enthusiastic days and nights (August 10–12, 1841) in a former Universalist church building that, with the addition of a decorative portico and a donated library, had become the island's Athenaeum. Garrison denounced racial discrimination in a firm resolution that assailed Northern segregationists for "acting as the bodyguard of slavery," but his most powerful statement was inspired by a former slave. As the August 11 session drew to a close, a tall young black man rose to his feet and hesitantly asked to be recognized. His name, though the secretary failed to catch it, was Frederick Douglass, and he worked as a stevedore and ship's caulker in New Bedford. He had done some preaching in the seaport's

Zion Chapel, and William Coffin, a bookkeeper who was part of the influential Nantucket Quaker family that included Lucretia Mott, had urged Douglass to come to the island meeting. He now felt moved to speak, and though he trembled in every limb and afterward could hardly remember two sentences of what he said, the young man did speak, explaining that he was a fugitive from bondage and telling of the cruelties he had witnessed and suffered.

Although a freeborn black man, a young barber from New Bedford, had spoken earlier in the meeting, and, indeed, remarks by black students eager to display their accomplishments were a staple item on many convention agendas, this was the first time many white abolitionists had heard an escaped slave speak in public for himself. Though Douglass seemed "green and awkward," a Boston woman recalled, he made such an earnest and straightforward statement that the audience was transfixed and "greatly moved." The emotion of the moment was, in fact, breathtaking, and Garrison, in a masterstroke of theater, capitalized upon it.

"Have we been listening to a thing, a piece of property, or to a man?" the editor quietly asked the awed congregation when Douglass had finished his testimony.

"A man! A man!" people responded.

"And should such a man be held a slave in a republican and Christian land?" Garrison asked, his voice rising.

"Never! Never!" came the answer.

Alluding to the risk Douglass had taken in making himself known, Garrison asked one more question.

"Shall such a man ever be sent back to slavery from the soil of old Massachusetts?" he roared.

No one who was there would ever forget the roar of "No! No! No!" that went up from the benches and set the walls and roof of the Athenaeum shuddering in the "wild enthusiasm" of the scene. "Taking me as his text," the overwhelmed Douglass said of his idol, whose newspaper had helped to forge his political consciousness, Garrison fused the meeting into "a single individuality" committed to freedom. Forty years later Parker Pillsbury could still tell Garrison's sons how their father had "carried the meeting into the sublime."

At the behest of the editor and other leaders, Douglass soon became an MAS agent. Four weeks later, on September 9, 1841, traveling on the Eastern Railroad in Essex County on his first speaking trip, Douglass was rudely separated from his coworker, John A. Collins, and forcibly escorted into the Jim Crow car. When Collins and several other passengers tried to go with him, they were blocked and their clothes torn. (The year before, after Garrison's return from London, he had quietly shared "the Negro pew" on the same line with William C. Nell, a worker in *The Liberator*'s office, who had been ordered from the first-class car. In taking his seat, Nell recalled, Garrison "remarked to me that he had become somewhat tanned since he left America and might perhaps be taken for a colored man; I told him that he always knew how to feel as one.")

Two weeks after the first assault, Douglass and Collins refused to get up from their seats when the same conductor harassed them at the depot in Lynn. They challenged his authority, demanded a vote among the passengers, and created such a commotion that the conductor brought a half-dozen toughs onto the coach to "snake out the damned nigger." Douglass and Collins sat impassively, hands gripped tightly to their bench, as the rain of blows fell. The ruffians expelled them only by ripping up the floor bolts and dumping the abolitionists—seat and all—upon the platform.

These incidents—which Douglass recounted with great effect in his lectures—stimulated a vigorous protest campaign in which the abolitionists tested conditions on every railroad in the state, sometimes integrating them without argument, sometimes creating a ruckus that led to community meetings, court cases, and—by February 1842—a full-dress hearing before the legislature. Though the senate rejected an antidiscrimination bill passed by the house, public opinion had shifted markedly on the issue. In April 1842, when the railroads announced their summer schedules, Garrison began publishing a weekly full-column "travelers' directory" that, along with departure times, noted—with a printer's fist—the degree of respect for "human rights" extended to passengers. Of the eight lines serving Boston, five offered "equality of privileges," while three still made "vile complexional distinctions" and displayed "a bullying propensity" to enforce them. Abolitionists continued to agitate the issue—Garrison made a point of always riding in the Jim Crow car "to remember those in bonds, as bound with them"—and within another year the three holdouts abandoned their segregationist policies. To mark the occasion, a Nantucket Quaker, Nathaniel Barney, who had refused to accept his dividends from the New Bedford & Taunton line during the struggle because he wanted no profit from evil, advised the railroad's treasurer to send the accumulated sum—$22.50—as a contribution to *The Liberator*.

The successful protest against segregation in transportation coincided with another victory for the antislavery movement: the release of three dozen Africans taken into U.S. custody in the aftermath of their dramatic shipboard revolt against their slave-trading captors. A Baltimore-built schooner, christened *Friendship*, had become a vehicle in the Caribbean slave trade under its Hispanicized name, *Amistad*. In the summer of 1839 it was carrying a cargo of newly purchased slaves between ports on the coast of Cuba when the captive Africans, under the leadership of a man known variously as Cinguez or Cinqué, commandeered the ship, killing its captain and ordering its navigators to return the ship to West Africa. By sailing into the sun by day and reversing course at night, the Spaniards deceived the rebels and gradually moved northwest until the *Amistad* washed up in Long Island Sound in late August 1839. A U.S. naval party seized it, charged the Africans with piracy and murder, and had them confined in a New Haven jail until the courts could hear a formal indictment and consider an array of salvage claims from the naval officers, the navigators, and the government of Spain.

Garrison published a lengthy account of the startling developments and declared that the case deserved "the sympathy of all true-hearted, impartial lovers of liberty." Cinqué and his associates were neither murderers nor pirates, he insisted, nor had they broken any U.S., Spanish, or international law. As in other cases of slave revolt, he abhorred the violence but insisted that it be regarded on a par with the heroic resistance of George Washington and the American Revolutionaries. The editor despaired of justice for the *Amistad* prisoners, however, because their case would be heard by the "infamous" Andrew T. Judson, the Canterbury selectman who had harassed Prudence Crandall in 1833 and earned a federal judgeship for his faithful service to the Democratic Party.

Something about the *Amistad* case won the hearts of people not previously friendly to abolition. As Africans who sought to return home, the captives struck a sympathetic chord with colonizationists; as rebels against Hispano-Catholic tyranny on the high seas, they seemed more heroic and less threatening than mutinous plantation slaves in Protestant America; as orphans of the storm, they appealed to clergymen and missionaries; as curiosities who spoke an exotic language and had survived a despicable commerce, they made good copy for the newspapers. It did not take long for abolitionists, organized in New Haven by Garrison's old friend Simeon Jocelyn and supported nationally under the benevolent aegis of Lewis Tappan, to hire attorneys, publish pamphlets, enlist Yale professors, and generally build a climate of opinion favorable to the prisoners' release. *The Liberator* regularly published the major documents in the case, extended accounts of the judicial proceedings, and reports on the history of the Africans as interpreters gradually pieced it together. The editor also brought to the committee's attention a visiting Englishman who had served on the joint British-Spanish commission charged with supervising the widely flouted ban on slave trading the countries had enacted in 1818.

Much to Garrison's surprise, Judge Judson quickly dismissed the murder and piracy charges, and after a well-conducted trial in January 1840, awarded the naval officers salvage rights to the ship itself, but not the prisoners. They were not slaves, Judson ruled, but kidnapped Africans—unlawfully traded and transported in Cuba and freed under the rule of self-defense in international waters. The United States, under the terms of its own laws against the slave trade, had an obligation to return them to Sierra Leone, said Judson, and he issued a writ commanding the president to transport them to their homeland.

The abolitionists' cheers did not ring out for very long, because President

Van Buren circumvented the ruling under intense pressure, both from Spain, which wanted the Africans extradited to Cuba as both property and assassins, and from Southern Democrats, who insisted that the United States had an obligation to return fugitive slaves to their masters. While the attorney general filed an appeal of Judson's ruling in the U.S. Supreme Court, the administration tried a number of clandestine maneuvers to wrench jurisdiction of the matter from the courts to the executive branch. Abolitionists protested the government's effort to assist in the "judicial murder" of the *Amistad* Africans by extraditing them to Cuba, and John Quincy Adams grew so angry at Van Buren's usurpation of power and willingness to serve as a Spanish "constable and catchpoll" that he joined the defense team and made a nine-hour argument before the high court that posed the broad issues in a manner both philosophical and theatrical.

In an opinion written by Justice Joseph Story of Massachusetts in March 1841, the court sustained Judson's view that the Africans were not slaves, but did not agree with his conclusion that the law required them to be returned to Africa. Principles of liberty and justice, Story reasoned, allowed them to decide that question for themselves. Story therefore revoked the order to the president and directed the release of the *Amistad* prisoners from custody. They were free at last, not by the universal principles of the Garrisonians perhaps, but free of the elaborate mesh in which admiralty law, diplomatic treaties, and the connivance of governments in an illegal commerce tried to ensnare them. After an additional six months of abolitionist fund-raising the twice-liberated Africans sailed east for good in November 1841.

The case was a triumph for humanitarianism, but not a strong blow against the constitutional system that sustained slavery. The decision turned on the complicated determination that the Spanish and Cuban traders had broken the laws against slave trading and had no legal claim to the *Amistad* Africans. Had such a claim been established at law (as it was in the single instance of a cabin boy on the *Amistad* who had lived in Cuba for years and manifestly belonged to its captain), Story made plain, the fugitives would have been returned. Indeed, the courts did order the cabin boy, Antonio, transported to Cuba, but abolitionist friends found him an underground passage to Montreal before the ruling could be enforced.

The *Amistad* campaign also proved a triumph of the abolitionists' ability to cooperate in an errand of mercy in the very years, 1839 to 1841, in which the movement rent itself in schism. Both old and new organizations kept a low profile in the work, allowing newcomers to bind themselves to the cause, and Garrison never hesitated to publish material from the rival *Emancipator* or the regular appeals issued by Lewis Tappan. Indeed, at the conclusion of the case, Garrison wrote a generous statement in praise of the "zeal and vigor" with which Tappan served as the Africans' "indefatigable and faithful friend." The abolitionists nonetheless realized that in gaining freedom for the *Amistad* rebels they had contended unsuccessfully with the brute fact of racial prejudice. Had the mutineers been Anglo-Saxons against pirates of the Algerine, declared a writer in *The Liberator*, they would not have spent two years in protective custody while outsiders tried to determine whether or not they were somebody's chattel.

It did not take long for the fugitive slave issue to occupy center stage in the abolitionist agitation. The *Amistad* case arose in special circumstances and dealt with a single boatload of displaced persons, but men and women who ran away from bondage in the Southern states posed a dramatic challenge to the entire system. For Garrison, simply sharing the platform with Frederick Douglass reminded him of every escapee's vulnerability and put a human face on the abstract constitutional provision [Article IV, Section 2] that "no person held to service or labor" in one state could be "discharged" from bondage by escaping to another state. Douglass was an example of that troublesome species of property, a runaway, whose masters advertised for return in almost every issue of every Southern newspaper. Douglass's very name was a protective alias, the editor learned, though as the young orator's reputation grew, it seemed inevitable that he would be recognized and an effort made to repossess him. Every runaway who did not go on to Canada stood in similar jeopardy of exposure and return, and the weight given by the law to the master's right of reclamation made all free black people subject to a kidnapper's false accusations and a court order that would send them south into the slave trade. Vigilance committees run by black leaders in New York and Philadelphia sprang up to protect their communities from such depredations, but the gathering controversy over abolition heightened fears and kept tension high. Douglass emphasized, too, that Southern slaves knew full well that the law would give them no protection in the North; the constitutional obligation to return fugitives thus discouraged escapes and stood as another "bulwark of slavery." "Every true abolitionist had to go against such a Union," Garrison heard Douglass exhort an 1841 Plymouth County meeting.

A few months later, when the U.S. Supreme Court upheld the constitutionality of the Fugitive Slave Law and ruled that the states had no power to impose safeguards—such as jury trials or other judicial supervision—on the process by which an owner or his agent claimed a black person as his runaway property, Garrison felt his allegiance pushed to the breaking point. Since seven justices wrote opinions in the case, *Prigg v. Pennsylvania* (1842), the holdings on a number of specific points remained uncertain, but the firmness of the leading opinion—by the venerable Justice Story—left no doubt that the Court had not only reinforced a major legal protection for slaveholders, but given fresh sanction to the constitutional compromise with slavery.

That this conclusion came from New England's most distinguished jurist, who had freed the *Amistad* captives and whose personal opposition to slavery reached as far back as the effort to bar slaveholding Missouri from entering the Union in 1819, came as a heavy blow. Story (1779–1845) had served on the Supreme Court for thirty-one years and had no peer as an expositor of American constitutional law. He had exerted a vast influence upon the Marshall Court's landmark decisions that helped to create a national commercial society by insulating entrepreneurs and property from regulation by the states. Through his systematic treatises and his lectures as Harvard's Dane Professor of Law, he had done as much as anyone to advance both national legal powers and the concept of an organic nation—the ideal of a sovereign people that politicians like Daniel Webster used to counter the states-rights, compact theories of government advanced in defense of slavery and local economic control by Calhoun and his allies.

The idea of *national* power, if turned against slavery, could have advanced the abolitionist agenda, which is why Calhoun exerted himself so strenuously against it, but in the *Prigg* case, Story construed the idea of an exclusive national power in favor of the slaveholders. In effect, he interpreted the slaveholders' federal right to recover their fugitive property without interference from the states as being of a piece with the work the Marshall-Story Court had accomplished for other vested economic interests. Slaveholders in pursuit of runaways had a right no different from the land speculators' contract rights to purchase land from a bribed legislature (*Fletcher v. Peck*, 1810), a steamboat owner's right to be free of state licensing laws that granted a monopoly to his competitors (*Gibbons v. Ogden*, 1824), the national bank's right to operate without being impeded by prohibitive state taxation (*McCullough v. Maryland*, 1819), or a private corporation's right to maintain its charter inviolate against subsequent modification by a state legislature (*Dartmouth College v. Woodward*, 1819). The states could not impair contracts or interfere with the explicit national power to regulate commerce or the implicit national power to undertake projects for the general welfare, and—similarly—the states could not interfere with the slaveholder's efforts to recapture his escaped chattel by imposing procedural hurdles more stringent than what Congress had laid out in 1793. The right to recover fugitives, Story held, was a national right guaranteed in the Constitution, and Congress had the necessary and exclusive power to regulate the process. By affirming the slaveholder's absolute right to have his property protected in every state of the Union, Story's decision laid the basis for the subsequent nationalization of slavery in the *Dred Scott* decision of 1857. In defending the summary procedures of the 1793 federal law, moreover, Story completely ignored that the state "personal liberty" laws invalidated in *Prigg* had an important protective function for free black citizens, and thus he opened the way for assertions in the *Dred Scott* decision that black people had no claim to citizenship at all.

Black abolitionists protested this fresh assault upon their liberty, and at least one radical black minister, Samuel R. Ward, wondered whether he ought to seek exile in Canada, since he had come to New York as a youngster with his fugitive parents and could not "prove" his freedom. Such cases were in Garrison's mind when he declared that "the enormity of this [*Prigg*] decision . . . cannot be exhibited in words." "If the slaveholding power is permitted to roam without molestation through the northern states, 'seeking whom it may devour,'" he predicted, it would be "the last turn of the screw." His was not an extreme opinion. Many lawyers remembered devoting an entire day to reading the troubling case and reluctantly concluding that while Story's reasoning was legally correct, the decision had made the 1793 law into "a grim fortress" for an assault upon civil liberty. The moderate *New York Tribune* pronounced *Prigg* the most important decision in the history of the Court and warned that it brought "the great question of Freedom or Slavery to all our doors."

The *Prigg* decision coincided with another highly publicized case that demonstrated a proslavery bias in the national government and revealed New England's subservience to it. Secretary of State Daniel Webster argued the Tyler administration's claim that Southern owners deserved compensation for a cargo of 135 slaves who had taken over their vessel, the *Creole,* and gained their freedom under British law by sailing it to Nassau. The situation paralleled the *Amistad* case, and once again the federal executive took the slaveholders' part. In a strongly worded protest to Great Britain, Webster claimed compensation for the property loss on the ground that the ship's deck should have been considered an extension of American soil. The argument shocked antislavery people, who contended that while explicit law could maintain slavery in a given state, the protection could not extend beyond its borders and certainly not to the high seas. Webster's reasoning "out Calhouns Calhoun himself," Samuel J. May complained. Even Dr. Channing, in the waning months of his life, found voice enough to attack Webster's "morally unsound and pernicious doctrine" for subordinating natural rights to the legal practices of a particular state. Natural law did not recognize slavery, Channing insisted, and the U.S. Constitution only offered protection for a preexisting property right. By extending the shield to the high seas or, by implication, to adjacent countries such as Texas, the administration was making slavery a matter of national, not merely local, interest, and bringing the North into greater connection with it. (This was the clear implication of the *Prigg* decision as well, although, interestingly, Justice Story had privately advised Webster not to push the *Creole* claim as far as he did.)

Although Garrison praised Channing's argument as "a logical, able, and eloquent effort" and reprinted it in pamphlet form himself, the editor had no patience with the remedy Channing proposed. The free states should be released by constitutional amendment, the minister said, from having anything to do with slavery, and should "make a treaty" with the South promising that except in the District of Columbia—which belonged to the entire nation—slave property would be as safe as if it "belong[ed] to foreign states" and no more subject to U.S. interference than were the serfs of Russia. The nation already had such a treaty, Garrison thought; it was the U.S. Constitution itself, and it would always be captive to the interests of the slaveholders. Channing's proposals, however heartfelt, demonstrated that far from becoming an immediatist, he still embraced the Union as an "inestimable good" which should not be sacrificed to the moral imperatives of emancipation as long as the slaveholders asked nothing more of their brethren in the free states.

Garrison, by contrast, thought the time had arrived for abolitionists to "come out" of the Union as they had the churches. In the name of the perfectionist ideal, he now attacked the shibboleth of constitutional compromise and the immorality of a union for politics' sake alone. He used an example drawn from the prophet Isaiah to show the folly of evading social responsibility with unholy alliances. Faced with an impending attack by the Assyrians, the people of Jerusalem had scoffed at the prophet's warnings and flaunted their wickedness: ". . . We have made a covenant with death, and with hell are we at agreement; when the overflowing scourge shall pass through, it shall not come unto us; for we have made lies our refuge, and under falsehood have we hid ourselves" (Isa. 28:15). But the prophet, Garrison went on, had warned them that the Lord would annul such sinful pacts and, in laying a cornerstone of righteousness for Zion, would use his line and his plummet to destroy their spurious shelter.

The editor would work variations on this passage for the remainder of his career. Sometimes he would apply it as a judgment upon the people of the North for remaining morally and politically complicit with slavery; at other times he would characterize the U.S. Constitution itself as the devil's pact. His point remained the same: the necessity of repudiating "the yoke of bondage" imposed by the Constitution in order to effect "a revolution . . . through the majesty of moral power." People of the free states had to "demand the repeal of the Union, or the abolition of slavery," he insisted, "not as a threat, but as a moral obligation" to purge their souls of guilt. "Repeal" became, for Garrison, a species of political come-outerism, and he became the prophet at the gate, warning people to leave the corrupt city or face destruction. It is significant, however, that Garrison always posed the issue as "Repeal *or* Abolition," for he was not so much threatening political secession as he was pointing out the inevitable collapse of a society built upon the great contradiction of slavery.

Unlike Garrison's attacks upon the colonizationists or his endorsement of women's rights, however, in which his intentions were clear and his gestures compelling, his assault on the Constitution began ambiguously as prophetic denunciation and only gradually developed into a political and philosophical critique. The confusion can be seen in the uncharacteristically scrambled syntax the editor tolerated in the slogan he placed at the head of his editorial column for many months in 1842–43: "The repeal of the Union between Northern liberty and Southern slavery is essential to the Abolition of the one, and the preservation of the other." Wendell Phillips put the phrases in a proper parallel sequence when the two agitators recast the proposition as a measure for adoption by various abolitionist bodies, but the lapse in Garrison's generally careful style suggests that disunion began as an angry change of attitude rather than a political remedy.

The editor tried to link his new idea with another complicated issue: the excitement generated by the Irish leader Daniel O'Connell's campaign to repeal the laws that bound Ireland to Great Britain. Garrison declared himself "an American repealer," but neither he nor his readers could develop the analogy in a powerful or telling manner. He wanted Northerners to feel themselves victimized by the power of the slave-owning oligarchy, but this never seemed a compelling parallel to the disenfranchisement of the Irish tenantry or the burden of discrimination against the Catholic Church. Indeed, both sides in the abolition controversy tried to get on the right side of Irish repeal. Many Democrats, including Southerners, were attempting to flatter the growing numbers of Irish immigrants in their ranks by supporting Irish repeal, a move that Garrison considered a species of "loathsome hypocrisy," though the states'-rights argument did have certain parallels with the Irish political situation. The Whig-minded abolitionists tried to counter with reminders of O'Connell's antislavery views. Indeed, at a Faneuil Hall meeting in January 1842, during which Garrison first put forward a repeal measure, Charles Remond, just returned from abroad, unfurled a scroll signed by O'Connell and sixty thousand Irishmen urging their countrymen in America to "unite with the abolitionists" and use their political power "for the sake of humanity." Nothing came of this "Irish address," for the immigrant vote was solidly racist and Democratic, and the urban violence directed against the abolitionists had poisoned their view of the immigrant question.

It was the shock value of repeal or "disunion," as the editor came to call his attack, that most appealed to Garrison. Disunion posed the issue as starkly as it could be, and it became a statement of the editor's moral and political priorities. It also offered the means—which no Northern politician had yet developed—of calling Calhoun's bluff.

While Calhoun threatened secession to frighten Northerners into maintaining the compromise, Garrison condemned the moral contradictions of union to shame citizens into resolving them. Garrison used the repeal idea as a means of "tearing off the mask" of political illusion that most Americans preferred to wear. He wanted to dispel the comforting idea that one could oppose slavery yet still be in political or spiritual fellowship with slaveholders. If enough Northerners became convinced that Calhoun's price was too high, then slavery would fall; if enough Northerners could see that the real choice was between Calhoun and Garrison, not Van Buren and Clay, then the abolitionists would penetrate the mainstream of political thinking; and if enough Northerners could accept Garrison's moral view of the question, even if they continued to distance themselves from the editor, then the days of a slavery-ridden union would be numbered.

The challenge of disunion proved a daunting one, even to abolitionists. Garrison antagonized a good many faithful friends in the AAS with his proposal that "repeal" be made "the grand rallying point" of the cause. Some thought that the editor now intended to impose the sort of ideological test he had long opposed during the schism, but he did not. Garrison deliberately absented himself from the 1842 AAS annual meeting to emphasize his commitment to open discussion, and when Chapman and others began to pressure Maria Child, who was in the midst of a successful effort to rejuvenate the *National Anti-Slavery Standard,* to write more fiery editorials, he expressed regard for her more "contemplative" approach and publicly celebrated the "diversity of tastes and temperaments" necessary to move the cause forward. Though Child shared Garrison's views about "peaceable separation for conscience' sake," she thought his disunionist exposition so "unguarded" that it would make enemies faster than it would win friends. The editor seemed content to wait. "I have not at any time supposed that a majority even of old organizationists are prepared openly to go for repeal," he told George Benson; "yet I have no doubt whatever, that, in the progress of the discussion, all who mean to be consistent, uncompromising abolitionists will ere long be found on the side of repeal." Over the next two years Garrison advocated disunion before the Massachusetts and American societies, as well as at the various local and regional conventions at which he spoke. He provoked vigorous debate, but gained no group endorsements. While the rabid New York papers rushed to characterize the editor's latest heresy as treason, others took his charges more thoughtfully. "People now talk about the value of the Union," Charles Sumner observed, "and the North has begun to return the taunts of the South."

Such was occurring even in Congress. John Quincy Adams, who had fought the gag rule for years, provoked a fresh storm early in 1842 by introducing a disunionist petition from taxpayers in Haverhill, Massachusetts, who thought the federal establishment cost them too much. The request had nothing to do with abolitionism, Adams said in mock innocence, and indeed he hoped the House would advise the petitioners that the time had not yet come to consider so fateful a step. Southern members took the bait, however, and howled that Adams was committing treason and should be disciplined for misconduct by the House. Adams then insisted upon a full hearing on the motion to censure him and boldly used the ensuing "trial" to lambaste Southern slaveholders for their violations of civil liberties and the imposition of a double standard that allowed them to hold the Union hostage to slavery but cry disloyalty when Northern people questioned any aspect of the relationship. After two weeks of Adams's far-ranging attacks, which made their way into newspapers throughout the country, the Southerners caved in and agreed to table "forever" the motion to censure.

Garrison cheered "the signal victory." Adams had "driven the slaveholding representatives to the wall," he wrote, and "frightened the boastful South almost out of her wits." From Washington, where he conducted an abolitionist lobbying effort, Theodore Weld told Angelina that from this "first victory over the slaveholders *in a body* . . . their downfall *takes its date*." The Southerners tried to recoup by censuring a less well known congressman, Joshua Giddings of Ohio, who had attacked Webster's *Creole* letter, but Giddings's constituents immediately returned him to Congress by a very large margin. Adams's grand battle and Giddings's reelection, which Garrison had fully supported in *The Liberator*, suggested that politicians who defied the South might do better at the polls than those who placated it. If such straws in the wind indeed proved indicators of a shift in public opinion, then the days of the gag rule were numbered and Congress, instead of avoiding debate on the slavery question, would find itself talking of little else.

The abolitionists formed a small but articulate element in American society, whose passionate critique drew upon the profound wellsprings of both the Christian and natural rights traditions. Each new set of converts to the cause expressed fresh outrage at the violation of their ideals and added momentum to the conviction that the nation had to undergo a fundamental change. Garrison understood that the "renovation" of the nation's understanding of itself would not occur until a majority accepted its necessity, and he saw his role as the permanent agitator, always pushing the well-intentioned to firmer statements and action. In a movement based on conscience, the perils of wrong or weak choices always had to be clarified, and Garrison had no hesitation at ripping into John Quincy Adams, for example, for his opposition to abolition of slavery in Washington, D.C., as inexpedient and impractical, even as he praised the former president for his heroic defense of free speech in Congress. Let them make a folk hero of Adams, Garrison thought, but let them not cease to judge him on grounds of conscience and not be seduced into the calculations of political and tactical expedience that governed even the indomitable old politician. As the cause became popular, Garrison realized, the ultra-abolitionists would have to coin "a stronger dialect" in which to express their dedication to immediatism and equality. Disunion became the latest innovation in Garrison's vocabulary of agitation. "In demanding equal and exact justice, we may get partial redress," the editor conceded. "In advocating the immediate, we may succeed in procuring the speedy abolition of slavery, but if we demand anything short of justice . . . if we ask for a part, we shall get nothing."

"Reform is commotion," Garrison liked to say, and he made the fugitive slave issue a striking means for generating it. In October 1842, the attempted recovery of a fugitive slave brought Boston to an unprecedented intensity of abolitionist excitement that drew new people into the cause and gave the editor an important opportunity to define a higher standard for political conduct. The furor began when George Latimer—a newcomer to Boston who had found lodgings on "the hill" with his young wife and child—was suddenly jailed on charges of theft. Word quickly went around that the charge was a pretext and that Latimer—described by the newspapers as "a very light good-looking mulatto"—had been incarcerated at the behest of a Norfolk, Virginia, planter named James Gray, who claimed him as a runaway slave. Gray applied, as the Fugitive Slave Law directed, to the federal courts for the certificate of removal that would sanction Latimer's return to bondage.

The case came before Justice Story himself, who was taking his annual turn at presiding over the federal circuit in Boston that quarter, and in the greatest of ironies, the author of the *Prigg* decision found himself trapped by the relentless logic of his opinion. Only federal officers had an obligation to enforce the act, Story had ruled, and as New England's highest-ranking federal officer, that is what he did. In accordance with the statute, Story gave Gray ten days in which to produce evidence for his claim and ordered Latimer to remain in Gray's custody until the hearing. The alleged fugitive was not to be removed from the state, the judge warned, and he further ordered that Latimer was to be allowed reasonable access to any legal counsel he might retain to argue his claim that he had been freed under his late mistress's will. Fearful that the abolitionists might "rescue" Latimer and spirit him away, Gray privately paid the county jailer to keep the young man in protective detention, an act which the abolitionists angrily denounced as a corrupt misuse of public resources.

That one man could be held as another's property in the city of Boston— under color of law and by order of a celebrated jurist—brought the fugitive slave issue home as nothing else had. Antislavery crowds gathered outside the jail, and excited talk filled the streets. At a Faneuil Hall rally Edmund Quincy denounced Story as "the slave-catcher-in-chief for the New England states," and a huge debate ensued about the conflicting obligations of Constitution and conscience. Despite his own abhorrence of slavery, however, Story had experienced little difficulty in following his own precedent. Like his Harvard classmate Dr. Channing, Story believed that emancipation could only gradually be accomplished and regarded the abolitionists as malicious obstacles toward that peaceful end. For Story, as for Channing and Harrison Otis and other fading relics of their generation, the Constitution and the Union, for all their compromises, represented the highest possible good. Story would shortly warn his Harvard students to repel the harsh attacks of abolitionists whose fanaticism threatened the undoing of fifty years of growth and prosperity and to transmit the Constitution *unimpaired* to their children. Story had not hesitated to make a revolution in the law on behalf of his class of commercial entrepreneurs, but when a bold view was required on behalf of racial justice, he held fast to the old ways of precedent and compromise.

Latimer's friends turned to attorney Samuel Sewall for help in preparing for the hearing, and Sewall immediately launched a collateral effort to have the man released from custody through habeas corpus and personal replevin petitions in the state courts. Mindful of the public clamor, the Massachusetts chief justice, the Bostonian Lemuel Shaw, came down to the jail to hear arguments on Latimer's plea. Garrison somehow managed to slip into the jailer's front parlor, which was closed to all but six observers, and gave his readers a memorable portrait that depicted the anguished victim Latimer and the preying claimant Gray appealing to the jurist, whose behavior struck the editor as "indifferent as if it were a case involving the ownership of an ox or an ass." While Shaw declared himself personally sympathetic to Latimer, the jurist ruled that the case was properly pending in federal court and that, following the *Prigg* decision, the state court could not interfere in a fugitive slave proceeding. Garrison reported—with his own furious exclamations of indignation—Shaw's dictum that an appeal to natural rights and the paramount law of liberty could not override an obligation to the Constitution and the laws, no matter how disagreeable they seemed, for the people were bound to them under a compact which could not have been secured on any other terms.

Shaw had acted "the part of Pilate" in thinking that a political calculation could "make wrong right." The forms of the law could not excuse the "vileness" of reducing a human being to slavery, said Garrison, who believed that Shaw ought to have resigned his position and borne a testimony against "legal diabolism." Conservatives defended Story and Shaw with an argument that the judicial oath was actually a contract that the officer would *not* intrude his own sympathies and beliefs into a process that had to remain impartial. A critique by one of Story's most distinguished students maintained that the public outcry against the jurists would either undermine the social order by fostering contempt for law or have the disreputable effect of "overawing" the bench and intimidating lesser judges into following the high road of popularity instead of the path of duty. Yet such critics had no remedy, other than the fullness of time, for the problem of slavery, and it was significant that the Latimer agitation exposed a cleavage between the older generation of Story and Channing (both of whom would be dead in three years) and the rising scions of the elite, not only the ultra-minded Phillips and Quincy, but the Bowditches and Danas and Sumners and Adamses, whose absorption in the Latimer case marked their first step toward a reconsidered politics.

While some attorneys believed that within the framework of impartiality the justices had sufficient discretion to interpret the law more generously in Latimer's favor, Garrison thought Story and Shaw had read the law correctly. That was his point; the law as corrupted by the fundamental compromise with slavery could not advance society to a just outcome. Citizens would have to face the naked truth about their government and undertake their own moral campaign to reform its premises. This would inevitably partake of the spirit of nonresistance, Garrison insisted, for the renovation would have to begin with the refusal to do evil. Social change would grow out of moral judgment and the popular demand for justice, not the contorted process of legal exposition.

The abolitionists transformed the legal complexities of the Latimer case into an examination of civic morality. They asked the city's ministers to read notices of a Faneuil Hall protest meeting from their pulpits, and *The Liberator* published a tally of those who had complied or refused. Three young men from pedigreed families produced an impromptu news sheet of Latimer developments, a feisty pamphlet in the spirit of Boston's Revolutionary days, which, with the help of Garrison's office, appeared three times a week in batches of five thousand copies. The earnest Charles Sumner told Mrs. Chapman that he would support a movement among members of the bar to withhold services from Southerners endeavoring to reclaim their runaways. Hundreds of people circulated a petition calling for a new state "personal liberty law" that would forbid all state officers from assisting in the recovery of fugitives and prohibit the use of state facilities either to hold hearings or incarcerate the alleged property. Such a law would be consistent with the *Prigg* decision, which held that the states had no obligation to aid in the return of fugitives under the federal law, though they could not block their seizure by federal agents. If the federal apparatus was inadequate, as many slaveholders feared, then the *Prigg* decision would be a Pyrrhic victory. Story himself had privately suggested the outlines of a stronger system of federal enforcement to a Georgia senator, and the Southern demand for a more stringent fugitive slave law would become a significant element in the controversy.

Anticipating the constitutional crisis, Wendell Phillips caused pandemonium in Faneuil Hall when he declared that the spectacle of people trampling on their consciences at the bidding of a piece of parchment prompted him to say, "My CURSE be on the Constitution of these United States." The shock of Phillips's words may have contributed to a nervous prostration that forced Story to withdraw from the case and necessitated an additional ten-day postponement in the scheduled hearing. Faced with mounting and unremitting opposition—and reports that contingents of protesters were coming to Boston for a "Grand Latimer Meeting" that might well result in a mass attempt to rescue him—the sheriff decided on November 15, 1842, that the jail could no longer be used at the behest of slave claimants and ordered Latimer released. The putative master conceded defeat, and the parties signed mutual quitclaims in which Latimer promised not to sue Gray for false imprisonment in exchange for Gray's acknowledgment of Latimer's freedom. The abolitionists had never before had so telling an effect upon

public opinion, and the mass movement had never before secured so rapid
an antislavery victory. Within a few weeks, John Greenleaf Whittier had
composed an ode, "Massachusetts to Virginia," that celebrated the public
outcry, though some citizens considered the "great popular whirlwind" of
protest more troubling than the case. The editor of Boston's *Law Reporter*
found it horrifying that the public sense of obligation to the fundamental
law of the nation could be so easily undermined by exaggerated language,
fanatical meetings and parades, and propaganda sheets put out by youngsters
whose opinions on public affairs no one of significance felt bound to consult.
In the very month (March 1843) that his eighteen-page critique appeared,
however, the Massachusetts legislature consolidated the Latimer victory by
passing the personal liberty law demanded by petitions (weighing 150
pounds and bearing 65,000 signatures) that the abolitionists rolled like barrels into the State House. Boston's elite was relearning what its Tory equivalent had learned in the 1770s: in the American polity, an aroused public
opinion could change the rules of combat and dominate the field.

Garrison felt enough emboldened by the Latimer protest to issue a public
address to "the slaves of the United States" urging them to emancipate
themselves by running away. Claiming that twenty thousand had already
successfully fled, Garrison promised that countless abolitionists in the free
states would succor fugitives and demand for them "all that we claim for
ourselves—liberty, equal rights, equal privileges." Condemning yet again the
idea of physical resistance and insurrection, Garrison in effect had extended
the come-outer's call to the people in bondage, making withdrawal from a
corrupt system an act of self-definition and moral witness. Whether his appeal had much specific influence in the South is impossible to determine,
though it surely strengthened the resolve of those abolitionists who had developed the subterranean network—later known as the underground railroad—that assisted runaways. For Garrison, however, the appeal was also a
declaration that abolitionists would take their own challenge to the established order yet another step. Increasing the tempo of escapes would demonstrate the vulnerability of the system, put a few more Frederick
Douglasses on the platform, arouse more Northern communities with sensational cases like Latimer's, and further abrade the political and religious
connection with slaveholders.

The conflict took on an increasingly sectional cast. In March 1843, John
Quincy Adams warned "the free states" that a fresh attempt at Texas annexation would undoubtedly be mounted in the next session of Congress.
Such a move would be an attempt by the South "to add new weight to her
end of the lever" and perpetuate both slavery and the political dominion of
"the slave power." To absorb a foreign nation, he warned, would violate the
constitutional compact of states and automatically dissolve the Union. To

Adams's surprise, and Garrison's applause, a dozen Northern congressmen cosigned the statement, and eight more endorsed it in the newspapers.

The movement seemed, at last, to have acquired a critical mass that could make itself heard and felt. The New England convention in May 1843 proved the largest—and liveliest—ever. The sessions had to be moved from the cramped Chardon Street Chapel, first to a come-outer tabernacle and then to venerable Faneuil Hall, and even Helen Garrison joined the throng. The vitality grew from the movement's mounting confidence and received further encouragement from the spirited participation of "the Hutchinsons," a large family of popular, commercially successful singers who had become absorbed in the cause. Singing in perfect harmony and with a dramatic flair previously seen only in the theater, the Hutchinsons offered their audiences a unique, homespun sound that drew deeply upon folk and gospel styles. Their appearances on the abolitionist platform proved galvanic, both in sentimental ballads such as "The Bereaved Slave Mother" and the jaunty rhythms of "There's a Good Time Coming." The earnest hymns of earlier gatherings gave way to foot-stomping and hand-clapping that some—Lucretia Mott, for one—found too emotional, but that Garrison considered a happy new dimension of the movement's culture.

The abolitionists felt rambunctious enough to bait President John Tyler when he came to Boston for commemorative exercises at the finally completed Bunker Hill Monument. Hundreds signed an appeal that called upon the chief executive, a Virginia planter who had assumed office when General Harrison died of pneumonia shortly after his inauguration in 1841, to liberate his slaves both as "an act of simple justice" and a recognition that the "speedy removal" of slavery was "essential to the preservation of the Union." The Virginia papers called the appeal to Tyler a "gross breach of hospitality," and one editor prayed that the president's adjutants would whip anyone who tried to introduce the chief executive to the "stolen" Latimer. This fantasy of confrontation found counterexpression by a black writer in *The Liberator* who dreamed that a trio of slaves escaped from the president's plantation and disrupted the Bunker Hill ceremonies. The pageant itself left Garrison unmoved. The whole affair, he said in disgust, bore "the impress of national hypocrisy." He found the military displays "painful," and, taking one look at the meretricious Webster on the rostrum, the editor realized that he had no patience for his speech and went home.

The Garrison household had endured an arduous winter. Everyone in it, including the editor, had endured lengthy periods of fever and sickness, which had nearly killed Grandmother Benson and had left her, and Helen's sister Anna, in fragile health. Their little house seemed like a hospital for weeks at a time, Garrison lamented, and friends implored the family to move from unhealthful Cambridgeport. Adding to the sadness, the editor's brother

James had died in October 1842, drifting out of life much as he had passed through it. The editor insisted that the funeral ceremonies be "as plain, simple, and *free* as possible," in keeping with his own nonsectarian principles, and from the depths of his heart he spoke a eulogy that inveighed against "the war system, the navy, and the intemperance" that had oppressed his hapless brother.

A few weeks before Jemmy's death, in September 1842, Helen had delivered a fourth son—named in honor of Charles Follen, the lonely abolitionist voice at Harvard who had died in an 1840 steamboat accident. The robust infant made it through the winter in good health and became the latest emblem of the editor's delighted boast that Garrisonism was on the rise. By spring 1843, however, Charlie was teething and irritable, and the long winter's upsets had told badly upon the older boys, especially seven-year-old Georgie, who had become cantankerous enough to tax even a nonresistant's patience.

Garrison himself had a painful swelling in his left side that caused him much distress. He went from one physician to another in search of a diagnosis and received varying opinions. Having never been wholly confident in conventional medicine, the editor also tried Thomsonian cures and spoke to clairvoyants, without success. When friends murmured that the editor might have the "hypos," he insisted, "The disorder which afflicts me I *feel* to be very serious."

The only remedy appeared to be rest and relaxation, but as summer approached, the option the Garrisons had long enjoyed—a sojourn at Friendship's Vale—no longer existed. Brother George had sold the lovely old farm, along with his Providence business concerns, in an effort to simplify his finances and devote his life more completely to reform. With friends, he had acquired the assets of a Northampton, Massachusetts, silk manufacturing enterprise, including a large brick factory building and a 420-acre farm, where, in 1842, they established a cooperative society, the Northampton Association and Industrial Community, as an alternative to the harsh inequalities of modern life. Within a year they had attracted sixty adults (with nearly as many children) to the place and appeared to be getting along tolerably well. The Garrisons had first thought of sending Georgie to live with his uncle's family in "the community," whose school attractively blended bookwork, practical skills, and pacifism, but then decided that the entire family ought to give up the Cambridgeport house, store the furniture, and live in Northampton for the summer.

Garrison had no intention, however, of adding utopian socialism to his "budget of heresies." Though he frequently said that mankind ought to "dwell together in unity" and deplored monopoly, favoritism, and inequalities of wealth and station, Garrison did not like the emphasis given to external arrangements in the writings of Owen, Fourier, and others on "the property question." If unfavorable circumstances could be modified by social reorganization, such changes should by all means take place, Garrison conceded, but not at the expense of "internal reorganization," the spiritual regeneration that would truly "put away the evil that is in the world." *The Liberator* gave polite attention to the conventions and manifestos of this latest phase of reform, but the editor allowed that he would "expend no thunder" on it. Nonetheless, over the next few years his columns remained open to socialists and land reformers. They witnessed extended debate over the large issues of economic organization and the tactical priority that elevated chattel slavery—wrongly, in the view of some persistent correspondents—over "wage slavery" as the most urgent social issue of the era.

Despite his philosophical reservations, Garrison enjoyed the summer's respite. In late June 1843, the family took simple lodgings close by "the community" in a cottage so small that the three older boys had to sleep crossways in one bed, but they took their meals in the group's hospitable dining hall. The place, with its stubby oaks and indifferent pasturage, did not look like much. The main four-story building and numerous shops grouped about a central commons gave the community the aura of a struggling little seminary, which, in a way, it was. Unlike the Transcendentalists' Brook Farm or Bronson Alcott's Fruitlands, which had more intellectual preoccupations, or Adin Ballou's Hopedale, with its more explicitly Christian orientation, the Northampton Association had an unusual combination of the practical and questing people who formed the backbone of *The Liberator*'s subscription list. The residents were artists and clerks, with a smattering of schoolteachers, all in search of a more uplifting life. The community also sheltered several fugitive slaves and an itinerant evangelist, Isabella Van Wagenen, who preached under the name Sojourner Truth. "The place and the people struck me as the most democratic I had ever met," said Frederick Douglass, visiting in the midst of a lecture tour. "There was no high, no low, no masters, no servants, no white, no black. I felt myself in very high society."

The family brightened in the congenial atmosphere. Helen always enjoyed country outings and a pleasant social circle, and the older boys rapidly grew tanner and taller as they roamed about the farm with their Benson cousins and the "tribe" of children in the community. Charlie, meanwhile, was learning to walk, and his father happily pronounced him "a bouncer indeed." Garrison's side still pained him, but he stopped worrying about it. He felt well enough to go "gypsying" about the countryside when N. P. Rogers came for a visit, and he climbed Mount Holyoke with Francis Jackson. He also spoke at the nonsectarian Sunday services and organized several abolition meetings in conservative Northampton, which he zestily reported for *The Liberator*.

The good times, however, came to a crashing halt on August 16, when Garrison took Wendy, Helen, and her mother out for a wagon ride. After the horse had drunk from a wayside stream, Garrison jumped down to guide the horse up the bank to the road. The horse started, and the wagon made "too short a curve" and spilled its passengers into the brook. The boy was only shaken up, but Helen sat in the mud, in considerable pain, cradling her right arm at an odd angle, and Mother Benson's hip hurt so badly that she could not walk.

A physician pronounced Helen's arm fractured and immobilized it, ordering her to rest completely, and Mrs. Benson was put to bed with a suspected broken hip. (This proved erroneous, and she made a good recovery.) Garrison lavished attention upon the patients, all the while lamenting his "unskillfullness" as a driver, and took on the care of the boys. Helen found it extremely difficult to nurse Charlie and endured a good deal of pain, while Garrison slept only in snatches and exhausted himself with worry. To darken the mood further, Helen's ailing sister Anna died, and Garrison received word of Isaac Knapp's death as well. "I am not sure that I could have commenced the printing of the Liberator without him," the editor sighed in tribute to this lost friend of his youth.

When Helen's cast was removed after five weeks, her arm had not healed. She had suffered a dislocation of the elbow, not a fracture, and her arm had now become ossified in a painful, virtually useless position. Urged to go at once to Boston for a surgical consultation, Garrison recoiled at the idea of compounding one professional blunder with another and thought it better to visit Stephen Sweet, a Connecticut "bone-setter" celebrated among the Brooklyn and Canterbury folk. In despair, Helen agreed, though the several weeks' separation from the children—her first—pained her almost as much as the injured arm. Their Boston friends worried about the editor's reliance upon country "quackery," but he persisted, though Wendy angrily slapped at his mother's bonnet when she kissed him goodbye. Dr. Sweet's initial attempts to move the bone proved so painful to Helen that they had to be stopped, but eventually he succeeded in restoring its position, and Garrison gave him a glowing testimony in *The Liberator* that affirmed the virtues of the self-taught against the myopia of the professional "faculty."

It was November 1843 before the Garrisons moved into their new Boston quarters at 13 Pine Street, a newly built red-brick row house in a working-class section just off Washington Street north of the Worcester Railroad tracks. The Johnsons, who would continue to share the living expenses, had brought some carpeting and brought the Garrisons' furniture out of storage and had the place ready for the patient's return. Helen began using her arm "with a good deal of freedom," and her mother and surviving sister, Sarah, settled in for another winter's visit. The editor fixed up the attic as his "sanctum sanctorum," though he seldom entered it, preferring to work on his letters and newspaper clippings downstairs amid his "active and blooming" family.

Garrison's sojourn in the community of believers had reanimated his perfectionist faith, and when he returned to *The Liberator* in November 1843, he suffused his editorials with the come-outer's vision of human brotherhood and spiritual freedom that would triumph in "the glory and renown of the SECOND REFORMATION." Week after week, Garrison insisted that abolitionists had to reimagine the social order and bravely cast aside all traditional forms of church and state. The editor's iconoclasm seemingly knew no limits. He dared to organize a series of free lectures on Sundays—timed to coincide with the hours of regular church services—at Amory Hall that would "vindicate the people's right to think for themselves" on ethical and religious subjects. Garrison himself led off on two successive Sundays with presentations on worship that once again challenged conventional views of the Sabbath and the established clergy. The series brought fresh denunciations of the editor's presumption from the authorities. The *Congregational Journal* sneered that Garrison had not only "turned Priest," but printed his own sermons and "would accept the triple crown of the popedom tomorrow, were it to be offered."

The reformers persisted, however, and for twelve weeks in the winter of 1844, seekers who had "emancipated themselves from sectarian bondage and ecclesiastical domination" filled the 275-seat hall each Sunday for presentations that included Adin Ballou on nonresistance, Charles Dana on utopian communities, the feminist and freethinker Ernestine Rose on social reform, Wendell Phillips on Texas and disunion, and John Pierpont on the influence of slavery upon religion and morals. The series gained some luster by pulling in the cautious Ralph Waldo Emerson for what proved to be a wry and stand-offish address titled "New England Reformers" that admired the dissenters' originality and independence but questioned their unseemly willingness to "assist the administration of the universe" rather than to nurture their own hearts and attune themselves to the beauty of the world. (Garrison missed the talk that Sunday, however, being obliged to speak at an abolitionist meeting in West Brookfield, and it was not written up in *The Liberator*.) Celebrating the conclusion of the series at the end of April 1844, the editor noted that it had paid its own way and, despite numerous requests to continue, was terminating as planned to avoid any imputation of "outward formality and sectarian imitation." For Garrison the Amory Hall lectures represented the culmination of a decade's antinomian inquiries, and he happily pointed out that the series had confirmed Sunday "as a convenient day on which to assemble for *reformatory* purposes."

In connection with Emerson's lecture and a dawning realization that he ought to take a hand in abolitionist work (this would take the form of an August 1 address on West Indian emancipation), the Concord philosopher had made a brief visit to Garrison's "dingy" office and shivered slightly at the editor's "demonic" energy and "animal spirits." Emerson respected Garrison for his "great ability in conversation" and "a certain long-sightedness in debate," he told friends, though the philosopher wondered whether it was necessary for the agitator to make such "immense demands" and "pay you only the one compliment of insatiable expectation."

One might have said that such expectations were Emerson's own message to humanity, but for the editor the question answered itself. Garrison always sounded "like a newly discovered chapter of Ezekiel," the young minister T. W. Higginson recalled, and he seemed to have attained the "original relation to the universe" Emerson had advocated. The editor never stopped pressing an ideal of citizenship that would have worked a moral revolution. In May 1844, with the annexation of Texas now formally before Congress, Garrison finally persuaded his organization "to hoist the banner of repeal." After a long debate that turned upon questions of expedience as much as philosophy, the AAS adopted the slogan "NO UNION WITH SLAVEHOLDERS!" and committed itself to a program of making the public realize that "nothing but the immediate abolition of slavery can make us a united people."

Garrison believed that he had gathered a saving remnant within the movement that would leaven the rest. He had come to regard the ballot box as "a pro-slavery argument" because it perpetuated the unjust compromise, and he insisted that the highest exercise of citizenship would be a refusal to vote. Certainly his opponents in the Liberty Party, which had absorbed the various advocates of the new organization, found his views provocative. As they prepared themselves for another Birney candidacy in the 1844 presidential election, the third-party men had begun to advance a counterinterpretation of the U.S. Constitution to justify their electoral efforts. Birney insisted the document had "incorporated" the Declaration of Independence and therefore could be construed as an antislavery text. Goodell held that "natural law" invalidated those clauses that protected slavery and thereby gave Congress the power to enact emancipation laws. The Ohio attorney Salmon P. Chase stressed the Framers' supposed antislavery intentions—manifested especially in the exclusion of slavery from the Northwest Territory—and maintained that they had made it a local, not a national institution; only positive law could sustain it, and abolitionists should ensure that the national government do nothing to uphold such local laws. Alvan Stewart attempted a number of ingenious readings, suggesting that in light of British common law precedents and the "due process clause" in the Fifth Amendment the slaves were being held unlawfully.

Such readings Garrison dismissed as naive wordplay or deceptive political contrivance. He insisted that the courts and the public had so uniformly accepted the proslavery protections of the Constitution for half a century that individuals could not dexterously conjure them out of existence. Frederick Douglass made a keen summary of the argument: "They looked at slavery as a creature of law; we regarded it as a creature of public opinion." Even if the document could be read as the Liberty men suggested, Garrison stressed, "such construction is not to be tolerated *against the wishes of either party*." Certainly the South would never agree that the three-fifths clause had to defer to some vague emanations that the preamble embraced antislavery philosophy, and the Prigg and Latimer cases demonstrated that stern

New England jurists would not substitute natural law for a strict construction of the fugitive slave clause. Political realism, he insisted, required people to recognize the Constitution as a corrupt "bargain and compromise" of which "no just or honest use . . . can be made, in opposition to the plain intention of its framers, *except to declare the contract at an end, and to refuse to serve under it.*"

Garrison distilled three years of thinking about repeal in an eloquent "Address to the Friends of Freedom and Emancipation in the United States" that occupied more than a full page of *The Liberator* in May 1844. He conceived the essay to be—like the Declaration of Independence—a defense of revolutionary ideas in a time of "solemn crisis," and thunderbolts crackled from his pen. "We rise in rebellion against a despotism incomparably more dreadful than . . . a three-penny tax on tea," Garrison declared. "Three millions of the American people are crushed under the American Union." To his familiar charges Garrison added a host of damning material culled from James Madison's recently published notes on the Philadelphia convention that revealed the Framers' deliberate attempts to placate the slaveholding interest. No matter what the Liberty Party wanted to believe about the high-sounding preamble, Garrison argued, it could not be read in a way that gainsaid "the very design of [the Framers'] alliance—to wit, *union at the expense of the colored population of the country.*" The harsh truth had to be faced that "our fathers were intent on securing liberty *to themselves,* without being very scrupulous as to the means they used," and whatever their occasional professions of brotherhood, "in *practice* they continually denied it."

Garrison took his readers through the Constitution passage by passage to demonstrate the protections extended to slaveholders and insisted that it would be "paltering with our consciences" to think that amendments could purge the evil so long as the slave states exercised their notoriously disproportionate power under the three-fifths clause. Rather, the time had come "to set the captive free by the potency of truth." Citizens should repent of their guilt and "secede from the government," hold no offices under it, send no representatives to it, sever all communion with slaveholders, and hold mass meetings to explain what they had done. He would counter the organic nationalism of Story and Webster with a universalism born of his commitment to the Golden Rule.

Just as he had taken antinomian perfectionism to the edge of ecclesiasticism, so, too, had he applied its imperatives to politics and reached the brink of American constitutionalism. By staying "in advance of those around you," his old friend George Thompson reassured him, the editor was "effecting by progressive steps the advancement of the public mind. . . . your last measure will always be an unpopular one. . . ." The young poet James Russell Lowell, inspired by the editor though he shied from disunionism, found the perfect American metaphor. Garrison was "like Daniel Boone," he said, "so used to standing alone that . . . he moves away as the world creeps up to him, & goes farther *into the wilderness.*"

On the day that Garrison's address appeared in *The Liberator,* the New England Anti-Slavery Convention endorsed disunionist principles by a vote of 250 to 24. That night, May 31, 1844, at a public celebration, Garrison received on behalf of the AAS a new banner for the movement. On a red ground it depicted a prostrate slave in shackles and an American eagle preying upon the Constitution. Under one of the eagle's wings stood the U.S. Capitol with a slave auction in progress in front of it; under the other wing stood a church, its congregation oblivious to the scourging of slaves on its doorstep. On the reverse side twin inscriptions in golden thread that seemed to be "letters of light" hailed "Immediate and Unconditional Emancipation" and "No Union with Slaveholders!"

"No hand is worthier to bear such a token of high esteem and deep trust," said the presenter, C. C. Burleigh, whose benign face, auburn curls, and tangled beard gave him a most apostolic appearance. Garrison stood ramrod straight with eyes aglow as the assembly rose in an overwhelming vote of confidence and tribute. Even after the cheers subsided, for some moments Garrison could not reply. Then he said, "Eighteen hundred years ago the sentiments were first promulgated of which this banner is but a repetition." For honoring them now the abolitionists could expect the brand of "traitor" to be added to the opprobrium they had previously endured. "Let it come, I say—let it come!" he cried. "We are not traitors to a free Constitution . . . our principles are the only ones on which a free government can stand." Garrison declared, "We will not play at this miserable farce of political union," but teach our fellow citizens how to make a moral revolution. It is now "incomprehensible" for people to conceive of a revolution without taking up arms and shedding blood, but we will demonstrate "how incomparably more glorious, triumphant, and permanent is the revolution of opinion." Ours will be the combat of "righteous principle in conflict with unrighteous practice," he promised, and with God as our captain, "we will go on to the end of the war in the fullest confidence that ere long we shall see the dawning day of his great deliverance!"

"Overwhelming applause" cascaded through the building, and the whole audience—several thousand strong—rose to its feet in enthusiastic cheering. Suddenly the Hutchinsons sprang to the platform and burst into their latest song, "Get off the Track." With their fiddles rippling the minstrel tune "Old Dan Tucker," they depicted emancipation as a railroad train with irresistible momentum. "Roll it along, roll it along through the nation/ Freedom's Car, Emancipation," they sang as the audience clapped.

Then Jesse Hutchinson swung into the verses. "First of all the train, and greater/ Speeds the dauntless Liberator . . ."

"Roll it along," chorused the crowd.

"Hear the mighty car wheels humming! Now look out the engine's coming! Church and statesmen, hear the thunder! Clear the track or you'll fall under."

On and on the song ran, with its louder and louder refrains, " 'Get off the track!' All are singing/ While the Liberty Bell is ringing . . ." *Roll it along!*

"All true friends of Emancipation/ Haste to freedom's railroad station;/ Quick into the cars get seated,/ All is ready and completed," Jesse sang, and then the crowd roared, " 'Put on the steam, put on the steam,/ Put on the steam' all are crying,/ And the liberty flags are flying."

There was Garrison, the crimson banner of revolution at his side, beating time with his hand in the air and booming, "Put on the steam, put on the steam," as the song reached its crescendo. The gathering dissolved into uproarious cheers and what Brother Rogers called "the jubilee cry of humanity." Slavery should have died of that music alone, the apostles said as they walked out into the sweetness of the evening, and all through the streets of Boston that night people could be heard whistling and singing snatches of the song. "Roll it along," "Put on the steam," "through the nation, Freedom's Car, Emancipation."

BOOK FOUR

A HEAVENLY RACE DEMANDS THY ZEAL

1844–1858

GARRISON AT FORTY-SEVEN

Daguerreotype by Broadbent Studio, Philadelphia, 1852
(Special Collections, Ablah Library, Wichita State University)

CHAPTER SIXTEEN

REVOLUTIONS NEVER GO BACKWARD

THE UNION THAT WILLIAM LLOYD GARRISON PROPOSED TO DISSOLVE CONSISTED OF TWENTY-SIX STATES IN 1844, HALF OF WHICH COUNTENANCED CHATTEL SLAVERY. ANY COMPETENT MAP, SUCH AS THE LARGE folded one tucked into the flyleaf of Samuel A. Mitchell's popular traveler's guide, displayed them in a rectangular mass stretching from Maine to Arkansas with their borders outlined in pastel shades. South of Georgia's purple lay the green-trimmed territory of the Florida panhandle, whose citizens now numbered themselves on the verge of statehood, and beyond the pale blue of Illinois lay patches of the Wisconsin and Iowa territories that seemed equally composed of rivers, tribes of Sioux, and a growing line of frontier settlements also nearing the threshold of statehood. Trailing off the left-hand edge of the map, beyond the golden yellow borders of Missouri and Louisiana, lay portions of the vaguely delimited Indian territory (marked with the names of the relocated Cherokee, Creek, and Choctaw) and, at the lower corner, a piece of independent Texas that did not extend far enough west to indicate the republic's capital at Austin.

Such was the picture of the United States that might have hung on Garrison's office wall or in his sons' schoolroom. Only the more comprehensive atlases displayed the "Louisiana" territory thrusting northwest from Missouri that Lewis and Clark had explored after President Jefferson had acquired it from France; it had not yet become part of the "magnificent parallelogram" that would soon form Americans' mental image of their country. Most mapmakers, moreover, like the diplomats, could not decide where the "Oregon" country beyond the Rockies passed from American claim to British control and thus positioned the label on both sides of the 49th parallel. To see what lay south of Oregon, one had to look at the atlas pages devoted to the neighboring nation of Mexico, which governed the coastal regions of New California, the intermountain areas of New Mexico, and the vast plains of Tamalpais and Tejas, each identified in block capital letters as provinces, though with internal boundaries so vague that they seemed to dwindle away into the desert that presumably rendered the center of the continent uninhabitable.

Boston was not completely oblivious to this Hispanic hinterland. One son of Harvard had written a popular account, *Two Years Before the Mast*, about an expedition to procure leather hides for New England's shoe industry from

This map, published in 1848 to celebrate the end of the Mexican War, demonstrates the expansionists' view that Cuba and northern Mexico were destined to fall under U.S. control and increase the domain of slavery.

the picturesque ranchos of California, and the sea captains of Boston and Salem had told their investors of the harbors at San Diego, Monterey, and San Francisco that might command the Pacific trade. Booksellers, indeed, could hardly keep up with the demand for a new title, *The Commerce of the Prairies*, that described the ripe trade in fur and precious metals centered upon Santa Fe. Only a few insiders knew, however, that a U.S. Army scouting party had reconnoitered the great western basins from the Rockies to the Sierra Nevada or that Presbyterian missionaries had brought the first wagon trains of Americans over the trail into the Columbia River basin. Yet before the decade ended, the territorial names *Texas! Oregon! California!* burst into the American lexicon, startling party politics out of customary patterns, rendering the maps obsolete, and pitching the antislavery controversy onto new ground.

The thirty months following Garrison's declaration of revolution stand as the most momentous in nineteenth-century American politics. In the summer of 1844 the Whig and Democratic parties fought a closely contested presidential election as national institutions; by February 1847, each party had fractured into sectional entities with incompatible goals, breaking traditional voting patterns and ensuring that every presidential election through 1860 would be fought among three or four candidates, each of whom had to address the once-forbidden question of slavery. In 1844 the presidential election took place in a republic whose states spanned the Appalachians and edged across the Mississippi; by February 1847 politicians had acquired a continental vision that reached from Vancouver to the Sea of Cortés, American soldiers had planted the Stars and Stripes in the halls of Montezuma, and the path seemed cleared for an extended empire of slavery. In 1844 the political consensus that slavery was a local matter beyond the reach of federal action still prevailed; by February 1847 the defenders and opponents of slavery each sought the political leverage necessary to commit the national government to their position, and for the first time the revolutionary confrontation Garrison envisioned between slavery and the Union seemed not remote, but palpable. As the conflicting approaches to the territorial issue and the partisan calculations underlying them bred crisis after crisis, in Texas, in Oregon and California, in Kansas, and in the realm of the Constitution itself, the nation seemed perpetually on the verge—in 1847, 1850, 1854, 1857—of the ultimate turning point. The fateful moment would come, as Garrison never ceased to insist, when one of the contestants decided that it would have to break up the Union in order to realize its fundamental premises. Either the partisans of slavery—certain that slavery was morally right, socially useful, and entitled to national protection—would secede to protest their declining power in the Union, or the advocates of liberty— convinced that slavery was morally wrong, economically threatening, and undeserving of further expansion—would dissolve the Union and reconstruct it on an antislavery basis. As an agitator the editor never lost his faith that the time would come, though the hour of Jubilee seemed to recede ever more into the future as Garrison's prime years slowly ebbed away. A career that had started in a young man's burning vision would persist into the ambiguities of middle age, and it seemed that immediatism would take a lifetime after all.

The road to civil war began in Texas. The abolitionist press had long pointed a warning finger at the unsavory alliance between the political leaders of the cotton South and the thousands of American settlers who had poured into the country west of the Sabine River and wrested control of the province from Mexico in 1836. When the demand quickly arose for the annexation of Texas by the United States, the pamphleteering of Benjamin Lundy, the pugnacious opposition of John Quincy Adams in Congress, and the striking success of an AAS petition campaign all made annexation politically untenable for the Van Buren administration, which sought always to avoid sectional issues that might divide the Democratic Party.

The issue would not die, however, and after years of private intrigue and diplomatic maneuvering, it burst upon the public in April 1844, with the revelation that the U.S. government had concluded a secret treaty of annexation with Texas that President Tyler would forward to the Senate for ratification. Tyler, a former states'-rights Democrat from Virginia who had balanced the Whig ticket in 1840 and assumed the presidency upon General Harrison's death, was the first "accidental" chief executive, and he had scant support in either of the national parties. In a desperate gamble to gain enough popular acclaim to win reelection, Tyler hit upon a flag-waving strategy that sought to exploit both the growing popular appetite for territorial expansion and the residual hostility toward powerful Great Britain, whose insistent claims on the Pacific coast and rumored antislavery activities in Texas could be portrayed as threats to American interests.

A bellicose popular leader like Andrew Jackson might have brought off such a strategy, but Tyler lacked the charisma and the skill to make it work for him. Instead, John C. Calhoun, who had come into the administration as secretary of state deliberately to exploit the opportunity, made it work for the South. He postulated a dreadful scenario in which British capital would subsidize abolition in Texas and make it a client state that would become a beacon for runaway slaves from across the South and, ultimately, the scene of Anglo-American warfare as slaveholders fought the British for the return of their fugitive property. Immediate annexation of Texas in his view had thus become a measure necessary for national security. In a letter to the British ambassador, Lord Pakenham, Calhoun emphatically tied annexation to the defense of slavery. Abolition might be a wise and humane policy for Great Britain, Calhoun declared, but a large number of the American states had reached a different conclusion, which both the federal government and Great Britain were obliged to respect. Those states which had chosen to alter by emancipation the long-standing relationship between the races, the Carolinian added gratuitously, had seen the condition of the blacks become sickly, impoverished, and degraded, while in the slave states "they have improved greatly in every respect." Calhoun buttressed his proposition with spurious data drawn from the 1840 census, but the endeavor was less to lecture the British (though he was happy to do that) and more to meld the racist defense of slavery with the annexation of Texas as a government policy.

While the Pakenham letter apparently rested upon the political cliché that slavery existed as a matter of local preference, the crafty Calhoun had in fact nationalized the question by making the protection of domestic slavery a reigning principle of American diplomacy. He had also devised a political trap for testing the resolve of free-state politicians. Those who opposed the Texas scheme could be characterized as soft on abolition; if there were a great number, then Calhoun would be able to advance the fortunes of the Southern sectional party he had long sought to propel himself into the presidency. If politicians ran for cover by supporting annexation, however, then Calhoun would have so dramatically enlarged the area of slavery and reinforced the political structure protecting it that he would have accomplished his slaveholder's mission even if the triumph did not carry him into the White House.

Calhoun seemed to have miscalculated, however, when the Senate unexpectedly rejected the Texas treaty in June 1844. Even mildly antislavery people proved offended by Calhoun's temerity and the administration's clandestine diplomacy, and seven Northern Democrats joined with Whigs from both sections to deny the annexation treaty the two-thirds vote required for passage. The vote was less a moral statement than a last-ditch effort to stamp out the sparks before they caused a brushfire that might work havoc on the looming 1844 presidential election. Both the leading candidates, the Whigs' Henry Clay and the Democrats' Martin Van Buren, had tried to keep the issue out of the campaign and opposed immediate annexation, though each envisioned circumstances under which it might be accomplished *after* the election—if Mexico agreed, said Clay; if a majority of the next Congress approved, said Van Buren. The Pakenham letter and the treaty's failure in the Senate ensured, however, that the election would become a referendum on the issue. Calhoun, it turned out, had placed a lingering fuse.

The Texas issue exploded because political leaders had already excited the country with the prospects of territorial expansion. Democratic editors, especially, proclaimed the "manifest destiny" of Americans to settle the entire continent, and Northerners eyed Oregon and California as hungrily as Southerners looked south to Texas and the Mexican Gulf Coast. Indeed, many Democratic leaders believed that in expansionism they had found the key to holding their party together on a national basis and absorbing a restless and growing constituency of Irish working-class immigrants with the prospect of fresh western land. Whig leaders, long the exponents of national market expansion, found the call of continental destiny hard to resist, and Tyler's message accompanying the Texas treaty cynically emphasized the commercial gain to the midwest in foodstuffs and New England in cotton from an enlarged Gulf Coast trade.

Once expansionism became intertwined with slavery, however, it became an agent not of national unity but sectional and political division. Clay's agility permitted him to obtain the Whig nomination, though in the course of the campaign he issued so many clarifications of his position, first to conciliate unhappy Southern annexationists and then to soothe nervous anti-Texas Northerners in his party, that he ended up badly discredited. Van Buren fared even worse. He proved unable to appease Southern and Western expansionist Democrats and lost the nomination to the Tennessee slave-holder James K. Polk, a loyal Jacksonian and former Speaker of the House whose continental vision would prove audacious indeed. The Democratic platform called for the "reannexation" of Texas (on the dubious premise that its vast domain had once been part of the Louisiana territory) and the "reoccupation" of Oregon (on the popular but equally dubious assumption that American traders had staked out the entire territory to the 54°40' border with Russian Alaska). The Democrats thus hoped that Anglophobia and a belligerent attitude toward the British in both Texas and Oregon would override the concern its Northern element felt about the further extension of slavery. The Whigs charged that the Democrats had sugar-coated Texas with Oregon, while embittered Van Burenites predicted that the "political insanity" of a war for slavery in Texas would be "the dose without the sugar."

The more Texas annexation threw conventional politics into confusion, the greater the opportunity it offered Garrison to advance the revolutionary issue of disunion and drive a deeper abolition wedge into the existing parties. Even before the Pakenham letter, *The Liberator* had given extensive coverage to proslavery maneuvering on Texas, and when the issue burst into flame, the local antislavery societies lost no time in calling protest meetings (New York's filled the Broadway Tabernacle) that denounced the "selfish machinations" of the slaveholders and their unsavory Texas cohorts and predicted that the treaty would be the death knell of the Union. Garrison readily capitalized on the profound conviction held by a great many citizens that Congress lacked constitutional power to annex a foreign country; in Congress, John Quincy Adams declared that Texas annexation would turn the Constitution into a "menstrous rag," and in the Massachusetts Senate his eldest son, Charles Francis Adams, drafted a powerful report contending that annexation would require, at the least, a constitutional amendment, or further, a new "Constitution of the United States and Texas." Such talk from reputable Whigs brought them very close to Garrison's disunionism, though they denied the intent.

Concurrently with the anti-Texas agitation, therefore, Garrison maintained his constitutional polemic that the slavery issue could not be solved within the prevailing framework. He gave over the entire front form of *The Liberator* to excerpts from the AAS pamphlet of extracts from James Madison's notes of the Philadelphia Convention of 1787, which demonstrated the Framers' expedient compromises with slavery—"not without some twinges of conscience, it is true," the editor conceded—but arrangements that nonetheless "sacrificed the slave population on the maxim that the end justifies the means." He also called attention to passages from Justice Story's definitive commentaries to demonstrate that whatever the Framers' private hopes for the diminution of slavery, the public record confirmed the compromise, in Story's words, as "a necessary sacrifice to that spirit of conciliation which was indispensable to the union of States."

Abolitionists countered Story's pleas for reverence with gestures of defiance. Francis Jackson resigned his commission as a Massachusetts justice of the peace, telling the governor that since the insidious virus of slavery was killing the Constitution, he felt obliged to consider himself dead to it. Garrison railed at the American Union as a "stupendous republican imposture" and pronounced it "accursed" for "its subtle and atrocious compromise," its "extermination" of the red men in the wilderness and the "despotism" of slavery, its "immolation of the individual to secure the general welfare," and its cruel power as "a mighty obstacle in the way of universal freedom and equality." Abolition would require a new constitution, he emphasized, because to expunge slavery from the existing one would be like removing the cornerstone from a building.

Disunion bore witness to the inability of the political parties to address moral issues and stripped away the illusion that an election could produce genuine change. It was his "special work to exhibit the corruption of politics," Garrison often said, and by demonstrating their alienation from a political system weighted in favor of slaveholders, reformers had the opportunity to influence the entire society rather than merely advance the fortunes of a political party. Garrison's "anti-politics," therefore, carried a strong political message. For those souls who could not imagine how one could discharge a civic duty without voting, the editor pointedly suggested that it was no different from meeting one's religious obligations without belonging to a church. For those who shrank from the come-outer parallel, Wendell Phillips found secular political equivalents. In a pamphlet widely circulated by the AAS he defended nonvoting as a patriotic withdrawal equivalent to Lafayette's refusal to acknowledge Napoleon or the democratic-minded Romans who retired to the Mons Sacer rather than submit to patrician authority. Changing the figure, Phillips said that disunionism was simply letting the gas out of the balloon.

The Texas issue would prove a significant leak. As was his practice, Garrison dismissed the 1844 presidential campaign, which ended in a narrow victory for Polk, as a distracting sideshow between "two monsters of tyranny." Though Garrison believed that Clay would have accomplished by "sorcery and manipulation" the annexation that the Democrats now claimed a mandate to pursue, he did not hesitate to blame Clay's defeat on Birney's Liberty Party, whose supporters in western New York drew enough votes away from the Whigs to give the state's decisive thirty-six electoral votes—and the presidency—to Polk. Other observers attributed the victory to the Democratic success at registering thousands of foreign-born voters in New York City, prompting more than one Whig to complain that "Ireland has reconquered the country which England lost." Some conservative Whigs began to call for tougher naturalization laws that would require a twenty-one-year residency before voting, a harbinger of the nativist sentiment that would further complicate the politics of the next decade.

With the election out of the way, the editor worked earnestly to build an anti-Texas coalition from disaffected elements in the old parties. It would require a dramatic protest to stop the Texas juggernaut, and Garrison promoted a fresh petition campaign that called upon Massachusetts to withdraw its delegation from Congress and call a convention to consider arrangements for a new union, should the existing one be traduced and dissolved by the admission of foreign territory. It is a measure of the depth of feeling on the issue that Garrison could get a respectable hearing for such a proposition. Annexationists, not surprisingly, tried to discredit all constitutional arguments with the smear of Garrisonian nonresistance. New Hampshire's Democratic senator Levi Woodbury, who supported Calhoun and yearned for a vice-presidential nomination, brandished *The Liberator* on the Senate floor and warned that it weekly did more violence to the Constitution than the treaty ever would. A Democratic paper in Boston charged that the mixed-race Garrison crowd of "superannuated men and antiquated spinsters" would not be satisfied until they had gained the "Kingdom of Massachusetts" with a constitution written by John Quincy Adams. Garrison had a good laugh over that one, but he wrote a stinging public rebuke to Woodbury as the most "loathsome" of hypocritical politicians, a proslavery democrat.

The anti-Texas protesters did not have much time. Hoping to salvage at least a smidgen of the credit, the lame-duck Tyler administration had asked the expiring Congress to annex Texas by a majority vote of both houses—a brazen subversion of the constitutional provisions that gave jurisdiction over foreign relations to the Senate and required a two-thirds vote for consent to treaties. With Calhoun willing to sacrifice his constitutional scruples and Polk working behind the scenes, the joint resolution passed the House in December 1844, though the negative votes of fourteen New York Democrats gave a momentous signal that the extension of slavery might fracture the party. Even more tellingly, a furious John Quincy Adams finally secured enough support from Northern Democrats with anti-Texas constituencies to repeal the hated gag rule and, at long last, clear the way for antislavery petitions in Congress.

The interval of several months during which the Senate debated the Texas resolution would give the critics in Massachusetts, Ohio, and New York a sterling opportunity to mobilize against it. For Garrison the tumultuous anti-Texas rally held at Faneuil Hall in January 1845 proved a major political landmark. For the first time his viewpoint found expression at a meeting called by a bipartisan group of "political gentlemen," and he exercised his talent for inspirational leadership upon a group that he neither convened nor controlled. A nucleus of respectable Whigs—including the prominent merchant Stephen C. Phillips, C. F. Adams, Story's ardent protégé Charles Sumner, and some of the young men galvanized earlier by the Latimer campaign—had organized the meeting in the form of a popular convention, with each of Boston's wards sending a batch of delegates. The abolitionists succeeded in getting many of their number chosen, including the editor himself, but most delegates proved to be the respectable attorneys, judges, ministers, and locally important political figures whom Maria Chapman liked to deprecate as "the reverend pastor from *Conformington* and the honorable senators of *Tarry-town* and *Mental Reserve*." Imagine, then, the mixture of shock and gratification the Garrison supporters felt when the editor took the rostrum to "deafening cheers" that emanated not only from the packed galleries where abolitionist women cheered and waved their handkerchiefs, but from the normally sedate gentlemen on the main floor.

Giving no sign of the pleasure he took in such vindication, Garrison offered typically direct and earnest remarks that challenged the convention to go further than it intended in opposition. C. F. Adams, fearing a radical takeover, listened with great anxiety as the editor announced that he represented not only Ward 10, but three million slaves and the "abolition party" of the country. Garrison explained his view that opponents of slavery ought not to "cling to the forms [of union] when the substance has vanished" and declared that he had agreed to serve in the convention because he thought that it would deal with this new political condition. The meeting should authorize the calling of a popular constitutional convention, he advised, if the Texas treaty was passed. He did not want the current generation to repeat the Missouri mistake in which "a farce of words words words" had protested its admission and only silent acquiescence had followed. If the delegates meant to oppose Texas but take no action once it was annexed, then they were manifestly still willing to be "the bodyguard of slaveholders." *His* motto, "No union with slaveholders," was well known, he said to great applause, and he insisted that the question was not support for the Constitution, but whether there was any constitution left to support. (When hisses broke out, he turned toward the sound and happily exclaimed that the noise demonstrated that he had hit the nail on the head.) Rapturous applause—

and a few cries of "treason"—rang through the hall when Garrison finished, and it appeared that the convention accepted him as its gadfly.

With tact, shrewdness, and restraint, Garrison had become, for the moment of crisis at least, a participant in mainstream politics without sacrificing either his radical views or his independent position. In a time of great tension and flux, politicians struggling to redefine themselves not only found inspiration in his vision, but saw a certain utility in paying respect to the editor while appearing to disassociate themselves from his more extreme positions. "New times demand new measures and new men," wrote the poet James Russell Lowell, a young Boston literary man who came into the abolitionist orbit during the furor and found himself transfixed by the idea of conscience in politics and the intellectual clarity Garrison had brought to the fight. Sumner, who revealed that he had been covertly reading *The Liberator* for years, praised Garrison's eloquence to his dying mentor Judge Story and found himself emboldened to make a Fourth of July address titled "The True Grandeur of Nations" that had a distinctly Garrisonian cast in its advocacy of peace principles and its condemnation of expansionism and war as ignoble. From Concord, where Wendell Phillips had addressed the town lyceum over the objections of its conservative officers, an unsigned account in *The Liberator* exulted in "the readiness of the people at large, of whatever sect or party, to entertain, with good will and hospitality, the most revolutionary and heretical opinions, when frankly and adequately, and in some sort cheerfully expressed." (Garrison knew the writer's mother and sisters, who were longtime subscribers and disunionists, but not the young man— Henry D. Thoreau—who, a few weeks later, would begin the sojourn at Walden Pond that would explore philosophical and literary independence to the fullest.)

When the Senate approved the Texas joint resolution on March 1, 1845, some people considered the struggle over. The treaty, however, only united the territories of the two republics; a second phase of the battle would be necessary to admit Texas formally to the Union as a state. Or states. The Mexican province of Tejas had extended only to the vicinity of modern San Antonio, but the American rebels claimed a vast sector of the western llano that embraced Santa Fe and much of modern New Mexico and Colorado. In addition to the slave plantations of eastern Texas, then, the United States was taking on a monumental border controversy that, if settled favorably, might gain enough territory to allow four or five more states to be carved from "Texas." Every politician in Washington had a political calculus to fit the situation. Many Southerners wanted two states from Texas, and two new states out of West and East Florida; Northerners sought to balance unitary slave states of Texas and Florida with Iowa and Wisconsin, though antislavery men pointed out that Iowa, filled as it was with white supremacist Democrats, would be a negligible weight in the free-state scale. The most zealous expansionists, however, looked to take over not only the Texas claim but Mexican California as well, and drafted resolutions of admission that would permit all new states south of an extended 36°30' (Missouri) line to sanction slavery, while abolitionist petitioners from New York and Michigan protested that it would take the annexation of Canada to counterbalance the looming threat of the slave empire of Texas. Under the resolution eventually adopted, however, Texas had the potential to become the guardian of sectional balance, since it would be able to hive off new states as needed to counter free-state expansion in the midwest and Oregon.

Garrison pronounced annexation "diabolism triumphant" and "the greatest crime of the age" and insisted that all of the various admission schemes involving Texas amounted to dissolution. *The Liberator* and the Massachusetts Anti-Slavery Society campaigned against statehood and circulated "peace" and "disunion" pledges that promised to withhold support for the anticipated war with Mexico and to boycott any election for offices that required an oath to support the U.S. Constitution. Over the next six months, hardworking abolitionists—dubbed the "moral revolutionary army" by Garrison—gathered at least 50,000 signatures on the pledges, which led the editor to boast that while there were not yet enough people to make a revolution, "we are enough to *begin* one, and once begun it never can be turned back." To reinforce the message of hope, he reprinted several times over the next few months James Russell Lowell's "The Present Crisis," with its stirring exhortation, "Once to every man and nation comes the moment to decide,/ In the strife of Truth with Falsehood, for the good or evil side . . ."

The editor's militancy attracted respectful attention from his moderate colleagues. The Whig editor Horace Greeley's *New York Tribune* published a long account from a correspondent who passed up the opportunity to hear Phillips and Emerson in order to get a good look at Garrison, who impressed the writer not as a great speaker or orator, "but a great character." He had an "indescribable look of healthy-mindedness," the reporter said, and spoke so logically and vigorously that he seemed not to be merely talking, "but doing something. You forget that these are only words that he is pouring out. They seem deeds—blows—orders—prophecies, by turns." The moral rigor Garrison had imparted to the abolitionists also stirred the reporter, who sensed "immense power" in their unwillingness to engage in the popular American practice of "splitting the difference" and playing politics.

By their forthright declarations, however, the abolitionists made themselves felt in politics, and indeed, the newly aroused anti-Texas political figures began to style themselves "Conscience Whigs" to distinguish themselves from the "Cotton Whigs," led by the prominent textile manufacturers Abbott Lawrence and Nathan Appleton, who did not consider it prudent to permit "abstractions" such as abolition to interfere with their customary political and commercial patterns. (In the summer of 1845, Lawrence had on his desk a proposal to extend a $30,000 mortgage to Calhoun in exchange for 100,000 pounds of his best cotton annually for five years, and the year before he had seriously considered financing the acquisition and stocking of a new Mississippi cotton plantation by the president-elect James K. Polk. Such dealings led Emerson to observe sourly, "Cotton thread holds the Union together.")

The Whig regulars had decided to recognize Texas as a *fait accompli* and resume politics as usual. Continued agitation would wreck both party and Union, Lawrence warned, and their acquiescence was signaled on the day of Charles Sumner's pacifistic speech, when Boston's congressman, Robert C. Winthrop, annoyed at Sumner's apparent flirtation with disunion, pointedly raised a Fourth of July toast to "Our country, however bounded." Winthrop had voted against annexation, but he had his eyes as fixed on the speakership as Lawrence did his on the vice-presidency and made an about-face that Garrison condemned as "a most shameful act of political profligacy." The toast was a warning reinforced by social ostracism. The literary arbiter George Ticknor excluded the cultured and well-traveled Sumner from his Park Street salon, and Sumner's long-anticipated elevation to Story's chair at Harvard was blocked because, it was said, he had become "an outrageous philanthropist . . . neglecting the law, to patch up the world."

Such measures, predictably, confirmed Sumner and his associates in their opposition, though C. F. Adams repeatedly cautioned against their becoming pawns of the abolitionists. Nonetheless, the Conscience Whigs became part of the anti-Texas effort that put forward "one last best effort" to gain a public gesture of resistance from Massachusetts. It began with a convention in Concord, with its Revolutionary associations, at which Garrison made one of those speeches in which his words rang out as prophetic blows. It continued with the publication of *The Texas Chain-Breaker,* a Latimer-style broadsheet edited by Sumner, and culminated with a massive rally at Faneuil Hall, for which two thousand people turned out in a torrential downpour to hear a range of speakers, including Garrison, that represented dissident Whigs, Democrats, disunionists, and the equivocal Liberty Party. A delegation would personally deliver the thousands of petitions to Washington, and a broad-based state committee would monitor late-breaking events. In the end, however, the agitation failed, and Texas was admitted to the Union in December 1845. (Florida and Iowa had already come in, and the admission of Wisconsin in 1848 would offset proslavery Texas, at least until it was partitioned further.)

Garrison, however, refused to be downcast. He considered the revolution well begun and pronounced himself satisfied that the "experiment" in coalition politics had demonstrated that the rising opposition—Conscience Whigs in Massachusetts, alienated New York Democrats, and disaffected Ohioans from both parties—could form a driving wedge against politics as usual and open the field to a broader range of antislavery activities. In a stirring editorial on free inquiry, which he offered deliberately as an antidote to the feeling of "moral paralysis" that followed defeat, the editor wrote an extraordinary tribute to the power of discussion in a democracy. Tradition, fashion, and authority all combined to chill independent thought and encourage hypocrisy, he argued, yet a moral revolution could take place only if people freely exercised their right to challenge authority, to vindicate the supremacy of reason, and to reach their own conscientious judgment. "We have too little, instead of too much dissent among us," he said bluntly.

The annexation emergency had allowed Garrison's ideas to register in politics, but it did not lead to an advance in the editor's fortunes. His monthly salary of $100 had not changed in a decade, though his expenses had greatly increased. As an editor who wore a frock coat instead of a leather apron (though he did set his editorials at the case and make up forms on the stone), he earned about twice as much as a master mason or other skilled craftsman, but less than a State Street bookkeeper, a minister, or the attorneys with whom he had begun to mingle. Though the young lawyer Richard Henry Dana, Jr., still affected the rolling gait and the long hair of the yeomen with whom he had sailed before the mast to California, he ended his first year of law practice in 1841 with a net profit of $1,375—greater than Garrison's annual income—after deducting all his business *and* living expenses. The editor, by contrast, ended each year in debt and had to borrow several hundred dollars from his patrons to clear the books. Since they frequently discounted or forgave the unpaid loans as a New Year's present in clearing the way for the next cycle, the amount probably should be counted as part of Garrison's income, although the publishing committee never raised his salary and the editor never counted on the reprieves, but rather felt himself continually oppressed by recurring debt. It was a curious pantomime that preserved the dignity of all in the belief that the newspaper ran on principles of economy, the publishers were not sentimental fools, and the editor was a proud mechanic, not an object of charity.

In many respects *The Liberator* was an old-fashioned small-scale proprietorship in a city that had transformed itself from the old trading town that Garrison had first known into a modern metropolis. By 1845, Boston had become a city of more than 100,000 people and had successfully reinvested its commercial and mercantile legacy in the new economy of manufacturing and railroads. A tight network of investors from the interbred families known as the Boston Associates controlled one-fifth of the nation's cotton spindles, one-third of the state's railroads, close to half of the city's banking institutions, and the insurance companies with their $6 million of capital to put into housing construction and business loans. Boston's port now exchanged more goods with New Orleans than New York did with Liverpool, which meant that, along with the ever-increasing trade in Southern cotton, the entire Ohio Valley could buy New England calicoes, furniture, and shoes in exchange for its beef, pork, flour, and wool. Boston's factories now refined sugar and distilled rum by steam power, and its foundries and metalworking establishments fashioned the machine tools that advanced industrial development throughout the northeast. The city had overnight mail and express service to New York, and with the advent of the Cunard Line in 1840, merchants could write orders for fine goods from the English midlands on June 1 and have the stock ready for sale on their shelves by August 1. Even more impressively, the news of Clay's and Polk's nominations clicked its way into Boston on the extraordinary new telegraph virtually as they occurred, reminding Garrison that when he was an apprentice on the *Herald* in 1818 the office had marveled that the text of President Monroe's annual message was but sixty-six hours in travel to Boston.

The city not only transformed its economy, but reconstructed its appearance. With the exception of the State House and the major public buildings and churches, Boston had torn down and rebuilt much of its central district, with new warehouses and commercial blocks built of stone and brick and decked out with gaudy signs and gilded letters. The newness fascinated the visiting celebrity Charles Dickens, who thought that the city resembled a brightly lit stage set that had been painted overnight and could be readily struck at a moment's notice.

The Garrisons lived on a new block of row houses in the South End that was itself a microcosm of rapidly shifting circumstances in the growing city. Pine Street formed a new diagonal connection between the main commercial thoroughfare of Washington Street and the more industrial Harrison Street corridor one block east. A large granite orthodox church with a dignified classical facade marked the Washington Street corner, and several older town houses, owned by well-to-do iron dealers and a lumber contractor, stood impressively on the adjoining lanes. Pine Street's block of flat-fronted, three-story red-brick dwellings had all gone up in 1843 as speculative ventures by downtown brokers, each of whom built on two or three lots. If they had expected quick sales in what they hoped would be an up-and-coming neighborhood, they were disappointed. Of the thirteen houses on the editor's side of Pine Street when the Garrisons took up residence at No. 13 in 1843, only one was occupied by its owner, an inspector at the Custom House, though a ship's chandler bought No. 23 in 1845; theirs were the only two families still living on the block at the time of the 1850 census. The remaining houses were rented to a succession of crockery dealers, merchant clerks, grocers, pump and block engineers, pianoforte workers, hat and cap makers, and, unfortunately for the teetotalling Garrisons, a brewer next door at No. 15. The small backyards abutted similar houses on Oak Street and Maple Place, rented by masons, housewrights, stonecutters, and paperhangers, that confirmed the neighborhood as a middling, ill-defined sort of place; it would either establish itself as an abode for skilled artisans and aspiring homeowners or be absorbed into the pool of cheaper boardinghouse and day-laborer accommodations that covered the blocks east of Harrison.

The street formed a border of sorts; it was the last street north of the big curve that brought the Worcester Railroad's tracks into the South Cove depot and shopping area several blocks to the east. Pine Street's southern side remained unbuilt, and one could look across an industrial expanse that included a rock quarry and linseed oil factory to the tracks and warehouse district beyond. The shrieking and chuffing of the locomotives, when added to the incessant clatter and rumbling of Washington Street's traffic, made it about the noisiest place the Garrisons had ever lived, while the distillery, along with a livery stable and an oyster house on Washington, made it the most odoriferous. Yet the editor was pleased to be living in a "wholly new" house on what he considered a "long and beautiful" block; for him, as for most of his neighbors, Pine Street was a step up in the world, and he praised the developers, including Francis Jackson, who had "improved" the marshy South End by "turning eel grass into dwelling houses . . . for the benefit of a great city."

Garrison occupied an anomalous position in Boston society, being possessed of a well-known name, yet living in a situation much like the anonymous class of artisans and mechanics from which he had emerged. The Garrisons may have had tolerable relations with their neighbors, though the boys reported some occasional teasing from schoolmates, but in a manner more familiar to city dwellers than small towners, their social connections reached beyond the neighborhood to their reform-minded associates across the city and beyond.

Abolitionist activity regulated the calendar. For Garrison the year began by hailing another volume of his newspaper and continued with the MAS annual meeting at the end of January. Early May brought the AAS meeting during New York's "anniversary week" gathering of all the great benevolent organizations, and late May saw a similar gathering, including the ad hoc New England Anti-Slavery Convention, in Boston. July featured an abolitionist picnic and rally at Abingdon or Framingham on the Fourth, and August meant a similar observance on the First to honor abolition in the British West Indies. Autumn brought the state society meetings in Ohio, Rhode Island, and other locales, and the year closed with the great Boston antislavery fair, which had developed under Maria Chapman's leadership from a quaint church bazaar into a sparkling combination of an antique show featuring donated prizes from Europe and a new-fashioned Christmas celebration dominated by a splendid New England evergreen. The event drew an audience that reached beyond the ranks of the faithful and raised thousands of dollars for the cause.

The abolitionist movement had its own sustaining culture. A "social reform bookstore" occupied the ground floor of *The Liberator*'s office on

Cornhill, and its proprietor kept a stock of the latest pamphlets and treatises not only on antislavery themes, but on temperance and health, peace, women's rights (including Maria Child's pioneering three-volume comparative history of the condition of women), education, and social reorganization. Similar bookstores existed in the other large cities, and volunteers in smaller places maintained reading rooms where such material could be perused. Local antislavery societies purposely bought extra subscriptions to *The Liberator* and other newspapers for such libraries, and one reader in Ohio told the editor that he kept a supply of tracts out by his roadside mailbox for the benefit of passing travelers. Abolitionist agents also did a brisk trade in pamphlets and popular iconography that included woodcuts of Garrison and other leaders, along with the famous insignia of the kneeling slave and the striking portrait of Cinqué, the leader of the captive Africans who commandeered the slaver *Amistad* and sailed themselves to freedom. Throughout the 1830s and 1840s, abolitionists and their friends wept over the movement cult novel *Memoirs of Archy Moore,* which affectingly described the humiliations of a free black man kidnapped into Southern slavery. Published anonymously and often thought to be a true story, the book was the work of a Whig gentleman-historian, Richard Hildreth, who was not otherwise an activist. It struck a chord with a public eager for direct information about Southern slavery and went through at least seven printings, anticipating the later success of genuine fugitive slave narratives and *Uncle Tom's Cabin*. One celebrated fugitive, Henry "Box" Brown, who had contrived to ship himself north concealed in a load of freight, capitalized on the vogue for "panoramas" by lecturing in front of a series of painted tableaus that both told his own story and held up "the mirror of slavery."

Music and poetry also played important roles in fostering the "homemade antislavery" of the schoolhouse and the sewing circle. The Hutchinsons toured regularly and found publishers for sheet music that allowed their songs to suffuse the parlor. The local and national societies published movement songbooks that grafted more pointed lyrics onto popular melodies from "Auld Lang Syne" to "Yankee Doodle" that would perk up many a meeting. "My country 'tis of thee, Stronghold of Slavery," began one verse from the folks in Hingham, concluding with a fervent hope that color would one day cease to be a crime.

Garrison filled *The Liberator's* poetry column—a fixture on page four—with earnest stanzas of modest literary merit, but with an uplifting intent that the editor judged would do some good; besides, he would say, "it will please the writer." In 1846, John Greenleaf Whittier published *Voices of Freedom,* a collection of a dozen years' worth of poetry in the cause that served as a moving historical album and abolitionist curriculum. Here were laments over the slave ships, a tribute to Toussaint L'Ouverture, scornful accounts of the Massachusetts pastoral letter of 1837 and clerical oppressors, poignant scenes of the havoc wrought upon slave families, tributes to British antislavery endeavors and the anthem hailing the purported world's convention, a figurative address from Massachusetts to Virginia on behalf of George Latimer and other fugitives, and—perhaps as a peace offering—the poet's 1833 salute to Garrison as an apostle of truth. Whittier's verse had great staying power and exemplified the union of artistic vision and spiritual assertiveness that Garrison had lauded from the outset of both their careers.

The abolitionists nurtured each other in a beloved community of reform shaped in earnest conversation and the stream of letters that flowed among them to be shared in the social circle and occasionally excerpted in print. When their views cut them off from old friends and their empty seats in the meetinghouse bore silent testimony to their ideals, abolitionists overcame their social isolation in their correspondence and conventions. Although the railroad and the telegraph had begun to shrink distance and quicken communication, it is astonishing to see how many antislavery friendships were sustained for years through letters and how close people felt to a man like Garrison whom they might have personally met perhaps once or twice or knew only through *The Liberator*. Less surprising, perhaps, but a rueful fact for both the editor and his wife, was the number of people who applied directly to the Garrisons for help and lodging and made their already crowded household into an "abolitionist hotel." They could have put an end to such presumed hospitality if they had truly wanted to, but recognizing the visitors as the movement's backbone and a tonic for them as well, they welcomed and drew sustenance from the company. Their lives were so busy, their house so full, and the talk so rich that the Garrison children said that they never realized until they were fully grown that their parents were social outcasts. When one of the boys was sent to bed early one evening, he sobbed disconsolately that it wasn't the supper he would miss but the conversation.

For well-intentioned abolitionists, sympathy for the slave led to an intense personal effort to overcome racism in one's personal life. The simple act of attending a racially mixed meeting, listening to a black speaker, or even reading an article by a black writer in *The Liberator* served as a solvent for prejudice and led many to testify that they had consciously overcome the stereotypes of racial inferiority they had unthinkingly absorbed from their society. Maria Child emphasized that in this sense, the movement—and *The Liberator* especially—served as a unique educational forum, for nowhere else could white people attend the work of black writers and nowhere else could blacks "utter themselves freely, with the certainty of a respectful hearing."

Such consciousness-raising could readily turn self-congratulatory and patronizing, especially as it laid stress on the accomplishments of black people that made them "deserving" of equal treatment. Yet, for much of the 1820s and 1830s black leaders themselves had emphasized a strategy of uplift and moral reform that similarly emphasized the acquisition of education and bourgeois manners as the key to racial success. As a self-made man, Garrison himself was very susceptible to the appeal of what might be called embourgeoisement, and although he often stressed that equal rights should obtain by condition, not by merit, he seldom missed an opportunity to laud black success. The columns of *The Liberator* hailed the accomplishments of black students in the schools the editor regularly visited, and the newspaper faithfully reported the musicales, oratorical contests, and self-improvement lecture courses in Boston's black community. *The Liberator,* too, could be counted on to promote and publish the proceedings of the growing number of black political conventions—local, state, and national—that independently sought to protest the infringements on suffrage and other civil rights that were common and rising in the Northern states.

The most famous self-help story belonged to the fugitive Frederick Douglass, and Garrison played a significant role in bringing it before the public. Not only had the editor enlisted the "self-emancipated" Douglass as an AAS agent, but his printing office issued, in June 1845, the *Narrative of the Life of Frederick Douglass, an American Slave,* with the byline "Written by Himself." Douglass had proved so potent a speaker that it seemed wise to extend his influence with a personal memoir, and, though records are scarce, it appears that the MAS subsidized its publication and Garrison saw it through the press in a labor that posterity has not fully credited. The leadership anticipated a propaganda document and got that and more: a memorable statement whose spare style and dramatic candor reproduced on paper the leonine power Douglass exerted on the lecture platform. Garrison contributed an introduction to the *Narrative* that vouched for its authenticity and recalled the powerful speech—as eloquent as any of Patrick Henry's, he said—Douglass had delivered at Nantucket in 1841. The pacifist editor passed silently over the writer's powerful account of the physical battle with the slave-breaker Covey that marked his psychological liberation but that stood in contrast to the nonresistance Douglass professed as an abolitionist lecturer. Instead, Garrison singled out for comment a soliloquy on freedom that poured from the young slave as he watched the sails of ships disappearing down Chesapeake Bay toward the ocean. In Douglass's meditation—the most overtly "literary" in the book—Garrison discerned "a whole Alexandrian library of thought, feeling, and sentiment . . . all that can, all that need be urged" against slavery's defilement of humanity, and by concentrating upon the Romantic moment of yearning, Garrison put the book in its broadest intellectual context.

The *Narrative* sold extremely well—4,500 copies in the next five months, 30,000 over the next five years—and earned Douglass an international reputation. Having revealed the details of his life in bondage (scanting only the particular details of his escape), the fugitive rendered himself more vulnerable to recognition and recapture, and he was encouraged to undertake a lecturing voyage to Great Britain to avoid arrest. Having told his "story" in the book, however, Douglass became liberated from the demands of a single required speech on the lecture circuit, which allowed him to express himself more freely on a range of issues and—ultimately—transformed him from an exemplary fugitive to a preeminent political figure.

Douglass's enlarged role reflected a general shift among black leaders in the 1840s away from the "moral uplift" talk of an older generation and toward direct political self-assertion, especially in the formation of the vigilance committees which, in the aftermath of *Prigg* and *Latimer,* supported a rising number of fugitives with shelter, jobs, transportation, and legal protection. While the Garrisonian AAS had always maintained that along with the stark contrast between slavery and freedom there went the need to insist upon enlarging the sphere of freedom for black citizens, in the 1840s black political associations in Northern cities and states raised their voices with a special urgency and experience that only they could provide. Although the movement never fractured along racial lines as did the civil rights movement of the late 1960s, there existed a continuum of integrationist and separatist tendencies that make any generalization about race relations in the movement both perilous and gratuitous. The two streams converged in many civil rights protests, and black agents such as the talented William Wells Brown worked successfully for the AAS. Abolitionists continually received public abuse for their integrated meetings and their efforts, not always successful, to maintain a color-blind social standard. Nowhere else in American life could the races mingle in even an approximation of equality, and nowhere else in American life did white people even embrace the idea that they should—a context that must be understood in weighing the accusations of racism scholars have sometimes levied against "white" abolitionism. It was Garrison, after all, who expressed from the outset of his career the vision of equal citizenship and consistently foretold the day when able black people would raise their voices as "Judges and Representatives and Rulers of the people—the whole people."

The viability of an independent black political identity would be a recurring question, but one on which Garrison and his colleagues could have but one opinion—the integrationist. They would respect separate organizations, of course, but to advocate them would open them to charges of prejudice from blacks and hypocrisy from reactionary whites. Garrison insisted that antislavery had "wholly confounded complexional differences," and he made the Biblical injunction "Remember them that are in bonds, as bound with them" the mandate not only for the abolitionists' empathy with the slave, but for their effort to transcend racial categories. When the editor once tried to stop overnight at his friend William Powell's seamen's hostel in New York and the desk clerk sought to turn him away with the admonition that it was not a house for whites, Garrison shrugged and said that he ranked himself as a colored man.

The color-blind ideal especially appealed to Garrison's religious understanding that slavery and racial prejudice "defaced the divine image" in which humankind was created, yet given the heightened consciousness he sought to generate, the ideal proved impossible to achieve. The propagandist in Garrison continually struggled with the utopian, who would have preferred to live by universal truths that his society refused to acknowledge, and he wrestled with the dilemma, not yet resolved, of talking about racial issues in order to proclaim and teach their irrelevance. The confusing swirl of emotions this generated can be seen in his account of the wedding of a young black couple in the home of his own patrons, Ellis and Louisa Loring, in May 1846, at which Garrison felt too overcome to speak. The groom was Robert Morris, whom the childless Lorings had taken in and encouraged to read law; he would serve as Loring's clerk and later become the first black attorney in Massachusetts. The bride, Catherine Mason, was a cook in another wealthy family who would become prominent in community affairs, and the wedding guests included Mayor Quincy himself. In the well-appointed setting, in the presence of such goodwill, and in the vista of long-denied opportunity opening before the young couple, Garrison said in *The Liberator,* he saw "a token . . . of the certain triumph of right over wrong, of virtue and merit over all opposing obstacles, of the ultimate banishment of an unnatural and vulgar prejudice from the land, [and] of the restoration of all who are enslaved to their just rights." He hoped that black youth would draw inspiration and determination from it and realize "how closely their elevation is tied to good manners and moral worth." Far from being patronizing, however, the editor was praising the very qualities that he believed had worked for himself, and though he had sentimentalized the occasion, to be sure, the event was a benchmark of progress in more than one sense. Not so many years earlier one of the wedding guests, the editor's black associate William C. Nell, had been excluded from the dinner given at Mayor Otis's house to laud the winners of academic honors in the Boston schools. While the white students received medals from the mayor, Nell's gift—ironically, a copy of *The Life of Benjamin Franklin*—was delivered to him at his segregated classroom at the Belknap Street Church. Nell went on to become one of the first writers to explore black history and culture, and within a few months of the Morris-Mason wedding, Garrison lent his support to the beginnings of Nell's nine-year effort to achieve equal school rights in the Boston public system.

The wedding at the Lorings' measured Garrison's ascent as well as Morris's. For much of the Boston elite, however, Garrison remained beyond its ken. When a young dissenting minister expressed admiration for the editor in the presence of Augustus Aspinwall, a gentleman of the old school famous for his rose garden, he calmly replied, between sips of his sherry, "It may be as you say. I never saw him, but I always supposed him to be a fellow who ought to be hung." Such bland indifference, which masked a frozen anger, permeated the highest echelons of Boston society throughout the antebellum period, though the rise of the Conscience Whigs and the notable defections into abolitionism of Phillips, Quincy, Bowditch, and several other patricians allowed Garrison to become a political reference point without becoming socially acceptable. Wendell Phillips's mother considered *The Liberator* to be a vulgar little sheet until the day she died, Edmund Quincy's wife was humiliated by rumors that she had to wait on Garrison and his black friends at her husband's table, and Richard Henry Dana, Jr., came home from his first visit to an abolitionist convention appalled at the easy familiarity with which a born "hater" like Garrison and "conceited shallow-pated Negro youths" like Douglass and Remond consorted with "a gentleman & a scholar" like Phillips.

Even among the wellborn folk who supported Garrison, there was a social gulf. The insouciant Edmund Quincy, who lightened his abolitionism with the mocking frivolity of an aristocratic flaneur, laughed up his sleeve at the editor's small and overheated house, his faith in the "hellbroths" of herbal medicine, and his frowning attitude toward Quincy's gaming with cards and dice. (To be fair, Quincy respected Garrison's work and generously took charge of the newspaper—though it cut into his languorous reading time—during Garrison's absences.) The Weston sisters made fun of Garrison's didactic taste in poetry, and when they managed to meet the visiting celebrity Charles Dickens, whom everyone thought rather theatrical and common, they pronounced his wife "as good-looking and as ladylike as Mrs. Garrison," a backhanded compliment that deftly put both the British and American journalists in their place.

Historians have routinely come to speak of "the Boston clique" that centered about Maria W. Chapman as if it included Garrison, but although he had a close working relationship with its members, he does not appear to have been in on its highjinks. The term was Quincy's joke, and it metamorphosed from "clique" to "cabal" to "the cab," as suited his mood; he awarded titles to the participants—Maria was "the Contessa" and Wendell was Lord "Arundel of Essex" (Street)—but, significantly, there was no pet term for Garrison, and the editor did not participate in the amateur theatricals with which the "clique" amused itself. Quincy visited the Chapman house almost daily, but his diary and letters suggest that several weeks passed between encounters with Garrison. When the widowed Maria, feeling the pain of social ostracism and worried about her children's prospects, exiled herself to Paris in 1849, Garrison mourned the loss of her indefatigable labors, while Quincy bemoaned the closing of her West Street salon where, he said, "my two lives met."

With Phillips, too, Garrison had a collaborative relationship in the cause that did not extend into the social world. Phillips liked to say that Garrison had made him a better person, and he displayed his gratitude with countless acts of charity toward his impecunious colleague. Phillips, however, had a

good deal of Quincy's hauteur and preferred his high-spirited collegiate bon-
homie to Garrison's more decorous and staid church-circle style. A bond
between their wives helped keep the men together. Helen Garrison struck
a sympathetic chord with Ann Phillips, housebound with a chronic nervous
malaise, and regularly pulled an armchair up to the invalid's couch for a cozy
"social chat." Both women evidently found the friendship, which continued
by letter when the Phillipses removed themselves to Nahant for the summer,
a rewarding one, though perhaps it meant more to the sociable Helen than
to the self-absorbed Ann. Occasionally Helen arrived at the Essex Street
door only to be informed that Mrs. Phillips had left town suddenly or
couldn't receive a visitor, which suggests that Helen might have been the
poor relation whose attentions to a bountiful lady were appreciated but not
fully reciprocated.

The Garrisons found themselves most comfortable socially among the
older Friends, people like Thankful and Joseph Southwick, or Lucretia and
James Mott, who resembled the senior Bensons in their simple humanitarianism, or with the Unitarian Francis Jackson, whose paternal kindness and
depth of character proved incalculably nurturing to Garrison for thirty years.
Theirs was a Bible-based sociability, rooted in a plain style and an ethic of
loving concern. When Lloyd or Helen spoke, as they frequently did, of getting up "a social circle," this was their ideal: an hour or two of quiet conversation that ranged among the events of the day and the issues of
conscience presented by them, the sharing of letters from absent friends and
relatives, the singing of hymns and songs including good-natured parodies
of folk songs that mocked their critics, and probing discussion of some of
the religious issues—the authority of Scripture, the tension between private
devotion and institutional piety, a growing interest in spiritualism—that preoccupied them.

Although they worked from premises of philosophical idealism that had
much in common with the Neoplatonists of the Transcendental movement,
they talked about issues without the formalist categories and critical rigor
that the intellectual circle around Emerson employed. Many have assumed
that Transcendentalism had an important bearing and influence upon abolitionism, but the two movements actually ran in separate channels. Indeed,
Maria Chapman had complained that Emerson's gift for beautiful language
had lulled "hundreds of young persons" into excuses for inaction, just as Dr.
Channing's soothing prose had dimmed the light a decade previously. Of
more than three hundred pieces in *The Dial*, the Transcendentalists' major
periodical, edited principally by the brilliant Margaret Fuller, only a handful
dealt with social issues, and none directly addressed abolitionism. Although
the Texas controversy had drawn Emerson into a more outspoken role as a
critic of the slave power, he still disdained any kind of organized opposition
as both an infringement upon his own intellectual and moral freedom and
a brush with odious people whom he found to be "the worst of bores and

canters." After a public meeting, Emerson said, he felt as if he needed to be "shampoo'd and in all other ways aired and purified." Though he admired Garrison's sincerity and unity of purpose, he considered *The Liberator* "a scold" and once called Bronson Alcott aside in the rarefied precincts of the Athenaeum to confide that he never felt entirely comfortable in the presence of "persons of Garrison's class." Similarly, Fuller had declined numerous requests to put the question of slavery on the agenda of the intellectual "conversations" she conducted among Boston women because she claimed not to have seen an intellectual exposition of the abolitionists' views sufficiently careful and rigorous to overcome her resistance to what seemed to be a purely emotional "hue and cry." Nor had the argument over women's rights in the movement struck her as significant, though the radical Harriet Martineau admonished her for talking so determinedly about Plato and Goethe while human liberty stood endangered. When, moreover, Fuller found herself moved to praise Frederick Douglass's *Narrative,* she made sure to criticize the "usual over-emphatic style" of Garrison's introduction. While praising the editor's motives, she complained that he had "spoiled his mind" with denunciation and, having screamed so long at deaf people, could no longer "pitch his voice on a key agreeable to common ears."

Garrison turned forty in December 1845, and his face had started to show signs of age, with wrinkles about the deep-set but still-glowing eyes and two long lines creasing his cheeks from nose to mouth. A daguerreotype taken in 1846 shows his head to be larger and squarer than earlier portraitists had conveyed, with a long jaw and a square, dimpled chin that relieved an otherwise thoughtful, even solemn, mien. Though Lowell sketched a memorable poetic portrait of Garrison as a blithe and busy spirit "beaming sunshine through his glasses," a British writer discerned beneath the editor's bright exterior "a shade of profound melancholy" and "strong traces" in his face "of the severe intellectual labor he has gone through." He joked that he was becoming as venerable as a Biblical patriarch. In addition to the four growing boys, he had fathered a daughter, born in December 1844, and named Helen Frances for the two most important women in his life. Fanny, as she would generally be known, would enjoy an unusually close relationship with her father and indeed prove his most conspicuous heir as a reformer, taking a prominent role in the women's suffrage and peace movements and in the founding of the NAACP. (In a photograph taken about the time of her marriage to the financier Henry Villard in 1866, Fanny—looking a great deal like her mother—is shown with her cheek pressed against her father's temple and her arm wrapped casually about his neck in a gesture of unsurpassed tenderness that speaks volumes about their bond. In her smile it is possible to see still the little girl who, riding gaily on the editor's shoulders and warming her cold hands on his large bald head, never failed to laugh at his jesting remark that a hot-blooded fanatic was good for something.)

There would be two more children, another daughter, Elizabeth Pease (born December 1846), and another son, Francis Jackson (born October 1848), an eleven-pounder with "cheeks like thumping red potatoes." Now that his garrison was "well-manned," the editor confided to Wendell Phillips, "we are prepared to say . . . Hold! Enough!" In fourteen years Helen bore seven children, and she conscientiously managed a complicated household with a blend of frugality and good cheer that made her a quiet but not unappreciated heroine of the movement. Though poised and affable in company, she often felt disheveled and distracted and more than once asked a friend not to pass her letters around because they had been written in stolen moments with the children clamoring about her and were consequently filled with "blunders." In their most anxious moments of financial distress, the editor would put his arm around his wife and walk up and down the room with her, saying, "My dear, the Lord will provide," as he had comforted from the outset of their marriage. The "dark clouds" always lifted, Helen remembered, and they "felt an inward peace which those who have an abundance can never feel."

Her husband paid tribute to Helen's devoted work in making their home the sentimental ideal of "a heaven on earth," but he was by no means a dour and remote Victorian patriarch. He took upon himself "burdens which most husbands and fathers shun," Oliver Johnson recalled. He carried in the water, chopped the wood (at least until the older boys took over), blacked the boots, and made the coffee, all the while singing or humming his favorite airs. "His shining quality was that of nurse," Fanny emphasized, feeding and tending the children with such "unbounded love" and skill that the little ones were "drawn to him as if by a magnet." He used to say, only half in jest, that he "was born into the world to take care of babies," and friends always remarked that when Garrison entered a social gathering he invariably went straight to the children and got down on the floor to play. (If there were no little ones to fuss over, he would stroke and play with the cat.) Elizabeth Cady Stanton, who had independently joined the MAS even as her own husband worked for the Liberty Party, remembered the editor taking responsibility for an impromptu postconvention gathering by taking off his coat to rock the baby to sleep, then dashing out with the market basket to pick up some refreshments while his wife took a few minutes to ready herself for company.

That Garrison took pleasure in the role of a nurturing father, and seemed not to insist overmuch upon patriarchal dignity, reveals the extent to which the ethic of nonresistance permeated his character and gave him a masculine identity—the Christian apostle—that varied considerably from the calculating character type that dominated the commercial and political culture. Many abolitionist men in the Garrisonian milieu strove to embody "the courage of Paul with the lovingness of John," as Oliver Johnson once described the universally beloved Samuel J. May, and their emotional expressiveness grew out of their shared appreciation of the rapturous union of man and God that characterized the primitive Christian sects that so many of them admired. The perfect abolitionist character, May himself said, would be a Christlike compound of masculine and feminine graces, and in their willingness to weep for the slave, welcome women into the realm of politics and power, and advocate a loving ethic as the touchstone of a just society, the abolitionists pioneered a different personal ethos as well.

Within the movement, however, Garrison's leadership did come increasingly to rely upon his paternal stature as a pioneer and founder. That the AAS maintained itself as a cohesive force in the decades after the schism of 1840 is a tribute, in part, to Garrison's ability to nurture the communal vision of an organization built upon the free expression of ideas. When the AAS relocated itself from New York to Boston in 1843, it seemed natural to install Garrison in the presidency, and although he *"nolo episcopari'*d a little at first," Quincy recalled, the editor accepted the post and retained it until 1865. Garrison's "great facility" for preserving the flow of a meeting with pointed and humorous interlocutory remarks contributed to his fatherly image, though when sessions turned into less structured debate, he was "rather apt, with all the innocence and simplicity in the world, to do all the talking himself," Quincy said. Critics, of course, took the less benign view that the domineering editor could not brook disagreement, but he learned to yield the gavel to the taciturn and judicious Francis Jackson at times when he wished to enter the lists, and the organization's affairs ran smoothly—with an admirable tradition of robust debate—for many years.

After the schism, the AAS operated on a much-reduced scale, maintaining the *Standard* as a national newspaper, issuing tracts and almanacs, keeping agents in the field, and conducting its annual week of public meetings, yet it successfully maintained itself as the national voice of immediate abolitionism. By contrast, Lewis Tappan's American and Foreign Anti-Slavery Society found its principal identity as a liaison with like-minded British evangelical abolitionists, and by the mid-1840s even Tappan conceded that the Liberty Party had become the domestic wing of the desire for new organization. While the party sustained a number of local newspapers and district election committees in New York, Ohio, and Massachusetts, it had enduring factional disputes between the moralistic "Bible politics" of a Gerrit Smith and the politically expedient tendencies of a Henry Stanton that blurred its identity and led to further splits and its demise before the decade ended. Yet its adherents, especially among the clergy, influenced both the continuing antislavery battle within their denominations and the established political parties. Because the party had evolved out of the effort to malign Garrison and separate him from the movement, the editor never acknowledged the Liberty Party's work in driving the first slender wedge into the party system that sustained slavery.

The AAS was not immune to fractious dispute. The most spectacular controversy of the 1840s destroyed the friendship between Garrison and his traveling companion Nathaniel P. Rogers, even though neither man was an original party to it. The New Hampshire state society, which sponsored Rogers's newspaper, had got into a financial squabble with its printer John R. French, who had apparently applied donations earmarked for the *Herald of Freedom* to some of his other projects. French was engaged to Rogers's daughter, and the cantankerous editor, who had retired in poor health, interpreted the society's efforts to bring French to order as an attack upon himself and supported the hot-tempered young man in challenging its authority. The movement's leading organizers, including Parker Pillsbury, Abby Kelley, and Stephen Foster, discerned in French's efforts to wrest control of the paper a parallel with the anti-Garrisonians' sale of *The Emancipator* in 1840 and feared that French might be trying to make over the newspaper into a third-party venture, a move that Rogers would never have countenanced.

When a committee of arbiters, including Garrison, came up from Boston in October 1844 to sort out the affair, it treated Rogers with deference, but found for the society, whereupon French refused to print its report and Rogers chose to interpret the committee's decision as a soul-killing attempt to enforce the coercive discipline of an organization upon his conscience. Garrison, who believed that he had devised a solution that respected his old friend's independence, was hurt by Rogers's hostility and responded with polemics that only intensified the argument. He was especially annoyed by Rogers's charge that Garrison had tried to "scuttle" the *Herald* when in fact he had worked to preserve it. Rogers believed that Garrison had become too political and bureaucratic, while Garrison thought that Rogers had become so "monomaniacal" in his antipathy to organization as to have lost all perspective on the work of reform. The personal breach grieved both men, but pride overcame affection and left them unable publicly to repair the damage. Garrison urged charity and forbearance toward his ailing old friend, while Rogers wrote an apologetic private note to Garrison that lamented the disruption of their bond and bade him an "affectionate goodbye." The two men did not meet again before Rogers's death in October 1846.

Though sad, the Rogers controversy had its chastening effect and may have fostered the moderation Garrison displayed during the coalition work of the anti-Texas movement. Nor did the fracas with Rogers sap the momentum of the AAS, which still provided institutional support for the radical grassroots spiritual and educational movement advanced by local agents and leaders. Historians who have narrowed the story of abolitionism after 1840 into a narrative tracing the rise of antislavery as a salient electoral issue have tended to regard immediatism and the AAS as irrelevant, but they are skimming the river's surface without attending sufficiently to the deeper moral currents flowing below. "I have long lost all confidence in ballot-box morality, and so have many of our thinking men," a farmer subscriber wrote to Garrison from Mecca, Ohio, in 1846; to abolish slavery the "public mind has to be better instructed on human rights" by the ultraism of "carrying out our principles in every subject of religion, politics, social relations. . . . Little, sir, do you know the amount of good you do by casting broad the seed of truth. . . . I thank God and I thank you."

As the abolitionists had prophesied, the annexation of Texas led to war with Mexico, yet the hostilities did not occur because that nation sought to recover its lost province, but rather because the United States boldly sought to take even more of its territory away. In May 1846, President Polk ordered American troops to cross the disputed Texas boundary and regarded the ensuing collision with Mexican troops as a cause of war, which he then pressured Congress to recognize and fund with $10 million. With Southern expansionists of both parties in support, and with Polk—having dispatched both a naval squadron and an overland force of dragoons to Mexican California with orders to seize that province as soon as feasible—emerging as a forceful commander of the continental destiny, Northern politicians found themselves caught in a conflict between flag and conscience. Under the spur of party discipline, Democrats supported the war measure; only fourteen Whig congressmen, led by an enraged John Quincy Adams, and two Whig senators voted nay.

The dissenters stood against a public primed for war, although many had expected it in another quarter. The president had kept General Zachary Taylor and half the U.S. Army at the ready in Texas for the better part of a year while he employed a wily combination of belligerence and diplomacy to settle the Oregon controversy with Great Britain and foreclose the prospect of a two-front war that might see British naval power in the Pacific frustrate his designs upon California. Having whipped up popular fury for seizing all of Oregon on the famous cry of "54°40' or fight" partly to intimidate John Bull into the obvious compromise at the 49th parallel, Polk had calculated that the expansionist war fever would extend to the Mexican venture, and this proved true enough. Northern Democrats later found themselves hard pressed to explain to their constituents why they had to settle for only half of the lush Pacific Northwest while Southerners fully gratified their appetite for the great southwest.

In the spring of 1846, however, Americans quickly rallied for war. Polk's home state of Tennessee saw thirty thousand men turn out for the three thousand places in the state's detachment of volunteers; Ohio filled its quota in two weeks, while Illinois provided enough men for fourteen regiments, when it only had to supply four, which critics said was a good thing because Polk had promised so many officers commissions in exchange for votes that he would need the extra places. Taylor's quick victories at Palo Alto and Reseca de la Palma further heightened the delirious mood and prompted the penny press to florid evocations of Andrew Jackson's heroic triumph over the British at New Orleans in 1815. In the public mind the war pitted the strength of a muscular republic against an inferior opponent mired in the corruptions of Latin politics, Roman religion, and feudal loyalties; the war would, in this racially condescending view, bring true freedom to Mexico while demonstrating the rising manhood of "Young America."

To oppose the tide of martial ardor and flag-waving aggression is always a formidable task, and critics of the Mexican War were repeatedly confronted with the slogan "My country, right or wrong" as a catch-all reason to suppress one's doubts. Garrison, however, detested such romantic nationalism and vehemently denounced the "diabolical" motto as "an impiety that defies Man and dethrones God." He was not alone. The two leading editors in New York City, the Democratic Bryant and the Whig Greeley, bitterly condemned the war, though across the river in Brooklyn young Walter Whitman of the *Eagle* supported it with an apostrophe to Santa Fe and California as the newest stars in the American firmament. All across New England, however, people laughed ruefully at the satires James Russell Lowell produced in the voice of rustic prophet Hosea Biglow that punctured the grandiose war rhetoric and gave antiwar and disunion views the sound of simple country common sense. "Ef you take a sword an' dror' it/ An' go stick a feller thru,/ Guv'ment aint to answer for it/ God 'll send the bill to you," Biglow warned. In poem after poem, which Garrison reprinted as fast as he could, Lowell sent a populist warning to Southern expansionists: "Ef I'd *my* way I hed ruther/ We should go to work an' part,—/ They take one way, we take t'other,—/ Guess it wouldn't break my heart;/ Man hed ough' to put asunder/ Them thet God has noways jined;/ An' I should n't greatly wonder/ Ef there's thousands o' my mind."

The abolitionist societies protested the war as an aggressive maneuver to justify the seizure of more territory for slavery and circulated pledges of noncooperation that attracted hundreds of signatures. In contrast to other states, Massachusetts took eight months to meet its quota of volunteers, and by then Garrison presented the state legislature with petitions from forty-three towns with 2,834 signatures calling for a separation from the Union. While the number seemed inconsequential, people had to realize that they were witnessing "one of those revolutions which never go backward," Garrison warned, for reconstruction of a new union on the basis of true freedom was the "only practicable remedy."

Yet there was a worrisome element in Garrison's dissent. His alienation ran deeply enough for him to sympathize with "plundered, stricken, inoffensive Mexico" and bend his nonresistance principles. He had broken with the American Peace Society in 1838 explicitly over the organization's willingness to tolerate defensive wars, but Garrison now seemed equally complaisant on the issue. He still recoiled from the sight of a soldier as he would from a rattlesnake, he said, but nonetheless confided to the English

Quaker Elizabeth Pease that given the iniquity of the present war, he considered it "a matter of justice to desire the overwhelming defeat of the American troops, and the success of the injured Mexicans." In the hubbub no one raised the underlying question: if Mexico was justified in taking up arms against the aggressions of the slave power, would Massachusetts, much less the slaves themselves, be equally justified in waging war to defend themselves against the incursions of slaveholders? Garrison's sympathy for Mexico, however, put him somewhat at odds with dissenters like Parker and Emerson who regarded the war as unnecessary because they assumed that the weaker Mexican civilization would eventually bow to the advance of the Anglo-Saxon.

Some Whig critics tried to sidestep the slavery issue by opposing any acquisition of territory. Senator Thomas Corwin of Ohio electrified the country with an antiwar speech that denounced the president's abuse of power, warned of the territorial ambitions that had ruined "every robber chief" from Tamerlane to Napoleon, and touched on the slavery question only as an issue that might provoke "internal commotion" and sectional collision if aggravated by further acquisitions of land. Among Whig politicians only the radical Ohioan Joshua Giddings, who was taking over the aged John Quincy Adams's role as the stalwart antislavery giant in the House, went as far as Garrison in describing the war as the "criminal murder . . . of an unoffending people." With his craggy face and mane of flowing white hair, Giddings loomed as a righteous figure in Congress and, spurred by his Garrison-minded daughter, advanced in speeches and nationally circulated public letters the doctrine that unlawful annexation and unconstitutional war had dissolved the Union and any obligation to defend slavery where it presently existed.

Texas had driven a wedge into the existing political parties, and the Mexican War loomed as the sledgehammer blow that would split them. The war caused political trouble for everyone but its successful generals—Zachary Taylor and Winfield Scott, both nominally Whigs, one of whom would ride into the presidency in 1848 and the other mount a successful campaign for the nomination in 1852. New York's dissident antislavery Democrats, whom Polk had snubbed in cabinet appointments, cut out of the patronage, and disappointed in Oregon, now verged on revolt. The rift between Conscience and Cotton Whigs in Massachusetts became a permanent division, symbolized by the frozen silence between Winthrop and Sumner, who slammed the Boston leader's famous toast with the rejoinder that their motto ought to be not "our party, however bounded," but "our party, bounded always by the Right."

The looming revolt of Northern Democrats erupted like a thunderbolt in the sweltering Washington summer when, at the tag end of the congressional session in August 1846, a Pennsylvania congressman named David Wilmot tacked onto an appropriation bill a rider that prohibited the introduction of slavery into any of the Mexican territory Polk planned to acquire with the money. The measure would shield vulnerable Democrats from charges of being proslavery and sought to neutralize the Whigs' powerful campaign argument that "Mr. Polk's War" was a high-handed attempt by slaveholders to augment their political power. The furious president dismissed the "foolish" amendment as a misbegotten product of factional intrigue and professed amazement that anyone could see a connection between "slavery and making peace with Mexico." Polk could not stop the defections, however, as the Wilmot Proviso passed the House on a strictly sectional vote with all but four of fifty-eight Northern Democrats supporting it. Though it could not pass the Senate, where Texas gave the South a two-vote edge, the proviso served notice that a Northern constituency for "free soil"—though manifestly not for abolition—had emerged in opposition to proslavery expansionism.

The election results confirmed the potency of antislavery and the shift in public opinion. Renegade Democrats forged successful coalitions with abolitionists in New Hampshire and Ohio, while Whig dissenters took over the governorships of New York and Connecticut, as well as Polk's own Tennessee, and animosity toward expansionist Democrats allowed the Whigs to gain control of the House of Representatives for the first time since 1840. The war, said Sumner, had brought the slavery question to a head twenty or thirty years sooner than it might have come otherwise.

When the House repassed the Wilmot Proviso by ten votes in February 1847, just as American troops gained the war's decisive victory at Buena Vista, Garrison hailed the measure as a landmark of antislavery resistance. The editor took his cue from John C. Calhoun, who also realized that the proviso had broken the historic alliance between Northern and Southern Democrats that had kept the political peace on slavery questions for a generation. Calhoun moved, therefore, to counter Wilmot with a proviso of his own: slaveholders had a right to migrate with their slaves into any commonly held territory, and any law that discriminated against them would be manifestly unconstitutional and an affront to the "perfect equality" of the states under the compact. By Calhoun's logic, not only was the Wilmot Proviso unconstitutional, but so was the Missouri 36°30' line. Anything less than permanent constitutional protection for slaveholders would destroy the Union and bring on a political revolution.

Garrison's appreciation of Calhoun's latest challenge was keen and immediate. He rushed the South Carolinian's resolutions into print, warning his readers that the Southerner had presented his most extraordinary demand yet "to eternize slavery under the star-spangled banner." Mark his words, Garrison advised, for "he is a man who means what he says and who never blusters," and if even so "calculating and stony-hearted [a] champion [as] . . . the Napoleon of slavery" felt pressed to new heights of constitutional blackmail to stave off the rising antislavery host, then abolition had—at long last—become a political possibility.

"Disunion must and will come," Wendell Phillips exclaimed. "Calhoun wants it at one end of the Union—Garrison wants it at the other." Yet, as practitioners of polarization, neither Calhoun nor Garrison considered dissolution as their primary goal; for one it was a threat to compel protection for slavery, for the other it was a tool for insisting upon a decision between incompatible values. Calhoun did not speak for the whole South any more than Garrison did for the entire North, but they represented the conflict between the Southern slaveholding elite and the yeomanry of the free states. Calhoun was determined to hold the Union hostage to slavery, but had begun to wonder how much longer it could be done; Garrison refused to hold abolition captive to the Union and, in the tumult created by Texas and the war, had an intimation that antislavery morality might yet override the settled habits of political compromise.

Both men knew that they had crossed into uncharted territory. Translating his anxiety into constitutional melodrama, Calhoun announced that a curtain had fallen between the past and the future; the war had closed "the first volume of our political history under the constitution, and opened the second, and no mortal could tell what would be written in it." Garrison would do everything he could to penetrate that curtain and show the republic a new vision of freedom. To write the second act of the drama, however, and bring the country to the revolutionary culmination he desired would still be a work of extraordinary labor and defiance that required, he said, "a good deal of nerve."

CHAPTER SEVENTEEN

SNAP THE CORDS OF PARTY

THE POST-WILMOT PHASE OF THE ANTISLAVERY STRUGGLE TESTED GAR-RISON'S METTLE AS AN AGITATOR. FOR THE FIRST TIME THE EDITOR COULD SEE A TRUE MIDDLE GROUND DEVELOPING IN PUBLIC OPINION, AND HE had to cope with its emergence without moderating either the substance or the intensity of his radical critique. The movement, in his judgment, had to heed the breaking up of winter's ice without succumbing to illusions of a false spring. As the editor well knew, the fresh surge of Northerners willing to speak out against the wrongs of slavery in no way signaled a consensus for immediate abolition. In the outburst of popular feeling against the annexation of Texas and the prospect of slavery's expansion into the newly conquered provinces of Mexico it seemed that Garrison had at long last won the moral contest with the South. Nonetheless, in the nation's desire to enlarge its domain of freedom, there loomed an equally difficult contest with the commercial destiny of the North, which as David Wilmot himself had said, required "a white man's proviso" that his future hopes in the fair country of the west be protected from degradation by the Negro race. The fusion of antislavery with racism would, over the remainder of the struggle, prove the abolitionists' most disquieting challenge, even more troubling than the political task of undoing the constitutional compromises that held the Union in thrall to chattel slavery.

Garrison's task had become more complicated because *antislavery* and *abolitionist* could no longer be regarded as synonymous terms. Against the tendency to regard an end to slavery expansion as the generation's most attainable and useful measure toward the ultimate extinction of slavery, Garrison still insisted upon immediatism and equality. In making himself heard, the editor now had to reach people whose ears, while unstopped, had become attuned to a different message. Faced with the contradiction of being willing to tolerate slavery in the existing states as a means of racial containment while seeking to exclude the peculiar institution from the beckoning western lands, people still endeavored to sidestep slavery as a moral issue. They preferred to believe that the technical problem of territorial regulation, once settled, would allay sectional strife and arrest the fragmentation of the national parties. While Garrison took advantage of every development that worked "to snap the cords of party" and thus loosen the bonds of union, he ran the risk of losing abolitionists to new coalitions in support of halfway measures. The movement became more vulnerable to the oscillations of the political process and an atmosphere of crisis and compromise that made it difficult to judge whether abolition had reached the beginning of the end or simply the end of the beginning.

Garrison began his new chapter in agitation with extensive work in Ohio in late summer 1847. He did not cross the Alleghenies fortuitously. There were as many antislavery societies west of the mountains as there were to the east, and he sought to direct this energy toward the radical abolitionist revolution he now considered possible. With his usual prescience the editor had realized that if continental expansion toward the southwest had opened a novel phase of constitutional history, then its outcome would be affected by the economic expansion that, within his own lifetime, had enabled the former Northwest Territory to grow twice as large as New England. (Since the editor's birth in 1805 the geographic center of the U.S. population had shifted from twenty miles west of Baltimore to Chillicothe, Ohio.) The transportation revolution had reoriented the northwestern trade from the Gulf to the Great Lakes as the Ohio-Mississippi river system gave way first to the canals and then the railroads that could take the heartland's wheat and corn and pork to New York, Boston, and Philadelphia more quickly than steamboats could bring cargoes to St. Louis and New Orleans. For a time in the 1840s the little inland town of Milan, Ohio, joined by canal to Lake Erie, was shipping more grain than any other freshwater port in the world except Odessa. Ohio had come into the Union only three years before Garrison's birth, but by 1840 it had grown twice as large as Massachusetts and would become the third-largest state in the Union a decade later. It had loomed as the harbor of opportunity for easterners and then become the hive from which swarms of pioneers set out, first for Illinois and Wisconsin, and then for Iowa, Minnesota, and Oregon. Its flourishing farms and prosperous towns epitomized the commercial culture—aggressively materialistic, on the one hand, and evangelically moralistic, on the other—that had transformed Jefferson's arcadian republic into Polk's enterprising nation committed to the ideals of self-improvement and continental greatness.

Ohio held the key to the booming midwest and to the spread of abolitionist ideas. The Garrisonians—always more numerous than historians' gibes about the "Boston clique" suggest—had signaled their intentions by renaming their Ohio state organization the *Western* Anti-Slavery Society, and in establishing their newspaper, the *Anti-Slavery Bugle*, they served notice that they meant to be heard throughout the region. For eighteen months beginning in June 1845, Abby Kelley had spearheaded the radical organization of Ohio, working closely with a young Oneida disciple, Jane Elizabeth Hitchcock, and the experienced lecturers Stephen Foster and Benjamin Jones, a Hicksite Quaker from Philadelphia. They started a newspaper, held countless meetings across the lakeside portion of the state, especially in the

northeast counties—known as the Western Reserve—which had been settled by New Englanders and had a reputation for spiritual intensity, and sold
hundreds of copies of the best AAS tracts against complicity in church and
state. Their affinities, it turned out, were social as well as ideological, and
by the end of the first year, Abby had married Stephen and Lizzie had
married Ben; the latter couple settled in Salem, Ohio, where they edited
the *Bugle* from a tiny two-room cabin, while the former continued itinerant
lecturing until Abby's pregnancy compelled her temporary retirement early
in 1847. Insisting that Garrison follow up their pathbreaking efforts, Kelley
emphasized that Ohio was to the entire west what the Bay State had been
to New England; they had done their best to give the new pivot "a Massachusetts character."

Garrison's tour began with racist hostility and ended in debilitating illness,
but steeped him in the excitement of a grassroots militancy that he believed
would ultimately carry the cause to victory. Accompanied by Frederick
Douglass, who had returned from England only a few weeks earlier, the two
men received a rousing send-off from Philadelphia's Bethel Church—the
largest black congregation in the country—and stopped first in Harrisburg.
The Pennsylvania capital had not previously seen a black speaker, and rowdies disrupted the meeting at its courthouse on August 7, 1847, with nasty
shouts, projectiles, and firecrackers. They managed to shout down Douglass
and grazed him with a brickbat, while Garrison, his head spattered with
sulfurous eggs that Douglass called the stink of slavery, shamed the crowd
into silence and condemned the city's feeble understanding of liberty. Writing to Helen, he shrugged off the incident and dwelt instead on the successful meetings held twice the next day in a black church and the
opportunity he had to meet old subscribers who had loyally supported the
cause in their inhospitable neighborhood.

Moving on to "dingy and homely" Pittsburgh, whose coal-blackened facades reminded the editor of the English factory towns, the speakers were
rousingly welcomed by a brass band and held open-air meetings with great
success. A steamboat took them down the Ohio to Beaver, Pennsylvania, and
meetings in New Brighton, where churches unexpectedly closed their doors
and the meetings took place in the loft of a store. Mice nibbled bags of
milled grain stored on planks above the rostrum, and the sprinkle of white
dust reminded the editor, he said, to make his talk "a little more floury." A
canal boat trip—Garrison's first—took them to Youngstown, Ohio, and
though the captain warned them that their racially mixed party (which included a young black physician—the son of an old subscriber—and the militant Pittsburgh editor Martin Delaney) might have trouble at the communal
supper table, none occurred, and the sympathetic proprietor of the "rum
tavern" where they were lodged in Youngstown entertained them without
charge. "The world presents some queer paradoxes," Garrison told his wife.
Their Sunday meetings in a beautiful grove drew so many hundreds from

the churches to "God's own temple" that Douglass declared that Ohio would be "a real anti-slavery revival."

Indeed it was. Between August 15 and September 12, Garrison spoke thirty to forty times across a checkerboard of fifteen towns in northeastern Ohio before a total of twenty thousand people. Dotted with red houses, red barns, and little district schoolhouses by the roadside, the prosperous countryside of dairy farms and orchards looked a great deal like Connecticut, and the well-built little towns, neatly laid out on rectangular plans with churches set on village squares, continued the Yankee pattern. In addition to the public addresses, the indefatigable editor spent hours in private conversation with his hosts and admirers and somehow seemed "as fresh at midnight as at midday," Douglass wrote. They met some extraordinary people, including the Ohio pioneer Ruth Galbreath, who had ridden a hundred miles on horseback to her first antislavery meeting in 1834; the constant reader Alpheus Cowles of Ashtabula, who told the editor their minds chimed so perfectly that it would be hard to say if the one were a Garrisonian or the other a Cowlesian; the come-outer C. F. Leffingwell, who had left the Methodist Church in 1844, resigned from the bar in 1846 with the outbreak of war, and built a network of seventy or eighty disunionists in Portage County; and the strong, friendly schoolteacher Betsey Mix Cowles, a protégée of Abby Kelley's, who would become the first female school superintendent in Ohio and whose activism was premised on the idea that women were "made for more than to flutter and to serve." The easterners generated such excitement that local abolitionist leaders drove ten miles out from town with their teams to give Garrison and Douglass a welcoming escort and a booster's sketch of their community's fame in peaches or raspberries or maple syrup or cheese. When the meetings were done, their hosts would escort them halfway to the next town, imploring them all the while to stay longer, so that the entire trip became one long festival of fellowship and excitement. With "monster" meetings attracting thousands in each place, moreover, Douglass exclaimed that it was marvelous "to see our cause *look* popular for once."

Many of the meetings took place in the "great Oberlin tent," a custom-made affair more than one hundred feet in diameter. The Tappan brothers had sent it west when the celebrated evangelist Charles Grandisson Finney took up his theology professorship at Ohio's Oberlin College in 1836 so that he could reproduce on the prairies the vast audiences he had reached in the spacious brick tabernacle they had built for him on Broadway. The tent became a conspicuous feature of the midwestern landscape for the next twenty years, dominating the horizon as people drew close, ten huge triangles undulating in the breeze, stout chains creaking under the strain, a long blue streamer rippling out from the flagstaff with the motto "Holiness to the Lord" inscribed in bold white letters. Used across the region for commencements, revivals, and conventions of the reform societies, the tent served as a physical refuge, a moral beacon, and a sign of the good time coming.

Garrison called the tent a "portable Faneuil Hall" and it so captivated his imagination that he said something about it in nearly every letter home. The sight of the great tent in a distant field with innumerable wagons and knots of pedestrians converging upon it from every direction impressed him as "a grand and imposing spectacle," as did the mechanical endeavors required to erect and transport the tent, the emotional and physical heat generated within it, and the overflowing multitudes—perhaps as many as four thousand persons—gathered under it in a union of feeling that surpassed anything in his previous experience and betokened the surging force of abolitionism itself. To speak to vast concourses while the tent throbbed with cheers and sighs of sympathy made the editor once again feel that, like Byron's Childe Harold, he had stirred the soul's secret springs and breathed all his thoughts "into the one word Lightning."

Garrison brought to Ohio his well-honed message of "come-outerism in church and state." While he cheered the Wilmot Proviso as a sign of fresh life in the Democratic Party, he hoped that its continuing failure to clear the U.S. Senate would convince the party-minded of the necessity for more radical measures. Everywhere he reiterated that the Constitution was a "Procrustean bedstead" that forced every political party to cut and twist moral principles to fit its narrow constraints. As for the Liberty Party, which retained so strong a clerical flavor in the midwest that its pockets of voting strength could be traced to the presence of particular ministers and congregations, Garrison continued to criticize its lack of rigor. In 1844 the party had dropped immediatism from its platform in favor of "the general divorce of the Federal government from slavery," and its theoreticians had developed the argument that when viewed through the "atmospheric medium" of the Declaration of Independence, the U.S. Constitution, whose text never employed the term "slavery," not only had a general antislavery purpose, but specifically gave Congress the power to abolish slavery in the existing states. Piling one strained assumption upon another, the Liberty men contended that the Framers not only intended to extinguish slavery at the earliest practicable moment, but anticipated that the task would take a maximum of fifty years. The proslavery compromises, Birney argued, were but temporary measures to "keep the peace" during slavery's period of demise, and the further admission of slave states had to be understood as a violation of the Framers' expectations. Garrison and Phillips repeatedly challenged such elaborate reasoning as wordplay that ignored both present reality and a half century of political practice. No amount of quibbling could "argue the seal from the bond," Garrison insisted; the corruption lay not so much in the words of the bargain, but in the bargain itself. The point was reinforced when the U.S. Supreme Court rejected the Liberty arguments in a fugitive slave case opinion written by the dough-faced New Hampshire

Democrat Levi Woodbury, whom Polk had appointed as Story's successor to join five Southerners on the bench. In *Jones* v. *Van Zandt* (1847) Woodbury declared that the Court had "a strait and narrow duty, to go where the Constitution and the laws lead, and not break both, by travelling without or beyond them."

It may seem ironic that Garrison should have criticized the Liberty Party for its naiveté, since it was his alleged lack of political realism that provoked the schism, but the party did seem to operate in a vacuum. Birney had frequently declared that, if elected, he would take the oath to support the Constitution, but once in office he would not enforce the Fugitive Slave Law, a position that the radical abolitionists derided as verging upon the conscientious objection for which they had endured censure. The party's cardinal assumption, moreover, that it could peaceably abolish slavery by congressional legislation was an idea that would "blow the union sky high," said Garrison, for the Southern states would never accede to it. In his view the Liberty Party functioned less as a dissenting minority and more as the purveyor of an apolitical fantasy in which abolitionists could take over the government and cut the Gordian knot that bound slavery and the Constitution without otherwise changing the system.

The come-outerism that Garrison and Douglass offered, by contrast, emphasized the necessity of making slaveholding so odious and wicked that every compromise with it—either in church organization or in politics— would suffer popular repudiation and encourage a fresh moral climate in which political reconstruction might become possible. In politics they ridiculed "doughfaces" and "flunkeys," and in religion they condemned as Pharisees the "south-side" apologists who tried to reconcile Christianity and slaveholding in the interest of union. In railing against the churches as bulwarks of slavery, moreover, the Garrisonians were also giving side blows to clerical supporters of the Liberty Party. In a shrewd division of labor on the tour, the "infidel" Garrison most frequently made the political critique, while the irreproachable Douglass offered an attack upon the pulpit as slavery's stronghold that included his famous parody of a minister admonishing the slaves to render cheerful service in accordance with God's law.

The Western Anti-Slavery Society had become the leading exponent of come-outerism and disunion in Ohio, and at the massive three-day WAS meeting at New Lyme, August 18–20, 1847, Garrison had the opportunity to debate his principles with the Whig congressional antislavery leader Joshua Giddings, home in nearby Ashtabula during the summer recess and happy to take the platform in his shirtsleeves and straw hat. So much was said of a radical nature, and so loudly did the meeting applaud sentiments that the nation "dare not prolong the experiment" of coexisting with slavery, that Giddings came as close to endorsing the disunion idea as a congressman could without surrendering his post on the grounds of conscience, and the minutes recorded somewhat charitably that the breadth of his remarks made it "difficult to know where to class him." One week later, in the large brick church at Oberlin College during graduation weekend, Garrison faced a more obdurate opponent in President Asa Mahan, who took Liberty Party ground, but the editor believed that he had spoken effectively to the three thousand people who jammed the all-day meeting.

In Oberlin, as at New Lyme, Garrison sensed a gathering undercurrent of disunion even where the surface appeared unmoved. He felt especially encouraged when he heard Mahan's most celebrated faculty member, the Rev. Charles G. Finney, tell the Oberlin seminary graduates that reflexive denunciations of come-outerism or rhetorical paeans to harmony in the churches would avail them nothing. If they weren't prepared to be "anti-devil all over," they ought to go back to their farms or workshops and not become ministers at all. The old evangelist had come to regard the Union as a "sinful abomination" for its compromises with slavery, and he insisted that since the present generation had received more light on the evils of slavery than any of its predecessors, it stood to incur the most guilt if it allowed the sinful practice to continue. Finney believed that in its selfish preoccupations slavery jeopardized the benevolent impulses that were the key to a life of practical holiness, and though he eschewed the Garrisonian term, he had plainly come to a disunionist position that would reverberate throughout the evangelical community. Yet as a bastion of the clerical abolitionism that had worked its way into the Liberty Party, Oberlin resisted identification with the editor, even as the Whig Giddings did in politics. Indeed, Garrison discovered when he met with Lucy Stone, a twenty-nine-year-old Massachusetts teacher (and admirer of the Grimké sisters) who had just become the first female to graduate from the general liberal arts curriculum, that the community had ostracized her for her admiration of Garrison, her public advocacy of *The Liberator*, and her sponsorship of the "vulgar infidel" Abby Kelley's appearances in the previous year. The undaunted Stone, who had "a soul as free as the air," the editor declared, was heading east to begin a lecturing and writing career in behalf of abolition and women's rights that would make them collaborators for the rest of their lives.

Throughout the tour, Garrison and Douglass strongly attacked Ohio's discriminatory "black laws" as emblematic of the racism that stood in the way of abolition. Although the Old Northwest had come to think of itself as *the* heartland of America and the purest realization of democratic ideals, its self-conception had a strictly racial cast that put the demand for "free soil" in a severely questionable light. Every state in the Old Northwest denied voting rights to black people, all except Wisconsin enacted exclusionary laws that prevented blacks from jury or militia service and, in some localities, from owning land or contracting for labor without posting bond, and several enacted complete prohibitions on black immigration. Ohio shared hundreds of miles of riverbank with slavery, and its pattern of settlement—Yankees in the northern counties and backcountry Scotch-Irish Virginians and Pennsylvanians in the southern—reproduced sectional antagonisms within its borders and extended them into Indiana and Illinois, where proslavery constitutional referenda lost by narrow margins in the 1820s. If hostility to the specter of aristocratic planter power and the competition of slave labor kept the region free-soil, then endemic racism made it a country for whites only. The WAS convention at New Lyme showed considerable courage in condemning Ohio's laws as "infinitely more proscriptive" than any tyranny imposed by George III, and Douglass told the Ohioans that if they cleansed their statute books, it would give a strong rebuke to pandering politicians and offer a moral beacon that would jeopardize the slave system across the river in western Virginia and Kentucky. That the WAS indeed waged a successful campaign over the next two years for repeal of all but the suffrage restriction is a substantial measure of both the practical effect of Garrisonian idealism and the rising political constituency that it fostered.

Garrison paid a high price for the success of the tour. In late September 1847, after speaking to three large meetings in one day in Cleveland, he collapsed from exhaustion. Chills and a fever followed, and after briefly indulging his experiments with Thomsonian remedies for several days, the editor's hosts sent for a physician, who feared typhoid and watched him carefully through three terrible days of delirium and fever. Continuing with his engagements in western New York proved impossible, and Douglass went on alone to Buffalo and Syracuse. The papers spread reports of Garrison's imminent death that severely alarmed Helen, and friends sent Henry C. Wright out to Cleveland so quickly that he had packed and gone before Helen received a reassuring letter from her husband that the crisis had passed. The weakened Garrison remained confined to bed for three additional weeks, and his hand shook so badly that he could hardly write. He lost twenty pounds and ran up expenses of nearly $100 that he despaired of paying, but he felt too embarrassed to leave on the strength of a promissory note. Wright and Stephen S. Foster, who had also hurried to Cleveland, managed to settle his affairs and bring the grateful invalid home by the end of October 1847. He had only one major complaint; he had heard nothing from Frederick Douglass during the entire convalescence and then learned at second hand that Douglass, reversing an earlier decision, had decided to start a newspaper of his own. In four weeks together on the tour Douglass "never opened his lips to me on the subject," Garrison lamented; such "inconsiderate" and "impulsive" conduct "grieves me to the heart."

The wound festered, and by the mid-1850s the preeminent spokesmen of radical abolition would find themselves consumed by a personal animosity so severe that they ceased speaking to each other. The relationship between

Garrison and Douglass could not have been anything but problematical. Two self-made men as determined and as proud as these would likely have clashed in any setting, but in the crucible of movement politics and the charged atmosphere of American race relations, their ability to forge a decade-long working relationship is as noteworthy as their inability to sustain it for a lifetime. Douglass, of course, had come into the movement under Garrison's aegis, and he had eloquently defended Garrisonian principles, including disunion—which resonated with his own profound alienation—and nonresistance—which perhaps fit less well with his self-assertive temperament and the insurgent rhetoric of new black spokesmen personified by the fiery minister Henry Highland Garnet.

Douglass, with his special authority as a fugitive slave enhanced by the publication of his book under Garrison's imprimatur, maintained his distance from the black convention movement and increased his prestige as an American abolitionist with his twenty-month tour of Great Britain, 1845–47. When Garrison joined him there on a brief three-month visit in 1846 to offset another evangelical counterattack on international abolition in the churches, they shared the platform many times with great success and deeply impressed British audiences with their power and sincerity. In social gatherings with editors and reformers, too, they made headway, though on these occasions Douglass was the lionized celebrity and Garrison the fondly admired veteran, a situation that surely grated on the older man's pride.

Yet when Douglass accepted the offer of some English friends to raise a purse and purchase his freedom—a complicated negotiation that ended with Douglass's legal owner selling him to a relative willing to manumit the fugitive—Garrison alone among the AAS leadership defended the "ransom" as a practical choice that enabled Douglass to return home safely. The editor emphatically disagreed with critics who shrugged off the danger that Douglass might be re-enslaved and who charged that the transaction amounted to an endorsement of compensated emancipation. The case was *sui generis,* he insisted, and if Douglass wanted his free papers, no one else could gainsay his choice. The ransom epitomized not complicity with evil but the "extortionate power" of the slaveholders. To liberate a loved one under coercion, as many black families found themselves obliged to do, was very different from a policy that legitimized the slaveholders' property right as a consideration in devising an emancipation program. The villainy lay not in paying the money, but in receiving it, Garrison pointed out, and he regarded the ransoming as a morality play that reenacted the crime of chattel slavery and dramatized its sinful covenant with American institutions. It would make a profound impression without jeopardizing Douglass's life. The editor's admirable defense—which belies his reputation for dogmatism—eventually prevailed.

Another gift from British philanthropists, however, opened a rift between the men. Douglass's admirers had gathered more than $2,000 which they had intended as an annuity that would free him from wage-earning and secure his full-time services for the cause, but the abolitionist declined the gift, partly with the jest that he was too young to become "superannuated" and partly with the astute observations that it would do him no good in America to be supported by Englishmen and that a guaranteed income would make him "so independent of my friends in the United States, as to disturb the sympathy which has resulted from mutual hardships in a common cause, and which is so necessary to successful cooperation." As an alternative, Douglass suggested that the money be used to purchase a printing press and equipment for a black-run newspaper, there being none at present in the United States, which would make the gift a "testimonial" to the race as well as the man.

Although Douglass shrewdly recognized the complexity of his relationship to the other prominent abolitionists, he did aspire to be more than a symbol and craved an independent role in the movement. When Douglass returned to the United States in May 1847 and floated the proposal for another newspaper, the AAS leaders reacted adversely, some pointing out that in his absence Thomas Van Rensellaer had started the *Ram's Horn,* and others demurring that a black-run venture threatened "to keep up the color distinction." Garrison said that from his experience in the printing business, he knew how difficult it was to sustain a venture that went against the grain of religious and political opinion, and he thought that *The Liberator's* decline in black subscribers indicated how crowded the field had already become. Douglass gracefully retreated, though his statements emphasized that he was setting aside the venture "for the *present*." In recompense he was offered a weekly column in the *National Anti-Slavery Standard* and the presidency of the 1847 New England convention. Illness prevented his accepting the ceremonial post, and an unseemly quarrel with Quincy and Chapman over piece rates for the column undid its placating effect. Though Douglass publicly stated that he had made his own decision and had not been cowed by the "Boston Board," the established leadership had dashed his expectations and left him in a sour frame of mind.

Much of the ensuing trouble can be traced to a protégé's inevitable resentment of a mentor. Garrison had started a newspaper on a shoestring with nary a subscriber in sight; Garrison had managed to combine editing and lecturing and parlayed his success in each field into enhanced prestige for both; Garrison exercised a moral and inspirational leadership which Douglass rightfully felt himself both capable of and suited for; Garrison, in short, had made himself a success by exactly the route that Douglass now proposed to follow, though it might be pointed out that Garrison did not have the sponsors and backers that Douglass enjoyed and had taken the lion's share in creating the institutional framework that supported Douglass's ascent. Inescapably, however, the younger man felt stifled and believed that his preceptor was trying to suppress a potential competitor. Perhaps he was, though Garrison had welcomed Van Rensellaer's effort in New York City, where a black newspaper stood the likeliest chance of success, and his tactical judgment that Douglass—fresh from his British tour—had an exceedingly valuable role to play as an AAS lecturer and organizer cannot be lightly discounted.

It is tempting, but dangerous, to discern a racial dimension in the conflict and regard the abolitionist establishment as endeavoring to keep Douglass "in his place." Yet, as Garrison had observed in the ransom controversy, Douglass's place was indeed *sui generis*. Although other fugitive slaves had become active in the movement, none had displayed Douglass's talent, attained his stature, or conducted himself with the tightly coiled, somewhat intimidating authority that Douglass commanded. The leadership for the most part dealt very gingerly with him (though Maria Chapman seemed capable of being as high-handed with him as with everyone else), for Douglass—like it or not—had become so potent a symbol of the abolitionists' vision of equality that no one wanted to antagonize, much less repress, him. It is difficult, however, to sustain a friendship with a symbol, and it is not at all surprising that as Douglass grew into his role, his relationships within the movement cooled or that Douglass himself drew a color line of sorts and kept himself deliberately aloof from white colleagues as he pondered the question of whether blackness was central or peripheral to his identity as a political leader.

Yet Douglass and Garrison had enjoyed a warm and cordial friendship, and their shared travel in both Great Britain and the midwest had put them on intimate terms for much longer than men, except in the military or merchant marine, generally experienced with each other. In the shared pain and excitement of the Ohio tour, which Douglass enthusiastically reported in weekly letters to the *Standard*, Garrison had every reason to think that the newspaper controversy had been laid to rest and to find vindication for his judgment that Douglass's spectacular contributions as an agent should not be sacrificed to a speculative flier into journalism. To rise from a sickbed to learn that Douglass had reversed his course without taking further counsel was a hurtful blow; he was sorry that Quincy—perceiving that he had no choice in the matter—had publicly welcomed the venture in *The Liberator*. "It is a delicate matter, I know, but it must be met with firmness," Garrison said, in the belief that Douglass had been enticed by some Ohio moderates to establish himself in Cleveland and supplant the Garrisonian *Bugle*. As events proved, Douglass began his newspaper in Rochester, New York, the heartland of Liberty Party supporters, which raised suspicions—unsupported by anything Douglass had said on the tour—that his political ideas might be changing. For now, however, the rift remained personal, though the anxiety occasioned by Douglass's about-face suggests that the radicals were afflicted not so much with racial bias as with the lingering effects of their sectarian warfare.

Garrison returned home to a wife determined to keep him there. Helen had remonstrated heavily against the 1846 trip to England. "I could not think of it with the least composure," she later told Ann Phillips, and grew reconciled only when she became convinced that her husband also suffered acutely the conflict between love and duty. The weeks before his departure became so filled with business and visitors, however, that the couple longed "for a quiet retreat for a few hours to be by ourselves without intruders" that never seemed to materialize. When he left, for the first time Helen felt virtually widowed by the cause and settled herself only with considerable emotional effort and self-discipline. Though she wouldn't have said it outright, Helen felt that the anguish over her husband's trip had generated the hardest quarrel of their marriage. The 1847 Ohio trip of four weeks rather than four months seemed more bearable, but its nearly fatal consequences made Helen adamant against further extended travel; it would be five years before he undertook a lecturing trip of more than a few days' duration, six before he revisited the Ohio Valley, and twenty before he returned to Great Britain.

The editor resumed direction of *The Liberator* in January 1848, but he lacked his accustomed zest and complained about having to labor "in the prison house of editorial life." His health remained weak for several months, the children all went through bouts of influenza, and Helen had a persistent cold and felt worn down as never before. At age thirty-seven she was in the early phase of her final pregnancy; Francis Jackson Garrison would be born in October. (In a note acknowledging his namesake, Francis Jackson graciously observed that while the rest of society scrambled to choose popular names, Garrison, in his odd consistency, even in matters of taste, "had selected an old-fashioned one.") The prospect of another child hardly eased the pain occasioned by the death of their sixteen-month-old baby Lizzie, who succumbed to chronic lung fever in April 1848. A large circle of friends gathered in the little parlor on Pine Street for a quiet funeral, and Garrison found himself turning to the Spiritualists for the language of bereavement. "No strange thing has happened unto us, more than unto others, in view of human mortality," Garrison said, and to know that their child now existed "in a spiritual body, subject to no sickness or decay, is an animating thought" that should reconcile all to "a temporary sojourn here." Helen, however, felt "an aching void" in her heart that would not go away, and she seemed "almost solitary" to her husband, staring into the empty cradle or waking in the night with the realization that there was "no little one nestling at her side." Only a daguerreotype of the child, taken before the burial, gave her bereaved mother any comfort, though she kept telling herself that "regrets will be of no avail to us."

Though it was a dark time for Garrison, he still paid attention to the rush of religious and political developments in the cause. The decade had witnessed continuing upheaval in the churches. Abolitionist come-outers had provoked controversies that fractured the established denominations on sectional lines, and the rifts had widened during the furor over the Mexican War. The conservative "Old School" Presbyterians had expelled four "New School" synods after a theological quarrel in 1837, but it was hardly coincidental that the offending bodies were all abolitionist strongholds in Ohio and New York and that the governing assemblies of each school experienced volcanic rumblings on the slavery issue at their regular meetings over the next ten years. The polarizing effect of the Texas controversy exerted itself in other churches as well, and in 1844–45 dramatic schisms occurred within both the Methodist and Baptist denominations. For the Methodists the crisis came over the refusal to install a slaveholding bishop, while for the less centralized Baptists it was a decision against the employment of slaveholding missionaries, but in both cases the result was the same: a secession that led to the formation of the Southern Methodist and Southern Baptist churches by clergymen and lay leaders who felt aggrieved that Northern fanaticism had led to a wholesale condemnation of slaveholders as sinners and the abandonment of the traditional policy of maintaining silence on divisive questions of social policy. That Northern clerical gradualists had moved closer to the immediatist brethren they had attacked for years made these denominational splits more than ecclesiastical events, and Southern leaders were neither slow nor wrong to regard "Free Soil Morality" as a consequence of the sectarian uproar.

The increasingly shrill defense of slavery by Southern clergymen, however, only intensified the commitment of Northern churchmen whose consciences had finally prompted them to speak out. In March 1848, more than six hundred Freewill Baptist ministers publicly declared that they would hold "no fellowship with slaveholders." Even among the orthodox Congregationalists, where Garrison had encountered his most obdurate critics, gradualists led by the formidable Leonard Bacon felt obliged to oppose Southern demands for expanded protection for slavery, and "abolitionist" ceased to be an abusive term. Bacon himself joined several other evangelical leaders close to Lewis Tappan in founding a new religious and political journal, called, significantly, *The Independent,* that favored the polity of Congregationalism and the politics of Wilmotism and free soil, and the Rev. Henry Ward Beecher, the most dynamic evangelist among old Dr. Beecher's six sons of the cloth, quickly became the new paper's leading antislavery columnist. Garrison's years of come-outer exhortation had obviously worked a cumulative effect; as in the political sphere, people were taking Garrisonian action against compromise and comity even as they disavowed Garrisonian intent.

With the middle shifting in Garrison's direction, the editor's "Daniel Boone-ism" asserted itself, and early in 1848 he became involved in a radical anti-Sabbatarian movement that revived the old charges of heresy and infidelity and put him on the far side of respectability once more. Garrison had often attacked the orthodox clergy's preoccupation with Sunday observances as an example of formalism that stood in the way of perfectionist holiness, but in calling for an "Anti-Sabbath Convention" to meet in Boston in March 1848, the editor wanted to strike a blow for freedom of conscience against the state laws in Massachusetts and elsewhere that by restricting nonreligious activities on Sunday seemed tantamount to compulsion. Phillips and Quincy did not regard the Sabbath issue as an evil in itself, as they regarded slavery, and thought Garrison was getting sidetracked into a theological dispute over divine inspiration, but he insisted that the spiritual tyranny represented by compulsory observances worked against abolition. C. C. Burleigh had recently been arrested in Connecticut for selling antislavery pamphlets on Sunday, he pointed out, which struck him as pharisaical in the extreme. Only by violating the petty restrictions of the priesthood did Jesus first perform his healing miracles, Garrison observed, and he further armed himself with quotations from Matthew (12:18) and Mark (2:27) that held it lawful to do good on the Sabbath.

Though the "clique" opposed the meeting, Garrison was supported in the endeavor by his spiritual mentor Lucretia Mott and by Henry C. Wright, the radical minister who had been Garrison's tutor in nonresistance and who remained, in effect, the gadfly's gadfly. Wright had forged a successful career for himself as an itinerant lecturer and pamphleteer (his nonresistance tract for children, *A Kiss for a Blow,* remained in print for decades), and the genial utopian made himself a much-loved member of the Garrison household for weeks at a time. Helen found him the most endearing and sweetest of the abolition friends and was moved beyond measure in the 1850s to learn that his will contained a legacy for her children. The editor's hospitality extended to the columns of *The Liberator,* where Wright's philosophical effusions and reports of his journeyings became a fixture of the newspaper's literary page. As in Garrison's case, his lamblike personality exerted a seductive appeal that made his intellectual belligerence all the more striking. Wright could wield a vitriolic pen and became a formidable exponent of "Man Above Theology! Conviction Above Authority! Nature Above Art! Self-evident Truth Above Bibles!"—a credo that matched the Romantic foundations of Garrison's own reform principles. Wright's anticlericalism especially appealed to Garrison, who had taken to quoting a black preacher's observation that "a minister who can preach and pray 12 months without speaking for the slave must be college-made, money-called, and devil-sent."

The anti-Sabbath meetings attracted a full house to Boston's Melodeon for three days of the intense conversation that Garrison cherished, but it also brought the orthodox press down on the editor as the "Prince of New England infidelity" who had begun to "out-Paine Tom Paine." The satirist, however, who predicted that soon there would be an anti-Monday convention under the auspices of the city's washerwomen put his finger on the underlying issue. Garrison did intend—in all his works—to subvert the social order. As in the controversy over the clerical abolitionists' appeal a decade earlier, his critics were less concerned with the substance of the editor's views than with his motives. Garrison and his followers considered themselves "born to be moral sovereigns . . . come to 'create all things new' . . . and wave over chaos the magic wand of reform," the *Christian Reflector* complained; their agitated hearts and rudderless souls needed "the sweet, bland rest of a Christian Sabbath." To Garrison, however, blandness stood very near blindness as a social disability, and he would forsake no opportunity to shatter complacency and coax a new order of holiness from what he perceived to be the moral chaos of American life. "New occasions teach new duties; Time/ makes ancient good uncouth," James Russell Lowell wrote in "The Present Crisis," a poem much loved and frequently reprinted by the editor. "They must upward still, and onward,/ who would keep abreast of Truth."

Insurgency in the churches reinforced the interplay of conscience and sectionalism in politics. Two events concurrent with the anti-Sabbath convention early in 1848 heralded a period of momentous struggle. The U.S. Senate received a treaty that would end the Mexican War with the cession of more than half a million square miles of land between the Rockies and the Pacific Ocean that would nearly double the size of the United States and make it the world's largest republic. Simultaneously, in France—once America's partner in revolution—an insurrectionary mob in the Tuilleries chased Louis Philippe from the throne and sought to remake the nation into a democratic republic that would enfranchise all men and protect workers' rights. Like a chain reaction, the revolution in France ignited explosions across Europe. In London, thirty thousand laborers marched to demand a charter of universal suffrage and the Duke of Wellington, who had vanquished Napoleon at Waterloo, assumed command of the capital's defense. Milan and Turin successfully rose against their Austrian rulers; the Bavarians deposed King Ludwig, and the Prussians forced their monarch to convene a pan-German parliament in Frankfurt; from Budapest the Magyars under Louis Kossuth sought autonomy for Hungary, and from Prague the Bohemians roused the aspirations of the Slavs for the liberal reforms (the use of national languages, the abolition of serfdom, an end to the nobility's exemption from taxes) that the Magyars had quickly won. Turmoil in the Hapsburg empire provoked uproar even in Vienna, where mobs of workers and students forced the resignation of Prince Metternich—for forty years the master diplomat of Europe and archdefender of the existing social order—and the temporary flight of Emperor Ferdinand. Before year's end, Italian nationalists had driven the pope from the Vatican and transformed the Papal States into a new Roman Republic headed by Giuseppe Mazzini, the prophetic voice of "Young Italy," who seemed now to have sired not only his own country but an entire "Young Europe" blossoming in a springtime of populism.

The collapse of absolutism generated Romantic enthusiasm among Americans. They saw in Europe's awakening a vindication of their own Revolution and their democratic aspirations for a "Young America" now enlarged to once-unimaginable grandeur, though Garrison protested that the American continental expansion—blighted as it was by the shadow of slavery—put the nation on the counterrevolutionary side. Tough-minded John C. Calhoun, however, warned his followers that the European insurgency could only profit the agitators who sought to unsettle the American social order, a point confirmed by Garrison, who called a special meeting of the AAS in Faneuil Hall to honor the provisional government of France for abolishing slavery in all its colonies. At last, he said, the world would know a people honorable enough to extend to all the rights they claimed for themselves and redeem the republican name from the odium cast upon it by the hypocrisy of slaveholding America. *The Liberator* also reprinted resolutions from a "large and enthusiastic" workingmen's meeting that rejoiced in the rise of "free institutions" in Europe and deplored "the despotic attitude of the slave power of the South and the domineering ascendancy of a Monied Oligarchy in the North as equally hostile" to the interests of labor and the "preservation of popular rights." Later in this momentous year, Garrison counted himself among the "friendly" editors and proprietors who supported the efforts of Boston's journeymen printers to organize against reductions in wages.

The Old World, apparently, still held lessons for the New. Garrison had spent an evening with the exiled Mazzini in London, and he recognized in the charismatic Italian leader's democratic idealism and soulful fervor a set of aspirations akin to his own. Mazzini was "trying to make the word bondage disappear from our living languages," wrote Garrison. They shared, too, the profound belief that the "revolution for truth" transcended national boundaries. "One God, one humanity, one law, one love from all for all," proclaimed Mazzini, much as Garrison had done from the time he broadcast "love to the whole world" from Baltimore Jail. Mazzini and his European counterparts contended with monarchical tyranny while Garrison fought against what he regarded as a moral despotism equally harsh in its suppression of freedom. In the European revolutions of 1848 he saw not only confirmation that the tide of history ran in his favor, but another opportunity to drive a wedge into conventional politics and compel attention to the great contradiction that beset American society.

Garrison posed too clear a choice for Americans in the rush of continental expansion, and they denied its revolutionary import by engulfing the issue in technicalities. The country underwent an excruciatingly long debate on what Garrison regarded as the peripheral question of whether slavery might be prohibited or protected in the newly acquired territories. While Europe erupted in a revolutionary conflict between hereditary privilege and workers' aspirations, democratic America tried to reconcile liberty and slavery in an argument over where to draw a line on a map and who would get to wield the pen. Worse yet, from the editor's perspective, people looked to the dubious mechanism of an impending presidential election for resolving a question of principle. He was certain that it couldn't be done, but held out the hope that people would learn better from the attempt and realize how thoroughly national party politics thwarted the imperatives of reform.

Five major positions could be discerned on the issue of slavery in the new territories. Northern antislavery politicians still favored the "free-soil" idea of outright congressional prohibition as exemplified in the Wilmot Proviso. Their Southern antagonists insisted upon Calhoun's new doctrine denying that Congress had any power to interfere with slavery as a matter of property rights and state equality; they advocated a position that was known as congressional noninterference, but verged increasingly into the blatantly contradictory demand that Congress, lacking the power to prohibit, nonetheless had the duty to protect slaveholding in the new lands. Between prohibition and protection lay two approaches to accommodation that attracted support from politicians trying to hold their parties together on a national basis. One sounded simple and direct: extend the Missouri Compromise line westward to the Pacific. The other sounded even simpler, but proved amorphous: let the people of each territory decide for themselves. The trouble with the 36° 30' line was that, striking the Pacific coast one hundred miles south of San Francisco at Monterey, it opened most of the Mexican acquisitions to slavery; the trouble with popular sovereignty was that it opened a host of collateral questions about how the decision would be made (by a handful of early settlers or when the population was numerous enough to apply for statehood? by the territorial legislature or by a statewide constitutional referendum?) that pointed down wide avenues of further manipulation, misunderstanding, and conflict.

Because these four territorial approaches—free soil, noninterference, compromise line, and popular sovereignty—accepted the basic proposition that Congress could not interfere with slavery in the states where it already existed, radical abolitionists rejected them for a fifth position—Garrison's disunionism—which dismissed the territorial question as "weaker than the spider's web" and rejected the entire constitutional compromise in favor of a thorough political reconstruction. To attempt to draw "the boundaries of sin" by driving slavery "back into its constitutional covert" was "an absurdity in morals," the editor argued, and to restrict it in one area while tolerating it in another was as futile as making bricks without straw or damming the Mississippi with bulrushes. The Garrisonian "abolition or disunion" position was seldom recognized in the political debates, except as an alternative all parties were eager to forswear, yet it exerted a subterranean influence on the discussion, and in the civil conflict a dozen years later the political paradigm wrenched toward Garrisonism in a shift more abrupt and violent than the editor either anticipated or desired.

The election of 1848 therefore proved a harbinger of political realignment. Both major parties turned to old soldiers as their standard-bearers and took evasive action on the slavery question. With the exhausted Polk having ruled out a second term, the Democrats rejected his uninspiring secretary of state, James Buchanan, who followed his chief in favoring the Missouri extension; they nominated instead a veteran Jacksonian politician, Michigan's Lewis Cass, who called himself a general on the basis of a western command in the War of 1812 and propounded a cryptic version of popular sovereignty that suited the party's vague platform promise to observe "the principles and compromises of the Constitution." The Whigs bested the Democrats in equivocation by passing over their aging heroes Henry Clay and Daniel Webster, whose frantic efforts to find the shifting middle ground proved too transparently opportunistic; they nominated instead a political neophyte, General Zachary Taylor, whose lack of a public commitment to any of the territorial formulas comported well with the party's crass decision to dispense with a platform entirely and whose national popularity as the victorious commander in Mexico was expected to compensate for his civilian status as a Louisiana sugar planter and master of three hundred slaves.

Antislavery politicians in the North who had committed themselves to Wilmotism and free soil found themselves isolated as extremists within their parties. Dissident "Barnburner" Democrats in New York faced a purge by their dough-faced "Hunker" rivals, and they angrily spoke of running "Prince" John Van Buren, the ex-president's son, as a protest candidate. New England's most prominent antislavery Democrat, John P. Hale of New Hampshire, agreed to head the Liberty Party ticket, much to the delight of Whittier, who, like many others, thought a revolutionary moment had arrived, and Henry Stanton, who crowed that the party's forty thousand votes were "a capital to trade upon." Hale soon proved unwilling to endorse more than nonextension, however, and embittered leaders such as Gerrit Smith and William Goodell who feared the corruptions of fusion politics split off into a Liberty League of their own. In writing the breakaway manifesto, Goodell seemed to have come full circle, conceding that if the Constitution could not be wielded against slavery, then his group would have to demand "either a new or amended constitution, and if this cannot be affected, a peaceful dissolution of the Union." In Massachusetts the Conscience Whigs, angry and miserable at the party regulars' willingness to swallow the slaveholding Taylor in their hunger for a national victory, pronounced themselves ready for forming a new organization that, in Sumner's words, would fuse "politics and morals . . . in the holy wedlock of Christian sentiment." Sounding a distinctly Garrisonian note, Sumner anticipated a revolution in American politics that would shatter the unholy alliance of "the lords of the lash and the lords of the loom" that perpetuated slavery.

The surge of antislavery dissent culminated in an astonishing "Free-Soil" convention at Buffalo in August 1848 that superseded the fractured Liberty

Party and produced the first significant break in the two-party system. Upward of ten thousand people sprawled across acres of city parkland and gathered in a huge tent for three days of rousing oratory and singing that looked and felt like the Ohio abolitionist festivals Garrison had addressed the previous summer. Yet these were not radical abolitionists, but conscience-driven moderates whose tolerance for evasion on an antislavery issue had so diminished that they were ready, as Garrison had long urged, to declare their independence from their traditional parties. Despite the revivalist-style euphoria in the park, the four hundred delegates (chosen by a complicated formula that allowed the Whig, Democratic, and Liberty tendencies each to have a voice) who met indoors for the actual convention engaged in some hard political dealing before fusing themselves into a new Free-Soil Party.

It is commonly said that at the Buffalo convention the dissident Democrats got the presidential nomination, the Conscience Whigs got the vice-presidency, and the Liberty Party got the platform, but this is subject to much qualification. A Democrat did become the nominee, but it was neither the outspoken Hale nor the popular Prince John but rather the old kingmaker Martin Van Buren who was now brought forward as a champion of freedom in revenge against the party regulars who had cast out his faction. A Whig did become the vice-presidential candidate, but it was neither the radical Sumner nor the congressional stalwart Giddings but the cautious and retiring Charles Francis Adams, who was named in tribute to his late father, John Quincy Adams, whose notable career in defense of antislavery petitions and against slavery's expansion into Texas had ended when he collapsed and died in the House of Representatives the previous February. Liberty Party ideas, however, did not much register in the platform. The convention affirmed the congressional power to prohibit slavery in the territories, but in promising not to interfere where it presently existed, the new party repudiated the Liberty assumption that slavery could be abolished everywhere. It so diluted the Liberty demand for the "unqualified and absolute divorce of the General Government from Slavery" that the vital key—abolition of slavery in the District of Columbia—was left to inference. Even more glaringly, from the abolitionist point of view, the platform completely ignored the Liberty Party's most notable feature: its stand as the first American political party pledged to remove—as vestiges of slavery—all inequalities of rights based upon color. In view of these limitations, the editor Joshua Leavitt's excited claim in Buffalo that the Liberty Party was "not dead, but translated" proved the last of its self-delusions.

Despite its expedient nominations and distinctly "lower standard," the Free-Soil Party drew a temperate and measured response from Garrison and his colleagues that, owing to the personal animosities of the schism, they had never extended to the Liberty Party. Taking the new coalition as a sign that their agitation had awakened people throughout the North, the veteran abolitionists welcomed the exodus from the "slavery parties" even as they emphasized that the real issue—immediate and universal emancipation— had not yet been reached. It was "an anti-Taylor, anti-Cass, and almost anti-slavery convention," said Samuel J. May, who had come over from Syracuse to observe the proceedings, but it would be "ungrateful and churlish," May told Garrison, "not to rejoice that so many thousands . . . representing no doubt millions more, have come so far upon anti-slavery ground, because they come as yet no further."

The editor fully concurred. "There is no teacher like experience," he said benignly, and anticipating that Free-Soilism would inevitably lead to a recognition of the great issue between the sections, he welcomed it publicly "as the beginning of the end," though he warned against taking the new party as anything more than "a token of progress." Nonextension was an issue "destitute of principle" that would not liberate a single slave, he emphasized, yet he believed that continuing moral suasion and the boundless aggression of the slaveholders would be sufficient to bring the deeper issues to the surface.

The Buffalo convention had barely ended before its influence was felt in Washington. Congress had wrangled itself into a hopeless deadlock on the question of organizing a government for the Oregon territory. Northern farmers led by evangelical missionaries had poured into the region, which embraced present-day Washington and Idaho as well. Few thought that slavery would take hold there, but Southerners in Congress blocked any territorial bill for Oregon that included a Wilmot-style prohibition. They wanted instead an abstract recognition of the Calhoun doctrine of noninterference, though in practice they would settle for an extension of the Missouri line and thereby set a precedent for the Mexican Cession yet to be addressed. The sides remained at loggerheads for months, in the face of Indian warfare in Oregon that took the lives of the missionary leaders, until the news from Buffalo of the rising Free-Soil tide produced a Northern majority strong enough to pass a territorial bill with a congressional prohibition of slavery. Polk dared not veto it, though he protected the slaveholders' position by claiming that he signed it in the recognition that the Oregon territory lay wholly north of the imaginary compromise line. *The Liberator* hailed "the first victory" over the slave power as the product of abolitionist fortitude, while the *New York Tribune*, though nominally committed to the national Whig ticket, credited the Buffalo meeting's emphatic message—"Free Soil first and Party Success afterward"—as a warning that General Taylor would have to heed the changing wind in the awakened North.

Unlike the Liberty Party, which had originated with movement defectors who hoped to draw party people into its fantasy of an abolitionist political takeover, the Free-Soil Party represented an exodus from the major parties by people who had become alienated by their traditional indifference and sought to build a practical new coalition for victory. The movement exuded so vibrant a spirit of righteousness and conscience that it proved easy to overlook the elements of expedience, ambition, and self-interest that made it work. Even the nomination of the dubious Van Buren, the architect of the New York–Virginia axis which sustained the Democratic Party for two decades by keeping abolitionism out of politics, was taken as a favorable sign that political managers were now willing to board the antislavery car, though Garrison did warn that Free-Soilers had bought the proverbial " 'pig in a poke.' " That the grand public meetings in the Buffalo park cheered stirring remarks by Frederick Douglass, Henry Highland Garnet, and other black leaders seemed more significant for the moment than the platform's silence on the principle of equal rights or the inherently racist tinge of the appeal to make the territories a haven for free labor against the "degrading" competition of slavery. To consider slavery bad policy because it threatened the dignity and ambition of white workers was a different matter from considering slavery a sin because it infringed upon the freedom God granted every soul. The Free-Soilers came dangerously close, moreover, to applying the morality of the latter position to the racism of the former, as instanced by the dissident Democratic editor Walt Whitman's free-soil exhortation that "the workingmen of the north, east, and west, come up, to a man, in defense of their rights, their honor . . . [and declare] . . . in tones as massive as becomes their stupendous cause, that their calling shall *not* be sunk to the miserable level of . . . Negro slaves." It was but a short step further to the spirit of the Ohio black laws and the complete exclusion of black workers— free or slave—from the territories and the body politic. In the headiness of the moment, however, those who believed in the politics of conscience— confident that they were gaining upon complacency—did not acknowledge the gravity of the threat. If the Free-Soil coalition was indeed the harbinger of the "great Northern party" capable of standing up to slavery, however, then the abolitionist vanguard still had much to do in "perfecting the moral vision of the people."

The election results proved ambiguous enough to encourage everyone but John C. Calhoun. As in 1844, the winner received fewer votes than his combined opponents. Taylor gained the presidency with forty-seven percent of the vote, carrying eight slave states and seven free states, while the Democrats carried seven slave and eight free states with forty-three percent of the vote, a five percent drop from 1844, when the victorious Polk—like Taylor—received less than a majority. The studied ambiguity of the major parties could evidently retain voters in each section, but the Free-Soil appeal suggested that the longer the slavery crisis continued, the less likely this would remain true. Van Buren took enough votes away from Cass in New York to give the state to Taylor, but in Ohio the third-party candidate drew off enough Whig voters to throw the state to the Democrats. More ominously for the regular parties, the Free-Soil vote tallied an impressive ten percent overall (compared with Liberty's two percent four years before), but in seven

Northern states its total exceeded the margin by which the state was won. Even more tellingly, the party elected nine congressmen, which would give it a pivotal role in the next Congress, otherwise closely divided 112–109 between Democrats and Whigs. No wonder that Calhoun, furious that a hard-core set of abolitionist agitators had succeeded in redefining the middle ground of the Northern electorate, had sat down immediately to draft a fresh appeal for Southern unity regardless of party: if Congress applied the Wilmot Proviso to the Mexican territories, he warned, the rupture of the Union would be assured. No wonder, too, that after the election Garrison's analysis emphasized that Free-Soil power was "not inherent, but [a] derivative" of the great moral struggle of the previous twenty years. Abolitionists, he promised, would continue to drive the Free-Soilers to higher ground. They would rewrite the Southern dictionary so that *compromise* did not mean "taking the whole" and *consistency* would not embrace the liberal endorsement of revolution in Europe and a reactionary effort to extend the domain of slavery in America.

By the fall of 1848, Garrison's financial problems had become dire again. It cost approximately $6,000 annually to produce *The Liberator*. If a minimum of 2,500 subscribers promptly paid their yearly $2.50 subscription, the paper could break even, but cash lagged far behind expenses, and in most years the fall became a pinched time in which money went out faster than it came in. In 1848, however, the publishing committee fell behind in meeting Garrison's salary in July, the earliest ever, while the newspaper, whose appearance and legibility were suffering from badly worn type, faced an expensive outlay to rehabilitate it. The situation worsened when the Garrisons returned to Pine Street in October after a retreat in which Garrison had hoped to restore his health. They could hardly afford the rent and felt oppressed by a dozen noisy boarders—hard-drinking ostlers, drivers, and laborers— packed in next door, yet they had run up such bills that they were in no position to consider a move. If he had cash, the editor told Wendell Phillips, he could buy in larger, wholesale quantities and not be so dependent upon credit at the retail shops. If they closed the printing office and hired out the work, he told the committee, they might end up with a better-looking paper at less cost. If the sponsors could persuade a few more friends to establish an annuity for the paper, he told Helen, no one would be unduly burdened and their minds would be relieved. This time, she had to remind him of the never-failing promise to trust in the Lord.

The crisis did get resolved. Unbeknownst to the Garrisons the faithful Francis Jackson had quietly begun to raise a trust fund that might help them purchase a house or aid the family in the event of the editor's untimely death. The effort had not borne enough fruit to make an immediate purchase, but a way was found for the Garrisons to rent smaller and cheaper quarters in one of Jackson's properties on the fringes of the South End. By the end of January 1849, Garrison had received nearly $400 in back pay from the committee, which then managed to stay current for the next six months. A new arrangement was negotiated with the printer James Brown Yerrinton, a man of sterling character, though his craftsmanship required the editor's careful supervision. Yerrinton agreed to pay the rent, buy the new type, and take over the printing office as his own business. He would do both composition and presswork on *The Liberator* for a fixed weekly fee of $34, while Garrison and the committee would supply the paper and retain office space in the Cornhill establishment. They had tried a similar scheme with Isaac Knapp, with unfortunate results, but Yerrinton was a better businessman and an easier fellow to work with, and the arrangement sufficed for the remainder of the newspaper's existence.

The new house at 65 South Suffolk Street, three blocks below Dover Street—the city's boundary line when Garrison had walked across the neck from Roxbury fifteen years before—was a tall flat-fronted brick dwelling with narrow oblong windows that accentuated its height and made it seem cramped. It formed part of a newly built row in the midst of a rapidly developing working-class district of cheap new housing. Across the way a contractor was wedging seven houses onto a square block meant for six, and on the adjoining streets numerous vacant lots were turning into building sites—noisy and attractive nuisances for the children. Only four families—headed by two furniture-makers, a locksmith, and a painter—on their stretch of South Suffolk owned their houses; a mixed lot of clerks, barbers, machinists, jobbers, pressmen, and grocers formed the bulk of the renters, with teamsters and day laborers, including a black family or two, at the older and cheaper end of the street. Most had young families, there was a school close by, and it seemed an encouraging change of situation.

Only a week after the move, however, a tragedy occurred that blighted the Suffolk Street house and made it impossible for the Garrisons to live there happily. Six-year-old Charlie—"our beautiful, affectionate, intelligent, large-hearted and noble boy"—became severely ill and died on April 8, 1849. He had apparently caught a cold (from running about without his overcoat during the exciting but cold and inclement days of the move, his parents thought), but by the weekend he felt feverish and sick to his stomach and ached terribly in his limbs. Winter influenza was so common in their household that Garrison was not alarmed, but Helen thought the boy had something out of the ordinary and considered him "a very sick child." Cold compresses and the usual homeopathic remedies seemed of no help, and by Wednesday afternoon (the day Garrison usually stayed very late at the office making the newspaper ready for the press), Charlie had grown lethargic and screamed so loudly whenever he moved that Helen sent her husband an urgent message to return home. When a friend offered to administer a medicated vapor bath that might sweat off the fever, the editor accepted, but she did it clumsily, scalding the child in the process, while Garrison stood by urging his poor son to be brave. Later that night Charlie became delirious, and over the next few days he sank lower and lower, until he died on Sunday evening, Mama and Papa whispering in his ear that he would soon be with baby Lizzie and receiving in return a gentle sigh and one last smile.

Charlie's death was "a staggering blow" that overwhelmed his parents and left them shocked and grieving for a very long time. Helen could hardly mention his name without weeping. "I try to be resigned," Helen told Henry C. Wright three months later, "I try to be cheerful, but it is all forced. My heart is ready to break." She was certain that the vapor bath had killed her son by sending the fever to his brain. If, as seems likely, the boy was already in the grip of rheumatic fever or another serious infection, then the scalding had but aggravated an already dangerous and likely fatal condition. Garrison felt miserably culpable in the horror of the vapor bath that had injured if not killed his son and berated himself for postponing, in their straitened circumstances, a call to the physician. He grieved in guilt, mourning his shining, beautiful, songful boy "born to take a century upon his shoulders, without stooping," while Helen grieved in anger, overwhelmed by loneliness, in a house that seemed "more like a tomb" than a home. When the boys started preparing for the Fourth of July, she remembered Charlie's happy face the previous year; when the bubbling baby Franky smiled, he reminded her of Charlie at that age; when Fanny clapped her hands and said that "if Charlie was only here we should be happy," Helen's heart would break all over again. She knew that her husband shared the sorrow and that he slept no better than she did and worked the days in the same fog of distraction, but reconciliation came very hard and slowly for her. When their old friend Samuel J. May, at his pastoral best, consoled them with the reminder that "you two have 'a strength of faith and a depth of love' that the world does not know," he tried instinctively to mend the bond that tragedy had severely strained and that only time could heal.

CHAPTER EIGHTEEN

THE MATHEMATICS OF JUSTICE

"DESPONDENCY IS NOT A WORD . . . ALLOWED IN OUR VOCABULARY," GAR-
RISON LIKED TO SAY, AND HE LITERALLY WILLED HIMSELF BACK INTO THE
STRUGGLE AFTER HIS SON CHARLIE'S DEATH, FORCING HIMSELF TO AT-
tend the annual spring meetings, accept lecturing invitations, and conduct
his newspaper with its customary polemical force. Solicitous care from the
Phillipses and the Jacksons helped greatly, as did the onrushing force of the
crisis itself. To coax the editor back to the office, Wendell gave him packets
of omnibus tickets on the pretext that he now lived at a greater distance
from 21 Cornhill, and Ann underwrote additional help for Helen with the
house and children, while Francis Jackson made sure that Garrison did not
get into one of his states of panic over the quarterly bills. Their ministrations
worked in part because the pace of movement activities quickened in 1849,
as it always did after the transitory excitement of the presidential election
dissipated, and Garrison found himself advocating revolutionary and religious
idealism in the face of a renewed and obdurate effort to suppress it.

Europe's liberal springtime proved ephemeral and faded rapidly under
the blazing force of monarchical armies that restored Bonapartism in France,
broke up the nascent Italian and German confederations, fractured Pan-
Slavism, and drove Kossuth and Garibaldi into exile. The revolutions of 1848
proved, in a famous phrase, "the turning point of the century upon which
the century failed to turn," and the collapse disheartened reformers everywhere. If humanity were to achieve its full birthright of freedom, it seemed
that the United States still afforded what Abraham Lincoln would call "the
last best hope" of mankind, an opportunity whose contradictions struck Garrison as both tantalizing and cruel. He could never share in the self-
congratulatory bombast that inflated American political rhetoric, yet he
cherished hope for a national redemption from the curse of slavery and racial
division. In his judgment, however, the United States also faced a reactionary
moment, for what he had hailed in 1848 as a bright new politics became
overshadowed in the next eighteen months by the gifted old practitioners
who tried to revive a coalition that could purge abolitionism from the political agenda. A fresh political crisis over the admission of California so far
exceeded the Texas uproar that the Union seemed on the verge of collapse
and threatened, as Garrison put it, to grind the abolitionists between the

"upper and the nether millstone" of constitutional compromise and a renewal of mob violence.

Abolitionists had to make "a moral impression on the heart of the country," the editor insisted, and their methods had to remain the homegrown agitation of schoolhouse discussions and neighborhood prayer meetings linked with local and regional county conventions and the intensive circulation of tracts—all aimed at generating talk that would make the "wickedness" of slaveholding so palpable that it would "shame politicians into decency" and "send a shudder throughout the universe." To counter the preoccupation with free soil, Garrison reasserted his radicalism on all counts—disunionism, racial integration, women's rights, and Christian nonresistance—and in many different venues. He addressed the state legislature on the latest round of petitioning for a state convention to consider severing relations with the Union; he spoke to an unusually well-to-do audience in New York's Broadway Tabernacle during which he disdained the conventional forms of national patriotism and distinguished, as he had done at Park Street in 1829, between America as the land of his nativity and freedom as the country of his heart; he appeared on platforms in the little towns of eastern Massachusetts with recently escaped fugitive slaves; and he energetically supported the boycott of Boston's segregated schools launched by his associate William C. Nell and other activists in the black community. His writing on the issue in *The Liberator* revealed his undiminished ability to puncture the fatuousness of the opposition with barbs of sarcasm and outrage.

The watchword, said *The Liberator*, had to be "organize! organize! organize!" The Massachusetts Anti-Slavery Society obliged with another "One Hundred Conventions" campaign that managed to put the experienced Fosters and Pillsbury in the field along with the talented newcomers William Wells Brown and Lucy Stone, both protégés of Garrison, who frequently joined them on the platform. They plowed the ground intensively. In the little town of Kingston in Plymouth County, a fifteen-year-old boy, Bradford Drew, who had first learned about slavery as a toddler by studying *The Liberator*'s masthead sketch, noted in his diary six abolition meetings in the first eight months of 1849 that afforded him both the opportunity of hearing the panoply of celebrated speakers and the special pleasure of meeting Garrison himself at his parents' supper table.

Brown, who also stayed overnight with the Drews, stepped forth as the latest in an endlessly renewing line of speakers and writers who had escaped from slavery. His memoir—which gave a more comprehensive portrait of slavery than Douglass's, since Brown had lived in Kentucky and Missouri and had seen firsthand the cruelties of the slave trade in the Mississippi Valley—had sold eighteen thousand copies in the two years since Garrison's office had published it in 1847, and it went into a fourth printing in August

1849. Like Douglass, Brown credited *The Liberator* for drawing him into the movement, and he demonstrated a gift for platform drama in organizing the appearances on the abolitionist circuit of William and Ellen Craft, runaways from Georgia who had ingeniously escaped with the light-skinned Ellen disguised as her husband's master. In the summer of 1849 the Crafts created a sensation in New England and helped the Garrisonians maintain their focus on Southern slavery itself.

Lucy Stone, who had become an MAS agent following her graduation from Oberlin, proved the first in a series of second-generation abolitionists who had literally grown up in the cause. She never forgot how her minister would not let her voice support for a deacon who had suffered censure by inviting Abby Kelley to their church; "You're not a *voting* member," the clergyman told her in a scornful voice that helped spur Stone to a lifetime of activism. Stone also proved an eloquent and forceful link with the quickening agitation for women's rights, to which she devoted a portion of her lecturing time, while the fresh demand for female suffrage reinforced the egalitarian dimension of the abolitionists' agenda.

The seed planted during Garrison's London protest at the world's convention in 1840 had germinated slowly as women took on influential roles in abolition without developing a program that addressed their own condition. When Lucretia Mott and Elizabeth Cady Stanton reencountered each other in western New York, where Mott was lecturing and Stanton presiding over a growing family while her husband pressed his career in New York politics, their passionate and searching conversations led to an impromptu women's rights convention in Seneca Falls—July 19–20, 1848—that laid the foundation for the modern feminist movement. (When she looked over reports of the London convention, Stanton "boiled" with humiliation, she said, and cried that she would "die of an intellectual repression, a woman's rights convulsion!" if she did not speak out.) First at Seneca Falls, then at Rochester in August, and afterward over the next two years at local meetings in Ohio and New England, Stanton, Mott, and their colleagues articulated a program of equality in voting, employment, property law, and domestic relations that they founded squarely in the natural rights tradition of the Declaration of Independence. Their Garrison-like "Declaration of Sentiments" also followed the tactic the editor had employed at Park Street by casting its demands in a paraphrase of Jefferson's own document. Garrison did not attend the hastily called local meeting at Seneca Falls, but in 1849 *The Liberator* promoted the first petition campaign for equal suffrage, and he and Helen both signed the call and attended the first national women's rights convention at Worcester, Massachusetts, the following year. The English feminist Harriet Taylor, reporting on the meeting in the *Westminister Review,* deemed it fitting that the men associated with extirpating "the aristocracy of colour" from democratic America should join "the first collective protest against the aristocracy of sex." When critics mocked Garrison for campaigning for a privilege that he himself declined to exercise, the editor defended himself with an exposition of his commitment to "impartial liberty." Everyone was entitled to civil rights regardless of sex or race, he said, and whether one chose to exercise them on grounds of conscience was immaterial to the tyranny manifested by their denial.

Garrison further emphasized the radical agenda with his extensive coverage of the campaign against segregated schools. The indefatigable William C. Nell, who combined his assistantship in the antislavery office with independent journalism and historical studies, became the driving force of the protest, which sought the closure of the woefully neglected Smith School—endowed in a previous generation to educate black youth throughout the city—and the admission of all students on a nonracial basis to their neighborhood schools. When the Boston School Committee demurred, the community undertook a lawsuit on behalf of Sarah Roberts, the daughter of a black printer who passed several white schools on her daily trip to the black one, and the conscience-minded attorney Charles Sumner argued the unconstitutionality of segregation before Chief Justice Lemuel Shaw in November 1849. The city, meanwhile, had begun to improve the Smith School, which was boycotted by a majority of black families, though a small number—professing the importance of "race schools" as a means of controlling their children's education—insisted upon keeping the segregated school open as a safe alternative to the spurious opportunities of the white schools. Garrison sided with the integrationists in the dispute and regretted that his former apprentice Thomas Paul, Jr., had taken a teaching position at the Smith School, in what the editor perceived as a divide-and-conquer strategy by the school committee. When Chief Justice Shaw upheld the committee's right to set school policy and rejected Sumner's claim that its racial distinctions were an unconstitutional denial of civil equality, the struggle became more clearly linked to the abolitionists' campaign against complicity with slavery and led to a five-year campaign to pass state legislation that would guarantee equal treatment in education.

Garrison worked steadily to contrast the abolitionists' vision with the complacency or shortsightedness of established leaders. When Henry Clay tried to smother the sparks of antislavery opinion that had flared among Kentucky Whigs by conceding the evil of slavery and proposing a gradual emancipation plan contingent upon resettlement in Liberia, the editor denounced Clay's myopia and termed Clay's crocodile tears more offensive than Calhoun's "monstrous" candor. Reminding the public that the incoming President Taylor was, to a certain extent, a surrogate for the slaveholding nationalism long represented by Clay and the Southern Whigs, Garrison condemned the old senator for the moral cowardice of "endeavoring to occupy a position half way between right and wrong."

Of a piece with Garrison's attacks upon Clay and the Whigs stood the editor's vigorous campaign against a visiting Irish temperance leader, the

Franciscan reformer Father Theobold Matthew, who had attracted crowds of thousands to his mass rallies, but who, in deference to the Democratic Party sympathies of his sponsors and his projected fund-raising tour through the South, declined to speak out on the slavery question. Garrison laid a trap for Father Matthew by inviting him to the MAS First of August celebration, calling on him privately when the priest failed to respond and finally revealing publicly that Father Matthew had told him that he had enough to do with saving men from the slavery of alcohol and could not meddle with a domestic issue. In a series of public letters to the popular visiting cleric, Garrison manufactured a controversy that lasted for several months. Yet Garrison's target was not so much Father Matthew as it was the religious and political press that leaped to his defense, for its abusive criticism of Garrison once again gave the editor an opportunity to indict dough-faced complicity and press the moral case for disunion.

The editor did not hesitate to criticize liberal heroes. In a long and thoughtful editorial on the Hungarian revolutionary Louis Kossuth, Garrison likened the popular leader to George Washington, but then undercut the compliment by assessing the moral limitations of militant nationalism. Territorial independence achieved through bloodshed taught a selfish lesson and manifested a primitive and vengeful form of retributive justice, Garrison maintained, and he contrasted the "local" patriotism of Kossuth and Washington with the "universal" principles of Jesus Christ, which envisioned the overthrow of tyranny "by a moral regeneration" more ennobling than the demand for national autonomy or free soil. The editor reinforced the point by commissioning a new engraving for his newspaper's masthead. It sharpened the details of the familiar contrasting scenes of the slave auction and the dream of freedom, but linked the two with a medallion that depicted the risen Christ—vigorous, muscular, and draped with a sash reminiscent of the European revolutionary costume—come to break the bonds of both slave and overseer. To draw the composition together the artist traced a flowing ribbon bearing the injunction "Thou shalt love thy neighbor as thyself."

When the first Congress of Zachary Taylor's administration convened in December 1849, the territorial controversy had ballooned into a civil crisis. In one of history's most rapid turnabouts the Mexican Cession had not remained a sparsely settled land of far-distant promise, but had become a beacon of immediate prosperity. With the discovery of gold in California a frenzied migration had begun that, over the course of 1849, carried ninety thousand people into the region, transformed San Francisco from a sleepy colonial outpost into a booming seaport, and created a mining district that quickly unearthed millions of dollars in wealth that would fuel a generation of rapid economic development. California no longer needed territorial government; it wanted statehood. It sought admission, moreover, on the basis of a newly drawn constitution that, despite the presence of many Southerners and pervasive white racism, had explicitly prohibited slavery. Calhoun insisted that the document was the covert work of abolitionists (*The Liberator* recorded its first San Francisco subscriber on February 17, 1849), and he pronounced the statehood application as a constitutional fraud that insulted an already injured South. He had cause for alarm. As the potential thirty-first state, California would tip the evenly balanced U.S. Senate toward free soil and guarantee the application of the Wilmot Proviso in the remainder of the Mexican Cession.

The potential loss of the southwest disturbed Southern leaders, but the pending shift of political power alarmed them even more, and throughout the South anger seethed over its looming vulnerability and the fear that with newfound leverage in national politics, Northern Free-Soilers would inevitably shift their attention to the eradication of slavery within the existing states. This may seem an extraordinary scenario to spin on the basis of two Senate seats, but a generation's worth of Garrisonian and Calhounite agitation had done its work, and by the end of 1849, more Southerners than ever before had come to believe that the fateful turning point in the struggle had been reached. It would no longer be enough to block the Wilmot Proviso and keep the territories open; now the South wanted "guarantees" that its constitutional position in the Union—that is, its power to protect slavery— would still be respected in the free states; otherwise the Union would be at an end. Indeed, if matters were not settled by June 1850, leading slaveholders warned, their states would meet in Nashville to consider independent means of protection. "The North must give way," Calhoun privately told his son-in-law, "or there will be a rupture." To Free-Soilers such demands and threats by "the slave power" seemed the height of arrogance: an attempt to defy both the power of numbers (the free states had a population three times greater than the slave states) and the weight of example that testified to the superiority of free labor in creating bourgeois economic prosperity in contrast to the feudal one-crop dependency of slavery. Let the South prosper with its slaves as long as it could, but let it not blackmail the nation into strengthening it through expansion. As more and more people came to think in such polarized terms, the territorial issue, as Garrison predicted, forced the question of the relationship between slavery and the Union itself.

So severe had sectional animosity become that Congress could not organize itself. With the parties closely divided and unwilling to concede anything to the maverick Free-Soilers, the House deadlocked for three weeks and fifty-nine ballots over the choice of Speaker, as Southern Whigs would not support even the cautious Robert C. Winthrop of Boston, Northern Democrats remained adamant against even the moderate Howell C. Cobb of Georgia, and the Free-Soilers' insistence upon David Wilmot aggravated the tension like a fingernail drawn along a chalkboard. In the corridors politicians cursed each other and brandished pistols across the sectional divide, while the press rehearsed the arguments in overheated fashion and could agree only that the nation faced a crisis more portentous than Missouri and more sinister than nullification. The abolitionists, however, regarded the stalemate as "cheering evidence" of an "awakened" public opinion. They had thrown a little free soil into the legislative machine, one Garrisonian gloated, and the paralysis offered opportunities for "re-educating a corrupt and besotted people." Eventually, the House chose the Southerner Cobb by a plurality, an expedient that would not be available to resolve the looming impasse over legislation.

In his first message to Congress, President Taylor revealed an old-fashioned nationalism that should have rallied the Whigs. He proposed that the crisis be faced directly by conceding the inevitable and standing tall against the complainers. He would admit California with its antislavery constitution and, rather than organize New Mexico as a territory, he would encourage it to proceed expeditiously to statehood with a constitution of its own devising. These measures would obviate the need for the proviso, yet recognize the political reality that Free-Soilers had gotten a head start in the territories. Since slavery in the existing states could best be secured by an end to sectional animosity, he would, Jackson-like, defend the Union against nullifiers and secessionists. Taylor, however, lacked two essential qualities enjoyed by his heroic predecessor, personal charisma and a unified party organization, and his plan seriously underestimated both the emotional fervor of Southern expansionism and the depth of anxiety generated by Free-Soilism. The South demanded something more than the harsh medicine Taylor offered, and in an audacious challenge the magnetic and charming Henry Clay upstaged him with a plan that would placate the South and settle the controversy at one stroke.

Harking back to the Missouri triumph that had made his reputation as "the Great Pacificator," Clay—still the most adroit of legislators and the most confident and persuasive of politicians—put forward in January 1850 an "amicable arrangement" that would effect "a reunion of the Union." Like Taylor, Clay would sidestep Wilmotism by admitting California as it had constituted itself, but unlike Taylor, he would create—without congressional intervention on the subject of slavery—two new territorial governments for the balance of the acquired land: one for New Mexico (which also included much of present-day Arizona) and another for Utah (also known as East California or Deseret, which embraced both the Mormon settlements around the Salt Lake and much of modern Colorado and Nevada). This proposal would checkmate the Free-Soil tendency in Congress, keep the area open to slavery under the ambiguous precept of popular sovereignty, and point the way to an eventual decision by the U.S. Supreme Court on the issues of if, how, and when territories might regulate slavery before statehood. Corollary measures would adjust the Texas–New Mexico boundary dispute in the latter's favor, but assuage Texas by federal assumption of its preannexation debt in exchange for relinquishment of its western border claims. On territorial matters, then, the cost to Northern antislavery interests of admitting California as a free state would be to accept an area theoretically open to slavery all the way to the southern border of Oregon at 42° north latitude (i.e., six degrees north of the imaginary Missouri line), along with enriching speculators in Texas bonds and revising the map of Texas in a process that might well produce the additional slave states permitted by the annexation law.

Clay was not finished, however. He also wanted to address the various issues of interstate comity that had arisen during the abolition controversy. His program would nod in the direction of free-soil restrictiveness by abolishing the commercial slave trade in the District of Columbia, a measure that would not impair the legal rights of resident slaveholders to transfer their chattels but would remove the awful slave pens and auction blocks that, as *The Liberator*'s masthead weekly reminded the public, stood within sight of the Capitol. Yet the price for this cosmetic change would be a stiff one. Congress would declare it "inexpedient" to abolish slavery in the District unless (or until) the state of Maryland and the voters of the District should agree to it and plans were made to compensate the owners. Congress would be formally denied jurisdiction over the interstate slave trade—as part of the constitutional understanding that the existing states had reserved powers on this subject despite the broad language of the commerce clause. At the same time, however, Congress would be asked to enact more stringent federal procedures for the recapture of runaway slaves—as part of the constitutional obligation reaffirmed in the *Prigg* decision, but undermined by the personal liberty laws enacted in some of the free states. Under the proposed law the alleged fugitive would be tried by federally appointed commissioners rather than in state courts and could be remanded south upon hearsay testimony and without benefit of a jury trial. As in the territorial portion of Clay's program, a small concession toward the antislavery divorce sought by Free-Soilers would be accompanied by a greater affirmation of principles that honored the Calhounite ideal of protection. Slave trade abolition in the capital, said Garrison, was nothing more than "a tub to the Northern whale."

The editor had always considered the wily Clay to be a dangerous opponent, and in the "adjustment" measures the seventy-three-year-old campaigner had struck his most clever and powerful blow yet against abolitionism. He stated quite openly his intention to deprive antislavery agitators of their occupation and welcomed their condemnation of the compromise as proof of its merits. Just as the abolitionists had begun to make their influence felt in Northern politics, Clay worked hard to push them to the margins once again, not only with the familiar epithet of fanaticism, but with the somewhat contradictory charge that their case was trivial. Northerners would have to sacrifice no principle, he said, for their controversy was on "matters of feeling merely," whereas the South's concerns went to the basis of its culture. "In the one scale, then, we behold sentiment, sentiment,

sentiment alone," he said, and "in the other, property, the social fabric, life, and all that makes life desirable and happy."

The Kentuckian had audaciously assumed the high ground of national patriotism, and by refusing to identify himself as a Southern partisan, he also opened himself to criticism from the region's ultraists, which they seemed happy to supply. (The volatile Henry Foote of Mississippi charged on the Senate floor that Clay had done more to abuse the South than the "far-famed Garrison," which allowed Clay to get a huge laugh from the gallery by retorting that he knew no man had received more abuse from the abolitionists than himself because they persisted in sending him copies of their papers.) Garrison suspected, however, that there was an element of sham in the ultraists' attacks upon Clay that was intended to camouflage just how much of their agenda the adjustment measures satisfied. Indeed, as Clay attracted praise for his "moral courage" from dough-faced Democratic editors such as James G. Bennett of the *New York Herald,* it seemed to Garrison that Clay had not only defined the legislative parameters of the issue, but found the means for reinvigorating a national coalition that could silence the freshly awakened antislavery public with the shibboleth of union.

It would take eight months of fractious debate and legislative dexterity before Clay's plan won congressional approval and, as the Compromise of 1850, received praise from relieved politicians as the "final settlement" of the slavery controversy. No one could remember a more anxious legislative session in which the entire nation—aided by the extraordinary new phenomenon of telegraphic news reports—had followed events in the capital with such undeviating attention. It was a season of inspired oratory from the oleaginous Clay, the dying Calhoun, the opportunistic Webster, and a host of rising new voices; a season of high drama as the demonic South Carolinian, only weeks from the grave and too ill to speak, glared in silence at the hushed chamber while a colleague read his last, grim, doom-laden review of the fractures in church and state caused by the abolitionists, and for which he believed no remedy short of constitutional amendments to perpetuate Southern power would suffice; a season of mourning, as President Taylor, struggling to regain his leadership, spoke for hours in the July Fourth sun, then downed so much ice water and cherries that he developed a stomach complaint and died within days; and a season of manipulation as the vice-president, New York's Millard Fillmore—"as pliant a piece of dough as was ever handled," said Garrison—threw his new administration's support to the compromise. The president collaborated with a rising northwestern Democrat, Stephen A. Douglas of Illinois, to pass the measures piecemeal by narrow margins after Clay's "omnibus" effort to make the California proposal draw the entire train derailed midway and threatened to deprive the old magician of his triumph.

From the outset Garrison had condemned the compromise as a surrender to injustice, but he gave thorough coverage to the debates, promptly printed the complete texts of the major speeches, and published several searching critiques of the proposals by Henry Ward Beecher and William Jay that decried the "two-headed, two-hearted" Constitution the compromisers sought to preserve at the expense of "public humanity." Clay's measures, however, presented Garrison with a major tactical challenge, for the sudden blaze of Southern secessionist talk made it difficult to press disunionism without further reinforcing Clay's position as a moderate. The editor needed to find a point of leverage that would convert the Kentuckian's pageant of patriotic nationalism into a drama of morality and conscience, and he brought considerable ingenuity to the task.

Garrison refused to engage the issue on legislative particulars, but sought to enlarge the moral framework of discussion. "What a travesty on the mathematics of justice to announce excitedly that two and two make six, to argue a bit about it, and then to shake hands on the number five!" he scoffed. Scorning "the compromising spirit and the compromising Constitution," he urged opposition not only as an act of individual duty, but as a mission to secure free expression against the intimidation of the national parties and religious denominations. He took the growing number of Democratic-organized pro-Union meetings—filled as they were with racist and anti-abolitionist vituperation—as a harbinger of 1835-style "mobocracy," and he warned that the compromise propositions contained implicit corollaries that would stifle further discussion. "Remember," he told his audiences, "we do not want the right to talk tonight only, but tomorrow also, in accordance with our convictions." Free-Soilers like Sumner echoed the argument, seeing in the compromise the wave of reaction that had overswept Europe now lapping at the American shore.

The editor restated his goal as "nothing less than a Reformation in the Religion and a Revolution in the Government of the country," and he worked up an important philosophical lecture on the process by which "old tests . . . vital in one age, become powerless in another" and necessitate a recognition of new truths in religion and politics. He charged that Christianity had lost its savor as "a test of character" and become merely "a fashionable appendage," while the Constitution had calcified into an idol not unlike the Golden Calf of the Israelites or the Juggernaut of the Hindus. To startle his audiences further, Garrison would intone, with grandiloquent fervor, the lines of Henry Wadsworth Longfellow's popular apostrophe to the Union—"Thou, too, sail on, O ship of State!/ Sail on, O Union, strong and great!/ Humanity with all its fears,/With all the hopes of future years,/Is hanging breathless on thy fate." As the audience, roused by the sentiments but puzzled by the editor's apparent endorsement, waited expectantly, Garrison would then charge that Longfellow had prostituted his gifts to perpetuate an image both historically and morally untrue; he would counter the figure with a description from Milton's "Lycidas" of "a perfidious bark,/Built i' th' eclipse, and rigged with curses dark," leaking from all its timbers, navigated by slaveholding pirates, and destined to sink, said Garrison, "to the joy and exultation of all who are yearning for the deliverance of a groaning world."

The issue, he insisted, was the manner in which the covenant with slavery tainted the Union and corrupted the very idea of liberty. "I am for union!" Garrison told abolitionist conventions to great effect, but "I am not for SLAVERY and UNION. . . . this is the issue we make before the country and the world." Though he posed it more starkly than anyone else, it was not Garrison's question that offended—Clay and Calhoun had put the same choice before Congress—it was his answer. Unlike conventional politicians and editors who insisted that slavery had to be accommodated, either out of justice or expediency, Garrison had pronounced the terms too severe and reached a moral judgment that he believed many Northerners shared but could not bring themselves to execute. To the degree that the abolitionists convinced people to regard the controversy not as a struggle over the status of new states but, in Theodore Parker's phrase, as "a great contest between the Idea of Freedom and the Idea of Slavery," they turned the debate from its cryptic preoccupation with technicalities into a more searching inquiry about civic morality.

Previously unsympathetic editors began to honor Garrison for his "plain-speaking" and to acknowledge the force of principled argument in politics. The *Tribune*'s Washington correspondent took exception to David Wilmot's claim that he had never discussed slavery as a moral question, noting that the Democrat had done so without realizing it, for the "moral assaults" of Garrison had opened the issue for discussion. Indeed, when Garrison finally found the key to dramatizing the spiritual poverty of the compromise, it turned out to be the spectacle of a politician slow to realize that the abolitionists had made moral judgment a political issue.

The device Garrison needed was fashioned for him by none other than Daniel Webster and handed over on the floor of the U.S. Senate. On March 7, 1850, the avatar of liberty made a three-hour address that he thought would crown his career and proved instead his political downfall. It was not so much that Webster endorsed the compromise, but that he truckled shamelessly to the South in so doing. With Olympian detachment he declared that slavery was a matter upon which conscientious and religious people had held differing opinions for centuries, and he blamed the unfortunate schisms in the major churches upon "absolutists" who "deal with morals as with mathematics" and think that "what is right may be distinguished from what is wrong with the precision of an algebraic equation." He condemned the abolitionists for having tightened the fetters of the slaves by roiling the political waters of the South, and he invited the South to seek federal support for underwriting a colonization scheme, observing that the abolition societies—in their "strange enthusiasm"—had spent enough money on their mischievous pursuits to have purchased all the slaves in Maryland and colonized them in Liberia. He reassured Southerners that, as a matter of conscience and morals, the North had an obligation to respect their constitutional right to recapture their runaway property and that he would support "to the fullest extent" the impending rigorous fugitive slave bill. He also argued that there was no need to "wound feelings unnecessarily" in the South with government action to exclude slavery from the territories because the laws of climate and geography had already barred it from the intermountain and Pacific regions the Free-Soilers sought to interdict. He endeavored to salve Southern irritation at the loss of California with a long exegesis on the Texas question, reaffirming that the congressional authorization of additional slave states stood as a "solemn understanding" that any so created would be guaranteed admission despite the growing sectional imbalance in Congress. Webster's only hard words for the South came in his rebuke of peaceable secession as a natural and political impossibility and his portrayal of the convulsions that would ensue if slaveholders abandoned the Union. His peroration, however, with its reiteration of the "liberty and union" appeal that had animated his memorable reply to Hayne twenty years before, contained a figure of speech that unwittingly resonated with an image of bondage: "Let us make our generation one of the strongest and brightest links in that golden chain which is destined, I fondly believe, to grapple the people of all the States to this Constitution for ages to come."

The Seventh of March speech achieved instant infamy among abolitionists and Free-Soilers. Webster had "bent his supple knees anew to the Slave Power," Garrison charged, and he immediately got up a petition campaign to have the state legislature censure the senator, whose "degrading" betrayal of liberty ranked him with Benedict Arnold. Adjacent to Webster's text, *The Liberator* published an eight-column analysis, deftly executed by Wendell Phillips on very short notice, that dealt with the technical issues but built its fundamental case upon the senator's moral indifference. "It would puzzle a jury of Philadelphia lawyers to tell, had nature given him a heart, to which side it would have leaned" in the contest between liberty and despotism, said Phillips, though in the ensuing weeks all New England and the Old Northwest had no trouble delineating Webster's "apostasy."

Nearly every Whig newspaper outside Boston so vehemently denounced the speech that Webster's foremost backers among the cotton and financial oligarchy felt obliged to issue a hurried letter of support; "so many sheep following their bell-wether," scoffed Garrison, though perhaps the reverse was truer, and the editor pounced with italicized delight when a collateral letter from Newburyport included the name of Francis Todd, the quondam slave carrier whose libel suit had, in a manner of speaking, launched Garrison's career. John G. Whittier's "Ichabod" lamented Webster's fall from glory with lines that embedded themselves in a generation's memory: "from those great eyes/ The soul has fled;/ When faith is lost, when honor dies,/ The man is dead." Equally indignant, the free-soil editor and aspiring poet Walt Whitman, with no paper of his own, published a volley of poems in the *New York Tribune*—reprinted by Garrison—that compared Webster to Judas, depicted freedom as "wounded in the house of its friends," and urged the "young North" to rise and repudiate the cowardly acts of its elders.

Webster had never enjoyed an unblemished reputation. He had always seemed to mix high statesmanship with unseemly avarice on behalf of corporate clients, but now people said that his ambition for the presidency had completely dulled his moral sensibility, deafened his ear to the changing tone of public opinion, and exaggerated the power of the sordid partnership between loom and lash to propel him into office. "The word *liberty* in the mouth of Mr. Webster sounds like the word *love* in the mouth of a courtezan," wrote Emerson in a widely echoed judgment. That Webster could endorse the new fugitive slave bill for the greater good of "liberty and Union" especially offended because it boded direct engagement in support of "kidnappers" in their midst rather than passive tolerance of a distant evil, and Garrison rang the changes on this theme at every opportunity. Webster's fundamental premise that humanity and policy could be silent because nature had spoken galled the abolitionists, and they countered it with much evidence about the slaveholders' efforts to establish a foothold in California. In Congress, only a few weeks before Webster's speech, Mississippi's Jefferson Davis had lauded the possibilities for irrigated cotton farming in the Central Valley, and this, when coupled with some ambiguous language in Clay's bill, hinted that a move might yet be made to detach the portion of California south of 36°30' from the projected state. Slaves could dig gold as well as cotton, Mary Grew pointed out in the *Pennsylvania Freeman,* and even Free-Soilers recognized that the discovery of a few flakes of silver in New Mexico or coal in Utah would utterly transform the situation in those territories. No one could permit "the fate of an entire race" to rest upon Webster's imperfect understanding of geography or his failure to comprehend slavery as a caste system that was not coterminous with the climate for cotton. Calhoun, too, pounced on the flaw in Webster's reasoning, exclaiming with virtually his dying breath that the South would happily leave the matter to nature—all it asked was scope and time and the removal of political impediments.

For six weeks Garrison filled *The Liberator* with commentary on Webster's speech from the political and religious press, and he could have published twice the amount had he had the room. With his propagandist's skill the editor instantly replaced Calhoun, who died on March 31, with Webster as the abolitionists' antihero. In Garrison's entire journalistic career, he said, no speech had "so powerfully shocked the moral sense, or so grievously insulted the intelligence of the people," and by devoting so much attention to it, he made Webster personify the moral deficiency of the compromise and the dough-faced complicity required for its success.

Forging the apostate Webster into a symbol of disreputable surrender stamped only one side of the coin; on the other, Garrison etched the counterimage of abolitionists as conscience-bound dissenters willing to suffer in the cause. In this effort, too, the defenders of compromise presented him an opportunity he could not fail to exploit. For several weeks before the annual American Anti-Slavery Society national meeting in New York City, the Democratic penny press, led by the incorrigible James Gordon Bennett of the *Herald,* had berated the abolitionists for jeopardizing the Union and urged the city's commercial leaders "to frown down the meetings of these mad people" if they would save their city's prosperity and reputation. The vituperation had steadily increased until, on the eve of the meetings, the papers were wildly denouncing the AAS president as a "mixed race Robes-Pierre," calling upon defenders of the Union to "enter the arena of discussion and send out the true opinion of the public," and denying that such "dangerous . . . treasonable assemblies" had any right to exist. To Garrison such talk harked directly back to the Boston mob of 1835, and he went to New York fully prepared to face disruption.

He was not disappointed. Tight knots of rowdy b'hoys pushed their way into the Broadway Tabernacle on May 7, 1850, and in the midst of Garrison's long disquisition on the inadequacy of institutional religion, they started to pepper him with questions. The editor patiently promised to answer them and resumed his discourse. When he declared that a belief in Jesus had become worthless as a test of goodness since His praises were sung in the South and a Christ-professing slaveholder sat in the White House, a pint-sized Tammany Hall captain named Isaiah Rynders dashed from his place, shouting and waving his arms, protesting the speaker's insult to President Taylor. Soon a clutch of ruffians had joined Rynders, who had won fame the previous year for a riotous demonstration in Astor Place that hounded the English actor William Macready from the city, and the boisterous crowd profanely demanded time for a rebuttal.

Unruffled, Garrison soon restored order by promising Rynders that he would make a place for him on the agenda. The politico accepted and stood menacingly with his band at the foot of the speaker's platform, but when the time arrived, Rynders ceded his place to a seedy-looking man billed as "Professor Grant," who launched into a racist harangue on the kinship between black people and monkeys. This was calculated by Rynders to enflame the audience into disrupting its own meeting, but the abolitionists put up a united cry for Frederick Douglass, and the cocky Rynders indicated that the ex-slave might speak after the dubious Grant.

Douglass sent the audience into thunderous applause by offering himself as refutation of the previous argument.

"Am I a man?" he asked, to a roar of approval.

"*You* are not a black man; you are only half a nigger," sneered Rynders when the din subsided.

"Then," replied Douglass blandly, "I am half-brother to you," and sent the Rynders crowd into furious expostulations that proved unavailing against Douglass's gift for repartee. The meeting "wound up with electrical effect," Garrison said, when the Rev. Samuel R. Ward—bigger, blacker, and even more eloquent—followed Douglass at the rostrum with such a triumphant vindication of civil equality that Garrison gaveled the session to conclusion in the gleeful belief that the abolitionists had bested their opponents on the honest battleground of free discussion. He boldly invited Rynders to return the next day.

Wednesday's session, however, found Rynders and his friends hell-bent on disruption and unwilling to go through the charade of debate. They shouted down Charles C. Burleigh, whose flowing locks and long red beard proved an irresistible target for the chants of "Go pay your barber's bill" and "Buy a wig for Garrison." They cursed and swore at Wendell Phillips, yelling "Traitor! Traitor!" while Rynders capered about, jerking his arms in an exaggerated patriotic salute. They sang "Old Garrison! Old Garrison! Are you Jesus?" during the chair's efforts to restore order, and when Garrison asked aloud if the chief of police was present, Rynders grew bug-eyed in mock fear and cried, "Oh, don't don't! You'll frighten us all to death."

The denouement was predictable. The police refused to intervene on the grounds that Rynders had an invitation to the meeting and that no violence had occurred, while the managers of the hall, fearing that violence would occur in the absence of the police, revoked their permission for the meeting and summoned the sheriff to shut it down. "Thus closed anti-slavery free discussion in New York for 1850," the *Tribune* reported sourly, while Garrison drew once more the familiar analogy between the early Christian apostles and the abolitionist martyrs who endured the scorn of modern-day Pharisees and the abuse of the rabble.

Only something as sensational as the Rynders mob could have driven Daniel Webster from *The Liberator's* pages, and Garrison had no trouble filling his columns with defenses of free speech that came flooding in from across the North. Newspapers from Philadelphia to Chicago took note of the ruckus and defended the abolitionists' right to assemble and speak in peace. Bennett's paper, however, described the affair under the heading "Garrison's Nigger Minstrels." For the most part, Garrison won praise in many quarters for his cool adherence to principle under fire, and John G. Whittier broke the decade of silence between the old friends to thank the editor for his "perseverance and firmness in vindicating rights dear to us all." In 1835 the newspapers had blamed Garrison for the mob that had nearly lynched him; in 1850 it seemed that the effusions of a racist mob had legitimized the abolitionists' claim to civil liberty.

When Clay's proposals came to a vote in late summer, the outcome demonstrated that the so-called compromise, far from being a meeting of the minds, had actually stiffened sectional antagonism. Regional identity counted for more than party loyalty in the tally, with only four senators and barely thirteen percent of the House (drawn largely from northwestern Democrats) voting for all the measures, which passed largely because unanimous Northern majorities supported the California and D.C. bills, while preponderant Southern votes pushed through the territorial and Texas bills. Given the lopsided sectional nature of the voting, the bloc of ten Free-Soil representatives had no pivotal influence upon the outcome. The Fugitive Slave Act, favored unanimously by the South, did not receive an absolute majority in either chamber and owed its passage to a significant number of Northern abstentions, including that of the Democratic leader, Senator Stephen Douglas himself. Though the legislative participants knew better than anyone else that they had gained no more than a truce, they celebrated with cannon salutes and serenades as if a war had ended. Douglas happily declared that he would never have to make another speech about slavery, for the question had been settled with such "finality" that the abolitionists would soon be "reduced to despair."

President Fillmore promptly signed each measure as it cleared Congress. "God knows that I detest slavery," he told Daniel Webster, "but it is an existing evil, for which we are not responsible, and we must endure it, and give it such protection as is guaranteed by the Constitution, till we can get rid of it without destroying the last best hope of free government in the world." His pledge to enforce the Fugitive Slave Law promptly and completely moved the conflict out of Congress and into the country before the ink had dried on the page. Huge "Union" meetings, organized by the commercial leaders in each party, took place in New York, Philadelphia, Boston, and even New Orleans, at which thousands pledged their support for an end to agitation. "To win the mighty good of the Constitution," said the respected Boston attorney Rufus Choate, it was not too much "to surrender the privilege of reviling the masters of slaves." In the Southern states, where secessionist talk had grown heated, the fall elections became a referendum on the compromise. Except for thirteen border state representatives who had backed at least four of the measures and voted against none, Southerners in Congress had not supported the breadth of Clay's settlement, but their constituents grudgingly accepted the result. Candidates pledged to a "conditional" acceptance of the measures won their races against those who advocated secessionist defiance. Yet the contingencies, as outlined by a Georgia convention, that would prompt repudiation included so many anticipated threats—Northern hostility that led to modification or repeal of the new Fugitive Slave Law, abolition of slavery in the federal district, a ban on slavery in New Mexico or Utah, the refusal to admit a new state or territory that had chosen to permit slavery—that it seemed plain that the fundamental requirement for Southern acquiescence had become an end to agitation by the abolitionists.

The calendar provided almost immediate evidence that such was impossible. The first day of 1851 marked the twentieth anniversary of the founding of *The Liberator,* and Garrison had no intention of either shutting down or shutting up. Indeed, three weeks later, on January 24, 1851, 350 people crammed into a banquet hall in downtown Boston for a "soirée" to honor the newspaper and its editor. James Russell Lowell had written a poem that described the journal's obscure origins: "In a small chamber, friendless and unseen,/ Toiled o'er his types one poor, unlearned young man;/ The place was dark, unfurnitured and mean,/ Yet there the freedom of a race began." The poem went on to compare Garrison's efforts to the solitary persistence of a Luther and a Columbus in possession of a new truth, and it enhanced the editor's reputation as the valiant pioneer whose conscientious stand had inspired a generation.

Garrison was nearly overcome at the outpouring of affection. He masked his feeling by philosophizing about the pendulum in all reform efforts that swings from "outrageous abuse" of the initiators to "excessive panegyric" as the cause "nears the goal" and arguing that, in his case at least, both were unmerited, for he had "simply stood up to discharge a duty. . . ." Then he tried to turn aside the adulation with humor. Presented with a gold watch, the editor joked that if it were a rotten egg, he would know better how to receive it, but graciously said that he wished he had a similar token for everyone in the room, for they had made the struggle possible. Finally, however, he sat back and relished the tributes, which took up nearly three pages of his next week's issue. He heard Wendell Phillips pronounce *The Liberator* a true Declaration of Independence, he heard Theodore Parker predict that when the slaves were free there would not be gold in California fine enough to write Garrison's name, and he heard his old British friend George Thompson, newly arrived for another lecture tour, ask the audience to render its verdict on Garrison's celebrated pledge. Had the editor been earnest? Had he equivocated, had he excused, or had he retreated a single inch? Thompson asked to increasingly thunderous cheers and the stamping of feet. When he came to the final clause in the creed, however, Thompson answered his own question. "Garrison has been heard from the coast of Maine to the mountains of California . . . and on both sides of the Atlantic," he said, and in the tumult of controversy, his voice had risen above the strife "demanding, in thunder tones, the freedom of the slave."

For weeks before the banquet, in speeches on the Fugitive Slave Law, Garrison had reminded his audiences of the Biblical story of Daniel, who had defied the unjust law of the Persians yet, secure in his faith, passed the night unharmed in the lion's den. The weak could confound the mighty, he insisted, and two weeks after the banquet, when a fugitive slave named Shadrach awaited judgment in a Boston courtroom, Garrison's maxim and his faith would, once more, move the controversy into another defiant and explosive phase.

CHAPTER NINETEEN

FUGITIVE SLAVE LAW: DENOUNCED, RESISTED, DISOBEYED

IF DANIEL WEBSTER PERSONIFIED THE SPIRIT OF COMPROMISE, THEN WILLIAM LLOYD GARRISON MADE SURE THAT THE FUGITIVE SLAVE DEFINED THE OPPOSITION. EACH WEEK'S *LIBERATOR* BROUGHT A FRESH headline about the enforcement of the new law. The first, from New York City in mid-September 1850, resulted in the return of a man named James Hamlet to Maryland as a slave; the next two, in Harrisburg and Bedford, Pennsylvania, returned ten more alleged fugitives to Southern claimants, and by the end of the year, the total had increased to nineteen, with only two dismissals. The beleaguered black communities, roiling with long-settled runaways suddenly rendered vulnerable to summary proceedings, immediately formed new vigilance committees, while hundreds of fugitives scrambled to conceal their whereabouts and flee to Canada. Strong new voices in the abolitionist ministry—Henry Ward Beecher in Brooklyn, Thomas Wentworth Higginson in Worcester, W. H. Furness in Philadelphia—joined Boston's Theodore Parker and Syracuse's Samuel J. May in declaring conscientious opposition to the law; if such a law was essential to the republic, May declared, then "let it be broken up, and some new form of government arise in its stead." Huge rallies against the law took place from the eastern seaboard to the Great Lakes. An August protest meeting in the little town of Cazenovia, New York, drew two thousand people and had to be moved from a local church to a sympathizer's orchard. In Chicago the city council resolved not to cooperate with federal marshals, and in New York City—where the police had allowed Rynders and his ilk free rein—the mayor declared that his officers would not assist in the capture and transport of fugitives. Thousands packed Faneuil Hall for an indignation meeting presided over by the venerable Josiah Quincy and addressed by Frederick Douglass, the nation's most celebrated fugitive, summoned by telegraph from Rochester, as he put it, "to appeal . . . in behalf of a suffering and terrified population." And an angry one, he made clear, for he hotly predicted that blood would flow in the streets before black people would suffer the return of anyone to slavery. The Massachusetts Anti-Slavery Society declared itself opposed to any compromise between right and wrong and considered it imperative that the law be "denounced, resisted, disobeyed . . . [and] its enforcement on Massachusetts soil . . . rendered impossible." Never had the nation been so "convulsed" on the subject of slavery, exulted Garrison, his columns so stuffed with news, resolutions, sermons, and editorials that he was certain not even a daily paper could have kept pace with the commotion.

It was clear to all parties that the 1850 Fugitive Slave Law was not so much a remedy for the South's chronic runaway problem as it was a deliberate condemnation of the abolitionist agitation that had unsettled traditional politics, and its strict enforcement became so passionately contested because, at the very moment that the antislavery tide had turned in Northern public opinion, the South demanded new pledges of fidelity to the old habits of compromise. The controversy over the law thus sharpened the ideological argument Garrison had long waged against the Constitution, underscored the contradictions of the Union, and fostered a period of proto-revolutionary thinking that pointed toward a violent resolution of the national dilemma.

As the measure's text, which Garrison printed in his "Refuge of Oppression" column, made plain, the new law articulated a clear congressional preference for harsh and summary enforcement over the protection of civil liberties. The owner, or his agent, could reclaim a fugitive either by securing a warrant beforehand or arresting the alleged runaway on the spot. The case for removal could be heard either by a federal judge or a court-appointed federal commissioner, who would be paid ten dollars if a certificate of removal was issued, but only five dollars if the claim was denied. Testimony from the fugitive was prohibited, no jury could be called, the commissioner's verdict could not be appealed, and other courts or magistrates were barred from issuing habeas corpus writs or other legal mandates that might postpone or override an order to remand the defendant into slavery. If the claimant persuaded the commissioner that an attempt to liberate or "rescue" the fugitive might occur during the return, moreover, the commissioner was authorized to appoint special deputies, call out a citizen's posse, and allow the arresting officer to hire additional help at federal expense. These provisions called forth denunciation of the law as a "kidnapping" machine, while the stiff penalties—up to six months in jail and a $1,000 fine—mandated for anyone aiding a fugitive or interfering with a return emphasized that the law also sought to suppress dissent and allow the courts wide latitude for harassing the opposition.

Boston seethed for months. The city's streets and squares filled with determined sentinels on the lookout for "slave-hunters"; its elegant homes and back-alley tenements forged a network for concealing, assisting, and relocating fugitives; its law offices busily studied the devices of obstruction and repeal; and its conservative mercantile elite became infuriated at hearing its support for the Union-saving compromise compared to the royalism of the city's Tory government in the Revolutionary crisis of the 1770s. Between October 1850 and April 1851, the city experienced three major confrontations that polarized public opinion and gave Garrisonians their most dramatic forum yet to protest complicity with slavery. Their activities, this time, looked to direct action as well as denunciation.

When two Georgians arrived in the city late in October 1850 with warrants to arrest the popular fugitive lecturers Ellen and William Craft, the vigilance committee hid the Crafts while abolitionist crowds dogged the hunters at every step. They blocked the way to Craft's cabinet shop, milled in the lobby and halls of the Georgians' hotel, set up a ruckus every time the "kidnappers" tried to meet with the local constabulary, and sought to have them arrested instead. A prominent Whig sent word to the Crafts that if they would submit to a peaceable arrest, guarantors would repurchase and free them immediately. The Crafts rejected the offer, saying that they represented hundreds of other fugitives and would not jeopardize their freedom by legitimizing the law's operation. After a fruitless week of maneuvering, with the city in an uproar, the agents gave up their quest as impossible, but taking no chances, the vigilance committee dispatched the Crafts on a speaking tour of Great Britain. Not since the Latimer case seven years before had the abolitionists so mobilized the city in defense of black freedom. The Rev. Theodore Parker, who had married the heroic couple in the formal ceremony denied them in bondage, dared President Fillmore to indict him for aiding his parishioners in defiance of the law.

Fillmore did not rise to the bait, but several months later, a more spectacular act of resistance drew a prompt and energetic presidential response. In February 1851, a waiter in a Cornhill coffeehouse named Frederick Jenkins was suddenly arrested and, still wearing his apron, rushed to court, where he was charged with being an escaped slave known as Shadrach to his Virginia master, whose high-priced Boston attorney now sought a certificate for his return. The vigilance committee hurried several attorneys, including Garrison's old friends Ellis Loring and Samuel Sewall, to the courtroom, while word spread through the streets that another judicial kidnapping was in progress. By the time an anxious crowd arrived at the building, the commissioner had granted the defense a postponement, the hearing room was nearly empty, and the marshal was preoccupied with turning away several newspaper reporters. It proved absurdly easy for a gang of black men to stream through the doors, shout "hurrah" to the startled prisoner, and quick-march out again with the liberated Shadrach safely in their midst. "Plucked as a brand from the burning," Garrison said later, evoking the trial of the fugitive's Biblical namesake in the fiery furnace. "Nobody injured, nobody wronged, but simply a chattel transformed into a man by unarmed friends of equal liberty."

The "rescue" of Shadrach, soon resettled in Montreal, severely embarrassed the Boston defenders of the "peace" measures and antagonized the administration. Daniel Webster, now secretary of state, heard the commissioner and the commercial press decry the action as "levying war," and he promptly pronounced the rescue as "strictly speaking, a case of treason." President Fillmore issued a wrathful proclamation—in the traditional phraseology of the riot acts—authorizing federal troops to quell dangerous "combinations" and ordering prosecution of those who aided so "flagitious" an offense. In the Senate, Henry Clay sought a congressional investigation and stiffer penalties for obstructing a fugitive's return. The outrage had been committed by "a band not of our people," said Clay, and therefore it raised the urgent question of whether "the government of white men is to be yielded to a government of blacks." (Clay did not know that Lewis Hayden, the black clothing dealer who had led the Shadrach rescue, had himself fled Kentucky bondage in 1844 with his wife and child and was in fact the son-in-law of one of the senator's own slaves.)

Clay's vicious remarks "threw off the mask," in Garrison's candid phrase; with one foot in the grave, the Kentuckian had made "his damnation doubly sure" by revealing the racist underpinnings of the compromise. Boston's Benjamin R. Curtis, an eminent member of the bar and likely nominee for a vacancy on the U.S. Supreme Court, followed Clay's lead by comparing the return of fugitive slaves to the extradition of criminals and insisted that the law appropriately regarded runaways as foreigners without legal standing in Massachusetts. Whatever the natural rights of black people might be, Curtis told a Unionist rally in Faneuil Hall, he did not consider Massachusetts the place to vindicate them. "This is *our* soil, sacred to *our* peace, on which we intend to perform *our* promises, and work out for the benefit of ourselves . . . the destiny which our creator has assigned to *us,*" he said. Ever since the fight against colonization in the early 1830s, Garrison had insisted that the abolition of slavery had to be accompanied by the inclusion of African-Americans in the political community. The callousness with which the Fugitive Slave Law disregarded the rights of black citizens in the North and blurred the distinctions between slave and free, chattel and criminal, revealed both the acuity of his insight and the limits of the abolitionists' achievement. Just as the rise of Free-Soilism exposed the white racism that might coexist with antislavery feelings, so did the defense of the "adjustment" measures reveal the prejudice that lay at the heart of the constitutional compromises. That the mobilization against the law produced an unprecedented degree of interracial cooperation as black and white abolitionists organized vigilance committees, sheltered fugitives, and engaged in public acts of defiance stood, by contrast, as a living demonstration of the radical definition of liberty for which the Garrisonians had long contended.

It also produced, especially in Boston, a close identification with the Revolutionary spirit of '76, with its traditions of a patriotic underground organization and a militant public opinion, that proved both inspiring and problematic. Theodore Parker termed the Shadrach rescue "the most noble deed done in Boston since the destruction of the tea," and in its aftermath Wendell Phillips thought that the Bostonians were experiencing the flavor of the liberal insurgencies of 1848, as well as the city's hallowed defiance of Lord North's edicts and King George III's redcoats. People everywhere used the old phrase "Liberty or Death" with a new ferocity, and Parker had publicly stated that the fugitive had the same natural right to defend himself against the slave-catcher that he had against a murderer or a wolf. Indeed, it was well known that the outspoken Lewis Hayden had barricaded and armed his house, long a major refuge for runaways, and threatened to blow it up if federal troops besieged it. The turn toward arms alarmed Garrison, who told a mass meeting that while each person had to be true to his own principles, as a nonresistant he hoped that the fugitive would be "more indebted to the moral power of public sentiment than to any display of physical resistance." His friends, hoping to distance the editor from some of the more militant activities, kept his name off the vigilance committee roster, yet Garrison could not help but feel an increasing tension between his conscientious opposition to force and the appeal of the revolutionary examples—from William Tell to George Washington and Toussaint L'Ouverture—that he repeatedly said the nation could not claim for itself and deny to those it enslaved.

The Shadrach rescue and the repressive threats it provoked gave the abolitionists a sense of triumph, but they knew that it would be short-lived. Boston remained filled with Southern agents; "All they want is *one from Boston,*" said Phillips, "to show the discontented ones at home that *it can be done. . . .*" The administration, too, felt pressured to put down the agitation in Boston in order to redeem its pledge of "finality." Eight men—four black, including Lewis Hayden, and four white, including Elizur Wright, now the editor of a Free-Soil newspaper—were indicted for abetting the Shadrach affair, but divided juries failed to convict anyone. While the trials wore on, however, yet another fugitive case gave the Fillmore administration an opportunity to make an example of Boston, although the measures it employed corroborated the abolitionists' charge that the law travestied the very liberty for which the Union stood.

Thomas Sims, a runaway bricklayer from Savannah, was arrested by city policemen on a trumped-up charge of disturbing the peace, but once in the courthouse, he was turned over to federal marshals for a hearing before the fugitive slave commissioner. Because the Latimer law forbade the use of state or county jails for detaining alleged fugitives, the officers confined Sims under close guard in the federal courtroom overnight, but they connived to transform the entire building into a federal prison. When crowds of abolitionists arrived at Court Square in the dawn light of April 4, 1851, they were flabbergasted to discover the courthouse itself girded with iron chains, its doorways fettered with ropes, and the entire city police force—reinforced by special deputies recruited among waterfront hooligans—ringing the building and patrolling the vicinity. The public was barred from entry, and even the attorneys and judges allowed to cross the threshold had to crouch quite low to get beneath the barrier. The spectacle of the state's aged chief justice—proud, stiff-necked Lemuel Shaw, who had refused to rule for Latimer and would shortly rule against Sims—stooping under heavy chains to enter the halls of justice appalled the abolitionists. Garrison termed it "one of the most disgraceful scenes ever witnessed in this city," for it made inescapably vivid how completely the legal system upheld the interests of slaveholders. Even Henry Wadsworth Longfellow, the poet laureate of Union and no friend to agitation, winced at the "degradation" imposed on Shaw and mourned, "Alas for the people who cannot feel an insult."

For an entire week the volunteer attorneys for Sims tried every conceivable device to interrupt the proceedings against the slender, frail mulatto, who looked younger than his twenty-three years and whose unwise but plaintive letter to his freeborn wife had tipped the authorities to his whereabouts. The lawyers filed several habeas corpus motions with Chief Justice Shaw, who refused to intervene, citing both a lack of jurisdiction based on the *Prigg* decision and his predisposition that the Fugitive Slave Law served the constitutional purpose of maintaining comity between the states. While the attorneys maneuvered, the abolitionists rallied, holding daily vigils at the courthouse and an open-air meeting on the Common, at which Wendell Phillips allowed that it would be a disgrace if Sims was deported without crowds blocking the streets and halting the machinery of an oppressive government. The impetuous young minister Thomas Wentworth Higginson talked with a few kindred spirits about a physical assault on the courthouse or hiring a privateer to intercept any Savannah-bound vessels, but nothing tangible materialized from such desperate fantasies. On Friday afternoon, April 11, 1851, the certificate of removal was issued, and before daylight the next morning a company of three-hundred policemen, armed with U.S. military sabers, formed a hollow square and slowly marched the weeping Sims down State Street to the Long Wharf and the ship hired to return him to bondage.

The *Boston Courier* spoke for the "cotton press" in lauding the city's "sound attachment" to the Union, while the *Mail* sank to minstrel-show vulgarity with what Garrison called the "depraved" fiction that Sims had sung "Carry Me Back to Old Virginny" as the boat's pilot beat a Jim Crow dance tune with castanets. Whittier countered with a lament, "Moloch in State Street," and the city's eldest statesman, Josiah Quincy, mourned that Boston had lost its moral sense and become "a mere shop." With his unwavering hope, Garrison predicted that the return of Sims would agitate the public and prove "a disastrous triumph" for the slave power. One week later, on the seventy-sixth anniversary of the British attack on Lexington and Concord, Massachusetts learned that the United States government had successfully returned Thomas Sims to Savannah, where he was given thirty-nine lashes in the public square. "Let the Heavens weep and Hell be merry!" wrote Frederick Douglass. "Daniel Webster has at last obtained from Boston . . . a living sacrifice to appease the slave god of the American Union."

It would be three years before Boston underwent another fugitive slave crisis, but in the interval more than one hundred prosecutions took place elsewhere and ninety-eight fugitives were remanded to their masters, with the government paying to complete the transfer without disruption in one out of every five cases. Commissioners ruled in favor of fugitives only twice, while one escaped and seven were "rescued" by opponents of the law. As in the Shadrach case, these were for the most part surprise rushes; Garrison's old friend Samuel J. May participated in a celebrated incident at Syracuse when an unarmed crowd charged the jail in September 1851 and spirited off a popular mulatto cooper named Jerry McHenry. The inevitable violence, however, had occurred earlier in the month at Christiana, Pennsylvania, when federal marshals tried to arrest two fugitives who had barricaded themselves in a black family's house. The slaves' owner and three black resisters died in the crossfire, while the fugitives escaped. (As proof of the hardening mood, Garrison needed to look no farther than across the breakfast table. Helen said that she couldn't help but think that the slaveholder had met with "a righteous retribution" and hoped that his demise would deter other masters from coming north and so be "the means of affecting some good.") Several dozen Quakers in the Christiana neighborhood who had refused to assist the marshals were indicted for treason, as were eight men, including May, in Syracuse, but the grave charge could not be sustained and all the proceedings were quashed.

It is likely that convictions could have been obtained for the obstructionist conduct described in the statute, but the administration had the more repressive intent of characterizing any dissent as subversion of the "peace measures" and hence as an assault upon the government itself. The Compromise of 1850 sought to impose a legislated silence upon an irreconcilable conflict, and its defenders stood upon the reactionary ground of preferring the suppression of tension to the creation of justice. The abolitionists' strategy of defiance entailed, therefore, along with direct assistance to fugitives, a concurrent debate upon the principles of civic obligation that dramatized the conflict between the authority of specific edicts and the sanctity of ethical principles. For defenders of the compromise the watchwords were obedience, order, and the necessity of complying with laws enacted by a democratic majority until they might be amended or repealed by the regular process of government. For the antislavery dissenters the watchwords were conscience, freedom, and the moral duty of opposing an oppressive exercise of power in a system so biased that the majority perforce did the bidding of a slaveholding minority. Although it was a debate whose terms had been defined long since in the ancient tragedy of Antigone and pondered by Aristotle and Cicero, both sides approached it in the framework of Christianity,. with the conservatives holding fast to the ethic of Biblical patriarchy and the radicals reiterating the principles of Protestant nonconformity.

Clerical apologists—finding their voice after years of declining to address the slavery issue—now insisted upon the spiritual necessity to return fugitives. Citing the familiar obligation to "render unto Caesar the things that are Caesar," a Presbyterian minister in Buffalo, President Fillmore's hometown, insisted in a nationally circulated sermon that "obedience to governments, in the exercise of their legitimate powers, is a religious duty, positively enjoined by God himself." To "interpose a private judgment" by resisting the compromise would invite infidelity, Jacobinism, and anarchy. Such self-indulgent disobedience, Satanic in its willfulness, would mock God and destroy the Union He had so generously blessed.

To the argument rooted in the Biblical injunction that "the powers that be are ordained of God," abolitionists replied with the Pauline injunction to "wrestle against principalities, against powers . . . against spiritual wickedness in high *places*." To the argument that a valid congressional enactment had to be obeyed until repealed by majority will, the New England Anti-Slavery Convention replied that by its "theory of civil disobedience," any argument on an important issue of conscience that bade "one man [to] submit his moral convictions, and square his actions by the votes of a majority, is anti-republican, tyrannical, unchristian and atheistical." The danger confronting the nation was not revolutionary excess, said Theodore Parker, but the despotism that would "enact injustice into law and with the force of the nation make iniquity obeyed." He shocked his audiences with the observation that the only apostle who had obeyed the Pharisees' command to reveal the fugitive Jesus to the marshals of Jerusalem was Judas Iscariot, whose thirty pieces of silver were equivalent to the ten Yankee dollars the Boston commissioner had received for performing his "constitutional obligation" to remand Sims.

In the lexicon of the 1850s, "the higher law" became the shorthand for antislavery opposition to the constitutional guarantees afforded slavery. The phrase had jumped out of a speech made in the Senate a few days after Webster's notorious Seventh of March effort by New York's antislavery Whig leader William E. Seward. He had tried to persuade the South that it had lost its battle to vindicate the justice of slavery and could not expect its constitutional protections to be sustained indefinitely in a climate of opinion influenced by "a higher law than the Constitution"—the universal principles of the Creator and the common heritage of mankind. In one of those strange reversals fostered by mass communications, Seward's philosophical appeal for the South to accept the inevitable and gradually dismantle the slave system on its own terms turned into a slogan that justified Northern opposition to the one compromise measure slaveholders had designated as proof that political morality had not changed.

The religious argument intensified the debate over moral and constitutional obligation that Garrison had all along intended to provoke with his slogan "No Union with Slaveholders." If, in the disjointed atmosphere of crisis and the disintegration of traditional party ties, individuals questioned their relationship to the constitutional system under the rubric of "the higher law" rather than "disunion," he could nonetheless register the examination as a sign of abolitionist progress. It is ironic, and even incredible, however, that the most profound and enduring inquiry stimulated by Garrisonian non-resistance played no direct role in the decade-long controversy over "the higher law." In 1848 the Concord writer Henry David Thoreau lectured at the town lyceum on the topic "The Rights and Duties of the Individual in Relation to Government," in which he expressed the belief that individuals had to live their lives "as a counter friction to stop the machine" of an unjust government. Born of his opposition to slavery and the Mexican War and nurtured by the Garrisonian milieu of his household, Thoreau's lecture was a passionate protest against the moral indifference that allowed such evils to continue and a plea to cultivate not "a respect for the law, so much as for the right." In its pacifism, its abolitionism, its confidence in the revolutionary effect of action from principle, and its whole-souled faith that "any man more right than his neighbors constitutes a majority of one already," the essay proved Garrisonian to the core. Yet Thoreau shifted the ground of the argument from Christian perfectionism to a set of ethical imperatives derived, in Transcendental fashion, from the perception of indwelling ideals. Published the following year, in May 1849, in the sole issue of one of the evanescent Emersonian journals, *Aesthetic Papers*, the essay—now titled "Resistance to Civil Government"—attracted scant attention, though the *Boston Courier* sourly advised the author to preach his views in revolutionary France if he couldn't learn to be "a better subject" here.

Garrison, astonishingly, took no printed notice of Thoreau's work. Its publication came just after Charlie's tragic death, which might account for the editor's inattentiveness to the periodicals on his exchange pile, but in June 1849, Garrison published both an appreciative notice of Thoreau's first book, *A Week on the Concord and Merrimack*, and a long obituary for Thoreau's sister Helen, which means that the writer was certainly within his field of vision. Equally astonishing, Thoreau made no effort to call Garrison's attention to his work, either at the time of publication or in the crisis of 1850–51, when the "higher law" debate intensified and Thoreau caustically followed the Boston fugitive slave cases in his journal. The essay, which was next reprinted in a posthumous collection of 1866 under the now-famous title "Civil Disobedience," has become a landmark document in the dissenting tradition and was a major influence upon the nonviolent protest campaigns of M. K. Gandhi and Dr. Martin Luther King, Jr., with scant awareness of its roots in Garrisonian fanaticism. That no one quoted Thoreau during the controversy over the Fugitive Slave Law does not mean that his iconoclastic ideas, like Garrison's, had not seeped into the discussion by osmosis. Prophets, however little they are honored in their time, are nonetheless connected to it. Garrison and Thoreau stood in the vanguard and spoke aloud what many could see, but were not yet prepared—or confident enough—to say. Under the stark pressure of events, however, thousands of individuals worked their way into a principled opposition that had seemed impossible only a few years earlier. "I cannot for an instant recognize that political organization as *my* government which is the *slave's* government also," Thoreau had written, and by 1851 many who shuddered at "No Union with Slaveholders" nonetheless agreed.

"This last year has forced us all into politics," said Ralph Waldo Emerson, who proved a shrewd judge of trends in the intellectual marketplace and responded favorably to his audiences' insistence that he turn himself at last to antislavery themes. Even some of Garrison's Liberty Party critics, most notably William Goodell, who had insisted for years upon an antislavery reading of the Constitution, now conceded that the editor's disunionism had "raised a serious and intelligible question . . . that comes home to the conscience and interests of every northern citizen" who opposed the Fugitive Slave Law. Goodell made a special trip to the annual MAS meeting in January 1851 to lay the old constitutional argument to rest. "We can all agree here, that whether slavery be in the Constitution or not, IT MUST CEASE; whether by revolution or otherwise. . . ."

No more convincing evidence of Garrison's success in reforming the ethical framework of politics could have appeared than the opposition to the law manifested by the newly founded (1848) Congregationalist journal, *The Independent,* which lost half of its original subscribers and gained twice as many new ones by its militant "higher law" stand. When the journal's senior editor, the old Beecherite Leonard Bacon, objected that his junior colleagues had embraced Garrisonian fanaticism during his absence in Europe, he was politely informed that the time for making fine distinctions and palliations had passed and there could be no overlooking "the great truths" the church held in common with the abolitionists. The radical shift in the mood of his constituency provoked Bacon to reconsider his own views, and in November 1851 he upheld the principle that "the eternal law of right . . . is higher than any constitution." If the law required us to worship idols, we would not obey it, Bacon said in a widely reprinted sermon; if it required us to extradite Hungarian exiles and subject them to reprisals from the Austrian tyrants, we would not do that either. "There is a higher law, and you know it," he said. "It is a rule for political action, and you know it. . . . You must obey it." To hear such words from Leonard Bacon—the epitome of the complaisant clergyman against whom Garrison had railed since the founding of *The Liberator,* a man who had lambasted *Thoughts on African Colonization* and supported the 1837 clerical abolitionists' appeal, who had rebuked disunionism and wanted to condemn as sinners only those slaveholders who did not treat their property with Christian charity, and who, in truth, had objected to everything Garrison had said and done for twenty years and more—had to be regarded as one of the most luminous "signs of the times" yet revealed.

Bacon's implied analogy between the popular cause of the Hungarian revolutionaries and American fugitive slaves suggested that the emotions roused by the abolitionists' campaign against the Fugitive Slave Law might penetrate the political culture more deeply than in previous controversies. Indeed, when the celebrated Hungarian leader Louis Kossuth made an American visit in search of U.S. assistance for his beleaguered revolution, every political tendency vied to align itself with the celebrated hero, but Garrison's polemical talent exposed the hypocrisy of the endeavor and turned it— against Kossuth's will—into an antislavery statement. The Fillmore administration had sent an American warship to Kossuth's rescue when he feared arrest in Turkey, and Secretary of State Webster crudely tried to boost Unionist pride with a letter to imperial Austria stating that the United States would recognize de facto revolutionary governments in Europe and make its moral influence felt for national freedom. The Democrats, for their part, also saw political capital in Kossuth as embodying both the nationalist fervor that fueled their crusade for Young America's expansion and the insurgent democracy reflected in their advocacy of popular sovereignty. Consequently, they supported intervention to revive Kossuth's struggle against Austrian tyranny, and their orators floated the new foreign policy slogan "Emancipation for Mankind." Free-Soilers and other antislavery people saw a domestic application of such a slogan and approved the idea of government intervention on behalf of moral principles, while the abolitionists thought that if Kossuth, who had been well briefed by British crusaders on a London stopover, linked their cause with his, the effect would be incalculable. Even Garrison, who oscillated between admiration for Kossuth as a martyred hero and distaste for him as a militaristic commander, wrote a sonnet hailing the visitor and prepared two pages of welcoming tributes in *The Liberator*.

All of these approaches converged to make Kossuth's December 1851 reception in New York the most tumultuous since Lafayette's. The Whigs' Seward and the Democrats' John L. O'Sullivan, who had coined the "manifest destiny" slogan, cochaired the welcoming committee, a quarter of a million people lined the parade route up Broadway, portraits of the bearded, handsome revolutionary with the sad, soulful eyes could be found everywhere, and the plumed Kossuth hat became a fashion craze as the excitement spread to other cities on the Hungarian's tour. As he began to negotiate the treacherous waters of American politics, however, Kossuth made a fateful decision to steer clear of the slavery question and announced—in response to a delegation of black leaders who appealed for a statement of support— that since he stood for national self-determination, he would "not meddle with any domestic concerns of the United States."

Garrison exploded in anger, and though the pages of tribute had gone to press, he added an editorial note that condemned Kossuth's "dishonorable" choice and promised further examination of the trimmer's course. As he had done with Father Matthew in 1849, Garrison now ferociously hammered Kossuth week after week and used the Hungarian's concession to excoriate the American political system. The attack culminated in a public letter to Kossuth in February 1852 that covered the entire front and back pages of *The Liberator* and then reappeared as an expanded 112-page pamphlet. In it Garrison returned to the tactic he had employed twenty years earlier in *Thoughts on African Colonization* of building a scaffold on which he could display massive amounts of incriminatory evidence derived from his antagonists' own writings. In parallel columns he matched Kossuth's adulation of American ideals with brutal extracts from Southern slave codes and crass advertisements for slave auctions and runaways. He then contrasted Kossuth's "sycophancy" with the forthright denunciations made by Daniel O'Connell, George Thompson, Giuseppe Mazzini, and Victor Hugo. The work closed with scenes that contrasted the recapture of fugitives in Washington, D.C., with Kossuth's praise of President Fillmore for having wrapped him protectively in the star-spangled banner and brought him to a capital "purified by the air of liberty."

The pamphlet stood as one of Garrison's Herculean efforts to fuse chapters of the documentary record that Americans preferred to read separately, if at all, and the Garrisonians' repudiation of Kossuth did a great deal to blunt his appeal to the national moral conscience. He raised only $90,000 of the $1 million subscription he sought, which financed not a renewed military campaign but Kossuth's retirement in London. The great irony is that while the Hungarian sacrificed his natural constituency among the abolitionists upon the reflexive advice of politicians accustomed to not alienating the South, the slaveholders also remained cool to his appeal, for they could hardly endorse a movement for intervention based on liberal morality without making themselves targets as well. Garrison's ideological attack nonetheless gave the abolitionists a triumph that was denied any of the mainstream party leaders who hoped to advance themselves on the wave of Kossuth's popularity. Like his book on colonization, however, Garrison's pamphlet did its job so thoroughly that it became obsolete, leaving posterity to wonder that he put such prodigious effort into what, in retrospect, seems to be a minor affair.

The revolutionary warrior Kossuth soon found himself supplanted in the public mind by a heroic Christian slave named Uncle Tom. First Bacon, then the Beechers. By the 1850s, Garrison's clerical nemesis Lyman Beecher, nearing eighty, had ceased to preach or write and lived quietly in his dotage, but his son Henry Ward became an exponent of "the higher law" and his daughter Harriet transmuted the uproar over the Fugitive Slave Law into the most popular antislavery novel the world would ever know. Married to an orthodox theologian who had taught for many years at the anti-abolitionist Lane Seminary in Cincinnati, Harriet Beecher Stowe had served a long literary apprenticeship in parlor sketches and domestic fiction for the women's magazines. Unlike Lydia Maria Child, who had sacrificed her popularity for the movement, Stowe had remained as remote from social agitation as her father and husband had long thought all Christians should be, though her personal convictions had grown too "Abolitiony" for her family's comfort. The distress over the Fugitive Slave Law, however, prompted her to speak out; she hoped that if she could present the issue in "a living dramatic reality," people who endorsed the recapture of fugitives might feel the agony and injustice of slavery itself.

The first sketches appeared in the leading journal of the party-minded abolitionists, the *National Era*, in June 1851 and drew upon Stowe's talent for domestic vignettes to contrast natural human sympathy in conflict with the "portentous shadow" of the law that transformed people into chattel. With a Dickensian mixture of social realism and sentimental comedy, she presented three couples in varying stages of distress: the Kentucky planter George Shelby, whose debts necessitate the sale of the trusted slave Tom, much to Mrs. Shelby's sorrow; the mulattos Eliza and George Harris, she a house servant and he nursing a grudge against the master who has returned him to field work after an interval of being hired out as a factory hand, and their son, who is also part of Shelby's deal with the slave traders; and Uncle Tom and Aunt Chloe, spiritual leaders among the slaves, whose cabin is a symbol of domestic accord and moral integrity.

When Eliza runs away with her little boy, the drama of the fugitive is set in motion, and in a sequence of weekly installments that adroitly combine heart-stopping melodrama, burlesque humor, and sharp-edged satire, Stowe depicted Eliza crossing the icy Ohio River while sympathetic blacks subvert, through feigned clumsiness and stupidity, her pursuit by professional slave-catchers. In a two-part colloquy, "A Senator Is But a Man," that ran July 24–31, 1851, Stowe portrayed a disagreement between an Ohio woman ready to disobey the Fugitive Slave Law and help Eliza as a Christian duty and her politician husband, whose defense of the law as sound public policy is overcome by "the real presence of distress." The husband, whose "idea of a fugitive was only the . . . image of a little newspaper picture of a man with a stick and a bundle," becomes "a political sinner" by driving Eliza and her son to a Quaker safe house, where she is reunited with the runaway George. With the kidnappers in pursuit, however, George declares himself free and ready to fight—like the heroic youths of Hungary, the author notes—for his independence.

It is not entirely clear when Stowe realized that her sketches had acquired the momentum of a novel. With the exception of one late episode (March 4, 1852) during which the Harrises, having adopted the cross-dressing sub-

terfuge made famous by the Crafts, board a Sandusky steamer for a successful escape into Canada, her fugitives' story had ended in early October
1851, while her tale of "The Man That Was a Thing" had barely progressed
beyond some horrifying scenes of slave auctions and traders hardened to
usages that, she said, national policy now wanted "our whole northern community used to . . . for the glory of the Union." In the episode of September
11, 1851, however, she contrived to have the betrayed Tom, on his downriver
voyage, rescue the angelic daughter of a New Orleans aristocrat and be
purchased by the grateful father as a just reward.

By making the planter, Augustine St. Claire, the Southern scion of a New
England family and introducing a sulky, hard-bitten wife and a schoolmarm
maiden aunt from Vermont, Stowe deftly created a new framework for an
examination of the full panoply of attitudes about the slave system that occurred as the story unfolded through the remainder of the year. The paternal
Tom offers young Evangeline an example of religious devotion more in tune
with her pious nature than her languid father's; the Yankee Aunt Ophelia
learns to transcend her own racial prejudice in coping with the mischievous
Topsy ("a funny specimen in the Jim Crow line," the author conceded); the
rudderless St. Claire comes to appreciate the Golden Rule as Tom nurses
poor little Eva through her last illness. With all this, Stowe had prepared
the way to free Tom in the Christmas 1851 episode, but she could not stop.
The penitent St. Claire is accidentally killed in a café brawl and dies with
Tom's hand clasped in his own.

Stowe had made the case against slavery with an abundance of sentiment
tempered by an astringent awareness of the contradictions between religious
truth and political expedience. Had her sketches, which had excited much
attention and swelled the *National Era*'s subscription list, ended at Christmastime, they would have done a good service in dramatizing the fugitive
issue and humanizing black people for a previously indifferent audience, but
Stowe had by now gotten hold of a profound literary vision. With the con-
trivances and coincidences endemic to the ramshackle construction of Victorian serial fiction, she pressed ahead, sending Tom into the hell of a Texas
plantation governed by the brutal Simon Legree, a coarse Yankee materialist
who had lost his moral compass in West Indian piracy. She then made the
last third of her story a three-way struggle in which Tom's religious faith
triumphs over both Legree's Satanic urge to dominion and the atheistic
despair of his black concubine, Cassie. Tom's spiritual grandeur—his willingness to be flogged rather than flog others, his steadfast vision of the
crucified Christ that allows him to endure punishment for refusing to throw
his Bible in the fire as Legree commands, his uplifting leadership of Legree's
sullen and downcast slaves, his refusal to betray Cassie after she makes her
escape—goads Legree into revealing more and more of his depravity until
the wicked master damns himself by beating Tom to death in a vengeful
fury. Young George Shelby, Jr., arrives too late to save Tom, but resolves

upon his old friend's grave to free all the family slaves. Cassie, meanwhile, is revealed to be Eliza's long-lost mother, and the Harris family embarks for a fresh start in Liberia. In a concluding chapter, significantly entitled "The Liberator," Shelby keeps his promise, crediting the slaves' release to the martyrdom of Tom, though his devastated widow, Chloe (who earned enough money for her own manumission by hiring out as a pastry chef), remains unconsoled, and the penitent master asks his newly emancipated hired hands to cherish Uncle Tom's Cabin as a symbol of black liberation and Christian faith.

The novel became America's greatest popular literary phenomenon of the nineteenth century. Published in book form on March 20, 1852, even before the last three installments had appeared in the newspaper, *Uncle Tom's Cabin* sold 10,000 copies within a week, 100,000 ten weeks later, 300,000 by the end of the year, and three million during its U.S. commercial life-time—with many British editions and translations into every European language doubling the total. Emphasizing that Stowe was moved to her work by the passage of the Fugitive Slave Law, Garrison observed: "So does a just God overrule evil for good."

As the editor's remark suggests, the work found its place on the religious bookshelf next to *Pilgrim's Progress* and the Bible itself, but it spawned a commercial sideshow in junky souvenirs that one critic complained made Uncle Tom the most frequently sold slave in the country. The novel also suffered the ambiguous tribute of being turned into an even more popular and accessible form, the stage melodrama, which drained the work of its ethical concerns and religious fervor, exaggerated the pathos while reducing the characters to stereotype, and, in some versions, introduced a coarse minstrel-show element that made the work popular even with racist defenders of slavery. These "treatments" completely undermined Stowe's central purpose of awakening "sympathy and feeling" for black people and exercising "a humanizing influence . . . favorable to developing the great principles of Christian brotherhood." Worse yet, they left a trashy cultural residue which detractors in our own time still mistake for the work itself.

Twentieth-century critics need to understand the book's nineteenth-century origins in a family and a culture that had resisted two decades of abolitionist effort to make civil equality the key to unlocking the political conundrum of slavery. Stowe's genius was to seize the hour of crisis and make palpable in concentrated fictional form the human problem that underlay the antislavery struggle. Her appeal lay principally with those people, like herself, who had bitten their lips and belittled the agitators rather than challenge received opinion. Critics once maintained that Stowe had idealized the slaves; now they complain that she patronized them. A truer measure of her achievement is that she made a vast white audience sympathize with the human aspirations of black people and in so doing made the unseen visible.

Garrison thought that *Uncle Tom's Cabin* would have a "prodigious effect

. . . especially upon the rising generation" in awakening compassion for the oppressed, and indeed his young admirer Brad Drew recalled his father bringing the book home from Boston the very week it was published. Although the editor claimed to have ignored the serialization in the rival paper, both his stature and the location of his printing office in the neighborhood of Stowe's publisher merited him an advance copy of the novel, which he read avidly and praised in an editorial of March 26, 1852. He had read with moistened eyes and trembling nerves, he confessed, and his study of the slave system only deepened his admiration for the author's thrilling descriptive powers and her moral acumen. He found in the character of Uncle Tom a "triumphant" illustration of the principles of Christian nonresistance, and he praised Stowe for the "rare religious perception" that had animated her creation. Yet Garrison recognized that intertwined with the parable of the suffering servant lay a secular freedom story that culminated in an act of armed resistance, and he wondered if Stowe fully grasped the point of nonresistance as an instrument of revolutionary transformation or whether she had fallen into the customary trap of teaching Christian submissiveness for enslaved blacks, while believing that Christianity sanctioned armed rebellion to vindicate the rights of white people. "Are there two Christs?" he asked, holding that Stowe's worth as "a religious teacher" depended upon the answer.

It was the same question he had posed about Kossuth, and she could answer it no more effectively than the Hungarian, or for that matter Garrison himself, for he had wrestled for twenty-five years with the dilemma his pacifism created for his politics. Stowe disputed the propriety of the question, and when the two finally met for the first of many searching philosophical discussions, she greeted him with a riposte worthy of Lyman Beecher's daughter: "Mr. Garrison, are you a Christian?"

Although they had each grown up in the hothouse of New England holiness, the beatific editor and the owlish author were a study in contrasts. The square and stalwart Garrison—dressed simply in his black frock coat and high stiff collar tied with a plain black cravat—glowed with a genial confidence that, as always, belied his reputation as a stern prophet; the diminutive Stowe—dressed fussily in thick brocade with puffs of lace at her wrists, a cameo at her collar, and her dark ringlets tricked out with cloth rosebuds and ribbons—had strong cheekbones and a jutting jaw that made her look more solemn and commanding than her reputation as a sentimental female scribbler implied. The novelist later told Frank Garrison that she had been "dreadfully afraid" of meeting his father, but the editor's tact and charm allayed her concerns, and they developed such a warm and confiding relationship that within a few months she would tell all comers that no one could know Garrison "and not love him—love him personally, love him for his earnestness and his faithfulness."

That Stowe liked Garrison proved important, because the evangelical abolitionists of the Lewis Tappan stripe in the United States and Joseph Sturge in Great Britain made a great pitch to bring Stowe into their church-based organizations, only to be frustrated by Stowe's unwillingness to commit herself wholly to any faction. Philosophically she inhabited the Tappanite universe, but she recognized her debt to the Garrisonians and would not put them down. Her novel, after all, had drawn upon the factual groundwork of a generation of radical pamphleteers—including Garrison, Weld, Grimké, and Douglass—and she had harvested an audience, as Wendell Phillips always emphasized, that the abolitionists had planted and cultivated. Her work, too, exalted the feminine ideals of nurturance and transcendence that Garrison had insisted lay at the heart of the abolitionist character, though she expected women's influence to be exerted solely in the domestic sphere and pointedly ignored the profound organizational efforts of Kelley, Stone, and the pioneering Grimké sisters that not only advanced abolition but were making the women's movement of the early 1850s a potent reform force of its own.

Though Stowe appreciated *The Liberator* as "a decidedly valuable" exponent of "the ultra progressive element in our times," she feared the unsettling effect of its religious discussions and raised with Garrison many of the same concerns her father had expressed about the deleterious influence of come-outerism and the editor's descent into heresy. "What I fear is, that [the newspaper] will take from poor Uncle Tom his Bible, and give him nothing in its place," she told Garrison, who replied that no one could take "the lamp from [Tom's] feet and the light from his path" and suggested that if a Simon Legree could not shake Tom's trust in his Savior, it was unlikely that free discussion of Bible issues in *The Liberator* would "induce him to throw that volume away." Garrison also pointed out that Stowe did not object to all the proslavery matter that appeared in his paper (indeed, Henry Ward Beecher had entered his own subscription with special praise for the scrupulous manner in which Garrison allowed the opposition to be heard) because she had complete faith in the antislavery cause. He ventured that it was her own religious uncertainty that led to her uneasiness about certain aspects of *The Liberator*. There were sentiments in the paper that *he* found distasteful, but that was an inescapable element of free discussion, he said; it was her dogmatism that was "fatal to the freedom of the human mind." It reminded him of the Romish priests who feared the circulation of the Bible among the laity. No, she retorted, it was not the fact of free discussion that bothered her; it was the hotheaded, passionate, wildly assertive *manner* of it that was hurting the cause and lessening the respect for religion among the masses, especially the "poor and lowly" who could not discriminate between passion and ideas as well as "intelligent, well-balanced minds."

Most of the Stowe-Garrison "free conversation" took place in private, and while the editor apparently enjoyed himself and the author was well enough pleased that she never condemned *The Liberator* or the AAS in public, their exchanges had an anachronistic ring. (When Garrison's Dublin friend Richard Webb met Stowe on her British tour in 1853, he pronounced her "a back number.") Stowe had written a work that was morally prescriptive—she wanted people to feel right on the slavery question—but politically naive. The assumptions of the book did not go much beyond Lundy's of 1829 that once slaveholders could be brought to the point of moral enlightenment, the genius of emancipation would unfold on an individual basis. These were assumptions that Garrison had long ago rejected, and the whiff of colonization that could be detected in the novel's denouement disturbed him greatly, though their private conversations must have cleared up the issue, for the author said no more about it. Indeed, Stowe refrained from taking political positions and exerted very little influence within the movement. Her greatest contribution remained *Uncle Tom's Cabin,* and its overall effect was more one of consolidation than trail-blazing. Coming as it did from the great font of clerical orthodoxy, the novel finally took the sting of fanaticism out of abolitionism, and its popularity gave incalculable weight to the idea of emancipation as a moral and historical inevitability. It confirmed Victor Hugo's observation, frequently quoted by Garrison, that "the light of the nineteenth century alone is enough to destroy [slavery]."

Continuing outrage at both the Fugitive Slave Law and the insidious pact of finality propelled the Garrisonians into several years of energetic and vociferous organizing. With a record number of agents, satchels of fresh pamphlets attacking the compromise and the demonic law, and the return of Abby Kelley Foster to full-time work as the field marshal, the AAS mounted from 1851 to 1853 its most extensive campaign since the anti-Texas drive of 1845. Kelley had developed an extraordinary cadre of young female organizers, the three most notable being Lucy Stone, whose dainty round face and soft voice contributed to her platform appeal, but whose strong intellect and pungent style made her a relentless advocate; Sallie Holley, another eloquent Oberlin graduate whose father Myron had started the Liberty Party, but who had taken Kelley as her mentor in the techniques of spiritual agitation; and Susan B. Anthony, an indefatigable Quaker schoolteacher from Rochester—cut from the same cloth as Kelley herself—who proved a wizard at the "cold hard labor" of securing halls, publicizing meetings, managing scarce funds, and coping with the myriad obstacles raised by the opposition in town after town. All three women spent time in the Garrison household as their routes crossed through Boston, and Anthony especially enjoyed a closeness with Helen. Stone's marriage in 1855 to the abolitionist Henry Blackwell, though she retained her own name, allied two of the earliest families to have backed Garrison and *The Liberator,* and her pioneering sisters-in-law, the physician Elizabeth Blackwell and the minister Antoinette Brown Blackwell, joined Stone in her forthright advocacy of women's rights.

Along with the female agents, who often made five or six appearances a week, went the leathery veteran Parker Pillsbury, a Baptist minister named Andrew T. Foss who had given up on the timidity of his church's missionary society, and a twenty-year-old Quaker newcomer, Aaron Macy Powell, who dropped out of teachers college under Kelley's inspiration to make a career of abolitionist agitation. After his return from a prudent interlude in Great Britain, the ex-slave William Wells Brown rejoined the staff, and from time to time Charles Lenox Remond and his talented sister, Sarah Remond, both undertook organizing tours. In 1850–51, moreover, the black evangelist Sojourner Truth, whom Garrison had met at the Northampton colony in 1843 and for whom he had printed an autobiographical narrative, also lectured for the AAS, armed with an indomitable spirit, an arsenal of "homemade" freedom songs, and a voice that matched Kelley's in both volume and passion.

The abolitionists' offensive took advantage of the different "tone" everyone had sensed in the wake of *Uncle Tom's Cabin*. The book had done "a marked work," said Abby Kelley Foster, "in clearing space in which abolitionists can speak to those who disagree," and they exerted a great deal of effort to keep the conversation going. Both Henry Clay and Daniel Webster died in 1852, and with them went the fervent but unreflective nationalism that had been the defining achievement of their generation of American leaders. Webster had gone to his grave much discredited for his insensitivity to the ethical claims of antislavery; indeed, the Free-Soilers in Massachusetts sold more than eighty thousand copies of Theodore Parker's daring eulogy that depicted the fall of the "God-like Daniel" as "the saddest sight in the western world." Although the Whigs tried to appropriate Clay's nationalism for the 1852 presidential campaign with a twelve-hundred-mile-long funeral pageant that returned the great compromiser's coffin to Kentucky via Philadelphia, New York, Albany, Buffalo, Cleveland, and Cincinnati, it was clear that an era had ended. Garrison had outlasted Clay, whose leadership he had severely criticized for two decades, and Webster and Calhoun as well. The rising generation, as Garrison had long insisted, would have to weigh the value of the Union against the imperatives of conscience in a manner that the old leaders had derided as disruptive and unnecessary.

Even in death, Garrison found occasion to attack Clay. When it became known that Clay's will provided for the emancipation and colonization of children born to his slaves after January 1, 1850, at age twenty-five for females and twenty-eight for males, it did not take long for *The Liberator* to publish calculations demonstrating the paucity of the gesture. If a Topsy on Clay's estate was five years old in 1850 and bore children until she were forty, her youngest would not be released from bondage until 1910 or 1913, and Topsy herself would never be free. No man had stood as a more implacable foe of black people, Garrison insisted one final time, and the pervasive respect paid Clay's memory could stand only as proof of the "universal demoralization" the abolitionists had to combat.

Although *Uncle Tom's Cabin* represented a convergence of abolitionist vision and antislavery sentiment, it nonetheless failed to fuse that potent combination into what Henry Clay would have termed a political interest, or, at least, failed to do so in time to influence the election at hand in the year of its publication, 1852. For all the emotional uproar created over the fugitive slave, the defenders of "finality" seemed to have prevailed with the party managers and the (white male) electorate; the Democrats had picked up 140 seats in the off-year congressional elections following the compromise, and by 1852 seemed well on the way to reconstructing the bisectional alliance that had made them dominant since Andrew Jackson's time. The antislavery fusion principle had withered in New York, where the dissident Van Burenites returned to the Democratic fold and abandoned their moralistic free-soil brides from the 1848 Buffalo convention for the easier liaisons of patronage and the spoils system. Though Free-Soilers were strong enough in Massachusetts and Ohio to forge legislative coalitions that sent the principled Charles Sumner and Benjamin Wade, Joshua Giddings's law partner, to the U.S. Senate, the momentum had so diminished nationally by 1852 that the disheartened remnant of the Buffalo gathering nominated token presidential candidates on a nonextension platform. The Democrats and Whigs both adopted "Southern" platforms for 1852 that endorsed the compromise as a "final adjustment" and promised an end to antislavery agitation, but there were enough Northern Whigs furious at the incumbent Fillmore's enforcement of the "peace measures" to block his renomination. The badly divided party turned yet again to its proven formula of running a Southern-born military hero—this time General Winfield Scott, leader of the victorious march on Mexico City—who had taken no previous part in the controversy. That the general seemed more plausible than Fillmore in the North alarmed slaveholding Whigs, who feared that Scott, like Taylor, would become the tail of the antislavery element's kite. The Democrats induced no such worry, for their nonentity, New Hampshire's dashing young brigadier Franklin Pierce, possessed an amiable temperament, shallow views, and a sound military record in the Mexican War, all of which left no doubt that he would prove a quintessential doughface ready to subordinate the slavery question to a renewed emphasis on national expansion. We will have "Pierce and Cuba" as we had "Polk and Texas," Southern editors gloated, as their region's Whigs defected to the Democrats, who recaptured the White House by winning twenty-seven of thirty-one states. Their candidate failed to win a popular majority in the free states, however, which meant that the election was not quite the mandate for "finality" that the victors claimed.

They asserted it nonetheless. "The question is now at rest," Pierce proclaimed in his inaugural address; his administration would protect the constitutional rights of slaveholders, including the recapture of fugitives, and expected all citizens to acquiesce "cheerfully" in the compromise. In Frank Pierce the nation gained a good-natured but weak-willed executive who put together a cabinet dominated by aggressive, even jingoistic slaveholders and anchored by Garrison's earliest political adversary, the ambitious and ever-adaptable Caleb Cushing of Newburyport, as attorney general. The Southerners immediately embarked on a fresh set of expansionist ventures, looking to the acquisition of Cuba either by diplomacy or invasion and covertly supporting filibustering expeditions into Sonora and Nicaragua, while Cushing tightened the machinery for enforcing the Fugitive Slave Law and left no doubt that he would demand political orthodoxy with equal rigor. In a high-handed "ukase" that set the tone for the administration, Cushing accused antislavery voters of subverting national policy and declared that "if there be any purpose more fixed than another in the mind of the President and those with whom he is accustomed to consult, it is that the dangerous element of Abolitionism, under whatever guise or form it may present itself, shall be crushed out."

It is hard to believe that one small-town printing office might have contained two such diametric personalities as Caleb Cushing and William Lloyd Garrison, the opportunist and the idealist, each so fixed in their attitudes that thirty years later they would find themselves reenacting their antagonisms on the national stage. Cushing, however, represented the most dangerous element in the North—the politician utterly indifferent to the moral issue and remarkably self-righteous about doing business as usual—and Garrison served notice that he would not be intimidated. He decked out *The Liberator* in fresh, crisp type to launch its twenty-third volume in January 1853 and declared himself "somewhat worn and battle-scarred," but with a spirit no less "cheerful and elastic." As for Pierce and Cushing, whose hearts pulsed in unison with the slave power, he said, they had to know that the only finality the friends of the slave would respect is "the eternal overthrow" of the institution.

Under Garrison's leadership the radical abolitionists made a deliberate attempt to rally the faithful and reiterate first principles. The year 1853 marked the twentieth anniversary of the AAS founding, and the editor and his colleagues took every opportunity to contrast the silent 1830s with the tumultuous 1850s and demonstrate that the movement had made slavery "the question of this generation." That the organization had survived for two decades itself became a lesson in the value of fidelity to truth and the impact that the nonpolitical reformer could have upon politics.

There seemed to be an intentional effort to put Garrison before the public and hail him as the exemplary pioneer. The AAS published a four-hundred page compendium of the editor's pivotal writings, which became part of the agents' arsenal and received from Horace Greeley's *Tribune* the appreciative notice "Bold, radical, earnest, eloquent, extravagant, denunciatory, egotistic, or it would not be Garrison." In addition to his heavy schedule of weekend convention speeches in New England, Garrison made two extensive western trips, one in the spring that took him across western New York and Ohio to Cincinnati for a convention called by antislavery women and a second in the fall that allowed him to work the ground in Michigan previously upturned by Abby Kelley and Stephen Foster. En route Garrison also attended a National Women's Rights Convention in Cleveland, where he emphasized that "the boasted human rights that we hear so much about are simply the rights of woman of which we hear so little . . ." and urged all reformers to contend for "the rights of humankind."

Garrison marveled at how much could be crowded into two weeks with the aid of steam power, and *The Liberator* saluted the manner in which the railroad had opened "new markets for Truth as well as merchandise." It was important for people to see Garrison themselves, said Edmund Quincy, for at least half the prejudices against the movement were rooted in misrepresentations of Garrison that seldom survived a meeting with him, and as for the remainder, "there is no man in it so able to brush them away." As in the Ohio visit of 1847, excitement rippled from town to town, and with the exception of hostility in Detroit that confined the meetings to black churches alone, Garrison's reception was enthusiastic and loving. At one meetinghouse in Adrian, Michigan, the editor spoke beneath a canopy of evergreen boughs in which were woven his initials and a commemorative plaque that depicted two hands—one white, the other black—clasped together. Everywhere people responded to his "apostolic" presence, cherishing their connection to him and returning to their own work with redoubled effort. His religious fervor, his sermonic style, and his heartfelt ability to speak of everything in relation to God without lapsing into cant proved as influential as Quincy had hoped. Garrison's religion is "the secret of his power," a Pennsylvania abolitionist concluded, and his long career as the prophetic agitator "seems to have earned for him a prescriptive right to speak where others are refused a hearing."

The zeal Garrison brought to the campaign of 1853 demonstrated his disregard for the electoral system and his underlying conviction that the movement had to work on the constituencies rather than the candidates. Yet the abolitionists also continued to prod and criticize the Free-Soil politicians their agitation had helped produce. When Charles Sumner cultivated his relationships in the U.S. Senate for sixteen months before making an antislavery address, Garrison tasked him severely for the delay; when Horace Mann, representing John Quincy Adams's former district, insisted that he could take the oath of office even though he would not countenance the return of fugitive slaves, Wendell Phillips questioned the contradiction in an illuminating if sometimes harsh exchange of letters that went on for months; when the perennial protest candidate Gerrit Smith, in a fluke produced by an unusual convergence of local issues, actually was elected to Congress, Garrison suggested that if he truly believed in the antislavery basis of the Constitution, the philanthropist ought to move for the expulsion of his twenty-five Southern colleagues who held their places by virtue of the three-fifths clause and thereby create "a hurricane of excitement." (Smith declined the venture and grew so discouraged in Washington that he resigned his seat after only five months.) Much of *The Liberator* was thus filled with continuing debate on the nature of the Constitution, the propriety of working within its assumptions, and conflicting appraisals of those who had gone too far and those who had not gone far enough. The controversies—some spontaneous, some contrived—all served the editor's purpose. As Garrison wrote in the call for the AAS twentieth-anniversary celebration, each pointed question, each hard-won conversion, added to the nucleus of moral power the abolitionists had created and, in the opposition provoked, revealed the true character of slavery and its apologists. Their publications had produced the gag law, their protests had exposed the proslavery bias of Texas annexation and the war with Mexico, their perseverance had ground Congress to a halt in 1849–50, and their opposition to the hateful fugitive slave bill had inspired *Uncle Tom's Cabin*. The dynamic of controversy was not the trivial shuttle-cock of politics, not a trial between attorneys who might shake hands afterward regardless of the verdict, not a contest between Democrats and Whigs or even North and South, but an absolute and profound moral confrontation between liberty and slavery. Even when the slave power seemed to triumph, in Garrison's keen appraisal, the abolitionists had found a way of spoiling the victory.

Only one serious problem blunted the anniversary well-being: political differences with Frederick Douglass, simmering for years, had degenerated into vituperative and personal feuding that did credit to no one. The trouble had first surfaced in May 1851, when Douglass shocked the annual AAS meeting by objecting to a ritualistic resolution praising the work of abolitionist newspapers. Presuming that the AAS would endorse only papers that shared the disunionist credo, he thought it fair to announce that he had undergone a change of views that would disqualify the *North Star* from the list. Speaking with unusual hesitation and apparent embarrassment, Douglass explained that after careful study of the writings of Goodell, Spooner, and Smith, he now believed that the Constitution—"construed in the light of well established rules of legal interpretation"—offered no protection to slavery, and he would henceforth advocate political action, including voting, for its abolition.

Garrison was shocked and hurt by Douglass's about-face. He had feared during the argument over the *North Star* in 1847 that Douglass might become captive to "Liberty Party thinking," but his colleague had subsequently advanced disunionism and the revolutionary critique of the compact so forcefully and so frequently that it was hard to imagine a more zealous, eloquent, or committed advocate of their point of view. The reversal struck him as intellectually implausible and emotionally suspect, especially given Douglass's fierce opposition to the enforcement of the Fugitive Slave Law. "There must be roguery somewhere," Garrison shouted angrily during the uproar that followed Douglass's statement, but to avoid proscribing the dissident the resolution was withdrawn.

While *The Liberator* reprinted strong criticism of the reversal from the other disunionist newspapers, Garrison and Douglass maintained a civil but chilly dialogue through their editorial columns. Each man expressed cordial respect for the other's talent, achievements, and integrity, and Garrison said that by "roguery" he meant only to refer to a level of deception that must necessarily be at work when every party faction from Calhounite Democrats to Smithite Liberty Leaguers found constitutional sanction for its views. This was lame, and everyone knew it, for postconvention events confirmed what Garrison had really suspected: Douglass had made an expedient conversion to save his newspaper. The *North Star* merged with a Syracuse Liberty sheet underwritten by Gerrit Smith to form a new weekly to be called *Frederick Douglass's Paper*.

Smith and Douglass had wooed each other for months. The philanthropist—one of the wealthiest men in New York, with a fortune derived from the Astor family's fur trade, upstate land grants, and railroad and milling investments—came out of the evangelical tradition of benevolent reform that had also produced Arthur and Lewis Tappan, but unlike the prim and narrow-minded brothers, Smith made his Mohawk Valley estate at Peterboro a haven for reformers of many schools. A man of volatile temperament and shifting enthusiasms, Smith was also an intellectual flibbertigibbet whose essays were so filled with preposterous statements and logical contradictions that Garrison, who had jousted with Smith in his columns for years, had stopped paying much attention to him. Yet Smith had several valuable attributes for the movement: sincerity, money, and a strong commitment to the welfare of black people. He supported a number of black educational and entrepreneurial ventures, he had given away many plots of land near North Elba in the central Adirondacks to fugitive slaves and impoverished city folk, and he had recently recruited a rugged abolitionist named John Brown, who was willing to exchange a failing wool brokerage for a pioneer farming venture, to bring some leadership and direction to the struggling resettlement effort there. To boost the journalistic career of the talented Douglass would further Smith's concern for black advancement and bring a forceful new advocate into his chimerical political enterprise.

Douglass, it seems clear, made a pragmatic change of views in order to maintain his journalistic platform. As their private correspondence reveals, the new partners had closed the deal for two years of monthly subsidies shortly before the AAS gathering. It had taken Douglass nearly five months to jettison his Garrisonian view that the Constitution had to be understood in its historical and political context and embrace instead the strained literalism that he had criticized for years as an effort to "mend old clothes with new cloth." His public disavowal—deliberately made "in open court" before his "old companions," Douglass said—provided a bold display of independence that gave some protective coloration to the opportunism that had prompted his conversion.

With his newspaper on the verge of collapse owing to a slender subscription list and the exhaustion of his British subvention, Douglass had too much pride to seek the aid of Garrison and the AAS leadership, who had warned him off the risky endeavor. He evidently regarded Smith as a more promising, sympathetic, and possibly malleable patron. Douglass might have defended his adoption of a more political stance as an effort to dramatize the principle of black citizenship, but his outrage at the injustices blacks experienced in the civic arena made him too alienated to pretend to be a model citizen trusting in the political process. How Smith's program of peaceful constitutional abolition would be accomplished without repeal of the three-fifths clause or without provoking a slaveholders' rebellion Douglass could explain no more successfully than his new partner. The radiance of the *North Star* would be "eclipsed," Garrison's friend William Powell predicted, when viewed through the "smoked optical instruments" Smith employed.

The argument was not entirely an intellectual one. Feeling that he stood in relation to Garrison "like that of a child to a parent," the public ideological break satisfied a compelling inner need for self-assertion. True to the role of the well-meaning but uncomprehending father, Garrison failed to hear Douglass's message. Wounded himself by the abrupt reversal of his colleague's course, Garrison did not appreciate how hurtful it was for Douglass to have *The Liberator* object to *Frederick Douglass's Paper* as too egotistical a name, lacking in the cultural associations that made *North Star* or *Ram's Horn* so resonant for the antislavery struggle. Garrison had always made sure that audiences appreciated Douglass—a man who had emancipated himself—as a living testament against slavery, but he did not seem alert to the ex-slave's own investment in that persona or Douglass's pardonable pride in making his name an artifact of struggle, much as Garrison reveled in his own reputation as a fanatic.

Yet Garrison himself was angered by the criticism from Samuel R. Ward, another prominent black editor supported by Smith, that the dispute with Douglass exposed the Garrisonians' hostility toward black "manliness" and independence. This was "a complexional distinction not to be tolerated for a moment," Garrison heatedly replied. "A 'black man' is to be criticized, rebuked, and 'denounced' as well as a white man, according to his position, failings or errors; and it is very absurd to make any outcry about it." Although Douglass had mistaken criticism of his views for impeachment of his motives, Garrison hoped that the movement could weigh the soundness and the vitality of their contending principles in an "amicable and magnanimous spirit."

Tempers did cool for a time. Douglass generously praised Garrison's new book and continued to honor the quality of moral agitation the Garrisonians brought to the struggle. Speaking to the Western Anti-Slavery Society in August 1852, Douglass so vigorously praised "truth-telling" as a duty superior to voting and so criticized party machines that Parker Pillsbury told Garrison that he couldn't figure out what Douglass hoped to accomplish in politics. (Abby Kelley Foster had no illusions; she warned that Douglass was "playing a double part in order to get aid from all parties.") Having spurned the organizational framework of the AAS and finding himself somewhat cramped in Smith's tiny circle of Liberty Leaguers, Douglass veered wildly in search of a new political base, becoming involved with the militant black convention movement, on the one hand, and searching for new support among the cautious evangelical abolitionists long uncomfortable with Garrison's religious radicalism.

Garrison had identified himself as a crusading editor and made his visionary newspaper the key element in his leadership. Less interested in journalism as a vocation, Douglass intended his newspaper as a personal platform for his leadership, yet the nature of his constituency remained unclear. Was he to be a representative of Northern blacks as well as the slaves, or was he an independent abolitionist voice who derived special authority from his experience in bondage? His newspaper subscribers were four-fifths white (black people, he said bitterly, expected free copies), and it survived on Smith's subsidy and the efficient efforts of a young Englishwoman named Julia Griffiths, who not only became the paper's business manager, but lived with the Douglasses and doted upon the editor in ways that generated a good deal of gossip. (The hardworking and neglected Anna Douglass, whose shyness and illiteracy had excluded her from her husband's intellectual and professional life, eventually ordered Miss Griffiths to find new lodgings. "I don't care anything about her being in the office," people heard her say, "but I won't have her in my house.")

To modern interpreters, the combination of ideological self-assertion and the sexual aggression of a presumed interracial love affair is an irresistible one that holds Garrisonian "racism" responsible for a purge of Douglass and the breach between the two leaders. Yet when hostilities flared again in 1853, they grew out of political differences that make so sensational an explanation dangerously oversimplified. Julia Griffiths was more than an abolitionist camp follower who had secretarial skills; she combined fierce loyalty to Douglass with a sectarian political outlook derived from close ties with the British evangelical abolitionists who had long opposed Garrison. Her support for Douglass—which ranged beyond fiscal management to the organization of a female antislavery society devoted to his newspaper and the creation of an annual gift album as a fund-raising souvenir—applied well-honed British techniques and struck no less a student than Abby Kelley as an ominous revival of "new organization" bias. "That miserable Julia Griffiths, making people think we're infidels, told Sallie Holley she had no self-respect if she hung out in such company [as ours]" Kelley fumed, adding that Douglass, too, was "slandering all our English and American friends." The Garrisonians had another sectarian fight on their hands, she warned, and "the sooner that battle is fought the better."

Kelley's prophecy seemed alarmist to Garrison, but in 1853, shortly after appearing at the annual meetings of both the AAS and Lewis Tappan's American & Foreign Anti-Slavery Society and declaring amiably that there could be "many societies but only one cause," Douglass unexpectedly lashed out at the Garrisonians. He accused the AAS of harboring "infidels" such as Foster, Pillsbury, and Wright, "who glory in their unbelief," an unmistakable signal that he would endeavor to fuse political abolition and evangelical piety into a new anti-Garrison coalition. At the same time Douglass advanced an ambitious separatist agenda that envisioned the creation of a National Black Council and a national black manual training school, both to be located in his hometown, Rochester, and he challenged the race loyalty of black Garrisonians who criticized the plan for both its excessive centralization and its racial exclusivity. Douglass regarded the opposition as factious and personal, charged that Garrison's hostility animated it, and claimed that his critics and the AAS sought to undermine him and his newspaper. When he attacked William C. Nell as a "contemptible tool," Charles L. Remond as an opportunist who had married a rich widow, and Robert Purvis as the inheritor of "blood-stained riches" whose wealth dulled his sympathies with ordinary people, Douglass sought to present himself as the victim of a rich and powerful organization with a spurious concern for the welfare of black people. Nell's friends deplored Douglass's attack, criticized his self-absorbed ambition, and warned that no black man could hope to advance himself very far by denying the value of Garrison's service to their cause. The atmosphere grew sulfurous with invective and abuse. By September 1853, the long-simmering hostility erupted into the nastiest factional quarrel the movement had ever known.

Garrison kept silent as long as he could, but eventually he responded, returning vitriol with vituperation that provoked more unseemly and damaging exchanges. He condemned Douglass as "an artful and unscrupulous schismatic" whose attacks had supplied fresh ammunition to the proslavery press while he basely presumed upon the color of his skin to shield himself from critics of his course. Angry, exasperated, and even bewildered by the fury of Douglass's attacks, Garrison admonished him not to cast aspersions upon those "who have been his best friends and to whom he is eternally indebted for his emerging from obscurity." No one had expelled Douglass from the movement for changing his views, Garrison insisted; he had "ostracized himself" in a "sectarian" spirit that derived from an "adviser" in his printing office who had never sympathized with the AAS and would rejoice to see it extinct. Furious that Garrison had made public insinuations about Julia Griffiths, Douglass insisted that the Englishwoman had "opened his eyes" to many things about his relationship to the movement, to which Garrison replied that the remark told "the whole story" in revealing the machinations of "a prejudiced, sectarian Delilah." It was Garrison and his "runners and whisperers," retorted Douglass, who aimed to destroy his "antislavery usefulness" and put "a fugitive slave to open shame."

Exasperated beyond measure, Garrison railed at the idea that fugitive slaves possessed superior wisdom. He angrily opined that perhaps the "sufferers' " special circumstances had transcended their ability as a class to understand all that the cause required. It was as nasty a gibe as Garrison had ever made, and if it is possible that there is a substratum of racism in every white American, then the months of polemical bitterness had finally laid it bare even in Garrison. It was a startling remark, made in fratricidal anger, which Douglass promptly termed a "stupendous insult" comparable to the colonizationists' charges of "natural inferiority," yet which, aside from a critical resolution passed by a black political organization in Chicago, attracted little public attention and faded away like the hurtful remnants of a family quarrel.

There is no telling how long the thunderous public feud would have continued, but by December 1853, Harriet Beecher Stowe had conducted earnest conversations with both Douglass and Garrison in which she tried to restore some measure of civility to their exchanges and drain the debate of its sectarian fury. "Silence in this case will be eminently *golden*," she emphasized, advising Douglass that there was "ample room" for him to work without "impeding the movements of his old friends" and hinting that her support for his training school depended upon a cessation of hostilities. To Garrison she suggested that his antagonist was still philosophically growing. "What Douglass *is* really, time will show," she counseled, and advised a magnanimous patience that would someday allow the rivals to meet "from opposing quarters of a victorious field . . . and shake hands together." Garrison grudgingly conceded that he would take no "special pains" to remedy matters, but would quietly await further developments. When the influential black Boston minister Leonard Grimes, who eschewed all organizations save his Baptist church, reliably suggested to the editor that Douglass regretted the nasty turn of affairs and wanted to clear the air, Garrison heard the message. The insulted Nell, however, who had once worked for Douglass in Rochester and had considered himself a friend, groused that if Douglass now sought to bury the hatchet, "it will only be because he thinks no more harm can be done with it." Though the wounds festered, the name-calling and editorial warfare subsided as abolitionists turned their energies to another urgent political controversy with another Douglas, the senator from Illinois who proposed a territorial act for Kansas and Nebraska that would repeal the Missouri Compromise.

The political vision of finality quickly proved a mirage. The Pierce administration's success so completely depended upon an end to agitation that it was comparatively easy for the radicals to frustrate it. As long as the abolitionists kept stirring, the slaveholders would remain uneasy, and as long as Southerners sought "reassurances" from the administration, their demands would continue to antagonize public opinion in the North. Generally the people in the free states who favored finality and defended the Fugitive Slave Law did so on the assumption that this would be the slave power's last exaction. To maintain "the Union as it is," even in their view, meant keeping slavery where it was, so the administration's expansionist moves in Cuba and Mexico jeopardized the compromise almost as much as the animosity generated by the return of fugitive slaves. Rather than a final adjustment, the Missouri Compromise was an unstable equilibrium that could be upset by any number of factors, yet, surprisingly, the stroke that wrecked it came from the very Democrats whose ascendancy rested upon an end to controversy.

The vectors that produced the 1854 Kansas-Nebraska Act and the portentous outcry of opposition can be traced ultimately to the imperatives of economic growth. The country had never known such boom times. Financed by a half billion dollars in California gold and the profits from the annual export of one billion pounds of cotton, railroad lines had advanced more than twenty thousand miles—with another ten thousand under construction—and reached the Mississippi at ten different points. Developments in iron and steel were beginning to give America's cities stronger, higher, and safer cast-iron buildings; Samuel Colt's small-arms factories had perfected a system of production based on the system of interchangeable machine-tooled parts, which led to a boom in toolmaking, clocks and watches, and literally the nuts and bolts of the industrial revolution; ingenious work in farm machinery had led to vastly increased yields with the aid of John Deere's plow and Cyrus McCormick's reaper and made the midwestern heartland the American breadbasket and butcher shop.

The prosperous excitement Garrison had seen in Ohio in 1847 had now spread to Illinois, whose population would surpass that of Massachusetts by 1860, and with four large railroad systems crossing the Alleghenies, the alluring prospect of a national market uniting the greater northwest and the northern Atlantic seaboard became reality. In 1850, two-thirds of the upper midwest's swelling trade left the region via lake ports and the Erie routes east, and ten years later Chicago, which had been little more than a palisaded trading post when Garrison began *The Liberator,* would become the railroad hub of five thousand miles of track and the ninth-largest city in the country, with grain elevators, stockyards, factories, and iron mills fueling an economy that would make its metropolitan region greater than Boston's in another two decades. Although the railroad had not penetrated the South as fully, its regional market flourished in the great age of Ohio-Mississippi steamboats, and both Memphis and St. Louis had rail connections with the east.

Though seventy-five percent of the nation's population remained rural, agriculture had become more commercial and specialized than ever before, and the urban economy (with New York and Brooklyn having a combined population exceeding one million and Philadelphia having passed the half-million mark) had become a bewildering medley of manufacturing, processing, transport, and financial enterprises. Not surprisingly, the United States had become a magnet for immigrants, especially refugees from the Irish potato famine and the failed German revolutions of 1848; in the first three years of the 1850s more than 300,000 immigrants annually had entered the country, and nearly half a million people would arrive in 1854 alone. In the eastern-seaboard cities and the newer areas of the upper midwest, foreign-born residents accounted for three out of every ten individuals and introduced fresh variables into the calculus of American politics. In 1860 the country would boast a population greater than Britain's—there would be 32 million Americans, including four million enslaved black people and four million foreign-born whites—and an economy growing even faster than its population. The rural, craft-based society of Garrison's boyhood had become a modern industrial nation; in the near half century since his birth the United States had doubled and redoubled its population, quadrupled its territorial domain, and septupled its gross national product.

Given the momentum of economic development, the territorial question could not remain dormant. Not only did population pressures in the heartland accelerate the need for opening the remainder of the Louisiana Purchase, but ambitious plans for transcontinental railroads also necessitated midcontinent territorial organization, unless the route was to be a southwestern one stretching from New Orleans across Texas and New Mexico and on to San Diego. For the Democrats' heir apparent, Senator Stephen A. Douglas of Illinois, a northern or central railroad became not only a matter of personal interest, given his involvement with major investors and land speculators, but a crucial element in his vision of the booming Mississippi Valley as the economic and political center of the Union. In moving to organize the region west of Iowa and Missouri as the Nebraska Territory, an area that extended from the 36°30' line north to the Canadian border and west to the Rocky Mountains, Douglas attempted a subtle sleight-of-hand that, once exposed, turned into a blatant change of policy that set the collision course toward civil war.

Because all of Nebraska lay within the area from which Congress had prohibited slavery in the Missouri Compromise, Douglas could not attract necessary Southern support for his measure without taking some evasive action. In a clever ruse, his bill therefore repeated the language of the 1850 New Mexico and Utah bills allowing states carved out of Nebraska to come into the Union "with or without slavery, as their constitutions may prescribe." This move substituted the ambiguous formula of popular sovereignty for the previous congressional restriction and amounted to a "silent repeal" of the Missouri formula. Douglas thought it would give him the crucial Southern votes he needed, and he intended to override the theoretical objections of Free-Soilers with the practical and confident argument that the economic strength of the northwest would quickly turn Nebraska into a free-soil commonwealth. A quartet of powerful Southern senators, however, including the very senior and very bellicose David Atchinson of Missouri, found the bill unacceptable for precisely that reason. If people thought the Missouri formula still applied, Free-Soilers would get the jump in territorial politics and slaveholders would not risk bringing their property into a region that, like California, would eventually prohibit slavery. Atchinson's caucus pressured Douglas relentlessly to make all of Nebraska explicitly open to slavery and refused his offer of some interpretative language that would declare the Missouri Compromise "superseded" by the 1850 measures. Though the midwesterner knew it would create "a hell of a storm," he felt obliged to submit a revised bill in January 1854 to create *two* territories— Nebraska, centered in the Platte River region, and Kansas, located in the river valleys directly west of Missouri—leaving the question of slavery for their residents to decide and repealing the previous congressional prohibition on slavery north of 36°30'. Pierce suggested that an explosion could be averted by referring the entire question of territorial slavery to the U.S. Supreme Court, but caved in to Douglas and his new Southern allies and pledged the administration's support. Cushing set the tone with a statement that Douglas's bill was a "practical extension" of the compromise and had to be regarded as a test of Democratic principles and party loyalty.

The storm proved even more ferocious than Douglas anticipated, and he said later that he could have traveled all the way home to Chicago by the light of his burning effigies. The handful of Free-Soilers in Congress, led by Chase and Sumner, issued an immediate denunciation that branded repeal as "an atrocious plot" by slaveholders to exclude free labor from the national domain and accused Douglas of transgressing sacred constitutional obligations for the sake of his presidential ambitions. (Had they known about the senator's railroad investments, their wrath might have reached apoplectic proportions.) Douglas retorted that Chase and Sumner were "the pure, unadulterated representatives of Abolitionism, Free Soilism, and Niggerism in the Congress of the United States," and in that astonishing remark lay the key to what happened.

Douglas, like Webster, made three mistakes. He greatly underestimated the power of antislavery morality; he overestimated the natural forces that were supposed to contain slavery; and he thought that winning a hard battle in Congress would be tantamount to convincing public opinion. Sharing the endemic prejudice against blacks and taking a purely materialistic view of slavery as an economic system suited to some regions and not others, Douglas would not condemn slaveholders for their choice, though it was one, he said, the people of Illinois had rejected. Yet he felt contemptuous of the reformers who pressed the claims of human rights and thought they had worked themselves up over a false issue, for white man's democracy and the superior strength of the free labor economy were destined by nature to overtake slavery in the territories. Such confidence might apply to distant, arid New Mexico, but the fertile prairies of eastern Kansas shared the ecology of contiguous western Missouri, where more than 100,000 slaves enriched their masters, and it was foolhardy to believe that slavery could not expand into Kansas or that an open competition among labor systems would not erupt into frontier warfare. However, by cracking the whip of party discipline and cranking the machinery of political patronage, Douglas in the Senate and Georgia's Alexander Stephens in the House waged a four-month campaign that produced a legislative triumph, but alienated the free-state public so profoundly that all but twenty-five Northern Democrats lost their seats at the next election.

No one could remember a surge of public anger that equaled the "anti-Nebraska" movement of 1854. In city after city, town after town, newspaper after newspaper, indignant meetings, outraged editorials, and vehement resolutions condemned what the dean of Democratic editors, William Cullen Bryant, called Douglas's "unholy, treacherous and monstrous proposition." Bankers and merchants, blacksmiths and ministers, all seemed united in outrage, for repeal of the Missouri Compromise struck at the heart of the political understanding that held the Union together. This was not a new compromise to save the Union, people complained; it was undoing a historic settlement meant to save it earlier. When viewed in light of the Pierce administration's dough-faced bias and the expansionist policy that verged on success in Cuba and Mexico, Douglas's craven submission to Southern demands confirmed fears that the "slave power" was reaching out to grab the Gulf of Mexico with one hand and squeeze the central prairies with the other. The constitutional guarantee of two generations that prohibited slavery in the northwest had ended; slave plantations would line the pathway of commerce and migration to the Pacific and turn the national domain of freedom into an imperial slaveocracy that would dominate the entire Mississippi Valley. For the sake of compromise in 1850, people said, they had agreed to substitute nonintervention for congressional restriction in a part of the Mexican Cession below the 42nd parallel, but now they were being asked to sanction the possibility of slavery all the way to the Canadian border in a region of 500,000 square miles with the capacity to form a dozen states as large as Ohio. Implicitly, too, the act would foreclose the possibility of imposing a Wilmot like prohibition on any further acquisitions from Mexico.

The power of the nation was being ceded to reckless adventurers and fili-busters, people said, in order to appease Southern Democrats long enough to make Douglas president. The "Nebraska fraud" appalled even the Cotton Whigs of New England. Their leader, Amos A. Lawrence, organized a Fan-euil Hall rally of thousands which denounced the renewal of controversy and protested the idea of repeal, though Garrison regarded their position as too preoccupied with restoring "finality" and too unsympathetic to the claims of the slave to count as abolitionism.

Many radicals expressed concern that the anti-Nebraska agitation, like the anti-Texas protests a decade previously, would shy from the hard political questions and collapse into an embittered acceptance that would prevail until the annexation of Cuba or Baja California came to the fore. Garrison, who never predicted failure, adopted a more affirmative approach and, taking advantage of a long-standing engagement to appear on a lecture series at New York's Broadway Tabernacle on February 14, 1854, exercised the abolitionists' special brand of moral leadership in a speech that reverberated throughout the country.

Realizing that he had a unique opportunity to influence the public re-sponse at the outset of the controversy, Garrison decided for the first time in years to speak from a prepared text, and he spent the entire day on the train writing out his lecture. The jolting of the cars proved frustrating, and the hours of crouching over his notebook aggravated his chronic back trou-ble, so that he arrived in New York at dusk feeling "more like going to bed than giving a speech." Worse yet, the weather was bad—"rainy, foggy, dis-piriting"—and had shut down both the Brooklyn and Jersey ferries. As he walked from the depot through the muddy streets with Oliver Johnson, the old friends despaired of having much of an audience.

The lecture series, a typical mixed offering that ran from December to March, had already featured several Free-Soil leaders, as well as the Gar-risonian radicals Lucy Stone and Charles Remond and newly indignant pulpit figures such as Henry Ward Beecher and William H. Furness; Garrison was the most celebrated speaker and he would be followed by Phillips, Parker, and Emerson. When Garrison arrived at the massive circular hall, he found a "large and substantial audience" awaiting him, and as the editor walked down the aisle toward the lectern, the entire room rose in a spontaneous ovation. The first time he had spoken in the tabernacle, in 1838, he had addressed a predominantly black audience, but this time the crowd was white, prosperous, and middle-of-the-road.

He would make "a clean breast of his ultraism," Garrison promised at the outset, and in his best "Daniel Boone" fashion he turned his back on the Nebraska issue and pointed his audience toward the moral wilderness of slavery itself. To readers of The Liberator, Garrison's argument would have seemed perfectly familiar, but even they might have been impressed by the clarity and eloquence he brought to the occasion. "My singularity is, that when I say that Freedom is of God, and Slavery is of the Devil, I mean just what I say," Garrison began, and he defended his absolutism as the only way of countering the majority in the churches and political parties who still retained cotton in their ears and padlocks upon their lips. He refuted a dozen popular arguments—rooted in racist attitudes toward blacks and tenderness toward property rights—frequently advanced against emancipation, and he reasserted the bedrock proposition that in its sinfulness slavery denied the rule that "God never made a human being for destruction or degradation." If slavery is not wrong, he asked the New Yorkers, why has your state abolished it? What his audience claimed as human right for themselves, he would demand for the enslaved, pointing out that abolitionists asked only for freedom and not the "complete justice" that would involve reparations for the slaves' suffering and deprivation.

Making only passing reference to Nebraska and repeal, he condemned as "moral quackery" the idea of protesting merely against slavery extension, as if halting the spread of a cancer would cure the disease. "If it would be a damning sin for us to admit another Slave State into the Union, why is not a damning sin to permit a Slave State to remain in the Union?" he asked; if one was allied with fifteen pickpockets, was it not "the acme of effrontery" to say that conscience required the exclusion of a sixteenth from the league? The logic of abolition required people to turn away from compromise, Garrison emphasized, and to repudiate as immoral the idea that if only slaveholders were restrained from further expansion, the fruit of their previous aggression could be retained. He would not allow a solitary slaveholder "to enjoy repose on any other condition than instantly ceasing to be one," he said. "I will not try to make as good a bargain for the Lord as the Devil will let me . . . and be thankful that I can do so much."

Devotion to the Union was "the latest and most terrible form of idolatry," Garrison declared, and it gave the South the power to crack the whip of secession at every rising of antislavery sentiment and make the North "cower and obey like a plantation slave." At this point one might have expected the editor to launch into his familiar denunciation of the covenant of death and repeat the slogans of disunion, but he issued instead a come-outer's appeal of crystalline simplicity. He pleaded with his audience not to sell its birthright for a mess of pottage, but rather to join the saving remnant—unwilling to compromise with evil—that contended for the reign of God, for the supremacy of "man above all institutions," and for "liberty for each, for all, forever!"

Garrison had spoken until his voice had grown hoarse, and during the entire ninety-minute address, he had heard no hissing or heckling, but only loud applause for his strongest expressions. The editor found himself cheered in New York for an argument that four years earlier had resulted in his organization's being chased from the city. Even more astonishing, the editors of the *New York Times*—a fairly new paper that had already attained a following for its sober restraint—asked for Garrison's text and printed it the next morning across four lengthy columns. "Was not that marvellous, as a work of despatch, and as a sign of the times?" he asked Helen. The AAS bought up five hundred copies for redistribution and later had the speech available nationally in a thirty-six-page tract.

Garrison's talk helped to stiffen the opposition as the debate in Congress approached its climax. In Washington, D.C., the editors of the *National Intelligencer,* who had condemned Garrison in 1831 for fouling the well-spring of American politics with his fanatical agitation, now threw all their weight and prestige into condemnation of repeal. Even more gratifying to Garrison, the New England clergy at last spoke out, issuing a statement signed by more than three thousand ministers, including Lyman Beecher and Leonard Bacon, that "in the name of Almighty God" protested any relaxation of the prohibition against slavery as a moral wrong, a breach of faith, and a danger to peace that would invite God's retribution. The work of collecting the signatures, printing the protest, and distributing it in Congress and across the country was underwritten by Harriet Beecher Stowe, who told Garrison that she rejoiced at the results of his New York talk and shared his conviction that the country would have to face "the root" of the question. At the final Broadway Tabernacle lecture a few weeks after Garrison's appearance, Ralph Waldo Emerson hoped that Americans had come "to the end of our unbelief" sufficiently to make "epic poetry" of the crusade for liberty and lauded Garrison and the AAS as "the Cassandra that has foretold all that has befallen us."

When the Kansas-Nebraska Act passed Congress at the end of May 1854, Garrison renewed "a thousand times" his curses on the Union that could support a deed so "diabolical" in the face of the strongest popular and religious remonstrance. The abolitionists intended to plan their next moves at the imminent New England convention, but received an unexpected boost from the government when—in the very midst of the meeting—the arrest of a fugitive slave turned Boston into a cauldron of resistance. For the first time *The Liberator* used headlines not as a label, but a narrative:

ANOTHER SIMS CASE IN BOSTON—SLAVE HUNTING
DEFENDED AT THE POINT OF THE BAYONET—CIVIL
LIBERTY PROSTRATE BEFORE MILITARY DESPOTISM—
MASSACHUSETTS IN CHAINS, AND HER SUBJUGATION
ABSOLUTE—THE DAYS OF SEVENTY-SIX RETURNED

The issue that had first roused opposition to the 1850 compromise had erupted again at the most combustible moment imaginable. A Virginia slave named Anthony Burns had stowed away on a Boston-bound vessel and worked undetected in a clothing store for several months before an incautious letter home gave him away. Arrested by federal marshals on May 24, 1854, Burns, like Sims, was jailed in the courthouse, which, once again, was wrapped in chains and ringed with police. Urged on by Caleb Cushing, President Pierce sent two artillery companies, a cavalry detachment, and a squadron of marines to Boston to symbolize his determination to execute the law, while he posted a federal revenue cutter in the harbor to transport Burns back to bondage once the court had done its part. With the streets jammed with angry protesters, with Faneuil Hall rocking nightly with indignant oratory, with militant abolitionists from all over New England already gathered in convention, with "conservative Compromise men" like Amos Lawrence footing the legal bills, and with the vigilance committee plotting a rescue attempt, Boston endured the most dramatic and emotional week in its history since the landing of the hated tea. There were differences from the Sims case. This time no prominent attorney aided the government's case; this time the owner offered to ransom Burns to a group ready to free him, but the U.S. attorney blocked a private settlement; this time the hot-headed Higginson and other whites joined furious blacks in a planned assault on the courthouse that was repulsed by club-wielding deputies, one of whom was fatally shot by an unknown assailant during the melee. Garrison candidly condemned the violence; if he bore no arms, he said, it was not because he was false to his principles, but true to them. James Forten's granddaughter, living with the Remonds in Salem while in school, remembered hearing the editor discuss nonresistance at his table that week, but she also recalled the cloud of despair that overwhelmed her as she returned to the depot and saw soldiers staring at her with "insolent authority" from the courthouse windows.

After nearly a week of desperate legal maneuvering, all avenues of redress had closed; the commissioner, Edward G. Loring, who considered his task merely administrative and not judicial, signed the certificate condemning Burns to servitude. The decision, wrote Garrison, converted a man into a thing "and makes the Declaration a lie . . . the Golden Rule an absurdity, and Jesus of Nazareth an impostor." He had thought "rendition" a harmless word, but in the Burns case it was a euphemism that concealed the horror of a kidnapping.

This time all Boston watched a lone black man marched down State Street completely surrounded by U.S. soldiers, eight artillery companies with fieldpieces, the county militia, and the Boston police augmented by a force of volunteer deputies armed with pistols and cutlasses. Liberty itself seemed handcuffed, thought Whittier, and his poem "The Rendition" portrayed "The Law" as an "unloosed maniac" coursing "blood-drunken" through the streets, shouting blasphemy in the ear of God. The police indeed forced the crowds of spectators from the sidewalks and chased the stockbrokers from their accustomed stand on the porch of the Exchange. Stores closed, church bells tolled, lampposts and windows were draped in black mourning; every ship in the harbor had spectators hanging from its rigging, hissing and groaning as the prisoner was transferred to the southbound naval cutter. Dressed in a new black suit, Burns looked meek and solemn and sent word that he was pleased that so many folks had turned out "for a black man." The "deed of infamy," said Garrison, demonstrated as nothing else could that only "the military power of the United States" could sustain slavery. The rendition of Anthony Burns, it was later calculated, had cost the government nearly $100,000.

And the respect of millions. When Thoreau wrote of the Burns case, "My thoughts are murder to the state," he voiced the common anger. On the day of Burns's removal, Boston, and in fact the entire North, truly awoke to Garrison's prophetic message. One conservative attorney said that the Webster Whigs felt betrayed by the South and blamed themselves for misleading others into complacency; another went back to his office, put his head on his desk, and wept. Amos Lawrence told his well-heeled colleagues that they would have to underwrite the migration of Free-Soilers to Kansas, and overnight it seemed that the Cotton Whigs had recovered the consciences whose political necessity they had denied for years. The Boston Vigilance Committee had helped three hundred fugitives escape during the past four years, but that success seemed negligible when measured against the government's show of force. So widespread was the reeling sense of confusion, anger, and bitter loss that the Massachusetts Anti-Slavery Society declared that it would make the Fourth of July a day of public mourning in the commonwealth.

CHAPTER TWENTY

IF KANSAS IS FREE SOIL, THEN WHY NOT CAROLINA?

AT NOON ON THE FOURTH OF JULY 1854, A GEORGIA MINISTER'S SON STUDYING LAW AT HARVARD HAPPILY WROTE HOME TO SAY THAT "THE ATTEMPT OF THE ABOLITIONISTS TO PREVENT A CELEBRATION OF THE DAY has signally failed." He had awakened to gunshots and band music; as he wrote he could hear cannon salutes booming from Cambridge Common and the Charlestown Navy Yard, and he looked forward to a fireworks display on the Boston Common that evening. "The patriotism of these Yankees seems, however, to manifest itself only in smoke," the young man complained, for he knew of no commemorative orations and would have much preferred a less noisy and "more intellectual" celebration. Had this South'ron only boarded one of the numerous special excursion trains heading for the outlying town of Framingham, sixteen miles west of Boston, he would have found not only abolitionists and ideas, but smoke and fire too.

More than six hundred abolitionists converged on the grove of young oaks beside Farm Pond that noontime for the customary Massachusetts Anti-Slavery Society picnic. It was a pleasant spot of shimmering sunlight and cooling shade, with a broad expanse of blue water glistening beyond, but, as at other abolitionist festivals, a somber awareness of the cause shadowed the joys of fellowship. Theirs was a counter-celebration which, after the Burns tragedy, they intended to make a day of "humiliation and sorrow" to accentuate the suffering of the slaves and the "recent triumphs and present designs of the slave power." A portion of the grove had been formed into a little amphitheater with benches banked into the hillside and a speaker's platform, festooned this day with two white flags labeled Kansas and Nebraska and banners depicting a downcast Massachusetts chained to a triumphant Virginia, though at the last minute William C. Nell improved the effect by hanging a portrait of Garrison between the two states, "to break the chain," he said. Completing the picture, an American flag turned upside down and edged with black crepe fluttered limply across the dais in the hot and humid air.

The Framingham picnic proved to be, in the activists' lexicon, a "whole-souled" gathering. Wendell Phillips spoke, as did Lucy Stone, and Sojourner Truth, who said that white people owed the slaves such a big debt that if they paid it all back they would have nothing left for seed, so that all they could do was to repent and have the debt forgiven. Abby Kelley Foster made her customary and fervent appeal for donations, and the unpredictable Henry D. Thoreau—his grim round face fringed with a wispy beard—insisted upon reading from a very sharp and spirited address he had been unable to deliver in Concord because, he said, his townspeople preferred to talk about slavery in Nebraska instead of slavery in Massachusetts. "I had thought the house was on fire, and not the prairie," he countered, going on to emphasize philosophical disunion in such a "racy and original" manner that Garrison asked to print the entire text in *The Liberator*. With his gift for aphorism Thoreau distilled a dozen years of Garrisonian criticism into a single sentence—"The law will never make men free; it is men who have got to make the law free." He offered the laconic reminder that citizens had "to be men first, and Americans only at a late and convenient hour," and, as the epitome of Garrisonian skepticism toward party politics, he warned that the fate of the republic depended not on "what kind of paper you drop into the ballot-box once a year, but on what kind of man you drop from your chamber every morning."

Of all the orations, however, Garrison's came closest to the theme of the Fourth of July itself. Twenty-five years had passed since his bold sermon at Park Street Church in 1829. Then he had spoken as an unheralded youth with the fervor of a convert; now he spoke as a celebrated leader with his convictions intensified by the passage of time. Then he had spoken into the void, facing a silent congregation and a complacent society; now he addressed two generations of apostles who were, as they liked to say, turning the world upside down to put it right side up. Yet there was a sorrowful tinge in the editor's oratory that most people had never heard before. He spoke gloomily of the evil in the world, of a Europe beset by reaction and an America compromised by slavery and deceived by the empty form of a republic. He spoke as grandly as always of the radical and universal promise of the Declaration, but, uncharacteristically, could not sustain a mood of hope as he looked out upon a world divided into hostile races, sects, and clans "incapable of recognizing among themselves a common brotherhood."

The talk was a melancholy recasting of the editor's familiar themes, yet save for readers of *The Liberator*, who would have the text to study, it was completely trumped by its author's next move. Reaching for a stack of documents, he said that he would now demonstrate with "the testimony of his own soul" his estimation of the nation's proslavery laws and deeds. He held aloft a copy of the Fugitive Slave Law and with a great flourish struck a match and set fire to the hated statute. As the flame quickened and the paper curled, Garrison called out, as revivalists often did, "And let all the people say, 'Amen.'" A great shout rang through the grove, as the editor picked up two more documents—Commissioner Loring's decision in the Burns case and the grand jury's indictment of the protesters who had charged the courthouse—and lit them aflame to another chorus of amens.

Then Garrison held aloft a copy of the U.S. Constitution. Pronouncing it "the source and parent of the other atrocities," he struck another match and watched in bright-eyed satisfaction as the paper burst into flame.

"So perish all compromises with tyranny," Garrison intoned, and again invoked the evangelist's cry, "And let all the people say, 'Amen.' "

A tremendous roar burst forth, mingled with applause and a few hisses, as the abolitionist leader completed his ritual. At this moment William Lloyd Garrison reached the pinnacle of his career in agitation. With a gesture harking back to Martin Luther's defiant burning of both the canon law and the papal bull that had excommunicated him for heresy, the editor made his most sensational and concentrated statement yet against "the parchment lies" and political idolatry of the visible world. With the apocalyptic enthusiasm granted only to the most visionary prophets, he sought to break the shell of a dead culture to liberate the inner life of conscience, to rend asunder the forms that kept both black and white people in bondage to false sovereigns, and to animate the ethical ideals of the beloved community. His was more than a symbolic protest; it was a substantial statement of what needed to be done.

No American before Garrison had so dramatically challenged his government's failure to realize and protect its ideals; no citizen before Garrison had staked the survival of the nation upon a spiritual revolution accomplished by a minority liberated from conventional politics and armed only with a righteous conviction of truth. In an intensely volatile and perplexing time, Garrison welcomed the growing polarization of the sections, insisted that the controversy turned upon a paramount issue of right and wrong, and labored steadily to bring the fundamental law into common contempt as the epitome of bondage. This confident absolutism remained his hallmark, and indeed his strategy, and he would not surrender it. When a moderate editor condemned the flamboyant protest at Framingham and sourly suggested that Garrison would have been outraged if the chairman of a Free-Soil meeting had burned a copy of *The Liberator*, Garrison demurred. If that person viewed the newspaper in the light he viewed the Constitution, as being hostile to the rights of the enslaved, why of course he would be justified in bearing a testimony against it. One crucial difference ought to be noticed, Garrison said: the Constitution was already destroying itself, but "*The Liberator* is fireproof." Yet, in the late 1850s, as the ramifications of the Kansas-Nebraska Act turned the prairie frontier blood-red with violence and murder and pushed the United States to the verge of civil war, Garrison's millennial vision became clouded and challenged by a growing determination to apply the militant principles of the First American Revolution to the moral necessity of the Second, and the twin pillars of the editor's creed—the Bible and the Declaration of Independence—threatened to collapse upon each other.

The battle for Kansas, somewhat to Garrison's regret, superseded the Fugitive Slave Law controversy as the centerpiece of antislavery agitation and brought sectional polarization to its apogee. Senator Seward challenged slaveholders to a righteous competition to fix the prairie's destiny by majority vote, and Senator Atchinson thundered in reply that Missourians would defend Kansas "with the bayonet and with blood" from abolitionist invaders. Congressional debate gave way to guerrilla warfare in Kansas and an unprecedented ideological battle in the nation's newspapers and pulpits. In the two years, from 1854 to 1856, following the passage of Douglas's Kansas-Nebraska Act, the territory endured a series of shamelessly rigged elections in which armed and loutish "border ruffians" from Missouri so badly distorted the outcomes in favor of proslavery legislative candidates that the free-state settlers formed a rival legislature of their own. With two local governments—one fraudulent, one extralegal—contending for supremacy, with governors and judges appointed by the Pierce administration reluctant to challenge the proslavery element for fear of upsetting the Democratic Party's precarious national balance, and with the essential frontier business of establishing land titles, validating timber claims, and settling water disputes subject only to the shotgun methods of frontier justice, the territory turned into a contested zone of sporadic violence and made "Bleeding Kansas" the newest watchword of the havoc wrought by the slavery issue in political life.

Garrison did not share the free-soilers' emotional commitment to Kansas as "a breakwater against the dark waters of oppression." The bogus legislature had passed a territorial slave code and harsh laws that punished anyone who advocated opposition to the Fugitive Slave Law, but the rival free-state assembly had passed noxious legislation of its own that followed the pattern of the older midwestern states in restricting emigration by free people of color and denying civil rights to those already settled there. As a redoubt of Free-Soil racism and a beacon for ten thousand pioneers from the lower Ohio Valley who resembled the Gold Rush emigrants in their materialist dreams, Kansas offered scant hope for abolitionists, Garrison concluded. The territory's leading free-state newspaper, he pointed out, favored only a distant and gradual emancipation, and the great majority of eastern settlers represented "the average sentiment of the North—and nothing more" on the issue of slavery and the Union. As an issue of principle, moreover, Garrison emphasized repeatedly the inconsistency of condemning slavery in a territory while tolerating it in a state. Over and over again he asked, "Why should Kansas be more entitled to freedom than Carolina?" and deplored the tendency to reduce a matter of conscience to the question, as he put it, of "the longitude and latitude of compromise."

Yet the editor could no more avoid the Kansas controversy than he could ignore a presidential campaign. People talked of little else. Sympathetic Northerners collected clothing, groceries, and supplies for the emigrants suffering in the guerrilla warfare; the National Kansas Committee shipped 762 boxes, more than a third from Massachusetts alone, in less than a year's time and raised nearly a quarter million dollars for the territory's "relief and protection." No previous crisis had stirred such resentment of the disproportionate power wielded by slaveholders in the Union. The administration had sent the army to Boston because one black man was loose, the familiar refrain went across the North and the west, but now refused to lift a finger to protect the free-staters in Kansas. Voicing a commonplace, one conservative minister said, "If Ohio had done to Kentucky, what Missouri has done to Kansas, the South would have risen as one" to redress the offense. The ministers were now free to speak out, Maria Chapman sourly observed, because the mercantile pillars were now speculating in northwestern lands and not Alabama lands, as was the case in the repressive 1830s. Stories from Kansas, week after week, month after month, trumpeted invasion, outrage, dictation, and civil war; they embittered the public and made credible, for the first time, the fearful idea that "the slave power" sought not only to protect its chattel within the Southern states but to legalize slaveholding throughout the nation. The public became so caught up in the excitement that Garrison had to walk a careful line between sympathy for the "undeniably trying" situation of the settlers and criticism of the discomfitingly narrow issue presented. His own headlines, ranging from the sarcastic to the cataclysmic, both told the darkening tale and revealed his rising level of engagement: "POPULAR SOVEREIGNTY ILLUSTRATED" (December 1854); "INVASION OF KANSAS" (May 1855); "A DUMB PRESIDENT" (August 1855); "THE GATHERING STORM" (August 1855); "MISSOURI DICTATION" (August 1855); "THE KANSAS INQUISITION" (September 1855); "BLOODSHED AND BURNINGS IN KANSAS" (December 1855); "MURDEROUS OUTRAGES" (December 1855); "THE KANSAS REBELLION" (February 1856); "SLAVE CODE PASSED BY BORDER RUFFIANS" (March 1856); "A CIVIL WAR IN KANSAS" (June 1856).

Yet, both as an abolitionist and as a pacifist, Garrison felt an obligation to enlarge the parameters of discussion. No issue, save Lovejoy's martyrdom in 1837, had jeopardized the connection between Garrisonian nonresistance and abolitionism more severely than the quarrel over Kansas, especially as the controversy gained dramatic identity as a frontier shoot-out between freedom and slavery. The evidence loomed menacingly across the spectrum of the movement. Gerrit Smith presided over a convention in Syracuse that collected money for pistols and ammunition in response to the appeal of a veteran abolitionist, John Brown, who intended to join his five sons already in Kansas and called for "armed means of defence." Thomas Wentworth Higginson returned to New England from reconnoitering Kansas to say that it had been "like waking up some morning and stepping out upon the battle of Bunker Hill" and urged the formation of a militia company for the defense of Kansas under the sensational slogan "peaceably if we can, forcibly if we must." Theodore Parker took up the cry (his grandfather, after all, had been the determined officer at Lexington in 1775 who had declared, "If they want a war, let it begin here") and announced that he would forgo a year's worth of purchases for his library to finance instead the acquisition of sharpshooting weapons and ammunition. He gaily recorded in his bibliographic journal the shipment of "twenty copies of Sharp's *Rights of the People*" intended to protect Kansas settlers from a proslavery government.

Even staunch Garrisonians began to falter. Angelina Grimké Weld broke fifteen years of public silence with the morose confession that she would renounce her pacifism and welcome the temporary bloodshed of servile and civil wars rather than endure the permanent triumph of slavery that now impended. Lydia Maria Child, who had stayed out of abolitionist polemics for a decade, became so caught up in the Kansas affair that she stayed up late night after night cutting and stitching cheap calico for the relief effort. Convinced that the final crisis with slavery had arrived, she symbolically repudiated her pacifism in a skillful newspaper serial, "The Kansas Emigrants," that depicted the murder of a nonresistant abolitionist and his colleagues' decision to redeem his sacrifice in a war that would liberate Kansas and establish racial justice.

Child's tale had its seedbed in fact. From Lawrence, Kansas, her distant cousin Charles Stearns, a young Garrisonian who had once served a jail term in Connecticut rather than conform to the militia law, confessed to *The Liberator* that the epidemic of cold-blooded murders in the vicinity of the free-state capital had become so severe that he now worked on the town's fortifications and shouldered arms in round-the-clock guard duty. When challenged by Garrison to be courageous in Christian faith rather than weaponry, Stearns shocked the editor by saying that his principles forbade the taking of human life, but he considered the proslavery ruffians such inhuman "devil's spawn" that he could kill them with no more compunction than he "would shoot a wild beast."

Extending the process of demonization, Henry Ward Beecher declared that "you might just as well read the Bible to buffaloes" as to the proslavery vigilantes and their political leaders, and the Brooklyn divine became a drum major for the parade of gospel ministers who gave their blessing to a militarized solution. Beecher so vigorously defended the "moral agency" of the Sharp's rifle over the Scriptures that Kansas arms shipments assumed the sobriquet "Beecher's Bibles." "Moral suasion has always been the better for a little something to stand on," he said.

Such talk shocked Garrison, who believed the minister's blithe words "made merry with evil," and it stimulated him to the most passionate defense of nonresistance he had made since drafting the manifesto of his society two decades earlier. With only a handful of followers, Garrison waged a quixotic struggle against an American culture in thrall to what he characterized as "the supremacy of the bowie knife, the revolver, the slavedriver's lash, and lynch law." Against the rule of violence he propounded nonresistance as "the reform of reforms," and he urged that people understand the magnitude of the abolition movement as a plea for human liberation from all coercive institutions and "the sanguinary code" that governed society by the rule of force rather than the laws of love and peace. Garrison joined his old friend the Christian utopian leader Adin Ballou in reconvening the dormant New England Non-Resistance Society for a symposium on the ethical dimensions of the resort to force. They rehearsed all the old arguments against the temptation to let the end justify the means and added a contemporary corollary: the price was too low. If he were going to sacrifice his principles, Ballou said, he would need a higher inducement than the spurious and restricted freedom promised for Kansas. If the Free-Soilers' "shuffling policy" had reaped the whirlwind, asked Garrison, why should abolitionists abandon their high ground to rescue them with carnal weapons?

Rather than exhorting people to fight to save the country, Garrison urged the belligerent clergymen to inspire the community with the Savior's injunction "not to fight, in order to save the world." Beecher's callous remarks about buffaloes placed a human being "on the level with the brutes, for the purpose of justifying his destruction," the editor retorted, and it followed from a mistaken regard for the "sanguinary" frontier tradition that had written American history in "characters of fire and blood." Garrison professed himself appalled at Beecher's inability to understand "the potency of suffering for righteousness' sake." Nonresistance did not guarantee safety, he conceded, but its spirit of self-sacrifice could purify the atmosphere of the brutalizing cycle of retaliatory violence. Christ lost His life, but that did not invalidate the gospel of peace that He preached.

The editor also tried to reverse the argument. If the ministers thought border ruffians deserved to be shot in Kansas, he taunted, should not the death sentence be extended to their employers in Missouri, to the president and his cabinet in Washington, and every Southern master who contributed to the "horribly depraved state of society" that tolerated both slavery and violence? Don't strain at a gnat and swallow a camel, the editor said, issuing Parker a challenge that everyone regarded as unthinkable: organize a military invasion of the South, or better yet, arm the slave population and make short work of it.

The editor naively believed that by driving the logic of forcible resistance to its implacable end in assassination, civil war, and slave revolt, he had made the case for its abandonment irrefutable. Throughout the Kansas controversy he adhered to the hope that a revolutionary social transformation could be accomplished by a religious awakening instead of raw-boned violence. Yet in the barbarous culture which he so eloquently censured, no other logic could take hold. Garrison had long understood that despite the genuine evangelical character of American society, the institutional church could not provide leadership for an abolitionist crusade. Now he had to face the realization that though Americans were susceptible to arguments from conscience as individuals, collectively they could understand revolution only in martial terms. Although Garrison lamented that Beecher and Parker would substitute Cromwell for Christ and exalt frontier Indian fighters and Concord minutemen over the apostles, the ministers had in fact chosen authentic heroes from the American political tradition. The comparison reveals that for most Americans the keystones of Garrison's creed, the Bible and the Declaration, could stand in isolation. While the visionary Garrison would make the dual imperatives of the Golden Rule and natural rights the foundation of a freshly conceived society, the conventional majority—even those convinced by moral and religious suasion to support abolition as a full realization of the Declaration's promise—pressed that understanding in the secular terms of the Revolutionary War. Garrison's radical vision of a "reformed" and morally renovated Union drew less upon American history than upon the broader tradition of Protestant nonconformity and the autonomous communities of primitive Christianity. His agitation, then, led to a terrible paradox: the more successful he became at persuading the society to take decisive action, the more it turned to modes that he rejected. His perfectionist vision would be overwhelmed by the weight of the republic's own history.

Garrison had to struggle not only to uphold the standard of nonresistance in the heat of the Kansas strife, but to preserve the integrity of the abolitionist vision in a period of political volatility. Two strong new party coalitions developed in the aftermath of the Missouri Compromise repeal to compete for the loyalties of disaffected Democrats and take the place left by the impotent and scattered Whigs. One grouping—the explicitly anti-Nebraska free-soil coalition—gradually took on the name "Republican" as an indication of its commitment to free institutions and focus upon the containment of slavery. The other grouping—emerging from clandestine social lodges opposed to the rising tide of immigration and Catholicism—took on the name "American" as symbolic of its appeal to traditional Unionist patriotism. It focused upon a grab bag of popular issues, especially nativist protective measures and reform of the political machinery that might unite the old Whig elite and anti-Irish Democratic mechanics against an outside enemy. The challenge for the Republicans would be to recast antislavery in a manner that appealed to the aspirations of enough Northern white men to offset the Democratic base in the South; theirs would be an exclusively sectional appeal. The challenge for the Americans (or the "Know-Nothings," as they were nicknamed for their once-secret character) would be to build a national following without becoming divided over the slavery question. The challenge for the abolitionists would be to hold fast to the moral idealism of their program during a period of shifting political movement that necessarily attempted to blur the issues and compromise them into a winning electoral formula.

Garrison and the abolitionists wasted little time on the Know-Nothings, even though the party scored its most stunning triumph in a fusion effort that secured it the Massachusetts governorship and control of the state legislature in 1854–55. No one could have predicted that a party "burrowing in secret like a mole in the dark" and relying upon the invidious object of "proscribing men on account of their birth and peculiar religious faiths" could have so sudden and complete a success, Garrison wrote. Such a whirlwind would prove no more than a "temporary excitement," he was confident, but to the degree that it eroded old party discipline and lured politicians and voters out of their accustomed paths, the populist insurgency would be a work of "beneficent destruction."

The rise of the Republicans, however, proved far more problematic for the abolitionists and raised all the old vexing questions about the lure and liabilities of fusion politics. Like the Know-Nothings, the Republicans appealed to a wide range of interests: the concerns of artisans and mechanics that the dignity of labor was being eroded by both slavery and the industrial revolution, a new faith in temperance and a fierce antagonism toward political corruption and self-seeking officeholders, the gathering sentiment for a transcontinental railroad, workingmen's interest in land reform and the prospect of homestead grants from the public domain, and an ambivalence about immigrants that at once feared the Roman Catholic (largely Irish) influx of the cities and lauded the Protestant (largely German and Scandinavian) migration to the prairies. The Republicans rose as a national party as they worked these issues, in various combinations, in a host of local and state campaigns so disparate and volatile that historians have had a hard time trying to weigh the cumulative impact of ethnographic, cultural, economic, and political factors in the party's success. Whatever the proportions, the cumulative impact of the Republican ascendancy elevated antislavery as the central political issue of the decade and made the party a transforming agent in national politics.

Garrison had no illusions about the narrowly "technical" brand of antislavery the Republicans supported: it was morally constricted, offering merely "a geographical aversion" to slavery bounded by the Missouri line and presenting itself as "a complexional party" limited by a racially restrictive idea of free soil. Though it had attracted many radical Free-Soilers, including Giddings and Sumner, even some of the most ardent political abolitionists of the old Liberty Party tendency feared that the Republicans represented a new low in opportunism and expediency. Yet the party seemed to be gaining the mass following denied the earlier Liberty and Free-Soil ventures, and its electoral potential had manifestly alarmed slaveholding leaders who regarded it as the abolitionists' stalking-horse and talked grimly of leaving the Union should the Republicans elect the next president in 1856. Would it therefore be better from the abolitionist standpoint to encourage the Republicans as an engine of destruction or criticize them as the latest exponents of an abhorrent compromise?

For Garrison the time for fusion had not yet arrived, but the time of wholesale condemnation had passed. While he told correspondents that the "relatively antislavery" Republicans had his good wishes, he considered the coalition composed of "very incongruous elements" who would be either "cheated or defeated in the end." Then they would be in a "listening condition" (as Abby Kelley put it) for the abolitionists' more principled demands. Rather than fall victim to the seductive appeal of easy victory themselves, abolitionists had to remain the teachers and leaders for the longer march. Political partisanship always made people worse abolitionists, Garrison argued, for the question became not how much, but how little antislavery feeling and principle would serve the temporary situation of the pending election, and the moral tone always succumbed to the scramble for office. Politicians made the best of existing circumstances while abolitionists, he said, had to create new ones.

Disunion remained Garrison's watchword, and he argued it with matchless persistency and fervor. Just as the glib turn toward violent rhetoric had prompted a fresh restatement of the nonresistance creed, so did the narrowness of what he termed "geographical" antislavery provoke Garrison to inspired advocacy of new-model politics. Not until citizens repudiated the bloodstained compact would they recognize that the "true union for freedom and a constitution that receives every emancipated slave and free person of color into the great American family on equal terms is ONE TO BE CREATED." We are making an extraordinary demand upon the American people, Garrison conceded, but we are talking, after all, not about "a question of parchment, but one of moral possibilities."

The editor's critics charged that disunion meant the abandonment of the slaves, but Garrison refused to accept their logic. We are leaving the slaveholders, not the slaves, he retorted. To break the constitutional bond with the masters would be like scourging the money changers from the temple and making a declaration of solidarity with the slaves. A free Northern republic—one that had no obligation to return fugitives—adjacent to Virginia and Kentucky would shift the border of liberty southward from Canada to the Ohio River and shine as a genuine moral beacon to the oppressed. The proximity of freedom would undermine slavery in the upper South, the loss of federal military power would make the slave states more vulnerable to insurrection and less able to conquer new territory, and the shockwaves of the separation would weaken the foundations of a despotism that could not peaceably coexist with a free Northern republic as it had with the states under the 1787 Constitution. To separate from the slaveholders was to make common cause with the slaves, said Garrison, even as discord with Belial was concord with Christ. In his arguments the editor often invoked Christ's precept "A house divided itself cannot stand," as an imperative for achieving the moral clarity of a nation purged of slavery. In Republican hands, however, the maxim became a sectional warning against the slave power's drive to make slavery national. The divided house would inevitably have to become "all free or all slave," Lincoln warned in 1858, and grimly wondered, "Have we no tendency to the latter condition?"

The editor's provocative gestures and prophetic vision had for twenty-five years exerted a subversive influence against the traditional power of the federal consensus and a gradual pressure upon mainstream politics. In the tumultuous reconfiguration of the 1850s, Garrison's insistence upon moral principle strengthened the radical antislavery element in the emerging Republican coalition, especially as the Kansas issue came to dominate the 1856 presidential campaign. Two concurrent events in May 1856 framed the issue with unprecedented drama and force. On the night of the 21st, an armed band of proslavery sympathizers, fortified by liquor and the writs of a sympathetic judge, stormed the free-state town of Lawrence, Kansas, on the pretext of taking its defiant leaders into custody, but actually mounting a preemptive strike against its munitions supplies. The skirmish left one raider dead, two printing presses smashed, the governor's house and barn in flames, and the South Carolina palmetto flag waving from the ruins of the hotel known as antislavery headquarters.

That same day in Washington, before any news had come of "the sack of Lawrence," Charles Sumner of Massachusetts had delivered a lengthy address—by turns ornate, lurid, and vituperative—in which he denounced "The Crime Against Kansas." Sumner's harsh diatribe, which included some nasty remarks about South Carolina's Senator Andrew Butler's embrace of the harlot slavery, roused the chamber to frenzied sectional animosity. It so infuriated Butler's kinsman and colleague Congressman Preston Brooks that he strode into the Senate chamber and beat Sumner into unconsciousness with a wickedly limber gold-headed walking stick. The combined shock of the fresh violence in Kansas, which triggered a summer's worth of reprisals and warfare, and the horrifying attack upon an antislavery leader in the conduct of his office produced a sensation in Northern politics. It solidified the position of the Republicans as the most credible opponent of the arrogant slaveholders who now made war upon free soil in Kansas and free speech in Washington. In the *New York Evening Post*, William Cullen Bryant expressed the common sense of outrage at the use of "plantation discipline" in the Senate: "Has it come to this, that we must speak with bated breath in the presence of our Southern masters?"

Emotions boiled further in the heat of the 1856 presidential campaign.

Another dough-faced Democrat, the veteran Pennsylvania politician James Buchanan, sought to hold the old proslavery party coalition together against the two rival aspiring parties. The Know-Nothings had, as expected, fractured over the free-soil question and could do nothing more adventurous than nominate former president Millard Fillmore to compete for the conservative Unionist vote. The Republicans, eager to enlist the eastern and midwestern Know-Nothings estranged by their national organization's refusal to take a stand against slavery extension, added the issue of land grants for homesteads and public education to their workingmen's appeal, challenged the slaveholders' repression of dissent in the South, in Kansas, and in Congress, and completed their "Free Soil, Free Labor, Free Speech" platform by nominating the intrepid John C. Frémont as their candidate. Celebrated for his exploration of the beckoning west, backed by disaffected Democrats (his father-in-law was the maverick Missouri senator Thomas Hart Benton), and possessed of nominal antislavery credentials gained as a proponent of free-state California in 1850, Frémont proved a potent symbol for an insurgent movement. While the Republican Party managers kept the candidate under wraps in New York, their propaganda machinery fashioned him into a defender of egalitarian economic opportunity against a greedy and despotic slave oligarchy. Though the Democrats tried to depict the Republicans as a collection of deluded reformers and lustful amalgamationists who had led the intrepid pathfinder into a political desert, the Republicans countered with a depiction of Buchanan as staggering under the weight of slave-power demands and portrayed their own platform as a gleaming rainbow that would span the country from the White House to California.

Even the most hard-core abolitionists became caught up in the excitement. The editor couldn't help laughing merrily when he learned that young Arnold Buffum Chace, grandson and namesake of the first NEAS president and anticolonization organizer, had torn down the Frémont flag his older brothers had raised over their house and substituted a "Liberator" standard bearing the slogan "No Union with Slaveholders." As in previous campaigns, however, he worried at the seductive and narcotic effect the election exerted upon the abolitionist dedication to principle. Even so staunch an advocate as Philadelphia's Mary Grew asked wonderingly, "Do you imagine Frémont *can* be elected?" And out in Illinois, a still-staunch teacher, Prudence Crandall Philleo, answered the call for female campaign volunteers. Maria Child declared a Republican victory so vital that if her husband did not return from a business trip in time, she would disguise herself in his old slouch hat and overcoat and attend the poll herself. (She did harbor reservations about Frémont personally, however, because he had been a filibuster who had led the aggressive war against Mexico and California, but like many politically minded women she admired Jessie, his outspoken and unabashedly antislavery wife, whose reputation campaigners were quick to exploit.) When Samuel J. May, the editor's oldest friend in the movement, declared himself in support of Frémont, it seemed that the abolitionist readiness to subsume itself in electoral politics had become complete. Even those who conceded that it would be "ridiculous" for Garrison to become "a party man" wondered if the editor couldn't see his way clear to voting for Frémont not as a believer in the Republicans or the Constitution, as one correspondent put it, but "from purely Christian motives—from the desire to prevent a *greater* evil, and to obtain a state of things more congenial for carrying forward the purely antislavery enterprise."

Earlier in his career Garrison might have denounced all such talk as heresy and chastised the advocates of Frémont for their delinquency. In 1856, however, the situation had grown so unstable and the editor's own strategic assessment so ambivalent that he took a much more measured approach and gave the issue of affiliation a calm and thorough airing in his columns. *The Liberator* offered a symposium on the fresh and urgent question of a reform movement's relationship to electoral politics, in the form of an extended public correspondence with the respected May in Syracuse, augmented by editorial responses to the extraordinary number of queries Garrison had received from abolitionists around the country.

Those advocating support for the Republicans lauded the party as the "first crack" in the system of national politics dominated by a coalition that gave slaveholders the upper hand; a Republican victory, said May, would be a "beginning to the great work" of abolition. Garrison and Phillips disagreed. The party platform called for an end to agitation, they insisted, as did the previous compromises of 1820 and 1850, and at best the Republicans looked to a practical settlement on traditional lines when the times demanded a revolutionary transformation. An antislavery Congress, countered May, could do a great deal of good, not only for Kansas and the cause of nonextension, but by abolishing slavery in the District of Columbia, restricting the interstate slave trade, recognizing black political achievement by establishing diplomatic relations with Haiti, and resisting Southern demands to reopen the international slave trade and annex Cuba and Nicaragua. True enough, Garrison replied, but the Republican Party had not endorsed any of those goals. May conceded the point, but emphasized that the party had not foreclosed such measures for the future. No party has ever done more than it promised, scoffed Garrison, adding that Republican support for the constitutional consensus and the "slave oligarchy" created by the three-fifths clause indeed blocked the more radical actions. When May argued that support for Frémont would bolster the position of the hard-core antislavery men within the Republican Party, Garrison disagreed. To go into the party would be to assume the burden of fighting against further dilution of principle rather than continuing to advocate immediatism and equality. May, however, insisted that a Frémont victory would at least "send a message" that the free states had drawn the line at further "aggression" by the slave power. That would be the wrong message, countered Garrison; if abolitionists contributed to a Frémont victory on the principle of preserving the Missouri Compromise, the country would only have retaken the ground of 1820 while the movement would have sacrificed the moral coherence that made it powerful.

Yet popular feelings could not be ignored. Garrison declared several times during the campaign that "if there were no moral barrier to our voting and we had a million votes to bestow, we should cast them for Frémont, as against Buchanan and Fillmore." His remark, however, was taken out of context by Democratic editors who tried to tar the Republicans with the brush of Garrison's endorsement and led to frantic efforts by Horace Greeley to secure *The Liberator's* disavowal of the ticket. The distorted accounts of these crosscurrents disturbed some of the editor's closest associates in the movement, notably Abby Kelley and Stephen Foster, who thought that he had gone soft and had accepted chaff for wheat.

Garrison agreed with them that the allure of the presidential campaign threatened the movement's identity. Abolitionists should not "bow down in the house of Rimmon," alluding to the parable (2 Kings 5:18) illustrating the dangers of false worship and conformity with outmoded rituals and reprehensible customs. The first duty of abolitionists, he concluded, was to avoid becoming Republicans. To the Fosters' intense annoyance, however, he argued that the "amount of conscience" in the party and the sectional basis of its opposition to the slave power made it a political entity that the movement had to take seriously. Kelley conceded that the party may be "the work of our hands," but she insisted that such "progeny," like other children, required "a great deal of reproof to bring it up in the way it should go." Garrison agreed, but sweetly added that, as in child-rearing, it was important to praise the party when it tried to do a good work, as it had on the issue of nonextension.

That Garrison accorded the Republicans a measure of respect he had never conceded to the Liberty Party remnant should come as no surprise. He always had more interest in politicians who lifted themselves toward an acknowledgment of moral principles than he had in moralists who lowered themselves into partisan activities. For the Republicans to support and elect candidates willing to condemn slavery as wrong would be productive agitation, for it created something where nothing had previously existed. For Gerrit Smith to advance himself as a presidential candidate was ludicrous, in Garrison's view, for he had no practical organization and demeaned himself in the futile process of making one. For Frederick Douglass to make persistent attacks upon Garrisonian abolition as passé—as a phase of moral education through which the movement had inevitably traveled en route to more enlightened forms of practical agitation—was more than a continuation of their personal feud; it was the old Liberty Party idea that a token candidacy offered a greater opportunity for moral agitation than did the prophetic apostleship of Garrison. While the Republican nonextensionist

NO SLAVERY!

FOURTH OF JULY!

The Managers of the

Mass. ANTI-SLAVERY SOC'Y

Invite, without distinction of party or sect, ALL who are ready and mean to be known as on LIBER-TY'S side, in the great struggle which is now upon us, to meet in convention at the

GROVE IN FRAMINGHAM,

On the approaching FOURTH OF JULY, there to pass the day in no idle glorying in our country's lib-erties, but in deep humiliation for her Disgrace and Shame, and in resolute purpose---God being our leader--- to rescue old Massachusetts at least from being bound forever to the car of Slavery.

SPECIAL TRAINS

Will be run on that day, TO THE GROVE, from Boston, Worces-ter, and Milford, leaving each place at 9 25 A. M.

RETURNING --Leave the Grove about 5 1-2 P. M. FARE, by all these Trains, to the Grove and back,

FIFTY CENTS.

The beauty of the Grove, and the completeness and excellence of its accommodations, are well known.

EMINENT SPEAKERS,

From different quarters of the State, will be present.

Earle & Drew, Printers, 212 Main Street, Worcester.

At this abolitionist Fourth of July event in 1854, Garrison burned a copy of the U.S. Constitution to protest the recent return to slavery of fugitive Anthony Burns.
(Courtesy of the Massachusetts Historical Society)

Frederick Douglass is seen at the right of the speaker's desk in this rare daguerreotype of an 1850 abolitionist meeting. Gerrit Smith, with upraised hand, stands behind him; the two women in plaid capes are the fugitives Mary and Emily Edmonson. (Courtesy of the Collection of Mr. and Mrs. Set Charles Momjian and the National Portrait Gallery, Smithsonian Institution)

Lucy Stone, the first woman to graduate from Oberlin College and a leading suffragist, was brought into the movement by the Grimké sisters and Abby Kelley Foster.
(Courtesy of the Massachusetts Historical Society)

Garrison is seen with Wendell Phillips (left) and British abolitionist George Thompson during an organizing campaign in 1851. (Courtesy of the Trustees of the Boston Public Library)

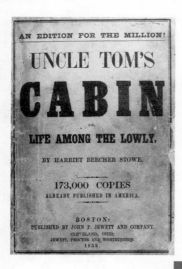

UNCLE TOM'S
CABIN

OR;

LIFE AMONG THE LOWLY.

BY HARRIET BEECHER STOWE.

173,000 COPIES
ALREADY PUBLISHED IN AMERICA.

BOSTON:
PUBLISHED BY JOHN P. JEWETT AND COMPANY.
CLEVELAND, OHIO;
JEWETT, PROCTOR AND WORTHINGTON.
1852.

The clergyman Lyman Beecher tried to suppress Garrisonian abolitionism in the 1830s, but his daughter Harriet Beecher Stowe, shown below with her father and brother Henry Ward Beecher, roused antislavery sympathies in the early 1850s with her best-selling protest novel, Uncle Tom's Cabin. *(Left: courtesy of the Boston Athenaeum; below: courtesy of the Library of Congress)*

James Redpath, a new breed of militant journalist, reported the guerrilla warfare in "Bleeding Kansas" and promoted the military reputation of Captain John Brown.

(Courtesy of the Kansas State Historical Society)

John Brown as he appeared upon his first visit to Boston in 1857, a few years before his famous raid on Harpers Ferry, Virginia, shown circa 1860.
(*Left:* courtesy of the Boston Athenaeum; *below:* courtesy of the Massachusetts Historical Society)

Thousands of people flocked to this war rally in Union Square, New York City, on April 20, 1861. The U.S. flag, lowered at the surrender of Fort Sumter one week earlier, is displayed from the statue of George Washington. (Collection of the New-York Historical Society)

Caricaturists challenged the abolitionist dimension of the war; these cartoons from Vanity Fair mocked both Garrison's commitment to equality and the idea that slavery had caused the war.
(Courtesy of the Library Company of Philadelphia)

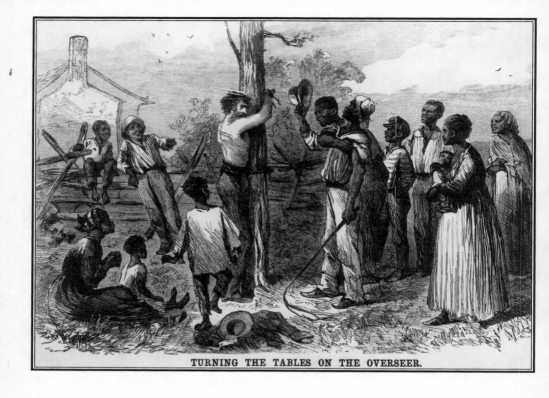

TURNING THE TABLES ON THE OVERSEER.

"STAND UP A MAN!"

VICTORY!

"HE DIED FOR ME!"

Black artists saw the war as an opportunity for self-assertion, as shown here in the woodblock print, "Turning the Tables on the Overseer," and three trading cards from a set of twelve published to honor black soldiers. (Courtesy of the Library Company of Philadelphia)

So many African Americans answered this call to join the 54th Massachusetts regiment that a second unit, the 55th Massachusetts, was formed. Its officers included George T. Garrison, the editor's eldest son.
(Courtesy of the Massachusetts Historical Society)

The regiments dug bomb shelters in the sandpits surrounding Charleston Harbor, and the 54th Massachusetts, led by Col. Robert G. Shaw, carried the battle flags shown at right on its brave but ill-fated charge against Fort Wagner in July 1863. (Courtesy of the Massachusetts Historical Society)

Garrison visited Hilton Head, South Carolina, in April 1865, and met families such as this one, which included five generations of liberated slaves, photographed by Timothy O'Sullivan.
(Courtesy of the Library of Congress)

Staff members dragged pews out of Massaponax Church for a war council on May 21, 1864, during the Wilderness campaign in Virginia. General Ulysses S. Grant (at left) is leaning over a bench to study a map. (Courtesy of the Library of Congress)

Fugitives from slavery, like the people pictured here in Virginia, often transported themselves to safety behind Union lines. (Courtesy of the Library of Congress)

Garrison was present as a guest of the Lincoln administration when the same U.S. flag lowered in 1861 was raised at Fort Sumter on April 14, 1865, to mark the end of the war. The enlarged section shows a man who might be Garrison, wearing a large hat, sitting in the front row to the right of Henry Ward Beecher, the standing figure in the midst of his oration. (Courtesy of the Library of Congress)

Garrison's family was an unusually close one. Shown here are Wendell, reading a newspaper; Lt. George T. Garrison in his uniform; and Frank as a young boy. The editor is seen sitting with his daughter Fanny. (Courtesy of the Sophia Smith Collection, Smith College)

See that pussy is put down cellar. You will find plenty of milk for her and for yourself.

A handwritten note from Garrison to Frank, who cared for him in his last years. (Courtesy of the Massachusetts Historical Society)

Helen Garrison, shown here in a Boston photograph made before she suffered a debilitating stroke in December 1863. (Courtesy of the Sophia Smith Collection, Smith College)

One of the last photographs of Garrison, taken in Scotland in 1877. (Courtesy of the Sophia Smith Collection, Smith College)

Garrison with some of his children and grandchildren at Rockledge in 1876. (Courtesy of Sophia Smith Collection, Smith College)

MR. GARRISON'S FUNERAL.

Dr. Putnam's Church, Eliot Square, Roxbury.

☞ Please hand this to one of the Ushers.

Wednesday, 2 P.M.

Friends received invitation cards to the abolitionist's funeral in Roxbury, May 28, 1879. Burial followed at Forest Hills Cemetery, alongside his wife, who had died three years earlier. (Top: courtesy of the Department of Special Collections, Ablah Library, Wichita State University; *bottom:* courtesy of the Massachusetts Historical Society)

WILLIAM LLOYD GARRISON
1805 — 1879
HELEN ELIZA GARRISON
1811 — 1876

approach had the virtue of exposing the constitutional compromises that prevented abolition, moreover, the Smithites continued to dwell, Garrison believed, in the realm of constitutional fantasy. They tried to claim the Framers as architects of an antislavery politics and advanced all sorts of schemes— a congressional repeal of the Fugitive Slave Law, a reconstruction of the federal judiciary through appointment of antislavery judges, the fixing of a date certain for abolition in the states and federal control of states in "default"—that had no chance of peaceably breaking the national political deadlock and, far from saving the Union, would make a military confrontation inevitable. Theirs was an oblique disunionism that masked itself behind the facade of constitutional interpretation. For Garrison the "special work" of abolition lay not in adopting the model of politics, but in creating a redemptive vision. "We see what our fathers did not see; we know what they did not know."

Powerful organizations never espouse great reforms, the editor told a December 1855 meeting called to celebrate the desegregation of Boston's public schools after a decade-long struggle by abolitionists of both races. Social reform, he said, begins "in the heart of a solitary individual" and grows strong among "humble men and humble women [who], unknown to the community, without means, without power, without station, but perceiving the thing to be done . . . and having faith in the triumph of what is just and true, engage in the work. . . ." He always regarded the abolitionists as a saving remnant who would create the preconditions for reform. Theodore Parker compared such "non-political reformers" either to the windlass that raises the anchor while the politicians haul in the slack or to the spinners and weavers who make the material from which politicians cut their clothes, but Garrison found the humblest metaphor of all in the baking of bread. By and by, he said with the apostle Paul, " 'the little leaven leavens the whole lump' . . . [and] this is the way the world is to be redeemed" (1 Cor. 5:6). The most popular metaphor for the progress of reform in the 1850s, however, drew from both mechanics and nature. "The world moves," people said, having found a shorthand way of remarking social change that evoked at once the lever of Archimedes and the stubborn faith of Galileo that the earth itself revolved in obedience to higher laws.

In the political crisis of the 1850s it became more difficult to distinguish Garrison's voice in the chorus of protest. Was he the disenchanted editor who said that the flag had become so stained by slavery that it should be dyed black and have "the light of [its] stars erased" and replaced with the devices of "the whip and the fetter"? Or was he the angry editor who decried the Northern politicians of 1856 as "swarms of doughfaces, office-vermin, kept-editors . . . body-snatchers, bawlers, bribers, compromisers . . . aware of nothing further than the drip and spoil of politics" who crawled from "political hearses, and from the coffins inside, and from the shrouds inside of the coffins; from the tumours and abscesses of the land" to the nominating conventions that chose "deformed, mediocre, snivelling, unreliable, false-hearted men" for the presidency? Though Garrison occasionally sounded like the first writer, the respectable William Cullen Bryant, he never went so far in slang-whanging denunciation as the second writer, the thunderously exuberant Walt Whitman. The editor of *The Liberator* still wrote with the prophetic censure and absolutist candor he had always employed; the rest of the press had merely caught up to him in a vociferous challenge to the old ways. He had, in fact, become renowned and admired for his adherence to principle and his salutary effect upon the nation's moral consciousness. In 1859 Garrison would receive more space in a major publisher's ambitious, definitive encyclopedia of American cultural and political life than Emerson, Thoreau, Stowe, Phillips, and Douglass *combined,* and, for good and ill, his name had become a household word.

Garrison's career in agitation had advanced the political instability of the decade, yet in the 1850s his personal life assumed the settled character that had previously eluded him. The family at last acquired a home of its own, and the newspaper's finances achieved an unwonted equilibrium. The three older boys came into independent manhood, while Fanny and Franky enjoyed a more comfortable bourgeois childhood replete with piano lessons and gymnasium exercises. Helen felt herself unburdened enough to take a larger role in the antislavery bazaar and accompany her husband to the annual conventions in New York and Philadelphia, and Garrison himself gracefully played the role of the pioneer whose longevity in the cause could now be seen as an admirable and constructive work of vision.

The Garrisons' new home on Dix Place a few blocks south of the Common was itself a tribute from a grateful constituency. The fund initiated after the editor's serious illness in 1847 had borne fruit. Pledges of $2,250, invested in shares of New England railroads and the State Street Bank by Francis Jackson, Samuel Philbrick, and Ellis Loring—the same trustees who managed *The Liberator's* affairs—had tidily compounded by November 1854 to $6,837, which more than covered the purchase of a house. The family had never grown comfortable on Suffolk Street, where the shadow of Charlie's death hung gloomily over the rooms, but straitened finances prohibited another move. Sensitive to their need, however, Jackson bought a house of the Garrisons' choice on Dix Place in 1852 and rented it back to them for the $400 a year he paid in mortgage interest and taxes.

The arrangement, Jackson reckoned, cut their expenses by at least $50 and gave them a more "permanent and pleasant home" than could be had on the open market. Professing "no friendship in trade," their benefactor insisted that the transaction was a proper business deal for him, and in the end it was. In October 1855, he sold the house at cost to the Garrison Fund trustees in exchange for $6,500 of their blue-chip railroad and bank shares.

Henceforth the editor would pay only the water bill and property tax, which totaled less than $100 a year. For Garrison, whose $1,200 annual salary had not changed in two decades despite a long-term upward trend in prices, the marked reduction in housing expenses would be the equivalent of a twenty-five percent raise in pay, and it left him feeling both prosperous and grateful. He told Jackson that he saw through the business fiction and knew that he had received a generous gift, yet in expressing his "poor, stammering acknowledgments" to the other friends who had made contributions to the fund, Garrison reiterated that he knew that they would continue to respect him only so long as they perceived him "faithful" to his own highest standards of conviction and duty. Iconoclasm thus had its own rewards and, for the editor, removed the sting of dependence from the transaction. Although the trustees formally held the title, Garrison, after his own fashion, had become a gentleman of property and standing.

Dix Place was a narrow cul-de-sac off bustling Washington Street about a quarter mile closer to downtown than the Garrisons' 1840s dwelling on Pine Street. At one time the section had been a fashionable neighborhood of merchants' residences on large tree-shaded lots; Francis Jackson himself occupied a substantial house in the adjacent street, and Garrison's immediate neighbors included a stockbroker, an iron dealer, and an importer of fine watches, all of whom had owned their homes there for a decade. Yet the city's steady growth (Boston's population rose thirty percent, from 138,788 to 177,840, between 1850 and 1860, with Irish immigration accounting for much of the increase) had made the central business district more congested than ever, and given Boston's elongated shape and lack of low-cost public transport, the adjacent residential areas experienced a wave of subdivision and new construction that both increased their density and changed their character. The Garrisons came to Dix Place at the same time as pattern-makers, machinists, leather and crockery salesmen, and dealers in vinegar and cigars. By 1860 only five of the fifteen houses on the row would be occupied by their owners, a majority of the rental units would be shared by two families, and four would be turned into boardinghouses. At the intersection with Washington Street, the shopping artery that ran the length of the city, there stood a furniture factory and a large bakery owned and operated by a Scots family named Kelt with the help of German immigrant bakers who lived on the premises. Unlike New York's Broadway, which had become an exclusively commercial corridor replete with square-block-sized department stores tricked out like Italianate palazzos, Washington Street remained a small-scale but hopelessly crowded avenue of three- and four-story brick or brownstone houses that combined street-level shops (the milliner's, the confectioner's, the cabinetmaker's) with upstairs apartments. With every firm displaying its wares and attracting business with large signs, with the roadway crowded with teamsters' wagons, hansom cabs, and horse-drawn omnibuses and the narrow sidewalk choked with pedestrians, Washington Street still resembled an old-fashioned market town's high street more than the thoroughfare of an industrial metropolis.

Though 14 Dix Place was scarcely two-hundred feet down the row, in real-estate parlance its location was "retired yet central," and the Garrisons regarded their house as a retreat from urban cacophony. The backyard had a southern exposure and room for a vegetable plot, a group of peach and cherry trees, and a good big currant bush, as well as a sweetwater grape vine the children planted under the kitchen window. The house fronted directly on the cobblestone sidewalk and had a small square entryway of several steps leading up to the first floor, while a boxy window recessed below pavement level admitted light to the cellar. Built of brick, three stories high with an attic dormer, the house had an unornamented facade save for the shutters framing the three windows on each floor, and it looked like a slightly larger replica of the plain dwellings they had previously occupied on Pine and Suffolk.

The children and the movement stood at the twin center of the family's social life. With the three older boys now mature, Fanny on the verge of womanhood, and Franky ("the Benjamin of the flock," Garrison called him) an exuberant and affectionate schoolboy, the household enjoyed a rich mixture of activity. Fanny played the piano, Wendy loved to put on amateur theatricals and read his literary parodies aloud, and Willie became an aficionado of the arts and insisted upon taking his mother to hear Adelina Patti in *Lucia di Lammermoor* ("exquisite") and Fanny Kemble in *Antony and Cleopatra,* which proved so thrilling that they went back another night for *Twelfth Night* and deemed it "masterly."

The whole family enjoyed candy scrapes after snowstorms and skating parties on the Back Bay. "Tremendous crowd on the ice. Crinoline, meerschaum, bad cigars, and moonbeams deliciously mixed," wrote Willie of one party, and Fanny considered the ice skates she received for her fifteenth birthday the most desirable present of her life. When Wendy had turned fifteen a few years before, however, he had hesitated even to ask for the jackknife he desired, since his parents had invested in some special drawing materials for him a few months before, but he was flabbergasted when Garrison sprang for a season ticket to Moorhouse's river bathing club on the Beacon Street shoreline. "Capital!" he told Willie. "Capital!"

By 1857 the older boys had all moved out. The second son, William Jr., had given up high school two years before to take a job as a bank teller in Lynn, where he boarded with Garrison's old friend James Buffum, earned a quick promotion to cashier, and developed a business acumen that would lead eventually to a successful career as a wool broker and real estate investor. The editor respected his son's commercial ambitions and felt confident that his loving, generous, and "self-forgetting" nature would lead him to practice the socially conscious philanthropy that distinguished the family's special friends. His younger brother, Wendell, carried the family's academic hopes. At seventeen, in his father's estimation "a model boy, mature beyond his years," Wendy passed the Harvard entrance examinations with scores high enough to earn him a small scholarship. With the remaining expenses of tuition, books, and board secured by Wendell Phillips's long-standing promise, the young scholar crossed the river to Cambridge, taking with him a beautiful five-volume dictionary of classical mythology presented by Theodore Parker, and joined the Harvard Class of '61 to ready himself for a career in *belles lettres*.

That left George. At twenty-one, Garrison's eldest son had not yet found himself. Always a slow student, he had left school at fifteen and lived for a time in Adin Ballou's utopian community at Hopedale. He then had a clerkship in Danvers that led nowhere and a bookkeeping job in a Boston music store that proved too hard. Quiet, conscientious, and exacting, George seemed more suited to mechanical work, and his father tried to find him a place as an apprentice jeweler with friends in Providence. He is "very diffident, and too distrustful of his own ability," Garrison explained, but "he is kind, faithful, steady, and upright—a good boy in all respects—though not calculated for a bustling, *driving* business."

When nothing had materialized by 1854, the editor took George into *The Liberator*'s office and taught him composition and presswork. For several years the young man performed capably, but he chafed inwardly at the situation, became more and more discouraged, and morosely talked of going to Kansas or to sea. Finally, in April 1857, he found gumption enough to attach himself to a friend's family bound for the Minnesota frontier, where he worked in a blind and sash factory until he got a compositor's job on a Republican newspaper. Though his parents fretted endlessly about the temptations he faced, George reassured them that he lived simply, reading and playing checkers in the evenings, save for Lyceum on Mondays and a ball at "the Frémont Hotel" on Thursdays. He hated to write and warned family members not to expect answers to every letter they wrote, especially as he heard in them only the exhortation to return home. After many anxious letters from his mother he burst out that he couldn't come home if it meant returning to *The Liberator*. "To go back and work in that office would settle my fate," he said. "I would have to stick to the paper as long as it lives and would never find a chance to better my condition." Garrison, who had taken his son into the office more in desperation than dynastic hopes, declared that George could be trusted "even in the far West" and respected his decision, though he would have preferred him closer to home. They exchanged letters about political developments, and when George lamented that the editor's views were not sufficiently understood in his region, Garrison bound up some remaindered sheets of his 1852 *Selections* and sent them west to his son.

For the younger children, life on Dix Place still held vitality and fascination. The Boston schools had undergone a wave of reform in the 1840s under Horace Mann's direction, which meant that unlike their older brothers, who had chanted lessons before a master in a large undifferentiated classroom much like that their father had known, Fanny and Franky attended a modern three-story grammar school divided into graded classes each with a teacher of its own. This reorganization followed the new principles of scientific classification and the factory model for division of labor, but the abolitionists charged that the moral price was too high, since school reformers like Mann refused to support the ongoing demand for racially integrated schools in order to maintain broad support for their building program. With centralized administration and nearly six hundred children in each building, the system was deemed highly efficient at "Americanizing" the growing numbers of immigrant children who made up half the school-age population of Boston, a higher priority for Mann than integrating classrooms for the small number of blacks. Though there was considerable hostility toward abolitionism among the Irish working class, the youngest Garrisons experienced no special difficulties among their schoolmates. The city made no provision for girls' education beyond eighth grade, but Fanny continued to study music and languages at home, which was just fine with Helen, who feared that competing for medals at school had "unstrung" her daughter's nerves. That concern did not extend to Frank, who became the first Garrison to attend the elite Boston Latin high school, where he felt "driven" by the rigorous program.

In the summers the youngsters frequently escaped the crowded and sweltering city for vacations with abolitionist families in the country, though their parents stayed in town and only traveled out on weekends in conjunction with the editor's lecture schedule. Throughout the year, Fanny and Franky, however, took their turns at bringing their father's dinner down to the newspaper office on Wednesday afternoons when the demands of going to press made it impossible for him to come home, and they loved being set up on a stool to play at distributing type. They also participated in the family ritual of proofreading when their father came home with a stack of galley slips and cried out, "Here's a chance to get *The Liberator* in advance of the mail." When Fanny wearied of the task, Garrison diverted her with a story paper pulled from his exchange pile, which, she later confessed, interested her a great deal more than her father's proofs.

Except for George, who labored under the burden of being the eldest son, the Garrison children grew up peaceably and charted their own paths with considerable aplomb. In the crisis-laden atmosphere of the 1850s, moreover, the children remained staunch abolitionists, as did the second generation of AAS apostles generally, and none turned against their parents' cause. Lloyd and Helen had endeavored to rear their children by example rather than indoctrination or rigorous discipline, and the fruit did not fall far from the tree. "If we do not teach by our lives," the editor told Willie as his twenty-first birthday neared, "we teach in vain."

As her children grew older, Helen Garrison enjoyed her newfound leisure. "I never saw a time since I was married when I could say before this I had no particular work to do," she marveled to Ann Phillips in 1851 when her youngest, Franky, was still a toddler, and as the decade went on, she felt comfortable enough to do more visiting and travel. In August 1854, they visited Brooklyn, Connecticut, for the first time in fourteen years and found the village so little changed that Garrison said it made possible the illusion that they had not grown any older themselves. In their courting days, he mused, the trip had taken fifteen hours, with the tedium relieved only by the expectation of seeing his sweetheart; now the railroad had brought them in an easy four hours, "and better than formerly . . . I had Helen all the way with me."

Occasionally Helen even ventured to Philadelphia or New York for the important conventions, where she charmed everybody with the simple grace that visitors to her home had appreciated over the years. Meeting the once-reclusive Mrs. Garrison at a Pennsylvania AAS meeting in 1852, the organizer Sallie Holley found her "a free and easy person with the least possible pretensions, and . . . a very natural, artless sort of way . . . no starched-up stiffness to scare a body out of their wits." Holley merrily recounted to her companion how Helen had asked to borrow a pocket dictionary as the two women shared a writing desk in Mrs. Mott's parlor. She didn't usually bother with one, Helen admitted, but she was writing to Ann Phillips and " 'Wendell is so particular.' "

In the exuberant mood of the Philadelphia trip, Helen even agreed to sit for a daguerreotype. She tensed up, however, and with her head thrust forward, her eyes peering warily into the camera, and her lips pressed into a thin line, the result did not project the cozy charm that was her hallmark, though the high contrast between her lovely pale complexion and her dark hair and eyes gave more than a hint of her attractiveness. Like most of the abolitionist women, she wore her hair in a severe style, parted sharply in the center, then looped over her ears and coiled and pinned at the back. Like most of the abolitionist women, too, she dressed in a style at least ten years behind the times, wearing in her portrait an open-fronted black silk dress with a white dickey and frilly lace collar pinned with an enameled floral cameo that might well have belonged to her mother.

For all the travel and an increasingly prominent role in the antislavery bazaar, Helen remained centered upon the domestic life of her husband and children and the movement's "social circle." She still worried about finances and worked closely with the Garrison trustees, who had given up on reforming the editor's helter-skelter way with his records and looked to his wife for sounder accounting. She could now make ends meet more easily, though the occasional gifts of barrels of flour, tubs of butter, and rounds of cheese helped her feed the steady stream of visitors that made Dix Place the "abolitionist hotel" of choice. And for the first time Helen could afford to worry more about appearances. The back blinds needed painting, and the carpets could not be turned and shaken anymore. They were "a disgrace," Helen lamented to Willie; even little Alla Foster had wondered aloud how people of their taste could have such a patchwork on the floor. When Garrison had the remaining stock of his book bound, Helen plotted with her sons to sell the volumes themselves (and use the profits for refurbishing the house) before the editor gave them all away.

Social life on Dix Place spanned the generations. When the older boys came home on holidays and family occasions, they brought along their friends, and Helen took great delight in serving scalloped oyster cake and oranges to the young people, who danced and played until nearly midnight. (Helen, however, worried that Francis Meriam, Mr. Jackson's grandson, talked so feverishly of going to fight the war in Kansas that she told George that his old school friend must have "a pin out somewhere" and prayed that her own son not indulge any similarly wild ideas.) The cadre of young women Abby Kelley had trained as organizers frequently came through Boston, lodging at Dix Place, and Helen offered them a motherly hospitality that offset the rigors of the road. She grew deeply fond of Susan B. Anthony and Sallie Holley, both of whom returned her affection and became much-loved "aunts" to the Garrison youngsters.

Holley, especially, refreshed Dix Place with her matchless enthusiasm. Her small blue eyes, dimpled cheeks, and rounded chin gave her a doll-like appearance that belied her toughness. She poked fun at the burdens of jouncy wagons, muddy roads, overheated kitchens, leaden pancakes, and cold attics, along with the overly curious hosts who taxed the patience of every lecture agent; perhaps, she joked, it would be well if Garrison posted answers to the most frequently asked questions in *The Liberator* to save her the business of saying umpteen times over that she was not married, that she had no sisters but lived with a dear friend, Caroline Putnam, who was a schoolteacher, that she had worked her way through Oberlin, that she had refused communion in Dr. Hosmer's church in Buffalo after Millard Fillmore had resumed his membership there, and that indeed she had never seen such tall wheat or such ripe berries as she had in this particular county.

On her visits, Holley delighted in bringing the Garrisons up to date on their mutual friends. Theodore Weld was a very popular teacher at a New Jersey commune, while Angelina had developed an interest in the harmonious spiritualism of Andrew Jackson Davis. Her sister Sarah, though her talk was "angels food," had grown "shockity in appearance," and her sharp-featured face was "like seeing Stonehenge." Gerrit Smith had conveyed his hopes for a closer alliance with Garrison, whom he regarded as "a beautiful spirit," while Harriet Beecher Stowe had confided that while she had once considered Garrison a wolf in sheep's clothing, she now knew that he was really a lamb in a wolf's disguise.

The report brought a great laugh from the editor, and he delightedly recounted his exchange with the celebrated author. When she had asked point-blank if he were a Christian, Garrison had responded that she could not have asked "a more indefinite question."

"Well, are you such a Christian as I am?" Stowe asked.

"That is, if possible, more indefinite than the other," Garrison quoted himself in reply. (Later, Stephen S. Foster said he would have answered, "I hope not.") The editor said Stowe paused for a while and then asked, "Well, Mr. Garrison, do you believe in the atonement?"

"Ah, that is a definite question," he said, and satisfied her by saying that he "did not believe that Jesus could not be good for me, nor good for you, but good only for Himself. Jesus is the hope of glory and the redemptive spirit of love."

Ironically, though the editor had satisfied Stowe's orthodox concerns for his piety, he and Helen had moved completely out of formal church life. They did sometimes attend Theodore Parker's weekly lectures in the new Music Hall delivered to a "congregation" with a nominal connection to Unitarianism, but that only confirmed the secular humanism of their orientation. When a teacher once asked Fanny if she had been baptized, she did not understand the question and said she would ask her father about it. "No, my darling," he told her, "you have had a good bath every morning and that is a great deal better."

Garrison did not think that his hostility toward the institutional church diminished his piety, and his conversation with Stowe was not a dissembling one. He believed in redemptive love, in the power of the Christian community of souls, in the injunctions of prophets and apostles, and in the righteousness and power of God. In the 1840s his religious quest had led him into the eclectic explorations of the Chardon Street meetings; in the 1850s the search brought him, and hundreds of thousands of others, into the diffuse movement known as Spiritualism. Although it began with well-publicized claims of "spirit rapping" and other efforts to communicate with departed souls, Spiritualism became a heterodox religious movement that offered an opportunity for individuals to establish rapport with more sublime levels of reality and gain access to divine truth without the mediation of clergy or church organization. A blend of animal magnetism, mesmerism, and Transcendentalism, it made men and women equally qualified "investigators" of spiritual life, offered a cosmic language that unified natural and spiritual phenomena, and regarded death—in the words of the popular writer Andrew Jackson Davis—"as a door leading to another room in the 'house not made with hands.'" Such "harmonial philosophy" encouraged a more affectionate and more personal religious style that comported well with a socially progressive outlook and skepticism toward authority. Helen had found Davis's "The Great Harmonium" the most consoling of works for years after Charlie's death, and the editor himself remained very open to the idea of spiritual communication and "new" religion long after some of the most publicized "rappings" had been exposed as frauds. For Garrison, however, Spiritualism was not so much a matter of seances as it was an appreciation that there might be truths not yet apprehended by established institutions, and it granted him, as it did countless others, an exhilarating sense of communion with the deepest powers of the universe.

Garrison was growing old in the cause. In February 1857 a Buchanan paper in Troy, New York, described the visiting editor, just past his fifty-first birthday, as "a tall, large-brained, clerical looking gentleman about sixty years old" who spoke earnestly but without the animation he had possessed ten years earlier. The local Republican sheet caricatured him in the usual style as a fanatic, who read at length from the Scriptures and peered over his spectacles to glare ferociously at the audience, but to Aaron Powell, the young organizer managing the tour, Garrison seemed the incarnation of a Biblical prophet returned to earth and an illustration of the saying that "one shall chase a thousand and two put ten thousand to flight." Sure signs that the editor was aging, however, came both from people everywhere telling him that he looked "as good as new" and Garrison's reporting such reassurances home to his wife.

To her budget of concerns Helen had added growing anxiety about her husband's long days at *The Liberator*. The printer James Yerrinton was five years Garrison's senior and not in good health. The editor no longer trusted him to read proof and stayed so late to do it himself that Helen feared his own eyes would give out. Yet Garrison cherished his long partnership with the sweet-tempered and gentle printer and would brook no changes. For a time Yerrinton's son, Winchell, who had joined the concern in 1849, took up the slack, but having mastered the new art of stenography, the young man developed a sideline career as a reporter of speeches and was often away. Garrison appreciated the accurate texts he supplied for the movement and did not complain about having to fill in for him, though Helen feared her husband had become "a complete drudge" and yearned for George's return. "Father does far more than he ought at the office I am certain," she sighed, but "it will always be thus."

The daguerreotypes taken of the editor during the 1850s support the friends' impressions of freshness more than his wife's anxiety about exhaustion. Garrison participated eagerly in the popular fad of having portraits made by the French process of exposing to light a chemically treated copper plate, developing it over heated mercury, and preserving the resulting image under glass in a fitted silver case. By 1853, New York's Broadway had more well-advertised studios and window displays than Paris or London, with

Mathew Brady's lavishly appointed portrait gallery merely one of many competing establishments, but every city had its famous practitioners, and Garrison seems to have tried them all without satisfaction. "Out of a hundred daguerreotypes that have been taken of me, not one is worth looking at a second time," he told Oliver Johnson in 1858. "The failure is absolute, whether it be Brady, in your city, or South[worth] or Whipple here. . . ." The problem, thought Garrison, lay in the mobility and "changeableness" of his face and the complications created by his spectacles, but verisimilitude may not have been the real issue. Garrison and his friends sought a physical image that would convey his moral stature, and while the best daguerreotypists prided themselves on their artistic talent for revealing character, the gap between Garrison's unprepossessing appearance and his visionary work proved too great to bridge. When Chief Justice Shaw marched into the Southworth & Hawes studio on Tremont Row, the camera made an awesome portrait of looming dignity tinged with shadows; when Southworth posed Harriet Beecher Stowe, draped in silk and bedizened with ringlets, next to a table and potted plant, he found the thoughtful woman beneath the decor of celebrated author; yet when Garrison sat next to the column used as a standard prop in political portraits, Southworth's camera showed only a bald middle-aged man, dark-eyed and thin-lipped, with a strong chin and jaw jutting above a stiffly starched white collar.

Other images made over the decade revealed some of the physical qualities that contributed to the abolitionist's appeal. In group portraits with Phillips and George Thompson in 1851, Southworth found the rapt attention and concern Garrison could bring to a conversation, and a cameraman in Rochester, though he posed the editor stiffly in his customary dark suit with his hand under his jacket, caught him peering over his glasses in the stern manner audiences knew so well. Broadbent's studio in Philadelphia produced an 1852 stereoscopic image that illuminated the bright, beseeching quality in Garrison's eyes and the tenderness of his half-smile. More daringly, the daguerreotypist flooded Garrison's head with an angled light so bright that it made his eyes seem to glow through his spectacles and gave him an aura of great exaltedness. An unknown operator tried a similar floodlit approach in full profile that, with the editor's collar informally turned down, illuminated something of Garrison's inner calm, with his head relaxed and his face remarkably innocent in repose. L. G. Chase in Boston made a three-quarter right profile, jaw and chin thrust forward, that produced an image of resoluteness and concern, though a frowning corner at the mouth gave an uncharacteristic impression of sadness. The editor's associates liked it well enough, however, to invite Louis Grozelier to make an engraving for publication, but the artist asked for additional sittings, reversed the profile, and achieved a considerably more sympathetic effect. William C. Nell supervised the production and sale of the lithograph with the motto "I Am in Earnest . . . I Will Be Heard."

The Grozelier image—serious, spirited, yet approachable—defined Garrison to the public in the late 1850s. His reputation rested entirely on his standing as the abolitionist pioneer, who now seemed more oracular than disruptive. While this view of the editor as a historical figure of consequence drained some of the militancy from his character, it did not turn him into a celebrity attraction. Unlike Wendell Phillips and Theodore Parker, who had capitalized upon stature gained in the movement to make thousands of dollars annually traveling the burgeoning lyceum circuit with set pieces on literary and cultural subjects, Garrison still proved too controversial for lecture bureau managers and local promoters. Though he could have used what popular speakers called "F.A.M.E" ("Fifty, and my expenses"), the editor stuck to his last and did not try to work up performances on "The Lost Arts" (Phillips) or "The Progress of Mankind" (Parker) that brought antislavery in sideways or relegated it to another evening and venue. Parker and Phillips, of course, spoke without charge countless times at abolitionist conventions, and the latter, with his dramatic platform delivery and pungent aphoristic style, far surpassed Garrison as an oratorical attraction.

The movement, however, looked to Garrison for leadership and polished the landmark view of him as it celebrated its own milestones: in 1855, the twentieth anniversary of the editor's mobbing; in 1857, the twenty-fifth anniversary of the founding of the New England Anti-Slavery Society; and, year by year, anniversaries of the other state societies and the AAS itself. Many abolitionist speakers took to displaying their well-preserved copies of the earliest numbers of *The Liberator* as sacred relics. In New York at a private meeting arranged for Garrison with Henry Ward Beecher and his most prominent parishioners, Oliver Johnson caused a stir by handing around the very first edition of the newspaper, and the minister insisted upon having the editor's famous credo read aloud so that the entire company could bask in its reflected glory. To have his defiant words endorsed in a wealthy salon amid tables laden with elegant cakes and creams left the editor with very mixed feelings, but Johnson assured him that the reception had done more good than any public speech he might have given in the city. The prophet was finding honor in his own country. An admirer in Ohio told Garrison that his voice had gone forth "like the low rumbling of a distant train, to an ear laid to an iron track."

Portions of the mainstream press, however, persisted in making fun of the multiracial tint of abolitionist events and ridiculing their speakers as moonbeams and Sambos and embittered spinsters. When Garrison spoke at a First of August celebration on Long Island, a reporter for the *New York Times* caricatured the spectacle as black people playing at politics, from which the respectable newspaper drew the lesson that "the sudden, and inconsiderate, and total abolition of Slavery, is only second as an evil to Slavery itself." For all the gain, the editor manifestly still needed to be heard.

"What historic denouements are these we are approaching?" Walt Whitman asked in his diatribe about the 1856 presidential campaign. "No man knows what will happen next, but all know that some such things are to happen as mark the greatest moral convulsions of the earth. Who shall play the hand for America in these tremendous games?" The electorate answered James Buchanan, but the voting trend exposed a stark sectional fissure in presidential politics that could not be bridged. Frémont carried eleven of the sixteen free states and won fifty-five percent of the popular vote in the North and west, while Buchanan took all the slave states except Maryland (the only state taken by Fillmore) with fifty-six percent of the popular vote in the South. Buchanan won the election only by holding the traditional Democratic vote in Pennsylvania, New Jersey, Indiana, Illinois, and California, and he would come into office as the president with the lowest proportion (forty-five percent) of the national vote since John Quincy Adams in 1824. For the Republicans their showing was more than encouraging; it offered the clear prospect of victory four years hence. The turnout in the North was an astonishingly high eighty-three percent of eligible voters; the Republicans had become the first party to reap political dividends from antislavery. They had prevailed over the Know-Nothing craze; to the bloc of states they had already lined up against the slave power, they had but to add Pennsylvania and either Indiana or Illinois to elect a president on a completely sectional basis. To attract voters in those states, however, the Republicans would feel compelled to dilute their antislavery statements in favor of the general appeal to workers' economic opportunity that had so far proven itself with disaffected Democrats and disillusioned Know-Nothings elsewhere.

For Garrison, who regarded the election as another triumph for "border ruffian democracy" and slavery's expansionist design on the Caribbean, the task of genuine abolitionism remained that of raising the consciousness of the Northern public to a moral standard that the Republicans would have to honor without subterfuge or delay. With a resilience that few could match, the editor countered postelection despair with a flurry of activity. To launch *The Liberator*'s twenty-seventh year in January 1857, he replaced its old worn-out type with a fresh set, the "new typographical dress" that was Garrison's recurring signal for renewed vigor, if not prosperity. Admitting that subscriptions had fallen off as they always did during campaign seasons, when some readers preferred newspapers "less stringent in their ethics," he nonetheless declared himself primed for further struggle and "as independent as if all the gold in California" were at his disposal. He stood with the Hutchinsons as they offered a rousing version of "Get off the Track" at the MAS twenty-fifth anniversary celebration and then personally launched the latest AAS organizing drive with a month of lecturing across the Mohawk Valley and western New York. He would maintain the abolitionist movement as a moral vector in the field of free-soil politics.

In the editor's lexicon this meant a renewed campaign for disunion to bring the nation's conscience into active conflict with its constitutional arrangements. The opposition to the Fugitive Slave Law had started the process, the larger debate over the "higher law" had continued it, but the next chapter—some direct effort at repudiation and reconstruction—had yet to be written. Garrison endorsed the effort of a group of abolitionists in Worcester led by T. W. Higginson who called a statewide convention to consider "the practicality, probability, and expediency" of repudiating the constitutional compromises and separating the free states from the slave. For Garrison the three-day meeting, January 15–17, 1857, represented "an experiment outside every organization" to probe support for radical defiance, and he was pleased that the conclave attracted the interest of several prominent Republicans, most notably Francis W. Bird, a paper manufacturer and state legislator who had engineered the martyred Sumner's election to the U.S. Senate. Sentiment ran high enough among the several hundred participants to initiate a national petition drive that by midsummer would attract more than seven thousand signatures calling for a "Great Northern Convention" to meet at Cleveland in October. Garrison rejoiced that disunion had become "an open question" among influential people who had previously condemned any such talk as verging upon treason. A few critics still invoked Webster's rallying cry of "Liberty and Union," but events had largely discredited the formula, and more often now people raised questions intended to expose the impracticality of the idea—where would you draw the line? what about tariffs and trade? could the North absorb a large population of runaway slaves?—but that revealed their having begun to think about the unthinkable.

Such could not be said about the new president. James Buchanan took the presidential oath on March 4, 1857, with a complacent address that denounced the abolitionist agitation. Antislavery people "can't expect much" from Buchanan, Bradford Drew noted in his diary, but he confidently predicted that the outgoing president's name would "rot." "Pierce's friends say 'history will do him justice,'" the young man wrote, "and I hope it will." Buchanan did not get a fresh start with history with his fatuous suggestion that tumult would cease if slavery were allowed to stand unmolested where it existed and if all good citizens would "cheerfully submit" to a judicial determination of the territorial question. This, he predicted with a confidence we now know to be a product of inside information, would be "speedily and finally settled" in a case pending in the Supreme Court. A scant two days later came a ruling in *Dred Scott v. Sandford* that instead fatally unsettled the nation.

Speaking for a 7–2 Court majority that included five Southerners and a Pennsylvania Democrat close to Buchanan, the chief justice of the United States delivered the dual opinion that (1) Congress had no authority to exclude slavery from the territories and (2) black people had no constitutional rights of citizenship.* The first ruling made the Missouri Compromise and any other restrictive legislation unconstitutional and thus took the most extreme Southern view of the territorial question. The second ruling reinforced the concept of chattel slavery and the constitutional recognition of a slavemaster's property rights and thus took the most extreme white supremacist view of the moral question. Roger B. Taney, an aged Marylander who had emancipated his own slaves decades before yet fiercely believed in the political sanctity of the institution and the Democratic Party he had helped to build, had written perhaps the most polemical and partisan judicial opinion in the nation's history. It marked a new aggressiveness in the campaign to defend slavery not on the familiar basis as an institution peculiar or local to the Southern states but as a national political entity entitled to protection everywhere under the flag. What Calhoun could not get from Congress in two decades, Taney delivered from the bench in fifty-five densely argued pages.

The *Dred Scott* decision proved a double-barreled attack upon abolitionism and Free-Soilism, but compared to the vituperation visited upon it by Republican editors, Garrison's reaction was remarkably understated. He of course placed excerpts from the Taney opinion in the "Refuge of Oppression"—the editor's traditional front-page place of obloquy for attacks upon the movement—and he filled many other columns with blistering excerpts from the Northern press, but he wrote no long statement himself. Like the Kansas issue, the Court's decision outraged the moderates who had more faith in constitutional antislavery than did Garrison, and with editors like Greeley and Beecher howling defiance, *The Liberator* hardly had to say a word. The Republican editors, however, devoted most of their energy to denouncing Taney's opinion as an effort to nationalize slavery, while Garrison directed most of his attention to the decision's exclusion of black people, "whether emancipated or not," from citizenship and the political community.

This was the most sinister aspect of *Dred Scott*, for Taney clearly sought to undercut the philosophical and moral basis of abolitionism by separating black people from the federal Constitution except in the degraded capacity of chattel. The corollary of this proposition, that manumitted slaves would have to be deported and colonized elsewhere, had long been recognized by Southern political figures as disparate as Jefferson, Calhoun, and Clay. In

---

*The case had originated in a routine petition for manumission by Dred Scott, a Missouri slave who claimed that he had become free after residing for several years in the Wisconsin Territory and Illinois with his owner, an army physician on assignments there. The Missouri courts had previously granted such petitions as a matter of comity with other states, and Scott had actually won a lower-court verdict, but proslavery politicians secured its reversal at a higher level and catapulted the case into the federal system, where political motives dictated a broad decision rather than a narrow one that might have rested on any number of jurisdictional issues. Although Dred Scott did not win his lawsuit for freedom, he was manumitted by his owner several months after the decision and worked as a hotel porter in St. Louis until he died of consumption in September 1858.

Taney's argument, which the judge had advanced without objection twenty-five years earlier as Andrew Jackson's attorney general, Garrison heard the voice of the colonizationist spirit of Judge Brice and the Taney political circle that had prosecuted him in 1830.

Taney held that at the time of the Declaration of Independence in 1776, blacks had "no rights that white men were bound to respect," a condition that, in the jurist's opinion, still prevailed in 1857. He committed serious errors of distortion and omission in this section of his opinion, and Garrison reprinted the important dissent by Justice Benjamin Curtis that corrected the chief justice's history, demonstrating that free blacks during the founding era had possessed political rights, including male suffrage, in at least five states. Curtis, formerly a Boston attorney who had earned the abolitionists' enmity a few years earlier by supporting the government's effort to return the fugitives Sims and Burns, did not press the issue of federal citizenship, however, and cautiously regarded the question of black civil rights as a matter for state determination.

For Garrison, the rebuttal could not be so limited, but had to defend equality to the fullest extent. *The Liberator* therefore reprinted a bitter attack from *The Independent,* with its lead sentence converted into a sensational headline, "THE DECISION OF THE SUPREME COURT IS THE MORAL ASSASSINATION OF A RACE, AND CANNOT BE OBEYED." The editor filled his columns with extracts from William C. Nell's recent historical studies of the patriotic role black people had played during the American Revolution, and he lent vigorous support to the black community's defiant response to Taney: a public commemoration of the death of a black man, Crispus Attucks, in the famous Boston Massacre that had presaged the Revolution. *The Liberator* also reported, as most papers did not, the mass protest meeting in Philadelphia at which Robert Purvis and Charles L. Remond insisted that the decision was "in perfect keeping" with the oppressive spirit of the Constitution and a political climate that made black civil rights a matter of "sufferance" alone.

The Garrisonians understood *Dred Scott* in the context of their disunionism. While the Republicans became drawn into the vortex of technicalities on the "incidental" issue of nonextension, the abolitionists advanced their view that slaveholders used the Constitution to control the government and that the entire liberation struggle had to be understood—in Garrison's phrase—as one of "conscience against organized injustice." In the editor's view, *Dred Scott* had delivered a crowning blow not only to the Republican idea that slavery could be extinguished by preventing its expansion but to the Smith-Douglass contention that the Constitution could be construed as carrying an antislavery mandate. No wonder that in their continuing polemical warfare Douglass insinuated that Garrison and Taney took identical views of the document. They shared, however, not so much a jurisprudence as a realistic appreciation that the Constitution conferred power upon the slaveholders sufficient to protect slavery aggressively and indefinitely.

It would be difficult to exaggerate the destructiveness of the *Dred Scott* decision, for it emboldened the South as deeply as it embittered the North. The court had given the slaveholding interest a constitutional counterweight to the moral arguments of the abolitionists and a powerful incentive not only to keep the Kansas question open, but to press Congress to enact a federal slave code that would protect rather than restrict slavery in the territories. The court had given Garrisonians a nasty reminder of the racist barriers that blocked the path toward abolition even more securely than the Constitution and had shown the Smith-Douglass tendency how chimerical were its hopes that a legislative transformation could occur once Northern majorities controlled both houses of Congress.

Dred Scott posed its cruelest dilemma, however, for the Republicans. To continue their advocacy of nonextension they had to discredit the decision, but the more extensively they attacked, the closer they came to the Garrisonian imperative. If Dred Scott had to remain a slave because he had no standing as a citizen to sue, then the Republicans had to stand up for black citizenship and risk alienating the racist portion of their constituency. If Dred Scott had to remain a slave because Congress had unconstitutionally prohibited slavery in a place where he had resided, then the central plank of the Republican platform collapsed and pitched them closer to abolitionism and disunion. As one editor in Maine put it, the Republicans had either to go out of business or become revolutionaries.

There was another way out, however. The party could portray itself as the sectional defender of the free states against a slave-power conspiracy to nationalize the institution. Southern leaders played into this fear by taking advantage of Taney's opinion to renew their demand that Congress enact a federal slave code for the territories. Such a law would override any "unfriendly" action by Free-Soil legislatures and raised the specter that the U.S. Army might be used to protect a master's right to hold slaves in Kansas or Colorado or Minnesota as it had protected Anthony Burns's master's right to have his fugitive returned from Boston. The *Dred Scott* decision, it was now argued, cast doubt upon the legality of abolition in the Northern states. If a master had a right protected by the Fifth Amendment not to be deprived of his chattel without due process of law, and if congressional exclusion was such an unlawful deprivation, was not state exclusion of slaveholding equally unconstitutional? One more *Dred Scott* decision could establish the principle, warned Abraham Lincoln, the 1858 Republican senatorial candidate in Illinois, that slavery was lawful in all the states; while the public mind wanted reassurance that the "house divided" would eventually become all free, the slave power—working through the Democratic Party—seemed bent on making the nation all slave.

The violent flashpoint remained Kansas. The prairie battle flared with renewed viciousness in spring 1857 as the proslavery element, spurred by the Taney opinion, boldly initiated another round of the politics of fraud and the terror of guerrilla warfare in a renewed effort to legitimize slavery. Although every week brought trainloads of midwestern migrants who swelled the free-staters into an overwhelming majority, slaveholding Southerners wanted to vindicate the principle that the territory remained open to them. The bogus legislature previously elected with the illegal votes of the border ruffians now called a constitutional convention based upon a faked census and a rigged election, and by October the meeting at Lecompton had produced a document so biased toward slaveholders and so fraudulent in its claim to legitimacy that it is hard to believe that anyone could have taken it seriously. Yet the complaisant Buchanan, bowing to his party's Southern power base, recommended in February 1858 that Congress admit Kansas to statehood on the basis of the Lecompton constitution, an egregious move so at variance with Northern opinion of the "swindle" that even Stephen A. Douglas felt obliged to oppose it and thereby risk both a sectional rift in the party and the forfeiture of his presidential nomination.

One of the Kansas "freedom fighters" took advantage of the public uproar to launch a clandestine war of his own. Early in 1857 a grizzled veteran of the border warfare, "Captain" John Brown, came to Boston in an ostensible effort to raise money and arms for the defense of liberty in Kansas. As old as the century, a knockabout entrepreneur who had suffered reverses in just about every line of work he had tried, and an abolitionist his entire adult life, Brown had organized a protective league for fugitives and served as leader of the community of resettled black people Gerrit Smith had subsidized in the Adirondacks. In 1855, with his second wife and young family left at North Elba, Brown had gone to Kansas with his older sons and earned a hero's reputation in the valiant defense against superior force of the doomed Osawatomie settlement. His scars, his bearing, and the knowledge that he had already lost one son in the warfare all vouched for his integrity, but Brown also came with character references from Smith and Salmon P. Chase, the Free-Soil governor of Ohio, and he promptly gained the confidence of the Boston and Concord men who ran the statewide committee that raised assistance for the Kansas settlers. They eagerly organized occasions at which the old soldier, his eyes gleaming with righteousness, spoke with intense eloquence of the epic battle for justice being fought on the prairie and with grim practicality discussed the $30,000 he needed to equip and train a home guard to protect free-soil communities and patrol the Missouri border. The committee's president, a wealthy manufacturer named George L. Stearns who had made a double fortune in linseed oil and lead pipe, took a great liking to the bluff, intense old soldier and introduced him to men like the wealthy Amos Lawrence, who readily pledged $1,000 annually until Kansas was free. The committee's secretary, a handsome and courtly Concord schoolteacher named Franklin B. Sanborn, took Brown to dinner at the Thoreaus and arranged an audience with Emerson, who blessed Brown's appearance in the town hall.

Garrison encountered Brown at a Sunday-evening reception organized by Sanborn at Theodore Parker's house. The meeting between the bespectacled, studious editor and Old Osawatomie—tall, spare, dressed in a cheap corduroy suit, his hair standing straight up from his scalp, his mouth drawn tight in a razor-straight line—offers so many possibilities for drama that it is a shame that there are no contemporary records of it. In one of the few fanciful passages in their memoir, Garrison's sons pictured the scene as a debate, with Garrison countering Brown's Old Testament wrath with his own adherence to New Testament love, and biographers have embroidered this conceit ever since. Yet there is reason to doubt that anything so formal took place or that Garrison at once recognized Brown as his polar opposite. The editor himself could quote the Hebrew prophets to great advantage, and his perfectionist hope for peace always contended with his pietistic fear of divine retribution, giving urgency and force to his work as an agitator, so it was not necessarily Brown's apocalyptic talk that put Garrison off. Brown, moreover, liked to say that he believed in only two things, the Bible and the Declaration of Independence, a statement of Garrisonian fundamentalism that could only have pleased the editor. Brown, for his part, might have balanced his general suspicion of benevolent religious reformers against the editor's longevity in the cause and the knowledge that his own father, Owen Brown of Ohio, had subscribed to *The Liberator* from the very beginning and, as a seminary trustee, had defended Elizur Wright and Beriah Green against harassment at Western Reserve for advocating Garrison's *Thoughts on African Colonization*.

If there were reasons for Brown and Garrison to find common ground, there were also factors that kept them apart. Garrison may have disliked the Cromwellian aura that so attracted warmongers like Higginson to Brown, for the editor preferred the posture of Christian sacrifice to the stance of Puritan enforcer. Garrison, too, remained lukewarm about Kansas as a sufficiently valuable organizing issue for abolitionists, but even more significant, he had no high regard for the Kansas men who had taken Brown under their wing. Stearns had never taken either a moral or a financial interest in the MAS, and Samuel Gridley Howe, a strong-minded authoritarian reformer who had fought in Greece and kept in his foyer an azure-plumed helmet said to have been worn by Lord Byron himself, had frequently and bitterly criticized disunionism on the usual third-party grounds. Whatever happened that night at Parker's, there is no question that the editor left without having developed any enthusiasm for Brown or his mission and took no notice of his presence in *The Liberator*.

John Brown did not raise the $30,000 he sought on his New England trip in 1857. He did wangle his two hundred rifles from the Massachusetts Kansas group and got a healthy $7,000 subsidy from George L. Stearns after he had appealed to Mrs. Stearns's guilty feelings at living in luxury while Kansans suffered and his own family made the sacrifices that permitted him to undertake the Lord's work against slavery. "Captain" Brown, it turned out, had a whining, petulant, self-pitying side that he shamelessly revealed when it served his purposes, and it turned out that his purposes were not what they seemed. For nearly a decade Brown had fantasized about commanding a mobile guerrilla force that could operate from the fastness of the Alleghenies, staging lighting raids upon plantations and moving the liberated slaves north through a network he called "the Subterranean Pass Way," while recruiting the bravest and strongest of the freed blacks into the band itself. He said nothing of this to his new Boston admirers, but when some skeptical members of the national committee for Kansas relief asked for more detail about what the Massachusetts men were financing, Brown imperiously refused to discuss his plans or make any guarantee that the weapons would not be used elsewhere. Sanborn and his colleagues took this to be a hint that Brown's measures might have to embrace "defensive" raids against the ruffians' strongholds across the border in Missouri, but others in New York and Chicago suspected something worse. There were disturbing reports that Brown and his sons had participated in the cold-blooded murder of five proslavery settlers at Pottawatamie, allegedly in "reprisal" for the attack upon Lawrence, but Brown flatly denied any knowledge of the affair to Sanborn, and the Boston men let the matter drop.

Brown spent the balance of the year recruiting soldiers, including an adventurer named Hugh Forbes who had fought with Garibaldi in Italy. With Kansas embroiled in political combat rather than open warfare, however, the captain brooded more and more upon the idea of "troubling Israel" with raids in the South and asked his eastern friends to help him raise money "for secret service, and no questions asked." At the end of January 1858, Brown came east to meld his black and white supporters into a revolutionary conspiracy. With magnetic fervor he sketched for Frederick Douglass the latest version of his plan to build a guerrilla strike force, and although Douglass had some tactical criticism, he agreed to help Brown raise some money and find recruits. From Douglass's house, Brown wrote manipulative letters to his best Boston prospects, making each out to be his most trustworthy friend, with news that he had "perfected arrangements for carrying out an important measure, in which the world has a deep interest," that lacked only money from people willing to give "practical shape" to their abolition theories. "Do you think any of my Garrisonian friends either at Boston, Worcester, or in any other place, can be induced to supply a little 'straw,' if I will absolutely make 'bricks'?" Brown asked Parker. While awaiting replies, Brown went on to Peterboro and persuaded his old patron Gerrit Smith to

support the idea, which had now metamorphosed from a slave-running operation ("railroad business on a somewhat extended scale," he called it) into
provocation of a full-fledged slave insurrection and establishment—under a
constitution he had drafted at Douglass's—of a provisional mountain republic of liberated slaves and freedom fighters.

There is absolutely no evidence that Parker or anyone else approached
Garrison about Brown's latest scheme, but Sanborn, Higginson, Howe, and
Stearns all manifested interest, and in the first week of March 1858, the
mysterious "Nelson Hawkins" from somewhere in Iowa or perhaps Ohio
registered at the American Hotel for a few days of conferences with his
business associates. Their discussion took place just as Congress was taking
up the Lecompton constitution for Kansas, and it appeared—despite Stephen Douglas's opposition—that the Buchanan administration would succeed in bringing another slave state into the Union. As it turned out,
Congress would reject the Lecompton plan in favor of a compromise that
promised a new referendum and a large land grant that would be contingent
upon Kansas's yet remaining a territory for several years.

The outcome of the Lecompton fight did not matter to Brown. He did
not want to talk about Kansas anymore; he had turned his mind to Virginia
and the idea of striking a blow that would be the signal for slave insurrection
everywhere and a war to the death for freedom. Parker found the appeal to
revolutionary violence irrefutable; Howe found great charm in the idea of
fighting, as the Greeks did, from mountain fortresses; for years the belligerent Higginson had thirsted for a bloody and cataclysmic triumph over the
slave power; Sanborn found a Byronic grandeur in the defiant scheme;
Stearns and Smith had come to admire Brown's personal bravery and, certain
that he would proceed at any hazard, simply went along, because as Smith
put it, "we cannot give him up to die alone." The group, which referred to
itself as the stockholders, agreed to start raising money for the venture,
though they did not know when or where Brown planned "to raise the mill."
History knows them as "the secret six," though in reality they were seven,
for Frederick Douglass was privy to the scheme, if not their deliberations,
and he undertook covert activity, similar to theirs, in recruiting and chan-
neling small amounts of money to Brown. They might in fact have been
eight, for on a recruiting trip among free blacks in Canada, Brown conferred
with the redoubtable Harriet Tubman, the most expert conductor of the
fugitives' long-standing underground railroad, who supplied him with information about the terrain and local allies and offered him help in building
his force. From Tubman, too, came a target date: the Fourth of July.

With a conspiratorial web of so many strands and a rhetorical atmosphere
growing more overheated by the day, it was not surprising that some people
beyond the circle caught wind of the pending action. Although the nonresistants had spurned any interest in Brown, and Old Osawatomie had told

Sanborn not to approach the tough-talking Wendell Phillips, whom he considered full of hot air, the Garrisonians felt something astir. Francis Meriam started pestering Wendy and Willie for advice about whether it would be better to help the slaves by giving his legacy to the antislavery societies or by participating in some kind of covert action aimed at an uprising, and a few months later he went out to Kansas in search of John Brown. A Boston-based journalist named James Redpath, a native Scotsman who had ably reported the Kansas struggle and developed close ties to Brown, was preparing to publish an incendiary tract, based on his travels in the slave states and dedicated to Captain Brown, in which he depicted the South as a powder keg on the verge of insurrection. The slaves needed only Northern allies to act as nobly as Lafayette had in the Revolution, Redpath maintained; the speediest way of abolishing slavery and "ending the eternal hypocritical hubbub in Congress and the country" was to incite "a few scores of rattling insurrections . . . and by a little wholesome slaughter to arouse the conscience of the people. . . ."

Even Garrison found his faith in "the omnipotence of peace" challenged by the raging talk. He remained bedeviled by the contradictions of slave rebellion and found himself arguing that disunion would allow the North to "stand aside" and "give the slave a chance to regain his feet, and assert his freedom!" The editor also applauded the rising tide of black militancy in Boston and endorsed the community's petition to authorize a black militia unit to be called the "Liberty Guard," yet at the annual Attucks celebration in March 1858, he devoted himself to a long appeal for "moral instrumentalies alone" and suggested that the boasting about Lexington and Concord should cease, as praise for a war devoted exclusively to political, not moral ends. A few weeks later, however, Garrison sent a message of applause to a liberal meeting in memory of Count d'Orsini, executed for the attempted assassination of Louis Napoleon, in which he argued that, judged by revolutionary standards, Orsini was no murderer, but a patriot and martyr. Had he known of Brown's plans, would he have endorsed them on similar grounds, or condemned them as either immoral or impractical for America?

The Brown conspiracy, meanwhile, began to unravel. Brown's drillmaster, the mercenary (and alcoholic) Hugh Forbes, had a falling out with the old man and threatened to betray the entire affair unless he was well compensated for his silence. He made enough noise in Washington by attacking Brown's reputation and dropping hints about military organization that in early May 1858, Senator Henry Wilson wrote a very strong letter to Dr. Howe advising him to take care that arms and matériel intended for Kansas not be diverted to other purposes, as rumored, but instead put into the custody of reliable persons other than Brown. So unmistakable a signal threw the committee of six into a frenzied effort to delay the attack and distance themselves from their friend's enterprise.

The Garrisonians held their annual New England Anti-Slavery Convention in the very week that the conspirators scrambled to contain the plot, and the conjunction of events throws an eerie shadow upon the two pacifist sermons Garrison delivered that week. On Sunday, May 30, 1858, he occupied Theodore Parker's pulpit and chose for his discourse the theme on which they differed most—the peace question! Parker, who had gone to speak at a progressive church meeting in Pennsylvania fresh from a secret meeting of the six, gratefully thanked the editor for enabling his congregation to hear a divergent point of view. Garrison's text does not survive, but the fervent remarks he made a few days earlier to the convention were transcribed by Yerrinton and reported in *The Liberator*, and they constitute too pointed a warning against the venture in which Parker had become embroiled to have been coincidental. Out of his own heart, and perhaps in response to the temptations his own rhetoric had tasted, Garrison bore once more his testimony to the power of conscience.

Addressing himself to the somber mood and the feelings of frustration and stalemate that permeated the proceedings, Garrison—as was his habit at such times—tried to remind the abolitionists of their origins. The movement was "baptized in the spirit of peace" and had dedicated itself to the use of spiritual weapons alone, he began, but decades of combating the relentless aggressions of the slave power had led to two sad changes—a premature turn to the "mania of politics" that diluted the work of conscience and a fearful temptation to violence. "We are growing more and more warlike," Garrison said, "more and more disposed to repudiate the principle of peace," more and more disposed to talk about cleaving the tyrant's neck and to inflame one another with the spirit of violence "for a bloody work." Such talk and such desires, if further indulged, would sap "the moral power" of the movement, he warned, because the abolitionist's power over the conscience and the heart relied upon invoking a spirit that countered the violence employed by despots. Much as he detested the oppression exercised by slaveholders, Garrison said, they were still men whose lives were sacred, though their sinful conduct deserved horrific rebuke; he wanted the crucial battle against their tyranny to occur not on their soil, but in the hearts of people of conscience everywhere until the condemnation grew so great that all the supports for slavery in church and state disintegrated and the evil system involuntarily collapsed. Summoning every ounce of authority that he possessed, Garrison made the most direct, plain-spoken, and personal appeal that he had ever issued. "I pray you, abolitionists, still to adhere to the truth. Do not get impatient; do not become exasperated . . . do not make yourselves familiar with the idea that blood must flow. Perhaps blood will flow—God knows, I do not: but it shall not flow through any counsel of mine."

Loud and sustained applause filled the hall when Garrison stopped speaking. He did not know that at that very moment the conspirators were preparing to tell John Brown to hie himself back to Kansas, lie low for several months, and then blind the informers and critics with a diversionary incident on the prairie. They would transfer title to the arms to him and continue to supply him with money, but they would confer no more. He was to complete his plans by himself and not "burden" them with inconvenient knowledge. July Fourth came and went without news of any railroad or milling business in Virginia.

William Lloyd Garrison's supplication for nonviolent revolution in 1858 ought to be as well known as his burning of the U.S. Constitution at Framingham in 1854, for one needs to understand the editor as both a holy fool and a defiant Protestant in order to measure his achievement as an agitator. As an abolitionist Garrison insisted that Americans redefine themselves as citizens and reconstitute their government in order to secure essential principles of justice. Because his vision was rooted in the idea of racial equality, it was socially more radical than any American had dared propose before him, and because his vision was rooted in the idea of moral transformation, it was politically more radical—more optimistic and more loving—than any process contemplated by the Framers and one that made the beloved community more influential than the party caucus. It did not prevail, but it proved the catalyst for a revolutionary social achievement nonetheless. He had made his newspaper a radical messenger, and he made himself a prophet of liberation and reconstruction.

The abolitionists had once thought that their condemnation would ring the South and destroy slavery as a scorpion stings itself to death within a circle of fire. By 1858, however, each section had encircled the other with imperatives that could not be met. New York's Senator Seward described the controversy as "an irrepressible conflict" between philosophical principles that abolition would ultimately win, while South Carolina's Senator Hammond declared that the South had "settled this question of emancipation against all the world, in theory and practice, and the world must accept our solution. . . . You dare not make war on cotton. No power on earth dares to make war upon it. Cotton is king."

Fifteen years after Garrison had first raised the disunion banner, people everywhere questioned the wisdom and viability of compromise for union's sake and recognized an inherent conflict between liberty and slavery that required a permanent resolution. "We shall surely be vindicated at the court of conscience and at the tribunal of God," Garrison declared in 1859, "and the verdict of posterity will be, *The abolitionists were in the right, and the nation was in the wrong.*" The compromise had come undone, for it was finally seen as a barrier to the full realization of American freedom and the liberation of black people. This was his achievement, a work of intellectual and moral force whose significance is obscured by the war that overtook it and the sentimental patriotism that yet regards that war as a tragedy of flag and not of the racist politics against which Garrison had set his soul and staked his life in spiritual combat. He had taken a "root out of dry ground" and tended it carefully for thirty years until it had grown ready to blossom, but whether the fruit would taste of sweet redemption or bitter retribution Garrison could not presume to know.

BOOK FIVE

AND AN IMMORTAL CROWN

1859–1879

GARRISON AT SIXTY

Mathew Brady Studio, c. 1865
(Library of Congress)

CHAPTER TWENTY-ONE

JOHN BROWN HAS TOLD US THE TIME

ONE MORNING IN MARCH 1858, A FAST-TALKING NERVY GENTLEMAN IN FANCY CLOTHES, KID GLOVES, AND PATENT LEATHER SHOES MARCHED UP THE STAIRS AT 21 CORNHILL AND SOUGHT A CONVERSATION WITH THE editor. Removing his silk hat to reveal a domed forehead and a high-flying thatch of jet-black hair, the visitor introduced himself as William H. Herndon, "but call me Billy," an attorney from Springfield, Illinois, who had yearned for years to meet the celebrated Garrison. Herndon considered himself a reformer, a freethinker, and a seeker of philosophic truth, and he loved nothing more than to talk effusively about the animating purposes of the universe with the snap and pep of a railroad promoter or a real estate man. The editor had his working day interrupted frequently by spiritual pilgrims from many sects, and truth to tell, he enjoyed the talk and never begrudged the time, but this Herndon fellow was not the usual sort of wayfaring stranger. Not only was he the temperance mayor of Springfield and the junior partner in the town's leading law firm, Lincoln & Herndon, but he was a member of the Republican central committee for Illinois, a presidential elector, and a putative candidate for governor. Herndon had come to philosophize, but he had politics on his mind as well.

After stiff confrontations with Stephen Douglas in Washington and Horace Greeley in New York, he had come to Boston to see "the places of revolutionary memory," he said, and to view "the three *living* institutions of Boston—Garrison, Parker, and Phillips." While the city had answered his expectations and he had found the female reformers both forthright and hospitable, the men had left him cold. Phillips brushed him off, and Parker had visibly winced at Herndon's "gaseous gush" and cut short the conversation the visitor had so longed to have. Garrison, however, welcomed Billy warmly and sat him right down to chat. Think of his disappointment, Herndon would say afterward, that the man he expected to be whining and insulting and "fanatically blind to the charities and equities of life" turned out to be approachably warm. When Garrison, eyes agleam, made his customary disclaimers about the dangers of talking with a fanatic, Herndon waved them away. "Never mind that," he said, "I'll take care of it. . . . I am not afraid of ideas, though they should blaze beneath fanaticism." Indeed. Herndon, it seemed, wanted to bottle some of Garrison's spirit and bring it home to Illinois.

Beyond the cheerful palaver and the musings about the cosmos, however, Herndon had a serious political goal to pursue. He had come east on behalf of Illinois Republicans to nip a budding enthusiasm among antislavery politicians to support Stephen A. Douglas in the pending Senate race there. In New York, Greeley had told him flatly, "The Republican standard is too high; we want something practical." Douglas, the reasoning went, had broken with the Buchanan administration by opposing the proslavery Lecompton constitution for Kansas and, if reelected in Illinois, might be just the candidate to fuse Northern Democrats and Republicans in a victorious free-soil coalition for 1860. To Herndon's way of thinking this was arrant nonsense: the need to appease its Southern constituency would always exert a proslavery influence upon the Democracy, and if there was to be a sectional breach, it would be far better for the cause if the great Northern party was headed by a sound antislavery Republican instead of the amoral and opportunistic Douglas, "the greatest demagogue in America." The party needed a man "as true as steel," Herndon thought, someone like his law partner and possible Senate candidate, Abraham Lincoln, who was "all right on slavery" and keenly understood the moral jeopardy in which *Dred Scott*, the designs upon Cuba, and the drive to reopen the slave trade had placed the entire country.

Herndon had not come to enlist Garrison in the nascent Lincoln campaign (years later he swore that his partner had not dispatched him east), but rather to signal the editor that the party not only remained susceptible to radical influence but required it. The visitor himself had not been radical for all that long, but the hard polarizing battle for Kansas had intensified his antislavery convictions and the *Dred Scott* decision had convinced him that the time had come "to cut through the Constitution" and curb the slave power. Herndon had once likened the slaveholding oligarchy to a gigantic corporation with overwhelming lobbying power in the capital, and Garrison had found his essay so "spirited" that he had excerpted it for *The Liberator*. It all came down to the Declaration of Independence, Herndon said; Southerners were now calling it "a lie," but if the founding document condemned slavery for one race, then it had to be wrong for all and the people had to get rid of it. Somehow.

Garrison listened to Herndon with great care. He fully recognized that a breach in the Democratic Party would ensure the election of a Republican in 1860; he understood that it would be preferable to have a candidate with at least the respectable antislavery credentials of a Seward or a Sumner (the editor didn't know anything about Herndon's partner) rather than Douglas, the architect of the entire Nebraska fiasco; and, as the visitor knew, he regularly derided the Republicans for diluting their platform in the quest for fusion. There was the rub, he told Herndon. As he saw it, the Republicans were still throwing up dust on the side issues of Kansas and Cuba and the alarming but abstract threat posed by *Dred Scott*. Yet the question for

1860 included all these incidentals and more—the nature of slavery as an institution and the evil incurred by the North in maintaining religious and political relations with it. Herndon had to understand that the abolitionists wanted to inspire people to do their religious duty to the slaves, not to frighten people into opposing the South with the specter of slavery nationalized.

Herndon shrugged off their disagreement on politics. "We are as we are," he said. "You hate Republicanism, but never mind *that:* it is a midlink," one that would eventually allow the abolitionists to "climb to heaven." Certainly God was working for abolition, Herndon conceded, but "through coarse forms and substances just now, my friend. I see what I see, and that is not much, but Republicanism is a condition—absolute and unannihilable to your march." There were going to be three tickets in 1860, Herndon predicted, and it didn't matter what Garrison thought of them, but the Republican ticket would be advancing his cause nonetheless. It would be a "hot" race, Herndon said, and "broader and deeper in *principle*" than the contest in 1856. He thought it would be a great help if Garrison printed up an edition of Phillips's speeches for use in the heartland, and he left the office with a copy of Garrison's *Selections,* an order for a stack of AAS pamphlets, and a subscription to *The Liberator*. With a tip of the hat he departed, having enjoyed their exchange and promising that he would drop the editor a line or two telling him "how politics are 'way out' in Illinois."

The colloquy with Herndon epitomized the political problem facing Garrison's leadership in the aftermath of *Dred Scott* and the growing influence of both a moderate party and a belligerent sectionalism. His visitor was not a Mephistopheles offering the editor all the gratification he ever wanted if he would only join the Republicans; the last thing the party needed was Garrison's endorsement! Rather, Herndon was telling Garrison that he had to persist in his necessary and telling criticism with the awareness that the Republican Party had become history's vehicle, the locomotive that would at last pull the abolition car into the station. If Garrison wanted to see his life's work crowned with success, he would have to see his agitation as part of the political dialogue and recognize himself as an independent participant, rather than an alien fanatic.

The editor had always understood—as his movement critics had not—that his special brand of moral suasion had political consequences, but he would now have to practice his "anti-politics" in an especially sophisticated fashion. For Garrison this meant walking a tightrope in which he balanced his high principles against the practical possibilities of Republicanism and maintained his criticism of the party's shortcomings without writing off as irredeemable the growing numbers of antislavery people willing to rally under its banner. The editor had, in fact, already won renown for his adherence to principle and his salutary effect upon the nation's moral consciousness. From many quarters now came praise for his consistency and his absolutism as a refreshing contrast to the "unprincipled" Republicans, who only wanted to rouse an antislavery sentiment strong enough to put the party in power but not disruptive enough to sunder the Union or free the slaves. To be lauded by those who refused to accept the rigorous consequences of his views, however, threatened to turn Garrison into a figurehead or house radical and impair his ability to inspire the small cadre of radical abolitionists who had shared the burdens of his fanaticism in the decades of darkness that had preceded the Republican dawn. For the first time since the schism, the editor's reformulation of the task would risk his leadership of the vanguard. Then the party-minded leaders in the movement feared that the editor's broadly radical views would repel voters; now the editor's closest colleagues feared that his indulgent approach to Republican shortcomings would narrow the issues, rob abolitionism of its purity and strength, and trade the immediatists' birthright for a mess of Republican/Free-Soil pottage.

For Garrison, however, there was no question that abolitionism had arrived at the threshold of a fresh relationship to politics. Indeed, in the calculus that an agitator tries to employ, Garrison realized that the new variables meant that he had already accomplished a sizable portion of his task. One by one the institutions that had collaborated to keep slavery out of politics had collapsed—the churches split, the press divided, the Whig Party died, and the Democratic Party ruptured—and now the sections had come to a standoff on the issue Garrison had so courageously raised. Southern slaveholders wanted guarantees that they would have an equal share in the western territories, that Congress would pass laws to protect slave property everywhere, that the Constitution would never be amended in ways that undid its protections of slavery, and that the abolitionist agitation would cease and they be permitted to live in peace. The Northern public wanted guarantees that the western territories would remain untainted by slave labor, that slaveholders would not seek to make their local institution a national one by pressing the logic of *Dred Scott* to its ultimate, and that the South would concede that while its present enjoyment of slave labor might continue, ultimately slavery would have to be extinguished. While the free states had fewer sweeping demands than the slave states and obviously asked for nothing that came close to immediate emancipation, they had taken a Garrisonian moral position that enraged the South and brought themselves to the point of no return.

By 1858–59 the country had reached a stalemate in which, as the Kansas controversy demonstrated, any political transformation—constitutional reconstruction, Free-Soilism, secession—would produce a militarized, physical conflict that would become civil war. The only untried path—a slave insurrection, either spontaneous or abetted by abolitionists—would also produce a war, though it might become a Haitian-style bloodbath that would destroy the slave power and leave the North to treat with the liberated black people, but Garrison loathed the idea of making so disturbing a vision the basis for prophetic agitation. He preferred to continue his high-minded appeal for a moral reformation that might yet break the impasse, and to accomplish this he had to engage in some kind of productive tension between Republican politicians and the abolitionist conscience. This would not be *"mere* Politics," as Garrison styled it, but "a common gathering of the people of the North to effect a common deliverance."

Within a few years, however, the editor would face questions more troubling than the relationship between moral agitation and a moderate anti-slavery party or its radical successor. He would have to cope with the shock waves created first by a terrorist attack in the South and then by an armed uprising against the outcome of the presidential election of 1860. He would have to wrestle with the radical pacifist's dilemma of endorsing a war in order to accomplish a revolution, and he would have to decide, having redirected his agitation, how and when to bring it to an end. Billy Herndon's law partner, Abraham Lincoln, would turn out to be the greatest democratic leader of the nineteenth century, and Garrison would have to decide whether that made him foe or friend, the voice of an intransigent racism or a fellow laborer in the long march to equality. The editor had forged a vision and a message in the evangelical revival of his youth and had never deviated from it, yet when the trumpet of war and Jubilee sounded, even Garrison was changed.

Garrison began his strategic reappraisal in the late 1850s because his disunionist campaign had not struck the sparks he had hoped. The "Great Northern Convention" planned for Cleveland in October 1857 had had to be canceled when a financial panic a few weeks earlier had thrown the economy into a severe tailspin that completely preoccupied the public mind. The continuing effort, moreover, to precipitate a crisis over the fugitive slave issue no longer yielded much political capital. There continued to be local controversies and protracted litigation, but none had the galvanic effect of the Burns case. In the celebrated Oberlin "rescue" case, the federal government tried to prosecute thirty-eight people who had helped spirit away fugitives to Canada, while the state of Ohio countered by arresting their pursuers as kidnappers, but the potentially dramatic confrontation ended with a standoff that saw all the proceedings quashed. In Wisconsin the state supreme court had freed an editor, Sherman Booth, who had been jailed under the Fugitive Slave Law for his role in a slave rescue, but Chief Justice Taney upheld both the constitutionality of the law and the supremacy of the national judiciary in its enforcement. Wisconsin's legislature protested the decision, but the state court did not issue another writ and Booth went to prison, only to be rescued, rearrested, and ultimately pardoned in a case that became too dense and complicated to serve as the rallying point for a popular movement as had the earlier cases of Sims and Burns. Indeed, in 1856, the most riveting fugitive episode since Burns only reinforced the sense of anguish felt by people of conscience. An escaping slave named Margaret Garner had killed the child in her arms rather than permit her to be recaptured and, once jailed, threatened to kill herself as well. The tragedy took the controversy beyond politics and bred a remorse among abolitionists that fed the brewing sense of apocalypse, which left even Garrison feeling that a country that could induce and tolerate such suffering might well have to endure untold retribution before its burden could be lifted.

The stalemate of the late 1850s forced Garrison into an explicit recognition of what had been true ever since the schism of 1840 and his embrace of disunion in 1844. The AAS could not be a mass organization itself, but a leavening agent that influenced the rise of other popular-based institutions. Political parties would always be "proportionate to the character of the people," Garrison argued, and in the confused and ambivalent state of public feeling about both the Union and the Negro race, the Republicans in their "pie-bald" diversity indeed reflected the gamut of opinion. The issue thus remained the state of popular feeling, and the editor posited a distinction between the timorous, narrow, opportunistic party and the "sound antislavery materials" in it.

Republicans rolled up their largest majorities in the abolitionist strongholds of rural and small-town New England and the "northern tier" of Great Lakes counties that some had dubbed "the Yankee West," and these numbers vindicated Garrison's contention that the best way to make antislavery felt in politics was to build an abolitionist public opinion. He had, moreover, long admired the role that the moralists within the party—Charles Sumner, Joshua Giddings, Ben Wade, and Owen Lovejoy (the martyred printer's brother)—had played in agitating the large questions of emancipation and the Union, and he could see that their efforts had borne fruit in the rise of newer men—Thaddeus Stevens in Pennsylvania, George Julian in Indiana, Charles Sedgwick in New York, John Andrew, the likely next governor of Massachusetts—who subscribed to *The Liberator* and were determined to prevent issues of conscience from being obliterated in the Republican rush to office. Unlike his heartland visitor Herndon, Garrison did not regard the Republican Party as the terminus of struggle, but rather the latest way station on the track to abolition. It was a party *pro tempore,* he thought, and he fully expected the Republican coalition of "incongruous elements" to break apart. It would likely jettison its opportunists after its presumed defeat in 1860 demonstrated the futility of compromising expedients and then build a new organization of sincere antislavery people receptive to the logic of disunion and the ideal of racial equality. Meanwhile, he thought that radical abolitionists had to face the fact—"and we are dealing with facts," he emphasized—that the Republican Party had drawn in the antislavery voters of America, save for Gerrit Smith Liberty League holdouts, and it would be the Garrisonians' task to bring such earnest antislavery folk, who wanted to "do something," to a higher understanding of what needed to be done.

This was the tack Garrison prepared to take with the Republicans. Phillips shared the approach, as did Chapman and Parker, who maintained a steady correspondence with Republican leaders even as he criticized their short-comings. For a time, even Abby Kelley Foster accepted the logic and un-dertook an AAS fund-raising campaign in 1857 among Boston Republican blue bloods, with the appeal (developed with some coaching from Chapman) that supporting the work of AAS agents and publications would enlarge the antislavery constituencies in the crucial band of Pennsylvania, Indiana, and Illinois counties the Republicans needed for victory in 1860. It was "tedious" work, waiting all day to talk to people who seemed either befogged or small-minded, and she considered herself lucky to come away with $500 from Sarah Shaw Russell and $50 from James Russell Lowell. Kelley gradually soured on the approach, especially when criticism started to appear in *The Liberator* that the vociferous anti-Republican attacks of her husband, Ste-phen Foster, and their sidekick Parker Pillsbury were alienating potential AAS supporters in the midwest. As a result, the trio began to feel that they were a beleaguered radical element in an organization that had gone soft. Maria Chapman assured her, however, that Garrison would "come right" as the debate ran its course, and Kelley herself predicted in December 1857 that the editor "will slide over into our position and not know he has changed a jot."

She couldn't have been more wrong. Garrison's sustained effort to distin-guish the shortcomings of the Republican platform from the promise of the Republican constituency did not abate, but steadily antagonized some of his oldest allies in the movement. For the first time since the 1830s, a portion of the abolitionist vanguard had come to doubt Garrison. He found himself bitterly criticized for abandoning the language of sin in order to extend "leniency" to Republicans. Garrison did not believe that he had abandoned the come-outer imperative, but he had certainly relaxed it—*pro tempore*, as he would say—to nurture the gradual illumination of political growth over the instantaneous conversion of revivalist prophecy. Though he never could have explained it this way, he was groping his way to a fusion of the old argument between moral agitation and electoral politics into an amalgam that might be called "political suasion," but the colleagues he had long in-spired by his adamant consistency heard in his new appeal only the accents of heresy.

The explosion came at the annual Massachusetts Anti-Slavery Society meeting in January 1859, twenty years after the vicious fight with Stanton, when Pillsbury, Kelley, Foster, and Higginson pressed to condemn the Re-publicans not only as being as "reprehensible" as the Democrats on the constitutional question of slavery, but as "more dangerous to the cause of freedom" owing to their party's false professions of friendship for the slave. Kelley reiterated her view that it was the Republicans' very nearness to genuine abolition that made it difficult but necessary to criticize them for their "unfaithfulness" and the duplicity with which the party "stealthily suck[ed] the very blood from our veins." Pillsbury insisted the Republicans embodied "the subtle and fiendish spirit of hostility to the cause" that was once the province of colonization, clerical abolitionists' appeal, and "new organization" efforts, and Higginson bemoaned the lack of public hostility toward abolitionism as a dangerous sign that the cause had become usurped by dangerous pretenders.

Garrison thought his colleagues "unduly desponding and lugubrious." He did not consider it wrongheaded or dangerous to reckon up the signs of progress. Something had surely changed for the better, he said, since the antislavery element in the old Whig Party had never caused a ripple of discomfort in the South, while the slaveholders now raised their old bluff of secession at the prospect of the Republicans winning the White House. Nor did he think that a recognition that the cause had advanced through other instrumentalities implied that there was nothing more for abolitionists to do. They had to keep aloft the standard of immediatism and disunion, as the Republicans "experimented" and learned for themselves—"as we have had to learn," Garrison said—that lesser, compromising expedients would not prevail against the aggressive and determined slave power. To paraphrase what he had told James G. Birney in the first great argument over the movement's relationship to electoral politics, he did not want all abolitionists to become Republicans, but rather sought to make all Republicans immediatists and disunionists.

His critics would have none of Garrison's pragmatism or optimism. Abby Kelley deplored it as "premature self-gratulation" in a time of crisis. "Nothing has been done," she insisted, "while anything remains to be done." The abolitionists had to do their work all over again, converting "those who think they are already converted." Garrison had become complacent and out-of-touch, she charged, sitting at a desk and only speaking by invitation, while field agents who had to force their way to a hearing knew that the path of true abolition was still a stony one and made more difficult by the Republican success at drawing people off with the erroneous idea that nonextension was an adequate response to evil.

In Kelley and Garrison one could see the temperament of the agitator dissolving into elements—denunciation and inspiration, pessimism and optimism, impatience and patience—that generally worked in combination. In Higginson one could hear the weariness of the militant who had given up on politics and only waited for the apocalypse, whose harbinger at the meeting proved to be a Kansan named Richard Hinton who hailed Osawatomie Brown as the Lafayette who would aid the slaves in revolution. Garrison grudgingly tolerated Hinton as part of the meeting's "free platform," though he took strenuous exception to such "speeches of death" and reiterated his faith in moral enlightenment. (Brad Drew of Plymouth came up afterward to thank the editor for his rebuke of Hinton, and the two had a long reminiscence about Drew's father as a pioneer in the cause.) In Pillsbury and Foster one could see the crankiness that impeded their ability to adapt to changing circumstances. They appeared stuck in the time warp of the schism, hearing the editor's changing perspective as a betrayal of principle rather than the tactical switch he intended. Ironically, it was Foster's pathetic insistence that the disunionists ought to form a political party of their own and triumph at the ballot box that most resembled the electoral preoccupations that had fed the new organization's move into politics.

The debate ended in hard feelings all around. Higginson charged into the cloakroom certain that Garrison had insulted him personally, and Pillsbury felt equally sure that the editor's "pleasantries," intended to lighten the tone of the meeting, had cast aspersions upon Abby Kelley's physical appearance. Grudging apologies did little to relieve the animosity, and the Garrisons' hospitality suddenly seemed suffocating to Kelley and part of the effort to stifle her dissent. Helen had sensed Kelley's distress, but Garrison shrugged it off as having no bearing on the vigorous and free discussion that had always characterized movement life.

When the same argument erupted at the New England convention in May 1859, this time over a Foster resolution of no-confidence in those professed abolitionists who gave countenance to the proslavery Republican Party, Garrison denounced the attack as "unjust and uncalled for." He pointed out the inconsistency of appealing to Republicans for funds, as Abby Kelley had done, while considering them the slave's worst enemy. She was not in the hall when Garrison spoke, but received secondhand reports that the editor had impugned her integrity and accused her of fraud. The next morning at seven o'clock, just as Garrison was coming down the stairs at Dix Place, he saw an infuriated Abby Kelley dashing out the front door, while Helen stood ready with breakfast on the dining table and Kelley's perplexed young daughter remonstrated that they needn't rush as they still had an hour to catch their train. Now it was Garrison's turn to be insulted at the breach of courtesy, and a two-month silence ensued before the editor wrote a stiff letter—part inquiry, part apology, and part self-defense—and received an unbending reply. There were two more fruitless exchanges before the veteran agitators lapsed into a social freeze that would not thaw until the slaves went free. Only with difficulty did Wendell Phillips smooth out matters so that Kelley agreed to take her seat on a special AAS committee, also including Garrison, charged with disbursing a legacy received from the late Charles Hovey for publishing a new series of propaganda tracts.

The infighting had grown so severe that Adin Ballou, the admired leader of the Hopedale community, felt obliged to admonish everybody. "Practical Christian Anti-Slavery" required not only the repudiation of violence but an end to the "excessive individualism" had disfigured the movement, he said. There had lately been too much "egotism, extremism, exaggerationism, antagonism, and contemptuous personality" in the abolitionist ranks, Ballou complained in September 1859, spelling out in great detail his distaste for rhetorical distortion and the notion that "the better a man is . . . the more dangerous [he is], so long as he is not a full saint." Ballou had sufficient moral authority to chasten all the participants, but his effort to mend the unraveling fabric of the movement was lost in the shouting a few weeks later when news of an attempted insurrection in Virginia electrified the country and set it on the trajectory of dissolution, war, and social revolution.

On Monday evening, October 17, 1859, Wendell Phillips called at Dix Place and spent an entertaining hour with Garrison and his son Willie merrily going over the poor showing Henry Ward Beecher had made in his Tremont Temple lecture on "bargain-making" a few days previously. The mood changed abruptly, however, when someone came in with a bulletin about a slave uprising in Virginia. One question sprang into their minds simultaneously—"Osawatomie Brown?"—and they looked at each other with "foreboding," Willie remembered, as the answer came, "Very like." (Willie kept to himself his own worst suspicion that Francis Meriam was involved, but wrote in his diary that his friend was "just reckless enough" to have become mixed up in such a business.)

The editor spent the next two days frantically redoing the inner form of *The Liberator* to include three columns' worth of newspaper dispatches: Monday's feverish reports that an armed band of several hundred "abolitionists and Negroes" had seized the federal armory at Harpers Ferry, the strategic rail and river junction at the confluence of the Shenandoah and Potomac rivers sixty miles northwest of Washington, D.C.; and Tuesday's equally hectic accounts that a detachment of U.S. Marines had subdued the assailants and mortally wounded their leader, who indeed had identified himself as Osawatomie Brown and declared that he had come solely to free the slaves. ("Sure enough," wrote Willie in his diary, "old Brown is at the bottom of this insane attempt. . . . The excitement all over the country is intense.") The last item Garrison had time or space to include was Wednesday morning's breathless story that materials found at Brown's nearby farmhouse had included incriminating letters from Frederick Douglass and a $100 check from Gerrit Smith. To all of this Garrison could only wedge in ten lines at the bottom of his editorial column that expressed an ambivalence that he would occasionally deny but never fully resolve. His first words described the raid (not the man) as "wild, misguided, and apparently insane," but then he added the qualifying phrase "though [a] disinterested and well-intended," effort to emancipate the slaves. The editor's views of "war and bloodshed, even in the best of causes, are too well known to need repeating here," he added, but again hedged by asserting that no one who took pride in the Revolutionary struggle of '76 could "deny the right of the slaves to imitate the example of our fathers." He was foundering on the shoals of a radical adventurism he had so long tried to avoid: if he condemned the action, would he be understood as having betrayed the cause?

Over the next week the outline of the story became clearer, though many details remained blurred. Brown and nineteen others, including five free black men, had stormed the federal armory and held the Virginia town for thirty-six hours after taking ten slaves and their owner hostage from an outlying plantation. Mob fighting had broken out in the streets, which resulted in several deaths even before the government troops staged their counterattack. In all, seventeen people had died: ten raiders, including two black men and two of Brown's sons, along with two slave captives, three townspeople, one plantation owner, and a marine. Brown, though wounded, did not die, but was taken prisoner with four of his soldiers and jailed in nearby Charlestown. Two more "invaders" who had escaped from Harpers Ferry were shortly recaptured in Pennsylvania and taken to Virginia, while five others remained at large. (Francis Meriam's name did not appear on lists of those imprisoned or killed, but since the captured correspondence included some hints that he had brought Brown money and helped in the purchase of arms, the Jacksons and the Garrisons feared that he must be among the fugitives.) The Virginia state government and the federal government engaged in frantic discussions about the unprecedented problem of overlapping jurisdictions: beyond the grim federal charge of treason, there were considerations of property destruction and disruption of the mail to set alongside the state accusations of murder, kidnapping, and slave incitement. The state had custody, however, and a grand jury and county court were already in session, so the ever-accommodating Buchanan administration proposed a compromise: Brown and his followers would be tried first by Virginia for murder and then by the United States for treason. Governor Henry A. Wise grandly declared that he had no objection to the general government proceeding against "what will be left of the prisoners by the time the Virginia authorities have done with them." No one doubted that the prisoners would be, as Willie Garrison put it, "judicially murdered." The trial date was set for seven days after the arrest, and Virginia added to the indictment the baseless charge of treason against the commonwealth. ("State-breaking is a new species of crime," declared the editor of the *Weekly Anglo-African;* a burglar breaks into your house to steal your goods, but John Brown broke into Virginia "to bring stolen goods out of the state.")

The Harpers Ferry raid shocked the entire country and produced an emotional furor without precedent in the nation's experience. Thanks to the telegraph, the news-gathering agencies, and the high-speed power press, more people had rapid access to both information and commentary than ever before, and the audacity of Brown's act "broke through the mask" in a moment of Byronic defiance that irrevocably moved the slavery controversy from the sphere of constitutional and moral abstraction to the visceral realm of feelings intensified beyond measure or reason. For the six weeks between

Brown's raid and his execution, the country could think or talk of little else, and the passions roused by the episode permanently influenced the political climate. No matter how quickly Virginia executed Brown or Congress investigated his collaborators, slaveholders felt themselves deeply threatened by subversion and conspiracy and became convinced that they could not inhabit a country governed by "black Republicanism" and abolitionists. No matter how loudly Republican politicians derided Brown as a lone madman whose action bore no relation to their platform, Democrats and residual Whig Unionists blamed his lawlessness and violence on the Republican belief in the immorality of slavery. No matter how often conservatives vowed to uphold "the Constitution, the Union, and the laws" by once more taking slavery out of politics with another compromise, there developed an abiding conviction in the free states that the fateful issue could not be settled without an epic and violent confrontation with the slavemasters.

The raid had freed not a single slave, nor had it conformed to the model of guerrilla action Brown had long advocated. No one could fathom why Old Osawatomie had boxed himself in or had allowed a railroad train to leave the junction to spread a rapid alarm before the invaders had accomplished their purpose, or why indeed they had shifted their presumed focus from liberating plantation slaves to capturing a federal fortress. Garrison found it difficult to puzzle out Brown's intentions. He must have intended "a desperate self-sacrifice for the purpose of giving an earthquake shock to the slave system," the editor told Oliver Johnson, "and thus hastening the day for a universal catastrophe." Others, including Johnson, criticized the affair largely on tactical grounds, arguing that from what had come out about the plan, the probability of success was far too low to justify the risk, which of course left open the question of whether or not old-line abolitionists would support a better-conceived or larger-scale assault. Brown himself gave conflicting statements to his captors, sometimes avowing and sometimes denying a revolutionary intent, and a lively contemporary debate ensued on the questions of Brown's sanity and his military competence, an argument that has echoed down the years with little chance of resolution. Southerners and abolitionists alike had a common interest in not regarding Brown as a lunatic: the slaveholders because they regarded the outlaw Brown as "the agent of wicked principals" and a product of the conspiratorial agitation they had denounced for decades, the abolitionists because they considered the attack the inevitable response to Southern intransigence and the violence the slaveholders had initiated in Kansas. Republican politicians and editors, however, very much wanted to portray Brown as a demented fanatic with delusions of grandeur in order to deflect Democratic efforts to smear their party with the thick brush of treason, disunion, slave insurrection, and amalgamationism. Yet even Horace Greeley, in condemning the "deplorable" affair as "the work of a madman," hedged the Republican line in deference to the antislavery backbone of the party. He would heap no "reproachful" words upon those who "dared and died for what they felt to be the right," he said, "though in a manner which seems to us fatally wrong."

Unlike the Republicans, most abolitionists, including Garrison, proudly claimed credit for heating "the fiery furnace" of agitation that had made slavery vulnerable after decades of quietude, but they regarded Brown's effort as "self-concocted" and ridiculed the idea of a conspiracy. An enterprise so "wild and futile . . . and lacking in common sense" could not have received "any countenance" from even the most devoted admirers of Brown's course in Kansas, Garrison declared in the face of suggestive evidence otherwise. Oliver Johnson conceded in the *Standard* that over the past two years he had "heard rumors" that Brown was planning a slave revolt, "but we little expected that he would lead an assault so desperate." Johnson's paper paid more attention than Garrison's to the evidence of conspiracy. Of the names so far fished out of John Brown's carpetbag, Smith, Howe, Stearns, and Sanborn all claimed that they believed themselves to have been supporting the defense of Kansas, though Smith prudently checked into a mental hospital and the latter two discovered urgent business in Canada. Douglass issued an ambiguous statement and accelerated the timetable for his winter schedule of lectures in Great Britain. Higginson's and Parker's complicity had not yet been exposed, but with Parker dying of consumption in Italy, only Higginson remained in place, brooding angrily at his colleagues' defections and entertaining the fresh fantasy of breaking Brown out of his prison cell.

Given Brown's abject failure to incite a revolt (he had picked a town dependent upon a federal payroll in a neighborhood of small-scale farms, rather than gang-style plantations), the disunionist implications of the Harpers Ferry raid loomed large. The gratuitous charge of treason against Virginia, in fact, enabled the abolitionists to link Brown's work with their own challenge to complicity. "Insurrection of thought always precedes insurrection of arms," Wendell Phillips said in a rousing speech from Henry Ward Beecher's pulpit in Brooklyn and boasted that two decades of radical abolitionist thought had at last produced a revolutionary deed. Virginia is a pirate regime, Phillips exclaimed in one of his typically extravagant metaphors, against which John Brown sailed as "a Lord High Admiral of the Almighty, with a commission to sink every pirate he meets on God's ocean of the nineteenth century." Henry D. Thoreau similarly extolled Brown's startling action as a challenge to conventional forms and contrasted his heroic religiosity with the stagnant Christian who is happy to say all the prayers in the liturgy provided he may go straight to sleep afterward. In "A Plea for Captain John Brown," delivered three times in one week in Concord, Worcester, and Boston, where he filled a commitment for the absent Frederick Douglass, Thoreau praised Brown as "a transcendentalist above all." No one would mistake John Brown for a Republican, scoffed Thoreau, yet from his "failure" millions would be persuaded to vote more correctly and nourish the "treason" that "an individual may be right and the government wrong." Those commonplace souls who condemned Brown as insane or foolish or inexpedient missed the point, Thoreau said, for his rebellion was both philosophical and practical; the issue was "not the weapon but the spirit in which you use it." (Listening to Thoreau's ninety-minute exposition, Willie Garrison thrilled to the writer's "radical, bold, uncompromising" stance but found his speech "tinged with extravagance which somewhat detracted from its justness.")

Ecstatic talk, however, could not eclipse stark fact. Brown represented— and Phillips and Thoreau endorsed—the principle of forcible intervention with slavery that the AAS and Garrisonian abolitionists had disavowed for decades. "God is now putting our non-resistance principles to a severe test," John Greenleaf Whittier told Maria Child, insisting that despite a deep personal sympathy for the noble-hearted Brown, believers in the Sermon on the Mount had to uphold Saint Paul's faith in "a more excellent way" (1 Cor. 12:31). Yet of the old apostles, only Adin Ballou joined Whittier in resolute condemnation of the turn to violence. Abby Kelley Foster agonized over the dilemma, but ultimately decided that individuals had conscientiously to choose their own means of opposing slavery. In moving from absolutism to relativism, Kelley joined Frederick Douglass, whose letter from exile had endorsed Brown's action with the French proverb "The tools to those that can use them." Her cantankerous husband, Stephen, for once went along with the others, saying tersely that he was "a non-resistant, but not a fool." Garrison himself continued to struggle ambivalently. He sent resolutions to a Worcester meeting declaring that abolitionists had "no apologies" to make for those antislavery men who had sought to break the oppressor's rod by the same measures the Revolutionary Fathers had used to secure national independence. A few days later, however, he explained in *The Liberator*, saying "once for all" that the "Bunker Hill standard" was not high enough for him. "We do not and cannot approve any indulgence of the war spirit," Garrison wrote; Brown might rank with Moses or Joshua, and Gideon, but he was "not on the same plain with Jesus, Paul, Peter, and John, whose weapons . . . were not carnal, though mighty to the pulling down of strongholds." He had said the same of Nat Turner in 1831 and Elijah Lovejoy in 1837 and had never regretted it, but in the powerful magnetic field created by the Brown affair, Garrison kept oscillating between the poles of soulforce and bloodshed.

It seemed that the editor could come to rest by discriminating, as Whittier and Child did, between personal admiration for the righteous hero and principled criticism of the dubious event, and Garrison contributed as much as anyone to the propaganda effort that turned "madness" to martyrdom. With the free states responding sympathetically to the piteous reports of Brown stretched out upon a pallet in the courtroom as the state launched its rush to judgment even before his wounds healed or his volunteer attorneys arrived from Boston, the movement had obviously acquired a powerful symbol. Two days before the court pronounced its inevitable sentence, Garrison called the Boston members of the AAS executive committee to Dix Place and suggested that "it would be a master-stroke of policy" to make the day of Brown's execution an occasion for "public moral demonstrations" to "consecrate" the abolitionist cause anew and bear fresh testimony against the "guilt and danger of slavery."

Even as Garrison helped to propagandize Brown as a martyr to the slave power, the editor became a victim of Brown's own efforts to influence the story. The AAS call for a day of solemn observance reached the public simultaneously with the news that Brown had been found guilty and sentenced to hang on December 2. In the text of the crusader's dramatic closing statement to the court Brown disingenuously claimed that he had come only to help slaves escape and disavowed any intent of incitement or insurrection, an assertion that the entire North accepted with relief, for it made him out to be more a railroad conductor than an assassin or provocateur. He explained himself as acting only in accord with the Golden Rule in behalf of God's despised poor and portrayed himself as the shepherd willing to suffer for the sheep. "If it is deemed necessary that I should forfeit my life for the furtherance of the end of justice," Brown said, "and mingle my blood further with the blood of my children and with the blood of millions in this slave country whose rights are disregarded by wicked, cruel, and unjust enactments, I say, let it be done."

The effect proved electrifying, and the four last weeks of John Brown's life witnessed a massive outpouring of sentiment—both spontaneous and orchestrated—perhaps never before lavished upon an individual American. Printers quickly made up broadsides of the speech; *The Liberator*'s office had one for sale that praised Brown with the traditional abolitionist watchwords that he had attempted "to give deliverance to the captives and to let the oppressed go free." The prisoner did his part, writing numerous letters to correspondents in the North, avowing his willingness to die for the cause and displaying the prophetic vision and the Christ-like composure that fused the dramaturgical strands of the movement. Virginia's unrighteous retribution would make "the gallows as glorious as the cross," Emerson told a cheering crowd in Boston, while Phillips mounted a macabre effort to have John Brown's body bequeathed to Garrison or Francis Jackson and buried in Boston within sight of Bunker Hill. The plan encountered opposition from Brown's wife, sixteen years his junior, who wanted her husband interred at their farm in the Adirondacks, and sensing that they had overstepped propriety, the abolitionists abruptly reversed course and organized large-scale meetings to raise funds for the support of Mary Ann Brown and her three young daughters.

Brown wanted to spare his wife the pain of a jailhouse visit, but after numerous Northern women—including Lydia Maria Child—had offered to go to Virginia to nurse him, the prisoner relented, and Mrs. Brown remained with him to the end. Child's public gesture of sympathy, however, yielded dividends of its own when first Governor Wise mocked her feelings as an accessory cause of the uprising and then Senator Mason's wife chided all Northern women as hypocrites who did not know how to care for the unfortunate as well as the Southerners, who nurtured their slaves like family. In an eloquent set of replies published in all the leading papers, Child memorably encapsulated the conflict of moral principles with the acerbic remark that of course free-state women performed all the charitable acts Mason had described with the exception that "here at the North, after we have helped the mother we do not sell the babies." Garrison had the entire correspondence bound as a pamphlet (five cents each or fifty cents a dozen) in the AAS series, and, with 300,000 copies in rapid circulation, it became the bestselling title of Child's long career. Although she did not go to Virginia, several other women did, including Helen Garrison's former schoolmate Rebecca Buffum Spring. Mary Stearns dispatched a sculptor to make a heroic bust of the soldier and, some said, sketch the jail setup for a possible escape. Brown, however, approaching the end with unsurpassed dignity, felt that the death sentence would redeem his military disaster: "I can recover all the lost capital," he told his wife, ". . . by only hanging a few moments by the neck; & I feel quite determined to make the utmost possible out of a defeat."

Friday, December 2, 1859, broke clear and summerlike over a nation solemn and awed by the grim ceremony taking place in Virginia. Southerners put up a facade of business-as-usual, but in the free states church bells tolled morning, noon, and night from Cape Cod to Kansas. In Concord, Thoreau argued with the narrow-minded selectmen who refused to endorse the ringing and threatened to fire off the town's minute guns as a countermeasure, but in Albany the council authorized a one-hundred-gun salute in tribute to Brown and in Syracuse the great fire bell in City Hall rang mournfully all through the day. In Hartford three men climbed to the top of the state capitol's dome and draped a statue of Liberty in mourning. Cleveland residents hung crepe banners in its streets, bankers closed their doors in Akron, and public prayer meetings took place in churches in New York and Philadelphia, the tabernacles of black congregations from Detroit to New Bedford, and the clapboard meetinghouses of New England and the Western Reserve. In Boston an interracial union service ran all day in the Twelfth Street Baptist Church, and when at four in the afternoon the telegraph confirmed that the execution had taken place a little before noon, many business places, black and white, closed and people put on mourning bands or rosettes studded with a likeness of the martyred Brown.

Willie Garrison that afternoon received a private shock. Stopping by the Phillipses' to meet his friend Phoebe Garnaut, he discovered her deep in conversation with George Hoyt, the young attorney who had defended

Brown, and he "unavoidably caught the information that Francis Meriam was in Boston." Let in on the secret, Willie learned that his old schoolmate had endured an eight-day escape on foot, pursued by baying hounds around him, hiding in thickets, and stumbling along a railroad track in a snowstorm before gaining fresh clothes and shelter among friends who helped him to Canada. Where he grew restless and struck out for home "under the insane idea that he must revenge Brown's death." Hoyt was convinced that the unstable young man had to be "gotten out of the way forthwith," and Phillips had gone to consult with Mr. Jackson about the arrangements. Overwrought, eyes filmed over, babbling incoherently, Meriam was a pitiable sight, but the old abolitionists dispatched him that night to Concord, where a nervous Sanborn, certain that Meriam would yet expose them all, got a friend—later identified as Thoreau—to drive the agitated young man to an out-of-the-way station and muscle him onto a westbound train and a second exile in the black colony at Chatham, Ontario, just across the river from Detroit.

If the editor knew that day of Meriam's presence, he never acknowledged it, but spent the afternoon overseeing the arrangements for the meeting at Tremont Temple. Lydia Maria Child had come in from Wayland the day before expressly to help him, and the two old apostles recalled their pioneering years in the movement as they decorated the platform and positioned placards and slogans around the barn-like auditorium—Saint Paul's "Remember them in bonds . . . ," Jeremiah's "Execute justice in the morning . . . ," Jefferson's "I tremble for my country . . . ," Henry's "Give me liberty . . . ," and other key statements of the American civil and spiritual litany. No funeral drapery, no black crepe, they decreed, and they made instead a lectern centerpiece of Brown's portrait supported by a cross and wreathed in evergreen and amaranth. Above the stage they hung a bright painted banner bearing the Great Seal of Virginia with its insurrectionary image of Liberty's soldier bestride a vanquished oppressor and the confident motto "Sic Semper Tyrannis." Just before the program began—half an hour early owing to the crush of four thousand people in the seats and three thousand more crowded in the street outside—a young man unfurled a banner from the gallery reading, "He dies by the mandate of the Slave Power, yet 'still lives' by virtue of his heroic deeds," and the temple erupted in an immense shout that gave the keynote for the evening.

There were many speakers, including the militant young fugitive slave John Sella Martin, who had recently assumed the pastorate of the Belknap Street Church. He first stunned the audience by charging that America had delivered up "the Barabbas of Slavery" and crucified "the John Brown of Freedom," and then brought the crowd to its feet by exclaiming that as a Christian and peace man, he would not quibble with John Brown for taking the revolutionary means extolled by white men and using them for black men instead. There were poems and tears and prayers and a collection for the Brown family taken up by a cadre of young men that included Willie

Garrison. The meeting, however, was his father's idea, and though the subject was Brown, the night belonged to the editor. It was Garrison who sounded the evening's theme: "Today Virginia has murdered John Brown; tonight we here witness his resurrection." It was Garrison who read aloud the victim's now-celebrated address to the court, and it was Garrison who, upon rising once more to give the eulogy, basked in the overwhelming affection that emanated from every part of the hall and fused the aura of Brown's martyrdom and the radiant energy of the pioneer into a beam of truth illuminated.

Garrison's speech, however, demonstrated the dishevelment that the Brown affair occasioned in the editor; that he was considered, by Willie's testimony, never to have spoken better or been received more enthusiastically in Boston only confirms how profoundly unhinged public opinion had become. The editor veered wildly from one vantage point to another, first describing his differences with the Cromwellian and Gideonite warrior and then asserting (against considerable evidence to the contrary) that Brown intended a "peaceful exodus" in which weapons would be used only for self-defense. He then changed tacks to condemn the judicial assassination of the lamb by the wolf and, declaring that he would try Brown "by the American standard," pronounced his intervention on behalf of the slaves a justifiable extension of the American Revolution. If Lafayette was justified in aiding Washington, then John Brown was "incomparably more so" in coming to the aid of Virginia's slaves.

Here was Garrison's attempt to subvert the conservative condemnation of Brown as an outlaw and, to borrow Thoreau's term, find a "transcendental" meaning in his act. The editor, however, lacked Thoreau's grounding in Platonic idealism and could only offer a literal inversion in the secular and martial terms of the Revolution that he had previously recognized did not serve his principles very well. Nor could he make his own Christian idealism serve the mood of the hour. Alluding to his own thirty years' moral warfare against the slave power, Garrison said that as a peace man, he would prefer to "disarm" not only Brown and the slaves but the masters as well and melt the fetters of bondage by the workings of conscience. That no longer seemed enough, he realized, and he felt obliged "as an 'ultra' peace man" to say, to immense applause, " 'Success to every slave insurrection at the South, and in every slave country."

Without warning and without premeditation, an ironic exchange of roles took place as Garrison, long identified as the movement's suffering servant, ceded his place to the martyred Brown and—for the moment—made himself the vengeful prophet, the Gideonite who would wield the sword in liberty's name. The editor argued that it was a sign of progress and "positive moral growth" that men who believed in carnal weapons were willing to take those weapons out of "the scale of despotism, and throw them in the scale

of freedom." His sympathies, Garrison said, would always lie with the oppressed, and since John Brown no longer needed their compassion, he would
hope the audience would give its "sympathies, prayers, and noblest exertions" to the "four million living John Browns" among the Southern slaves.
He didn't think that he compromised or stained his peace principles by
envisioning slaves "breaking the head of the tyrant with their chains," he
said, for it was a way to get up to "the sublime platform of non-resistance."
John Brown, it seemed, had reduced him to double-think, or perhaps the
heat of the moment had swept him along into contradictory overstatement.

The Harpers Ferry raid had brought to the foreground the specter of
slave revolt that had always lurked behind the editor's disunionist idea that
the masters could not survive once Northern support for their oppressive
social order was withdrawn. Even though he denied Brown's insurrectionary
intent in one passage, he endorsed the idea in another. Now John Brown
had made him a forceful and open advocate of slave revolt, but had it made
him an advocate of more invasions of the South by abolitionists? The logic
of the speech went in one direction, the emotion in another, and the peroration—a moving evocation of a reconstructed and peaceable union—in a
third. Far from offering counsel and direction for a movement brought to a
new pinnacle of emotional commitment, Garrison was trapped between his
vision of reformation and the tactics of revolutionary warfare. Later he explained to Adin Ballou, who consistently deplored Brown's "seductive" influence and wished "the speediest failure" for any contemplated slave revolt,
that he could not believe that perfectionist principle required that "the
wrong triumph over the right," which would be the case if the oppressor
prevailed over insurgent slaves. Even if freedom is gained by the sword,
Garrison argued gamely, it fosters a place where peace and justice can flourish, which is impossible under slavery. To the staunch Ballou this simply
meant that the editor now brooked the relativist possibility that good might
come from doing evil and had forsaken his absolutist standard. The confusion
of Garrison's speech seemed to be a confession of failure, an admission that
history's course had shifted and that he would have to sail with wind and
tide as best he could.

Yet his oratory may have been an aberrant response to a complex moment.
No journal outside Boston took note of it, and he never said anything quite
like it again. Ten days later, at an important lecture series organized in
tribute to the late Theodore Parker, Garrison's topic was "The Irrepressible
Conflict and the Higher Law" and the editor's treatment a standard attack
on slavery and an exposition of disunion with only a passing word about the
martyred Brown and no word at all about revolutionary violence. A few
weeks later, in advocating sales of Maria Child's high-minded and loving
Virginia correspondence, the editor claimed that a copy in every home would
go far to change public sentiment and abolish slavery by "the majesty of
moral power without the aid of invasion or insurrection." When the editor

was asked on the first anniversary of Brown's execution to outline his program for abolishing slavery, Garrison responded with the answers he had given for thirty years: brand slavery unjust, make slaveholders odious, break up the institutions that are complicit with them, and extend equal rights and protections to black people. As for revolutionary measures, Garrison said that *if* he were a convert to the forcible resistance doctrines of '76, then he would plot insurrection and "deal more in blows and less in words," but as a nonresistant he confined himself to "spiritual weapons" and did not seek the overthrow of slavery by "a bloody process."

On the day after the execution, people read the newspaper accounts from Charlestown and absorbed the details that forever fixed John Brown's saintly image in the popular mind. He had faced death with courage and serenity, courteously thanking his keepers for their kind treatment, and kissing a little slave child as he left his jail cell. He rode to the execution ground in a wagon seated upon his own coffin, remarking pleasantly upon the beauties of the Blue Ridge countryside, surveying the scene with a nerveless smile and expressing surprise that the public had been excluded from the field packed with more than a thousand troops, and nonchalantly tossing his black slouch hat aside just before the white hood was placed over his leonine head. The state of Virginia allowed his body to dangle from the gallows for thirty-eight minutes before it was cut down, replaced in the wagon, driven to Harpers Ferry and turned over to Mrs. Brown for the slow journey north. When the coffin reached Philadelphia, the train station overflowed with black people, singing hymns and seeking to comfort the martyr's widow.

The public fascination with John Brown continued unabated for many weeks. The news reports never let up, with accounts of his funeral procession and burial, the execution and funerals of his subordinates, and the seemingly endless flow of tributes and sermons and poetry that required—for the first time ever—an extra edition of *The Liberator* at the end of the year to accommodate the volume of material. Forty thousand pre-publication orders poured in before James Redpath's rapidly produced biography hit the stands in February 1860, and a brisk trade went on in reprints of the address to the court and cheaply printed portraits of the hero, with proceeds from all sales announced as going to the benefit of the family. The story of the kiss, especially, caught the Northern imagination at its most sentimental point, making John Brown at the gallows infinitely more appealing than John Brown at the arsenal and turning him into an iconic figure to set beside Harriet Beecher Stowe's Uncle Tom. "Without the rash and bloody hand/ within the loving heart," ran Whittier's popular tribute; "Not the raid of midnight terror, but the thought which underlies;/ Not the borderer's pride of daring but the Christian sacrifice."

The *New York Times* scoffed that it only took a few hands to ring a church bell and that the "great majority" of Northerners still respected Southern rights and were not ready, despite widespread personal sympathy for John Brown, to wage warfare upon slavery, but the abolitionists believed that the tide had turned enough that both public morality and sectional loyalty required standing up to Southern demands even if resistance put the Union in jeopardy. "Years are no longer required for a revolution," Thoreau remarked. "Days, nay hours, produce marked changes." Fifty people who had been ready to hang John Brown when they went into a meeting would no longer say that when they came out. If John Brown had fired his gun twenty years ago, Garrison told the MAS annual meeting in January 1860, the entire country would have judged that he indeed had died a madman and fool; now even the thousands who ten years before could not endure the editor's rebuke of the South "easily swallow John Brown whole, and his rifle in the bargain." His gunshot "merely" told us the time of day, said Garrison. "It is high noon, thank God!"

The showdown would come in stages, first in the most splintered presidential campaign of the century and then in a cataclysmic challenge of the results. Though John Brown was no Republican, his canonization redounded to the party's benefit in several ways. The intensified antislavery moral climate in the free states, as Garrison had long predicted, created the wind before which Republican congressional and presidential candidates had to sail, and even though they continued to decry Brown as an extremist—an Orsini-like assassin with a divine appointment to counter injustice personally—they profited immensely from the overwhelming Northern feeling that the power of the slaveholders had to be checked and repudiated. (A divinely inspired agent would end slavery long before a political appointee ever did, scoffed Thoreau, who advised the Republicans to count the John Brown vote as more powerful than Pennsylvania's, not realizing perhaps how deftly the party would retain the one while courting the other.) That great numbers of Northerners mourned a reckless and murderous invader and condemned Virginia for punishing him infuriated the slaveholders' leadership even more than the raid itself. This realization drove an angry and fearful Southern public into a wave of repression that made every Yankee in its midst subject to violent harassment and brought the mood of sectional antagonism to the boiling point.

From December 1859 to March 1860, Garrison filled nearly a page of his newspaper each week with accounts of how the slaveholding states, long shut to genuine abolitionist advocacy, had moved into a coercive phase that he regarded as hysterical in origin and ruthless in effect. Merchants in Richmond boycotted Northern houses that did not advertise in their "white lists" of businesses respectful of Southern rights, and the *Charleston Mercury* vowed to embarrass those who did not cut off trade with New York companies headed by members of Henry Ward Beecher's church. Local postmasters refused to deliver such mainstream periodicals as *Harper's Weekly* or *The Independent,* much less Republican sheets like Greeley's *Tribune.* In Washington, D.C., a Quaker physician was fined for disturbing the peace after a private discussion of the Brown raid, the judge applying the Dogberry-like reasoning that if the defendant had uttered the remarks before slaves it would have endangered the community. (Garrison's friend Charles Burleigh couldn't resist the retort that the judge ought to be indicted for kindling a fire in his office stove, for if he had kindled it in a powder magazine, it would have blown somebody up.)

Most of the incidents, however, produced not levity but outrage. In North Carolina, an elderly Methodist minister, Daniel Worth, was sentenced to a year in jail for circulating a volatile antislavery work by a Southern yeoman, but spared the public whipping also prescribed by law so that the abolitionists would be less able to make a martyr of him. Mobs chased two Connecticut book salesmen out of several piedmont towns in the Carolinas, which prompted the hounding of dozens of book peddlers across the region, the tar-and-feathering of a Yankee shoe dealer in Savannah who was accused of allowing slaves to read in his shop, and the brutal flogging of an Irish stonecutter working on the new statehouse in Columbia, South Carolina, who supposedly said that slavery degraded white labor and who returned north to bare his scars before antislavery groups. In Kentucky a peaceable antislavery religious community at Berea was broken up, its newspaper press smashed, and its preachers driven from the state. By April 1860, Garrison had printed hundreds of such reports and, following the principle he had followed ever since *Thoughts on African Colonization* that slaveholders could be convicted by evidence of their own making, compiled the mountain of dispatches into a 144-page pamphlet, *The New Reign of Terror in the South.* The AAS published an edition of ten thousand copies that the editor said ought to become "household reading" everywhere in the free states. It would "stir a fever in the blood," he predicted, and cause thousands to ponder the value of a union in which slaveholders might swagger into Boston and freely advocate their twisted morality in Faneuil Hall yet bully into silence every hint and whisper of criticism in their own backyards.

Intimidation found support in the Democratic Party. Senator Mason's committee pushed the investigative powers of Congress to unprecedented lengths, but lost an effort to have Franklin Sanborn arrested in Massachusetts when he refused to come to Washington to testify. The episode enabled abolitionists to dramatize further the "inquisitorial" hand of the slave power and ultimately foil Mason's effort to make political capital of the conspiracy. The Buchanan administration, however, did sustain the discretionary power of local officers to restrain periodicals they considered a hazard to the peace, and Senator Douglas joined a Southern colleague in sponsoring a new federal sedition act that would have allowed the government to suppress "conspiracies and combinations" intended to "assail" the governments or institutions of any state. Though couched as a measure to prevent another

John Brown raid, it obviously was drawn broadly enough to use as a battle-ax against every abolitionist organization in the country. It was also intended to provide Douglas with some cover in his pursuit of the Democratic presidential nomination, but the mood in the North had so shifted that the proposal was stymied by the bloc of radical Republicans in Congress. New York's Charles Sedgwick led the effort and displayed *The Liberator* on the floor of the House as the epitome of free speech, thus offering the first praise of Garrison ever delivered in that body.

The editor took the broadest view of the polarization as a prelude to a disunionist transformation. Southern repression had made a truly free election so impossible that either party might contest the result, Garrison thought, while Maria Chapman predicted that within a year the Union would either be dissolved or a Republican majority would be reconstructing it with constitutional amendments. The AAS prepared for battle. After twenty years under the eaves at 21 Cornhill, the organization rented much larger quarters for itself and *The Liberator* in an uptown office building at 221 Washington Street, the city's commercial center. Having raised over $6,000 from an evening gala in Boston arranged by Maria Chapman, the organization increased its publication of tracts and by midsummer had in circulation a half-dozen fresh items, including an abolitionist appeal by Victor Hugo, a reassuring study of West Indian emancipation—*The Right Way, the Safe Way*—by Lydia Maria Child, and a historical review of slave insurrections by Garrison's old friend Joshua Coffin. After ten years of somewhat desultory relations with abolitionists in Great Britain, the Garrisonians refurbished their connections. They assembled a collection of more than 250 volumes for a library in London and hired George Thompson as their British agent.

Two dramatic turns in the oncoming presidential campaign helped convince Garrison that he had a significant political role to play. First the Democrats split, which elated the abolitionists, and then the Republicans made a feint toward the middle that discouraged them. In April, 1860, the alliance of Northern and Southern Democrats—for thirty years the Democratic Party's key to national power—collapsed under the cumulative weight of the controversy. Infuriated that the free-state majority at the party nominating convention would not yield to their demand for a platform committed to a federal slave code for the territories, the belligerent slaveholding bloc staged a walkout, which, under the two-thirds rule, left the putative candidate Douglas in limbo. After six weeks of frantic maneuvering a second convention took place, only to end with another "bolt" and rival sectional tickets, a popular sovereignty one led by Douglas and a slave code protectionist alternative headed by Buchanan's vice president, John C. Breckenridge of Kentucky. The party that for so long opposed all agitation was now the most agitated party in the country, Garrison joked, but he knew that Herndon's scenario for a Republican victory had come to life.

The Republicans, meanwhile, sought to exploit the Democratic breach by rejecting the long-anticipated nomination of its most prominent antislavery leader, New York's William H. Seward, in favor of a less polarizing candidate, the obscure Illinois attorney Abraham Lincoln. The party platform, moreover, muted the clarion tone of the 1856 document, fuzzing the language even on the Republicans' bedrock issue of nonextension and plainly conceding that it would not challenge sovereignty over slavery in the states where it presently existed. Only a threatened floor fight by Giddings stopped the party, eager to dispel the "Black Republican" slur, from deleting in 1860 the equal rights credo from the Declaration of Independence that it had quoted prominently in 1856. The diminution of nativism, however, and the growing population of antislavery German Protestants in the upper midwest made viable a pledge of "full and efficient protection to the rights of all classes of citizens," though, as Garrison was quick to point out, the platform remained silent about the threat *Dred Scott* posed to the rights of black citizens.

Although Kansas had now regularized its government and stood on the verge of statehood with an antislavery constitution, nonextension remained a live issue. Mining booms in Nevada and Colorado had attracted thousands of prospectors (including the sojourner George Garrison, who horrified his parents with requests for the expensive equipment necessary for an expedition from Kansas to Pikes Peak), putting those regions in need of territorial government, and there was the likelihood that another gold rush would pose another California-style admission crisis. There were new schemes afloat to manufacture additional states by subdividing Texas and California, by fusing portions of northern Mississippi with western Tennessee and Kentucky into a new state, or by reclaiming the Indian Territory, not to mention the persistent Southern designs upon Mexico and Cuba. The Republican commitment to freedom in the territories, therefore, could not be sloughed off as irrelevant.

The slaveholding Democratic ticket blustered that the Southern states would secede if the Republicans came to power, while the Northern Democratic ticket could appeal only to those who shared Douglas's premise that the slavery issue was a needlessly disruptive one that a growing economy would resolve for itself if politicians left the choice of labor systems to local communities. Democrats of both tendencies remained "eager and venomous" in their insistence that antislavery agitation be suppressed, Garrison emphasized, and he had little patience with the faction of movement "growlers," who saw no difference between Democrats and Republicans. It was "too palpable for denial," he said, that the Republican ranks were filled not only with products of the abolitionist crusade, but with thousands of sincere, if timid and inconsistent, people who earnestly wanted "something done" at least to stop the spread of slavery, if not (yet) to emancipate the slaves. They had to be dealt with justly.

Justice required fidelity to "bedrock principles," however, and Garrison insisted far more clearly than he had in 1856 that abolitionists had no business endorsing any party. From March 1860, when he sharply criticized Seward's opportunistic, but belated, efforts to moderate his position, to the major AAS meetings in New York and Boston in May, the annual Framingham picnic on the Fourth of July, and long editorial statements in the autumn, Garrison endeavored to keep abolitionists focused upon their higher goals and prevent a sacrifice of moral vision to the constraints of Republican expediency.

Parties, not candidates, drove presidential campaigns in the antebellum era. Party organizers forged the tickets and made the promises, party newspapers spread the slogans and slammed the opposition, party loyalists went to the polls in numbers that repeatedly broke the previously recorded turnout, and the party favorites reaped the spoils of victory in postmasterships, custom house clerkships, and government contracts. It was a system that Garrison watched taking shape at the outset of his career with mounting disgust, and it was a system that, far from repudiating, the Republicans mastered in technique even as they realigned its direction. The editor's warning against too close an association with an inadequate party involved more than the issue of ideological purity; it represented a statement of character as profound as one's identification with a church. The party, like the church, placed dogmatic limits upon conscience, reduced one's independence, and subordinated private judgment to the needs of institutional preservation. Garrison had challenged both church and party system as ties that bound the nation to slavery, and he had made "snapping the cords" part of his life's work.

Now that the last old institution, the Democratic Party, had sundered, Garrison saw new possibilities in politics, but he remained extremely cautious about fusing the movement's goals with the fortunes of a new party, especially one that accepted slavery where it presently existed and ran away from the issues—immediate emancipation and civil equality—that he considered fundamental. "It may not be in all respects as bad as another party, but it is *so* bad that I cannot touch it, and will not give it any countenance whatsoever," the editor said at Framingham. Yet it was remarkable that six years after he had burned the Constitution on that very spot, he had a colloquy about the constitutional compromises with a U.S. senator, Henry Wilson, who felt it necessary to honor the abolitionist constituency with his attendance. That was the problem with Republicans, people said; while reminding the abolitionists that they hated slavery as much they did, they tried to convince the public that they weren't abolitionists. The paradox was deeper yet. The party hoped to walk into the White House in 1860 on the narrow plank of being both antislavery and anti-Negro, which made abolitionists fearful that Republican rule would change too little while Southern slaveholders grew certain that it would change too much.

In an age of party, the candidates, with the exceptions of a celebrated hero like Andrew Jackson or an eminent national political figure like Henry Clay, mattered less as people of character and more as mechanical parts of the electoral system. To the abolitionists in 1860, Abraham Lincoln was just another in the parade of unfamiliar names—Polk, Cass, Pierce, Buchanan, Taylor, Tyler, Fillmore, Scott, Frémont—whose pedestrian reputations and indistinct views made them convenient flag-bearers for their parties rather than magnets of attraction themselves. "Who is this county court advocate?" Wendell Phillips sneered of Lincoln, while the AAS annual report termed him "a good enough Republican for the party's purposes, but far from being the man for the country's need."

Garrison, of course, had Herndon's continuing assurance that his partner condemned slavery as a basic violation of the Declaration of Independence, and Herndon's paid-up subscription to *The Liberator* meant that Lincoln was the first and only presidential candidate ever to have Garrison's paper coming into his law office on a regular basis. Sumner, too, passed the word that Lincoln was "a good honest antislavery man" who generated confidence among those who knew him as "a person of positive ability and of real goodness." Such private assurances counted for little with the editor, however. He always judged by the public record, and Lincoln's single term in Congress and equivocal views made him seem another in the long line of timorous time-servers who would, in Garrison's estimation, "do nothing to offend the South." Lincoln's views on abolition in the District of Columbia (he was for it, but only if the residents concurred), on the Fugitive Slave Law (he considered slave-catching distasteful, but promised to enforce all congressional enactments), and on racial discrimination (he thought blacks had an equal right to labor freely, but ought to remain politically and socially subordinate to whites) led abolitionists to regard him as nothing more than "a Henry Clay Whig," as a young black Illinoisan, H. Ford Douglass, described him at Framingham. Like Clay, Lincoln believed that slavery could not be eradicated at once without producing even greater evil to the cause of human liberty.

Yet the South considered Lincoln so "black" an abolitionist and so bent on invading their states to drag their slaves right out of the fields that its leaders pronounced themselves ready to secede from the Union rather than accept his election. In part this was political demonology, a symbolic representation of the serious loss of power slaveholders would experience with a sectional party and a president they did not control. In part, however, this was a recognition of the major difference between Lincoln and every other presidential candidate since John Quincy Adams: Lincoln was willing to regard slavery as a moral issue—as a question, in other words, that could have only one right answer—and therefore, as much as Seward, he understood the sectional conflict as an "irrepressible" one to be resolved in accordance with the "higher law" of conscience.

That Garrison and the abolitionists did not emphasize this about Lincoln can only have been a deliberate decision, for the evidence stared them in the face, both in the text of the debates Lincoln had held with Douglas during their hard-fought Senate campaign in 1858 and in a series of widely reported speeches Lincoln had made in New York and New England on an eastern swing in February and March 1860, several months before the Republican convention. Although the Lincoln-Douglas debates have become a justly famous episode in the narrative of democratic politics, they did not rivet a national audience at the time, and the texts did not become available until 1860, when the Republicans reprinted them as a campaign document. Studying them for clues to Lincoln's position, the abolitionists came away appalled at the racism Lincoln had manifested and published examples of his *"white-man-ism"* in *The Liberator* and other papers. They ignored, however, the numerous instances in which Lincoln attacked Douglas's devotion to popular sovereignty as a feigned moral indifference that masked real zeal for slavery and Lincoln's reiteration that the Republicans' willingness to condemn slavery as an evil marked the true difference between the parties. Even more tellingly, in his New England speeches, which Garrison, an assiduous reader and clipper of exchange newspapers who prided himself on knowing the public pulse, most certainly had seen, Lincoln had said at every stop that "the whole controversy hinges" upon each section's moral view of slavery. "If it is right, we may not contract its limits. If it is wrong, they cannot ask us to extend it . . . All they ask, we could readily grant, if we thought Slavery right; all we ask, they could as readily grant, if they thought it wrong . . . Thinking it right as they do, they are not to blame for desiring its full recognition, as being right; but, thinking it wrong, as we do, can we yield to them?"

Here spoke a different voice in American politics, and in accents that would prove persuasive in their homeliness and simplicity. It was a voice that, as yet, the abolitionists did not want to advertise or commend, lest they give away all leverage and settle for what the party would accept. On the outside, Lincoln would be an agitator, Wendell Phillips said, but in office he would be forced to make the usual concessions. Oliver Johnson was sure that the South would immediately test a victorious Lincoln by precipitating another crisis over the return of fugitive slaves, and, like most abolitionists, he was certain that Lincoln would do exactly as Fillmore and Pierce had done. The abolitionists very deliberately chose to judge the man by his party, not the party by the character of its nominee, and the history of presidential politics bore them out. Except for Andrew Jackson, no president had loomed larger than his party or brought its principles into accord with his own.

Abolitionists resolved their ambivalence about the 1860 election in a variety of ways. Some followed Garrison in a rigorous but charitable critique that said, in effect, that a presidential choice need not be made. Others, such as the Fosters and Pillsbury, ripped into the Republicans and ferociously advocated the righteousness of rejecting the lesser evil. The Liberty remnant, including Frederick Douglass, who had suppressed his first impulse to support Lincoln, put forward Gerrit Smith, yet again, as a token candidate in order to differentiate themselves from the Garrisonians, whose sympathetic critique of the Republicans could be taken as tacit encouragement to vote for them. A great many movement men indeed held their noses and voted for Lincoln, "just this once," telling themselves that the rank and file of the party had more antislavery backbone than the leadership and that a more thoroughgoing abolitionist party was impossible to build under the present Constitution. Abolitionists for Lincoln embraced veteran Liberty and Free-Soil organizers such as Henry Stanton and Elizur Wright, as well as old-line Garrisonians such as David Child, and even "John Brownists" such as Higginson and Stearns. Such voters persuaded themselves, said the AAS general agent, Samuel J. May,° himself a nonvoter, that in going for the party "the slaveholder most fears," they were moving the cause in the right direction.

The Republicans ran a razzle-dazzle campaign that fed the impression of movement. John Hutchinson contributed campaign songs in the jaunty and inspirational style his family had popularized for a generation, and thousands of young voters eagerly enrolled in "Wide-Awake" clubs that staged vast torchlight parades, which rolled along to endless choruses of the party theme song, "Ain't You Glad You Joined the Republicans?" Lincoln made no speeches, but campaign biographies spread the genuine story of his rise from humble frontier beginnings (epitomized by the split fence rail that became the campaign's symbol) as an example of the American opportunities jeopardized by the extension of slavery. The party had also opportunely loaded its platform with a number of bread-and-butter issues that enabled it to run on the promise of homesteads for the landless, a transcontinental railroad for Mississippi Valley growers, harbor improvements on the Great Lakes, tariff protection for seaboard industries, and the dignity and dreams of free labor everywhere. By 1860, in fact, "free labor" had become an even more significant element in the Republican appeal than "free soil." In speaking of a major shoemakers' strike in February, 1860, Lincoln had said that he *liked* the system that let a man quit when he wanted to improve himself—the answer Garrison had given for years to apologists who charged that there was no difference between Southern chattel slavery and Northern "wage" slavery. Republicans, said Lincoln, sought for "the humblest man an equal chance to get rich with everybody else"; in the debates with Douglas he had explicitly said that in the right "to eat the bread, without leave of anybody else, which his own hand earns," the black slave had to be consid-

---

°Samuel J. May, Jr. (1810–1899), was the cousin of Garrison's old friend Samuel J. May, Jr. (1797–1871), and a very effective manager of the MAS/AAS from the late 1850s through the close of the war. To avoid confusion the younger man, also a minister, will be referred to as "Agent May" in the text and as "SJM(A)" in the reference notes.

ered "my equal, and the equal of Judge Douglas, and the equal of every living man."

By October 1860, the Republican campaign machine was on the verge of victory, and even Garrison began to feel some enthusiasm for the prospect. *If* the Republicans succeeded in taking the reins of government and preserving the territories "absolutely and beyond a peradventure from the designs of the Slave Power," he said, "it will do no slight service to the cause of freedom." Two weeks before the election the editor and his family all went down to a friend's house on Dover Street to watch the grand finale of the Massachusetts campaign, a nighttime march of ten thousand "Wide-Awakes" through the streets of Boston. For an hour and half Garrison stood, bundled against the evening chill, as wave after wave of young men rolled along, carrying torches and clad in dark blue oilcloth capes and gold caps, their voices clattering in the narrow street—"Wide-Awake! Wide-Awake!"— as they danced in the zigzag pattern of a split-rail fence. It was hard not to tap one's feet to the jaunty rhythms of ". . . Joined the Republicans, Joined the Republicans, Ain't You Glad You Joined the Republicans, Down in Boston Town" and feel stirred by the glowing display of idealistic youth. (The family's friend Brad Drew had come up to march with the group from Plymouth and went back home on an extra train at three in the morning.) Fireworks boomed all around as Garrison took note of the linen banners bearing free-labor and antislavery mottoes, but groused at the many slogans of support for the Constitution and the plaintive sign "We are Republicans but not Abolitionists." For the editor the happiest moment of the night came when a West Boston group of two hundred black men strode by under a banner reading, "God never made a tyrant or a slave," and he made special note of their presence in his report for *The Liberator*. For Willie, standing next to his father, the procession was significant not for the electoral triumph it portended, but for the remarkable achievements of free speech and a free press. The date was three days shy of being the twenty-fifth anniversary of Garrison's mobbing, and looking at his father amid the tumult and the flaming golden light of the torches, Willie could only murmur, "Verily the world does move."

Lincoln carried every free state except New Jersey and gained 180 electoral votes, twenty-eight more than necessary for victory. He had only forty percent of the national vote, but fifty-four percent of the Northern vote and lost fewer than two dozen counties in the swath that reached across New England and its Great Lakes Yankee extension. Although the Republicans fell a few votes shy of working majorities in Congress, public opinion hailed the election as a revolution. Everyone understood, said Garrison, that although the campaign was ostensibly about nonextension, it signified a "much deeper sentiment" in the North which "in the process of time must ripen into more decisive action." "It was a test of strength," said Agent May, "and slavery was for once borne to the wall." Although they had spent the campaign feeling like repudiated parents, the abolitionists quickly claimed the Republican triumph as owing to their own decades-long effort to build an antislavery constituency. If the election was not yet a gain for freedom, it was nonetheless a blow to slavery, and Lincoln stood as a "pregnant symbol" of the slaveholders' loss of power. For the first time in our history, Wendell Phillips told a cheering multitude in Tremont Temple on November 7, "the *slave* has chosen a President of the United States," and, with matchless audacity, he crowed, "Lincoln is in *place, Garrison in power.*"

It would never be that simple. The Republican victory precipitated a crisis far graver than anyone had imagined, as the cotton states, led by South Carolina, erupted in fury and made military preparations to repudiate the election, leave the Union, and counter what they regarded as a "Black Ab-olitionist" revolution with one of their one. Garrison took the turmoil as a sign that the South was driving itself mad in a whirl of guilt and fear, and he first ridiculed the secession threats as the latest in the tradition of slave-holder bombast and bluff. As he published the grim news, however, that hundreds of free black families were fleeing Charleston to escape a legal crackdown that sought to reenslave them, the editor realized that the inten-sified pressure was more than rhetorical. By early December 1860, *The Lib-erator* reported that secessionist banners and the palmetto flag waved throughout the city—including a great silk standard over the slave market that proclaimed "South Carolina—Going, Going Gone!"—while the Stars and Stripes could only be seen from the ramparts of Fort Moultrie on the shoreline flanking the harbor. For the second year in a row, Garrison had to publish an extra edition, on Monday, December 31, this one containing South Carolina's Declaration of Independence, enumerating among its chief grievances the existence in the nonslaveholding states of abolitionist socie-ties, bent upon disrupting the peace, that had now obtained control of the common government in order to pervert the constitutional guarantees that protected slavery. The headlines blared of "treason consummated" and told how the U.S. commander at Fort Moultrie, fearful of a land-based attack upon the rear of his installation, had abandoned the place for the greater security of newly constructed Fort Sumter on an island athwart the harbor entrance.

Garrison reacted to the accelerating crisis with ambivalence. He wel-comed the break in the covenant and dared to hope that the Jubilee might be at hand, but fresh eruptions of mob violence and a surging compromise movement in Washington made him fearful of new concessions to placate the slaveholding states and repress the abolitionist movement. In December 1860, an unruly crowd of ruffians, egged on by the State Street merchants fearful of a commercial break with the South, attacked a John Brown anni-versary meeting in Boston and forced it to relocate in the Belknap Street Church. Public opinion rallied to the side of abolition—as it had not in

1835—but the Democratic mayor and police chief winked at the disruption, which continued over the next few weeks every time Wendell Phillips spoke in Boston and culminated with two days of disturbances that curtailed the January 1861 MAS annual meeting. Similar outbreaks occurred in Buffalo, Albany, and Detroit, as part of the blame-shifting strategy pursued by the diehard Democrats who still sought the basis for national compromise in the silencing of abolitionism.

These events distressed Garrison not only by their virulence, but by his inability to participate in the confrontation. The editor lay in the shadow of illness. His chronic bronchitis had grown more severe, and in September 1860 his physician warned grimly that pneumonia or a wasting disease like Parker's might be Garrison's fate as well. He immediately canceled all speaking engagements for the balance of 1860, difficult enough in the heat of the campaign, but made more frustrating by the need to decline an invitation that had finally come from a national lecture bureau that wanted to put him on its roster of lyceum speakers. "Better save your strength for editorials," Henry C. Wright advised, and Garrison indeed made no speeches for ten months.

During the long interregnum between Lincoln's November 1860 election and his March 1861 inauguration, the country looked on with mounting anxiety as Georgia, Florida, and the four Gulf states joined South Carolina in renouncing their ratification of the Constitution and declaring first their independence and then their intention to confederate in a new government that would extend "national" protection to slavery. "The argument is exhausted," Mississippi's Jefferson Davis told the U.S. Senate as he walked out, and "all hope of relief in the Union . . . is extinguished." A few weeks later, Davis, whom Sam Houston considered "as ambitious as Lucifer and cold as a lizard," took the oath as president of the new confederation and assumed office with a message that spoke grandly of rights and posterity and the refusal to bow before "the despotism of numbers," but said nothing about slavery, though he had devoted his political career to its continental expansion and considered it as the cornerstone of the way of life his Confederate States sought to protect.

Meanwhile, Washington experienced "a strange and bewildering chaos," recalled young Henry Adams, serving as his father's congressional secretary, in which conscience-bound New Englanders and noisy, brawling northwesterners contended with "demented" Southerners either "agog with the idea of dissolution" or rapt in contemplation of slave-empire "fancies oriental in their magnificence." Privately James Buchanan mourned to friends that he would be the last president of the United States. Amid the undercurrent of rumors that rebel troops would disrupt Lincoln's inaugural and perhaps stage a military coup, Congress was awash with proposals for compromises that would stop the exodus of states and reconcile the issues. All of these were premised upon the passage of constitutional amendments that would not only protect slavery in the territories but hamstring the effort to abolish it in the federal capital and designate all the slave-related clauses in the Constitution (including the powerful guarantee of sixty percent more representation on the basis of slave property) as forever beyond the reach of subsequent amendment.

Garrison condemned all "Union-saving" measures as "simply idiotic," and abolitionists generally joined him in regarding any "compromise" as a shameful surrender to the usual Southern bluster. The slaveholders had at last broken the covenant when the agreement no longer worked to their advantage, and the free states would now have an opportunity to reconstruct it on a moral basis while the seceding states grappled with slaves bent on exercising revolutionary rights of their own. The editor's long-standing confidence that slavery could not survive without the protection of the Union seemed unshaken by the repressive power the South had displayed in the months since John Brown's raid, and even Frederick Douglass now agreed that dissolution of the Union would advance the cause of abolition.

The abolitionist refusal to be cowed by the imperatives of Union and compromise proved important in stiffening the backbone of the Republican Party. Herndon passed the word to his Boston friends that Lincoln, a man of "superior will and moral courage," would stand "firm as a rock" and would not cower in the face of rebellion. Sumner said the same; he had private assurances from those close to Lincoln who represented the president-elect as convinced that "the tug" had to come now, or else everything gained by the election would be lost and the next election would likewise be held hostage to the demands of the South. Even so, a number of prominent Republicans, including Charles Francis Adams and William Seward, seemed poised for compromise, and even Lincoln indicated that he could accept a proposed Thirteenth Amendment (the only piece of a compromise package to pass Congress) that permanently guaranteed the protection of slavery in states where it presently existed. That was his present understanding, Lincoln said, and he saw no harm in spelling it out, though he wished the seceding states would, in exchange, agree to suspend their disruptive work until the new administration committed acts of offense.

Such "shivering in the wind" grieved Garrison. Though he insisted that "dark as the times are, beyond them all is light," his thoughts took an increasingly gloomy turn. The crisis presaged "God's judgment day with our guilty nation," he wrote, which would likely be visited "with civil and servile war [and] . . . turned inside out and upside down, for its unparalleled iniquity." En route to his inauguration, Lincoln had to sneak through Baltimore under cloak of night as if he were a felon, the editor fumed, and no one knew if the new president would meet an assassin's bullet as he rose to take the oath. "What terrible times," Helen exclaimed to Mary Grew, who replied that they were not half so terrible "as the times of moral stagnation" the abolitionists had already dispelled.

In a long editorial Garrison described "the conflicting hopes and fears" of Inauguration Day and praised the miracle of the telegraph for relieving the "feverish anxiety" that murder or a coup d'état would interrupt the transfer of power. Dispatches brought the details of how a bronzed statue of Freedom lay on the ground awaiting the completion of the Capitol dome and how the ancient and cadaverous Roger Taney, eighty-four years old, could not stop his hands from shaking as he administered the oath to his ninth president. Garrison admired Lincoln's courageous self-possession and the brevity of his address, though the new president's efforts to reassure the South gave renewed evidence that the Republicans were far from being "the Garrison party" that the slaveholders feared.

Having listened to the grown-ups' conversation around him, twelve-year-old Franky Garrison concluded in his diary that Lincoln's address had been "pro-slavery" and "bad." The nub of the whole controversy, his father said, was Lincoln's pledge to maintain the Union and exercise federal authority without invading the errant states. It wouldn't work, Garrison predicted, and either blood would flow or the North would have to back down. Six weeks later, after intricate diplomatic maneuvering in which the president tried to resupply the beleaguered command at Fort Sumter without an aggressive move against South Carolina, the slaveholders lost patience and launched a cannonade upon the outpost in Charleston Harbor. On Sunday afternoon, April 14, Franky went out for a walk on the Common with his eldest brother, George, home at last from the west, only to race back with the news that Fort Sumter had fallen under the Confederate bombardment. On Wednesday, Franky read galley proofs for his father with headlines set in the largest type ever seen in *The Liberator*:

CIVIL WAR BEGUN!

FORT SUMTER CAPTURED

THE FEDERAL CAPITAL IN DANGER

THOUSANDS OF TROOPS MUSTERING

THE NORTH UNITED AT LAST

CHAPTER TWENTY-TWO

THE COVENANT ANNULLED

SUDDENLY FLAGS WAVED EVERYWHERE. THE EDITOR AND HIS YOUNGEST SON WATCHED WITH ASTONISHMENT AS THE MERCHANTS OF FRANKLIN STREET RAISED THE STARS AND STRIPES ON A FLAGPOLE 140 FEET HIGH directly in front of *The Liberator*'s office. The more the dealers in human flesh trampled upon the flag, said Garrison, the more handsome it looked in his eyes. Oliver Johnson added a flag engraving to the editorial column of the *Standard*, and Wendell Phillips told a rapturously cheering crowd in the Music Hall that the slaves craved sight of the star-spangled banner and henceforth he would regard it as the pledge of their redemption. A jam-packed meeting in the Rev. Sella Martin's Baptist church "most vociferously" greeted a flag unfurled in its midst and resolved to start forming volunteer companies while agitating to lift the ban on black enlistments in the militia.

Not all abolitionists agreed with such heady patriotism. William Wells Brown warned the Baptist meeting that those in attendance could expect no more from Abraham Lincoln than they could from Jefferson Davis. Espousing a similar sentiment, Maria Child said that she would only wear a flag pin and mount the Stars and Stripes in her great-elm tree when she was certain that the United States would treat oppressed slaves with justice and humanity; until then she'd as soon wear a rattlesnake upon her bosom as the eagle. Indeed, the "sensitiveness" of many readers of the *Standard* led Oliver Johnson, prodded by Garrison, to withdraw the flag from his columns after only two appearances. By June 1861, with Lincoln having called out 75,000 militiamen for ninety days to suppress an insurrection that now included four more states from the upper South, *The Liberator* reprinted a long debate, "The Flag of Our Union—What Does It Symbolize," which questioned whether "our troops" would be fighting for freedom or slavery. Would this be a war to restore the Union as Jackson, Clay, and Webster knew it, or would it be a war to reconstruct a nation on a moral basis less compromised than the Constitution that had so evidently failed? Could the rebellious states be brought to heel and yet retain their "sovereign" right to slave property, or had their rebellion in fact dissolved the Union, as Garrisonians had advocated, and presented the opportunity for a new birth of freedom? These were radical questions, and only the abolitionists raised them at the outset of the war. They believed that the logic of events favored them, despite the outpouring of a conservative patriotism that repudiated any hint of social revolution, but it would take Garrisonian abolitionists six months of earnest discussion to clarify the movement's strategy and many months of agitation after that to bring the country to the year of Jubilee.

Faced with the outbreak of a war he had never believed would come, Garrison reacted in unaccustomed fashion: he preached gloom and he counseled hesitation. Too ill to speak before the late Theodore Parker's congregation at the Music Hall on the Sunday after Sumter, the editor instead chose the texts to precede a discourse by Phillips. Intuitively, Garrison turned to the prophet Jeremiah. For the lesson he provided an expertly rendered condensation of chapters 50 and 51 that told of how the Lord sent "an assembly of great nations from the north country" to punish sinful Babylon when that kingdom had refused to renounce iniquity and became forsaken by God. For an epigraph Garrison proposed Jeremiah 34:17, "Therefore thus saith the Lord: Ye have not hearkened unto me in proclaiming liberty every one to his brother, and every man to his neighbor; behold I proclaim a liberty for you, saith the Lord, to the sword, to the pestilence, and to the famine." The passage, said Garrison, not only summed up "the cause and consequence" of our national trouble, but "vindicated" the abolitionists whose counsel, if heeded, would have averted the bloodshed. Not only did Phillips employ the passages with striking success, but they became the texts for scores of sermons across the free states in the next few months as people tried to make sense of what Garrison insisted—in the midst of martial ardor—be recognized as a national "visitation" or catastrophe.

For abolitionists, with the American Anti-Slavery Society scheduled to hold its annual meeting three weeks after Sumter, Garrison had a different text: "Stand still and see the salvation of God" (Ex. 14:13). The editor persuaded the AAS executive committee to postpone indefinitely both the New York meeting and the traditional New England convention at month's end in Boston. "So mighty and irresistible is the popular feeling," wrote Garrison of the great outpouring that followed Lincoln's call for volunteers, "that nothing can stand before it," and he worried that a full-bore abolitionist discussion of the "anomalous," "paradoxical," and "confusing" issues presented by the war might bring down more violence upon them or invite charges of "treason" that would hound them from the political arena.

If the editor had felt himself unalterably opposed to the war, he undoubtedly would have defied the mob and the government to assert himself. He recommended a period of watchful waiting, however, because he needed time to work out a strategy for making the war serve an abolitionist purpose. It was no time for "minute" criticism of Lincoln and Republicanism, the editor counseled. To combine sympathy for the government against the "Southern desperadoes and buccaneers" without compromising abolitionist principles would be a challenging task that required "great circumspection and consummate wisdom," Garrison told his closest associates, but he could see no other course.

Thirty years of struggle had brought Garrison to a fateful conflict between his abolitionism and his pacifism. Agitation and politics had converged in a manner that made emancipation so viable a prospect that Garrison believed himself compelled to subordinate perfectionism and contend in the practical arena. Another pacifist leader, Adin Ballou, who had lived for years within his own utopian community, would strike a different calculus and uphold the light of nonresistance amid the darkness of war, but Garrison would not sacrifice his voice for abolition at the culminating moment of struggle, even if that meant acceptance of the violent measures he had always deplored. The wound dealt to his pacifism by John Brown had now proved fatal. He held an antislavery war to be a stronger good than a proslavery peace, and he felt a higher obligation to support that war on behalf of the slaves than to oppose it on behalf of nonresistance ideals. He knew that the people were not in "a listening condition" for the gospel of peace, but he believed—he had to believe—that they were ready to accept the gospel of liberation.

If Garrison had to accede to war, he understood his choice as part of the dark toll imposed by God for two centuries of racial oppression. At a moment when both sides had high confidence in their prowess and felt certain that a bloodless victory lay within their reach, Garrison preached a different lesson. Let there be no illusions about war. Even a simple thank-you note to Brad Drew for his annual basket of May flowers turned into a somber disquisition on the "severe scourge" that lay ahead. "There will be desolation and death on a frightful scale, weeping and mourning, and lamentation for the slain and wounded in thousands of families," the editor prophesied, "but if it shall end in the speedy and total abolition of slavery, the fountain-source of all our national difficulties, it will bring with it inconceivable blessings, and the land will have rest, and the old waste places be restored." If the war ended in more compromise, however, Garrison predicted a further wrathful apocalypse that would lead to "the extinction of the Republic." For all his gloom, though, the editor never felt that the abolitionists had failed either God or the nation, but rather that the nation had failed abolitionism and God. The war, however dreadful, would be a terrible and final chance to repent.

Many abolitionists who had no religious scruples about the war nonetheless withheld full-hearted support because it lacked an antislavery purpose. Garrison, however, considered such a stance both shortsighted and counterproductive. He endorsed the war for the same reason he had sympathized with the Republicans in the late 1850s: the struggle presented a historic political opportunity too great and too insistent to ignore. "Facts are mightier than syllogisms," Oliver Johnson had written in support of Garrison's watchful policy, for both men were certain that with the South even temporarily out of the Union, the political ground rules could be altered and the purposes of the war enlarged. Their task—the creation of a public demand for abolition—had not changed, but the framework for it had shifted. Instead of a national party disposed toward compromise, they had to influence a sectional party whose bedrock principles stood challenged by rebellion. At the moment of Lincoln's victory, George Thompson had presciently warned Garrison that he would face a different sort of political challenge in grappling with the near-enemy of "Republican conservatism" rather than the minions of the slave power. Abolitionists, said Thompson, would have to contend with those who had obtained power with their assistance but would be likely to "regress" into "mere *white-manism*," if not made "genuine converts" to the "true gospel." Garrison's policy of discriminating criticism had already reflected this insight, but the war enhanced its applicability. The gap between abolitionists and the Republican antislavery majority was narrow enough to bridge by means of political discourse and critical advocacy if the movement focused itself properly. They had nearly arrived at the point of convergence, Maria Chapman told Garrison, when "the reformer's work and the statesman's work are one." The abolitionists had "all the disunion they needed" to create a new kind of nationality and invite the popular majority to join in the process of reconstruction. In her exceedingly elliptical manner Chapman declared, "Now we must step upon the vantage ground and without ceasing to be priests and prophets, the circumstances compel us to be kings." Public opinion, though not yet all that could be desired, was sounder than the abolitionists had ever dared to hope.

The armies squared off for what Unionists expected to be a short and sharp rebuke to rebellion and Confederates anticipated as a brief and decisive strike for independence. Garrison, meanwhile, mobilized to vest the war with an abolitionist purpose. Still laboring under respiratory difficulties that prevented him from public speaking, the editor drove himself hard between April and July 1861 to produce a series of articles on the questions that perplexed him most, and he made *The Liberator* an important forum for the issues neglected in the patriotic frenzy. (President Lincoln would have ready access to the discussion; three days after his inauguration the editor's old friend Nathaniel White ordered a paid subscription for the president to be sent to the White House.)

Garrison had a genius for exposing the flaws in his opponents' arguments which he employed to identify the essence of issues. Yet his logical and disciplined cast of mind did not always extend to his editorial writing, in which he tended to argue several points simultaneously, to stud his columns with quoted passages, to peg his themes as bristling ripostes to the "flings" of other editors, and to plead lack of time and space as reasons for breaking off before he had explored an issue fully. These habits stamped his work with the journalist's urgency rather than, say, the Emersonian calm of a formal essay. Nonetheless, taken together, in the spring of 1861 his work concentrated upon three large tasks. First, the effort to distinguish disunion from secession and refute the canard that the abolitionists were responsible for the war. Second, the endeavor to compel recognition of slavery as the cause of the war and to make abolition one of its goals. Third, the challenge of finding a constitutional approach to emancipation compatible with the tenets of Republican conservatism and Lincoln's reluctance to antagonize the four slaveholding border states (Missouri, Kentucky, Maryland, and Delaware) still in the Union.

From the outset, Garrison regarded the cotton states' departure as an extralegal act of rebellion, and in denying a constitutional right of secession, he stood on common ground not only with Lincoln and the Republicans, but with the maligned Daniel Webster, whose words on national supremacy he quoted without a shred of embarrassment. "State sovereignty" in the hands of Calhoun and his successors had always been a blind for "slave sovereignty," the editor contended, and he had no patience with the fog of obfuscation intended to cloak the secessionists with constitutional legitimacy. The rebels would have to defend their departure in revolutionary terms, Garrison maintained, and by the tests propounded in the Declaration of Independence, he found the act unwarranted. The government still had the consent of the majority, and the minority, far from being abused, had previously dominated the political process. South Carolina and Georgia had dictated the terms of Union to suit their desire to protect slavery, and—in contrast to the long train of usurpations that had motivated the colonists in '76—all the proslavery guarantees mandated by the Constitution had remained in force until the day the states had departed. The South, moreover, had always possessed "the lion's share" of power in the government, and if its leaders now protested the loss of an election by taking up arms, it seemed to Garrison that they had put themselves in the position of the apostate angels who thought it better, as Milton put it, "to reign in hell than serve in heaven."

The universal condemnation of secession in the North made it inevitable, however, that conservatives and racists would try to discredit the abolitionist effort to add an egalitarian dimension to the struggle by charging them with being the moral equivalent of secessionists and therefore disqualified from patriotic discussion. It was precisely in the "moral point of view," however, that Garrison explained the diametric opposition between abolitionist disunion and Southern secession. Disunion was a moral effort to reveal the national complicity with sin; secession was an illegitimate grab for political power to perpetuate a sinful institution. Disunion looked to the creation of equality through peaceful agitation and political reconstruction; secession aimed at the perpetuation of aristocratic privilege through violence. The secessionist movement was a political repudiation of constituted authority that turned into a war against peaceful democratic institutions; disunion was a moral repudiation of constitutional compromise, and it had employed the democratic and religious measures of protest and witness. If disunionists had sought a confrontation between state and federal authority, it was in the name of "the higher law" and directed toward effectuating a nonviolent revolution for justice. To blame the abolitionists for the outbreak of war, said Garrison, was like blaming lambs for the ravages of wolves. With the fanatic's delight, Garrison proudly turned the charge around. Without slaveholders, there could have been no abolitionists, and if people believed that they had provoked the secession he would take the reproach "as a splendid tribute to the power of truth, the majesty of justice, and the advancement of the age."

The editor's emphasis upon the peaceful intent of disunion as transformative protest, however, gave fresh weight to the concurrent charge that abolitionists had hypocritically forsaken their peace principles by endorsing the war, and this question generated a great deal of concern within the movement as well as among its most malicious critics. Garrison tried several exculpatory arguments, none of which fully met the charge. He did point out that most radical abolitionists, including many Garrisonians, were not in fact nonresistants in the formal sense, and emphasized that, in thirty years, the AAS had never in any way violated its promise to employ only peaceful and constitutionally protected means of agitation. That the war had come unsought by them and represented the nation's moral failure was true enough, though this defense conveniently ignored both the "forcibly if we must" frenzy of the late 1850s and the foreshortened ethical debate over the John Brown raid. To claim, however, that the war did not diminish the beauty of nonresistance ideals nor make it more difficult to realize them stretched credulity. Slavery epitomized endemic violence, Garrison ventured, and any endeavor that purged it from society had to be understood as advancing the cause of peace. By this argument, even though the government employed violent weapons, it did so in righteousness and innocence, whereas the slaveholders embodied "diabolism" and guilt. The editor had the same problem with the Civil War that he had with John Brown; those Northerners who were prominently against it were no friends of the slave, and he preferred to readjust his principles rather than have himself confused with an opposition that he regarded as disreputable and immoral.

Garrison's effort to reconcile nonresistance and warfare rested upon the premise that the war was indeed being waged against the oppressive and violent institution of slavery, an assumption that ran against both a strong current of Unionist public opinion in the North and the tide of Southern rhetoric that submerged the peculiar institution beneath the gallant waves of honor, patrimony, sovereignty, and self-defense. With the latter Garrison had no patience, of course, and he found it no difficult chore to interpret the secessionists' war as a counterrevolutionary effort to perpetuate the chattel slavery that they erroneously believed to be no longer safe in the Union.

In this he was much aided by the candid statement of Georgia's Alexander Stephens, the Confederate vice-president, who had declared "the corner-stone" of his new government to be "the great truth that the negro is not equal to the white man . . . [and] slavery . . . is his natural and normal con-dition." This meant, said the Georgian, that the Confederacy had rectified the fundamental "mistake" of the Declaration of Independence. Garrison both applauded his candor and brandished the statement as irrefutable ev-idence which "convicted" the rebels, as he liked to say, "from their own mouths."

It was easy to show that the South fought *for* slavery, but it was difficult to show that the North fought *for* abolition, since the administration and a substantial portion of the Republican Party denied such a purpose. Even before the attack upon Sumter, James Russell Lowell had given the New England elite's definition of the controversy to the readers of his influential new magazine, *The Atlantic Monthly*. The secessionists' quarrel was not "with the Republican Party, but with the theory of Democracy," he said, and defenders of the Union had to "beware of being led off upon th[e] side issue" of slavery. The "matter now at hand," intoned Lowell, was "the re-establishment of order," and he insisted that "the violent abolition of slavery" would not compensate for "the evil that would be entailed upon both races by the abolition of our nationality." Maria Chapman and Agent May dis-missed Lowell as a product of the "change-hating complacency of the Col-lege [Harvard] and its Boston circles," but similar views could be found in many other sectors of Northern opinion. In a sermon that occupied the entire front page of *The Liberator*, for example, Henry Ward Beecher laid out a ringing endorsement of the war as a defense of "constitutional liberty" without once alluding to emancipation. The force of such expressions led President Lincoln, in his message to Congress in July 1861, to justify the war in narrow terms as the military suppression of rebellion and more broadly as a defense of the cardinal principle of free government that bullets could not overrule a decision fairly and constitutionally made by ballots. The president disavowed conquest or subjugation and stated only an aim "to preserve the government, that it may be administered for all, as it was ad-ministered by the men who made it."

Garrison shared Lincoln's concern for the defense of democratic govern-ment, but he wanted to enlarge its meaning from the "verbal and technical" protection of form to the substantive guarantee of civil equality. To challenge the limited definition of the war's purpose, Garrison, paradoxically, had to maintain his "disunionist" view of the Constitution. He did not have to burn once more a constitution that the seceding states had attacked for him; he had to argue instead that the rebellion had betrayed the compromise and released the loyal states from their pledge to maintain slavery. Disunion, as he had always meant it, had triumphed. "The covenant is annulled," Garrison proclaimed. "The relation of things has essentially changed, and a new definition of terms is needed. . . ." He would endow the war with a transcendent purpose, lifting it from a struggle undertaken in resentment for insults to the flag and putting it on the higher plane of righting the injustices perpetuated in the flag's name. The argument was not one of states' rights or federal supremacy, he said, but an opportunity to "to extract the root of bitterness" and "to remove the cause which had brought us to our doom." If the war put an end to "that execrable system" of slavery, said Garrison, it would be "more glorious in history" than the American Revolution; if slavery remained intact, even though Southern "treason" was temporarily quashed, the community could expect "heavier judgments" and "irrevocable" destruction.

By the Fourth of July 1861, Garrison had forged his argument and found his voice. At the annual Framingham picnic he and Phillips defined the abolitionists' political task as one of shaping the unprecedented situation to the ends of freedom. The "masses" had to decide this battle, said Phillips, by awakening the administration to its real task. Lincoln and the Republicans, clinging to the idea of being "a constitutional administration" instead of an antislavery one, were not yet strong enough to declare an emancipation policy; only the people could make them—and, Phillips added, there were sufficient antislavery men among the Republicans willing to be led. The editor, speaking in public for the first time in ten months, offered the assembly a fresh definition of Garrisonian abolitionism premised on the application of the Golden Rule and the repudiation of "colorphobia." "Let us see, in every slave, Jesus himself," he cried, and plead for those in bonds as brothers.

It wouldn't have been an abolitionist meeting, however, without a challenge from Parker Pillsbury, who said he had no more confidence in Lincoln than he did in Jefferson Davis, or from Stephen S. Foster, who moved that abolitionists withhold their support from Lincoln and the military effort until the administration had committed itself to an emancipation policy. As such a course might have opened the movement to the charge of disloyalty, Garrison, Phillips, and a large majority voted it down. Abolitionists could still uphold their principles and sympathize with the government, Garrison said; the time to criticize would come when and if—against the tendency of events—the administration insisted upon enforcing the old proslavery compromises. The meeting ended harmoniously, with Abby Kelley Foster's conciliatory observation that since Garrison and Phillips each looked to outside forces to weigh heavily upon the administration, they really had no more faith in the government than her husband did, and therefore there was "no confusion of tongues," "no confusion of heart," and they "all stood together" on the immediatist, moral suasionist platform of the old AAS.

In pronouncing the covenant annulled, Garrison spoke out of a broader moral universe than the world of law inhabited by the president and Congress. To make a bridge between them, the editor advanced an alternative view that did not rest upon his disunionist premises but simply pressed the logic of warfare to its ultimate conclusion. In a time of national peril, Garrison argued, the commander in chief had the constitutional authority to regard slavery as a military threat and could emancipate the slaves as a means of depriving the enemy of an important military and economic resource. Forced labor supplied the food for the Confederate army. ("Arrest that hoe in the hands of the negro," Frederick Douglass said, and you attack the rebellion in its stomach.) If justice could not prevail with the public, perhaps "military necessity" would be more persuasive, if less ennobling. John Quincy Adams had advanced the "war power" argument during the Texas annexation quarrel two decades earlier, and Garrison now revived it, printing extracts from Adams and other nonabolitionist authorities in *The Liberator* and offering David Lee Child extensive column space for a lengthy three-part review of the legal issues that later became a broadly circulated AAS pamphlet.

The argument began to take hold over the course of the summer, especially after the Union forces sustained a humiliating defeat at Bull Run in July 1861, and even conservative Republicans began to see some practical wisdom in depriving the Confederacy of its slave resources. From Washington the *New York Times* correspondent—writing in a cold fury in a report that appeared next to a page-long list of casualties—said that it seemed "Quixotic" and absurd to protect slavery in the South while the rebels were killing loyal citizens. "There is a point of time beyond which forbearance ceases to be a virtue," he wrote, ". . . and the war-making power, as expounded by John Quincy Adams, suggests a short cut to the solution of present troubles." This was an oblique but unmistakable sign to abolitionists that public opinion had begun to shift their way.

Sad and bloody as was Bull Run, David Child told Garrison, that "disgraceful rout" had done more for the cause than "a dozen victories." That judgment was borne out early in August when Congress passed a "Confiscation Act" that permitted the seizure by Union forces of all property—including slaves—used "in aid" of the rebellion. This meant that slaves who had built fortifications for the Confederacy, worked in its arms factories, hauled its armies' wagonloads of food, or loaded its naval vessels might be captured and held as "contraband," an ambiguous twilight status in which their masters had forfeited a right to reclaim them as property, but their captors did not gain them as prizes. The law did not make them free, but it left them masterless and able to work for wages, though life in refugee camps—fed on army rations, clothed in the spoils of war, and sheltered in tattered tents—underscored their tentative and precarious situation.

No sooner had the Garrisonians sounded their keynote, however, than Lincoln acted in a manner that suggested he might be tone deaf. At the end of August 1861, the U.S. commanding general in Missouri, John C. Frémont, faced with holding for the Union a state bitterly divided in opinion and beset with an aggressive guerrilla insurgency, took the military necessity argument at face value and, with a declaration of martial law, emancipated all the slaves owned by Missourians in rebellion. "Laus Deo!—'the beginning of the end,'" Garrison headlined the text of Frémont's proclamation, and the movement erupted in joy, especially as it became known that Captain Edward M. Davis, a Philadelphia Garrisonian and the son-in-law of Lucretia and James Mott, served on Frémont's staff and had directly influenced the dramatic action. President Lincoln, however, deeply concerned that the edict would alienate public opinion in another crucial border state, Kentucky, privately asked Frémont to modify his order to make it consistent with the congressional confiscation policy. When Frémont refused to accede without a direct order, Lincoln "cheerfully" gave it, publicly countermanded the proclamation, and, six weeks later, removed Frémont to an obscure post in western Virginia.

Abolitionists reacted furiously. "The soldiers are *mad*," Franky Garrison wrote in his diary, without mentioning his own father's anger. The editor put thick black rules around Lincoln's message, branded it as "timid, depressing, suicidal," and, breaking the self-imposed moratorium on criticism, blasted the president for his "dereliction" in not extending Frémont's order to areas in rebellion. Lincoln's reactionary course would prolong the war and subvert the government, Garrison charged in a fervent editorial, and he might well deserve impeachment for his failure to take the military steps most vital to the republic's security. In private, Garrison expressed even greater disgust. Lincoln might be six feet four inches tall, he groused, but "he is only a dwarf in mind."

Though Congress had settled for "only a tenth of the loaf" in the Confiscation Act, said David Child, *The Liberator*'s expert on the war powers issue, it meant to put the president on "the right track," but instead Lincoln had wrongly inferred that he could proceed no further. If the president could "ride his war horse" over secessionists in Maryland by suspending habeas corpus in Baltimore and ordering preventive detention as a war measure, Child reasoned, surely he could sustain his field commander in a general emancipation for Missouri. Child's backhanded reference to Lincoln's arbitrary treatment of dissent exposed a serious problem in the abolitionists' advocacy of martial law as a weapon against slavery. It evidently "gagged" them on an important issue of civil liberty that, in other circumstances, would have drawn heated criticism from a conscience-minded editor like Garrison. There was, instead, an unaccustomed silence, the most telling measure of his willingness to adjust his convictions to altered circumstances.

While many blamed Lincoln's constricted antislavery policy upon his preoccupation with retaining the border states, Garrison saw a deeper political motive. Lincoln, he believed, was trying to placate the very conservative Democratic element which had given only nominal support to the war and clearly looked to a rapid negotiated settlement that would preserve the Constitution as it was and bring the erring sister states back into the fold. All of this was designed, Garrison believed, to send the reunited Democrats back to the White House in 1864 on a platform of national reconciliation. Democratic editors, as epitomized by Garrison's ancient enemies at the *New York Herald* and the *Journal of Commerce,* were still filled with "pro-slavery venom" and hissed and shook their rattles at every mention of emancipation, the editor pointed out, and they (not Kentucky) were the president's real source of concern. Lincoln might well abandon the slaves and make an "atrocious compromise" with the South in order to restore the Union and secure his reelection with racist rather than abolitionist votes.

In retrospect, both the fantasies of the Democratic editors and Garrison's pessimistic scenario appear far-fetched, but in late 1861 there were ominous "signs of the times" that the editor could not ignore. Many Republicans reacted with hostility as Sumner, Julian, Lovejoy, and the other radicals began to advocate an emancipation policy, and party regulars, in fact, tried to restrict the radicals' participation in conventions and denied them coverage in their newspapers. On the evangelical front, so reliable a bellwether as Henry Ward Beecher condemned a wartime abolition as an unconstitutional "revolution" and warned that "the conflict must be carried on *through* our institutions and not over them." Unionist editors praised Lincoln's firm rebuke of Frémont, loudly charged the abolitionists with seeking to prolong the war in behalf of their amalgamationist fantasies, and called for Garrison's arrest as an enemy of the administration. In Newburyport, where public antagonism had kept the editor away from his birthplace for nearly thirty years, the *Herald* decried the "simple theories of Lloyd Garrison" and, calling for one crusade at a time, urged a rapid restoration of the Union without going into "any great humanity schemes for blacks." It would be "quite enough," sniffed the *Herald,* "to attend to the well-being of America, without looking after Africa."

To counter such hostility, abolitionists redoubled their own propaganda effort, but tried to make it a broad-based affair. Garrison and the AAS turned down the idea of holding a national antislavery convention in the wake of the Frémont affair, in part from lingering concern about mob violence and in part from a shift in tactical perspective. Stimulated by Maria Chapman's earnest advocacy that the time to go it alone had passed and that the "enlarged fraternity" of the war made it possible to build a truly mass movement, Garrison advocated that abolitionists "merge ourselves, as far as we can without a compromise of principle, in the onward sweeping current of Northern sentiment." Chapman worked hard among her family connections in the Boston and New York mercantile communities to promote public support for emancipation, and by late fall, a number of prominent commercial men (including "War Democrats") had begun to speak out. "Start the thing by others & then fall in, is our best plan," she told Miller McKim in

Philadelphia, as Republicans along the entire seaboard engaged in joint ventures with abolitionists they had once shunned.

Garrison went along with the creation of a new "Emancipation League," drawn from the Boston mercantile elite and headed by a former Democratic governor, George S. Boutwell. Intended as a mainstream lobbying effort, financed by George L. Stearns and staffed by Frank Sanborn and Samuel G. Howe, the group undertook public lobbying and educational efforts, including an intensive petition campaign directed toward the next congressional session. In keeping with the strategy, Garrison did not press very hard for the broadside the AAS had intended to issue as its own reiteration of principles.

In going along with the Emancipation League's petition, Garrison followed the example of the British antislavery leaders he had observed in 1833, who successfully combined a radical mass movement with a Parliamentary lobbying group at the climactic moment. He also followed the British example in not putting up a fuss about the details. The petition, which demanded "under the war power, the total abolition of slavery throughout the country" as a response to the root causes of the rebellion, nonetheless contained an escape clause that "while not recognizing the right of property in man, allow[ed] for the emancipated slaves of such as are loyal to the government a fair pecuniary reward." Such a promise of compensated emancipation, not unlike the "loan" to the planters accepted by British abolitionists that had so annoyed Garrison in 1833, proved tolerable this time to the editor, who regarded it as "a conciliatory measure" that might ease the passage of those coming into the movement from the Unionist rather than the abolitionist point of view.

Such a concession, which once would have seemed horrifying to the Garrisonian apostles, did not occasion much of a stir in the new mood of pragmatism. Oliver Johnson in the *Standard* compared it to the expedient purchases of individual fugitives, including Frederick Douglass, in order to put their "self-ownership" beyond legal doubt, but Robert Purvis objected that he wouldn't give a dollar to so-called loyal slaveholders whose devotion remained contingent upon the government's protecting their rascality. No one really thought that the provision was anything but camouflage, but it did epitomize the concern of many abolitionists that a soulless and expedient "emancipationism" would, at the last minute, overwhelm the moral grandeur of the abolition they had envisioned for decades. Nevertheless the movement's organizers rallied to collect signatures in the greatest mobilization since the original drives of the late 1830s. As Mary Grew told Helen, abolitionists ought not to complain that politics had entered the work. "Sane reformers" could not expect grandeur, she said, but should be thankful that "by events over which the government has or has not control; from motives pure, selfish, or commingled, the abolition of slavery is at hand."

For the Garrisons, as for countless other families, the campaign became an occasion for everyone to share in the movement's work, with Fanny and Franky taking their share of door-to-door soliciting, along with their parents and elder brothers. Helen had also taken on more work in the movement, assuming direct charge of the annual AAS fund-raising by national subscription and an evening affair in Boston after Maria Chapman had scotched the old bazaar and antique sale as old-fashioned and too burdensome. In 1861 and 1862 the affair raised record amounts, all of which went into the fund for publishing and circulating pamphlets.

The Liberator, too, had become a family concern, with George home from Kansas and associated with the Yerrintons in the printing office and Wendell and Willie contributing occasional articles. It startled the editor to look around and see his three older boys turned into "full-bearded adults," and he was unstinting in his praise and affection. Franky, too, was a joy and became a regular hand for Wednesday proofreading and other chores. He became friends with the office boy, Willie Wright, and when he went off to the country for a few weeks in midsummer took the opportunity of sending him a letter in the striking "Liberty Bell" envelopes they had helped to print and distribute.

Helen fretted as always about the effort the newspaper required. She knew that her husband would never give it up, even though the rising cost of newspaper (given the shortage of cotton rags) had made its finances precarious again and would require an increase in the subscription price. *The Liberator* had passed its thirtieth anniversary in January 1861. It had started as a handout in black barbershops and now went to Congress and the White House and was mailed to subscribers in Peoria and Beloit, Winona and Yam Hill, San Francisco and Placerville and Steilacoom, as well as England, Scotland, and Canada. Few newspapers in the country could match *The Liberator*'s record of continuous publication, and even fewer editors had maintained their connection with a single venture as long as Garrison had. Though his newspaper was still printed on one sheet, it now folded to make a page twice as large as in the beginning, and the proprietor's only regret at the start of his fourth decade proved to be the fiscal inability to enlarge the sheet to match the size of the leading Republican journal, Greeley's *Tribune*.

To ease her husband's burden Helen pressed for family vacations. The family enjoyed the sojourn in New Hampshire undertaken for the editor's health in 1860, though Garrison said that walking in the mountains was not as easy at fifty-four as it had been at twenty. In 1861 and 1862 they made shorter trips to Plymouth, where the older sons could pal around with Brad Drew, and to Valley Falls, Rhode Island, where Elizabeth Buffum Chace gathered a social circle for relaxing days of walking and visiting, earnest evening conversations, and a great deal of singing. Fanny and her friend Lillie Chace spent the time reading, with their parents' approval, Elizabeth Barrett Browning's *Aurora Leigh,* a long narrative poem about an orphan girl who marries a strange reformer, and of course found it fascinating. There were huckleberry expeditions, though Helen teased that her husband got so burned on his nose that he looked like "an old toper." "Only think of it," said one of the Chace girls, "going berrying with a man whose name shall live fresh and green when the Napoleons are forgotten." Her mother retained happy memories of the editor standing on her piazza, rejoicing in the sunshine and exclaiming, " 'This is a day that the Lord hath made.' "

When Congress opened in December 1861, Garrison took the dramatic step of changing *The Liberator*'s banner. He removed the disunionist "covenant with death" slogan from the place it had occupied since 1844 and replaced it with the Biblical command "Proclaim Liberty throughout the land, to all the inhabitants thereof" (Lev. 25:10). When rabid New York editors chided him for inconsistency in supporting a Union that still contained slaves, Garrison made a memorably witty reply. Recalling Benedick's explanation in *Much Ado About Nothing* that when he said that he would die a bachelor he did not think that he would live to get married, the editor said that when he had vowed not to sustain the Constitution because it was "a covenant with death and an agreement with hell," he had "no idea that [he] would live to see death and hell secede." It was a retort that drew deafening applause every time the editor repeated it before an audience that winter.

Week after week the petitions poured into Congress in such profusion— ten in one day, each bearing thousands of names—that the newspapers began to compare the volume to the memorials that flooded Parliament in 1833. The numbers were not close, but the comparison was apt. Radical Republicans managed to get seven different bills relating to confiscation and emancipation reported out of committee by the second week of January 1862, despite the president's warning in his annual message to Congress that he did not want the war to "degenerate" into a "remorseless revolutionary struggle" and his pallid suggestion that contraband slaves be colonized overseas. "President Lincoln may colonize himself if he choose," fumed Garrison, "but it is an impertinent act, on his part, to propose the getting rid of those who are as good as himself." The "wishy-washy" message convinced the editor that Lincoln had "not a drop of anti-slavery blood in his veins" and lacked any capacity for leadership.

It seemed, however, that the president would have to follow his people, for the emancipation campaign appeared to have acquired irresistible momentum. Aided by the rise of sympathetic editors, including Garrison's friends Sydney Howard Gay and Theodore Tilton, at influential publications such as the *New York Tribune* and *The Independent*, the abolitionist argument gained a respectable and extended hearing. Emancipation leagues, patterned on the Boston example, blossomed in a number of cities, including Washington, D.C., where even Abraham Lincoln attended several of the antislavery talks at the Smithsonian Institution and Wendell Phillips made a triumphant appearance unthinkable twelve months earlier. The enthusiastic crowds Phillips drew on a northwestern tour (aside from one surly mob of Kentucky thugs in Cincinnati), along with the favorable receptions accorded Frederick Douglass and other black speakers in places that had previously mobbed them, demonstrated beyond doubt that public opinion had swung round to confer heroic stature upon the abolitionists and protect their meetings. Garrison spoke repeatedly before Pennsylvania and New York groups, and his major address—"The Abolitionists and Their Relations to the War"—carried his well-honed message to an audience of prominent Republicans at Manhattan's Cooper Union that interrupted him more than sixty times with laughter, cheers, and applause. The speech was reported in full by the reputable New York papers and then circulated in *The Pulpit and Rostrum,* a national periodical that more generally republished the works of conservative clergymen and politicians. A few weeks earlier, Garrison had met the elder Dr. Beecher in his son's Brooklyn church and cordially shaken hands with the orthodox leader who had tried to suppress him. The aged minister seemed desirous of an earnest talk with Garrison, but the editor declined, explaining to Helen that Beecher's broken memory and impaired speech had reduced him to "a state of second childhood" that made serious conversation impossible.

Replete with acceptance and brimful of righteous confidence, the editor nonetheless was incredulous when fifteen correspondents from major newspapers slogged through "the slush and mush" of Boston's streets to cover the thirtieth-anniversary meeting of the Massachusetts Anti-Slavery Society in January 1862. The writer for the *New York Times* apologized for the ridicule his paper had previously heaped upon the organization for its "promiscuous and somewhat peculiar features" of interracial sociability and mixed-gender participation. Circumstances had changed, he explained, and given the antislavery societies "an importance which hitherto has not been theirs, and which justifies the most wide circulation of their sayings, doings, prophecies and lamentations." The reporter took a good look at Garrison, "the Moses and David of the antislavery cause," and liked what he saw. Even slouched in his seat and wrapped in a shaggy overcoat against the chill of the hall, the editor emanated a sense of strength and majesty. "He sits, a more than middle-aged man, with gold spectacles, no beard, a stern though not cross visage, a mouth indicative of resolution and determination, a chin prominent, a fighting neck, a chest full and competent, and an entire physique of more than ordinary capacity," the journalist wrote, adding that Garrison's pertinacious thirty years' martyrdom had earned him "at least the respect of all, while it has gained for him the absolute love of thousands throughout the world."

The winter's triumphs, especially the editor's success at Cooper Union, raised hopes that Garrison might participate in the Washington, D.C., lecture series that had attracted Lincoln's interest. After some delicate negotiations among intermediaries, however, the radical Indiana congressman George W. Julian had to confess that "one or two tender-footed members of the committee" had blocked the invitation. We "must have you" next winter, Julian vowed, adding that with "the current running in our direction . . . a pretty fair confiscation bill can now go through."

In the first five months of 1862, the 37th Congress indeed completed a budget of antislavery business that the now-departed Southern members had blocked for a decade. A national prohibition on slavery in the territories? Passed. More effective suppression of the international slave trade? Passed. Diplomatic recognition of Haiti and Liberia? Approved. Immediate abolition of slavery in the District of Columbia? Passed. Repeal of the Fugitive Slave Law? Not formally passed, though by approving an article of war that forbade army officers to return fugitives, Congress committed itself to a reversal of policy where it counted most—on the military frontier with slavery. By spring 1862, Union forces had taken control of significant coastal areas in North and South Carolina and portions of the Tennessee Valley, and with strenuous combat taking place in Virginia and the lower Mississippi, the number of "contrabands" was ballooning week by week until thousands of black refugees from slavery had sought the protection of the Stars and Stripes. The new article of war offered the minimal guarantee that they would not be sent back to bondage, although until Congress enacted a more comprehensive Confiscation Act (which, despite Julian's confidence, would not come until midsummer) the U.S. government could be regarded as, technically, the largest holder of slaves in the country.

Abolitionists regarded the rush of congressional action with subdued enthusiasm. In the grand light of great wartime expectations, the legislation seemed like old business—forward steps, to be sure, but tiny ones. "Well, it is something to get slavery abolished in ten miles square [D.C.], after thirty years of arguing, remonstrating, and petitioning," Lydia Maria Child remarked to *The Liberator*'s business agent, Robert Wallcut, as they sorted and exchanged pamphlet orders. Though the editor himself granted the "historic importance" of the act, he marked its advent with scant fanfare, concerned as he was by Lincoln's acceptance of the legislation on the grounds that his twin policy concerns—compensation for loyalists and support for voluntary colonization—had found expression in the bill.

A few weeks earlier the president had asked Congress to pass a joint resolution offering compensation to states that adopted plans for "gradual abolishment" of slavery. Lincoln had offered a stone when bread was needed, Garrison complained, and his message evinced neither sympathy for the enslaved nor recognition of the moral evil involved. While the president was dithering, Garrison fumed, Tsar Alexander was emancipating the Russian serfs. Given public support for the freedom bills pending in Congress, the president's proposal was "a cowardly and criminal avoidance of the one great saving issue" that even failed to indicate what Lincoln would do if the slave states could not be bribed into surrendering the property (and the cause) for which they fought.

Although other abolitionists, including Phillips, thought that the president, in the mildest of ways, had conceded the significance of the slavery issue and was gradually "turning toward Zion," Garrison failed to be convinced, and in May 1862, his pessimism was borne out when Lincoln once again prohibited his field commanders from issuing edicts of emancipation. The president overruled General David Hunter, who had first proclaimed martial law in the South Carolina, Georgia, and Florida coastlands controlled by his Union forces and then declared the slaves within that jurisdiction "forever free." He sternly told Hunter that the questions of the legal authority and military necessity for emancipation were ones he had "reserved" to himself as commander in chief; they were too important to be left to the discretion of field officers. Although he tried to blunt the sting of veto with beseeching remarks to the slave states that they heed "the signs of the times" and accede to his gradualist offer, the abolitionists took no comfort from the heavily veiled suggestion that the president might be running out of patience.

Garrison feared, however, that the Union might be running out of time. The news from the battlefield had a few bright spots, but none that portended anything but stalemate. In February 1862, the Union had acquired its first major hero when Brigadier General Ulysses S. Grant had seized Fort Henry and Fort Donelson on the Tennessee River and seemed poised for a major advance into the heart of the cotton belt. Eight weeks later, in the muddy fields and wooded hillsides between Pittsburgh Landing and Shiloh Church just north of the Mississippi border, two days of sickeningly bloody fighting stymied the drive. Shiloh buried, along with 3,477 dead, the illusion that the war could be anything other than a long, slow wearing down of the enemy in which the relentless laws of arithmetic—which side could outlast the other in troops and matériel—would dictate the outcome. One out of every four soldiers in combat at Shiloh became a casualty (killed, wounded, or missing), and the total, 23,741, exceeded the losses in the country's three previous wars combined. Grant said later that the fierce fighting at Shiloh convinced him that the war could only end with "complete conquest."

Obstacles remained everywhere for the Union troops. Even though Admiral Farragut forced his way into New Orleans a few weeks later and regained control of the vital entrepôt for military operations, a ribbon of hundreds of miles of muddy river and impenetrable terrain still lay northward, which meant that the campaign to sever the Confederacy would be nothing other than long and brutal. In the eastern theater, the Union had a commanding general, George B. McClellan, with dashing popularity among his troops but conservative political and military instincts. His brilliant plan for a roundabout surprise attack in May 1862 on the Confederate capital at Richmond had come undone in delays and literally bogged down in the tidewater flats of the Chickahominy Peninsula. Extraordinary countermoves by the Confederate generals Robert E. Lee and Stonewall Jackson had pushed aside the western flank of the Union army in Virginia, and by early summer Lincoln's worst nightmare about McClellan's plan, that it would leave Washington too lightly defended and subject to assault, appeared to be coming true.

With the Mississippi Valley campaign a standoff and Lee's Army of Northern Virginia poised for an invasion of the North, the Confederacy's bid for international recognition of its independence gained credibility. Great Britain held the key, and its interests were divided. Although its cotton imports had dropped by ninety-seven percent, a backlogged supply had kept its mills operating while capital sought new sources of textiles and mill workers expressed solidarity with the free labor of the North. The upper classes evinced much sympathy for the Southern aristocracy, though why Europe's leading imperialists looked favorably upon a revolt against central authority remains something of a puzzle. The Palmerston government had officially remained neutral, despite several contretemps with the Lincoln administration that had nearly provoked war, but the tenacity and growing strength of the Southern military effort in 1862—just as the loss of cotton was really beginning to pinch the economy—led it to consider diplomatic recognition more seriously. Whether the British middle-class reform public would accept the extension of support to a slaveholding regime remained a crucial question; with the Union still pledged not to disturb slavery, the moral issue seemed irrelevant to the government's calculation of its self-interest.

Garrison could do little with the diplomats, but a great deal with British public opinion. It was fortunate, in retrospect, that the AAS had rejuvenated its ties with friends in Great Britain in 1859–60 and had brought the redoubtable George Thompson back into the struggle, for Garrison's dear comrade had a far shrewder understanding of American political affairs than most of his countrymen. Indeed, the editor had grown alarmed at the exceedingly "muddled" view taken by many of the British reform papers, which had developed the impression the American abolitionists had abjectly surrendered their principles and had become cheerleaders for a sectional war of conquest that lacked moral justification. Throughout the first year of the war, *The Liberator* had tracked and refuted a number of specific British editorials, but early in 1862, Garrison decided upon a bolder approach that would transform a nagging sectarian quarrel into a new transatlantic alliance. He would endeavor to rally British opinion from afar with a dramatic message to George Thompson that his old friend, with his matchless tactical ingenuity, could employ as the basis for a campaign paralleling the American abolitionists' effort to pressure the Lincoln administration. Garrison's appeal, which saturated the press as a set of three public letters to Thompson in February–March 1862, advanced the abolitionist argument with the cogency and moral clarity of the editor's ablest polemical style, and it met with important success. Thompson used the letters to launch his own campaign, contending with "Toryism and Mammon" as if it were 1833 all over again, and gradually built up a demand from the British reform public that the Palmerston government withhold support for the Confederacy pending the outcome of the Garrisonians' sustained drive to broaden the Union war aims. Other American writers, notably Harriet Beecher Stowe in the vigorous "An Appeal to the Christian Women of Great Britain," joined the effort to bring British opinion into play. The rising chorus of overseas voices that tied the Union's diplomatic fortunes to the administration's emancipation policy became another crucial element that Lincoln, thanks initially to Garrison and Thompson and later to the leadership of the great John Bright, had to take into account.

Garrison's overseas work with Thompson seemed to bear fruit just as the domestic springtime mobilization reached its culmination. The editor had helped to forge a coalition of truly impressive breadth that had blended the movement with the Republican rank and file as never before. The party's disparate constituencies seemed to draw more closely toward the radical pole, and veteran abolitionists everywhere seemed roused to a last great burst of activity. From Illinois, Prudence Crandall sent orders to *The Liberator*'s office for more copies of Mrs. Child's pamphlet *The Right Way, the Safe Way*, while another name from the past, Theodore Dwight Weld, responded to Garrison's entreaties and tried his frail voice on the lecture platform once again. Even more gratifying, the movement's factions came together. Gerrit Smith marveled that the public had "converted" to Garrisonism, donated fifty dollars to the AAS, and publicly told the editor that their conflicting interpretations of the Constitution no longer mattered. An old Liberty Party man, now working for the AAS in New Hampshire, told Garrison, "Dear Brother, there never was but an imaginary chasm between us, and the providential events of the last few months have bridged it all over." A close relationship between a pugnacious New York minister, George Cheever, and Garrison bridged the very real gap that yawned between the AAS and the Tappanite evangelical wing of the movement, and even Frederick Douglass declared an end to the old hostilities, writing in his newspaper that "a common object and a common emergency" prompted him to set aside all differences "for the time at least" and recognize all antislavery workers—voters and nonvoters, Garrisonians and Smithites, blacks and whites—as "kinsmen." For the first time in a decade, favorable notices of Douglass's speeches appeared in *The Liberator*, and the following year Garrison would invite many of the old colleagues to share the platform at the thirtieth-anniversary celebration of the AAS in Philadelphia.

The veterans were joined in 1862, moreover, by a striking new recruit, a young woman named Anna Dickinson, whom Garrison had heard speak at meetings in Philadelphia and immediately enlisted for major service in New England. A cunning blend of youthfulness and theatricality, heightened by her flaring eyes, sensual mouth, and daringly stylish bobbed hair, Dickinson brought a different look to the movement platform. She could speak in tones that ranged from the spiritual to the sardonic and perfected a heroic platform manner that inevitably led her audiences to consider her the abolitionist Joan of Arc. It was the Grimké phenomenon revisited, as the editor engineered first a tumultuous debut in Boston's Music Hall and then a triumphant tour across Massachusetts that generated a conviction that Jubilee was at hand and sent her audiences home ready to work even harder for the cause. Republican Party leaders would eventually capitalize upon the Dickinson phenomenon, but in 1862 her appearances contributed, as Garrison shrewdly understood, to the aura of inevitability the abolitionists sought to create for an emancipation decree. Dickinson's appearances set civilians marching like soldiers to "the John Brown" song, and Garrison, among others, tried his hand at fashioning new verses for that hypnotic hallelujah chorus. He unveiled them at Framingham on the Fourth of July.

For the sighing of the needy, to deliver the oppressed,
Now the Lord our God arises, and proclaims his high behest;
Through the Red Sea of his justice lies the Canaan of [our] rest:
Our cause is marching on.

They didn't catch on, though Julia Ward Howe's "Battle Hymn" eventually did, at least among choirs and public chorales, if not with the soldiers.

The excitement of springtime had, by August 1862, yielded to a summer of despondency for abolitionists. Delegations went to the White House week after week to press their case with Lincoln, who received them wearily but courteously and represented himself as the victim of cross-pressures that he could not reconcile. He told a group of Progressive Friends, headed by Oliver Johnson and bearing a memorial drafted by Garrison, that an emancipation decree could not be more binding upon the South than the Constitution, which the slaveholders were presently defying; when Johnson remonstrated that Lincoln nonetheless had committed his administration to enforce the Constitution everywhere, the president just shrugged. A few weeks later he once again pleaded with border-state congressmen to accept his plan for gradual and compensated emancipation or else risk slavery's becoming eliminated in the "mere friction and abrasion" of war, but simultaneously told Horace Greeley, in reply to the editor's impassioned "prayer of twenty million people" for emancipation, that regardless of his personal desire for universal freedom, if he could save the Union without freeing a single slave, he would do it. By saying that he would do whatever was necessary—consistent with his sense of official duty—to save the Union, whether that meant freeing some, none, or all the slaves, he gave heart to some abolitionists that he truly had the matter under consideration. Phillips, however, pronounced the reply "disgraceful," while the acerbic Edmund Quincy wrote in the *Standard* that having failed to save the Union without freeing any slaves, perhaps the president ought to see if freeing some would produce better results. Pessimism seemed confirmed in early September 1862 when the president told an interdenominational delegation of ministers from Chicago bearing petitions (in German as well as English) signed by thousands of Lincoln's heartland constituents that the decree they sought would have no more effect against slavery than the pope's bull had exerted against the comet. Optimists, however, found a ray of hope because in this conversation Lincoln conceded that emancipation had to be considered as "a practical war measure" and allowed that he "supposed" he had the power to make such a decree if and when he considered it advisable, a matter, he said, that occupied his mind, "by day and night, more than any other."

Garrison did not take these hints that the abolitionists had been heard because he had completely soured on Lincoln after reading his discouraging remarks to a delegation of free black people from Washington, D.C. He had asked them to the White House to promote the idea of pioneering a new colony in Central America for manumitted slaves. "But for your race among us," the president said, "there could not be a war," which was both a perverse way of recognizing the abolitionist argument that slavery lay at the root of the controversy and an offensive suggestion that black removal would resolve it. Racial differences, said the president, would always impose disadvantages and inequality upon black people in the United States, and they had best recognize this as an inescapable fact that he could not alter even if he desired. It was taking "an extremely selfish view," the president admonished the group, to think that they might live advantageously here, when the urgent needs of their race so clearly pointed to the need for building a homeland elsewhere. Lincoln hoped that "for the good of mankind" his visitors would assist him in finding twenty-five or fifty families willing to become pioneers in shaping the ultimate solution to the conundrum that the conditions of American life permitted black people to live here only as slaves and subordinates, never as equal citizens.

Nothing Lincoln had previously said or done infuriated Garrison as did this minatory lecture, which he flung into *The Liberator*'s "Refuge of Oppression" column under the headline "The President of African Colonization." No more "humiliating . . . impertinent . . . untimely" spectacle could be found in all Christendom than this extraordinary meeting, stormed Garrison, which brought the editor full circle to confront once more the exclusionist assumptions he had battled at the outset of the struggle. During the campaign, people had derided Lincoln as no better than a Henry Clay Whig, but Garrison never imagined how blinded by Clay's colonizationism the Republican had remained. To brand the blacks as the cause of the war, moreover, when they were in fact martyrs to the cupidity and arrogance of white people only demonstrated for the editor that Lincoln's "education (!) with and among 'the white trash' of Kentucky was most unfortunate for his moral development," as it prevented him from recognizing the natural right and redemptive justice of black citizenship. The issue remained civil rights, not race, the editor insisted, as he had since the Park Street Address and *Thoughts on African Colonization:* "[I]t is not their color, but their being free, that makes their presence here intolerable." Had the president the nobility and vision to comprehend this, "he would sooner have the earth opened and swallowed him up, than to have made the preposterous speech he did. . . ."

If some of the president's midsummer comments were intended to string along those in the Republican and abolitionist ranks who craved decisive action, then his separatist message to blacks also sent a political signal to the portion of the public who feared it. It is conventional wisdom to say that Lincoln superbly attuned his actions to what public opinion would bear and gradually shaped support for an emancipation policy, but this is an easy sort of retrospective admiration. Viewed through the lens of the news dispatches of the sanguinary summer of 1862, what seems remarkable is how little the president did to educate people to the justice of the act (he left that to the abolitionists) and how much he did to legitimate racial hostility. In Lincoln's defense it is also said that he was able to lead the public to emancipation because he mirrored and understood its fears, but this is too sentimental. The public by this time was deeply divided, and Lincoln had no leeway to build a consensus. The war had brought slavery to the point of ultimate extinction several generations earlier than the nonextension theory (draw a line and gradually strangle slavery with it) had anticipated, and now Lincoln had to make a choice. One way pointed to an emancipation that would bring down the wrath of the "Peace Democrats," possibly cost him his job, but probably keep Europe out of the war and make it more likely that the Union would win it. The other way pointed to a negotiated settlement. Slavery could not be abolished without some political risk, but the war could not be won without emancipation. If Lincoln refused to confront the racists who opposed emancipation, then he would have to make some accommodation with the slaveholders and end the war where it began, with a nation half slave and half free. Since colonization was a fantasy and not a practical solution, Lincoln's feints in that direction won no friends for emancipation and allayed no fears, but encouraged the worst element in American life without gaining him any leverage on the problem. They were not part of Lincoln's education process, but evidence of his paralysis.

Lincoln's continuing reluctance to act, together with the standstill of Mc-Clellan's Peninsula campaign, the long delay in securing a tough new confiscation bill in the House, and strong signs that the European powers might aid the Confederacy with a call for international mediation of the dispute all combined to make Garrison fear that the administration might go for a negotiated settlement. (So despairing had abolitionists become of Lincoln that on August 19, 1862, Nathaniel White advised *The Liberator* to stop the gift subscription he had been sending to the White House.) Indeed, the editor was not alone in suspecting that the unusually partisan McClellan had deliberately slowed his military efforts in order to create the basis for stalemate and truce. Had Garrison known that McClellan privately called Lincoln "the gorilla" and joked with intimates that the sweatstains on the president's shirt, as seen during their war conferences in Virginia, resembled a map of Africa, the editor would have had his suspicions confirmed.

A truly malignant campaign against emancipation by conservative Democrats greatly enhanced this impression, as week after week their newspapers preyed upon fears of a black population unleashed and decried the "lunatic" abolition press that thought "the Negro of more consideration that the Nation." The humor magazine *Vanity Fair* (an aspiring New York version of the British *Punch*) purveyed racist caricatures of unspeakable vulgarity. The contention that emancipation was essential to a Union victory was ridiculed with a cartoon depicting a key whose teeth formed an ape-like profile; the plight of the contrabands was mocked in brutal verses; a "monotonous minstrel" (Horace Greeley) was shown playing his pipe for an uncertain Lincoln as a midget Sambo begged for coins. The magazine's cover, which weekly featured satiric engravings of prominent literary and political figures, finally rounded on Garrison in August 1862, when the talented Henry Louis Stephens lampooned the editor as a dreamy idealist besotted by his vision of racial equality. Garrison was depicted puffing on a long, carved fetish pipe filled with a popular black tobacco, colloquially known as "niggerhead," that released clouds of dancing African totemic figures.

Such ugliness told on Garrison more than ever before. He railed that the "Satanic democracy of the North" had captured Lincoln, who was either dishonest or "nothing better than a wet rag," and who would be forced into a settlement or face overthrow by a military cabal. The editor seemed to be losing heart. He had worked hard to prepare a written address for a debating society at Williams College, the first invitation he had ever received from an educational institution, but no faculty had attended the event, the audience proved thin, owing to the sultry August weather and the twenty-five-cent admission charge for nonmembers, and the newspapers expressed surprise at the amount of Scripture the speaker had quoted. The speech, "Our National Visitation," was one of his best, said Maria Child, "which is saying a good deal," but the editor shrugged off the compliment. "One gets weary," he told his son Wendell, "in the constant affirmations of those moral truisms which would seem to be as plain to every mind as the midday sun is to the vision."

By early September 1862, his spirits had fallen as low as they ever had, and Helen vented the somber mood at Dix Place in a letter to Fanny on September 14. "We are feeling extremely anxious about the country," she wrote. "We have come to the conclusion that Lincoln will not declare emancipation and that our Generals have so far shown themselves entirely unequal to the task of subduing the rebels and the North are so divided among themselves that there seems little in reserve for us as a nation." Senator Sumner had called the day before, she added by way of news, and had a long talk with Father, the substance of which was surely reflected in her letter. Eight days later occurred a stunning turnabout.

The military situation first worsened, then improved enough for Lincoln to show his hand, though if General McClellan had done what had been expected of him, perhaps Lincoln would not have played the card he did. On August 30 the Union had suffered a second grievous defeat at Bull Run. Three weeks later, while Helen was writing to Fanny, Lee's army crossed the Potomac into Maryland, and McClellan frantically wheeled his forces around to block the invasion route. The armies met at Antietam Creek on September 17 in a battle that stands yet as the single bloodiest day of fighting in American military history. With losses of six thousand dead and seventeen thousand wounded, the carnage equaled the two-day horror of Shiloh. When Mathew Brady's stark photographs of bodies piled in front of a small meetinghouse and strewn in a sunken road were shown in his Broadway gallery a few weeks later, the *New York Times* said that the cameraman had virtually "laid bodies in our doorways and along [our] streets." Indeed, the war had come home.

The Union—at fearful cost—had repulsed Lee's advance, which was a strategic accomplishment if not a victory, but Lee's achingly slow retreat had made his entire army vulnerable to hot pursuit and capture. Though Lee was slow, McClellan was slower, and the Union commander dawdled in the borderland between commendable concern for his troops' safety and politically motivated insubordination until his prize got away. Ironically, had McClellan caught Lee and forced the surrender of his army, the war might arguably have ended then and there with the status of slavery in the rebellious states unchanged. Lee, however, survived to fight again, but the war turned into an abolition one. Lincoln announced on September 22 that to meet the exigencies of war the slaves in the areas still in rebellion one hundred days hence on January 1, 1863, "shall be then, thenceforward and forever, free. . . ."

"Is not Father joyous?" asked Fanny in a letter from New York. "I have felt like dancing every moment for the simple reason that I cannot keep still." Her host, Theodore Tilton, wondered whether Garrison had laughed or cried and admitted that he himself had done both. A day later, Tilton wrote that he remained in a "bewilderment of joy . . . half crazy with enthusiasm."

The moment had come, or at least the president had promised that it would come in one hundred days. The moment would come, at least for the three-quarters of the slave population who lived and toiled in the Confederacy, for the president had said nothing about disturbing the institution in the states that had not seceded. The moment had perhaps already come, for Lincoln had premised his decree upon the provisions of the Second Confiscation Act, passed in July 1862, which freed slaves captured from rebels or simply found in areas occupied by Union forces, and so it was possible that the significance of the president's statement lay in its commitment that the executive department, including the military and naval forces, would henceforth "recognize and maintain the freedom of such persons. . . ." The moment might well be delayed, for the prefatory clause of the president's message promised that he would renew his request that Congress appropriate money for a voluntary and gradual compensated emancipation in the border states. The moment might not last, for the very same clause also promised a continuation of the administration's effort to "colonize persons of African descent, with their consent," in some other country. The moment might not come at all if the South accepted the offer to give up the war and keep its slaves. Was the president's proclamation a promise or an ultimatum, a giant's stride or a pygmy's step, the realization of a dream or the continuation of an ambiguous voyage whose outcome remained uncertain?

Garrison didn't know, which is why a visitor hurrying to Dix Place to congratulate the pioneer found him curiously subdued, worrying over the text, and distinctly lacking in enthusiasm. Of course it was an act of "immense historic consequence," and the people who were rejoicing, he said, were justified "as far as it goes." He could not be jubilant, however, when "what was wanted, what is still needed, is a proclamation, distinctly announcing the total abolition of slavery." Still, it was a commitment, "an important step in the right direction," and so he would praise it publicly and hope for the best, though he told Fanny how infuriated he felt that Lincoln "can do nothing for *freedom* in a direct manner, but only by circumlocution and delay. How prompt [by contrast] was his action against Frémont and Hunter!"

It was unusual, to say the least, for Garrison to grouse while the movement cheered. He was not alone. Many of the old apostles privately complained of the stinting and chilly nature of the proclamation, which failed to surround "the politic act with a halo of moral glory," as Maria Child put it. The desire for rhetoric stemmed from the abolitionist need to see the signs of conversion; pragmatic politics had gained results, however gratifying, that nonetheless lacked the "whole-souled" authority that they deeply sought. All in all, though, people praised the deed and forgave the document, declaring with Agent May that they would forbear the "oughts" in gratitude and relief.

Garrison's tepid reaction gave confirming evidence of both the deep investment he had made in the cause and the toll taken of him by the exertions of the seventeen months since Sumter. That the Democratic press unleashed an excoriating and vicious attack upon Lincoln pleased him insofar as it unmasked the hypocrisy of which the editor had long complained, but he had lost so much confidence in the president that he fully expected him to cave in. The caricaturists who had depicted the pipe-smoking editor now drew Lincoln as an itinerant bird peddler with cages of blackbirds slung across his back, lamenting that "if nobody won't buy 'em I'll have to open the cages and let 'em fly." The British *Punch* depicted Lincoln as a Satanic gambler attempting to trump the Confederacy with the ace of spades.

The president, however, did not flinch. His firmness in dismissing McClellan, who had coupled a terse notice that the army comply with the presidential edict with the provocative observation that "the remedy for political error" lay at the polls, gave Garrison hope that Lincoln had abandoned any effort to placate the Democrats, and indeed the president told many confidants that there could be no turning back even though the Republicans would pay for it at the polls in the impending 1862 congressional elections. With the newspapers and party men in full roar that Lincoln had become an abolitionist dictator while the military situation remained unsatisfactory, it was not surprising that the Democrats gained back many of the traditional districts in Pennsylvania, Indiana, and Illinois that they had lost to Lincoln in 1860, but the opposition also made such inroads in New York, Ohio, and Wisconsin that the Republicans very nearly lost their majority in Congress.

In the aftermath the president did another about-face that this time distressed not only Garrison but the entire antislavery movement. In his annual message to Congress, Lincoln recommended a package of three constitutional amendments that offered a federal compensation plan to any state (in rebellion or not) that formulated a gradual plan to abolish slavery voluntarily by 1900. Individual slaves liberated by the fortunes of war would remain free, but the remainder would have to await the favorable action of their masters or the workings of the various plans, which historically had manumitted only slave children born after a certain date and then only at their legal coming-of-age. The president characterized his proposal as a compromise of "mutual concessions" that would cost less than the war, that would engage the entire country in expunging by a common charge the evil that the old Union had mutually accepted, and that would postpone abolition long enough for the present generation of diehards to pass away and the present generation of slaves to be spared the "vagrant destitution" an immediate liberation would engender. After pages and pages of densely argued prose, Lincoln attained unmatched heights of eloquence in his closing passage, which implored Congress and the public to rise to the occasion and accept his proposal as a generous, honorable, and peaceful settlement. "The dogmas of the quiet past are inadequate to the stormy present," he said. "In giving freedom to the slave, we assure freedom to the free. . . . we shall nobly save, or meanly lose, the last best, hope of earth."

Posterity has chosen to read Lincoln's closing words as a reference to the promised proclamation of January 1, 1863, rather than to the thirty-seven-year deferral (with compensation) that he proposed in December 1862. Perhaps the president knew that his latest alternative plan would gain few adherents and his earnest melting phrases might soothe a different set of ears. But it is understandable that the abolitionists reacted in outrage, terror, and astonishment that the president, like all his dough-faced predecessors, was asking them once again to compromise universal liberty for the sake of Union. "The President is demented—or else a veritable Rip Van Winkle," Garrison raged, and his proposal, with its odious elements of bribery and colonization, "borders upon hopeless lunacy" and offered grounds for impeachment.

It was evident, if the president meant to achieve serious discussion of his proposed amendment, that he would have to renege on his promise to issue a permanent emancipation decree on January 1, 1863. Certainly the Democratic press crowed that the blackbirds were going to remain caged after all, and the abolitionists feared the worst. Given the editorial reaction from Republicans, however, the threat of abandonment eased, and before the weeks ran out Sumner passed the word that Lincoln had told him personally, and the phraseology sounded authentic, that he would not stop the proclamation if he could and that he could not if he would. Garrison, however, remained skeptical until the very end. He thought the president realized that he would incur the moral opprobrium of the world and risk the loss of the war if he faltered, but nonetheless the editor feared some last-minute surprise. "A man so manifestly without moral vision, so unsettled in his policy, so incompetent to lead, so destitute of hearty abhorrence of slavery, cannot be safely relied on in any emergency," the editor wrote on December 26 in his last issue of the year. Nonetheless he intended to delay putting *The Liberator* to bed the following week in order to accommodate the longed-for news. They normally locked up the inside form on Wednesdays, printed on Thursdays, and distributed on Fridays, but for the first time since the delays engendered by the mobbing in 1835, the newspaper would hold one full column open until Friday morning, January 2, and scramble to set the type, lock up the form, and go to press as rapidly as possible with whatever the news from Washington on New Year's Day should be.

Willie Garrison played charades on New Year's Eve at a "rather spiritless" party whose number included a wounded veteran of Antietam. His parents, as customary, passed the evening at home, but they allowed Fanny, her houseguest Lizzie Powell (sister of Aaron, the organizer), and Franky to go out to the midnight watch-meeting with the Bethel Methodists on Beacon Hill. Like other black congregations throughout the Union, the group raised up impassioned prayers for the consummation of the promise, the young Garrisons joining, with mingled awe and thanksgiving, as the people clapped and sang their way into the dawning year of Jubilee.

Next morning, no one quite knew what to expect. No text had come in advance from Washington for the morning papers. Would word perhaps arrive at noon, after the president had communicated with Congress? The hour struck and passed in silence. The entire Garrison family prepared to attend an afternoon Jubilee concert at the Music Hall, sponsored by a committee of distinguished literary figures headed by Henry Wadsworth Longfellow, Francis Parkman, and Oliver Wendell Holmes, that would raise money for the contraband relief effort. As the fashionable crowd streamed into the building, the mood was festive but edgy, as no bulletin had yet arrived to justify the celebration. People applauded Garrison as the editor entered the gallery, and they clapped as well when Harriet Beecher Stowe, in her black silk and bonnet, was spotted across the way.

This was a society gathering—of the people of property and standing, who had come so slowly and grudgingly to abolitionism that it seemed not quite the right place for the editor to be at the anticipated moment of triumph. Yet Garrison had elected to attend, though William C. Nell had invited him to a meeting going on simultaneously at Tremont Temple sponsored by a black political association at which John S. Rock and Frederick Douglass were to speak. The editor had turned him down, Nell said, "for reasons satisfactory to himself," but which no one ever disclosed. Poor voice alone would not account for it, nor would feelings of political delicacy, for it was an interracial meeting at which Garrison's name was loudly cheered and the alliance with abolitionists broadly praised. It is tempting to posit lingering ill will with Douglass as a reason to hang back, but it is just as easy to suggest that Garrison did not want to crowd (or be charged with crowding) Douglass on a day that surely belonged to him as much as anyone. Perhaps it was simply the current of the broad-based strategy that carried him to the Music Hall. In any event, Garrison that day mingled with the upper crust who now gloried in a cause they had spurned too long.

The chilly light of winter filtered through the semicircular windows high above the hall, though the gas lamps at the cornices would provide warmer illumination before the concert ended. Flags and shields hung from the columns, and the pale blue ceiling squares seemed like the canopy of heaven itself. The orchestra sat massed on the risers of the stage, behind which loomed the seven-foot gleaming bronze statute of the titan Beethoven, his face all earnestness and his hands cradling the score of the Choral Symphony, opened to the opening passage—*Freude, schöne Götterfunken*—of Schiller's "Ode to Joy."

After the conductor had tapped his baton for silence, Josiah Quincy, Jr., the old mayor's son, came forward with a surprise announcement, not the news everyone yearned to hear, but a literary coup. Ralph Waldo Emerson had arrived to deliver a poetic prologue entitled "Boston Hymn"! The writer meant it as a companion piece to his immensely popular "Concord Hymn" memorializing the Revolution, but it was a turgid, feeble effort—nineteen stanzas long, spoken in the voice of God bringing a providential message of freedom to the Pilgrims—and unmemorable save for a dramatic thrust against the idea of compensation ("The slave is owner/ And ever was. Pay him") that stirred the audience to applause.

Then the music began. Mendelsohn's "Hymn of Praise" thrilled its listeners with its plaintive question "Watchman, will the night soon pass?" and the stirring choral response "The night is departing, the day is approaching." The audience sat attentively through a Beethoven piano concerto, but milled about restlessly in the interval that followed. No word had come from Washington.

The chorus resumed the program with a rousing musical setting of Oliver Wendell Holmes's "Army Hymn," and Dr. Holmes himself had just finished reading several additional stanzas when Quincy rushed to the platform with the joyous news. The president had just signed the proclamation! The text would be coming over the wire later in the evening. The Music Hall erupted in pandemonium, with a shouting and screaming and crying and roaring that the staid assembly had never in its life experienced. The boys tossed their hats, and Lizzie Powell felt such hot tears in her eyes that she could not see the tears in Fanny's. Amid the cheering and the waving of handkerchiefs and the hugging and kissing and great loud sighs, the editor sat alone with his thoughts.

The cacophony in the hall became a chorus of its own. "Three times three for Lincoln" went the call, and the floor shook as people stamped their feet and nine great shouts welled up from three thousand voices all at once. "Three cheers for GARRISON!" someone else yelled. Suddenly every head turned to find the editor, who leaned out over the latticed gallery wall to wave and smile. The cheers burst into the air, first crisp, then swelling and echoing and swelling again, for the backstreet Baptist boy who had flung his words into the whirlwind and survived a Boston mob to print and preach and call from the depths of his prophetic soul this hour into life.

At last the hall fell quiet, shaken and spent with emotion. The orchestra, however, pounded out the opening chords of Beethoven's Fifth Symphony— the motif the composer had described as fate knocking on the door—and for the next half hour took the company on yet another pilgrimage of struggle and spiritual grandeur, the bassoons and trombones blaring out the martial notes of triumph and exhilaration and driving off the flickering phantoms of doubt as the piece built—and built—and built—to its heroic and jubilant conclusion.

That evening, after the concert, the Garrisons went to a soirée at the mansion George and Mary Stearns had built in suburban Medford. Emerson again read his poem, Julia Ward Howe recited her "Battle Hymn," and Wendell Phillips unveiled a marble bust of John Brown, commissioned by Mary Stearns from the sculptor who had visited the old soldier in jail, which the company lavishly praised as reminiscent of Michaelangelo's *Moses*.

Early the next morning Garrison rushed to *The Liberator*'s office. The proclamation was better than expected. It did more than free the confiscated slaves of rebels; it emancipated all the slaves in the rebel states. Not only would the nation regard all those people as free, but it would extend military protection to them and accept their enlistment "in the armed service of the United States." Though the document remained as cumbersome and prosaic as its September predecessor, Lincoln's eloquence had flared momentarily in the concluding lines describing the decree as "an act of justice, warranted by the Constitution upon military necessity" for which he asked "the considerate judgment of mankind and the gracious favor of Almighty God." The editor put the text into the form under three lines of stacked boldface type:

THE PROCLAMATION.
THREE MILLION OF SLAVES SET FREE!
GLORY HALLELUJAH!

He had room for only a few lines of comment, in which he hailed the epochal event as "sublime in its magnitude, momentous and beneficent in its far-reaching consequences, and eminently just and right alike to the oppressor and oppressed."

In the years to come the editor would pronounce this day the "turning point" that fixed slavery's destiny. "The stars in their courses fought against Sisera," he would say, likening the Confederacy's doom to the fall of an ancient oppressor of the Hebrews (Jg. 5:20). Yet before he left the office that morning, Garrison sent word to the AAS executive committee that he wanted to meet the following week. Even though he believed that abolitionists had come from "midnight darkness to the bright noon of day," they had to address the danger that remained and define their duty to the one million black people still enslaved in the border states exempted from the proclamation. Joy had to be tempered with determination, for the mighty work was not yet done.

CHAPTER TWENTY-THREE

EVERYTHING GRAVITATES TOWARD FREEDOM

In October 1862, a twenty-three-year-old soldier named Jacob Allen, bivouacked in Western Virginia and feeling bereft of purpose, wrote a long letter to William Lloyd Garrison in search of guidance. He introduced himself as the son of a veteran Garrisonian abolitionist from Clinton County, Ohio, who had subscribed to *The Liberator* from the beginning, and said that he himself had read the paper ever since he had been old enough to study and comprehend the picture on the masthead. Having now served thirteen months in the army, Allen said, he felt himself "swept as it were by a violent hurricane into a foggy valley where I stand enveloped in mystery. . . ." So much carnage, so many fractured opinions, the administration and generals dragging their feet, the Christian sanction for the conflict in doubt, Allen said, all made him worry that they were either standing still or going backward. He would be more willing to suffer privation and death, the young man said, if Garrison could "reconcile" him to the idea that the war would indeed free the slaves, restore harmony to the distracted land, and "bring mankind up to the standard you and your school" had advocated for so many years. Allen thought he could see a change in some men who came into the army with bitterness toward black people but now were the very ones shouting " 'Confiscate! Annihilate! Emancipate!' " in order to put a stop to the war and get home. Yet Allen feared the possibility that "at some not very distant day, these old rank prejudices that are now lulled to sleep by selfish motives, may again possess these men and *work evil* when we think all is *safe.*" The proclamation of September 22 "suits the majority of the men in the army to the letter," he said, but he was not at all sure what that portended. "Are we progressing?" Allen wondered.

The editor's reply, if any, to the troubled soldier has not come to light, but almost everything Garrison undertook in 1863 could be taken as an answer that elevated hope over despair, though his work demonstrated that like the war itself, the abolitionists' struggle was far from concluded. The Emancipation Proclamation endowed the war with a fresh and hallowed purpose, but those who had pressed so diligently for it possessed few illusions. Anxiety about the fiat, as George Thompson put it, gave way to concern about the fruit. Lincoln had signed a promissory note, Garrison believed, that only victory in war could make good. He understood that

Lincoln had committed the nation to free its slaves by military force and, by opening the door to the enlistment of black troops, had extended an official sanction to the long battle for equal citizenship that had been concomitant to the antislavery struggle. This was progress, and it more firmly than ever—in Garrison's view—put the government on the side of the historic movement toward liberty and nationalism that had coursed over the western world during the editor's lifetime. "Everything must gravitate toward freedom, and free institutions by an irresistible law," he liked to say, without negating the historic labors of the people—black and white, soldier and civilian—who do God's work.

The link between military necessity and emancipation, though crucial in persuading Lincoln and the public opinion he represented to act, remained—as Jacob Allen so well knew—an uncertain foundation for social transformation. Emancipation depended not simply upon winning the war, which in January 1863 itself seemed doubtful, but making a devastating conquest of the slaveholding states that would enormously complicate postwar settlement of the labor and racial issues and the eventual transition from military occupation to civilian government. Universal and lasting freedom, moreover, required further action not only to end slavery in the "loyal" states, but to establish a firmer constitutional foundation for abolition than an executive wartime edict, which might be overturned by a lenient successor or a hostile court or set aside in a negotiated truce. Slavery had to be put on the road to "utter annihilation," Garrison told the January 1863 MAS meeting, and declared that the abolitionists' watchword had not changed from the old cry "Agitate, agitate, agitate!" While as philanthropists and agents of uplift they had to concern themselves with the work of assisting newly freed slaves in acquiring land and education and protecting their rights, their "special work" would remain that of raising the moral sentiment of the North to sustain the birth of a free people in a nation redeemed.

Moral work in 1863, for Garrison, meant war work, and he accepted the paradox with unruffled composure. *The Liberator* began a regular feature, "Chronicle of the War," which featured a detailed calendar of political and military events since the secession of South Carolina, and the newspaper now frequently carried reports from the battlefield culled from the correspondents' dispatches that filled the major daily newspapers. Franky liked to study the accounts with the help of the large topographical views *Harper's Weekly* published, based on the work of balloonists. In April 1863, Willie brought as a guest to Dix Place one of the most dashing of the war journalists, Henry Villard, a young German émigré who had covered Lincoln's political rise in Illinois and then filed courageous field reports from Bull Run, Shiloh, and Fredericksburg. Villard's tales of the desperate measures, including a wild night-long horseback ride from Manassas and a frantic row in a boat manned by two fugitives, undertaken to file stories ahead of the competition, held the entire family transfixed and fed a war enthusiasm that, before emancipation, they were loath to express.

Villard had just returned from the Sea Islands, where he had studied the communities emerging among the first freedmen—the black people liberated in the 1861–62 confiscation of plantations in General Hunter's district around Port Royal Sound, Hilton Head, and Beaufort, South Carolina—and he was most impressed by the difficult transition that lay ahead. He saw, he said, a population of farmworkers who worked hard and were well-behaved, but tattered and dirty in appearance, though they appeared well-fed. He thought education would be a difficult task (New England had already organized battalions of teachers to go south to help) because the people were "embruted" by slavery and, in their isolation, had retained a high degree of their African culture and spoke a jargon of their own. He did, however, report favorably about the process of making soldiers out of the contraband men, which, like schoolteaching, took place under the aegis of abolitionist officers from the North.

The editor took the keenest possible interest in the recruiting of black soldiers. The abolitionist minister Thomas Wentworth Higginson had taken command of one of the regiments of volunteer freedmen Villard had observed, and Francis Meriam, recovered from his narrow escape at Harpers Ferry, had worked to recruit another. The success of the South Carolina volunteers had markedly influenced Lincoln's determination to open the ranks with the Emancipation Proclamation. Hardly an issue of *The Liberator* went by without some crosscurrents of discussion on the propriety and fitness of black participation in combat or the historic role of Toussaint L'Ouverture, along with bulletins on the ongoing effort led by Frederick Douglass to enroll black volunteers for regiments being formed in Massachusetts, Pennsylvania, Ohio, and other states. "Men of Color, to Arms!" became the rallying cry as Douglass, Remond, Rock, and other leaders argued that participation in the struggle would advance the national cause, rebuke racist contempt, vindicate black manhood, and offer a model of self-advancement that would enhance and ennoble the claims of the freedmen in the South. Douglass often quoted Byron's verse "They who would be free must themselves strike the blow," and Garrison several times reprinted Wordsworth's ode to Toussaint, with its stirring Romantic credo "Thy friends are exultations, agonies, and love/ And man's unconquerable mind."

The pioneering effort—the 54th Massachusetts Volunteer Infantry, led by Robert Gould Shaw, the son of patrician abolitionists close to the Childs and the Chapmans—attracted the editor's special attention, and he went out to the training camp at Readville with Franky several times to watch the drilling exercises by which raw recruits became molded into troops of soldiers. At the invitation of the war governor of Massachusetts, John A. Andrew, Garrison attended the ceremony at which the chief executive presented the regiment its flags and swore that his own reputation as both "man and magistrate" was indissolubly yoked to theirs. On May 28, 1863, the day of the regimental review on the Boston Common, Garrison adjourned the sitting New England Anti-Slavery Convention so that the entire abolitionist contingent could join the throng gathered on the Common to give the troops the most ardent send-off the city had yet witnessed. The chief of police mounted at the head of sixty city patrolmen led the parade through the downtown streets, a sight that the abolitionists found "remarkable" and that by itself was enough to silence the "venomous" racist newspapers the next day, Franky reported to his new friend the correspondent Villard. Willie Garrison, after leaving the family on the green, returned to his bank office on State Street, where he watched the regiment march with brisk pride toward the wharf, its band playing "the John Brown song" while people waved flags and roared their approval of the valorous black men. There couldn't have been a "broader contrast," thought Willie, between this grand moment and the dreadful day nine years before when a solitary Anthony Burns was marched back to slavery through Boston's mournful streets.

The extravagant response to the creation of the 54th Massachusetts had fateful ramifications for the Garrison family. A second regiment, the 55th Massachusetts, had to be formed for the abundance of recruits—more than three hundred—closed out of the 54th, and its commander, Norwood Hallowell, who came from a Philadelphia Quaker family close to the editor, offered a second lieutenant's commission to George Garrison. Like many young abolitionists, George had not felt himself eager to volunteer for the war while its purpose remained narrowly conceived as the restoration of the old Union, but with the advent of the Emancipation Proclamation, he had felt both the pull of duty and the push of discontent in his situation as Mr. Yerrinton's hardworking junior partner at the paper. The editor, in his travels, had found many of his Quaker and nonresistant friends deeply troubled by their sons' decisions—despite their upbringing—to enlist in the military, and he had counseled them to respect the work of conscience and at least be grateful that if their boys had discovered themselves to be only "birthright" Quakers, they did not shrink from duty consistent with their values. They had imagined themselves to be on the plane of the Sermon on the Mount, he said, but having found themselves only up to the level of Lexington and Bunker Hill, they were honoring the commitment. It was the ambivalent message he had delivered ever since Harpers Ferry, but now it was his turn to live with its implications as a parent.

Father and son talked at length. Garrison made no secret of his wish that George had adopted peace principles, but candidly acknowledged that "much would be lost" by attempting to interfere with his son's own convictions of duty. Unlike their family friend Elizabeth Buffum Chace, who had forbidden her eldest son to enlist, the editor promised that he "would not lay a straw" in George's way. (Sam Chace was only seventeen, of course, while George, ten years older, had passed beyond any formal parental control.) Yet, even after George had begun training a few days before the 54th's parade, the editor could not help himself from applying a little moral suasion. He "tenderly" hoped that George would "seriously review the whole matter" before the point of irrevocability was reached. Garrison wanted him to consider the prejudices with which the black regiments would contend, including the widely held and sinister impression that the government intended to employ them in the most desperate situations. Worse yet, the editor feared that if captured, George might incur additional risks as the fanatic's son. Though Garrison could be very direct about his own feelings for his children, in this instance he retreated into a more conventional masculine mode and reminded George how much his perilous situation would affect his mother. "Her affection for you is intense, her anxiety beyond expression. . . ."

When George maintained his position, Garrison respected it. "I wish my children to know themselves," he had told Elizabeth Chace the year before, and he and Helen, like other parents of soldiers, found a way to live with their mingled sense of pride and fear. The family went out to the Readville camp several times to visit. Over half the regiment came from Ohio and Pennsylvania, with a goodly sprinkling of men born in Virginia, Kentucky, and North Carolina; the great majority had been farmers and laborers, though at least one hundred had held jobs as cooks and waiters and there were teamsters and blacksmiths, as well. George was the only printer in the ranks of officers, and although there were other mechanics and artisans, most of the officers had come from jobs as bookkeepers, clerks, teachers, or students. Franky found the sight of his brother in full uniform immensely stirring, and at the dress parade during which George received his officer's sword, his father was unexpectedly called upon for a speech, which evoked long and enthusiastic cheers from the regiment.

Enlistment posed one set of decisions, the draft another. While George made himself and his men ready for war at Readville, his brothers planned to bear witness for the nonresistant conscience. For the first two years of the war, the Union met its need for military manpower with calls for volunteers; in 1863, however, with war-induced employment high and the grim costs of combat all too evident in the shocking casualty rates, the deaths felt in every community, and the grim battlefield photographs by Brady and others on display in city galleries, the supply of volunteers dwindled away. The government had to turn to conscription. Unlike the Selective Service System of the mid-twentieth century, the Civil War draft was less a means of commandeering men than it was a crude set of devices to encourage volunteering. From the enrollment acts compiled in each congressional district, quotas were assigned to communities which, if met by enlistments, exempted their section of the list from the draft. Those "drafted," moreover, had the traditional option of hiring a substitute or the novel one of paying a "commutation" fee of $300, intended by Congress as a cap on the price of substitutes and a means of raising revenue for paying enlistment bounties to volunteers. Many communities paid commutation fees for poorer men out of their tax revenues, and factories and railroad companies paid the commutation for drafted workers from a subsidy fund raised through employer contributions and a tax on wages. Of the 133,000 men drafted in 1863, sixty percent paid the fee. (Intended as an equalizing device, the commutation fee roused serious opposition, however, and was abandoned in 1864 in favor of an expanded bounty system, which developed abuses of its own.) A compulsory draft ran against the popular grain: the system was detested, cordially or otherwise, across the Union, and there was both great diversity in its operation and considerable evasion, fraud, flight, and physical resistance to its operation. The riots that broke out in New York City in July 1863 originated in grievances against the draft system but exploded rapidly into horrendous mob violence directed against black people, who were scapegoated as the cause of the war.

For principled nonresistants, the draft posed a special burden. While many states had recognized religious scruples as a basis for exemption from militia service, the federal draft law did not. Drafted pacifists who refused to comply received varying treatment from the provost marshals—some sympathetic, but many harsh and abusive—until appeals to President Lincoln and War Secretary Stanton led to reforms in 1864. These provided noncombatants with alternate forms of service, a solution acceptable to some sects, but other noncooperationists still regarded it as an infringement of conscience. For those, like the Garrisonians, for whom nonresistance was a perfectionist creed unsanctioned by an institutional church, there were no exemptions.

Both Willie and Wendell considered themselves to be nonresistants in their father's understanding of the term. Their belief in the inviolability of human life led them to withhold allegiance (by refusing to vote or hold office) from a war-making state and thus to make a testament of faith in the possibilities of a higher form of society. It was a form of moral witness that did not extend to nonpayment of taxes, however; Garrisonians paid taxes passively as a submission to superior force, a rendering unto Caesar that coerced from them what they would not volunteer. For the sons, as for the father, nonresistance did not comport well with the existence of a war whose purposes, if not methods, they regarded as just and necessary. Though they could not serve and would not hire a substitute, they pondered whether they could submit to the commutation fee as they did to other taxes and allow, in effect, their property to be confiscated as a form of passive suffering. In an editorial their father argued that the responsibility for the use of the money adhered to the government, not the person taxed, but conceded that others might choose "a more afflicting alternative" of tax refusal in order to mount the issue before the community.

Under the press of the war, however, Garrison had come to believe that there was "a time to be silent as well as to speak," and though he continued to publish opposing points of view, he had decided that the middle of a war against slavery was a poor time to be debating the "abstract" issues of non-resistance. His critics, however, promptly insisted that "the time to rebuke sin is when it abounds," and the debate in fact continued. It is a measure of the havoc wrought by the war upon Garrison's ethics that, for the first time in his career, he preferred a muddled silence to the conscientious exploration of issues that he had made his touchstone. Garrison had made the serious and practical institutional compromise he had long deplored and justified it, in fact, by his absolutism. He cited Jesus's maxim "He that is not with me is against me" for his willingness to support an imperfect government rather than, by passivity, to abet the enemies of freedom.

And his sons did likewise. Wendell Garrison was drafted on July 18, 1863, in Ward 10, and, with an earnest and cogently argued public statement, explained that he would pay the commutation fee. He had a point to make, but he would not martyr himself for it. "The value of a protest depends much upon the spirit in which it is made, and much upon the time at which it is presented," Wendell wrote. He did not want to be accused of indifference to a war "which is to extinguish the greater war which gave it birth," nor did he "wish to be identified with those who cry Peace, and mean Rebellion." (The same issue of *The Liberator* that printed Wendell's letter also carried an eloquent one from a family friend, the Philadelphia Quaker Alfred H. Love, who did not share Wendell's tactical reservations and by refusing induction willingly subjected himself to civil penalties as an act of conscience. His enrollment board would not rise to the bait, however, and reclassified him as ineligible based on a diagnosis of nearsightedness, though Love had refused to take an exam.)

"We are coming, Father Abraham, three hundred dollars more," ran the popular parody lines that Willie copied into his journal after his brother paid the fee. "My turn on Friday. Small chance of escape." Yet he did. At the draft in Dorchester, where Willie lived in a boardinghouse, his name was not called in the lottery, and his protest letter went unposted.

That night, after the whole family had gone out to Readville to see the regiment's final dress parade, George came back to Dix Place for a farewell dinner. Three days later, on July 21, 1863, the 55th Massachusetts Volunteer Infantry marched through the streets of Boston, colors flying, drums beating, and band playing "John Brown's Body." Bouquets from the women and enthusiastic cheers greeted them, including wild yelling from a detachment of white soldiers lined up in front of Park Street Church, but the drizzly day, the burden of being the second group rather than pioneers, and the considerable threat of a violent racial and antiwar outbreak similar to New York's, made the send-off a "very tame" affair compared to the 54th's two months before. The jittery authorities canceled the scheduled review on the

Common, which embittered the men whose families had reserved tickets and who expected to bless and hug their boys one last time after the ceremony. Instead the friends and relatives, including all the Garrisons, had to press forward on the Tremont Street mall, hoping for a quick wave from their soldier and one last glimpse of his face.

Franky spotted George, his sad eyes dark beneath heavy brows, and George gave them a salute. Then the youngster ran ahead to intercept the parade up by the State House, with Fanny, Willie, and Wendy close behind. They waited for George, then rushed out to shake his hand and say goodbye one last time. Franky wouldn't leave George's side and walked the entire route down to the wharf with him. Willie cut through side streets and got back to his office before the parade reached State Street. Franky spotted him at the window and prompted George to look up and salute once more before passing out of sight, Willie said, "perhaps never to reappear to us."

The other children had stayed with their mother near the Common, but the editor had dashed after the parade, only to become jostled in the crowds and pushed to the wrong side of the street. Because of the thronged sidewalk and the continuous line of march, he found it impossible to get back across, and when they reached the transport vessel the crowd pressed him so far back that he could not catch sight of his son. Garrison scrambled over to the next wharf, waiting forlornly in the worsening rain, to wave a last farewell and give his firstborn a parting benediction and handclasp. The delay proved too long, however, and sadly, the editor said, he had to "beat a retreat" with the keenest regret. What he could not voice in person came out in a letter a few days later. "I miss you by my side at the table, and at the printing office," Garrison told George, "and cannot get reconciled to the separation."

By then Boston knew that on the very day of George's farewell dinner, Robert Gould Shaw and half his regiment had died in a courageous but doomed assault on Fort Wagner, one of the island strongholds on the southern edge of Charleston Harbor. George's willingness to risk his life—the 55th Mass., they had learned, was also bound for that theater—now seemed to his father the height of heroism, and he hoped that fortune would give his son the opportunity to participate in the conquest of Charleston. "The fall of that city," he said, with a vindictive tinge that only hinted at the rage and sorrow he felt over the 54th's tragic encounter, "will give more satisfaction to the entire North than that of any other place, not excepting Richmond itself."

The month of July illustrated how rapidly the emotional pendulum could swing in wartime. At Framingham on the Fourth, the editor announced from the platform news of the great victory at Gettysburg, which had repulsed Lee's second and final attempt to invade the North. Two days later came news that Grant, after a brilliant, dogged campaign and a six-week siege, had finally taken Vicksburg, the last Confederate citadel on the Mississippi, a victory that divided the rebel nation in two and meant that, as Lincoln phrased it in the soulful meter of national destiny, "the Father of Waters again goes unvexed to the sea." From Great Britain, moreover, came news of spectacular rallies held by the London Emancipation Committee (led by John Bright, George Thompson, and Thompson's son-in-law F. W. Chesson) that reflected the great turnabout in sentiment after the news of emancipation and ensured that their country would not assist or recognize the Confederacy. Yet by the end of the month it appeared that the Union troops would have a difficult time pressing their military advantage to a quick conquest, and sentiment rose once more for a negotiated settlement. The riotous attacks upon black people in New York epitomized the resurgence of a Democratic-led "peace" movement that viciously disparaged the abolitionist war at every opportunity. The vanguard regiment of black soldiers had met its terrible fate, with Shaw reportedly buried in a ditch "with his niggers" and some of the survivors imprisoned in Charleston awaiting death in accordance with Jefferson Davis's order that all armed black men would be shot as presumptive slave insurrectionists. No wonder that at the MAS's traditional First of August observance the veteran apostle Theodore Dwight Weld spoke for all abolitionists in pronouncing their most vital work to be cultivating "true sympathy with the black man."

The Liberator became both the chronicler of the black soldiers' success and an advocate for their interests. Although recruiters had promised them equal pay and bounties, Congress had authorized their enrollment under a law providing for the hiring of contraband cooks and laborers at a lesser rate, and the discrimination rankled bitterly. George had already said that the men of the 55th Mass. had marched off disgruntled at their chilly send-off, and now the controversy over pay threatened to subvert morale further. The black regiments refused to accept any pay, including a compensatory supplement offered by the state legislature, until the problem could be remedied by Congress, and their officers (George included) joined the boycott until the enlisted men insisted that they take their pay at the end of 1863. As the political fight wore on, George several times warned that he expected a "serious outbreak" of discontent, but in mid-1864 equal (and partially retroactive) pay was approved in Congress and the crisis abated.

Meanwhile, the 55th Mass. engaged in onerous fatigue duty on Folly and Morris islands, carrying shells and powder, throwing up earthworks, digging trenches, all the while remaining cool under desultory enemy shelling and coping with the hazards of bad drinking water. The units received praise for their work, and morale remained high. George reported the entire regiment consumed by a desire to vanquish Charleston and avenge the 54th's defeat. "If we succeed in taking Charleston," he wrote, "the intention is . . . not to leave one stone upon another, but to level it to the ground." In December 1863, George advanced in rank to first lieutenant and became acting regimental quartermaster. The job taxed his organizational capacity to the maximum when he had to oversee the regiment's transfer to Jacksonville, Florida, for two months of rearguard action early in 1864, before it returned to Charleston and more preparations for the final siege and bombardment of the city.

The valiant performance of black soldiers impressed the country. Mathew Brady stirred his exhibition galleries with before-and-after photographs of a ragged and barefoot contraband boy transformed into a crisply uniformed regimental drummer, and Garrison called his readers' attention to a *Harper's Weekly* engraving that famously fixed the image of a transformed people in three panels depicting, in turn, a slave whose naked back was scarred by whippings, a refugee in mangy clothes, and a resolute, uniformed soldier equipped with knapsack, cartridge case, and rifle.

The political focus of the AAS in the autumn of 1863 drew not only on a new petition drive but on women's activism as well. Earlier in the year, Elizabeth Cady Stanton had directed the formation of a "Women's National Loyal League." The idea seemed to be a complement to the propaganda work of the Union Leagues that had sprung up among Republican Party men to sustain the war effort. The redoubtable Stanton, herself liberated for political work by the completion of her family and its move from upstate Seneca Falls to New York City, where her husband, Henry, had a patronage job in the Custom House, also intended the league as a vehicle for women's rights. It would create opportunities for women to make a civic contribution that went beyond nursing, bandage-rolling, and other war-related charitable efforts and might indeed broaden the political agenda of the movement to embrace gender as well as racial equality. Stanton's allies proved to be the second generation of abolitionist women—Lucy Stone, Susan B. Anthony, Antoinette Brown Blackwell, Ellen Wright, and Frances Gage—which was not surprising, given that the comparable second generation of abolitionist men—Chase, Sumner, Lovejoy, Julian, Stevens, Andrew—had found their outlet in the radical wing of the Republican Party. Certain that women, too, could be "Soldiers of the Second Revolution," the Women's National Loyal League harked back to the first great female success in the movement, the abolitionist petition campaign against the gag rule, for a tactical model. The women would present to Congress a "Mammoth Petition" bearing one million signatures and pressing the abolitionists' demand for a congressional emancipation act that would free slaves everywhere. In December 1863, at the urging of both Sumner and Garrison, the AAS sharpened its focus and called for an abolition amendment to the Constitution, and the Loyal League's petition was accordingly adjusted, since by that time the AAS had agreed to subsidize the campaign. Stanton was miffed because she thought her more generally worded version afforded greater tactical flexibility, but an amendment—as Sumner evidently signaled—was the most practicable approach and the one most likely to enlist the president's support.

The petition drive began the remarkable collaboration of Stanton, whose imperious yet inspiring leadership combined intellect, nobility, and asperity in a manner reminiscent of Maria Chapman's, with Susan B. Anthony, whose tireless and ingenious grasp of detail enabled her to wage the war of ideas in the trenches of movement organizing. Stanton wrote and lectured and exhorted, while Anthony figured out how to distribute and retrieve petitions, raise money for printing and postage, and tabulate the results and forward them to Congress in the most dramatic manner possible. They suggested that each signer donate a penny along with her name; they sold badges that depicted a black man, half risen, breaking his own chains; they printed the names of larger donors in *The Liberator* and the *Standard;* they made liberal use of Sumner's congressional franking privilege; and they implored women everywhere to "magnetize" their neighborhoods and obtain signatures from both women and men. Even children were mobilized; Stanton told Franky and Fanny Garrison, whom she hadn't seen since their infancy, that her own son was working two or three hours a day and she expected them to circulate petitions at the next set of antislavery meetings and get "any little black boys and girls" they knew to help as well. They would get a free badge for every hundred names and participate in the competition of the states for the most signatures. By February 1864, Anthony had assembled petitions with 100,000 names into a mammoth roll that two black men carried into the Senate and deposited at Sumner's desk in the first of four installments that would total 400,000 names by the time Congress adjourned. The monumental effort proved the largest and most successful drive yet in American political history and demonstrated both the continued vitality of the movement and the fresh imperatives of a feminist political participation that the AAS had pioneered thirty years before. The right of petition, Stanton told Sumner, was "the only political right woman has under the Constitution," and she served notice that in the era of reconstruction looming ahead that inequity would have to be addressed.

In the midst of the petition mobilization, the AAS celebrated the thirtieth anniversary of its founding with a return to Philadelphia in December 1863. Garrison intended the observances to serve as a measure of progress, a beacon of inspiration, and an opportunity to renew the original crystalline demand for immediate emancipation. He sought congratulatory letters from prominent civic figures; he invited the forty-five surviving signers of the Declaration of Sentiments to return, which led to a cordial reconciliation by mail with the aged Arthur Tappan; and he arranged a commemorative program that gave equal place to the reminiscences of the founding spirits—including Robert Purvis, Lucretia Mott, Mary Grew, and Samuel J. May—and the voices of the younger leaders—Frederick Douglass, Susan B. Anthony, and Theodore Tilton—who had emerged from the AAS milieu. Some popular figures who had risen to prominence in the antislavery ranks but had kept themselves at arm's length from AAS radicalism came to pay their respects, including Senator Henry Wilson, who hailed the once-reviled organization for its pivotal influence upon contemporary politics, and Henry Ward Beecher, who penetrated to the heart of the AAS achievement by praising it as "an uncanonical Church . . . of the very best and most apostolic kind, held together by the cohesion of a rule of faith, and an interior principle. . . ."

Meeting in the largest assembly hall in the city, with a squad of black soldiers as honored platform guests, Garrison recalled the founding sessions in the humble black clubhouse three decades before and proclaimed that they now stood so "very near the Jubilee" that no one could doubt that the AAS would not need to hold a fortieth-anniversary meeting in 1873. Though the labor to abolish slavery seemed drawing to an end, Garrison said, "our labors in the field of a common humanity, and in the cause of reform, are never to terminate here, except with our mortal lives." The vast work of protection and uplift that lay ahead would permit people of all denominations and parties to make "a common atonement" for the "wrongs and outrages" inflicted by generations of bondage. In paying tribute to the pioneering Benjamin Lundy, moreover, Garrison reverted to the religious vision that had animated the movement and portrayed the impending victory over slavery into a triumph of redemption. They would not curse the South, but rather bless it with freedom; they would not repay the South in vengeance for its oppression, but rather extend it "love and goodwill."

Garrison's vision now found representation in the popular mind. *Harper's Weekly* published a drawing entitled *Emancipation* done in the tripartite medallion style of *The Liberator's* familiar masthead. A large central oval depicted a prosperous freed family gathered contentedly at a "Union" woodstove in their parlor. Below the scene rested an oval portrait of Abraham Lincoln and above it was the Thomas Crawford statue of Freedom intended for the Capitol dome. In the left-hand panels Cerberus presided over the terrible scenes of slave auctions and floggings, while on the opposite side Justice introduced scenes of well-tended fields, public schools, and the paymaster's window. An archway of clouds and sunbeams framed the entire drawing, which was executed by Thomas Nast, a young German-born artist whose deft pen had quickly earned him a reputation for combating the Democratic caricaturists with telling work of his own. *Emancipation* became a celebrated piece, often reprinted and made available in lithographed form suitable for framing.

The two days of meetings turned into a combination of family reunion and revival meeting that found Garrison, despite the grim cloud of war, in his warmest element, greeting old friends and sharing memories—perhaps too many, he feared—about the good old days of eggs and brickbats. Helen had come along, as had Willie and Wendy, and Samuel J. May told her that she looked just as bright and cheerful as she had looked thirty years before in the midst of the crisis over Prudence Crandall's school. The editor had written his first courtship letter to Helen shortly after the AAS founding meeting, yet it scarcely seemed possible that the couple would be celebrating *their* thirtieth anniversary come September.

The observances drew exceedingly complimentary attention from the press. The Philadelphia papers used the occasion to make atonement for the burning of Pennsylvania Hall and cite the widespread understanding that in 1838 the abolitionists had been right and the civic establishment wrong. The *New York Tribune* likened the reformers' thirty-year direct march toward abolition to the parallels of latitude that cross oceans, climb mountains, and traverse deserts and prairies "without variableness or shadow or turning." It required no spirit of "divination," the paper said, to perceive that the founding of the AAS in 1833 and the election of a Republican president in 1860 stood toward each other "as remote cause and ultimate effect." The *New York Times* disagreed, and taking the occasion a few months later of George Thompson's return to the United States, berated the abolitionists for the "demoralization" their anti-Constitution views had created. The antislavery cause would have advanced further and faster if Garrison, Phillips, and Thompson "had never existed," the newspaper said.

It was a minority view. From the presidency of Andrew Jackson to the incumbency of Abraham Lincoln, the AAS, it was now clear, had helped inspire the transformation of American political culture. Jackson had affirmed the Union framed by the Constitution of 1787; Lincoln had come to represent the mystic ideal of a nation committed, as he had said at Gettysburg two weeks before the anniversary, to "a new birth of freedom" under the aegis of the Declaration of 1776. It was Garrison and the movement embodied by the AAS that formed the bridge between the two conceptions, and as the editor fondly embraced the old black caterer in whose Philadelphia home he had penned the AAS declaration, there could be no doubt that abolitionism had forged a revolutionary change in constitutional practice. An amendment that would everywhere and forever abolish slavery now seemed within their grasp, only three years after the U.S. Congress had endorsed the idea of an amendment that would have forever barred such action. Other amendments that would negate the three-fifths and fugitive-slave clauses lay on the horizon, as did the protection of black citizenship in a constitution that the chief justice, now on his own deathbed, had nine years earlier read as devoid of such a concept. (When Taney finally passed away in October 1864, the editor observed that the country would accept his death "in perfect resignation.")

For Garrison the thirtieth anniversary demonstrated that the world had moved and that, with faith and work, it would move some more. Yet there was an undercurrent of doubt in the discussions, a questioning of the editor's purpose, that would not stay still. Where many heard fresh resolve, a few heard hints of retirement. Some people said that Wendell Phillips had stayed away to protest the weakening of Garrison's purpose, and Pillsbury had done the same, while other naysayers pointed to the absence of Whittier, Chapman, and others as signs of slackening and contentment. Abby Kelley splashed cold water upon the congratulatory tone of the gathering by repeating Napoleon's maxim "Nothing is done while anything remains to be done." The emancipation achieved thus far owed more to "Jeff Davis and the terrible persistency of the rebels," she said, than it did to Lincoln's alleged "conversion," and she warned against a possible fall from grace. Garrison replied that it was not their province to question the motives of recent sympathizers with the cause, but to rejoice in the "miraculous change" and hail anyone as a friend who was willing to work for freedom. It was the old argument between the broad platform and the narrow, between pressure-group politics and sectarian exhortation, between the beacon of hope and the goad of despair, and it was an argument that would not disappear.

Like her husband, Helen Garrison had enjoyed herself greatly at the anniversary. Franky remembered her coming home abloom with delight and declaring that when the war finally ended, when the slaves all went free and George came safely home, she would look forward to more travel with her husband. Before any of those longed-for moments came to pass, however, the course of her life changed for the worse.

On Tuesday, December 30, 1863, Helen had spent the afternoon on errands for the subscription fund-raiser and then gone out to an evening lecture with the editor and their children. She looked radiant in the cause and content in the midst of the quiet family talk they had enjoyed upon returning home. Shortly after midnight, however, Garrison awakened the household with a loud cry for help. Helen had collapsed as they were getting into bed, and she now lay on the floor, her mouth distorted in a grimace and her entire left side, arm, and leg rigid with paralysis. Wendell ran at once for the doctor, while Willie and Frank tried to help Father lift Mother onto the bed. Suddenly Garrison cried out in pain; he had wrenched his back in the effort to help Helen, and Fanny had to make him lie down while the boys dealt with their mother, who had quite evidently suffered a stroke. She was conscious and murmuring incoherently by the time the doctor came, and he said that if she survived, it might be some time before they knew the extent of the damage. "It was a fearful night," Willie wrote in his diary, "and its consequences horrible to think of. . . ."

The next day seemed brighter. Helen could speak, she knew the family, and she recognized the succession of friends who stopped in all day with sympathetic words and offers of help. They helped arrange for an adjustable bed, which made her more comfortable, and the smile she offered to Willie for the hot lemonade he brought reassured him greatly. The editor's back-strain, too, improved, but he collapsed emotionally and could do little but sit by his wife's bedside. Helen did not yet comprehend what had happened to her; she thought her stiffened, unresponsive arm belonged to someone else. By the day after New Year's, however, she had regained her understanding and the doctor declared that she would live and quite possibly recover a good deal of movement in her limbs.

Fanny took over management of the household in addition to her paying work with nine piano students, Franky resumed his demanding routine at the Boston Latin School, with at least four hours of studying a day, and their father (after nearly two weeks' absence) went back to *The Liberator*. With Wendell off lecturing in the petition campaign and trying his hand at journalism with Theodore Tilton at *The Independent* in New York, with Willie returned to boardinghouse life, and with the usual passel of visitors unwilling to impose in a time of illness, their dining table seemed empty: only Garrison and the two younger children, with Helen taking her meals upstairs. Not until the end of March 1864 would she be able to walk a few steps unassisted, and it would be mid-April before she could be helped into the parlor to visit or could take meals at table with the family. Her husband, however, had recovered his optimism. With the fair weather on its way, he predicted, Helen would be able to get outdoors and "will doubtless recuperate more rapidly."

From domestic crisis Garrison plunged directly into political controversy. The editor's critics marched into the MAS meeting in late January 1864 intent upon making a scene, and they succeeded. This time, instead of the usual grousing from Foster or Pillsbury, the challenge came from none other than Wendell Phillips, who wanted to condemn the Lincoln administration as "ready to sacrifice the interest and honor of the North to secure a sham peace" that would betray the cause of civil rights. Garrison objected to the imputation of bad motives, though he conceded that he had areas of concern about policy, and he sought to modify the resolution by saying that the administration was "in danger of sacrificing" crucial principles. Phillips would not accept the amendment, and a caustic discussion ensued, which quickly deviated from the alleged surrender into a wrangle over Lincoln's character that seemed, at times, a throwback to 1860. Phillips charged that the president remained only "a half-converted, honest Western Whig, trying to be an abolitionist," and Foster called Lincoln "the very embodiment of the Dred Scott decision" who was yet keeping a million slaves in bondage. Garrison, on the other hand, announced that he had modified his opinion of Lincoln and believed that the president had made an irrevocable commitment to emancipation that justified continued faith in the administration. No one else, however, took the editor's position in debate, and though the voice vote proved too close to call, the show of hands went against him. Not only did Garrison's amendment lose, but his political judgment had become suspect.

The press coverage now extended to MAS meetings meant that the disagreement between Garrison and Phillips became a major political story as the harbinger of a new schism in the ranks, but abolitionist editors downplayed its significance. Debate in the movement was always robust, they explained, and the two leaders exemplified polar temperaments that would eventually find a happy medium. Garrison was the optimistic man of faith, while Phillips, as a student of history, took a more measured view of the dangers ahead. "The cheerful caution of Mr. Garrison, and the less hopeful doubtings of Mr. Phillips," said Oliver Johnson in the *Standard,* "work well together for good."

However true, all this was irrelevant, for the eruption was not so much a substantive disagreement over the movement's direction or identity as it was a tactical quarrel over whether Abraham Lincoln should be nominated for reelection. For the first time, abolitionists stood close enough to the center of power to think that they could directly influence the course of a presidential campaign. For critics of the administration to consider the possibility of an alternative candidate was by no means out of the ordinary. No incumbent president since Andrew Jackson had won reelection, and no incumbent since Martin Van Buren had gained renomination. The sectional basis of the Republican Party and the wide range of opinion within it, moreover, when combined with the unusual circumstances of wartime, upset traditional political calculations and offered fresh opportunities for ambitious and dexterous men to maneuver themselves into consideration. For those impatient with Lincoln or suspicious of his motives, there were a number of seemingly radical alternatives among prominent antislavery generals such as Frémont and Butler, conscience-minded cabinet officers such as Chase (an old Liberty man), or even an apolitical military hero such as Grant. To a certain extent, Phillips's maneuver at the MAS meeting was intended as a probe in behalf of one or several of these available noncandidates.

Garrison, however, had no patience with such schemes. In the past, of course, he had stayed completely out of presidential politics and concentrated upon advocacy of the principles that would redefine the context of public opinion. To the degree that Phillips's criticism of Lincoln was an endeavor to raise the standards for the president's performance, Garrison could hardly object, especially since he considered Lincoln's ability to understand and respond to public opinion to be one of his greatest strengths. To hear the absolutist Garrison now say that Lincoln had moved about as far and as fast as the public would sustain and that he had to be judged on the basis "of his possibilities, rather than by our wishes, or by the highest abstract moral standard" provoked either an astonishment that bordered upon disbelief or a sense of betrayal.

The editor adopted so expedient a view for two reasons. First, he had developed a genuine respect for Lincoln, based largely upon the way he had grown in office and met the challenge of both secession and abolition. The contrast between the president's December 1863 message in which he reiterated his unequivocal commitment to emancipation and the gradualist, colonizationist statement of the year before was too striking for Garrison to ignore, as was Lincoln's deep understanding, as manifested in his address at Gettysburg, that the war had occasioned a moral transformation that would bring the nation closer to the ideals of the Declaration. Second, Garrison saw the gravest danger emanating not from the administration's present shortcomings, but from the "Peace Democrat" opposition that had vilified Lincoln ever since emancipation and who might yet capitalize upon antiblack sentiment and war-weariness to mount a poisonous "Copperhead" campaign that would unseat the Republicans and undo a half-completed abolition in the negotiated settlement that Phillips feared. As they had in 1860, abolitionist hopes rested with the Republicans, Garrison believed, and he considered it the height of folly to jeopardize the administration's reelection with an untried nominee.

By mid-March 1864, however, that threat had eased. Chase's manipulations had come to light prematurely, and the treasury secretary had to disavow the moves made on his behalf. Lincoln, meanwhile, had moved adroitly to mobilize enough support in the state legislatures and the party machinery to all but guarantee victory at the Baltimore nominating convention in June. Many Republican editors felt that Garrison's support had played a crucial role in consolidating Lincoln's position. "Everything that identifies the Government with Abolitionism is a benefit," declared the influential editor of the *Philadelphia Press,* adding that the surest way of making Lincoln the captive of the most conservative Republicans would be for radical abolitionists to withdraw their support.

Garrison's concern shifted from protecting Lincoln's renomination to squelching the idea of abolitionist support for an independent candidate, probably Frémont, on a platform that looked beyond abolition to the protection of the freed slaves' economic and political rights. The policy disputes among Republicans should be addressed in ways that gave no opening to the Copperheads and their Confederate sympathizers to divide and conquer, Garrison warned, and at all costs, the argument should not find its expression in rival tickets. "There must be but one candidate," the editor wrote in a March 18 editorial, "The Presidency," that marked the first political endorsement he had ever made. No man had as strong a hold upon the mass of people as Lincoln, he said, and for all the president's inconsistencies and hesitations, no public official had done more to advance the antislavery cause than Lincoln had with his edict of emancipation, his willingness to place 100,000 black soldiers in the field, and his understanding that slavery had to be permanently expunged from the Constitution.

Garrison had virtually declared himself to be a Republican, and he opened himself to a bruising counterattack by Phillips that completely preoccupied the spring meetings of the AAS and ultimately threatened the continued existence of both *The Liberator* and the *Standard*. "A million dollars would have been a cheap purchase for the Administration of *The Liberator's* article on the Presidency," Phillips sneered, and he redoubled his effort to portray Lincoln's administration as "a civil and military failure" and the president himself as hostile to black citizenship.

This was an extravagant claim that the public found hard to accept, though many hard-core abolitionists cheered Phillips on. The May 1864 meetings of the AAS and the New England convention took place against the backdrop of some of the hardest fighting of the war at the Wilderness and Cold Spring Harbor in Virginia, and Phillips drew upon the sadness of stalemate to complain that the sacrifices of the war demanded a "thorough" revolution that would eliminate all vestiges of slaveholding aristocracy from political life. In the same weeks, however, the Senate repealed the Fugitive Slave Law and approved a draft Thirteenth Amendment that would prohibit slavery throughout the country and thus provide a constitutional sanction for the military emancipation already substantially achieved. Lincoln's attorney general, Edward Bates, moreover, had defied the *Dred Scott* decision with a memorandum that made an irrefutable case for black citizenship, which in turn had broken the logjam in Congress and led to a measure that settled the military pay controversy. These developments left nothing for the administration's critics to "harp upon," thought Garrison, except for the political status of the Louisiana freedmen and the broader question of reconstruction. These "new issues," he thought, would have to be settled upon "a new basis" after a great deal more analysis and political preparation. Whatever happens, the editor told Johnson, "let *us* possess our souls in patience."

The editor's expectations proved naive, as the meetings witnessed stormy oratory and clashes of personality that turned what might have easily become a victory celebration into a bitter party caucus that belied the abolitionists' reputation for high-minded and respectful debate. The mood had become so sour that just about the only thing people could agree on was the futility of holding the annual Fourth of July picnic at Framingham. "I never imagined the Fosters & Co. should show me that it would require more virtue to rejoice with them than to suffer with them," Maria Chapman dryly told Garrison, "but we live and learn. . . ." Resolutions and counterresolutions came and went, and although the galleries cheered Garrison's temperate views of Lincoln and the tasks ahead, the critics narrowly prevailed in the voting and in effect directed the movement to oppose Lincoln and nurture the budding protest candidacy of Frémont. (Elizabeth Cady Stanton told the editor that he could speak at the Loyal League's meeting only if he was "sound on the presidential question" and hinted that his son Wendell's hesitations about Lincoln put him "ahead" of his father.)

The editor tried to remain serene in the midst of vituperation, though he was sorely tested when Phillips tried to disqualify George Thompson's eloquent defense of Lincoln as the uninformed work of a foreigner. Garrison deplored the effort to disrupt the organization on political grounds and tried, for the final time, to summon his constituency of apostles. "We all go for equal rights, without regard to race or color," he said on the last night of the Boston convention. "We have not relaxed our vigilance or our testimony, and I am sorry to hear any intimation thrown out that we do not call for the amplest justice." The movement still demanded everything that is just, "as of old," he said pointedly, pronouncing the signs of the times as more favorable and encouraging than ever before and concluding with the words of a song from the Port Royal contrabands, "Da massa run—ha, ha!/ De darkies stay—ho, ho!/ It must be now de kingdom's comin'/ And de year ob jubilo!" The loud and prolonged applause demonstrated that Garrison still had his public.

It was an unusual debate in that Garrison the visionary occupied the expedient ground that the election had to be won in order to consolidate the victory of emancipation, while Phillips, the counterpuncher and sensationalist, took the visionary position that unless the long-run issues of reconstruction and civil rights were addressed, the immediate victory would be a worthless one. Phillips's strongest suit lay in the manifest shortcomings of the administration's first efforts at restoration: field regulations in the occupied areas of Louisiana that seemed to put the freedmen in a heavily restricted state of apprenticeship and an amnesty proclamation that looked to restoring the state to the Union when only ten percent of its white males had taken loyalty oaths (including a pledge to respect the executive action against slaveholding). These policies, as Garrison readily conceded, were "pregnant with evil consequences," and he questioned Lincoln's authority over the issue and argued that the entire question of reconstruction had to await the more extensive conquest of the South. Yet, to Phillips, the editor was dodging important and troubling matters for political reasons. Even when Garrison did speak about "the reconstruction of society on the basis of political equality in the rebel states" and the duty of the president "to use his utmost constitutional power to secure equal rights for all under the national flag, without regard to complexional distinctions," Phillips's invective and sarcasm had a way of making the editor sound vague and inadequate.

Garrison's strongest suit, however, lay in the moral progress that Lincoln had demonstrably made, which made an expression of confidence seem less fatuous and more sagacious than Phillips charged. Confidants of the president, moreover, now divulged the story that the president had decided early in July 1862 upon an emancipation policy and had used the summer to prepare the public for it. The information made more plausible the argument that Lincoln could indeed be influenced by abolitionist agitation even though he would craftily behave in a way that seemed to deny its force. Another telling point proved to be the public understanding that the war had undeniably wrought an irreversible social change. "We have advanced a quarter of a century in a single year," the editor exulted, and those who had once considered Lincoln a "slow coach" had to admit that the president had "beaten the Birmingham train." If reliance upon Lincoln was the surest way to make 1864 the year of military victory and approval of the antislavery constitutional amendment, then Garrison's political instincts were sound, and his willingness to risk his leadership of the radical abolitionists on Lincoln's behalf would be recognized as an uncommon act of statesmanship.

Garrison consolidated his emerging reputation as "a radical with a substratum of common sense and practical wisdom" by making a triumphant appearance at the Republican convention in Baltimore on June 8, 1864. Traveling with his admiring friend Theodore Tilton of *The Independent,* the editor, who had been jailed there over three decades before, turned the visit into a homecoming and festival of vindication. The two stayed with the family of John Needles, the Quaker cabinetmaker who had supported Garrison and Lundy in the days of the *Genius* and who welcomed him with good-hearted joy. It had taken over thirty years for Maryland to make itself free enough for the prodigal editor's return, but the recent passage of a state constitutional amendment had abolished slavery and permitted nearly all the able-bodied slaves to emancipate themselves by enrolling in the military. A black regiment, the editor wrote, marched on the spot where pro-secession vandals had assaulted Massachusetts troops at the outset of the war. Garrison walked all about the city, marveling that its growth since his boyhood had outstripped Boston's, but he was dismayed to find among the many signs of progress a brand-new jail instead of the gloomy old hulk in which he had served his sentence for libel. Frustrated in the hope of adding a postscript to the poetry he had scrawled on the walls of his cell in 1830, Garrison called upon the presiding judge—an antislavery loyalist named Hugh Bond—who good-naturedly looked up the old trial record and offered to summon the eight surviving jurors into court so that they might reconsider their verdict and allow Garrison to bestow his public forgiveness upon them. Amid much laughter, Tilton insisted that his paper receive the photographic rights.

Merriment gave way to a deep exultation when Garrison mingled with the immense crowd that crammed into the Front Street Theater to hail Lincoln's nearly unanimous nomination and roar its approval of a platform resolution that condemned slavery as the cause of the war and called for a constitutional amendment that would abolish it forever. There were loud calls for Garrison, but he could do no more than wave from the gallery. The platform was "the first NATIONAL VERDICT ever recorded, in form and fact, in letter and spirit, against slavery, as a system 'incompatible with the principles of republican government,'" he said in *The Liberator,* and he regarded it as a public endorsement of all the abolitionist fanaticism and incendiarism he had practiced since he had walked out of Baltimore Jail thirty-four years and three days before.

From Baltimore, Garrison and Tilton joined the crowds of politicians heading to Washington to congratulate the president upon his renomination. He thought that he must be dreaming, the editor told his wife, as they rode past the buildings of the capital city and onto the grounds of the White House. Then, suddenly, he was face to face with the tall, sad-eyed commander in chief, whose face lit up with unfeigned pleasure as he heartily pumped the editor's hand. Lincoln lost no time in displaying his famous wit. Upon hearing that Garrison had found his old Baltimore prison demolished, the president wisecracked, "Then you couldn't get out; now you cannot get in," and broke up the crowd. Amid the hubbub the president invited the editor to return the next morning for a private talk and passed him along to the war secretary, Edwin Stanton, who told him of his own father's close connection to Benjamin Lundy in the old crusader's Ohio days and swore that he admired no character in public life more than he did Garrison.

The whirlwind of flattering attention continued with a visit to the Capitol, its huge dome now securely in place and topped by the heroic figure of Freedom. Sumner and Wilson instantly came out to the lobby as soon as Garrison's card announced him and forthwith conducted the editor onto the floor of the U.S. Senate. He was offered the chair of an absent member and sat astonished in the hallowed chamber that once echoed with the voices of Clay and Webster and Calhoun as the present senators came up, one by one, to pay their respects. "Quite a sensation was produced by my presence," Garrison told Helen afterward, and added, "Let nothing be said in *The Liberator* about this."

The next morning, June 10, Garrison started a note to Helen from the White House lobby, but had to break it off when the president called him in. They spoke privately for an hour, with Garrison recounting something of the change of heart he had undergone and Lincoln retelling his own difficulties in steering toward an antislavery harbor. Lincoln had developed quite a reputation for diverting visitors, especially critics, with folksy stories and sympathetic wit, and he evidently performed to expectation for the editor, who told Helen of his pleasure in "the familiar and candid way in which he unbosomed himself." Lincoln told Garrison that he had personally insisted upon the abolition amendment plank in the Baltimore platform, and he professed himself anxious to secure its rapid adoption so that the issue would not be linked either to the fortunes of war or his own reelection or death. The editor came away convinced that Lincoln would "do all that he can see it right and possible for him to do to uproot slavery, and give fair-play to the emancipated." Garrison made no mention of any flattering remarks the president may have extended to him, but later Lincoln was known to have told one of his generals, Daniel H. Chamberlain, that he considered himself "only an instrument" in the antislavery struggle. "The logic and moral power of Garrison," said Lincoln, "and the antislavery people of the country and the army, have done it all."

The more closely the editor identified himself with Lincoln and the Republicans, the more abuse he received from his antagonists within the movement who condemned him as a political opportunist. He certainly sought no office himself, much less patronage or favor for others. The accolades from prominent Republicans, the chorus of public adulation, and the rituals of vindication he regularly performed all gratified him deeply, but there is no evidence that he prostituted his convictions to receive them. It is true that Garrison had decided to make 1864 an occasion for consolidation rather than the agitation of fresh demands, but he genuinely believed that abolitionism should partake of the historic moment that presented itself. Was it not Wendell Phillips four years earlier who hailed Lincoln's election as Garrison's triumph? Nevertheless, the tempo of personal attacks increased dramatically as supporters of Frémont excoriated the editor as a fallen angel, a lost leader, and a vindictive and jealous old man endeavoring to crush the brighter star of Phillips for shameful partisan ends.

If anyone had become drunk with popularity, however, it was Phillips, who had indeed emerged as the foremost abolitionist orator of the war years and whose collected lectures sold more than 100,000 copies in a few months, and who now behaved in a manner both high-handed and naive. He persuaded a majority of the committee in charge of spending Charles Hovey's generous bequest for movement publications to discontinue the $300 subsidy it had granted The Liberator to distribute gratuitous copies to leading public figures. The argument that the paper had become too partisan and was no more deserving of support than any other Republican paper not only insulted Garrison but jeopardized the newspaper's precarious health by sparking a flurry of cancellations. Over the course of the summer, however, generous donors (including Gerrit Smith and Theodore Tilton) made up the cash deficiency and letters from sympathetic and loyal readers buoyed the editor's spirits. One woman sent extra money to extend the life of the subscriptions others wanted to cancel, while William Still, the black Philadelphian widely admired for his skillful management of fugitive escapes, entered two gift subscriptions, one for the black soldiers training at Camp Penn and the other for a military hospital. It was most significant, said another reader, that when President Lincoln reviewed Grant's army in Virginia, the black soldiers cried out, "Three cheers for The Liberator."

Phillips coupled his slam at Garrison's paper with a direct attack upon Oliver Johnson and the *Standard* by forbidding (on no clear authority) the AAS treasurer from paying the newspaper's bills or salaries until the executive committee had the opportunity of reviewing the charges of excessive partisanship he proposed to bring. Garrison and Phillips had a bitter conversation preceding the meeting, after which the editor warned Johnson to prepare himself for censure or worse. At the meeting Phillips maintained that he had thrice obtained an anti-Lincoln mandate from the society and that its newspaper had to conduct itself in accord with it, but the committee, which included others who shared Phillips's hostility toward the administration, was not prepared to press the issue to a disruptive conclusion and expressed confidence in Johnson's ability to canvass the issues impartially. The result proved a triumph for Garrison and left Phillips in a "heated state," the editor said, and regrettably determined "to leave us."

The real problem for Phillips, however, lay not with critical editorials in the abolitionist press but in the growing rancidness of the Frémont movement. The Great Pathfinder had accepted the nomination of an ad hoc convention in Cleveland composed of anti-Lincoln abolitionists, disgruntled War Democrats, and a cadre of German-Americans interested in land reform and appreciative of Frémont's antislavery moves in Missouri. Calling itself the "Radical Democratic Party," the convention adopted a platform that endorsed Phillips's civil rights demand in language no more specific than Garrison's, but ignored much more of the radical agenda while taking up the Peace Democrats' favorite charge that Lincoln had become a military dictator. When the convention named a dough-faced supporter of Pierce, Buchanan, and Breckenridge as Frémont's running mate and the campaign started up a newspaper organ in New York headed by one of the general's subordinates who actively courted Democratic support, many abolitionists (including Wendell Garrison and Frederick Douglass) once sympathetic to Frémont felt obliged to reconsider. One by one, they distanced themselves from the candidacy that increasingly seemed to be a cat's-paw for a Copperhead effort to subvert the administration, just as *The Liberator* and the *Standard* had warned earlier in the year.

Phillips persisted, but critics, led by Theodore Tilton in *The Independent,* charged Phillips with extraordinary naiveté in thinking that a fresh and provocative issue such as voting rights could be profitably raised as an adjunct to a political campaign, even if his candidates were truly pledged to it, as they increasingly seemed not to be. If the abolitionists had learned anything from their third-party misadventures, it was that issues should not be pushed to premature defeat at the ballot box. Nor should an admirable moral stance be considered an effective substitute for a practical political organization, Garrison added as a corollary; to identify a provocative issue with a candidate who lacked a constituency was both poor agitation and poor politics. The question of universal suffrage, the editor told a critic in midsummer, would be "hard to win and to hold, without a general preparation of feeling and sentiment," and the victory would come, not in one election, but "only by a struggle *on the part of the disenfranchised,* and a growing conviction of its justice."

The summer of 1864 wore on, with Grant stalemated in central Virginia and Sherman creeping into northern Georgia, and by late August, even Lincoln thought that war-weariness might cost him the election. Phillips was certain that Frémont and the War Democrats could yet forge an effective coalition, but when the Democratic Party turned to the discredited George

McClellan and a platform that pledged the continuation of slavery in the coded language of "immediate armistice" and "restoration of unimpaired states rights," there was no question that champions of abolition and a more egalitarian nation had to support Lincoln. Frémont gracelessly withdrew, and, as almost every prominent abolitionist joined Garrison in the Lincoln camp, Phillips even more gracelessly sat on the sidelines and angrily declared that he would "cut off both hands before doing anything to aid Lincoln's re-election."

The Republicans, it turned out, did not need the abolitionists' sulking Achilles; they had a new hero in William Tecumseh Sherman, who severed the southeast by taking Atlanta in September, then launching a devastating march to the sea that would put him in Savannah before Christmas. If Lee and Grant remained stalemated on the James, Sherman—it was clear to all—could tear through the Carolinas and attack the Army of Northern Virginia from below. Lincoln received boosts from two more military "campaign managers." Admiral David Farragut damned torpedo attack boats and victoriously steamed full-speed into Mobile Bay, while Grant's cavalry leader Phil Sheridan chased Jubal Early from the Shenandoah Valley and laid waste to an important Virginia breadbasket.

With military victory now firmly in view, the election ceased to be a doubtful one, and Lincoln won it by half a million votes, carrying all but three states (Kentucky, Delaware, and New Jersey) and flaunting coattails long enough to make the next Congress seventy-five percent Republican. The Garrison men gathered in Faneuil Hall with the rest of Boston to hear the election returns come in by telegraph, and even after midnight, the streets and squares of the city resounded with jubilant voices singing "Old Hundred" ("Praise God from whom all blessings flow") and "the John Brown song," to which the editor himself might have added a few bars of "Ain't You Glad You Joined the Republicans."

While the sectarian election campaign had strained old friendships in the movement, the season witnessed the growth of new relationships in the family. In February 1864, Willie announced that he had become engaged to Ellen Wright, the niece of Lucretia Mott and the daughter of faithful Garrisonian abolitionists in central New York. They had known each other for years, but the relationship had blossomed only in the last year or so, as both had become involved in the Loyal League's petition campaign and Willie had traversed the Mohawk Valley. In writing a benediction to the young people, the editor rejoiced that they found themselves "warmed by the same electric flame," and looking over at Helen, he shook his head and exclaimed that it seemed only yesterday that they had united their own hearts. It was only fitting that their dear friend Samuel J. May performed their son's ceremony, which took place in September 1864, two weeks and thirty years after May had united Lloyd with Peace and Plenty.

Even before his brother's wedding, Wendell had declared himself betrothed to Ellen's very close friend Lucy McKim, the daughter of Pennsylvania abolitionists who had stood very close to Garrison throughout the struggle. Lucy had worked in the Port Royal community of freed slaves, had published transcriptions of several slave songs as a signal element in black culture, and spoke glowingly of the grand heartswell she had experienced in hearing a congregation of three hundred black people sing "Roll, Jordan, roll!" as a triumphal anthem in a church of their own.

The couple's announcement caught the editor by surprise, though the rest of the family had tumbled to the romance early on, but he couldn't have been more delighted at the formal enlargement of the abolitionists' family circle. He joked that he had once thought his sons would all remain bachelors, but now he felt certain that soldier George, if spared to return, would find a sweetheart, and Franky, suddenly gangling at sixteen and graduated to coat and vest, would soon have lassies hanging about. And Fanny, of course, would be a catch without parallel, though for now, he teased, gentlemen had better not ask her hand in marriage.

Fathers are the last to know. Fanny had already rejected one suitor, a conceited young man who had turned in her direction after Lucy McKim had spurned him for Wendell, but her younger brother was doing his best to remedy the situation. Franky had stayed in regular correspondence with the journalist "Harry" Villard, sharing the letters with his sister. When Villard joked that Franky's brothers had done well in the matrimonial line and casually hinted that his sister must also be "under bonds," Franky leaped at the bait. Oh no, he replied as Villard's "special correspondent," she was "wonderfully destitute of beaus" save for the self-infatuated one she had curtly dismissed; she was very likely to be an old maid. When Harry then asked Franky to see whether Fanny would permit him to correspond with her, the youngster related the entirely proper reply that his sister was flattered but thought an exchange of letters might be unsuitable, and then blurted out an entirely improper postscript. "But let me tell you, dear Villard, that Fanny loves you as much as you love her," her brother added, and advised his friend to keep writing and "go in and win her." Mother probably knew what was afoot, but certainly brother and sister agreed that there was nothing to tell Father—yet.

As romance among her children bloomed, Helen's condition had somewhat improved. By July 1864, she could walk, with a companion, the few blocks north to the Boylston Street edge of the Common, and when she and Franky spent several weeks at Samuel Sewall's farm in Melrose, she managed to walk outdoors for nearly half a mile. As much as Helen enjoyed sociable visiting, she hated to impose herself and her need for special attention upon her hosts, and with great regret she declined to go west for Ellen and Willie's wedding, but had a nursing companion and a homeopathic healer come in to keep her company while the rest of the family was away. She managed to write letters to keep up with friends and became resigned to her lack of mobility, insisting that it not restrict her husband and children from their active social life.

For Helen's sake, however, the family uprooted itself. The Dix Place house had become very uncomfortable: its limited cross-ventilation made it "sweltering" in the summer, and it had stairs that were too steep for an invalid, rooms that were too dark for a shut-in, and a well-beaten path to its door, which meant that the regular stream of callers—however well-meaning—frustrated Helen's sensitivity as a hostess more than it overcame her feelings of isolation. It took the entire summer to find a suitable replacement, however, that the family could afford, but at last a lovely two-story frame house turned up on the hillside in Roxbury (just transforming itself into the suburb of "Boston Highlands") not far from the old fort and water standpipe at the summit. Perched on a rocky outcrop and painted a buttery yellow with ornamental stonework at the corners, the house at 125 Highland Street occupied a half-acre lot with many trees and a nice green lawn at the rear. The snug, airy quality of the place led everyone to call it "the bird's nest," though later the estate became formalized as "Rockledge."

The house had many grace notes: the front doorway formed a triptych arch with glass side panels that gave a churchly effect, the second-story front bedroom had a bay window from which one could see the harbor, the parlor had a black marble fireplace and an inlaid pine floor, the staircase—though narrow—had a gracefully curving walnut banister, and the interior doorways had raised floral carvings in the freshest Victorian ornamental style. There was also a good-sized front porch that permitted Helen to get outside easily to enjoy the air, and the location, only a few blocks from the old Freedom's Cottage, filled them with recollections of their honeymoon days and made the move something of an affectionate homecoming. The editor professed no discomfort at being a half hour's horsecar ride from his office, and, though they never lacked for company, the flow of unanticipated visitors came under control. The Highland Street house would suit them for the rest of their lives; the grandchildren would crowd into its attic and romp in its yard, and Lloyd and Helen would be borne to their graves from its parlor.

The family had a terrible scare in December 1864 when the news flashed that the 55th Massachusetts had taken a beating. It had comprised a leading element in a force of five thousand men dispatched from Hilton Head, South Carolina, to sever the Charleston & Savannah Railroad in aid of Sherman's advance. Unfortunately, a contingent of Georgia militia had rushed up by rail to defend the tracks at Honey Hill, and eight companies of the 55th ran into a fierce attack as they attempted to advance over the swampy ground while three others participated in a flanking attack that was stopped when the rebels set fire to a field of broom sedge and forced them back. The 55th lost nearly a hundred men, and its commanding officer, Alfred S. Hartwell, was seriously wounded. "George safe—so far," Willie wrote in his diary on December 11, but it was several weeks before they knew for certain.

Other than that brief, unfortunate foray into combat, the 55th Mass. had spent the fall in fatigue and support activity for the bombardment of Charleston. A black private boasted to Garrison that the editor's principles were "strongly represented" in the battery of white soldiers that loaded the 100-pounder gun that initiated the attack. "No. 1 is a strong abolitionist," he wrote. "No. 2 is now in favor of emancipation, though he don't think the negro is his equal. No. 3 was an emancipationist years ago, and always took your paper. And the gunner is a Republican."

In some ways the most problematic element in the family remained *The Liberator*. Helen and the children fretted endlessly about the drudgery the editor underwent weekly. Fanny's description of a "busy Wednesday" in which a "half-sick" Garrison labored into the night to get out the paper prompted her brother Wendell to declare "there must be a revolution in the office." Yet Garrison persisted in his work habits though he was vexed and weary. He promised to be "more methodical" about correcting copy and teaching the others how to make up the forms, but that fooled nobody. The family had to acquiesce, though Willie kept an eye on the books and contributed an occasional editorial, while Wendell became the paper's first New York correspondent and turned in a creditable set of weekly dispatches throughout the presidential campaign.

Phillips's attack, however, brought the situation to a climax. Garrison simply would not let the paper die at the hands of its former friends, and even the family agreed that it would be a shame for *The Liberator* to close before the end of the year. From South Carolina, George offered the suggestion that the size be cut in half and filled simply with articles by Garrison. If the paper had to die a natural death, he said, its loss "would be a severe blow to Father," but his standing with the public would not diminish; if the end to mechanical drudgery gave him more time to write, his influence might even increase. (Whatever happened, make it clear, George told Willie, that he would not be returning to the printing office after the war, so there could be no hope of rescue from his quarter.)

The editor had no intention of keeping *The Liberator* going indefinitely, but, with the end of the protracted struggle in view, he very much wanted the satisfaction of recording "the consummation" in his own paper. Nevertheless he listened seriously when Oliver Johnson suggested a merger with the *National Anti-Slavery Standard,* the combined journal to be published in New York with Garrison contributing as much as he wanted from Boston. For more than a month the editor mulled the idea, pulling out the subscription ledgers to see just how much overlap existed among their customers (not a great deal, it seemed) and talking earnestly with the friends, including Maria Chapman, George Thompson, and Agent May, who supported the idea. Johnson himself lobbied with Helen, who thought the plan would avert her husband's fast-declining health, and Willie, who believed in October that Garrison had decided to go for the merger.

They misread their man. In late November 1864, Garrison advised the executive committee that he did not want to consider an amalgamation, at least until the spring meetings. By that time, he thought, the struggle would be over and the AAS could discontinue the *Standard* and he could let *The Liberator* close with its "distinctive identity" preserved. He had started without any subscribers, and if he ended that way, so be it. His paper had "an historic position and a moral prestige," he told Johnson, that the merger would obscure, and there was no guarantee that his subscribers would follow him to the other paper and make good the added expense of his salary. He told Johnson that while he appreciated the compliment intended by the assurance that it was his writing alone that interested the readers of *The Liberator*, he could not accept it at face value. "I am not willing to believe, after an editorial experience of thirty-eight years, that, aside from my own lucubrations, I have neither the tact nor the talent to make an interesting journal," he said. "This touches me too closely." He had worked hard to make *The Liberator* a "complete" newspaper, with carefully selected matter and a large number of original letters and literary work that satisfied his readers' interests from week to week and year to year, he said, and he was proud of it as an institution. Come what may, Garrison vowed, he would publish *The Liberator* "until the Jubilee Bell is rung. . . ."

Abraham Lincoln promptly redeemed his pledge to Garrison and gave the passage of the Thirteenth Amendment his immediate and urgent attention. He conceded in his annual message that the lame-duck Congress meeting in December contained the same members who had failed to muster the requisite two-thirds vote in the House in June, but with an election having occurred and the next Congress certain to approve, it would be both prudent and honorable to respect the majority view and go ahead. To this mild-mannered appeal the president added the muscle of political hard-dealing. He and Seward made up a list of twelve to sixteen retiring Democrats whom they considered reasonable targets and worked them very hard, with invitations to the White House, religious and patriotic exhortation, and certain understandings, never revealed, about favors and patronage.

The lobbying worked, and when the roll was called in the House on January 31, 1865, sixteen Democrats joined all 103 Republicans in voting aye, while eight other Democrats absented themselves, and the measure passed with two votes to spare, 119–56. The packed galleries, which included many black people formerly excluded by congressional rules, burst into the delirious cheering and weeping that had previously occurred at mass meetings but never before in the House itself, where members embraced and literally danced with joy in a raucous display of emotion. George Julian of Indiana felt, he said, as if he had awakened "in a new country." *Harper's Weekly* published an engraving that made the House look like an evangelical prayer meeting and congratulated itself that the country "has now seen what some men have always seen. . . ." As for the "contemptible" fifty-six in opposition, the magazine predicted that any of their descendants would a thousandfold rather say that his ancestor voted against separation from the Crown than to admit that he had voted "against giving a lawful, peaceful chance of freedom to the slaves in America."

In Boston, the news was greeted with a one-hundred-gun salute on the Common. "It is the greatest and most important event in the history of Congressional legislation," Garrison wrote the next day. "Lord, now let thy servants, the abolitionists, depart in peace," said Mary Grew "in blessed communion" from Philadelphia, telling the Garrisons how much she regretted not being able to hold hands in their family circle to share the feeling of joyful relief. In Plymouth, Brad Drew celebrated the historic change and wrote, "This is a glorious day to live in. How rejoiced I am that *Garrison* still lives to see the death blow given to that infernal system. . . ."

At the end of the week the editor himself joyfully told a Jubilee meeting in the Music Hall that he felt in "a thoroughly Methodistical state" and yearned to shout at the top of his voice, "Glory! Hallelujah! Amen! Amen!"— whereupon the crowd did it for him, over and over again. The editor praised the "anti-slavery phalanx" who had labored for decades in the wilderness of contumely and ridicule, and he hailed the popular majority that at last decided upon a "radical change" that made "the Declaration CONSTITU-TIONALIZED" and the "supreme law of the land." They were celebrating, he said, the emancipation not only of four million black people, but 34 million whites as well. With the old Constitution "purged" and liberty at last become the birthright of all Americans, he said, he felt stirrings of a patriotism he had never known before. After years in moral alienation from his country, the editor had come home.

Charleston fell three weeks later near the end of February. With General Sherman's columns laying waste to the interior country fifty miles west, the city became cut off from vital supplies and the Confederate command, after maintaining itself against a twenty-two-month siege and bombardment, realized that it must evacuate. On February 21, 1865, the 55th Massachusetts, singing "the John Brown song," marched into the city, once the hotbed of secession but now streaked with smoke and ashes, to be greeted by thousands of cheering black people who had survived the war and now had charge of their destinies. In the *Harper's Weekly* engraving of the triumphal scene, Franky tried unavailingly to spot George among the mustachioed officers, but it did not take long to have his presence established. James Redpath, the war correspondent of the *Tribune*, reported that, amid the joyful noise, he heard a lieutenant give the order "*Shoulder* arms," thought he recognized the voice, and turned to shake the officer's hand. "Who do you think he was?" the writer asked. "The son of William Lloyd Garrison!"

The Northern papers hailed the occupation of Charleston as the end of the war, even though Lee had not yet surrendered and Jefferson Davis still held office in Richmond. "Jubilate!"; "Glorious Tidings!"; "The Old Flag Waving over Sumter!" headlined the *Boston Journal,* to which *The Liberator* added, "Babylon Is Fallen!" The correspondents searched out the slave market district, pressed into one of the abandoned establishments, and explored it with the mingled awe of the charnel house and the maliciousness of looters. They scrawled abolitionist Bible texts on the chalkboard and seized account books, manacles, pieces of broken signs, and a small set of auction steps that, with great bravado, "Carleton" of the *Journal* declared must be sent to Boston, just as the key to the Bastille hung at Mount Vernon. And sure enough, on March 9, at a crowded fund-raising event for the Freedman's Aid Society, the journalist (Charles Carleton Coffin) displayed his relics beneath a trophy "Stars and Bars" in Boston's Music Hall and invited Garrison to deliver a talk from the captured steps.

There would be a grander moment of triumph. The Lincoln administration decided to make the regained Fort Sumter the place for a dramatic pageant to commemorate the symbolic end of the rebellion. The secretary of war invited Major General Robert Anderson to return to Charleston on April 14 to raise over the fort the very same flag that he had lowered when surrendering it exactly four years before. Stanton asked Henry Ward Beecher to deliver an address and, at the president's suggestion, included William Lloyd Garrison on the list of dignitaries invited as the government's guests. The editor quickly accepted, but asked Stanton if George Thompson might also be included to acknowledge his work in thwarting British recognition of the Confederacy. Stanton agreed, adding that the Briton's namesake, Lieutenant Garrison, would be furloughed for a reunion with his father in Charleston. They always taunted us, "Why don't you go South?" Thompson reminded the editor merrily as they departed, and at long last they could answer that the government wanted us there to celebrate the triumph of Garrisonian abolitionism in the capital of secession and slaveholding. By the time they arrived, Lee had surrendered to Grant at Appomattox and the war was over.

Dawn broke blue and gentle over Charleston Harbor on Friday, April 14, 1865. Every vessel hauled out the regalia and bunting that signaled celebration, and the national flag could be seen from every fortification around the broad estuary, save the 150-foot-high flagpole at Fort Sumter, the Gibraltar-like structure at the harbor entrance. All morning long, small craft of every description carried visitors from the city across the three miles of water to the fort, the boats so crammed in at the narrow landing place that people had to walk and jump from deck to deck in order to disembark. The government mail steamer *Arago*, carrying Major General Anderson, Beecher, Garrison, and eighty other distinguished guests, lay outside the bar. It had arrived during the night from Savannah, after a four-day sail from New York with stopovers at Fortress Monroe and Hilton Head, where the passengers visited the black village of Mitchellville, a neat and new-built settlement that had recently elected its own town council and rapturously received the abolitionists in a joyous church service.

The dignitaries were to land at the fort after the spectators had gathered themselves, and so their small transport vessel hovered for hours alongside the *Arago*, with the swells increasing, while flotillas from the city made their passages to the fort. Of all the craft, none stirred more interest than the *Planter*, once a Confederate side-wheeler that its young black pilot, Robert Smalls, had daringly delivered to the Union navy in 1862, and that now brought a festive company of liberated slaves to the ceremony.

Not until eleven o'clock did the official party get underway, everyone jammed on the ferry's decks, eager for first sight of the storied locale. On the north shore they could see low-lying Sullivans Island and Fort Moultrie. To the south lay Morris Island, the marshy tidal flat where Shaw and the gallant 54th Massachusetts had fallen in the initial effort to establish a beachhead against Sumter. The company grew silent for a moment, gazing at the scene of carnage now washed clean.

Then, as the vessel came around to the northwest, a large, dark earthen mound loomed up like a beached whale. It was Sumter, not the trim, three-story red-brick pentagonal fortress of their imaginings, but a hulking ruin. Two years of intermittent shelling had destroyed three of the five sides, as the second and third stories had collapsed upon the first, but the determined Confederate force had remolded the debris into a high earthwork twenty feet thick, an irregular curved pile reinforced on the inside with charred timbers and long wicker baskets filled with sand. The company sailed by the intact right face, then swung around to the left flank, which also retained some of the original brick, to approach the landing wharf. Disembarking, they crossed an apron of broken iron, cannonballs, and rubbish and formed up into a procession that would ascend a long flight of stairs up to the parapet, and then proceed across a sandy walkway and down another staircase to the parade ground.

An honor guard of soldiers, white and black, who had taken part in the Charleston campaign, lined the route, the band played ruffles and flourishes, and cheers welled up from the spectators grouped on the benches below, when William Lloyd Garrison paused on the parapet, bright blue water all around, Charleston at his back, to wait his turn. He didn't have to wait long. The department's commanding officer, Major General Quincy Gillmore, escorted Major General Anderson and his daughter down to the platform; the Beechers went next, followed by Anderson's brother with Theodore Tilton. Then, arm in arm with his comrade in agitation George Thompson, the editor of *The Liberator* walked into Fort Sumter, past the stones and brickbats and into the bright noon of glory and the embrace of a grateful crowd.

They took their places on a platform carpeted with greenery and already crowded with officers of rank, with schoolteachers from the Sea Islands, and with a delegation from Washington including the president's private secretary, John Nicolay. Four pillars, fifteen feet high and wrapped in bunting, rose from the corners of the platform, and from their tops sprung arched poles, also decorated, forming a slender canopy topped with a gold eagle emblem at the center. Three to four thousand people—including a chartered boatload of Beecher's parishioners—crowded before them on bleachers that covered the acre of parade ground, and all eyes kept drifting up to the huge white flagpole that dominated the scene. Looking around, Garrison could now see the brick chimneys of the old fort standing against the earthwork made of rubble and stack after stack of sand baskets; it seemed as if they had come to hold a service of consecration at a construction site.

The exercises began with a prayer by the chaplain who had served with Anderson when he shifted his command from Moultrie to Sumter and continued with the responsive reading of psalms. *The Lord hath done great things for us. . . . O clap your hands, all ye people, shout unto God with the voice of triumph. . . . O sing unto the Lord a new song: for he has done marvelous things. . . . Some trust in chariots, and some in horses; but we will remember the Name of the Lord our God.* The assistant adjutant general read the dispatch in which Major Anderson had, four years earlier, announced the surrender of the fort, and then called the officer forward. The moment had come.

Anderson stepped up. From the Sumter leather mailbag he and a former staff sergeant withdrew the old flag, which had reposed during the war in a New York bank vault. A three-man crew attached it to the halyards with wreaths of evergreen as the crowd started to cheer, then hushed itself. Anderson, a tall and gaunt Kentuckian with a thatch of stiff gray hair (he looked like John Brown, Garrison thought), stood in a breathless silence for a long minute. He had in his pocket a letter from his former junior officer William Tecumseh Sherman, who was on campaign in North Carolina and had sent a fire-breathing message of vindication to his old commander, but Anderson made no reference to it. He simply thanked God that he had lived to perform his last act of duty to his country.

The old officer grasped the halyards and gave a great pull. The immense flag—it measured thirty-six by twenty feet—started to rise and unfurl, then caught the breeze and suddenly revealed itself, as soldiers and sailors snapped their salutes and the assemblage stood as one and began to cheer. Anderson passed the halyards along, and Gillmore, Garrison, Thompson, Beecher, and the other guests at center stage took their turn at hauling Old Glory high. The band struck up "The Star-Spangled Banner," playing it slowly, in almost dirgelike time, as the stained and shot-torn ensign made its long climb. At the instant the flag reached the peak, six immense guns on the parapet started to boom a hundred-gun salute, jolting everyone with the sound, promptly answered with shorter tributes from all the fortifications in the harbor that had fired on Sumter in 1861. The explosions went on for nearly a half hour, and the rejoicing nearly that long, the air growing thick with smoke, before the crowd composed itself to resume the exercises, people certain that whatever joy later came into their lives would be inevitably compared to the drama they had just witnessed. "It was the most exciting moment of my life when that flag went up," one clergyman said; it was "the rainbow sign" that the deluge of blood had ended and "the Ark of Freedom had rested at last upon its Ararat." The only word Garrison could utter was "sublime."

Beecher followed gamely with a long address. The wind came up and rattled his pages so badly that he had to clamp his hat back on his head and hold his text with both hands. A photograph shows Garrison, seated to the speaker's left, legs extended, wearing a large campaign hat and listening attentively, and he later told Helen the discourse was "a good one." Some felt disappointed that the minister had read a speech rather than preached a sermon, and others did not think he addressed the question of citizenship emphatically enough. Beecher would never be a ground-breaker, however, and his was a task of celebration. He declared that the flag Anderson had just returned was "more and better" than when he had hauled it down because the land was purged of slavery and four million people now emancipated could claim it as their own. He pronounced the lessons of the war as "no more secession" and "no more slavery," hailed the supremacy of national government, and observed that there would be "a new dispensation" in the South which would make for an easy reconstruction that would need "neither architect, nor engineer." Leaving the fort, one of the abolitionist schoolteachers from Port Royal felt vaguely let down, but looked forward to the morrow as the truly "grand day" when Garrison would speak in Citadel Square to the black people of Charleston.

As cities, Boston and Charleston had much in common. Both lay on peninsulas between broad rivers and the sea; both had proud and insular aristocracies and traditions of civic engagement and statesmanship reaching deep into the colonial and Revolutionary eras; both had vibrant commercial economies rooted in old mercantile assumptions that had not quite kept pace with their more aggressive midcentury rivals, New York and Philadelphia, Baltimore and New Orleans. Both cherished the past and still retained an English look, with Georgian public buildings and gracefully spired churches. Yet Boston and Charleston had become the antipodes of the sectional conflict, the capital of abolition posed against the nerve center of slaveholders' sovereignty. The Grimké sisters had exiled themselves from Charleston's gracious streets and become famous in Boston's public halls. Charleston had burned mailbags full of Boston's propaganda and hung Garrison in effigy. Charleston's senator had sworn that he would call the roll of his slaves at Bunker Hill, and Boston had sent black soldiers to Charleston, where many died reviled and lay in unmarked graves.

The antagonism of decades turned to solemn awe when the visitors from the North walked Charleston's battered streets in those April days of conquest and, looking at the shattered walls and shivered glass, the toppled columns and the broken archways, spoke in hushed tones of the ruins of Nineveh and Thebes and Rome, other civilizations that had fallen in their pride. Sheaves of documents lay strewn about the courthouse floor, and worthless heaps of Confederate money littered the deserted stock exchange. The city was under military occupation; there was a curfew; black soldiers were barracked in the old citadel; businesses required licenses to open, and only those who took a loyalty oath could receive them. The upper squares near the railroad station and the black neighborhoods showed a good deal of life, but the mile-long lower part of the town—where the antebellum aristocracy had lived in unmatched elegance—seemed a ghostly place of abandoned, looted houses and gardens gone rank and wild.

Yet the visitors had come in triumph, and they would not be denied. Introducing Garrison at a festive banquet on Friday night, Theodore Tilton had quipped that the war had begun with Fort Sumter standing on a foundation of New England granite, and it would end with "South Carolina standing upon a foundation of New England ideas." The leading speaker, Judge Advocate General Joseph Holt, made a very firm declaration of the stern measures that would be required to enforce emancipation, but it was not clear how directly he spoke for the administration. In his own remarks Garrison took a more subdued approach, but one that reinforced the abolitionist definition of the war. He had come to fallen Charleston not as an enemy, he explained, but as one who had tried to save her from retribution with the demand that the oppressed go free, and he had come to witness, with the city that had reaped the whirlwind, the unfurling of the flag of a universal freedom that would be guaranteed by the Constitution.

The editor bore himself with a becoming dignity in Charleston and performed two gestures that epitomized his career in agitation. On Friday evening, en route to the banquet, he happened by the printing office of the *Charleston Courier*, long a rabid slaveholders' mouthpiece but now licensed to loyalists, and dropped in to look around. His fellow "typos" were flabbergasted and invited him to step up to the case, where he dexterously set a stickful of Beecher's address, then read it aloud three or four times (it dealt with the common religious and political heritage of the two sections) and remarked that it was "singular" that those sentiments had fallen to him. They all mused on what the printers before the war would have thought to find Garrison setting type beside them in this shop, bade farewell, and let the editor resume his tour. "Mr. Garrison did the work like one who understood his business," the *Courier* reported.

The next morning Garrison paid another call. With Thompson, Tilton, and others, he walked up to St. Philip's Church, its bells melted down for gun barrels, but its spire—so much like the stacked cupolas of Park Street Church in Boston—standing tall and unharmed. They sought the graveyard that lay between St. Philip's and the hulking ruin of a fire-stricken church in the next block. Following a narrow path among the crepe myrtle and the brambles, they came to a plain oblong brick tomb, covered with a slab of flat marble and inscribed with the single name Calhoun. They stood quietly at the great adversary's resting place for a moment, then Garrison murmured, "Down into a deeper grave than this slavery has gone, and for it there is no resurrection." A long and profound silence followed. He had, as always, hit the nail on its head.

At the typecase and at the tomb, Garrison had symbolized the core of his achievement: an absolute and unswerving confidence in his principles, a belief in the power of ideas advocated with the relentless urgency of an independent press, and a faith in the moral and religious transformation of both a people and its politics. Of very few individuals can it be said that they purged an evil from the world, but Garrison, in conjunction with others and at a dreadful cost, had done it, and what more solemn place to acknowledge it than in the graveyard where Calhoun lay buried and in the city where the Constitution he defended received its *coup de grâce*.

From the past represented in St. Philip's churchyard the editor walked into the future personified a few blocks north where thousands of black Carolinians flocked to a political rally. Organized by the propagandist James Redpath and the black abolitionist Martin Delaney, now an army officer and recruiter, the meeting had the blessing of General Rufus Saxton, the district commander most experienced in resettlement and reconstruction, and it was billed as a welcoming event for Garrison, Senator Wilson, and the other visiting dignitaries. It was, however, intended as a statement of civic intent and to impress the visiting journalists with the capacity of the black community for incorporation into the body politic. The crowd spilled so far into the side streets that Garrison could not get anywhere close to the platform until he was physically lifted onto the shoulders of the spectators and passed from one to another until he reached the stand to deafening cheers and rejoicing.

No sooner had the crowd on the square settled itself than General Saxton sent word to move the meeting to Zion's Church, a block away, since Senator Wilson was too indisposed to speak in the open air. What seemed foolishly disruptive and logistically impossible happened quickly enough, and two or three thousand people crammed themselves into the sanctuary of the large barnlike tabernacle, while hundreds of children were shepherded into ground-floor schoolrooms for a service of their own.

Seated in the pulpit, Garrison watched intently as a stately black man advanced down the aisles, accompanied by two young girls bearing a large floral wreath. His name was Samuel Dickerson, he had a reputation as a slave preacher, and he had something to say. "I have read of you," he said to the editor. "I have read of your mighty labors . . . and here is your handi- work," he said, pointing to the children at his side. They were his daughters, he explained, who had been stolen from him in slavery days, and now he stood here in gratitude to God that "through your instrumentality, under the folds of that glorious flag . . . you have restored them to me."

With moist eyes and a tremulous voice, Garrison recalled the Psalmist, "Not unto us, not unto us, but unto God be all the glory" (Ps. 115). Then he said that he had worked in the slave's cause for almost forty years, that he had hated slavery as he hated nothing else in all the world, not only as a crime and an affront to humanity, but as "the sin of sins." He had made their cause his cause, they were children of a common father, and he thanked God that they were now free. He had done all this in pursuit of justice, he said, "but I never expected to look you in the face, never supposed you would hear of anything I might do in your behalf." It was the most "un- speakably satisfying" moment of his career.

Addressing himself to the entire congregation, he made a solemn pledge that "the American Government will stand by you to establish your freedom against whatever claims your former masters will bring" and that he would demand for them, for as long God gave him "reason and strength," every- thing claimed "for the whitest of the white in this country."

There is no way of knowing how, for the first time in his life, Garrison came to speak in the government's name, unless he meant it as an imperative he would demand, but the political speakers who followed—Senator Wilson of Massachusetts and Congressman William Kelley of Pennsylvania—also spoke most emphatically of government protection, of black citizenship, of the people's preference for "a loyal black man [over] a white traitor." Amid homilies about the great dream of self-improvement (Wilson, Kelley, Gar- rison, and Lincoln, it was pointed out, were all self-made men) and the need to refute those who disparaged black ability, Wilson drew an explicit analogy. Just as black soldiers had proved themselves with the bayonet, so would the liberated slaves "use the ballot in the cause we have maintained." The visitors had come to celebrate the flag on Friday, but on Saturday they set the agenda for Reconstruction in Zion's Church. The congregation rose to sing "Roll, Jordan, Roll," and poured out of the building in a mighty stream that flowed for a mile down Meeting Street and bore the guests to their lodgings.

A bulletin came later that afternoon that George Garrison's company had just returned from an inland mission, and the editor hurried three miles out of the city to the 55th Mass. encampment for a reunion with his son. Taller, he seemed, weather-worn and wiser, too, but ready for a rest; he would be granted thirty days' leave to return home with his father. George's company had spent the last month bringing the word of freedom to plantations along the Cooper River. Masters had abandoned many places; at some the able-bodied had long gone to soldiering; at others overseers were ordered to summon the people and deliver the news. Some people grabbed their bundles to join the march back to the city, others guided the soldiers to hidden valuables and fodder and allowed that they would be all right in place with their cabins and their gardens.

On his last mission, George had gone out into the country to help rescue ex-slaves who found themselves lost and homeless in the wake of Sherman's march, uprooted from their plantations but vulnerable to the murderous animosity of diehard rebel guerrillas. Gradually the refugee train had stretched longer than a mile, as more than twelve hundred people joined the exodus. They drove everything from one-mule carts and four-ox wagons to creaking plantation wagons hauled by spavined horses in patched and pegged-up harnesses, every conveyance piled high with feather beds, tinware, cooking pots, farm tools, and dozens of children too small to walk. The 55th Mass. safely brought the procession into the sanctuary it maintained at Rickersville, where the editor visited on April 15. In the faces of the refugees Garrison could see the wretchedness of the slavery they had shed not more than days or weeks before. Some of the officers told the people that Garrison was their friend, and there were expressions of affection and gratitude, but the exchange was deeply unsettling. When the editor, in parting, said, "Well, my friends, you are free at last—let us give three cheers for freedom," they stared at him in numb wonder. The editor led off the first cheer, but there was no response. He gave a second, and a third—alone—then waved and walked away.

A great human drama—the birth of a free people—had begun in the war-torn South, and in his few days in Charleston the editor had seen various manifestations of it. In the plantation lowlands near Hilton Head, in a region under military occupation for most of the war, he had seen the first fruits of reconstruction in a model village, built with government supplies, in which black people had directed the work, organized their land and crops, and taken on a civic life. Whether they could hold on to what they had achieved when the former owners of the land (and the people) returned to make their claims remained an open question. In Charleston, also under occupation but a lighter one, a multifaceted black community, composed of skilled workers who had either hired out as slaves or won their freedom long before, had a semi-autonomous tradition and a structure of leadership, as represented in Zion's Church, originally sponsored by white missionaries but taken over and directed by the largely black congregation itself. In the countryside, however, as epitomized in George's camp, conditions were far more grim and unsettled, especially in areas still in combat. More than half a million black people had seized their own freedom by running away to the Union lines over the course of the war, and as the conquering troops spread over more and more territory, those people who had stayed at home gained the chance to assert themselves. For the liberated slaves in refugee camps, there would have to be a long process of resettlement; for those who remained in place, there would be challenges of adjustment and adaptation with their former masters; for all, there would be the assumption of civil rights for self-protection and common governance. Lincoln had declared the slaves free and made the national commitment to a revolutionary transformation, but it was not an abstract or automatic process. It had happened with the sword or without it, with the consent of the owners and without it, by running away or staying put. In the midst of a war of conquest and the creation of a powerful new national government, chattels had taken freedom for themselves.

Garrison had looked into the face of freedom and had promised to protect it and enlarge it. He went to bed that night in Charleston believing that he had played a leading role in the moral pageant that had closed the war and pointed the way to a righteous peace. He did not yet know that Fate, the universal dramatist, had composed a different ending. Early that morning, while the editor had communed at Calhoun's grave, Abraham Lincoln had breathed his last and become abolition's final and greatest martyr.

CHAPTER TWENTY-FOUR

MY VOCATION HAS ENDED

"NO ONE KNOWS WHAT TO SAY OR DO," BRADFORD DREW WROTE IN HIS DIARY ON THE MORNING AFTER LINCOLN'S ASSASSINATION, HAVING FIRST CAREFULLY INKED A MOURNFUL BLACK BORDER AROUND THE PAGE. THE newspapers, including *The Liberator,* lined their columns with black rules as well, but there was no shortage of words to remark the unprecedented public sadness and lamentation. As was said of Wilberforce, Agent May wrote in *The Liberator,* the president "has gone up to the bar of God with millions of broken fetters in his hand." All seemed to regard Lincoln's murder as the last vengeful act of the vanquished slave power and, as Garrison's friend Charles K. Whipple put it, a lethal blow from the same arm that had wounded Sumner in the Senate nine long years before. The editor himself received the news on the southward-bound *Arago,* heading for visits to Beaufort and Savannah, but the vessel reversed course immediately. The passengers transferred at Hilton Head to a fast government steamer that brought them into New York by Friday, April 21, in time for Henry Ward Beecher to preach a eulogy in his Brooklyn pulpit on Sunday, but not in time for Garrison to attend Boston's memorial meeting at Faneuil Hall. There Wendell Phillips, with bland disregard for his vehement dissent in the 1864 campaign, praised Lincoln's presidency as "the natural growth of democratic institutions" and rejoiced that "he sleeps in the blessings of the poor." Other abolitionists spoke with greater frankness about their ambivalence. Lydia Maria Child told *The Independent* that she had sworn after Lincoln's First Inaugural Address that she would never forgive him, but found herself unable to keep such an "un-Christian vow." Year by year the president had gained her respect and confidence, she allowed, and although his deficiencies "sorely tried the patience of radicals," she now considered him "a gift from providence" whose addresses at Gettysburg and the second inauguration had a "simplicity" that approached the "sublime."

Although Garrison came so late to the eulogies that he felt there was nothing left to say, he remained the only public figure candid enough to recapitulate in detail the excruciatingly circumspect approach Lincoln had taken toward an emancipation policy. Lincoln could not be judged as "either a philanthropist or a reformer," the editor said pointedly, but within his chosen sphere of politics "no man ever did so large a business on so small a capital in the service of freedom and humanity. . . ." From the day the president had issued the Emancipation Proclamation, Garrison declared, Lincoln had grown "in grace and knowledge" and had understood "that he was to be an instrument in the hand of God to bring about great and glorious ends." The passage about retributive justice in Lincoln's "grandly phenomenal" Second Inaugural Address deserved "to be written in starry letters upon the sky," and since it expressed his own understanding of the war the editor quoted it in full:

> If we shall suppose that American slavery is one of those offenses which, in the Providence of God, must needs come, but which, having continued through His appointed time, He now wills to remove, and that He gives to both North and South this terrible war as the woe due to those by whom the offense came, shall we discern there is any departure from those divine attributes which the believers in a living God always attribute to him? Fondly do we hope, fervently do we pray that this mighty scourge of war may speedily pass away. Yet, if God wills that it continue until all the wealth piled by the bondmen in two hundred and fifty years of unrequited toil shall be sunk, and until every drop of blood drawn with the lash shall be paid by another drawn with the sword—as was said three thousand years ago so it still must be said, that the judgments of the Lord are true and righteous altogether.

Lincoln, it seemed to Garrison, had written his own best epitaph.

Three weeks after the president's funeral procession filled New York's Broadway with thousands of mourners, Garrison walked down the thoroughfare to his last meeting of the American Anti-Slavery Society. The Sumter celebration had ended the war; he had already announced that he would stop publication of *The Liberator* at the end of 1865, confident that the Thirteenth Amendment would be fully ratified in time to make his newspaper's thirty-five volumes a complete record of the antislavery agitation; the dissolution of the AAS would mark the accomplishment of its special work as an abolitionist organization. He believed that these events would mark the close of a chapter: not the end of the story of American freedom or the realization of racial equality, but the end of the special task—the abolition of slavery—to which Garrison had pledged himself from the pulpit of Park Street Church in 1829, from Baltimore Jail in 1830, and from the cramped and chilly Boston garret from which he had published the first issue of *The Liberator* in 1831. He was worn out, having pushed himself on nervous energy for most of the war years; he had an invalid wife, who had nurtured him throughout the struggle, but now needed his tender care more than ever before; he had received, at last, the praise and vindication he had longed for during his decades of principled opposition; and he had instigated a revolution that, at the outset of his career, had seemed a social and political impossibility. Yet, when he walked into Dr. Cheever's Church of the Puritans that morning in May 1865, he faced not gratitude but abuse; he was told that nothing had been accomplished, that the work had just begun, that he was an old fogy, that a dissolution would violate the founding charter, and that his retirement amounted to a betrayal of black people. It would be the last fight of his life in the movement, and it would make him peripheral to the momentous political struggle of the postwar era.

The trouble stemmed directly from the fault lines exposed in the 1864 election campaign. Garrison's antagonists considered him so hopelessly in thrall to the Republican Party as to have either lost or deliberately suppressed his critical faculties, while the editor regarded the opposition as so dogmatic and fault-finding as to be squandering the best opportunity in thirty-five years to influence mainstream politics without the necessity for martyrdom or third-party machinations. Almost everything the contentious factions said in their meetings, editorials, and letters reinforced the negative views each held of the other and bred an atmosphere of distrust that made the quarrel not only unpleasant, but stubbornly irrational and not amenable to compromise. After an acrimonious session in January 1865, Agent May had termed it "the least pleasant A.S. meeting" he had ever attended, and by mid-April, after letters had flown up and down the seaboard for weeks, Oliver Johnson told May that the "incessant quarreling" had gotten to him. Dissolution was only a question of expedience, not principles, and he was ready to let the factionalists "have it all to themselves."

Garrison operated on the assumption that the wartime strategy had worked. Abolitionists had not hesitated to be critical of the Republicans and had exerted a steady moral pressure for emancipation. They had educated both public opinion and the president through nonexclusive popular leagues and petition drives. Their broad-based efforts found success in the liberation of the slaves by military conquest and the abolition of slavery by constitutional amendment. With the pulpits and the religious journals open to egalitarian views, with the radical wing of the Republican Party responsive to issues of principle, with the national press proud of its role as agents of enlightenment, it seemed both feasible and appropriate for abolitionists to "mingle with the millions" and form new agencies to lobby on the challenges of Reconstruction that did not perpetuate either the old sectarian divisions within the movement or the stigmatizing identification that had prevented cooperation with centrists during the sectional crisis.

The AAS, he pointed out, had allowed itself to decline during the war; its state and local affiliates had collapsed, its pamphleteering had stopped after 1861–62, it maintained no agents in the field, and it had issued no annual report—always a major propaganda piece in itself—since 1861. The nationalizing tendencies of the age, moreover, militated against the small-scale grassroots organizing—quarterly meetings, published resolutions, local conventions—that had filled the small-town papers and served as the backbone of the AAS agency work since 1835. The texts of speeches now crackled over the telegraph wires and could reach millions at once instead of thousands over the course of many weeks; well-established magazines, such as *The Independent, The Atlantic Monthly,* and *Harper's Weekly,* had large national audiences, welcomed the work of Garrison and Phillips, Child and Douglass, and made *The Liberator* and the *National Anti-Slavery Standard* look like relics of a bygone age. The editor's bittersweet decision to discontinue *The Liberator* at the end of 1865 made both economic and political sense, although some of the critics irritated the editor enormously by insinuating that he was making a selfish, personal decision instead of considering the greater good of the movement. They had not struggled "against wind and tide" for thirty-five years to maintain his paper, he replied, and as it had begun as an independent venture, so would it end. (He might also have pointed out that with the death of Francis Jackson in November 1861, he had lost his last and most loyal benefactor.)

The AAS was a different matter, however. If Garrison had compelling personal reasons to retire, why did he want the organization to dissolve itself as well? He evidently believed that the symbolism of a mission accomplished carried a potent political message for the future. Just as his own vindication symbolized that the world could move, so did the completion of the "special work" of the AAS bear witness to the viability of moral suasion as a method for social change. To continue the agitation for equal rights under the rubric of antislavery struck him as an unfortunate solecism, a slantwise approach that would blur the focus of the new movement and narrow its potential constituency. There was precedent in the dissolution of the Anti–Corn Law League, a friend suggested, which managed to end its specific agitation without compromising the spirit of free trade.

There was something else at work, too, so fundamental to the editor's approach that he could not articulate it, and yet it contains the key to the events that unfolded. Garrison considered slavery to be a sin and the AAS to be an instrument of reformation and redemption. Reconstruction, by contrast, posed a host of vexing political issues that, for all their profundity, did not carry a theological burden. The questions were ones of desirable social policy that not only could be approached in more overtly political ways, but had to be adapted to circumstances. They were, in other words, matters of political choice, not sin and damnation. Whereas the moral imperatives of immediatism and disunion were appropriate to dramatizing the question of abolition, the complexities of Reconstruction would not so readily fit the absolutist dichotomies upon which the movement had generally proceeded. When Garrison spoke the language of political realism, his opponents thought they heard the accents of partisan expediency; when they articulated absolute principles for purposes of agitation, he heard a sectarian demand for purity that threatened to abandon hard-won ground and make the movement more isolated than it needed to be. The editor evidently did not think that the AAS—given its history and its makeup—could approach the issues of Reconstruction with the intellectual and tactical flexibility that they required.

Yet for as keen a student of dramaturgy and symbolism as Garrison had been throughout the struggle, he disabled himself badly in this last fight. Not only had he already announced his intention to discontinue *The Liberator* and resign the AAS presidency, which put him beyond the reach of compromise, but the only new symbol he offered was the spectacle of himself as a vindicated prophet. If he had proposed the formation of a "Universal Suffrage Association" or an "Equal Rights League," he might at least have underscored his continuing commitment to the issues, but of course the editor's whole point was that new organizations would grow from new coalitions and it was not his intention to be a founder again. His vagueness, however, did leave him vulnerable to the charge that he had forsaken the necessity of a continuing agenda.

Garrison might well have abdicated in favor of Wendell Phillips had the latter's poor political judgment in 1864 not alienated the editor and made him fear for the success of an organization under so erratic and impulsive a leader. The editor also feared that Phillips saw the AAS preeminently as a platform for his own inspired advocacy rather than an organization with a variety of programs and concerns for building a constituency for reform. Phillips might have helped Garrison to withdraw from the organization without insisting that it be dissolved if he, in turn, had not become convinced that the editor had turned apostate and needed to be rebuked.

Were there issues beyond the editor's support for Lincoln in 1864 that had so deeply soured Phillips that he insisted upon discrediting Garrison and taking over his role as the personification of abolitionism? The two most controversial points proved to be General Banks's wartime labor regulations in Louisiana and the postwar question of whether the rebellious states could be readmitted to the Union before they granted voting rights to the former slaves. On both these issues, Garrison, in fact, had moved more slowly than Phillips and other colleagues. His fidelity to the Lincoln campaign had shown itself most tellingly in his willingness to defend the Banks apprentice-like program as a well-intentioned though not entirely successful first step in coping with conditions of terrible hardship and disorder. He had also, in 1864, hesitated briefly upon the question of immediate enfranchisement, drawing the traditional distinction between the protection of universal personal rights to conscience, property, and due process and the granting by social convention of rights, such as voting, to certain classes of people. Two questions gave him pause: the daunting problem of granting the vote to people so badly disadvantaged by slavery and the constitutional problem that in the old federal system the matter of voting rights had been left to the states.

By the end of the war, however, Garrison had fully endorsed the idea of universal suffrage. The problems of illiteracy and the other disabilities of slavery could be remedied with a large-scale freedmen's relief effort, he thought, and the constitutional issues would have to be met as part of the national Reconstruction that the war had set in motion. The only point on which he differed with Phillips in the first six months of 1865 concerned the question of whether or not the states should be readmitted before they had instituted black suffrage. Lincoln's first draft of a Reconstruction policy had envisioned a quick restoration with few impositions by conquest (acceptance of the Thirteenth Amendment being one), but if that proved unsound, Garrison was certain that the Republican Party could be moved to a more stringent policy. As for the constitutional process by which racial equality in voting might be achieved, Garrison had qualms about imposing on the seceded states by presidential regulation a policy that also had great implications for the loyal states, where ninety-three percent of the regional black population remained disenfranchised. Partisans of equal rights should contend for a constitutional amendment, he argued, that would make electoral conditions uniform and nondiscriminatory throughout the country, and not press for a policy in Louisiana that it refused to impose on Connecticut.

There was nothing simple about Reconstruction. Phillips contended that the army had made a pathway for him to reach Louisiana, whereas the way to Connecticut was blocked by the constitution and politics, and that he would therefore go where he could. The attitude of conquest and swagger, however, offended Garrison, who regarded Reconstruction as the opportunity to regenerate the constitutional framework or, as he put it in language borrowed from Milton, to "have a soul created . . . under the ribs of death." In the polemical warfare the editor was nonetheless said to favor admitting Louisiana on the same discriminatory basis as Connecticut, which seriously distorted his intentions.

If the war had annulled the covenant, then the remaking of the Constitution became the highest piece of national business. With Congress in adjournment until December 1865, an opportunity existed for a continuation of the presidential leadership that Lincoln had demonstrated with the Thirteenth Amendment. Would his successor, Andrew Johnson, the War Democrat and Unionist governor of Tennessee placed on the ticket for his border-state appeal, be adequate to the task? Garrison, four weeks into the new president's tenure, was not as ready as Phillips to make a wholesale condemnation. Johnson had distinguished himself for firmness and courage during the war, had supported the recruitment of black soldiers, and professed a deep opposition to the slaveholding aristocrats of the old regime. Phillips distrusted him because he appeared to be continuing Lincoln's lenient policy of readmission, and within six months, Garrison lost confidence in Johnson because he lacked Lincoln's deep moralism, had proved stubborn and unyielding in the face of criticism, and had demonstrated his reversion to the antebellum Democratic credo of states' rights and white supremacy. Instead of the creative tension between Lincoln and the Radical Republicans, there developed one of the most vicious power struggles of the century between an accidental president who, like John Tyler, tried to build a coalition to reverse his predecessor and a Congress bent upon a radical Reconstruction that the president opposed. Yet the editor's failure to discern this pessimistic scenario from the outset hardly amounted to a repudiation of the cause; he may have been wrong about Johnson, as he admitted by calling for his impeachment in February 1866, more than two years before it occurred, but he was not so wrong in May 1865 to think that the wartime political process might still be a workable framework for reform. Phillips was loud and bellicose in his denunciation of Johnson from the outset, but when the president did commit overt offenses—his veto of the Freedman's Bureau, his opposition to guarantees of suffrage and citizenship, his indulgence of the intimidation and violence directed against black people in the South— that deserved abolitionist condemnation and dismissal, Phillips had no choice but to oppose him, in the same way that Garrison did, within parameters devised by the Radical Republicans.

If the ground on specific matters of policy shifted so rapidly and offered no fair litmus test for heresy or radicalism, why did Garrison become identified as an apostate? The editor and his friends considered it the culmination of the long vendetta conducted by Pillsbury and the Fosters, now intensified by the influence and weight of the disgruntled Phillips. Garrison had changed, but the alteration had occurred in the late 1850s and they had mistrusted it then and ever since. They would not accept his effort to outline a discriminating middle ground. They pushed him into a closer identification with the Republicans than he intended, which did not hamper him on the ascendant curve of the party's acquisition of power and response to the war, but in the complexity of postwar politics it made him more vulnerable to attack. The editor's proposal for dissolution, given the Manichaean tendency of abolitionist thought and the colossal problem of Reconstruction, led to an unfortunate polarization.

In part, it was, as always, a question of temperaments. Garrison believed in the inevitability of progress; his critics—recalling the European failures of 1848—decided that revolutions could indeed go backward. Garrison believed that the satisfaction of a job well done would breed confidence for attacking the next; his critics feared the onset of complacency and a collapse of energy. Garrison believed that this could be countered by inspired leadership and a new vision of the tasks to be accomplished; his critics believed that "the freshness of fanaticism" required exhortation and harangue about the tasks left undone.

Ultimately the debate turned on the question of whether or not the AAS had, in fact, completed its "special work" of abolishing slavery. For Garrison this was a self-evident truth. The war had annulled the covenant with death, Lincoln's proclamation had made emancipation a goal of the war, and the Thirteenth Amendment had translated the military liberation into a constitutional mandate that none could deny. Phillips and the critics were not so sure; the death of Chief Justice Chase and a Democratic victory in 1868 might lead to an effort of revocation, they predicted, and the AAS would have to remain vigilant.

In practical terms, the critics went on, much work remained undone to secure the rights and working conditions of black people in the South, and until that was accomplished, the slaves could hardly be said to be free. Had not the AAS pledged itself to the "elevation of free people of color" in its declaration of 1833? Was that not a sufficient mandate to continue in existence? This argument infuriated Garrison in two ways. He had written the charter and knew well that immediate abolition and civil equality went hand in hand, but the huge first task had received precedence and taken nearly a lifetime to accomplish, and the second task now had to be addressed, he thought, in a manner appropriate to the circumstances, even if that meant letting go of the organization. More profoundly, however, the editor thought no good could come of disparaging emancipation as a hollow act. Granted that it imposed a new set of social and political challenges, it nonetheless represented the advent of light for darkness, the fulfillment of a dream and a promise against the nightmare of oppression and the denial of opportunity. Surely when Frederick Douglass crossed safely into Pennsylvania and secured a job in New Bedford, he believed that he had achieved something that he had never had before, Garrison said with some asperity, and it was a great disservice, and an unfair reproach to the entire abolitionist phalanx, to pretend otherwise. Furthermore, there was no need for it. The mandate for justice was too strong, the coalition committed to it too broad, the participants in the job too numerous for the AAS to continue to set itself up as the agency with a unique mission to bring an immoral people to their duty. Douglass had done the subsequent work of making something of his freedom himself, Garrison argued, whereas the millions of black people in the South would be aided by a host of organizations in the North, by a temporary military presence in the South and the newly created government bureau for resettlement, and by the long political process of reconstituting the government. Abolitionists had much work to do, especially in the realms of education and philanthropy, he thought, but they could take up the burden in the context of a transformed public opinion. Since advocates of civil rights still had to confront the persistence of prejudice within the loyal states, moreover, it would be even more preferable to work within the enlarged stream of enlightened opinion rather than stand aloof in condemnation of everyone but themselves.

However much sense Garrison's strategy made, it nonetheless required abolitionists to give up an institutional identity that they held dear, and although the editor seemed ready to do it, as did his closest associates—Johnson, Quincy, Chapman, McKim, Wright, May—there were many others—such as Mary Grew, Sallie Holley, and Aaron Powell—not affiliated with the perennial critics, who did not see the harm of maintaining at least the symbolism of the old organization and its commitments. The editor had found a moderate constituency during the war and, in the process, sacrificed his ability to lead his more radical colleagues. In the end they repudiated his motion to dissolve the AAS by a vote of 118–48. He declined a pro forma offer to remain as its president and let the office pass to Wendell Phillips, saying pointedly that he had taken the office when it was highly unpopular to hold it and saw no need to keep it now that it had become a popular post. "My vocation, as an Abolitionist, thank God, has ended," he said, and went home to Boston.

"So be it," he told Helen. "I regard the whole thing as ridiculous." It was a wound, part gratuitous and part self-inflicted, that hurt deeply and would fester for years. He paid close attention to the calendar, however, and as the cycle came around, he always managed to tell someone that he was *not* going to the next set of meetings. Maria Chapman told him sourly that the sessions now featured "Anna Dickinson and W. P. swearing by each other as the greatest man and woman of the 19th century."

For the remainder of 1865 Garrison conducted *The Liberator* exactly as he always had. He devoted nearly a month's worth of issues to the climactic set of debates and the valedictory editorials that followed from Johnson and Quincy as they relinquished the *Standard* to Parker Pillsbury. He published articles and letters from a variety of sources on the suffrage question that by the end of the year pointed to a general argument that racial discrimination in voting had to be ended in the North and the franchise had to be extended to blacks in the reconstructed states before readmission. (Most of the material came not from the AAS but from an independent effort by George Stearns, who spent thousands of dollars putting half a million pages of pamphlets into circulation. Stearns also put together a partnership to underwrite a new journal of opinion, *The Nation,* which would be headed by a British-born editor, Edwin L. Godkin, with Wendell Garrison as his assistant. Capitalization for the new venture ran more than $100,000.)

The Liberator followed the fall campaigns to remove restrictions against black voters in Connecticut, Minnesota, and Wisconsin, and from the failure of the referenda Garrison realized that the task of rallying Northern opinion in support of black suffrage would be more formidable, and take longer, than anybody had thought. He also devoted considerable space and effort to the unification of the various private agencies and commissions to organize aid to freemen by raising money to relieve poverty and develop an education system staffed by Yankee volunteers. Phillips derided such work as "an old clothes movement," but Garrison considered it the kind of benevolent work that had important political concomitants, and he would not be deterred. "Knowledge is power," he said of the Freedman's Commission work that had organized by December 1865 more than seven hundred schools, with twelve hundred teachers to serve seventy thousand pupils. He seemed oblivious, however, to both the potential for community organizing and the problems of missionary-style paternalism inherent in the dispatch of outside teachers; he regarded the project as the first step toward the self-advancement that would eventually obliterate racial distinctions.

Garrison found himself "longing for rest, but willing to toil." He complained frequently about feeling foggily confused and jaded in the wearied state that he described as "flabby-dabby." He underwent a series of tooth extractions in July 1865 that left him struggling for months with an ill-fitting temporary dental plate, and he fretted endlessly about Helen's disability, especially when a course of highly touted electromagnetic treatments did little to strengthen his wife's weakened limbs. He also had begun to realize how hard it would be to discontinue *The Liberator*, and he had begun to worry about what he would do without the newspaper to give order to his days and significance to his labor.

In the midst of such travail, he found himself disturbed by the news that Fanny had agreed to marry Henry Villard. Of course, he said, he knew that an "interest" had developed but the "hasty and impulsive" move left him startled and worried. Villard seemed honorable, but he was of foreign birth and family, and they really knew very little about him. Even if Fanny had turned twenty-one, she was his only daughter. "My love for Fanny is so strong, and my estimate of her so high," he told Wendell candidly, "that I have not been willing to entertain the thought of her cleaving to another in this manner." Yet he had no choice but "to tenderly acquiesce," and, after a talk with Harry that cleared up the sensitive matters of family references and the editor's inability to provide a dowry, Garrison blessed the union and said that he and Helen hoped that the young couple would consider living at Rockledge until they had a more permanent plan. "We feel sure that you and Fanny were born for each other," he told his future son-in-law.

The editor had signed on with a lecture bureau for an autumn speaking tour in the midwest, but the concern went bankrupt in September 1865 and left Garrison without firm plans. He had counted on the money, however, to square *The Liberator*'s accounts, and he somewhat hastily decided to improvise a tour himself. It proved to be arduous and uncertain work that sent him rattling on trains for five weeks on a circular route that took him to Syracuse and Lockport, New York; Erie and Meadville, Pennsylvania; Warren, Akron, Cleveland, and Toledo, Ohio; Detroit, Adrian, and Hillsdale, Michigan; La Porte, Indiana; Chicago, Princeton, Springfield, and Jacksonville, Illinois; Lafayette, Indianapolis, and Richmond, Indiana; and Cincinnati and Pittsburgh, before he ended up in Philadelphia for his son Wendell's wedding to Lucy McKim. He had his pocket picked once and his trunk misdirected twice; he shivered in unheated halls and strained his eyes in dimly lit ones; he struggled to keep his shirts pressed and his mind from growing stupid with fatigue and repetition; he lost one audience to the humorist Artemus Ward, another to the actor Charles Kean, and a third to a timid YMCA director who feared a disturbance; he hated reading from a text; he feared that he would get sick and worried so about Helen that he wrote her thirteen times in thirty-four days. "How I long to get home," he told her, only nine days into the tour, though when he returned he pronounced the tour a success and declared himself convinced by the boosters' slogan " 'This is a great country.' " He made $1,400 above expenses, kept every engagement, and, he said proudly, "never missed a train."

At almost every stop he met movement veterans and people who introduced themselves as loyal subscribers to *The Liberator,* but for the most part he spoke to the respectable middle-class audiences that had shunned him in the antebellum years. In Springfield he stayed with Billy Herndon, still an enthusiast of the cosmos, and Herndon arranged an appearance before the Illinois legislature and took him to visit the temporary crypt in which Lincoln's coffin lay, still draped and festooned with mourning crepe. The guest book already contained thousands of names, the editor told Helen, and he mingled solemnly with throngs of visitors of both races.

Garrison's elastic topic, "The Past, Present, and Future of Our Country," gave him ample opportunity to reminisce about his career and the remarkable transformation of public opinion. He praised the expansive spirit of the west and linked the economic development of the country with the moral improvement he confidently expected as equal civil and educational rights for the former slaves vanquished prejudice and produced a more soulful and righteous nation. He did not discuss Reconstruction policy in great detail, nor did he expatiate at length on freedmen's relief efforts, though he emphasized the principles of civil equality and impartial protection of the laws as the touchstones. Yet from his discussions in dozens of situations, he returned with a firm belief that public opinion favored a "thorough" Reconstruction in which the South would be held "firmly by the strong arm of the General Government until she can be safely [re]admitted by the adoption of free institutions." A "longer probation" under the "direct omnipresent power of the U.S. Government," he told Sumner, would be necessary to reform the spirit of the South, and to George W. Julian he added that "the ballot must be insisted upon . . . for the loyal blacks as a sine qua non to the recognition of state independence."

The speech, with variations, seemed to go over well, though Garrison did not have much confidence in it and considered it "crude and disjointed." The editor decided that the platform arts were not for him. "Lecturing is not to my taste," he told Helen, and admitted that "it always worries and annoys me when I speak for pay." He disliked the loss of independence that came with the need to please the sponsor and audience and much preferred the free outpourings of the heart that characterized his oratory in the movement. Even when he had delivered the same message night after night and, indeed, year after year, he had always felt the flash of righteous inspiration, adapting his remarks to immediate circumstances and never feeling jaded or dull or a failure. He thought that the new style of celebrity lecturers had a sensationalist interest in "bringing down the house," while he much preferred the satisfaction of "bringing the house up" to a higher consciousness. The fling at Wendell Phillips was unmistakable.

Suddenly the calendar had turned to December 1865, and the time had come to close out the newspaper. Garrison had wanted to record the ratification of the Thirteenth Amendment in *The Liberator,* but as with so many of the unprecedented actions flowing from the war, a controversy sprang up that threatened to deprive the editor of the justly poetic ending that he craved. The old 1861 flag Garrison had seen raised at Fort Sumter contained thirty-three stars, but during the war Congress had admitted three more states—Kansas (finally), West Virginia (the Unionist counties that had refused to secede), and Nevada (mineral-rich, population-thin, but rushed in to provide three more electoral votes for Lincoln in 1864)—so that the total number of states had grown to thirty-six. However, eleven of those states had withdrawn their representatives from Congress, waged war against national authority, and now lay occupied in the limbo of military defeat. If they had disqualified themselves from constitution-making, then ratification by nineteen of the twenty-five loyal states would be sufficient to make the amendment legal and binding. An influential line of thinking, even among many radicals, held that so solemn an alteration of the supreme law ought to be approved by three-quarters of the whole number of states, looking forward to the time (by whatever route) that the seceded states would be readmitted and the nation joined on a different premise. On the basis of twenty-five states, the amendment had gained ratification when New Hampshire had voted its approval in June; the three states carried by McClellan in 1864 had declined to ratify, and three other legislatures, in California, Oregon, and Iowa, would not meet until December or January. On the basis of thirty-six states, and assuming that the three states not yet met would ultimately ratify, it would take a minimum of four seceded states to add their approval before the measure could become part of the Constitution. A tall order, it seemed, until Andrew Johnson, continuing the work of executive leadership begun by Lincoln on this issue, made the Thirteenth Amendment a precondition of his readmission policy, and by the end of November, eight former slave states had acquiesced in the national constitutional prohibition of slavery that they had gone to war to prevent. On December 18, 1865, Secretary of State Seward proclaimed the Constitution so amended.

Two days later, William Lloyd Garrison tied on an apron, put Seward's statement in his copy stand, set the measure of his typestick, and reached into his case. "With our own hands," he wrote, "we have put into type this unspeakably cheering and important official announcement that, at last, the old 'covenant with death' is annulled. . . ." Following the official text, the editor of *The Liberator* launched an apostrophe to the abolitionist ideal that rang with the undiminished vigor of his youthful songs. "Hail, redeemed, regenerated America! Hail, North and South, East and West! Hail, the cause of Peace, of Liberty, of Righteousness. . . . Hail, the present. . . . Hail, the future. . . . Hail, ye ransomed millions. . . . Hail, all nations, tribes, kindreds and peoples 'made of one blood'. . . . Hail, angels in glory and spirits of the just made perfect, and tune your harps anew, singing 'Great and marvelous are thy works, Lord God Almighty. . . .' "

There would be only one more issue. Its dateline ran, "Volume XXXV, No. 52, Boston, Friday, December 29, 1865, Whole No. 1803," a set of numbers astonishing for an editor whose four previous newspapers had lasted but six months each and whose credo defied the settled wisdom of the nation. Garrison read the proofs and made up the forms as usual, though he allowed Winchell Yerrinton to insert some of the congratulatory letters that filled the editorial page, while he completed his farewell address for the two columns that remained. He began by reaching back to 1831 to reprint the burning resolves of his first issue; then he launched into a review of his passage from being one of the youngest editors in the country to being, next to Mr. Bryant of the *New York Evening Post,* "the oldest, not in years, but in continuous service." He reiterated his pride at having conducted a journal more open to the words of his opponents than any before him and insisted that no other newspaper in the country had gone beyond his in advocating the equality of human rights. He had founded his newspaper to exterminate chattel slavery, and with that task accomplished, he said, it seemed appropriate to "let its existence cover the historic period of the great struggle." Garrison affirmed, however, that he saw "a mighty work of enlightenment and regeneration yet to be accomplished at the South, and many cruel wrongs done to the freedmen yet to be redressed." He expressed himself "most happy" not to be "in conflict" anymore with the mass of his countrymen on the subject of slavery, but took satisfaction in having been "in a minority of one with God" so long as the multitude insisted upon doing evil. With a grateful heart he took leave of his faithful subscribers, feeling the poignancy of losing their "weekly method of communicating with each other," but confident that they still shared their principles and cherished the same hopes for the future.

The editor set the final paragraph himself, tied it off, and carried it to the ancient slate imposing table—the printer's "stand" that had traveled with him from Merchants' Hall to Cornhill to Washington Street (and that now reposes in the Massachusetts Historical Society)—where he transferred it to the vacant place in the column. He pulled one last proof and declared the form ready to lock up. Darkness had fallen outside, and the gas lamps gave a twilight glow to the last moment. While the senior Yerrinton fiddled with the make-ready, his son Winchell looked sadly at George and Frank Garrison, who turned with a sense of bereavement toward their father, who was smiling. He never was anything but cheerful at the end of a good day's work, and he always smiled when he put his newspaper to bed, even now, when it would be forever. The men shook hands, and while the others stood forlornly, the editor of *The Liberator* got his coat and announced that he was off to a meeting of a freedmen's relief group, "his face," as Frank wrote later, "towards the resurrection and the life of Freedom."

For weeks afterward the tributes flowed in. Editors recognized the stern conscience and single-hearted devotion that had distinguished their colleague's achievement. Maria Child in *The Independent* spoke for the old apostles in declaring that *The Liberator,* having kept faith with freedom, "has finished its course, and impartial posterity will award to it a crown of righteousness." One reader called the newspaper "a perpetual Quaker meeting where each spoke as the spirit moved him," and many more wrote to thank Garrison, not only for his service, but for the role *The Liberator* had played in their own moral and spiritual growth. Brad Drew mused on the inspiration that the newspaper had brought during the darkest days of slavery's reign and swore that if he lived to be one hundred, he would never forget the impression made on him as a small child by the picture of the auction block in the title banner. Harriet Beecher Stowe mourned the passing of "a staunch and faithful friend," though a leading minister contended that *The Liberator* had not died, but rather was "translated" and had disappeared in the light of its own victory. From Tennessee an army officer asked for a copy of the last issue "as a relic . . . that our tale is true." Without such proofs, he said, future generations would never believe "that there was once such a thing as slavery."

For thirty-five years Garrison had persisted, for eighteen hundred issues, week in and week out, and his newspaper became the correlative of his tenacity. *The Liberator* never changed. Its page grew larger but its layout and typeface remained the same. Save for the banner, it never contained graphic art, never added amusing features, never abandoned the country almanac formula of squibs and flings and curiosities, and never varied its tone of high purpose and propulsive movement. Its poetry hardly qualified as art; its literary criticism remained patchy and unsophisticated; its polemical exchanges ran on too long. For all its faults, *The Liberator* became an institution that offered far more than Garrison's adamant soliloquies; it made manifest an editorial vision, an animated sense of possibility, a collective statement of the freedom to be won in lives of faithful obedience to conscience. His paper was a portrait of the community of reformers at work. People liked to say *The Liberator* was "a terror to evil-doers," but it was also, to complete the phrase and to understand the full nature of its genius, "a praise to them that do well."

New Year's Day 1866 found Garrison at his desk engaged in the customary task of settling his household accounts and sending annual greetings to a select company of friends. He could not quite close *The Liberator*'s books. Subscription money trickled in from places as far away as San Francisco for two and a half months; the big ledger in the Boston Public Library still has a blotter placed on the final entry page, March 8, 1866, that records $3.50 received from Josepheus Harris of Boston. The editor could not bring himself to write many letters either, for he felt debilitated by the loss he had steadfastly refused to acknowledge at the press a few days before.

He forced himself to write three brief notes. One reflected upon his deep ties of craft and friendship with James B. Yerrinton. "The little printing office has daily brought us together, and enabled us to know each other as intimately as it is possible," Garrison wrote. He wanted to acknowledge, first, "the unfailing good temper and kindness of spirit" the printer had manifested through twenty-five years of "the annoyances and perplexities" attendant upon the newspaper trade and, next, the "liveliest interest" Yerrinton had taken in the paper's principles that made his work more than "a mere mechanical performance." The second note similarly recognized Winchell Yerrinton, whom Garrison had known since he was a little boy, and whose contributions at the paper and as a reporter of speeches, the editor declared, made him "a public benefactor."

The third and final note went to Wendell Phillips. Warmly and forthrightly Garrison renewed his expressions of gratitude for the "numerous acts of kindness, and the generous pecuniary aid you have rendered to me and mine, through so many years of personal friendship and anti-slavery cooperation." Phillips, he said, had helped to sustain the editor's labors, put a roof over his head, keep the wolf from the door, and shape his namesake's destiny by sending Wendell to Harvard. "Though, my dear P., you and I have differed somewhat in our judgment of the bearing of events and the action of public men upon that cause which has been equally dear to our hearts," Garrison wrote, he felt comforted in the secure belief that they still shared the same commitment to "equal and exact justice" and he hoped that their friendship would remain "as perpetual as sun, moon and stars." He added admiring greetings for "dear and noble Ann," hoped that they would be present at Fanny's wedding, and signed himself "your affectionate and grateful friend."

Fanny Garrison married Henry Villard in the parlor at Rockledge two days later. Ellen and William stood up with them; Helen's old friend Sarah Fayerweather (the first pupil enrolled in Prudence Crandall's school) sent a huge wedding cake by express from Providence; the caterer Joshua Bell Smith, soon to be one of the first black members of the Massachusetts legislature, prepared, as a gift, an elegant luncheon for a large company that included the elders of the movement—the Quincys, the Mays, the Sewalls, and the Phillipses. The next day, from Worcester, their daughter wrote an exuberant and grateful letter to her "dearest of mothers, noblest of fathers." People called her "Mrs. Villard," she said wonderingly, "but I will always be Fanny Garrison."

In closing his newspaper, Garrison had ended his vocation as an editor and printer, and he found himself rudderless. For the first few weeks he went down to the office space *The Liberator* had shared with the MAS to collect the mail and the bundles of exchange newspapers that still came his way. From these he assiduously made clippings as if nothing had changed and kept neat fan-shaped piles of materials in the "literary" room he had fixed up in the attic at Rockledge. He would use them as best he could in his speeches and articles, but he had not fully realized how much he had depended upon the regular weekly platform his newspaper had provided.

Garrison told his family that he felt "like a hen plucked of its feathers," and it grieved Helen, who had yearned for her husband's release from toil, to see how poorly he coped with the loss of routine. "If I only had my health," she kept saying, the couple could travel together "and feel more free than ever before in our married life." Instead she felt bound to the house and her seat by the window; her hair became streaked with gray, her weight ballooned, and her spirits drooped. The editor, meanwhile, seemed determined to join her in misery. Within three months of his retirement he had taken two bad winter falls—one on the ice and one while running to catch a train—that bruised or fractured his collarbone and severely wrenched his arm. For months he experienced recurring pain that left him sleepless and unable to write, except in short spells and with much difficulty. Only the birth of their first grandchild, Ellen and Willie's Agnes, in June 1866, freshened their spirits. Helen delighted in the little "star and sunbeam," the first of the eleven grandchildren she would know, and by Christmastime the editor felt well enough to march around with the little one perched on his shoulder and declare that he felt thirty years younger.

He nevertheless worried about money. Aside from intermittent fees for lectures and articles, he had the income from a $4,000 legacy Francis Jackson had provided (a portion of which was reserved for the benefactor's namesake, Frank, to attend Harvard), and the nominal amount William and Ellen, who boarded at Rockledge, contributed to the household. The student Frank was the only nonemployed child left at home; Fanny lived in Washington, D.C., with her journalist husband; Wendell was well situated at *The Nation* and had found a place there for George as a bookkeeper; yet there still were expenses to be faced. They had a small mortgage on Rockledge, Helen's disability required help in the kitchen and carried recurring medical expenses, and while they lived frugally and had no social pretensions, prices had risen dramatically during the war and the editor's salary had not.

Faced with these pressures, but against his better judgment, Garrison signed a book contract in April 1866 with Ticknor & Fields for a two-volume history of the abolitionist struggle. He received a $2,500 advance for each book, in addition to a promised ten percent royalty; the publisher anticipated sales in the neighborhood of 25,000 sets and advertised the first installment (which would carry the story to 1850) for Christmas giving before the ink had dried on the agreement. The project was doomed from the start. The editor felt incompetent to write a history, correctly believing that he lacked perspective, yet he felt diffident about a memoir that would seem too egotistical, and after forty years of writing to the measure of a newspaper column, the thought of an endless stream of blank white paper made him frantic with worry and led him to procrastinate. He made a pass at collecting materials, and he rented a studio downtown, but he never got to work. Eventually he abandoned the project and returned the advance. By then a group of celebrated admirers, including Sumner, Wilson, Chase, and Andrew, organized a national subscription drive that by 1868 raised nearly $30,000 as a testimonial and annuity for Garrison that not only made his retirement secure but implicitly confirmed his standing with the radical wing of the Republican Party.

For all his good intentions, Garrison never managed to play an influential role in the drama of Reconstruction. Without the discipline of the weekly newspaper he did not find the means to express himself, and poor health remained a hindrance. No sooner had Garrison resoundingly declared himself against the president and in support of "thorough" Reconstruction in February 1866 than he suffered the bad falls that took him out of action for the six months that encompassed the passage of the Civil Rights Act and the drafting of the Fourteenth Amendment. Another round of illness—his own, and Frank's, who verged on consumption—led father and son to a long convalescence with the Villards in Europe from May to November 1867, during the interval that saw the initial defeat of the Fourteenth Amendment and the imposition of black voting under congressionally mandated military rule in the South. The editor did not return until the climactic showdown between president and Congress in the impeachment crisis of 1867–68, which he followed in a series of regular columns for *The Independent* that lent support to the Radical Republicans.

Reconstruction did not suit the tactics of exhortation and polarization that he knew so well. Unlike the movement to abolish slavery, which took decades of single-minded agitation simply to force the question onto the political agenda, the issues—the protection of freedom through citizenship, land, education, and the ballot—readily presented themselves. The challenges stemmed from the multiplicity of constitutional problems posed by the collapse of the old system, the legacy of bitterness and mistrust engendered by the rebellion and war, and the poisonous politics of race that made liberated black people subject to violent intimidation in the South and their white allies subject to restorationist political reprisals in the North and the west. For the partisans of equal justice the perplexity came in deciding whether the agenda could best be pursued through executive action or congressional legislation, whether additional constitutional amendments would be necessary to insulate policies from later reversal, and whether the desired protection for the rights of former slaves could be attained through a rejuvenated political process in the South or imposed as a conqueror's peace, either as the political prerequisites for readmission or under the promulgated rules of a military occupation. The polarization, in other words, already existed, and the problem became one of choosing the surest and most manageable way to take advantage of it.

For the Republican Party, the medium through which these questions had to be filtered, two underlying questions recurred and dominated: how much change public opinion would bear and how long the party could maintain itself before being overtaken by a reconstructed national Democratic Party bent on restoring the old Union on a nonslave but thoroughly white supremacist basis. Put another way, this question became one of whether to broaden the party's base with black voters in the South and risk losing its most conservative and racist voters in the North, or to take a partial victory as a promissory note and expand the party's strength on the basis of other issues, such as national finance and postwar economic development.

This was the old antislavery political dilemma of the 1850s, but with a significant difference. The South remained temporarily out of the Union, which meant that the Republicans had a historic but brief moment in which to rewrite the rules and consolidate the political revolution begun by the war. How such changes would further the civic revival or moral refounding of the nation anticipated by the old abolitionists and many Radical Republicans became the question of most urgent concern, but it was one susceptible only to political rather than ideological solutions. Having staked out voting rights for the former slaves as the indispensable precondition for readmission, the old apostles could only reiterate the principle and condemn as missteps or cheer as progress the partial measures by which the Republican majority gradually approached the goal.

The second great principle of Reconstruction—land reform—never got past the talking stage. Phillips and others, including some Radical Republicans, spoke forcibly about the destruction of the old slaveholding aristocracy and the redistribution of land, but beyond the protection of some titles to confiscated plantations worked out by the Freedman's Bureau, the land issue—the mythical promise of "forty acres and a mule"—did not register on the congressional agenda. Garrison, as usual, concentrated upon the constitutional issues and took scant interest in economic matters, assuming that under conditions of political equality blacks as well as whites could make opportunities for themselves in a laissez-faire economy. Similarly, he paid little attention to the stirrings of organized protest intended to gain greater bargaining power for Northern industrial workers in the war-induced centralizing economy. He did, however, in 1866, endorse the movement for an eight-hour day and told its organizers that he supported measures to improve the conditions of "all overtasked working classes, without regard to complexion or race."

In the absence of a new, broad-based civil rights organization, Garrison comfortably blended in with the Radical Republicans and moved at their pace, just as his critics had predicted, but the critics in turn found themselves unable to move more quickly, which made them even more shrill and despairing. Phillips often acted as if he could single-handedly split or defeat a Republican Party insufficiently responsive to his demands, but most of his followers recognized that course as both impossible and unwise. For all his impressive thunder, Phillips found himself in the political bind of having to accept the half-loaves he had vigorously condemned as more dangerous than no bread at all. Garrison willingly accepted the paradigm of practical politics, and Phillips found himself unwillingly bound by it. He had believed himself Garrison's successor in agitation—and in the 1870s he would develop a radical economic program that challenged many prevailing assumptions about the social order—but on the pressing civil rights issues for which he insisted upon preserving the AAS, he did not exercise the commanding position that he anticipated. Garrison's true successors in the agitation of the broad constitutional issues turned out to be the radical women, Elizabeth Cady Stanton and Susan B. Anthony, who broke with abolitionism and laid the foundation for a very different feminist movement that they would bring to fruition in the early twentieth century.

The controversy unfolded from an earnest attempt to remedy one grievous wrong without foreclosing future attention to another wrong. Congressional policy in 1866 simultaneously addressed the two most glaring constitutional anomalies created by the abolition of slavery: the holding in the *Dred Scott* decision that black people could not be citizens and the clause (Article I, Section 2) that allowed three-fifths of the chattel slaves in a state to be included in the population count that determined the size of a state's delegation in Congress. With the partially reconstructed Southern states bent on passing "black codes" that greatly restricted the freed population's labor, mobility, and status at law, and violence already on the rise against the former slaves in many localities, it seemed imperative that the national government secure their personal rights to make contracts, to have access to the courts to enforce the payment of wages and the protections of due process and habeas corpus, and to protest racial discrimination with the traditional rights of freedom of speech, press, assembly, and petition. This was done first in a statutory definition of citizenship and civil rights (vetoed by President Johnson and overridden by Congress) and then, for greater security, in Section 1 of the omnibus proposal that became the Fourteenth Amendment. Because the statement has become the fundament of twentieth-century antidiscrimination policy, it deserves full quotation:

> All persons born or naturalized in the United States, and subject to the jurisdiction thereof, are citizens of the United States and of the State wherein they reside. No State shall make or enforce any law which shall abridge the privileges or immunities of citizens of the United States; nor shall any State deprive any person of life, liberty, or property, without due process of law; nor deny to any person within its jurisdiction the equal protection of the laws.

This statement not only superseded *Dred Scott* but consolidated the abolitionists' victory in the Civil War by creating a national guarantee of equality before the law that could be enforced against the states in the federal courts even after Congress changed hands or the military no longer occupied the South. It drew out and made explicit what abolitionists like Garrison had thought implicit in the Thirteenth Amendment, and it so completely represented the consensus of opinion that it occasioned relatively little debate in the North. Because Section 1, however, did not include a protection for voting rights, the one principle upon which the Republicans remained deeply divided, Wendell Phillips denounced the Fourteenth Amendment as a "swindle" that would permit reentry of the South on less than satisfactory terms, and he pledged himself to its defeat.

The second section of the amendment addressed the issue of congressional representation and aroused more controversy and opposition. Abolition of slavery had created the startling constitutional result that the Southern states would gain sixteen seats in Congress because free black people would be counted equally with whites instead of at the former three-fifths rate for slaves. Such a windfall, in combination with the broad amnesty proposed by President Johnson, would most certainly make the Democrats the majority party once more, allowing them to take over Congress, where they might mandate compensated emancipation or repudiate the war debt, and putting them in position to win the 1868 presidential election with either Grant or Lee as their candidate. If the black population were allowed to vote, matters would be different, but their exclusion from the ballot would be inevitable unless the Republicans coerced it with national legislation, a step the moderates in the party could not bring themselves to take.

The alternative would be to come up with some device that would reduce the South's congressional delegation without having a corresponding effect in the North. To base representation upon the number of "legal voters" instead of the whole population would allow the states to control enfranchisement and would offer, in effect, a bonus for adding blacks to the rolls. It would, however, also have the effect of reducing the delegations of

Northern states with large female and foreign-born populations, unless sex and naturalization requirements were lifted. Since that approach presented problems, Congress debated a second proposal that would have excluded the entire black population from the enumeration in any state that denied the right to vote on the basis of race. That would not seriously inconvenience discriminatory Northern states with small black populations but would reduce the Southern presence in Congress. Abolitionists led by Sumner—and cheered on by Garrison—opposed such a scheme as putting an open invitation to discriminate in the Constitution and offering the crass bargain of local white autonomy for the South in exchange for Northern control of Congress. A third (and the ultimately successful) proposal tried a different tack. It assigned congressional representation upon the "whole number of persons" in each state, but mandated a reduction in the size of a state's delegation in proportion to the number of "adult male citizens" denied the suffrage. This would prevent the South from devising literacy or property tests that might be covert forms of racial discrimination, for states would still be penalized for the potential voters excluded. The clause also meant that states outside the South had an incentive to remove whatever lingering restrictions they imposed upon male suffrage. Finally, the clause meant that the only form of suffrage discrimination that would not be penalized with a reduced delegation in Congress was the denial of the ballot to women.

The Fourteenth Amendment thus combined a noble philosophical commitment to the civil equality of all persons before the law with a candid political contrivance that tacitly recognized two forms of franchise discrimination but punished only the one that directly jeopardized the Republican political ascendancy.° The measure aroused the furious opposition of President Johnson, who actively campaigned in the states against its ratification, and the middle-ground policy it represented became the platform for the Republicans in the 1866 congressional elections.

This posed a cruel dilemma for the old abolitionists in several ways. For Phillips the amendment represented a "fatal and total surrender," because he was certain that it would end the Reconstruction effort and readmit the Southern states without the imposition of black suffrage. Focused upon the ballot as the only true means of protection, he ignored entirely the civil rights protections of Section 1 and assumed that the prescriptive penalties of Section 2 would not effectively reduce the South's power. He therefore hoped that the Republicans would be defeated, and he made speeches under the slogan "Reject the Amendment, Depose the President." Yet to purge the worst evil, a white supremacist Democratic-leaning president, it would

---

°Other sections of the omnibus proposal dealt explicitly with two other political problems. Section 3 dismantled the old Southern political leadership by excluding from federal or state office any prior officeholders who had fought in the rebellion, and Section 4 barred both state and federal governments from repudiating the Union war debt, assuming the Confederate debt, or paying compensation for the loss of slaves.

be necessary to accept the lesser evil of a Republican victory, and so many of the old abolitionists told him so that by midsummer he confessed that people had no place to work except within the Republican Party. Garrison, like Sumner, was there already, having decided that the amendment was a halfway measure en route to suffrage, and worthy of support in part because of the enemies it had among "rebels and copperheads."

For abolitionists who subscribed to the principle of women's suffrage, however, the Fourteenth Amendment posed even graver problems. For the first time it would introduce the word "male" into the Constitution, and as Elizabeth Cady Stanton warned, once there it would take a century to get it out again. It was not that the amendment introduced a new form of discrimination, but that it implicitly compromised with an existing one, much as the three-fifths clause had acknowledged the reality of slavery without mentioning the word. Although Stanton had the most astute legal mind among her generation of reformers, she did not regard the inherent conflict between Sections 1 and 2 as a fruitful source of agitation and did not sense how the equal protection clause might be advantageous to women. She condemned the amendment outright as fundamentally insulting and harmful and actively campaigned against it, frequently making the overheated charge that it placed an absolute prohibition against female voting in the Constitution, which it did not. Nonetheless, her broader point could not be denied, only infuriatingly deferred.

Stanton and Susan B. Anthony directly contested the political premise of Reconstruction. They pressed the logic of constitutional annulment farther than anyone else and insisted that the question of suffrage be regarded as a truly universal one. Working from their old base in the Women's National Loyal League in fall 1865, they obtained ten thousand signatures on a petition to eliminate sex discrimination in voting. When informed by staunch friends, including Sumner and Phillips, that such a proposal could not get anywhere politically and would have to defer to "the Negro's hour," Stanton publicly questioned the preferential treatment. The disenfranchised "all make the same demand," she wrote, "and the same logic and justice which secures suffrage for one class gives it to all." Women needed to "press in through that constitutional door the moment it is opened for the admission of Sambo," she told her colleagues, arguing that "we have fairly boosted the negro over our own heads, and now we had better to remember that self-preservation is the first law of nature." In affirmative terms she argued that Reconstruction offered the opportunity for truly radical and comprehensive change, but in negative terms she contended that women were more deserving of the vote than black men. In a public letter to Phillips in December 1865, the prelude to a quarrel that would estrange her from the AAS, Stanton wrote that wrangling politicians had unjustly placed "the black man . . . far above the educated women of the country" and expressed concern that "once intrenched in all his inalienable rights," there was a significant danger that the black man would become "an added power to hold us at bay. Have not 'black male citizens' been heard to say they doubted the wisdom of extending the right of suffrage to women?" Raising the question of the two million black women in the South, moreover, she asserted that Africans would be no more generous than Saxons and declared that "it is better to be the slave of an educated white man, than that of a degraded, ignorant black one." "The real fact," added Anthony, "is that we have so long held woman's claims in abeyance to the Negro's that the naming them now is reckoned an impertinence."

Philosophically this position set Stanton and Anthony on a course that would see them break completely with abolitionism by the end of the decade and formulate a feminist basis for women's rights rooted more in attacks upon the social assumptions of patriarchy than in the mandate of natural rights. Tactically their position led them into tenuous alliances with Democrats and racists that antagonized many of the old abolitionists, females as well as males, who believed that after thirty years of struggle and four years of war, the Negro's hour had indeed struck.

An earnest and extraordinarily loving exchange between Lucy Stone and Abby Kelley Foster, both products of the Garrisonian movement and pioneers in women's advocacy, reveals the dilemma in all its poignancy. There could be no stronger example of the conflict between the politics of self-empowerment and the politics of altruism that this conversation between two abolitionist mothers about their daughters' fates. In January 1867, Stone confessed her despair at the indifference and counsels of patience she had encountered from male abolitionists and the movement's periodicals when she tried to raise the issue of women's suffrage. How could Foster give precedence to the ballot for black men alone and countenance such "strange blindness" on the part of the staunch workers who for thirty years had said "let justice be done though the heavens fall"? To Stone it seemed that the abolitionist veterans now believed that 'the nation's peril could be averted if it can be induced to accept the poor half loaf of justice for the Negro, poisoned by its lack of justice for every woman in the land—as if the application of a *universal* principle to a single class *could* suffice for the necessity of this hour!" She pleaded, "O Abby, it is a terrible mistake you are making . . . " with a cry that "a nail goes through my heart akin to that which I should feel if I saw my little daughter drowning before my eyes with no power to help her."

In her reply Foster said that from the very beginning of the struggle she believed that all her abolitionist work—including her bold claim to speak by right, not sufferance—advanced the cause of women's equality, and Garrison and Phillips both sustained her in that conviction. She conceded that they had never made a "specialty" of the woman question but pursued it as an "incidental" issue for the very reason that "the slave in this country is more deeply wronged than woman and while a nation can be so infernal as to keep him a chattel, it cannot be induced to allow political rights to woman." Arguing that thousands of ex-slaves, female and male, were still in an oppressive, violence-prone, and "unspeakably worse condition than if 'drowning,' " Foster said that she would consider herself "a monster of selfishness" if she should turn from helping her neighbor's daughter to escape brutal treatment in order to secure political equality for her own. The question of woman's equality was "more comprehensive" and would take longer than their lifetimes to resolve, but "the Negro's hour" had arrived after thirty years of struggle and she felt obliged to work "until all in this country shall be secured in their humanity. . . ." "If you see a different path to pursue," Foster concluded, "I say to you today, as I said to you nearly twenty years ago, 'pursue it,' and God bless your efforts now as heretofore."

Garrison had grasped Stanton's point from the beginning and had begun to use a bracketed qualifier, "universal [male] suffrage," to indicate the practical limitation he had temporarily accepted. He also expressed, as did Phillips, his dissatisfaction with the use of the word "male" in the penalty device of the Fourteenth Amendment, but he had gone too deeply into the politics of Reconstruction to make it the touchstone of opposition that Stanton desired. He thought the cause of women's suffrage was still in its prepolitical phase of preparing the ground and believed that much would be lost and little gained by inverting the Fourteenth Amendment issue to make a moral point similar to the disunionist challenge that he had pursued for decades with respect to slavery. Stanton and Anthony had, in 1865, taken inspiration from a radical intuition that would take them years to elaborate. Phillips had an intimation of what they were getting at, and he maintained a jocular tone about it in his exchanges with Stanton, but on the immediate question of black suffrage he displayed the same pragmatism for which he criticized Garrison: one issue at a time, Phillips told Stanton; we can't have a coach with uneven wheels. He did say, however, that he would "never so ask for negro voting as to put one single obstacle" in the way of women's suffrage, though later he labored hard to keep the women's issue off the AAS agenda and out of its newspaper. Stanton condemned him as a politician who had forfeited an opportunity to be a statesman.

Though making an eloquent declaration that she "would not talk of Negroes or women, but of citizens," Stanton nonetheless fell into the single-issue fallacy by acting upon her belief that abolitionists and Republicans had chosen the wrong one. "If Mr. Garrison may judge parties by their action on slavery alone," she asked, "is it not equally fair for us to judge them by their action on woman alone?" In 1866 Stanton found congressional Democrats willing to introduce the women's suffrage petitions as a purely obstructionist tactic, and in 1867 Stanton and Anthony accepted funding from an eccentric, politically ambitious speculator named George F. Train, a Copperhead Democrat during the war who had an additionally dubious reputation as a platform quack. With Train's help, Stanton and Anthony campaigned hard for a Kansas state ballot measure on women's suffrage that the Republicans refused to endorse, while Train offended other women in the campaign, including Lucy Stone, with his outrageously racist participation in the Democrats' campaign against a Republican-sponsored ballot measure that would allow blacks to vote. Both propositions lost, and it seemed obvious to everyone but the two feminist campaigners that Train and the Democrats had used them as cat's-paws to draw off support for the black voting measure with their appeal for an "educated suffrage." Lucy Stone found herself so appalled by the episode that she went over to Abby Kelley's point of view and, without abandoning a broad-based women's rights agitation, decided that black suffrage deserved its political priority.

Undeterred, Stanton declared that in Kansas they were abandoned by the Republicans and had learned to fight alone, and a few months later accepted more of Train's money to launch their new journal, *Revolution,* with its forthright slogan "Men Their Rights and Nothing More—Women Their Rights and Nothing Less." Intent upon offering a comprehensive vision of female emancipation, Stanton promised to talk about "bread and babies" as well as the ballot and published the work of Mary Wollstonecraft along with contemporary political analysis. *Revolution* bid fair to be *The Liberator* of the incipient feminist movement, but Garrison utterly failed to appreciate it. He privately wrote a "friendly" remonstrance to Susan Anthony, an old friend and a woman whom he considered a genuine daughter of the abolitionist movement, which warned that the misalliance with Train and the Democratic Party jeopardized their "true self-respect" and brought "contempt" upon their movement. Stanton published the letter and a stinging rejoinder that expressed astonishment at having been seized by Garrison's "metaphysical tweezers" and held up as a specimen of error. She defended the association because Train, "an efficient worker," appreciated, as the Republicans so evidently did not, that "it is infinitely more important at this hour to secure the rights of 15,000,000 women, black and white, Saxon and Celt, than to bring 2,000,000 more men to the polls." The abolitionist platform had attracted some awfully strange characters in its early days, she reminded the venerable editor, and she dismissed his use of "the Negro question" litmus test as the "natural infirmity" of someone who had played such a great role in the antislavery drama. However, she said acidly, Garrison now "lags superfluous" on the stage, unaware that the "the curtain has fallen upon the last act, that the lights are extinguished, and the audience gone to their homes." Garrison did not subscribe to *Revolution,* though he kept an eye on it, and in the brewing sectarian controversy he later asked Oliver Johnson to send him a file of back issues, sub rosa in care of Willie's office, in case it became necessary to prepare a comprehensive review of the journal's "objectionable features."

The Republicans gained ground in the elections of 1866, and the swindle Phillips feared did not occur. Ten Southern states followed Andrew Johnson's lead and rejected the Fourteenth Amendment as an unjustified and unconstitutional infringement upon states rights, and as the chasm between president and Congress widened, emboldened radicals pushed through an even more thorough proposal to remodel the South politically. The Reconstruction Acts of 1867 divided the South into five military districts and directed the twenty thousand occupying troops to enroll black voters and oversee the creation of new state governments that would ratify the Fourteenth Amendment and enact black male suffrage. On the model of the previous two years, this remarkable legislative and political advance ought to have been coupled with the preparation of another constitutional amendment to protect the voting rights that Congress had initiated, but the Republicans, still divided on the black suffrage question and mindful that efforts to remove franchise discrimination in northern and western states had once again gone down to defeat, held back. Ratifying the Fourteenth Amendment, which was accomplished by July 1868, and preventing the president from undermining other portions of the civil rights program had a higher priority. Garrison, though he supported the idea of a suffrage amendment, regarded the Reconstruction Acts as a vast practical accomplishment that would transform the South county by county and legislature by legislature as black leaders, born into slavery, took the reins of free government.

This assessment, however, led to another quarrel with Phillips that revealed, in its furious preoccupation with personalities, just how inward and peripheral the old abolitionists had become. The issue this time was not ideas or organizational strategy, but money. When the editor's great friend and benefactor Francis Jackson died in 1861 he had bequeathed $10,000 "to be used to create a public sentiment in favor of putting an end to Negro slavery" and designated the inner circle of Garrison, Phillips, Foster, May, Quincy, Chapman, and several others as a board of trustees to administer the fund. Because Jackson's will was contested by his heirs on other grounds, the matter was tied up in court for years and the money did not become available until after the Thirteenth Amendment had abolished slavery. When asked in 1867 by the master in chancery for advice on how to proceed, the trustees evenly divided on the new sectarian lines, with Phillips and his allies wanting the money to underwrite the *Standard* and the suffrage campaign as the true abolition of slavery, and Garrison and his supporters eager to subsidize the freedmen's education program as the benevolent next step that surely would have attracted Francis Jackson's concern. To avoid further controversy, the editor proposed a compromise that would have awarded nearly equal amounts to each party, but after the Reconstruction Acts had established black voting and officeholders in the Southern states, Garrison reversed himself, withdrew from the compromise, and petitioned the court to direct the entire amount to education. This brought a barrage of criticism down upon Garrison, in which the terms "Iscariot" and "Arnold" were frequently used, and when the court decided in favor of Garrison, Phillips organized a campaign of such vituperation that the trustees by a 4–3 vote refused to release the money and rehashed the argument endlessly in the *Standard* with charges and rebuttals that filled five or six columns at a time. The court eventually removed the obstinate trustees and a more compliant board transferred the money to the education project, but it left the remnant of the movement in a shambles of name-calling and pettifoggery that honored no one's reputation and sent Garrison and Phillips's already cooled friendship into an icy silence.

The Fifteenth Amendment, which forbade both federal and state governments from denying or abridging the right to vote "on account of race, color, or previous condition of servitude," finally passed Congress in 1869. The failure to convict Andrew Johnson and remove him from the presidency in 1868 meant that the proposed amendment had to await the end of his term and the intervening election, which put the Republicans back into the White House with the Union's hero, General U.S. Grant, at the head of the ticket.

By the time Congress put forward the proposal, the abolitionist phalanx had fractured yet again. In 1866 the group of traditional abolitionists associated with the pre-war women's rights conventions reformed itself into the Equal Rights Association which, for a time, seemed able to shelter both the women committed first to ending racial discrimination in voting and the Stanton-Anthony agitation for an "educated universal suffrage." In 1867 the ERA did not actively oppose the Fourteenth Amendment but concentrated upon campaigns, such as the Kansas venture, to remove both race and gender barriers from state election laws. Stanton's and Anthony's challenge to the Fourteenth Amendment led them in a different direction, however, and by 1868–69 the shaky coalition had collapsed.

The abolitionist-minded women concentrated their efforts in the New England Woman Suffrage Association, led by Stone and Foster with genteel support from Julia Ward Howe, Louisa May Alcott, and prominent male abolitionists including Higginson and Garrison, which advocated the medium-term goal of women's suffrage but declared itself first in support of the pending Fifteenth Amendment. Stanton and Anthony, however, working first through *Revolution* (which lost its subsidy and collapsed in 1870) and then through a women's caucus in New York, launched the National Woman Suffrage Association, which opposed the Fifteenth Amendment unless accompanied immediately by a Sixteenth Amendment that would enfranchise women. In short order the New England group enlarged itself into the American Woman Suffrage Association, which based its agitation on the abolitionist natural rights argument, and the two organizations conducted parallel enterprises for more than twenty years until a merger was effected in the 1890s.

In this schism, a more profound division than the temperamental battle between Garrison and Phillips, the editor sided with Stone and Foster. He accepted an honorary office in their organization (AWSA) and agreed to help them for a few months in starting up a new paper, the *Woman's Journal,* that Stone would edit for a generation. The ironies abounded. As a reticent honeymooning bride, Elizabeth Cady Stanton had witnessed firsthand Garrison's dramatic protest against the exclusion of women at the London antislavery conference in 1840, and it was her husband, Henry Stanton, who had led the effort in 1839–40 to purge the editor from the AAS because he had insisted upon the linkage between abolition and women's rights. Now, in 1869–70, it was the confident, outspoken visionary Elizabeth Cady Stanton who contended that the broader issues of social and economic subordination had to be faced, and the old organization's leaders, Garrison and Kelley, who urged a practical concentration upon the single remaining point of the old crusade.

The ratification of the Fifteenth Amendment allowed Wendell Phillips and the AAS to declare their task at an end "as far as law can accomplish it," and a meeting of dissolution and celebration took place in New York on April 9, 1870. Although Mary Grew and other old friends told Garrison how grand it would be to have him join the gathering so that they might set aside all differences at least for a day of shared thanksgiving, the editor would not go to a meeting he thought should have occurred five years previously. He received in absentia two small gestures of respect, however. One speaker said that Garrison had to be acknowledged for attacking slavery in its citadel; it was Abby Kelley Foster, wearing a new dress and declaring happily that she felt as if she had lived a thousand years. Another speaker proposed that to avoid hurt feelings, people ought to refrain from referring to individuals in their remarks, but then exempted from his stricture Benjamin Lundy and William Lloyd Garrison "as the pioneers whose names America will add to the benefactors of the world." The speaker was Wendell Phillips.

Garrison had turned down invitations to speak at ratification celebrations in Baltimore, Richmond, and Vicksburg, but he did participate in a grand two-hour procession, organized by the Boston black community, that featured veterans of the 54th and 55th Massachusetts regiments and culminated with oratory at Faneuil Hall. In his speech the editor, who looked quite feeble but spoke in a strong voice, said that he felt as if he had seen "a miracle performed" and "a nation born as it were in a day." A black man, Hiram Revels, occupied Jefferson Davis's seat in the U.S. Senate, he exclaimed, and he declared that no parallel in history could be found for the "wonderful, quiet, and sudden transformation . . . from the auction block to the ballot box." He praised the names of Lincoln, Grant, and Sumner, and closed with a fervent appeal for black people to support women's right to vote.

Garrison threw himself into the women's suffrage issue with an infusion of energy that he had not demonstrated in years. He made several speaking trips—at some peril to his health, the family believed—and could always be counted on for lively statements to the conventions that he could not attend. He took the nominal post of associate editor on the *Woman's Journal* for much of 1870, wrote regularly for it over the next few years, and "improved" every opportunity to make a point. Garrison evidently had no further dealing with Stanton, but he occasionally corresponded with Anthony, declining her invitiation to launch another campaign for a Sixteenth Amendment as "quite premature." "Even as a matter of 'agitation,'" he said, "I do not think it would pay" until a "mighty primary work" had built a more enlightened and sympathetic public opinion.

Such primary work he knew how to do. In the women's rights campaign of the 1870s he acted almost as if he were back in the old days, freed of the partisan constraints that had muffled his voice during the Reconstruction controversies, and in possession of a clear and irrefutable argument that he would advance against all comers. It seemed appropriate that his affectionate reunion with Wendell Phillips and Frederick Douglass should take place in Faneuil Hall, on December 20, 1873, the hundredth anniversary of the Boston Tea Party, when all three men shared the platform at an AWSA rally organized by Lucy Stone and Abby Kelley Foster under the women's suffrage slogan "Taxation Without Representation Is Tyranny." Six months later Garrison attended, for the first time in a decade, the movement's Fourth of July picnic at Framingham, twenty years after he had burned the Fugitive Slave Law and the U.S. Constitution on that very spot. Having consigned one covenant to the flames and witnessed the revolutionary transformation of the national charter, he seemed to radiate confidence in the progress of reform.

Yet the holiday had, throughout his career, tended to be one of those occasions upon which Garrison deliberately chose to go against the grain, not only in challenging the conventional wisdom but in granting himself leave to vent his pessimism rather than press his hope. In 1876, on the centennial Fourth of July, he reflected upon the national history in a jeremiad not unlike the one he had delivered in Park Street Church nearly fifty years before. He reviewed the long-standing compromises with slavery, the national guilt incurred in the campaigns against the Indians and the war with Mexico, the lack of political equality for women, and the continuing caste prejudices that blighted the effort at political reconstruction. "If we rejoice at all," the editor warned in all his prophetic dignity, "let it be with contrite hearts that we have not been utterly consumed."

CHAPTER TWENTY-FIVE

I Miss Mr. Garrison

———— • ◆ • ————

GARRISON OUTLIVED THE MOVEMENT TO WHICH HE HAD DEVOTED HIS CAREER. THROUGHOUT THE 1870S THE EDITOR HAD TO STAND BY IN ISO-LATED OUTRAGE AS THE NATION DRIFTED AWAY FROM "OUR OLD BUT SUB-lime conflict" and into "another dark period" of compromise and corruption. The "era of moral politics" had ended, the *New York Times* said approvingly, while Wendell Phillips lamented that the abolitionists' day was slipping away. "Once let public opinion float off from the great issue of the war," he warned, and "it will take perhaps more than a generation to bring it back again."

Part of the reaction can be explained as the onset of an inevitable war-weariness and a return to the standard political preoccupation with economic policy, especially in an era that first witnessed a postwar industrial expansion of spectacular dimensions and then an equally unparalleled collapse follow-ing a financial panic in 1873. The partisan realignments occasioned by the sectional crisis and the war, when coupled with the growth of urban centers and the rise of both new money and new claimants for spoils, had redesigned the political machinery. A novel series of interlocking, well-financed "rings" now controlled candidacies and contracts at the municipal and state level and brought national politics as well into a pattern of favor-seeking, influence-peddling, graft, and corruption unmatched in the antebellum period.

In the headlong rush of enterprise and jobbery that became known as "the great barbecue" and the preoccupation with materialism that led Mark Twain to mock the decade as "the gilded age," the moralists lost out to the promoters and the cause of civil rights dwindled in significance. The Radical Republicans lost their ideological unity and fractured into competing interest groups after the passage of the Fifteenth Amendment. They could no longer mobilize majority support for the use of federal troops to protect black voters from the intimidation that Southern Democrats in cahoots with violent as-sociations such as the Ku Klux Klan and the White League increasingly employed in an effort to overturn the fledgling multiracial governments in the reconstructed states. By 1872 an influential group of "Liberal Republi-cans" had decided that only an amnesty with the South that restored the old elite to power could end the violence and permit economic development to go forward peacefully under the leadership of the "best men" of both sections. In 1875 when the beleaguered, scandal-ridden Grant administration intervened to prevent egregious violence and fraud in the Louisiana state elections, a Faneuil Hall meeting jeered Phillips as "played out" when he endeavored to defend the administration. The *New York Times* correctly observed that while men like Phillips and Garrison were "not exactly extinct," they represented ideas toward the South that the majority of Republicans had "outgrown," and *The Nation* declared that politics had passed "out of the region of the Civil War."

Garrison fought the reactionary tendencies as long as he lived. In essays for *The Independent* and open letters to the *Boston Journal* that the newspapers in New York picked up and recirculated, the old editor inveighed against the abandonment of black people and the new constitutional guarantees. In column after column he took every opportunity to attack manifestations of racism and to denounce the rising violence in the South. He also protested the U.S. Army's massacres of the Plains Indians that marked the new wave of western expansion, and he inveighed against the jingoists' efforts in 1871 to annex Santo Domingo. "Our true policy," he said then, "is to mind our own business, get rid of all egotism and self-sufficiency; crucify the passion for national aggrandizement; cultivate amicable relations with all mankind; and, finally, beat our swords into ploughshares and our spears into pruning-hooks, and learn war no more." He passionately denounced the dissident Liberal Republicans who ran Horace Greeley against the incumbent Grant in 1872, fusing with the Democrats on a platform of reconciliation with the South. Garrison regarded the venture as an expedient surrender to violence and a betrayal of the abolitionist values that Greeley, in Garrison's opinion, had never fully comprehended.

Although Grant won in a landslide and Greeley died less than a month after the election, the new mood gradually took hold. The Democrats regained control of the House in 1874 and in 1876 would have won the presidency had the electoral vote in three bitterly contested, fraud-ridden contests not been awarded to the Republican candidate, General Rutherford B. Hayes. In exchange, the new administration agreed to withdraw federal troops from the South and turned a blind eye to the violence-scarred elections that put Democratic "redeemer" state governments back in power. Garrison followed these developments with "unabated vigilance" and attacked them with undiminished vehemence, but to no avail. Once more he was a voice crying in the wilderness, no longer confident that he could rally people to a set of values they did not yet embrace, but gamely exhorting them to return to the values they once had shared. As an occasional columnist he was but one voice among many, and the contrast illuminates just how much *The Liberator* as a weekly manifestation of its editor's vision had enlarged his sphere of influence.

Garrison explained the shift in public opinion as the "melancholy" consequence of having emancipated the slaves as a response to military necessity rather than as "an act of general repentance." "Expediency on selfish grounds, and not right with reference to the claims of our common humanity, has controlled our action," he lamented in a national centennial address for the Fourth of July 1876, and this condition allowed the South to remain "insolent and brutal" to the former slaves and permitted the North to contemplate restoring "the palmy days" of the old and fatally compromised Union. Without a profound moral appreciation of "the terrible wrongs done to the colored race," Garrison told Theodore Dwight Weld, the public remained insensitive to the consequences of withdrawing federal troops from the South. Just as circumstances had led the editor to support emancipation by means he abhorred, so too did the politics of Reconstruction compel him to defend long past practicality a policy that sought to impose wholesale social change by physical coercion. Even as he did this, however, he extolled the purity of the abolitionist crusade and told its dwindling band of apostles that the nation would only progress in proportion to "our willingness to contemplate the causes of our fearful visitations" and to "study the things that make for peace." "We must give up the spirit of complexional caste," he declared, "or give up Christianity."

Once scorned but heard, now honored yet ignored, Garrison found the admixture of success and failure difficult to bear. He knew in his heart that the abolitionists had not exaggerated the wickedness of slavery, or overstated the guilt of the nation, or erred in calling for immediate emancipation and repentance. He knew, too, that they had won a great victory and righted a great wrong even though, in his waning days, the achievement seemed to be one more of form than practice. He no longer had the energy, however, to generate a new evangelical revival, nor did he have a church interested in such an enterprise or a constituency thirsting for new light. It seemed that the best that he could offer the public now was the historical inspiration of a moral crusade that had demonstrated "the efficacy of spiritual weapons against the strongholds of Satan" and would prove worthy of study for those who undertook the "innumerable" righteous battles yet to come. Yet in glorifying the fight well waged and in accepting honor as its prophetic leader, Garrison allowed self-congratulation to obscure the limitations of the abolitionist achievement and to insulate himself from the exhaustion of its spirit.

The editor took refuge in his household and fashioned a domestic routine that allowed him to remain active, feisty, and loving to the end. He and Frank walked down to the post office every morning that his rheumatic knee and the weather permitted, and at least once a week he rode the cars into Boston to visit the *Woman's Journal* office on Park Street or deliver statements to the daily papers. Whenever he had an article in a periodical he spent several hours buying up armloads of the issue and several days clipping and sending it, with a covering note, to a specially tailored list he had constructed for the occasion. He was imperious with other editors, brooking no changes in his copy or punctuation without his clearance and regularly advising them to follow his old method of vigilantly consulting their exchanges to document the abuses to which he addressed his protest. He thrived on controversy. When his son Wendell casually mentioned the importance of the movement to preserve the Old South Church from demolition, his father was ready with six specific reasons why preserving relics stifled free thought and why that particular meetinghouse, whose pastor had opposed the abolitionists for decades, had no superior standing to occupy a space that might well be used for something more progressive.

Honors still came his way. Harvard elected him to Phi Beta Kappa, and the leading reformers of Great Britain gave him a testimonial breakfast in London during his voyage of 1867 at which John Stuart Mill and John Bright hailed him as the preeminent agitator of the century. "If you aim at something noble and succeed," Mill declared, "you will generally find that you have succeeded not in that alone," and he therefore praised Garrison for emancipating not only the slaves but the American mind as well. "The whole intellect of the country has been set thinking about the fundamental questions of society and government," Mill said, marveling that the editor had saved his country from "intellectual and moral stagnation."

Some thought he merited a political reward. When Charles Sumner died in 1874, some Republican leaders bruited the editor's name as a possible successor in the Senate. "Birnam wood will come to Dunsinane" before he would be elected to the U.S. Senate, Garrison joked, but were so strange an occurrence to take place, he added, his conscientious scruples would prevent his taking the oath. He preferred to be remembered as a moralist and cooperated readily in 1869 when the popular American sculptor John Rogers asked for a week of sittings so as to include him in a sentimental group piece. *The Fugitive's Story* depicted him, with Henry Ward Beecher and John Greenleaf Whittier, listening intently to an escaped slave mother. The family thought the sculptor had made Garrison too thin and stiff, but if the editor had any reservations about having become a piece of Victorian kitsch he kept them to himself.

If anything, Garrison enjoyed his standing as an icon, for in truth it was the only political identity left him. He chose instead to cultivate the role of paterfamilias. He and Helen wrote regular weekly letters to the children who were not presently living at home, though for several years they were delighted to have the Villards at Rockledge as well as Willie and Ellen around the corner. He greeted each grandchild—there would be thirteen by the time of his death and eighteen all told—with his musty pun "Our Garrison increases." As the grandchildren grew old enough, the editor wrote them charming little notes reminiscing about his own boyhood or describing the latest misadventures of the latest household pussycat. He spent a great deal of time contriving little presents: a music box for Helen, a "chatterbox" juvenile magazine for Fanny's daughter, or newfangled adding machines for

George, who had returned to Boston to take a bookkeeper's job in Willie's firm, and Frank, who had joined the Riverside Press in Cambridge as an assistant manager. Helen and the children, in turn, made a ritual of his birthday, December 12, with gifts of photo albums, a dressing gown, or a lap robe, along with a special oyster stew, followed by ice cream and cookies and singing of the old favorites. There would be games of whist and charades and, in summers, endless rounds of croquet. A cherished family photograph shows three generations of Garrisons on the lawn at Rockledge, Fanny and her daughter seated demurely, Willie's son on a hobbyhorse, Fanny's boy with a hoop and ball, the fathers in light summer coats, and proud Grandpapa in his habitual black suit, but sporting a straw boater and leaning on a doll carriage.

Helen especially loved the years with Fanny and her children at home, before Harry made his fortune in western railroads and they moved on to a wealthy and fashionable life in New York. She advised Fanny through several pregnancies, reminding her that her own morning sickness had always ended by the third month and left her "perfectly well" afterward, even carrying George right through the mob. Mother and daughter put their heads together for many cozy chats. "Won't we have good times," Fanny said in anticipation of a visit to Rockledge. "I will tell you everything I can think of, the minutest detail shall be poured into your greedy ears." "A little gossip . . . is good fun sometimes," Helen agreed. When she tumbled to the secret that "our staid boy" George was courting a young lady in Cambridgeport, she rushed to share the news ("upon the peril of your life") with Fanny.

Helen was sure that her daughter would inherit Garrison's mantle as a reformer. "Much as I idolize you," she said, "I don't want you ever to walk in my steps." Fanny had her father's "best qualities of heart and mind" and could put them to good use. The editor did not disagree, but also saw in Fanny Helen's sterling character. "You inherit in full measure your mother's affectionate nature, and her disinterested and self-sacrificing spirit. . . . my love for you is to be found in the very core of my heart." Fanny proved her parents both correct, as she extended her "very determined" support to a variety of charitable and educational ventures, including the founding of Barnard and Radcliffe colleges, the Consumers' League, and a long career in the women's suffrage movement and the Woman's Peace Society until her death in 1924. Her son, Oswald Garrison Villard, continued the family tradition, serving on the founding committee of the NAACP and as editor of *The Nation* from 1918 to 1940.

The vicissitudes of old age began to tell. Helen became very forgetful and started referring to herself as "your crazy old ma." Garrison was known to get off the train at the wrong stop and endeavor to walk home, only to lose his way and arrive several hours late and worn out by the detours. He became even more obsessive and particular about details, writing two paragraphs of elaborate instructions to Wendell about how to send him baskets of peaches by express from New York (Helen loved peaches and used to cherish the annual gifts from Susan Anthony's family in the old days), only to pause in mid-lecture to declare that perhaps the business would be too extravagant after all. He fretted, too, over news of a grandchild's earache or sniffles and his children's health as well. To his father every cough threatened pneumonia, Frank said, in one of his rare moments of irritation, and long after Willie recovered from serious injuries received in a railway accident, Garrison still winced and sighed about his son's scarred hands. (When Willie turned forty in 1878 and his own children left him far behind at ice skating parties, however, the editor was quick and kindly in his commiseration.) The editor worried, too, that Fanny, while living for several years with Harry's dour family in Heidelberg, did not have enough opportunity to engage in discussions of reform and that her young children would come home to Boston more fluent in German than English.

The 1870s became the decade of funerals. Garrison had always served as the unofficial minister of the abolitionists' come-outer flock and brought a ceremonial gravitas to weddings, anniversaries, and, now, funerals. In 1871, despite poor health, he traveled to Syracuse to bury his oldest friend and "brother beloved" in the movement, Samuel J. May, who had come forward to enlist on the night of Garrison's first lecture in Boston in 1830 and had remained a steadfast and nourishing friend for forty years. The editor saluted him for the final time as Wordsworth's "Happy Warrior," an appellation that May had often applied to Garrison.

The procession continued. Henry C. Wright. Charles Lenox Remond. David Child. Thankful Southwick. James Yerrinton. Sarah Grimké. James Miller McKim. Edmund Quincy. Abby May Alcott. William C. Nell. When Garrison could not be present, Phillips performed a similar office, and sometimes they both spoke. Garrison had a serene belief in death as merely "an exchange of spheres," a "translation" to another realm of union with departed friends. He would meet "the inevitable hour," he told Maria Child, "with gratitude to the Divine Being for the life I have here enjoyed, and with unquestioning faith and lively hope as to the life to come."

His ideas received their most severe test when death came to Rockledge. Helen had endured another small stroke in 1871 and gradually became housebound and immobile, though she had her genial and companionable times until the very end. Wife and husband both developed severe colds in January 1876. The doctor feared pneumonia and confined them to bed, but they did not seem to recover. Helen's condition worsened, and by Monday the 24th she was finding it very hard to breathe. She got so restless and disoriented that Frank seemed always to be moving her from bed to chair and back again, until she finally became prostrate and slipped into semiconsciousness. Fanny stayed up with her all that night, and in the morning the doctor said the end was near. Willie and Ellen were summoned, Frank alternately rubbed his mother's swollen feet and held her perspiring hand, and Fanny brought their sick and grieving father to sit by his wife's bedside, where he fanned her brow and stroked her tenderly. At about ten o'clock on the morning of January 25, 1876, one month short of her sixty-fifth birthday, Helen Garrison died. "Although we could not help weeping," her youngest son, Frank, wrote of the close family group at the deathbed, "we could not but rejoice and be thankful for her great release from suffering and pain." Family members cherished the image of a placid Helen seated patiently at the front window awaiting their return. Frank, however, could not get out of his mind the sight of his determined mother dragging herself upstairs, the folds of her long skirt gathered in her teeth, intent upon fending for herself and not summoning Fanny from the task of putting her own child to sleep.

They planned a quiet funeral at home. The boys cleared the two front rooms of furniture and hung her portrait with smilax, a twining greenbrier that she loved for the sweetness and simplicity that people loved in her. The neighbors brought violets that added a dainty note of color to the pallid light of the winter afternoon. People said that Helen looked easy and peaceful in her casket, but Garrison could not come downstairs to see. He lay prostrate with grief, fever, and a bronchitis so severe that the doctor feared that they might lose him as well. Wendell Phillips came to speak Helen's eulogy, going upstairs to condole privately with the editor, as did Lucy Stone and one or two others. With the doors ajar, however, he had little difficulty in hearing the heartfelt tributes. Phillips praised not only Helen's dignity and cheer, but her courage and capacity to serve the cause by making her home its spiritual center and giving her husband the strength to serve. Lucy Stone said that Helen "took things as they came and [was] working in her waiting," while C. W. Denison said that Helen's life "was one of those that made other lives possible." Everyone agreed that she wisely refrained from what she could not do and threw herself "whole-souled" into the many things she could and always kept her common sense and human sympathy. Only four carriages made the long cold journey up the ridge to Jamaica Plain to the receiving vault at Forest Hills. In May, when Garrison had recovered and the trees had come into bud, he and Frank chose a plot on the broad hilltop of the cemetery, and they quietly buried their Peace and Plenty, wife and mother, among the greening boughs she loved.

It took Garrison a long time to recover from Helen's death. He wandered from room to room in bewilderment and loss, and when Fanny turned up a packet of the old courtship letters, he read them over and over again. In some ways he never did recover. He resumed the practice of attending Spiritualist "circles" at which he sought communication with Helen, with his mother, and with little Charlie. He wanted to ask Helen whether she thought the wagon accident at the Northampton Association had later caused her paralysis, and he wanted to know if his long-lost boy thought that any other treatment than the vapor bath might have saved his life. He confessed to Wendell that even though his mother had died at forty-seven and he was beyond seventy, he felt like a child again when he thought of meeting her on the other side.

In his vulnerability Garrison grew even more dependent upon Frank, who readily, even eagerly, assumed the burden of his father's care. In July 1876, he took him to the Centennial Exhibition in Philadelphia, pushing him about in a wheelchair until the editor had had enough of celebration and complained as of old that the Founders did not deserve the worship they received. In 1877, after another winter of poor health and sagging morale, Frank—at Fanny's urging and perhaps with her subsidy—escorted Garrison on a last visit to England, which included many sentimental encounters and a surprise visit with the dying George Thompson. "He could not speak when he tottered into the room and embraced Father in silence, the tears coming into his eyes," Frank recalled. "We were shocked at his altered appearance and difficulty of speech, and were deeply affected."

During Garrison's intervals of good health, he remained vigorously engaged with public affairs and kept up a lively social life. He and Frank went to the theater and read Dickens aloud. They went to a "parlor" lecture by Emerson at which many of the old Transcendentalists had gathered. The experience was "distinctively Emersonian," Garrison told Fanny, "unique, discursive, disjointed and kaleidoscopic, interspersed with wise suggestions and pithy utterances. Yet I could get no very tangible idea as to the drift of it." They listened to Alexander Graham Bell demonstrate his remarkable telephone: they distinctly heard in the Music Hall, through a single wire, a cornet solo played in Somerville three and a half miles away! They also saw the typewriter demonstrated. Lucy Stone was using one at the newspaper, and the editor one day tried it and, not surprisingly, proved fairly accurate on the keys. He typed a favorite quotation at one end of the paper and then reinserted the page from the bottom and drafted a note to Frank, suggesting a Christmas visit to Fanny in New York. "You have been so much with me in my various excursions, near and remote," he said fondly, "that I have come to lean upon you as my main stay."

Garrison worried, however, that he had taken up too much of Frank's attention and prevented him from having a proper social life of his own. The editor tried to make more independent arrangements for himself, spending the summer of 1878 with the Villards at a summer estate near Tarrytown, New York, and he enjoyed it greatly when Maria Child moved into the city for the winter and they had more opportunities for the long speculative conversations they both loved. He resumed as well his rich and soulful friendship with John G. Whittier, frequently visiting his farm and recalling how the young editor had launched the young poet's career. Whittier thought that time had made Garrison "gentler and more charitable" and retirement had allowed his old love of nature to blossom with "renewed strength and keenness."

Through Child, the editor gained the friendship of Anne Whitney, the daughter of an abolitionist family who had turned to art in her forties and, after studying sculpture in Florence and Rome, had earned an important reputation for her grand renditions of historic subjects, including Samuel Adams and Toussaint L'Ouverture. Garrison enjoyed much earnest talk at her Mount Vernon Street studio on Beacon Hill, and eventually he agreed to a sitting. The formal portrait bust Whitney created in 1878 captured, as few other artists had, the sweet serenity of the man as well as the dignity of the reformer, though she was honest enough not to ignore the severe signs of fatigue and aging that she perceived. (A few years after the editor's death, Anne Whitney gave the Garrison family a lovely plaster statuette of the editor, seated in his inimitable style, slouched slightly in his chair, legs extended, arms relaxed at his sides, but his head held firmly erect in an attitude at once alert, thoughtful, and kindly. Wendell and Frank were so charmed by the piece that they urged the sculptor to enter the Boston civic competition for a Garrison bronze figure to be placed in Commonwealth Avenue. Miss Whitney boycotted the contest, however, because she had won an earlier competition for a statue of Charles Sumner but then the commission had been revoked when it was discovered that she was a woman.)

With his penchant for dates, Garrison made ceremonial capital out of one more event that took him back to his origins. On October 12, 1878, he rose before dawn to catch a train to Newburyport to mark the sixtieth anniversary of his apprenticeship. The *Herald* still occupied a little brick printing office on State Street, though it now had a steam press. One of the old-timers recalled that there were but three places in town that autumn of 1818: a storekeeper's assistantship went to some worthy's son, a hatter's apprenticeship went to the teacher's boy, and printer's devil was the only spot left when Deacon Bartlett came looking to help his poor little charge. The editor stepped up to the case and set three of his own poems from memory, though the nonpareil type taxed him somewhat. Yet he didn't "squabble a line," he said proudly, and when the proof was pulled, no one could find a single mistake.

Two nights later, an association of Boston printers, the Franklin Typographical Club, honored the editor at an affectionate and good-humored testimonial dinner. The Rev. E. W. Allen, the son of his old master, came to pay his respects, and Toby Miller's son came as well, to speak warmly about his father's memory of the inspiring association with Garrison. The editor reiterated his pride and delight in the printer's craft and how it had literally "put into his hands" the means of overthrowing the slave system. He reminisced about his earliest days as an apprentice and declared that "no graduate of Harvard or Yale can take more pride in his Alma Mater than I do in the printing office." All crafts were honorable, he allowed, but printing "has the power to move the world." With "a well-assorted case and a compositor at that case with active brains and active hands putting 'thoughts that breathe and words that burn' into type," he said, "the age is bound to move 'onward and upward.'" The lesson of his career, Garrison suggested, was that "by speaking the truth and applying it boldly to the conscience of the people, there is no need of despair. . . ."

He knew the struggle would go on. For the first time in our history, he said, "all races of men on our soil are looking each other in the face and asking the question whether they can dwell together in unity, whether they cannot stand by one another in regards to their rights and liberties. . . . It is the sublimest spectacle on earth . . . and my hope is boundless."

The family had a grand reunion for Thanksgiving 1878, with everyone but Wendell and his children able to attend. Garrison danced the Virginia reel with his granddaughters and made plans to spend Christmas in New York. A few weeks later, on December 12, he received a new library chair and a host of callers who came to surprise him for his seventy-third birthday.

Even after he caught a bad cold in New York that persisted for the rest of the winter, the old editor kept up such a schedule of activity that no one suspected how sick he had become. He continued to write energetic public letters—full of the "old fire and ring," Frank said—on the Republican Party's abandonment of the South and its surrender to terror and white supremacist government. The expedient bargain that had settled the 1876 presidential election was "an abomination," Garrison railed, that was tantamount to renewing the old "covenant with death." He went to the State House with Lucy Stone to testify before a legislative committee on women's suffrage. In February 1879, he wrote another dramatic statement protesting the "caste spirit—vulgar, conceited, and contemptible" manifest in pending congressional attempts to exclude Chinese immigrants, which was published all over the country and received a good deal of praise. He was so "morally incensed," he told Fanny, that he "was nerved" to write not only the letter but a stinging rejoinder to his critics that further defended "those fundamental principles which as a nation we profess to be guided by." In March and April he undertook a fund-raising campaign for the hundreds of black families fleeing the violence in Mississippi and Louisiana for new settlements in Kansas. (A worn pocket diary with a list of donors' names was found in his suit coat after his death.) One of the last letters he ever received came from Prudence Crandall Philleo, who had gone to Kansas to assist the "Exodusters," thanking him for his aid in the cause. He wanted very much to stand up at a public meeting on the subject in Faneuil Hall on April 24, but he was much too weak. Instead he sent a resonant statement to the chairman, Robert Morris, the distinguished attorney who had begun his career as Ellis Loring's first black clerk.

The letter proved Garrison's valedictory. "It is clear . . . that the battle for liberty and equal rights is to be fought over again," he wrote, and added, "Let the edict go forth, trumpet-tongued, that there shall be a speedy end put to all this bloody misrule; that no disorganizing Southern theory of state[s'] rights shall defiantly dominate the Federal Government, to the subversion of the Constitution; that the millions of loyal colored citizens at the South, now under ban and virtually disfranchised, shall be put in the safe enjoyment of their rights—shall freely vote and be fairly represented—just where they are located. And let the rallying-cry be heard from the Atlantic to the Pacific coast, 'Liberty and equal rights for each, for all, and forever, wherever the lot of man is cast within our broad domains!' "

Four weeks later he was dead. He had paid for each one of those last efforts in days of pain and exhaustion. Suddenly his various complaints—catarrh, rheumatism, bladder and kidney troubles, swollen legs—descended upon him at once, weakening his resistance and making him frantic and miserable. Frank gave him rubdowns and read aloud to him in the evenings, copied over the drafts of his articles, and, on Easter Sunday 1879, shyly told him that he had met a young woman named Mary Pratt from Philadelphia who had accepted his proposal of marriage. The editor wrote immediately to Mary to tell her that she had drawn the "first-class prize" of the sweetest, most equable and unselfish man alive.

A few weeks before he had had another surprise. An elderly black churchwoman called upon him who turned out to be Maria W. Stewart, the exhorter whose soulful messages the editor had published more than forty years before. She had come to Boston in search of evidence to support her federal claim to a widow's pension and homestead grant, and the two veterans of the movement's pioneering decade passed a long afternoon in happy reminiscence. Mrs. Stewart had worked for years in New York and then had become the matron of the Freedman's Hospital in Washington, D.C., where she also won a name for herself as the director of a large Sunday school movement in the capital's free black community. Garrison insisted upon writing then and there a generous testimonial letter in support of both her pension claim and a private effort to publish an augmented edition of her "Meditations and Prayers." The old friends parted, marveling at the changes they had witnessed and grateful for their improbable but rich reunion after a separation of so many years.

The editor's career had come full circle, and the end approached. When Garrison's condition continued to worsen, Fanny insisted that he come to New York to consult her medical specialists. On April 28, Frank put his father, looking pale and run-down and feeling wretched beyond belief, on the train. The physician, Dr. Leonard Weber, thought at first that a regimen of catheterization would ease the bladder obstruction that seemed to be the most immediate cause of distress, pain, and sleeplessness, but within a few days it became apparent that underlying kidney disease had so weakened the editor that his life was ebbing way.

The Villards had a huge, elaborately furnished duplex suite of eleven rooms in the Westmoreland House just above Union Square at Seventeenth Street and Fourth Avenue. Fanny turned a corner bedroom and parlor into a light and airy sickroom for her father, and over the next few weeks his condition improved, then worsened, then improved again, only to sink once more. The telegrams raced back and forth to Boston; poor Frank would pack a suitcase after one message, only to unpack after the next. Finally, on May 21, the bulletins became uniformly urgent, and Frank rushed to catch the 8:30 A.M. train to New York. At 4:40 P.M. he reached the Westmoreland and found Wendell and Fanny dissolved in tears. "You are almost too late," his sister sighed.

Frank ran into the sickroom and saw his pale and stricken father on a bed by the open window, looking exhausted. "Father, does thee know me?" he asked, grabbing Garrison's hand. The editor opened his eyes, nodded weakly, and asked his son which train he had caught. The voice was faint, and Frank had to bend low to catch it, but they spoke quietly for an hour. Willie and Ellen and George had arrived by then, and the grandpapa asked after George's infant daughter. When Garrison dozed off, the children retired for supper, after which Frank came back into the room and stretched out alongside him on the bed. His father murmured something, then "suddenly turned and throwing his left arm over me, embraced me closely, holding my left hand with his right, and fell into a sleep. . . ."

The next morning the editor's mind began to wander, but when Dr. Weber asked him what he wanted, the reply was vintage Garrison: "To finish it up!" He spent an uncomfortable day but seemed calmer at night. Fanny asked him if he would enjoy singing some hymns, and he nodded happily. Holding hands and not stopping to hold back their tears, the editor's five living children sang and sang and sang the favorite melodies of their family life together. Four tall bearded men with long Garrison faces and one petite woman with the full Benson cheeks and deep dark eyes stood in an opulent room of the metropolis, singing praise and glory to the Lord as their grandmother had sung before them in the crowded little boardinghouse of Newburyport with her hungry children at her side. Garrison lay there on the bed, the grand old tunes marching and gathering around him, and though his voice was stilled, there was no doubt that he could hear, for looking down, brothers and sister could see their indomitable father beating time with his hands and with his feet. They sang until they were hoarse and dry and the patient dozed. By Saturday morning, May 24, 1879, he had become comatose, but he lingered all day and into the evening as callers joined the watch. Then, in the hour before midnight, his capacious heart gave up at last, his whispered breaths faded into nothingness, and William Lloyd Garrison died.

The editor's body returned to Rockledge in a rosewood coffin with a silver nameplate. The family first announced that the funeral would be private, intending to have the old friends come to the house as they had for Helen's memorial three and a half years earlier. An outpouring of editorial tributes had, by Monday afternoon, produced such a wave of popular feeling—"an apotheosis!" exclaimed Maria Child—that such a plan would no longer do. Though Garrison would have abhorred a religious service, he had spent much of his career in meetinghouses. After some consultation, during which Wendell Phillips warned that the "priestcraft" would gloat that having denounced churches all his life Garrison was buried from one at last, the children accepted an offer from the First Religious Society of Roxbury to hold a public remembrance in its venerable church on Eliot Square. (Observances would also take place in many cities over the next few weeks, but of all the tributes Fanny most cherished the report from Atlanta that told of an interracial service held in the shadow of the capitol building where a reward had once been posted for her father's head.)

Flags flew at half-staff all across Boston and the state of Massachusetts on Wednesday, May 28, 1879, the day of William Lloyd Garrison's funeral. The sky shone so blue and the sunlight gleamed so brightly off the bright yellow walls and steeple of the church that it seemed to herald the editor's ascent to glory. Carriages surrounded the village green hours before the service, and more than fifteen hundred people sat close together in the stately boxes of the main floor and jammed even more closely together on the benches of the encircling gallery. Great sprays of lilac adorned the pulpit; with the blinds thrown open, the four long rows of windows admitted an abundance of spring sunshine, in keeping with the family's desire to avoid a mournful atmosphere and honor the editor's belief in translation to another sphere. Among the guests could be seen two generations of abolitionists, black and white, and a large number of young people drawn, said Lucy Stone, in "loving sympathy" to savor the spirit that would be among them one last hour.

A few minutes past two o'clock, Garrison's casket was carried into the church, and with a sudden rush the congregation rose spontaneously to its feet in tribute. The pallbearers moved slowly down the aisle into the light and the silence with the body of their old friend on their shoulders: Oliver Johnson, who said that he felt a void in his heart that could never be healed; Samuel Sewall, who had made a donation to *The Liberator* even before Garrison had set a line of it; Robert F. Wallcut, who had managed the office on Cornhill for two decades; Lewis Hayden, born a slave and escaped to lead the black community of Boston; Charles Mitchell, once a typesetter on *The Liberator* who had gone on to become the first black man to serve in the legislature and who limped from wounds suffered as a member of the 55th Massachusetts Regiment; the Rev. Samuel May, the MAS agent, who would preside; and Theodore Dwight Weld and Wendell Phillips, who would speak the eulogies.

Agent May began the exercises with some of the texts Garrison liked to read at abolitionist meetings.

"Cry aloud and spare not; lift up thy voice like a trumpet, and show my people their transgression."

"The Spirit of the Lord God is upon me; because He hath sent me to bind up the broken-hearted, to proclaim liberty to the captives, and the opening of the prison to them that are bound."

"And Jesus said:—'Inasmuch as ye have done it unto one of the least of these, my brethren, ye have done it unto me.' "

Then a quartet of gospel singers, led by Mrs. Mitchell, burst into the editor's favorite hymn, "Awake my soul! Stretch every nerve, and press with vigor on; A heavenly race demands thy zeal, and an immortal crown," taking the short and simple phrases and making them an exaltation and a praise such as few had ever heard before. Again and again their voices would embrace and twine around the house, punctuating the interval between speakers with the harmonies of sacred love.

Lucy Stone came next to say that Garrison had left an example "grand like the hilltops against a clear evening sky" and had stood as the tower of strength for the cause of women's rights. "I can think of no funeral in the history of the world," she said, "where those left behind had so much reason to rejoice" at their legacy of inspiration and faith. (A few weeks later, after learning that the editor's will had contained a $500 bequest to the *Woman's Journal*, Stone exclaimed that it would be doubly valuable "because *he* gave it," since the editor knew better than anyone else the struggle it took to keep alive a contentious and unpopular newspaper. Feeling the personal loss more keenly with each passing day, she told Frank, "All the time I miss Mr. Garrison, all the time something seems gone. There is nowhere a man left that takes his place in the need the world had of him.")

John Greenleaf Whittier was too sick to attend the gathering, but Agent May read the verses the poet sent to praise his friend of fifty years for his unselfish labor:

> From lips that Sinai's trumpet blew
> We heard a tenderer undersong;
> The very wrath from pity grew,
> From love of man thy hate of wrong.

Theodore Dwight Weld, his white beard looking massive above his frail and wispy frame, next stood up and took Garrison's life as a text to illustrate "the power of a single soul, *alone*," to ignite the world with "sacred fire." In a shaking voice, the fabled evangelist evoked the power of the movement as he described, in phrases broken by the catch in his throat, the gathering of souls—"here and there, and thick and fast, too, not merely one, and another, and another, of the great mass, the multitudes of souls ready to receive the truth and welcome it, to incorporate it into their thought and feeling, to live and die for it."

Finally, Wendell Phillips ascended the pulpit raised high above the floor and looked out over the rapt and somber congregation. In the pungent phrases Phillips had employed so often in Faneuil Hall, in the modulated tones that threatened always to explode into melodramatic oratory, the editor's flamboyant coadjutor fixed the dimensions of Garrison's achievement. The eulogist's theme could not have been simpler: Garrison understood *agitation,* and *movement.* He "announced the principle, arranged the method, gathered the forces, enkindled the zeal, started the argument, and finally marshalled the nation" against slavery, Phillips said, piling verb upon verb in tribute to the editor's unwearied activism. "John Brown stood on the platform Garrison had built," Phillips said, his voice rising; Mrs. Stowe charmed an audience that *he* had gathered with words that *he* had inspired. The orator made a great dramatic point of the editor's youth—only twenty-three when he went to jail in Baltimore, not yet twenty-five at the founding of his newspaper—and hailed "this boy without experience" who had defied the nation. Warming to his task, Phillips enumerated the forces arrayed against Garrison, and speaking of the opposition he faced from the churches, said grimly, "The very pulpit where I stand saw this apostle of liberty and justice sore beset . . . yet it never gave him one word of approval or sympathy."

Wendell Garrison shot a look at his brother William and sat livid with embarrassment. They were guests in the late Dr. Putnam's church, and Phillips had insulted the memory of the man who had occupied its pulpit for nearly fifty years. The eulogist's namesake seethed through the rest of the service.

Phillips went on, marveling at "this boy," "this stripling," "this solitary evangelist" daring "to make Christians of twenty millions of people!" As logical as Jonathan Edwards, as brave as Martin Luther, Garrison stood up to Calhoun when Webster and Clay shrank away; only Garrison met him face to face, branded slavery a sin and risked the Union to right a moral wrong. Peering down from the pulpit into the casket set below, Phillips addressed the editor for the final time and spoke his epitaph: "Your heart, as it ceased to beat, felt certain, *certain,* that whether one flag or two shall rule this continent in time to come, one thing is settled—it never henceforth can be trodden by a slave!"

In the long silence that followed Phillips's grand apostrophe, Wendell glared at the orator and at Agent May, who finally rose and smoothly offered the thanks of the Garrison family and friends for "the great courtesy" granted in the use of "this spacious house." Wendell sat back mollified, but later asked the stenographer he had hired to delete the offending sentence from the report given the newspapers. (The family spent weeks discussing the matter before overruling him and restoring the remark in the pamphlet version of the services. Lucy Stone assured them that everyone understood that it was "like Phillips" to satisfy his own mind—"and after all though it did not seem courteous, it was true and said in the finest way that Phillips could say it." She added, "Several old abolitionists said to me that they thought it just.")

After the congregation was invited to file past the open casket to look Garrison in the face one last time, the body was carried from the church. A long, long line of carriages began the procession up through Roxbury and onto the ridge above the city, en route to Forest Hills. They passed through the incongruous Egyptian gateway of the cemetery and ascended the greening hillcrest where a grave alongside his wife's awaited Garrison. In the slanting light of late afternoon the company could look back toward Boston, down past Rockledge, toward Suffolk Street where Charlie died and Pine Street and Dix Place where the family flourished, toward the spire of Park Street Church where Garrison first sounded abolition's trumpet.

Some thought of Bunyan's *Pilgrim's Progress* and the story of Mr. Valiant-for-Truth, who had fought alongside Great-Heart and Stand-Fast on the Enchanted Ground and who, when he had received the summons that his pitcher was broken at the fountain, called his friends together and said, " 'I am going to my fathers. . . . My sword, I give to him that shall succeed me in my pilgrimage, and my courage and skill to him that can get it. My marks and my scars I carry with me.' . . . many accompanied him to the riverside, into which, as he went, he said, *'Death, where is thy sting?'* And as he went down deeper, he said, *'Grave where is thy victory?'* So he passed over, and the trumpets sounded for him on the other side."

"I cannot always trace the way," the quartet sang, "but this I know, that God is love." The sky turned pink and gold and the company bowed their heads in tribute. Then, in twos and threes, they walked away from the grave and into an evening that seemed at once ennobled and empty. The editor and leader had transformed their lives and their epoch and now he was gone.

William Lloyd Garrison left not only the benefaction his eulogists extolled of slavery annihilated, freedom of the press vindicated, and a social movement forged in the crucible of a nation's soul. He left something else, so powerful and yet so fragile that it could hardly be mentioned, though it was the heart of his action and the challenge before us still, the realization of the beloved community, the vision of a nation that has transcended the phobia of color and the barriers of race. He not only stood up against slavery when no one else would accept the consequences of the condemnation; he stood up for a humane vision of equal citizenship when no one else dared publicly to imagine an America truly so conceived. It was for this vision, as much as for the heroic years of protest and the hard-won path out of bondage, that black hands reached across with white to bear his coffin and black voices crooned him to his rest. "This is a sad and mournful hour," Frederick Douglass told a memorial service at a church in Washington, D.C. "It was the glory of this man that he could stand alone with the truth, and calmly await the result." We await it still.

In the long struggle to achieve equality in the United States, William Lloyd Garrison occupies a place as central in the history of the nineteenth century as that of Dr. Martin Luther King, Jr., in the history of the twentieth. Both men willingly understood themselves as radicals and used the integrity of their spiritual vision as an independent political force. Both men epitomized the power of a social movement built upon thousands of individual acts of moral witness. Both men exemplified the courage necessary to expose the injustice of established institutions and illuminate the darkness with the beacon of irrefutable truth. Garrison and King both faced, as did their companion in spiritual agitation M. K. Gandhi, the agony of seeing the strategy of soul-force lost in a spiraling violence that would, in course, claim the lives of the latter two.

Garrison and King are both remembered for only a portion of their achievement. Dr. King is extolled today principally as a dreamer and not as the extremist and agitator that he most assuredly was, while Garrison (when recalled at all) is known primarily as a firebrand and not as the prophet of a society transformed. Yet they both fused the politics of radicalism with the language of love to provoke confrontations with oppressive authority in the name of a nobler fellowship of equals. It was Garrison's vision as much as his agitation that elevated him to Lincoln's plane, and it was King's agitation as much as his vision that enabled him to make his celebrated oration in front of the Lincoln Memorial. For the culminating image of his dream, it must not be forgotten, Dr. King renewed the egalitarian words of Isaiah beloved by Garrison that envisioned humanity made one with every valley exalted, the crooked made straight, and the rough places plain. Given their comparable roles in our history and the compatibility of their thinking, it is striking that Dr. King made no public mention of Garrison and traced his own pilgrimage to nonviolence through Gandhi to Thoreau and the New Testament concept of Christian love (*agape*) without a recognition of how these ideas had manifested themselves in Garrisonian abolitionism.

Yet the editor's reputation had faded badly in the twentieth century. Boston had installed a statue of Garrison in the Commonwealth Avenue esplanade in 1886, and in 1905 a remnant group of friends and admirers had conducted a centenary observance of Garrison's birth marked by several days of oratory and reminiscence in the old African Meeting House, which by then had become a synagogue. About that time, Justice Oliver Wendell Holmes, walking on Commonwealth Avenue, paused at the Garrison statue and told his wife that nothing could induce him "to do honor to a man who broke the condition of social life by bidding the very structure of society perish rather than he not have his way—expressed in terms of morals, to be sure, but still, his way."

Holmes's harsh judgment of fanatics and come-outers influenced history's verdict. Garrison's formidable combination of romantic will and religious zeal came to be regarded as a menacing egotism, and his absolutism sounded extreme and dangerous to a modern society grown relativistic in its judgments and suspicious of ideology. Even within the constitutional tradition of free speech, Justice Holmes's narrower views came to prevail over Garrison's implacable commitment to free expression. Holmes had sent several radical orators and pamphleteers to jail before he became persuaded that the government ought to be more circumspect in its repression of dissent. He then developed his famous credo that truths ought to be allowed to contend in "the marketplace of ideas," grounded in the realization that time had upset many "fighting faiths" that had once commanded a popular majority. Yet even in his great dissents, Holmes belittled the fanatical utterances at issue as being too insignificant to worry about and left open the possibility of suppressing speech that presented, in his famous phrase, "a clear and present danger." In narrowing the doctrine of free speech from the unbridled conflict of absolutes to a problem in market regulation and the assessment of national security, Holmes, who scorned fanatics, became for decades the popular embodiment of dissent. The public forgot Garrison, who had epitomized truly unfettered speech and had reshaped the Constitution it was Holmes's sworn duty to interpret.

It is therefore not surprising that as a doctoral student at Boston University in the early 1950s, Martin Luther King, Jr., found scant trace of Garrison in his milieu. Not until Boston tried to build a new city hall did the editor's reputation become a matter of civic concern. In 1962 a group of historians, led by Harvard's Arthur M. Schlesinger, Sr., belatedly learned that the building on Cornhill that had housed Garrison's printing office was scheduled to be demolished to make way for the redevelopment of Scollay Square and the new Government Center. They managed to stir controversy enough for a few newspaper editorials and a stirring letter from a Salem man who told the *Boston Globe* that if the planners couldn't move the new building, then they should "take the Liberator building down, brick by brick, and carefully restore the structure in the very heart of the government center, as a memorial to William Lloyd Garrison and that undying spirit of the free press in this country." The demand came too late. On March 3, 1963, a blaze of mysterious origin roared through the dilapidated old building, and the imprint it bore of Garrison and *The Liberator* disappeared into the unrelenting heat and smoke of a three-alarm fire.

REFERENCE NOTES

All on Fire is built upon the primary sources of Garrison's journalism and correspondence. Garrison's own file of *The Liberator* is preserved in the Rare Books Collection of the Boston Public Library. It is also available on microfilm as part of the Nineteenth-century American Periodicals Series. In addition to his published work, there are several important collections of manuscripts relating to Garrison. The bulk of the editor's papers were donated by his children to the Boston Public Library. In addition, there are valuable family papers in the Sophia Smith Collection at Smith College; among the Villard Papers at Houghton Library, Harvard University; at the Massachusetts Historical Society; and in the Eunice McIntosh Merrill Collection at Wichita State University. The notes reflect my indebtedness to these sources, as well as many other manuscript collections dealing with collateral figures in the story. Permissions and acknowledgments will be found below.

Citations are supplied for most direct quotations and for my narrative when I feel some readers may want to know more about my sifting of the available evidence. I have especially tried to supply such information in cases in which my reading corrects a misunderstanding or my interpretation differs from those of previous biographers. I have not thought it necessary to annotate topics generally covered in the standard histories and biographies of the period, and I have not tried to duplicate the bibliographies and notes found in specialized monographs. Biblical references are to the King James Version. Readers well versed in Scripture will notice that occasionally Garrison, reciting or quoting from memory, slightly varies a phrase, such as substituting "God" for "the Lord," and I have let these alterations stand uncorrected. I have referred to secondary sources principally to alert the reader to works that I have found exceptionally stimulating or that offer a very different perspective on the topic. In referring to works by major American writers, I have tried wherever possible to use editions published in the Library of America series, on the assumption that they are most readily available to readers of a book such as this one. Abbreviations are used as shown in the list below. For Garrison letters whose texts are taken from Walter M. Merrill and Louis Ruchames, eds., *The Letters of William Lloyd Garrison,* 6 vols. (Cambridge, 1971–81), I have provided the volume and page number in brackets, following the date, e.g., WLG to HBG, 14 Nov. 1835 [1:555]. When I have grouped citations by topic, they occur insofar as possible in the sequence used in the text. I have not always cited in the notes passages from letters or articles that are dated precisely in the text, nor have I cited incidental detail on individuals or locales derived from biographical dictionaries, city directories, and local histories. Passing details on Garrison not otherwise cited may be presumed to come from *Life.*

A word about previous biographies. Garrison's close associate Oliver Johnson wrote a sympathetic account shortly after the editor's death based largely on the biographical information Garrison had offered to journalists during his career. The four-volume work produced by Wendell and Frank Garrison filled out the narrative with a great many documents from the editor's files. Though the biography appreciates the editor's radicalism, its style is rather grave and stuffy. Yet the volumes stand as both a useful starting point and a ready reference tool; the personal reminiscences that dot the pages are invaluable. The two modern studies by academic historians are more problematic.

Walter M. Merrill, *Against Wind and Tide* (Cambridge, 1963), adds a great deal to the documentary record, but fails to grasp the religious dimension of Garrison's radicalism. John Thomas, *The Liberator* (Boston, 1963), identifies the perfectionist side of Garrison, only to condemn it as both politically ineffective and subversive of the "controlled change" the author regards as socially indispensable. A recent short study, James Brewer Stewart, *William Lloyd Garrison and the Challenge of Emancipation* (Arlington Heights, Ill., 1992), has a better understanding of Garrison as an agitator but engages in more psychological generalization than the evidence will bear. Not surprisingly, interesting treatments of Garrison have come from outsiders. John Jay Chapman, *William Lloyd Garrison* (N.Y., 1913), is a biographical essay of great discernment; Ralph Korngold, *Two Friends of Man* (Boston, 1950), is a somewhat dated popular treatment that nonetheless appreciates abolitionism as a social movement; Truman Nelson, *Documents of Upheaval* (N.Y., 1966), is a pioneering anthology of excerpts from *The Liberator*, with a stirring introduction that comprehends both Garrison's radical and prophetic leadership and the "Sophoclean" tragedy that overtook his pacifism. The most recent collection is William L. Cain, ed., *William Lloyd Garrison and the Fight Against Slavery: Selections from "The Liberator"* (N.Y., 1995).

ABBREVIATIONS FOR FREQUENTLY CITED TITLES AND COLLECTIONS

AAS=American Anti-Slavery Society

ACS/DLC=American Colonization Society Papers, Library of Congress

AmAqS=American Antiquarian Society, Worcester, Mass.

BAP=Peter Ripley, ed., *The Black Abolitionist Papers*, 55 vols. (Chapel Hill, 1991–)

BC=*Boston Courier*

BPL=Boston Public Library, Boston, Mass.

BT=*Boston Transcript*, Boston, Mass., 1826–30

CJCC=*Correspondence of John C. Calhoun*, ed. J. Franklin Jameson, *Annual Report of the American Historical Association*, 1899, Part Two (Washington, 1900)

DJBL=Dwight L. Dumond, ed., *Letters of James Gillespie Birney, 1831–1857*, 2 vols. (Washington, D.C., 1938)

DLC=Library of Congress, Washington, D.C.

DWGL=Gilbert H. Barnes and Dwight L. Dumond, eds., *Letters of Theodore Weld, Angelina Grimké Weld, and Sarah Grimké*, 2 vols. (Washington, D.C, 1934)

ECSL=*Elizabeth Cady Stanton as Revealed in Her Letters, Diary and Reminiscences*, ed. Theodore Stanton and Harriot Stanton Blatch, 2 vols. (N.Y., 1922)

EELA=[Ralph Waldo] *Emerson: Essays and Lectures*, Library of America ed. (N.Y., 1983)

FDLT=Frederick Douglass, *Life and Times of Frederick Douglass*, 1892 revised ed. (reprinted N.Y., 1965)

FDLW=Philip S. Foner, *Life and Writings of Frederick Douglass*, 5 vols. (N.Y., 1950)

FDPS=John W. Blassingame, ed., *The Frederick Douglass Papers, Series One, Speeches, Debates, and Interviews*, 3 vols. (New Haven, 1979–)

FHL=Friends Historical Library of Swarthmore College, Swarthmore, Pa.

FJGDi=Francis Jackson Garrison, Diaries, 1868–1879, WSU

GCL=Grimké Papers, Clements Library, University of Michigan

GFP/SSC=Garrison Family Papers, Sophia Smith Collection, Smith College, Northampton, Mass.

GUE=*Genius of Universal Emancipation*, Baltimore, Md., 1826–30

HHL=Houghton Library, Harvard University, Cambridge, Mass. (B/HHL=Blagden Collection, b Ms Am 1953; FG/HHL=Frances M. Garrison Papers, b Ms Am 1906 (655); V/HHL=Villard Papers, b Ms Am 1321)

JGWL=*Letters of John Greenleaf Whittier*, ed. John B. Pickard, 3 vols. (Cambridge, 1975)

JMN=*The Journals and Miscellaneous Notebooks of Ralph Waldo Emerson*, ed. William H. Gilman et al., 16 vols. (Cambridge, 1960–1982)

JT=*Journal of the Times*, Bennington, Vt., 1828–29

Lib.=*The Liberator*, Boston, Mass., 1831–65

Life=Wendell P. Garrison and Francis Jackson Garrison, *William Lloyd Garrison, 1805–1879: The Story of His Life Told by His Children*, 4 vols. (N.Y., 1885)

LMCMf=Microfiche Collected Correspondence of Lydia Maria Child, ed. Milton Meltzer, Patricia Holland, and Francine Krasno (Amherst, 1982)

LCSL=Alma Lutz Collection, Arthur and Elizabeth Schlesinger Library on the History of Women in America, Radcliffe College, Cambridge, Mass.

MAS=Massachusetts Anti-Slavery Society

MHS=Massachusetts Historical Society, Boston, Mass. (G/MHS=W. L. Garrison Papers)

NAS=*National Anti-Slavery Standard*, New York, N.Y., 1840–70

Nat.Phil.=*National Philanthropist*, Boston, Mass., 1826–28

NFP=[Newburyport] *Free Press*, Newburyport, Mass., 1826

NPH=*Newburyport Herald*, Newburyport, Mass., 1818–79

NPL=Newburyport (Mass.) Public Library

NYHS=New-York Historical Society, New York, N.Y.

NYTi=*New York Times*, New York, N.Y., 1853–79

NYTr=*New York Tribune*, New York, N.Y., 1850–59

OJBi=Oliver Johnson, *William Lloyd Garrison and His Times* (Boston, 1880)

PASP=Pennsylvania Abolition Society Papers, Historical Society of Pennsylvania

R&W=Maria Weston Chapman, *Right and Wrong in Massachusetts* (Boston, 1839)

SLCS=*Selected Letters of Charles Sumner*, ed. Beverly Wilson Palmer, 2 vols. (Boston, 1990)

SJMREC=Samuel Joseph May, *Some Recollections of Our Anti-Slavery Conflict* (Boston, 1869)

TBDDi=Thomas Bradford Drew Diaries, 1849–79, T. B. Drew II Papers, MHS

WCB=*Power for Sanity: Selected Editorials of William Cullen Bryant*, comp. William Cullen Bryant II (N.Y., 1994)

WLG(J)Di=William Lloyd Garrison, Jr., Diaries, 1855–65, GFC/SSC.

WSU=Eunice McIntosh Merrill Collection of William Lloyd Garrison Papers, Department of Special Collections, Ablah Library, Wichita State University, Wichita, Kan.

For permission to quote from manuscripts in their collections I am grateful to Thomas Knoles, Director of Reference Services and Curator of Manuscripts, American Antiquarian Society; Gunars Rutkovskis, Assistant Director, Research Library Services, Boston Public Library; Mary Ellen Chijioke, Curator, Friends Historical Library of Swarthmore College; David de Lorenzo, Curator of Manuscripts and Archives, Harvard Law School; Amy Fleming, Historical Society of Pennsylvania; David S. Zeidberg, Director, The Huntington Library; Leslie A. Morris, Curator of Manuscripts, The Houghton Library, Harvard University; Louis L. Tucker, Director, Massachusetts Historical Society; John C. Davis, Director, William L. Clements Library, University of Michigan; Margaret Heilbrun, Library Director and Curator of Manuscripts, New-York Historical Society; Sylvia McDowell, Arthur and Elizabeth Schlesinger Library on the History of Women in America, Radcliffe College; Amy Hague, Assistant Curator, Sophia Smith Collection, Smith College; Paul A. Carnahan, Librarian, Vermont Historical Society; Michael Kelly, Curator, Special Collections, Wichita State University.

CHAPTER ONE: A PRAYING PEOPLE

forced march/*Narrative of Captain William Owen, R. N.* (N.Y., 1942), 123. **transatlantic movement**/ Bernard Bailyn, *Voyagers to the West* (N.Y., 1986), esp. 3–28, 355–429. Like most migrants, the Lawless family had already moved once before—from the Protestant enclave in Limerick, County Cork, to the English Midlands—before undertaking the voyage to North America. For the Liverpool slave trade, see Elizabeth

Donnen, *Documents Illustrative of the History of the Slave Trade* (Washington, D.C., 1931) 2:536, 545–46, 626–27. **voyage and settlement/** Owen, *Narrative*, esp. 114, 121, 122, 125, 149, and the Lloyd marriage, 151 n. 581. A bill of lading (6 Dec. 1781) for the *Managuash* is in W. O. Raymond, "The James White Papers," *Collections of the New Brunswick Historical Society* 2 (1895): 34. **Frances's mind/** Peter Vose to Wendell P. Garrison, 21 May 1890, GFP/SSC. For daily life see J. B. Brebner, *The Neutral Yankees of Nova Scotia: A Marginal Colony During the Revolutionary Years* (N.Y., 1937), 175–82. **I had enough/** FMG to Maria Elizabeth Garrison, 20 May 1820, WSU. **boundary dispute/** William H. Kilby, *Eastport and Passamaquoddy: A Collection of Historical and Biographical Sketches* (Eastport, Me., 1888), 51, 111–12. **religious revolution/** Maurice Armstrong, *The Great Awakening in Nova Scotia 1776–1809* (Hartford, 1948), 64–65, 81–88; William James, *The Varieties of Religious Experience* (1902), in *Writings*, Library of America ed. (N.Y., 1987), 148, 200–202; George A. Rawlyk, *Ravished by the Spirit: Religious Revivals, Baptists, and Henry Alline* (Kingston, Ont., 1984). **great religious festivals/** Kilby, 313 ff. **Frances as preacher/** Peter Vose to Wendell P. Garrison, 21 May 1890, GFP/SSC; *Life* 1:13. The story of the Lloyds' enmity toward religious dissenters was first recounted in an interview with WLG by Mary Howitt, *People's Journal* (London), 12 Sept. 1846, but because it doesn't square with the peaceful impression of 'Quoddy's religious life derived from other sources and FMG, in her copious writing, never mentioned this conflict, I report it only as legend. **Maugerville/** Alline, q. Armstrong, 74; William O. Raymond, *The River of St. John: Its Physical Features, Legends, and History from 1604 to 1784* (Sackville, N.B., 1910; reprint 1943), 173–74, 165–195, 274; and "The Maugerville Settlement," *Collections of the New Brunswick Historical Society* 1 (1894): 63–87. **naturalized/** "Registry of American Seamen from July 1806 to April 1810," Mss., Newburyport Custom House Records, Essex Institute; Henry Adams, *History of the United States During the Administrations of Thomas Jefferson*, Library of America ed. (N.Y., 1986), 527–31. **sailing-master/** Most biographers have understood "sailing-master" to mean "captain," but there is no evidence that Abijah Garrison was enrolled in the Newburyport Marine Society, the town's much-admired association of ship captains. For him "sailing-master" evidently meant a lesser rank referring to the officer in charge of navigation. See Marcus Rediker, *Between the Devil and the Deep Blue Sea: Merchant Seamen, Pirates, and the Anglo-American Maritime World, 1700–1750* (Cambridge, Eng., 1987), 83–93. **Lady Fr—/** Abijah Garrison to Benjamin Jones, 14 July 1798, GFP/SSC. **following the rule/** AG to parents, 4 April 1805, *Life* 1:18–19; Charles Hutton, *A Course of Mathematics* (N.Y., 1812) 1:135. **Newburyport/** Caleb Cushing, *The History and Present State of the Town of Newburyport* (Newburyport, 1826), 85; Newburyport Custom House Records, 1807, Essex Institute; AG to Joseph Garrison, 3 April 1806, GFP/SSC. See, generally, E. Vale Smith, *History of Newburyport* (Newburyport, 1854); John J. Currier, *History of Newburyport, Massachusetts, 1764–1905* (Newburyport, 1906), vol. 1; Sarah Emery, *Memories of a Nonagenarian* (Newburyport, 1879); Benjamin W. Labaree, *Patriots and Partisans: The Merchants of Newburyport, 1764–1815* (Cambridge, 1962). **Baptists/** "Outline History of the Baptist Church: Centennial Anniversary 8 May 1905," pamphlet, NPL; *Diary of Isaac Backus*, ed. William McLoughlin (Providence, 1979), 1483 [9 Dec. 1802]. **commonplace topics/** John Quincy Adams, *Diary* (Cambridge, 1981) 2:321. As a young law clerk in the town Adams had observed backstreet prayer meetings which he mocked as "calling upon God in every tone of voice, and repeating a number of texts of Scripture incoherently huddled together, so as to make an unintelligible jumble of nonsense, which they think is a proper method of seeking the Lord." *Diary* 2:444 (20 Aug. 1788). **Whitefield & Presbyterians/** Whitefield died after preaching in the church, which had been founded in the 1750s by "new lights" inspired by his earlier revivals in the town. His remains were placed in a crypt beneath the pulpit and became an attraction for evangelically minded tourists. John J. Currier, *Ould Newbury* (Boston, 1896), 509–23. **Martha Farnham/** Newburyport Cemetery Records, City Hall. MF died 14 Sept. 1830, aged 52. **birthdate/** "Newburyport Vital Records: Births," Special Collections,

NPL, gives WLG's birthdate as 12 Dec. 1804, but biographers now—and his sons in 1879—all accept 1805 as the correct year. **mother's religion/** Frances M. Garrison to [?], 29 Mar. 1807, GFP/SSC; FMG, misc. corr., n.d., WSU; FMG to Martha Farnham, 22 Oct. 1815, WSU, including the hymn lines quoted. Except as noted, religious references by FMG in the next few pages are taken from these undated manuscript fragments. For the religious context, see Stephen A, Marini, *Radical Sects of Revolutionary New England* (Cambridge, 1982), 1–40; Nathan O. Hatch, *The Democratization of American Christianity* (New Haven, 1989), chs. 1–4. **It seems seven years/** AG to FMG, 12 Nov. 1806, *Life* 1:23–24. **Embargo protest/** Smith, 181; George Wood, "Recollections of Early Newburyport, No. 9," NPH, 10 Feb. 1863. **name change/** Passing references throughout her correspondence substantiate this. A certificate made out to "Francis Meriah Garrison" by her pastor [5 Sept. 1815, HHL, b Ms Am 1906 (184)] tells us how the name was pronounced. **father's hourglass/** WLG to WPG, 29 Mar. 1878 [6:515]; WLG to WPG, 31 Oct. 1877 [6:485]. **female prayer meetings/** FMG to [?], 29 March 1807, GFP/SSC. **John Peak/** *Memoir of Elder John Peak Written by Himself* (Boston, 1832), 102–11. **Baptists' procession/** Peter Schlemhil [George Wood], "Early Recollections of Newburyport," NPH, 27 Jan. 1863. **Great Fire/** Peak, 112–17, and untitled pamphlet (5 June 1811) in Currier 1:646–47.

CHAPTER TWO: THE ART AND MYSTERY OF PRINTING
We appoint/ FMG to WLG, 12 May 1820, WSU. **parting advice/** FMG to WLG, 2 Aug. 1814, WSU; 18 July 1814, GFP/SSC. **practiced reading/** See facsimile of *The New England Primer* (1727 version), ed. Paul L. Ford (N.Y., 1899). **mother in Lynn/** FMG to MF, 5 Apr. 1814, WSU; FMG to MF, 26 May, 28 June 1814, GFP/SSC; FMG to Dear Brother, 21 Aug. 1814, GFP/SSC. **Bartletts/** "Newburyport Vital Records: Marriages," NPL. **mother wrote/** FMG to WLG, 2 Aug. 1814, WSU; FMG to WLG 18 July 1814, GFP/SSC. **schooldays/** JMN 1:46; Peter Schlemhil, "Early Recollections," NPH, 27 January 1863. **mother's quandary/** FMG to MF, 11 Sept. 1814, 28 Feb. 1815, GFP/SSC. **James/** James Holley Garrison, *Behold Me Once More*, ed. Walter M. Merrill (Boston, 1954), 7–10. **tolerable shoe/** WLG recalled his apprenticeship in an obituary notice for Gamaliel Oliver, *Lib.*, 2 Feb. 1849. **letter of dismission/** 5 Sept. 1815, HHL. **voyage/** FMG Log, 9–22 Oct. 1815, from notes copied by WPG, FG/HHL. **James's grog/** *Behold*, 11. **Everything seems/** FMG to MF, 22 Oct. 1815, WSU. **You won't/** FMG to MF, 7 Sept. 1816, GFP/SSC. **Baptists/** FMG to MF, 7 Jan. 1816, GFP/SSC; 18 Apr. 1816, HHL. Like Newburyport's congregation, Baltimore's First Baptist Church drew adherents primarily from the ranks of artisans and day laborers. Terry D. Bilhartz, *Urban Religion and the Second Great Awakening: Church and Society in Early National Baltimore* (Rutherford, N.J., 1986), 159. **if he learned/** WLG's reasoning is recounted by his mother in a letter to James, presumably lost, but excerpted in *Life* 1:35; reply, FMG to WLG, 29 Aug. 1817, HHL. **Allen and printing/** Newburyport Tax Roll, 1811, City Hall Records; Ezekiel Bartlett, by contrast, had his house listed at one-tenth the value of Allen's. J. T. Buckingham, *Personal Memoirs and Recollections of Editorial Life* (Boston, 1852) 1:40, says EWA accumulated "a handsome property." Milton W. Hamilton, *The Country Printer: New York State, 1785–1830* (N.Y., 1930), 56–63; Rollo G. Silver, *The American Printer, 1787–1825* (Charlottesville, 1967), 32–35, 65–82. Newspaper figures from Isaiah Thomas, *The History of Printing in America* (1810), ed. Marcus McCorison (N.Y., 1974), 15–16, and Richard D. Brown, "The Emergence of Urban Society in Rural Massachusetts, 1760–1820," *Journal of American History* 61 (1974): 43. Allen q.NPH, 10 June 1823, 20 Oct. 1818; the town historian's assessment is in E. Vale Smith, *History of Newburyport* (1854), 259. **apprenticeship/** WLG reminiscences to Franklin Club, *Boston Daily Evening Traveller*, 15 Oct. 1878; WLG to Frank W. Miller, 30 Apr. 1870, *Life* 1:41; Horace Greeley, *Recollections of a Busy Life* (N.Y., 1868), 63. The classic account of the craft is Joseph Moxson, *Mechanick Exercises on the Whole Art of Printing* (1683–84), ed. Herbert Davis and Harry Carter (N.Y., 1978). See also Thomas F. Adams, *Typographia, or The Printer's Instructor* (Philadelphia, 1857),

and Parke Rouse, Jr., *The Printer in 18th Century Williamsburg* (Williamsburg, Va., 1955). **return to Baltimore/** FMG to WLG, 5 Oct. 1819, WSU. **but one printing press/** NPH 3 Nov 1818, 1 Jan 1822. **no formal articles/** More than eight months after Lloyd began work at the *Herald* Maria Garrison was writing, "I should like to have Mr. Allen specify in writing what he intends to do." FMG to WLG, 5 May 1819, HHL. **weary with excitement/** WLG described the effect of Byron on him in JT, 7 Nov. 1828. For similar comments on Hemans and other Romantic poets, see JT, 10 Oct. 1828 and 16 Jan. 1829. For Scott and other novelists, see NPH, 17 Oct., 14 May 1825. **A.O.B./** NPH 21 May, 24 May, 31 May 1822. **quizzing:** FMG to WLG, 1 July 1822, HHL. **rather a great signature/** WLG to FMG, 26 May 1823 [1:10–11]. **authors generally starve/** FMG to WLG, 3 June 1823, WSU. **mother's health/** FMG to WLG, 24 Mar. 1823, WSU. **problems with visit/** WLG to FMG, 26 May 1823 [1:10–13]. **sister/** FMG to WLG, 12 May, 24 May, 13 June 1820, WSU; his sister died in Sept. 1822. **mother's appeal/** FMG to EWA, 3 Jun 1823, GFP/SSC. **so altered/** WLG to EWA, 7 July 1823 [1:14–15]. **should your father/** FMG to WLG, 30 Dec. 1821, GFP/SSC. Other phrases in this scene are from FMG Mss., n.d., WSU; FMG to WLG, 7 Apr 1821, GFP/SSC; 30 Dec. 1821, WSU. **obituary/** NPH, 9 Sept. 1823.

CHAPTER THREE: A NEW RACE OF EDITORS
passion for reading/ J. F. Otis recollections, 1833, BPL. **compact physique/** *Life* 1: xv, 123. **speech/** *An Address Delivered before the members of the Franklin Debating Club on the morning of the 5th of July, Being the Forty-Eighth Anniversary of American Independence*, By a Member (Newburyport, 1824), BPL. The author is identified in ink as William L. Garrison. See also NPH, 9 July 1822. **Lafayette visit/** E. Vale Smith, *History of Newburyport* (1854), 219; *Life* 1:57; Marian Klamkin, *The Return of Lafayette, 1824–1825* (N.Y., 1975), 41; NPH, 3 Sept. 1824. The Tracy mansion now houses the Newburyport Public Library. **era of good feelings/** q. *Boston Centinel*, NPH, 13 Dec. 1818. **campaign/** WLG, "Our Next Governor," I-III, NPH 14 Mar., 1 Apr., 3 Apr., 1823. **election/** WLG attack on Jackson, *Salem Gazette*, 27 July 1824; see also A.O.B., "Political Reflections," NPH, 25 Jan. 1825. **one more satire/** NPH, 3 Jan. 1826. **birthday poem/** NPH, 16 Dec. 1825. For the problem of the confused birth year, see Walter H. Merrill, *Against Wind and Tide* (Cambridge, 1963), 335 n. 1. My references to WLG's age are based on 1805, but occasionally, as here, I have referred to the age as WLG believed it to be. Confusion also existed as to whether his birth date was Dec. 10 or 12; early in his life WLG thought the 10th, but later the family observed Dec. 12, which squares with the Newburyport records. **sailing to Greece/** NPH, 20 Jan. 1826. **pacifism/** When the pacifist William Ladd lectured in Newburyport in July 1826, WLG enthusiastically reprinted Ladd's text in his newspaper. **sendoff/** NPH, 17 Mar. 1826; ad, NPH, 10 Mar. 1826; for Knapp's complaints, see *Essex Courant*, 17 Nov. 1825. **salutation/** NFP, 22 Mar. 1826. Impressionistic quotations from the next few issues are not cited individually. **drive out to Haverhill/** WLG tells the story himself in *Nat. Phil.*, 11 Apr. 1828; *Life* 1: 67–68. On vocational choice, see Bertram Wyatt-Brown, "Conscience and Career: Young Abolitionists and Missionaries," in Christine Bolt and Seymour Drescher, eds., *Antislavery, Religion, and Reform: Essays in Memory of Roger Anstey* (Folkestone, Kent, 1980), 183–203; Perry Miller, "John Greenleaf Whittier: The Conscience in Poetry," *Harvard Review* 2 (1964): 8–24. **new race of editors/** JT, 27 Mar 1829. **Gould on Cushing/** John J. Currier, *Ould Newbury: Historical and Biographical Sketches* (Boston, 1896), 662–67. **public story/** WLG to *Haverhill Gazette*, 1 Nov. 1826 [1:32]; NFP, 21 Sept. 1826. For the campaign, see NPH, 31 Oct. 1826; BC, 4 Nov. 1826. Cushing's own opportunism—as manifested in an extremely self-serving promotional letter—was the most controversial issue of the campaign, but WLG's later notoriety made him a convenient scapegoat for Cushing's apologists and biographers. See Claude M. Fuess, *Life of Caleb Cushing* (N.Y., 1923) 1:72–79. **Harris/** NFP, 9 Dec. 1826. **thoughts that breathe/** The fragment from Thomas Gray, *The Progress of Poesy* (1757), had become a catchphrase that WLG and many other journalists used without attribution.

CHAPTER FOUR: MY SOUL WAS ON FIRE THEN
Boston/ Walter Muir Whitehill, *Boston: A Topographical History*, 2nd ed. (Cambridge, 1968), chs. 1–4; Peter B. Knights, *The Plain People of Boston, 1830–1860* (N.Y., 1971), 10–21; William Pease and Jane Pease, *The Web of Progress: Private Values and Public Styles in Boston and Charleston, 1828–1843* (N.Y., 1985), 1–7; Robert A. McCaughey, "From Town to City: Boston in the 1820s," *Pol.Sci.Q.* 88 (June 1973): 191–211. The Boston City Hall and JFK Federal Office Building now cover the ground once occupied by numerous printing establishments, including several of Garrison's workplaces. **office to office/** WLG, *Boston Daily Evening Traveller*, 15 Oct. 1878. **Collier/** William B. Sprague, *Annals of the American Pulpit* (N.Y., 1855) 6:376–79. **awake/most interesting/** *The Journals of Bronson Alcottt*, ed. Odell Shephard (Boston, 1938), 17–18. **Beecher/** Milton Rugoff, *The Beechers: An American Family in the 19th Century* (N.Y., 1981), 84–108; Lyman Beecher, *Autobiography*, ed. Barbara Cross (Cambridge, 1981), q. 1:65, 2:48, 1:86; on benevolence, see Beecher's *Sermons Delivered on Various Occasions* (Boston, 1828), 280–85, and *The Bible A Code of Laws: A Sermon First Preached at Park Street Church, 3 September 1817* (Boston, 1818). **Tappan conversion/** Bertram Wyatt-Brown, *Lewis Tappan and the Evangelical War Against Slavery* (Cleveland, 1969), 33–36; Paul Goodman, *Towards a Christian Republic: Antimasonry and the Great Tradition in New England 1826–1836* (N.Y., 1988), 169. **what a harp/** Rugoff, 96, also describes daughter Harriet and her brothers reciting passages from Scott's novels while making applesauce with their parents. **Channing/** Arthur W. Brown, *Always Young for Liberty: A Biography of William Ellery Channing* (Syracuse, 1956), 128. WLG comparison, JT, 30 Jan. 1829. **light of the sun/** Alcott, *Journals* [26 Oct. 1828], 15; WLG on Boston, *Lib*, 4 June 1831. **temperance/** Lyman Beecher, *Six Sermons on the Nature, Occasions, Signs, Evils, and Remedy of Intemperance*, 6th ed. (Boston, 1826); Alice Felt Tyler, *Freedom's Ferment*, (St. Paul, 1943), 324–25; Horace Greeley, *Recollections of a Busy Life* (N.Y., 1868), 98–102. **raise moral tone/** *Nat.Phil.*, 4 Jan. 1828; other q. 18 Apr., 21 Mar., 1 Feb. 1828. **impudent young man/** BC, 13 July 1827; reply, WLG to BC, 14 July 1827 [1:50]. For WLG on Boston politics see NPH, 24 Apr., 8 May, 12 June 1827 [1:38–46]. **a great moral influence/** *Nat.Phil.*, 18 Jan. 1828. **Lundy/** *Lib.*, 20 Sept. 1839; *Boston Daily Evening Traveller*, 15 Oct. 1878; Thomas Earle, *Life of Benjamin Lundy* (Philadelphia, 1847), 1–26; Merton M. Dillon, *Benjamin Lundy and the Struggle for Negro Freedom* (Urbana, 1966), chs. 1–8; GUE, July 1822. Lundy's influence on WLG may be seen in *Nat.Phil*, 21 Mar., 28 Mar., 4 Apr. 1828. **Channing advisory/** WEC to DW, 14 May 1828, *Papers of Daniel Webster*, ed. Charles M. Wiltse (Hanover, N.H., 1974) 2:347–48. **Liberty does not consist/** *Nat.Phil.*, 4 Apr. 1828. Beecher's credo, q. Perry Miller, *The Life of the Mind in America* (NY, 1965), 36. **Neal quarrel/** WLG to JN, 30 July, 15 Aug. 1828 [1:61–63, 68–69]. **Negroes the last/** BL diary notes, in Earle, 27. **Lundy appeal/** WLG reported the Boston talk under his old byline of "A.O.B.," BC, 11 Aug., 12 Aug. 1828 [1:64–68]; Howard Malcolm to WLG, *Lib.*, 25 Aug. 1835. The follow-up meeting was promoted by David L. Child in *Massachusetts Journal*, 21 Aug. 1828. The editor of the *Christian Watchman & Baptist Register*, in a column-long account (15 Aug. 1828) of Lundy's "very sensible and pertinent" address, also reported that an organization was imminent. *Freedom's Journal*, 9 Sept. 1828, noted a Boston meeting friendly to abolition but made no mention of the leaders. **soul on fire/** *Lib.*, 20 Sept. 1839. BL reaction based on diary, in Earle, 28; GUE, 13 Sept. 1828; *Life* 1:99. **carte blanche/** *Life* 1:101. **village newspaper/** *Nat.Phil.*, 23 May 1828. **his new vehicle/** JT, 3 Oct. 1828. Greeley's praise, q. *Life* 1:112; BL q. GUE, 27 Dec. 1828 *Massachusetts Journal*, 7 Oct. 1828, welcomed the advent of a "neat and well-conducted Adams paper" for the people of Vermont and urged its "liberal support." **election/** verse, JT, 10 Oct. 1828; Richards, *The Life and Times of Congressman John Quincy Adams* (NY, 1986), 9–14. Jackson's 200,000 Southern voters gave him 105 electoral votes; Adams's 400,000 Northern votes earned him only 73 electoral votes. **antislavery petition/** JT, 24 Oct 1828, reprinted GUE, 8 Nov. 1828. **editor made fun/** *Vermont Gazette*, 31 Mar. 1829. **forswore immediatism/** JT, 7 Nov 1828. **inaction**

ruinous/ JT, 9 Jan., 16 Jan. 1829. **windy, vain/** *Vermont Gazette*, 10 Feb. 1829.
Athenaeum/ JGW to Edwin Harriman, 18 May 1829, JGWL 1:20. **love poems/** JT, 3
Oct., 17 Oct., 7 Nov., 12 Dec. 1828, 9 Jan. 1829. **Mary paints/** WLG to Stephen Foster,
30 Mar. 1829 [1:78–79]. **resignation/** JT, 27 Mar. 1829; WLG to Foster, 30 Mar. 1830
[1:79]. **Lundy had turned up/** The documentary record is confused. The dates in the
unreliable *Life, Travels, and Opinions of Benjamin Lundy* are off-kilter, but William
Clinton Armstrong, *The Lundy Family and Its Descendants . . . with a Biographical
Sketch of Benjamin Lundy* (New Brunswick, 1902), 365–67, reproduces a section of BL's
diary that puts him in Bennington on 6 Dec. 1828 after a trip from Baltimore (on foot,
stage, and steamboat) that began on 11 Nov. 1828 and included stops in Frederick and
Port Deposit, Md.; New Castle and Wilmington, Del.; Philadelphia; Burlington and
Mount Holly, N.J., and New York City. In GUE 3 Jan. 1829 BL thanks the friends who
have conducted the paper during his lengthy absences of the past eight months. A list of
agents for the paper includes for the first time WLG in Bennington and other new names
in Brattleboro, Portsmouth, N.H., and Providence, which suggests the remainder of his
itinerary. A few weeks later, BL told a supporter in Philadelphia that while he was
suspending the paper for a time in order to undertake a fact-finding mission to the South,
by the following summer he expected "to have a very suitable partner . . . [and to] improve
the paper, both in matter and manner of mechanical execution." BL to Isaac Barton, 21
Jan. 1829, PASP. **Boston social life/** JGW to Edwin Harriman, 18 May, 26 June 1829,
JGWL 1:20, 27. **double mistake/** For a typical view regarding WLG as a colonizationist,
see Donald M. Jacobs, ed., *Courage and Conscience: Black and White Abolitionists in
Boston* (Bloomington, 1993), 1–20. The notices of the Boston observances in *Christian
Watchman*, 3 July, 10 July 1829, and *Columbian Centinel*, 8 July 1829, make absolutely
clear that the ACS did not sponsor the Park Street service. For WLG's criticism of
misrepresentations in the *American Traveller* see his letter to BC, 9 July 1829 [1:84–86].
Leonard W. Bacon, "A Forgotten Glory of Park Street Church," *Congregationalist and
Christian World*, 9 July 1904, misleadingly characterizes ACS lectures given at the
church as pioneering antislavery ventures. **preparations/** WLG to Jacob Horton, 27 June
1829 [1:83]; JGW described WLG's editorial style in *American Manufacturer*,
2 Apr. 1829. **Boston 4th of July/** *American Traveller*, 7 July 1829; *Columbian Centinel*,
8 July 1829. For Park Street Church see *Bowen's Picture of Boston* (1831), 159–60; pew
controversy, 132–33; OJBi, 100–101. **Park Street Address/** *Nat.Phil.*, 22 July, 29 July
1829, AmAqS, contains the most complete text of the Park Street Address, and my
quotations are taken from this source. Excerpts in *Life* 1: 127–37. John Jay Chapman
compares the radical nature of the Park Street Address to Emerson's Phi Beta Kappa
address six years later, emphasizing WLG's social concerns against RWE's aesthetic and
intellectual ones; John Jay Chapman, *William Lloyd Garrison* (N.Y., 1913), 44–45.
Jefferson/ "Notes on the State of Virginia," query xiv, query xviii, in *Thomas Jefferson:
Writings*, Library of America ed. (N.Y., 1984), 264–70, 288–89. Elsewhere in the address
WLG quoted TJ's analysis of how slavery degraded both master and slave as well as his
famous evocation of the spectre of slave revolt: "I tremble for my country when I reflect
that God is just. . . ." **Whittier/** JGW to FJG, 21 Oct. 1885, Whittier Mss. 004, FHL.
Months later WLG learned of a New Hampshire woman who had been so moved by his
Park Street Address that she had persuaded her family to curtail its use of butter and tea
until they had raised $5 for the ACS! GUE, 12 Feb. 1830. For the ACS return to Park
Street in 1830, see *Christian Watchman*, 11 July 1830. WLG later recalled that the ACS
leaders disliked both his emphatic denunciation of slaveholders and his failure to devote
more than one sentence to the society; WLG, *Thoughts on African Colonization* (Boston,
1832), p. 4. **dig on/** WLG to Jacob Horton, 27 Jun. 1829 [1:83]. **freedom jubilee/** The
story of the July 14, 1829, celebration is related by an anonymous correspondent (almost
certainly Garrison himself) in WLG's first issue of GUE, 2 Sept. 1829. For an example
of the ridicule directed at such events, see the broadside "Grand Bobalition, or 'Great
Annibersary Fussible,' " in *Courage and Conscience*, 153. The interracial dimension of
the Boston benevolent community of the 1820s has not yet been adequately studied.

early prejudice recalled/ 20th anniversary celebration, *Lib.*, 31 Jan. 1851. **although a slave/** FMG to WLG, 12 May 1820, WSU. **immediatism/** *Boston Daily Evening Traveller*, 15 Oct. 1878; George Bourne, *The Book and Slavery Irreconcilable* (Philadelphia, 1816), 3, 4, 7–8. For praise of Bourne, see *Lib.*, 17 Mar., 25 Aug 1832; Elizabeth Heyrick, *Immediate, Not Gradual Abolition* (1824), reprinted in GUE, 7–21 Jan. 1826.

CHAPTER FIVE: IN BALTIMORE JAIL
trudge on foot/ GUE, 25 Sept. 1829. **Baltimore/** Raphael Soames, *Baltimore as Seen by Visitors, 1783–1860* (Baltimore, 1953), 60, 83, 90; Robert J. Brugger, *Maryland: A Middle Temperament* (Baltimore, 1988), 186–93. **like Boston/** Ralph L. Rusk, *Letters of Ralph Waldo Emerson* (N.Y., 1939) 1:196; **low spirits/** JGW to [?], Sept. 1829, JGWL 1:30. **editorial statement/** WLG, "To the Public," GUE, 2 Sept. 1829. As a matter of policy he thought the sooner freed slaves received "the benefits of instruction" the better it would be "for them and us," but in no way, he promised, would he "excuse those pseudo-philanthropists who find an apology for slavery's continuance in the [degraded] condition of the slaves." **odious distinctions/** BL to Isaac Barton, 8 Mar. 1825, Box 9A, PASP. **signed editorials/** *Boston Daily Evening Traveller*, 15 Oct. 1878; Dillon, *Benjamin Lundy*, 159. **advocates of slavery/** GUE, Dec. 1830; also *Life* 1:406. **rotten politics/** GUE, 4 Dec. 1829. **that they will create/** GUE, 25 Sept. 1829. **Black List/** GUE, 16 Sept., 2 Oct. 1829; on the interregional slave trade see Peter Kolchin, *American Slavery, 1619–1877* (N.Y., 1993), 94, and Michael Tadman, *Speculators and Slaves: Masters, Traders, and Slaves in the Old South* (Madison, 1989), 6–7, 41–45. **Woolfolk/** GUE, 6 Nov. 1829. **BL assault and trial/** GUE, 29 July 1826, 20 Jan., 24 Feb., 31 Mar. 1827; Frederic Bancroft, *Slave Trading in the Old South* (Baltimore, 1931), 31–42, 370–71. The jurors in that instance, BL said, "could not be prevailed on to convert the truth into a libel, nor set itself up as an editorial tribunal for the censorship of the Press." **criticism of Todd/** GUE, 13 Nov., 20 Nov. 1829. **Pinckney/** GUE, 30 Oct., 6 Nov. 1829. **confronted issue candidly/** GUE, 16 Sept., 25 Sept., 2 Oct., 27 Nov. 1829, 12 Feb. 1830. **attacks on Clay/** GUE, 19 Feb.–5 Mar. 1830; also 26 Oct. 1829. **free blacks/** Barbara Jeanne Fields, *Slavery and Freedom on the Middle Ground: Maryland During the Nineteenth Century* (New Haven, 1985), 1–5, 40–62; Ira Berlin, *Slaves Without Masters: The Free Negro in the Antebellum South* (N.Y., 1974), 88–95; Leroy Graham, *Baltimore: The Nineteenth Century Black Capital* (Lanham, 1982), 93–105. The young slave Frederick Douglass lived and worked in Baltimore, 1828–32, and said later that it "opened the gateway" to freedom for him. Robert G. Harper to Elias Caldwell, q. Carolyn Weekley et al., *Joshua Johnson: Freeman and Early American Portrait Painter* (Baltimore, 1987), 29. Brice, q. GUE, 1 Mar. 1828; Daniel Raymond, *The Missouri Question* (Baltimore, 1819), 7. **the time is to come/** GUE, 5 Feb. 1830. **we call things/** GUE, 9 Oct. 1829. **If somebody must suffer/** GUE, 16 Oct. 1829; Dillon, 155–56. **Walker/** *Walker's Appeal, in Four Articles, together with A Preamble to the Colored Citizens of the World, but in particular, and very expressly to those of the United States of America, Written in Boston, in the State of Massachusetts, Sept. 28, 1829* (reprint N.Y., 1969); Peter P. Hinks, *To Awaken My Afflicted Brethren: David Walker and the Problem of Antebellum Slave Resistance* (University Park, Pa., 1997). **attacks on Walker/** Clement W. Eaton, *The Freedom-of-Thought Struggle in the Old South*, 2nd ed. (NY, 1964), 121–25. WLG's views on Walker are in GUE, 15 Jan., 26 Feb., 5 Mar. 1830; *Lib.*, 1 Jan. 1831; *Life* 1:159–62. BL's view, GUE, April 1830. **civil suit/** GUE, 8 Jan 1830. **indictment text/** 19 Feb. 1830, q. *Life* 1: 167. **criminal libel/** Blackstone's *Commentaries* 4:150–51; "An Act authorizing any person prosecuted for a libel to give the truth in evidence," Ch. LIV, *Laws of Maryland Made and Passed at a Session of Assembly* (Annapolis, 1804). *Norvel v. Safeway Stores*, 212 Md. 14, 128 A.2d 591 (1957), reviews criminal libel cases in Maryland and, ignoring the Garrison prosecution, asserts that the charge had never been brought except in cases involving public officials. I am grateful to Llewellyn C. Thomas for advice on the legal background and for turning up the Maryland

statute of 1804. **politically inspired prosecution/** Whether Todd took the initiative in the lawsuit or whether his anger was exploited by the Baltimore colonizationists opposed to Garrison cannot now be determined. The Newburyport histories all ignore Todd, and no evidence about his business dealings has ever come to light. For WLG criticism of Woolfolk's political power, see GUE, 16 Oct. 1829. **Ritchie's editorial/** *Richmond Enquirer*, 28 Jan. 1830. If Taney had indeed tacitly encouraged the libel proceeding, it would have represented a change of opinion for him, since in 1819 he had defended—on free speech grounds—a minister who had been indicted for preaching an antislavery sermon. Carl B. Swisher, *Roger B. Taney* (N.Y., 1935), 95. **muzzle the press/** GUE, Oct 1830. **antagonized Todd/** GUE, June 1830. **libel trial/** WLG, *A Brief Sketch of the Trial of William Lloyd Garrison for an Alleged Libel on Francis Todd of Massachusetts* (Baltimore, 1830), 1. The ensuing account of the trial is based on this pamphlet in AmAqS, the only surviving record of the proceeding. I have occasionally changed indirect discourse into direct. Also see the 2nd ed. of the pamphlet, BPL, published by WLG in 1834, and his account, *Lib.*, 1 Jan. 1831, of the civil suit proceedings in October 1830. **Brice manumission/** Nicholas Brice to Moses Sheppard, 20 May 1834, FHS. **sided with Woolfolk/** GUE, 3 Mar., 12 May 1827. WLG later claimed Judge Brice had told Mitchell after the trial that there was nothing actionable in the column and if it had been submitted to the court and not the jury, he would have thrown it out, a statement that, if true, only confirms Brice's willingness to lend his court to the politics of repression. *Lib.*, 15 Jan. 1831. **juror opinions/** *Proceedings Against William Lloyd Garrison for a Libel* (Baltimore, 1847), 15–20, contains copies of their affidavits, which were gathered by prominent colonizationists in an effort to discredit Garrison's charges of "slave-ite" repression. Manuscript material about this project is in Moses Sheppard Papers, FHL. Information about juror occupations is from the 1829–30 Baltimore City Directory. **buzzing fly/** WLG to R. W. Gill, 13 May 1830 [1:95]. **power, not justice/** *Brief Sketch*, 8. **farewell editorials/** GUE, 5 Mar. 1830. **wages/** W. J. Rorabaugh, *The Craft Apprentice: From Franklin to the Machine Age in America* (N.Y., 1986), 85, reports that Horace Greeley made $6 a week, working 14 hours a day, in New York City in 1831. **voluntary inmate/** BL to *Baltimore Minerva*, 24 June 1830, in GUE, July 1830. Brice q. WLG to NPH, 1 June 1830 [1:102]. **preferment/** WLG to BC, 13 May 1830 [1:96]. **no rent/** [1:91]. **jail conditions and Hudson/** Mss. "Minutes of Visitors and Governors, Baltimore County Jail, 1829–30," Maryland Hall of Records. For WLG cards and remarks from jail see his letters 13 May–1 June 1830 [1:92–97], **Love to the whole world/** WLG to Harriet Farnham Horton, 12 May 1830 [1:92]. Garrison's words recall Schiller's "Ode to Joy"—*Seid umschlungen, Millionen! Diesen Kuss der ganzen Welt* ("O you millions, let me embrace you; Let this kiss be for the whole world")—which Beethoven had set to music in 1824 as the finale of his Ninth Symphony. **court may shackle/** WLG to NPH, 1 June 1830 [1:102]. **Tappan offer/** AT to BL, 29 May 1830, in *Life* 1:190–91. There is no credible evidence to support the often-cited story that Whittier persuaded Henry Clay to intercede with his Baltimore friends on Garrison's behalf. For conflicting recollections, see JGWL 3:59–60, 62–65; Lewis Tappan, *Life of Arthur Tappan* (N.Y., 1870), 167. **everyone who comes/** WLG to NPH, 1 June 1830 [1:101]. **warden's receipt/** WLG Papers, BPL. **It is my shame/** *Brief Sketch*, 8. On the process by which "dissidents" are made, see Vacel Havel, "The Power of the Powerless," *Living in Truth*, ed. Jan Vladislav (London, 1989), 83: "It begins as an attempt to do your work well, and ends with being branded an enemy of society."

CHAPTER SIX: A NEW ENGLAND MECHANIC

centennial observance/ BT, 16–18 Sept. 1830; Josiah Quincy, *A Municipal History of the Town and City of Boston* (Boston, 1852), 318–57; q. 319, 357; Charles Sumner to J. F. Stearns, 28 Sept. 1830, *Selected Letters of Charles Sumner*, ed. Beverly Wilson Palmer (Cambridge, 1990) 1:6. The City Hall building has resumed its former designation as the Old State House and is part of the National Historical Park in downtown Boston. **Walter welcomed/** BT, 2 Oct. 1830. **enable us both/** GUE, May 1830. **decision to**

leave Baltimore/ WLG to Ebenezer Dole, 14 July 1830 [1:104]; GUE, Oct. 1830. **a fine lad/** GUE, Jan. 1833, q. altered slightly, as Lundy spoke in the plural, referring also to William Swaim. **Public Liberator/** *Life* 1:199–202; mss., BPL. **Tappans/** Bertram Wyatt-Brown, *Lewis Tappan and the Evangelical Crusade Against Slavery* (Cleveland, 1969), 31–43; LT to WLG, 29 Jan. 1870, *Life* 4:255. WLG had in his pocket an appeal from the two editors for supporting a revival of the *Genius* as a weekly, but it is not clear that he showed the proposal to Tappan. BL Mss., "To the Friends . . ." 7 June 1830, BPL. **Tappan reply/** AT to WLG, 9 Aug. 1830, BPL. **for heaven sake/** Elliott Creeson to R. R. Gurley, 28 Sept. 1830, ACS/DLC. **lecture tour/** WLG to Oliver Johnson, 5 Feb. 1874 [6:293]; *Philadelphia Inquirer*, 2 Sept. 1830. WLG to George Shepard, 13 Sept. 1830 [1:110]. **Do you know/** WLG to BL, q. GUE, Dec. 1830. **perfect silence/** T. H. Gallaudet to R. R. Gurley, 24 Sept. 1830, ACS/DLC. **Allen critique/** NPH, 25 May, 11 June, 1830; WLG to editor, 1 June 1830, in NPH, 11 June 1830 [1:97–103]. **Newburyport closed/** WLG to NPH, 30 Sept. 1830 [1:111]. Today a statue of Garrison stands in Newburyport's Brown Square in front of the church that had shut him out. **Boston columns/** BT, 12 Oct., 13 Oct. 1830. **Julien Hall lectures and May's conversion/** *Life* 1: 212–14; SJMREC, 17–20; *The Journals of Bronson Alcott*, ed. Odell Shephard (Boston, 1938), 24 [15–16 Oct. 1830]. NPH, 28 Sept 1830, contains an account of three appearances in Amesbury, Mass., from which I have extrapolated the outline of the Boston talks. Since Garrison always recycled material, and his letters and proposals over these months repeat many passages and themes, I am confident that the Julien Hall lectures followed this format. **May/** Thomas J. Mumford, *Memoir of Samuel Joseph May* (Boston, 1882); Donald Yacovone, *Samuel Joseph May and the Dilemmas of the Liberal Persuasion* (Philadelphia, 1991); SJMREC, 20–24, describes the pro-Garrison sermon and ensuing censorship; Sewall to WLG, 27 Oct. 1830, BPL, outlines arrangements for the Athenaeum lecture. **Beecher/** OJBi, 45. **falling out/** BT, 6 Nov., 8 Nov. 1830; WLG letter reprinted [1:111–14]. **Webster-Hayne debate/** Merrill D. Peterson, *The Great Triumvirate: Webster, Clay, and Calhoun* (N.Y., 1987), 170–79; GUE, 5 Mar. 1830. **contempt more bitter/** *Lib.*, 1 Jan. 1831. **moral phenomenon/** SJMREC, 25. Alcott describes an effort by May, Collier, Sewall, and Blanchard to form an antislavery society, *Journals*, 26 [8 Nov. 1830]. **the Childs' support/** LMC, "The Liberator and Its Work," *Independent*, 28 Dec.1865; Carolyn L. Karcher, *The First Woman in the Republic: A Cultural Biography of Lydia Maria Child* (Durham, 1994), 174–75. **choice of name/** Sewell, q. *Life* 1:217. Although Garrison never explained his choice, that his romantic ardor led him to link the venture with Bolívar and O'Connell seems obvious. Byron wrote of his admiration for Bolívar and almost went to South America instead of Greece, and Lafayette sent Bolívar a gold medal from George Washington's descendants. O'Connell deliberately chose the South American "Liberator" as a model and ended up also bearing the title himself; the Irishman was charged for sedition for saying publicly that he hoped "a new Bolívar may be found" to free Ireland from its persecution. Gerhard Masur, *Simon Bolivar*, 2nd ed. (Albuquerque, 1969), 123, 399, 489; Oliver MacDonagh, *The Hereditary Bondsman: Daniel O'Connell, 1775–1829* (London, 1988), 170–71, 214. Bolívar was dying as *The Liberator* was being born, and WLG published Bolívar's farewell message in *Lib.*, 29 Jan. 1831. **black community/** James Oliver Horton and Lois Horton, *Black Bostonians: Family Life and Community Struggle in the Antebellum North* (N.Y. 1979), 1–87; William D. Piersen, *Black Yankees: The Development of an Afro-American Subculture in Eighteenth Century New England* (Amherst, 1988); George A. Levesque, "Black Boston: Negro Life in Garrison's Boston, 1820–1860," Ph.D. dissertation, SUNY Binghamton, 1976. **Walker legacy/** Donald M. Jacobs, "David Walker and William Lloyd Garrison," in *Courage and Conscience: Black & White Abolitionists in Boston* (Bloomington, 1993), 1–20, regards WLG as an "artful accommodationist" who endorsed some of Walker's views as a tactical maneuver to attract black support. Peter B. Hinks, *To Awaken My Afflicted Brethren* (University Park, Pa., 1997), 269–70, compares the folklore about Walker's demise with the municipal death records and an obituary in the *Boston Courier*. For continuing suspicion, see *Lib.*, 22 Jan. 1831. **black newspapers/** In

1827 Cornish had published the country's first black newspaper, *Freedom's Journal*, in New York, with John Russworm, the first black graduate of Bowdoin College, as editor. When Russworm took the paper into the colonization camp, however, Cornish started *The Rights of All* as an abolitionist alternative. David Walker was the Boston agent for *Freedom's Journal*. **December 10 meeting/** John G. Barbadoes to *Lib.*, 12 Feb. 1831; WLG reminiscence on *Lib.* 20th anniversary, *Lib.*, 31 Jan. 1851; WLG, *An Address delivered before the free people of color, in Philadelphia, New York, & other cities, during the month of June, 1831* (Boston, 1831). John T. Hilton recalled the women's efforts in *Lib.*, 27 July 1849. John Peak, *Memoirs*, 185. For Paul and Snowden's approval see Nell, *The Colored Patriots of the American Revolution* (Boston, 1855), 344–45. The phrase "against wind and tide" was a familiar reference from *Pilgrim's Progress*. **Forten gift/** JF to WLG, 31 Dec.1830, BPL. From the date it is clear that WLG had gone to press before the money came to hand, but he later blurred the chronology to give more honor to Forten. **Surely, no man/** James Russell Lowell, "The Day of Small Things," reprinted in *Selections from the Writings and Speeches of William Lloyd Garrison* (Boston, 1852), ix–x. **office/** WLG to Oliver Johnson, 1 Mar. 1874 [6:301]; OJBi, 51–52. **I have six days/** WLG to SJM, 14 Feb. 1831 [1:114–15]. For the lovelorn poetry, see *Lib.*, 2 Apr., 9 Apr., 23 Apr., 4 Jun. 1831. **Todd's civil suit/** *Lib.*, 1 Jan., 15 Jan. 1831. **attacks on prejudice/** *Lib.*, 8 Jan., 15 Jan., 5 Feb. 1831. I am indebted to Walker's biographer, Peter Hinks, for calling my attention to WLG's deliberate attempt to establish continuity with Walker's militancy. Peter Hinks to author, 2 Oct. 1994. For the campaign to overturn the ban on interracial marriage see *Lib.*, 8 Jan., 13 Aug. 1831; *Life* 1:254–55. **Watkins/** *Lib.*, 19 Feb. 1831. **Forten/** *Lib.*, 22 Jan. 1831. The newspaper, said Forten, had "roused up a spirit in our young people that had been slumbering for years [and would] produce writers able to vindicate our cause." **black support/** *Lib.*, 22 Jan, 12 Feb. 1831; JF to WLG, 21 Mar. 1831, BPL. J. T. Hilton et al. to WLG, 7 Aug. 1831, *Lib.*, 20 Aug. 1831; WLG reply, 13 Aug. 1831 [1:126–27]. The editor requested that the generous donation that accompanied the endorsement be used to establish a public reading room where copies of the newspaper would be readily available. He also provided 100 copies of the *Address* for complimentary redistribution by the group. WLG to SJM, 14 Feb. 1831 [1:115]; WLG to Simeon Jocelyn, 30 May 1831 [1:119]. **labor issues/** *Lib.*, 1 Jan. 1831, 13 Oct., 20 Oct. 1832 [also 1:168]; 6 Aug. 1836. For an overview see Eric Foner, "Abolitionism and the Labor Movement," in Christine Bolt and Seymour Drescher, ed., *Antislavery, Religion, and Reform: Essays in Memory of Roger Anstey* (Folkestone, 1980), 254–71. **few foolish whites/** *Lib.*, 9 July 1831. **Gurley/** *Lib.*, 23 July 1831. Gurley insisted that he had represented Garrison's views fairly, RRG to WLG, *Lib.*, 10 Sept. 1831. For warnings about WLG in ACS files, see Gabriel P. Disoway to RRG, 23 June 1831; Charles Tappan to RRG, 18 Aug. 1831, ACS/DLC. **anonymous letters/** *Tarborough* (N.C.) *Free Press*, in *Washington National Intelligencer*, 15 Sept. 1831, and *Lib.*, 15 Oct. 1831; "A Freeman" to WLG, 26 Aug. 1831, in *Lib.*, 10 Sept. 1831. **no neutrals/** WLG, *An Address to the Free People of Color* (Boston, 1831), preface. **as smooth/** WLG to HBG, 17 Sept. 1846 [3:412]. The pharmacist analogy is in OJBi, 55. **office atmosphere/** *Life* 1:221; OJBi, 52–54. **editorial jibes/** *Lib.*, 15 Jan., 29 Jan., 26 Feb. 1831. Noah's remark from *New York Courier*, q. *Lib.*, 20 Aug. 1831. **reform the reformers/** *Lib.*, 26 Mar. 1831. For a discussion of the era's "slang-whanging" editorial style, see David S. Reynolds, *Walt Whitman's America* (N.Y., 1995), 130. **"all on fire" conversation/** SJMREC, 36–37. **Southampton Insurrection/** *Lib.*, 3 Sept. 1831; WLG to La Roy Sunderland, 8 Sept. 1831 [1:129]; Henry I. Tragle, ed., *The Southampton Slave Revolt of 1831* (Amherst, 1971); Stephen B. Oates, *The Fires of Jubilee: Nat Turner's Fierce Rebellion* (N.Y., 1975). **editorial reaction/** BT, q. *Lib.*, 3 Sept. 1831; *New York Journal of Commerce*, q. *Lib.*, 10 Sept. 1831; *Alexandria Gazette*, Sept. 1831, in Tragle, 88. The *New York Journal of Commerce* even condoned the indiscriminate white reprisals, saying that "when the lives of a whole community are in jeopardy, severe measures are not only justifiable, but necessary" even if the "comparatively innocent" are injured by them. **Governor's file/** Oates, 130; "L.M.Q." to Gov. of Va., 15 Oct. 1831, Virginia State Library; John Floyd to

J. C. Harris, Orange County Postmaster, 27 Sept. 1831, Tragle, 274–75. **assassination threats/** LaRoy Sunderland to WLG, in *Lib.*, 10 Sept. 1831; reply [1:129]; *Lib.*, 15 Oct., 22 Oct. 1831. **Tappan gift/** AT to WLG, 12 Sept. 1831, BPL. When Southern states sought to indict WLG on sedition charges, Tappan increased his support. AT to WLG, 18 Oct. 1831, BPL. **Washington editors' attack/** *National Intelligencer*, 15 Sept. 1831. While editing the GUE, Garrison had attacked the *National Intelligencer* for its "black spots" of slave auction advertisements, and in a column adjacent to the notorious attack on Francis Todd, Garrison had called the editor Joseph Gales "a plausible specious hypocrite." Gales did not sue for libel. GUE, 20 Nov. 1829. **blistering reply/** WLG to Joseph Gales and William W. Seaton, 23 Sept. 1831 [1:130–35]. **too severe/** q. *Lib.*, 15 Oct. 1831. **riposte for each attack/** WLG to Henry Benson, 19 Oct. 1831 [1:139]; *Lib.*, 22 Oct., 24 Dec. 1831. **Floyd/** Diary entries, 8 Oct., 11 Oct., 16 Oct., 18 Oct. 1831, excerpted in Tragle, 256–59; annual message, 6 Dec. 1831, in Tragle, 460. **Otis heard/** texts in Samuel Eliot Morison, *The Life and Letters of Harrison Gray Otis, Federalist, 1765–1848*, 2 vols. (Boston 1913) 2:259–61; 276–81. *Life* 1:242–44. **the paper you/** Francis Wayland to WLG, 1 Nov. 1831, q. *Life* 1:242–44. **amend his definition/** *Lib.*, 12 Nov. 1831. **must we now begin/** *Lib.*, 1 Jan. 1832. **extract a root/** WLG to Gales and Seaton, *Lib.*, 15 Oct. 1831. **masthead illustration/** *Lib.*, 23 Apr. 1831. Sewall regarded the new ornamental heading as unnecessarily provocative and offered to pay the cost of suppressing it. *Life* 1:232. **popular medallion/** Hugh Honor, *The Image of the Black in Western Art* (Houston, 1989) 4:62, depicts the medallion devised by Josiah Wedgwood; organizers sold the cameos to raise money for the cause, though Wedgwood himself gave them away because he never wanted it said that he had sold a Negro. Betty J. Fladeland, *Men and Brothers: Anglo-American Antislavery Cooperation* (Urbana, 1972), 49. Honor's discussion [4:62–64] overinterprets the kneeling posture as an enshrinement of "pathetic, docile subservience and black inferiority." For a different perspective see the poem in *Lib.*, 21 Jan. 1832, celebrating Wilberforce kneeling alongside a black man at a communion service. **work of Christianity/** *Lib.*, 9 Apr., 28 May 1831; WLG to J. T. Hilton et al., 13 Aug. 1831 [1:126–27]. **fantasy/** [T. T.], "A Dream," *Lib.*, 2 Apr. 1831. **agitate the subject/** *Lib.*, 24 Dec. 1831.

CHAPTER SEVEN: SCATTER TRACTS LIKE RAINDROPS
scatter tracts/ *Lib.*, 26 Mar., 30 July 1831. **ability to do good/** AT to WLG, 12 Oct. 1831, BPL. **NEAS Founding/**OJBi, 82–86; SJMREC, 30–32. "Records of the NEAS, Boston 1832" (BPL), a bound volume of minutes largely in the handwriting of Joshua Coffin, is the only contemporary source other than *Lib.* Pasted in the back of the volume—and ignored by previous writers—is Coffin's letter (29 Dec. 1831) to the drafting committee, which was read aloud at the meeting of 1 Jan. 1832. WLG, *Lib.*, 13 Aug. 1831, 21 Jan. 1832, 7 Jan. 1832; SJM to WLG, 20 Feb. 1832, BPL. For the founding documents see *Lib.*, 18 Feb. 1832. WLG recalled the dispute over the preamble in *Lib.*, 3 Jan. 1835. **move to meeting house/** At the 25th anniversary celebration WLG recalled the black presence, *Lib.*, 9 Jan. 1857. William C. Nell, in 1832 the 15-year-old son of a black political leader, recalled that he observed the event through the vestry window, but made no mention of the stormy weather; perhaps he was referring to an inside partition. *Lib.*, 16 Jan. 1857. William C. Nell, *The Colored Patriots of the American Revolution* (Boston, 1855), 345, notes the desire of both races for separate political organizations. In the 1980s the African Meeting House was restored to its 1806 appearance and made the centerpiece of the Boston African American National Historic Site. **separate signing/** The signatures of the "founders" are in a right-hand column on the page below Coffin's text. In a parallel column are the signatures of 11 important leaders in the black community, including John G. Barbadoes, John B. Cutler, Thomas Cole, Coffin Potts, and John E. Scarlett. It seems unlikely that they were added on a subsequent occasion, as the following page contains parallel columns of signatures of men who presumably enrolled at the next opportunity, with white and black names intermingled—including Samuel J. May and John T. Hilton, one below the other. "Records of the N.E.A.S.,

Boston, 1832," bound notebook, BPL. If the black leaders signed next to the "founders" in some ceremonial fashion, why was it not later commemorated as such? It seems more likely that there was a mutual understanding not to do so, for surely William C. Nell, in his efforts to promote black history during the 1850s (see Chap. 20), would have made more of the episode than he did. It would be facile to regard this as an instance of racial discrimination within the movement, however, since the Jan. 6 meeting obviously went as the black leaders chose. To confuse the issue further, there is in the MAS file at NYHS an undated, unsigned memorandum on the early history of the NEAS that lists the participants at each of the organizational meeting and notes after the voting on Jan. 6 that "the Constitution was then signed by 72 persons." I believe that this sentence is an erroneous inference drawn by the writer from a perusal of the minute book; at least one of the 72 signatories, Samuel J. May, is known to have been absent that night. No additional evidence has yet come to light that might resolve the puzzling aspects of this extraordinary event; Francine Farr, curator African Meeting House/Museum of Afro American History, to author, 6 Sept. 1991. The Mass. General Colored Association sent a delegate, Joshua Easton, to the first annual NEAS meeting in Jan. 1833 with a resolution of support and an offer to become an "auxiliary." NEAS, *First Annual Report* (Boston, 1833), 7. **storm/** OJBi, 84–85. **Friends, we have met/** OJ, *Lib.*, 9 Jan. 1857, at the 25th anniversary celebration. **Virginia debate/** *Lib.*, 7 Jan., 14 Jan., 4 Feb., 25 Feb. 1832. **We must satisfy/** *U.S. Telegraph*, 5 Dec. 1835; see generally, Charles Sellers, "The Travail of Slavery," in Charles Sellers, ed., *The Southerner as American* (Chapel Hill, 1960), 40–71. Figures on slave ownership are from Kenneth Stampp, *The Peculiar Institution* (N.Y., 1956), 29–33. **Stewart/** q. *Lib.*, 7 Jan 1832. For the pamphlet *Religion and the Pure Principle of Morality . . .* see the reprinted text in Marilyn Richardson, ed., *Maria W. Stewart: America's First Black Woman Political Writer* (Bloomington, 1981), 28–41. **Boston judge tried/** q. *Lib.*, 7 Apr. 1832; criticism in *Lib.*, 5 May, 28 July, 2 Aug. 1832. **book-length refutation/** WLG gives the outline of his first eight charges in *Lib.*, 5 May 1832; WLG, *Thoughts on African Colonization . . .* (Boston, 1832). *Life* 1:301 notes that 2,750 copies were sold within nine months; a second edition was announced in *Lib.*, 29 Dec. 1833. For the ACS, see P. J. Staudenraus, *The American Colonization Movement 1816–1865* (N.Y., 1961). **Innocent birds/** *Lib.*, 12 Mar. 1831. **May on ACS/** SJM to WLG, 26 Mar. 1831, BPL; SJM to WLG, 10 July 1831, BPL; Henry Benson to SJM, 4 Aug., 2 Sept., 20 Dec. 1831, BPL; WLG to Benson, 12 Nov. 1831 [1:139–40]. **Thoughts/** q., in order, preface, i, ii, 90, 66, 141, 143, 154; Pt. 2, p. 5. Production and sales: WLG to Henry Benson, 31 May 1832 [1:150]; WLG to *London Patriot*, 6 Aug.1833 [1:258]; AT to WLG, 20 June 1832, BPL. J. Miller McKim recoll., *Lib.*, 25 Dec. 1863. For Amos Beman's descriptions of oral reading at political gatherings in black communities, see Peter B. Hinks, *To Awaken My Afflicted Brethren* (University Park, Pa., 1997), 154. I am grateful to the late Paul Goodman for allowing me to read his unpublished manuscript "Of One Blood: Origins of Racial Equality and the Emergence of Abolitionism," which contains the most thorough analysis yet of the ACS ideology and the abolitionist response. **kindled a fire/** Elizur Wright recollections, 1 June 1879, q. *Life* 1:298–99. **Buffum tour/** *Lib.*, 1 Sept., 8 Sept. 1832. For Danforth's response see *Lib.*, 1 Sept. 1832; Danforth to RRG, 10 June, 7 July 1832, ACS/DLC; WLG to Henry Benson, 21 July 1832 [1:159]. The NEAS attack is outlined in 30 Apr.–25 June 1832, Minute Book, BPL. The conservative ministers' view is recounted in the journal of Henry C. Wright, in Truman Nelson, *Documents of Upheaval* (N.Y., 1966), xiii. For the affinities between anti-Masonry and abolition in Massachusetts, see Paul Goodman, *Towards a Christian Republic: Antimasonry and the Great Transition in New England 1832–1836* (N.Y., 1988), 147–76, 187–88, 239–42. **people pressed forward/** Lester A. Miller to WLG, 5 Sept. 1832, BPL; also [?] to WLG, 2 Sept. 1832, BPL. Colby College, q. *Lib.*, Oct. 1832; the Western Reserve fight received full coverage in *Lib.*, Oct. 1832–March 1833. **to do justice/** *Lib.*, 7 Sept. 1832; opening lecture gambit, q. *Lib.*, 16 July 1831. **grand Miltonic poem/** Harriet Beecher Stowe, *Oldtown Folks*, Library of America ed. (N.Y., 1982), 1314. **ACS reaction/** Asa Cummings to Danforth, 14 Dec. 1832; Thomas Adams to Danforth, 26

Dec. 1832; Danforth to Matthew Carey, 6 Nov. 1832; Danforth to Gurley, 21 Dec. 1832, ACS/DLC. Danforth described *Thoughts* as nothing more than "a labored concentration of the mass of volcanic matter which for two or three years has been belched forth from that Vesuvius of the press—*The Liberator.*" **Gurley review/** *African Repository* 7 (Nov. 1832): 271–76, reprinted in *Lib.*, 8 Dec. 1832, with WLG reply. Additional q., RRG to Birney, 20 Feb. 1833 [1:56–57]. For ACS counterattack see Staudenraus, 204–11; Danforth, q. *Lib.*, 4 May 1833. **Nullification/** *Lib.*, 22 Dec. 1832, 5 Jan. 1833. **financial problems/** *Lib.*, 13 Oct., 24 Nov. 1832; Henry Benson to WLG, 23 Nov. 1832; Benson to SJM, 11 Dec. 1832; Tappan to WLG, 12 Dec. 1832. For WLG notes of gratitude see [1:192–98]. **My life/** WLG to Robert Purvis, 10 Dec. 1832 [1:196]. The Cunningham-Porter marriage was recorded in *Columbian Centinel*, 19 May 1832. **to see Whittier/** WLG to Harriet Minot, 3 Apr. 1833 [1:216]; to Harriott [sic] Plummer, 18 Mar. 1832 [1:214]. See generally, Donald Yacovone, "Abolitionists and the Language of Fraternal Love," in Mark C. Carnes and Clyde Griffen, eds., *Meanings for Manhood* (Chicago, 1990), 85–95; David S. Reynolds, *Walt Whitman's America* (N.Y., 1995), 198–99, 391–99. **English trip/** *Life* 1:325–30; *Lib.*, 9 Mar. 1833; WLG to George Benson, 8 Mar. 1833 [1:213]; WLG to Harriet Minot, 19 Mar. 1831 [1:215]. The editor had wanted George Bourne to be his substitute, but the minister wanted only to write a weekly column entitled "The Firebrand against the Ecclesiastical Man-Stealers." Bourne to WLG, 20 Mar. 1833, BPL. **confidential letter/** PC to WLG, 18 Jan. 1833, q. Rena K. Risby, "Canterbury Pilgrims," typescript, 1947, Crandall Museum. **Boston meeting/** PC to WLG, 29 Jan., 12 Feb. 1833, q. *Life* 1:316–17. PC described the evolution of her thinking in a letter to *Brooklyn Advertiser*, 7 May 1833, in *Lib.*, 25 May 1833. *Lib.*, 2 Mar. 1833, announced the school. Susan Strane, *A Whole-Souled Woman: The Story of Prudence Crandall* (N.Y., 1990), is a striking biography and major source for this section; also helpful is Marvis Olive Welch, *Prudence Crandall: A Biography* (Manchester, Conn., 1983). **reaction/** George Benson to WLG, 5 Mar. 1833, in *Lib.*, 9 Mar 1833; WLG to Benson, 8 Mar. 1833 [1:212]. The town meeting is reported in *Lib.*, 16 Mar. 1833; SJMREC 45–46; PC to WLG, 19 Mar. 1833, q. *Life* 1:322. **Boston farewells/** *Lib.*, 30 Mar. 1833; E. L. B. Cutler to WLG, 2 Apr. 1833; WLG to Samuel Snowden et al., 4 Apr. 1833 [1:217]; the silver medal is in the Garrison Collection, BPL. **Providence farewell/** Henry Benson to Isaac Knapp, 9 Apr. 1833, BPL; *Address Before the Free People of Color* (N.Y., 1833), 11; Helen Benson to Rebecca Buffum, 11 May, 1833, G/MHS. **Brooklyn visit/** WLG to Knapp, 11 Apr. 1833 [1:221–22]; Prudence Crandall to Simeon Jocelyn, 9 Apr. 1833, in *Journal of Negro History* 18 (Jan. 1833): 81–82; GWB to WLG, 30 Mar. 1833, BPL; Henry Benson to Isaac Knapp, 10 Apr. 1833, BPL; George Benson, Sr., to George Benson, Jr., 11 Apr. 1833, BPL; Almira Crandall to Henry Benson, 30 Apr. 1833, BPL. SJMREC, 47–50, describes his conversation with Judson. Nathan Winslow to Garrison & Knapp, 13 July 1833, BPL, emphasizes that people in his region saw the connection between Judson's views and the harassment of Crandall. **escape from sheriff/** WLG to Harriet Minot, 22 Apr., 1 May 1833 [1:223–26]; AB to *Lib.*, 6 May 1833, in *Lib.*, 11 May 1833. **dreamlike vision/** WLG to Harriott Plummer, 4 Mar. 1833 [1:206–207].

CHAPTER EIGHT: AMBASSADOR OF ABOLITION
international abolition/ Robert W. Fogel, *Without Consent or Contract: The Rise and Fall of American Slavery* (N.Y., 1989), 205–7; Robin Blackburn, *The Overthrow of Colonial Slavery* (London,1988); Herbert S. Klein, *African Slavery in Latin America and the Caribbean* (N.Y., 1986), 243–71. The Brazilian abolitionist Joaquim Nabuco used the *nom de plume* "Garrison" in his influential pamphlets of 1884: *Abolitionism: The Brazilian Antislavery Struggle*, ed. Robert Conrad (Urbana, 1977), xiv. For WLG's tributes to British abolition, see his *Address on the Progress of the Abolition Cause, delivered before the African Abolition Freehold Society, of Boston, July 16, 1832* (Boston, 1832), 9–10. **Liverpool arrival/** WLG to *Lib.*, 23 May, 24 May 1833; WLG frag., 27 May 1833 [1: 228–34]. **railroad/** WLG, "Mission to England," NEAS, *Second Annual Report* (Boston,

1834), 35, which is the source for other quotations not specifically cited. **Guildhall breakfast/** WLG to NEAS Board of Managers, 20 June 1833 [1:237–38]. For the development of the abolition bill in Parliament, see Izhak Gross, "The Abolition of Negro Slavery and British Parliamentary Politics, 1832–33," *Historical Journal* 23 (1980): 63–85. The standard treatment of the period, Asa Briggs, *The Age of Improvement* (London, 1959), has a good account of the reform bill, pp. 236–68, but pays only scant attention to abolition. **Buxton compliment/** *Life* 1:351. **true charity/** q. C. Duncan Rice, *The Scots Abolitionists, 1833–1861* (Boston Rouge, 1981), 3. **all the amends/** Charles Stuart to *London Patriot*, 11 Jan. 1833, in *Lib.*, 12 Apr. 1834. **Devonshire Chapel meeting/** *Lib.*, 10 Aug., 19 Oct. 1833, reprints proceedings from *London Patriot*, 12 Jun., 19 Jun. 1833; NEAS *2nd Annual Report*, 38–41; WLG to NEAS, 20 June, 1 July 1833 [1:238, 244–45]. **Wilberforce/** WLG impressions, *Lib.*, 9 Jan. 1836; account of meeting, NEAS *2nd Annual Report*, 44–45; John Pollock, *Wilberforce* (London, 1977), and Garth Lean, *God's Politician: William Wilberforce's Struggle* (London, 1980). **Thompson/** Rice, *The Scots Abolitionists*, 54–58; W. L. Garrison, *Lectures of George Thompson & A Brief History of His Connection with the Anti-Slavery Cause in England* (Boston, 1836), viii–ix. **sin will lie/** q. Howard Temperley, *British Antislavery, 1833–1870* (Columbia, S.C., 1972), 16. **the people love/** Stuart to Arnold Buffum, 29 June 1833, in *Lib.*, 31 Aug. 1833. **Exeter Hall/** *Lib.*, 9 Nov., 16 Nov., 23 Nov. 1833, reprints most of the speeches, including WLG's, which takes up eight full columns. GT's speech is in WLG, *Lectures*, q. 188, 179; JGW to WLG, 12 Nov. 1833 [1:133]. **Clarkson visit/** WLG version, NEAS, *2nd Annual Report*, 46–47; Clarkson version, TC to Mr. [?] Crisp, 24 Oct. 1833, Clarkson Papers [CN 76]. Huntington Library. On the lack of prejudice in England see NEAS, *2nd Annual Report*, 33–35; Nathaniel Paul to WLG, 10 Apr. 1833, *Lib.*, 22 June 1833. **John Bright/** q. Briggs, 260. **Wilberforce funeral/** *Lib.*, 21 Sept. 1833. **give us Thompson/** *Life* 1:437–38; Temperley, 22–23. **farewell present/** *Lib.*, 12 Oct. 1833; WLG to *London Christian Advocate*, 10 Aug. 1833 [1:260]. WLG left London at the end of August in the *Hannibal* for New York. To underwrite his passage Garrison had to negotiate a cash advance from Nathaniel Paul with a note permitting the minister to draw upon the Tappans' credit for repayment. There was much later confusion about the maneuver, which resulted from WLG's casual aproach to finance, and his critics attempted to make a scandal out of it. The actual correspondence with the Tappans on the matter is amiable in tone. LT to WLG, 29 May 1835, 25 Feb. 1836, BPL; AT to WLG, 2 Mar. 1833, BPL.

CHAPTER NINE: THE MOST EVENTFUL YEAR IN MY HISTORY
   New York reception/ *New York Gazette*, 2 Oct. 1833; *New York Courier & Enquirer*, 2 Oct. 1833; *New York Standard*, 2 Oct., 1833; *New York Evangelist*, 5 Oct., 1833; *Lib.*, 19 Oct. 1833; *Life of Arthur Tappan*, 169–75; *Lib.*, 12 Oct. 1833; John Neal to R. R. Gurley, 2 Oct. 1833, ACS/DLC. Cresson's reports are in *New York Commercial Advertiser*, 27 Aug., 9 Sept. 1833; *New York Evening Post*, 30 Aug. 1833. **misguided young gentlemen/** *New York Commercial Advertiser*, 3 Oct. 1833. **Garrison countered/***Lib.*, 12 Oct. 1833. More sympathetic editorials are *Journal of Commerce*, 3 Oct. 1833, and *Workingman's Advocate*, 5 Oct. 1833. **Martineau/** Harriet Martineau, *The Martyr Age* (N.Y., 1839), 3–4. **population figures/** *Negro Population in the U.S. 1790–1915* (Washington, D.C., 1918); Robert W. Fogel, *Without Consent or Contract: The Rise and Fall of American Slavery* (N.Y., 1989), 29–30, 44–45. **Child/** Lydia Maria Child, *An Appeal in Favor of That Class of Americans Called Africans* (Boston, 1833), esp. preface, 109–28, 141, 149. **national organization/** Edwin Atlee to Arthur Tappan, 7 Oct. 1833, PASP. WLG's letters on the necessity of an early meeting do not survive, but the story is summarized in Elizur Wright's correspondence; see especially the call (29 Oct. 1833) and EW to his father, 2 Nov. 1833, DLC. **finances/** *Lib.*, 2 Nov., 30 Nov. 1833; WLG to John B. Vashon, 5 Nov. 1833 [1:267–68], thanking him for an advance of $60. **Canterbury visit/** *Lib.*, 2 Nov. 1833; WLG to George Benson, 2 Nov. 1833 [1:266–67]. The house, now a museum, is open to the public under the auspicies of the

Connecticut Historical Commission. On the court case see Susan Strane, *A Whole-Souled Woman: The Story of Prudence Crandall* (N.Y., 1990), 61–69, 80–89. *Lib.*, 26 Oct. 1833, reprints the judge's charge and critical commentary. **no never/** PC to Simeon Jocelyn, 17 Apr. 1833, in *Journal of Negro History* 18 (Jan. 1933): 83–84. **delightful attractions/** WLG to George Benson, 25 Nov. 1833 [1:272]; on village gossip, Strane, 96. **Philadelphia/** Russell F. Weigley, *Philadelphia: A 300-Year History* (N.Y., 1982), 208–306; Gary B. Nash, *Forging Freedom: The Formation of Philadelphia's Black Community, 1720–1840* (Cambridge, 1988), 212–79. **run at once/** SJMREC, 287. **AAS convention/** JGW reminiscence, *Commemoration of the Fiftieth Anniversary of the American Anti-Slavery Society* (Philadelphia, 1884), 8–15; SJMREC, 81–97; *Proceedings at the Third Decade of the AAS* (Philadelphia, 1863), 32–49; Declaration of Sentiments, *Lib.*, 14 Dec. 1833, also *Life* 1:408–12. The desk is preserved in BPL; convention proceedings, *Lib.*, 21 Dec., 28 Dec. 1833; JGW to Harriet Minot, 4 Dec. 1833, JGWL 1:135. **give in/** Robert B. Hall to WLG, 21 Jan. 1834, BPL. To preserve his independence WLG relinquished his secretarial post and a seat on the executive committee before the first annual meeting in May 1834. **first courtship letters/** WLG to HB, 18 Jan. 1834 [1:279–80]; HB to WLG, 11 Feb. 1834, V/HHL; WLG to HB, 18 Feb., 1834 [1:283–84]. The Merrill edition unfortunately publishes only WLG's side of the correspondence; Helen Benson's replies must be read at HHL b Ms Am 1906 (13). Quotations from the ensuing letters are not separately cited, since the key dates are given in the narrative. **low mood/** WLG to SJM, 18 Feb. 1834 [1:285–86]; WLG to Henry Benson, 26 Feb. 1834 [1;287–88]. **Friendship's Vale/** Wendell Phillips Garrison, *The Benson Family of Newport, R.I.* (N.Y., 1872), GFP/SSC. The Benson house, now known as Friendship Valley, still stands a few hundred yards north of the village green in Brooklyn, Connecticut. **poem/** WLG quoted his stanza, "She was the masterpiece of womankind," to HB in 21 June 1834 [1:368], but he had published it in *Lib.*, 4 June 1831, as part of an extended tribute to an unidentified woman, obviously Mary Cunningham. **good abolitionist/** WLG to HB, 1 May 1834 [1:337]; WLG to GWB, 4 Sept. 1835 [1:493]. Lawrence J. Friedman's suggestion that WLG turned on PC after she "openly defied him by marrying Philleo" disregards chronology and is misguided. See "Racism and Sexism in Antebellum America: The Prudence Crandall Episode Reconsidered," *Societas: A Review of Social History* 4 (1974): 224. James Brewer Stewart, *William Lloyd Garrison and the Challenge of Emancipation* (Arlington Heights, 1992), 75–80, 101, speculates about WLG's fear of a dominant spouse. **condolences/** PCP to WLG, 20 Apr. 1879, BPL. Before moving to La Salle County, Ill., in 1847, Crandall taught an experimental "phonotypy" class in adult literacy at Boston's Belknap Street Church. PCP to WLG, 22 Apr. 1846, in *Lib.*, 1 May 1846. **wedding and housekeeping plans/** HB to WLG, 16 June, 23 June, 1834, V/HHL; WLG to HB, 21 June, 25 June, 11 Aug. 1834 [1:368–73, 394–95]. **opinions of Philleo/** WLG to HB, 18 Aug. 1834 [1:398–99], HB to WLG, 13 Mar., 9 June, 13 Aug. 1834, V/HHL. **eventful year/** WLG to GWB, 12 Sept. 1834 [1:411–12], which also contains an account of the wedding ceremony itself. On New England country weddings in this era, see Jack Larkin, *The Transformation of Everyday Life 1790–1840* (N.Y., 1988), 63.

CHAPTER TEN: BRICKBATS IN THE CAUSE OF GOD
strife of Christ/ WLG to Henry Benson, 11 Aug. 1836 [2:155]. **Bunyan/** *Lib.*, 8 Nov. 1834; *The Pilgrim's Progress*, Penguin ed. 1965), 136–47; **be of good cheer/** David Child to WLG, 23 Sept. 1835, BPL. **words blistered/** SJM to WLG, in *Lib.*, 20 Sept. 1834. On the closing of the school see WLG to SJM, 15 Sept. 1834 [1:415]. **signs of the times/** Like many of Garrison's catchphrases, the origin is Biblical. Christ mocks the Pharisees who can forecast the weather by the color of the sky but cannot understand the message of God: "O ye hypocrites, ye can discern the face of the sky, but can ye not discern the signs of the times?" Matt. 16:3. **Lane Seminary/** SJMREC, 102–108. T. D. Weld to LT, 18 Mar. 1834, DWGL 1:133, describes the creation of five day schools, evening schools, a lyceum, a reading room, a library, and Bible classes. **Colonization is dead/** q. P. J.

Staudenraus, *The American Colonization Movement 1816–1865* (N.Y., 1961), 234. **if our people**/ *New York Courier*, 23 Sept. 1834 q. *Life* 1:451. The Thompson family was hounded out of a New York hotel, but found hospitable lodging in a Roxbury boardinghouse near the Garrisons. GT to WLG, 24 Sept. 1834, BPL. **Groton & Boston talks**/ SJMREC, 117–19; *Lib.*, 18 Oct. 1834; *Lib.*, 31 Jan. 1835; memoir, C. K. Whipple to FJG, Oct.1885, GFC/SSC. **Emerson**/ JMN 5:90–91; Aunt Mary, q. SJMREC, 25. **I am almost afraid**/ WLG to HB, 21 June 1834 [1:369]. **home-body**/ WLG to Anna Benson, Oct. 1834 [1:420]. For the neighborhood, see Francis S. Drake, *The Town of Roxbury: Its Memorable Persons and Places* (Boston, 1905). **Boston's growth**/ William Pease and Jane Pease, *The Web of Progress: Private Values and Public Styles in Boston and Charleston, 1828–1843* (N.Y. 1985), 37–39, 66 ff; Walter M. Whitehill, *Boston: A Topographical History*, 2nd ed. (Cambridge, 1968), 73–103; BT 30 June 1836. **great locomotive**/ WLG to N. P. Rogers, Sept. 1840 [2:692]. **newspaper affairs**/ *Life* 1:430–34; Arnold Buffum to Garrison and Knapp, 31 [?] 1835, BPL, offers, in friendship, "a severe scolding" on sloppiness in business matters. GT to Robert Purvis, 10 Nov. 1834, BPL. **holy indignation**/ AT to Amos A. Phelps, 17 Jan. 1835, BPL. **not phraseology:** *Lib.* 27 Dec. 1834. **plan of cooperation**/ *Lib.*, 14 Feb. 1835; Wright's views: EW to AAP, 20 June 1834, BPL; AAS, *2nd Annual Report*, [May 1835], 59–62. Printing plans are outlined in EW to Weld, 10 June 1835, DWGL 1:224; Wyatt-Brown, *Lewis Tappan*, 143 ff. For the technological changes in printing, see W.J. Rorabaugh, *The Craft Apprentice: From Franklin to the Machine Age in America* (N.Y., 1986), 76–77; Rollo G. Silver, *The American Printer, 1787–1825* (Charlottesville 1967), 55–56. **nightmare**/WLG to HBG, 13 Mar. 1835 [1:464]. **new house**/ WLG to HBG, 4 May 1835 [1:471–72]. **Nova Scotia trip**/ WLG to HBG, 21 July, 25 July, 31 July 1835 [1:476–84]. **postal censorship**/ *Life* 1:492–94; Russell Nye, *Fettered Freedom: Civil Liberties and the Slavery Controversy* (East Lansing, 1949), 56–62; Tyler q. Leonard Richards, *"Gentlemen of Property and Standing": Anti-Abolition Mobs in Jacksonian America* (NY, 1970), 56–57; Amos Dresser narrative, *Lib.*, 26 Sept. 1835; Amos Kendall to Postmaster of Charleston, S.C., 4 Aug. 1835, in *Lib.*, 22 Aug 1835; Andrew Jackson to Amos Kendall, 9 Aug. 1835, *Correspondence of Andrew Jackson*, ed. John S. Bassett (Washington, D.C., 1931) 5:360. The two officials invited mob action by saying that if postmasters delivered "inflammatory papers" only to those who publicly insisted upon receiving them, the problem would take care of itself. **New York mood**/ LMC to Louisa Gilman Loring, 15 Aug. 1835, LMCMf. **Thompson escape**/ LMC wrote increasingly embroidered reminiscences of the affair in NAS, 18 Aug. 1842, 27 Feb. 1864, that suggest a full-fledged mob scene, though the contemporary Boston papers do not report one, nor does LMC's 15 Aug. 1835 letter describing her safe passage to N.Y. with GT. **guaranteed rights**/ BT, 3 Aug. 1835. **if the mob**/ Henry Benson to GWB, 19 Aug. 1835, BPL. **wire-worked**/ JGW in *Lib.*, 3 Oct. 1835. **if we are beaten**/ *Lib.*, 22 Aug. 1835. **incendiary matter**/ WLG to Knapp and Benson, 29 Aug–3 Sept. 1835 [1:486–492]. **Faneuil Hall meeting**/ *Lib.*, 29 Aug., 5 Sept., 12 Sept. 1835. **Concord**/ JGW to Erastus Brooks, 9 Sept. 1835, in *Lib.*, 3 Oct. 1835. **gallows**/ *Lib.*, 19 Sept. 1835; WLG to Henry Benson, [15 Sept.], and GWB, 17 Sept. 1835 [1:528–29]. Black sentinels recalled by John T. Hilton, *Lib.*, 27 July 1849. **shifting opinion**/ *Lib.*, 29 Aug. 1835, reprints *New York Evening Post editorial; Lib.*, 10 Oct. 1835; SJM to WLG, 2 Sept. 1835 BPL. **Boston mobbing**/ Preliminary events are summarized in *Lib.*, 17 Oct. 1835; statements of Mayor Lyman and Deputy Marshal Wells in Theodore Lyman, Jr., ed., *Papers Relating to the Garrison Mob* (Cambridge, 1870), 15–16, 67–68. There are three contemporary accounts: C. C. Burleigh, *Lib.*, 24 Oct. 1835, and WLG, dated 25 Oct. 1835, in *Lib.*, 7 Nov. 1835; [Maria Weston Chapman], *Right and Wrong in Boston: Annual Report of the Boston Female Anti-Slavery Society* (Boston, 1836). *Papers Relating to the Garrison Mob*, 14–24, contains a memoir by Mayor Lyman that is undated, but clearly written as a rebuttal to abolitionist criticism of his conduct. James Homer's recollections about the handbill are reprinted in *Life* 2:10–11. My account is a synthesis of this material, the Boston newspaper comments, and miscellaneous items from *Life* 2:12–30; Henrietta Sargent to

Angelina Grimké, 21 Jan. 1837, in DWGL 1:358; WLG to G. W. Benson, 21 Oct. 1835 [1:540]; WLG to Samuel E. Sewall, 24 Oct. 1835 [1:541]; Helen B. Garrison to Caroline Weston, 31 Oct. 1835, BPL; Anne Weston to Mary Weston, 22 Oct., 27 Oct., 30 Oct. 1835, BPL; Deborah Weston Diary, [October 1835], BPL; [anon.] to WLG, Oct. 1835, BPL; EQ Diary, 21 Oct. 1835, MHS. WLG's remark "I am passive in your hands" is recalled in WLG to Wendell Phillips, Nov. 1870, B/HHL; George Benson, Jr., to Henry Benson, 26 Oct. 1835, BPL; Knapp to WLG, 26 Oct. 1835, BPL; WLG to George Benson, Jr., 30 Nov. 1835; *Proceedings of the 20th Anniversary of the Boston Mob* (Boston, 1855), 72–73, has W. C. Nell's recollection of the black coachman and other details. **Ephesian uproar/** Imprisoned at Ephesus, the apostle Paul wrote a letter to the Ephesians describing the church as an instrument of social redemption. The passage, Ephesians 6:11–12, exhorts the faithful to "put on the whole armour of God. . . . For we wrestle not against flesh and blood, but against principalities, against powers, against the rulers of the darkness of this world, against spiritual wickedness in high *places*." It was often quoted by WLG's mother. **I did not prove/** WLG to HBG, 4–14 Nov. 1835 [1: 546–557]; WLG to GWB, 30 Nov. 1835 [1:566]. **Such a mob/** Sarah Southwick, *Reminiscences of Early Anti-Slavery Days* (Cambridge, 1893), 14. GT was transported secretly to St. John, N.B., where he boarded the Liverpool packet on 9 Nov. 1835. **one house at least/** SJMREC, 160–62. **Harriet Martineau/** on Boston indifference, *Retrospect of Western Travel* (NY, 1838) 2:159; WLG interview, *Retrospect* 2:218–20; E. G. Loring to WLG, 5 Dec. 1835, *Life* 2:55–56; Martineau, "The Martyr Age," *Westminster Review*, Dec. 1838, recapitulates her assessment. **five year comparison/** *Lib.*, 19 Dec. 1835, 2 Jan. 1836.

CHAPTER ELEVEN: A UNIVERSAL EMANCIPATION FROM SIN
Christian revolt/ WLG to Elizabeth Pease, 28 Feb. 1843 [3: 125]. **missionary work/** LMC to Sarah B. Shaw, [?] 1860, LMC to SJM, [?] 1867, LMCMf. Fifty years later Theodore Dwight Weld still closed his letters in the bond of "the old abolition love that never waneth," TDW to Dear Friends, 31 Mar. 1884, LCSL. **her savior/** Frances H. Drake to FJG, 2 Nov. 1899, Misc. Coll., MHS. I discovered this note—previously uncatalogued—tucked into the flyleaf of FJG's inscribed copy of Sarah H. Southwick's *Reminiscences of Early Anti-Slavery Days* (Cambridge, 1893). **attempted diary/** The 1836 pocket almanac with notes in WLG's hand is preserved in the Garrison Collection, BPL. **not a philosopher/** V. L. Parrington, *Main Currents in American Thought* (N.Y., 1927) 2:344–53, appreciates WLG as "a religious soul rather than a speculative intellect" and cautions against seeking "a political philosopher in a Hebrew moralist." **contradictory advice/** WLG to Henry Benson, 16 Jan., 26 Jan. 1836 [2:9,23]. **birth of son/** WLG diary, 13 Feb. 1836; WLG to GWB, 10 Apr. 1836 [2:72]. **sonnets/** *Lib.*, 20 Feb. 1836. **largest state/** New York had 1.9 million people in 1830, Pennsylvania 1.3 million, Ohio 937,000; Massachusetts, with 610,000, ranked 4th in the North and 8th overall, behind slave states of Virginia, North Carolina, Kentucky, and Tennessee. **ding dong'd/** TDW to EW, 6 Oct. 1836, in DWGL 1:237–39. **gag rule/** For good examples of Northern editorials on free speech, see W. C. Bryant, *New York Evening Post*, 21 Apr., 20 May 1836. For Clay see *Lib.*, 26 Mar. 1836, and HC to James T. Austin, 5 Jan. 1836, in *Papers of Henry Clay*, ed. Robert Seager II (Lexington, 1984) 8:815–16. **Calhoun/** JCC speech in *Lib.*, 27 Feb. 1836; assessment of Calhoun, *Lib.*, 8 Oct. 1836, 21 Jan. 1848. *Cong. Globe*, 24th Cong., 1st Sess., 1103–8, 1136–71, 1721–37. **Phillips/** *Tributes to William Lloyd Garrison at the Funeral Services, May 28, 1879* (Boston, 1879), 46. **We have blasted/** WLG to AAP, 16 Dec. 1835 [1:578]. **Channing**: *Slavery* (Boston 1835), q. 13, 11, 25, 119, 135, 140–41, 148. Theodore Bacon, *Leonard Bacon* (N.Y., 1931), 245–47; LMC to *Lib.*, 2 Apr. 1836; SJMREC, 175; *Lib.*, 9 Jan. 1836; WLG to SJM, 5 Dec. 1835 [1:572]. **still for gradualism/** *Lib.*, 27 Feb. 1836. **your eldest child/** HCW to WLG, 6 April 1836, BPL; WLG to HCW, 11 Apr. 1836 [2:73–75]. **needed no more/** WLG to HBG, 25 May 1836 [2:108]. **a challenging puzzle/** WLG to David Child, 6

Aug 1836 [2:153–54]. WLG assumed a larger role in the subsequent anti-Texas petition campaigns; *Lib.*, 7 July 1837, and [2:266–67]. **other great subjects/** WLG to Mary Benson, to GWB, both 27 Nov. 1835 [1:561–63]. For the pacifist conversation, see HCW Journal, 29 Dec. 1835, BPL. **truth for authority/** q. Blanche K. Hersh, *The Slavery of Sex: Feminist-Abolitionists in America* (Urbana, 1978), 15. WLG always credited the Motts for having "liberalized" his mind and freed it from sectarian bondage. *Lib.*, 9 Nov. 1849; WLG to HBG, 19 Mar. 1835 [1:467–68]. **Hicksites/** Walt Whitman, "Elias Hicks," in *Whitman: Poetry and Prose* (Library of America ed., N.Y. 1982), 1234–35. See GUE, 6 Mar. 1830, for Lundy's memorial tribute to Hicks. On the split see Bliss Forbush, *Elias Hicks* (N.Y, 1956), 112, 120–21, 136 ff. The painter Edward Hicks, known today for his "Peaceable Kingdom" series, was a nephew of Elias Hicks. **prevalent heresy/** *Lib.*, 4 July, 12 Dec. 1835. **perfectionism/** For contemporary criticism by a Presbyterian minister, see Joseph L. Foot, "The 'New Dispensation,' or Modern Antinomianism, Commonly Called Perfectionism," *Literary and Theological Review* 1 (Dec. 1834): 554–83. J. H. Noyes, *The Way of Holiness* (Putney, Vt., 1838), reprints articles from *The Perfectionist*; see also George W. Noyes, ed., *Religious Experience of John Humphrey Noyes* (N.Y., 1923), esp. 100–196. Noyes to WLG, 22 Mar 1837, in *Lib.*, 13 Oct. 1837, recounts their conversation. Noyes did not found his uptopian colony at Oneida, where his anti-institutional thinking found expression in group marriages and sexual freedom, until 1848, long after WLG had ceased to have connections with him. **make havoc/** WLG to HCW, 16 Apr. 1837 [2:258]; see also *Lib.*, 23 June, 22 July 1837. For Boyle, see two long letters from him to WLG, *Lib.*, 22 Mar., 29 Mar. 1839; also a letter from Laura Boyle, *Lib.*, 5 Apr. 1839. Paul E. Johnson and Sean Wilentz, *The Kingdom of Matthias: A Story of Sex and Salvation in 19th Century America* (Oxford, 1994), explores another, more lurid phase of millennial experience in this era. **blasts against Beecher/** *Lib.*, 23 July, 30 July, 6 Aug. 1836. Jabs against Beecher from other newspapers are reprinted in *Lib.*, 20 Aug., 5 Nov. 1836. For Beecher's attempts to suppress abolitionists, in conjunction with Leonard Bacon, see *New York Evangelist*, 9 July, 16 July 1836; William Goodell, *Slavery and Anti-Slavery* (N.Y., 1852), 430; Lyman Beecher, *Autobiography*, ed. Barbara Cross (Cambridge, 1981) 2:260; *Lib.*, 3 Sept. 1836. **replies to critics/** WLG to *New England Spectator*, 30 July 1836; to E. L. Capron, 24 Aug. 1836 [2:147–48, 172–73]; WLG to Henry Benson, 21 Aug. 1836 [2:166]; *Lib.*, 27 Aug., 10 Sept. 1836. **looks tolerable/** Lucretia Cowing to Debora Weston, 30 Sept. 1836, BPL. **Only Moses/** Garrison Centenary Committee of the Suffrage League of Boston, *Celebration of the 100th Anniversary of the Birth of William Lloyd Garrison* (Boston, 1906), 26, GFP/ SSC. **newspaper arrangements/** committee circular, 12 Jan. 1836, NYHS; WLG to SJM, 26 Dec. 1835 [1:586]. On MAS support see *Lib.*, 10 Dec. 1836, 4 Feb., 11 Feb. 1837; WLG to Anna Benson, 4 Feb. 1837 [2:206–8]. **"seventy" convocation/** The campaign drew inspiration from Luke 10:1, "After these things the Lord appointed other seventy also, and sent them two and two before his face into every city and place, whither he himself would come." Only fifty had been appointed by the time of the conference, however, and not all of them took the field. WLG to HBG, 22 Nov. 1836, to Henry Benson, 3 Dec. 1836 [2:184–189]; *Lib.*, 3 Dec. 1836; Sarah and Angelina Grimké to Jane Smith, 19 Nov. 1836, AG to JS. Nov. 1836, GCL. Weld's principles of organization are laid out in TDW to J. F. Robinson, 1 May 1836, DWGL 1:295–96. **Grimké sisters/** Biographical sketch based on Gerda Lerner, *The Grimké Sisters from South Carolina: Rebels Against Slavery* (Boston, 1967); Katherine Du Pre Lumpkin, *The Emancipation of Angelina Grimké* (Chapel Hill, 1974). AEG to WLG, 30 Aug. 1835, in *Lib.*, 19 Sept. 1835; AEG and Concord Female A-S Soc., in *Lib.* 25 Feb. 1837; AEG convention resolution, *Lib.*, 16 June 1837. **tour/** Lumpkin, 109–128; q., AEG to JS, 26 June, 25 July 1837, GCL; *Lib.*, 9 June 1837, AEG to JS, 29 May–5 June 1837, GCL. **pastoral letter/** approved at Brookfield, Mass., 28 June 1837; reprinted *Lib.*, 11 Aug. 1837; replies, *Lib.*, 11 Aug 1837; SMG, "Letter III on the Equality of the Sexes," July 1837, in *Lib.* 6 Oct. 1837; JGW poem, *Lib.*, 20 Oct 1837. **Lucy Stone/** q. Hersh

25, **Kelley/** AK to WLG, 20 Oct. 1837, BPL. **Emersons/** q. Robert Richardson, *Emerson: The Mind on Fire* (Berkeley, 1995), 270. **Appeal of Clerical Abolitionists/** *Lib.*, 11 Aug., 18 Aug. 1837; other attacks, *Lib.*, 1 Sept. 1837, with WLG reply [2:292–97]. **lack of church membership/** *New England Spectator*, 18 Oct. 1837, and WLG reply, *Lib.*, 27 Oct. 1837 [2:314–20]. **crazy superstructure/** *Lib.*, 25 Aug. 1837; my analysis of the "gospel differences" is based on Donald M. Scott, *From Office to Profession: The New England Ministry 1750–1850* (Phila., 1978), 95–111. **black support/** *Lib.*, 15 Sept., 6 Oct. 1837. **hands of laymen/** WLG to GWB, 20 Oct. 1837 [2:313]; R&W, 30; *Lib.*, 15 Sept. 1837. **New York office/** EW to WLG, q. in WLG to GWB, 23 Sept. 1837 [2:305–6]; WLG to LT, 13 Sept. 1837 [2:298–300]; EW to Amos Phelps, 29 Oct. 1837, BPL; TDW to AEG/ SMG, 15 Aug. 1837, DWGL 1:425–26; JGW to AEG/ SMG, 14 Aug. 1837, DWGL 1:423–24. As Southerners the sisters had a unique advantage in lecturing on abolition, Weld argued, which they forfeited in taking up other subjects. Whittier suggested that they were forsaking the slave for "a selfish crusade against some paltry grievance" of their own. For replies, see AEG to both, 20 Aug. 1837, DWGL 1:427–28; SMG to Amos Phelps, 3 Aug. 1837, BPL. **mutually strengthened resolve/** SMG/AEG to HCW, 27 Aug. 1837, DWGL 1:437–38; AEG to JS, 26 Aug., 15 Sept., 26 Oct. 1837, GCL. SMG noted her enthusiastic reading of "The Perfectionist," 11 June 1837, DWGL 1:400–403, saying that its sentiments "are in many respects as transcripts of my heart." **Lovejoy/** *Lib.*, 24 Nov.–8 Dec. 1837; Faneuil Hall speeches; *Lib.*, 15 Dec. 1837; in *New York Evening Post*, 18 Nov. 1837. **their own reservations/** *Lib.*, 5 Jan. 1838; SMG to Anne Weston, 1 Dec. 1837 in *Lib.*, 5 Jan. 1838; SJM to WLG, 18 Dec. 1837, BPL; reply, 30 Dec. 1837 [2:326]. **universal emancipation/** *Lib.*, 16 Dec. 1837, 5 Jan 1838.

CHAPTER TWELVE: THE EDITOR AS ISHMAELITE
prize worth seeking/ MAS, *7th Annual Report* (Boston, 1839), 7; AAS Proceedings, *Lib.*, 13 May 1838; R&W, 43–47. **everybody seemed delighted/** WLG to HBG, 7 May 1838 [2:350–53]. **Pennsylvania Hall/** *History of Pennsylvania Hall, which was destroyed by a mob on May 17, 1838* (Philadelphia, 1838), 12–35, 70–72, 117–20, 123–26; *Lib.*, 21 Sept. 1838, contains the Fall River delegate's report. Other details come from WLG to Sarah Benson, 19 May 1838 [2:362–63]; press accounts reprinted in *Lib.*, 25 May, 1 June 1838; BL to WLG, 18 May 1836, in *Lib.*, 9 Oct. 1840; Merton M. Dillon, *Benjamin Lundy and the Struggle for Negro Freedom* (Urbana, 1966), 254. **wedding/** WLG to HBG, 12 May 1838 [2:358–59]; Gerda Lerner, *The Grimké Sisters from South Carolina: Rebels Against Slavery* (Boston, 1967), 240–42. **New England Convention/** *Lib.*, 8 June 1838; JGW to *Pennsylvania Freeman*, 31 May, 3 June 1838, JGWL 1:297–302; *A Collection of the Miscellaneous Writtings of Nathaniel Peabody Rogers*, ed. John Pierpont (Manchester, N.H., 1849), 44–47; Goodell "manufactory," *Lib.*, 23 June 1837; James Mott to Anne Weston, 7 June 1838, BPL; a postscript from Mrs. Mott discusses "half-way abolitionists." A good example of WLG's answer to critics is his letter to Erasmus D. Hudson, 8 Sept. 1838 [2:384–85]; also *Lib.*, 26 Oct. 1838. **Douglass/** FDLT 213–14; FDPS 4:508–9. **Broadway Tabernacle speech/** *Lib.*, 17 Aug 1838; Knapp had the text published as a pamphlet before the month was out. **Cornish/** *Lib.*, 25 May 1838. **founding non-resistance society/** SJM to WLG, 22 July 1838, BPL; Peter Brock, *Pacifism in the United States: From the Colonial Era to the First World War* (Princeton, 1968), 523–58; LMC to E. Carpenter, 20 Mar. 1838, LMCMf; EELA, 73–92; MWC to WLG, 30 Aug. 1838, BPL; WLG to HBG, 21 Sept. 1838 [2:390–91]; text of declaration in *Lib.*, 28 Sept. 1838; LMC to AK, 1 Oct. 1838, LMCMf. Leo Tolstoy, "Introduction to a Short Biography of William Lloyd Garrison" (1904), *The Works of Leo Tolstoy*, ed. Aylmer Maude (London, 1935), 20:575–77. Tolstoy's own nonresistance essay, *The Kingdom of God Is Within You*, profoundly influenced M. K. Gandhi, whose philosophy inspired Dr. Martin Luther King, Jr., though neither of the latter apparently knew of Garrison's prior contributions. Judith M. Brown, *Gandhi: Prisoner of Hope* (New Haven, 1989), 78–80. **domestic details/** WLG to HBG, 21 Sept., 23 Sept. 1838 [2:391–98]; WLG to Mary Benson, 23 Dec. 1838 [2:409]. **newspaper arrangements/** Mss. signed

agreement, 17 Nov. 1838, BPL; *Lib.*, 4 Jan. 1839; handwritten appeal signed by committee, 1839, GFP/SSC; "Donations to the Liberator," 1939, mss. list, NYHS. **antislavery steward/** WLG to Harriet Foster, 14 Jan. 1839 [2:423–24]. **Truly Jack Cade/** q. Brock, 550; R&W, 64ff., reviews the rumors. **a talented woman/** q. James B. Stewart, *Wendell Phillips: Liberty's Hero* (Baton Rouge, 1986), 128. **clerical snake/** WLG to GWB 5 Jan. 1839 [2:418]. **political action as Christian duty/** circular letter, 4 Jan. 1839, q. in Richard H. Sewell, *Ballots for Freedom* (N.Y., 1976), 30. **Gurley/** q. *Life* 2:249. **Spiritual Quixotism/** EW to WLG, 6 Nov. 1837, DLC. **Stanton-Birney position/** MAS Quarterly Meeting at Worcester, Mar. 1839, in *Lib.* 29 Mar., 5 Apr. 1839; WLG to *Emancipator*, 31 May 1839 [2:465–82]. **Ishmaelitish editor/** WLG to Knapp, 9 Aug. 1837 [2:273] **public support**; David and Maria Child to MAS, 15 Jan. 1839, in *Lib.*, 8 Feb. 1839; SJM to Abolitionists of Mass., 10 Jan. 1839, in *Lib.*, 25 Jan. 1839; MWC to Rhode Island A-S Soc., 4 Nov. 1838, in *Lib.* 11 Jan. 1839. **If the South/** "Truth-Teller," *Lib.*, 1 Mar. 1839. **MAS meeting and aftermath/** MAS, *7th Annual Report*; *Lib.* 1 Feb. 1839, R&W, 96–115; Hilton speech reported in *Ipswich Register*, q. *Lib.*, 22 Feb. 1839; Stanton to Birney, 26 Jan. 1839, in DJBL 1:481–83; WLG to Mary Benson, 10 Feb. 1839, to GWB, 19 Mar. 1839 [2:433, 443]. On Stanton's mendacious reputation and abuse of WLG's hospitality, see OJ to Elizur Wright, 19 Apr. 1881, Johnson Papers, Vermont Historical Society. Sewell, *Ballots for Freedom*, 30, regards WLG's answer to Stanton as "the boast of an unquestioned egotist and true believer" that cleverly articulated an "implied standard of *true* abolitionism." **historical fact/** *Lib.*, 7 June 1839. **Child's report/** LMC to Caroline Weston, 7 Mar. 1839, to MWC, 10 Apr. 1839, LMCMf. **hold fellowship/** Vermont Antislavery Society, q. *Lib.*, 1 Mar. 1839. **pierced to heart/** George Bourne to WLG, 2 Mar. 1839, BPL. **Boston quarrel/** JGW to Elizabeth Neall, 10 Feb., 26 Feb., 12 Mar. 1839, to WLG, 24 Feb. 1839, to TDW, 10 Apr. 1839, JGWL 1:323–48; replies, *Lib.*, 22 Feb., 8 Mar. 1839; R&W, 115. **Fitch apology/** *Lib.*, 24 Jan. 1840. WLG replied that he would plant "the kiss of forgiveness" upon his cheek.

CHAPTER THIRTEEN: SCHISM

ideological differences/ WLG's views are drawn primarily from two major documents: an open letter to *The Emancipator*, 31 May 1839, reprinted in *Lib.*, 28 Jun. 1839 [2:464–85], that refuted Birney's attacks upon the nonresistants, and an open letter to the abolitionists of Massachusetts, written by WLG for the MAS, 17 July 1839, in *Lib.*, 19 July 1839 [2:497–516], that responded to the new organization. For the 1839 AAS meeting that serves as the context for this discussion see WLG to HBG, 5 May 1839 [2:457]; *Lib.*, 10 May, 17 May 1839; David L. Child in *Lib.*, 31 May 1839. Aileen S. Kraditor, *Means and Ends in American Abolitionism: Garrison and His Critics on Strategy and Tactics, 1834–1850* (N.Y., 1967), is a thoughtful examination that has influenced my approach. **Birney/** *Emancipator*, 2 May 1839, reprinted in *Lib.*, 28 June 1839. For Child's dualism, see NAS, 20 May 1841. **when doctors disagree/** William Powell, BAP 1:299–300. **if impudence/** OJ to Elizur Wright, 19 Apr. 1881, Johnson Papers, Vermont Historical Society. **men will no longer/** DWGL 1:146. **even while professing** R&W, 158. **farmers, mechanics/** *Lib.*, 19 July 1839 [2:504]. **it was Tappan/** For the struggle within the executive committee over political nominations, see AAS Executive Committee Minutes, vol.1, BPL, esp. 11 Dec., 18 Dec. 1839, 6 Feb. 1840. WLG's replies are from the major 1839 documents cited above. **woman question/** Dorothy Sterling, *Ahead of Her Time: Abby Kelley and the Politics of Antislavery* (N.Y., 1991), 20–93; Child, q. Kraditor, 47. **sickened/** Rev. Horace Moulton to Amos Phelps, 8 May 1839, BPL. **opposed to hens/** Elizur Wright to Phelps, 11 July, 17 Aug. 1838, BPL. **men or persons/** 1839 AAS Proceedings, *Lib.*, 17 May, 24 May, 31 May 1839. **new organization/** MAS, *9th Annual Report* (Boston, 1841), 5–7; for organized expressions of support for WLG and the old organization, see pp. 22–23, 30–31, also *Lib.*, 7 June, 14 June, 19 July 1839. **Amazons/** MAS, *9th Annual Report*, 7–8. **BFAS spilt/** *Lib.*, 1 Nov. 1839; WLG to MWC and BFASS, 13 Oct. 1840 [2:714–17], and *Lib.*, 16 Oct. 1840. Debra Gold Hansen, *Strained Sisterhood: Gender and Class in the Boston Female Anti-Slavery Society*

(Amherst, 1993) fails to recognize the sectarian context of the split, for most of the members seeking a dissolution were members of Phelps's and Fitch's congregations. **Welsh blood/** C. Weston to Anne Weston, 20 Nov. 1838, BPL. **children and finances/** WLG to GWB, 30 Sept. 1839, 4 Jan. 1840 [2:533–34, 555]. SJM to WLG, 15 June, 25 July 1839, BPL. **brother's return/** WLG to J. K. Paulding, 14 Dec. 1839; WLG to Caleb Cushing, 16 Dec. 1839, 10 Feb. 1840 [2:549–52; 558–559]; James H. Garrison, *Behold Me Once More* (N.Y., 1954). To be strictly accurate, James had turned up very briefly in the summer of 1835 but fled again before the relationship could be reestablished, so I have elected to treat the 1839 encounter as the beginning of resumed relations. **Knapp/** WLG to GWB, 4 Jan. 1840 [2:555–56]; WLG to Elizabeth Pease, 15 May 1842 [3:79–82]. J. C. Smith to WLG, 10 Dec. 1841, BPL, protests Knapp's "mistreatment" and accuses WLG of "living in princely stile literally surrounded by friends of wealth and influence faring sumptuously every day" while his old partner remained in poverty. IK to WLG, Sept. [1841], BPL, is a piteous appeal to speak privately away from the printing office. **finances/** Liberator Committee Ledger, 1840, BPL; "Donations to the Liberator," 1839–40, Mss., NYHS; WLG to EQ, 14 Dec. 1844 [3:271], recalls that Jackson, Loring, and Philbrick each advanced $200 to capitalize the printing office. E. G. Loring to Friend Robson, 27 Dec. 1839, NYHS, describes *Lib.* as "the free-est paper in the world." FJ to WP, 11 Nov. 1842, NYHS, says that *Lib.* met its expenses in 1841 for the first time ever, though $500 would be needed to meet the 1842 deficit. **prostituted press/** *Lib.*, 3 Jan. 1840. **The new year/** WLG to GWB, 4 Jan. 1840 [3:555]. **Thomsonian medicine/** For the regimen, WLG to GWB, 10 Mar., 7 Apr. 1838 [2:341–44]; for background, Alex Berman, "The Thomsonian Movement and Its Relation to American Pharmacy and Medicine," *Bull. Hist. Med.* 25 (Sept.–Oct. 1951): 405–28. **political transformation/** Charles Sellers, *The Market Revolution: Jacksonian America, 1815–1846* (N.Y., 1991), 297–300, 348–53. **Clay/** speech, 7 Feb. 1839, in *Lib.*, 15 Feb. 1839; Merrill D. Peterson, *The Great Triumvirate: Webster, Clay, and Calhoun* (N.Y., 1987), 286–88. **funeral sermon** [Francis Philpott], *Facts for White Americans*, c. 1839, Rare Book Collection, DLC. **Birney/** The argument is laid out in *Emancipator*, 2 May 1839, reprinted in *Lib.*, 29 June 1839. **critique of nominations/** WLG to OJ, 5 Aug. 1839 [2:523–25]; MAS Statement [drafted by WLG], *Lib.*, 25 Oct. 1839; David L. Child, *Lib.*, 20 May 1839; "A Plain Man," *Lib.*, 27 Mar. 1840. **abolition made easy/** *Lib.*, 10 Apr. 1840. **Jay/** Kraditor, 145. **wade to their armpits/** Stanton to Birney, 21 Mar. 1840, DJBL 1:542–43. **downplayed election/***Lib.*, 13 Mar., 24 Apr. 1840. **new organization's Boston sheet/** *Lib.*, 29 Nov. 1839. **small but talented/** WLG, "To the Abolitionists of the United States," *Lib.*, 28 Feb. 1840; Henry Wright's report, *Lib.*, 21 Feb. 1840; HCW to GWB, 20 Feb. 1840, BPL. **snobbery/** Birney's son recalled his father's disinterest in socializing with WLG. William Birney to Samuel Willard, 11 Nov. 1885, Chicago Historical Society. **every minister/** LMC to Ellis G. Loring, 7 May 1840, LMCMf. For evidence of Stanton's plotting, see his scribbled notes to Amos Phelps, 15 Feb., April [?] 1840, on the backs of British circulars, BPL. **If you would preserve/** *Lib.*, 24 April 1840. **New York trip/** WLG to *Lib.*, 12 May 1840; OJBi, 289–90; Sarah H. Southwick, *Reminiscences of Early Anti-Slavery Days* (Cambridge, 1893), 26; J. H. Garrison, 110. **world's convention plans/** JGW's poetic salute to the meeting, *Lib.*, 10 Jan. 1840, for WLG's doubts, see William Chace to George Benson, 6 May 1840, BPL; WLG to HBG, 19 May 1840 [2:615–19]; **New York reception/** WLG to HBG, 15 May 1840 [2:612]; q. New York papers all from *Lib.*, 29 May 1840. **business meeting/** AAS Minutes, OJ and HCW reports, all in *Lib.*, 22 May 1840; Anne Weston to MWC, 23 May 1840, BPL; WLG to HBG, 15 May 1840 [2:611–613]; Parker Pillsbury, *Herald of Freedom*, reprinted *Lib.*, 12 June 1840; Address of A&F Society, *Lib.*, 19 July 1840, and AAS Exec. Com. reply, *Lib.*, 31 July 1840; JGW to Elizabeth Whittier, 30 May 1840, JGWL 1:412; LT to TDW, 26 May 1840, DWGL 2:836; EQ Diary, 13 May 1840, MHS; LMC to L. B. Child, 7 June 1840, LMCMf; *Lib.*, 22 May 1840, contains the resolutions. Only in the condemnation of ministers who refused to testify against slavery did they sound a harsher note than the

Tappanites would have permitted. For an argument that underplays the schism, see Ronald Walters, *The Antislavery Impulse* (Baltimore, 1976), 3–18. **did not bring/** LMC, "The Liberator and Its Work," *Independent*, 28 Dec. 1865; see also LMC, "To Abolitionists," NAS, 20 May 1841, which puts the schism in the context of the duality inevitable in "every new application of old principles to exsting institutions." **living in the world/** q. in Lillie B. C. Wyman and Arthur C. Wyman, *Elizabeth Buffum Chace 1806–1899: Her Life and Its Environment* (Boston, 1914) 2:63–64.

CHAPTER FOURTEEN: GARRISONIZED TO THE BACKBONE

protest plans/ WLG to OJ, 22 May 1840 [2:627]; Bourne's view, WLG to HBG, 19 May 1840 [2:616]. **our good feeling/** Charles B. Ray to Birney and Stanton, 20 May 1840, in BAP 3:331–35; *Lib.*, 5 June. 1840. **farewell statements/** WLG to OJ, 22 May 1840, *Lib.*, 29 May 1840; *Emancipator*, q. in *Lib.*, 3 July 1840. Leavitt's joke is repeated in JL to JGB, 1 June 1840, DJBL 1:581. **voyage/** WLG to HBG, 19 May–15 June 1840 [2:615–53], and an extract from a letter by William Adams in *Lib.*, 7 Aug. 1840. **Sometimes you have hinted/** WLG to HBG, 14 June 1840 [2:642]. **world's convention/** Primary sources for the London convention include WLG to HBG, 29 June, 3 July 1840; WLG to OJ, 3 July 1840 [2:654–66]; WP to OJ, [25?] June 1840, in *Lib.*, 24 July 1840; *Slavery and the Woman Question: Lucretia Mott's Diary . . . of the World's Antislavery Convention in 1840*, ed. Frederick B. Tolles (Philadelphia, 1952), 14–66; N. P. Rogers to Parker Pillsbury, 24 July 1840, *Lib.*, 21 Aug. 1840; C. L. Remond to C. B. Ray, 30 June. 1840, BAP 1:71–74; William Adams, extract from a letter in *Lib.*, 7 Aug. 1840; Ann G. Phillips to WP, note on back of convention program, B/HHL; Maria Waring, mss. notes, June 1840, BPL, reprinted in Clare Taylor, *British and American Abolitionists* (Edinburgh, 1974), 97. The convention agenda was based upon a comprehensive outline of the subject prepared by the leadership, which then assigned aspects to different speakers, so that the meeting was more like a professional symposium than a plenary debating session. Though policy resolutions were offered, the convention occupied most of its time listening to a series of reports. See annotated Order of Business, Antislavery Convention, 12 June 1840, in B&FASS Papers, Rhodes House, Oxford, micro. ed., Reel 58. **forth came much folly/** Elizabeth Cady Stanton to AGW & SG, 25 June 1840, DWGL 2:845–49. **Haydon sitting/** B. R. Haydon to WLG, 30 June 1840, BPL; Abby Kimber to RDW, 25 Aug. 1840, BPL; the painting, which hangs in the National Portrait Gallery, London, is reproduced in Hugh Honour, *The Image of the Black in Western Art* (Cambridge, 1989), vol. 4, part 1, p. 169. **English social conditions/** WLG to SJM, 6 Sept. 1840 [2:696–97]; WLG to HCW, 23 Aug. 1840 [2:680]; *Lib.*, 23 Oct. 1840. The British leaders are criticized in *Lib.*, 24 July, 23 Oct. 1840, 15 Jan. 1841. **Boston convention/** N. P. Rogers to J. H. Tredgold, 3 Aug 1840, Rhodes House Mss., Oxford. **Garrisonized/** RDW to Sarah Poole, 3 Aug. 1840, BPL, in Taylor, 101. **Edinburgh and Glasgow speeches/** *Lib.* 21 Aug., 28 Aug., 18 Dec. 1840. **Dublin/** RDW to WLG, 1 Aug., 2 Sept. 1840, BPL. **no longer surprising/** RDW to Sarah Poole, 3 Aug. 1840, BPL, in Taylor, 100. **Boston reception/** *Lib.*, 28 Aug. 1840; WLG to Elizabeth Pease, 1 Sept. 1840 [2:685]. **campaign atmosphere/** CS to George Sumner, 30 Oct. 1840, SLCS 1:94; WLG to Joseph Pease, 1 Sept. 1840, to John A. Collins, 16 Oct. 1840 [2:690, 719]. Collins estimated that 70% of voting abolitionists intended to go with the Whigs. JAC to WLG, 1 Sept. 1840, BPL. *Lib.*, 16 Oct., 23 Oct. 1840; WLG to JAC, 16 Oct. 1840 [2:718–19]. For the antiparty arguments see *Lib.*, 23 Oct., 30 Oct., 13 Nov. 1840. **family life/** WLG to JHG, 17 Sept., 1840, to JAC, 16 Oct. 1840, to GWB, 1 Nov. 1840 [2:702,719, 721]; Irving H. Bartlett, *Wendell and Ann Phillips: The Community of Reform, 1840–1880* (N.Y., 1979), 32. While at the world's convention in London, Phillips had told his mother of the flattering attentions he had received from eminently respectable British abolitionists. "I tell you all this to show you how far from vulgar *The Liberator* would be, Ma, in London." Bartlett, 30. **anniversaries/** *Lib.*, 11 Dec., 25 Dec. 1840, 1 Jan. 1841. **Carlyle/** The lectures were delivered in London, 5–22

May 1840; Thomas Carlyle, *On Heroes, Hero-Worship, & the Heroic in History* (1841), ed. Michael K. Goldberg (Berkeley, 1993), q. 100, 116. **working for a new world**: Hannah Webb notes, June 1840, q. RDW to Sarah Poole, 3 Aug. 1840, BPL.

CHAPTER FIFTEEN: NO UNION WITH SLAVEHOLDERS
Alcott/ Bronson Alcott to SJM, 10 Aug. 1840, to Junius Alcott, 28 Sept. 1841, *Letters of Bronson Alcott*, ed. Richard L. Herrnstedt (Ames, Iowa, 1969), 54, 57. **a people's movement/** T. W. Higginson, *Cheerful Yesterdays* (Boston, 1898), 119. Theodore Parker believed that "a great revolution went on [in] New England's spiritual history . . . so silent that few men knew it was taking place." See his important "Letter to the Members of the Twenty-Eighth Congregational Society of Boston, 19 April 1859," *The Works of Theodore Parker* (Centenary ed.), 15 vols. (Boston 1907–13), 13:275–413. **seekers/** Higginson, 115–16; Charles Sellers, *The Market Revolution: Jacksonian America, 1815–1846* (N.Y., 1991), 157–61, emphasizes the protest against commercial culture embodied in the new religious groups; E. P. Thompson, *The Making of the English Working Class* (London, 1965), ch. 2, "Christian and Apollyon," demonstrates the centrality of Bunyan's imagery in the dissenting tradition. Lewis Perry, *Radical Abolitionism: Anarchy and the Government of God in Antislavery Thought* (Ithaca, N.Y., 1973), ch. 4, locates come-outerism in the tradition of "Christians without Churches" that extends back to sectarian conflicts against the Roman Catholic hierarchy and the second phase of the Protestant Reformation in which radical 17th-century sects opposed the churches of the Protestant states. **little heretical meeting/** *Lib.*, 10 Sept. 1841. **Chardon St. convention/** The call for the convention is in *Lib.*, 23 Oct. 1840; WLG views are in *Lib.*, 6 Nov., 4 Dec., 18 Dec. 1840; WLG to Collins, 1 Dec. 1840 [2:724–25]. **Emerson's report/** EELA, 1210–13; Joel Meyerson, "A Calendar of Transcendental Club Meetings" [1836–40], *Amer. Lit.* 44 (May 1972): 197–207. **detractors/** *Lib.* 29 Jan. 1841, reprints Colver's letter and WLG's refutation; Pease to Collins, 25 Dec. 1840, q. *Life* 2:430. The proximate goal of Colver's campaign was the disruption of a fund-raising mission undertaken by John A. Collins for the MAS, so there was an organizational as well as a personal basis for WLG's concern. **religious views/** WLG to Elizabeth Pease, 1 Mar., 1 June 1841 [3:17, 23–24]; *Lib.*, 15 Oct., 19 Nov., 26 Nov. 1841. Views similar to WLG's are expressed in Lucretia Mott's address, Marlboro Chapel, Boston, 23 Sept. 1841, in *Lib.*, 15 Oct. 1841. **Oberlin perfectionism/** WLG to GWB, 19 Mar. 1839 [2:443], approved President Asa Mahan's discourses; see also *Lib.*, 27 Dec. 1839. Oberlin's historian is at pains to distinguish Mahan's and Finney's views from Garrisonian ultraism, Robert S. Fletcher, *A History of Oberlin College from its Founding through the Civil War* (N.Y., 1943), 223–34. **church withdrawals/** AK to WLG, 28 Sept. 1841, with 22 Mar. 1841 letter to Uxbridge Meeting, in *Lib.*, 8 Oct. 1841. Also see Eliza and Mary Kenny to WLG, 30 Aug. 1841, with accompanying church correspondence, in *Lib.*, 3 Sept. 1841. Rhoda Bement's case (1843) is summarized in Dorothy Sterling, *Ahead of Her Time* (N.Y., 1991), 182–85; a complete transcript is in Glenn C. Altschuler and Jan M. Saltzgaber, *Revivalism, Social Conscience and Community in the Burned-Over District: The Trial of Rhoda Bement* (Ithaca, N.Y., 1983). For the rise of new church groups, see John R. McKivigan, *The War Against Proslavery Religion: Abolition and the Northern Churches, 1830–1865* (Ithaca, N.Y., 1984), 94ff. **the strongest proof/** C. K. Whipple, "How It Operates," *Lib.*, 26 Nov. 1841. **Parker/** *Theodore Parker: An Anthology*, ed. Henry Steele Commager (Boston: 1960), 38–62; *Lib.*, 26 Nov. 1841. **Foster disruptions/** Parker Pillsbury, *Acts of the Anti-Slavery Apostles* (Concord, N.H., 1883), 123ff., 281–82; WLG to HBG, 27 Nov. 1842 [3:113–14]; Beach: *Lib.*, 3 Dec. 1841. **Ruggles incidents/** *Lib.*, 9 July, 23 July, 6 Aug. 1841; steamship protest, NAS, 20 Aug. 1841. **Nantucket convention/** *Lib.*, 20 Aug. 1841; FDLT 214–15; Sarah H. Southwick, *Reminiscences of Early Anti-Slavery Days* (Cambridge, 1893), 30; Pillsbury, 324–27; Pillsbury to WLG(J), 11 May 1879, GFP/SSC; NAS, 20 Aug. 1841. **Douglass incidents/** *Lib.*, 15 Oct. 1841. **remarked to me/** WCN to WP, 31 Aug 1840, BAP micro. **travelers' directory/** *Lib.*, 8 Apr. 1842; stock dividend, *Lib.* 1 Dec. 1843. Barney was a son-in-law of the first NEAS president, Arnold Buffum.

Amistad case/ *Lib.*, 6 Sept. 1839. WLG to LT, 1 Nov. 1839 [2:535], introduces the British expert. For typical coverage, see *Lib.*, 13 Sept., 27 Sept., 11 Oct., 18 Oct., 6 Dec., 13 Dec. 1839; for the Judson decision see *Lib.*, 17 Jan., 24 Jan. 1840; for the U.S. Supreme Court phase, *Lib.*, 12 Mar., 19 Mar., 26 Mar. 1841; Tappan praise, *Lib.*, 12 Nov. 1841. **fugitive slave issues/** FD, *Lib.* 26 Nov. 1841; Prigg case: *Lib.*, 11 Mar. 1842; Samuel R. Ward to Gerrit Smith, 18 Apr. 1842, in BAP 3:383–84; Charles Sumner to C. F. Adams, 1 Mar. 1843, SLCS 1:128; NYT, q. *Lib.*, 18 Mar. 1842; *Prigg v. Pennsylvania* 41 U.S. 539 (1842); Kent Newmyer, *Supreme Court Justice Joseph Story: Statesman of the Old Republic* (Chapel Hill, 1985), 370–78. **Creole case/** *Lib.*, 18 Mar. 1842; SJM to J. A. Collins, 28 Feb. 1842, BPL; "The Duty of the Free States," *The Works of William E. Channing*, 6 vols., (Boston, 1867) 6:233–373; q. 235, 251, 318–19. **disunion/** See the resolutions prepared for Faneuil Hall (28 Jan. 1842), in *Lib.*, 4 Feb. 1842; Essex County (8 Feb. 1842), *Lib.*, 25 Feb. 1842. WLG's major statement is in *Lib.*, 6 May 1842. **American repealer/** WLG to GWB, 22 Mar. 1842 [3:62]. Oliver MacDonagh, *The Emancipist: Daniel O'Connell 1830–47* (N.Y., 1989), 80–84, emphasizes that O'Connell's repeal slogan was "a stab in the dark," more a rallying cry than a specific blueprint for social and political reorganization. Younger nationalists in O'Connell's coalition wanted him to soft-pedal abolition issues and support the American annexation of Texas as both an anti-British and pro–Democratic Party issue, but O'Connell remained firm in refusing American support that "came across the Atlantic stained with human blood." Text of the "Irish Address" in *Lib.* 11 Mar. 1842. **grand rallying point/** *Lib.* 22 Apr., 6 May, 1842. **he did not/** *Lib.*, 27 May, 3 June 1842; LMC to WP, 3 May 1842, LMCMf; WLG to GWB, 13 May 1842 [3:72]. **People now talk/** CS to George Sumner, 29 Mar. 1842, SLCS 1:112. **Adams victory/** Leonard L. Richards, *The Life and Times of Congressman John Quincy Adams*, (N.Y., 1986), 140–45, (includes Weld quote); WLG to RDW, 27 Feb. 1842 [3:53]. **criticism of Adams/** *Lib.*, 19 July 1839, 2 Feb. 1844. For the Grimké sisters' distress at Adams's "political morality," see SMG to TDW, 11 June 1837, DWGL 1:403 and AEG to JS, 29 May 1837, GCL. **in demanding/** WLG, Fourth of July Address, in *Lib.* 19 July 1839. **reform is commotion/** *Lib.* 19. Nov. 1841. **Latimer case/** *Lib.*, 28 Oct.–25 Nov. 1842; Story's views, Newmyer, 375–78; WLG's account of Justice Shaw's hearing, *Lib.*, 4 Nov. 1842; CS to MWC, 30 Nov. 1842, SLCS 1:121; Peleg W. Chandler, "The Latimer Case," *Boston Law Reporter*, Mar. 1843. See also, Robert M. Cover, *Justice Accused: Antislavery and the Judicial Process* (New Haven, 1975), 169–71, and William M. Wiecek, "Latimer: Lawyers, Abolitionists, and the Problem of Unjust Laws," in Lewis Perry and Michael Fellman, eds., *Antislavery Reconsidered* (Baton Rouge, 1979), 219–35. These writers, noting that Justice Shaw's daughter married the writer Herman Melville, regard Shaw as the possible model for the conflicted Captain Vere in *Billy Budd*. **Story suggested/** Story to John M. Berrien, 29 Apr. 1842, q. in Newmyer, 376–77. **Phillips/** *Lib.*, 11 Nov. 1842. **all that we claim/** WLG, "Address to the Slaves of the United States," *Lib.* 2 June 1843; **Adams warning/** "Address to the People of the Free States of the Union," *Lib.*, 19 May 1843. David M. Potter, *The Impending Crisis, 1848–1861* (N.Y., 1976), 135–36, points out that census data do not substantiate abolitionist claims on the number of slave escapees. **New England convention/** *Lib.*, 23 June 1843. Information on the Hutchinsons comes from the program booklet accompanying the Smithsonian Institution's recording "There's a Good Time Coming," a replica performance, 1978. **Tyler appeal/** *Lib.*, 2 June, 9 June, 23 June 1843; slave disruption dream, *Lib.*, 21 July 1843; WLG to GWB, 20 June 1843 [3:167]. **brother's death/** WLG to George Benson, 11 Oct., 14 Oct. 1842; WLG to HCW, 1 Mar. 1843 [3:105–7, 132]; obituary, *Lib.*, 21 Oct. 1842. **The disorder/** WLG to GWB, 15 Apr. 1843 [3:153]. **property question/** *Life* 3:95; WLG to Louisa Humphrey, 15 Dec. 1843, WLG to HCW, 1 Apr., 16 Dec. 1843 [3:145, 235, 240–41]. For examples of the continuing debate, see *Lib.*, 19 Mar., 26 Mar., 5 Apr. 1847, and, generally, Philip S. Foner and Herbert Shapiro, eds., *Northern Labor and Antislavery: A Documentary History* (Westport, Conn., 1994). **Northampton Association/** Charles A. Sheffield, *History of Florence, Mass., including a complete account of the Northamption Association* *of Education & Industry* (Florence, Mass., 1895), 73–130, FD q. 130; Alice Eaton McBee, "From Utopia to Florence: The Story of a Transcendental Community in Northampton, Mass., 1830–52," *Smith College Studies in History* 22 (1947): 46–71. The wagon accident and subsequent medical treatment may be followed in WLG letters of 16 Aug.–14 Oct. 1843 [3:197–224]. In Boston the gossips said that WLG had been trying to show off his hitherto unsuspected talents as a horseman, and the waspish Anne Weston observed, "It may be well enough to talk about 'every man his own priest,' but 'every man his own driver' is another thing." q. *Life* 3:84. **death of Knapp/** *Lib.*, 17 Sept. 1843. **come-outer editorials/** *Lib.*, 22 Dec. 1843, 19 Jan. 1844. **series of free lectures/** *Lib.*, 9 Feb., 26 Apr. 1844; EELA, 591–609. **Emerson shivered/** JMN, 7:281; 8:116, 523; 9: 132–34. Henry Thoreau was advertised as a speaker in the series, but there is no evidence that he actually appeared. **Ezekiel/** Thomas Wentworth Higginson, *Contemporaries*, (Boston, 1899) 246; **AAS resolution/** *Life* 3:99–100, *Lib.*, 24 May 1844. **Liberty Party constitutional arguments/** Alvan Stewart, *Writings and Speeches of Alvan Stewart on Slavery* ed. Luther R. Marsh (N.Y., 1860), 255–57; Wiecek, 208–215; Aileen S. Kraditor, *Means and Ends in American Abolitionism: Garrison and His Critics on Strategy and Tactics, 1834–1850* (N.Y., 1967), 188–91. **they looked at slavery/** FDLT 229. **Address to Friends of Freedom/** *Lib.*, 31 May 1844. **Thompson/GT** to WLG, 27 Jan. 1845, BPL. **Lowell/** q. Martin Duberman, *James Russell Lowell* (Boston, 1966), 110. **banner ceremony/** *Lib.*, 7 June 1844; WLG speech, *Lib.*, 16 Aug. 1844; "Get Off the Track" lyrics, *Lib.*, 19 Apr. 1844.

CHAPTER SIXTEEN: REVOLUTIONS NEVER GO BACKWARD

maps/ Samuel A. Mitchell, *Traveller's Guide Through the U.S.* (Philadelphia, 1845); Sidney E. Morse, *Cerographic Atlas of the United States* (New York, 1843). **Hispanic hinterland/** Richard Henry Dana, *Two Years Before the Mast* (Boston, 1840), sold 10,000 copies soon after publication. D. W. Meinig, *The Shaping of America: Continental America, 1800–1867* (New Haven, 1993) is a fresh look at the territorial issues, esp. pp. 128–46 on Mexico and Texas. William R. Brock, *Parties and Political Conscience: American Dilemmas, 1840–1850* (Millwood, N.Y., 1979), surveys the political transformation. **Calhoun and Texas/** JCC to Richard Pakenham, 18 Apr. 1844, in Arthur Schlesinger, Jr., and Fred Israel, eds., *History of American Presidential Elections, 1789–1968* 4 vols. (N.Y., 1971), 818–21. "If our safety and the great interest we have in maintaining the existing relation between the two races in the south are of no estimation in the eyes of our northern friends . . . it is time that we should know it," Calhoun told his political associates. JCC to Francis Wharton, 28 May 1844, CJCC, 596. From Washington David L. Child reported in *Lib.*, 3 May 1844, Calhoun's fear that the British would buy the freedom of Texas slaves. For Lewis Tappan's efforts to interest the British in such a scheme, see Bertram Wyatt-Brown, *Lewis Tappan and the Evangelical War Against Slavery* (Cleveland, 1969), 250–51. **political insanity/** *New York Evening Post*, 25 July 1844, in WCB, 231–32. **anti-Texas opposition/** *Lib.*, 23 Feb., 5 Apr., 3 May, 10 May, 6 Sept., 4 Oct. 1844; Leonard L. Richards, *The Life and Times of Congressman John Quincy Adams* (N.Y., 1986), 182. **constitutional polemic/** *The Liberator* was filled with constitutional discussion throughout 1844–46, but see especially *Lib.*, 19 Aug. 1844 (FJ), 13 Sept. 1844 (Madison Papers), 10 Jan. 1845 (curses), 17 Apr., 24 Apr. 1846 (political action), 12 Feb. 1847 (church analogy). For Phillips, see *The Constitution a Pro-Slavery Document* (AAS, 1844) and *Can an Abolitionist Vote or Hold Office Under the Constitution* (AAS, 1845). For Story's views, see *Commentaries on the Constitution of the United States* (Boston, 1833), sections 642, 1282, 1334, 1811, 1913. **election/** Polk received 49.6% of the vote to Clay's 48.1%, the closet election yet in U.S. history; the best account is Charles Sellers, "The Election of 1844," in Schlesinger and Israel 1:747–98, q. at 796. **Woodbury brandished/** 1 Mar. 1845, *Cong. Globe*, 28th Cong., 2nd sess., 299–300; he called the newspaper the "highest authority" of the opposition; reply, *Lib.*, 14 Mar. 1845. **superannuated men/** *The Olive Branch*, q. *Lib.*, 14 Feb. 1845. **Faneuil Hall convention/** *Lib.*, 31 Jan., 7 Feb. 1845; WLG to *Boston Daily Mail*, 1 Feb. 1845, in [3:277–79]. CS to Story, 5 Feb. 1845, CS to Sarah Perkins Cleveland, 31 Jan. 1845, in SLCS 1:142, 152; CS considered the editor's very participation in the meeting a statement of "eloquent" significance. MWC remark, *Lib.*, 23 Jan. 1846; **new times demand/** James Russell Lowell, "The Times, the Manners, and the Men," *Lib.*, 28 Feb. 1845. On his views of conscience politics, see JRL, *Pennsylvania Freeman*, 16 Jan., 30 Jan. 1845, in *Antislavery Papers* (Boston, 1902) 1:2–13, 67. **Sumner/**David Donald, *Charles Sumner and the Coming of the Civil War* (N.Y., 1961), 106–11; WLG to CS, 23 Aug. 1845 [3:319]. **Thoreau/** "Wendell Phillips Before Concord Lyceum," *Lib.*, 28 Mar. 1845, reprinted in *Writings of Henry D. Thoreau: Reform Papers*, ed. Wendell Glick (Princeton, 1973). Robert Richardson, *Thoreau: A Life of the Mind* (Berkeley, 1986), 150–51, emphasizes the anti-Texas agitation as the political context for Thoreau's experiment at Walden. The Thoreau women (mother Cynthia, sisters Sophia and Helen) are recorded as voting in favor of WLG's disunion resolution at the 1844 New England convention, *Lib.*, 14 June 1844; their names also appear in the newspaper's subscription books, BPL. **Texas admission/** *Lib.*, 7 Mar. 1845; draft resolutions in BT, 28 Jan. 1845; for examples of political calculus, see *Lib.*, 28 Feb. 1845, on Iowa and Florida; Meinig, 454–56. **protest pledges/** *Lib.*, 11 July 1845; see also WLG to SJM, 17 July 1845 [3: 303]. The abolitionist William Jay, a distinguished attorney and son of the nation's first chief justice, produced a learned treatise—widely excerpted in the press—that supported Garrison's contention. *Lib.*, 11 Apr. 1845. **enough to begin one/** *Lib.*, 3 Oct. 1845. Lowell, "The Present Crisis," *Lib.*, 20 Dec. 1845. **a great character/** *Lib.*, 15 Aug. 1845, reprinting NYTr report of 2 Aug. 1845; I have been unable to identify the author. **cotton thread/** JMN 7:232. For the Calhoun deal see JCC to AL, 13 May 1845, CJCC 2:654; for Polk, see Sellers, "Election of 1844," 791. **Winthrop toast/** *Lib.*, 25 July 1845; ostracism, Donald, 128–129. **stirring editorial/** *Lib.*, 30 Jan. 1846; See also WLG form letter, 25 July 1845 [3:310–11] and a lengthier editorial on free inquiry written during the Mexican War, *Lib.*, 2 Apr. 1847. **editor's fortunes/** Samuel Philbrick to WLG, 21 Jan. 1846, BPL; WLG to FJ, 12 Jan. 1846 [3:330–31]; Richard Henry Dana, *The Journal* ed. Robert F. Lucid, 3 vols. (Cambridge, 1968) 1:97; he was ten years younger than WLG. Charles Dickens, *American Notes* (1842), ch. 3, is a vivid portrait of the city. **neighborhood/** This impressionistic sketch is based on study of the manuscript census returns of 1850 (microfilm), the Boston tax assessors' manuscript "street volumes," 1843–50, (Boston City Archives), and the Boston city directories for the period. I am grateful to the late Dr. Peter R. Knights, York University, for valuable guidance in using these materials and for providing copies of the templates he devised to correlate census and assessors data. **praised the developers/** FJ to WLG, 26 July 1843, BPL; WLG to FJ, 2 Aug. 1843 [3:186]. **movement culture/** The Ohio reader was Amos Gilbert, in *Lib.* 6 Apr. 1848. *Lib.* 12 Jun. 1846 notices the 6th edition of *Archy Moore*, which WLG emphasizes preceeded FD's *Narrative* and is "fully sustained by it" as an accurate exhibition of slavery's horror. *Lib.* 3 May 1850, advertises Brown's panorama. Jarius Lincoln, comp., *Anti-Slavery Melodies for the Friends of Freedom, Prepared for the Hingham Anti-Slavery Society, 1843* p. 28. **social isolation/** Agnes Crain to AK, 26 Mar., 20 May 1847, Kelly-Foster Papers, AmAqS, portrays the loneliness of the movement worker and the support network the leaders helped to sustain. When Crain visited Boston, she came with a letter of introduction from Mary Grew in Philadelphia and expected to lodge with the Garrisons. **Douglass/** *Narrative of the Life of Frederick Douglass, an American Slave* (Boston, 1845), ix; sales figures, William McFeely, *Frederick Douglass* (N.Y., 1991), 116–17. Contrast McFeely's suggestion that Garrison's introduction is an instance of the "great white father" endeavoring "to commandeer [the book] for the cause" with the book's provenance in the movement and the role played by the MAS and the Cornhill printing office in its production. Note, too, that the editors of the Frederick Douglass Papers (FDPS 1:xlviii) discount the frequently repeated canard that the abolitionists counseled Douglass not to appear too learned. **seamen's hostel/** *Lib.*, 26 Oct. 1849. **wedding/** *Lib.*, 1 May 1846. **social distinctions/** John T. Moore, *Life and Letters of Oliver Wendell Holmes* (1896) 2:157; T. W. Higginson, *Cheerful Yesterdays*

(Boston, 1898), 125; WP to Sarah Phillips, 24 July 1840, B/HHL; Richard Henry Dana, Jr., 1 June, 1843, *Journal*, 1:161–62. **as good-looking/** Anne Warren Weston to Deborah Weston, 4 Feb. 1842, BPL; she also quotes another friend's depiction of Dickens as "her beau ideal of an Italian valet." **Quincy/** Edward F. Payne, *Dickens Days in Boston* (Boston, 1927), 128. Robert Vincent Sparks, "Abolition in Silver Slippers: A Biography of Edmund Quincy," Ph.D. thesis, Boston College, 1978, esp. 113, 209–216; Quincy-Webb Letters, BPL, esp. 29 Jan, 26 Mar., 27 June 1843, 13 Dec. 1845, 1 Feb. 1849. **Phillips relationship/** WP & AGP to WLG & HBG, 6 Jan. 1846, BPL; James B. Stewart, *Wendell Phillips: Liberty's Hero* (Baton Rouge, 1986), 128–129. Helen's letters to Ann Phillips, c. 1846–51, are in HHL. Ironically, Ann saved what Helen had asked her to destroy, while Helen seems not to have preserved the letters from Ann, so we know less about her side of the friendship, though Wendell told the Garrisons how much he appreciated their attentiveness to his wife. **social circle/** Sarah H. Southwick, *Reminiscences of Early Anti-Slavery Days* (Cambridge, 1893), 34–36. **hundreds of young persons/** MWC, 1844 fragment, BPL. Reviewing Emerson's address on West Indian Emancipation (1 Aug. 1844), Whittier said that he had felt indignant that while abolitionists were struggling, "such a man should be brooding over his pleasant philosophies, writing his quaint and beautiful essays, in his retirement on the banks of the Concord, unconcerned." JGWL 1:649 n.2. Joel Myerson, *The New England Transcendentalists and the Dial* (Rutherford, N.J., 1980), 289–301, lists the contents of each volume. **odious people/** shampoo'd, JMN 9:71; never felt comfortable, *The Journals of Bronson Alcott* ed. Odell Shephard (Boston, 1938), 225 [14 Feb. 1850]. **Fuller/** MF to MWC, 26 Dec. 1840, BPL, reprinted in Bell Gale Chevigny, *The Woman and the Myth: Margaret Fuller's Life and Writings* (Old Westbury, N.Y., 1976), 238–39; on FD, NYTr 10 Jun. 1845. **marriage and family life/** WLG to SJM, 19 Dec. 1846 [3:461]; Fanny Garrison Villard, *William Lloyd Garrison on Non-Violence, together with a Personal Sketch by His Daughter* (N.Y., 1924), 2–10; HBG to Ann Phillips, 8 Aug. 1846, B/HHL; HBG to Henry C. Wright, 10 Sept. 1861, WSU; E. C. Stanton, *Eighty Years and More: Reminiscences 1815–1897* (N.Y., 1898), 128–129; OJ, NYTr, 26 May 1879. **Hold enough!/** Though WLG is likely being merely witty, it is possible that birth control was on his mind. Jack Larkin, *The Transformation of Everyday Life 1790–1840* (N.Y., 1988), 200–201, suggests a Grahamite influence toward abstinence, but Peter Knights, *Yankee Destinies: The Lives of Ordinary Nineteenth-Century Bostonians* (Chapel Hill, 1991) 58, points out that the average age of last birth for women with five children was 37 (exactly HBG's age at Franky's birth). **presidency/** EQ to RDW, 27 June 1843, BPL. **Rogers fight/** The endless polemic may be followed in *Lib.*, 5 July–27 Dec. 1844. WLG to RDW, 1 Mar. 1845 [3:286–88], EQ to RDW, 14 Dec. 1844, BPL, and NPR to Elizabeth Pease, 23 Dec. 1844, in *Life* 3:127–28, offer conflicting viewpoints to British friends; NPR to WLG, 3 Jan. 1845, BPL, is an affectionate apology and farewell. Stewart, *Wendell Phillips*, 131–32, sees class animosity as well as ideological bias at work. **I have long lost/** John Smith to WLG, 24 June 1846, pub. *Lib.*, 17 July 1846, under heading "Reform Movements of the Age." **Mexican War/** Robert W. Johannsen, *To The Halls of the Montezumas: The Mexican War in the American Imagination* (N.Y., 1985), is a trove of information, esp. pp. 7–8, 10–11, 16–18, 53–61, 214–15, 275–76, 310, but it minimizes the significance of dissent by accepting Polk's premise that the war had nothing to do with the extension of slavery. **my country/** *Lib.*, 26 June 1846; WLG to RDW, 1 July 1847 [3:489] **Lowell/** *Lib.*, 3 July 1846; this poem proved the first of "The Biglow Papers." Lowell explained that he based the character upon the "upcountry" men he had frequently seen at antislavery meetings. Thomas Wortham, ed., *James Russell Lowell's "The Biglow Papers": A Critical Edition* (DeKalb, Ill., 1973), xxii–xxiii. **revolutions never go backward/** *Lib.*, 19 Mar. 1847; for other uses of the phrase see WLG to Louisa Loring, 7 Jan. 1847 [3:466], WLG to Heman Humphrey, 15 June 1847 [3:481], CS to Francis Lieber, 22 Mar. 1847, SLCS 1:189. For New England opposition, see *Lib.*, 5 June 1846; Parker, "A Sermon of War," excerpts in *Lib.*, 26 June 1847; WLG to HCW, 1 June 1846 [3:338–39]. **sympathy for Mexico/** WLG to CKW, 19 July 1846 [3:352];

WLG to Elizabeth Pease, 1 Apr. 1847 [3:476]. **Corwin/** speech, 11 Feb. 1847, text in *Lib.*, 19 Mar. 1847. **criminal murder/** J. R. Giddings, *Speeches in Congress* (Boston, 1853), 201. His disunionist letter is excerpted in *Lib.*, 31 July 1846. **Sumner rejoinder/** Donald, 141–47. **Calhoun/** speech of 24 Feb. 1847, *The Collected Works of John C. Calhoun* ed. Richard Crallé, 6 vols. (N.Y., 1851–57) 5:371; speech of 11 Feb. 1847, in *Lib.*, 26 Feb. 1847, with WLG remarks. Other quotations are from WLG to RDW, 1 Mar. 1847 [3:470].

CHAPTER SEVENTEEN: SNAP THE CORDS OF PARTY
Wilmot/ *Cong. Globe*, 29th Cong, 2nd sess., 1847, p. 317; Eugene H. Berwanger, *The Frontier Against Slavery: Western Anti-Negro Prejudice and the Slavery Extension Controversy* (Urbana, 1967), 3–8, 30–45. **population changes/** By 1860, the five states of the former Northwest Territory (Ohio, Indiana, Illinois, Michigan, and Wisconsin) would have 6.9 million inhabitants, twice the population of New England, and would be nearing parity with the three Middle Atlantic states that, at 7.5 million, formed the most populous region of all. *Statistical History of the U.S.* (Washington, D.C., 1965), 13. See generally, Andrew R.L. Cayton and Peter S. Onuf, *The Midwest and the Nation: Rethinking the History of an American Region* (Bloomington, 1990), 15–16, 29, 35, 84–85. **western tour/** WLG to HBG, 9 Aug.–18 Sept. 1847 [3:506–28]; FD dispatches to NAS, 9 Aug.–23 Sept. 1847, in FDLW 1: 256–69; C. W. Leffingwell, in *Lib.*, 19 Feb. 1847; Alpheus Cowles, in *Lib.*, 30 Jan. 1846; Ruth Galbreath obit., *Lib.*, 28 Jan. 1853; Linda L. Geary, *Balanced in the Wind: A Biography of Betsey Mix Cowles* (Lewisburg, Pa., 1989), 30. On the Oberlin tent, see James H. Fairchild, *Oberlin: The Colony and the College* (Oberlin, 1883), 73–74. There are no surviving texts for the speeches WLG and FD made on the tour, but I have reconstructed the message from the correspondence cited, as well as from FD speeches made just prior and just following the Ohio tour. See FDPS 2:84–95, and the manuscript "Minute Book of the Western Anti-Slavery Society, 1845–57," DLC, which summarizes the 18–20 Aug. 1847 New Lyme meeting. For Finney's views, see James David Essig, "The Lord's Free Man: Charles G. Finney and His Abolitionism," *Civil War History* 24 (Mar. 1978): 25–45. Henry Howe, *Historical Collections of Ohio* (Cincinnati, 1907), is a treasure house of general information. **Liberty Party/** Aileen S. Kraditor, "Liberty and Free Soil Parties," in Arthur M. Schlesinger, Jr., *History of U.S. Political Parties* (N.Y., 1973) 1:741–63, is a good overview. Vernon L. Volpe, *Forlorn Hope of Freedom: The Liberty Party in the Old Northwest, 1838–1848* (Kent, Ohio, 1990), emphasizes the clerical influence. A good example of Birney's thinking is JGB to TP, 27 Oct. 1848, in DJBL 2:1113. For Garrisonian critiques see *Lib.*, 2 July, 17 Sept., 22 Oct. 1847. **strait and narrow duty/** Leon Friedman & Fred Israel, *The Justices of the U.S. Supreme Court: Their Lives and Major Opinions*, 5 vols. (Washington, D.C., 1969) 2:869. **never opened/** WLG to HBG, 20 Oct. 1847 [3:533]. FD expressed great concern for the editor's health when he arrived in Syracuse on Sept. 24 and later said that he had discussed the newspaper matter with WLG in Cleveland just before the editor was taken ill. SJM to WLG, 7 Oct. 1847, to Mary Carpenter, 4 Mar. 1848, BPL. **brief English visit/** It is a measure of the significance the editor attributed to ferment in the churches that he proved willing to leave the country in July 1846, at the height of the protest against the Mexican War, in answer to George Thompson's call for help in fending off the combined efforts of British and American evangelical leaders to arrest the advance of radical abolition. This campaign tied in with another abolitionist effort to persuade the Free Church of Scotland, which was endeavoring to maintain itself independently of the established national church, to "Send Back the Money" donated to it by slaveholding Southerners eager to preserve fellowship in the denomination. Garrison's three-month tour generated a great deal of emotional heat, many columns of text, and a brief flurry of enthusiasm for the fusion of British abolitionists into a one grand antislavery league. Details are in *Lib.*, Aug.–Oct. 1846 and *Letters* [3:346–451]. **situation that grated/** Howard Temperley, *British Antislavery, 1833–1870* (Columbia, S.C., 1972), 219, suggests WLG's jealousy. **ransom of Douglass/**

WLG's views are expressed in *Lib.*, 15 Jan., 5 Mar. 1847; WLG to Elizabeth Pease, 1 Apr. 1847[3:476]. For other comments, including FD himself, also see *Lib.*, 29 Jan., 19 Feb. 1847. One of WLG's critics told him that he was "getting too presumptuous about the infallibility of your opinions." A. Brooke to WLG, 28 Jan. 1847, BPL. For details of the transaction, William McFeely, *Frederick Douglass* (N.Y., 1991), 143–45. **so independent/** FD to *Boston Daily Whig*, 27 June 1847, in *Lib.*, 9 July 1847. **for the present/** FD to WLG, 18 July 1847, in *Lib.*, 23 July 1847. **a delicate matter/** WLG to HBG, 20 Oct. 1847 [3:533]. There are sotto voce remarks in the private correspondence suggesting that people sometimes bit their lips rather than criticize Douglass. After FD had harshly criticized a convention colleague, Rogers groused that having been a slave "does not entitle him to play the master, though it undoubtedly has a tendency to make him want to . . ." (q. FDPS 1:xxxviii). Webb confided that while he vastly admired Douglass, he did not "feel much freedom" around him and found Garrison "twenty times a pleasanter body." RDW to WLG, 31 Mar. 1847, BPL. There are also the uglier remarks of Quincy, who grudgingly conceded the merit of Douglass's claim for higher pay as an agent, but feared that to meet it would "set all the flax to flame—or, at least, all the *wool*." EQ to RDW, 30 July 1847, BPL. For MWC highhandedness, see McFeely, 107–8, 121. For an earlier instance, see the controversy between MWC and the militant Henry H. Garnet, whose Liberty Party tendencies affected the dispute more deeply then the racism perceived by modern critics. *Lib.*, 22 Sept., 8 Dec. 1843; William H. Pease and Jane H. Pease, "Boston Garrisonians and the Problem of Frederick Douglass," *Canadian J. Hist.* 2 (Sept. 1967): 29–33. **I could not think/** HBG to AP, 18 July 1846, B/HHL. She apologized to her friend for talking so much about "ourselves . . . but I beg you will excuse it at this particular time when I feel so much." **prisonhouse/** WLG to GWB, 29 Oct. 1848 [3:600]. **FJG birth/** FJ to WLG, 5 Nov. 1848, G/MHS. **no strange thing/** WLG, variously, to MWC, GB, TP, 20 Apr. 1848 [3.550–52]; for Helen's grief, see HBG to GWB, 3 May 1848, GFP/SSC, and WLG to Elizabeth Pease, 3 May 1848 [3:556]. **church splits/** Donald J. Matthews, "The Methodist Schism of 1844 and the Popularization of Antislavery Sentiment," *Mid-America* 51 (Jan. 1968): 3–23, declares that "the schism was one of the most important events leading to the Civil War." Free Will Baptists petition, *Lib.*, 24 Mar. 1848. Louis Filler. "Liberalism, Anti-Slavery, and the Founders of *The Independent*," *New England Quarterly* 27 (Sept. 1954): 291–306, describes the shift toward abolition among the Congregationalists. **Wright/** Lewis Perry, *Childhood, Marriage, and Reform: Henry Clarke Wright 1797–1870* (Chicago, 1980), 165 (credo). **minister who can/** *Lib.*, 15 Aug. 1845. **born to be moral sovereigns/** *Boston Christian Reflector*, q. *Lib.*, 5 May 1848. For other commentary, including the anti-Monday jest, see *Lib.*, 21 Apr. 1848. Text of the Anti-Sabbath Convention Call, *Lib.*, 21 Jan. 1848. A correspondent who declined to sign the call thought it would have been preferable to delimit the meeting as "An Anti-Sabbath Superstition and Legal Enforcement Convention" and declared himself "not for destroying the Lord's Day but reforming it." D. Judd, Jr., to WLG, 17 Jan. 1848, BPL. **European Revolutions/** For WLG reactions, see *Lib.*, 31 Mar., 14 Apr. 1848. Workingmen's Resolutions, *Lib.*, 26 May 1848. Printers, *Lib.*, 15 Dec. 1848. For Calhoun, see CJCC 2:745–54. See Mazzini's letter to the British Anti-Slavery League, *Lib.*, 21 July 1854, for his internationalist principles. WLG introduction to *Joseph Mazzini: His Life, Writings, and Political Principles* (N.Y., 1872), xviii. **weaker than spider's web/** *Lib.*, 26 May, 14 July 1848. **capital to trade/** Stanton q., *Life* 3:214; JGW to CS, 20 June, 31 July 1848, JGWL 2: 103, 112. **breakaway manifesto/** draft enclosed in William Goodell to James G. Birney, 1 Apr. 1847, JGBL 2:1054. **Sumner/** David Donald, *Charles Sumner and the Coming of the Civil War* (N.Y., 1961), 166. **free-soil convention/** NYTr, 10–12 Aug. 1848; Allan Nevins, *The Ordeal of the Union* (N.Y., 1947) 1:203–8. Instead of the Liberty Party's "divorce" plank, the Free-Soil Party platform held it "the duty of the federal government to relieve itself from all responsibility for the existence or continuance of slavery wherever that government possess constitutional power to legislate on that subject, and is thus responsible for its existence." This language implied D.C. abolition, partisans claimed, but the commitment was never made explicit, and Van Buren would say only that he was no longer opposed to such an idea. Kirk H. Porter and Donald H. Johnson, eds., *National Political Party Platforms* (Urbana, 1970), 13. **measured response/** SJM to WLG, 10 Aug. 1848, in *Lib.*, 25 Aug. 1848; WLG to HBG, 26 July 1848 [3:574], WLG to EQ, 10 Aug. 1848 [3:581–2]; WLG to WP, 21 Aug. 1848, B/HHL. **Oregon/** *Lib.*, 18 Aug. 1848, NYTr., 15 Aug. 1848. **Whitman/** "American Workingmen vs. Slavery," 1 Sept. 1847, in *Uncollected Poetry and Prose of Walt Whitman*, ed. Emory Holloway (Gloucester, 1972) 1:171–72. **perfecting moral vision/** *Lib.*, 23 Feb. 1849. **not inherent/** *Lib.*, 17 Nov. 1848; dictionary, *Lib.*, 15 Dec. 1848. **finances/** Liberator Cash Books, BPL. WLG to Sidney H. Gay, 25 May 1849, Gay Papers, Columbia University, contains a copy of the carefully drawn four-year contract with Yerrinton that commenced on 1 Jan. 1849. WLG to HBG, 18 Oct. 1848 [3:598]; WLG to WP, 20 Nov. 1848, B/HHL; WLG to Committee, 20 Nov. 1848, B/HHL. The records of the trust fund are in a small folder of MAS material, G/MHS. **Charlie's death/** WLG to TP, 9 Apr. 1848 [3:613]; WLG to E. Pease, 20 June 1848 [3:618–22]; HBG to HCW, 15 July 1849, WSU; HBG to AP, [n.d., but c. 4 July 1849], B/HHL; SJM to WLG/HBG, 17 Apr. 1849, BPL. See HBG to AP, 30 Sept. 1850, HHL, for renewed expression of anger after her sister's death: "one after another my family circle have been removed by death till I feel I am not submissive I cannot say 'Thy will Heavenly Father not mine be done.' "

CHAPTER EIGHTEEN: THE MATHEMATICS OF JUSTICE
solicitous care/ WLG to AP, 27 Apr., 13 Aug. 1849, B/HHL. **millstones/** WLG to AKF, 25 Mar. 1851 [4:53]. **moral impression/** *Lib.*, 12 Jan. 1849. **shame politicians/** *Lib.*, 19 Oct. 1849. **shudder/** WLG to SJM, 13 Jan. 1850 [4:3–4]. **organize!/** *Lib.*, 19 Oct. 1849. See *Lib.*, 1 June 1849, for a report on the conventions. TBDDi, MHS, entries for 7 Jan., 3 Feb., 8 May, 4 July, 21 July, 26 Aug. 1849. WLG's talk, the young man said, was "very good indeed." **Brown/** *Narrative of William Wells Brown* (Boston, 1847); WWB to WLG, 15 Sept. 1848, BPL. **women's rights/** Stone anecdote, q. Andrea Ker Moore, *Lucy Stone: Speaking Out for Equality* (New Brunswick, 1992), 25. *Lib.*, 25 Aug., 15 Sept. 1848, reports the Seneca Falls and Rochester conventions. Elizabeth Cady Stanton, *Eighty Years and More* (1898), reprint ed. (N.Y., 1971). Boiling point, q. ECS to SBA, 2 Apr. 1852, Ellen Dubois, ed., *Stanton-Anthony: Correspondence, Speeches, Writings* (N.Y., 1981), 55. For the Garrisons' support of the national conventions see *Lib.*, 6 Sept., 8 Nov. 1850. In March 1853 they both signed a petition calling for the elimination of the word *male* from the Massachusetts constitution. *Lib.*, 4 Mar. 1853. Harriet Taylor, q. Blanche K. Hersh, *The Slavery of Sex: Feminist-Abolitionists in America* (Urbana, 1978), 59. **impartial liberty/** *Lib.*, 11 Jan. 1850; also 14 Dec. 1849. **Boston school/** James Oliver Horton and Lois Horton, *Black Bostonians: Family Life and Community Struggle in the Antebellum North* (N.Y., 1979), 71–76. *Lib.*, 10 Aug., 21 Sept., 16 Nov., 14 Dec. 1849, covers the important phases of the controversy. Nell believed the Boston School Committee represented "the pro-slavery public." WCN to Amy Post, 1 June 1849, Post Papers, BAP micro. **attack on Clay/** *Lib.*, 16 Mar. 1849. **Father Matthew/** *Lib.*, 10 Aug.–12 Oct. 1849. **Kossuth/** *Lib.*, 31 Aug. 1849. **new engraving/** *Lib.*, 31 May 1850. The artist, Hammatt Billings, donated the piece, valued at $20; he later was chosen to illustrate the first edition of *Uncle Tom's Cabin*. James F. O'Gorman, *A Billings Bookshelf* (Wellesley, 1983), 16–17. **gold rush/** WLG's second cousin Andrew Garrison set out for California, but died of cholera beyond Fort Laramie. Ann Garrison to WLG, 25 Oct. 1852, HHL. Brad Drew carefully noted dates and names of young men from his neighborhood who left for California, TBDDi, MHS. J. S. Holliday, *The World Rushed In* (N.Y., 1981), offers a fresh firsthand account of the Gold Rush. **North must give/** JCC to T. G. Clemson, 8 Dec. 1849, CJCC 2:776. For Calhoun's views on California statehood see JCC to James H. Hammond, 4 Jan. 1850, to A. P. Calhoun, 12 Jan 1850, CJCC 2:779–80, 785. **cheering evidence/** *Lib.*, 28 Dec. 1849, 1 Feb. 1850. **Clay's program/** The resolutions and speech are in *Lib.*, 8 Feb. 1850. In a later speech of 22 July, reported in *Lib.*, 9 Aug. 1850, Clay said that in the adjustment

measures abolitionists "see their doom as certain as there is a God in heaven, who sends his providential dispensations to calm the threatening storm and tranquilize agitated man." WLG condemned the speech as "specious, dictatorial clap-trap." **Foote**/ *Cong. Globe*, 31st Cong. 1st sess., 1:403–4 (20 Feb. 1850). **moral courage**/ Bennett, q. Merrill D. Peterson, *The Great Triumvirate: Webster, Clay, and Calhoun* (N.Y., 198), 458. **as pliant a piece**/ *Lib.*, 2 Aug. 1850. **two-headed**/ *Lib.*, 8 Mar. 1850. **what a travesty**/ James Brewer q. Stewart, *Holy Warriors: The Abolitionists and American Slavery* (N.Y., 1976), 122. **Remember**/ WLG to New England Anti-Slavery Convention, 30 May 1850, in *Lib.*, 28 June, 1850. **Sumner**/ CS to Wm. Bates and James W. Stone, 12 Aug. 1850, SLCS 1:306. **nothing less**/ *Lib.*, 1 Feb. 1850, which also reports the Longfellow reading. **old tests**/ WLG to BT, *Lib.*, 31 May, 1850 [4:26]; WLG to *London Morning Advertiser*, in *Lib.*, 19 Sept. 1851 [4:82]. **I am for union**/ *Lib.*, 28 June 1850; also source for Parker's "great contest." **moral assaults**/ q. *Lib.*, 23 Aug. 1850. **Webster**/ *Lib.*, 15 Mar., 22 Mar. 1850, reprints the speech, along with the WLG/WP criticism quoted. For an admiring account of Webster's speech, see Allan Nevins, *The Ordeal of the Union* (N.Y., 1947) 1: 288–91. **so many sheep**/ *Lib.*, 12 Apr. 1850. **Todd**/ *Lib.*, 10 May 1850. **Ichabod**/ *Poetical Works of John Greenleaf Whittier* (Boston, 1888), 146. **Whitman**/ Whitman, *Early Poems and Fiction*, ed. Thomas L. Brasher (N.Y., 1963), 36–48; *Lib.*, 17 May, 22 Nov. 1850. **The word liberty**/ q. Peterson, 465. **Davis**/ *Cong. Globe*, 31st Cong. 1st sess., App. 154 (14 Feb. 1850). For Free-Soiler criticism, see William H. Seward, speech of 11 Mar. 1850, *Cong. Globe*, 31st Cong., 1st sess., App. 266ff. *Lib.* carried warnings throughout 1849 about slaveholders' efforts to bring their property to California; see, e.g., 18 May, 22 June 1849. **so powerfully shocked**/ *Lib.*, 3 May 1850. **New York disruption**/ *Life* 3:282–99 reproduces many of the documents from which quotations are taken; NYTr, 8 May, 9 May 1850, has a narrative of events; *Lib.*, 17 May 1850, contains many newspaper extracts; WLG to HBG, 7 May 1850 [4:6–7], WLG to NYTr, 13 May 1850, and WLG to BT, 17 May, 31 May 1850, all in *Lib.* and [4:12–27], also refer to the event. JGW to WLG, 13 May 1850, LJGW 2:155. **compromise voting pattern**/ Roger L. Ransom, *Conflict and Compromise: The Political Economy of Slavery, Emancipation, and Civil War* (N.Y., 1985), 111–16. Roll call tabulations in Holman Hamilton, *Prologue to Conflict* (Lexington, Ky. 1964), 191–200. Douglas q. from Nevins 1:349. **God knows**/ Fillmore to DW, 23 Oct. 1850, *Letters of Daniel Webster, from Documents Owned Principally by the New Hampshire Historical Society*, ed. C. H. Van Tyne (N.Y., 1902), 437. **Choate**/ q. William Brock, *Parties & Political Conscience: American Dilemmas, 1840–1850* (Millwood, N.Y., 1979), 325. **20th anniversary**/ *Lib.*, 31 Jan. 1851; JRL, "The Day of Small Things," reprinted in WLG, *Selections* (Boston, 1852), ix–x. "Oh how did I long to be at that Liberator festival," Oliver Johnson told the Fosters, who were also working too far away to attend. OJ to AKF/SSF, 6 Feb. 1851, Kelley-Foster Papers, AmAqS.

CHAPTER NINETEEN: FUGITIVE SLAVE LAW: DENOUNCED, RESISTED, DISOBEYED
let it be/ SJMREC, 360. **Cazenovia**/ *Lib.* 16 Aug., 30 Aug. 1850, for reports of the meeting, which was attended by a group of fugitives and issued an appeal for more runaways and resistance that was written by Gerrit Smith. A daguerreotype taken by Ezra Greenleaf Weld is the only known image of an abolitionist gathering. A complete account of the meeting and the image is Hugh C. Humphreys, " 'Agitate! Agitate! Agitate!' The Great Fugitive Slave Law Convention and Its Rare Daguerreotype," *Madison County Heritage*, no. 19 (Oneida, N.Y., 1994). **FD and MAS**/ *Lib.*, 27 Sept, 1850. **text of law**/ *Lib.*, 27 Sept. 1850. Enforcement statistics based on Stanley Campbell, *The Slave Catchers* (Chapel Hill, 1970), 199–207. **Boston seethed**/ *Lib.*, 1 Nov. 1850; SJM to J. B. Estlin, 10 Nov. 1850, BPL; Theodore Parker to Millard Fillmore, 21 Nov. 1850, in *Life and Correspondence of Theodore Parker*, ed. John Weiss, 2 vols. (Boston 1864), 2:100–101. **Shadrach case**/ *Lib.*, 21 Feb., 28 Feb. 1851; T. W. Higginson, *Cheerful Yesterdays* (Boston, 1898), 135–36; *Life* 3:326–27; Curtis, q. BT, 25 Nov. 1850; *Lib.*, 20 Dec. 1850; Parker Journal 16 Feb. 1851, in Weiss, 2:103; WP to Elizabeth Pease, 9 Mar. 1851, BPL;

"more indebted," *Lib.*, 11 Oct. 1850. For Hayden's connection to Clay see Stanley J. and Anita W. Robboy, "Lewis Hayden: From Fugitive Slave to Statesman," *New England Quarterly* 46 (Dec. 1973): 604. **all they want/** WP to Elizabeth Pease, 9 Mar. 1851, q. *Life* 3:324. **Sims case/** *Lib.*, 11 Apr., 18 Apr., 25 Apr. 1851; Higginson, *Cheerful Yesterdays*, 139–46; Paul Finkelman, *Slavery in the Courtroom: An Annotated Bibliography of American Cases* (Washington, D.C., 1985), 68–75; Quincy, q. *Life* 3:328; *North Star*, 17 April 1851, FDLW 5:180–82. **righteous retribution/** HBG to ATP, 21 Sept. 1851, B/HHL. **higher law debate/** John C. Lord, *"The Higher Law" in Its Application to the Fugitive Slave Bill: A Sermon on the Duties Men Owe to God and to Governments* (N.Y., 1851), 5–6, 10–11; New England convention credo, *Lib.*, 6 Jun 1851; Theodore Parker, "The Function and Place of Conscience, in Relation to the Laws of Men," September 22, 1850, in *Speeches, Addresses, and Occasional Sermons* (Boston, 1867), 131–179, esp. 133–35; Judas, q. *Lib.*, 13 Dec. 1850. **Thoreau/** "Resistance to Civil Government," in *Reform Papers*, ed. Wendell Glick (Princeton, 1973), 63–90, 313–21; BC, q. *Henry David Thoreau: A Reference Guide, 1835–1899*, comp. Raymond R. Borst (Boston, 1987), 11; Robert Richardson, *Henry Thoreau: A Life of the Mind* (Berkeley, 1986) 175–79; WLG review, *Lib.*, 15 June 1849, obit., *Lib.*, 22 June 1849; HDT Journals, 174–79. **this last year/** Robert Richardson, *Emerson: The Mind on Fire* (Berkeley, 1996), 497. "If our resistance to this law is not right," said Emerson, "there is no right." *Lib.*, 18 Apr. 1851. **Goodell/** *Lib.*, 7 Feb. 1851, William Goodell, *Slavery and Freedom* (N.Y., 1852), 526–27. **Bacon/** Theodore D. Bacon, *Leonard Bacon* (New Haven, 1931), 342–7. **Kossuth/** *Lib.*, 20 Feb. 1852 [4:97–186] **Stowe/** Joan D. Hedrick, *Harriet Beecher Stowe* (N.Y., 1994), is a general source for personal details; "Abolitiony" q., 93; 202–53. *Uncle Tom's Cabin* is republished in *Stowe: Three Novels* (N.Y., Library of America, 1982), q., 110–11, 157, 278. WLG review in *Lib.*, 26 Mar. 1852; "so does God" q., 11 June 1852. Robert Purvis thought WLG had been too tame in his critique of Stowe's colonization views. Purvis to OJ, 24 Apr. 1852, BAP 4:124; TBDDi, 30 Mar. 1852, MHS; meetings with WLG, *Life* 3:401; are you a Christian q. *Life* 3:363 n.3. HBS view of WLG is paraphrased by Sarah Pugh to Anne W. Weston, 6 June 1853, BPL; WP to Elizabeth Pease, 10 Jan. 1853, q. *Life* 3:363. HBS to WLG, [Nov. 1853], BPL; WLG to HBS, 30 Nov. 1853, in *Lib.*, 23 Dec. 1853 [4:280–86]; HBS to WLG 12 Dec. 1853, BPL (excerpts in *Life* 3: 395–400); RDW to Mary Estlin, 11 July 1853, BPL; Victor Hugo letter, in *Lib.*, 8 Aug. 1851. **printed a narrative/** Sojourner Truth to WLG, 28 Aug. 1851, BPL, discusses book orders; this tour affords the first documented version of her famous "Ain't I a Woman" speech. BAP 4:81. **marked work/** AKF in *Lib.*, 4 Feb 1853. **Clay's death/** *Lib.*, 2 July, 9 July 1852; will, *Lib.*, 1 Oct. 1852. Merrill D. Peterson, *The Great Triumvirate: Webster, Clay, and Calhoun* (N.Y., 1987), 488–89, terms Clay's plan "a testament of faith not only in the colonization scheme but in the survival of the Union." **question at rest/** *Lib.*, 11 Mar. 1853. **ukase/** Claude M. Fuess, *Life of Caleb Cushing* (N.Y., 1923), 2:139–45; Cushing to *Boston Post*, 29 Sept. 1853. **somewhat worn/** *Lib.*, 7 Jan., 21 Jan. 1853. **bold, radical/** NYTr, 17 Jan. 1852. *Selections from the Writings and Speeches of William Lloyd Garrison* (Boston, 1852) appeared under the imprint of R. F. Wallcut, *The Liberator*'s general manager, and was printed in the 21 Cornhill office by J. B. Yerrinton. In reprinting excerpts from the Park Street Address, the passage advocating gradual emancipation was silently omitted. *Selections*, 59. **boasted human rights/** *Lib.*, 28 Oct. 1853. **markets for truth/** WLG to HBG, 17 Oct. 1853 [4:273]; tour details in WLG letters home [4:258–76]; EQ in *Lib.*, 7 Oct 1853. **secret of his power/** J. Miller McKim to Sarah Pugh, 1 Nov. 1852, q. *Life* 3:374–75. **hurricane of excitement/** *Lib.*, 12 Nov. 1852. **differences with Douglass/** The controversy at the 1851 AAS meeting may be followed in *Lib.*, 23 May 1851 and subsequent issues. William McFeely, *Frederick Douglass* (N.Y., 1991), 169, asserts that the delegates "passed a resolution forbidding support by any member of the society of any paper that did not specifically condemn the Constitution," but the proceedings refer only to Quincy's motion, subsequently withdrawn, "recommendatory of *The Liberator, Pennsylvania Freeman, Ohio Bugle, and North Star* to the support of Anti-Slavery people." For examples of FD's

Garrisonian views see *North Star*, 30 Mar. 1849, in FDLW 1: 374–79; FDPS 2:217–33 (17 Jan. 1850), also 193–97. On the new arrangement see FD to GS, 21 Jan., 1 May, 15 May, 21 May 1851 in FDLW 2:149–57; smoked optical instruments, William Powell in NAS, 14 Aug. 1851, q. BAP 4:89–90; child to parent, FD to CS, 2 Sept. 1852, in FDLW 2: 210; complexional distinction, *Lib.*, 4 July 1851. **praise for book**/ FDLW, 5:220–22. **truth-telling**/ FDPS 2:393–96; Pillsbury, *Lib.*, 10 Sept. 1852. **a double part** AKF to WLG, 30 Mar. 1852, BPL. **gossip**/ GT to AWW, 17 Mar. 1851, BPL. **Anna Douglass**/ Anna Douglass, q. in SBA to WLG, 13 Dec. 1853, BPL. **new org**/ AKF to WLG 30 Mar. 1852, BPL. FD on infidels, *Lib.*, 10 June 1853; on black Garrisonians, *Lib*, 26 Aug. 1853, and see also BAP 4:174–186; *Lib*, 29 July, 5 Aug. 1853, gave extensive coverage to the report of the National Colored Convention, which had discussed both the council and school proposals. Nell's friends are quoted in WCN to Amy Post, 22 Dec. 1853, BAP micro. The harsh exchanges are in *Lib*, 23 Sept., 18 Nov., 16 Dec. 1853. BAP 4:180–81 reprints the 28 Dec. 1853 Chicago resolutions. **cessation of hostilities**/ HBS to WLG, 19 Dec. 1853, BPL; WCN to Amy Post, 22 Dec. 1853. **Cushing**/ *Washington Union*, 24 Jan 1854, q. Fuess, 147. **pure unadulterated**/ q. Allan Nevins, *The Ordeal of the Union* (N.Y., 1947) 2:114. **reaction**/ *New York Evening Post*, 27 Feb. 1854, in WCB, 275; *Lib*, 17 Feb., 13 Mar. 1854. **New York speech**/ WLG to HBG, 16 Feb. 1854 [4:292]; WLG, *No Compromise with Slaveholders: An Address delivered in the Broadway Tabernacle, New York, February 14, 1854* (N.Y., AAS, 1854); text also in *Lib.*, 24 Feb. 1854. **clergy petition**/ *Lib*, 7 Apr., 14 Apr. 1854; HBS to WLG, 18 Feb. 1854, BPL. **Emerson**/ *Lib.*, 17 Mar. 1854. **Burns case**/ *Lib*, 2 June. 9 June 1854; Higginson, *Cheerful Yesterdays*, 147–66; LMC to Francis Shaw, 3 June 1854, LMCMf; *Journal of Charlotte L. Forten*, ed. Ray Allen Billington (N.Y., 1961), 45–46; JGW, "The Rendition," in *The Panorama and Other Poems* (N.Y., 1856), 144. Thoreau, *The Journal of Henry David Thoreau*, ed. Bradford Torrey and Francis H. Allen, 14 vols. (Boston, 1906) 6:358. Richard Henry Dana, *Journal*, ed. Robert Lucid, 3 vols. (Cambridge, 1968) 1:637; Lawrence, q. Abbott, 26; Vigilance Committee figures, FJ to TP, 11 June 1854, BPL. TBDDi, 31 May–2 June 1854, MHS, recounts Drew's own indignation at hearing his parents' report of the Burns agitation. "The Slave Power rules this nation," he concluded. In Concord a few weeks later, a meeting attended by the Emersons, the Thoreaus, and nine others agreed that all present would aid escaping fugitives and do everything possible to help them attain their "God-given rights." William Whiting to Theodore Parker, 10 July 1854, in Weiss 2: 143.

CHAPTER TWENTY: IF KANSAS IS FREE SOIL, THEN WHY NOT CAROLINA?

the attempt/ Charles C. Jones, Jr., to the Rev. and Mrs. C. C. Jones, 4 July 1854, in Robert Manson Myers, ed., *The Children of Pride* (N.Y., 1972) 1:53–54. **Framingham**/ *Lib.*, 7 July, 14 July 1854. The Grove, which was used by many church, school, and temperance societies, was created by a retired Boston merchant, Lathrop Wright, in 1852; description in NAS, 14 July 1860. For Thoreau's text see *Lib.*, 21 July 1854, and "Slavery in Massachusetts," in Henry D. Thoreau, *Reform Papers*, ed. Wendell Glick (Princeton, 1973), 91–109. The talk was based largely on the journal entries Thoreau had made during the Burns case. When compared to the "Higher Law" speeches of Seward and other politicians, said the *New York Tribune*, 2 Aug. 1854, Thoreau's speech was "the Simon-Pure article." **turning the world**/ Not to be confused with the British marching tune, "The World Turned Upside Down" was a traditional evangelical hymn that praised the religious agitation of prophets and apostles. Nathan O. Hatch, *The Democratization of American Christianity* (New Haven, 1989), 230. WLG and his correspondents used it frequently as a catchphrase. WLG to FJ, 16 Aug. 1843 [3:195]; E.A.W. in *Lib.*, 26 May 1856. **let the people**/ The phrase originates in Deut. 27:15 in an episode in which Moses condemns idolatry. **Martin Luther**/ James Atkinson, *Martin Luther and the Birth of Protestantism* (London, 1968), 194–97, identifies Luther's dramatic gesture outside the gates of Wittenberg as the "fiery signal of emancipation" and says that "if the Reformation can be dated, the date must be 10 Dec. 1520." *Life* 3:412 describes the Framingham ceremony as "Lutheran incendiarism," and it is plain that WLG understood his action in the context of Reformation history. **Liberator is fireproof**/ *Lib.*, 21 July 1854. On polarization, see WLG's speech to Penn. Anti-Slavery Society, 23 Oct. 1854, *Lib.*, 3 Nov. 1854. **Kansas**/ For typical expressions of WLG's view, see *Lib*, 28 July 1854, 1 June 1855, 27 May, 6 June 1856. WLG thought that even if admitted as a free state, Kansas would be like California, a pro-Democratic, conservative state and a weak element in antislavery politics. Eli Thayer, *The New England Emigrant Aid Company* (Worcester, 1887), is bitter in its denunciation of the Garrisonians as "mountebanks" whose skepticism and impracticality undermined Kansas work and retarded the cause. **If Ohio**/ Charles Hodge, q. Richard Carwardine, *Transatlantic Revivalism: Popular Evangelicalism in Britain and America 1790–1865* (Westport, Conn., 1978), 243. A typical expression of the contrast with the Burns case is *Ashtabula Sentinel*, in *Lib.*, 3 Aug. 1855. **ministers are free**/ MWC to Samuel Sewall, 9 Aug. 1857, Robie-Sewall Papers, MHS. **undeniably trying**/ WLG to SJM, 21 Mar. 1856 [4:391]. **headlines**/ *Lib.*, 29 Dec. 1854, 11 May, 3 Aug., 24 Aug., 21 Sept., 14 Dec. 1855, 15 Feb., 28 Mar., 13 June. 1856. **the evidence loomed**/ for Smith see *Lib*, 6 July 1855, and *Life* 3:440; for Higginson see Jeffrey Rossbach, *Ambivalent Conspirators: John Brown, the Secret Six, and a Theory of Slave Violence* (Philadelphia, 1982), 72; for Parker see Edward J. Renehan, Jr., *The Secret Six: The True Tale of the Men Who Conspired with John Brown* (N.Y., 1995), 92–93. Weld, *Lib.*, 7 Jul. 1854, and replies, *Lib.*, 28 July 1854. Child, "The Kansas Emigrants," NYTr, 23–28 Oct. 1856; LMC to David Child, 27 Oct. 1856; Stearns, *Lib.*, 24 Dec. 1855, 4 Jan., 15 Feb. 1856; relief totals, F. B. Sanborn, *Life and Letters of John Brown* (Concord, 1910), 352– 53. **defense of nonresistance**/ *Lib.*, 2 Feb., 30 Mar., 13 Apr., 25 May, 15 June 1855, 2 May 1856. On Beecher and Parker, *Lib.*, 29 Feb., 14 Mar., 4 Apr., 11 Apr. 1856. **Know-Nothing estimate**/ *Lib.*, 10 Nov., 17 Nov. 1854. **view of Republicans**/ WLG to Ann R. Bramhall, 8 Aug. 1856 [4:400–401]; *Lib.*, 15 June, 28 Sept. 1855, 4 Feb., 11 July 1856; MWC, *How Can I Help to Abolish Slavery*, AAS Tract No. 14 (1855), *Revolution the Only Remedy for Slavery*, AAS Tract No. 7 (1855); WLG to SJM, 27 Jan., 1856 [4: 378]. For disunion, also see *Lib.*, 11 Apr. 1856; on conflicting views of the Republicans, *Lib.*, 6 June, 20 June 1856. **presidential election**/ For political caricatures of the 1856 campaign see Bernard F. Reilly, Jr., *American Political Prints, 1776–1876: A Catalog of the Collections in the Library of Congress* (Boston, 1991), 405–10. For the crucial exchanges with May and Kelley see *Lib.*, 5 Sept., 12 Sept., 19 Sept., 17 Oct., 31 Oct. 1856. See also WLG to J. M. McKim, 14 Oct. 1856 [4: 404–10], which was read on his behalf to the 20th anniversary meeting of the Penn. Anti-Slavery Society. *Life* 3:446–47 describes Greeley's efforts. For Chace, *Virtuous Lives: Four Quaker Sisters Remember Family Life, Abolitionism, and Women's Suffrage*, ed. Lucille Salitan and Eva Lewis Perera (N.Y., 1994), 111. TBDDi, 30 June 1856, MHS; Mary Grew to WP, 23 June 1856, B/HHL; LMC to David Child, 27 Oct. 1856, LMCMf; W. G. Babcock to WLG, 20 Oct. 1856, BPL. **social reform begins**/ *Lib.*, 28 Dec. 1855. For Parker see *Lib.*, 16 May 1856. **Bryant**/ *New York Evening Post*, 9 Mar. 1857, in WCB, 311; **Whitman**/ "The Eighteenth Presidency," *Whitman: Poetry and Prose* (N.Y., Library of America, 1982), 1309–13. **encyclopedia**/ *The New American Cyclopaedia: A Popular Dictionary of General Knowledge*, ed. George Ripley and Charles A. Dana (N.Y., 1859–70). **house purchase**/ FJ to WLG, 9 Mar. 1852, BPL; FJ to WLG, 1 Oct. 1855, G/MHS; WLG to FJ, 11 Oct. 1855 [4: 347]; pledge list (27 Nov. 1847), account ledger, and schedule of investments (1854), MHS; Suffolk County Grant Deeds 630/258 to FJ, 31 Mar. 1852. Having purchased the house in 1852, FJ did not want to evict the tenant in residence, and so he helped to situate the Garrisons until March 1853 in another of his rental properties at 125 Concord St., on the far edge of the South End. That house still stands, but Dix Place is now covered by the New England Medical Center. The shabby conditions under which the Suffolk County records were kept prevented a complete study of FJ's transactions. Author to Paul Tierney, Registrar of Deeds, 21 May and 22 June 1993; Tierney to author, 10 June 1993, and *Boston Globe*, 2 June 1993. **house and**

neighborhood/ photographs and WPG to WLG(J), 10 June 1855, GFP/SSC; *Lib.*, 7 Oct. 1864; the neighborhood profile is based upon the manuscript census return (1850–1860) and the tax assessor "street volumes," 1853–64, Boston City Archives. **family life/** WLG(J)Di 27 Jan. 1856, 5 Feb. 1857, 5 Dec., 16 Dec. 1859, 3 Jan., 25 Jan., 20 Feb. 1860, GFP/SSC; WPG to WLG(J), 10 June 1855, WLG to WLG(J), 31 Dec. 1858 [4: 601–602], characterizes each of his children. WP to WLG, 12 Sept. 1855, HHL/b Ms Am 1169 (135), renews the offer for Wendy's expenses. Parker's gift, WLG to TP, 17 June 1858 [4: 535–36]. For George's travail see WLG to Thomas Davis, 6 Oct. 1854 [4: 319–20]; GTG to WLG, 8 July, 9 Aug. 1857, GTG to HBG, 7 Feb., 14 Feb. 1858, GTG to WLG(J), 14 Mar. 1858, all in GFP/SSC. WLG to FJG, 13 Aug., 17 Aug. 1857 [4: 467–69, 474–75]; Fanny Garrison Villard, *William Lloyd Garrison on Non-violence, Together with a Personal Sketch by His Daughter* (N.Y., 1924), 7–9. WLG to WLG(J), 7 Jan. 1858 [4: 503]. On Fanny's becoming "unstrung" if she goes for a school medal, HBG to WLG, 22 Oct. 1858, BPL. Stanley K. Schultz, *The Culture Factory: Boston Public Schools, 1789–1860* (N.Y., 1973), 116–38, 187–95, 282–83. **I never saw/** HBG to ATP, 2 Aug. 1851, B/HHL. **Brooklyn trip/** WLG to Charlotte Newell, 19 Aug. 1854 [4: 305]. **free and easy person/**Sallie Holley to Caroline Putnam, 24 Oct. 1852, in John White Chadwick, ed., *A Life for Liberty: Anti-Slavery and Other Letters of Sallie Holley* (N.Y., 1899), 96. Dorothy Sterling, *Ahead of Her Time: Abby Kelley and the Politics of Antislavery* (N.Y., 1991), 270, cites newspaper criticism of Kelley for similarly unfashionable attire. **household worries/**HBG to WLG(J), [?] Mar. 1858, GFP/SSC. **a pin out/** HBG to GTG, 12 Dec. 1858, WSU. **Stowe anecdote/** Holley to Caroline Putnam, 21 May 1853, in Chadwick, 123–24. For other remarks see Chadwick, 99–100, 107, 139–40. **a good bath/** Villard, 7. **growing old/** *Lib.*, 6 Mar. 1857; Aaron M. Powell, *Personal Reminiscences of the Anti-Slavery Movement* (N.Y., 1899), 37–41. **overwork/** HBG to GTG, 23 Feb. 1858, WSU; HBG to WLG(J), 9 Jan. 1859, GFP/SSC; WLG to HBG, 29 Oct. 1858 [4: 595]. **daguerreotypes/** WLG to OJ, 1 May 1858 [4: 523–24]. The most complete catalog of WLG images is Harold Fister, *Facing the Light: Historic American Portrait Daguerreotypes* (Washington, D.C., 1978), 320–22. The 1850 Southworth & Hawes daguerreotype is shown in Beaumont Newhall, *The Daguerreotype in America* (N.Y., 1975), Plate 98; Shaw and Stowe appear as Plates 95 and 100. The 1854 Chase daguerreotype is the frontispiece to Walter M. Merrill, *Against Wind and Tide* (Cambridge, 1963), but is misdated as 1849; it is also in Fister, fig. 29. **heart-stirring festivals/** WLG to Charles Hovey, 15 Sept. 1855 [4:344]; *Proceedings of the 20th Anniversary of the Boston Mob* (Boston, 1855), 30; *Lib.*, 9 Jan. 1857, for MAS celebration in Faneuil Hall. **reading at Beecher's/** WLG to HBG, 17 Dec. 1856 [4: 415–16]. **low rumbling/** L. C. Todd to WLG, *Lib.*, 25 Dec. 1857. **reporter's caricature/** NYTi, 2 Aug. 1855. **state-wide convention/** *Lib.*, 16 Jan., 23 Jan., 30 Jan. 1857. **can't expect much/** TBDDi, 4 Mar. 1857, MHS. **Dred Scott decision/** For Greeley and Curtis, *Lib.*, 20 Mar. 1857; Cheever and Philadelphia, *Lib.*, 10 Apr. 1857; Don E. Fehrenbacher, *The Dred Scott Case: Its Significance in American Law and Politics* (N.Y., 1978), 340–41, 417–48. **Attucks celebration/** *Lib.*, 5 Mar. 1858; WLG to SJM, 6 Mar. 1858 [4: 516–18]. **John Brown/** This section is a synthesis of material in Oswald Garrison Villard, *John Brown 1800–1859: A Biography Fifty Years After* (Boston, 1910); Stephen B. Oates, *To Purge This Land with Blood: A Biography of John Brown* (N.Y., 1970); Franklin B. Sanborn, *Life and Letters of John Brown* (Concord, Mass., 1885); and Edward J. Renehan, Jr., *The Secret Six: The True Tale of the Men Who Conspired with John Brown* (N.Y., 1995). **reception at Parker's/** The only source is *Life* 3: 487–88, but the "debate" described therein is a literary conceit of the authors. Their only citation is a passing reference to Sanborn, 445, which in turn is a casual mention that says nothing about the discussion. **disturbing reports/** Documents fixing Brown's involvement in the Pottawatomie killings did not become generally known until late in the 19th century. Reports at the time were very sketchy. See, for example, excerpts in *Lib.*, 30 May, 13 June 1856, which contain the only two references that might conceivably refer to the massacre: "Four new murders have come to light" and "100 U.S. troops have started in pursuit of some Free State men who shot five pro-slavery men for attempting to hang a free-state man." **do you think/** JB to TP, 11 Sept. 1857, 2 Feb. 1858, in *Life and Correspondence of Theodore Parker,* ed. John Weiss, 2 vols. (Boston, 1864) 2:163–64; Sanborn to Higginson, 11 Sept. 1857, in Villard, 303. **they were seven/** FD gave many accounts of his relationship with John Brown; see especially, FDLT, 314–21, and "Did John Brown Fail?" in FDPS 5:7–35. **Tubman/** Oates, 241–42. **started pestering/** Francis Meriam to WPG, 22 Sept. 1858, O. G. Villard Papers, Columbia University. **incendiary tract/** James Redpath, *The Roving Editor, or Talks with Slaves in the Southern States* (N.Y., 1859), iv, 84–85, 129–32. Redpath described his own plan for creating secret lodges of apostles who could promote escapes by groups in the border states. **Orsini/** WLG to John W. Le Barnes, 29 Apr. 1858 [4:521–22], also in *Lib.*, 7 May 1858. **two pacifist sermons** WLG to Parker and reply, 3 June 1858 [4: 534–35]; *Lib.*, 4 June 1858. **Seward/** NYTr., 26 Oct. 1858, reprinted in *Lib.*, 5 Nov. 1858. **Hammond/**"settled question," *Lib.*, 19 Nov. 1858; "cotton is king," 4 Mar. 1858, *Cong. Globe*, 35th Cong., 1st sess., App. 70–71. **we shall be vindicated/** WLG, *No Fetters in the Bay State*, Speech Before the Committee of Federal Relations, Massachusetts Legislature, 24 Feb. 1859 (Boston, 1859), 7.

CHAPTER TWENTY-ONE: JOHN BROWN HAS TOLD US THE TIME

Herndon/ William H. Herndon to WLG, 16 Apr., 29 May 1858, BPL; Herndon to Parker, 7 Apr., 29 May 1858, University of Iowa; Herndon to Lincoln, 24 Mar., 1858, Herndon-Weik Coll., DLC; WLG to Vermont Anti-Slavery Convention (25 Jan. 1858) in *Lib.*, 19 Mar. 1858; Herndon extract in *Lib.*, 2 May 1856; Herndon to Jesse W. Weik, 23 Dec. 1885, in Emanuel Hertz, ed. *The Hidden Lincoln* (N.Y., 1938), 115–16. **common gathering/** WLG to *Lib.*, 15 Oct. 1858 [4:569]. **Garner case/** *Lib.*, 8 Feb., 29 Feb. 1856. **view of Republican Party/** See esp. WLG speeches at the 1859 meetings of MAS and New England convention, *Lib.*, 4 Feb., 3 June 1859; WLG to AKF, 8 Sept. 1859 [4: 650–51]; AKF to SSF, 7 Aug., 4 Dec. 1857, AmAqS. For the Radical Republicans generally, see Eric Foner, *Free Soil, Free Labor, Free Men: The Ideology of the Republican Party Before the Civil War* (N.Y., 1970), 103–48. **Kelley fight/** Debates in *Lib.*, 4 Feb., 3 June 1859; TBDDi, 28–29 Jan. 1859, MHS; AKF to SSF, 14 Dec. 1857, Kelley-Foster Papers, AmAqS; HBG to WLG, 17 Oct. 1858, WSU; WLG to AKF, 22 July, 25 July, 8 Sept. 1859 [4:639–45, 649–53]; AKF to WLG, 24 July, [?] Sept. 1859 (marked reply to No. 2), Kelley-Foster Papers, AmAqS. **Kelley agreed/** AKF to WP, 21 June 1859; WP to AKF, 30 June, 20 July 1859, B/HHL; MAS Minutes and Proceedings of the Board of Managers, 19 July 1859, BPL. **Ballou/** *Lib.*, 16 Sept. 1859. **John Brown raid/** WLG(J)Di, 17–20 Oct. 1859, GFP/SSC; *Lib.*, 21 Oct. 1859. **Meriam/** "John Brown's Carpet Bag," NAS, 29 Oct. 1859. **jurisdiction/** NYTr., 18 Oct., 19 Oct. 1859. **state-breaking/** Thomas Hamilton, *Weekly Ango-African*, 19 Nov. 1859, in BAP 5:41. **desperate self-sacrifice/** WLG to OJ, 1 Nov. 1859 [4:660–61]. **wicked principals/** *Richmond Enquirer*, 2 Nov. 1859. **Greeley/** NYTr, 19 Oct. 1859. **heard rumors/** NAS, 22 Oct. 1859; **wild and futile/** *Lib.*, 28 Oct. 1858. **Douglass/** FD to *Rochester Democrat and American*, 31 Oct. 1859, in *Lib.*, 11 Nov. 1859. Douglass denied that he had ever promised to join the Harpers Ferry brigade, but avoided comment on any prior knowledge of the event; he had in fact conferred with Brown near his hideout only a few days before the raid, when he expressed skepticism about the plan and declined an invitation to participate. **Phillips/** *Lib.*, 11 Nov. 1859. **Thoreau/** "A Plea for Captain John Brown," in *Reform Papers*, ed. Wendell Glick (Princeton, 1973), 111–43; the lecture was reported in the Boston and New York papers and reprinted in James Redpath, *Echoes of Harper's Ferry* (Boston, 1860), an instant compilation of Brown material that had 30,000 copies in print by February 1860. WLG(J)Di, 1 Nov. 1859, GFP/SSC. **nonresistants' dilemma/** JGW to LMC, 21 Oct. 1859, JGWL 2:435–36. Dorothy Sterling, *Ahead of Her Time* (N.Y., 1991), 326; Worcester County Resolutions, 23 Oct. 1859, in *Lib.*, 4 Nov. 1859; *Lib.*, 25 Nov. 1859. **martyrdom campaign/** WLG to OJ, 1 Nov. 1859 [4:660–61]; WLG to unidentified correspondent, 18 Dec. 1859 [4: 665], *Lib.*, 4 Nov., 11 Nov. 1859; the LMC correspondence with Wise and Mason is reprinted in

Lib., 11 Nov., 25 Nov., 31 Dec. 1859; the broadside is in the collection of the Boston Athenaeum, Bro 1.21; Paul Finkelman, "Manufacturing Martyrdom: The Antislavery Response to John Brown's Raid," in Finkelman, ed., *His Soul Goes Marching On: Responses to John Brown and the Harpers Ferry Raid* (Charlottesville, 1995), 41–66. All modern writers quote the statement Brown is said to have handed to a guard on the morning of his execution: "I John Brown am now quite *certain* that the crimes of this *guilty land: will* never be purged *away;* but with Blood. I had *as I now think: vainly* flattered myself that without *verry* much bloodshed; it might be done." Stephen B. Oates, *To Purge This Land with Blood: A Biography of John Brown* (N.Y., 1970), 351, from the document in Chicago Historical Society. However, this passage does not appear in the contemporary material and evidently came to light much later. **I can recover/** JB to Mary Ann Brown, 10 Nov. 1859, in Oswald Garrison Villard, *John Brown 1800–1859: A Biography Fifty Years After* (Boston, 1910), 540–41. **Meriam return/** WLG(J)Di, 2 Dec. 1859, GFP/SSC; HDT *Journal*, 3 Dec. 1859; FJ to TWH, 6 Dec. 1859, BPL. Jackson's letter declines an offer from Higginson to shelter the fugitive in Worcester and is cast in the present tense, which suggests that Meriam was still in Boston on 6 Dec. If so, Thoreau must have helped someone other than Meriam in the dawn hours of 3 Dec. **memorial meetings/** *Lib.*, 9 Dec., 16 Dec. 1859; Oates, 354–56; HDT, "The Martyrdom of John Brown," in *Reform Papers*, 139–43; LMC to MWC, 28 Nov. 1859, BAP 5:51; WLG's debate with Ballou, *Lib.*, 13 Jan. 1860. **Fraternity Lecture/** *Boston Atlas & Bee*, 21 Dec. 1859, clipping in WLG(J)Di, GFP/SSC. Willie called the talk "radical and Garrisonian" but said he didn't "enjoy it so well as I should have had I been less anxious for Father to do well." **pamphlet endorsement/** *Lib.*, 17 Jan. 1860. **outline his program/** WLG to James Redpath, 1 Dec. 1860 [4: 702–4], in *Lib.*, 7 Dec. 1860. **execution reports/** *Lib.*, 9 Dec. 1859. **Whittier poem/** *Lib.*, 13 Jan. 1860. **high noon/** *Lib.*, 17 Feb. 1860. **Orsini-like/** Lincoln made the comparison in his Cooper Union speech, 27 Feb. 1860, Roy P. Basler, *Collected Works of Abraham Lincoln* (New Brunswick, 1953) 3: 541. **wave of repression/** *Lib.*, 23 Dec., 30 Dec. 1859; AAS, *Anti-Slavery History of the John Brown Year* (N.Y., 1861), 166ff. **stir a fever/** *Lib.*, 13 Apr. 1860. **sedition act/** *Lib.*, 3 Feb., 10 Feb. 1860; *Cong. Globe*, 36th Cong., 1st Sess., 26 Mar. 1860, App. 178. **Chapman predicted/** *Lib.*, 10 Feb. 1860. **AAS prepared/** *Lib.*, 11 May 1860; AAS Minutes, 9 Nov. 1859, BPL; MAS Minutes, 26 Apr. 1860, BPL; SJM(A) to RDW, 15 Apr., 6 May 1860, BPL. **Democratic split/** *Lib.*, 4 May, 18 May 1860. **Republican platform/** Kirk H. Porter and Donald H. Johnson, eds., *National Political Party Platforms* (Urbana, 1970), 27–28, 32–33. **too palpable/** *Lib.*, 28 Sept. 1860. **It may not/** *Lib.*, 20 July 1860, which contains the proceedings of the Framingham Fourth of July rally. **estimates of Lincoln/** WP, *Lib.*, 8 June 1860; AAS, *28th Annual Report, 1860–61*, 25, BPL (this report is not included on the microfilm edition of AAS Annual Reports); Sumner to Duchess of Argyll, 22 May 1860, SLCS 2:23–24; Liberator Mail Books, BPL; WLG to OJ, 9 Aug. 1860 [4: 687]. **Lincoln in New England/** Basler 4:8–29, 5–6 Mar. 1860. **just this once/** NAS, 29 Sept. 1860. **slaveholder most fears/** SJM(A) to RDW, 6 Nov. 1860, BPL. **no slight service/** *Lib.*, 28 Sept. 1860. **Wide-Awake parade/** WLG(J)Di, 18–21 Oct. 1860, GFP/SSC; TBDDi, 16 Oct. 1860, MHS. **much deeper sentiment/** WLG to J. M. McKim, 21 Oct. 1860 [4: 698]. **test of strength/** AAS, *28th Annual Report*, 43. **slave has chosen/** *Lib.*, 16 Nov. 1860. **Charleston crackdown/** *Lib.*, 23 Nov., 30 Nov. 1860. Michael Johnson and James L. Roark, eds., *No Chariot Let Down: Charleston's Free People of Color on the Eve of Civil War* (Chapel Hill, 1989), is an excellent collection of documents. **argument is exhausted/** Shelby Foote, *The Civil War* (N.Y., 1958) 1: 3, 13. **strange and bewildering/** Henry Adams, *The Great Secession Winter of 1860–61 and Other Essays*, ed. George E. Hochfield (N.Y., 1958), 3–4. **simply idiotic/** *Lib.*, 4 Jan. 1861; WLG to CS, 26 Feb. 1861 [5: 10–11]. **reassurances/** Herndon to Samuel Sewall, 1 Feb. 1861, BPL; WH to WP, 28 Dec. 1860, 1 Feb. 1861, B/HHL; CS to John Andrews, 18 Jan. 1861, to JGW, 5 Feb. 1861, SLCS 2:53, 69. **dark times/** WLG to OJ, 19 Jan. 1861 [5: 5–6]. **what terrible/** HBG q. in Mary Grew to WP, 15 Mar. 1861, B/HHL. **conflicting hopes/** *Lib.*, 8 Mar. 1861; FJGDi, 4 Mar. 1861, WSU; **war headlines/** *Lib.*, 19 Apr. 1861.

CHAPTER TWENTY-TWO: THE COVENANT ANNULLED
flags/ FJGDi, 25 Apr. 1861, WSU; NAS, 27 Apr. 1861; *Lib.*, 26 July 1861; Baptist meeting, *Lib.*, 26 Apr. 1861; LMC to Sarah Shaw, 5 May 1861, LMCMf; flag debate, *Lib.*, 7 Jun. 1861. **texts/** WLG to WP, 21 Apr. 1861, B/HHL; *Lib.*, 26 Apr. 1861. **meetings postponed/** WLG to OJ, 19 Apr., 9 May 1861, and to James S. Gibbons, 28 Apr. 1861 [5:17–22]; OJ to WLG, 22 Apr. 1861, BPL; Aaron Powell to WLG, 8 May 1861, BPL; WLG to Aaron Powell, 14 May 1861 [5: 27–28]; Lucretia Mott to WLG, 8 May 1861, BPL. **thank-you note/** WLG to T. B. Drew, 25 Apr. 1861, BPL. **facts are mightier/** NAS, 17 Apr. 1861. **Republican conservatism/** GT to WLG, 23 Nov. 1860, in *Lib.*, 14 Dec. 1861. **Chapman/** MCW to WLG, 12 Aug. 1861, and fragment, Fall 1861, BPL. **secession vs. disunion question/** *Lib.*, 19 Apr., 10 May, 19 July, 4 Oct. 1861; splendid tribute, WLG to GT, *Lib.*, 7 Mar. 1862. **peace principles/** *Lib.*, 10 May, 14 June 1861. **no difficult task/** *Lib.*, 3 May, 10 May, 24 May, 28 June, 12 July, 4 Oct. 1861. **Lowell/** "E Pluribus Unum," *Atlantic Monthly*, Feb. 1861, 235–46; SJM(A) to RDW, 26 Mar. 1861. **Framingham/** *Lib.*, 12 July 1861. **war powers/** *Lib.*, 5 July, 23 Aug., 6 Sept. 1861. **Bull Run aftermath/** NYTi, 25 July 1861; David Child to WLG, 29 July 1861, BPL. **Frémont rebuked/** *Lib.*, 6 Sept., 20 Sept., 4 Oct. 1861; WLG to OJ, 7 Oct. 1861 [5:37]; FJG Diary, 6 Nov. 1861, WSU. **negotiated settlement/** WLG to OJ, 6 Dec. 1861 [5: 47–48]. For samples of Democratic editorials, see "Refuge of Oppression," *Lib.*, 4 Oct., 11 Oct. 1861, which includes NPH excerpt. **Emancipation League/** petition in *Lib.*, 27 Sept., 4 Oct. 1861; MWC to WLG, Fall 1861, BPL; NAS, 5 Oct., 2 Nov. 1861; MG to HBG, 20 June 1862, BPL. **family affairs/** WLG contract with J. M. Yerrinton and GTG, 1 Jan. 1861, BPL; FJG Diary, 1861 *passim*, WSU; HBG to Dear Friend, Sept. 1861; HBG to MWC, Oct. 1861, WSU; WLG to OJ, 9 Aug. 1860 [4: 685–87]; Lillie B. C. Wyman and Arthur C. Wyman, *Elizabeth Buffum Chace 1806–1899: Her Life and Its Environment* (Boston, 1914) 1:222–23, including Lillie B. Chace to Lucy F. Lovell, 13 Aug. 1861; TBDDi, 7–28 Aug. 1863, MHS. **removed slogan/** *Lib.*, 13 Dec. 1861; for the witty reply, see WLG, "The Abolitionists and Their Relations to the War," *Lib.*, 24 Jan. 1862. **President's message/** *Lib.*, 6 Dec. 1861; WLG to OJ, 6 Dec. 1861 [5:47]. **Cooper Union speech/** *Pulpit and Rostrum*, 15 Feb. 1862. TT to WLG, 3 Apr. 1862, BPL. **Beecher/** WLG to HBG, 21 Oct. 1861, in *Life* 4: 36. **writer apologized/** NYTi, 25 Jan. 1862. **tender-footed members/** George W. Julian to WLG, 16 Apr. 1862, BPL. **it is something/** LMC to Wallcut, 20 Apr. 1862, LMCMf. **cowardly avoidance/** *Lib.*, 21 Mar. 1862. **Hunter veto/** *Lib.*, 23 May 1862. WLG called the veto "a wet blanket thrown over the flame of popular enthusiasm." WLG to Charles B. Sedgwick, 20 May 1862 [5:93]. **war situation/** Military information throughout these chapters is based on James M. McPherson, *Battle Cry of Freedom: The Civil War Era* (N.Y., 1988), the best general history of the period, and Shelby Foote, *The Civil War*, 3 vols. (N.Y., 1958–74), an epic literary narrative. **British initiatives/** WLG to GT, *Lib.*, 21 Feb., 28 Feb., 7 Mar. 1862 [5:64–82]; *Life* 4:65–67. **Crandall/** *Lib.*, 23 May 1862. **Weld/** *Lib.*, 14 Nov. 1862. **Gerrit Smith/** GS to WLG, 16 Apr. 1862, in *Lib.*, 9 May 1862. **Dear Brother/** C. W. Dension to WLG, 24 Feb. 1862, BPL. **Douglass/** q. in James M. McPherson, *The Struggle for Equality: Abolitionists and the Negro in the Civil War and Reconstruction* (Princeton, 1964), 104–6, not reprinted in *Lib.* **Dickinson/** WLG to Anna E. Dickinson, 22 Mar.–3 Apr. 1862 [5:85–90]. **battle hymns/** WLG lyrics, *Lib.*, 11 July 1862; Howe's verses, *Lib.*, 24 Jan. 1862, reprinted from *Atlantic Monthly*. **delegations/** NAS, 24 June 1862; OJ to SJM(A), 25 July 1862, SJM(A) to Charles Burleigh, 17 July 1862, BPL; NAS, 30 Aug. 1862; *Lib.*, 3 Oct. 1862. **reply to Greeley/** *Lib.*, 22 Aug. 1862. **colonization/***Lib.*, 22 Aug. 1862. **cancel subscription/** Liberator Mail Books, BPL. **WLG caricature/***Vanity Fair*, 23 Aug. 1862. The caption described Garrison as someone "whose eloquence would soon wither but for his beloved Dhudeen or Black Pipe." For other *Vanity Fair* attacks see, e.g., 18 Jan, 5 July, 6 Sept. 1862. **wet rag/** WLG to OJ, 9 Sept. 1862 [5:112]. **Williams College talk/** WLG to WPG, 1 Aug. 1862 [5:103–4]; *Lib.*, 22 Aug., 29 Aug. 1862. **Helen despair/** HBG to Fanny, 14 Sept. 1862, WSU. **Photographs/** Roy Meredith, *Mr. Lincoln's Cameraman: Mathew B. Brady*

(N.Y., 1946), 111–12, 129. **proclamation reactions/** FG to HBG, 24 Sept. 1862, B/ HHL; TT to WLG, 23 Sept. 1862, BPL; *Life* 4:62; WLG to FG, 25 Sept. 1862 [5:114–15]; *Lib.*, 26 Sept. 1862; LMC to Sarah Shaw, 30 Oct. 1862, LMCMf; SJM(A) to RDW, 23 Sept. 1862, BPL. **caricatures/** *Vanity Fair*, 4 Oct., 25 Oct., 1 Nov. 1862. **president is demented/** *Lib.*, 5 Dec. 1862. **Emancipation Day/** WLG(J)Di, 31 Dec. 1862–1 Jan. 1863, GFP/SSC; *Lib.*, 2 Jan., 9 Jan., 16 Jan. 1863; Elizabeth Powell Bond to Henry Stearns, 13 Feb. 1906, which contains an undated memoir of the day's events, Stutler Collection, West Virginia Dept. of Archives and History. In Plymouth, where church bells rang morning, noon, and night, Brad Drew said the celebration was "mingled with the sadness" of a funeral for a local boy killed at Fredericksburg. TBDDi, 1 Jan. 1863, MHS.

CHAPTER TWENTY-THREE: EVERYTHING GRAVITATES TOWARD FREEDOM
soldier's letter/ Jacob H. Allen to WLG, 23 Oct. 1862, BPL. Allen served his full three-year enlistment and survived hard fighting with his regiment (the 40th Ohio) at Chickamauga, Lookout Mountain, and the Georgia campaign. He was mustered out of service on 7 Oct. 1864 in Atlanta, after Sherman's conquest. *Official Roster of the Soldiers of the State of Ohio in the War of the Rebellion, 1861–1866* (Akron, 1887) 4: 138. **everything must gravitate/** WLG to LMC, 10 July 1865 [5:282]. **Villard report/** *Memoirs of Henry Villard, Journalist and Financier 1835–1900* (Boston, 1904) 2:15–24, 53–54. **54th parade/** FJG to HV, 30 May 1863, HHL; WLG(J)Di, 28 May 1863 GFP/ SSC; *Lib.*, 5 June 1863. Luis F. Emilio, *A Brave Black Regiment: History of the Fifty-fourth Regiment of Massachusetts Volunteer Infantry, 1863–65* (Boston, 1891), 32, claims that WLG was seen on the balcony of Wendell Phillips's house on Essex St. watching the parade with one hand resting on a bust of John Brown. Emilio was an officer in the regiment who compiled his history from reminiscences and documents, so this should carry some weight. The report is presented in third-person narrative, however, not as eyewitness testimony. Even though many modern writers have repeated the story, I have set it aside as apocryphal and have offered instead an account based on the family diary. While the parade route did include Essex St., it would seem that the abolitionists were in a downtown convention hall and adjourned directly to the Common, where Willie recorded that he had met his parents, who had obtained a pass that permitted them inside the lines. *Life* 4:81 places WLG "by chance" at the corner of State St. and Wilson Lane, the scene of his 1835 mobbing. Of course, WLG could have hurried downtown from Essex St. after the parade had passed, but this seems doubtful. Also, the Essex St. house was very small and had only an ornamental balcony that, at least in photographs, does not appear large enough for a reviewing party. **George enlistment/** WLG to GTG, 11 June 1863; on other families' experience, WLG to HBG, 21 Oct. 1861, *Life* 4:37; WLG to Elizabeth B. Chace, 7 Aug. 1862 [5:106–7]; Lillie B. C. Wyman and Arthur C. Wyman, *Elizabeth Buffum Chase 1806–1899: Her Life and Its Environment* (Boston, 1914) 1:219–20; WLG(J)Di, 3 June 1863, GFP/SSC; Charles B. Fox, *Record of the Service of the 55th Regiment of Massachusetts Volunteer Infantry* (Cambridge, 1868). **the draft and nonresistants/** WLG views, *Lib.*, 19 Sept., 26 Sept. 1862, 31 July 1863; WPG protest, 10 July 1863, in *Lib.*, 21 Aug. 1863; A. H. Love to WLG, 7 Jan. 1864, in *Lib.*, 29 Jan. 1864; WLG(J)Di, 13 July, 18 July 1863, GFP/SSC. Eugene C. Murdock, *One Million Men: The Civil War Draft in the North* (Madison, 1971), 197–217. For an account of a nonresistant's harsh treatment, see J. Wesley Pratt to WLG, 16 Mar. 1864, in *Lib.*, 1 Apr. 1864. On Lincoln's liberal use of his powers of pardon, see Edward Needles Wright, *Conscientious Objectors in the Civil War* (Philadelphia, 1931), 83–121. **George departure/** WLG(J)Di, 21 July 1863, GFP/SSC; *Lib.*, 24 July 1863; WLG to GTG, 6 Aug. 1863 [5:166–67]; GTG to HBG, 3 Aug. 1863, GFP/SSC. **Framingham/** *Lib.*, 10 July 1863, which also reprints a major speech by John Bright. **Weld/** *Lib.*, 7 Aug. 1863. **55th Mass experience/** GTG to HBG, 3 Aug. 1863, GFP/SSC; excerpts from GTG to WLG, 1 Sept., 6 Sept. 1863, in *Lib.*, 18 Sept. 1863; GTG to WLG(J), 10 Dec. 1863, 10 Feb. 1864, GFP/SSC; *Lib.*, 3 July 1863. **Loyal League petition drive/** ECS

to FJG/FG, 25 May 1863. *Lib.*, 2 Oct. 1863, has an address from ECS and a typical weekly appeal by WLG in support. ECS to E. S. Miller, 1 Sept. 1863, ECSL 2:95; ECS to WLG, 13 Dec. 1863, in *Lib.*, 1 Jan. 1864; ECS to CS, 1 Feb. 1864, ECSL 2: 97. *Lib.*, 11 Mar. 1864, contains SBA's summary of the work accomplished. **AAS 30th anniversary**/ WLG to J. M. McKim, 14 Nov. 1863 [5:175–76]; *Lib.*, 11 Dec. 1863; WLG remarks, *Lib.*, 18 Dec. 1863, 29 Jan. 1864; Beecher, *Lib.*, 8 Jan. 1864; Kelley, *Lib.*, Jan. 1864; other speeches reprinted in *Lib.* throughout Jan. 1864. NYTr q. *Lib.*, 18 Dec. 1863. *New York Times*, 9 Feb. 1864. **Nast drawing**/ *Harper's Weekly*, 24 Jan. 1863. For printed engraving, see Bernard F. Reilly, Jr., *American Political Prints, 1776–1876:A Catalogue of the Collections in the Library of Congress* (Boston, 1991), 551. **Helen's stroke**/ WLG(J)Di, 30 Dec. 1863–2 Jan. 1864, GFP/SSC; FJG to HV, 25 Mar. 1864, HHL; WLG to WPG, 14 Apr. 1864 [5:196]; *Life* 4:93–94. **Phillips challenge**/ *Lib.*, 5 Feb., 29 Feb., 18 Mar. 1864; McKim to WLG, 9 Feb. 1864, BPL. **endorsing Lincoln**/ *Lib.*, 18 Mar. 1864; WLG to McKim, 27 Feb. 1864, in *Philadelphia Press,* 17 Mar. 1864; McKim to WLG, 18 Mar. 1864. **division at meetings**/ AAS proceedings, *Lib.*, 15 Apr., 20 May 1864; Convention proceedings, *Lib.*, 3 June, 10 June 1864; NAS, 11 June 1864; WLG to OJ, 28 Apr. 1864 [5:201], 5 May 1864, BPL; MWC to WLG, n.d. [May 1864?], BPL; ECS to WLG, 22 Apr. 1864, BPL. **Baltimore visit**/ WLG to HBG, 8 June 1864 [5:207–8]; *Lib.*, 24 Jun. 1864. **Lincoln conversations**/ WLG to HBG, 9 June, 10 June, 11 June 1864 [5:209–12], which also recount the Senate visit; *Life* 4:117. Chamberlain is quoted in *Life* 4:132 n.1, with citation to NYTr, 4 Nov. 1883. **personal attacks**/ *Lib.*, 24 June 1864. For editorial defense of WLG see *Plymouth Memorial* and *Rochester Express* extracts in *Lib.*, 29 July 1864. **moves against newspapers**/ WLG to OJ, 17 June, 20 June 1864 [5:213–15], OJ to WLG, 20 June 1864, BPL; WLG to SJM(A), 17 June 1864, BPL. OJ to SJM(A), 23 June 1864, BPL. *Lib.*, 30 Dec. 1864, describes the Hovey Fund action; WLG to CKW, 13 Mar. 1865 [5:260–62] announces his resignation from the fund board. OJ to WP, 22 June 1864, BPL, tried to smooth over the hurt feelings and sought to avoid "personal unkindness," but Phillips later refused to speak with him. OJ to SJM(A), 15 Oct. 1864, BPL. **Frémont candidacy**/ *Lib.*, 3 June, 10 June 1864. Also see George W. Smalley to WP, 15 Mar. 1864, B/HHL, for a severe assessment of Frémont's character. **Tilton charged**/ *Lib.*, 1 July, 8 July, 15 July 1864, reprints the editorials from *The Independent* and WP's reply. **hard to win**/ WLG to Francis Newman, 22 July 1864 [5:229]. **cut off both hands**/ WP to ECS, 27 Sept. 1864, ECSL 2:100 n.1. **election night**/ *Lib.*, 11 Nov. 1864. **engagements**/ WLG to Ellen Wright, 19 Feb. 1864 [5:188–89]; WLG to Lucy McKim, 30 June, 11 July 1864 [5:216–18]; FJG to HV, 18 Aug., 25 Sept. 1864, HV to FJG, 10 Aug., 14 Sept. 1864, HHL; Lucy McKim, "Songs of the Port Royal Contrabands," *Dwight's Journal of Music*, 8 Nov. 1862, in Irving Sablosky, ed., *What They Heard: Music in America, 1852–1881* (Baton Rouge, 1986). **move to Roxbury**/ FG to FJG, 31 July 1864, B/HHL; *Life* 4:163. By 1870 all but three families from the Dix Place of the Garrisons' decade had moved to suburban addresses. **regimental news**/ For details of Honey Hill, see Fox, 43–44; Emilio, 236–53; gun battery, *Lib.*, 15 July 1864. **newspaper problems**/ FG to FJG, 29 July 1863, B/ HHL; WPG to WLG, 8 Aug. 1863, GFP/SSC; *Lib.*, 29 July, 12 Aug., 19 Aug., 26 Aug., 16 Sept., 16 Dec., 30 Dec. 1864; GTG to WPG, 12 Aug. 1864, GTG to WLG(J), 14 June 1864, GFP/SSC; OJ to SJM(A), 15 Oct., 31 Oct. 1864, BPL; WLG to OJ, 26 Nov. 1864 [5:239–42]. AAS Minutes, 25 Nov. 1864, reported about 350 names as overlapping subscribers, with NAS having a total of 2,000 paid subscriptions and *Lib.* 1,875. **Thirteenth Amendment celebrations**/ *Harper's Weekly*, 18 Feb. 1865; Mary Grew to WLG, 1 Feb. 1865, BPL; *Lib.*, 3 Feb., 10 Feb. 1865; extract from Miss [?] Manning's Diary, 4 Feb. 1865, GFP/SSC; TBDDi, 31 Jan. 1865, MHS. **fall of Charleston**/ NYTr, 22 Feb. 1865; *Lib.*, 3 Mar., 10 Mar., 17 Mar. 1865; *Boston Journal*, 21 Feb., 2 Mar., 4 Mar., 10 Mar. 1865; Charles Carleton Coffin, *Boys of '65* (Boston, 1883), 469–75; *Harper's Weekly*, 18 Mar. 1865; Fox, 56. **Sumter invitation**/ Stanton to WLG, 7 Apr. 1865, in *Life* 4:136–37; GT to Robert Wallcut, 8 Apr. 1865, in *Lib.*, 14 Apr. 1865. **flag-raising ceremony**/ The account is based on NYTi, 18 Apr. 1865; *Philadelphia Press*, 18

Apr. 1865; *Charleston Courier*, 16 Apr. 1865; *Lib.*, 28 Apr. 1865; *New York Evangelist*, excerpted in *Lib.*, 5 May 1865; WLG to HBG, 9 Apr., 15 Apr. 1865 [5:266–70]; NAS, 6 May, 1865; Laura Towne to [?], 14 Apr., 23 Apr. 1865, in *Letters and Diary of Laura M. Towne*, ed. Rupert Sargent Holland (Cambridge, 1912), 159–61; *The Trip of the Steamer Oceanus to Fort Sumter...*" (Brooklyn, 1865); W. T. Sherman to Robert Anderson, 5 Apr. 1865, *War of the Rebellion: A Compilation of the Official Records of the Union and Confederate Armies* (Washington, D.C., 1895), ser. 1, vol. 47, ch. 59, pp. 107–8; National Park Service, *Fort Sumter: Anvil of War* (Washington, D.C., 1984.) **Charleston/** *Lib.*, 28 Apr., 5 May 1865, and NAS, 6 May 1865, have several accounts of the banquet speeches, the Zion's Church meeting (reprinted from *Charleston Courier*), and the visit to Calhoun's grave. Of the several versions of WLG's remark, I have chosen the pithiest, as reported by the Rev. A. D. Putnam in *The Independent*, q. *Lib.*, 12 May 1865. Charleston legend holds that Calhoun's body wasn't in his tomb that day; patriots had surreptitiously removed it to another part of the churchyard to forestall vandals and grave-robbers. **Printing office/** *Charleston Courier*, 17 Apr. 1865. **Refugee camp/** *Life* 4:149. For the regiment's work in the countryside and the exodus train see the excerpted letter (presumably from GTG) in *Lib.*, 31 Mar. 1865, and Fox, 71–72. For the visit to Mitchellville, see *Lib.*, 12 May 1865. On the city generally, see Robert Rosen, *Confederate Charleston: An Illustrated History of the City and the People During the Civil War* (Columbia, S.C., 1995), and the photograph file, South Carolina Historical Society. For the reactions of an exiled Charleston aristocrat, see *The Diary of Miss Emma Holmes, 1861–1866*, ed. John F. Marszalek (Baton Rouge, 1979), which describes the "fooleries" of the Fort Sumter celebration and the "promiscuous" meetings that followed. Complaining that liberated slaves had taken to wearing hand-me-down "finery," Miss Holmes wrote, twelve days before the Sumter flag-raising, this astonishing statement: "If I ever own negroes, I shall carry out my father's plan & never allow them to indulge in dress. It is ruin body and soul to them." 2 April 1865, p. 428. For an eloquent account of the emancipation process, see Leon Litwack, *Been in the Storm Too Long: The Aftermath of Slavery* (N.Y., 1979).

CHAPTER TWENTY-FOUR: MY VOCATION HAS ENDED

no one knows/ TBDDi, 15 Apr. 1865, MHS. Other remarks on Lincoln's death are taken from *Lib.*, 21 Apr., 28 Apr. 1865; LMC, 6 May 1865, in *Independent*, 11 May 1865, reprinted *Lib.*, 28 May 1865. WLG eulogy, delivered at the Providence Union League, 1 June 1865, in *Lib.*, 7 July 1865. See also WLG to OJ, 28 May 1865 [5:281]. **AAS controversy/** This account synthesizes the debates at three meetings: MAS, Jan. 1865, in *Lib.*, 17 Feb. 1865, NAS, 21 Jan. 1865; AAS, May 1865, in *Lib.*, 19 May, 26 May, 2 June. 1865, NAS, 8 Apr. 1865; MAS, Jan. 1866, in NAS, 3 Feb. 1866. In addition to the proceedings, see *Lib.*, 22 Jan., 2 Dec. 1864, 13 Jan., 24 Mar., 31 Mar. 1865. AAS Executive Committee Minutes, 16 Mar. 1865; SJM(A) to RDW, 14 Feb. 1865, BPL; OJ to WLG, 24 Jan. 1865, BPL; MG to SJM(A), 7 Mar. 1865, BPL; S. H. Gay to SJM(A), 12 Mar., 27 Mar. 1865, BPL; OJ to SJM(A), 24 Apr. 1865, Johnson Papers, Vermont Historical Society; OJ to WLG, 24 Apr., 18 May 1865, BPL; WLG to HBG, 10 May 1865 [5:271–72]; WLG to LMC, 10 July 1865 [5:282]; WLG to FGV, 27 Jan. 1866 [5:374–75], MWC to J. M. McKim, 4 June 1865, BPL. See James M. McPherson, *The Struggle for Equality: Abolitionists and the Negro in the Civil War and Reconstruction* (Princeton, 1964), 287–307, for an overview. **Stearns effort/** McPherson, *Struggle*, 322–26, 338–39; Frank P. Stearns, *Life and Public Services of George Luther Stearns* (Philadelphia, 1907), 332–38, describes Stearns's dissatisfaction with Godkin and the moderate course adopted by *The Nation*. **longing for rest/** WLG to J. M. McKim, 14 Sept. 1865 [5: 294]. **Fanny's engagement/** WLG to WPG, 25 May 1865 [5:276–77], WLG to HV, 10 Aug., 12 Sept. 1865 [5:286–88, 291–92]. **lecture tour/** Based on WLG to HBG, 31 Oct.–3 Dec. 1865 [5:311–54]. For lecture reports see *Chicago Tribune*, 17 Nov. 1865, and *Chicago Times*, 17 Nov. 1865. For the political conclusions see WLG to CS, 14 Dec. 1865 [5:361–62], and WLG to G. W. Julian, 11 Feb. 1866 [5:382], which unaccountably omits the crucial sentence referring to the ballot. See DLC Microfilm edition (5857E) of the Giddings-Julian Correspondence for a photostat of the complete manuscript. **Liberator closing/** *Lib.*, 22 Dec., 29 Dec. 1865; *Life* 4: 169–70. Tributes include LMC, *Independent*, 28 Dec. 1865; *Nation*, 4 Jan. 1866; TBDDi, 29 Dec. 1865, MHS; NYTr, 4 Jan. 1866; Stowe to WLG, 2 Jan. 1866, BPL; N. P. Atkinson to WLG, 1 Jan. 1866, BPL; John Ruhm to WLG, 8 Jan. 1866, BPL. Liberator Day Book, BPL. **New Year's letters/** WLG to JBY, 1 Jan. 1866 [6:369–70]; WLG to JWY, 1 Jan. 1866, q. *Life* 4:169 n. 2; WLG to WP, 1 Jan. 1866 [6:368–69]. **Fanny's wedding/** WLG to FGV, 7 Jan. 1866, [6:371]; WLG to FGV, 1 Feb. 1867 [6:453] details the gift of a John Rogers sculpture, *The Wounded Scout*, to J. B. Smith as a token of gratitude. TBDDi, 3 Jan. 1866. FGV to HBG & WLG, 4 Jan. 1866, B/HHL. **book contract/** FJG to HV, 30 Mar. 1866, B/HHL. On his anxieties, see WLG to John Keep, 11 July 1868, DLC. **all overtasked/** WLG to Ira Steward, 20 Mar. 1866 [6:401–2]. For a letter more typical of WLG's resistance to any argument that likened the circumstances of free workers to the institution of chattel slavery see WLG to W. G. H. Smart, 18 Aug. 1875 [6:388–90]. **Fourteenth Amendment/** For a guide to the vast literature on the intent of the framers, see Robert J. Kaczorowski, "To Begin the Nation Anew: Congress, Citizenship, and Civil Rights after the Civil War," *American Historical Review* 92 (Feb. 1987): 45–68. For WLG's general views, see his two important New York speeches, NYTi, 28 Feb. 1866, and NAS, 9 Mar. 1867; also WLG to CS, 11 Feb. 1866 [6:383–84], and WLG to WPG, 22 Feb. 1866 [3:391–92]. For WP, see NAS, 3 Nov. 1866; WLG to OJ, 25 Jan. 1867 [6:450–51]. See generally, Eric Foner, *Reconstruction: America's Unfinished Revolution, 1863–1877* (N.Y., 1988). **Stanton challenge/** ECS to WP, 26 Dec. 1865, ECSL 2:109–11; ECS to Martha C. Wright, 20 Dec. 1865, 6 Jan., 20 Jan. 1866, ECSL 2:108–13. On the feminist break with abolitionism, see Ellen C. DuBois, *Feminism and Suffrage: The Emergence of an Independent Women's Movement in America, 1848–1869* (Ithaca, N.Y., 1978). **earnest and loving exchange/** LS to AKF, 24 Jan. 1867, Blackwell Family Papers, DLC; AKF to LS, 10 Feb. 1867, National American Woman Suffrage Papers, DLC. **Kansas campaign/** Andrea Ker Moore, *Lucy Stone: Speaking Out for Equality* (New Brunswick, 1992), 123–30; Elisabeth Griffith, *In Her Own Right: The Life of Elizabeth Cady Stanton* (N.Y., 1984), 127–31. **Revolution controversy/** WLG to SBA, 4 Jan. 1868 [6:28–29]; *Revolution*, 20 Jan. 1868; WLG to Isabella Beecher Hooker, 12 Nov. 1869, WLG to OJ, 14 Nov. 1869 [6:144–50]; LS to WLG, 6 Mar., 22 Oct. 1868, 22 Aug., 27 Sept. 1869, all in BPL. **Jackson bequest/** WLG to SJM(A), 24 Jan., 7 May 1867 [6:448–49, 474–75]; SJM(A) to Editor of the *Standard*, 26 Aug. 1867, BPL. WLG to Editor, NAS, 14 Mar. 1868. **AAS dissolution/** NAS, 16 Apr. 1870. **a miracle performed/** *Boston Journal*, 15 Apr. 1870; FGV Diary, 14 Apr. 1870, HHL. **quite premature/** WLG to SBA, 4 Jan. 1877, Huntington Library [HM 10564]; SBA to WLG, 1 Jan. 1877, BPL. **reunions/** *Woman's Journal*, 20 Dec. 1873, 11 July 1874; *Growing Up in Boston's Gilded Age: The Journal of Alice Stone Blackwell, 1872–1874*, ed. Marlene Deahl Merrill (New Haven, 1990), 211–12. Fifteen-year-old Alice, who thought her mother had never spoken more eloquently, was thrilled to exchange a few words with Mr. Garrison. She scoffed at the rival centennial party given the next night by a more traditional ladies' group, who served tea wearing colonial dress and listened to an array of male speakers. "Found it very stupid," she wrote, and "was glad to come away and get home." **If we rejoice/** WLG, "Centennial Reflections," *Independent*, 6 July 1876.

CHAPTER TWENTY-FIVE: I MISS MR. GARRISON

old but sublime/ WLG to OJ, 13 Jan. 1873 [6:266]. **another dark period/** WLG to George Downing et al., 30 Dec. 1876 [6:445]. **era of moral politics/** NYTi, 30 Dec. 1874, q. Eric Foner, *Reconstruction: America's Unfinished Revolution 1863–1877* (N.Y., 1988), 527. Foner, 412–563, traces the reactionary change in opinion. **once let public opinion/** NAS, 13 Nov. 1869. **played out/** James B. Stewart, *Wendell Phillips: Liberty's Hero* (Baton Rouge, 1986), 309–10. **Garrison fought/** For examples of WLG's articles on racial issues see *Independent*, 27 Feb. 1868, 16 Apr. 1874; for warfare against Indians, see *Independent*, 31 Mar. 1870, 1 May 1873; on Santo Domingo, *Independent*, 27 Apr. 1871. **1872 presidential campaign/** WLG to Charles Sumner, 3 Aug. 1872 [6:238–47]; *Boston Journal*, 23 Aug. 1872; *Independent*, 9 May, 6 June, 4 Oct., 24 Oct., 31 Oct. 1872. **unabated vigilance/** WLG to George W. Stacy, 31 Aug. 1874 [6:344]. **explained the shift/** *Independent*, 27 Feb. 1868, 6 July 1876; WLG to Cyrus Donagan, 9 Sept. 1876 [6:415–17]; WLG to TDW, 1 Feb. 1875 [6:371]; WLG to William Still, 12 Apr. 1875 [6:380]. **knew in his heart/** WLG to Henry Wilson and the Antislavery Reunion Convention, 5 June 1874 [6:328–30]. **historical inspiration/** WLG to Alexander M. Ross, 18 Aug. 1875 [6:385–86]; WLG to Edmund Quincy et al., 17 Mar. 1873 [6:272]. **domestic routine/** These impressions are based largely on WLG correspondence and FJGDi, 1870–79, WSU. **imperious with editors/** WLG to W. W. Clapp, 14 Oct. 1876 [6:24]. **Old South/** WLG to WPG, 21 July 1876 [6:411]. **If you aim/** J. S. Mill, in *Proceedings of the Public Breakfast Held in Honor of William Lloyd Garrison* (London, 1868), 34. **Birnam Wood/** WLG to Edwin Atkinson, 28 Mar. 1874, q. *Life* 4:261. **cherished photograph/** Rockledge, Aug. 1876, GFP/SSC. **cozy chats/** Based on FGV to HBG, 27 Mar. 1866; HGB to FGV, Jan. 1868, 20 Feb., 29 Mar. 1872, 27 Aug. 1875, WSU. **you inherit/** WLG to FGV, 16 Sept. 1878 [6:528]. **very determined/** Author interview with Lloyd K. Garrison, New York, 26 Jan. 1989. **lost his way/** FJGDi, 7 Apr. 1868, WSU. **view of death/** WLG to LMC, 25 Oct. 1874 [6:354]; WLG to WPG, 12 Dec. 1878 [6:538]. **Helen's death/** FJGDi, 23–26 Jan. 1876, WSU; *Helen Eliza Garrison: A Memorial* (privately printed, 1876), 55, 69, BPL; *Life* 4:342. **bewilderment and loss/** WLG to WPG, 27 Feb. 1876 [6:400], WLG to Hannah Cox, 2 Apr. 1876 [6:404]; WLG to FGV, 25 Jan. 1877 [6:452]; WLG to WPG, 12 Dec. 1878 [6:539]. **Thompson/** FJGDi, 11 July 1877, WSU. **Emerson lecture/** WLG to FGV, 31 Jan. 1879 [6:551]. **telephone/**FJGDi, 8 May 1877, WSU. **typewriter/** WLG to FJG, 9 Dec. 1877, G/MHS. **friendships/**LMC to Anne Whitney, 25 May 1879; LMC to WLG, 22 Apr. 1879; LMC to Mrs. S. S. Russell, 28 May 1879, LMC to Sarah Shaw, 20 July 1879, all in LMCMf. **Whitney statuette/** WPG and FJG, *The Words of Garrison: A Centennial Selection* (Boston, 1905), 117–18. The piece itself is in the Museum of Art Collection, Smith College. **apprenticeship anniversary/** NPH, 14 Oct. 1878; the Rev. E. W. Allen to WLG, 16 Jan. 1879, BPL; FJGDi, 12 Oct., 14 Oct. 1878, WSU; Franklin Club Dinner, reported in *Boston Traveller*, 15 Oct. 1878. See also WLG to John D. Whitcomb, 14 Jan. 1874 [6:290]. **energetic public letters/** BT, 24 Jan. 1878 [6:500–508]; NYTr, 17 Feb. 1879 [6:556–60]; WLG to Robert Morris, 22 Apr. 1879 [6:578–81], reprinted in *Boston Traveller*, 24 Apr. 1879; Prudence Crandall Philleo to WLG, 20 Apr. 1879, BPL; WLG to FGV, 20 Feb. 1879 [6:562]. **Frank's engagement/** FJGDi, 13 Apr., 1879, WSU; WLG to Mary Pratt, 14 Apr. 1879 [6:574]; LMC to FJG, 30 May 1879, LMCMf. **Maria Stewart visit/** WLG to Maria W. Stewart, 4 Apr. 1879, BPL; Marilyn Richardson, ed., *Maria W. Stewart: America's First Black Woman Political Writer* (Bloomington, 1981), 88–97. **final illness/** FJGDi, 14 May–21 May 1879, WSU; telegrams, May 1879, G/MHS; NYTr, 26 May, 27 May 1879; *Life* 4:304–5. **Atlanta memorial/** NYTr, 12 June 1879; FGV to FJG, 13 June 1879, B/HHL. **funeral/** WLG(J) to WPG, 25 May 1879, GFP/SSC; LMC, "William Lloyd Garrison," *Atlantic Monthly*, August 1879, 234–38; *Woman's Journal*, 31 May 1879; *Tributes to William Lloyd Garrison at the Funeral Services, May 28, 1879* (Boston, 1879); FD, 2 June 1879, FDPS 4:505. For Lucy Stone's bequest see LS to FJG, 7 June, 15 Aug. 1879, LCSL. The controversy over Phillips's remark is revealed in WPG to WLG(J), 3 June, 6 June 1879, GFP/SSC; LS to FJG, 5 July 1879, LCSL Microfilm Reel 2, folder 25. The passage from *The Pilgrim's Progress* appeared in *Independent*, 29 May 1879. **Holmes/** The remark is recalled in Oliver Wendell Holmes, Jr., to Learned Hand, 24 June 1918, Holmes Papers, Harvard Law School Library, Box 103, Folder 24. I am indebted to Robert C. Post of Boalt Hall, School of Law, University of California, Berkeley, for bringing this letter to my attention. **Scollay Square demolition/** John Beresford Hatch to *Boston Globe*, 17 Feb. 1962; *Boston Globe*, 22 June 1961 (Schlesinger protest); 3 Mar. 1963 (fire); clippings in GFP/SSC.

ACKNOWLEDGMENTS

A book as long (and as long in the making) as this one is built upon the efforts of many people and institutions. My research could not have been accomplished without the substantial assistance of librarians throughout the country who guided me through their collections, answered urgent inquiries, supplied photocopies, helped me locate photographs, and made many helpful suggestions. Because the list is very long I want to express my appreciation collectively, but special thanks are in order for the following: Roberta Zonghi, Curator of Rare Books, Giuseppe Bisaccia, Curator of Manuscripts, and Eugene Zepp, Reference Librarian, at the Boston Public Library; David Nathan, Boston City Archivist; Phil Lapsansky, Reference Librarian, Library Company of Philadelphia; Susan Boone and Amy Haig, curators, Sophia Smith Collection, Smith College; and Michael Kelly, Curator of Special Collections, Ablah Library, Wichita State University. For assistance in assembling the photographs I am especially grateful, in addition, to Catharina Slautterback, Associate Curator of Prints and Photographs, Library of the Boston Athenaeum; Chris Steele, Curator of Photographs, Massachusetts Historical Society; Noah Dennen, Medford Historical Society; Ann Shumard, Assistant Curator of Photographs, National Portrait Gallery; and Cecile Pimental, Special Collections, Newburyport Public Library. The book is also richer for the efforts of people who guided me through some of the historic places that figure in this story: Kaz Kozlowski, curator, Prudence Crandall Museum; Leslie and Dick Wendel, former owners of Friendship Valley, the Benson homestead; Barbara Nash, the African Meeting House and National Historic Site, Boston; Deborah Easterbrook, curator, and Bill Martin, ranger, at Fort Sumter National Monument; Sister Esther of the Society of St. Margaret, present owners of Rockledge; and Robert Neiley, architect for the restoration of the First Church, Eliot Square, Roxbury. I was also immeasurably aided on particular matters by the expertise of many others, especially Walter Dellinger, Susannah Driver, Cynthia Gorney, Peter Hinks, the late Peter R. Knights, Charles V. Peery, Robert Post, Eva Shade, Susan Strane, Llewellyn C. Thomas, and Harold R. Worthy. Three people, now sadly deceased, who occupied varying places on the spectrum of twentieth-century social movements, all contributed by example to my understanding of abolitionism; the influence of Sarah Crome, Frances Herring, and Mario Savio will be apparent to all who knew them.

All on Fire has enjoyed the luxury of two agents and two editors. Glenn Cowley influenced the genesis of the project, but when circumstances forced his withdrawal from business, Sharon Friedman, first with the John Hawkins agency and now with Ralph Vicinanza Ltd., represented this book with great dedication and care. At St. Martin's Press, Bill Thomas guided the early manuscript with wonderful insight, but when his talents earned him opportunities elsewhere, I had the immense good fortune of coming into the editorial care of Robert Weil, whose understanding of my work was instantaneous and profound, and whose gifts of intellect and sympathy have sustained and improved it at every juncture. Also at St. Martin's, Andrew Miller, associate editor, minded the production details with efficiency and enthusiasm; Ted Johnson proved a copy editor of great distinction; Henry Sene Yee designed a jacket completely suited to Garrison's boldness; and Diane Hobbing designed a book to match.

Many friends offered encouragement and help, and the following deserve special mention. Leroy Votto encouraged this project from its inception, several times undertook research assignments to move the cause along, and enthusiastically read drafts both early and late. Bill Sokol cheered me for years even as we cheered the Bushrod and Rockridge Cougars from the sidelines. Jim Reston brought thirty-five years of friendship to our hikes in the Tetons and the Sierra Nevada and to the task of getting this book finished at last. Candace Falk stepped up time and again with important support, Marge Frantz and Eleanor Engstrand read the manuscript at a crucial time, as did Charles Sellers, while the entire company at Chamokome Ranch sustained a climate of intellectual inquiry and social activism in which the Garrisons would have been right at home. During the decade of work on this book the Mayer family's house rattled in the Loma Prieta earthquake and withstood the threat of the Oakland Hills fire at the head of our block, but the joys of our life together have never dimmed. Eleanor and Tom have grown up during the decade of work on the manuscript and, like this book, are ready to make their own way in the world. For me there is world enough with Betsy, always.

H. M.

INDEX